The Eastern District Manual

Third Edition

Judicial Practice and Procedure
in the United States District Court for the
Eastern District of Pennsylvania

*To Ed Mullinix —
A truly great lawyer, teacher,
partner and friend —
With deep gratitude for
all you taught me and
all the help you gave me.
Chuck Bruton
January 2014*

The Eastern District Manual

Third Edition

Judicial Practice and Procedure
in the United States District Court for the
Eastern District of Pennsylvania

Editor
Charles R. Bruton

Associate Editors
Donald W. Myers
Samuel W. Silver

© 2013, THE PENNSYLVANIA BAR INSTITUTE.
ALL RIGHTS RESERVED.

Printed in the United States of America.

ISBN 978-1-57804-001-8

PBI Number 7919

PENNSYLVANIA BAR INSTITUTE
5080 RITTER ROAD
MECHANICSBURG, PENNSYLVANIA 17055
800/932-4637 OR 717/796-0804
E-MAIL: info@pbi.org
WEBSITE: http://www.pbi.org

The Pennsylvania Bar Institute does not render any legal, accounting, or other professional services. The Institute's programs and publications are designed solely to help attorneys maintain their professional competence. Commentary, opinions, or views expressed by the authors are not necessarily the views of PBI. In dealing with specific legal matters, the attorney using PBI publications or orally conveyed information should always research original sources of authority.

This book is part of the Pennsylvania Bar Institute's Automatic Update Service. Under this service, PBI makes a commitment to keep this book up to date through new editions as appropriate, and to send these updates to everyone who purchases the book. You will receive each update with an invoice for less than the normal price.

It is PBI's mission to provide Pennsylvania lawyers with continuing legal education (in the form of seminars, books, and electronic media) that is timely, practical, cost effective, and of the highest possible quality. You can count on us to keep you up to date in this important area of practice.

If you do not want to be part of this service, please call Customer Service at 800-247-4724, ext. 2288, and ask that we remove your name from the list of those who will receive updates to this book.

The Pennsylvania Bar Institute

PBI is a self-supporting nonprofit corporation chartered in 1965 under the guidance of the Pennsylvania Bar Association for the following purposes:

The design, promotion, and administration of cooperative programs in legal research, to the end of furtherance and betterment of the administration of justice in Pennsylvania and elsewhere.

The development, promotion, and administration of cooperative programs for continuing legal education and education of the interested public in law and related subjects.

PBI is dedicated to excellence in continuing legal education and aims to provide a comprehensive curriculum of post-admission studies under competent instructors with course materials of immediate and continuing use in practice.

PENNSYLVANIA BAR INSTITUTE
5080 RITTER ROAD
MECHANICSBURG, PENNSYLVANIA 17055-6903
800/932-4637 OR 717/796-0804
E-MAIL: info@pbi.org
WEBSITE: http://www.pbi.org

PENNSYLVANIA BAR INSTITUTE
BOARD OF DIRECTORS
MAY 2013–2014

OFFICERS

President:	Penina Kessler Lieber, Pittsburgh
Vice President:	Mark A. Kearney, Blue Bell
Secretary:	Seth A. Mendelsohn, Hershey
Treasurer:	Gail P. Granoff, Philadelphia
Immediate Past President:	Sara A. Austin, York
Past President:	Paul C. Troy, Norristown

DIRECTORS

Norris E. Benns, Jr.
Harrisburg

Hon. Mark I. Bernstein
Philadelphia

Pamela F. Cross
Harrisburg

Sayde J. Ladov
Philadelphia

Hon. Maureen Lally-Green
Pittsburgh

Hon. Bonnie B. Leadbetter
Blue Bell

Brenda K. McBride
Grove City

C. Dale McClain
Worcester

Jeffrey A. Mills
Lancaster

Jill E. Nagy
Reading

William H. Pugh, V
Norristown

David G. Ries
Pittsburgh

David E. Schwager
Wilkes-Barre

Barry M. Simpson
Harrisburg

Donald F. Smith, Jr.
Reading

Prince A. Thomas
Philadelphia

Rhodia D. Thomas
Harrisburg

Dennis A. Whitaker
Harrisburg

Kathleen D. Wilkinson
Philadelphia

Brett M. Woodburn
Harrisburg

PAST PRESIDENTS (HONORARY DIRECTORS)

Susan L. Anderson
Bryn Mawr

John J. Bagnato
Johnstown

William G. Boyle
Pittsburgh

G. Daniel Carney
Pittsburgh

Chester C. Corse, Jr.
Pottsville

H. Robert Fiebach
Philadelphia

Joseph P. Flanagan, Jr.
Philadelphia

Richard H. Galloway
Greensburg

F. Hastings Griffin, Jr.
Newtown Square

James L. Hollinger
Norristown

Hon. Lawrence W. Kaplan
Pittsburgh

Stephanie F. Latimore
Harrisburg

Hon. Francis J. Leahey, Jr.
Ebensburg

James R. Ledwith
Berwyn

Marvin S. Lieber
Pittsburgh

Thomas S. Mansell
New Castle

Jane R. Maughan
Stroudsburg

Edwin L.R. McKean
Erie

William H. Murray
Cape May, NJ

Herbert R. Nurick
Harrisburg

Hon. William H. Platt
Allentown

Robert Raphael
Pittsburgh

Marvin J. Rudnitsky
Selinsgrove

William Z. Scott, Jr.
Bethlehem

Ruth M. Siegel
Hershey

Stanley H. Siegel
Lewistown

Ralph S. Snyder
Bala Cynwyd

Lee C. Swartz
Lemoyne

Nancy Hopkins Wentz
Norristown

Thomas G. Wilkinson, Jr.
Philadelphia

EXECUTIVE DIRECTOR

Richard L. McCoy
5080 Ritter Road, Mechanicsburg, PA 17055
717-796-0804 or 800-932-4637 ext. 2285
rmccoy@pbi.org

Preface

Preparation of this third edition of the *Eastern District Manual* would not have been possible without the cooperation and support of each of the district judges, bankruptcy judges, and magistrate judges sitting in the Eastern District of Pennsylvania. In particular, the guidance and encouragement provided by our extraordinary clerk of court, Michael E. Kunz, was invaluable and deeply appreciated.

With the exception of the Clerk's Office Procedural Handbook, all the information contained in this manual comes directly from this distinguished group of jurists. Each section was drafted on the basis of information provided by the judge it concerns. While there were numerous discussions about procedural matters between individual judges and the editors, the final decision as to the content of each section was made by the judge, not the editors. As such, this manual is an accurate resource on what is the right thing to do in most circumstances in typical matters pending before the judges sitting in the Eastern District of Pennsylvania.

Although it has a number of objectives, the primary purpose of the *Eastern District Manual* is to level the playing field for all lawyers—junior and senior, local and out-of-state, experienced and inexperienced—who find themselves serving as counsel in matters pending before the United States District Court for the Eastern District of Pennsylvania and the United States Bankruptcy Court for the Eastern District of Pennsylvania. This manual is intended to be a standard reference tool for trial lawyers handling real cases before the judges sitting in the Eastern District of Pennsylvania. It is designed to be an accurate source of important information that can be relied on when time is short and serious decisions have to be made.

To assist trial lawyers in determining what an individual judge prefers or requires in pretrial and trial practice and procedure, the format and content of the manual strongly favor the practical over the theoretical. The goal is to give busy lawyers an efficient way to locate the specific information needed to handle problems from A to Z in federal litigation. For example, among other things, the manual informs the reader whether the judge to whom a case is assigned:

A. permits correspondence from counsel;
B. allows counsel to communicate with his or her law clerks;
C. uses telephone conferences in lieu of requiring counsel to appear in person for status conferences;
D. requires submission of a formal motion for pro hac vice admissions;

E. permits oral argument on motions;
F. wants counsel to send courtesy copies of motion papers to chambers;
G. requires counsel to submit written proposals on initial scheduling;
H. uses a standard form of scheduling order;
I. follows different procedures in arbitration cases than in cases certified as involving more than $150,000;
J. requires a particular form of pretrial memorandum;
K. handles cases involving requests for injunctive relief differently from other cases;
L. uses a trial pool rather than dates certain for scheduling trials;
M. gives special consideration to out-of-town parties, attorneys, and witnesses;
N. allows note-taking by jurors;
O. permits counsel to participate in voir dire;
P. has any special policy regarding sidebar conferences;
Q. imposes time limits on opening statements or summations;
R. uses special procedures for videotaped testimony;
S. requires pre-marking and exchange of documentary and photographic exhibits and demonstrative evidence such as graphics and charts;
T. has a special policy on when counsel should offer exhibits into evidence;
U. requires the submission of proposed jury instructions in any particular form or at any particular time;
V. normally sends the exhibits admitted into evidence into the jury room during deliberations;
W. allows counsel to return to their offices rather than waiting in the courtroom during jury deliberations;
X. submits written interrogatories to the jury;
Y. permits counsel to interview jurors after the verdict has been recorded; and
Z. prefers to receive copies of the appellate briefs when an appeal is taken from a decision he or she renders.

This manual is intended to help trial lawyers solve real problems in the time-pressured world of federal litigation. Its true value will be determined by the lawyers who use it and the judges of the Eastern District of Pennsylvania before whom they appear. It is the sincere hope of the editors that it will serve them well.

Charles R. Bruton, Editor-in-Chief
Philadelphia, Pennsylvania

September 2013

Foreword and Caveat of the Chief Judges

This third edition of the *Eastern District Manual* is intended to be an aid to all those who practice before the United States District Court for the Eastern District of Pennsylvania and the United States Bankruptcy Court for the Eastern District of Pennsylvania. Its main purpose is to advise attorneys of what is expected and required of them in the administration of a typical case by the individual district court judges, bankruptcy judges, and magistrate judges now sitting in this district. It is important, however, for all who will use this manual to recognize that it is an aid to practice, not a rulebook. Accordingly, counsel should carefully review the following caveats.

1. The information and guidance provided in this manual do not constitute "rules of court," "rules of procedure," "rules of practice," or "guidelines" as those concepts are commonly understood. They are informal aids and suggestions intended to assist lawyers appearing in this district to prepare and present their cases efficiently and effectively.

2. The information contained in this manual is not binding on any judge. The practices and procedures described here are those currently being used by individual judges in typical cases assigned to them. In any given case, whether by reason of its complexity, simplicity, facts, or other circumstances, the practices and procedures discussed here may be modified without notice.

3. Nothing contained in this manual is intended to conflict with, supplant, or supersede the United States Code, the United States Bankruptcy Code, the Federal Rules of Civil Procedure, the Federal Rules of Criminal Procedure, the Federal Rules of Evidence, the Local Rules of Civil Procedure of the United States District Court for the Eastern District of Pennsylvania, the Local Rules of Criminal Procedure of the United States District Court for the Eastern District of Pennsylvania, or the Local Bankruptcy Rules of the United States Bankruptcy Court for the Eastern District of Pennsylvania. In the event that any practice or procedure discussed in this manual conflicts or is inconsistent with any official source, the official source is to be followed.

4. The information contained in this manual is *not* to be cited as authority or precedent.

Foreword and Caveat of the Chief Judges

5. The information contained in this manual may be modified or revised by any judge without notice. Such modifications or revisions may include any additions, deletions, or changes in practice or procedure that the judge may consider appropriate at the time.

On behalf of each of the judges now sitting in the Eastern District of Pennsylvania, we extend our appreciation to the Federal Courts Committee of the Philadelphia Bar Association for its sponsorship of this important and valuable project, and to Charles R. Bruton, Esquire, Donald W. Myers, Esquire, and Samuel W. Silver, Esquire, whose hard work and persistence made this publication possible.

/s/ Petrese B. Tucker

Petrese B. Tucker
Chief Judge,
United States District Court
for the Eastern District
of Pennsylvania

/s/ Eric L. Frank

Eric L. Frank
Chief Judge,
United States Bankruptcy Court
for the Eastern District
of Pennsylvania

/s/ Carol Sandra Moore Wells

Carol Sandra Moore Wells
Chief Magistrate Judge,
United States District Court for
the Eastern District of Pennsylvania

Philadelphia, Pennsylvania

September 2013

About the Editors

Charles R. Bruton, Esquire

Mr. Bruton is a member of Dentons US LLP, an international law firm, and is a trial lawyer in the firm's Intellectual Property and Technology Practice, based in Washington, DC. Mr. Bruton received a BA with honors from Northwestern University in 1968 and a JD from Stanford Law School in 1971, where he served as a member of the Stanford Law Review. From 1971 to 1975, Mr. Bruton served in the Judge Advocate General's Corps of the United States Navy, where, among other duties, he represented POWs returning from Vietnam and served as a United States military judge. In private practice since 1975, Mr. Bruton has served as trial and appellate counsel in dozens of cases in federal and state courts throughout the United States. He has handled major cases involving pharmaceuticals, generic drugs, medical devices, semiconductors, communication systems, software security systems, elevators, flooring products, bulk transfer technology, and a wide range of other products, systems, and technologies. He has also served as trial counsel in cases involving antitrust claims, class actions, construction disputes, toxic torts, franchises, trade secrets, and the Lanham Act.

Donald W. Myers, Esquire

Mr. Myers is a shareholder in Buchanan Ingersoll & Rooney PC, and is a member of the firm's Litigation Section, based in Philadelphia. Mr. Myers received a BA with honors from Michigan State University in 1994, a JD cum laude from Wayne State University in 1997, and an MBA from Wayne State University in 2000. From 1997 to 1999, Mr. Myers served as a law clerk for the Michigan Court of Appeals and from 1999 to 2001 he served as a law clerk to Chief Judge Lawrence P. Zatkoff of the United States District Court for the Eastern District of Michigan. In private practice since 2001, Mr. Myers has significant trial experience in all phases of federal and state court cases, as well as major commercial arbitrations, class actions, securities litigation, and injunctive proceedings. He also has extensive experience in the area of electronic discovery, and he frequently advises and assists clients in developing cost-effective strategies for e-discovery and litigation involving the preservation, collection, review, and production of electronically stored information.

About the Editors

Samuel W. Silver, Esquire

Mr. Silver is a partner in Schnader Harrison Segal & Lewis LLP, based in Philadelphia, where he chairs the Litigation Department, and has served on the firm's Executive Committee. Mr. Silver received an AB magna cum laude from Middlebury College in 1986 and a JD from the University of Michigan Law School in 1989. A commercial litigator, Mr. Silver has tried to verdict a wide variety of cases involving intellectual property, health care, securities, banking, insurance coverage, restrictive covenants, and theft of trade secrets. He concentrates on representing global manufacturers of products in litigation and product safety matters, and he has extensive experience in representing top members of the equestrian sport. Mr. Silver is a Fellow of the American College of Trial Lawyers, and has received numerous honors and awards for his pro bono and public interest work and efforts to improve the administration of justice.

Summary of Contents

Preface ix
Foreword and Caveat of the Chief Judges xi
About the Editors xiii
Table of Contents xvii

Part I
Practice and Procedures of Judges and Judges' Forms and Orders 1

        District Court Judges   *3*
        Bankruptcy Judges   *367*
        Magistrate Judges   *431*

Part II
Standing Orders *509*

Part III
Clerk's Office Procedural Handbook *521*

Table of Contents

Preface ix
Foreword and Caveat of the Chief Judges xi
About the Editors xiii
Summary of Contents xv

Part I
Practice and Procedures of Judges and Judges' Forms and Orders

District Court Judges

    Chief Judge Petrese B. Tucker 5

    Judge Harvey Bartle III 11

    Judge Michael M. Baylson 17
        Conference Information Report 22

    Judge Anita B. Brody 23
        Scheduling Order 29
        Attachment A 31
        Notice 32
        Attachment A - Proposed Discovery Plan Under Rule 26(f) 34
        Attachment B - Default Scheduling Order 35
        Rule 16 Conference Information Report 36

    Judge Ronald L. Buckwalter 37
        Pretrial and Trial Procedures 42

    Judge Stewart Dalzell 44
        Scheduling Policy Statement 50

    Judge Legrome D. Davis 51

    Judge Paul S. Diamond 57

    Judge J. William Ditter, Jr. 59
        Notice 64
        Scheduling Information Report 65

    Judge Jan E. DuBois 66
        Notice 73
        Rule 16 Conference Information Report 74
        Notice to Counsel—Scheduling and Discovery Policy 75
        Scheduling Order (Jury Trial) 77
        Scheduling Order (Nonjury Trial) 79

    Judge James Knoll Gardner 81
        Application for Continuance 101
        Jury Trial Attachment Order 102

Table of Contents

  Nonjury Trial Attachment Order 105
  Criminal Jury Trial Attachment Order 108
  Standing Order 110
  Rule 16 Telephone Conference Scheduling Order 111

Judge Mitchell Goldberg 113

Judge C. Darnell Jones II 119
  Report of Rule 26(f) Meeting 128

Judge J. Curtis Joyner 130
  Scheduling Order 135

Judge Robert F. Kelly 137
  Pretrial Order 142
  Cover Page 143
  Pretrial and Trial Procedure 144

Judge Edmund V. Ludwig 146
  Civil Trial SOP 152
  Case Management Policy Statement 153
  Use of Electronic Filing System 155
  C A S E Management Program 156
  Rule 16 Trial Scheduling Order 159
  Arbitration Scheduling Order 160
  Pretrial Preparation SOP 161
  SOP on Oral Argument 162
  Joint Discovery Schedule 163
  Format for Joint Submission 164

Judge Mary A. McLaughlin 165
  Courtroom Procedures 171
  Procedures for Voir Dire in a Civil Case 172
  Procedures for Voir Dire in a Criminal Case 173

Judge Thomas N. O'Neill, Jr. 174
  Notice Scheduling an Initial Pretrial Conference 180
  Standard Order Issued After Pretrial Conference 181

Judge John R. Padova 183
  Notice to Counsel 190
  Scheduling Information Report 192
  Fed.R.Civ.P. 16 Pretrial Scheduling Order (Standard Track) 193
  Trial de Novo for Arbitration Case 196
  Fed.R.Civ.P. 16 Pretrial Scheduling Order (Trial De Novo) 198

Judge Gene E.K. Pratter 200
  Criminal Continuance Form 212
  Sample Pro Se Order 213
  Guidelines for Trial and other Proceedings in the Courtroom 215
  Pilot Project Regarding Initial Discovery Protocols for
    Employment Cases Alleging Adverse Action 218
  Model Protective Order 225

Judge Nitza I. Quiñones Alejandro 228

Table of Contents

Judge L. Felipe Restrepo... 229
   Order Governing Electronic Discovery 237

Judge Eduardo C. Robreno... 240
   Joint Status Report Pursuant to Rule 26(f)........................ 247

Judge Cynthia M. Rufe.. 248
   Sample Scheduling Order... 253
   Scheduling Order Attachment 1 255
   Scheduling Order Attachment 2 256

Judge Juan R. Sánchez... 257
   Joint Rule 16 Conference Information Report...................... 268

Judge Timothy J. Savage 269
   Report of Rule 26(f) Meeting 276
   Order Governing Electronic Discovery 278

Judge Berle M. Schiller... 280
   Scheduling Order 284
   Rule 16 Conference Information Report 287

Judge Jeffrey L. Schmehl 288
   Joint Status Report Pursuant to Rule 26(f)........................ 295

Judge Norma L. Shapiro... 296
   Pretrial Conference Order 303
   Pretrial Scheduling/Status Conference Report..................... 304
   Adaptation of Form 35. Report of Parties' Planning Meeting 305
   Order Pursuant to Fed.R.Civ.P. 16 and 26,
      Local Civil Rules 16.1 and 16.2, and Civil Justice Expense
      and Delay Reduction Plan 307
   Special Management Track Case—Case Management Policy 310
   Pretrial Order No. 1 312
   Service List 314
   RICO Case Standing Order 315
   Code of Civility 317
   Working Rules of Professionalism 320

Judge Joel H. Slomsky 321
   Report of Rule 26(f) Meeting 330
   Order Governing Electronic Discovery 332
   Speedy Trial Act Acknowledgment of Rights 335

Judge Lawrence F. Stengel.. 336
   Joint Status Report Pursuant to Rule 26(f)........................ 344
   Order Governing Electronic Discovery 345

Judge R. Barclay Surrick 347

Judge William H. Yohn, Jr... 352
   Scheduling Order 358
   Trial Guidelines 361
   Notice to Counsel Regarding Court's Scheduling and Discovery Policy ... 364

Table of Contents

Bankruptcy Judges

Chief Bankruptcy Judge Eric L. Frank 369
    Pretrial Order #1 376
    Order Granting an Expedited Hearing 379
    Order Granting Extension of Automatic Stay under § 362(c)(3)
        Without Opposition 380
    Order Approving Allowance of Compensation to Debtor's Counsel
        (Chapter 13) 381
    Order Granting Motion for Leave to Conduct 2004 Examination 382
    Order Converting Case under Chapter 7 to Case under
        Chapter 13 383
    Order Approving Debtor's Motion to Modify Confirmed
        Chapter 13 Plan 384
    Order Granting Motion to Avoid Judicial Lien on Real and
        Personal Property—§ 522(f) 385

Bankruptcy Judge Magdeline D. Coleman 386
    Pretrial Scheduling Order 392

Bankruptcy Judge Richard E. Fehling 395
    Pretrial Order #1 402
    Appendix "B-1"—Order Setting Expedited Hearing to Consider
        Motion 405
    Appendix "B-2"—Order on Avoidance of a Lien
        Pursuant to 11 U.S.C. § 522(f) 406

Bankruptcy Judge Jean K. FitzSimon 407
    Pretrial Scheduling Order 414
    Order on Avoidance of a Lien Pursuant to 11 U.S.C. § 522(f) 417
    Order Setting Expedited Hearing 418

Bankruptcy Judge Bruce Fox 419

Bankruptcy Judge Stephen Raslavich 423
    Pretrial Order 428

Magistrate Judges

Chief Magistrate Judge Carol Sandra Moore Wells 433

Magistrate Judge M. Faith Angell 438
    Scheduling Order 444

Magistrate Judge Linda K. Caracappa 445
    Settlement Conference Order 450
    Settlement Conference Summary 451

Magistrate Judge Jacob P. Hart 452
    Standing Order re Pretrial Stipulation (Jury Trial) 456
    Standing Order re Pretrial Stipulation (Bench Trial) 457
    Scheduling Order 458
    Backup Scheduling Order 459
    Courtroom Rules 460
    Settlement Conference Schedule 461

Magistrate Judge Elizabeth T. Hey 462
    Scheduling Order—Jury 465
    Scheduling Order—Bench 466
    Standing Order—Jury 467
    Standing Order—Bench 468
    Settlement Schedule Order 469

Magistrate Judge Henry S. Perkin 470
    Settlement Conference Scheduling Order 476
    Consent To Have Ex Parte Communication With United States
        Magistrate Judge 477

Magistrate Judge Arnold C. Rapoport 478

Magistrate Judge Timothy R. Rice 482
    Rule 16 Pretrial Scheduling Order—Standard Track Cases 485
    Settlement Conference Notice 488
    Settlement Conference Summary 489

Magistrate Judge Thomas J. Rueter 490

Magistrate Judge Lynne A. Sitarski 494
    Settlement Conference Order 500
    Confidential Settlement Conference Summary 501

Magistrate Judge David R. Strawbridge 502

Part II
Standing Orders

Court Approval of Reporters Required for Taking of Depositions 511
Calendar Control 511
Civil Suspense Docket 512
Bankruptcy Administration Orders 512
Assignment Procedure for Habeas Corpus and Social Security Cases
    for United States Magistrates 513
Order Adopting Civil Justice Expense and Delay Reduction Plan 514
Order Extending Civil Justice Expense and Delay Reduction Plan 514
Approval of Pre-Judgment Notice of 28 U.S.C. § 3101(d) 515
Standing Orders Re: 1993 Amendments to Federal Rules of Civil Procedure 516
Presentence Investigations and Time Limits 517
Standing Order Re: Sentencing Reform Act of 1984 518

Part III
Clerk's Office Procedural Handbook

Table of Contents 525
    Electronic Case Filing System 529
    Filing a Civil Action 532
    Documents 537

Motions 542
Summons 542
Jurisdiction 542
Subpoenas 543
Foreign Subpoenas 544
Discovery 544
Temporary Restraining Order (T.R.O.) 545
Writs of Garnishment, Attachment and Execution 545
Filing of Judgment by Default 545
Multidistrict Litigation 545
Arbitration 546
Appeals 547
Certification of Judgment (AO 451) 548
Referral to United States Magistrate Judge 548
Post Judgment Interest Rate 549
Taxation of Costs 549
Courtroom Deputy Clerks 589
Standing Order Re: Sentencing Reform Act of 1984 594
After-hours Contact for Emergency Matters 594
After-hours Filing Depository 594
Opinions/Correspondence Clerk 594
How to Find a Case Number 594
Clerk's Index File by Nature of Suit 595
Copywork 595
Records Room 595
Credit Card Collection Network 595
Required Check Conversion Disclosure 596
Depositing/Withdrawing Monies 596
Fines 597
Central Violations Bureau (CVB) 597
Bail Bonds 597
Attorney Admissions 598
Court Reporting/Recording Services 598
Electronic Transcripts of Court Proceedings 598
Digital Audio File Electronic Access 599
Videotape Services 599
Video Teleconferencing 599
Courtroom Technology 599
Interpreters' Services 599
Jury Selection 600
Inclement Weather 600
PACER—Public Access to Court Electronic Records 600
Internet Website 601
Local Rules 602
Portable Electronic Devices and Public Telephone Locations .. 602
Directory of Public Telephone Locations 602

Personnel Directory 604

List of Appendices 613

Index 615

Appendix A:	Electronic Case Filing Procedures	617
Appendix B:	PDF File Information	624
Appendix C:	Validation of Signature Form, Local Rule 5.1.2	625
Appendix D:	Electronic Case Filing Account Registration Form	627
Appendix E:	ECF Training Application Form	631
Appendix F:	Designation Form	633
Appendix G:	Disclosure Statement Form	634
Appendix H:	Civil Cover Sheet	636
Appendix I:	Civil Case Management Track Designation Form	638
Appendix J:	Modification or Redaction of Personal Identifiers, Local Rule 5.1.3	640
Appendix K:	Consent to Facsimile Transmission of Notices of Orders	641
Appendix L:	Mail Information Form	644
Appendix M:	Judges' Room Numbers and Zip Code + 4-Digit Extension Numbers	646
Appendix N:	Summons in a Civil Action, Proof of Service	648
Appendix O:	Writ of Execution	650
Appendix P:	Appellate Transcript Purchase Order	656
Appendix Q:	Consent to Proceed before a United States Magistrate Judge	657
Appendix R:	Bill of Costs	659
Appendix S:	Special Listing Agreement	661
Appendix T:	Busy Slip	662
Appendix U:	Standing Order Re: Sentencing Reform Act of 1984	663
Appendix V:	Credit Card Collection Network Authorization Form	664
Appendix W:	Bail Bond Secured by Property or Real Estate Bond	669
Appendix X:	Attorney Admissions Application	673
Appendix Y:	Transcript Order Form	678
Appendix Z:	Tape Order Form	680
Appendix AA:	Amendment to Local Rule 5.1.2 and Notice of Electronic Availability of Transcripts	681
Appendix BB:	Digital Audio File Electronic Access Pilot Program	685
Appendix CC:	PACER—Public Access to Court Electronic Records Registration Form	686
Appendix DD:	Directory of Court-Automated Services	687
Appendix EE:	ECF Electronic Filing of Complaints Information Form	695

Part I

Practice and Procedures of Judges and Judges' Forms and Orders

District Court Judges

Chief Judge Petrese B. Tucker

Chief Judge Tucker was nominated by President William J. Clinton to the United States District Court for the Eastern District of Pennsylvania in 1999, and was sworn in on July 14, 2000. She became Chief Judge on May 1, 2013. Prior to becoming a federal judge, Judge Tucker served 13 years as a state judge in the First Judicial District of Pennsylvania. During her tenure in the Pennsylvania Common Pleas Court, Judge Tucker served in the Family Court Division, the criminal and civil sections of the Trial Division, and was appointed by the Pennsylvania Supreme Court as the administrative judge of the Orphans' Court Division. Before becoming a member of the judiciary, Judge Tucker was assistant chief of the Rape Unit and assistant chief of the Child Abuse Unit of the Philadelphia District Attorney's Office. In addition, her prior work experience includes positions as senior trial attorney for the Southeastern Pennsylvania Transportation Authority (SEPTA), and adjunct professorships at the Great Lakes College Association and trial advocacy courses at Temple University School of Law. Judge Tucker is a member of the Barristers Association of Philadelphia, past member of the Pennsylvania Conference of State Trial Judges, and the National Council of Juvenile and Family Court Judges. As a member of the Philadelphia, Pennsylvania, National, and American Bar Associations, Judge Tucker has chaired and worked on numerous committees. She has received many meritorious distinguished service awards for her significant contributions to the community. Judge Tucker is also a board member of the Avenue of the Arts, Incorporated.

PRELIMINARY GENERAL MATTERS

1. **Correspondence with the Court.** Judge Tucker permits correspondence with the court concerning scheduling, other routine matters, and to advise the court that a case has been settled or dismissed. Otherwise, all communications with the court should be made by the filing of pleadings, motions, applications, briefs, or legal memoranda.

2. **Communications with Law Clerks.** Judge Tucker permits counsel to speak with her law clerks about administrative or scheduling matters.

3. **Telephone Conferences.** Judge Tucker may hold telephone conferences to resolve scheduling matters or discovery disputes. Counsel will be notified of the date and time for the telephone conference. It will be the responsibility of counsel for the moving party to initiate the conference and to contact chambers after all parties are present on the call.

4. **Oral Arguments and Evidentiary Hearings.** Judge Tucker does not set aside certain days or times for oral argument, motions, or evidentiary hearings. Hearings and argument are scheduled when warranted.

5. **Pro Hac Vice Admissions.** Judge Tucker prefers that a written motion for admission be made by associate counsel of record. The admission of pro hac vice counsel does not relieve associate counsel of responsibility for the matter before the court.

CIVIL CASES
Pretrial Procedures

1. **Pretrial Conferences.** Judge Tucker regularly schedules an in-person initial pretrial conference soon after the answer is filed or the case is transferred to her. Counsel is required to submit a Rule 16 pretrial conference information report prior to the pretrial conference.

At the pretrial conference, counsel will be expected to be prepared to discuss those topics listed in Local Rule of Civil Procedure 16.1(a) and Rule 16(b) and (c) of the Federal Rules of Civil Procedure as well as other appropriate matters. Counsel should also be prepared to discuss the progress of self-executing disclosures pursuant to Rule 26(a)(1) of the Federal Rules of Civil Procedure.

A scheduling order will be issued after the pretrial conference setting forth deadlines for the completion of discovery, the filing of dispositive motions, the filing of pretrial submissions, and a date when the case will be placed in the trial pool.

Continuances and Extensions

1. *General Policy.* Judge Tucker has a general policy of adhering to originally scheduled dates unless a compelling reason is presented that justifies a change. This policy applies to briefing schedules, oral argument, evidentiary hearings, discovery deadlines, and trial dates.

2. *Requests for Extensions and Continuances.* Counsel should advise the court immediately, and *before the date has run,* of any compelling reason justifying an extension or continuance of any originally scheduled date. Any request for extension or continuance may be made by letter and set forth in detail the reason or basis for the request and noting the agreement or disagreement of all other counsel as well as the period of delay requested.

General Motion Practice

1. *Oral Argument on Motions.* Judge Tucker generally schedules oral argument on motions if requested by counsel and if she believes it will be helpful in the court's decision-making process.

2. *Reply and Surreply Briefs.* Judge Tucker generally discourages the filing of reply and surreply briefs. Requests for time to do so should be made by written motion.

3. *Chambers Copies of Motions.* Judge Tucker does not require courtesy copies of motions.

4. *Timing.* The parties *must not* file any dispositive motions before attending a settlement conference with Magistrate Judge Caracappa. All motions to amend the complaint, join or add additional defendants, or name John Doe defendants should be filed on or before the date set by the court. All motions in limine should be filed and served at least five business days before the trial date. All other motions should be filed and served prior to the close of the discovery period. Any motions filed in violation of this order will be deemed waived unless good cause is shown.

5. *Page Limitations and Numbering. All* briefs must be on 8.5 by 11 inch sequentially numbered pages. The text must be double-spaced. Headings and footnotes may be single-spaced. The font must be 12 point. The margins must be one inch on all four sides. No brief filed in support of or in opposition to *any* motion may exceed 25 pages in length without prior leave of court. Any brief filed in support of or in opposition to any motion that exceeds 10 pages in length *must* be accompanied by a table of contents. Reply briefs are generally not helpful and are discouraged by the court; as such, reply briefs cannot be filed without prior leave of court. A reply brief is limited to a maximum of seven pages, and must be filed within five business days of the filing of the opposing party's response.

6. **Motions for Summary Judgment.** A party against whom a claim, counterclaim, or cross-claim is asserted or a declaratory judgment is sought may, at any time, move with or without supporting affidavits for a summary judgment in the party's favor as to all or any part of them. All motions for summary judgment or partial summary judgment should be filed and served on or before the date set by the court.

7. **Initial Filing of Moving Party.** A party referred to and moving under Fed.R.Civ.P. 56(b) may move without reference to supporting affidavits or other evidence and, in doing so, the party making the motion should:

    (1) identify in outline form the issues and/or sub-issues as to which the motion is directed, for example, referring to the pleadings;

    (2) affirm, on the basis prescribed in Fed.R.Civ.P. 11, that there is no legally sufficient evidentiary basis to support the issues so identified; and

    (3) request judgment as provided in Fed.R.Civ.P. 56(c).

    The initial filing by the moving party *should not exceed three double-spaced, typewritten pages.*

8. **Response of Non-moving Party.** The party against whom the motion for summary judgment is addressed should file and serve a response on or before the close of two weeks from the initial filing of the moving party. The response, subject to provision of Fed.R.Civ.P. 56(e) and (f), should be supported with affidavits, depositions, documents, or other evidence permitted by those provisions. Where applicable, references to such evidence must include *specific* citations to exhibit, page, and line number.

9. **Reply of Moving Party.** The movant should file a reply as permitted by Fed.R.Civ.P. 56(e) and (f). Such a reply must be filed no later than 10 days after the response is served. The reply must *specify* the relevant exhibit, page, and line numbers when referring to the record.

Discovery Matters

1. **Length of Discovery Period and Extensions.** Judge Tucker generally permits 90 to 120 days for discovery unless a longer period of time is dictated by the nature of the case.
    Judge Tucker generally allows extensions of 30 to 60 days when warranted.

2. **Discovery Disputes and Dispute Resolution.** Judge Tucker is available to schedule discovery disputes by telephone conference or may forward the matter to a magistrate judge for resolution.
    Judge Tucker encourages alternate dispute resolution at all stages of the case.

3. **Expert Witnesses.** The time for disclosure of the identity of experts and for discovery pursuant to Fed.R.Civ.P. 26(a)(2)(B) will be set forth in the scheduling order issued at the conclusion of the Rule 16 pretrial conference.

Settlement

1. **General Approach to Settlement and Nonjury Cases.** Judge Tucker encourages settlement at all stages of a case. Settlement conferences may be initiated by counsel for either party.

2. **Referral of Settlement Negotiations to a Magistrate Judge.** Judge Tucker generally refers cases to a magistrate judge for settlement negotiations.

Trial Procedure

1. Scheduling Cases. Judge Tucker's practice is to assign a date for placing a case in the trial pool at the time of the initial pretrial conference. Once a case is placed in the trial pool, counsel, parties, and witnesses should be ready to start trial upon 24 hours telephone notice. Counsel will not be required to commence trial less than 24 hours after completing trial in another case.

It is the responsibility of counsel (or pro se or unrepresented parties) to contact Judge Tucker's courtroom deputy with respect to the status and movement of Judge Tucker's trial pool.

2. Conflicts of Counsel. Judge Tucker requires that counsel notify the court immediately of any unavoidable and compelling professional or personal conflicts affecting the trial schedule.

3. Cases Involving Out-of-Town Parties or Witnesses. Judge Tucker schedules the trial of cases involving out-of-town counsel, parties, or witnesses the same as all other cases. Judge Tucker leaves the scheduling of witnesses to counsel.

4. Note-taking by Jurors. Judge Tucker generally decides on a case-by-case basis on whether to permit jurors to take notes.

5. Trial Briefs. Judge Tucker requires the submission of a trial brief no later than five days before the trial pool date.

6. Voir Dire. Judge Tucker generally permits counsel to conduct the voir dire in civil matters. Judge Tucker conducts the voir dire in all criminal cases.

7. Sidebars. Judge Tucker permits sidebar conferences when appropriate.

8. Motions in Limine. Judge Tucker requires motions in limine to be submitted no later than five days before the trial pool date.

9. Examinations of Witnesses Out of Sequence. Judge Tucker generally will permit counsel to take the testimony of a witness out of turn for the convenience of the witness unless it is objected to by opposing counsel.

10. Opening Statements and Summaries. Judge Tucker generally does not place time limits on opening statements or summations by counsel. However, Judge Tucker believes that 20 to 30 minutes is usually adequate for an opening and 30 to 45 minutes is usually adequate for summations in routine cases.

11. Offers of Proof. Judge Tucker requires counsel to inquire of each other privately as to offers of proof regarding any witness or exhibit expected to be offered. If counsel cannot resolve such matters, Judge Tucker will rule on them upon application before a witness testifies or an exhibit is offered into evidence and at a time when the jury will not be inconvenienced.

12. Examination of Witnesses by More Than One Attorney. Judge Tucker will permit more than one attorney for a party to examine different witnesses or to argue different points of law before the court. Ordinarily, Judge Tucker will not permit more than one attorney to examine the same witness, or to address the jury during the opening statement or summation.

13. Examination of Witnesses Beyond Redirect and Recross. Judge Tucker has no general policy regarding further examination of a witness after redirect or recross has been completed. Where appropriate, she will allow it.

14. Videotaped Testimony. Videotaped testimony should begin with the witness being sworn. Judge Tucker requires that a list of all objections to videotaped trial testimony and a copy of the transcript should be submitted to the court well in advance of the offering of such evidence.

15. Reading of Material Into the Record. Judge Tucker has no special practice or policy regarding reading stipulations, pleadings, or discovery material into the record. When appropriate, she will allow it.

16. Exhibits. Exhibits must be pre-marked and pre-exchanged. A bench copy of trial exhibits should be provided to the court on the first day of trial. The trial exhibits should be accompanied by an exhibit list that describes each exhibit.

As long as each exhibit is offered and admitted into evidence before it is shown to the jury, Judge Tucker has no particular preference as to when counsel should offer exhibits into evidence. At the conclusion of a party's case-in-chief, counsel should make sure that all exhibits intended to be offered into evidence either have been or are offered into evidence.

Unless there is an objection from opposing counsel placed on the record, exhibits are released at the close of trial to the custody of the party who offered them and must be picked up within 48 hours after the close of trial or they will be destroyed.

17. Directed Verdict Motions. Motions for judgments as a matter of law in jury trials under Fed.R.Civ.P. 50(a) and motions for judgment on partial findings in nonjury trials under Fed.R.Civ.P. 52(c) may be oral or written. Judge Tucker will hear oral argument on such motions if counsel request it.

18. Proposed Jury Instructions and Verdict Forms. Judge Tucker requires proposed jury instructions and verdict forms to be filed with the clerk and served on the court at least three days before the case is placed on the trial list.

A courtesy copy of the proposed jury interrogatories, jury instructions, and verdict forms will be submitted to the chambers of Judge Tucker on a clearly labeled disk in WordPerfect format and/or by electronic mail.

Jury Deliberations

1. Written Jury Instructions. Ordinarily, Judge Tucker will provide counsel with a draft of the proposed instructions, but does not provide a copy to the jury.

2. Exhibits in the Jury Room. After the close of the charge, counsel will review the exhibits among themselves to determine which exhibits will go out to the jury *if and when requested by the jury*. Any disputes will be resolved by the court.

3. Handling of Jury Requests to Read Back Testimony or Replay Tapes. At the jury's request, if the transcript is available, Judge Tucker will consider allowing the reading of the appropriate portions back to the jury and replaying of audiotapes and videotapes.

4. Availability of Counsel During Jury Deliberations. Counsel should be available on 10 minutes notice during jury deliberations. As a practical matter, this means that counsel must stay in or very near the courthouse or have an associate present.

5. Interviewing the Jury. Post-trial discussions with jurors by counsel will not be permitted.

CRIMINAL CASES

1. Approach to Oral Argument and Motions. Judge Tucker will grant oral argument on motions in criminal cases if she believes it will assist her in her decision-making process. Hearings on motions to suppress evidence and *Starks* hearings will usually be held in advance of trial.

2. Pretrial Conferences. Judge Tucker conducts pretrial conferences in criminal cases as needed.

3. Voir Dire. Judge Tucker conducts voir dire in all criminal cases. Judge Tucker requires counsel to submit proposed voir dire questions at least three days prior to the trial date.

4. Proposed Jury Instructions and Verdict Forms. Judge Tucker requires that counsel for each party submit to the court and serve upon each other, proposed points for charge and any proposed jury interrogatories at least five days before the trial date. Each point for charge and proposed jury interrogatory should be numbered and on a separate sheet of paper identifying the name of the requesting party. Supplemental points for charge will be permitted during and at the conclusion of the trial. Points for charge should be accompanied by appropriate citations of legal authority.

5. Guilty Plea Memoranda. Judge Tucker requires counsel for the government to submit a guilty plea memorandum at least two days prior to the date of the plea hearing. Such a memorandum must include the elements of each offense to which the defendant is pleading guilty and legal citations for those elements.

6. Sentencing Memoranda. Judge Tucker encourages the submission of sentencing memoranda by both counsel for the government and the defendant(s).

OTHER GENERAL MATTERS

Judge Tucker expects counsel to be punctual for all conferences, hearings, and trials. She also expects counsel at all times to be civil to one another as well as to all parties, witnesses, and court personnel.

In all courtroom proceedings, Judge Tucker expects counsel to stand when addressing the court or when examining witnesses as well as when the jury is entering or exiting the courtroom. Counsel also may approach the witnesses with the permission of the court.

In general, Judge Tucker expects counsel to bring matters to her attention only after they have been discussed with opposing counsel.

Judge Harvey Bartle III

Judge Bartle was born on June 6, 1941, in Bryn Mawr, Pennsylvania. He graduated cum laude from Princeton University with an A.B. in 1962 and received his LL.B. cum laude from the University of Pennsylvania Law School in 1965. Judge Bartle was admitted to the Pennsylvania Supreme Court in 1965. From 1965 to 1967 he served as a law clerk to the Honorable John Morgan Davis of the United States District Court for the Eastern District of Pennsylvania. After engaging in private practice with the law firm of Dechert Price & Rhoads in Philadelphia from 1967 to 1979, he served as the Pennsylvania insurance commissioner from 1979 to 1980. He was the Pennsylvania attorney general from 1980 to 1981. He then returned to private practice at Dechert Price & Rhoads. Judge Bartle was appointed to the United States District Court for the Eastern District of Pennsylvania on September 16, 1991. He assumed senior status on October 1, 2011.

PRELIMINARY GENERAL MATTERS

1. **Correspondence with the Court.** Counsel may write to Judge Bartle to request an extension of time and for all matters pertaining to scheduling. Judge Bartle does not permit correspondence in lieu of formal discovery or contested motions or other substantive matters that should be made of record.

2. **Communications with Law Clerks.** Judge Bartle has no objection if law clerks are used as vehicles for relaying information to the court. He does not permit law clerks to give advice to counsel.

3. **Telephone Conferences.** Judge Bartle will use telephone conferences for scheduling changes, extensions of time, and similar matters. He often has conference calls on discovery motions. Judge Bartle requests that counsel or a conference call operator place the call.

4. **Oral Arguments and Evidentiary Hearings.** Judge Bartle does not set aside specific days or times for oral arguments or evidentiary hearings. Arguments and hearings are scheduled on an ad hoc basis.

5. **Pro Hac Vice Admissions.** Judge Bartle expects motions for pro hac vice admissions to be in writing. He requires the attorney seeking such admission to submit a signed affidavit or certification stating that he or she is a member in good standing of the bar of another state.

CIVIL CASES
Pretrial Procedure

1. **Pretrial Conferences.** After the entry of appearance by defense counsel in civil actions, Judge Bartle schedules a status conference in chambers. At this status conference, counsel are expected to be prepared to discuss jurisdictional defects; possibility of amicable settlements; alternative dispute resolution; time limitations for joining additional parties and amending pleadings, if necessary; scheduling for discovery deadlines, filing of motions, filing of pretrial memoranda, and future pretrial conferences; scheduling a date for trial; and any other appropriate matter. Judge Bartle enters a scheduling order following this conference.

Prior to attending this conference, parties are expected to have conferred with each other about each of these items, including discussion of settlement.

Continuances and Extensions

1.   General Policy.   Since trial dates are set well in advance, normally at the time of the initial conference, Judge Bartle is extremely reluctant to grant continuances—especially if the attorneys have not been diligent in moving the case forward. The court will not accept accommodations counsel may extend to each other during the discovery period as a reason to extend the discovery deadline or the trial date.

Judge Bartle will permit extension of discovery deadlines only upon showing of good cause.

General Motion Practice

Except as set forth herein, motion practice will be conducted in accordance with Local Civil Rule 7.1.

The originals of all motions and briefs must be filed with the clerk. *A copy of them must be delivered to Judge Bartle's chambers, including documents that are submitted using the Electronic Case Filing (ECF) system.*

A reply brief, addressing arguments raised in the brief in opposition to the motion, may be filed and served by the moving party *within seven days* after service of the brief in opposition to the motion unless the court sets a different schedule. However, the court will not necessarily delay its decision while awaiting a reply brief.

No further briefs may be filed, and no extension of time will be granted without leave of court for good cause shown.

Except with leave of court for good cause shown, no supporting brief and no brief in opposition may exceed 25 pages and no reply brief may exceed 15 pages. *Every factual assertion in a brief must be supported by a citation to the record where that fact may be found.* Both legal citations and citations to the record must include pinpoint cites.

Judge Bartle does not routinely hear oral argument on motions, but will consider it on request of counsel or if he believes it will assist him in deciding the motion.

Discovery Matters

1.   Length of Discovery Period and Extensions.   The length of time permitted for discovery depends upon the nature of each case. Judge Bartle generally permits up to six months of discovery, except for more complex litigation.

2.   Discovery Disputes.   When a discovery dispute arises, counsel are strongly urged to settle it among themselves. However, if after making a good-faith effort, counsel are unable to resolve a disputed issue, counsel for the aggrieved party must file with the court a motion in conformity with Local Civil Rule 26.1(b), with a form of order, and short brief not to exceed five pages describing the disputed issue(s). The court will normally schedule a telephone conference with counsel to discuss the motion before the filing of any responsive brief. In most cases, the court expects to rule promptly on discovery motions and often decides such motions during the telephone conference. *All motions must contain the certification required under Local Civil Rule 26.1(f).*

3.   Confidentiality Agreements.   Judge Bartle will approve a confidentiality order if the order includes a detailed statement demonstrating that good cause exists for the protective order. See *Pansy v. Borough of Stroudsburg,* 23 F.3d 772, 786 (3d Cir. 1994). All such orders must contain the following language or language substantially similar:

> The court retains the right to allow disclosure of any subject covered by this stipulation or to modify this stipulation at any time in the interest of justice.

4.   **Expert Witnesses.** Parties should identify expert witnesses and provide the experts' written reports pursuant to the scheduling order entered in the particular case. Failure to do so will bar the use of the expert's testimony at trial.

Settlement

1.   **General Approach to Settlement.** Judge Bartle strongly encourages settlement. He believes that the court's involvement in settlement conferences is generally helpful and will become involved in settlement of jury cases. In nonjury cases and sometimes in jury cases, Judge Bartle will refer settlement negotiations to a magistrate judge.

2.   **Referral of Settlement Negotiations to Another District Court Judge.** Judge Bartle rarely refers settlement negotiations to another district court judge.

Arbitration

1.   **General Approach to Arbitration Cases.** In arbitration cases, Judge Bartle normally does not schedule a status conference or settlement conference unless requested by counsel to do so. Appeals from arbitration are scheduled for trial promptly.

Proposed Final Pretrial Memoranda

1.   **Required Form of Pretrial Memoranda.** Judge Bartle requires the parties to submit pretrial memoranda addressing the subject matter set forth in Local Civil Rule 16.1(c)(1) through 16.1(c)(7). Counsel should carefully review and follow the terms of Judge Bartle's scheduling orders.

Injunctions

1.   **Scheduling and Expedited Discovery.** Judge Bartle will schedule hearings for preliminary injunctions promptly. He permits (or orders) expedited discovery in injunctive matters.

2.   **Proposed Findings of Fact and Conclusions of Law.** Judge Bartle permits the submission of proposed findings of fact and conclusions of law in injunction cases.

Trial Procedure

1.   **Scheduling of Cases.** Each case on Judge Bartle's calendar is assigned a month when it will be placed in the trial pool. He often specially lists cases for a day certain and, in any event, will advise counsel as soon as possible when each case will be called for trial. The court may start as early as 9:00 a.m. and may sit until 5:00 p.m. or later.

2.   **Conflicts of Counsel.** When counsel become aware of professional or personal conflicts that may affect the trial schedule, they should notify Judge Bartle and opposing counsel immediately.

3.   **Cases Involving Out-of-Town Parties or Witnesses.** Judge Bartle has no special policy for cases involving out-of-town attorneys, parties, or witnesses.

4.   **Note-taking by Jurors.** Judge Bartle permits note-taking by jurors.

5.   **Trial Briefs.** Judge Bartle encourages the submission of trial briefs when they are necessary or likely to be helpful to the court.

6.   **Voir Dire.** Judge Bartle's usual practice in civil matters is to conduct voir dire himself and, if appropriate, will ask questions submitted by counsel.

7.   **Sidebars.** Judge Bartle holds sidebar conferences when necessary.

8. In Limine Motions. Judge Bartle normally hears any necessary in limine motions immediately prior to trial or during trial unless an earlier ruling will assist settlement discussions or the trial of the case. He prefers such motions to be in writing and filed sufficiently in advance of trial, so that he can consider the motion and make an appropriate ruling.

9. Examination of Witnesses Out of Sequence. Judge Bartle is willing to take witnesses out of turn for their convenience, particularly when there is no objection by opposing counsel.

10. Opening Statements and Summations. Judge Bartle is flexible but will place time limits on opening statements and summations. He will discuss the time needed with counsel prior to the speeches.

11. Examination of Witnesses or Argument by More Than One Attorney. Judge Bartle will not permit more than one attorney for a party to examine the same witness.

12. Examination of Witnesses Beyond Redirect and Recross. Judge Bartle does not have any general policy concerning examination beyond redirect and recross.

13. Videotaped Testimony. Judge Bartle requires counsel to view all videotaped depositions for the purpose of editing the videotape and resolving material objections before offering the videotape as evidence.

14. Reading of Material Into the Record. Judge Bartle has no special practice on reading stipulations, pleadings, or discovery materials into the record.

15. Preparation of Exhibits. Before commencement of trial, exhibits are to be pre-marked and exchanged by counsel. Counsel should provide Judge Bartle with two copies of each exhibit and a schedule of exhibits that briefly describes each exhibit.

16. Offering Exhibits Into Evidence. Judge Bartle has no general policy as to when exhibits should be offered into evidence. When the number of exhibits in a case is large, Judge Bartle prefers counsel to reach advance agreement as to the admission of as many exhibits as possible.

17. Directed Verdict Motions. Judge Bartle hears directed verdict motions outside the hearing of the jury.

18. Proposed Jury Instructions and Verdict Forms. Judge Bartle's usual practice is that at least five working days before the case is placed in the trial pool or listed for trial, each party will submit to the court, and serve on each other, two copies of proposed points for charge and any proposed special jury interrogatories. Each point for charge and proposed jury interrogatory must be numbered and on a separate sheet of paper identifying the name of the requesting party. Supplemental points for charge will be permitted during and at the conclusion of the trial. Points for charge should be accompanied by appropriate citations of legal authority.

19. Proposed Findings of Fact and Conclusions of Law. Judge Bartle requires the submission of proposed findings of fact and conclusions of law in nonjury cases. Counsel are to submit them in accordance with the scheduling order entered in each action.

20. Decisions in Nonjury Cases. Counsel should be prepared for oral argument immediately following the close of all the evidence in a nonjury trial. Except in complex cases, it is Judge Bartle's usual practice to issue his ruling from the bench within a few days. Normally, Judge Bartle does not allow post-trial briefs.

Jury Deliberations

1. **Written Jury Instructions.** Judge Bartle provides counsel with a copy of proposed jury instructions for review in advance of a charge conference. After reading the charge to the jury, he provides each juror with a copy. Judge Bartle permits counsel to put objections to the charge on the record before the jury retires.

2. **Exhibits in the Jury Room.** Judge Bartle's general rule is that (except for weapons and drugs) if an exhibit is admitted into evidence, it goes into the jury room.

3. **Availability of Counsel During Jury Deliberations.** Judge Bartle prefers counsel remain in the courthouse during jury deliberations. Counsel should be available in case questions arise from the jury during its deliberation.

4. **Taking the Verdict and Special Interrogatories.** In most civil cases, Judge Bartle submits written interrogatories to the jury. A copy of such interrogatories is given to each juror.

5. **Polling the Jury.** If there is a request to poll the jury, the deputy clerk polls the jury.

6. **Interviewing the Jury.** Judge Bartle permits counsel to interview the jurors after the verdict has been recorded and the jury has been discharged. However, jurors are told they are under no obligation to speak with counsel.

CRIMINAL CASES

1. **Approach to Oral Argument and Motions.** Judge Bartle will grant oral argument on motions in criminal cases if he believes it will assist him in deciding the motions. Hearings on motions to suppress evidence and *Starks* hearings will usually be held in advance of trial.

2. **Pretrial Conferences.** Judge Bartle holds pretrial conferences in criminal cases as needed.

3. **Voir Dire.** Judge Bartle conducts the voir dire in criminal cases, and he encourages counsel to submit proposed voir dire questions.

4. **Proposed Jury Instructions and Verdict Forms.** Judge Bartle requires that at least seven working days before the date the case is set for trial, each party must submit to the court and serve on each other, two copies of proposed points for charge and any proposed jury interrogatories. Each point for charge and proposed jury interrogatory must be numbered and on a separate sheet of paper identifying the name of the requesting party. Supplemental points for charge will be permitted during and at the conclusion of the trial. Points for charge should be accompanied by appropriate citations of legal authority.

5. **Guilty Plea Memoranda.** Judge Bartle requires the government to submit a guilty plea memorandum two days prior to the guilty plea. Such a memorandum must include the elements of each offense to which the defendant is pleading guilty and legal citations for such elements.

6. **Sentencing Memoranda.** Judge Bartle encourages the submission of sentencing memoranda by both the government and the defendant.

OTHER GENERAL MATTERS

Judge Bartle expects counsel to be punctual for all conferences, hearings, and trials. He also expects counsel at all times to be civil to one another as well as to all parties, witnesses, and court personnel.

In all courtroom proceedings, Judge Bartle expects counsel to stand when addressing the court. However, counsel may remain seated when examining witnesses. Counsel also may approach the witnesses with permission of the court.

Stipulations should be sent to Judge Bartle's chambers for review and not to the clerk. Judge Bartle requires that all stipulations be submitted to him for his approval. If approved, Judge Bartle forwards the stipulations to the clerk for filing, and the clerk mails copies to counsel.

In general, Judge Bartle expects counsel to bring matters to his attention only after they have been discussed with opposing counsel.

Judge Michael M. Baylson

Judge Baylson was born on May 29, 1939, in Philadelphia, Pennsylvania. He received a B.S. from the University of Pennsylvania in 1961 and an LL.B. from the University of Pennsylvania in 1964. From 1965 to 1966, Judge Baylson served as a law clerk to the Honorable Joseph Sloane of the Court of Common Pleas of Philadelphia County. After serving as an assistant district attorney for the Philadelphia District Attorney's Office from 1966 to 1970, Judge Baylson entered private practice. From 1988 to 1993, Judge Baylson served as the United States Attorney for the Eastern District of Pennsylvania. He then returned to private practice. Judge Baylson was appointed to the United States District Court for the Eastern District of Pennsylvania on June 19, 2002. He assumed senior status on July 13, 2012.

PRELIMINARY GENERAL MATTERS

1. **Correspondence with the Court.** Correspondence on scheduling is accepted, but correspondence on substantive matters is not accepted and will not be considered. Other than scheduling issues or to advise that a case has been settled or discontinued, requests for court action, or opposition to court action, must be made by a pleading filed with the clerk of the court.

2. **Communications with Law Clerks.** Telephone calls to law clerks are discouraged. Law clerks are not permitted to render advice and have no authority to grant continuances or to speak on behalf of the court. All scheduling matters should be discussed with the deputy clerk.

3. **Scheduling Questions.** Any scheduling questions or issues should be addressed to the deputy clerks as follows:
   Joanne Bryson, 267-299-7520, all civil cases.
   Janice Lutz, 267-299-7291, all criminal cases.

4. **Chambers Copies of Submissions.** Courtesy copies of pleadings to chambers are not required, but are accepted.

5. **Electronic Case Filing.** Judge Baylson requires the use of Electronic Case Filing (ECF). ECF provides greater efficiency and timeliness in the filings of pleadings, automatic e-mail notice of case activity, and electronic storage of documents for remote access by the court, the bar, and the litigants. Attorneys appearing before Judge Baylson are required to register as ECF users in accordance with Rule 5.1.2 of the Local Rules of Civil Procedure, referencing the Procedural Order on Electronic Case Filing. If motions are accompanied by lengthy or multiple exhibits, a paper copy of the exhibit, tabbed, must be mailed or delivered to chambers. Counsel may, particularly with summary judgment papers, submit an extra copy to chambers by mail or hand delivery. Pro se parties are not required to use ECF.

6. **Pro Se Parties.** Pro se parties are expected to adhere to the Federal Rules of Civil Procedure and the Local Rules of Civil Procedure and to file all of their pleadings with the clerk of the court, rather than directly with chambers.

CIVIL CASES
Pretrial Procedure

1. **Pretrial Conferences.** A preliminary pretrial conference as described in Fed.R.Civ.P. 16(a), (b), and (c) will be held, usually by telephone, approximately 60 to 90 days after an action is filed, or after an answer is filed, or shortly after a case is reassigned to Judge Baylson's calendar.

    The preliminary pretrial conference will take approximately 10 minutes. If it is truly impossible for trial or associate counsel to attend the preliminary pretrial conference, counsel should call to reschedule.

    Pursuant to Fed.R.Civ.P. 26(f), counsel are required to discuss the following topics among themselves prior to the preliminary pretrial conference and to submit (by fax to chambers) a Conference Information Report in the form found on page 22 of this book:

    a. jurisdictional defects, if any;
    b. prospects of settlement;
    c. establishing schedules for remaining pretrial proceedings including discovery, dispositive motions, exchange of expert reports, pretrial memoranda, etc.;
    d. conduct of discovery; and
    e. setting a date for entry of the case into the trial pool.

    Additional conferences should be requested by counsel if desired for exploration of settlement or for trial management or trial preparation purposes. A final pretrial conference will be scheduled.

Continuances and Extensions

If counsel determine that a change in the scheduling order is necessary, they should attempt to agree on new dates and submit a letter or stipulation to that effect, following the format of the court's original scheduling order. If there is no agreement, a telephone conference should be requested. Counsel are welcome to suggest appropriate dates for entry of the case into the trial pool.

General Motion Practice

1. **Timing.** Motions to dismiss, amend, transfer, add parties, and other threshold motions should be filed, whenever possible, before the preliminary pretrial conference.

2. **Expert Witnesses.** Motions relating to expert testimony should be made promptly after the close of discovery, and in any event, prior to the filing of dispositive motions, or if none, prior to entry of the case into the trial pool.

3. **Dispositive Motions**

    a. **Briefing Schedule.** The parties may stipulate to a briefing schedule.

    b. **Components of Opening Brief.** The party filing a motion for summary judgment should include, preferably as a separate document, or, if short, within the memorandum of law, a "Statement of Undisputed Facts," which sets forth, in numbered paragraphs, all material facts that the moving party contends are undisputed, with record references.

    c. **Components of Response Briefs.** The responding party should include, preferably as a separate document, or within the memorandum of law, a "Statement of Disputed or Undisputed Facts" responding to the numbered paragraphs set forth in the moving party's statement, either admitting that the paragraph is not disputed, or if disputed, setting forth those facts contended to be in dispute, with record reference to where the party's contention is supported in the papers filed with the court on the dispositive motion.

The responding party may also set forth, in additional numbered paragraphs, any additional material facts that the responding party contends preclude the granting of the dispositive motion, with record references.

 d.   ***Reply and Surreply Briefs.***   A party desiring to file a reply in support of any motion may do so within seven days of service of the brief responding to the motion, limited to 15 pages, and limited to refuting arguments made in the opposition brief. Surreply briefs are not accepted without leave of the court.

For both motions to dismiss and motions for summary judgment, a reply brief must be filed by the moving party within seven days following receipt of the responding party's papers, should be limited to 15 pages, and limited to refuting arguments in the responsive brief. For summary judgment motions, the moving party must also respond to the responding party's statement of additional material facts, following the numbered paragraphs. Surreply briefs should be filed in the same manner as reply briefs if there are cross-motions; otherwise, surreply briefs are not accepted without leave of the court.

 e.   ***Statements of Material Facts.***   Statements of material facts in support of or in opposition to a motion for summary judgment should include specific and not general references to the parts of the record that support each of the statements, such as the title or numbered reference to a document, or the name of a deponent and the page(s) of the deponent's deposition, or the identity of an affidavit or declaration and the specific paragraph relied upon.

 f.   ***Exhibits.***   Exhibits should be listed in an index and preferably tabbed.

 g.   ***Oral Argument.***   Oral argument may be requested or may be required by the court.

Discovery Matters

1.   ***Length of Discovery Period and Extensions.***   In an uncomplicated case, discovery should be completed within 120 days after appearances have been filed for all defendants. The date for completing discovery will be set at the preliminary pretrial conference. In complex cases, following the preliminary pretrial conference, counsel will be directed to file a joint discovery schedule.

Counsel are expected to initiate discovery immediately following the preliminary pretrial conference, and to complete discovery within the stated deadline. Unless specifically ordered, counsel need not file a discovery report.

The discovery deadline means that, unless otherwise specified, all reasonably foreseeable fact and expert discovery must be served, noticed, and completed by that date. Discovery may take place after that date only by agreement of the parties, as long as the trial will not be delayed and trial preparation will not unreasonably be disrupted.

Unexcused violations of scheduling orders are subject to sanctions under Fed.R.Civ.P. 16(f), upon motion or the initiative of the court.

2.   ***Initial Disclosures and Document Production.***   Initial disclosures under Rule 26(a) should be made prior to the Rule 16 conference. As a general rule, once the initial disclosures have been completed, the parties should serve document requests immediately and arrange for the production and copying of documents in a cooperative manner. Documents produced should be stamped showing their origin with an appropriate numbering system.

3. **Discovery Disputes.** Counsel must discuss any problems that arise concerning discovery with each other and make good-faith attempts to resolve those problems before filing any discovery motions with the court.

When discovery is not forthcoming after a reasonable attempt has been made to obtain it, a motion to compel should be filed promptly. See Local Rule 26.1(f). Discovery motions are usually resolved by telephone conference, often before a response is filed.

4. **Confidentiality Agreements.** Agreements on "confidentiality" may be made between counsel without court approval. If submitted for court approval, the agreement must specifically define the type of materials to be protected as "confidential" and may not place any restrictions on the use of "confidential" materials by the court or in any hearing or trial in court.

Settlement

A settlement conference is required in every case by a court-appointed mediator, an independent mediator, a magistrate judge, or Judge Baylson. The timing of the settlement conference is to some extent in the hands of counsel. Early settlement conferences are encouraged because they have the potential of saving expenses. In some cases, however, counsel legitimately want to undertake some discovery before engaging in settlement discussions. Counsel should not hesitate to request a settlement conference when it is the mutual desire of all parties.

Arbitration

1. **Scheduling of Trial De Novo From Arbitration.** After arbitration, requests for trial de novo will result in the case being placed in the trial pool promptly. No discovery will be allowed after the arbitration except by order of the court upon good cause shown as to why the discovery requested could not have been reasonably anticipated and completed prior to the arbitration.

Proposed Final Pretrial Memoranda and Final Pretrial Conference

1. **Required Form of Pretrial Memoranda.** The filing of a pretrial memorandum as described in Local Rule 16.1(c) will be required. The requirements of Local Rule 16.1(d)(2) will only be used when specially ordered.

2. **Final Pretrial Conference.** The court will generally hold a final pretrial conference (in court or by telephone) with all counsel at or about the time the case is placed into the trial pool. The final pretrial conference must be attended by trial counsel. Any logistical issues that may impede the smooth flow of the trial, such as taking witnesses out of order, using video depositions, etc. should be raised. Counsel should also be prepared to discuss significant or unusual legal issues concerning the case and evidentiary issues that may arise during the trial. Any objections to admissibility of documents on the opposing party's exhibit list must be raised at the final pretrial conference. Both parties should have a realistic view of how long it will take to present their case, and, in some cases, the court may impose time limits on the presentation of evidence by a particular party, or on the length of time that may be taken for examination of specific witnesses.

Trial Procedure

1. **Scheduling of Cases.** The court intends that most cases should be tried (if not settled) within one year of filing. If extended pretrial proceedings are necessary, every case should reach trial no later than two years after the date of filing. Exceptions will be necessary only when there have been interlocutory appeals or other unusual pretrial procedures.

2. Objections. Any party having an objection to (a) the admissibility of any exhibit based on authenticity, (b) the adequacy of the qualifications and/or admissibility of testimony of an expert witness expected to testify, or (c) the admissibility of any opinion testimony from lay witnesses pursuant to Federal Rule of Evidence 701, should set forth separately each such objection in its pretrial memorandum. Each objection should describe with particularity the ground for the objection.

3. Offers of Proof. If any party desires an "offer of proof" as to any witness or exhibit expected to be offered, that party should inquire of counsel *prior to trial* for such information. If the inquiring party is dissatisfied with any offer provided, he or she should file a motion seeking relief from the court prior to trial.

4. Oral and Videotaped Deposition Testimony. Because a witness may be unavailable at the time of trial, as defined in Fed.R.Civ.P. 32(a)(3), the court expects use of oral or videotape depositions at trial of *any witness* whose testimony a party believes is essential to the presentation of that party's case, whether that witness is a party, a non-party, or an expert. The unavailability of any such witness *will not be a ground to delay* the commencement or progress of an ongoing trial. In the event a deposition is to be offered, the offering party should file with the court, prior to the commencement of the trial, a copy of the appropriate portions of the deposition transcript, but only after all efforts have been made to resolve objections with other counsel. Unresolved objections should be noted in the margin of the deposition page(s) where a court ruling is necessary, along with a covering list of the objections with page and line numbers.

5. Submissions to the Court in Jury Cases. At least three days before a jury case is listed for trial or appears on the trial pool list, each party must file (a) proposed jury voir dire questions, (b) proposed jury instructions with *pinpoint* citations of authority for each point (*one point per page*), (c) proposed jury interrogatories, and (d) a trial memorandum on the legal issues involved in the case. Copies may be delivered to chambers if any documents are lengthy.

6. Submissions to the Court in Nonjury Cases. At least three days before a nonjury case is listed for trial or appears on the trial pool list, each party must submit to the court (Chambers, Room 3810) two copies of (a) proposed findings of fact and conclusions of law, (b) motions in limine, and (c) a trial memorandum on the legal issues involved in the case. The originals must be filed with the clerk of the court.

7. Motions in Limine. Motions in limine may be filed after dispositive motions, if any, have been decided or close to the trial pool date, and should be answered within seven days unless a different briefing schedule is agreed upon or ordered.

CONFERENCE INFORMATION REPORT

CIVIL ACTION NO. _____

JURY TRIAL _____ NON-JURY TRIAL _____ ARBITRATION _____

SERVICE OF PROCESS MADE _____ (Date)

SHORT CAPTION:

TRIAL COUNSEL _____

REPRESENTING _____

LAW FIRM _____

ADDRESS _____

TELEPHONE & FAX _____

DISCOVERY COMPLETED _____ IF NOT, WHEN? _____ (Date)
                                Yes

PROTRACTED DISCOVERY REQUIRED? _____
                                          Yes/No

IF YES, DESCRIBE PROPOSED DISCOVERY SEGMENTS BY SUBJECT MATTER OR PARTIES AND SUGGEST DATES FOR SEGMENTS:

OTHER PRETRIAL MATTERS:

SETTLEMENT CONFERENCE REQUESTED? _____

TRIAL TIME: TIME TO PRESENT YOUR CASE _____

                TIME FOR ENTIRE TRIAL _____

OTHER COMMENTS:

DATE: _____

                                                      _____
                                                        SIGNATURE OF COUNSEL

                                                        _____
                                                        TYPE OR PRINT NAME

This form should be faxed to Chambers at 267.299.5078 or mailed or hand delivered to Chambers, Room 4001, U.S. Courthouse, 601 Market Street, Philadelphia, PA 19106-1741.

Judge Anita B. Brody[*]

Judge Brody received her A.B. from Wellesley College and her J.D. from Columbia Law School. She served as a deputy assistant attorney general in New York, then took time out to raise her children. She was in private practice, and was a lecturer in law at the University of Pennsylvania Law School. Judge Brody served as a judge on the Court of Common Pleas, Montgomery County. On October 20, 1992, she was appointed to the United States District Court for the Eastern District of Pennsylvania by President George H.W. Bush. Judge Brody assumed senior status on June 8, 2009.

PRELIMINARY GENERAL MATTERS

1. Correspondence with the Court. Judge Brody permits correspondence by e-mail, letter, and fax from counsel concerning urgent administrative matters such as scheduling hearings and conferences or their continuances. All other matters should be addressed by motion, including requests for extensions of time to file, requests to file reply and surreply briefs in non-dispositive motions, and all discovery controversies. If counsel improperly submits a letter to the court to which opposing counsel would like to respond, opposing counsel is not to respond via letter, but rather should file the letter on CM/ECF with a response.

2. Communications with Law Clerks. Judge Brody permits counsel to e-mail and speak with her law clerks about administrative or scheduling matters.

3. Telephone Conferences. Judge Brody will often arrange for a telephone conference to deal with less complex matters, including discovery disputes involving no more than three attorneys and less complex issues.

4. Chambers Copies of Submissions. Judge Brody expects counsel to send two courtesy hard copies of all submissions (including copies of the complaint and answer) to her chambers. Chambers copies should include the ECF docket entry number on the first page. Double-sided copies to save paper are encouraged. Points for charge should also be e-mailed to the law clerk.

5. Filings with the Clerk of Court. Judge Brody insists that all parties appearing before her register on ECF and submit official filings with the court directly through ECF. All orders, opinions, and other docket entries generated from chambers will likewise be filed directly on ECF. Notice of the entry will be communicated to counsel by ECF.

6. Naming of Responses and Replies to Motions. Particularly in complex cases with multiple parties and dispositive motions, Judge Brody encourages parties to title motions and responses in a logical and helpful manner by including both descriptive titles and docket entry numbers. For example: "Opposition to Plaintiff's Motion # 35 (Res Judicata) and Motion # 42 (Statute of Limitations)" and "Reply in Support of Plaintiff's Motion # 35 (Res Judicata) and Motion # 42 (Statute of Limitations)."

CIVIL CASES
Pretrial Procedure

1. Pretrial Conferences. Judge Brody notices an initial pretrial scheduling conference as soon as counsel for all parties have entered appearances. A copy of the standard notice is shown on page 32. The notice establishes certain guidelines that Judge Brody will

---

[*] <u>Disclaimer</u>: This document is not intended to be read as a statute but rather as a compilation of best intentions.

follow throughout the litigation and outlines the matters that will be considered at the scheduling conference. The judge expects trial counsel to attend the conference in person. As stated in the notice, counsel must submit a joint proposed discovery plan via ECF to the court no later than three days prior to the conference. After the scheduling conference, Judge Brody issues a scheduling order. (See page 29 for a copy of the standard scheduling order.) Judge Brody will arrange for additional pretrial conferences if necessary, and conduct a final pretrial conference close to the date for trial.

2.   Scheduling Policy. Judge Brody tries to accommodate reasonable requests from counsel regarding scheduling. If counsel agree on a scheduling issue, a letter requesting Judge Brody's approval is often sufficient. If time does not permit a letter, an attorney may fax the request to the law clerk.

3.   Continuances and Extensions. Judge Brody is generally accommodating with respect to initial requests for extensions; she is less accommodating with respect to subsequent requests. Although Judge Brody adheres to the general policy that no associate should be forced to "pull an all-nighter" to comply with a scheduling deadline, once the dates are established, reasonable compliance is expected. It is unlikely that Judge Brody will grant a continuance once a case has been called for trial.

General Motion Practices

1.   Chambers Copies of Motion Papers. As stated previously with respect to all submissions, counsel should send two courtesy hard copies of motion papers to her chambers.

2.   Reply and Surreply Briefs. With respect to dispositive motions, Judge Brody encourages submission of a reply brief. Parties need not move for permission to file a reply. For nondispositive motions, parties must file a motion for leave to file a reply. If the moving party has filed a Rule 56 motion in accordance with Judge Brody's "preferred procedure," then a reply and surreply brief are required. Otherwise, surreply briefs are discouraged and will be accepted only if the judge grants a motion for a surreply. When no order or applicable rule imposes a deadline for filing a reply brief, replies are due 10 days after the related response is filed.

3.   Motions for Summary Judgment. Both the brief accompanying a motion for summary judgment and the responding brief must identify the material facts that are not in dispute, preferably in outline form including specific citations to the underlying record. In addition to the standard summary judgment procedure under Fed.R.Civ.P. 56, instructions on Judge Brody's "preferred procedure" on summary judgment are appended to the scheduling order (see attachment A on page 31).

4.   Motions for Pro Hac Vice Admission. Motions for admission pro hac vice should be filed with the court.

5.   Oral Arguments and Evidentiary Hearings. Judge Brody will hold oral argument if she believes it will assist her in deciding the motion. Judge Brody will also consider requests from counsel to hold oral argument on a particular motion. The law clerk assigned to the case, in conjunction with the judge's secretary/civil deputy, handles scheduling for oral arguments and evidentiary hearings. Unless arrangements for more time are made in advance through the law clerk, counsel should assume a 20-minute limit.

Discovery Matters

1.   Length of Discovery Period. Except in complex cases, Judge Brody will allow 90 to 120 days for discovery. She will grant additional time upon request if necessary.

2. Discovery Conferences and Dispute Resolution. Judge Brody expects the parties to resolve discovery disputes on their own. If they cannot, she will hold a telephone conference or in-chambers conference depending on the number of counsel and issues. Judge Brody requires that all discovery disputes be addressed by motion.

3. Confidentiality Agreements. Parties are free to reach a confidentiality agreement among themselves. If the parties request that the court enter the agreement as an order, it must include a proviso clearly indicating that Judge Brody is not bound by the terms of the agreement and may alter them sua sponte.

4. Expert Witnesses. Counsel should arrange for the exchange of written expert reports without the assistance of the court. Judge Brody will permit counsel to depose experts when appropriate. Furthermore, Judge Brody expects that counsel will identify expert witnesses well in advance of trial, and that the parties will videotape the deposition of any expert who will be unavailable at trial.

Settlement

Whether requested to or not, Judge Brody will inquire as to settlement at every opportunity. Unless the parties opt for a particular method of ADR, Judge Brody will refer the case to the magistrate judge for a formal settlement conference immediately upon the close of discovery and before the pretrial submissions are due. If counsel would like to attend a settlement conference earlier, they can request at the pretrial conference that such a provision be included in the scheduling order.

Arbitration

Judge Brody does not hold pretrial scheduling conferences in arbitration cases. She expects that discovery will be completed before the arbitration date. If a trial de novo is demanded, Judge Brody will hold a pretrial conference to explore settlement and will schedule the trial as soon as possible.

Pretrial Requirements

In an order setting the date for trial, Judge Brody will require that parties submit short, final pretrial memoranda pursuant to Local Rule 16.1. The parties should submit the following with their memorandum: voir dire questions, proposed jury instructions, proposed verdict sheets, and motions in limine. In nonjury cases and criminal cases in which a suppression hearing will be held, she also requires submission of proposed findings of fact and conclusions of law. Additionally, in preparation for a final pretrial conference, Judge Brody expects counsel to communicate with each other on a number of matters, including objections to exhibits, expert depositions, and stipulations of fact.

Injunctions

1. Scheduling and Expedited Discovery. When a temporary restraining order is requested, Judge Brody will immediately schedule a conference to decide the TRO. Unless the urgency of the circumstances precludes notice to opposing counsel, Judge Brody requires that all counsel be present. Judge Brody rarely grants ex parte temporary restraining orders. Judge Brody schedules preliminary and permanent injunction hearings as soon as possible and combines the two hearings if feasible. Usually, she permits expedited discovery for injunctive matters.

2. Proposed Findings of Fact and Conclusions of Law. As in all nonjury trials, Judge Brody requires the submission of tentative findings of fact and conclusions of law, in accordance with Fed.R.Civ.P. 52(a).

Scheduling of Trials

1. Scheduling Conflicts. Judge Brody prefers that counsel notify her by letter concerning professional and personal scheduling conflicts affecting the trial schedule. If absolutely necessary, counsel may contact Judge Brody's secretary/civil deputy by telephone and then confirm the request in writing.

2. Cases Involving Out-of-Town Parties or Witnesses. Judge Brody does not generally change her trial schedule for the convenience of out-of-town parties or witnesses; however, she will consider special requests if brought to her attention before the case enters the trial pool.

Trial Procedure

1. Pretrial Briefs. Judge Brody prefers that parties submit pretrial briefs.

2. Voir Dire. Judge Brody requires the submission of proposed voir dire questions prior to trial. Proposed voir dire should not exceed 15 questions. In civil cases, Judge Brody permits counsel to conduct the voir dire. Initial questioning, however, is limited to the questions that are submitted.

3. Sidebars. Judge Brody permits sidebar conferences during trial to address matters that were unanticipated prior to trial. To the extent possible, counsel are directed to raise potential issues prior to trial to ensure that sidebars are kept to a minimum.

4. Motions in Limine. Judge Brody expects all issues that can be anticipated prior to trial to be raised in motions in limine. Motions in limine should be accompanied by a memorandum and will usually be addressed at the final pretrial conference. Judge Brody may, however, defer ruling on motions in limine until trial.

5. Examination of Witnesses Out of Sequence. Judge Brody makes every effort to accommodate counsel regarding the scheduling of witnesses. Depending upon the circumstances, Judge Brody may permit counsel to take the testimony of a witness out of turn.

6. Note-taking by Jurors. Judge Brody decides whether note-taking will be permitted on a case-by-case basis and accepts requests from counsel or from the jurors themselves.

7. Opening Statements and Summations. Generally, Judge Brody will not impose time limits on opening statements or summations and does not require use of the lectern. Judge Brody expects counsel to refrain from objecting during closing argument if the objection can wait until counsel has finished. If an objection is necessary, it should be stated softly and will usually be ruled upon at the conclusion of the summation. Judge Brody may, if requested, cure the objectionable statement in her charge.

8. Offers of Proof. All offers of proof as to the testimony of witnesses or the admissibility of documents must be raised and addressed at the final pretrial conference. If other evidentiary issues arise and an offer of proof is necessary, counsel will usually be called to sidebar.

9. Use of Multiple Attorneys During Trial. The parties may use several different attorneys during the trial to examine witnesses and argue legal points. The parties may not, however, use more than one attorney to examine a particular witness or argue a specific legal point.

10. Examination of Witnesses Beyond Redirect and Recross. Upon request, Judge Brody may permit further examination of a witness after redirect or recross has been completed.

11. Disputes over Videotaped Testimony. Objections to videotaped testimony should be submitted before the final pretrial conference. A transcript of the testimony should also be provided.

12. Exhibits. Judge Brody requires that exhibits be marked and exchanged prior to trial. Judge Brody encourages the use of computerized and other electronic devices to present evidence. Two courtesy copies of all trial exhibits should be submitted to the judge at the pretrial conference. If the exhibits are voluminous or difficult to reproduce, counsel should bring this to the court's attention before trial. Counsel must also provide the court with three copies of an exhibit list.

13. Reading of Material Into the Record. Judge Brody has no overall practice or policy on reading stipulations, pleadings, or discovery materials into the record.

14. Offering Exhibits Into Evidence. Judge Brody has no overall policy regarding the offering of exhibits into evidence. Unless otherwise necessary, counsel may wait until the close of his or her case to move for the admission of exhibits.

15. Directed Verdict Motions. Counsel may move for a directed verdict either orally or in writing. Judge Brody usually conducts oral argument on such a motion.

16. Jury Instructions and Verdict Sheets. As stated in the section concerning final pretrial conferences, counsel are required to submit proposed jury instructions (one point per page) and a proposed verdict sheet in advance of trial. These must also be submitted via e-mail attachment to the law clerk assigned to the case (WordPerfect format is preferred but Microsoft Word is acceptable). Normally, Judge Brody will distribute a copy of her proposed charge early in the trial, and then conduct a conference to review the revised proposed charge, including any critiques from counsel on substantive issues. If a new issue arises, Judge Brody will permit submission of supplemental jury instructions up until the close of evidence. It is Judge Brody's usual practice to distribute to all counsel a written copy of the final version of the charge before closing arguments.

17. Proposed Findings of Fact and Conclusions of Law. In nonjury cases, Judge Brody requires submission of tentative proposed findings of fact and conclusions of law in advance of trial. After trial, counsel must amend and this must include citations to the notes of testimony.

Jury Deliberations

1. Written Jury Instructions. Judge Brody does not routinely give the jury a copy of her instructions; however, if requested by counsel or the jury, she will consider doing so.

2. Exhibits in the Jury Room. Counsel are instructed to confer as to which exhibits should go out with the jury. Judge Brody will rule upon disputed exhibits.

3. Handling of Jury Requests to Read Back Testimony or Replay Tapes. Judge Brody will evaluate jury requests to play back portions of recorded or videotaped testimony on a case-by-case basis.

4. Availability of Counsel During Jury Deliberations. Judge Brody permits counsel to leave the courthouse during deliberations but expects them to be available by telephone and within close distance to the courthouse.

5. Taking the Verdict and Special Interrogatories. The courtroom deputy usually takes the verdict. In most cases, Judge Brody will submit special interrogatories to the jury.

Practice and Procedures of Judges and Judges' Forms and Orders

6. **Polling the Jury.** Judge Brody will poll the jury upon request.

7. **Interviewing the Jurors.** After the verdict has been recorded and the jury discharged, Judge Brody permits counsel to speak with the jurors. Judge Brody advises the jurors that they are permitted to speak with counsel, but instructs them that it is their personal choice and that they are not required to do so. She expects all counsel to respect each juror's choice in this regard.

CRIMINAL CASES
(To the Extent Different from the Procedures in Civil Cases)

1. **Voir Dire.** Judge Brody conducts the entire voir dire but receives proposed questions. After voir dire, where necessary, jurors will be called to sidebar to respond to any unanswered questions or for further questioning by the judge or counsel.

2. **Other Practices and Procedures.** Judge Brody issues the standard pretrial order shown on page 29.

3. **Sentencing Memoranda.** Judge Brody expects the submission of sentencing memoranda by both the government and the defendant well in advance of the sentencing.

OTHER GENERAL MATTERS
Appellate Briefs

Judge Brody appreciates receiving copies of the appellate brief when a decision she renders is appealed.

Judge Anita B. Brody

**IN THE UNITED STATES DISTRICT COURT
FOR THE EASTERN DISTRICT OF PENNSYLVANIA**

	:	CIVIL ACTION
V.	:	
	:	NO.

<u>SCHEDULING ORDER</u>

AND NOW, this _____ day of _____, 20___, **IT IS ORDERED** as follows:

1. Pretrial timetable:
   - All discovery shall be completed by _____;
   - Plaintiff's expert reports due _____; Defendant's reports due _____; depositions of all experts to be completed by _____;
   - Dispositive motions due _____;
   - Pretrial hearing, such as *Markman* or *Daubert,* will be scheduled if needed;
   - After all dispositive motions have been decided or when no dispositive motions have been filed and the time for filing dispositive motions has elapsed, the parties will be given notice of a trial date, a Final Pretrial Conference, and deadlines for pretrial findings.

2. Unless the parties agree to another form of ADR, United States Magistrate Judge David Strawbridge will be in touch with you regarding settlement. Judge David Strawbridge requires that lead counsel and parties with full settlement authority attend the conference.

3. With the exception of employment discrimination cases and cases in which the plaintiff is *pro se,* I prefer that a party moving for summary judgment under F.R.C.P. 56 follow the instructions set forth in **Attachment A.** The parties in employment discrimination cases and cases in which the plaintiff is *pro se* should file traditional summary judgment motions. For those following the instructions set forth in Attachment A, all responses and replies to summary judgment motions shall contain a statement of undisputed and disputed facts. For those using the traditional summary judgment procedure, all summary judgment motions and responses shall contain a statement of undisputed and disputed facts. For me to consider any filing made in conjunction with a motion for summary judgment, all references to affidavits, depositions, documents or other evidence ***must*** cite specifically to the exhibit, page, and line number.

4. In a jury trial, each party shall submit with the pretrial memoranda:
   (a) a trial memorandum on the legal issues in the case,
   (b) proposed *voir dire* questions **(limited to 15 questions),**
   (c) proposed jury instructions (one point per page). Failure to submit proposed jury instructions may result in the forfeiture of a right to object to omissions in the jury charge, and
   (d) proposed jury verdict sheet and special interrogatories.

In addition to the items above, in non-jury cases, each party shall file:
   (e) a trial memorandum on the legal issues in the case and
   (f) proposed findings of fact and conclusions of law.

5. In preparation for the final pretrial conference, counsel are expected to communicate with each other on the following matters in an effort to reach agreement. At the final pretrial conference, counsel must be prepared to present a report on the following matters:
   (a) agreed to and disputed facts;
   (b) objections to any proposed witnesses;
   (c) objections to any proposed exhibits (including objections to genuineness and authenticity);
   (d) objections to any depositions to be read at trial;
   (e) disputed legal issues;
   (f) amendments to pleadings;
   (g) stipulated to and disputed points for charge;

(h) verdict sheet and special interrogatories; and
(i) number of days required for trial.

6. **If you fail to object to proposed voir dire questions, exhibits or witnesses prior to trial, then you have waived any objection.**

7. Three copies of the schedules of exhibits and, if practicable, two copies of the exhibits themselves shall be prepared for my use at trial.

8. **REMINDER:** All official filings submitted to the Clerk of Court must be filed by the attorney directly onto ECF. Counsel must submit to chambers **TWO** courtesy copies of *all* papers filed with the clerk. The submissions to chambers must be in hard copy with a copy of the ECF docket entry number on the first page. Double-sided copies are encouraged to save paper. *Note:* This requirement also applies in ECF cases.

9. Your case has been assigned to:

_____ Law Clerk Maya Sosnov, maya_sosnov@paed.uscourts.gov

_____ Law Clerk Adam G. Yoffie, adam_g_yoffie@paed.uscourts.gov

_____ Law Clerk John C. Eason, john_c_eason@paed.uscourts.gov

10. Counsel are reminded that all submissions given directly to Judge Brody in the courtroom or chambers must also be filed by counsel onto ECF.

11. Judge Brody's Policies and Procedures can be accessed via the U.S. District Court's website at www.paed.uscourts.gov.

12. Throughout the course of the litigation, counsel shall provide the courtroom deputy clerk, Jim Scheidt, with current telephone and FAX number(s).

_____
Anita B. Brody, J.

Chambers Fax: 215-580-2356

XC: Magistrate David R. Strawbridge

COPIES VIA ECF on _____ to: COPIES MAILED on _____ to:

Judge Anita B. Brody

ATTACHMENT A

PREFERRED PROCEDURE

Brody Instructions on Summary Judgment for those moving under Rule 56*

Rule 56(a) of the Federal Rules of Civil Procedure provides in part that:

> "A party may move for summary judgment, identifying each claim or defense—or the part of each claim or defense—on which summary judgment is sought. The court shall grant summary judgment if the movant shows that there is no genuine dispute as to any material fact and the movant is entitled to judgment as a matter of law."

- This Preferred Procedure is applicable to all motions for summary judgment.
- A party moving under Rule 56(a) shall comply with the procedures set forth in Rule 56(c) and (d) and, in doing so, the party making the motion shall:
  (1) identify in outline form the issue(s) and/or sub-issue(s) as to which the Motion is directed, for example, referring to the pleadings;
  (2) affirm, on the basis prescribed in Rule 11, that there is no legally sufficient evidentiary basis to support the issues so identified; and
  (3) request judgment as provided in Rule 56(e)(3).
- The party against whom the Motion for Summary Judgment is addressed shall file a Response not later than 20 days after the Motion for Summary Judgment is received. The Response must include a statement of undisputed and disputed facts. The Response, subject to the provisions of Rule 56(c) and (d), must be supported with affidavits, depositions, documents, or other evidence permitted by those provisions. Where applicable, references to such evidence must include **specific** citations to exhibit, page, and line number.
- The movant shall file a Reply as permitted by Rule 56(c) and (d). Such a Reply must be filed not later than 10 days after the Response is received. The Reply must state the undisputed facts, address the disputed facts, and **specify** the relevant exhibit, page, and line numbers when referring to the record.
- The party against whom the Motion for Summary Judgment is directed may, within 10 days after the Reply is received, file a Sur-reply to the Reply. The Sur-reply must **specify** the relevant exhibit, page, and line numbers when referring to the record.

The purpose of these *Instructions* is to encourage the parties in their dispositive motion to track the natural order of trial where the plaintiff sets forth its case and the defendant then responds.

---

* THE PARTIES SHOULD NOT USE THIS PREFERRED PROCEDURE IN EMPLOYMENT DISCRIMINATION CASES OR IN CASES IN WHICH THE PLAINTIFF IS *PRO SE*.

IN THE UNITED STATES DISTRICT COURT
FOR THE EASTERN DISTRICT OF PENNSYLVANIA

DATE MAILED

                    :   CIVIL ACTION

v.

                    :   No.

NOTICE

This case has been assigned to Judge Anita B. Brody.

ANY NONGOVERNMENTAL CORPORATE PARTY SHALL FILE FORTHWITH A STATEMENT WITH THE COURT (WITH A COPY TO CHAMBERS) IDENTIFYING ALL ITS PARENT CORPORATIONS AND LISTING ANY PUBLICLY HELD COMPANY THAT OWNS 10% OR MORE OF THE PARTY'S STOCK. A PARTY SHALL SUPPLEMENT THE STATEMENT WITHIN A REASONABLE TIME OF ANY CHANGE IN THE INFORMATION.

    1. A pretrial scheduling conference as described in Fed. R. Civ. P. 16 (a), (b) and (c) and Local R. Civ. P. 16.1(a) and (b) will be held in chambers on _____ at _____. Unless otherwise specified, Judge Brody will follow the procedure at the conference as outlined in the federal and local rules.

    2. Not later than **3** days prior to the conference, counsel must submit to the court a joint Proposed Discovery Plan under Rule 26(f). Disagreements concerning the timetable of discovery or other discovery-related matters must be highlighted in bold-face type. For assistance in developing the Proposed Discovery Plan counsel shall follow the example set forth in **Attachment A**.

    3. Motions to dismiss, transfer, add parties and other threshold motions should be filed, whenever possible, **before** the conference.

    4. Prior to the conference, counsel shall evaluate the case for settlement purposes. Plaintiff's counsel shall make a demand on opposing counsel no later than **five days** prior to the conference. Defense counsel shall respond to the demand no later than one day prior to the conference. All counsel shall arrive at the conference with *settlement authority* from the client and arrange for the client to be available by telephone for the duration of the conference.

    5. Unless the factual or legal issues are complex, the conference will last approximately thirty minutes. Judge Brody expects trial counsel to attend this conference. If unable to attend, trial counsel must appoint other counsel familiar with the case and with authority to discuss settlement to attend the conference. Trial counsel shall notify Judge Brody and opposing counsel of a substitute appearance at the earliest possible date.

    6. At the conference the following matters will be considered (See Fed. R. Civ. P. 16(b) and (c) and Local R. Civ. P. 16.1(b)):
        (a) jurisdiction;
        (b) recitation of the facts, claims, and applicable law;
        (c) settlement;
        (d) setting dates for pretrial matters (see **Attachment A**);
        (e) any other matters that may arise.

    7. The parties should be prepared at the conference to argue all outstanding motions.

    8. In an uncomplicated case, Judge Brody will set the discovery deadline for between 90 and 120 days after the conference. Discovery shall be served, noticed and completed by the discovery deadline. Requests for extension of discovery deadlines or trial pool entry dates must be made by motion or stipulation.

    9. All cases that are appealed from court-annexed arbitration will be set for trial as soon as possible.

    10. All attorneys appearing before Judge Brody **must be** registered on ECF. All official filings submitted to the Clerk of the Court must be filed directly by the attorney onto ECF. All orders, opinions, and

Judge Anita B. Brody

other docket entries generated from chambers will likewise be filed directly onto ECF. Notice of these chamber entries will be communicated to counsel either by ECF or ordinary mail.

11. Counsel must submit **TWO courtesy hard copies** to chambers of all papers filed with the clerk. *Courtesy copies should include the ECF docket entry number on the first page. Double-sided copies to save paper are encouraged. **Note**:* This requirement also applies in ECF cases.

12. Briefs or memoranda of law filed with the court shall not exceed 50 pages. Substantially less than 50 pages would be appreciated.

13. Your case has been assigned to:

_____ Law Clerk Adam G. Yoffie, adam_g_yoffie@paed.uscourts.gov

_____ Law Clerk Maya Sosnov, maya_sosnov@paed.uscourts.gov

_____ Law Clerk John Eason, john_c_eason@paed.uscourts.gov

14. Counsel are reminded that all submissions given directly to Judge Brody in the courtroom or chambers must also be filed by counsel with the Clerk of the Court to assure proper docketing.

15. Requests to reschedule a conference or other appearance before the court may be made by letter, fax, or e-mail to the law clerk assigned to the case, stating the reasons and noting the agreement or disagreement of all counsel. Counsel must also provide the court with five alternative dates that are acceptable to all parties.

16. Request for a hearing or conference may be made by letter, fax, or e-mail to the law clerk assigned to the case. Counsel must provide the court with five potential dates that are acceptable to all parties.

17. Judge Brody's Polices and Procedures can be accessed via the U.S. District Court's website at **www.paed.uscourts.gov**.

Throughout the course of the litigation, counsel shall provide the courtroom deputy clerk, Jim Scheidt, with current telephone numbers, fax numbers, and e-mail addresses. Judge Brody's fax number is **215-580-2356**.

Marie O'Donnell
Civil Deputy/Secretary to
Judge Anita B. Brody

xc:

Civil Action No. _____ Jury Trial _____ Bench Trial _____
Arbitration _____
Caption: _____
Trial Time Estimates: Time to present your case_____
                        Time for entire trial_____

Attachment A - Proposed Discovery Plan Under Rule 26(f)

I. Rule 26(a) Disclosures
Counsel anticipate completing the self-executing disclosures on _____, as required by Rule 26(a).

II. Discovery Subjects
(A) Counsel agree that unless otherwise stipulated by the parties or ordered by the court, discovery shall proceed in accordance with the Federal Rules of Civil Procedure. This includes the amendments to the Federal Rules regarding electronic discovery effective December 1, 2006. If the parties agree to modifications to this default position, please list:

(B) Counsel agree that the subjects for discovery include:

(C) Counsel anticipate that the following depositions will be necessary (identify parties if known at this point):

III. Pretrial Timetable
(A) The Court will enter the default scheduling order, a copy of which is attached as **Attachment B**, unless the parties request an alternate discovery schedule. The parties request a close of discovery date of _____.
(B) Counsel may set forth below an alternative proposed scheduling order if agreed to by all parties. Counsel should use dates certain rather than contingent dates; if a date is difficult to specify, counsel should estimate it to the best of their ability.

IV. Alternative Dispute Resolution
(A) type of ADR, settlement conference, etc.
(B) timing of ADR
(C) unless otherwise recommended, a settlement conference will be scheduled upon the close of all discovery.

V. Other Pretrial Issues
(e.g. protective orders, etc.)

Signed,

_____
Counsel for Plaintiff

_____
Counsel for Defendant

Judge Anita B. Brody

Attachment B - Default Scheduling Order

AND NOW, this _____ day of _____, 20_____,

IT IS ORDERED as follows:

1. Pretrial timetable:

    - All discovery shall be completed by _____.

    - Plaintiff's expert reports due **[4 weeks before close of discovery (COD)]**; Defendant's reports due **[2 weeks before COD]**; depositions of all experts to be completed by: **[COD]**.

    - Dispositive motions due normally **[2 weeks after COD]**.

    - Pretrial hearing, such as *Markman* or *Daubert,* will be scheduled if needed.

    - After all dispositive motions have been decided or when no dispositive motions have been filed and the time for filing dispositive motions has elapsed, the parties will be given notice of a trial date, a Final Pretrial Conference, and deadlines for pretrial filings.

2. Unless the parties agree to another form of ADR, United States Magistrate Judge David Strawbridge will be in touch with you regarding settlement. Judge David Strawbridge requires that lead counsel and parties with full settlement authority attend the conference.

Practice and Procedures of Judges and Judges' Forms and Orders

[*Counsel*: Please bring completed form to the conference. Do not mail.]

RULE 16 CONFERENCE INFORMATION REPORT

Caption: _____

Civil Action No. _____ Jury Trial ____ Bench trial ____ Arbitration ____

    Trial counsel   _____

    Representing   _____

    Law Firm   _____

    Address   _____

        _____

    Telephone   _____ Fax _____

    Email   _____

Are there threshold motions? _____
                                (identify motion(s))

When will discovery be completed? _____
                                    (date)

Will motion for summary judgment be filed? _____
                                          (yes or no)

Ready for trial by? _____
                            (date)

Has settlement been discussed? _____ If not, why not? _____
                        (yes or no)

Future settlement conference requested _____
                                              (yes or no)

Novel issues or special problems? _____ Describe overleaf.
                                 (yes or no)

Trial time estimates
        Time to present your case   _____
        Time for entire trial   _____

Date: _____   _____
                                                  Signature of counsel

                                                  _____
                                                  Typed or printed name

Judge Ronald L. Buckwalter

Judge Ronald L. Buckwalter was born on December 11, 1936, in Lancaster, Pennsylvania. He received an A.B. from Franklin & Marshall College in 1958 and a J.D. from the College of William and Mary in 1962. Judge Buckwalter was in private practice in Lancaster from 1963 to 1977. He served as the district attorney of Lancaster County from 1977 to 1980, when he was elected to the Court of Common Pleas, Second Judicial District. Judge Buckwalter was appointed to the United States District Court for the Eastern District of Pennsylvania on March 12, 1990. He assumed senior status on December 11, 2003.

PRELIMINARY GENERAL MATTERS

1. **Correspondence with the Court.** Judge Buckwalter has set forth in his standard pretrial and trial procedures his policy with regard to contacting chambers during pendency of litigation. (See page 42 of this book for Judge Buckwalter's standard procedures.)

2. **Communications with Law Clerks and Chambers Staff.** Judge Buckwalter permits his law clerks to speak to counsel with regard to administrative matters only. Law clerks may not render advice to counsel and have no authority to grant continuances or to speak on behalf of the court.

3. **Telephone Conferences.** Judge Buckwalter will conduct telephone conferences concerning any matter appropriately before him rather than requiring all parties to appear in person, unless for good cause one of the parties objects to a telephone conference or Judge Buckwalter decides that the matter before him can be more fairly and effectively resolved by a personal conference.

4. **Oral Arguments and Evidentiary Hearings.** Judge Buckwalter will set special times for oral argument and evidentiary hearings as the particular case requires.

5. **Pro Hac Vice Admissions.** Judge Buckwalter has no fixed policy with regard to pro hac vice admissions.

CIVIL CASES
Pretrial Procedure

1. **Pretrial Conferences.** Judge Buckwalter requires the filing of a status report on a form that is sent to counsel by his courtroom deputy. When a completed form has been returned by all parties, he will issue a Fed.R.Civ.P. 16 scheduling order. He will, upon request and for good cause, hold scheduling, discovery, settlement, pretrial and final pretrial conferences. Judge Buckwalter's regular agenda are those matters referred to in Fed.R.Civ.P. 16, local civil rules, and the court's Civil Justice Expense and Delay Reduction Plan, specifically, chapter 3 of that plan.

Continuances and Extensions

1. **General Policy.** Judge Buckwalter expects adherence to the dates that have been established in the scheduling order because that order is entered based upon counsels' assessment of the time needed for discovery as well as counsels' proposed trial date as set forth in the status report.

2. **Requests for Extensions and Continuances.** Counsel should immediately notify the courtroom deputy after contacting opposing counsel of any request for change in schedule, together with the compelling reasons necessitating the change. If counsel can agree on the

extension, a stipulation requesting approval by the court should be sent to the courtroom deputy. If no agreement can be reached, counsel should file an appropriate motion in accordance with local rules motion practice.

General Motion Practice

1.   Oral Argument on Motions.   Judge Buckwalter does not normally hold oral argument on motions.

2.   Reply and Surreply Briefs.   Judge Buckwalter follows local rules motion practice, which contains no specific reference to reply or surreply briefs. Counsel should immediately notify the court of his or her intention to file a reply brief or surreply by letter addressed to the judge's secretary.

3.   Chambers Copies of Motions Papers.   Judge Buckwalter prefers to receive courtesy copies of motion papers in chambers, but he does not require it.

Discovery Matters

1.   Length of Discovery Period and Extensions.   Judge Buckwalter expects discovery to be completed in accordance with his scheduling order. In the normal case, that date would be approximately six months from the date the case is filed.

2.   Discovery Conferences and Dispute Resolution.   Judge Buckwalter does not normally hold discovery conferences but will do so upon request of all counsel or when required by the Civil Justice Expense and Delay Reduction Plan of this court. Telephone conferences to resolve disputes during depositions are permitted. Other discovery disputes are normally resolved through local rules motion practice.

3.   Confidentiality Agreements.   Although Judge Buckwalter generally disfavors confidentiality orders, he may hold a conference to discuss their entry even if the parties have agreed to such an order.

4.   Expert Witnesses.   Judge Buckwalter requires a party to disclose the identity of any person who may be used at trial to present evidence under Rules 702, 703, or 705 of the Federal Rules of Evidence in accordance with the terms of F.R.C.P. 26(a)(2), unless otherwise directed by the scheduling order or other order of this court.

Settlement

1.   General Approach to Settlement and Nonjury Cases.   Judge Buckwalter will become involved in settlement negotiations in jury cases. It is not Judge Buckwalter's practice to participate in settlement negotiations in nonjury cases. A settlement conference will be scheduled upon request of all parties.

2.   Referral of Settlement Negotiations to Another District Court Judge.   Judge Buckwalter has no fixed policy in this regard. In certain nonjury cases, Judge Buckwalter may refer settlement negotiations to another district judge or a magistrate judge. The latter may be used for settlement conferences in jury cases as well.

Arbitration

1.   General Approach to Arbitration Cases.   At this time, Judge Buckwalter has no fixed policy involving arbitration cases other than to schedule the trial de novo as soon as possible.

2. **Scheduling of Trial De Novo from Arbitration.** When de novo trial is demanded, it will be scheduled promptly. Judge Buckwalter has no special practices or procedures regarding de novo trials.

Proposed Final Pretrial Memoranda

1. **Required Form of Pretrial Memoranda.** Judge Buckwalter's final pretrial memoranda requirements are set forth in his standard pretrial and trial procedures (see page 42 of this book).

Injunctions

1. **Scheduling and Expedited Discovery.** Judge Buckwalter promptly schedules hearings, but he may limit the time of initial hearings. He may permit expedited discovery depending upon the circumstances.

2. **Proposed Findings of Fact and Conclusions of Law.** At a hearing on a petition for a TRO or preliminary injunction, Judge Buckwalter prefers to have proposed findings of fact and conclusions of law before the hearing. Recognizing that the emergency nature of such a hearing may make this difficult, he requires proposed findings of fact and conclusions of law no later than 24 hours after such a hearing.

Trial Procedure

1. **Scheduling of Cases.** Judge Buckwalter's usual practice in the scheduling of cases for trial is to place all cases in his trial pool.

2. **Conflicts of Counsel.** Counsel should immediately notify the courtroom deputy of professional and personal conflicts affecting the trial schedule.

3. **Cases Involving Out-of-Town Parties or Witnesses.** In cases involving out-of-town witnesses or parties, Judge Buckwalter may assign the case a date certain for trial.

4. **Note-taking by Jurors.** Judge Buckwalter has no objection to note-taking.

5. **Trial Briefs.** Judge Buckwalter encourages the submission of trial briefs if the pretrial memorandum raises genuinely disputed legal issues that are better presented in a brief separate from the pretrial memorandum.

6. **Voir Dire.** Judge Buckwalter permits counsel to conduct all voir dire. The courtroom deputy is present during voir dire. Disputes will be handled by Judge Buckwalter in chambers. Sixty to ninety minutes should be sufficient time to conduct voir dire.

7. **Sidebars.** Judge Buckwalter discourages the use of sidebar conferences for reasons set forth in paragraph 11 of his pretrial and trial procedures (see page 43 of this book).

8. **In Limine Motions.** Motions in limine must be filed no less than 10 days before trial. Responses must be filed no less than five days before trial.

9. **Examination of Witnesses Out of Sequence.** Judge Buckwalter allows witnesses to be examined out of turn for the convenience of the witnesses.

10. **Opening Statements and Summations.** Judge Buckwalter feels that 30 minutes is sufficient for opening statements and 45 minutes is sufficient for closing.

11. **Examination of Witnesses or Argument by More Than One Attorney.** Judge Buckwalter allows more than one attorney for a party to examine different witnesses or to argue different points before the court.

12. Examination of Witnesses Beyond Redirect and Recross. Judge Buckwalter feels that direct examination and cross-examination should be adequate in a well-prepared trial. He will permit redirect on issues brought up in cross-examination, but not to bring up matters that counsel neglected to cover on direct. Recross is limited to matters brought up on redirect. No further examination is normally permitted.

13. Videotaped Testimony. All objections will be ruled upon in advance of playing videotapes to the jury. To accomplish this, all objections to videotapes must be filed no less than 10 days before trial. Responses must be filed no less than five days before trial.

14. Reading of Material Into the Record. Reading of material into the record may be done in a manner agreed upon by court and counsel.

15. Preparation of Exhibits. Judge Buckwalter requires that exhibits be pre-marked and pre-exchanged. Counsel need only provide one set of trial exhibits to the court.

16. Offering Exhibits Into Evidence. Judge Buckwalter requires exhibits to be placed in evidence at the close of each party's case-in-chief.

17. Motions for Judgment as a Matter of Law. Motions for judgment as a matter of law (F.R.C.P. 50(a)) may be made orally. Such motions may be made in writing if counsel desire and must be in writing when the court deems it necessary or applicable rules require a written motion.

18. Proposed Jury Instructions and Verdict Forms. Counsel should submit points on each matter he or she wishes to have covered by the court. (See paragraph 8 of Judge Buckwalter's pretrial and trial procedures on page 42 of this book). Each instruction should be on a separate page. Supplemental instructions may be submitted at any time prior to the closing of the evidence. Pursuant to Fed.R.Civ.P. 51, the court conducts a charging conference.

19. Proposed Findings of Fact and Conclusions of Law. Except at hearings on petitions for TRO or preliminary injunction, Judge Buckwalter prefers that an initial proposed findings of fact and conclusions of law be submitted to him at least 24 hours before the start of the trial. Judge Buckwalter further expects that counsel will submit an amended proposed findings of fact and conclusions of law at a reasonable time after the close of the evidence. Normally, the time for such submission is determined at the conclusion of the case by agreement of counsel.

Jury Deliberations

1. Written Jury Instructions. Judge Buckwalter does give a copy of instructions to the jury, when the complexity of the law involved requires it.

2. Exhibits in the Jury Room. At the conclusion of trial, an on-the-record determination is made by the court as to which exhibits go out with the jury.

3. Handling of Jury Requests to Read Back Testimony or Replay Tapes. Judge Buckwalter decides each such request according to the facts of the particular case.

4. Availability of Counsel During Jury Deliberations. Judge Buckwalter permits counsel to return to their offices only if they are able to return to the courtroom within 15 minutes.

5. Taking the Verdict and Special Interrogatories. The nature and requirements of the case dictate whether Judge Buckwalter takes a general or a special verdict or submits interrogatories to the jury.

6. Polling the Jury. Judge Buckwalter permits polling of the jury.

7. Interviewing the Jury. Judge Buckwalter will permit counsel to interview jurors.

CRIMINAL CASES

Judge Buckwalter does not handle criminal cases at this time.

OTHER GENERAL MATTERS

Judge Buckwalter does not expect to receive appellate briefs if a decision rendered by him is appealed.

PRETRIAL AND TRIAL PROCEDURES
BEFORE JUDGE RONALD L. BUCKWALTER

PRETRIAL

1. As soon as reasonably practicable after an action is filed or a case is reassigned to Judge Buckwalter's calendar, the courtroom deputy will mail to counsel a status report form which is to be completed and returned to this office within 10 days. Based substantially upon those reports, the court will issue a scheduling order as prescribed by F.R.C.P. 16. In some cases, either upon request of counsel or pursuant to Section 3:01 of the Civil Justice Expense and Delay Reduction Plan of this court or *sua sponte*, the court will set a scheduling conference to establish the terms of the F.R.C.P. 16 scheduling order.

2. The court expects discovery to be conducted promptly, diligently and fairly. Because they have been established after careful consideration of the status reports of each party, *discovery deadlines as set forth in the scheduling order will be enforced.* Counsel should seek discovery enforcement or relief only by filing a motion promptly.

3. The court will establish a specific trial date if counsel have persuaded the court that such a special listing is an indispensable requisite to an expeditious trial. Normally, all cases shall be listed in the trial pool. Every case in the trial pool will be deemed ready to proceed to trial upon 24 hours telephone notice to counsel. The court will attempt to attach cases for trial as they are listed in the trial pool.

4. Counsel should call the COURTROOM DEPUTY regarding any matters relating to the scheduling of pretrial conferences or hearings in any civil or criminal case, as well as any matters related to pretrial and post-trial motions in any CRIMINAL case. Counsel should call the JUDICIAL SECRETARY regarding any matters relating to pretrial and post-trial motions in any CIVIL case.

5. Contacting the court by letter or phone during the pendency of litigation is normally not appropriate for the following reasons: (a) Pretrial matters involving discovery disputes or case dispositive motions should normally be handled by motion practice in accordance with Local Rules; and (b) Questions about scheduling whether involving dates or times of hearings or possible conferences with the court about any matters related to the case should be communicated orally or in writing to the courtroom deputy.

6. Because *ex parte* communications are normally inappropriate, if counsel must contact the court, such contact should be made only after consulting with opposing counsel. If opposing counsel objects to the proposed contact with the court, then counsel should file a motion. Merely sending opposing counsel a copy of a letter sent to chambers does not fulfill this directive.

7. Law clerks may not render advice to counsel and have no authority to grant continuances or to speak on behalf of the court.

8. Upon completion of discovery, but no later than ten (10) days before a case is to be listed in the trial pool, counsel shall file a pretrial memorandum which may be supplemented up to 24 hours before the trial begins. The pretrial memorandum shall include the following:

   (a) A brief, concise summary of the nature of the case.
   (b) A list of all witnesses to be presented with a brief statement of the nature of their testimony. Witnesses not listed may not be called in the party's case-in-chief.
   (c) A list of all exhibits pre-numbered and pre-exchanged among all counsel, including those exhibits whose introduction into evidence is objected to and the reasons for the objections.
   (d) Claimant's itemized statement of damages or other relief sought.
   (e) A statement of any anticipated legal issues on which the court will be required to rule, together with counsel's single best authority (case citation, Rule of Civil Procedure, Rule of Evidence, statute, etc.)
   (f) All stipulations of counsel and an itemized list of any admissions to be read into evidence.
   (g) In all jury cases, proposed points for charge and in all non-jury cases, proposed findings of fact and conclusions of law. Counsel have the right to file supplemental points, findings and conclusions upon the close of testimony.
   (h) The court requires that all submissions to it be in duplicate. An exception to this requirement is exhibits, a single court copy of which is sufficient at the time of trial. In certain instances, the court will excuse its requirement for copies of exhibits if the making of the same is unduly burdensome.

9. Motions *in limine* must be filed no less than ten (10) days before trial. Responses must be filed no less than five (5) days before trial.

10. All objections will be ruled upon in advance of playing videotapes to the jury. To accomplish this, all objections to videotapes must be filed no less than ten (10) days before trial. Responses must be filed no less than five (5) days before trial.

TRIAL

11. Because side bar conferences interrupt the flow of the trial and interfere with the jurors' understanding of a witness' testimony, the court intends to avoid side bar conferences. Under most circumstances this is accomplished by virtue of counsel having anticipated the legal issues and objections and raised them during pretrial proceedings or at a recess or after adjournment.

12. Court sessions involving jury trials will commence daily at 9:30 a.m. and continue until 12:30 p.m., with a short mid-morning break. Court will reconvene at 1:45 p.m. and continue until 4:30 p.m., with a short mid-afternoon break. The 4:30 p.m. adjournment may be extended depending upon the transportation considerations of the jurors.

13. Counsel has the responsibility to have all witnesses available in court as scheduled. Failure to do so may result in sanctions.

14. Except for good cause shown, counsel shall be limited in the examination of a witness to direct, cross, redirect and recross. As to redirect and recross, counsel are not entitled to these as a matter of right.

15. Whenever a deposition or portion thereof is to be read into evidence, a written designation of the pages and lines shall be furnished to opposing counsel and to the court at least 24 hours before commencement of trial. Opposing counsel shall submit any counter designations in a similar fashion within 24 hours.

16. In conducting videotape recordings, counsel should do so with acute sensitivity realizing that the videotape may be shown to a jury. Thus, skillful organization of the testimony, elimination of unnecessary objections and conservation of time are essential in videotape recordings.

17. Whenever a deposition or videotape is to be used, a transcript of the testimony shall be furnished to the court in advance.

18. All exhibits, once identified, shall be placed and kept at all times on the exhibit table in sequential order arranged according to each party except when being used during examination of a witness. Each exhibit should be offered into evidence at the conclusion of a party's case. Normally, it is the court's policy to send out all exhibits admitted into evidence with the jury when they retire to deliberate. The only exceptions will be those exhibits which all parties agree or which the court, upon motion, determines should not go out with the jury. The court's policy on exhibits reflects its belief that well organized and identified exhibits are of great value to counsel in their efficient presentation of the case as well as to jurors in their understanding of the case.

19. Counsel shall conduct examination of witnesses from counsel table or from the lectern.

20. When necessary to an intelligent understanding of the testimony, counsel may display an exhibit specifically to the jury upon its admission by holding it directly in front of all jurors at once or by circulating the exhibit among the jurors. In either case, counsel should request the court's permission before doing so.

21. Opening statements should be *brief* and *outline only (not argue)* the evidence counsel intends to present.

22. Summations should not exceed forty-five (45) minutes unless a shorter or longer time is established by the court. Rebuttal argument by plaintiff shall ordinarily not exceed ten (10) minutes.

These Pretrial and Trial Procedures are effective as of August 1, 1995.

Judge Stewart Dalzell

Judge Dalzell was born on September 18, 1943, in Hackensack, New Jersey. He received a B.S. in Economics from the University of Pennsylvania, Wharton School, in 1965. He thereupon worked at the National Broadcasting Company in New York City before returning to the University of Pennsylvania Law School, from which he received a J.D. in 1969. Judge Dalzell then was a visiting lecturer in law at the Wharton School at the University of Pennsylvania for one year before entering the private practice of law in Philadelphia in June of 1970. He was appointed to the United States District Court for the Eastern District of Pennsylvania on September 16, 1991.

PRELIMINARY GENERAL MATTERS

1. Correspondence with the Court. Judge Dalzell permits correspondence for scheduling an extension of time, but discourages correspondence that raises substantive issues that should be brought to the court's attention by motion. See Fed.R.Civ.P. 7(b)(1). All correspondence should include the action number of the case.

2. Communications with Law Clerks. Judge Dalzell permits communications with his law clerks concerning administrative aspects of cases but never on the merits of cases. Scheduling matters or requests for extensions of time should initially be directed to his courtroom deputy.

3. Telephone Conferences. Judge Dalzell rarely holds telephone conferences. All pretrial conferences are held in person.

4. Oral Arguments and Evidentiary Hearings. Judge Dalzell does not set aside certain days or hours for oral arguments or evidentiary hearings.

5. Pro Hac Vice Admissions. Judge Dalzell has no preference as to how counsel present requests for pro hac vice admissions, but, consistent with the local rule, expects local counsel to remain knowledgeable about the case.

CIVIL CASES
Pretrial Procedure

1. Pretrial Conferences. Judge Dalzell normally conducts a Rule 16 pretrial conference two weeks after the defendant answers the complaint. A copy of Judge Dalzell's scheduling policy statement (shown on page 50 of this book) accompanies the letter scheduling the conference. Counsel should be prepared to discuss settlement, or the barriers to it, at the conference, and therefore, trial counsel should attend this conference. Judge Dalzell will conduct status conferences, settlement conferences, and final pretrial conferences as needed or as requested in a particular case.

Continuances and Extensions

1. General Policy. Judge Dalzell adheres to the spirit of the Civil Justice Expense and Delay Reduction Plan of the court. Although Judge Dalzell tries to accommodate counsel with regard to minor amendments regarding the scheduling of briefs, oral arguments, and the like, discovery deadlines and trial dates set at the Rule 16 conference are only changed for weighty cause shown.

2. Request for Extensions and Continuances. Requests for extensions of time should be made as far in advance as possible. Judge Dalzell does not grant unopposed requests for extensions of time as a matter of course and strictly adheres to the requirement of

Fed.R.Civ.P. 6(b) that such requests be made "before the expiration" of the originally set deadline. Absent grave emergencies, requests for extensions of trial dates submitted within a month of trial will not be favorably considered.

General Motion Practice

1.   Oral Argument on Motions.   Judge Dalzell holds oral arguments on motions only when he believes it will assist him in deciding the motion. Thus, in all but the rarest of cases, no oral argument is ordered.

2.   Reply and Surreply Briefs.   Judge Dalzell disfavors reply or surreply briefs. Before filing a reply or surreply brief, counsel should obtain permission from the judge.

3.   Chambers Copies of Motion Papers.   Judge Dalzell prefers that courtesy copies of motion papers be delivered to his chambers.

4.   Appendices or Exhibits to Briefs or Motions.   For briefs or motions submitted to Judge Dalzell, counsel should affix tabs to each appendix or exhibit.

Discovery Matters

1.   Length of Discovery Period and Extensions.   Counsel should recognize that the median time from filing through disposition in the Eastern District of Pennsylvania is eight months, and counsel should manage their caseloads accordingly. Except in cases placed on the Special Management Track, or where extraordinary circumstances exist, Judge Dalzell sets a relatively short discovery deadline, seldom more than 90 days after the Rule 16 conference. Judge Dalzell considers the merits of motions for extension of discovery deadlines, whether opposed or unopposed.

2.   Discovery Conferences and Dispute Resolution.   Judge Dalzell expects counsel to resolve discovery disputes between them, and holds discovery conferences only upon request. Except in rare emergencies, Judge Dalzell does not permit telephone conferences to resolve discovery disputes. With respect to discovery motions, Judge Dalzell enforces the local rules regarding discovery. Additionally, pursuant to the local rule, Judge Dalzell often summarily grants all these discovery motions without waiting for a response, and therefore the burden is on counsel opposing the discovery motion to advise Judge Dalzell's chambers at once that he or she seeks to file a response.

3.   Expert Witnesses.   At the Rule 16 conference, Judge Dalzell sets a separate deadline for the exchange of expert witness reports. Judge Dalzell expects that counsel will identify expert witnesses well in advance of trial and that an unavailable expert witness will be videotaped for use at trial. Judge Dalzell does not continue trials because experts are unavailable.

Settlement

1.   General Approach to Settlement and Nonjury Cases.   Judge Dalzell takes a very interventionist approach to settlement unless the case is nonjury. In the latter event, Judge Dalzell will refer settlement negotiations to his magistrate judge, an agreed-upon district judge, or some other mutually acceptable party. Sometimes Judge Dalzell will invite the parties' consideration of creative alternatives to trial resolution of their dispute.

Arbitration

1.   General Approach to Arbitration Cases. Judge Dalzell typically does not conduct Rule 16 pretrial conferences in arbitration cases. He does expect, however, that arbitration trials will be conducted in the "meaningful manner" Local Rule of Civil Procedure 53.2(5)(C) requires.

2.   Timing of Motion Practice in Arbitration Cases. Judge Dalzell will normally deny as untimely any motion filed within 15 days of a scheduled arbitration, other than motions in limine.

3.   Settlement in Arbitration Cases. Judge Dalzell is available for settlement discussions in arbitration conferences, at the request of any party.

4.   Scheduling of Trial De Novo from Arbitration. When a trial de novo is granted, Judge Dalzell schedules the case for trial promptly. He will typically hold a pretrial conference within 10 days of the filing of the trial de novo demand, and will schedule the trial for a date shortly afterwards.

Proposed Final Pretrial Memoranda

1.   Required Form of Pretrial Memoranda. Judge Dalzell provides counsel with the appropriate form of pretrial memoranda at the Rule 16 conference. The date for submission of the pretrial material (stipulations, exhibits, proposed jury instructions, etc.) is provided for in the scheduling order entered at the Rule 16 conference. Motions in limine must be filed no later than one week before trial.

2.   Common Deficiencies in Pretrial Memoranda. Judge Dalzell is disappointed at the frequent failure of counsel to make a serious effort to stipulate to as many facts in advance of trial as possible.

Injunctions

1.   Scheduling and Expedited Discovery. Judge Dalzell schedules preliminary and permanent injunction hearings promptly, and he attempts to combine the two hearings where possible. He permits expedited discovery on injunctive matters.

2.   Proposed Findings of Fact and Conclusions of Law. Judge Dalzell sometimes requires that proposed findings of fact and conclusions of law be submitted to him before the beginning of an injunction hearing. At a minimum, he will require prehearing memoranda of law.

Trial Procedure

1.   Scheduling of Cases. Judge Dalzell sets firm trial dates for each case unless his criminal docket precludes it. Civil jury trials typically begin on Tuesdays, though sometimes jury selection is done on Fridays. The only event that prevents the actual beginning of a civil trial on the date scheduled would be the interposition of a criminal trial.

2.   Conflicts of Counsel. Judge Dalzell expects counsel to advise him at the Rule 16 conference about any conflicts that may affect the trial schedule. If several counsel are involved in a particular case, Judge Dalzell will specially list the case to assure that all counsel will be available.

3.   Cases Involving Out-of-Town Parties or Witnesses. Generally, Judge Dalzell makes no distinction in scheduling because either counsel or witnesses are from outside the Philadelphia metropolitan area.

4. **Note-taking by Jurors.** Judge Dalzell permits jurors to take notes, and jurors have availed themselves of that opportunity in every case.

5. **Trial Briefs.** Judge Dalzell allows counsel to submit trial briefs if such briefing would assist the court.

6. **Voir Dire.** Absent an anticipated problem, Judge Dalzell permits counsel to conduct all voir dire in civil cases. If disputes arise during the voir dire, Judge Dalzell handles them in chambers. Except in complex cases, Judge Dalzell expects counsel to complete voir dire in no more than one hour.

7. **Sidebars.** Judge Dalzell actively discourages sidebars because he, juries, and his court reporter loathe them. Counsel should anticipate problems and discuss with each other the objection and its resolution before bringing it to Judge Dalzell's attention. Except in the rarest of cases, matters to be discussed outside the jury's hearing can be covered during natural breaks in the trial.

8. **In Limine Motions.** Judge Dalzell requires that all motions in limine be filed no later than one week before the commencement of trial.

9. **Examination of Witnesses Out of Sequence.** Judge Dalzell will permit counsel to take witnesses out of turn for the convenience of the witnesses.

10. **Opening Statements and Summations.** Judge Dalzell encourages counsel to be brief in opening statements. For summations, he expects counsel in civil cases not to exceed 20 to 30 minutes.

11. **Examination of Witnesses or Argument by More Than One Attorney.** Judge Dalzell will permit more than one lawyer to examine different witnesses; however, only one lawyer for a party may examine a particular witness. More than one lawyer for a party may argue different points in a motion.

12. **Examination of Witnesses Beyond Redirect and Recross.** Generally, Judge Dalzell does not allow further examination of witnesses after redirect and recross.

13. **Videotaped Testimony.** Rulings on disputes or objections should be sought in advance through submission to Judge Dalzell of a written transcript of the relevant testimony. Counsel should edit the videotape in advance of trial.

14. **Reading of Material Into the Record.** While Judge Dalzell has no special practice or policy on reading material into the record, he encourages counsel to minimize the time required for reading to the jury.

15. **Preparation of Exhibits.** Exhibits should be pre-marked and pre-exchanged and two copies of the exhibits should be delivered to chambers in advance of trial in three-ring binders with tabs to identify each exhibit.

16. **Offering Exhibits Into Evidence.** Judge Dalzell prefers to have exhibits admitted at natural times during the course of the trial, typically at the close of each party's case.

17. **Motions for Verdict as a Matter of Law.** Motions for judgment as a matter of law under Rule 50 may be made either orally or in writing.

18. **Proposed Jury Instructions and Verdict Forms.** As part of the pretrial submission, Judge Dalzell requires that counsel submit proposed jury instructions. Unless the trial is very short, Judge Dalzell will share with counsel his draft jury charge in advance of the charge conference. During the charge conference Judge Dalzell considers counsels' suggestions for improvement in his draft.

19. Proposed Findings of Fact and Conclusions of Law. Judge Dalzell requires the submission of proposed findings of fact and conclusions of law a week in advance of the commencement of trial, and encourages counsel to stipulate to as many findings of fact as possible.

Jury Deliberations

1. Written Jury Instructions. Judge Dalzell invariably gives the jury at least two copies of the jury charge.

2. Exhibits in the Jury Room. All exhibits go out with the jury unless counsel agree that some should not be included for reasons, typically, of bulk or possible confusion because of excessive detail.

3. Handling of Jury Requests to Read Back Testimony or Replay Tapes. Judge Dalzell will allow short portions of testimony to be read back or tapes to be replayed if this is practical under all the circumstances.

4. Availability of Counsel During Jury Deliberations. Counsel should remain in the courthouse except when the jury takes its lunch.

5. Taking the Verdict and Special Interrogatories. Judge Dalzell typically submits interrogatories to the jury in civil cases, and each juror takes with him or her a copy of the questionnaire.

6. Polling the Jury. Judge Dalzell permits polling of the jury if counsel makes a timely request.

7. Interviewing the Jury. After the verdict is recorded, Judge Dalzell advises the jurors that they are under no obligation to speak with counsel, but may do so if they so elect.

CRIMINAL CASES

1. Approach to Oral Argument and Motions. Judge Dalzell has no policy on the scheduling of oral argument on motions. He tries to consolidate such arguments with a pretrial conference. Hearings on motions to suppress, or on *Starks* motions, are held as far in advance of trial as possible; they are rarely held the morning of trial.

2. Pretrial Conferences. Generally, Judge Dalzell does not hold pretrial conferences in every criminal case. He often finds it most helpful to hold a motions hearing at least one or two weeks before the start of trial.

3. Voir Dire. Judge Dalzell conducts voir dire in criminal cases. He requests that counsel submit proposed voir dire questions at least a day in advance of trial for his consideration.

4. Other Practices and Procedures. If either the government or defense counsel takes exception to any aspect of the presentence-investigation report, Judge Dalzell encourages the submission of sentencing memoranda at least one week in advance of the sentencing hearing. He also encourages the government to file section 5K1.1 motions as far in advance of sentencing hearings as possible.

OTHER GENERAL MATTERS

1. Appellate Briefs. Counsel may submit appellate briefs to Judge Dalzell if they wish.

2. Courtroom Decorum. Judge Dalzell expects counsel to be punctual and courteous to each other at all times. He has no patience for posturing, grandstanding, or contesting evidentiary rulings after they are made.

3.   Ex Parte Temporary Restraining Orders. Absent exceptional circumstances, Judge Dalzell has a strong policy against granting ex parte temporary restraining orders.

4.   Stipulations. Judge Dalzell energetically enforces the local rule regarding written stipulations.

JUDGE DALZELL'S SCHEDULING POLICY STATEMENT

1. Judge Dalzell orders Rule 16 scheduling conferences about two weeks after the defendant responds to the complaint. Settlement invariably appears on the agenda of this conference.

2. Absent compelling circumstances, counsel should file motions to dismiss, transfer, add parties or seeking other threshold action before the conference. Counsel should file summary judgment motions so as not to delay trial, and in any event at least thirty days before the trial date. Counsel should note the prospect of Rule 56 motions at the conference.

3. The conference usually takes ten to twenty minutes. Absent extraordinary circumstances, the conference will not be held by telephone. Absent extraordinary circumstances approved in advance of the conference, trial counsel must attend.

4. In an uncomplicated case, discovery should be completed in sixty to ninety days, with a trial listing shortly thereafter. In complex cases, longer periods of discovery may be permitted. The discovery deadline is in no sense a hypothetical date. It will only be changed for weighty cause shown.

5. The trial listing will be for a specific date, typically a Monday, for jury trials. These trial listings do not constitute a "pool". The case will be called for trial on the date assigned unless Speedy Trial Act constraints in a criminal case are preemptive.

6. Judge Dalzell typically does not hold a further conference unless counsel requests one to discuss settlement or a special trial issue. Judge Dalzell always seeks to help the parties achieve the settlement of their disputes.

7. Counsel should make requests for continuance by motion, with a concise explanatory memorandum appended. Judge Dalzell will grant a continuance only for the most compelling reasons; in any event, Judge Dalzell considers motions for continuances on their merits, whether opposed or unopposed. In any motion for continuance, Judge Dalzell reserves the right to require a written statement, signed by the plaintiff, that the plaintiff consents to the continuance.

8. Foreseeable discovery problems, including noncompliance or tardiness, will not constitute an acceptable ground for continuance of the trial. Counsel should act promptly to enforce the discovery schedule.

9. When timely discovery is not forthcoming after a reasonable attempt to obtain it, Judge Dalzell will act under Local Rule 26.1(g), subject to the movant's good faith compliance with Local Rule 26.1(f).

10. Trial depositions must be scheduled so as not to delay trial or disrupt trial preparation. They may not be taken later than fourteen days before the trial date unless the parties agree or the Court approves. Continuance applications because of refusal of an expert witness to appear for trial or to be available for trial deposition will not be granted unless notice of the trial date was given to the witness at least sixty days in advance or at the earliest reasonable opportunity.

11. A Pretrial Stipulation is required, signed by all counsel.* Although counsel should consult Local Rule 16.1(c) for guidance, they should tailor the Pretrial Stipulation to be commensurate with the needs of the case. The foregoing sentence is intended to encourage brevity and simplicity. The Stipulation should be submitted at least fourteen days before the trial date or as specified in the Scheduling Order. Absent cooperation, counsel may file a separate pretrial memorandum with the permission of the Court. If the Pretrial Stipulation is not submitted on time or in proper form, the Court may consider the case not ready for trial.

12. Unexcused violations of scheduling orders are subject to sanctions under Fed.R.Civ.P. 16(f), upon motion or the Court's initiative. The Court will normally sanction counsels' failure to appear at a Rule 16 pretrial conference by awarding costs to counsel who do appear.

13. Direct all communications regarding the trial calendar to Judge Dalzell's courtroom deputy clerk, Eileen Adler: (267) 299-7399.

Judge Stewart Dalzell

04/00

---

* A Pretrial Stipulation is not required in arbitrations, but is required in arbitration appeals. See Arbitration Scheduling Order form.

Judge Legrome D. Davis

Judge Davis was born in 1952 in Columbus, Ohio. He received a B.A. from Princeton University in 1973 and a J.D. from Rutgers University School of Law in 1976. Judge Davis served as an assistant district attorney in Philadelphia from 1977 to 1980, and again from 1981 to 1987. Judge Davis was an attorney with the Pennsylvania Crime Commission from 1980 to 1981, and he worked as an attorney in the Office of the General Counsel of the University of Pennsylvania in 1987. Judge Davis served as a judge on the Court of Common Pleas, First Judicial District of Pennsylvania, from 1987 to 2002. He was appointed to the United States District Court for the Eastern District of Pennsylvania on April 23, 2002.

PRELIMINARY GENERAL MATTERS

1. Correspondence with the Court. All communication with the judicial chambers should occur by letter or formal motion. Letters to the court are permitted only if they pertain exclusively to administrative and/or scheduling matters. For parties represented by counsel, communication shall be made only by those attorneys who have entered an appearance and who are identified on the docket sheet.

All other written communications with the court concerning any case assigned to the court's calendar shall be by the filing of a pleading, motion, application, brief, legal memorandum, or other similar filing permitted by the Federal Rules of Civil or Criminal Procedure or the Local Rules of Civil or Criminal Procedure.

2. Communication with Law Clerks. All questions concerning matters on Judge Davis's docket should be directed to Mia Harvey, the civil deputy, or Donna Croce, the criminal deputy. Communication with law clerks is not permitted.

3. Telephone Conferences. Judge Davis rarely schedules telephone conferences. Counsel desiring to schedule a telephone conference should contact Judge Davis's chambers by letter and advise the court of the reason for the request. Judge Davis will consider requests on a case-by-case basis.

4. Electronic Case Filing. Upon service of the complaint and summons, counsel must promptly file proof of service on ECF.

5. Oral Arguments and Evidentiary Hearings. Judge Davis does not reserve specific days or times for oral arguments or evidentiary hearings. Counsel may request oral argument or an evidentiary hearing on pending motions. Judge Davis will consider the request and determine whether to schedule argument.

6. Pro Hac Vice Admissions. Counsel not admitted to practice in the Eastern District of Pennsylvania must be sponsored for pro hac vice by a member of the bar of this court. Strict compliance with Rule 83.5.2(b) of the Local Rules of Civil Procedure for the United States District Court for the Eastern District of Pennsylvania is required.

CIVIL CASES
Pretrial Procedure

1. Pretrial Conferences. Judge Davis schedules an initial Rule 16 conference within 30 days of the filing of the answer. Rule 16 conferences are normally held in chambers, but sometimes are conducted on the record in open court. The chambers deputy schedules the initial pretrial conference.

At least three business days prior to the initial Rule 16 conference, counsel must submit a completed scheduling information report. The court's processes and procedures rely upon the good faith of counsel and the diligent compliance with Rule 26(f). The Rule 26(f) meeting should take place as soon as possible, and at least 10 days prior to the Rule 16 conference. Counsel should file the Rule 26(f) report on ECF.

The attendance of lead counsel at the Rule 16 conference is required; attendance by telephone is not permitted. If lead counsel is unavailable, upon written request, substitute counsel may appear at the Rule 16 conference. All counsel attending the Rule 16 conference are expected to be fully conversant with the factual background of the action, anticipated legal issues, and potential procedural impediments to timely resolution of the action.

Topics addressed at the initial Rule 16 conference frequently include those listed in Local Rule 16.1(b), Fed.R.Civ.P. 16(b) and (c), and the status of self-executing disclosures under Fed.R.Civ.P. 26(a). Counsel participating in Rule 16 conferences should be prepared to address these concerns and are expected to have authority from their clients to address settlement. In complex cases, counsel may be requested to prepare an agenda for the Rule 16 conference. Following the Rule 16 conference, the court will enter a scheduling order that sets firm dates for the completion of discovery, the exchange of expert reports, and the filing of dispositive motions.

Continuances and Extensions

General Motion Practice

1. *Oral Argument.* Counsel may request oral argument on pending motions. Judge Davis will consider the request and determine whether to schedule argument.

2. *Page Limitations and Page Numbering.* Original motions and responses are limited to 25 double-spaced pages each, excluding exhibits. All motions, responses, briefs, or memoranda must be submitted on numbered pages.

3. *Reply and Surreply Briefs.* Reply and surreply briefs may be filed only with leave of the court. Generally, they will be permitted only when necessary to rebut an issue or factual assertion not covered by the party's original submission. Counsel should file a motion requesting leave to file any additional document, attaching the proposed reply or surreply as an exhibit. When permitted, reply and surreply briefs are limited to 10 pages each and should be filed within seven days of the filing of the document to which it replies.

4. *Citations to the Record and Exhibits.* Every factual assertion contained in a brief or memorandum must be supported by a specific page citation to the record. All exhibits must be individually labeled and identified, and exhibits that contain multiple pages must be numbered.

5. *Chambers Copies of Motions.* Judge Davis requests that parties send to chambers by mail a single courtesy copy of all motions and exhibits. All proposed orders consisting of these or more pages should be submitted on a computer diskette or CD, in WordPerfect format.

6. *Rule 56 Motions.* Upon motion for summary judgment pursuant to Fed.R.Civ.P. 56, counsel should also submit, in numbered paragraphs, a separate, concise, and explicit statement of the material facts as to which the moving party contends no genuine issue exists.

The brief in opposition to a summary judgment motion should include a separate, concise, and explicit statement of the material facts, in numbered paragraphs, responding to the numbered paragraphs required of the movant in the above paragraph, as to which it is contended genuine issues exist.

Statements of material facts in support of, or in opposition to, a summary judgment motion should include citations to the record in support of the party's contentions.

All material facts set forth in the statement required to be served by the moving party may be taken by the court as admitted unless challenged, with a specific citation to the record, by the opposing party.

Discovery Matters

1.   Consultation with Opposing Counsel. While Judge Davis believes that the active participation of the court in the pretrial process is an important factor in the prompt, efficient, and fair resolution of disputes, it is expected that counsel will bring matters to his attention only after they have been discussed with opposing counsel. Moreover, the judge believes discovery to be a process in which counsel secures, in a timely and cooperative manner, information legally relevant to the fair resolution of a dispute; it is not a vehicle for securing an unfair tactical advantage.

2.   Discovery Conferences and Dispute Resolution. Judge Davis does not normally conduct further discovery conferences. The court expects discovery to be voluntary and cooperative in accordance with the Federal Rules of Civil Procedure.

3.   Confidentiality Agreements. Parties may agree privately to keep documents and information confidential. The court may enter an order of confidentiality only after making a specific finding of good cause based on a particularized showing that the parties' privacy interests outweigh the public's right to obtain information concerning judicial proceedings.

4.   Expert Witnesses. Counsel are required to identify expert witnesses and provide the curriculum vitae for their experts. Counsel are also expected to voluntarily exchange expert reports, and to conduct interrogatories and depositions in accordance with the dates outlined in the court's scheduling orders. See Fed.R.Civ.P. 26(a)(2)(B). Except for good cause, expert testimony will be limited at trial to the information provided.

Settlement

1.   Settlement Conferences. Judge Davis works with Magistrate Judge Timothy R. Rice. Settlement conferences on matters assigned to Judge Davis typically occur before Judge Rice. Requests for settlement conferences should be presented in writing to Judge Davis, and only upon the existence of a reasonable belief by both parties that the case might be resolved at a settlement conference. Depending upon the particulars of a case, a settlement conference might occur at the inception of the case, after the completion of discovery, or after the resolution of dispositive motions. Counsel's views as to the most opportune time for a settlement conference will be solicited at the Rule 16 conference.

Final Pretrial Conference and Proposed Final Pretrial Memoranda

1.   Final Pretrial Conferences. Judge Davis typically holds a final pretrial conference sometime during the month prior to the anticipated trial date. A firm trial date (at least two weeks in the future) will be established at the final pretrial conference. Counsel should therefore be familiar with the schedules of all necessary witnesses and parties. Settlement and trial procedure will also be addressed at the final pretrial conference.

Practice and Procedures of Judges and Judges' Forms and Orders

2. *Required Form of Pretrial Memoranda.* Final pretrial memoranda must be received by the court at least three business days before the final pretrial conference. One copy of each pretrial memorandum should be filed with the clerk of court and one copy should be sent to Judge Davis's chambers.

In accordance with Local Rule of Civil Procedure 16.1(c), the pretrial memoranda must also be filed with the clerk of court. In addition to compliance with Local Rule of Civil Procedure 16.1(c), the pretrial memoranda should include the following:

    a. the identity of each expert witness the party anticipates calling at trial;
    b. a curriculum vitae for each expert witness;
    c. the identity of each fact witness to be called in the party's case-in-chief and a brief statement of the nature of the witness's expected testimony;
    d. an itemized statement of the claimant's damages or relief sought; and
    e. a statement of any anticipated important legal issues on which the court will be required to rule, accompanied by the best single authority on any such issue.

Injunctions

1. *Injunctions.* Judge Davis usually conducts a conference with counsel before scheduling hearings for temporary restraining orders and injunctive relief.

Judge Davis requires the submission of proposed findings of fact and conclusions of law for TRO and injunction hearings. The schedule for document submission will be set at the initial conference.

Trial Procedure

1. *Cases Involving Out-of-Town Witnesses or Parties.* Trial scheduling will not substantially change merely because of the involvement of out-of-town witnesses. Counsel are expected to control the availability of their witnesses.

2. *Note-taking by Jurors.* Judge Davis permits jurors to take notes and will issue an instruction on juror note-taking.

3. *Submissions of Proposed Voir Dire Questions, Jury Instructions, and Jury Interrogatories.* It is expected that counsel will work cooperatively and submit joint proposed voir dire questions, jury instructions on substantive issues, and proposed special interrogatories or verdict forms. In the event that counsel cannot agree upon the substantive jury instructions or the verdict forms or interrogatories, each counsel should submit a proposed jury instruction or interrogatory on the points in dispute. Citations to relevant case law or pattern jury instructions should be included.

Counsel should submit one copy of the joint and/or individual submissions to Judge Davis's chambers at least three days prior to the commencement of trial. The parties should also submit a computer disk or CD containing their instructions or verdict form in WordPerfect for Windows format. Each proposed jury instruction should be double-spaced on a single piece of paper. The parties should submit jury instructions with respect to substantive issues in the case. Proposed instructions on procedural matters such as the burden of proof and credibility are not required. Judge Davis may accept supplemental jury instructions until the start of closing argument.

4. *Voir Dire.* Judge Davis conducts voir dire and asks a standard set of voir dire questions. Parties should file proposed voir dire questions consistent with the schedule established at the final pretrial conference.

5. *In Limine Motions.* Motions in limine must be submitted at least seven days prior to the trial date, and will be resolved prior to the commencement of trial.

6. **Questioning of Witnesses.** As Judge Davis uses the electronic sound recording system, all examinations of witnesses must be conducted from counsel table or the lectern.

7. **Opening and Closing Statements.** The agreement of counsel on the time limits for opening statements and summations is appreciated. Judge Davis believes 20 minutes to be sufficient to comprehensively outline a party's anticipated proofs in an opening statement. Thirty to forty-five minutes is usually sufficient for a party to adequately present a closing argument.

8. **Examination of Witnesses or Argument by More Than One Attorney.** More than one attorney for a party may examine different witnesses or present argument on different issues before the fact finder. Multiple attorneys for the same party may not examine the same witnesses or present argument on the same point.

9. **Videotaped Testimony.** Counsel should videotape the testimony of witnesses unavailable to testify before the jury consistent with the schedule established at the final pretrial conference. As a general matter, the court is not inclined to delay a trial, or to recess prematurely, merely because a witness's personal or professional schedule does not allow his or her presence at the most opportune time for counsel.

Videotaped testimony should begin with the witness being sworn. Counsel are expected to provide the court with a transcript of the witness's testimony in advance of the tape being offered at trial. Objections must also be given to the court in advance of the tape being offered into evidence. The court will rule on all objections well in advance of the submission of the videotaped testimony to the jury. As a general matter, Judge Davis believes the resolution of legal issues should not delay the presentation of evidence to the jury.

10. **Trial Exhibits.** All exhibits should be marked and exchanged among counsel prior to trial. Two bound copies of trial exhibits must be provided to the court as soon as practicable, but in no event later than the commencement of trial. In addition, each party is required to provide a schedule of its exhibits. At the conclusion of the trial, original exhibits will be returned to the proponent.

11. **Motions for Judgment as a Matter of Law and Motions for Judgment on Partial Findings.** Rule 50 motions should be in writing. Oral argument, if necessary, will be scheduled by the court.

12. **Bench Trials.** Judge Davis requires the submission of proposed findings of fact and conclusions of law in nonjury cases. The schedule for the submission of the proposed findings of fact and conclusions of law is set at the conclusion of the bench trial, and is typically no more than two to three weeks. Two copies of the proposed findings and conclusions should be submitted and should be accompanied by a computer disk in WordPerfect format.

Counsel are expected to submit trial memoranda in bench trials. The memoranda must be received by the court, and filed with the clerk of court, at least three days prior to the commencement of trial. Exhibit notebooks should be provided at the commencement of trial, at the latest.

Jury Deliberations

1. **Exhibits in the Jury Room.** Judge Davis permits the jury to take many exhibits admitted into evidence into the deliberation room. A discussion with counsel will occur before any exhibit is sent out with the jury.

2. **Availability of Counsel During Jury Deliberations.** Unless excused by the court, counsel must remain in the courthouse during jury deliberations.

3. **Polling the Jury.** All requests to poll the jury will be granted.

CRIMINAL CASES

1. **Motions to Suppress.** Hearings on motions to suppress are usually conducted separate from, and in advance of, the trial date.

2. **Trial Dates.** Trial dates are assigned by the courtroom deputy.

3. **Pretrial Conferences.** Judge Davis generally does not hold a final pretrial conference in criminal cases.

4. **Motions in Limine.** It is generally expected that all disputed evidentiary matters will be brought to the attention of the court well in advance of the trial. Motions in limine should be filed at least seven days prior to the trial date.

5. **Proposed Voir Dire and Proposed Final Jury Instructions.** Written proposed voir dire and final instructions must be provided to the court at least three business days prior to the trial date. Proposed instructions on procedural matters such as the burden of proof, presumption of innocence, and the credibility of witnesses are not required. Instructions need only be submitted with respect to the substantive issues in the case. Each proposed instruction should be on a separate piece of paper, double-spaced, and must include citation to specific authority. The parties should also submit a computer disk or CD containing their instructions or verdict forms in WordPerfect format.

Counsel will have the opportunity to submit supplemental points following the conclusion of the testimony.

6. **Voir Dire.** Judge Davis conducts voir dire in all criminal matters.

7. **Written Jury Instructions.** Judge Davis generally does not provide the jury with a copy of the instructions.

8. **Exhibits in the Jury Room.** Upon agreement of counsel, and at Judge Davis's discretion, the jury may be provided with relevant and legally appropriate trial exhibits during deliberations.

9. **Availability of Counsel During Deliberations.** Unless excused by Judge Davis, counsel must remain in the courthouse during deliberations.

10. **Sentencing Memoranda.** Judge Davis requires the timely submission of objections to the presentence-investigation report. Judge Davis also encourages the submission of sentencing memoranda by both the defendant and the government.

Judge Paul S. Diamond

Judge Diamond was born in 1953 in Brooklyn, New York. He received a B.A. from Columbia University in 1974 and a J.D. from the University of Pennsylvania School of Law in 1977. Judge Diamond served as an assistant district attorney in the Philadelphia District Attorney's Office from 1977 to 1979 and from 1981 to 1983. He served as a law clerk to the Honorable Bruce W. Kauffman on the Pennsylvania Supreme Court in 1980. From 1983 to 2004, Judge Diamond was in private practice in Philadelphia, and he served as an adjunct professor of law at the Temple University School of Law from 1990 to 1992. He was appointed to the United States District Court for the Eastern District of Pennsylvania on June 22, 2004.

PRELIMINARY GENERAL MATTERS

1. **Communication with Law Clerks.** Judge Diamond prefers that counsel communicate with his civil or criminal deputy clerk. If they are not available, then Judge Diamond permits counsel to speak with his law clerks on scheduling and procedural issues only.

2. **Copies of Items Filed with the Court.** Judge Diamond would appreciate one courtesy copy of all items filed with the court. Judge Diamond also encourages electronic filing. Counsel need not provide courtesy copies of those items that have been filed electronically.

3. **Appellate Briefs.** Judge Diamond wishes to receive a courtesy copy of any briefs filed in appeals of his decisions.

CIVIL CASES
Pretrial Procedure

1. **Service of Complaint.** Judge Diamond expects plaintiffs to serve their complaints as expeditiously as possible.

2. **Pretrial Conferences.** Judge Diamond will hold a Rule 16 pretrial conference as soon as possible after the answer to the complaint is served. If trial counsel is absolutely unable to attend, the conference will be rescheduled.

3. **Settlement Discussions and the Rule 16 Conference.** Judge Diamond actively encourages settlement and will discuss settlement at the Rule 16 pretrial conference. Counsel should be prepared to discuss the strengths and weaknesses of the case and, therefore, should be completely conversant in the essential issues and facts of the case. Counsel must have full authority to negotiate or settle the case or should bring a client representative to the conference who does have such authority.

Motion Practice

1. **Oral Arguments.** Judge Diamond ordinarily will not require oral argument on motions.

2. **Reply and Supplemental Briefs.** Unless so ordered, Judge Diamond will accept reply or supplemental briefs, but normally will not await a reply brief before ruling on a motion.

Discovery Matters

1. **Discovery Disputes Should be Settled by the Parties.** Judge Diamond believes that discovery should begin as soon as possible. In ordinary circumstances, Judge Diamond requires that discovery be well underway by the time of the Rule 16 conference. Although Judge Diamond requires the parties to meet the conciliation requirements of Local Rule

26.1(f), he expects counsel to bring unresolved discovery disputes to his attention as soon as possible. Counsel should provide the court with a brief letter or motion and attach the disputed discovery request.

Ordinarily, Judge Diamond will schedule a telephone conference to resolve the discovery motion promptly after it is filed, usually before any response is due. If a dispute arises during a deposition, Judge Diamond expects counsel to phone his chambers during the deposition so that he can resolve the dispute immediately.

2. **Length of Discovery Period and Deadline Compliance.** Judge Diamond believes the complexity of the case should dictate the amount of time allowed for discovery. This will normally be determined at the Rule 16 conference. Generally, 45 to 75 days should be sufficient time for discovery unless the case is complex or otherwise out of the ordinary.

Judge Diamond looks unfavorably on attempts to ambush opposing counsel with the production of evidence or witnesses past the appropriate cutoff date in the case management order. Judge Diamond takes the dates seriously and expects counsel to do so as well.

Trial Procedure

1. **Scheduling of Cases.** Ordinarily, Judge Diamond will schedule a trial date immediately after the Rule 16 conference.

2. **Conflicts of Counsel.** When counsel become aware of professional or personal conflicts that may affect the trial schedule, they should notify the civil deputy clerk immediately.

3. **Trial Date Extensions.** Judge Diamond is extremely reluctant to grant continuances of trial dates.

4. **Stipulations of Counsel.** Judge Diamond encourages counsel to agree on or stipulate to as many matters as possible before trial. If, for instance, counsel can agree on jury instructions, exhibits, and the like, it will make trial less burdensome for everyone.

5. **Order of Proof.** Normally, Judge Diamond requires counsel each day to inform the court and opposing counsel of the witnesses he or she expects to call the next trial day.

Judge J. William Ditter, Jr.

John William Ditter, Jr. was born in Philadelphia, Pennsylvania, in 1921. He graduated from Ursinus College in 1943. From 1943 to 1946, and again from 1951 to 1953, Judge Ditter served as a captain in the United States Navy Reserves. He received his LL.B. from the University of Pennsylvania Law School in 1948. Judge Ditter clerked on the Court of Common Pleas for Montgomery County, Pennsylvania, from 1948 to 1950. In 1951 he worked as an assistant district attorney in Montgomery County, a position he would return to from 1953 to 1955. In 1956 he was promoted to first assistant district attorney. From 1953 to 1963 he also worked in private practice in Ambler, Pennsylvania. In 1964 he became a judge on the Court of Common Pleas for Montgomery County, a position he held until 1970, when President Richard Nixon appointed him to the Eastern District. Judge Ditter assumed senior status on October 19, 1986.

PRELIMINARY GENERAL MATTERS

1. *Correspondence with the Court.* Counsel or pro se parties may correspond with Judge Ditter concerning scheduling, routine matters, or to advise that a case has been settled or discontinued. All correspondence should include the case number and must be copied to opposing counsel.

2. *Communications with Law Clerks.* Judge Ditter permits communications with law clerks with respect to ministerial matters such as scheduling. Law clerks are not permitted to give legal advice or explain the reasons for the court's rulings.

3. *Telephone Conferences.* Judge Ditter will hold telephone conferences to resolve scheduling or discovery disputes. Counsel requesting the conference will be responsible for initiating the telephone call and contacting chambers after all parties are present on the call.

4. *Electronic Case Filing.* Judge Ditter prefers that all documents be filed electronically using the Electronic Case Filing (ECF) system. Attorneys should register as ECF users at the Office of the Clerk of the Court or at the court's website at www.paed.uscourts.gov.

A copy of the "Pretrial and Trial Procedures" for Judge Ditter is available on the court's website.

5. *Oral Arguments and Evidentiary Hearings.* Judge Ditter does not set aside certain days or times for oral arguments, motions, or evidentiary hearings.

6. *Pro Hac Vice Admissions.* To be admitted pro hac vice, associate counsel of record should submit a written motion for admission. The admission of counsel pro hac vice does not relieve associate counsel of responsibility for the matter before the court.

7. *Faxes.* Unless specifically requested, parties should not transmit pleadings, motions, or other filings by fax.

8. *Courtesy Copies.* Courtesy copies to the court are not required if the document has been electronically filed. In all other circumstances, the court should be provided one courtesy copy at the time of filing.

9. *Courtroom Assignment.* Judge Ditter does not have an assigned courtroom. Counsel will be notified of the courtroom to be used the day before the hearing/trial.

CIVIL CASES
Pretrial Procedure

1. *Rule 16 Conference.* Judge Ditter will schedule a preliminary pretrial conference shortly after a defendant has filed an appearance or pleading. A copy of the order used by Judge Ditter is shown on page 64. At least three days prior to the conference, counsel must submit to chambers the scheduling information report and a proposed discovery plan pursuant to Rule 26(f).

At the initial pretrial conference, the parties should be prepared to address all topics listed in Local Rule of Civil Procedure 16.1(b) and Federal Rule of Civil Procedure 16(b) and (c), the progress of self-executing disclosure under Federal Rule of Civil Procedure 26(a), and any settlement or alternative dispute resolution proposals. Counsel participating in the conference must be prepared to discuss all claims and defenses, must have a thorough understanding of the facts, and must be prepared to discuss settlement and have authority from their clients to do so. Judge Ditter will issue a Rule 16 Scheduling Order at the conclusion of the conference.

2. *Continuances and Extensions.* When possible, Judge Ditter tries to accommodate counsel with regard to scheduling and requests for continuances or extensions. If counsel have agreed to a continuance or an extension (other than that of a trial date), they should request a continuance by letter and include the reasons for the extension, the amount of additional time needed, and that all parties agree.

Requests for continuance of trial should be made as early as possible. A request submitted on the eve of trial is not favored.

General Motions Practice

1. *Oral Argument.* Judge Ditter will grant oral argument if he believes it will assist him in deciding the motion. A request for oral argument may be made by letter or in the body of the motion.

2. *Reply and Surreply Briefs.* Judge Ditter has no formal policy on reply or surreply briefs. If filed, they should be concise and not repetitive. Decision of the motion will not be delayed for the receipt of such briefs.

Discovery Matters

1. *Length of Discovery Period and Extensions.* Except in complex cases, Judge Ditter sets relatively short discovery deadlines—usually not to exceed 90 days from the date of the Rule 16 conference. Extensions will be granted if necessary.

2. *Discovery Conferences and Dispute Resolution.* Judge Ditter expects parties to resolve most discovery disputes without involving the court, and holds discovery conferences only if requested. Judge Ditter permits telephone conferences to resolve discovery disputes if not excessive.

If a motion to compel is filed, it should include the specific attempts counsel has made to resolve the issue with opposing counsel. See *Crown Cork & Seal Co. v. Chemed Corp.*, 101 F.R.D. 105 (E.D. Pa. 1984). A response should be filed within five days. Judge Ditter will schedule a conference (via telephone or in-person) to resolve the dispute as soon as possible.

3. *Confidentiality Agreements.* Requested confidentiality agreements should be submitted to Judge Ditter and will be reviewed pursuant to *Pansy v. Borough of Stroudsburg*, 23 F.3d 772 (3d Cir. 1993).

4. Expert Witnesses. Judge Ditter expects counsel to identify experts and exchange expert reports in a timely manner, and will permit depositions where appropriate. Trial will not be continued because of the unavailability of an expert witness.

Settlement

Settlement will be discussed at the initial pretrial conference and at any subsequent conference. Judge Ditter will refer a case to a magistrate judge for a settlement conference if the parties request it.

Arbitration

Judge Ditter does not use any special practices or procedures for arbitration cases.

Final Pretrial Memoranda

Unless otherwise ordered, the pretrial memorandum should be prepared in accordance with Local Rule of Civil Procedure 16.1(c) and should also include:
1) all stipulations of counsel;
2) a statement of objection (describing with particularity the ground and the authority for the objection) to the admissibility of any exhibit or evidence; to the adequacy of the qualifications of an expert; or the admissibility of any opinion testimony from lay witnesses; and
3) deposition testimony (including videotape deposition testimony) that the party intends to offer during its case-in-chief.

Injunctions

1. Scheduling and Expedited Discovery. Judge Ditter schedules preliminary and permanent injunction hearings quickly and will combine the two hearings where possible. He permits expedited discovery and will hold a prehearing conference to discuss discovery issues and narrow the issues of contention.

2. Proposed Findings of Fact and Conclusions of Law. Judge Ditter requires proposed findings of fact and conclusions of law. The time for the filing of these submissions will be set at the pre-hearing conference.

Trial Procedure

1. Scheduling Cases. Once discovery has been completed, Judge Ditter will send notices to counsel listing the case for trial.

2. Conflicts of Counsel. Counsel should notify the court immediately upon learning of any unavoidable and compelling professional or personal conflicts affecting the trial schedule.

3. Cases Involving Out-of-Town Parties or Witnesses. When possible, Judge Ditter tries to schedule cases involving out-of-town parties or witnesses for a date certain and to give substantial advance notice of the trial date.

4. Note-taking by Jurors. Judge Ditter permits jurors to take notes.

5. Trial Briefs. Judge Ditter encourages counsel to submit trial briefs.

Practice and Procedures of Judges and Judges' Forms and Orders

6. **Voir Dire.** Judge Ditter conducts voir dire. Counsel will submit proposed questions for voir dire and Judge Ditter will incorporate those questions as he deems appropriate. At the conclusion of Judge Ditter's voir dire, he will hold a sidebar conference and give counsel the opportunity to suggest additional or follow-up questions. If circumstances require, Judge Ditter may also conduct individual voir dire at sidebar.

7. **Sidebars.** Judge Ditter permits sidebar conferences.

8. **Motions In Limine.** Generally, the time for filing motions in limine will be determined at the pretrial conference and will be required in advance of trial.

9. **Examination of Witnesses Out of Sequence.** Judge Ditter will permit counsel to take witnesses out of turn for the convenience of the witnesses or for other good reason.

10. **Opening Statements and Summations.** Counsel are to make their opening statements and summations at the lectern using a microphone. Judge Ditter encourages brevity and will usually set time limits for openings and closings based on discussions with counsel.

11. **Examination of Witnesses or Argument by More Than One Attorney.** Judge Ditter will permit more than one attorney to try the case on behalf of a party; however, only one attorney for each side may examine a particular witness. More than one attorney for a party may argue different points in a motion before Judge Ditter.

12. **Examination of Witnesses Beyond Redirect and Recross.** Judge Ditter will permit limited recross examination on matters not previously covered by cross-examination or in special circumstances.

13. **Videotaped Testimony.** Rulings on disputes or objections should be sought in advance through submission to Judge Ditter of a written transcript of the relevant testimony and the videotape should be edited accordingly prior to trial.

14. **Reading of Material Into the Record.** Judge Ditter does not have any special practice or policy regarding reading stipulations, pleadings, or discovery materials into the record. He encourages counsel to stipulate to as many facts as possible.

15. **Preparation of Exhibits.** Judge Ditter requires that the exhibits be marked and exchanged prior to trial. One copy of the exhibits and an exhibit list should be provided to the court.

16. **Offering Exhibits Into Evidence.** Unless the parties have an agreement as to the admissibility of a proposed exhibit, a witness may not testify as to its content until it has been admitted into evidence.

17. **Directed Verdict Motions.** Judge Ditter usually conducts a short oral argument on motions for judgment as a matter of law and motions for involuntary dismissal. He does not have a preference as to whether such motions are written or oral.

18. **Proposed Jury Instructions and Verdict Forms.** Counsel should submit comprehensive proposed jury instructions in advance of trial. Counsel need not submit charges on standard matters unless specifically directed to do so. If not electronically filed, the jury instructions should be submitted in hard copy and on a disk in WordPerfect format. Cases and pattern jury instructions that are cited should be quoted accurately and without change and specific page references should be given. Judge Ditter conducts a charging conference prior to instructing the jury and will accept supplemental proposed jury instructions as necessary. At the end of his charge, counsel will be given the opportunity, at sidebar, to take exception, make corrections, or suggest additions.

19. Proposed Findings of Fact and Conclusions of Law. Judge Ditter requires proposed findings of fact and conclusions of law in nonjury trials, and citations to the evidence should be included. The proposed findings of fact and conclusions of law must be filed one week prior to trial. Counsel will have the opportunity to file a supplement at the end of trial. If not electronically filed, the proposed findings of fact and conclusions of law should be submitted in hard copy and on a disk in WordPerfect format.

Jury Deliberations

1. Written Instructions. Judge Ditter does not give the jury a written copy of the jury instructions.

2. Exhibits in the Jury Room. All exhibits (except for weapons, drugs, and the like) will go with the jury unless counsel agree otherwise or they contain matters that would be confusing or prejudicial.

3. Handling Jury Requests to Read Back Testimony or Replay Tapes. If the requested portion of testimony is available, Judge Ditter will permit it to be read back or played for the jury.

4. Availability of Counsel During Jury Deliberations. Unless excused by the court, counsel must remain in the courthouse during jury deliberations.

5. Taking the Verdict and Special Interrogatories. Depending on the nature of the case, Judge Ditter will take a special or general verdict. He frequently submits interrogatories to the jury.

6. Polling the Jury. Judge Ditter will permit the polling of the jury if requested.

7. Interviewing the Jury. Judge Ditter will permit the jury to be interviewed at the conclusion of trial but he will instruct the jurors that they are not required to speak to counsel.

CRIMINAL CASES

At present, Judge Ditter is not handling any criminal matters.

OTHER GENERAL MATTERS

1. Appellate Briefs. Judge Ditter expects to receive a courtesy copy of appellate briefs.

2. Consultation with Opposing Counsel. Judge Ditter expects counsel to bring matters to his attention only after they have been discussed with opposing counsel.

3. Courtroom Decorum. Judge Ditter expects counsel to be punctual and courteous. The examination of witnesses should be conducted from the lectern. Counsel should stand when addressing the court and should seek permission to approach a witness or the bench. To the extent possible, counsel should notify Judge Ditter of any issues that will need to be ruled on at the start of the day's proceedings or during a recess out of the jury's presence. Sidebar conferences are permitted when necessary.

4. Chambers Contacts. Counsel should not hesitate to contact Judge Ditter's chambers with questions about his courtroom practices or procedures.

Secretary: Mrs. Dale Ballard-Hill
215-597-9640
Deputy Clerk: Mr. Stephen Iannacone
267-322-6029
Law Clerks: Patricia M. Furlong, Esquire
Rebecca E. Lacher, Esquire
215-597-9640

Practice and Procedures of Judges and Judges' Forms and Orders

**IN THE UNITED STATES DISTRICT COURT
FOR THE EASTERN DISTRICT OF PENNSYLVANIA**

		:	CIVIL ACTION
		:	
vs.		:	
		:	
		:	NO.

NOTICE

    AND NOW, this _____ day of _____, 20__, you are hereby notified that a [Pre-Trial/Settlement Conference] before the Honorable J. William Ditter, Jr. in this matter will be held on _____ at _____M, in Chambers, Room 3040, United States Courthouse, 601 Market Street, Philadelphia, Pennsylvania. The Conference is being called to discuss the present status of the action, to consider time requirement for discovery, and to agree on further pre-trial procedures.

    Counsel are reminded of the duties imposed on them by Fed. R. Civ. P. 26(a)(1) and 26(f), each shall complete the scheduling information report (copy attached), and together shall submit the discovery plan required by Fed. R. Civ. P. 26(f) to me[*] on or before three (3) days prior to the conference.

    At this conference, counsel shall be prepared and authorized to discuss the matters referred to in Local Rule 16.1(b), Fed. R. Civ. P. 16(b) and Fed. R. Civ. P. 16 (c), and settlement.

    The Conference will be continued to another date only in exceptional cases.

                                                                Very truly yours,

                                                                 Stephen J. Iannacone
                                                                 Deputy Clerk to the
                                                                 Honorable J. William Ditter, Jr., S.J.

cc:

---

[*]   There is no need to file the scheduling information report or discovery plan with the Clerk of Court.

Judge J. William Ditter, Jr.

SCHEDULING INFORMATION REPORT

(To be completed and returned to Judge Ditter's Chambers three (3) days before Conference)

Caption: _____

Civil Action No.: _____

Jury Trial: _____ Non-Jury Trial: _____ Arbitration: _____

Plaintiff's Counsel: _____

Address: _____

Phone: _____ Fax: _____

Defendant's Counsel: _____

Address: _____

Phone: _____ Fax: _____

Have you complied with the duty of self-executing disclosure under Federal Rule of Civil Procedure 26(a)?

_____ When? _____ If not, why? _____

_____

Have you filed a discovery plan pursuant to Federal Rule of Civil Procedure 26(f)? _____

_____ When? _____ If not, why? _____

_____

If you contend the discovery period should exceed four months after the last appearance by all Defendants is filed, please state reasons:

_____

Ready for trial by: _____
                      (Date)

Is a Settlement Conference likely to be helpful? _____

If so, when: Early _____ (Yes/No) After discovery _____

Do you expect to file a case-dispositive motion? _____

If so, by what date? _____

Trial time estimate: _____

Time to present your case: _____

Time for entire trial: _____

Date: _____   _____
                                                                      Signature of Counsel Preparing Form

                                                                     _____

                                                                     Type/Print Name

Judge Jan E. DuBois

Judge DuBois received a B.S. from the University of Pennsylvania in 1952, and an LL.B. from Yale University Law School in 1957. From 1957 to 1958, Judge DuBois was law clerk to the Honorable Harry E. Kalodner of the United States Court of Appeals for the Third Circuit. From 1958 until 1988, he was in private practice in Philadelphia. He was appointed to the United States District Court for the Eastern District of Pennsylvania on July 27, 1988. Judge DuBois assumed senior status on April 15, 2002.

PRELIMINARY GENERAL MATTERS
Pretrial and Trial Procedures*

1. Correspondence with the Court. Judge DuBois permits correspondence under the circumstances set forth in his standard notice to counsel, which is routinely sent to counsel promptly after a case is assigned to Judge DuBois. A copy of the notice is shown on page 73 of this book. All other communications with the court should be by the filing of pleadings, motions, applications, briefs, or legal memoranda.

2. Communications with Law Clerks. Judge DuBois permits communications with his law clerks concerning the administrative aspects of cases, but not on scheduling matters or requests for extensions of time, which must be directed to Judge DuBois.

3. Telephone Conferences. Judge DuBois usually finds telephone conferences a preferred method of handling matters such as discovery disputes, scheduling matters, and requests for extensions of time. A pretrial conference with counsel participating by telephone may be held upon timely request to the court.

4. Oral Arguments and Evidentiary Hearings. Judge DuBois determines in any given case whether to schedule oral argument or an evidentiary hearing. If counsel prefer either an oral argument or an evidentiary hearing, they should request it. The scheduling of all such matters is handled by Judge DuBois's courtroom deputy. Judge DuBois does not set aside any certain days or times for oral arguments or evidentiary hearings.

5. Pro Hac Vice Admissions. Judge DuBois does not have a preference as to how counsel should submit a pro hac vice motion to the court.

CIVIL CASES
Pretrial Procedure

1. Pretrial Conferences. Judge DuBois regularly conducts pretrial conferences except in arbitration cases. His pretrial conference policy is set forth in the notice to counsel shown on page 75. A conference information report (see the form on page 74) and Rule 26(f) report must be forwarded to the court at least two days before the scheduled preliminary pretrial conference.

2. Pretrial Memoranda. Unless specifically provided for by separate order in a particular case, in jury and nonjury cases Judge DuBois requires the use of the short-form pretrial memorandum described in Local Rule of Civil Procedure 16.1(c) with three modifications—he requires that objections to (a) the admissibility of any exhibit based on authenticity, (b) the admissibility for any reason (except relevancy) of any evidence expected to be offered, and (c) the admissibility of any opinion testimony from lay witnesses pursuant to Federal Rule of Evidence 701, be set forth separately in the pretrial memorandum.

---

* A copy of the pretrial and trial procedures for Judge DuBois is available on the court's website at http://www.paed.uscourts.gov under the heading "Documents" and the subheading "Judges' Procedures."

Continuances and Extensions

1.   General Policy. Judge DuBois has a general policy of adhering to originally scheduled dates unless a compelling reason is presented that justifies a change. This policy applies to briefing schedules, oral argument, evidentiary hearings, discovery deadlines, and trial dates.

2.   Requests for Extensions and Continuances. Counsel should advise the court immediately, and *before the date has run,* of any compelling reason justifying an extension or continuance of any originally scheduled date. Any request for an extension or a continuance may be made by letter, setting forth the reasons and noting the agreement or disagreement of all other counsel, or by telephone conference with all counsel participating.

General Motion Practice

1.   Oral Argument on Motions. Judge DuBois schedules oral argument on motions when he believes it will be helpful in the court's decision-making process.

2.   Reply and Surreply Briefs. Reply and surreply briefs should be filed only if absolutely necessary. Requests for time to do so should be directed to Judge DuBois.

3.   Chambers Copies of Motion Papers. Judge DuBois requires that two courtesy copies of motion papers be sent to his chambers when the originals are filed. Any motion papers that include exhibits or attachments should be properly tabbed.

4.   Dispositive Motions and **Daubert** *Motions.* The court generally schedules the filing of dispositive motions and *Daubert* motions after completion of discovery. When dispositive motions do not require complete discovery, Judge DuBois orders an earlier filing.

Judge DuBois generally schedules a *Daubert* conference after a *Daubert* motion is completely briefed. At the conference, Judge DuBois determines, among other things, whether a *Daubert* hearing is required.

5.   Motions for Summary Judgment. A motion for summary judgment filed pursuant to Federal Rule of Civil Procedure 56 must be accompanied by a separate, short, and concise statement of the material facts, in numbered paragraphs, as to which the moving party contends there is no genuine issue of material fact to be tried. The response to the motion for summary judgment must include a separate, short, and concise statement of material facts, responding to the numbered paragraphs set forth in the moving party's statement, as to which it is contended that there exists a genuine issue of material fact. The responding party may also set forth, in additional numbered paragraphs, any additional material facts that the responding party contends preclude the granting of a motion for summary judgment.

Statements of material facts in support of, or in opposition to, a motion for summary judgment should include specific references to the parts of the record that support the statements. All material facts set forth in the moving party's statement will be deemed to be admitted unless controverted in the opposing party's statement.

Discovery Matters

1.   Length of Discovery Period and Extensions. In uncomplicated cases, Judge DuBois usually allows four months to complete discovery, measured from the date appearances are filed for all defendants. If counsel have been diligent and genuinely need more time for discovery, he will usually grant additional time. In arbitration cases, the discovery should be completed by the arbitration date.

2. Discovery Conferences and Dispute Resolution. Judge DuBois prefers that discovery disputes be resolved by discovery conferences, either by telephone or in chambers, if the parties are unable to resolve them without court assistance. Where the discovery dispute is complex, a motion should be filed.

3. Confidentiality Agreements. Judge DuBois has no standard practice or policy concerning confidentiality orders. He does not favor confidentiality orders that place virtually all discovery materials under a confidentiality nondisclosure status, even those agreed upon by counsel. All confidentiality agreements must comply with the Third Circuit opinion in *Pansy v. Borough of Stroudsburg*, 23 F.3d 772 (1994).

4. Expert Witnesses. The conduct of expert witness discovery is covered by Judge DuBois at the pretrial conference and is the subject of a scheduling order. In most cases, Judge DuBois requires that plaintiffs serve expert reports and/or responses to expert witness discovery before a defendant is required to do so.

Settlement

1. General Approach to Settlement. Judge DuBois requires the parties to jointly report by letter to chambers regarding settlement by a date selected by the parties. In the event a case is not settled by that date, Judge DuBois requires the parties to advise whether they believe a settlement conference before a magistrate judge, mediation under Local Civil Rule 53.3, and the mediation protocol under Local Civil Rule 53.3 or some other form of alternative dispute resolution might be of assistance in resolving the case. If the parties agree on such alternative dispute resolution, Judge DuBois orders it.

2. Referral of Cases to Magistrate Judges for Settlement Conferences and to Mediator under Local Civil Rule 53.3 and the Mediation Protocol Under Local Civil Rule 53.3
Judge DuBois does not generally conduct settlement conferences himself. He favors use of a magistrate judge for settlement conferences or a mediator under Local Civil Rule 53.3 and the mediation protocol where the parties agree that such referral might be helpful in resolving the case.

3. Referral to Another District Judge for Settlement Conferencing. Judge DuBois sometimes refers a case to another district judge for a settlement conference.

Arbitration

1. General Approach to Arbitration Cases. Judge DuBois has no standard procedures or practices for arbitration cases except that pretrial conferences are not normally held in such cases and, except in unusual cases, scheduling orders are not issued.

2. Scheduling of Trial De Novo After Appeal From Arbitration Award. Once a trial de novo is demanded, Judge DuBois schedules a status conference. At the status conference, he issues a scheduling order covering all further proceedings including, but not limited to, limited additional discovery, the filing of pretrial memoranda, and the filing of proposed voir dire questions and proposed points for charge or proposed findings of fact and conclusions of law.

Final Pretrial Conferences

The court schedules final pretrial conferences and requires the filing of final pretrial memoranda only in complex cases or cases in which the court determines that such proceedings are necessary in order to expedite the trial.

Injunctions

1. Scheduling and Expedited Discovery. Judge DuBois will promptly list any injunction matters assigned to him. The scheduling of injunction matters is conducted at an initial conference attended by all counsel. In appropriate cases, Judge DuBois will require expedited discovery.

When the plaintiff requests a temporary restraining order, Judge DuBois expects prompt service of the motion and complaint upon the opposing party and notice to opposing counsel unless, for good cause shown, this is impossible.

2. Proposed Findings of Fact and Conclusions of Law. Judge DuBois requires submission of proposed findings of fact and conclusions of law in injunction cases as early as possible.

Trial Procedure

1. Scheduling of Cases. Judge DuBois routinely places all cases on his trial list. Cases are not assigned a date certain and very rarely are they specially listed. Counsel whose cases are in the pool must maintain telephone contact with his courtroom deputy.

2. Conflicts of Counsel. Counsel should notify Judge DuBois of any professional or personal conflicts affecting the trial schedule by telephoning or writing to his courtroom deputy. Busy slips should be timely filed and withdrawn.

3. Cases Involving Out-of-Town Parties or Witnesses. Trial scheduling by Judge DuBois is not generally affected by the presence of out-of-town parties or witnesses. Judge DuBois leaves the scheduling of witnesses to counsel.

4. Note-taking by Jurors. Judge DuBois permits note-taking by jurors.

5. Trial Briefs. Judge DuBois requires the submission of trial briefs in unusual or complex cases and in cases where unusual evidentiary problems are anticipated.

6. Voir Dire. Judge DuBois conducts the voir dire in civil cases and requires the submission of proposed voir dire questions at least three days before the case is placed on his trial list. In appropriate cases a jury questionnaire will be used.

7. Sidebars. Judge DuBois prefers that sidebars be infrequent and sought only when truly necessary.

8. In Limine Motions. In limine motions that require resolution in order to allow opening statements and trial to proceed should be filed as early as possible. Other in limine motions may be filed before trial or during trial but generally will not be ruled upon until an appropriate time during the trial.

9. Examination of Witnesses Out of Sequence. Judge DuBois will generally grant a request by counsel to take the testimony of a witness out of turn for the convenience of the witness, subject to objection by opposing counsel.

10. Opening Statements and Summations. No time limits are placed on opening statements or summations by counsel. However, Judge DuBois believes that 20 to 30 minutes is usually adequate for an opening and 30 to 45 minutes is usually adequate for a summation in routine cases.

11. Offers of Proof. Judge DuBois requires the parties to inquire of each other privately as to offers of proof regarding any witness or exhibit expected to be offered. If counsel cannot resolve such matters, Judge DuBois will rule on them upon application before a witness testifies or an exhibit is offered into evidence.

Practice and Procedures of Judges and Judges' Forms and Orders

12. **Examination of Witnesses or Argument by More Than One Attorney.** More than one attorney for a party may examine different witnesses or argue different legal points before Judge DuBois. Ordinarily, more than one attorney for a party may not examine a single witness or argue the same legal point.

13. **Examination of Witnesses Beyond Redirect or Recross.** Judge DuBois has no general policy regarding further examination of a witness after redirect or recross has been completed. Where appropriate, he will allow it.

14. **Videotaped Testimony.** Judge DuBois requires that a list of all objections to videotaped trial testimony and a copy of the transcript be submitted to the court well in advance of the offering of such evidence.

15. **Reading of Material Into the Record.** Judge DuBois has no special practice or policy for reading stipulations, pleadings, or discovery material into the record. He permits it when appropriate.

16. **Preparation of Exhibits.** Judge DuBois requires that exhibits be marked and exchanged in advance of trial. Two copies of trial exhibits should be provided to the court on the first day of trial. The trial exhibits should be accompanied by an exhibit list that describes each exhibit. Copies of exhibits used only in cross-examination need not be marked and exchanged in advance of the trial, but copies must be made available for the court, opposing counsel, and the witness at the time of cross-examination.

17. **Offering Exhibits Into Evidence.** Counsel may choose the timing of their offer of exhibits into evidence.

18. **Motions for Judgment as a Matter of Law and Motions for Judgment on Partial Findings.** Motions for judgment as a matter of law in jury trials under Fed.R.Civ.P. 50(a) and motions for judgment on partial findings in nonjury trials under Fed.R.Civ.P. 52(c) may be oral or written. Judge DuBois will hear oral argument on such motions if counsel request it.

19. **Proposed Jury Instructions and Verdict Forms.** Judge DuBois requires proposed jury instructions and verdict forms to be filed with the clerk, and served on the court (Chambers) in duplicate, at least three days before the case is placed on the trial list. It is not necessary that counsel submit standard points normally given in civil cases. Judge DuBois will permit submission of supplemental jury instructions up to the time he charges the jury. He will rule on proposed jury instructions at a conference before closing speeches.

If a model jury instruction taken, for instance, from O'Malley, Grenig & Lee, *Federal Jury Practice and Instructions,* or Sand, *Modern Federal Jury Instructions,* is submitted, the parties should state whether the proposed jury instruction is unchanged or modified. If a party modifies a model jury instruction, the modification must be set forth in the following manner: additions must be underlined and deletions must be placed in brackets.

20. **Proposed Findings of Fact and Conclusions of Law—Nonjury Cases.** Judge DuBois requires that proposed findings of fact and conclusions of law in nonjury cases be filed with the clerk, and served on the court (Chambers) in duplicate, three days before the case is placed on the trial list.

21. **Stipulations.** Judge DuBois requires the parties to meet in an effort to reach agreement on the facts. In the event an agreement is reached, a stipulation of uncontested facts must be filed at least three days before the case is placed on the trial list. Two copies of the stipulation must be served on the court (Chambers) when the original is filed.

22. Joint Statement of the Case for Reading to the Jury. Judge DuBois requires filing of a joint statement of the case for reading to the jury at least three days before the case is placed on the trial list. The joint statement of the case is read to the jury as part of Judge DuBois's preliminary jury instructions immediately after the jury is sworn and immediately before opening statements. Two copies of the joint statement must be served on the court (Chambers) when the original is filed.

The joint statement must include (a) a brief statement of the facts, (b) the essential elements of the plaintiff's causes of action, (c) a brief statement of the defendant's position on liability, (d) the essential elements of any affirmative defenses, (e) the essential elements of any counterclaims, cross-claims or third-party claims, and (f) a brief statement of the position of the defendant on any counterclaims, cross-claims, or third-party claims. It is generally limited to three pages.

Jury Deliberations

1. Written Jury Instructions. Judge DuBois generally gives the jury copies of his charge.

2. Exhibits in the Jury Room. Judge DuBois usually permits all exhibits received in evidence to go out with the jury unless there is an objection.

3. Handling of Jury Requests to Read Back Testimony or Replay Tapes. In cases where transcripts are available, Judge DuBois will consider reading appropriate portions requested by the jury. He will generally allow audiotapes and videotapes to be replayed in open court if necessary.

4. Availability of Counsel During Jury Deliberations. Counsel should be available on 10 minutes' notice during jury deliberations.

5. Taking the Verdict and Special Interrogatories. Judge DuBois usually submits interrogatories to the jury in civil cases.

6. Polling the Jury. Judge DuBois has no standard practice for polling the jury in civil cases, but will permit it when requested.

7. Interviewing the Jury. After a verdict has been recorded and a jury has been discharged, Judge DuBois usually permits counsel to interview jurors in the courtroom, or immediately adjacent to the courtroom. Each juror is told that they are permitted to talk to counsel and others, but they need not do so.

CRIMINAL CASES

1. Approach to Oral Argument and Motions. Judge DuBois has no preference regarding oral arguments on motions in criminal cases.

2. Pretrial Conferences. Judge DuBois only holds pretrial conferences in complex criminal cases.

3. Voir Dire. In criminal cases, the voir dire is conducted by Judge DuBois. Judge DuBois requires the filing of proposed voir dire questions by counsel at least two weeks before trial. Two copies of the proposed voir dire questions must be served on the court (Chambers) when the original is filed.

4. Proposed Jury Instructions and Verdict Forms. Judge DuBois requires proposed jury instructions and verdict forms to be filed with the clerk, and served on the court (Chambers) in duplicate at least two weeks before trial. It is not necessary that counsel submit standard points normally given in criminal cases. Judge DuBois will permit submission of supplemental jury instructions up to the time he charges the jury. He will rule on proposed jury instructions at a conference before closing speeches.

If a model jury instruction taken, for instance, from O'Malley, Grenig & Lee, *Federal Jury Practice and Instructions,* or Sand, *Modern Federal Jury Instructions,* is submitted, the parties should state whether the proposed jury instruction is unchanged or modified. If a party modifies a model jury instruction, the modification must be set forth in the following manner: additions must be underlined and deletions must be placed in brackets.

5. **Trial—Other Procedures.** Generally, Judge DuBois uses the same procedures in criminal trials that are used in civil trials except that criminal trials are scheduled for a date certain.

6. **Sentencing Memoranda.** Judge DuBois requires the submission of sentencing memoranda by the government and the defense no less than seven days before sentencing. Two copies must be served on the court (Chambers), and one copy on the United States probation officer, when the original is filed.

7. **Sentencing Motions.** Motions for downward departure under U.S.S.G. § 5K1.1 and 18 U.S.C. § 3553(e) must be filed no less than seven days before sentencing. All other sentencing-related motions must be filed and served no less than 14 days before sentencing; responses to any such motions must be filed no less than seven days before sentencing. Two copies of all such motions and responses must be served on the court (Chambers), and one copy on the United States probation officer, when the originals are filed.

OTHER GENERAL MATTERS

Judge DuBois would like to receive copies of appellate briefs when a decision rendered by him is appealed.

Judge Jan E. DuBois

DATE OF NOTICE: _____

IN THE UNITED STATES DISTRICT COURT
FOR THE EASTERN DISTRICT OF PENNSYLVANIA

vs.	:	CIVIL ACTION
	:	NO.

NOTICE

Please be advised that a **PRELIMINARY PRETRIAL CONFERENCE** will be held by telephone on _____, with the Honorable Jan E. DuBois. Counsel for Plaintiff will initiate the telephone conference and when all counsel are on the line, call Chambers at (215) 597-5579.

Attached is the Court's Scheduling and Discovery Policy and a Conference Information Report which counsel are required to complete and forward to the Court **at least two days prior to** the day of the conference. Do not docket the Report.

Counsel are also required to comply with the provisions of Federal Rule of Civil Procedure 26(f) by conferring before the Preliminary Pretrial Conference for the purpose of preparing a joint proposed case management plan. The joint proposed case management plan should be submitted to the Court before the Preliminary Pretrial Conference.

In the event trial counsel in this case is on trial in a Court of record at the time of the Preliminary Pretrial Conference, another attorney in that trial attorney's office, who should be familiar with the case, is required to appear at the Preliminary Pretrial Conference. The Conference will be continued to another date only in exceptional circumstances.

Any attorneys who are not admitted to the Bar of this Court, and who want to participate in the Preliminary Pretrial Conference, should arrange to have local counsel file on their behalf, before the Conference, a motion for leave to appear *pro hac vice*.

_____
Milahn Hull,
Deputy Clerk to Judge DuBois
267-299-7339

cc:

Practice and Procedures of Judges and Judges' Forms and Orders

CONFERENCE INFORMATION REPORT
FEDERAL RULE OF CIVIL PROCEDURE 16

CIVIL ACTION NO. _____

JURY TRIAL _____ NON-JURY TRIAL _____ ARBITRATION _____

SERVICE OF PROCESS MADE _____
                                        Date

CAPTION:

TRIAL COUNSEL _____

REPRESENTING _____

LAW FIRM _____

ADDRESS _____

TELEPHONE _____

DISCOVERY:

    COMPLETED   Yes ___ No ___

    IF NOT, WHEN?   _____
                                    Date

SETTLEMENT:

    CONFERENCE BEFORE MAGISTRATE JUDGE REQUESTED   Yes ___ No ___

    MEDIATION UNDER LOCAL CIVIL RULE 53.3 AND
    MEDIATION PROTOCOL REQUESTED   Yes ___ No ___

IF YES TO SETTLEMENT CONFERENCE OR MEDIATION, AFTER WHAT DATE? _____
                                                                                                                                                    Date

TRIAL:

    READY FOR TRIAL _____
                              Date

    TIME TO PRESENT YOUR CASE _____

    TIME FOR ENTIRE TRIAL _____

SPECIAL COMMENTS

DATE _____   _____
                                                                    SIGNATURE OF COUNSEL

                                                                  _____
                                                                  TYPE OR PRINTED NAME

This Form Should Be Faxed to Chambers at 215-580-2141 or Hand Delivered to Chambers, Room 12613, United States Courthouse, Philadelphia, Pennsylvania, at least two (2) days before the scheduled Preliminary Pretrial Conference.

Judge Jan E. DuBois

NOTICE TO COUNSEL
SCHEDULING AND DISCOVERY POLICY

1. A Preliminary Pretrial Conference as described in Fed. R. Civ. P. 16(a), (b) and (c) will be held in Chambers approximately 60 to 90 days after an action is filed, or shortly after a case is reassigned to my calendar.

2. Motions to dismiss, transfer, add parties and other threshold motions should be filed, whenever possible, before the Conference. The prospect of motions for summary judgment should be noted at the Conference. Two (2) courtesy copies of motion papers should be sent to chambers when the originals are filed. Any motion papers that include exhibits or attachments should be properly tabbed.

3. The Conference will take twenty (20) to thirty (30) minutes. If it is truly impossible for trial or substitute counsel to attend the Conference, it may be held by telephone upon timely request to the Court. In a complex case, it is required that trial counsel be present.

4. At the Conference the following matters, among others, will be considered and acted upon:

   A. Jurisdictional defects, if any;

   B. Time limits to join other parties and to amend pleadings;

   C. Prospects of amicable settlement;

   D. Establishing schedules for remaining pretrial proceedings including discovery, pretrial filings, exchange of exhibits, exchange of expert reports, etc.; and,

   E. Setting a date for trial.

5. No further conferences will be held unless requested by counsel for exploration of settlement or for trial management or preparation purposes. Conferences of this type are encouraged provided counsel believe they will be useful.

6. In an uncomplicated case, discovery should be completed within 120 days after appearances have been filed for all defendants. The date for completing discovery will be set at the Preliminary Pretrial Conference. In more complex cases, at the Conference counsel will be directed to file a joint discovery schedule setting forth the dates, time intervals and subjects of discovery to be completed by the deadline.

7. The discovery deadline means that all reasonably foreseeable discovery must be served, noticed and completed by that date. Discovery may take place thereafter only by agreement of the parties, so long as the trial will not be delayed and trial preparation will not unreasonably be disrupted; provided however, that the Court will not entertain Motions to Compel discovery after the deadline date for the failure to timely serve the discovery or file such Motion before the deadline (absent a showing of good cause).

8. When timely discovery is not forthcoming after a reasonable attempt has been made to obtain it, the immediate assistance of the Court should be sought. See Local Rule 26.1(f) & (g). The Court encourages the submission of discovery disputes by telephone conference. Also discovery Motions may be disposed of promptly by a telephone conference in lieu of the usual Motion practice even before a response is filed.

9. Requests for extension of discovery deadlines or trial pool entry dates can be made by letter, stating the reasons and noting the agreement or disagreement of all other counsel, or by telephone conference with all counsel participating.

10. The filing of a Pretrial Memorandum described in Local Rule 16.1(c) will be required. The requirements of Local Rule 16.1(d)(2) will only be utilized when specially ordered by the Court.

11. After Arbitration, requests for trial de novo will result in the case being placed in the trial pool promptly. No discovery will be allowed after the Arbitration except by order of the Court upon good cause shown as to why the discovery requested could not have been reasonably anticipated and completed prior to the Arbitration.

12. Unexcused violations of scheduling orders are subject to sanctions under Fed. R. Civ. P. 16(f), upon Motion or the initiative of the Court.

13. Letters or written communications (which are discouraged) shall be directed to the Court and not to law clerks or to the Deputy Clerk. Telephone calls to law clerks are discouraged. Law clerks are not permitted to render advice to counsel and have no authority to grant continuances or to speak on behalf of the Court. All scheduling matters should be discussed with Andrew J. Follmer, Deputy Clerk, 267-299-7339.

14. For a complete listing of chambers' policies, counsel should consult Judge DuBois's *Pretrial and Trial Procedures,* which is available online at: http://www.paed.uscourts.gov/documents/procedures/notices/dubpol.pdf.

JAN E. DUBOIS, J.

Judge Jan E. DuBois

**IN THE UNITED STATES DISTRICT COURT
FOR THE EASTERN DISTRICT OF PENNSYLVANIA**

Plaintiff,	:	CIVIL ACTION
	:	
vs.	:	NO.
	:	
Defendants.	:	

SCHEDULING ORDER (JURY TRIAL)

    AND NOW, this ___ day of _____, 20___, following a Preliminary Pretrial Conference on said date, the parties, through counsel, having reported that they are interested in discussing settlement after completion of certain discovery, **IT IS ORDERED** that the parties, through counsel, shall jointly report to the Court in writing (letter to Chambers, Room 12613) on or before _____, with respect to whether the case is settled. In the event the case is not settled on or before _____, counsel shall include in their joint report a statement as to whether they believe a settlement conference before a magistrate judge or mediation under Local Civil Rule 53.3 and the Mediation Protocol Under Local Civil Rule 53.3 might be of assistance in resolving the case and, if so, on what form of alternative dispute resolution they agree and by what date they will be prepared to begin such proceedings.

    IT IS FURTHER ORDERED that the case shall proceed on the following schedule:

1. Initial Disclosure under Federal Rule of Civil Procedure 26(a)(1) shall be completed by _____; All remaining fact-discovery shall proceed forthwith and continue in such manner as will assure that all requests for, and responses to, discovery will be served, noticed and completed by _____;

2. All trial exhibits shall be marked and exchanged on or before _____;

3. On or before _____, plaintiff shall identify and submit curriculum vitae for all expert witnesses on liability, injuries and other damages who have not yet been identified. On or before _____, plaintiff shall serve defendants with reports and/or responses to expert witness discovery for all expert witnesses on liability, injuries and other damages.
   On or before _____, defendants shall identify and submit curriculum vitae for all expert witnesses on liability, injuries and other damages. On or before _____, defendants shall serve plaintiff with reports and/or responses to expert witness discovery for all such expert witnesses;

4. If requested by defendants, plaintiff shall present herself for physical and/or mental health evaluations by physician(s) of defendants' choice at a mutually convenient time on or before _____;

5. Any party expecting to offer opinion testimony from lay witnesses pursuant to Federal Rule of Evidence 701 with respect to the issues of liability and damages shall, at the time required for submission of information and/or reports for expert witnesses on liability, injuries and other damages, serve opposing parties with details and/or documents covering the lay opinions of the Rule 701 witnesses;

6. Any discovery depositions of expert witnesses may be taken between _____, and _____;

7. Any motions for summary judgment or *Daubert* motions shall be filed and served on or before _____. Pursuant to the Court's Pretrial and Trial Procedures, moving parties shall include with any motion for summary judgment a separate, short and concise statement of the material facts as to which the moving party contends there is no genuine issue of material fact. Responses to any such motions shall be filed and served within the time provided under the Local Civil Rules of this Court. The response to a motion for summary judgment shall include a separate, short and concise statement of material facts, responding to the numbered paragraphs set forth in the moving party's statement, as to which it is contended that there exists a genuine issue of material fact. The responding party may also set forth, in additional numbered paragraphs, any additional material facts which the responding party contends preclude the granting of a motion for summary judgment. Two (2) copies of any such motions and responses shall be served on the Court (Chambers, Room 12613) when the originals are filed;

8. All parties shall prepare and file with the Clerk of Court their Pretrial Memoranda, in accordance with this Order and Local Rule of Civil Procedure 16.1(c) as follows:
   a. Plaintiff—on or before _____.
   b. Defendants—on or before _____.

One (1) copy of each Pretrial Memorandum shall be served on the Court (Chambers, Room 12613) when the original is filed;

9. The case will be placed on the Court's trial list on _____;

10. Any party having an objection to: (a) the admissibility of any exhibit based on authenticity; (b) the admissibility for any reason (except relevancy) of any evidence expected to be offered; or, (c) the admissibility of any opinion testimony from lay witnesses pursuant to Federal Rule of Evidence 701, shall set forth separately each such objection in their Pretrial Memorandum. Each objection shall describe with particularity the ground and the authority for the objection;

11. If any party desires an "offer of proof" as to any witness or exhibit expected to be offered, that party shall inquire of counsel prior to trial for such information. If the inquiring party is dissatisfied with any offer provided, such party shall file a motion seeking relief from the Court prior to trial;

12. Because a witness may be unavailable at the time of trial as defined in Federal Rule of Civil Procedure 32(a)(3), the Court expects use of oral or videotape depositions at trial of any witness whose testimony a party believes essential to the presentation of that party's case, whether that witness is a party, a non-party or an expert. The unavailability of any such witness will not be a ground to delay the commencement or progress of an ongoing trial. In the event a deposition is to be offered, the offering party shall file with the Court, prior to the commencement of the trial, a copy of the deposition transcript, but only after all efforts have been made to resolve objections with other counsel. Unresolved objections shall be noted in the margin of the deposition page(s) where a Court ruling is necessary and a covering list of such objections supplied therewith;

13. The parties shall meet to prepare a complete and comprehensive stipulation of uncontested facts pursuant to (d)(2)(b)(2) of Local Rule of Civil Procedure 16.1; two (2) copies of such stipulation shall be submitted to the Court (Chambers, Room 12613) at least three (3) days before the case appears on the trial list. The original shall be filed with the Clerk of the Court;

14. At least three (3) days before the case appears on the trial list, each party shall submit to the Court (Chambers, Room 12613) two (2) copies of (a) proposed jury voir dire questions, (b) proposed jury instructions with pinpoint citations of authority for each point (ONE POINT PER PAGE), (c) proposed jury interrogatories, (d) motions in limine (excepting *Daubert* motions); and, (e) a trial memorandum on the legal issues involved in the case. The originals shall be filed with the Clerk of the Court.

If a model jury instruction taken, for instance, from O'Malley, Grenig & Lee, *Federal Jury Practice and Instructions,* or Sand, *Modern Federal Jury Instructions* is submitted, the parties shall state whether the proposed jury instruction is unchanged or modified. If a party modifies a model jury instruction the modification shall be set forth in the following manner: additions shall be underlined and deletions shall be placed in brackets;

15. At least three (3) days before the case appears on the trial list, the parties shall submit to the Court (Chambers, Room 12613) a joint written statement of the case for reading to the jury at the commencement of the trial which shall cover (a) a brief statement of the facts; (b) a brief statement of plaintiff's causes of action and the essential elements of each cause of action; and, (c) a brief statement of the defenses and the essential elements of each affirmative defense. The statement of the case shall not exceed two (2) pages in length; and,

16. At the commencement of trial, the Court should be supplied with two (2) copies of each exhibit, and three (3) copies of a schedule of exhibits which shall briefly describe each exhibit.

BY THE COURT:

_____
JAN E. DUBOIS, J.

Judge Jan E. DuBois

IN THE UNITED STATES DISTRICT COURT
FOR THE EASTERN DISTRICT OF PENNSYLVANIA

Plaintiff,   :   CIVIL ACTION
                          :
vs.   :   NO.
                          :
Defendants.   :

SCHEDULING ORDER (NON-JURY TRIAL)

AND NOW, this _____ day of _____, 20___, following a Preliminary Pretrial Conference on said date, the parties, through counsel, having reported that they are interested in discussing settlement after completion of certain discovery, **IT IS ORDERED** that the parties, through counsel, shall jointly report to the Court in writing (letter to Chambers, Room 12613) on or before _____, with respect to whether the case is settled. In the event the case is not settled on or before _____, counsel shall include in their joint report a statement as to whether they believe a settlement conference before a magistrate judge or mediation under Local Civil Rule 53.3 and the Mediation Protocol Under Local Civil Rule 53.3 might be of assistance in resolving the case and, if so, on what form of alternative dispute resolution they agree and by what date they will be prepared to begin such proceedings.

IT IS FURTHER ORDERED that the case shall proceed on the following schedule:
1. Initial Disclosure under Federal Rule of Civil Procedure 26(a)(1) shall be completed by _____;
All remaining fact-discovery shall proceed forthwith and continue in such manner as will assure that all requests for, and responses to, discovery will be served, noticed and completed by _____;
2. All trial exhibits shall be marked and exchanged on or before _____;
3. On or before _____, plaintiff shall identify and submit curriculum vitae for all expert witnesses on liability and damages who have not yet been identified. On or before _____, plaintiff shall serve defendants with reports and/or responses to expert witness discovery for all expert witnesses on liability and damages.
On or before _____, defendants shall identify and submit curriculum vitae for all expert witnesses on liability and damages. On or before _____, defendants shall serve plaintiff with reports and/or responses to expert witness discovery for all such expert witnesses;
4. Any party expecting to offer opinion testimony from lay witnesses pursuant to Federal Rule of Evidence 701 with respect to the issues of liability and damages shall, at the time required for submission of information and/or reports for expert witnesses on liability and damages, serve opposing parties with details and/or documents covering the lay opinions of the Rule 701 witnesses;
5. Any discovery depositions of expert witnesses may be taken between _____, and _____;
6. Any motions for summary judgment and *Daubert* motions shall be filed and served on or before _____. Pursuant to the Court's Pretrial and Trial Procedures, moving parties shall include with any motion for summary judgment a separate, short and concise statement of the material facts as to which the moving party contends there is no genuine issue of material fact. Responses to any such motions shall be filed and served within the time provided under the Local Civil Rules of this Court. The response to a motion for summary judgment shall include a separate, short and concise statement of material facts, responding to the numbered paragraphs set forth in the moving party's statement, as to which it is contended that there exists a genuine issue of material fact. The responding party may also set forth, in additional numbered paragraphs, any additional material facts which the responding party contends preclude the granting of a motion for summary judgment. Two (2) copies of any such motions and responses shall be served on the Court (Chambers, Room 12613) when the originals are filed;
7. All parties shall prepare and file with the Clerk of Court their Pretrial Memoranda, in accordance with this Order and Local Rule of Civil Procedure 16.1(c) as follows:
    a. Plaintiff—on or before _____.
    b. Defendants—on or before _____.

One (1) copy of each Pretrial Memorandum shall be served on the Court (Chambers, Room 12613) when the original is filed;

8. The case will be placed on the Court's trial list on _____.

9. Any party having an objection to: (a) the admissibility of any exhibit based on authenticity; (b) the admissibility for any reason (except relevancy) of any evidence expected to be offered; or, (c) the admissibility of any opinion testimony from lay witnesses pursuant to Federal Rule of Evidence 701, shall set forth separately each such objection in their Pretrial Memorandum. Each objection shall describe with particularity the ground and the authority for the objection;

10. If any party desires an "offer of proof" as to any witness or exhibit expected to be offered, that party shall inquire of counsel prior to trial for such information. If the inquiring party is dissatisfied with any offer provided, such party shall file a motion seeking relief from the Court prior to trial;

11. Because a witness may be unavailable at the time of trial as defined in Federal Rule of Civil Procedure 32(a)(3), the Court expects use of oral or videotape depositions at trial of any witness whose testimony a party believes essential to the presentation of that party's case, whether that witness is a party, a non-party, or an expert. The unavailability of any such witness will not be a ground to delay the commencement or progress of an ongoing trial. In the event a deposition is to be offered, the offering party shall file with the Court, prior to the commencement of the trial, a copy of the deposition transcript, but only after all efforts have been made to resolve objections with other counsel. Unresolved objections shall be noted in the margin of the deposition page(s) where a Court ruling is necessary and a covering list of such objections supplied therewith;

12. The parties shall meet to prepare a complete and comprehensive stipulation of uncontested facts pursuant to (d)(2)(b)(2) of Local Rule of Civil Procedure 16.1; two (2) copies of such stipulation shall be submitted to the Court (Chambers, Room 12613) at least three (3) days before the case appears on the trial list. The original shall be filed with the Clerk of the Court;

13. At least three (3) days before the case appears on the trial list, each party shall submit to the Court (Chambers, Room 12613) two (2) copies of (a) proposed findings of fact and conclusions of law, (b) motions in limine (excepting *Daubert* motions), and (c) a trial memorandum on the legal issues involved in the case. The originals shall be filed with the Clerk of the Court; and,

14. At the commencement of trial, the Court should be supplied with two (2) copies of each exhibit, and three (3) copies of a schedule of exhibits which shall briefly describe each exhibit.

BY THE COURT:

_____
JAN E. DUBOIS, J.

Judge James Knoll Gardner

Judge Gardner was born on September 14, 1940, in Allentown, Pennsylvania. He received a B.A. magna cum laude from Yale University in 1962 and a J.D. from Harvard Law School in 1965. From 1966 to 1969 Judge Gardner served on active duty with the United States Navy Judge Advocate General's Corps, and he served in the Navy Reserve from 1969 to 1993, including sitting as an appellate judge on the United States Navy and Marine Corps Court of Military Review. He retired in 1993 with the rank of captain. From 1965 to 1966, and 1969 to 1970, Judge Gardner was an associate in the law firm of Duane, Morris and Heckscher in Philadelphia, Pennsylvania. From 1972 to 1981, Judge Gardner served in the Lehigh County District Attorney's Office, initially as an assistant district attorney, and subsequently as first assistant district attorney. From 1970 to 1981, he also maintained a general civil practice as a partner in the firm of Gardner, Gardner and Racines in Allentown, Pennsylvania. From 1981 to 2002, Judge Gardner served as a judge of the Court of Common Pleas of Lehigh County, Pennsylvania, and he served as president judge from 1997 to 2002. In 1996 and 1997, Judge Gardner served as president of the Pennsylvania Conference of State Trial Judges. Judge Gardner was appointed to the United States District Court for the Eastern District of Pennsylvania on October 2, 2002.

PRELIMINARY GENERAL MATTERS

1. **Chambers.** Judge Gardner's primary chambers and courtroom are located in the federal courthouse in Allentown, Pennsylvania. Judge Gardner's mailing address is United States District Court for the Eastern District of Pennsylvania, Edward N. Cahn United States Courthouse, 504 West Hamilton Street, Suite 4701, Allentown, Pennsylvania, 18101. Chambers telephone numbers are 610-434-3457 (secretary and law clerks) and 610-434-3765 (courtroom deputy clerk). The fax number is 610-434-3459.

2. **Courtrooms.** Judge Gardner's primary courtroom is Courtroom B, on the fourth floor of the federal courthouse in Allentown. Judge Gardner also presides regularly at the James A. Byrne United States Courthouse at 601 Market Street, Philadelphia, Pennsylvania. Trial and hearing attachment orders will specify the location of the proceeding. Courtroom assignments vary in the federal courthouse at Philadelphia. A member of Judge Gardner's staff will advise counsel and unrepresented parties of the specific Philadelphia courtroom assignment as soon as it is known.

3. **Jury Selection and First Day of Jury Trials.** Currently all juries are selected at the United States Courthouse in Philadelphia. On jury selection days, counsel for the parties and unrepresented parties should be prepared to make their opening statements and, if time permits, to present witnesses. Customarily, jury selection, and the rest of the first day of a jury trial, will take place in Philadelphia, and the second and subsequent days of the trial will occur in Allentown.

4. **Magistrate Judge Assignment.** Magistrate Judge Henry S. Perkin is assigned to Judge Gardner. Magistrate Judge Perkin's chambers and courtroom are located in the federal courthouse in Allentown. His chambers are located in Suite 4401. Other than the suite number, Magistrate Judge Perkin's mailing address is the same as Judge Gardner's mailing address. Magistrate Judge Perkin's chambers' telephone number is 610-434-3823. His fax number is 610-434-5152.

5. **Correspondence with the Court.** Judge Gardner permits correspondence from counsel and unrepresented parties in the following circumstances: (a) when letters of transmittal accompany documents required to be sent to, or filed with, the court or in another official office in the courthouse, (b) when specifically requested by the court to communi-

cate information to the court by letter, (c) when requesting permission to exceed the page limitation for briefs or to file reply or surreply briefs, and (d) to advise the court that a case has been settled, dismissed, or otherwise finally resolved.

Other correspondence is not prohibited. However, all requests for a judicial ruling, order, decree, extension, continuance, or other formal judicial relief should be made by the filing of a motion, petition, application, or other appropriate pleading, accompanied by a proposed order and a brief or memorandum of law, or other similar filing provided for in the Federal Rules of Civil or Criminal Procedure or the Local Rules of Civil or Criminal Procedure for the United States District Court for the Eastern District of Pennsylvania. Ordinarily, Judge Gardner will not entertain, or grant, such requests made by letter.

Moreover, unless otherwise authorized by statute, case law, or rule of court, correspondence with the court about a case or other matter pending before Judge Gardner is not appropriate unless copies of the letter and all enclosures are simultaneously provided to at least one counsel of record for each party and to all unrepresented parties. The letter to Judge Gardner should indicate that those copies have been provided to each of those persons.

6. Communication with Law Clerks. Counsel may speak directly to Judge Gardner's law clerks regarding scheduling and similar administrative matters, with the understanding that counsel must carefully observe ethical considerations and avoid discussion of the merits of pending cases or any proposed or pending motion with any member of Judge Gardner's staff. Law clerks may advise counsel and unrepresented parties concerning Judge Gardner's requirements, policies, procedures, and practices, but may not give substantive, procedural, or legal advice to counsel. Counsel and unrepresented parties may relay information concerning a case to the court through the law clerks, but only after all counsel of record and all unrepresented parties have been advised of the intention to communicate that information to the court.

7. Telephone Conferences. Judge Gardner permits, and uses, telephone conferences in appropriate circumstances. Ordinarily, Judge Gardner will require the lead trial counsel of record for each party and all unrepresented parties to participate in all telephone conferences concerning a case or other matter pending before Judge Gardner. No substitutions will be permitted unless authorized by Judge Gardner at least 48 hours prior to the conference. Unless directed otherwise by Judge Gardner, only one counsel will speak on behalf of each represented party. Customarily, it is not necessary for more than one counsel per party to be listening in on the conference call. Frequently, one of Judge Gardner's law clerks will listen to telephone conference calls by speaker phone or telephone extension. (See the sample Rule 16 telephone conference scheduling order on page 111 of this book.)

8. Pro Hac Vice Admissions. Judge Gardner requires a formal motion and proposed order for pro hac vice admission to be filed by any attorney not formally admitted to practice before the United States District Court for the Eastern District of Pennsylvania. The motion must be signed by an attorney admitted to practice before the United States District Court for the Eastern District of Pennsylvania and filed prior to the day the attorney seeking admission first appears in court or participates in a telephone conference.

9. Courtesy Copies of All Papers Filed. Judge Gardner welcomes and requests receipt in his chambers in Allentown of courtesy *paper* copies of all papers filed in all matters pending before him, regardless of whether the original papers were filed electronically or in hard copy, including all complaints, counterclaims, cross-claims, amendments, motions, petitions, applications, answers, replies, briefs, memoranda of law, and supporting exhibits.

10. ***Courtesy Copies of Appellate Briefs.*** Judge Gardner appreciates receiving courtesy copies of all appellate briefs concerning any case or decision of Judge Gardner that is appealed.

CIVIL CASES
Pretrial Procedures

1. ***Rule 16 Status Conferences and Conference Memoranda.*** A status conference pursuant to Fed.R.Civ.P. 16 will normally be conducted by Judge Gardner shortly after the case has been assigned, or reassigned, to him. The conference is usually held after the issue has been joined or the pleadings are otherwise closed.

Counsel and unrepresented parties will be notified of the date, time, location, and requirements for the status conference by the entry of a formal scheduling order. Counsel and unrepresented parties are to be prepared to discuss the items enumerated in the scheduling order. Not later than seven days prior to the conference, counsel and unrepresented parties must provide Judge Gardner with an informal memorandum, which should not exceed two pages in length and should include the information specified in the scheduling order. (See the sample Rule 16 telephone conference scheduling order on page 111 of this book.)

Ordinarily, deadlines will be set at the status conference for completion or amendment of pleadings, discovery, expert reports, dispositive motions, and motions in limine. Customarily, a trial date will be set at the conference. In that regard, trial counsel are required to have their trial schedules and appointment calendars with them at the Rule 16 status conference.

Customarily, the dates and deadlines set at the Rule 16 status conference will be memorialized in a Rule 16 status conference order. However, counsel and the parties will be bound by all dates and deadlines set at the status conference, whether or not such an order is filed or received prior to the expiration of those dates and deadlines.

Lead trial counsel of record for each party and each unrepresented party must attend the Rule 16 conference. No substitutions will be permitted unless authorized by Judge Gardner at least 48 hours prior to the conference. Co-counsel for a party may attend in addition to the lead trial counsel, but ordinarily Judge Gardner will permit only one counsel per party to speak on behalf of the client at the conference. Parties who are represented by an attorney of record are ordinarily not permitted to attend the conference (even if the client is also an attorney), whether in person or by speaker phone.

Counsel and unrepresented parties must be prepared to discuss settlement at the Rule 16 conference, unless the matter is to be tried without jury before Judge Gardner. (Nonjury cases may be referred to Magistrate Judge Perkin for a settlement conference.)

At the discretion of Judge Gardner, status conferences may be held in the courtroom, in chambers, or by telephone conference call. Normally status conferences are not proceedings of record, or otherwise recorded.

At his discretion, Judge Gardner may schedule additional status conferences, on his own initiative, or at the request of counsel or unrepresented parties.

Unless the case is particularly complex, status conferences customarily last approximately 30 minutes.

2. ***Pretrial Conferences and Trial Memoranda.*** As noted above, many pretrial dates and deadlines are set in a Rule 16 status conference order. In addition, a jury trial attachment order or nonjury trial attachment order will be issued. These attachment orders contain all of the deadlines customarily set at a pretrial conference. (See the samples of Judge Gardner's trial attachment orders starting on page 102 of this book.)

Such deadlines include the deadlines for submitting trial memoranda, which should include, among other things, witness lists, exhibit lists, and an itemized statement of damages and other relief sought. In jury trials, the trial memoranda should also include proposed voir dire questions and a proposed verdict slip (including any requested interrogatories to the jury). In nonjury trials, the trial memoranda must also include proposed findings of fact and conclusions of law.

The jury trial attachment order also contains deadlines for requesting points for charge and for making objections to such requests. Both jury trial, and nonjury trial, attachment orders include deadlines for requesting a hearing concerning the proposed testimony of any expert witness pursuant to *Daubert v. Merrell Dow Pharmaceuticals, Inc.*, 509 U.S. 579 (1993).

Because pretrial matters are covered extensively by these pretrial orders, a formal pretrial conference (as opposed to Rule 16 status conferences, discussed above) may not be scheduled. However, Judge Gardner may, nevertheless, schedule formal pretrial conferences in complex or other appropriate cases. In addition, Judge Gardner may meet informally with trial counsel and unrepresented parties, either by telephone or in person, during the week prior to trial or immediately prior to jury selection to discuss voir dire and other trial procedures.

3. Witness Lists. In their trial memoranda, counsel should list those witnesses whom they intend to call in their cases-in-chief. Plaintiff's rebuttal witnesses and defendant's surrebuttal witnesses need not be listed. Listing a witness does not constitute a certification that the witness will testify or be present at trial. Unless authorized by Judge Gardner for good cause shown, witnesses not listed may not be called by that party in its case-in-chief.

4. Common Deficiencies in Pretrial Memoranda. Judge Gardner considers the most common deficiency in pretrial memoranda to be overkill, which is typically exhibited by listing hundreds of exhibits and dozens of witnesses, when considerably fewer witnesses and exhibits will actually be presented at trial.

5. Continuances. All requests for continuances of scheduled proceedings, except for criminal jury trial continuance requests, must be made on a continuance form approved by Judge Gardner. (See the sample application for continuance on page 101 of this book.) Oral or letter requests for continuance will not be considered. Approved continuance forms are available in Judge Gardner's chambers, in the Office of the Clerk of Court in the Allentown federal courthouse (telephone 610-434-3896), or on the Internet at http://www.paed.uscourts.gov (click [single left click] on "Judges' Procedures").

Continuance forms must be signed by one counsel of record for each party and by all unrepresented parties. Prior to submitting the continuance form, applicants for continuance must obtain a new date and time for the proceeding from Judge Gardner's secretary or courtroom deputy clerk, and insert the new date and time where indicated in the court-order portion at the bottom of the continuance form. Obtaining a new date and time does not imply that the continuance will be granted. However, failure to do so may result in denial of the request.

Because trial dates are ordinarily set many months in advance with the approval of all counsel and unrepresented parties, continuance of the trial date should not be expected. Scheduled oral arguments, hearings, and trial dates are strictly enforced, and continuances are unlikely absent extraordinary circumstances. Obtaining new counsel will not ordinarily justify a continuance, nor justify revisiting prior deadlines or rulings.

The unavailability of a witness at the time of trial in the manner defined in Fed.R.Civ.P. 32(a)(3), or otherwise, will not be a ground to delay the commencement, or progress, of a trial. In such circumstances, Judge Gardner anticipates the use of oral or videotape depositions at trial of any unavailable witness whose testimony a party believes essential to a presentation of that party's case, whether that witness is a party, a non-party, or an expert.

6. **Extensions.** Requests for extensions of discovery, pleading, or briefing deadlines must be made by motion or stipulation. Judge Gardner may grant a first request for extension that is unopposed and does not affect the deadline for filing dispositive motions or the trial date. Motions or stipulations for extensions must include all current deadlines, the number of previous extensions, and all currently scheduled trial, hearing, and argument dates.

If unopposed, requests for extensions of briefing schedules may be made informally through Judge Gardner's law clerks, but only after counsel has obtained, or attempted to obtain, the agreement of all parties.

7. **Motions in Limine.** Judge Gardner does not require motions in limine. He neither encourages, nor discourages, the filing of such motions. However, Judge Gardner sets specific deadlines for the filing of motions in limine. Customarily, this deadline is set at the initial Rule 16 status conference. The deadline for filing motions in limine, accompanied by a brief, is usually five to seven weeks before trial.

At the discretion of Judge Gardner, motions in limine may be disposed of prior to trial, or at trial. They may be disposed of on briefs, after hearing, or after oral argument. The filing of a formal motion in limine is not a prerequisite to making an objection to inadmissible evidence or testimony at time of trial.

Because the purpose of a motion in limine is to dispose of evidentiary matters out of the hearing of the jury, motions in limine are not appropriate, and customarily will not be heard, in connection with nonjury trials.

Motion Practice

1. **Stipulations.** Judge Gardner encourages the parties to stipulate to as many facts as possible, as early as possible, in each legal proceeding—whether oral argument, hearings, nonjury trials, or jury trials. Judge Gardner also encourages stipulations concerning the applicable law and the procedures to be followed.

Whenever possible, stipulations should be reduced to writing and accompanied by a brief proposed order approving the stipulation. Unless otherwise directed by Judge Gardner, written stipulations must be signed by one counsel of record for each party and all unrepresented parties. All parties in the case must execute the written stipulation, whether or not they have an interest in the subject matter of the stipulation.

Counsel's signature on the stipulation constitutes a representation that his or her client fully understands, and agrees to, the stipulation. When oral stipulations are placed on the record during legal proceedings, Judge Gardner will customarily conduct a colloquy on the record with each party, whether or not represented by counsel, to ascertain whether the party understands and agrees to the stipulation.

2. **Oral Argument, Evidentiary Hearings, and Submission on Briefs.** Judge Gardner determines in the case of all motions and petitions whether to schedule oral argument or an evidentiary hearing, or whether to decide the matter based upon the briefs of the parties and the record. Counsel may request oral argument, a hearing, or acceptance of the issue on briefs and the record. However, Judge Gardner will determine which procedure to follow.

Counsel and unrepresented parties will be advised of the date, time, and location of all hearings, arguments, and trials by means of an attachment order issued by Judge Gardner. (See the samples of Judge Gardner's attachment orders starting on page 102 of this book.)

Judge Gardner will generally conduct oral argument on motions involving complex matters and on many dispositive motions. Not later than seven calendar days before the argument date, each party must submit to Judge Gardner a written summary of the issues and of that party's argument; the summary should not exceed two pages in length.

Ordinarily each party will have 20 minutes to present oral argument, unless more time is allotted, or less time is directed, by Judge Gardner. Irrespective of any time limit, counsel are expected to present argument in a concise manner and to be prepared to answer questions by the court concerning the argument and the case.

Rebuttal and surrebuttal argument is ordinarily not permitted unless requested by the court.

At the conclusion of oral argument, hearing, or trial without jury, in open court, on the record, and in the presence of counsel and the parties, Judge Gardner frequently announces his decision and reasons, including citation of legal authority. This may be accomplished by dictating a formal order and bench opinion, or by means of an informal narrative explanation. At the conclusion of oral argument, Judge Gardner may take a recess for deliberation before reopening court to announce his decision. Counsel are invited, but not required, to remain and be present for the announcement of the decision and analysis.

Because Judge Gardner frequently announces his decision at the conclusion of oral argument, hearing, or nonjury trial, counsel should not expect to be permitted to submit additional documents, briefs, citations, or arguments subsequent to the proceeding.

3. Briefs. Pursuant to Rule 7.1 of the Local Rules of Civil Procedure for the United States District Court for the Eastern District of Pennsylvania, the movant's brief must be filed at the time the motion or petition is filed. Response briefs must be filed 14 calendar days after service of the movant's brief.

Briefs and response briefs must not exceed 25 pages, absent leave of court. Requests to present a brief in excess of 25 pages are to be made either by formal motion and proposed order, by letter request to the court, or by oral request to the law clerk assigned to the matter being briefed. Judge Gardner will grant permission only for good cause shown.

4. Reply Briefs and Surreply Briefs. Reply briefs and surreply briefs are not allowed unless requested, or permitted, by Judge Gardner. If permitted, reply briefs and surreply briefs must not exceed seven pages, absent leave of court. Requests to file a reply brief or surreply brief or to exceed the page limit must be made either by formal motion and proposed order, by letter request to the court, or by oral request to the law clerk assigned to the matter being briefed. Judge Gardner will grant permission only for good cause shown.

5. Proposed Order. Each motion, petition, answer, or reply must be accompanied by a proposed order in the following format.

[Caption]

<u>ORDER</u>

NOW, this *[leave date blank]* day of *[insert month]*, *[insert year]*, upon consideration of *[insert the exact title of the motion, petition, answer, or reply]* filed *[insert the date of filing]*, *[add, as appropriate, either* "which motion is unopposed," *or* "upon consideration of the briefs of the parties," *and if oral argument has been scheduled, add* "and after oral argument held *[insert date, month, and year of oral argument],"]*

IT IS ORDERED that the [motion] [petition] is [granted] [denied].

BY THE COURT:

_____
James Knoll Gardner
United States District Judge

6. **Legal Citations.** Citation of all legal authority—including published and unpublished opinions, statutes, codes, regulations, executive orders, legislative history, and other sources—in briefs, memoranda of law, pleadings, and other documents must conform with the standards promulgated in *A Uniform System of Citation,* commonly referred to as "The Bluebook," published by The Harvard Law Review Association, Eighteenth Edition (2005), or the most recent subsequent edition.

Opinions of the United States Supreme Court should be cited to the United States Reports ("U.S."), the Supreme Court Reporter ("S.Ct."), and the Lawyers' Edition Reports ("L.Ed."), in that order. Where applicable, citations to state court opinions should include parallel citations to the official and unofficial reporters (e.g., "Pa." and "A.2d").

Pinpoint citations should be provided for all direct quotations from an opinion, and are encouraged for all references to a lengthy opinion (e.g., "224 F.Supp.2d 950, 959 (E.D. Pa. 2002))."

All statutes located in titles of the Pennsylvania statutes that have been officially codified should be cited in the following format: 42 Pa.C.S.A. § 913. Use the full citation of the legislative act for reference to all statutes located in titles of the Pennsylvania statutes that have not been codified, in the following format: Act of April 3, 1987, P.L. 43, art. VI, sec. 342, as amended, 43 P.S. § 7342.

7. **Citation of Unpublished Opinions.** Unpublished opinions that are available through the LexisNexis or Westlaw computer legal research programs may be cited to their computer locations in the following format: *Smith v. Jones,* 2002 U.S. Dist. LEXIS 15425, August 15, 2002; 2002 WL 121 (3d Cir. 2002).

Unpublished opinions that are not available through Lexis or Westlaw may be cited in the following format: *Smith v. Jones,* No. Civ. A. 05-1234 (Gardner, J.) (E.D. Pa. January 3, 2005). Attach to the brief or other document a complete copy of any unpublished opinion not available through Lexis or Westlaw.

Do not cite, or rely upon, any unpublished opinion where rules of the jurisdiction promulgating the opinion prohibit citation of, or reliance upon, such opinion.

8. **Courtesy Copies of Motion Papers.** Judge Gardner welcomes and requests receipt in chambers of courtesy copies of motions, petitions, applications, answers, replies, briefs, memoranda of law, proposed orders, and supporting exhibits in matters pending before him.

Discovery

1. **Mandatory Informal Discovery Disclosures.** Counsel and unrepresented parties must comply with Fed.R.Civ.P. 26 concerning mandatory informal self-executing disclosures prior to the Rule 16 status conference.

2. **Discovery Deadlines.** Judge Gardner expects discovery to commence at the close of the pleadings, and counsel and unrepresented parties should commence discovery before the initial Rule 16 status conference. Judge Gardner establishes discovery deadlines at the initial Rule 16 status conference. He does not usually conduct separate discovery conferences, but he may do so in special circumstances or complex cases.

3. **Discovery Period.** Judge Gardner generally permits 90 to 120 days to complete all discovery including interrogatories, requests to produce documents, depositions, and independent medical examinations. Judge Gardner may establish longer discovery periods in special circumstances or exceedingly complex cases. All liability and damages discovery must be completed during a single discovery period. Judge Gardner does not normally establish separate liability and damages discovery periods.

4. **Expert Discovery.** At the Rule 16 status conference, Judge Gardner establishes deadlines to identify expert witnesses and to provide a curriculum vitae and a signed, written expert report from each expert witness. Plaintiff's expert reports are generally due on the last day of the discovery period; defendant's expert reports, 30 days after that; and third-party defendant's expert reports, 30 days after that. Customarily, Judge Gardner does not permit rebuttal expert reports. In appropriate cases, Judge Gardner may permit a brief separate subsequent discovery period for deposing expert witnesses.

5. **Discovery Disputes.** On January 2, 2003, Judge Gardner promulgated a standing order providing that if discovery disputes cannot be amicably resolved, or if additional depositions or other discovery is required, such disputes or requests should immediately be brought to the attention of Magistrate Judge Perkin by letter or other informal means. Any party contending that an order of the magistrate judge is clearly erroneous or contrary to law may file a petition to reconsider, together with a proposed order, directed to Judge Gardner, pursuant to 28 U.S.C. § 636(b)(1)(A). A copy of the standing order is shown on page 110 of this book. The standing order is also available on the Internet at http://www.paed.uscourts.gov.

6. **Confidentiality Agreements.** In matters concerning trade secrets, rights of privacy, privileged information, or similar confidential matters, the parties are encouraged to execute written confidentiality agreements, and may submit such agreements, together with a proposed order, by stipulation to Judge Gardner for approval.

7. **Daubert Hearings.** Any party who contends, or may contend, that the proposed testimony of any expert witness requires a hearing at, or before, trial to challenge the qualifications of an expert to render certain opinions, or to challenge the methodology of the expert, or to make other challenges, pursuant to *Daubert v. Merrell Dow Pharmaceuticals, Inc.,* 509 U.S. 579 (1993), must notify the court of this contention in writing at least 60 days prior to the trial date, or at such other time as directed by Judge Gardner. (See the samples of Judge Gardner's attachment orders starting on page 102.)

Settlement

1. **General Approach to Settlement.** Judge Gardner strongly encourages settlement in civil cases. He believes that court involvement often facilitates settlement agreements.

Judge Gardner refers many cases to Magistrate Judge Perkin for settlement conferences. At the request of the parties, or sua sponte, Judge Gardner personally conducts settlement negotiations in some jury trial cases. In nonjury cases, settlement conferences are handled by Magistrate Judge Perkin. Occasionally, a case will be referred to another district court judge or magistrate judge for settlement.

2. **Alternative Dispute Resolution.** Pursuant to Rule 53.3 of the Local Rules of Civil Procedure for the United States District Court for the Eastern District of Pennsylvania, Judge Gardner requires the parties to consider the use of an alternative dispute resolution (ADR) process at an appropriate stage in the litigation. ADR processes include mediation, conciliation, private arbitration, and court-annexed mediation under Local Rule 53.3.

Arbitration

1. **Consensual Arbitration.** In all appropriate cases, Judge Gardner encourages the parties to consent to federal arbitration pursuant to the provisions of Rule 53.2(3)(B) of the Rules of Civil Procedure of the United States District Court for the Eastern District of Pennsylvania.

Except where prohibited by law, Judge Gardner will approve agreements of the parties to submit cases to federal arbitration containing any one or more of the following provisions: (1) subject to the statutory monetary jurisdictional limitation on arbitration awards, (2) waiving the statutory monetary jurisdictional limitation on arbitration awards, (3) agreeing to the finality of the award of the arbitrators and waiving the right to demand a trial de novo before the district court after arbitration, (4) waiving pretrial discovery, in whole or in part, prior to arbitration, (5) waiving the application of certain evidentiary rules at the arbitration hearing, and (6) other appropriate agreements.

Ordinarily, federal arbitrators are not empowered to award injunctive or declaratory relief, even by consent.

2.   Nonconsensual Arbitration.   In appropriate cases Judge Gardner will direct the parties to submit to federal arbitration, either sua sponte or upon the request of one or more parties, over the objection of a party or parties. All such nonconsensual arbitrations should be conducted subject to the statutory monetary jurisdictional limitation on arbitration awards, the right of all parties to demand a trial de novo before the district court after arbitration, and all procedural and evidentiary rules applicable to federal arbitration, unless otherwise agreed to by all parties.

3.   Scheduling Arbitration Hearing.   Judge Gardner will consider the agreements and preferences of the parties, the schedule of the court, and the interests of justice and efficient case administration in determining whether to schedule arbitration hearings before commencement of discovery, during the discovery period, or after completion of discovery. If the scheduling of the arbitration hearing occurs before, or during, the Rule 16 status conference, Judge Gardner may also schedule a trial date at the status conference, to be used in the event any party makes a timely demand for a trial de novo before the district court after arbitration.

Injunctions

1.   Temporary Restraining Orders.   Consistent with the nature of the emergency involved, Judge Gardner will promptly schedule hearings and/or arguments on requests for temporary restraining orders. Except in cases where the nature of the emergency precludes it, Judge Gardner requires the petitioner to notify the respondent of the nature of the request for a temporary restraining order; and to serve the petition and proposed order upon the respondent, if practical; and to provide the respondent with notice of the date, time, and location of the hearing or argument.

2.   Filing Requirements.   Except in cases of the most extreme emergency, Judge Gardner will not entertain a petition for a temporary restraining order unless a case has been formally commenced by the filing of a separate complaint seeking permanent injunctive relief or other permanent equitable relief. The petition for a temporary restraining order must be filed under the same caption and case number as the complaint for permanent relief.

3.   Preliminary Injunctions.   In cases seeking a preliminary injunction (as opposed to an emergency petition for a temporary restraining order), a hearing and/or argument will be scheduled in due course consistent with the nature of the relief requested. As in the case of a request for a temporary restraining order, a petition seeking a preliminary injunction must be accompanied by a separate complaint seeking permanent relief under the same caption number.

4.   Service.   The complaint, petition for preliminary injunction, proposed order, and notice of hearing or argument must be formally served on all parties as in the case of other civil litigation.

5. Proposed Findings of Fact and Conclusions of Law. Prior to the hearing (or argument, if there is no hearing) in all preliminary injunctions and final injunctions, Judge Gardner requires all parties to submit proposed findings of fact, conclusions of law, and a legal memorandum or brief.

6. Expedited Discovery. In appropriate cases, Judge Gardner permits expedited and intensive discovery in injunctive matters.

7. Consolidation of Hearings on Preliminary and Final Injunctions. When appropriate and consistent with the nature of the case, Judge Gardner favors advancing and consolidating the trial of the action on the merits of the request for a final injunction with the preliminary injunction hearing pursuant to Fed.R.Civ.P. 65(a)(2).

CIVIL AND CRIMINAL TRIAL PROCEDURE
Trial Attachment Procedures

1. Scheduling of Trials. Each jury and nonjury trial on Judge Gardner's calendar is attached to a specific trial term. Ordinarily the trial date is set at the initial Rule 16 status conference. Whenever possible, Judge Gardner accommodates the professional and personal schedules of trial counsel in assigning cases to a particular trial term.

2. Trial Terms. Customarily, cases will be tried during a one- or two-week trial term. Both jury and nonjury cases are assigned to the same trial term. Ordinarily, both civil and criminal cases are assigned to the same trial term. Pursuant to federal law, criminal cases take precedence over civil cases.

3. Trial Continuances. Because all case-related deadlines are customarily set at the initial Rule 16 status conference—including deadlines for amendment of pleadings, discovery, expert witness disclosure, dispositive motions, and motions in limine—counsel generally have six to twelve, or more, months advance notice of the trial date. Because Judge Gardner will ordinarily not schedule a trial unless counsel certify their availability for that date; because counsel have sufficient advance notice to resolve witness scheduling conflicts, or to preserve the testimony of unavailable witnesses for presentation at trial by means of videotaped, or oral, depositions; continuances of trial are rarely granted, and only for the most unexpected, or unforeseen reasons.

Problems locating witnesses, witness scheduling problems, unavailability of witnesses, discovery problems, withdrawal or dismissal of counsel, recent entry of appearance by new counsel, continuing medical problems of plaintiff in a personal injury case, and similar circumstances, ordinarily will not result in postponement of trial.

4. Disposition of Trials. Because statistically a high percentage of cases settle at or before trial, it is necessary to somewhat overbook the number of cases scheduled during a trial term. However, Judge Gardner does not excessively overbook the cases. The customary experience is that all cases listed for a particular trial term will be reached during that trial term.

5. Cases Not Reached. If for any reason a case is not reached (by commencement of jury selection, or by starting a nonjury trial) during the trial term, counsel and the parties will be released from their trial attachment at the end of the last day of the trial term. In that event, the case will be reattached, with priority, for the next trial term for which all counsel are available.

6. **Completion of Cases.** Customarily, a jury trial that has commenced, but is not completed, by the end of a trial term, will continue into the next week, and beyond, if necessary, until its conclusion. A nonjury trial that has commenced, but not concluded, before the end of the trial term, will, at the discretion of Judge Gardner, continue uninterrupted into the next week, or be rescheduled for completion at a future date.

7. **Order in Which Cases are Called.** Cases are not necessarily called for trial in the order in which they are attached for trial. The cases scheduled for each trial term will be prioritized by Judge Gardner approximately one week prior to commencement of the trial term.

Criminal cases will be disposed of before civil cases are reached. Ordinarily, any case not reached in a previous term (for reasons other than a continuance) will be tried before any cases on the list for the first time are reached.

Factors considered by Judge Gardner in prioritizing cases for the trial term include the age of the case, the length of the trial, the complexity of the case, circumstances involving parties, witnesses, and counsel who reside outside of the Eastern District of Pennsylvania, and other relevant factors.

Ordinarily, all cases attached for trial in the first week of a multi-week trial term will be disposed of before any cases attached for the second week of the term are reached.

8. **Communication with the Court Concerning Trial Schedule.** Lead trial counsel for each represented party and each unrepresented party are directed to contact Judge Gardner's chambers by telephone each business day, commencing Wednesday of the week immediately preceding their trial attachment. In these daily calls counsel and unrepresented parties will be advised of the order in, and estimated date on, which their case will commence. Counsel and unrepresented parties should keep their clients and witnesses on standby, and continue the daily calls until advised of a specific time and date to appear to commence the trial.

9. **Location of Jury Trials.** Currently, juries for all trials throughout the Eastern District of Pennsylvania are selected at the James A. Byrne United States Courthouse, 601 Market Street, Philadelphia, Pennsylvania. Accordingly, the first day (including, but not limited to, jury selection) of all jury trials will take place in that federal courthouse in Philadelphia.

Counsel and unrepresented parties will be advised in advance of a specific courtroom assignment for the first day of trial in Philadelphia. If such notification is not received, counsel and unrepresented parties should contact Judge Gardner's chambers in Allentown at 610-434-3457, or inquire on the first day of trial at the jury selection office in Philadelphia (Room 2208 (next to the snack bar)) for the courtroom assignment.

Depending upon the time of completion of jury selection, counsel should be prepared to give their opening statements and to begin witness presentation on the first day of trial in Philadelphia.

After completion of the first day of the jury trial in Philadelphia, the case will ordinarily resume the next business day, and proceed until its conclusion, at the federal courthouse in Allentown. However, in the event jury selection is not completed on the first day, jury selection will resume in Philadelphia on the second day of trial, and the trial will remain in Philadelphia until the end of the day on which jury selection is completed. On the next business day after completion of jury selection, the trial will resume in Allentown until its conclusion.

10. **Location of Nonjury Trials.** Unless otherwise directed by Judge Gardner, all nonjury trials will be tried in their entirety in Courtroom B on the fourth floor of the Edward N. Cahn United States Courthouse at 504 West Hamilton Street, Allentown, Pennsylvania.

Courtroom Protocol

1. **Counsel Tables.** In civil proceedings plaintiffs are assigned the counsel table on the left (from the perspective of the judge). Defendants and third-party defendants are assigned the counsel table on the right. Additional counsel tables may be added to accommodate a large number of parties.

In criminal proceedings defendants are assigned the counsel table closest to the entrance to the prisoner's retaining cell. The government is assigned the other counsel table.

In argument court, counsel occupy the counsel tables. In all other court proceedings, counsel and the parties occupy the counsel tables.

2. **Presence of Parties During Court Proceedings.** The parties are expected to be present for all courtroom proceedings of record except argument court. The parties are welcome, but not required, to attend argument court.

Parties desiring to be excused from part, or all, of a courtroom record proceeding must request in advance from Judge Gardner permission to be excused and formally waive their presence on the record.

3. **Voir Dire.** Judge Gardner always conducts the preliminary, introductory, and informational portion of voir dire. Case-specific voir dire is sometimes conducted by Judge Gardner and sometimes, at Judge Gardner's discretion, by counsel. This subject is normally discussed at the final pretrial conference. Objections to proposed voir dire questions will be heard, and rulings made, at the final pretrial conference.

4. **Length of Opening Statements and Closing Arguments.** Judge Gardner will generally impose an appropriate time limit for opening statements and closing arguments after considering the requests of counsel and the type and complexity of the case.

5. **Order of Presentation.** In the absence of contrary agreement approved by the court, the parties' opening statements, cases-in-chief, rebuttal cases, and closing arguments should be presented in the order in which the parties appear in the caption of the case. For this purpose, multiple parties may be grouped according to their similarity of interest in the litigation. In the event of such grouping, the order of a group's presentation will be determined by the caption placement of the first party in that group to be listed in the caption.

The order of closing arguments in a civil case are the plaintiff's closing, followed by defendant's closing, followed by plaintiff's rebuttal argument. The order of closing arguments in a criminal case are the government's closing, followed by defendant's closing, followed by the government's rebuttal argument.

6. **Order of Examination of Witnesses.** In the absence of contrary agreement approved by the court, witnesses are cross-examined in the order in which the parties appear in the caption (in circular fashion).

In other words, in a case with three parties (a plaintiff, defendant, and third-party defendant), in the plaintiff's case-in-chief, the order of examination of witnesses is direct examination by plaintiff, cross-examination by defendant, and cross-examination by third-party defendant. In the defendant's case-in-chief, the order of examination of witnesses is direct examination by defendant, cross-examination by third-party defendant, and cross-examination by plaintiff. In the third-party defendant's case-in-chief, the order of examination is direct examination by third-party defendant, cross-examination by plaintiff, and cross-examination by defendant.

7. ***Location of Counsel During Interrogation of Witnesses, Opening Statements and Closing Arguments.*** Counsel may interrogate witnesses from counsel table (standing or seated), from a lectern, from the far end of the jury box, standing next to an easel when questioning about an exhibit placed on the easel, or briefly next to the witness stand when handing a document or exhibit to a witness and referring to it.

Because Judge Gardner's courtroom is equipped with an electronic sound recording system, counsel must be located near a microphone. Microphones will be placed at counsel tables, the lectern, and the witness stand, and standing floor microphones will be placed where needed.

Counsel may make opening statements and closing arguments to the jury from behind the lectern, beside the lectern, or standing at a floor microphone in front of the center of the jury box without a lectern. Counsel may not touch the jury box rail or place notes, documents, or exhibits on it.

If opening statements and closing arguments are invited in a nonjury trial, counsel must make those addresses from behind the lectern.

8. ***Avoiding Downtime.*** Judge Gardner expects counsel to have a sufficient number of witnesses present each trial day to fill each day with testimony and to avoid "downtime" at trial.

9. ***Note-taking by Jurors.*** Judge Gardner does not usually permit note-taking by jurors. However, in complicated or lengthy cases, or at the request of counsel, he may permit note-taking in appropriate circumstances.

10. ***Sidebars.*** Judge Gardner requests or permits sidebar conferences as needed. Only one attorney per client or client group will be permitted to speak at sidebar. When the sidebar discussion concerns an objection made during the testimony of a witness, the attorney addressing that objection at sidebar for each client group should be the attorney who is conducting the direct or cross-examination of that witness.

Requests to approach sidebar are to be kept to a minimum. Such requests will be granted only when the law requires a matter to be discussed out of the presence of the jury, in circumstances where Judge Gardner requires sidebars (such as requests to display weapons, illegal drugs, contraband, physical features, or to present a demonstration), or where otherwise appropriate in the discretion of Judge Gardner.

Ordinarily, objections to testimony or exhibits will be briefly made, argued, and ruled upon in the presence of the jury without approaching sidebar.

In nonjury trials, sidebar conferences will not often be appropriate or necessary.

Witnesses

1. ***Examination of Witnesses or Argument by More Than One Attorney.*** Judge Gardner will not permit more than one attorney for a party to examine the same witness. The attorney examining, or cross-examining, a witness will be the only attorney making, or responding to, objections concerning that witness on behalf of that attorney's client.

2. ***Examination of Witnesses Beyond Redirect and Recross.*** Judge Gardner does not have any specific policy concerning examination of witnesses beyond redirect and recross. The rules of evidence will be followed concerning the scope of cross-examination, re-direct, re-cross, and subsequent examination, if any.

3. ***Examination of Witnesses Out of Sequence.*** Judge Gardner will permit counsel to call witnesses out of turn, even during another party's case if necessary, for the convenience of the witnesses upon agreement of opposing counsel or when appropriate in his discretion.

4. Approaching Witnesses. In a jury trial, counsel must request advance permission from Judge Gardner each time counsel wishes to approach a witness during testimony.

In a nonjury trial or hearing, counsel must request advance permission from Judge Gardner the first time counsel wishes to approach a witness during testimony that day. If permission is granted, counsel may approach the witness in a nonjury trial or hearing the remainder of that day without seeking permission each time.

5. Requesting Witnesses to Step Down from the Witness Stand. In a jury trial, counsel must request advance permission from Judge Gardner each time counsel wishes a witness to step down from the witness stand to demonstrate something to the jury or to draw or mark something at the easel. Permission to draw or mark something at the easel may be requested in the presence of the jury. Permission for the witness to demonstrate something must be made in advance at sidebar out of the hearing of the witness and audience.

If permission to draw or mark is granted, the witness must complete the drawing or marking without comment and then step aside from the easel for questioning. If a witness is permitted to demonstrate something, the demonstration will be carried out only in the precise manner approved in advance by Judge Gardner.

6. Displaying Physical Features. Any party wishing to display scars, injuries, birthmarks, tattoos, or other physical features of a person to the jury must request permission from Judge Gardner in advance at sidebar out of the hearing of the jury and audience. After giving each party an opportunity to object and be heard, Judge Gardner will rule on such requests. If permitted, such physical features will be displayed to witnesses or jurors only in the precise manner approved in advance by Judge Gardner.

Pre-recorded Testimony

1. Videotaped Testimony and Oral Trial Depositions. Judge Gardner requires that prior to trial, he be provided with the original and one copy of the complete transcript of any videotaped testimony that will be played at trial and any oral deposition that will be read at trial. Portions of the videotaped or oral deposition that the plaintiff intends to offer at trial must be marked on the copy in blue; portions intended to be offered by defendant, in red.

In addition, at trials conducted in Allentown, counsel must supply their own video playback equipment and operator. Sufficient equipment must be provided to enable Judge Gardner, all jurors, counsel, parties, and the audience to clearly see and hear the videotaped testimony. The equipment must be set up in the courtroom when court is not in session, at a time pre-approved by Judge Gardner.

2. Transcripts and Videocassettes. Judge Gardner will seek the agreement of counsel and the parties to substitute the original transcript of the videotaped or oral deposition in the record as the official record of the trial testimony of the deponent, in lieu of transcription of the testimony of that witness by the court reporter or the court's typist.

At the conclusion of the trial, counsel for any party presenting videotaped testimony must take possession, and maintain custody, of the videocassette of that testimony until the final disposition of all appeals and retrials, if any.

3. Objections to Videotaped Testimony and Oral Trial Depositions. Prior to commencement of trial, parties intending to offer videotaped testimony or oral trial depositions must make reasonable efforts with all counsel and unrepresented parties to resolve each objection made on the record at the time of the deposition. Ordinarily, objections not made on the record at the time of the videotaped or oral trial deposition will be deemed to be waived.

Where a court ruling is necessary, the basis for unresolved objections must be written in 10 words or less in the margin of the copy of the deposition, accompanied by a separate written index of such objections.

4.   Reading Materials Into the Record.   Parties desiring to read stipulations, pleadings, discovery materials, or other matters into the record must provide Judge Gardner and all parties in advance of the reading with a copy of the matters to be read. Parties intending to read such materials into the record must make reasonable efforts to obtain the agreement of all other parties. A record will be made of such agreements. Any unresolved objections should be argued and ruled upon before the reading is permitted.

Any reasonable proposal concerning the reading procedure, to which there is no objection, will be approved. Subject to any objections, counsel may provide the readers, do the reading, or request Judge Gardner to do the reading. However, counsel should not request members of Judge Gardner's staff to read materials into the record.

5.   Manner of Reading Materials Into the Record.   All materials are to be read clearly and accurately in a professional, not overly-dramatic, fashion. Unless otherwise prohibited by the rules of evidence, prior to the formal reading, counsel must briefly identify the source of the material being read, the identity of any persons being quoted (including the attorney-questioner and witness), and the date and location of the original testimony or deposition being read.

When testimony is read, two readers may be provided: one to read the attorney's questions, and the other to read the answers of the witness. The person portraying the witness may sit on the witness stand, if desired.

If only one person is provided for reading testimony, the reader should state "Question" before each question and "Answer" before each answer.

6.   Submission of Materials Read Into the Record.   All materials read into the record are to be marked as exhibits and formally offered into evidence. If only a portion of such exhibit is being read or offered into evidence, the proponent of the exhibit must clearly delineate for the record (by page and line number, or other appropriate designation) which portions are being read into the record and which portions are not.

Exhibits

1.   Preparation of Exhibits.   Before commencement of trial, exhibits are to be pre-marked and exchanged by counsel and unrepresented parties. Prior to opening statements, the parties must provide Judge Gardner with a copy of each exhibit together with an index briefly describing each exhibit.

2.   Offering Exhibits Into Evidence.   Prior to trial, counsel and unrepresented parties must attempt to agree to the admission of as many exhibits as possible.

To the extent possible, exhibits should be pre-numbered prior to trial. It is not required that exhibits be presented in numerical order during trial. Nor is it necessary that all pre-marked exhibits be used at trial.

Whether or not pre-marked, no exhibit may be referred to at trial until it has been presented to the court reporter for dating, initialing, and recording and, if not already done, for assignment of a number and affixing an evidence sticker or tag.

Counsel are encouraged to meet with the court reporter prior to the commencement of each court session for the tagging, dating, initialing, and recording of each exhibit to be presented that morning or afternoon for the first time.

3. ***Displaying Exhibits to the Jury During Trial.*** In the absence of agreement, no exhibit may be referred to at trial until shown to all counsel and unrepresented parties for examination and possible objection. No exhibit or portion thereof may be shown or read to the jury until after the exhibit has been formally offered and received in evidence, and a request has been made and granted to display or publish the exhibit.

With advance permission of Judge Gardner, an exhibit may be read to the jury, displayed on an easel, projected on a movie screen, displayed on a video or VCR screen, displayed in a shadow box (x rays), demonstrated by a witness, or personally examined by the jurors in the jury box. Only Judge Gardner or members of his staff will hand exhibits to the jury or retrieve them from the jury.

4. ***Weapons, Ammunition, and Other Dangerous Items as Evidence.*** No firearms, explosives, weapons, ammunition, or dangerous items should be brought into the courtroom as evidence without first presenting them to the United States marshal in an unloaded or disengaged condition. The marshal will inspect the items and render all firearms, explosives, and other similar items inoperable.

With approval of the marshal, the items may be transported to the courtroom by the marshal, court security officer, law enforcement case agent, or counsel. All such items must be concealed in an evidence envelope, box, bag, briefcase, or other appropriate container until Judge Gardner grants permission to display the items in the courtroom. Such permission must be requested in advance at sidebar out of the hearing of the jury and the audience.

5. ***Illegal Drugs and Other Contraband as Evidence.*** No illegal drugs or other contraband will be brought into the courtroom without first advising the United States marshal and, if the marshal requests, presenting the items to the marshal for inspection. After that, the items may be transported to the courtroom by the same category of individuals authorized to transport firearms into the courtroom.

All such items must be concealed in appropriate containers in such a fashion as to prevent spillage or other destruction or modification of the evidence, and until Judge Gardner grants permission to display the items in the courtroom.

Permission to display any such item must be requested of Judge Gardner in advance at sidebar out of the hearing of the jury and audience. Judge Gardner will inspect the item before granting permission to display it. Such items will be displayed to witnesses, the jurors, or others in the courtroom only in the precise manner approved in advance by Judge Gardner.

Ordinarily, jurors will not be permitted to touch or handle such items. However, with advance permission of Judge Gardner requested out of the hearing of the jury, the items may be displayed to the jury in a manner approved by the court.

6. ***Custody of Weapons, Ammunition, Other Dangerous Items, and Contraband During and After Trial.*** All firearms, explosives, weapons, ammunition, dangerous items, or contraband referred to during trial, whether or not admitted into evidence, must remain in the custody of the law enforcement case agent or other appropriate law enforcement official, or other authorized person, both during trial and during recesses and adjournment of the trial. After conclusion of the trial, those items are to remain in the custody of the appropriate official until after the appeal period expires (if no appeal is taken), and until the final disposition of all appeals and retrials (if an appeal is taken).

The custodian will secure the items in an evidence locker or other appropriate secure storage facility with limited access, maintain a written chain of custody record, and will not permit the evidence to become lost, destroyed, damaged, altered, or modified in any fashion.

Prior to conclusion of the trial, the party who offered those exhibits into evidence must provide the court reporter with 8-1/2" x 11" color photographs of the exhibits for retention in the record in lieu of the actual items.

7. **Custody of Tangible Property, Blow-Ups, Enlargements, and Other Large Items After Trial.** At the conclusion of the trial, counsel for any party that offered into evidence tangible property, blow-ups or enlargements, or other large or bulky items, must take possession and maintain custody of those items until the final disposition of all appeals and retrials, if any.

Prior to conclusion of the trial, the party who offered those exhibits into evidence must provide the court reporter with 8-1/2" x 11" color photographs of the exhibits for retention in the record in lieu of the actual items.

8. **Custody of Exhibits After Trial.** At the conclusion of trial, any exhibits not returned to counsel or the parties will remain in the possession of the court reporter for a period of 60 days if no appeal is taken, or for 60 days after disposition of all appeals and retrials, if any. Counsel and unrepresented parties have 30 days after expiration of this time period in which to retrieve their trial exhibits. Any exhibits not retrieved by that time will be destroyed by the court reporter.

Trial Submissions

1. **Trial Briefs.** Trial briefs will not be required, unless Judge Gardner specifically directs their production in order to address some unique or complex issue. However, the materials and information required by the trial attachment order must be provided by the deadlines established in that order.

2. **Proposed Findings of Fact and Conclusions of Law.** In nonjury trials, counsel for plaintiffs must initiate a meeting of all counsel of record and unrepresented parties to be held at least 40 days before commencement of trial, at which counsel will meet and discuss and submit to the court at least 30 days before commencement of trial, one complete set of agreed-upon findings of fact and conclusions of law.

If the parties cannot agree upon one complete set of findings of fact and conclusions of law, they are required to submit to the court at least 30 days before commencement of trial, one set of those findings and conclusions that have been agreed upon, and each party must submit to the court at least 15 days before commencement of trial, proposed findings of fact and conclusions of law that are not agreed upon, and a legal memorandum in support thereof.

The original of each document should be filed with the clerk of court. If a good-faith effort is not made to comply with these directives, sanctions may be imposed, the trial may be continued, or both.

3. **Proposed Jury Instructions.** In civil jury trials, counsel for the parties and unrepresented parties are required to jointly submit one set of agreed-upon jury instructions. To accomplish this, the parties are required to serve their proposed instructions upon each other one month prior to trial. The parties should then meet, confer, and submit to the court one complete set of agreed-upon jury instructions. Sanctions may be imposed if a good-faith effort to comply with this directive is not made.

If the parties cannot agree upon one complete set of jury instructions, they are required to submit one set of those jury instructions that have been agreed upon, and each party must submit a supplemental set of jury instructions that are not agreed upon.

These joint instructions and supplemental instructions must be filed two weeks prior to trial. Each party must then file, one week before trial, its objections to the non-agreed-upon instructions proposed by all other parties. All objections must be in writing, setting forth the objectionable proposed instruction in its entirety.

The objection must specifically set forth the objectionable material in the proposed instruction. The objection must contain citation of legal authority explaining why the instruction is improper and a concise statement of argument concerning the instruction. Where applicable, the objecting party must submit a correct alternative instruction covering the subject or principle of law, with citation of legal authority supporting the alternative instruction.

All proposed supplemental jury instructions must be numbered and must have citation of authority for each point (one instruction per page). If a model jury instruction is submitted, for example, from *Pennsylvania Suggested Standard Civil Jury Instructions,* or from Sand, Siffert, Reiss, and Batterman, *Modern Federal Jury Instructions,* Lexis-Nexis (originally published in 1984 and updated annually), counsel must indicate whether the proposed jury instruction is modified or unchanged.

If counsel modifies a model jury instruction, additions must be underlined and deletions placed in brackets. If a model jury instruction is unchanged, it must be submitted by title and paragraph number reference only, and must not be retyped verbatim.

4. **Jury Interrogatories.** In all civil jury trials, Judge Gardner requires each counsel to submit a proposed verdict slip not later than five weeks before trial. In most civil trials Judge Gardner provides the jury with a verdict slip containing written jury interrogatories that the jury must answer.

After the jury responds to the written interrogatories and delivers the completed verdict slip to the clerk in the courtroom, Judge Gardner will mold the verdict on the record as appropriate considering the jury's interrogatory responses.

Motions During Trial

1. **Motions for Judgment as a Matter of Law and Motions for Judgment on Partial Findings.** Motions for judgment as a matter of law in jury cases, and motions for judgment on partial findings in nonjury cases may be made orally, or in writing, at the appropriate time or times during trial. Judge Gardner will customarily hear oral argument and decide such motions at the time they are made.

Jury Deliberations

1. **Written Jury Instructions.** Judge Gardner does not give the jury or counsel a copy of his jury charge.

2. **Exhibits in the Jury Room.** No exhibit will be submitted to the jury during deliberations that was not admitted into evidence during the trial. However, admission of an exhibit into the record during trial and submission of an exhibit to the jury during deliberations are two separate procedures. Merely because an exhibit has been received into evidence during trial does not necessarily mean that it will be submitted to the jury during deliberations.

A separate request to submit admitted exhibits to the jury during deliberations must be made at the charge conference conducted prior to closing arguments. After hearing and deciding any objections, Judge Gardner will indicate which exhibits will be sent to the jury during deliberations. Judge Gardner will also discuss and decide during the charge conference whether approved exhibits will be automatically sent to the jury room at the beginning of deliberations, or only if and when the jury requests to see particular exhibits.

Firearms, explosives, other weapons, dangerous items, illegal drugs, other contraband, or perishable goods will ordinarily not be sent to the jury deliberating room.

3.   Handling Jury Requests.   The jury is instructed to communicate all requests during deliberations to Judge Gardner in writing. All written requests will be made part of the record.

Prior to responding, Judge Gardner discusses the request with counsel and the parties on the record and out of the hearing of the jury in an effort to reach agreement on the preferred way to respond. In the absence of agreement, Judge Gardner will respond to the request in a manner that he deems appropriate.

4.   Jury Requests to Re-hear Testimony.   If the jury requests to re-hear testimony presented at trial, Judge Gardner will discuss the request with counsel and the parties on the record and out of the hearing of the jury. He will discuss whether or not it is appropriate to grant the request in whole or in part, and how much, if any, of the testimony will be played for the jury on the court's electronic court-reporting equipment.

If Judge Gardner grants any jury request to re-hear audiotape or videotape recordings previously admitted into evidence, the recordings will be replayed for the jury in the courtroom in the presence of the parties and their attorneys, unless the parties agree to permit the jury to hear or watch the recordings privately in the courtroom or jury room. The parties are responsible for providing appropriate equipment and an operator for the playing of any audiotapes or videotapes, both during trial and during deliberations.

5.   Availability of Counsel and the Parties During Jury Deliberations.   At the commencement of jury deliberations counsel must provide Judge Gardner with the cell phone number for a working cell phone in their possession.

During deliberations, counsel and the parties are to remain in the courthouse, or within four blocks of the courthouse. With the exception of incarcerated criminal defendants, counsel must be aware of the whereabouts of their clients at all times during deliberations and are responsible for the prompt return of their clients to the courtroom upon being summoned to respond to a jury request or to receive the verdict.

At all times during deliberations, counsel must advise Judge Gardner's courtroom deputy of counsel's whereabouts inside the courthouse or on the outdoor courthouse plaza immediately adjacent to the courthouse. No counsel will be permitted to depart from the courthouse or beyond the area of the courthouse plaza, without first obtaining the personal permission of Judge Gardner (not a staff member or deputy) and then informing the courtroom deputy of their destination and of the fact that they have obtained Judge Gardner's permission to go there.

At all times during deliberations when counsel are outside of the courthouse, they must be in possession of their cell phones, which must be turned on, operational, and ready to receive calls without delay.

6.   Polling the Jury.   If there is a request to poll the jury, the jury will be polled on the record by Judge Gardner or a courtroom deputy.

7.   Interviewing the Jury.   Immediately prior to their discharge, the jury will be told that they are now at liberty to discuss the case if they wish to, but that it is their personal choice whether or not to talk about the case, and that they are under no obligation to do so. In addition, the jurors will be instructed that while they may discuss their own thoughts and impressions, they may not disclose the thoughts, impressions, views, discussions, or statements of any other jurors, or reveal the details of the confidential jury deliberations, unless directed by the court to do so.

Subject to those limitations and consistent with those instructions, Judge Gardner does not prohibit jurors from discussing the case with counsel, after they have been formally discharged as jurors in the case, nor requires them to do so.

CRIMINAL CASES

1. Criminal Jury Trial Attachment Order. In all criminal cases, Judge Gardner will file a criminal jury trial attachment order. (See the sample of Judge Gardner's criminal jury trial attachment order on page 108 of this book.) This order will schedule a date formally attaching the case for trial, establish deadlines for filing and responding to pretrial motions, and schedule a hearing on all pretrial motions.

The attachment order will set deadlines for submitting proposed jury instructions, and for filing objections to proposed jury instructions. The order will establish a deadline for submitting proposed jury selection voir dire questions, and for objecting to proposed voir dire.

Finally, the attachment order will set deadlines for each party to submit a brief two-page written summary of its contentions regarding the facts and that party's theories concerning the case. The order will also establish a deadline for all other parties to submit written objections or alternatives to this summary.

2. Oral Argument. Judge Gardner will grant or require oral argument on motions in criminal cases if he determines that it will assist him in deciding the motions, regardless of whether or not argument has been requested by counsel.

3. Hearings. Hearings on all pretrial motions will be conducted, and decisions rendered, in advance of trial.

4. Pretrial Conferences. Judge Gardner holds pretrial conferences in criminal cases as needed or at the request of counsel.

5. Continuances. All requests for continuances of criminal jury trials must be submitted no later than 10 days prior to the commencement of trial by motion accompanied by a proposed order and memorandum of law containing a brief recitation of the applicable facts, and a concise statement of the legal contentions together with the authorities relied upon in support of such motion.

6. Plea and Sentencing Memoranda. Judge Gardner invites the submission of guilty plea and sentencing memoranda at change-of-plea and sentence hearings, respectively. These memoranda should be submitted to Judge Gardner not later than five business days before the plea or sentencing hearing, as appropriate.

7. Written Guilty Plea Agreement. In cases where the parties have executed a written guilty plea agreement and accompanying acknowledgment-of-rights document, the United States attorney assigned to the case must submit a copy of the final version of the fully executed originals to Judge Gardner in chambers not later than five business days before the change of plea hearing. Government counsel must present the fully executed originals of those documents to Judge Gardner on the record at the guilty plea hearing.

Judge James Knoll Gardner

IN THE UNITED STATES DISTRICT COURT FOR THE EASTERN DISTRICT OF PENNSYLVANIA
JAMES KNOLL GARDNER, DISTRICT JUDGE

APPLICATION FOR CONTINUANCE

INSTRUCTIONS:
1. Please type or print legibly.
2. Counsel of record and unrepresented parties must sign.
3. Applying counsel or unrepresented party shall (a) complete Sections I, II and III; (b) obtain a new date certain from Judge Gardner's chambers; (c) obtain agreement of all counsel and unrepresented parties to the new date; and (d) insert new agreed date and time on the "DATE/TIME" line in Section V.
4. Other counsel of record and unrepresented parties shall complete Section IV, indicating whether "UNOPPOSED" or "OPPOSED", and specifying the reasons for any opposition.
5. This form may be submitted in multiple parts.

I. **APPLICATION IS MADE TO CONTINUE THE FOLLOWING CASE(S):**

　　　　　　　　　　　　　　　　　　　　　　　　　CASE NO: _____
　　　　　　　　VS　　　　　　　　　　　　　　　**COMPANION CASE NO(S):** _____

CASE SCHEDULED ON　　DATE _____　　TIME _____
BEFORE JUDGE JAMES KNOLL GARDNER
TYPE OF PROCEEDING **(CHECK BELOW)**

☐ ARGUMENT　　　　☐ NON-JURY TRIAL　　　☐ RULE 16 OFFICE PRE-TRIAL CONFERENCE　　☐ SENTENCING

☐ HEARING　　　　　☐ PLEA HEARING　　　　☐ RULE 16 TELEPHONE STATUS CONFERENCE　　☐ SETTLEMENT CONFERENCE

☐ JURY TRIAL　　　　☐ RULE 16 OFFICE STATUS CONFERENCE　　☐ RULE 16 TELEPHONE PRE-TRIAL CONFERENCE　　☐ OTHER _____

II. **NUMBER OF PREVIOUS CONTINUANCES** _____　**BY PLAINTIFF** _____　**BY DEFENDANT** _____
　　BY THIRD PARTY PLAINTIFF _____　**BY THIRD PARTY DEFENDANT** _____

III. **APPLICATION IS MADE FOR THE FOLLOWING REASON(S):**

_____　　_____　　_____
APPLYING PARTY: PLEASE PRINT AND SIGN　　DATE　　REPRESENTING
Telephone: _____

IV. **APPLICATION IS UNOPPOSED/OPPOSED FOR THE FOLLOWING REASON(S):**

_____　　_____　　_____
OPPOSING PARTY: PLEASE PRINT AND SIGN　　DATE　　REPRESENTING
Telephone: _____

_____　　_____　　_____
OPPOSING PARTY: PLEASE PRINT AND SIGN　　DATE　　REPRESENTING
Telephone: _____

V. **ACTION TAKEN BY THE COURT:**　　NOW, _____
　　☐ APPLICATION IS GRANTED AND THE CASE IS CONTINUED　　☐ APPLICATION DENIED
　　　　　　　　　　　　　　　　　　　　　　　　　　　　　　☐ NO FURTHER CONTINUANCES

　　☐ TO _____
　　　　　　　DATE/TIME

　　　　　　　　　　　　　　　　　　_____
　　　　　　　　　　　　　　　　　　JUDGE

IN THE UNITED STATES DISTRICT COURT
FOR THE EASTERN DISTRICT OF PENNSYLVANIA

```
                    )
                    )   Civil Action
      Plaintiff     )   No.
                    )
vs.                 )
                    )
                    )
      Defendant     )
```

JURY TRIAL ATTACHMENT ORDER

NOW, this _____ day of _____, 20___,

IT IS ORDERED that a jury trial of the within case shall commence before **[Judge Gardner] [the undersigned]** on **[day of week], [date]**, 20___, at _____ o'clock **[a.m./p.m.]**, or as soon thereafter as the schedule of the court permits, with the selection of a jury at the James A. Byrne United States Courthouse, 601 Market Street, Philadelphia, Pennsylvania. After completion of jury selection, the trial shall continue in Courtroom B, Edward N. Cahn United States Courthouse, 504 West Hamilton Street, Allentown, Pennsylvania. This Order shall serve as a formal attachment for trial.

IT IS FURTHER ORDERED that counsel for the parties[*] are required to jointly submit one set of agreed-upon jury instructions. To accomplish this, the parties are required to serve their proposed instructions upon each other one month prior to trial. The parties shall then meet, confer, and submit to the court one complete set of agreed-upon jury instructions. Sanctions may be imposed if a good faith effort to comply with this directive is not made.

If the parties cannot agree upon one complete set of jury instructions, they are required to submit one set of those jury instructions which have been agreed upon, and each party shall submit a supplemental set of jury instructions which are not agreed upon.

These joint instructions and supplemental instructions must be filed two weeks prior to trial. Each party shall then file, one week before trial, its objections to the non-agreed upon instructions proposed by all other parties. All objections shall be in writing and shall set forth the objectionable proposed instruction in its entirety. The objection shall specifically set forth the objectionable material in the proposed instruction. The objection shall contain citation(s) of legal authority explaining why the instruction is improper and a concise statement of argument concerning the instruction. Where applicable, the objecting party shall submit a correct alternative instruction covering the subject or principle of law, with citation(s) of legal authority supporting the alternative instruction.

All proposed supplemental jury instructions shall be numbered and shall have citations of authority for each point (one instruction per page). If a model jury instruction is submitted, for example, from *Pennsylvania Suggested Standard Civil Jury Instructions,* or from Sand, Siffert, Reiss and Batterman, *Modern Federal Jury Instructions,* LexisNexis (originally published 1984 and updated annually), counsel shall indicate whether the proposed jury instruction is modified or unchanged. If counsel modifies a model jury instruction, additions shall be underlined and deletions shall be placed in brackets. If a model jury instruction is unchanged, it shall be submitted by title and paragraph number reference only, and shall not be retyped verbatim.

IT IS FURTHER ORDERED that on or before **[five weeks before trial date]**, counsel for the parties and all unrepresented parties shall submit to **[Judge Gardner] [the undersigned]** and serve on all counsel of record and unrepresented parties a trial memorandum which shall include:

---

[*] Whenever used in this Order, the terms "counsel" and "counsel for the parties" shall also refer to any unrepresented parties.

(a) A list of all exhibits to be used at the trial. Not later than one month prior to trial all exhibits shall be pre-marked and counsel and unrepresented parties shall exchange with each other copies of all documentary and photographic exhibits and shall provide an opportunity for opposing counsel to view any models or videotapes.

(b) A list of the name, address, and field of expertise of each expert witness to be called at trial by the party.

(c) A curriculum vitae for each expert witness listed.

(d) A list of the name and address of each fact witness to be called at trial, together with a brief statement of the nature of his or her expected testimony. (Unless authorized by **[Judge Gardner] [the undersigned]** for good cause shown, witnesses not listed may not be called by that party in its case-in-chief.)

(e) An itemized statement of claimant's damages and/or other relief sought.

(f) A statement of any anticipated significant and/or unique legal and procedural issues on which the court will be required to rule, together with counsel's single best authority on each such issue.

(g) Names and addresses of all parties at the time the cause of action arose and presently.

(h) Name, address and telephone number of trial counsel, and, if applicable, the name and telephone number of the firm with which he or she is affiliated.

(i) Proposed voir dire questions.

(j) Proposed verdict slip.

(k) Any other matters of importance for the efficient trial of the case.

IT IS FURTHER ORDERED that not later than three weeks prior to trial, counsel for the parties and all unrepresented parties shall submit to **[Judge Gardner] [the undersigned]** and serve on all counsel of record and unrepresented parties any objections to proposed voir dire questions and the proposed verdict slip. Objections not made pursuant to this provision may be deemed waived.

IT IS FURTHER ORDERED that any party who contends that the proposed testimony of any expert witness is inadmissible in whole or in part, pursuant to *Daubert v. Merrell Dow Pharmaceuticals, Inc.,* 509 U.S. 579, 113 S.Ct. 2786, 125 L.Ed.2d 469 (1993), shall file a *Daubert* motion and proposed Order, accompanied by a brief, at least sixty days prior to the trial date.

IT IS FURTHER ORDERED that not later than three weeks prior to trial any party having an objection to: (a) the admissibility of any exhibit based on authenticity, (b) the adequacy of the qualifications of an expert witness expected to testify, (c) the admissibility for any reason (except relevancy) of any item of evidence expected to be offered, or (d) the admissibility of any opinion testimony from lay witnesses pursuant to Federal Rule of Evidence 701, shall set forth separately in writing each such objection, clearly and concisely. The objection shall describe, with particularity, the grounds for the objection and the authority relied upon.

IT IS FURTHER ORDERED that unless stipulated to by all affected parties and approved by the court, or by Order of court so as to avoid manifest injustice, only those exhibits, discovery items and expert witnesses identified in the manner set forth in this Order shall be considered by the court for admission into evidence at trial.

IT IS FURTHER ORDERED that the unavailability of a witness at the time of trial in the manner defined in Federal Rule of Civil Procedure 32(a) (3), will not be a ground to delay the commencement, or progress, of a trial. In such circumstances, the court anticipates the use of oral or videotape depositions at trial of any unavailable witness whose testimony a party believes essential to the presentation of that party's case, whether that witness is a party, a non-party or an expert.

IT IS FURTHER ORDERED that any party offering a deposition at trial shall provide the court, prior to commencement of trial, a copy of the deposition transcript, but only after all efforts have been made to resolve objections with all counsel and unrepresented parties. Portions of the deposition offered by plaintiff shall be marked in blue; portions offered by defendant, in red. Where a court ruling is necessary, the basis for unresolved objections shall be written in ten words or less in the margin of the deposition, accompanied by a separate written index of such objections.

IT IS FURTHER ORDERED that at least ten business days before commencement of trial, each party shall submit to the court a written summary, not to exceed two pages in length, in plain language, of its contentions regarding the facts and that party's theories concerning liability and damages. Not later than five days prior to the beginning of voir dire, all other parties may submit in writing objections or alternatives to this summary. The summary may be used by the court in jury voir dire and in its preliminary and final instructions to the jury to familiarize the jurors with the general framework of the factual and legal issues and contentions in the case.

IT IS FURTHER ORDERED that counsel shall familiarize themselves with the Local Rules of Civil Procedure of the United States District Court for the Eastern District of Pennsylvania. Failure to comply with the within Order or the Local Rules may result in the imposition of sanctions.

IT IS FURTHER ORDERED that continuances will be granted only in extraordinary circumstances. Continuance requests shall be filed by one counsel of record for each represented party and by each unrepresented party. Continuance requests shall be submitted at least ten days prior to the commencement of trial on a form approved by **[Judge Gardner] [the undersigned]**.

By:

CHERYL E. SINCLAIR
Civil Deputy Clerk to
Judge James Knoll Gardner
Phone: (610) 434-3457

or

BY THE COURT:

James Knoll Gardner
United States District Judge

Judge James Knoll Gardner

IN THE UNITED STATES DISTRICT COURT
FOR THE EASTERN DISTRICT OF PENNSYLVANIA

Plaintiff	)	Civil Action
	)	No.
vs.	)	
	)	
	)	
Defendant	)	

NON-JURY TRIAL ATTACHMENT ORDER

NOW, this _____ day of _____, 20___,

IT IS ORDERED that a non-jury trial of the within case shall commence before **[Judge Gardner] [the undersigned]** on **[day of week], [date]**, 20___, at _____ o'clock **[a.m./p.m.]** in Courtroom B, Edward N. Cahn United States Courthouse, 504 West Hamilton Street, Allentown, Pennsylvania, or as soon thereafter as the schedule of the court permits. This Order shall serve as a formal attachment for trial.

IT IS FURTHER ORDERED that on or before **[five weeks before trial]**, counsel for the parties[*] shall submit to **[Judge Gardner] [the undersigned]** and serve on all counsel of record and unrepresented parties a trial memorandum which shall include:

(a) A list of all exhibits to be used at the trial. Not later than one month prior to trial all exhibits shall be pre-marked and counsel shall exchange with each other copies of all documentary and photographic exhibits and shall provide an opportunity for opposing counsel to view any models or videotapes.

(b) A list of the name, address, and field of expertise of each expert witness to be called at trial by the party.

(c) A curriculum vitae for each expert witness listed.

(d) A list of the name and address of each fact witness to be called at trial, together with a brief statement of the nature of his or her expected testimony. (Unless authorized by **[Judge Gardner] [the undersigned]** for good cause shown, witnesses not listed may not be called by that party in its case-in-chief.)

(e) An itemized statement of claimant's damages and/or other relief sought.

(f) A statement of any anticipated significant and/or unique legal and procedural issues on which the court will be required to rule, together with counsel's single best authority on each such issue.

(g) Names and addresses of all parties at the time the cause of action arose and presently.

(h) Name, address and telephone number of trial counsel, and, if applicable, the name and telephone number of the firm with which he or she is affiliated.

(i) Any other matters of importance for the efficient trial of the case.

IT IS FURTHER ORDERED that counsel for plaintiff(s) shall initiate a meeting of all counsel of record and unrepresented parties to be held at least forty days before commencement of trial, at which counsel shall meet and discuss and submit to the court at least thirty days before commencement of trial, one complete set of agreed-upon findings of fact and conclusions of law. If the parties cannot agree upon one complete set of findings of fact and conclusions of law, they are required to submit to the court at least thirty days before commencement of trial, one set of those findings and conclusions which have

---

[*] Whenever used in this Order, the terms "counsel" and "counsel for the parties" shall also refer to any unrepresented parties.

been agreed upon, and each party shall submit to the court at least fifteen days before commencement of trial, proposed findings of fact and conclusions of law which are not agreed upon, and a legal memorandum in support thereof. The original of each document shall be filed with the Clerk of Court. If a good faith effort is not made to comply with these directives, sanctions may be imposed, the trial may be continued, or both.

IT IS FURTHER ORDERED that any party who contends that the proposed testimony of any expert witness is inadmissible in whole or in part, pursuant to *Daubert v. Merrell Dow Pharmaceuticals, Inc.,* 509 U.S. 579, 113 S.Ct. 2786, 125 L.Ed.2d 469 (1993), shall file a *Daubert* motion and proposed Order, accompanied by a brief, at least sixty days prior to the trial date.

IT IS FURTHER ORDERED that not later than three weeks prior to trial any party having an objection to: (a) the admissibility of any exhibit based on authenticity, (b) the adequacy of the qualifications of an expert witness expected to testify, (c) the admissibility for any reason (except relevancy) of any item of evidence expected to be offered, or (d) the admissibility of any opinion testimony from lay witnesses pursuant to Federal Rule of Evidence 701, shall set forth separately in writing each such objection, clearly and concisely. The objection shall describe, with particularity, the grounds for the objection and the authority relied upon.

IT IS FURTHER ORDERED that unless stipulated to by all affected parties and approved by the court, or by Order of court so as to avoid manifest injustice, only those exhibits, discovery items and expert witnesses identified in the manner set forth in this Order shall be considered by the court for admission into evidence at trial.

IT IS FURTHER ORDERED that the unavailability of a witness at the time of trial in the manner defined in Federal Rule of Civil Procedure 32(a) (3), will not be a ground to delay the commencement, or progress, of a trial. In such circumstances, the court anticipates the use of oral or videotape depositions at trial of any unavailable witness whose testimony a party believes essential to the presentation of that party's case, whether that witness is a party, a non-party or an expert.

IT IS FURTHER ORDERED that any party offering a deposition at trial shall provide the court, prior to commencement of trial, a copy of the deposition transcript, but only after all efforts have been made to resolve objections with all counsel and unrepresented parties. Portions of the deposition offered by plaintiff shall be marked in blue; portions offered by defendant, in red. Where a court ruling is necessary, the basis for unresolved objections shall be written in ten words or less in the margin of the deposition, accompanied by a separate written index of such objections.

IT IS FURTHER ORDERED that at least ten business days before commencement of trial, each party shall submit to the court a written summary, not to exceed two pages in length, in plain language, of its contentions regarding the facts and that party's theories concerning liability and damages. Not later than five days before commencement of trial, all other parties may submit, in writing, objections or alternatives to this summary.

IT IS FURTHER ORDERED that counsel shall familiarize themselves with the Local Rules of Civil Procedure of the United States District Court for the Eastern District of Pennsylvania. Failure to comply with the within Order or the Local Rules may result in the imposition of sanctions.

IT IS FURTHER ORDERED that continuances will be granted only in extraordinary circumstances. Continuance requests shall be filed by one counsel of record for each represented party and by each unrepresented party. Continuance requests shall be submitted at least ten days prior to the commencement of trial on a form approved by **[Judge Gardner] [the undersigned]**.

By:

_____

CHERYL E. SINCLAIR
Civil Deputy Clerk to
Judge James Knoll Gardner
Phone: (610) 434-3457

or

BY THE COURT:

_____

James Knoll Gardner
United States District Judge

IN THE UNITED STATES DISTRICT COURT
FOR THE EASTERN DISTRICT OF PENNSYLVANIA

UNITED STATES OF AMERICA	)	
	)	Criminal Action
	)	No.
vs.	)	
	)	
JOHN DOE,	)	
	)	
Defendant	)	

CRIMINAL JURY TRIAL ATTACHMENT ORDER

NOW, this _____ day of _____, 20___,

IT IS ORDERED that a jury trial of the within case shall commence before the undersigned on **[day of week], [date]**, 20___, at _____ o'clock **[a.m./p.m.]**, or as soon thereafter as the schedule of the court permits, with the selection of a jury at the James A. Byrne United States Courthouse, 601 Market Street, Philadelphia, Pennsylvania. After completion of jury selection, the trial shall continue in Courtroom B, Edward N. Cahn United States Courthouse, 504 West Hamilton Street, Allentown, Pennsylvania. This Order shall serve as a formal attachment for trial.

IT IS FURTHER ORDERED that on or before _____, 20___, defendant shall file and serve any motions pursuant to Federal Rule of Criminal Procedure 12(b) in accordance with Rule 12.1 of the Local Rules of Criminal Procedure for the Eastern District of Pennsylvania.

All motions shall be filed with the Clerk of Court, served upon counsel for all parties, and a copy sent to the undersigned. Each motion shall be accompanied by a memorandum of law containing a brief recitation of the applicable facts and a concise statement of the legal contentions, together with the legal authorities relied upon.

IT IS FURTHER ORDERED that within five days after receipt of a motion, any party desiring to oppose such motion shall file and serve on all parties, the Clerk of Court and the undersigned a legal memorandum in opposition to such motion pursuant to Local Rule 12.1.

IT IS FURTHER ORDERED that a hearing on all motions is scheduled before the undersigned on _____, 20___, at _____ o'clock ___.m. in Courtroom B, Edward N. Cahn United States Courthouse, 504 West Hamilton Street, Allentown, Pennsylvania.

IT IS FURTHER ORDERED that on or before **[two weeks before trial]**, counsel for the parties[*] shall file and submit proposed jury instructions to the undersigned and serve them on all counsel.

All proposed jury instructions shall be numbered and shall contain citation(s) of legal authority for each point (one instruction per page). If a model jury instruction is submitted counsel shall cite the source of the model instruction and shall indicate whether the proposed jury instruction is modified or unchanged. If counsel modifies a model jury instruction, additions shall be underlined and deletions shall be placed in brackets. If a model jury instruction is unchanged, it shall be submitted by title and paragraph number reference, and shall not be retyped verbatim.

IT IS FURTHER ORDERED that on or before **[one week before trial]**, each party shall file and submit to the undersigned and serve on all counsel any objections to the jury instructions proposed by all other parties. All objections shall be in writing and shall set forth the objectionable proposed instruction in its entirety. The objection shall specifically set forth the objectionable material in the proposed instruction. The objection shall contain citation(s) of legal authority explaining why the instruction is improper and a

---

[*] Whenever used in this Order, the terms "counsel" and "counsel for the parties" shall also refer to any unrepresented parties.

concise statement of argument concerning the instruction. Where applicable, the objecting party shall submit a correct alternative instruction covering the subject or principle of law, with citation(s) of legal authority supporting the alternative instruction.

IT IS FURTHER ORDERED that on or before **[two weeks before trial]**, all counsel and unrepresented parties shall file and submit to the undersigned and serve on all counsel proposed jury selection voir dire questions.

IT IS FURTHER ORDERED that on or before **[one week before trial]**, each party shall file and submit to the undersigned and serve on all counsel any objections to the voir dire questions proposed by any other party. All objections shall be in writing and shall set forth the objectionable voir dire question in its entirety. The objection shall specifically set forth the objectionable material in the proposed voir dire question. The objection shall contain citation(s) of legal authority explaining why the proposed voir dire question is improper and a concise statement of argument concerning the objection. Objections not made pursuant to this provision may be deemed waived.

IT IS FURTHER ORDERED that at least ten business days before commencement of trial, each party shall submit to the court a written summary, not to exceed two pages in length, in plain language, of its contentions regarding the facts and that party's theories concerning the case. Not later than five days prior to the beginning of voir dire, all other parties may submit in writing objections or alternatives to this summary. The summary may be used by the court in jury voir dire and in its preliminary and final instructions to the jury to familiarize the jurors with the general framework of the factual and legal issues and contentions in the case.

IT IS FURTHER ORDERED that counsel shall familiarize themselves with the Local Rules of Criminal Procedure of the United States District Court for the Eastern District of Pennsylvania. Failure to comply with the within Order or the Local Rules may result in the imposition of sanctions.

IT IS FURTHER ORDERED that continuances will be granted only in extraordinary circumstances. Continuance requests shall be filed by one counsel of record for each represented party and by each unrepresented party. Requests for a continuance of trial shall be submitted not later than ten days prior to the commencement of trial by motion accompanied by a proposed Order and memorandum of law containing a brief recitation of the applicable facts, and a concise statement of the legal contentions together with the authorities relied upon in support of such motion.

IT IS FURTHER ORDERED that if a defendant is currently incarcerated, the defendant or his counsel shall notify the undersigned in writing immediately so that the necessary procedures can be taken to have the defendant present in the courtroom for any proceedings.

BY THE COURT:

_____
James Knoll Gardner
United States District Judge

IN THE UNITED STATES DISTRICT COURT
FOR THE EASTERN DISTRICT OF PENNSYLVANIA

STANDING ORDER RE:)
) STANDING ORDER #2
1993 AMENDMENTS TO FEDERAL)
RULES OF CIVIL PROCEDURE)

STANDING ORDER

NOW, this 19th day of March, 2007,

IT IS ORDERED that if discovery disputes cannot be amicably resolved, or if additional depositions or other discovery is required, such disputes or requests shall immediately be brought to the attention of United States Magistrate Judge Henry S. Perkin by letter or other informal means, or by such other means as directed by Magistrate Judge Perkin. Any party contending that the Order of the Magistrate Judge is clearly erroneous or contrary to law may file a Petition to Reconsider, together with a proposed Order, directed to the undersigned, pursuant to 28 U.S.C. § 636(b)(1)(A). As to matters other than discovery, all counsel are directed to comply with Rule 7.1 of the Rules of Civil Procedure for the United States District Court for the Eastern District of Pennsylvania. A written response to all motions must be filed with the court and served on opposing parties within fourteen days of the filing and service of a motion.

This Standing Order supersedes the Standing Order dated January 2, 2003, which is hereby revoked.

BY THE COURT:

/s/ James Knoll Gardner
James Knoll Gardner
United States District Judge

Judge James Knoll Gardner

IN THE UNITED STATES DISTRICT COURT
FOR THE EASTERN DISTRICT OF PENNSYLVANIA

JOHN SMITH,	)	
	)	Civil Action
Plaintiff	)	No.
	)	
vs.	)	
	)	
JANE DOE,	)	
	)	
Defendant	)	

RULE 16 TELEPHONE CONFERENCE SCHEDULING ORDER

NOW, this _____ day of _____, 20___,

IT IS ORDERED that a Rule 16 conference by telephone conference call is scheduled on _____, 20___, at _____ o'clock ___.m. with Judge James Knoll Gardner.

IT IS FURTHER ORDERED that lead trial counsel for plaintiff* shall initiate the telephone conference call with lead trial counsel for all other parties and with all unrepresented parties. Counsel for plaintiff shall initiate the call five minutes in advance of the scheduled conference, and when all counsel and unrepresented parties are on the line, shall call chambers at (610) 434-3457.

IT IS FURTHER ORDERED that the lead trial counsel of record for each party, and each unrepresented party, shall participate in the conference. No substitutions will be permitted unless authorized by Judge Gardner at least 48 hours prior to the conference.

IT IS FURTHER ORDERED that at the conference counsel† and unrepresented parties shall be prepared to discuss (where applicable) the following:

1. Deadlines (if applicable) for:

    (a) filing and responding to pleadings;
    (b) amendment of pleadings;
    (c) discovery, including the submission of expert reports;
    (d) motions, and cross-motions, for summary judgment, and responses;
    (e) other dispositive motions;
    (f) motions in limine;
    (g) pre-trial memoranda.

2. Proposed trial dates. (Counsel shall have their trial calendars available).

3. Length of trial.

4. Attachments of trial counsel before other courts in this and other jurisdictions during the trial term.

5. Witness availability.

6. Other scheduling considerations.

7. Whether the case shall be tried with or without a jury.

---

* If there are multiple plaintiffs represented by different counsel, counsel for plaintiffs shall determine which plaintiff's counsel shall initiate the call. If there are both represented and unrepresented plaintiffs, the call shall be initiated by counsel for one of the represented plaintiffs. If the only plaintiff, or each of multiple plaintiffs, is unrepresented, the call shall be initiated by an unrepresented plaintiff.

† Ordinarily, only one counsel per party will be permitted to speak at the conference.

Practice and Procedures of Judges and Judges' Forms and Orders

8. Number of jurors.
9. Juror voir dire.
10. Legal issues to be resolved prior to trial.
11. Any unique or unusual factual, legal, or procedural, aspects of the case.
12. Logistical problems requiring court attention.
13. Settlement negotiations history (in jury trial cases).
14. Settlement (in jury trial cases).
15. Status of pending motions.

IT IS FURTHER ORDERED that counsel and unrepresented parties shall provide Judge Gardner[*] by mail, delivery service, or fax to be received by Judge Gardner and served on all opposing counsel and unrepresented parties not later than seven days prior to the conference, an informal memorandum which shall not exceed two pages in length and which shall include the following information:

1. A brief statement of the facts.
2. The party's liability contentions.
3. The party's damages contentions.
4. Enumeration of all special or liquidated damages claimed.
5. History of settlement negotiations, including all demands and offers.[†]

IT IS FURTHER ORDERED that continuances will be granted only in extraordinary circumstances. Continuance requests shall be signed by one counsel of record for each represented party and by each unrepresented party. Continuance requests shall be submitted at least ten days prior to the conference on a form approved by Judge Gardner.

By:

_____
CHERYL E. SINCLAIR
Civil Deputy Clerk to
Judge James Knoll Gardner
Phone: (610) 434-3457

---

[*] The memoranda may be forwarded to Judge Gardner by mail at Edward N. Cahn United States Courthouse, 504 West Hamilton Street, Suite 4701, Allentown, PA 18101; or by fax at (610) 434-3459.

[†] History of settlement negotiations shall be provided only in cases in which a jury trial has been requested. Settlement negotiation history should not be provided in cases in which the trial will be conducted without a jury.

Judge Mitchell Goldberg

Judge Mitchell Goldberg received his B.A. from Ithaca College in 1981 and his J.D. from Temple University Beasley School of Law in 1986. Upon graduation from law school, Judge Goldberg joined the Philadelphia District Attorney's Office as an assistant district attorney serving in both the trial and appellate divisions. In 1990, he joined the law firm of Cozen O'Connor, eventually being promoted to senior partner. In 1997, Judge Goldberg returned to the public sector as an Assistant United States Attorney for the Eastern District of Pennsylvania, where he handled mostly white-collar cases. In February 2003, Judge Goldberg was appointed by the governor of Pennsylvania to a position on the Bucks County Court of Common Pleas, and in November 2003, he was elected to a 10-year term. Judge Goldberg was appointed to the United States District Court for the Eastern District of Pennsylvania on October 31, 2008.

PRELIMINARY GENERAL MATTERS

1. ***Correspondence with the Court.*** Written communication is permitted by regular mail or facsimile regarding scheduling and other non-substantive matters. Before communicating with the court on scheduling, counsel should ascertain the position of opposing counsel and include that position in the correspondence. All substantive issues must be addressed by an appropriate motion or other filing. Judge Goldberg does not wish to receive copies of correspondence between counsel.

Law clerks may not render advice to counsel and have no authority to grant continuances or any other relief. Telephone inquiries should be directed as appropriate to either of the following:

For matters related to civil scheduling and case management, requesting telephone conferences, and general procedures:

Civil Courtroom Deputy/Judicial Secretary: Carole J. Ludwig
Telephone: 267-299-7500
Facsimile: 267-299-5056

For matters related to criminal scheduling and case management, and obtaining transcripts of civil and criminal proceedings:

Criminal Courtroom Deputy/ESR: Steve Sonnie
Telephone: 267-299-7509
Facsimile: 267-299-7058

2. ***Telephone Conferences.*** Counsel may request a telephone conference to resolve straightforward discovery disputes, but the resolution of complicated discovery matters should be initiated through the filing of a formal motion. Counsel must attempt to resolve all discovery disputes with opposing counsel before requesting the court's assistance.

3. ***Stipulations/Consent Decrees.*** Any stipulations, consent decrees, or other documents requiring court approval or the judge's signature must be submitted in a form containing original signatures.

4. ***Electronic Case Filing.*** Counsel should file all pleadings electronically, through the Electronic Case Filing (ECF) system. In the unusual case where counsel does not file using ECF, courtesy copies of all pleadings and motion papers should be delivered to Chambers, United States Courthouse, 601 Market Street, Philadelphia, Pennsylvania 19106.

CIVIL CASES
Pretrial Procedure

1. Rule 26 Conferences. The Rule 26(f) conference between counsel will take place as soon as possible and, in any event, at least 14 days before the Rule 16 scheduling conference. Outstanding motions will not excuse counsel from timely holding this meeting and submitting a Rule 26 plan.

2. Rule 16 Conferences. A preliminary pretrial conference pursuant to Fed.R.Civ.P. 16 will be scheduled shortly after a defendant has filed an appearance or pleading. At least three business days before the Rule 16 conference, a joint report of the Rule 26(f) meeting with a proposed discovery plan should be submitted to chambers.

Topics addressed at the initial pretrial conference will be those listed in Local R.Civ.P. 16.1(b) and will also include the progress of self-executing disclosure under Fed.R.Civ.P. 26(a), discovery, the preservation and production of electronically stored information, settlement, and mediation proposals.

Lead trial counsel must attend the Rule 16 conference and must enter an appearance prior to the conference. All applications to appear pro hac vice must be approved prior to the conference. For the convenience of out-of-state counsel, in some instances, the Rule 16 conference may be conducted via telephone.

Any attorney appearing at the conference must have a thorough understanding of the facts, be prepared to discuss all claims and defenses in detail, have evaluated the case for settlement purposes, and have settlement authority from the client. Motions to dismiss, transfer, add parties, and other threshold motions should be filed before the conference. Counsel must be prepared to present argument at the conference on any pending motions.

At the conclusion of the Rule 16 conference, a scheduling order will be issued by the court.

Counsel may not extend discovery deadlines set forth in the court's Rule 16 scheduling order without court approval.

3. Discovery. The Federal Rules of Civil Procedure call for voluntary, cooperative discovery in a timely manner. The information required to be disclosed pursuant to Fed.R.Civ.P. 26(a) is required to be exchanged no later than 14 days after the date of the order scheduling the Rule 16 conference.

Counsel should be prepared to report on the progress of discovery at the Rule 16 conference. Pending motions do not excuse counsel from proceeding with discovery.

The court encourages the submission of routine discovery disputes through the scheduling of a telephone conference. If a motion to compel is filed under Local R.Civ.P. 26.1(g), the motion should not exceed five pages, contain exhibits, or include a brief or memorandum of law, unless the motion involves the invocation of a privilege. The certification required under Rule 26.1(f) must state what efforts were made to resolve the dispute.

If the court's intervention is required, the court may impose sanctions in favor of the prevailing party, if warranted.

Judge Goldberg permits telephone conferences to resolve disputes during depositions in situations where the deposition would otherwise have to be adjourned.

4. Confidentiality Agreements. Judge Goldberg will consider entry of stipulated confidentiality or sealing orders if the proposed order includes a statement demonstrating that good cause exists. See *Pansy v. Borough of Stroudsburg*, 23 F.3d 772, 786 (3d Cir. 1994). All such orders must contain the following language (or language substantially similar):

> The Court retains the right to allow disclosure of any subject covered by this stipulation or to modify this stipulation at any time in the interest of justice.

5.   Settlement Conferences. Except in nonjury trial matters, the issue of settlement may be raised at all stages in the proceedings. Consistent with Local R.Civ.P. 53.3, Judge Goldberg directs all parties to consider the use of an alternative-dispute-resolution process at an appropriate stage in the litigation.

In most cases, a settlement conference will be scheduled before United States Magistrate Judge David R. Strawbridge. Judge Goldberg strongly encourages litigants to avail themselves of Judge Strawbridge's skillful assistance regarding settlement throughout the course of the litigation.

6.   Requests for Extensions of Time. Where compelling circumstances exist, counsel may request an extension of a filing or other deadline. Extension requests should be made through correspondence, and the counsel requesting the extension must state the position of opposing counsel. Any counsel opposing the extension must submit a responsive correspondence setting forth the reasons for opposition. Counsel may not extend any deadlines without court approval.

7.   Pretrial Settlement. Upon reaching a settlement, counsel must notify Judge Goldberg's chambers immediately and request dismissal of the action pursuant to Local R.Civ.P. 41.1(b) or propose some other procedure that will effectively terminate the litigation.

8.   Length and Content of Briefs or Legal Memoranda. All grounds for relief should be set forth in a single, comprehensive motion. A motion to dismiss, for example, should not be divided into separate motions for each count, but rather should include all bases for relief. Any brief or memorandum filed in support of the motion should be limited to 25 pages. Any brief or memorandum filed in opposition or in response to a motion is subject to the same page limitation. If a party requires more than 25 pages to explain its position to the court, a motion to exceed the page limit should be filed prior to the memorandum deadline, setting forth good cause for granting an exception to this rule.

Judge Goldberg appreciates courtesy copies of significant motions, memoranda of law, and other pleadings, along with attachments/exhibits, but requests that counsel send to chambers only one courtesy copy. All attachments and exhibits must be submitted in bound form. Transmittal of courtesy copies by facsimile is not permitted.

9.   Reply and Surreply Briefs. Reply briefs for motions for summary judgment may be filed without leave of court. Leave of court is required to file surreply briefs regarding motions for summary judgment. All other reply and surreply briefs may only be filed with leave of court. Generally, reply and surreply briefs will only be permitted when necessary to rebut an issue or factual assertion not covered by the party's original submission. Counsel should file a motion requesting leave to file any additional document, attaching the proposed reply or surreply as an exhibit. When permitted, reply and surreply briefs are limited to 10 pages each and should be filed within 14 days of the filing of the document to which it replies.

10.   Rule 56 Motions. Any motion for summary judgment filed pursuant to Fed.R.Civ.P. 56 must include a short and concise statement of undisputed facts as a separate exhibit. The statement must set forth, in numbered paragraphs, all material facts that the moving party contends are undisputed and entitle the movant to judgment as a matter of law. Only those facts that bear on dispositive material issues should be included.

The papers opposing a motion for summary judgment must include as a separate exhibit a short and concise statement of the material facts, which respondent contends present genuine issues for trial. This statement should respond to the numbered paragraphs set forth in the moving party's statement of undisputed facts. The responding party also must set forth, in separate numbered paragraphs, any additional facts that the respondent contends preclude summary judgment. The court will accept all material facts set forth in the moving party's statement as admitted unless controverted by the opposing party.

Statements of material facts in support of or in opposition to a motion for summary judgment should include specific and not general references to the parts of the record that support each statement. Each stated fact must cite the source relied upon, including the page and line of any document to which reference is made.

Pursuant to Fed.R.Civ.P. 56, reply briefs regarding motions for summary judgment may be filed without leave of court. Leave of court is required for responsive surreply briefs regarding motions for summary judgment.

11. Injunctions. Judge Goldberg will promptly list any request for a temporary restraining order (TRO) or a preliminary injunction assigned to him. When possible, a pre-hearing conference will be scheduled to discuss discovery issues, and allocate a time for the hearing. Expedited discovery will also be discussed and, when appropriate, ordered at the conclusion of the pre-hearing conference.

12. Pretrial Conferences. A pretrial conference date will be set in the scheduling order. Motions in limine, objections to exhibits, voir dire, other pretrial matters, and trial procedures will all be discussed and resolved at the pretrial conference.

Trial and Trial Procedures

Judge Goldberg's scheduling order will typically assign a date certain for trial. Because trial dates are established well in advance and continuances will rarely be granted, counsel should be prepared to proceed on the scheduled trial date.

Prior to trial, counsel must supply the court and opposing counsel with a tabbed exhibit binder and exhibit index. An additional binder must also be prepared for the deputy clerk and for use with witnesses.

Other miscellaneous trial procedures are listed below.

1. Note-taking by Jurors. Judge Goldberg permits jurors to take notes.

2. Trial Briefs. Parties should submit a trial brief only if a new or unique point of law is involved.

3. Examination of Witnesses Out of Sequence. The court will permit counsel to examine his/her own witnesses out of sequence for the convenience of a witness.

4. Opening Statements and Summations. Judge Goldberg will typically be flexible regarding time limits for opening statements and summations and will discuss the time needed with counsel prior to the speeches.

5. Examination of Witnesses or Argument by More Than One Attorney. More than one attorney for a party may examine different witnesses or argue different points of law before the court. Only one attorney for each side may examine the same witness or address the jury during the opening statement or summation.

6. Videotaped Testimony. Videotaped testimony should begin with the witness being sworn. Counsel should bring objections to the court's attention at the time of the final pretrial conference. After the court rules on any objections, counsel should edit the tapes before offering the videotaped testimony at trial.

7. Offering Exhibits into Evidence. Unless the parties have an agreement as to the admissibility of a proposed exhibit, it may not be published to the jury, nor may a witness testify as to its content, until it has been admitted into evidence.

8. ***Directed Verdict Motions.*** Motions for judgment as a matter of law in jury trials and motions for an involuntary dismissal in nonjury trials must be in writing. Oral argument on the motions is ordinarily permitted.

9. ***Written Jury Instructions.*** In an appropriate case, the court will give the jury a copy of the written jury instructions.

10. ***Exhibits in the Jury Room.*** After the jury has been instructed and taken to the jury room to begin deliberations, the court and counsel will discuss which exhibits should go out with the jury for their consideration during deliberations.

11. ***Interviewing the Jury.*** Judge Goldberg may allow counsel to interview jurors but will instruct the jury that they are not required to talk to the attorneys.

CRIMINAL MATTERS

1. ***Motions Practice.*** All pretrial motions must be filed no later than 20 days in advance of trial date and, except in rare circumstances, will be heard on a date prior to the scheduled trial date.

   All post-trial motions must be filed in accordance with the Federal and Local Rules of Criminal Procedure. Supporting memoranda for such motions and response memoranda should not exceed 25 double-spaced pages. Reply and surreply memoranda may be filed only with leave of the court.

2. ***Continuances of Trial.*** Any request for a continuance must be filed no later than 14 days in advance of the scheduled trial date. Requests for a continuance must be filed as a motion stating the reasons for the request. Any such motion must be accompanied by a proposed order consistent with the requirements of the Speedy Trial Act, 18 U.S.C. § 3161. The order must include a proposed finding that explains in reasonable detail why the ends of justice served by granting the requested continuance outweigh the best interest of the public and the defendant in a speedy trial. Continuance requests by letter in criminal cases are not permitted.

3. ***Pretrial Hearings.*** Suppression, *Starks,* and *Daubert* hearings are typically held at least 14 days prior to trial. Following a motion to suppress hearing, counsel may be requested to submit a post-hearing brief or proposed findings of fact and conclusions of law to the court. A schedule of these submissions will be established at the conclusion of the motion to suppress hearing.

4. ***Pretrial Conferences.*** Pretrial conferences with counsel will be scheduled at least three days prior to trial and may be conducted by telephone. Any issues relating to voir dire, motions in limine, jury instructions, and jury verdict forms will be addressed at that time.

5. ***Voir Dire.*** Counsel may submit proposed voir dire questions. Judge Goldberg will conduct most of the voir dire in criminal jury matters. Counsel are permitted to address the venire with follow-up questions, but only after approval by the court.

6. ***Trial Memorandum.*** At least seven days prior to the trial date, the government must file a trial memorandum setting forth the essential elements of the offenses, the facts that it intends to present, the identity of each witness it intends to call, a statement of the substance of each witness's testimony, and any legal issues. The defendant is not required to file a trial memorandum but may do so.

7. ***Proposed Jury Instructions and Verdict Forms.*** Each party must submit to the court and serve on opposing counsel proposed points for charge and any proposed jury interrogatories no later than seven days prior to the trial date. Each point for charge and proposed

jury interrogatory must be numbered and on a separate sheet of paper identifying the name of the requesting party. Each proposed instruction must be submitted with authority. If a model jury instruction is used, the party submitting it must state whether the proposed instruction is unchanged or modified. If a party modifies a model instruction, additions are to be underlined and deletions are to be placed in brackets.

8. *Guilty Plea Memorandum.* The government must submit a guilty plea memorandum at least two days prior to the change of plea hearing. The memorandum must include the elements of each offense to which the defendant is pleading guilty and legal citations for the elements, the maximum statutory penalties for each offense, the terms of any plea agreement, and the factual basis for the plea.

9. *Sentencing.* Sentencing motions and supporting memoranda must be filed at least seven days prior to the scheduled sentencing date, and any response thereto must be filed at least seven days prior to the scheduled sentencing date. Motions filed pursuant to U.S.S.G. § 5K1.1 must be filed no later than seven days prior to sentencing.

Sentencing memoranda (exclusive of motions) must be filed no later than seven days prior to the scheduled sentencing date, and any response thereto must be filed at least five days prior to the scheduled sentencing date.

A sentencing date will be selected at the time the court accepts a guilty plea or there is a conviction at trial. Requests for continuances from sentencing are discouraged, and sentencing will be continued for good cause only. Judge Goldberg will not consider any request for a continuance exceeding 90 days.

In the rare event of a 90-day continuance, if counsel for both the government and the defendant(s) believe that good cause exists for an additional continuance beyond the initial 90-day period, counsel may jointly request in writing an additional continuance. Any such request must state why good cause exists for an additional continuance. If Judge Goldberg grants such a request, counsel are required to submit in writing a joint status update every 45 days until judgment of sentence is entered.

If a defendant is responsible for restitution, the government must submit sufficient information in its sentencing memorandum to enable the court to determine entitlement, the name and the address of each victim, the amount of loss for each victim, and documentary support for each amount. If liability for restitution is joint and several, the government must itemize the restitution amount for which each defendant is responsible.

Judge C. Darnell Jones II

Judge C. Darnell Jones II received his B.A. from Southwestern College in 1972 and his J.D. from the Washington College of Law at American University in 1975. Upon graduation from law school, he served as an attorney with the Defender Association of Philadelphia, which represents indigent defendants charged with criminal offenses, until 1987. In 1979, he became assistant chief of the Family Court Division, which represents indigent juvenile defendants charged with delinquent, criminal offenses, and rose to chief of the division in 1985. Between March and November 1987, he served as an associate on the Citizens Crime Commission. Governor Casey appointed him to be a judge on the Philadelphia Court of Common Pleas in 1987. He was elected to a ten-year term in November 1987 and was retained in 1997 and in 2007. He served as president judge of the Philadelphia Court of Common Pleas from 2006 to 2008.

PRELIMINARY GENERAL MATTERS

1. **Correspondence with the Court.** Counsel may write to Judge Jones to request an unopposed extension of time and for unopposed requests pertaining to scheduling. However, Judge Jones does not permit correspondence in lieu of opposed extension requests, contested discovery or substantive motions, or other disputed substantive matters that should be made of record via motion practice. Correspondence may be faxed to 267-299-5057 (maximum five pages by fax, otherwise by mail or hand delivery).

Judge Jones does not accept carbon copies of letters to opposing counsel.

Judge Jones does not permit ex parte communication with the court, written or otherwise.

Usually, communication with chambers will occur via Judge Jones's civil deputy, Ms. Betty Harper, at 267-299-7750.

2. **Communications with Law Clerks.** Judge Jones generally does not permit counsel to directly communicate with law clerks. If a law clerk contacts counsel, it is at Judge Jones's direction.

3. **Telephone Conferences.** Judge Jones uses telephone conferences for scheduling changes and similar matters. He also holds telephone conference calls on discovery and other motions as necessary. Judge Jones usually requests that counsel initiate any such call.

4. **Oral Arguments and Evidentiary Hearings.** Judge Jones does not set aside specific days or times for oral arguments or evidentiary hearings. Judge Jones will hear oral argument on a motion if he believes argument will assist him in deciding the motion. A party may request argument in writing. Arguments and hearings are scheduled on an ad hoc basis.

5. **Pro Hac Vice Admissions.** Judge Jones expects applications for pro hac vice admissions to be submitted in writing using the forms found on the court's website at www.paed.uscourts.gov. He requires the attorney seeking such admission to (1) submit the signed affidavit or certification stating that he or she is a member in good standing of the bar of another state, and (2) pay all pro hac vice admission fees.

6. **Thorough Review of Filings.** In order to avoid confusion, when counsel receives an electronic notification of a court order filed in a case, counsel is directed to open the order on the docket and review the contents of the order. Occasionally, the docket's description of an order is inaccurate; counsel are responsible for making themselves aware of the actual content of every docket entry.

7. Communication with Opposing Counsel. In general, Judge Jones expects counsel to bring matters, including those that arise during trial, to his attention only after they have been discussed with opposing counsel.

8. Cases Involving Out-of-Town Parties or Witnesses. Judge Jones has no special policy for matters involving out-of-town attorneys, parties, or witnesses. Counsel are free to raise any issues they deem necessary.

Motion Practice

1. In General. Except as set forth in Judge Jones's policies and procedures, motion practice will be conducted in accordance with Local Civil Rule 7.1.

2. Courtesy Copies. Unless otherwise directed, Judge Jones requires that counsel deliver to chambers, via U.S. mail or hand delivery, two courtesy copies of any dispositive motion, response, or reply. Courtesy copies of other motions or responses are discouraged where the pleadings have been filed electronically.

3. Proposed Orders. Judge Jones requires a proposed order to be filed along with every motion and response. Proposed orders should not contain an attorney's name or address.

4. Motions for Summary Judgment. All summary judgment motions and oppositions to such motions must contain a recitation of facts with complete and accurate citation to the record. To this end, Judge Jones requires the parties to file *separate* statements of material facts (not simply a factual narration section of a brief), as follows:

   a. Any motion for summary judgment should include a *separate* statement of undisputed material facts that sets forth, in numbered paragraphs, the material facts that the moving party contends are undisputed and entitle the movant to judgment as a matter of law. Only those facts that bear on dispositive material issues should be included in the statement of undisputed material facts.

   b. The papers opposing a motion for summary judgment must include a *separate* statement of undisputed and/or disputed material facts that responds to the numbered paragraphs set forth in the moving party's statement of undisputed material facts, either admitting those facts are undisputed or contending that they are disputed and, as such, are genuine issues to be tried. The responding party may also set forth, in separate numbered paragraphs, any additional disputed material facts that the respondent contends preclude summary judgment.

   If a responding party sets forth additional disputed material facts, the moving party must, within seven business days, file a response either admitting those facts are disputed or contending they are undisputed and, as such, are not genuine issues to be tried.

   Without exception, all facts set forth will be deemed admitted unless addressed by the opposing party as set forth above.

   c. The court will not consider any description of a fact that is not supported by citation to the record. Statements of material facts in support of or in opposition to a motion for summary judgment must include *specific* and not general references to the parts of the record that support each of the statements, such as the title of or numbered reference to a document, the name of a deponent and the page(s) of the deponent's deposition, or the identity of an affidavit or declaration and the specific paragraph relied upon. *Pinpoint citations are required.*

Summary judgment motion practice that fails to follow these procedures to the letter will not be accepted.

4. Reply and Surreply Briefs. A party may move to file a reply or surreply brief. A motion for leave to file such a brief must be accompanied by (1) a *short* memorandum indicating why the party wishes to supply the court with *additional* information and (2) the proposed reply or surreply brief itself. Judge Jones will not accept repetitive pleadings. Any motion for leave to file a reply or surreply brief must be filed within 5 business days of service of the brief in opposition. Except with leave of the court for good cause shown, no reply or surreply brief should exceed 10 pages.

5. Joinder in Motion. Judge Jones strongly disfavors joinder in the substantive motions of other parties and normally does not permit them.

6. Motions in Limine. As noted above, motions in limine usually are due three weeks before trial. A response to any motion in limine is due within five business days of the filing of the motion. Judge Jones will usually rule on outstanding motions in limine prior to or during the final pretrial conference.

7. Pretrial Submissions. Unless otherwise specified, Judge Jones requires the parties to submit the following by a date set by the court, which is normally approximately three weeks prior to the trial date:

1. Jointly proposed voir dire questions;
2. Jointly proposed jury instructions;
3. Jointly proposed verdict sheet;
4. Motions in limine; and
5. Final pretrial memoranda pursuant to Local Civil Rule 16.1(c).

Parties should submit to the court two copies of proposed points for charge and special jury interrogatories, along with a disk containing the documents.[*]

The proposed points for charge and special jury interrogatories should be prepared and submitted *jointly*. Counsel are expected to work together to achieve agreement on as many items as possible before submission to Judge Jones. Proposed points for charge should be accompanied by appropriate citations of legal authority—including use of the Model Civil Jury Instructions for the Third Circuit, where applicable (see http://www.paed.uscourts.gov, "Third Circuit Model Jury Instructions" bullet).

Each proposed point for charge must be numbered and on a separate sheet of paper.

Where counsel cannot agree on a particular point for charge or interrogatory, the joint submissions should provide the alternative version proposed by each party and the rationale for each.

Where one party proposes a point for charge or interrogatory, and the other party objects to the proposal in its entirety (wishes nothing be used, as opposed to an alternative version), the joint submission should note such and include the objecting party's rationale.

Supplemental points for charge will be permitted during and at the conclusion of trial.

---

[*] Documents must be submitted in WordPerfect or Microsoft Word formats—PDF format is not acceptable.

CIVIL CASES
Pretrial Procedure

1. Pretrial Conferences. Judge Jones may schedule a Fed.R.Civ.P. 16 conference to occur via telephone, in chambers, or in a courtroom. Judge Jones requires the parties to commence discovery immediately upon receipt of the order scheduling the Rule 16 conference, and he expects the parties to conduct substantial discovery before the Rule 16 conference.

The court's procedures rely upon the good faith of counsel and diligent compliance with Fed.R.Civ.P. 26(f). A Rule 26(f) meeting will take place as soon as possible, and at least *10* days prior to the Rule 16 conference. Without exception, counsel must, at least *5 business days* prior to the Rule 16 conference, file with the clerk of court a completed report of their Rule 26(f) meeting.

At the Rule 16 conference, counsel are expected to discuss jurisdictional defects; the possibility of amicable settlement (including by referral for settlement discussions facilitated by a U.S. Magistrate Judge); alternative dispute resolution; time limitations for joining parties and amending pleadings, if necessary; scheduling for discovery deadlines, expert reports, motion practice, pretrial memoranda, and future pretrial conferences; scheduling a trial date; and any other appropriate matter. In addition, Judge Jones usually inquires whether the parties would be amenable to having the entire matter transferred to the jurisdiction of a U.S. Magistrate Judge pursuant to 28 U.S.C. § 636(c) and Fed.R.Civ.P. 73. Parties are expected to have conferred with each other about each of these items prior to the conference (especially as to settlement and transfer to the jurisdiction of a U.S. Magistrate Judge).

Judge Jones usually enters a comprehensive case management order following the Rule 16 conference that sets firm dates for the completion of discovery, the exchange of expert reports, the filing of dispositive motions, and the commencement of trial.

2. Continuances and Extensions. Since trial dates are set well in advance, Judge Jones is extremely reluctant to grant continuances—especially if the attorneys have not been diligent in moving the case forward. However, the court will consider motions for extension of discovery deadlines upon showing of good cause.

3. Final Pretrial Conferences. Judge Jones usually holds the final pretrial conference in chambers approximately two weeks prior to the trial date. In preparation for the conference, Judge Jones expects counsel to communicate with each other on a number of matters, including exhibit designations, objections to exhibits, use of expert depositions, and stipulations of fact. The parties should be prepared to once again discuss the possibility of settlement or alternative dispute resolution in lieu of trial.

Discovery

1. Length of Discovery. The length of time permitted for discovery depends on the nature of each case. Judge Jones generally permits three to six months of discovery, except for more complex litigation.

2. Discovery Disputes. When a discovery dispute arises, counsel are strongly urged to settle it among themselves. However, if, *after making a good-faith effort*, counsel are unable to resolve a disputed issue, counsel for the aggrieved party should file with the court a motion in conformity with Local Civil Rule 26.1(b), with a proposed order and a brief not to exceed 10 pages. After a response, also limited to 10 pages, is filed, the court will (1) issue a ruling, (2) hold a telephone conference or hearing, (3) refer the dispute to a U.S. Magistrate Judge for determination, or (4) order additional briefing. The court normally rules promptly on discovery motions.

As a reminder, all discovery motions must contain the certification required under Local Civil Rule 26.1(f). Lack of civility between counsel during discovery and depositions will not be tolerated.

3. **Confidentiality Agreements.** Judge Jones will approve a confidentiality order if the order includes a detailed statement demonstrating that good cause exists. All such orders must contain the following language or language substantially similar: "The court retains the right to allow disclosure of any subject covered by this stipulation or to modify this stipulation at any time in the interest of justice."

4. **Expert Witnesses.** Parties should identify expert witnesses and engage in expert discovery pursuant to the scheduling order entered in the particular case. Failure to do so may bar the use of the expert's testimony at trial.

Injunctions

1. **Scheduling.** When a temporary restraining order is requested, Judge Jones will schedule a conference as soon as counsel have appeared and it is possible to properly consider the request. Judge Jones requires all counsel to be present unless the urgency of circumstances precludes notice to opposing counsel. Judge Jones rarely grants ex parte temporary restraining orders.

2. **Hearings.** Prior to any formal hearings, Judge Jones holds a conference with counsel. Judge Jones schedules preliminary and permanent injunctions hearings as soon as practicable and combines the two hearings if appropriate. Judge Jones usually permits expedited discovery when preliminary injunctive relief is requested.

3. **Proposed Findings of Fact and Conclusions of Law.** Judge Jones requires the submission of proposed findings of fact and conclusions of law in injunction cases, in accordance with Fed.R.Civ.P. 52(a).

Settlement

Judge Jones usually refers settlement conferences to a U.S. Magistrate Judge. However, if warranted, Judge Jones may refer a matter to a settlement master with the parties bearing the cost.

Trial Procedure

1. **Trial Briefs.** Counsel may submit trial briefs when they are likely to be helpful to the court.

2. **Proposed Findings of Fact and Conclusions of Law.** Judge Jones may require the submission of proposed findings of fact and conclusions of law in nonjury cases.

3. **Examination of Witnesses Out of Sequence.** Judge Jones is willing to take witnesses out of turn for their convenience, particularly when there is no objection by opposing counsel.

4. **Videotaped Testimony.** Judge Jones requires counsel to view all videotaped depositions for the purpose of editing the videotapes and resolving material objections *before* offering any videotape as evidence.

5. **Hearing and Trial Dates.** The court's calendar is generally set well in advance. Parties and counsel rely on assigned hearing and trial dates and Judge Jones is reluctant to reschedule set dates without good cause. If counsel becomes aware of a professional or personal conflict that may affect any significant scheduled event (including trial), they should *immediately* notify Judge Jones and opposing counsel.

Judge Jones generally sets a firm trial date for all matters. On the day of trial, court promptly convenes at 9:30 a.m. and may sit until 5:00 p.m. or later. Dependent on juror transportation concerns, Judge Jones adjusts the schedule for subsequent trial days as necessary.

Counsel may contact chambers the day prior to any hearing or trial to ascertain the assigned courtroom.

6.   Voir Dire. Judge Jones's practice in civil and criminal matters is to personally conduct the voir dire. Counsel are free to submit proposed questions (at least three business days prior to the trial date) and supplemental questions (on the trial date) to Judge Jones. Should the need for follow-up questioning arise, Judge Jones permits counsel to either do so themselves or submit follow-up questions for Judge Jones to ask.

7.   Courtroom Procedure. Unless counsel have secured the court's permission, Judge Jones expects counsel to stand when addressing the court, the jury, or when examining witnesses. Counsel may stand where they choose, except that they may not crowd the witness or the jury.

Counsel has the responsibility to advise their witnesses that no witness should talk to any jury member at any time.

Judge Jones considers a jury trial a formal affair and asks all counsel to act accordingly. Extraneous clothes and food or containers should not be left within sight of the jury. Boxes of exhibits or briefcases should not be on counsel table. Bottled water should be poured into a paper cup and the bottle removed from counsel table.

Opposing counsel should not engage in extended conversations with each other in front of a jury without the court's permission. The court will allow counsel to have a private conversation if it is requested and efficient. *However, lawyers absolutely should never argue with either opposing counsel or the court in front of the jury.*

8.   Approaching Witnesses. Counsel may approach a witness with the permission of the court. If counsel needs to approach the witness many times, Judge Jones may instruct the attorney that he or she need not continue to ask. Nonetheless, once the attorney has accomplished his or her reason for approaching the witness (however many times), he or she should return to the place from which he or she is questioning.

9.   Objections. Judge Jones does not permit speaking objections in front of a jury. Counsel should give the basis for the objection in a word or phrase (for example, "hearsay").

Judge Jones does not allow "continuing objections"; counsel must state *every* objection for the record. If counsel wishes to have a sidebar to argue on an objection, the court will usually grant the request as long as the number of sidebars remains reasonable. Counsel are strongly encouraged to bring evidentiary questions to the attention of the court outside the presence of the jury.

10.   Examination of Witnesses Beyond Redirect and Recross. Judge Jones does not have a strict policy concerning examination beyond redirect and recross. However, "beyond the scope" and "asked and answered" will be strictly enforced.

All counsel are reminded that redirect is still direct examination and not cross.

11.   Examination of Witnesses by More Than One Attorney. Judge Jones does not permit more than one attorney for a party to examine the same witness.

12.   Reading of Material Into the Record. Judge Jones does not have a specific practice as to reading stipulations, pleadings, or discovery materials into the record. If counsel request the court to read such, the written material must be prepared and submitted in advance of trial.

13.   Exhibits. Counsel must mark and exchange exhibits before commencement of a hearing or trial. Counsel should provide Judge Jones with two copies of each exhibit and a schedule briefly describing each exhibit. These must be submitted in binders for ease of use by the court.

Judge Jones has no strict policy as to when exhibits should be offered into evidence. When the number of exhibits in a case is large, Judge Jones strongly prefers counsel to reach advance agreement as to the admission of as many exhibits as possible.

Judge Jones will always have a clerk in the courtroom during a jury trial who will give the jurors any exhibits or other items that counsel requests be given to them. Counsel should never approach the jury to distribute exhibits unless permitted by Judge Jones.

14.   Opening and Closing Statements. While Judge Jones is flexible with regard to time limits on opening statements and summations, he does not allow open-ended presentations. Judge Jones usually will discuss the time needed with counsel in advance.

Counsel should be prepared to begin closing arguments immediately following the close of all evidence.

15.   Note-taking by Jurors. Judge Jones allows jurors to take notes.

16.   Directed Verdict Motions. Judge Jones permits motions for a directed verdict outside the hearing of a jury.

17.   Written Jury Instructions. Judge Jones provides counsel with a copy of his final jury instructions for review prior to trial (and in advance of a charge conference if any changes have been made). Judge Jones permits counsel to put objections to the jury charge on the record before the jury retires.

Jury Deliberations

1.   Exhibits in the Jury Room. Judge Jones will evaluate requests from a jury for particular exhibits on a case-by-case basis. Counsel will always be contacted prior to a decision on any such requests.

2.   Availability of Counsel During Jury Deliberations. Counsel must be available in case questions arise from the jury during its deliberations. Judge Jones prefers counsel to be within 15 minutes' distance of the courthouse during jury deliberations.

3.   The Verdict Form and Special Interrogatories. In most civil cases, Judge Jones submits written interrogatories to the jury. In criminal cases, Judge Jones submits a verdict form to the jury with interrogatories, as necessary.

CRIMINAL CASES

1.   Pretrial Conferences. Judge Jones holds pretrial conferences in all criminal cases.

2.   Pretrial Motions. The parties must file any pretrial motions, including *Starks* motions or motions to suppress evidence, as soon as possible and no later than three weeks prior to the commencement of trial (or as otherwise permitted by the court's case management order). The opposing party must respond to any pretrial motion no later than seven days after the motion is filed.

Judge Jones will consider requests for oral argument on *Starks* motions or motions to suppress. If Judge Jones grants any such request, he will hold argument separate from and in advance of trial. Counsel for the moving party is required to file proposed findings of fact and conclusions of law no later than two days after a motion hearing.

Judge Jones normally rules upon any motions in limine in advance of trial.

3. **Pretrial Submissions.** At least three weeks before the case is listed for trial, the parties should submit to the court two copies of proposed points for charge and proposed jury verdict form, along with a disk containing the documents.* Proposed points for charge should be accompanied by appropriate citations of legal authority. If a proposed point for charge is a model jury instruction, the submission should state whether the model jury instruction is unchanged or modified. If counsel modifies a model jury instruction, additions must be underlined and deletions placed in brackets.

The proposed points for charge and jury verdict form must be prepared and submitted *jointly*. Counsel are expected to work together to achieve agreement on as many items as possible before submission to Judge Jones.

Each proposed point for charge should be numbered and on a separate sheet of paper.

Where counsel cannot agree on a particular point for charge or on the verdict form, the joint submissions should provide the alternative version proposed by each party and the rationale for each.

Where one party proposes a point for charge or element of the jury verdict form and the other party objects to the proposal in its entirety (wishes nothing be used, as opposed to an alternative version), the joint submission should note such and include the objecting party's rationale.

Supplemental points for charge will be permitted during and at the conclusions of trial.

5. **Trial Memorandum.** At least three weeks before the case is listed for trial, the government must file a trial memorandum. At a minimum, the trial memorandum should specify the essential elements of the crime(s) charges, discuss any anticipated evidentiary issues, and contain a witness list. Any defense response to the government's trial memorandum should be filed within seven days.

The government must file any motion to admit evidence under F.R.E. 404(b) at least 14 days before trial. Any defense response is due within 5 business days.

6. **Guilty Plea Memoranda.** Judge Jones requires the government to submit a guilty plea memorandum *no later than seven business days prior to the guilty plea*. A guilty plea memorandum must include the elements of each offense to which the defendant is pleading guilty and legal citations for the elements, the maximum (and mandatory minimum, if any) statutory penalties for each offense, the terms of any plea agreement, and the factual basis for the plea.

7. **Motions for Downward Departure or Variance.** A motion for downward departure or variance, except a motion filed under § 5K1.1 of the United States Sentencing Guidelines, must be filed no later than 14 days prior to the sentencing date. The motion should include legal and factual support for the proposed departure.

The government must file any motion pursuant to § 5K1.1 no later than seven days prior to the sentencing date.

8. **Sentencing Memoranda.** Judge Jones requires both the government and the defendant to submit sentencing memoranda *no later than seven business days prior to the sentencing date*. Sentencing memoranda must set forth any legal authority relied upon by the party.

---

* Documents must be submitted in WordPerfect or Microsoft Word formats—PDF format is not acceptable.

OTHER GENERAL MATTERS

1. ***Punctuality and Civility.*** Judge Jones expects counsel to be punctual for *all* conferences, hearings, and trials. Judge Jones also expects counsel *at all times* to be civil to one another as well as to all parties, witnesses, and court personnel—whether in front of a jury or the court.

Judge Jones expects all counsel and all parties they represent to maintain the highest ethical standards at all times and to strictly adhere to the opportunities, requirements, limitations, and deadlines set forth in his policies and procedures.

FORM

**IN THE UNITED STATES DISTRICT COURT
FOR THE EASTERN DISTRICT OF PENNSYLVANIA**

PLAINTIFF	:	CIVIL ACTION
v.	:	NO. _____
DEFENDANT	:	

REPORT OF RULE 26(f) MEETING

In accordance with Federal Rule of Civil Procedure 26(f), counsel for the parties conferred on (____date____) and submit the following report of their meeting for the court's consideration:

1. Discussion of Claims, Defenses and Relevant Issues

    You should assume that the court has read the complaint and is familiar with the claims. However, the facts supporting those claims and defenses are unknown. Therefore, **counsel shall set forth concisely the factual background that the parties contend support their claims and defenses.**

    Summarize your discussion of primary issues, threshold issues and those issues on which the parties will need to conduct discovery. Identify what information each party needs in discovery as well as when and why. Also indicate likely motions and their timing.

2. Informal Disclosures

    State the parties' agreement on timing, form and scope of informal disclosures. Specifically identify not only the information listed in Rule 26(a)(1), but any additional information the parties agree to disclose informally.

    Keep in mind that self-executing discovery must not be delayed until the pretrial conference. If the parties have not made the Rule 26(a) initial disclosures within the time required by the Court's Order scheduling the pretrial conference, they should explain why not.

3. Formal Discovery

    Indicate nature, sequence and timing of formal discovery, as well as any need to conduct discovery in phases to prepare for the filing of motions or for settlement discussions. Specifically delineate what discovery will be conducted formally.

    The discovery deadline should normally be no more than 120 days from the date of the Rule 16 pretrial conference. If the parties believe there are compelling reasons for a longer period of discovery, state them.

    The parties are required to address procedures to preserve electronically stored information, to avoid inadvertent privilege waivers, and to determine the form in which electronic information will be produced. The cost of producing the information must be discussed.

    The parties shall discuss the parameters of their anticipated e-discovery at the Rule 26(f) conference and shall be prepared to address e-discovery at the Rule 16 scheduling conference with the court. It is expected that the parties will reach an agreement on how to conduct e-discovery.

4. Expert Witness Disclosures

    Indicate agreement on timing and sequence of disclosure of the identity and anticipated testimony of expert witnesses, including whether depositions of experts will be needed.

The parties should expect that the court requires expert reports to be exchanged simultaneously. If there are compelling reasons to stagger the production of expert reports, state them.

5. Early Settlement or Resolution

   The parties must familiarize themselves with Local Rule 53.3. Recite the parties' discussion about early resolution through ADR and state what steps were taken by counsel to advise the client of alternative dispute resolution options. Explain any decision not to seek early resolution. State what mediation options the parties may consider and when mediation would be appropriate.

6. Trial date

   State the parties' agreement on the three or four week range of time during which a firm trial date will be scheduled.

7. Other Matters

   Indicate discussion and any agreement on matters not addressed above.

_____
(Attorney Signature)

_____
(Attorney Signature)

CDJ, Rev 12.4.08

Judge J. Curtis Joyner

Judge Joyner was born on April 18, 1948, in Newberry, South Carolina. He received a B.S. from Central State University in Wilberforce, Ohio, in 1971, and a J.D. from Howard University in 1974. Judge Joyner served in the Chester County District Attorney's Office for 12 years as an assistant district attorney, chief deputy district attorney, and lastly, as first assistant district attorney. He also maintained a small general civil practice simultaneously. Judge Joyner was appointed and subsequently elected to the Chester County Court of Common Pleas in 1987. Judge Joyner was appointed to the United States District Court for the Eastern District of Pennsylvania on April 13, 1992. He assumed senior status on May 1, 2013.

PRELIMINARY GENERAL MATTERS

1. **Correspondence with the Court.** Judge Joyner permits correspondence on scheduling issues and requests for extensions of time. Copies of such correspondence should be sent to all counsel of record. He discourages correspondence that raises substantive issues properly handled by motion.

2. **Communications with Law Clerks.** Judge Joyner permits communications with his law clerks concerning the administrative aspects of cases, but not on scheduling matters, extensions of time, and the like, which must be directed to his courtroom deputy.

3. **Telephone Conferences.** Judge Joyner uses telephone conferences for non-complex pretrial conferences, scheduling, discovery disputes, settlement conferences, and other like matters. Judge Joyner requires that the time for telephone conferences be arranged through his deputy clerk. Counsel have the responsibility to initiate telephone conferences and to contact Judge Joyner through his secretary after all other parties are present on the call.

4. **Oral Arguments and Evidentiary Hearings.** Judge Joyner determines in any given case whether to schedule oral argument or an evidentiary hearing. If counsel prefer either an oral argument or an evidentiary hearing, they should request it. The scheduling of all such matters is handled by Judge Joyner's courtroom deputy. Judge Joyner does not set aside any certain days or times for oral arguments or evidentiary hearings.

5. **Pro Hac Vice Admissions.** Judge Joyner prefers a written motion for admission to be made prior to the day of the first appearance of out-of-state counsel.

CIVIL CASES
Pretrial Procedure

1. **Pretrial Conferences.** Judge Joyner regularly conducts status conferences, settlement conferences, and final pretrial conferences, depending on the complexity of the cases. He will usually schedule a pretrial conference upon request of counsel. Judge Joyner uses Rule 16 of the Federal Rules of Civil Procedure as the agenda for a typical pretrial conference. Judge Joyner has a standard form of order that is entered after the pretrial conference. A copy is shown on page 135 of this book.

Continuances and Extensions

1. **General Policy.** Judge Joyner has a general policy of adhering to originally scheduled dates unless a compelling reason is presented that justifies a change. This policy applies to briefing schedules, oral argument, evidentiary hearings, discovery deadlines, and trial dates.

2. Requests for Extensions and Continuances. Counsel should advise the court immediately, and *before the date has run,* of any compelling reason justifying an extension or continuance of any originally scheduled date. Any request for an extension or a continuance may be made by letter, setting forth the reasons and noting the agreement or disagreement of all other counsel, or by telephone conference with all counsel participating.

GENERAL MOTION PRACTICE

1. Oral Argument on Motions. Judge Joyner hears oral argument on motions only when it is requested by the court.

2. Reply and Surreply Briefs. Reply and surreply briefs should be filed only if absolutely necessary. Requests for time to do so should be directed in the first instance to the courtroom deputy.

3. Chambers Copies of Motion Papers. Judge Joyner appreciates having courtesy copies of the motion papers.

Discovery Matters

1. Length of Discovery Period and Extensions. In uncomplicated cases, Judge Joyner usually allows four months to complete discovery, measured from the date appearances are filed for all defendants. If counsel have been diligent and genuinely need more time for discovery, he will usually grant additional time. In arbitration cases, the discovery should be completed by the arbitration date.

2. Discovery Conferences and Dispute Resolution. Judge Joyner prefers that discovery disputes be resolved by discovery conferences, either by telephone or in chambers, if the parties are unable to resolve them without court assistance. Where the discovery dispute is complex, a motion should be filed.

3. Confidentiality Agreements. Judge Joyner has no standard practice or policy concerning confidentiality orders. He does not favor confidentiality orders that place virtually all discovery materials under a confidentiality nondisclosure status, even those agreed upon by counsel.

4. Expert Witnesses. The conduct of expert witness discovery is covered by Judge Joyner at the pretrial conference and is the subject of a scheduling order. In most cases, Judge Joyner requires that plaintiffs serve expert reports and/or responses to expert witness discovery before a defendant is required to do so. Generally, Judge Joyner orders that all expert witness discovery be completed by the time fact discovery is concluded.

Settlement

1. General Approach to Settlement and Nonjury Cases. Judge Joyner will become involved in settlement negotiations at the request of the parties, but he refers most cases to a magistrate, especially nonjury cases, preferring not to participate in negotiations in nonjury cases unless specifically requested by all parties.

2. Referral of Settlement Negotiations to Another District Court Judge. Judge Joyner rarely refers settlement negotiations to other district court judges.

Arbitration

1. General Approach to Arbitration Cases. Judge Joyner has no standard procedures or practices for arbitration cases except that pretrial conferences are not normally held in such cases and, except in unusual cases, scheduling orders are not issued.

2. Scheduling of Trial De Novo from Arbitration. Once a trial de novo is demanded, Judge Joyner will give counsel a 30-day discovery period, after which time counsel will have 20 days to file joint pretrial motions. The case will be placed in the trial pool on the same day motions are filed.

Proposed Final Pretrial Memoranda

1. Required Form of Pretrial Memoranda. Unless specifically provided for by separate order in a particular case, in jury and nonjury cases Judge Joyner requires the use of the pretrial memorandum described in Local Rule 16.1(c) with two modifications—he requires that any objections to the qualifications or testimony of expert witnesses be set forth in the pretrial memorandum, and he requires a stipulation of uncontested facts as described in Local Rule 16.1(d)(2)(b)(2)(A) through (E).

Injunctions

1. Scheduling and Expedited Discovery. Judge Joyner will promptly list any injunction matters assigned to him. The scheduling of injunction matters is conducted at an initial conference attended by all counsel. In appropriate cases, Judge Joyner will require expedited discovery.

When a plaintiff requests a temporary restraining order, Judge Joyner expects prompt service of the motion and complaint upon the opposing party and notice to opposing counsel unless, for good cause shown, this is impossible.

2. Proposed Findings of Fact and Conclusions of Law. Judge Joyner requires submission of proposed findings of fact and conclusions of law in injunction cases as early as possible.

Trial Procedure

1. Scheduling of Cases. Judge Joyner routinely places all cases on his trial list. Cases are occasionally assigned a date certain and given a special listing. Counsel whose cases are in the pool must maintain telephone contact with his courtroom deputy.

2. Conflicts of Counsel. Counsel should notify Judge Joyner of any professional or personal conflicts affecting the trial schedule by telephoning or writing to his courtroom deputy.

3. Cases Involving Out-of-Town Parties or Witnesses. Trial scheduling by Judge Joyner does not generally change by the presence of out-of-town parties or witnesses. Judge Joyner leaves the scheduling of witnesses to counsel.

4. Note-taking by Jurors. Judge Joyner permits note-taking by jurors in extremely complicated cases.

5. Trial Briefs. Judge Joyner encourages the submission of trial briefs.

6. Voir Dire. Voir dire in civil cases is conducted completely by counsel, with the deputy clerk present. If disputes arise, Judge Joyner usually handles them in chambers. Judge Joyner prefers that counsel not spend more than one hour on voir dire.

7. Sidebars. Judge Joyner prefers that sidebars be infrequent and sought only when truly necessary.

8. In Limine Motions. Judge Joyner prefers that motions in limine be submitted before trial, rather than on the day trial begins.

9. Examination of Witnesses Out of Sequence. Judge Joyner permits counsel to take witnesses out of turn for the convenience of the witnesses.

10. Opening Statements and Summations. Judge Joyner places no time limit on opening statements or summations. He urges counsel to remember that opening statements are not for argument, but for presentation of an outline of what the parties intend to prove.

11. Offers of Proof. Judge Joyner requires the parties to inquire of each other privately as to offers of proof regarding any witness or exhibit expected to be offered. If counsel cannot resolve such matters, Judge Joyner will rule on them upon application before a witness testifies or an exhibit is offered into evidence.

12. Examination of Witnesses or Argument by More Than One Attorney. Only in an extreme and rare circumstance will Judge Joyner permit more than one attorney for a party to examine different witnesses or argue different points before the court.

13. Examination of Witnesses Beyond Redirect or Recross. Judge Joyner generally does not permit further examination of a witness after redirect or recross has been completed.

14. Videotaped Testimony. Judge Joyner requires that a list of all objections to videotaped trial testimony and a copy of the transcript be submitted to the court well in advance of the offering of such evidence.

15. Reading of Material Into the Record. Judge Joyner has no special practice or policy for reading stipulations, pleadings, or discovery material into the record. He permits it when appropriate.

16. Preparation of Exhibits. Judge Joyner requires that exhibits be pre-marked and pre-exchanged. Two copies of trial exhibits should be provided to the court on the first day of trial. The trial exhibits should be accompanied by an exhibit list that describes each exhibit.

17. Offering Exhibits Into Evidence. Judge Joyner leaves this decision to counsel.

18. Directed Verdict Motions. Judge Joyner prefers, but does not require, that directed verdict motions be in writing. He will hear oral argument on such motions.

19. Proposed Jury Instructions and Verdict Forms. Judge Joyner prefers that counsel submit proposed jury instructions at the beginning of trial. Proposed jury instructions must include citation to proper authority. Judge Joyner always conducts a conference on proposed jury instructions. Submission of supplemental proposed jury instructions is permitted up to the time the charge is given. Toward the end of the charge, Judge Joyner always solicits suggestions and amendments from counsel.

20. Proposed Findings of Fact and Conclusions of Law. Judge Joyner requires that proposed findings of fact and conclusions of law in nonjury cases be filed with the clerk, and served on the court (Chambers) in duplicate, three days before the case is placed on the trial list.

Jury Deliberations

1. Written Jury Instructions. Judge Joyner has never given the jury a copy of the instructions.

2. Exhibits in the Jury Room. Judge Joyner usually permits all exhibits received in evidence to go out to the jury unless there is an objection.

3. Handling of Jury Requests to Read Back Testimony or Replay Tapes. In cases where transcripts are available, Judge Joyner will consider reading appropriate portions requested by the jury. He will generally allow audiotapes and videotapes to be replayed in open court if necessary.

4.   Availability of Counsel During Jury Deliberations. Counsel should be available on 10 minutes' notice during jury deliberations. As a practical matter, that means that counsel must either stay in the courthouse or have an associate present.

5.   Taking the Verdict and Special Interrogatories. Judge Joyner has no usual practice for taking a special or general verdict. Interrogatories are submitted to the jury in most civil cases.

6.   Polling the Jury. Judge Joyner grants all requests to poll the jury.

7.   Interviewing the Jury. Judge Joyner permits counsel to interview jurors after the verdict has been recorded and the jury has been discharged. The jury is instructed that they may speak with counsel, but are not required to do so.

CRIMINAL CASES

1.   Approach to Oral Argument and Motions. Judge Joyner permits oral argument on motions in criminal cases. Oral argument normally takes place prior to jury selection.

2.   Pretrial Conferences. Judge Joyner will hold pretrial conferences depending on the circumstances of the particular case. He will also hold a conference at the request of counsel.

3.   Voir Dire. Judge Joyner conducts the entire voir dire in criminal cases. He encourages submissions of proposed voir dire questions by counsel. He permits counsel to follow up and ask individual questions, where warranted.

4.   Sentencing Memoranda. Judge Joyner permits and encourages the submission of sentencing memoranda by both the government and the defense.

OTHER GENERAL MATTERS

Judge Joyner employs no procedures in criminal cases that differ significantly from those he uses in civil cases.

Judge Joyner does not wish to receive copies of the appellate briefs if a decision he renders is appealed.

Judge Joyner expects punctuality, as well as courtesy, from counsel regarding each other, both in the presence of the court and otherwise. He is of the view that vigorous, robust advocacy need not be rude.

Judge J. Curtis Joyner

IN THE UNITED STATES DISTRICT COURT
FOR THE EASTERN DISTRICT OF PENNSYLVANIA

PLAINTIFF, : CIVIL ACTION
:
v. : ____ - _____
:
DEFENDANT :

SCHEDULING ORDER

AND NOW, this ____ day of _____, following Conference with the parties and pursuant to Fed.R.Civ.P. 16(b), it is hereby ORDERED as follows:

1. All discovery shall proceed forthwith and continue in such manner as will assure that all requests for, and responses to, discovery will be served, noticed, and completed by _____.

2. All trial exhibits shall be marked and exchanged on or before _____.

3. Plaintiff shall identify and submit Curriculum Vitae for all expert witnesses on or before _____.

4. Defendant shall identify and submit Curriculum Vitae for all expert witnesses on or before _____. Reports and/or responses to expert witness discovery for all such expert witnesses shall be served by defendant on plaintiff on or before _____.

5. All <u>DAUBERT</u> MOTIONS AND MOTIONS FOR SUMMARY JUDGMENT ARE DUE BY _____.

6. The parties shall prepare and file with the Clerk of Court their Joint Pretrial Memoranda, in accordance with this Order and Local Rule of Civil Procedure 16.1(c) and any and all motion *in limine* on or before _____.

7. The case will be placed in the Court's trial pool on _____.

8. Any party having an objection to: (a) the admissibility of any exhibit based on authenticity; (b) the admissibility for any reason (except relevancy) of any evidence expected to be offered; or (c) the adequacy of the qualifications of an expert witness expected to testify shall set forth separately each such objection in their Pretrial Memoranda. Such objection shall describe with particularity the ground and the authority for the objection.

9. If any party desires an "offer of proof" as to any witness or exhibit expected to be offered, that party shall inquire of counsel <u>prior to trial</u> for such information. If the inquiring party is dissatisfied with any offer provided, such party shall file a motion seeking relief from the Court prior to trial.

10. Because a witness may be unavailable at the time of trial as defined in Federal Rule of Civil Procedure 32(a)(3), the Court expects use of oral or videotape depositions at trial of any witness whose testimony a party believes essential to the presentation of that party's case, whether that witness is a party, a non-party, or an expert. The unavailability of any such witness <u>will not be a ground to delay the commencement or progress of an ongoing trial</u>. In the event a deposition is to be offered, the offering party shall file with the Court, prior to the commencement of trial, a copy of the deposition transcript, but only after all efforts have been made to resolve objections with other counsel. Unresolved objections shall be noted in the margin of the deposition page(s) where a Court ruling is necessary and a covering list of such objections supplied therewith.

11. The parties shall meet to prepare a complete and comprehensive stipulation of uncontested facts pursuant to paragraph (d)(2)(b)(2) of Local Rule of Civil Procedure 16.1; two (2) copies of such stipulation shall be submitted to the Court (Chambers, Room 8613) at least three (3) days before the case appears on the trial list. The original shall be filed with the Clerk of Court.

12. At least three (3) days before the settlement conference, or in certain cases where there is to be no settlement conference, then three days before the day of trial, each party shall submit to the Court two (2) copies of proposed *voir dire* questions, proposed jury instructions with citations of authority for each point (ONE POINT PER PAGE AND WITH PIN CITES), proposed jury interrogatories, and a trial memorandum on the legal issues involved in the case. The originals shall be filed with the Clerk of the Court.

13. At the commencement of trial, the Court should be supplied with one (1) copy of each exhibit, and two (2) copies of a schedule of exhibits which shall briefly describe each exhibit.

14. **IF DOCUMENTS ARE FILED ELECTRONICALLY, THE PARTIES SHALL SEND A COPY OF CHAMBERS.**

15. Unexcused violations of scheduling orders are subject to sanctions under Fed.R.Civ.P. 16(f), upon motion or the initiative of the Court.

16. Letters or written communications shall be directed to the Court and not to law clerks or to the deputy clerk. Telephone calls to law clerks are discouraged. Law clerks are not permitted to render advice to counsel and have no authority to grant continuances. All scheduling matters should be discussed with Angela J. Mickie, Deputy Clerk, (267-299-7419). Only in the event that the deputy clerk is unavailable should counsel contact Chambers directly.

BY THE COURT:

_____
J. CURTIS JOYNER, J.

Judge Robert F. Kelly

Judge Robert F. Kelly was born on June 17, 1935, in Rosemont, Pennsylvania. He received a B.S. in economics from Villanova University in 1957 and LL.B. from Temple University in 1960. Judge Kelly was in private practice in Media and Chester, Pennsylvania, from 1961 to 1976. In 1976, he was elected to serve as a judge of the Court of Common Pleas, Thirty-second Judicial District. Judge Kelly was appointed to the United States District Court for the Eastern District of Pennsylvania in 1987. He assumed senior status on July 17, 2001.

PRELIMINARY GENERAL MATTERS

1. **Electronic Case Filing.** Judge Kelly requires that all documents be filed electronically by the attorney by using the Electronic Case Filing (ECF) system. ECF provides greater efficiency and timeliness in the filing of pleadings, automatic e-mail notice of case activity, and electronic storage of documents for remote access by the court, the bar, and the litigants. Attorneys appearing before Judge Kelly are required to register as ECF users at the Office of the Clerk of the Court or at the court's website at http://www.paed.uscourts.gov.

A copy of the pretrial and trial procedure for Judge Robert F. Kelly is available on the court's website at http://www.paed.uscourts.gov under the heading "Documents" and the subheading "Judges' Procedures."

2. **Correspondence with the Court.** Judge Kelly permits correspondence under the circumstances set forth in his standard notice to counsel, which his courtroom deputy routinely sends to counsel after a case is assigned. A copy of the notice is shown on page 143 of this book. Otherwise, all other communications with the court should be by the filing of pleadings, motions, applications, briefs, or legal memoranda.

3. **Communications with Law Clerks.** Judge Kelly permits communications with his law clerks concerning the administrative aspects of cases, but not on the merits of a case.

4. **Telephone Conferences.** Judge Kelly encourages the use of telephone conferences for matters such as pretrial conferences, scheduling, and minor discovery disputes. He prefers that such matters be managed by his courtroom deputy or the law clerk if the courtroom deputy is not available.

5. **Oral Arguments and Evidentiary Hearings.** Judge Kelly does not set aside any certain days or times for oral argument on motions or evidentiary hearings.

6. **Pro Hac Vice Admissions.** Judge Kelly prefers a written motion for admission to be made on the day of the appearance of out-of-town counsel.

CIVIL CASES
Pretrial Procedure

1. **Pretrial Conferences.** When all defendants have entered appearances in the case, Judge Kelly's courtroom deputy will arrange a conference call with counsel. The purpose of this is to give the court information from which it can prepare a scheduling order. The matters discussed will be time needed to complete fact and expert discovery, likelihood of dispositive motions, and a specific trial date. At that time, the judge also advises counsel that he is willing to hold a settlement conference at any time, providing that all counsel feel it might be fruitful.

Continuances and Extensions

1. General Policy. Judge Kelly has a general policy of adhering to originally scheduled dates unless a compelling reason is presented that justifies a change. This policy applies to briefing schedules, oral arguments, evidentiary hearings, discovery deadlines, and trial dates.

2. Requests for Extensions and Continuances. Counsel should advise the court immediately of any compelling reason justifying an extension or a continuance of any originally scheduled date. Any request for an extension or a continuance should be made by a formal motion.

General Motion Practice

1. Oral Argument on Motions. Judge Kelly hears oral argument on motions only when he requests it.

2. Reply and Surreply Briefs. Reply and surreply briefs should be filed only if absolutely necessary.

3. Chambers Copies of Motion Papers. Judge Kelly prefers to receive courtesy copies of motion papers in chambers, and he encourages this practice.

Discovery Matters

1. Length of Discovery Period and Extensions. Judge Kelly's general policy is to allow four months to complete discovery.

2. Discovery Conferences and Dispute Resolution. Judge Kelly normally does not hold discovery conferences other than the usual Rule 16 conferences. He encourages the use of telephone conferences to resolve disputes arising during depositions. At times, he will initiate discovery conferences if he observes that counsel are having continuing difficulty getting through the procedure.

3. Confidentiality Agreements. Judge Kelly has no standard practice or policy concerning confidentiality orders. Counsel may submit stipulated confidentiality orders for consideration.

4. Expert Witnesses. Judge Kelly does not generally require written expert reports or expert depositions. He usually leaves these matters for agreement by counsel. It is the judge's policy to have experts identified 60 to 90 days after the filing of a complaint.

Settlement

1. General Approach to Settlement and Nonjury Cases. Judge Kelly believes the court's involvement in settlement conferences is generally helpful, and he will become involved in settlement conferences in jury cases at the request of both counsel when they feel there is a possibility of a settlement. Judge Kelly participates in settlement negotiations in nonjury cases, and he will only do so if counsel for both parties consent. Otherwise, in nonjury cases, he refers settlement negotiations to a magistrate judge.

2. Referral of Settlement Negotiations to Another District Court Judge. Judge Kelly has never referred settlement negotiations to another district court judge.

Arbitration

1. General Approach to Arbitration Cases. Judge Kelly has no standard procedures or practices for arbitration cases that differ from cases certified as involving more than $100,000. He handles motions and conferences the same as in other cases.

2. Scheduling of Trial De Novo from Arbitration. Upon demand for trial de novo from an arbitration award, Judge Kelly places the matter in his trial pool immediately. Judge Kelly has no special practices or procedures concerning motions, pretrial memoranda, exhibits, or additional time for discovery for de novo arbitration cases.

Proposed Final Pretrial Memoranda

1. Required Form of Pretrial Memoranda. In jury cases, unless specifically provided for by separate order in a particular case, Judge Kelly has no requirements for pretrial memoranda other than those set forth in Rule 16. Any other requirements are set forth in paragraph 4 of his standard notice to counsel (see page 144 of this book).

2. Common Deficiencies in Pretrial Memoranda. The most common deficiencies in pretrial memoranda noted by Judge Kelly are incomplete lists of proposed witnesses and inaccurate estimates of the number of days for trial. Incomplete witness lists frequently cause disputes at the time of trial.

Injunctions

1. Scheduling and Expedited Discovery. Judge Kelly's usual practice is to give priority and expedited treatment to the scheduling of preliminary and permanent injunction hearings. Judge Kelly has no standard policy for handling expedited discovery in injunction matters.

2. Proposed Findings of Fact and Conclusions of Law. Judge Kelly prefers to have proposed findings of fact and conclusions of law submitted prior to trial if possible. He accepts them after the testimony, but does not wish to wait for the transcript to be prepared.

Trial Procedure

1. Scheduling of Cases. Judge Kelly's practice is to give a specific trial date at the time of the scheduling conference.

2. Cases Involving Out-of-Town Parties or Witnesses. Judge Kelly will usually accommodate out-of-town parties or witnesses.

3. Note-taking by Jurors. Judge Kelly permits note-taking by jurors in most cases.

4. Trial Briefs. Judge Kelly encourages the submission of trial briefs.

5. Voir Dire. Judge Kelly allows counsel to conduct voir dire in civil cases. Judge Kelly's courtroom deputy is present during voir dire. Judge Kelly will intervene if he notices that counsel will not be able to handle the voir dire themselves in an orderly fashion. Counsel may come to chambers if a dispute arises during voir dire. At a later time, the problem, and Judge Kelly's decision, will be put on the record. There is no time limit on the conduct of voir dire, although it is Judge Kelly's experience that the entire process takes one hour or less.

6. Sidebars. Judge Kelly allows sidebar conferences when absolutely necessary.

7. In Limine Motions. Judge Kelly views motions in limine as a great help in making him aware of evidentiary problems that will arise during trial. He prefers they be served in advance of trial in order to be properly studied. He will, however, accept them at any time.

8. Examination of Witnesses Out of Sequence. Judge Kelly usually grants requests by counsel to take the testimony of a witness out of turn for the convenience of the witnesses.

9. Opening Statements and Summations. Judge Kelly places time limits of one-half hour on both opening statements and summations by counsel.

10. Examination of Witnesses or Argument by More Than One Attorney. Judge Kelly permits more than one attorney for a party to examine different witnesses or argue different points before the court.

11. Examination of Witnesses Beyond Redirect or Recross. Judge Kelly does not generally allow further examination of a witness after redirect or recross are completed.

12. Videotaped Testimony. Videotaped testimony should start with the witness being sworn. Objections should be given to the court well in advance of the tapes being offered, and they should be accompanied by a copy of the transcript for the court that is tabbed to indicate the exact location of the various objections.

13. Reading of Material Into the Record. Judge Kelly has no special practice or policy for reading stipulations, pleadings, or discovery material into the record. Counsel may do it at any point.

14. Preparation of Exhibits. Judge Kelly requires that exhibits be pre-marked and pre-exchanged. Two copies of trial exhibits should be provided to the court in cases involving large numbers of documents and in nonjury cases.

15. Offering Exhibits Into Evidence. Judge Kelly has no preference concerning when an exhibit is offered into evidence.

16. Motions for Judgment as a Matter of Law and Motions for Judgment on Partial Findings. Judge Kelly prefers that motions for judgment as a matter of law (or motions for judgment on partial findings) be in writing. Judge Kelly normally hears oral argument on motions for judgment as a matter of law and motions for judgment on partial findings.

17. Proposed Jury Instructions and Verdict Forms. Judge Kelly normally requests that jury instructions for all points covered in the case be submitted prior to the start of trial. He will allow counsel to submit supplemental jury instructions up to the time of closing arguments. At the end of his charge to the jury, counsel will be given the opportunity, at sidebar, to take exception, make corrections, or suggest additions. Judge Kelly usually conducts a conference on proposed jury instructions.

18. Proposed Findings of Fact and Conclusions of Law. Judge Kelly prefers that proposed findings of fact and conclusions of law in nonjury cases be submitted before trial, if possible. If so submitted, he will give counsel, upon request, an opportunity to submit additional proposed findings at the close of the testimony.

Jury Deliberations

1. Written Jury Instructions. Judge Kelly does not give a written copy of his instruction to the jury.

2. Exhibits in the Jury Room. Judge Kelly generally permits all exhibits received in evidence to go out to the jury unless they contain matters that would be confusing or prejudicial.

3. Handling of Jury Requests to Read Back Testimony or Replay Tapes. Judge Kelly's courtroom is equipped with an electronic court reporting system. Upon request by the jury, he will have the electronic court reporter locate that portion of the tape requested by the jury and simply play it back for them. He allows tapes and videotapes to be replayed if necessary.

4. Availability of Counsel During Jury Deliberations. Judge Kelly requires counsel to remain in the courthouse during deliberations. If counsel can assure him that they can get to the courtroom within five minutes, Judge Kelly will allow them to return to their offices.

5. Taking the Verdict and Special Interrogatories. Judge Kelly generally takes a special verdict. On simple, uncomplicated cases he allows a general verdict. He usually submits interrogatories to the jury.

6. Polling the Jury. Judge Kelly will, upon request, allow the jury to be polled.

7. Interviewing the Jury. After a case is concluded, Judge Kelly usually advises the jury that they are free to talk to anyone about the case, including counsel for the parties. He also tells the jury that they are not obligated to do so.

CRIMINAL CASES

1. Approach to Oral Argument and Motions. Judge Kelly will normally allow oral arguments on motions in criminal cases prior to selection of the jury on the first day of trial.

2. Pretrial Conferences. Judge Kelly rarely holds pretrial conferences in criminal cases.

3. Voir Dire. Judge Kelly conducts voir dire in criminal cases. He requests that counsel submit suggested questions to him two or three days prior to the start of trial. When finished with his questions, Judge Kelly will allow counsel an opportunity to submit follow-up questions to him to be given to the jury as a whole. When follow-up questions are to be asked of individual jurors, he normally brings the juror to sidebar to allow the questioning of the juror on the record, but out of the hearing of the remainder of the panel.

Judge Kelly instructs the jury panel that if any of their answers would be embarrassing to them, they may come to sidebar and respond to questions on the record at sidebar in the presence of counsel.

4. Sentencing Memoranda. Judge Kelly permits and encourages the submission of sentencing memoranda by both the government and the defense.

OTHER GENERAL MATTERS

If a decision rendered by Judge Kelly is appealed, he does not care to receive copies of appellate briefs.

Counsel should not hesitate to contact Judge Kelly's courtroom deputy or law clerks if they have a question about his courtroom practices or procedures.

Practice and Procedures of Judges and Judges' Forms and Orders

UNITED STATES DISTRICT COURT
EASTERN DISTRICT OF PENNSYLVANIA

CHAMBERS OF JUDGE ROBERT F. KELLY	: : : : : : :	11613 U.S. COURTHOUSE PHILADELPHIA, PA 19106 215-597-0736 CIVIL ACTION NO.

PRETRIAL ORDER

AND NOW, this _____ day of _____, 20___, it is **ORDERED**:

1. All discovery in this case is to be completed by _____.

2. This case will be tried on _____.

3. Final Joint Pretrial Order pursuant to Fed. R. Civ. P. 16 and Local Rule of Civil Procedure 16.1(d)(2) due: _____.

4. Changes in the foregoing schedule may be obtained only by written application to the Court, for cause shown.

_____
Thomas Garrity
Deputy Clerk to
Judge Robert F. Kelly

HONORABLE ROBERT F. KELLY
Senior United States District Judge

U.S. Courthouse
601 Market Street, Room 11613
Philadelphia, Pennsylvania 19106-1765
215-597-0736
Secretary: Maureen Mattern
Courtroom Deputy Clerk: Thomas Garrity
267-299-7319

MAGISTRATE JUDGE ASSIGNMENT:
  Magistrate Judge Strawbridge

STANDING ORDERS:
  None

COMMUNICATIONS WITH LAW CLERK:
  Judge Kelly permits counsel to communicate with his law clerks on administrative matters.

PROBATION REPORT:
  Judge Kelly does not permit the defendant or counsel to review the Probation Department's written recommendations as to sentence.

PRETRIAL AND TRIAL PROCEDURE
Before Judge Robert F. Kelly

1. Counsel shall be familiar with the provisions of F.R.C.P. 16.

2. Discovery shall be conducted promptly and diligently. Deadlines will be enforced and neither unnecessary discovery nor obstructionism will be tolerated. Discovery enforcement or relief should be sought promptly by motion only. Telephone inquiries relating to scheduling should be directed to the court deputy clerk.

3. A specific trial date will be established at the scheduling conference. The court will make every effort to commence trial as scheduled.

4. Pretrial memoranda required to be delivered to the court as per court order shall include the following:

    a. All things as required in the Final Joint Pretrial Order pursuant to Fed. R. Civ. P. 16 and Local Rule of Civil Procedure 16.1(d)(2), if applicable.

    b. A list of all exhibits pre-numbered and pre-exchanged among all counsel. If exhibits are numerous, they should be suitably tabbed to facilitate ease and speed in locating an exhibit.

    c. In all jury cases, proposed points for charge and in all non-jury cases, proposed findings of fact and conclusions of law. Counsel have the right to file supplemental points, findings and conclusions upon the close of testimony (counsel is reminded that the originals of these documents should be filed in the Clerk's Office, Rm. 2609, and that the Court should be provided a copy).

    d. A statement of any anticipated legal issues on which the Court will be required to rule together with counsel's single best authority (case citation, Rule of Civil Procedure, Rule of Evidence, Statute, etc.).

    e. All stipulations of counsel and an itemized list of any admissions to be read into evidence.

5. Court sessions will commence daily at 9:30 a.m. and continue until 12:30 p.m. with a short mid-morning break. Court will reconvene at 1:30 p.m. and continue until 4:30 p.m. (unless a juror from one of the outlying counties has a transportation schedule to meet) with a short mid-afternoon break. The court will adhere to this schedule and counsel must fit *all* witnesses into that time frame and not seek exceptions.

6. Counsel has the responsibility to have all witnesses available in court as scheduled. Failure to do so may result in sanctions.

7. All videotape recordings shall be conducted with an acute sensitivity that the videotape will be shown to a jury. Skillful organization of the testimony, elimination of unnecessary objections and conservation of time are strongly urged.

8. Counsel may conduct examination of witnesses from counsel table or from the lectern. Counsel is reminded that the courtroom is equipped with an electronic sound recording system. Therefore, counsel should always be near a microphone when speaking.

9. Opening statements shall be *brief* and *outlines only (not argument)* of the evidence counsel intends to present.

10. Summations shall *not* exceed thirty minutes except upon special exception allowed by the court in a complex case. Rebuttal argument by plaintiff shall ordinarily not exceed five minutes and shall be confined strictly to a response to *unanticipated* argument by opposing counsel. Re-argument will not be permitted.

11. Except for letters of transmittal that accompany documents that are required to be sent or filed at the Courthouse, counsel should not include the court as an addressee or as a party designated to receive copies of letters among and between counsel, except in the following instances:

    a. Where the court specifically invites counsel to advise the court of some matter by letter; or

    b. When the cause of counsel's participation in the case is expected to be affected by a personal matter concerning counsel, a party, a witness, or counsel's immediate family, such as a medical problem, vacation plans, or other similarly personal problems or questions; or

    c. To confirm or advise the court that a case has been settled, dismissed or otherwise finally disposed of.

All other communications with the court concerning cases before the court should be by the filing of pleadings, motions, applications, briefs, legal memoranda, or other similar filings provided for in the Federal Rules of Civil or Criminal Procedure or our Local Rules of Civil or Criminal Procedure.

Judge Edmund V. Ludwig

Judge Ludwig was born in Philadelphia on May 20, 1928. He received an A.B. in 1949 from Harvard College and an LL.B. in 1952 from Harvard Law School. Judge Ludwig was admitted to practice in Pennsylvania in 1953. He was a member of the Army Judge Advocate General's Corps from 1953 to 1956 and served in Korea. He was in private practice in Philadelphia from 1956 to 1959, and in Doylestown from 1959 to 1968. From 1968 to 1985, he was a judge of the Court of Common Pleas of Bucks County. Judge Ludwig was appointed to the United States District Court for the Eastern District of Pennsylvania on October 17, 1985. He assumed senior status on May 20, 1997.

PRELIMINARY GENERAL MATTERS

1. Correspondence with the Court. Judge Ludwig permits correspondence on minor scheduling matters, but where an order is sought on a contested issue, counsel should file a formal motion.

2. Communications with Law Clerks. Judge Ludwig permits counsel to speak with his law clerks.

3. Telephone Conferences. Judge Ludwig finds telephone conferences to be a convenient method of handling matters such as discovery disputes, scheduling changes, and extensions of time, but prefers in-chambers conferences for settlement discussions and complex issues.

4. Oral Arguments and Evidentiary Hearings. Judge Ludwig does not set aside certain days or times for oral arguments or evidentiary hearings. Oral argument may be requested by counsel or the court. In practice, it occurs infrequently.

5. Pro Hac Vice Admissions. Judge Ludwig does not require a formal motion and order to be presented for pro hac vice admissions. The motion may be made in open court when the attorney to be admitted first appears.

6. Courtroom Practice. Judge Ludwig has no hard-and-fast special restrictions on courtroom practice. A general standard operating procedure (SOP) to that effect, which is given to counsel at trial, is shown on page 152 of this book.

7. Changes in Office Procedure. Judge Ludwig revises his office's scheduling procedures from time to time. His law clerks and courtroom deputy are available to discuss procedural questions with counsel.

CIVIL CASES
Pretrial Procedure

1. Pretrial Conferences. Judge Ludwig usually conducts a Rule 16 scheduling conference 30 to 60 days after an action, including arbitration, is filed. Before the conference, he sends counsel a scheduling policy statement, a copy of which is shown on page 153 of this book. At the conference, he issues a scheduling order either fixing an early trial date or another Rule 16 conference after a two- to three-month discovery period. Copies of his scheduling orders for jury and nonjury trials and arbitrations are shown on pages 159 to 160. He conducts informal pretrial conferences and encourages counsel to request settlement and other conferences. He does not use a standard agenda for conferences.

Continuances and Extensions

1.   General Policy. Judge Ludwig grants continuances and extensions of briefing schedules, discovery deadlines, oral arguments, hearing dates, and trial dates only for cause. Hearing and trial dates ordinarily will not be continued because of discovery problems.

2.   Requests for Extensions and Continuances. Judge Ludwig will schedule a conference to discuss most requests for continuances and extensions of time. When requests for continuances or extensions are contested, he prefers that they be made by motion.

General Motion Practice

1.   Oral Argument on Motions. Judge Ludwig will schedule oral argument if it appears likely to be helpful to the court. In addition, he usually will hold oral argument on counsel's request. Each party is allocated 15 minutes unless more time is deemed necessary. A portion of time may be reserved for rebuttal. Each party submits a one-page summary of argument in a joint submission at least three days before the argument date. An SOP for oral argument is shown on page 162 of this book.

2.   Reply and Surreply Briefs. Judge Ludwig permits reply and surreply briefs but allows only a short period of time for their submission.

3.   Chambers Copies of Motion Papers. Counsel are encouraged to submit a chambers copy of motion papers but are not required to do so. Receipt of the original may not occur for a day or two after filing.

Discovery Matters

1.   Length of Discovery Period and Extensions. For most cases, Judge Ludwig allows a discovery period of 90 days to 120 days with trial scheduled a month or so thereafter. He allows a longer period for complex cases, but then segments discovery into stages of 60 to 90 days, with scheduling conferences to follow. For each discovery phase, counsel are asked to submit a joint discovery schedule, a copy of which is shown on page 163 of this book. The main purpose of the joint discovery schedule is to reserve deposition dates well in advance. When a properly completed joint discovery schedule is returned to his office, Judge Ludwig will sign a Rule 16(b) order at the bottom approving the schedule and fixing the date of the next Rule 16 conference. He expects counsel to take all steps necessary to enforce compliance with the discovery schedule.

2.   Discovery Conferences and Dispute Resolution. Judge Ludwig does not regularly hold discovery conferences after the initial Rule 16 conference. However, he encourages the use of telephone conferences, in lieu of motion practice, to resolve discovery disputes. When a discovery *default* occurs, he encourages counsel to file a motion to compel, which he will grant forthwith pursuant to Local Civil Rule 26.1(g). When a discovery *dispute* occurs, and counsel have been unable to resolve it themselves or with Judge Ludwig's assistance by telephone, he requires a special format for a motion to compel. A copy of the format instructions is shown on page 164 of this book.

3.   Confidentiality Agreements. Judge Ludwig prefers to deal with confidentiality agreements and stipulations on a case-by-case basis.

4.   Expert Witnesses. Judge Ludwig requires that expert reports be exchanged on or before the dates set by the scheduling order unless counsel otherwise agree. He does not have a special policy as to when the depositions of expert witnesses will be permitted, excepting that all trial depositions must be taken at least 10 days before trial unless counsel otherwise agree or court approval is granted. He requests that expert witnesses be identified in a timely manner pursuant to properly propounded interrogatories.

Settlement

1. General Approach to Settlement and Nonjury Cases. At the earliest convenient point, Judge Ludwig takes an active role in settlement discussions. He may hold an early resolution hearing in court at which individual parties, or principals, are present. He usually recommends settlement figures. He discusses alternative methods of dispute resolution. He will participate in settlement negotiations in nonjury cases if counsel approve.

Judge Ludwig's scheduling order requires plaintiff's counsel to report, in writing, by a certain date—usually the end of discovery—on "serious settlement efforts." He requires counsel to conduct negotiations before he holds a settlement conference and, if possible, to resolve the case without the court's assistance.

2. Referral of Settlement Negotiations to Another Judge. If counsel request, or sua sponte in cases he considers appropriate, Judge Ludwig will refer settlement negotiations to a magistrate judge. He will also refer settlement negotiations to another district court judge in certain circumstances.

Arbitration

1. General Approach to Arbitration Cases. Judge Ludwig conducts Rule 16 conferences in arbitration cases but encourages counsel to keep pretrial practice as simple as possible. His scheduling order in arbitration cases designates the week of the arbitration—the specific date is fixed by the clerk of court—and the date for plaintiff's counsel to report on settlement efforts. He does not permit an arbitration date to be continued without his approval.

2. Scheduling of Trial De Novo from Arbitration. Judge Ludwig does not permit delay of de novo trials. He generally schedules such trials 30 to 60 days after the demand for trial de novo. Judge Ludwig requires counsel to submit a proposed final pretrial stipulation at least 10 days before the scheduled trial date.

Proposed Final Joint Pretrial Stipulation

1. Required Form of Joint Pretrial Stipulation. Except in arbitration cases, Judge Ludwig requires that counsel submit a proposed joint final pretrial stipulation. The contents of the stipulation appear on the reverse side of his scheduling order. The intent is to simplify the requirements of Local Civil Rule 16.1(d)(2) by making the final pretrial submission commensurate with the needs of the case.

2. Common Deficiencies in Pretrial Memoranda. Judge Ludwig notes that the parties' proposed joint final pretrial stipulation often is not submitted on time and that counsel have not prepared their exhibits for trial, as required by Local Civil Rule 16.1(d)(2). He also finds that counsel sometimes do not make a genuine attempt to agree on facts not in dispute. In addition, he finds that when counsel do not cooperate, they may end up submitting separate pretrial papers that violate the scheduling order, often necessitating another submission.

Injunctions

1. Scheduling and Expedited Discovery. Judge Ludwig's usual practice is to hold a conference before the issuance of a temporary restraining order or the scheduling of preliminary and permanent injunction hearings. If practicable, he will consolidate the preliminary and permanent injunction hearings. His practice is to hold a conference on contested requests for expedited discovery. Usually he will grant such requests.

2. Proposed Findings of Fact and Conclusions of Law. Judge Ludwig requires that proposed findings of fact and conclusions of law be submitted at the start of an injunction hearing.

Trial Procedure

1. Scheduling of Cases. Judge Ludwig schedules civil jury cases for a specific date, usually listing three to five cases for every other or third Monday. All cases must be ready for trial on the date scheduled. He does not use a "pool" system. His courtroom deputy will give counsel at least 24 hours notice of attachment for trial. Judge Ludwig does not recognize a trial listing that is set after the date of his scheduling order. He suggests that if such a conflict is about to occur, counsel should notify his courtroom deputy so that she may attach the case for trial.

2. Conflicts of Counsel. Counsel should immediately notify Judge Ludwig's courtroom deputy as to professional and personal conflicts affecting the trial schedule.

3. Cases Involving Out-of-Town Parties or Witnesses. Judge Ludwig does not have any special policies regarding the scheduling of out-of-town parties or witnesses.

4. Note-taking by Jurors. Judge Ludwig ordinarily permits note-taking by jurors if a request is made at the start of trial.

5. Trial Briefs. Judge Ludwig encourages counsel to submit trial briefs.

6. Voir Dire. Unless a problem is anticipated, Judge Ludwig permits counsel to conduct all voir dire in civil cases. If disputes arise during the voir dire, they are handled by Judge Ludwig in chambers. Except in complex cases, he expects counsel to complete voir dire in 45 minutes to an hour.

7. Sidebars. Judge Ludwig allows sidebar conferences if they are necessary, but often asks counsel to talk to each other informally first in an effort to resolve an objection or problem without a sidebar conference.

8. In Limine Motions. Judge Ludwig prefers that counsel submit in limine motions at least 10 days before the scheduled trial date as part of the final joint pretrial stipulation.

9. Examination of Witnesses Out of Sequence. Judge Ludwig will permit counsel to take witnesses out of turn for the convenience of the witnesses.

10. Opening Statements and Summations. Judge Ludwig does not have standard time limits for opening statements and summations, and he tries to tailor any time limits to the requirements of the case. He asks that at trial, counsel request specific amounts of time for such speeches.

11. Examination of Witnesses or Argument by More Than One Attorney. More than one attorney for a party may examine different witnesses or argue different points before the court, as long as counsel notify Judge Ludwig before the start of trial of their desire to divide such examination or argument. Ordinarily, more than one attorney for a party per witness or issue will not be permitted.

12. Examination of Witnesses Beyond Redirect and Recross. Judge Ludwig does not have a general policy as to further examination of witnesses after redirect and recross, but usually will sustain an objection to further examination if it exceeds the scope of the previous examination by opposing counsel.

Practice and Procedures of Judges and Judges' Forms and Orders

13. Videotaped Testimony. When counsel intend to introduce videotaped testimony, Judge Ludwig encourages them to resolve, between themselves and well in advance of trial, any objections that were made or reserved when the videotaped testimony was taken.

14. Reading of Material Into the Record. Judge Ludwig has no special practice or procedure regarding the reading of stipulations, pleadings, or discovery material into the record.

15. Preparation of Exhibits. Judge Ludwig prefers that exhibits be pre-marked and pre-exchanged. Counsel should provide one set of trial exhibits to Judge Ludwig. Exhibits should be itemized in the joint pretrial stipulation.

16. Offering Exhibits Into Evidence. Judge Ludwig does not have a preference as to when counsel should offer exhibits into evidence during their case. He may refuse to consider an offer made when it is not during counsel's case.

17. Motions for Judgment as a Matter of Law and Motions for Judgment on Partial Findings. Motions for judgment may be made either orally or in writing. Oral argument on such motions is usually permitted.

18. Proposed Jury Instructions and Verdict Forms. Judge Ludwig suggests that counsel submit proposed jury instructions only as to case-specific or unusual issues of law and that they do so on the first day of trial. He will permit counsel to submit supplemental proposed jury instructions at any time before the jury is charged, but he requests that such submissions be made before the day of the charge. He uses jury verdict forms and requests that counsel submit proposed verdict forms with proposed jury instructions. A sample verdict form is available from Judge Ludwig's courtroom deputy. Judge Ludwig conducts a conference on proposed jury instructions and the jury verdict form.

19. Proposed Findings of Fact and Conclusions of Law. Proposed findings of fact and conclusions of law should be submitted before the start of a nonjury trial.

Jury Deliberations

1. Written Jury Instructions. Judge Ludwig rarely gives the jury a copy of his instructions.

2. Exhibits in the Jury Room. This issue—which exhibits go out to the jury—is usually resolved by counsel. Judge Ludwig will rule on any dispute.

3. Handling of Jury Requests to Read Back Testimony or Replay Tapes. Judge Ludwig will allow portions of testimony to be read back or tapes to be replayed if doing so is practicable. Otherwise, he will ask the jurors to rely on their recollections. As to jury requests in general, he will consult with counsel before responding.

4. Availability of Counsel During Jury Deliberations. Judge Ludwig permits counsel to return to their offices during jury deliberations, but he requires that they be available on telephone notice within 10 minutes.

5. Taking the Verdict and "Special Interrogatories". Whether Judge Ludwig takes a general or a special verdict depends on the facts of the case. Judge Ludwig usually submits interrogatories to the jury, but he refers to them, collectively, as a "jury verdict form" and, individually, as "jury questions" and does not call them "interrogatories."

6. Polling the Jury. Judge Ludwig permits polling of the jury if a timely request is made.

7. ***Interviewing the Jury.*** After the verdict is recorded, Judge Ludwig will permit counsel to interview any juror who agrees to be interviewed. Judge Ludwig instructs the jurors that it is up to each of them to decide whether to allow an interview by counsel. Judge Ludwig advises jurors that they should not disclose their deliberations. Counsel should not question jurors with a view to challenging or impeaching the verdict.

OTHER GENERAL MATTERS

Judge Ludwig likes to receive copies of appellate briefs when a decision of his is appealed.

Civil Trial SOP
Judge Edmund V. Ludwig

General Information:

Jury of eight • Three strikes each • Unanimous verdict • Counsel conduct voir dire—in about one hour • I will be available for rulings.

The following policies and procedures are intended to simplify the conduct of the trial.

1. **Where to stand? Stand or sit?**

   In Courtroom 12A, the proceedings are recorded electronically. Counsel should position themselves so that the microphones will pick up what they say. Otherwise, they are free to speak to the jury or to me from wherever they choose. Also, counsel may stand or sit, as they believe appropriate.

2. **Length of openings and closings.**

   Counsel should advise me beforehand how long they expect to speak. Counsel are requested to limit the length of speeches commensurate with the case. Openings—ordinarily 10–15 minutes. Closings 30–45 minutes. Plaintiff argues first and has brief rebuttal.

3. **Objections to questions.**

   If counsel are objecting to a question, they should say so—i.e., use a word with "object" in it. They should give an F.R.E. reason for the objection—such as "hearsay," "relevance," etc. They should not make explanation or argument unless invited.

4. **Approaching the witness.**

   Ordinarily, counsel need not request permission to approach a witness. In instances where the witness might be intimidated by counsel's approach, counsel may want to request permission.

5. **Sidebar conferences.**

   Counsel should try to resolve issues with each other before requesting a sidebar. That can often be done in an informal huddle next to counsel table. Some simple clarification or assurances may be enough.

6. **Trial depositions.**

   Whenever possible, objections should be eliminated in advance.

   Any unresolved objections should be called to my attention before the outset of trial. If more than a few objections are left unresolved, the objector should submit a statement setting forth the questions objected to, an explanation of each objection, together with a response from the party calling the witness. The statement should be signed by both counsel.

7. **Demonstrative evidence: Display of exhibits.**

   Matters not in evidence should of course be kept out of sight of the jury. When matters have been received, they should be displayed only during the times when they are being actively used.

8. **Talking to jurors after discharged.**

   I will advise jurors that it is up to them whether to talk to counsel. This is not intended to open up the sanctity of a jury's deliberations, and counsel should be careful not to delve into that area.

If counsel have any questions—or suggestions—they should feel free to bring them to my or my staff's attention.

Judge Edmund V. Ludwig

Judge Edmund V. Ludwig

Case Management Policy Statement—Judge Ludwig

1. A Rule 16 scheduling conference will be held within 60 or so days after an action is filed, and a Case Management order will be entered. Fed.R.Civ.P. 16. Counsel will be asked to outline the specific discovery and trial preparation needs of the case and alternative dispute resolution possibilities. *See* Rule 16 Conference Information Report form.

2. Motions to dismiss, transfer, add parties and other threshold motions should be filed, whenever possible, before the conference. Summary judgment motions must be received by the court and nonmovants at least 30 days before trial date unless otherwise permitted.

3. The initial conference will usually take 15 minutes. If inconvenient for counsel to appear in person, a telephone conference may be held. In a complex case, or where settlement is practicable, counsel should attend.

4. In an uncomplicated case, discovery is to be completed in 90 days. In more protracted cases, discovery will be divided into 60–90 day intervals, and counsel will be directed to file a Joint Discovery Schedule, or successive Schedules, on a form supplied, until the case is ready for a trial listing. Arbitration appeals will receive early trial listings, usually within 30–60 days.

5. The trial listing will be for a specific date—ordinarily Monday for jury trials, with up to five other cases, and Thursdays for bench trials. These listings are not "pool" assignments. The case will be called for trial on the date specified or as soon thereafter as practicable. A special listing will not be recognized if entered after the date of the scheduling order.

6. The discovery deadline means that all known discovery must be concluded by that date. Discovery may take place thereafter only by agreement or with court approval.

7. Foreseeable discovery problems, including noncompliance or tardiness, ordinarily will not constitute a ground for continuance of the trial listing. Counsel should act promptly to enforce the discovery schedule and should not permit depositions, medical and other examinations, or discovery in general to be postponed.

8. Counsel are responsible for compliance with the Scheduling Order.

9. In a discovery default—*i.e.,* when timely discovery is not forthcoming after an attempt to obtain it—the Court's immediate assistance should be employed, by a motion for an order to compel. A conference call is an option. *See* Local Civil Rule 26.1(g). However, as to discovery disputes, a motion is the last recourse. If counsel cannot resolve, a telephone conference is the next step. If a discovery dispute motion to compel becomes necessary, contact the courtroom deputy to obtain guidelines for special format. A discovery dispute motion must be by joint submission.

10. Trial depositions are to be scheduled so as not to delay trial or disrupt trial preparation. They may not be taken later than 10 days before the trial date unless agreed to by the parties or approved by the Court. Continuance applications because of refusal of an expert witness to appear for trial or to be available for trial deposition will not be considered unless notice of the trial date was given to the witness at least 60 days in advance or at the earliest reasonable opportunity thereafter.

11. A Pretrial Stipulation is required, signed by all counsel.[*] The detailed provisions of Local Civil Rule 16.1(d)(2) are simplified, and the stipulation should be commensurate with the needs of the case. It should be submitted at least 10 days before the trial date. Counsel may file a separate pretrial memorandum pursuant to Local Civil Rule 16.1(c) only with permission of Court. If the Joint Pretrial Stipulation is not submitted on time or in proper form, the case may be continued or put in suspense as not ready for trial.

---

[*] A Pretrial Stipulation is not required in arbitrations, but is required in arbitration appeals. *See* Arbitration Scheduling Order form.

Practice and Procedures of Judges and Judges' Forms and Orders

12. Unexcused violations of scheduling orders are subject to sanctions under Fed.R.Civ.P. 16(f), upon motion or the court's initiative.

13. Note: Continuances of trial listings will be granted sparingly and only for compelling reasons.

14. Communications regarding the trial calendar should be directed to the courtroom deputy clerk: (267) 299-7589.

15. Electronic Filing System. *See* Use of Electronic Filing System—Judge Ludwig (attached).

Judge Edmund V. Ludwig

Use of Electronic Filing System
Judge Ludwig

As recommended by the Clerk of Court, Judge Ludwig supports and encourages the use of the Court's Electronic Filing System for the submission of complaints, notices of appeal, notices of removal and other civil documents. The Electronic Filing System allows greater efficiency and timeliness in the filing of pleadings, as well as electronic storage of documents for remote access by the Court, the bar and the litigants. Applications are available from the Office of the Clerk of Court 601 Market Street Room 2609, Philadelphia, Pennsylvania, 19106-1797 or (267) 299-7061.

Counsel are advised that current telephone and FAX number(s) and any changes are to be submitted to the courtroom deputy clerk.

The use of the Electronic Filing System will result in the following benefits:

- expedient filing by litigants;
- instantaneous receipt of documents for filing;
- immediate availability of documents after filing for both the Court and the public remote access.

C A S E MANAGEMENT PROGRAM

Court-Annexed Savings & Efficiency Management Program
Rule 16 Conference Report to Judge Ludwig

_____

___ Trial counsel are requested to meet together and to fill out the following Rule 16 Conference Report and to FAX it to Judge Ludwig—FAX (215) 580-2142—at least one week before the Conference. A copy is also to be given to each counsel's principal before the conference. Counsel should review the accompanying Case Management Policy Statement.

___ The Rule 16 Conference should be attended by trial counsel or by counsel fully authorized to speak for them. Principals should be available by telephone. Exceptions will be made for out-of-town counsel in appropriate cases. Contact Courtroom Deputy (267) 299-7589.

___ In filling out this joint report, counsel should attempt to reach agreement. If they cannot do so, each counsel's separate answer should be identified.

___ It is the aim of this C A S E Management Program to effectuate litigation expense and delay reduction.

Case Caption: _____ C.A. No. _____

Jury _____ Non Jury _____ Arbitration _____

1. Before deposition discovery, which ADR process do you prefer? Please rank the first two—1 and 2—and submit your comments, if any, below.

    ___ Voluntary arbitration under present system.

    ___ Mediation using court's present system.

    ___ Mediation in which counsel select mediator.

    ___ Meeting with Judge Ludwig.

    ___ Meeting with Magistrate Judge Caracappa.

    ___ Meeting with other judicial officer selected by counsel.

    ___ Other ADR to be selected by counsel.

    ___ Other ADR to be selected by Judge Ludwig.

Comments, if any:

2. After deposition discovery, which ADR process do you prefer? Please rank the first two—1 and 2—and submit your comments, if any, below.

    ___ Mediation using court's present system.

    ___ Mediation in which counsel select mediator.

    ___ Meeting with Judge Ludwig.

    ___ Meeting with Magistrate Judge Caracappa.

___ Meeting with other judicial officer selected by counsel.

___ Summary hearing (one hour) before Judge Ludwig.

___ Summary hearing before three attorneys.

___ Mini-Trial with six jurors.

___ Other ADR to be selected by counsel.

___ Other ADR to be selected by Judge Ludwig.

Comments, if any:

3. Can all discovery be completed within 90–120 days after the first Rule 16 Conference?

   Yes   No   (circle)

   If No, state estimated total number of depositions. _____

   (If necessary, give range)

4. Are Rule 12 or other threshold motions pending or contemplated?

   Yes   No   (circle)

   If Yes, please identify by title, date filed or to be filed.

5. If an IME is to be done, has the exam, or exams, been scheduled?

   Yes   No   (circle)

   If not, give reason:

6. Will a dispositive motion or motions be filed?

   Yes   No   (circle) (identify movant(s))

7. Estimate of trial time.

   Plaintiff(s) case: _____

   Defendant(s) case: _____

8. (This question may be answered *ex parte* by a separate, confidential submission before Rule 16 conference.)

   What do you project will be the total cost to your principal to prepare this case and to take it through trial?

   ___ $ 10,000 to $ 25,000   (If representation is on a contingency
   ___ $ 25,000 to $ 75,000   or non-billable basis, total time and
   ___ $ 75,000 to $ 150,000   expenses should be projected on a
   ___ $ 150,000 to $ 500,000   separate page.)
   ___ Excess of $ 500,000

9. What is settlement demand?* _____

(Include any non-monetary issues)

   What is settlement offer? _____

---

* Ordinarily, demand should be made before Rule 16 conference.

10. At this point, do counsel know of any reason why they cannot cooperate with each other in bringing this case to resolution either by settlement or trial?

        Yes   No   (circle)

If Yes, please explain.

Date of submission of this form _____.

Plaintiff attorney(s)*   Defendant attorney(s)*

_____

Name of attorney filling out this form   Name of attorney filling out this form

_____

Name of trial counsel   Name of trial counsel

_____

Name of law firm   Name of law firm

_____

Mailing address   Mailing address

_____

Telephone number   Telephone number

_____

Fax number   Fax number

---

*   If there is more than one representation of plaintiffs or defendants, additional sheets should be submitted identifying counsel and parties represented.

Judge Edmund V. Ludwig

SO _____

RULE 16 TRIAL SCHEDULING ORDER

C.A. No. _____ Filed: _____   Jury _____   Non-jury _____

IN THE UNITED STATES DISTRICT COURT
FOR THE EASTERN DISTRICT OF PENNSYLVANIA

Trial Counsel:

_____

_____

v.

_____

_____

ORDER

It is ORDERED:

1. Discovery deadline: _____, 20___

2. Exchange of experts reports: Plaintiff   _____, 20___

                                                       Defendant   _____, 20___

3. Pretrial Order signed by all counsel.
(See Standing Order on pretrial
preparation—on back of this page.)   _____, 20___

4. Trial date: _____, 20___

                                                                                               Monday list no. _____

Note: A special listing entered after this Order will not be recognized.

- Contact courtroom deputy for instructions before filing a discovery motion as to a discovery dispute. (267) 299-7589. If total default, file under Local Rule 26.1(g) for immediate order.

- No final pretrial conference unless requested.

- Trial depositions no later than 10 days before trial date unless by agreement or Court approval.

- See Scheduling Policy Statement.

- Summary judgment motions must be received by the Court and nonmovants at least 30 days before trial date unless otherwise permitted.

By _____, 20___, plaintiff will report in writing on counsels' serious settlement efforts. Any party may request another conference.

Date: _____   _____

                                                           Edmund V. Ludwig, J.

ARBITRATION
SCHEDULING ORDER

C.A. No.: _____   Filed: _____   Jury: _____   Non-jury: _____

IN THE UNITED STATES DISTRICT COURT
FOR THE EASTERN DISTRICT OF PENNSYLVANIA

Trial Counsel:

v.

ORDER

It is ORDERED:

Arbitrate during week of _____, 20___. No continuance without order.

- Contact courtroom deputy for instructions before filing a discovery motion as to a discovery dispute. (267) 299-7589. If total default, file under Local Rule 26.1(g) for immediate order.

- See Scheduling Policy Statement.

- Trial depositions no later than 10 days before trial date unless by agreement or court approval.

- Summary judgment motions must be received by the court and nonmovants at least 30 days before arbitration date unless otherwise permitted.

By _____, 20___, plaintiff will report in writing on serious settlement efforts. Any party may request another conference.

[If arbitration decision is appealed, a Pretrial Stipulation signed by all counsel must be submitted 10 days before the trial date. (See Standing Order on pretrial preparation - on back of this page.)]

Edmund V. Ludwig, J.

Date: _____

**Pretrial Preparation SOP
for Trials Before
Judge Ludwig**

In lieu of pretrial memoranda or a Final Pretrial Order, under Local Rules 16.1(d) (2), a Pretrial Stipulation shall be submitted, containing the following:

1. Agreed facts. A conscientious effort should be made to narrow the areas of dispute.
2. Each party's disputed facts.
3. Each party's witnesses and the subject matter of the witness's testimony.
4. Each party's exhibits, as marked for trial.
   - Any objections to authenticity should be noted or will be considered waived.
5. Unusual issues - contentions and authority.
6. Brief description of any motions *in limine* - and nonmovant's position.
7. The signed approval of trial counsel for each party.

Plaintiff's counsel should circulate initial draft at least one week before date due.

To be submitted by first day of jury trial:

- Requests for jury instructions.
- Proposed jury verdict form ("special interrogatories"—contact courtroom deputy for format).

By first day of nonjury trial:

- Requests for findings and conclusions.

Judge Ludwig

SOP on Oral Argument
Judge Ludwig

1. Each party shall have 15 minutes to present argument unless more time is allocated. A portion of time may be reserved for rebuttal.

2. The parties shall submit a joint summary of the issues and their arguments at least three (3) days before the argument date. Ordinarily, a summary of the issues and of each party's argument should be set forth on a separate page.

Judge Edmund V. Ludwig

Judge Edmund V. Ludwig

IN THE UNITED STATES DISTRICT COURT
FOR THE EASTERN DISTRICT OF PENNSYLVANIA

: Civil Action
:
:
:
: No.

Joint Discovery Schedule

The following schedule of discovery is submitted pursuant to Scheduling Order of _____, 20___.

1. Counsel are to reserve specific dates for depositions. Names of deponents are unnecessary. (Dates may be substituted by agreement as long as same number are utilized within same time period.)

   Deposition dates:

2. If interrogatories or requests are outstanding, give date(s) when answers will be provided or documents produced. not yet served, deadline dates for service and for compliance should be shown.

   Other discovery dates:

Check one:

____ No motion for summary judgment is contemplated.

____ Summary judgment may be moved for by _____.

(fill in party or parties)

Date: _____ _____
signed by counsel for plaintiff after consultation with all counsel

---

ORDER - Fed.R.Civ. P. 16(b)

Approved and so ordered: _____ _____, 20___

Edmund V. Ludwig, J.

Next Rule 16 Conference: _____, 20___ _____ m.

Note: This action will be listed for trial based on this and any future discovery schedule. If a schedule is not followed, action may be listed for trial as though there had been compliance. *Also see* Fed.R.Civ.P. 16(f) Sanctions.

IN THE UNITED STATES DISTRICT COURT
FOR THE EASTERN DISTRICT OF PENNSYLVANIA

Judge Ludwig

**Motion for Order to Compel in Discovery Disputes
<u>Format for Joint Submission</u>**

A joint statement of the dispute should be submitted either as part of or accompanying the motion to compel. The format of the statement should be as follows:

1. As to each discovery item in dispute: The interrogatory or document request, the applicable answer or response, or objection, and the respective positions of the parties should be set forth in that sequence and, if possible, on a single page. Case citations and other authority should be included. (This joint briefing obviates the need for separate briefs.)

2. Unless items in dispute can be consolidated because they involve the same issue and contentions, each item in dispute should begin with a new page.

3. The joint statement should be drafted initially by the movant and circulated to the nonmovant(s) for completion.

4. The statement should be signed by all counsel involved in the dispute.

If there is any question, please be in touch with the assigned law clerk.

Judge Edmund V. Ludwig

Judge Mary A. McLaughlin

Judge McLaughlin was born in 1946 in Philadelphia, Pennsylvania. She received a B.A. from Gwynedd-Mercy College in 1968, an M.A. from Bryn Mawr College in 1969, and a J.D. from the University of Pennsylvania in 1976. Judge McLaughlin served as law clerk to the Honorable Stanley Brotman, United States District Court for the District of New Jersey, from 1976 to 1977. She was in private practice from 1977 to 1980, and again from 1986 to 2000. Judge McLaughlin served as an assistant United States attorney in the District of Columbia from 1980 to 1984. She worked as an assistant professor at Vanderbilt University Law School from 1984 to 1986. In 1995, Judge McLaughlin served as chief counsel for the Subcommittee on Terrorism, Technology, and Government, Committee on Judiciary, to the United States Senate. She was appointed to the United States District Court for the Eastern District of Pennsylvania on May 31, 2000.

PRELIMINARY GENERAL MATTERS

1. **Correspondence with the Court.** Counsel may write to Judge McLaughlin to request an extension of time and for all matters pertaining to scheduling. Judge McLaughlin does not permit correspondence in lieu of formal discovery or contested motions or other substantive matters that should be made of record. Correspondence may be faxed to Judge McLaughlin at 267-299-5071. (Maximum 25 pages by fax, otherwise by mail or hand delivery.)

2. **Communications with Law Clerks.** Judge McLaughlin permits counsel to speak with her law clerks about administrative or scheduling matters.

3. **Telephone Conferences.** Judge McLaughlin will use telephone conferences for scheduling changes, extensions of time, and similar matters. She often has conference calls on discovery motions, and requests that counsel or a conference call operator place the call.

4. **Oral Arguments and Evidentiary Hearings.** Judge McLaughlin does not set aside specific days or times for oral arguments or evidentiary hearings. Arguments and hearings are scheduled on an ad hoc basis.

5. **Pro Hac Vice Admissions.** Judge McLaughlin expects motions for pro hac vice admissions to be submitted in writing using the forms found on the court's website at www.paed.uscourts.gov by clicking on the "Documents" file and "Forms" tab. Judge McLaughlin requires the attorney seeking such admission to submit the signed affidavit or certification stating that he or she is a member in good standing of the bar of another state.

6. **Orders.** In order to avoid confusion, when counsel receives an e-mail notification of a court order filed in the case, counsel is directed to open the order on the docket and review the contents of the order. At times, the docket's description of an order is inaccurate.

CIVIL CASES
Pretrial Procedure

1. **Pretrial Conferences.** After the entry of appearance by defense counsel in civil actions, Judge McLaughlin schedules a Rule 16 conference on the telephone. Counsel for the plaintiff or a conference call operator will be required to initiate the call. At this status conference, counsel are expected to be prepared to discuss jurisdictional defects; possibility of amicable settlement; alternative dispute resolution; time limitations for joining additional parties and amending pleadings, if necessary; scheduling for discovery deadlines, filing of

motions, filing of pretrial memoranda, and future pretrial conferences; scheduling a date for trial; and any other appropriate matter. Judge McLaughlin enters a scheduling order following this conference.

Prior to attending this conference, parties are expected to have conferred with each other about each of these items, including discussion of settlement.

Continuances and Extensions

1. General Policy. Since trial dates are set well in advance, normally at the time of the initial conference, Judge McLaughlin is extremely reluctant to grant continuances, especially if the attorneys have not been diligent in moving the case forward. The court will not accept accommodations counsel may extend to each other during the discovery period as a reason to extend the discovery deadline or the trial date.

Judge McLaughlin will permit extension of discovery deadlines only upon showing of good cause.

General Motion Practice

1. General Policy. Except as set forth herein, motion practice will be conducted in accordance with Local Civil Rule 7.1. *Every factual assertion in a brief should be supported by a citation to the record where that fact may be found.* Both legal citations and citations to the record must include pinpoint cites.

2. Chambers Copies of Motion Papers. *A copy of all motions and briefs must be delivered to Judge McLaughlin,* either by mail, hand delivery to the clerk's office, or fax at 267-299-5071. Motions and briefs may be faxed only if they are 25 pages or less (including exhibits). There is no page limit for materials that are not faxed. Motions and briefs not faxed are to be bound, stapled, or in a binder; motions and briefs with more than two exhibits are to be tabbed.

3. Reply and Surreply Briefs. A reply brief, addressing arguments raised in the brief in opposition to the motion, may be filed and served by the moving party *within seven calendar days* after service of the brief in opposition to the motion unless the court sets a different schedule. However, the court will not necessarily delay its decision while awaiting a reply brief. Except with leave of court for good cause shown, no reply brief should exceed 15 pages.

No further briefs may be filed, and no extension of time will be granted without leave of court for good cause shown.

4. Motions for Summary Judgment. All summary judgment motions and oppositions to such motions must contain a recitation of facts with citation to the record. The court will not consider any description of a fact that is not supported by a citation to the record. A party opposing summary judgment must state whether it agrees or disagrees with each fact the moving party lists as undisputed. The opposing party must explain why the fact is in dispute with citations to the record. If a party contends that a fact is in dispute, it must cite to the record evidence that supports the party's view of that particular fact.

5. Oral Arguments and Evidentiary Hearings. Judge McLaughlin will hear oral argument on motions, if she believes it will assist her in deciding the motion. Counsel may request to be heard on a motion, and this request will be considered.

Discovery Matters

1. Length of Discovery Period and Extensions. The length of time permitted for discovery depends upon the nature of each case. Judge McLaughlin generally permits up to six months of discovery, except for more complex litigation.

2. Discovery Disputes. When a discovery dispute arises, counsel are strongly urged to settle it among themselves. However, if after making a good-faith effort, counsel are unable to resolve a disputed issue, counsel for the aggrieved party should file with the court a motion in conformity with Local Civil Rule 26.1(b), with a form of order, and a *short brief not to exceed five pages* describing the disputed issue(s). The court will normally schedule a telephone conference with counsel to discuss the motion before the filing of any responsive brief. In most cases, the court expects to rule promptly on discovery motions and often decides such motions during the telephone conference. *All motions must contain the certification required under Local Civil Rule 26.1(f).*

3. Confidentiality Agreements. Judge McLaughlin will approve a confidentiality order if the order includes a detailed statement demonstrating that good cause exists for the protective order. See *Pansy v. Borough of Stroudsburg*, 23 F.3d 772, 786 (3d Cir. 1994). All such orders must contain the following language or language substantially similar:

> The court retains the right to allow disclosure of any subject covered by this stipulation or to modify this stipulation at any time in the interest of justice.

4. Expert Witnesses. Parties should identify expert witnesses and provide the experts' written reports pursuant to the scheduling order entered in the particular case. Failure to do so may bar the use of the expert's testimony at trial.

Settlement

Judge McLaughlin usually will refer settlement conferences to a magistrate judge.

Arbitration

In arbitration cases, Judge McLaughlin normally does not schedule a status conference or settlement conference unless requested by counsel to do so. Appeals from arbitration are scheduled for trial promptly.

Proposed Final Pretrial Memoranda

Unless otherwise specified, Judge McLaughlin requires the parties to submit short pretrial memoranda pursuant to Local Rule 16.1(c). Judge McLaughlin requires the submission of voir dire questions, proposed jury instructions, proposed verdict sheets, and motions in limine. In nonjury cases, she requires submission of proposed findings of fact and conclusions of law.

In preparation for a final pretrial conference, Judge McLaughlin expects counsel to communicate with each other on a number of matters, including objections to exhibits, expert depositions, and stipulations of fact.

Injunctions

1. Scheduling and Expedited Discovery. When a temporary restraining order (TRO) is requested, Judge McLaughlin will immediately schedule a conference as soon as possible to decide the TRO. She requires all counsel to be present unless the urgency of the circumstances precludes notice to opposing counsel. Judge McLaughlin rarely grants ex parte temporary restraining orders.

Judge McLaughlin schedules preliminary and permanent injunction hearings as soon as possible and combines the two hearings if feasible. Usually, she permits expedited discovery for injunctive matters.

2. Proposed Findings of Fact and Conclusions of Law. Judge McLaughlin requires the submission of findings of fact and conclusions of law in injunction cases, in accordance with Fed.R.Civ.P. 52(a).

Trial Procedure

1. Scheduling of Cases. Each case on Judge McLaughlin's calendar is assigned a specific trial date. The court may start as early as 9:00 a.m. and may sit until 5:00 p.m. or later.

2. Conflicts of Counsel. When counsel become aware of professional or personal conflicts that may affect the trial schedule, they should notify Judge McLaughlin and opposing counsel immediately.

3. Cases Involving Out-of-Town Parties or Witnesses. Judge McLaughlin has no special policy for cases involving out-of-town attorneys, parties, or witnesses.

4. Note-taking by Jurors. Judge McLaughlin allows jurors to take notes.

5. Trial Briefs. Judge McLaughlin encourages the submission of trial briefs when they are necessary or likely to be helpful to the court.

6. Voir Dire. Judge McLaughlin's usual practice in civil matters is to conduct the voir dire.

7. Sidebars. Judge McLaughlin holds sidebar conferences when necessary.

8. In Limine Motions. Judge McLaughlin normally hears any in limine motions during the final pretrial conference. She prefers such motions to be in writing and filed sufficiently in advance of trial so that she can consider the motion and make an appropriate ruling.

9. Examination of Witnesses Out of Sequence. Judge McLaughlin is willing to take witnesses out of turn for their convenience, particularly when there is no objection by opposing counsel.

10. Opening Statements and Summations. Judge McLaughlin is flexible with regard to time limits on opening statements and summations. She usually will discuss the time needed with counsel prior to the speeches.

11. Examination of Witnesses or Argument by More Than One Attorney. Judge McLaughlin will not permit more than one attorney for a party to examine the same witness.

12. Examination of Witnesses Beyond Redirect and Recross. Judge McLaughlin does not have any general policy concerning examination beyond redirect and recross.

13. Videotaped Testimony. Judge McLaughlin requires counsel to view all videotaped depositions for the purpose of editing the videotape and resolving material objections before offering the videotape as evidence.

14. Reading of Material Into the Record. Judge McLaughlin has no special practice on reading stipulations, pleadings, or discovery materials into the record.

15. Preparation of Exhibits. Before commencement of trial, exhibits are to be premarked and exchanged by counsel. Counsel should provide Judge McLaughlin with two copies of each exhibit and a schedule of exhibits that briefly describes each exhibit.

16. Offering Exhibits Into Evidence. Judge McLaughlin has no general policy as to when exhibits should be offered into evidence. When the number of exhibits in a case is large, Judge McLaughlin prefers counsel to reach advance agreement as to the admission of as many exhibits as possible.

17. Directed Verdict Motions. Judge McLaughlin hears directed verdict motions outside the hearing of the jury.

18. Proposed Jury Instructions and Verdict Forms. Judge McLaughlin's usual practice is that at least five working days before the case is listed for trial, each party must submit to the court, and serve on each other, two copies of proposed points for charge and any proposed special jury interrogatories, along with a disk containing the documents. Each point for charge and proposed jury interrogatory must be numbered and on a separate sheet of paper identifying the name of the requesting party. Supplemental points for charge will be permitted during and at the conclusion of the trial. Points for charge should be accompanied by appropriate citations of legal authority. Judge McLaughlin will use the Model Civil Jury Instructions for the Third Circuit, where applicable (they can be accessed at http://www.paed.uscourts.gov by clicking on the "Third Circuit Model Jury Instructions" bullet under "Miscellaneous").

19. Proposed Findings of Fact and Conclusions of Law. Judge McLaughlin may require the submission of proposed findings of fact and conclusions of law in nonjury cases.

20. Decisions in Nonjury Cases. Counsel should be prepared for oral argument immediately following the close of all the evidence in a nonjury trial.

Jury Deliberations

1. Written Jury Instructions. Judge McLaughlin provides counsel with a copy of proposed jury instructions for review in advance of a charge conference. Judge McLaughlin permits counsel to put objections to the charge on the record before the jury retires. Judge McLaughlin usually gives the jury a copy of her instructions.

2. Exhibits in the Jury Room. Counsel are instructed to confer on which exhibits should go into the jury room. Judge McLaughlin will rule upon any dispute.

3. Availability of Counsel During Jury Deliberations. Judge McLaughlin prefers counsel to remain in the courthouse during jury deliberations. Counsel should be available in case questions arise from the jury during its deliberation.

4. Taking the Verdict and Special Interrogatories. In most civil cases, Judge McLaughlin submits written interrogatories to the jury. A copy of such interrogatories is given to each juror.

5. Polling the Jury. If there is a request to poll the jury, the court will poll the jury.

6. Interviewing the Jury. Judge McLaughlin permits counsel to interview the jurors after the verdict has been recorded and the jury has been discharged. However, jurors are told they are under no obligation to speak with counsel.

CRIMINAL CASES

1. Approach to Oral Argument and Motions. Judge McLaughlin will grant oral argument on motions in criminal cases. Hearings on motions to suppress evidence and *Starks* hearings will usually be held in advance of trial.

2. Pretrial Conferences. Judge McLaughlin holds pretrial conferences in criminal cases as needed.

3.   *Voir Dire.* Judge McLaughlin conducts the voir dire in criminal cases, and she encourages counsel to submit proposed voir dire questions.

4.   *Pretrial Filings.* Judge McLaughlin requires that at least three working days before the date the case is set for trial, each party must submit to the court and serve on each other, two copies of proposed points for charge and a proposed verdict form, along with a disk containing the documents. Each point for charge must be numbered and on a separate sheet of paper identifying the name of the requesting party. Supplemental points for charge will be permitted during and at the conclusion of the trial. Points for charge should be accompanied by appropriate citations of legal authority.

The government should also deliver to Judge McLaughlin's chambers on that date a trial memorandum. At minimum, this memorandum must specify the essential elements of the crime charged, discuss any anticipated evidentiary issues, and contain a witness list. Any defense response to the government's trial memorandum should be delivered to Judge McLaughlin's chambers on the date of the commencement of trial.

The government must file any motion to admit evidence under F.R.E. 404(b) at least 10 days before trial.

A form of verdict slip, agreed upon by all parties, must be delivered to Judge McLaughlin's chambers on the date of the commencement of trial.

5.   *Guilty Plea Memoranda.* Judge McLaughlin requires the government to submit a guilty plea memorandum two days prior to the guilty plea. The memorandum must include the elements of each offense to which the defendant is pleading guilty and legal citations for such elements.

6.   *Sentencing Memoranda.* Judge McLaughlin encourages the submission of sentencing memoranda by both the government and the defendant.

OTHER GENERAL MATTERS

Judge McLaughlin expects counsel to be punctual for all conferences, hearings, and trials. She also expects counsel at all times to be civil to one another as well as to all parties, witnesses, and court personnel.

In all courtroom proceedings, Judge McLaughlin expects counsel to stand when addressing the court or when examining witnesses. Counsel also may approach the witnesses with permission of the court.

In general, Judge McLaughlin expects counsel to bring matters to her attention only after they have been discussed with opposing counsel.

Judge McLaughlin's Courtroom Procedures

1. Counsel should stand whenever speaking, that is, counsel should stand when addressing the Court, the jury, or the witness.

2. Counsel may stand anywhere he or she chooses when questioning the witness or talking to the jury, except that counsel should not crowd the witness or the jury.

3. If counsel wishes to approach the witness, counsel should ask for permission to do so. "Your Honor, may I approach the witness." If counsel needs to approach one witness many times, the Court will at some point tell the lawyer that the lawyer need not continue to ask. When counsel approaches the witness, he or she should accomplish the reason for approaching and then return to the place from which he or she is questioning.

4. If counsel wishes to make an objection, he or she should stand and say objection, Your Honor. Counsel may give the basis for the objection in a word or phrase, like "hearsay." Counsel may not make a speech. If counsel wishes to have a sidebar, the Court will usually grant the request if counsel does not ask for too many sidebars. Counsel is encouraged to bring any evidentiary questions to the attention of the Court outside the presence of the jury.

5. All counsel, but especially prosecutors, are reminded that redirect is still direct examination, and not cross.

6. Counsel has the responsibility to advise their witnesses that no witness, especially government witnesses in a criminal case, should talk to the jury at any time. For example, if the witness has stepped down from the witness stand to testify from an exhibit, the witness should not have any private conversation whatsoever with any juror. The witness may, of course, direct his or her answers to the jury's direction but the witness is still answering the lawyer's questions.

7. In opening or closing statements, no lawyer, especially criminal prosecutors, may call a witness, especially a criminal defendant, a "liar" or say that the witness "lied." Such conclusions are for the jury to make. Using such language is giving your opinion and inflammatory. Similarly, lawyers are not to give their own opinions during opening or closing statements. For example, you should not say "I believe," or "I think."

8. The Court will always have a clerk in the courtroom during a jury trial who will give the jurors any exhibits or other items that counsel requests be given to them. Counsel should not walk up to the jury and start handing them things out. Nor should counsel ask the jurors if they can see or hear something. If counsel is concerned, he or she should say something like: "Your Honor, would the Court ask if the jury can see or hear."

9. Judge McLaughlin considers a jury trial a very formal affair and asks all counsel to act accordingly. Coats, coffee cups, water bottles should not be left within sight of the jury. Boxes of exhibits or briefcases should not be on counsel table.

10. Opposing counsel should never talk to each other in front of the jury, without the Court's permission. The Court will allow counsel to have a private conversation if requested and if it will move things along. Lawyers should never talk to each other in front of the jury. Lawyers absolutely should not argue with either opposing counsel or the Court.

Judge McLaughlin's Procedures for Voir Dire in a Civil Case

The Court will conduct the voir dire with input from counsel for the plaintiff and the defendant. The panel of approximately 25–40 prospective jurors will enter the courtroom and sit according to the number that appears next to their names on the printout from the jury office. This number is different from their "juror number." They will sit according to their order number—the number that reflects the order in which they were selected downstairs in the jury room. The order numbers are 1 to 25–40. They will then be asked to give their order number as they stand to respond to questions. This will allow the lawyers to keep track more easily of the prospective jurors' responses.

The Court will explain the purpose of voir dire and then begin questioning. The Court will ask questions in a way that calls for panel members to raise their hand only if their answer to the question is yes. For example, "is there anyone who for any reason thinks that they could not be fair and impartial if he or she sat as a juror in this case." I will tell the panel that if the answer to this question is yes, they should raise their hand and, when called on, state their juror number and nothing else. I will then follow up privately with that panel member.

With some questions, I will follow up on the prospective juror's answer in open court. For example, "is there anyone who has had any legal training." If a panel member raises his or her hand to say yes, I will follow up with questions about the prior legal training.

After asking the questions to the full panel, the Court will go to sidebar with counsel for follow-up as necessary. The Court will ask the questions but will ask the lawyers if they would like the Court to do any follow-up. The lawyers will not talk directly to the panel member. If any party wants to request a strike for cause, he or she should do so right after the panel member leaves the sidebar, rather than waiting until all the panel members have been questioned.

After any individual questioning is complete, the peremptory challenges begin. A panel of 14 is needed for 8 jurors. The deputy clerk will give to plaintiff's counsel the list of jurors from which the peremptory challenges will be taken. Plaintiff takes the first strike and will pass the list to defense counsel until both parties have taken their 3 peremptory challenges.

The jurors selected will then be called to the jury box by the deputy clerk. After they are all seated, the Court will ask counsel if the jurors in the box are the ones they selected, meaning only did the deputy clerk call the correct jurors into the box. Any previous objections that have been made to any decisions by the Court will be preserved.

Judge McLaughlin's Procedures for Voir Dire in a Criminal Case

The Court will conduct the voir dire with input from counsel for the government and the defendant. The panel of approximately 50–60 prospective jurors will enter the courtroom and sit according to the number that appears next to their names on the printout from the jury office. This number is different from their "juror number." They will sit according to their order number—the number that reflects the order in which they were selected downstairs in the jury room. The order numbers are 1 to 50–60. They will then be asked to give their order number as they stand to respond to questions. This will allow the lawyers to keep track more easily of the prospective jurors' responses.

The Court will explain the purpose of voir dire and then begin questioning. The Court will ask questions in a way that calls for panel members to raise their hand only if their answer to the question is yes. For example, "is there anyone who for any reason thinks that they could not be fair and impartial if he or she sat as a juror in this case." I will tell the panel that if the answer to this question is yes, they should raise their hand and, when called on, state their juror number and nothing else. I will then follow up privately with that panel member.

With some questions, I will follow up on the prospective juror's answer in open court. For example, "is there anyone who is, or has ever been, or has a close friend or family member, who is a member of any law enforcement agency." If a panel member raises his or her hand to say yes, I will follow up with questions about the relationship and what law enforcement agency is involved.

After asking the questions to the full panel, the Court will go into the jury room with the parties and counsel for follow-up as necessary. In the jury room, the Court will ask the questions but will ask the lawyers if they would like the Court to do any follow-up. The lawyers will not talk directly to the panel member. If any party wants to request a strike for cause, he or she should do so right after the panel member leaves the jury room, rather than waiting until all the panel members have been questioned.

Under Fed. R. Crim. Pro. 24(b), the government gets 6 peremptory challenges in a felony case and the defendant gets 10. If we seat two alternates, as I usually do, each side gets 1 additional peremptory (Rule 24(c)(4)).

After any individual questioning is complete, the peremptory challenges begin. A panel of 32 is needed for 12 jurors and two alternates. The deputy clerk will give to the prosecutor the list of jurors from which the peremptory challenges for the first 12 will be taken. The order of taking the challenges is as follows:

Government	Defendant
1	2
1	2
1	2
1	2
1	2
1	

The government gets the first and last strike.

Counsel will then take the peremptory challenge(s) for the alternates. If there are two alternates, and therefore one peremptory for each side, the defendant takes the first strike and then the government.

The jurors selected will then be called to the jury box by the deputy clerk. After they are all seated, the Court will ask counsel if the jurors in the box are the ones they selected, meaning only did the deputy clerk call the correct jurors into the box. Any previous objections that have been made to any decisions by the Court will be preserved.

Judge Thomas N. O'Neill, Jr.

Judge O'Neill was born on July 6, 1928, in Hanover, Pennsylvania. He received an A.B. from Catholic University of America in 1950 and an LL.B. from the University of Pennsylvania in 1953. Judge O'Neill served as a law clerk to Judge Herbert F. Goodrich of the United States Court of Appeals for the Third Circuit from 1953 to 1954 and as law clerk to Justice Harold H. Burton during the October 1954 term of the United States Supreme Court. From 1955 to 1956, Judge O'Neill was a Fulbright Scholar at the London School of Economics. Judge O'Neill was in private practice in Philadelphia, Pennsylvania, from 1956 until 1983. He was chancellor of the Philadelphia Bar Association in 1976. He is a Fellow of the American College of Trial Lawyers. He was appointed to the United States District Court for the Eastern District of Pennsylvania on August 30, 1983. Judge O'Neill assumed senior status on July 6, 1996.

PRELIMINARY GENERAL MATTERS

1.   Correspondence with the Court. Judge O'Neill permits correspondence for scheduling and extensions of time, but ordinarily not in lieu of discovery motions. All correspondence directed to the court should include the action number of the case, and a copy of such correspondence should be served upon opposing counsel.

2.   Communications with Law Clerks. Judge O'Neill permits counsel to speak with his law clerks with respect to ministerial matters such as scheduling. They are not, however, permitted to give legal advice or to explain the reasons for the court's rulings.

3.   Telephone Conferences. When appropriate, Judge O'Neill will entertain telephone conferences for matters such as pretrial conferences, scheduling changes, and extensions of time. Ordinarily, the first conference in a case should take place in chambers.

4.   Oral Arguments and Evidentiary Hearings. Judge O'Neill does not set aside certain days or times for oral arguments or evidentiary hearings.

5.   Pro Hac Vice Admissions. Judge O'Neill has no preference as to how counsel present requests for pro hac vice admissions.

6.   Requests for Default and Default Judgment. Judge O'Neill requires that all requests for default and default judgment be served upon the parties that are in default.

7.   Motions to Dismiss Pro Se Complaints. If a pro se plaintiff does not respond to a motion to dismiss within the response time prescribed by Local Rule 7.1(c), Judge O'Neill will enter an order granting the plaintiff an additional 30 days within which to respond. Should the plaintiff not respond to the motion within the additional time, Judge O'Neill will dismiss the action without prejudice.

CIVIL CASES
Pretrial Procedure

1.   Pretrial Conferences. Judge O'Neill normally conducts an initial pretrial conference 60 days after the filing of the complaint. (In FELA cases, the conference usually is done by telephone.) A copy of the form of order used by Judge O'Neill to schedule such conferences is shown on page 180 of this book. Judge O'Neill also will conduct status conferences and final pretrial conferences as needed or as requested in a particular case. He will not hold a settlement conference until after the parties have engaged in extensive negotiations, and prefers to schedule a conference only if all counsel agree that a conference may be helpful.

Judge O'Neill does not follow a standard agenda for pretrial conferences. A copy of the standard form of order normally issued by Judge O'Neill following the initial pretrial conference is shown on page 181 of this book.

Continuances and Extensions

1.   General Policy. When possible, Judge O'Neill tries to accommodate counsel with regard to the scheduling of briefing, oral arguments, evidentiary hearings, discovery deadlines, trial dates, and requests for continuances or extensions.

If counsel have agreed to a continuance or an extension (other than that of a trial date), they should so inform Judge O'Neill by letter, which should state that all parties agree to the extension, the reasons for the extension, and the reasonable amount of additional time to which counsel have agreed. Approval of such an agreement usually follows, but is not automatic.

2.   Requests for Extensions and Continuances. Judge O'Neill does not have any particular requirement as to how far in advance of a due date counsel should submit a request for an extension of time. However, a request for extension of a trial date that is submitted on the eve of trial usually is not favorably considered.

General Motion Practice

1.   Oral Argument on Motions. Judge O'Neill will grant oral argument on a motion only if he believes it will assist him in deciding the motion.

2.   Reply and Surreply Briefs. Judge O'Neill has no formal policy on reply or surreply briefs. Such briefs should be concise, and counsel should evaluate carefully whether a reply or surreply brief is necessary. Decision of the motion will not be delayed for the receipt of such briefs.

3.   Chambers Copies of Motion Papers. Judge O'Neill prefers that courtesy copies of motion papers be sent to his chambers.

4.   Appendices or Exhibits to Briefs or Motions. For briefs or motions submitted to Judge O'Neill, counsel should affix tabs to each appendix or exhibit.

Discovery Matters

1.   Length of Discovery Period and Extensions. Except in complex cases, Judge O'Neill sets relatively short discovery deadlines—usually 60 or 90 days after the initial pretrial conference. He then extends the discovery deadline in individual cases if it becomes necessary.

Judge O'Neill permits counsel to engage in discovery past the deadline if the additional discovery does not delay the trial.

2.   Discovery Conferences and Dispute Resolution. Judge O'Neill expects parties to resolve most discovery disputes without coming to him, and he usually holds discovery conferences only if requested. Judge O'Neill will permit telephone conferences to resolve discovery disputes that arise during a deposition, but if too many disputes arise during a particular deposition or case, he will stop accepting the telephone calls. If a discovery motion is filed, Judge O'Neill expects the parties to brief the relevance of the information sought and the validity of the asserted objection.

3.   Confidentiality Agreements. Requested confidentiality agreements should be submitted to Judge O'Neill and will be reviewed pursuant to the *Leucadia* and *Pansy* cases, 998 F.2d 157 (3d Cir. 1993), and 23 F.3d 772 (3d Cir. 1994).

4. Expert Witnesses. Because counsel normally exchange expert reports, Judge O'Neill usually does not have to direct them to do so. If necessary, he will. Judge O'Neill will permit expert depositions where appropriate. Judge O'Neill expects that counsel will identify expert witnesses sufficiently in advance of trial to permit adequate preparation by all parties. Judge O'Neill will not continue trial because of the unavailability of an expert. He expects that the deposition of an expert who will be unavailable at trial will be videotaped.

Settlement

1. General Approach to Settlement and Nonjury Cases. Judge O'Neill favors judicial involvement in settlement negotiations, but he expects counsel to conduct in-depth negotiations before coming to him. Judge O'Neill refers settlement negotiations to a magistrate judge if the parties request it.

2. Referral of Settlement Negotiations to Another District Court Judge. In nonjury cases, Judge O'Neill normally will refer settlement negotiations to another district court judge or to his magistrate judge. On rare occasions, he will participate in settlement negotiations in a nonjury case if the parties agree. In such instances, Judge O'Neill's involvement normally is limited to cases where only questions of law and no factual disputes are involved. When Judge O'Neill refers a case to another judge, he asks counsel to agree on the identity of the judge to conduct the negotiations.

Arbitration

Judge O'Neill does not use any special practices or procedures for arbitration cases that differ from cases certified as involving more than $150,000, except that he does not conduct an initial pretrial conference in arbitration cases.

Proposed Final Pretrial Memoranda

1. Required Form of Pretrial Memoranda. Unless Judge O'Neill specifies otherwise, he requires the parties to submit only short-form pretrial memoranda. Judge O'Neill requires long-form memoranda only in those few cases in which they are genuinely necessary.

2. Common Deficiencies in Pretrial Memoranda. Judge O'Neill notes that he does not find significant deficiencies in most proposed final pretrial memoranda he receives.

Injunctions

1. Scheduling and Expedited Discovery. Judge O'Neill schedules preliminary and permanent injunction hearings quickly, and he attempts to combine the two hearings where possible. He permits expedited discovery on injunctive matters.

2. Proposed Findings of Fact and Conclusions of Law. Judge O'Neill may not require proposed findings of fact and conclusions of law if the parties waive Rule 52(a) of the Federal Rules of Civil Procedure.

Trial Procedure

1. Scheduling of Cases. Once discovery has been completed, Judge O'Neill will send notices to counsel listing the case for trial.

2. Conflicts of Counsel. Judge O'Neill prefers that counsel notify him by letter about professional and personal conflicts affecting the trial schedule.

Judge Thomas N. O'Neill, Jr.

3. **Cases Involving Out-of-Town Parties or Witnesses.** When possible, Judge O'Neill tries to schedule cases involving out-of-town parties or witnesses for a date certain and to give substantial advance notice of the trial date.

4. **Note-taking by Jurors.** Judge O'Neill permits jurors to take notes.

5. **Trial Briefs.** Judge O'Neill encourages counsel to submit trial briefs.

6. **Voir Dire.** Judge O'Neill permits counsel to conduct all voir dire in civil cases with the deputy clerk present and Judge O'Neill not present. If there is a dispute, counsel go to Judge O'Neill's chambers. He does not generally place a time limit on voir dire, but he prefers that counsel not spend more than one hour on voir dire.

7. **Sidebars.** Judge O'Neill permits sidebar conferences.

8. **In Limine Motions.** If possible, in limine motions should be submitted in advance of trial.

9. **Examination of Witnesses Out of Sequence.** Judge O'Neill will permit counsel to take witnesses out of turn for the convenience of the witnesses or for other good reason.

10. **Opening Statements and Summations.** Counsel are to make their opening statements and summations at the lectern using a microphone. Judge O'Neill encourages brevity in opening statements, and he will cut off counsel if he or she goes on too long. For summations, he also encourages brevity. He usually will discuss with counsel the time they need and try to get agreement on the length of time for summations.

11. **Examination of Witnesses or Argument by More Than One Attorney.** Judge O'Neill will permit more than one attorney to try the case on behalf of a party; however, only one attorney for a party may examine a particular witness. More than one attorney for a party may argue different points in a motion before Judge O'Neill.

12. **Examination of Witnesses Beyond Redirect and Recross.** Judge O'Neill does not have any general policy on further examination of witnesses after redirect and recross have been completed.

13. **Videotaped Testimony.** Ruling on disputes or objections should be sought in advance through submission to Judge O'Neill of a written transcript of the relevant testimony. Counsel should edit the videotape in advance of trial.

14. **Reading of Material Into the Record.** Judge O'Neill does not have any special practice or policy on reading stipulations, pleadings, or discovery materials into the record. He encourages counsel to stipulate to as many facts as possible.

15. **Preparation of Exhibits.** Judge O'Neill requires that exhibits be pre-marked and pre-exchanged. Counsel should provide one copy of the marked exhibits to him, except for exhibits that are voluminous or difficult to reproduce.

16. **Offering Exhibits Into Evidence.** Judge O'Neill does not have a general policy regarding the offering of exhibits into evidence.

17. **Directed Verdict Motions.** Judge O'Neill usually conducts a short oral argument on directed verdict motions and Rule 41(b) motions to dismiss nonjury trials. He has no preference as to whether such motions are written or oral.

18. **Proposed Jury Instructions and Verdict Forms.** Counsel should submit comprehensive proposed jury instructions in advance of trial as provided in the form order shown on page 181 of this book. Counsel need not, however, submit charges on standard matters unless specifically directed to do so. Each proposed instruction should be on a separate sheet of paper and double-spaced. Cases and pattern jury instructions that are cited should be

quoted accurately and without change, and specific page references should be given. Judge O'Neill conducts a conference on proposed jury instructions and will accept supplemental proposed jury instructions until the case goes to the jury.

19. Proposed Findings of Fact and Conclusions of Law. Judge O'Neill usually requires proposed findings of fact and conclusions of law in a nonjury case and prefers citations to the evidence to be included. He may not require proposed findings of fact and conclusions of law if the parties waive Rule 52(a) of the Federal Rules of Civil Procedure.

Jury Deliberations

1. Written Jury Instructions. Judge O'Neill ordinarily gives the jury a copy of the charge.

2. Exhibits in the Jury Room. All exhibits (except for weapons, drugs, and the like) usually go out with the jury unless counsel agree otherwise.

3. Handling of Jury Requests to Read Back Testimony or Replay Tapes. If the requested portion of testimony, tape recording, or videotape is available, Judge O'Neill will have it read or played back.

4. Availability of Counsel During Jury Deliberations. Counsel may return to their offices during jury deliberations if their offices are within easy reach of the courthouse.

5. Taking the Verdict and Special Interrogatories. Depending on the nature of the case, Judge O'Neill will take a special or general verdict. He frequently submits interrogatories to the jury in civil cases.

6. Polling the Jury. Judge O'Neill will permit polling of the jury. If counsel request polling of the jury, each juror may refer to the verdict sheet.

7. Interviewing the Jury. Judge O'Neill will permit the jury to be interviewed only after their service in the courthouse has been completed. He instructs the jurors that they are not required to speak to counsel.

CRIMINAL CASES

1. Approach to Oral Argument and Motions. Judge O'Neill will grant oral argument on a motion in a criminal case, but only if he believes it will assist him in deciding the motion.

2. Pretrial Conferences. Judge O'Neill does not hold pretrial conferences in criminal cases as a matter of course, but he will do so if needed.

3. Voir Dire. Judge O'Neill conducts the entire voir dire in criminal cases and he encourages submissions of proposed voir dire questions by counsel.

4. Other Practices and Procedures. Other than those discussed here, Judge O'Neill employs no practices or procedures in criminal cases that differ significantly from those he uses in civil cases. In particular, Judge O'Neill encourages stipulations of fact in all cases.

5. Sentencing Memoranda. Judge O'Neill encourages the submission of sentencing memoranda by both the government and the defendant. He prefers that letters that are in handwriting in the original be typed for submission to him.

OTHER GENERAL MATTERS

1. Appellate Briefs. Judge O'Neill usually does not want to receive copies of the appellate briefs if a decision he renders is appealed.

2. Courtroom Decorum. Judge O'Neill expects counsel to be on time and to be courteous to each other.

3.   ***Ex Parte Temporary Restraining Orders.***   Judge O'Neill is strongly disinclined to grant ex parte temporary restraining orders.

4.   ***Stipulations.***   Stipulations should be sent to Judge O'Neill's chambers for review and not to the clerk. If approved, Judge O'Neill forwards the stipulation to the clerk for filing, and the clerk mails copies to counsel.

5.   ***Consultations with Opposing Counsel.***   In general, Judge O'Neill expects counsel to bring matters to his attention only after they have been discussed with opposing counsel.

NOTICE SCHEDULING AN INITIAL PRETRIAL CONFERENCE

IN THE UNITED STATES DISTRICT COURT
FOR THE EASTERN DISTRICT OF PENNSYLVANIA

NOTICE

A pretrial conference will be held on _____ at ____ a.m. in Chambers, Room 4007.

It is the obligation of counsel for plaintiff to serve a copy of this notice upon counsel for all defendants and upon counsel for any other parties joined prior to the date of the conference, as soon as the identity of such counsel is learned.

(DATE)

_____
Charles J. Ervin,
Deputy Clerk to Judge O'Neill

cc:

Judge Thomas N. O'Neill, Jr.

STANDARD ORDER ISSUED AFTER PRETRIAL CONFERENCE

IN THE UNITED STATES DISTRICT COURT
FOR THE EASTERN DISTRICT OF PENNSYLVANIA

<u>ORDER</u>

AND NOW, this _____, it is hereby ORDERED:

1. Additional parties, if any, must be joined within the time specified in Local Rule 14.1. All discovery, and any other activity within the provisions of Rule 16(b)(1)–(3), is to be completed by _____.

2(a). The party filing a dispositive motion shall include, preferably as a separate document, or, if short, within the memorandum of law, a "statement of undisputed facts", which sets forth, in numbered paragraphs, all material facts that the moving party contends are undisputed, with record references.

(b). The responding party shall include, preferably as a separate document, or, within the memorandum of law, a "statement of disputed or undisputed facts" responding to the numbered paragraphs set forth in the moving party's statement, either admitting that the paragraph is not disputed, or if it is disputed, setting forth those facts contended to be in dispute, with record reference to where the party's contention is supported in the papers filed with the Court on the dispositive motion.

(c). The responding party may also set forth, in additional numbered paragraphs, any additional material facts which the responding party contends preclude the granting of the dispositive motion, with record references.

(d). A reply brief may be filed within seven days following receipt of the responding party's papers, and shall be limited to fifteen pages, and limited to refuting arguments in the responsive brief. The moving party may respond, following the numbered paragraphs, to the responding party's statement concerning factual issues. Surreply briefs are not accepted without leave of the Court.

(e). Statements of material facts in support or in opposition to a dispositive motion shall include specific and not general references to the parts of the record that support each of the statements, such as the title or numbered reference to a document, or the name of a deponent and the page(s) of the deponent's deposition, or the identity of an affidavit or declaration and the specific paragraph relied upon.

(f). Exhibits should be listed in an index and preferably tabbed.

(g). The parties may stipulate to a briefing schedule.

3. Counsel for plaintiff(s) will file a final pretrial memorandum, points for charge, any notices pursuant to Fed. R. Evid. 902(11) and (12), and any dispositive motion(s) by _____. Counsel for defendant(s) will file a final pretrial memorandum, points for charge and any dispositive motion(s) by _____. The defendant(s) points must designate those plaintiff points not objected to.

4. Absent extraordinary circumstances, in its case in chief a party will not be permitted to offer a witness or exhibit not listed in its final pretrial memorandum.

5. Counsel will mark and exchange all exhibits in advance of trial.

6. The testimony of expert witnesses should be videotaped. A trial date will not be continued because of the unavailability of an expert witness.

7. In a jury case, if requested by counsel, the Court or Magistrate Judge Carol Sandra Moore Wells will hold a settlement conference. In non-jury cases, counsel should notify the Court whether a settlement conference before another District Judge or Magistrate Judge Wells is desired.

8. This case will be placed in the trial pool on _____.

_____
THOMAS N. O'NEILL, JR., J.

Judge John R. Padova

Judge Padova was appointed United States District Judge for the Eastern District of Pennsylvania on March 13, 1992, and entered duty on March 31, 1992. On February 11, 2008, Judge Padova assumed senior status. He received his B.A. degree from Villanova University in 1956 and a J.D. degree from Temple Law School in 1959. Judge Padova was in private practice concentrating in civil litigation until his appointment as a district judge.

Judge Padova is a past faculty member of the National Institute for Trial Advocacy and a lecturer at Temple Law School. He is a past member and former vice chairperson of the Disciplinary Board of the Supreme Court of Pennsylvania, having chaired the committee that proposed and introduced the Pennsylvania Rules of Professional Conduct adopted by the Supreme Court of Pennsylvania in 1987. Judge Padova has been certified as a specialist in civil trial advocacy by the National Board of Trial Advocacy. He is a diplomat of the National Board of Trial Advocacy, and past member of the Philadelphia Bar Association's Professional Guidance Committee and Judicial Selection and Evaluation Committee. He has also been a member of the Pennsylvania Chief Justice's Advisory Committee on Comprehensive Education.

From 1999 through 2002, he served as a member of the Advisory Committee on Civil Rules of the Judicial Conference of the United States. Judge Padova is a past chairperson of the Jury Selection Committee for the United States District Court for the Eastern District of Pennsylvania and past co-chairperson of the Third Circuit Death Penalty Task Force.

Presently, Judge Padova is chairperson of the court's Disciplinary Panel.

PRELIMINARY GENERAL MATTERS

1. ***Correspondence with the Court.*** Judge Padova permits correspondence under the following circumstances:
    - a. When letters of transmittal accompany documents required to be sent to, or filed with, the court, or in another official office in the courthouse;
    - b. When counsel are specifically requested by the court to communicate some information to the court by letter;
    - c. When there is a request for a continuance of the preliminary pretrial conference (see paragraph titled "Continuances and Extensions" on page 185);
    - d. When there is an uncontested request for a continuance of the Rule 16 scheduling order deadlines not affecting the trial date or pool placement (see paragraph titled "Continuances and Extensions" on page 185);
    - e. When the participation of counsel in the case is expected to be affected by a personal matter concerning counsel, a party, a witness, or counsel's immediate family, such as medical problems, vacation plans, or other similarly personal problems or questions; or
    - f. To confirm or advise the court that a case has been settled, dismissed, or otherwise finally disposed.

All other communications with the court should be by the filing of pleadings, motions, applications, briefs, or legal memoranda.

2. ***Communications with Law Clerks.*** Judge Padova strongly discourages communication with his law clerks. All telephone inquiries should be directed to one of Judge Padova's deputies.

3. **Electronic Filing System.** Judge Padova requires that all documents be filed electronically through Electronic Case Filing (ECF). ECF provides greater efficiency and timeliness in the filing of pleadings, and electronic storage of documents for remote access by the court, the bar, and the litigants. Applications are available from the Office of the Clerk of the Court, 601 Market Street, Room 2609, Philadelphia, PA 19106-1797; by calling 215-597-5711; or by accessing the court's website at www.paed.uscourts.gov.

4. **Telephone Conferences.** Judge Padova sometimes uses telephone conferences for non-complex pretrial conferences, scheduling, discovery disputes, settlement conferences, and other like matters. Telephone conferences should be arranged through the deputy. Judge Padova expects counsel to bring matters to his attention only after they have been discussed with opposing counsel. All parties must be represented on any telephone conference with Judge Padova.

Counsel have the responsibility to initiate telephone conferences and to contact Judge Padova through his deputy after all other parties are present on the call.

5. **Oral Arguments and Evidentiary Hearings.** Judge Padova does not set aside any certain days or times for oral argument on motions or evidentiary hearings.

6. **Pro Hac Vice Admissions.** Counsel not admitted to practice in the Eastern District of Pennsylvania must be sponsored for admission pro hac vice by a member of the bar of the court. Judge Padova requires a written motion for admission on or before the day of the first appearance of counsel seeking admission.

CIVIL CASES
Pretrial Procedure

1. **Preliminary Pretrial Conference (Scheduling Conference).** Judge Padova regularly schedules an initial pretrial conference within 35 days of the filing of answers or pre-answer motions by all defendants in cases assigned to the standard management track. Such a conference is always scheduled within 30 to 60 days of the filing of the complaint in cases assigned to the special management track.

At least three days prior to the pretrial conference, counsel must submit to chambers a completed scheduling information report. Counsel must also timely submit the discovery plan adopted at the Rule 26(f) conference in accordance with the Federal Rules of Civil Procedure, but no later than three days prior to the scheduled pretrial conference. (It is not necessary to docket these submissions.) The court's processes and procedures rely on counsel's good faith compliance *in all respects* with Rule 26(f). The Rule 26(f) meeting will take place as soon as possible and, in any event, at least 14 days before the scheduling conference. Such compliance is of the highest degree mandatory. *Parties who do not comply will have no voice at the scheduling conference and may be subject to additional sanctions.*

Topics that are frequently addressed in an initial pretrial conference include those listed in Local Rule 16.1(b), Fed.R.Civ.P. 16(b) and (c), and the progress of self-executing disclosure under Fed.R.Civ.P. 26(a). Judge Padova further requires that counsel taking part in all pretrial conferences be prepared to speak on the subjects to be covered, including settlement, and have authority from their clients to do so. A Rule 16 scheduling order is issued at the conclusion of the conference. Judge Padova uses a standard form of scheduling order for standard track cases, a copy of which is posted on the court's website under Judge Padova's policies and procedures.

Counsel must be prepared to present argument at the conference on any pending motions.

2. **Final Pretrial Conference.** Judge Padova typically holds a final pretrial conference sometime during the month before trial is scheduled. At that time, outstanding topics that were the subject of the initial pretrial conference are typically addressed, as well as settlement, resolution of motions in limine, and trial procedure.

Continuances and Extensions

Judge Padova has a general policy of adhering to originally scheduled dates unless a compelling reason is presented that justifies a change. This policy applies to briefing schedules, oral argument, evidentiary hearings, discovery deadlines, and trial dates.

Counsel should advise the court immediately, and *before the date has run,* of any compelling reason justifying an extension or continuance of any originally scheduled date. Any request for an extension or continuance should be made in writing by letter or formal motion for cause shown. If there is an agreement, a stipulation of counsel should be submitted; however, court approval is required.

A letter request is acceptable when there is an uncontested request for a continuance of the Rule 16 scheduling order deadlines not affecting the trial date or pool placement, when the continuance of a preliminary pretrial conference is requested, or when there is an uncontested request for an extension of time to respond to a motion.

Motion Practice

1. **Oral Argument on Motions.** If Judge Padova determines that oral argument will aid in deciding the matter, he will order argument or grant a request by counsel to be heard. Requests should be made in writing at the time of filing a motion or reply as part of the moving papers.

2. **Reply and Surreply Briefs.** Judge Padova considers motions "ripe" when a response has been filed. Reply and surreply briefs may only be filed with leave of the court. A motion for leave to file a reply or surreply brief must be filed within 14 days of the previous filing, and counsel should attach as an exhibit the proposed reply or surreply brief.

3. **Chambers Copies of Motion Papers.** Judge Padova requires that one courtesy copy of motion papers be sent to his chambers. Courtesy copies should be stapled or neatly bound, with dividers between exhibits.

4. **Rule 56 Motions.** Upon any motion for summary judgment pursuant to Fed.R.Civ.P. 56, there must be filed with the motion a separate, short, and concise statement of the material facts, in numbered paragraphs, as to which the moving party contends there is no genuine issue to be tried.

The papers opposing a motion for summary judgment must include a separate, short, and concise statement of the material facts, responding to the numbered paragraphs set forth in the statement required in the paragraph above, as to which it is contended that there exists a genuine issue to be tried.

Statements of material facts in support of, or in opposition to, a motion must include references to the parts of the record that support the statements.

All material facts set forth in the statement required to be served by the moving party may be taken by the court as admitted unless controverted by the opposing party.

The pendency of a Rule 56 motion does not stay the deadlines contained in the court's scheduling order. Counsel must apply by letter or by motion if they wish an extension to the scheduling order deadlines.

Judge Padova requires that one courtesy copy of motion papers be sent to his chambers. Courtesy copies should be stapled or neatly bound, with dividers between the exhibits.

Discovery Matters

1. Length of Discovery Period and Extensions. At the initial pretrial conference, Judge Padova will set a discovery period. Judge Padova usually allows 60 to 90 days to complete discovery from the date when all defendants have entered their appearance.

2. Discovery Conferences and Dispute Resolution. Judge Padova normally does not hold discovery conferences, but encourages the use of telephone conferences in lieu of motion practice to resolve discovery disputes. When a *discovery default* occurs, Judge Padova encourages counsel to file a motion to compel, which he will usually grant upon presentation pursuant to Local Civil Rule 26.1(g). When a *discovery dispute* occurs, and counsel have been unable to resolve it themselves or with Judge Padova's assistance by telephone, he requires a motion to compel. Judge Padova expects discovery to be voluntary and cooperative in accordance with the Federal Rules of Civil Procedure and the Plan.

3. Confidentiality Agreements. Parties may agree privately to keep documents and information confidential. The court may enter an order of confidentiality only after making a specific finding of good cause based on a particularized showing that the parties' privacy interests outweigh the public's right to obtain information concerning judicial proceedings. See *Pansy v. Borough of Stroudsburg,* 23 F.3d 772, 786 (3d Cir. 1994).

4. Expert Witnesses. Counsel are required to identify expert witnesses and provide curriculum vitae and, as to all experts, voluntarily exchange the information referred to in Fed.R.Civ.P. 26(a)(2)(B) by expert report, deposition, or answer to expert interrogatory in accordance with the dates outlined in the court's scheduling orders. Except for good cause, expert testimony will be limited at trial to the information provided.

Settlement

1. General Approach to Settlement. At the earliest appropriate point, Judge Padova takes an active role in settlement discussions. This point is typically reached in the initial pretrial conference. Judge Padova may hold an early resolution hearing in court, at which individual parties, or the principals of corporate parties, are present, and he often recommends settlement figures or alternative methods of dispute resolution. Judge Padova prefers not to participate in settlement negotiations in nonjury cases. He typically refers such cases to a magistrate judge for settlement.

2. Referral of Settlement Negotiations to Another District Court Judge. Judge Padova will occasionally refer a case to another district court judge for settlement.

Arbitration

1. Scheduling of Trial De Novo from Arbitration. Once a trial de novo is demanded, Judge Padova issues a standard form scheduling order, a copy of which is on the court's website under Judge Padova's Policies and Procedures and is also included on page 198 of this book. If counsel believe that a settlement conference would be helpful, Judge Padova is willing to meet with the parties upon their request. Ordinarily, Judge Padova does not allow additional discovery. Counsel can expect the case to be placed in the trial pool within 30 days.

Proposed Final Pretrial Memoranda

The Rule 16 scheduling order will specify the items to be included in all pretrial memoranda and the filing dates. Judge Padova uses a standard form order, which can be found on the court's website under Judge Padova's Policies and Procedures and is also included on page 193 of this book.

Injunctions

1. Scheduling and Expedited Discovery. Judge Padova's usual practice is to hold a conference with counsel before scheduling hearings for temporary restraining orders and preliminary and permanent injunctions. Judge Padova usually handles requests for expedited discovery by telephone conference. When a complaint is accompanied by a motion for a temporary restraining order or preliminary injunction, Judge Padova will contact counsel and schedule a hearing.

2. Proposed Findings of Fact and Conclusions of Law. Parties must submit proposed findings of fact and conclusions of law in accordance with the deadlines set forth in the Rule 16 scheduling order. *One courtesy copy should be sent to chambers. Judge Padova also requires that the parties submit a computer diskette in WordPerfect format.*

Trial Procedure

1. Scheduling Cases. Cases may be placed in the trial pool or assigned a date certain for commencement of trial.

2. Cases Involving Out-of-Town Parties or Witnesses. Trial scheduling by Judge Padova does not change by the presence of out-of-town parties or witnesses. Judge Padova leaves the scheduling of witnesses to counsel.

3. Conflicts of Counsel. When counsel become aware of professional or personal conflicts that may affect the trial schedule, they should notify Judge Padova and opposing counsel immediately. Such notice may be given to Judge Padova's deputy by telephone, but it must be confirmed in writing.

4. Note-taking by Jurors. Judge Padova permits jurors to take notes and will issue an instruction on juror note-taking similar to that found in *United States v. MacLean,* 578 F.2d 64 (3d Cir. 1978).

5. Voir Dire. Judge Padova ordinarily asks a standard set of voir dire questions. Parties should file proposed voir dire questions by the deadline set forth in the Rule 16 scheduling order for the submission of proposed jury instructions. *Judge Padova also requires that the parties submit voir dire questions on a computer diskette in WordPerfect format.*

6. Trial Briefs. Judge Padova requires the submission of one courtesy copy of trial briefs.

7. In Limine Motions. Judge Padova requires counsel to submit one courtesy copy of motions in limine in accordance with the deadlines set forth in the Rule 16 scheduling order.

8. Examination of Witnesses Out of Sequence. Judge Padova will permit counsel to take witnesses out of turn for the convenience of the witness, subject, of course, to objection by opposing counsel.

9. Opening Statements and Summations. Judge Padova normally attempts to obtain the agreement of counsel regarding time limits to be placed on opening statements and summations. However, Judge Padova believes that 20 to 30 minutes is usually adequate for an opening statement and 30 to 45 minutes is usually adequate for a summation.

10. Examination of Witnesses or Argument by More Than One Attorney. Judge Padova will permit more than one attorney for a party to examine different witnesses or to argue different points before the court, but he will not permit two attorneys for a party to examine the same witness or argue the same point.

11. Examination of Witnesses Beyond Redirect and Recross. Judge Padova does not have a general policy regarding further examination of a witness after redirect or recross have been completed. Where appropriate, he will allow it, but he will not permit any repetition or rehashing.

12. Videotaped Testimony. Videotaped testimony should begin with the witness being sworn. Objections should be given to the court well in advance of the tapes being offered so that the tapes may be appropriately edited. Objections should be accompanied by a copy of the transcript in order for the court to issue a ruling.

13. Reading of Material Into the Record. Judge Padova has no special practice or policy of reading into the record stipulations, pleadings, or discovery material. He will permit it when necessary.

14. Preparation of Exhibits. Judge Padova requires that exhibits be pre-marked and pre-exchanged. At the commencement of trial, the parties must provide the court with three copies of a schedule of exhibits that briefly describes each exhibit. *At the trial, the parties must provide the court with two copies of each exhibit at the time of its first use at trial.*

15. Offering Exhibits Into Evidence. Judge Padova prefers that counsel offer exhibits into evidence at the close of testimony by the first witness testifying about the exhibit unless the exhibit is objected to, in which event it should not be testified to unless it is received into evidence.

16. Motions for Judgment as a Matter of Law and Motions for Judgment on Partial Findings. Judge Padova prefers that Rule 50 motions be in writing. Oral argument, if necessary, will be requested by the court.

17. Proposed Jury Instructions and Verdict Forms. As set forth in his standard form of pretrial order, Judge Padova expects counsel to work together in submitting joint proposed jury instructions on substantive issues and proposed verdict forms or special interrogatories to the jury. In addition, Judge Padova requires that counsel submit individual proposed jury instructions on substantive issues and proposed verdict forms or special interrogatories to the jury on those issues that counsel cannot agree upon in their joint submissions. In all cases, one copy of the joint and/or individual submissions should be submitted to the court (chambers) *no later than the date provided in the Rule 16 scheduling order.* Judge Padova also requires that the parties submit jury instructions and verdict forms on a computer diskette in WordPerfect format. Each proposed instruction should be double-spaced on a separate sheet of paper. Cited cases and pattern jury instructions should be accurately quoted and specific page references should be given. Jury instructions need only be submitted with respect to substantive issues in the case. Proposed instruction on procedural matters such as the burden of proof, unanimity, and credibility are not required. Judge Padova may accept supplemental jury instructions until the start of closing argument.

18. Proposed Findings of Fact and Conclusions of Law. Judge Padova requires that proposed findings of fact and conclusions of law in nonjury cases be submitted in accordance with the date set forth in the Rule 16 scheduling order. One courtesy copy should be sent to chambers along with a diskette with the document in WordPerfect format.

Jury Deliberations

1. Written Jury Instructions. Judge Padova generally does not give the jury written instructions, but may do so in complex cases.

2. Exhibits in the Jury Room. Judge Padova generally permits all trial exhibits to go out to the jury unless a well-founded objection is asserted.

3. Handling of Jury Requests to Read Back Testimony or Replay Tapes. Judge Padova will advise the jury that testimony is usually not in transcript form to give them. However, if a transcript is available, he will consider reading appropriate portions requested by the jury. He will usually allow tapes and videotapes to be replayed.

4. Availability of Counsel During Jury Deliberations. Counsel must remain in the courthouse during jury deliberations.

5. Taking the Verdict and Special Verdicts. Whether Judge Padova takes a general or special verdict depends on the case. If useful, Judge Padova will submit interrogatories to the jury.

6. Polling the Jury. Judge Padova grants all requests to poll the jury.

CRIMINAL CASES

1. Speedy Trial Act Continuances. Motions requesting a trial continuance should be accompanied by a proposed order in Speedy Trial Act language, containing findings of fact and conclusions that would justify a continuance under the Speedy Trial Act.

2. Sentencing Memoranda. Judge Padova encourages the submission of sentencing memoranda by both the government and defendants, but notes that they must be within the framework provided by the Sentencing Guidelines in order to be useful.

Sentencing memoranda should be submitted at least three days before the scheduled sentencing date.

OTHER GENERAL MATTERS

1. Cases on Appeal. Judge Padova generally expects to receive copies of appellate briefs when a decision rendered by him is appealed.

Practice and Procedures of Judges and Judges' Forms and Orders

UNITED STATES DISTRICT COURT
Eastern District of Pennsylvania
U.S. Court House
Independence Mall West
601 Market Street
Philadelphia, PA 19106-1797

Revised September, 2011

NOTICE TO COUNSEL:

This notice sets forth my policy on discovery, my guidelines for communication with the Court and my Chambers staff, and a brief overview of the manner in which this case will generally progress in my Court. In addition to this Notice, I expect counsel to become familiar with my "Policies and Procedures," which can be found on the Court's website at **www.paed.uscourts.gov.** On the Court's home page, click on "Judges' Procedures." Before calling Chambers with procedural questions, please consult this publication.

I. Communication with Chambers

I strongly discourage communication with law clerks. Telephone inquiries should be directed to my Deputy, Gerrie Keane (215-597-1178).

Please do not write letters directly to the Court, or send or designate copies of correspondence among and between counsel to the Court, except:

(1) When letters of transmittal accompany documents required to be sent to, or filed with, the Court or in another official office in the Courthouse;

(2) When counsel are specifically requested by the Court to communicate some information to the Court by letter;

(3) When there is a request for a continuance of the Preliminary Pretrial Conference (see paragraph entitled "Continuances and Extensions");

(4) When there is an uncontested request for a continuance of the Rule 16 Scheduling Order deadlines not affecting the trial date or pool placement (see paragraph entitled "Continuances and Extensions");

(5) When the participation of counsel in the case is expected to be affected by a personal matter concerning counsel, a party, a witness, or counsel's immediate family, such as medical problems, vacation plans, or other similarly personal problems or questions; or

(6) To confirm or advise the Court that a case has been settled, dismissed, or otherwise finally disposed.

All other written communications with the Court concerning any case assigned to my calendar should be by the filing of a pleading, motion, application, brief, legal memorandum, busy slip, or other similar filing provided for in the Federal Rules of Civil or Criminal Procedure or our Local Rules of Civil or Criminal Procedure. **Do not write letters to the Court that are properly the subject of these filings.**

When a written communication concerning a case cannot timely address a problem, counsel may initiate necessary telephone communications with my Chambers. Issues appropriately addressed by telephone contact include:

Scheduling of conferences or proceedings, including pretrial and trial conferences; attendance of witnesses;

Exhibit handling or arrangements for video replay;

Arrangements for telephone conferences regarding discovery disputes; and

Requests for absolutely necessary extensions of time to file any response, reply, brief, memorandum of law, or the like.

Judge John R. Padova

All such inquiries should be directed to my Deputy.

II. Discovery

Discovery rules are not intended to create strategic advantages for any party and should *never* be used to play games. The Federal Rules of Civil Procedure call for voluntary, cooperative discovery in a **timely** manner. Federal Rule of Civil Procedure 26(a) requires disclosure of certain types of information. Compliance with the Rules is mandatory. I expect that counsel will act in accordance with both the **letter** and the **spirit** of the Rules. Discovery disputes should be presented to the Court in the manner provided for in my "Civil Action Procedures."

III. Pretrial Procedure

My Deputy typically sends counsel notification of the scheduling of a pretrial conference to be held within 35 days after all defendants have answered or filed pre-answer motions. At least three days prior to the pretrial conference, counsel must submit a completed Scheduling Information Report.

Counsel must also timely submit the discovery plan adopted at the Rule 26(f) conference in accordance with the Federal Rules of Civil Procedure, but no later than three days prior to the scheduled pretrial conference. The Court's processes and procedures rely on counsel's good faith compliance *in all respects* with Rule 26(f). The Rule 26(f) meeting shall take place as soon as possible and, in any event, at least fourteen days before the scheduling conference. Such compliance is of the highest degree mandatory. **Parties who do not comply will have no voice at the scheduling conference and may be subject to additional sanctions.**

Topics which are frequently addressed in an initial pretrial conference include those listed in Local Rule of Civil Procedure 16.1(b), Federal Rule of Civil Procedure 16(b) and (c) and the progress of self-executing disclosure under Federal Rule of Civil Procedure 26(a). Counsel taking part in pre-trial conferences should be prepared to speak on the subjects to be covered, including settlement, and have authority from their clients to do so. A Rule 16 Scheduling Order is issued at the conclusion of the conference containing either a specific trial date or pool listing, and dates and form of pretrial memoranda.

With the exception of a final pretrial conference (which usually takes place sometime during the month before trial is scheduled), no other conferences are normally scheduled unless requested by counsel. Settlement conferences are encouraged, provided counsel believe that they will be useful.

IV. Motions Practice

I consider a motion "ripe" when a response has been filed. Reply and surreply briefs may only be filed with leave of the Court. Counsel should file a motion requesting leave to file additional briefing and attach the proposed reply as an exhibit.

V. Rule 56 Motions

Upon any motion for summary judgment pursuant to Fed. R.Civ.P. 56, there shall be filed with the motion a separate, short and concise statement of the material facts, in numbered paragraphs, as to which the moving party contends there is no genuine issue to be tried.

The papers opposing a motion for summary judgment shall include a separate, short and concise statement of the material facts, responding to the numbered paragraphs set forth in the statement required in the foregoing paragraph, as to which it is contended that there exists a genuine issue to be tried.

Statements of material facts in support of or in opposition to a motion shall include references to the parts of the record that support the statements.

All material facts set forth in the statement required to be served by the moving party may be taken by the Court as admitted unless controverted by the opposing party.

Your cooperation is **expected** and **appreciated**.

Honorable John R. Padova, J.

SCHEDULING INFORMATION REPORT
(To be completed and returned to Judge Padova's
Chambers three (3) days before the pretrial conference)

Caption: _____

Civil Action No.: _____

Jury Trial _____ Non-Jury Trial _____ Arbitration _____

Plaintiff's Counsel: _____

Address: _____

Phone: _____ Fax: _____

Defendant's Counsel: _____

Address: _____

Phone: _____ Fax: _____

Have you complied with the duty of self-executing disclosure under Federal Rule of Civil Procedure 26(a)?

_____ When? _____ If not, why? _____

Have you filed a discovery plan pursuant to Federal Rule of Civil Procedure 26(f)?

_____ When? _____ If not, why? _____

_____

Discovery completed?_____ If not, when? _____

If you contend the discovery period should exceed four months after the last appearance by all defendants is filed, please state reasons:

_____

Ready for trial by: _____
                    Date

Is a settlement conference likely to be helpful? _____

If so, when: Early_____(yes/no)   After discovery_____

Do you expect to file a case-dispositive motion? _____

If so, by what date?_____

Trial time estimate: _____

Time to present your case: _____

Time for entire trial: _____

Date: _____   _____
                                                   Signature of counsel preparing the form

                                                   _____
                                                   Typed or printed name

Judge John R. Padova

IN THE UNITED STATES DISTRICT COURT
FOR THE EASTERN DISTRICT OF PENNSYLVANIA

: CIVIL ACTION
:
v. :
:
: NO.

FEDERAL RULE OF CIVIL PROCEDURE 16 PRETRIAL SCHEDULING ORDER
STANDARD TRACK CASES

AND NOW, TO WIT, this _____ day of _____, 20___, following a preliminary pretrial conference, IT IS ORDERED as follows:

1. All discovery shall proceed forthwith and continue in such manner as will assure that all requests for and responses to discovery will be served, noticed and completed by _____.

2. Unless the parties agree to another form of ADR, they shall participate in a settlement conference to be scheduled and held before United States Magistrate Judge Timothy R. Rice on or about _____. If the parties believe that a settlement conference would be helpful at an earlier time, they are directed to contact Magistrate Judge Rice to schedule the same. Magistrate Judge Rice will require that lead counsel and parties with full settlement authority attend the conference.

3. On or before _____, counsel for each party shall serve upon counsel for every other party the information referred to in Federal Rule of Civil Procedure 26(a)(2)(B) by expert report, deposition, or answer to expert interrogatory. If the evidence is intended solely to contradict or rebut evidence on the same subject matter identified by another party, counsel shall serve the information on counsel for every other party on or before _____.

4. Dispositive motions shall be filed no later than _____. Upon any motion for summary judgment pursuant to Fed. R.Civ.P. 56, there shall be filed with the motion a separate, short and concise statement of the material facts, in numbered paragraphs, as to which the moving party contends there is no genuine issue to be tried.

The papers opposing a motion for summary judgment shall include a separate, short and concise statement of the material facts, responding to the numbered paragraphs set forth in the statement required in the foregoing paragraph, as to which it is contended that there exists a genuine issue to be tried.

Statements of material facts in support of or in opposition to a motion shall include references to the parts of the record that support the statements.

All material facts set forth in the statement required to be served by the moving party may be taken by the Court as admitted unless controverted by the opposing party.

5. On or before _____, counsel for each party shall serve upon counsel for every other party:

(a) the original or a copy of each exhibit they expect to offer at trial in furtherance of their respective contentions. Each party shall mark its trial exhibits *in advance of trial* with consecutive numbers appropriately prefixed with an identifying letter of counsel's choice (i.e., P-1, P-2; D-1, D-2);

(b) curriculum vitae for each expert witness expected to testify; and

(c) a specific identification of each discovery item expected to be offered into evidence.

6. All parties shall prepare and file with the Clerk of Court their pretrial memoranda in accordance with this Order and Local Rule of Civil Procedure 16.1(c), as follows:

Plaintiffs - on or before _____.

Defendants - on or before _____.

All motions in limine shall be filed on or before _____.

Responses thereto are due on or before _____.

In addition to compliance with Local Rule of Civil Procedure 16.1(c), the parties shall include the following in, or attached to, their pretrial memoranda:

    a. A listing of the identity of each expert witness to be called at trial by the party;

    b. A curriculum vitae for each expert witness listed;

    c. A listing of each fact witness to be called at trial with a brief statement of the nature of their expected testimony (witnesses not listed may not be called by that party in its case-in-chief);

    d. An itemized statement of claimant's damages or other relief sought;

    e. A statement of any anticipated important legal issues on which the Court will be required to rule, together with counsel's single best authority on each such issue.

One copy (1) of the pretrial memoranda shall be filed with the Clerk of the Court and two (2) copies shall be sent to the Court (Chambers).

7. A final pretrial conference for this matter will be held on _____, at _____ in chambers (Room 17613).

8. (a) If a jury trial is scheduled, the parties shall file in writing with the Clerk of Court one (1) copy of *joint* proposed jury instructions on substantive issues and proposed verdict forms or special interrogatories to the jury. The parties shall also file one (1) copy of proposed jury instructions, verdict forms, or special interrogatories on those issues not agreed upon by the parties in their joint submission. These filings shall be made **on or before** _____. Jury instructions shall be submitted each on a separate sheet of paper, double spaced, with accurate quotes from and citations to cases and pattern jury instructions where appropriate. A courtesy copy of these filings shall be submitted to chambers in hard copy, **as well as on a disk in WordPerfect format.**

(b) If a non-jury trial is scheduled, the parties shall file one (1) copy of proposed findings of fact and conclusions of law with the Clerk of the Court on or before _____. One (1) copy of the proposed findings of fact and conclusions of law shall be sent to the Court (Chambers).

9. **No later than three days** before the date trial is scheduled to commence if a date certain, or three days before case appears in the trial pool, the parties shall file a complete and comprehensive stipulation of uncontested facts pursuant to paragraph (d)(2)(b)(2) of Local Rule of Civil Procedure 16.1; the original shall be filed with the Clerk of the Court, and two (2) copies shall be submitted to the Court (Chambers).

10. At the commencement of trial, the parties shall provide the Court with three (3) copies of a schedule of exhibits which shall briefly describe each exhibit. At the trial, the parties shall provide the Court with two (2) copies of each exhibit at the time of its first use at trial.

11. This case will be listed for trial as follows:

Date Certain: _____ at 10:00 a.m. in Courtroom **17-B.**

Civil Trial Pool: _____

Counsel should consider themselves attached as of this date.

COUNSEL PLEASE NOTE: This Scheduling Order will be the only written notice counsel receive of the date this case will be tried. Counsel and all parties shall be prepared to commence trial on that date and as soon thereafter as counsel receive telephone notice that trial is to commence. If the case is a pool case, counsel should have the responsibility to maintain contact with the deputy clerk once the case goes into the pool. Every effort will be made to give counsel at least 24 hours notice and hopefully 48 hours notice of commencement of trial. Pool cases are to be ready for trial as of the date they are placed in the pool and are frequently not called in the order in which they appear.

12. Any party having an objection to: (a) the admissibility of any exhibit based on authenticity; (b) the adequacy of the qualifications of an expert witness expected to testify; (c) the admissibility for any reason (except relevancy) of any item of evidence expected to be offered, or (d) the admissibility of any opinion testimony from lay witnesses pursuant to Federal Rule of Evidence 701 shall set forth separately each such objection, clearly and concisely, in their pretrial memorandum. Such objection shall describe with particularity the ground and the authority for the objection. Unless the court concludes at trial that manifest injustice will result, the Court can be expected to overrule any objection offered at trial in respect to any matter covered by (a), (b), (c) and/or (d) above, if the Court concludes that the objection should have been made as required by this Order.

13. Only those exhibits, discovery items and expert witnesses identified in the manner set forth in this Order shall be considered by the Court for admission into evidence at trial, unless stipulated to by all affected parties and approved by the Court, or by Order of Court so as to avoid manifest injustice.

14. Because a witness may be unavailable at the time of trial in the manner defined in Federal Rule of Civil Procedure 32(a)(3), the Court expects use of oral or videotape depositions at trial of any witness whose testimony a party believes essential to the presentation of that party's case, whether that witness is a party, a non-party or an expert. The unavailability of any such witness will not be a ground to delay the commencement or progress of an ongoing trial. In the event a deposition is to be offered, the offering party shall file with the Court, prior to the commencement of the trial, a copy of the deposition, but only after all efforts have been made to resolve objections with other counsel. Unresolved objections shall be noted in the margin of the deposition page(s) where a Court ruling is necessary.

_____
JOHN R. PADOVA, J.

UNITED STATES DISTRICT COURT
Eastern District of Pennsylvania
U.S. Court House
Independence Mall West
601 Market Street
Philadelphia, PA 19106-1797

NOTICE TO COUNSEL:

TRIAL DE NOVO FOR ARBITRATION CASE

This notice sets forth my guidelines for additional discovery and communications with the Court and my Chambers staff, and provides a brief overview of the manner in which this case will generally progress in my Court. In addition to this Notice, I expect that counsel will become familiar with my "Policies and Procedures," which can be found on the Court's website at **www.paed.uscourts.gov.** On the Court's home page, cursor down to and click on "Judges' Procedures." Before calling my Chambers, please consult this publication for answers to any procedural questions you might have.

I. Communication with Chambers

Judge Padova strongly discourages communication with law clerks. All telephone inquiries should be directed to my Deputy, who will then direct the call as appropriate.

Please do not write letters directly to the Court or send or designate copies of correspondence among and between counsel for the Court except:

(1) When letters of transmittal accompany documents required to be sent to or filed with the Court or in another official office in the Courthouse;

(2) When counsel are specifically requested by the Court to communicate some information to the Court by letter;

(3) When there is an uncontested request for a continuance of the Rule 16 Scheduling Order deadlines not affecting the trial date or pool placement;

(4) When the participation of counsel in the case is expected to be affected by a personal matter concerning counsel, a party, a witness, or counsel's immediate family, such as medical problems, vacation plans, or other similarly personal problems or questions; or

(5) To confirm or advise the Court that a case has been settled, dismissed, or otherwise finally disposed.

All other written communications with the Court concerning any case assigned to my calendar should be by the filing of a pleading, motion, application, brief, legal memorandum, busy slip, or other similar filing provided for in the Federal Rules of Civil Procedure or our Local Rules of Civil Procedure. *Do not write letters to the Court which are properly the subject of these filings.*

When a written communication concerning a case cannot timely address a problem, **necessary** telephone communications with my Chambers, regarding such things as scheduling of a conference or proceeding, including pretrial and trial conferences; attendance of witnesses; exhibit handling; arrangements for video replay; arranging telephone conferences; and requests for absolutely necessary extensions of time to file any response, reply, brief, memorandum of law or the like, should be directed to the Chambers Deputy at (215) 597-1178.

II. Discovery

I am of the view that after a case has been tried at an arbitration hearing, no additional discovery is necessary. Therefore, absent a compelling reason to do so, no further discovery is permitted. Counsel should bring any compelling reason to permit additional discovery to the Court's attention by formal motion as soon as possible, and in no event beyond one week after receiving this notice.

III. Pretrial Procedures

Enclosed is a Rule 16 Scheduling Order which will direct proceedings throughout this case. No conferences are scheduled unless requested by counsel. Settlement conferences are encouraged, provided counsel believe they will be useful.

Your cooperation is *expected* and *appreciated*.

_____
JOHN R. PADOVA, J.

IN THE UNITED STATES DISTRICT COURT
FOR THE EASTERN DISTRICT OF PENNSYLVANIA

	:	CIVIL ACTION
	:	
v.	:	
	:	
	:	NO.

FEDERAL RULE OF CIVIL PROCEDURE 16 PRETRIAL SCHEDULING ORDER
FOR TRIAL DE NOVO FROM ARBITRATION

AND NOW, TO WIT, this _____ day of _____, 20__, IT IS ORDERED as follows:

    1. On or before _____, counsel for each party shall serve upon counsel for every other party:

(a) the original or a copy of each exhibit they expect to offer at trial de novo in furtherance of their respective contentions. Each party shall mark its trial de novo exhibits in advance of trial with consecutive numbers appropriately prefixed with an identifying letter of counsel's choice (i.e., P-1, P-2; D-1, D-2); (b) curriculum vitae for each expert witness expected to testify; (c) the information referred to in Federal Rule of Civil Procedure 26(a)(2)(B) by expert report, deposition or answer to expert interrogatory; and, (d) a specific identification of each discovery item expected to be offered into evidence.

    2. All parties shall prepare and file with the Clerk of Court their pretrial memoranda, in accordance with this Order and Local Rule of Civil Procedure 16.1(c), as follows:

Plaintiffs—on or before _____;

Defendants—on or before _____.

In addition to compliance with Local Rule of Civil Procedure 16.1(c), the parties shall include the following in or attach to their pretrial memoranda:

    a. A listing of the identity of each expert witness to be called at the trial de novo by the party;

    b. a curriculum vitae for each expert witness listed;

    c. a listing of each fact witness to be called at the trial de novo with a brief statement of the nature of their expected testimony (witnesses not listed may not be called by that party in its case-in-chief);

    d. an itemized statement of claimant's damages or other relief sought;

    e. a statement of any anticipated important legal issues on which the Court will be required to rule, together with counsel's single best authority on each such issue.

One copy (1) of the pretrial memoranda shall be filed with the Clerk of the Court and one (1) copy shall be sent to the Court (Chambers).

    3. (a) If a jury trial de novo is scheduled, the parties shall file in writing with the Clerk of Court one (1) copy of joint proposed jury instructions on substantive issues and proposed verdict forms or special interrogatories to the jury. The parties shall also file one (1) copy of proposed jury instructions, verdict forms, or special interrogatories on those issues not agreed upon by the parties in their joint submission. **These filings shall be made no later than** _____. Jury instructions shall be submitted

Judge John R. Padova

each on a separate sheet of paper, double spaced, with accurate quotes from and citations to cases and pattern jury instructions where appropriate. Two copies should be sent to the Court (Chambers). The Court also encourages that the parties submit a computer diskette in WordPerfect 6.1 for Windows format.

    (b) If a non-jury trial <u>de novo</u> is scheduled, the parties shall file one (1) copy of proposed findings of fact and conclusions of law with the Clerk of the Court no later than _____. One (1) copy of the proposed findings of fact and conclusions of law shall be sent to the Court (Chambers). The Court also encourages that the parties submit a computer diskette in WordPerfect 6.1 for Windows format.

    4.   No later than three days before the date the trial <u>de novo</u> is scheduled to commence, the parties shall file a complete and comprehensive stipulation of uncontested facts pursuant to paragraph (d)(2)(b)(2) of Local Rule of Civil Procedure 16.1; the original shall be filed with the Clerk of the Court, and two (2) copies shall be submitted to the Court (Chambers).

    5.   At the commencement of trial, the parties shall provide the Court with three (3) copies of a schedule of exhibits which shall briefly describe each exhibit. At the trial <u>de novo</u>, the parties shall provide the Court with two (2) copies of each exhibit at the time of its first use at trial.

    6.   This case will be tried on _____.

    <u>COUNSEL PLEASE NOTE:</u> This Scheduling Order will be the <u>only</u> written notice counsel receive of the date this case will be tried. Counsel and all parties shall be prepared to commence the trial <u>de novo</u> on that date and as soon thereafter as counsel receive telephone notice that the trial <u>de novo</u> is to commence.

    7.   Any party having an objection to: (a) the admissibility of any exhibit based on authenticity; (b) the adequacy of the qualifications of an expert witness expected to testify; (c) the admissibility for any reason (except relevancy) of any item of evidence expected to be offered, or (d) the admissibility of any opinion testimony from lay witnesses pursuant to Federal Rule of Evidence 701 shall set forth separately each such objection, clearly and concisely, in their pretrial memorandum. Such objection shall describe <u>with particularity</u> the ground and the authority for the objection. Unless the court concludes at the trial <u>de novo</u> that manifest injustice will result, the Court can be expected to <u>overrule</u> any objection offered <u>at the trial de novo</u> in respect to any matter covered by (a), (b), (c) and/or (d) above, if the Court concludes that the objection should have been made as required by this Order.

    8.   Only those exhibits, discovery items and expert witnesses identified in the manner set forth in this Order shall be considered by the Court for admission into evidence at the trial <u>de novo</u>, unless stipulated to by all affected parties and approved by the Court, <u>or</u> by Order of Court so as to avoid manifest injustice.

    9.   Because a witness may be unavailable at the time of the trial <u>de novo</u> in the manner defined in Federal Rule of Civil Procedure 32(a)(3), the Court expects use of oral or videotape depositions at the trial <u>de novo</u> of <u>any witness</u> whose testimony a party believes essential to the presentation of that party's case, whether that witness is a party, a non-party or an expert. The unavailability of any such witness <u>will not be a ground to delay</u> the commencement or progress of an ongoing trial. In the event a deposition is to be offered, the offering party shall file with the Court, prior to the commencement of the trial <u>de novo</u>, a copy of the deposition, but only after all efforts have been made to resolve objections with other counsel. Unresolved objections shall be noted in the margin of the deposition page(s) where a Court ruling is necessary.

                                                  JOHN R. PADOVA, J.

Judge Gene E.K. Pratter

Judge Gene E.K. Pratter was born in Chicago, Illinois. She grew up in Southern California, earned an A.B. from Stanford University, and earned a J.D. from the University of Pennsylvania Law School. From 1975 to 2004, Judge Pratter was in private practice in Philadelphia, Pennsylvania, engaging in general civil litigation with a concentration in professional liability matters. She served as general counsel to a multi-state 500-lawyer firm from 1999 to 2004. While in practice and now in public service, Judge Pratter has been active in a host of diverse community activities, charities, and projects. She is an adjunct instructor of trial advocacy at the University of Pennsylvania Law School. Judge Pratter was inducted into the United States District Court for the Eastern District of Pennsylvania on June 18, 2004.

PRELIMINARY GENERAL MATTERS[*]

1. *Professionalism and Civility.* Counsel and their clients should be polite, courteous, and otherwise civil to one another as well as to all parties, witnesses, and court personnel at all times. Gratuitous hyperbole, deliberate or reckless misstatements, uncooperative attitudes, "Rambo" tactics, overreaching in discovery or other demands, pointless personal insults, refusals to accommodate reasonable requests for scheduling adjustments, and the like are deleterious to the efficient and fair conduct of litigation and detract from the effectiveness and reputation of those who engage in such conduct, as well as their colleagues, affiliates, and clients. Written material of similar ilk, when included in submissions to the court is rarely—if ever—relevant to the matter at issue, much less persuasive, and *may be cause for the submission to be returned to counsel for appropriate editing and possible resubmission without the offending material.*

Judge Pratter expects counsel to confer with and keep their respective clients up to date (1) with respect to substantive submissions to the court, (2) in advance of court appearances, and (3) as to material developments in the client's case.

In general, counsel should bring matters to the judge's attention only after they have been discussed with opposing counsel and a reasonable effort has been made to resolve a dispute and the positions of all interested counsel on the matter needing the court's attention have been shared with all other counsel.

Counsel and their clients should be punctual for all conferences, hearings, oral arguments, and trials.

2. *Correspondence with the Court.* Correspondence may be directed to the court concerning scheduling, or other very routine matters. Correspondence to advise the court that a case has been settled or dismissed is also appropriate,[†] as is correspondence on any matter when specifically requested by the court. Any written communication requesting action by the court on such subjects should include at a minimum: (1) a very brief description of the situation requiring the court's attention, (2) the position of the opposing party(ies) (i.e., consent or opposition), and (3) the specific relief sought. All counsel should, at the same time, be sent a copy of all correspondence sent to the court. *All* other communications with the court should be made by the formal filing of pleadings, motions, applications, briefs, or legal memoranda. For example, discovery or other disputes should be

---

[*] All of the matters addressed in these procedures apply to all counsel *and all pro se litigants* in any matter pending before Judge Pratter.

[†] Indeed, the Court expects to be promptly advised in writing whenever any case has been resolved.

handled by formal motion, not by correspondence unless specifically invited by the court. Counsel *should not* send Judge Pratter copies of letters sent to each other unless specifically invited by the court to do so.

3. Communication with Law Clerks. Judge Pratter permits communications by counsel with her law clerks on appropriate matters. Counsel should avoid adopting an overly familiar tone with the law clerks or deputies and, for example, should always address them by their surnames. Unless directed otherwise by the court, counsel should *never* contact law clerks for advice on substantive or procedural matters other than of a very rudimentary nature (such as to confirm the court's administrative policies and procedures or to alert the court of some actual emergency that cannot be timely handled by correspondence or formal filings). Communications with the court about scheduling matters should be directed to Judge Pratter's courtroom deputy for criminal matters or to the judicial secretary/deputy clerk for civil matters.

Communications from counsel purporting to justify counsel's conduct because "Your Honor's law clerk [or Deputy] said ..." are highly disfavored and are never appropriate as an explanation of counsel's strategic or tactical choices.

4. Telephone Conferences. Telephone conferences with all counsel may be used at the court's discretion to resolve scheduling matters, time extensions, or certain discovery disputes. Counsel will be notified of the date and time for the telephone conference. It will be the responsibility of counsel for the moving or initiating party to arrange the telephone conference and to contact Judge Pratter through her judicial secretary/civil deputy after all parties are present on the call. Counsel are reminded to be especially careful to avoid being discourteous during phone conferences by failing to listen to other speakers, failing to identify themselves prior to each statement, failing to speak loudly or slowly enough to be heard, and the like. In that regard, counsel should be mindful that cell phones typically do not perform well for multi-party conference calls. Failure to observe basic phone courtesy will result in the court's refusal to use phone conferences in matters involving the offending participants.

5. Oral Arguments and Evidentiary Hearings. Judge Pratter does not set aside specific days or times for oral argument, motions, or evidentiary hearings. Hearings and arguments are scheduled on an ad hoc basis as warranted. They typically are conducted in the courtroom. The court endeavors to provide counsel with appropriate advance notice of scheduled hearings, arguments, and conferences and expects counsel to refrain from last-minute (i.e., less than 48 hours) requests to cancel, postpone, or reschedule such matters in the absence of actual emergencies.

6. Pro Hac Vice Admissions. All motions for the pro hac vice admission of counsel must be made by an attorney who is (1) admitted to practice and in good standing before the United States District Court for the Eastern District of Pennsylvania and (2) whose appearance has been entered in the case in which the motion is made. Judge Pratter does not accept merely the standard form made available from the offices of the clerk of court. Each such motion must be accompanied by the affidavit or similar declaration of each attorney being proposed for pro hac vice admission in which the affiant/declarant includes the following information and undertakings:
    a. Year and jurisdiction of each bar admission;
    b. Status of the attorney's admission(s), i.e., active or inactive, in good standing, etc.;
    c. Whether the attorney has ever been suspended from the practice of law in any jurisdiction or received any public reprimand by the highest disciplinary authority of any bar in which the attorney has been a member;

d. That the affiant/declarant (i) has in fact read the most recent edition of the Pennsylvania Rules of Professional Conduct and the Local Rules of the Court, and (ii) agrees to be bound by both sets of rules for the duration of the case for which pro hac vice admission is sought; and
e. That, if granted pro hac vice status, the affiant/declarant will in good faith continue to advise counsel who has moved for the pro hac vice admission of the current status of the case for which pro hac vice has been granted and of all material developments therein.

The admission of out-of-the-jurisdiction counsel pro hac vice does not relieve associate local counsel of responsibility for the matter before the court.

7. Use of Electronic Court Filings (ECF). Counsel are also advised that the court expects all counsel to be registered on the ECF system of the district court. All official filings submitted to the clerk of the court must be filed directly by the filing attorney onto ECF. The court's orders, opinions, and other docketed materials will be filed onto ECF and notice thereof will be communicated to counsel either by ECF or ordinary first-class mail. Requests to be excused from ECF registration must be made in writing directly to Judge Pratter.

8. Pro Se Litigants—Assistance from a Lawyer. Pro se litigants who have received substantive assistance (i.e., help, guidance, direction, or the like with the development of strategy or tactics, drafting pleadings, motions, or briefs, etc.) from an attorney for any material filed with the court must, at the time the material is filed, identify the attorney, the attorney's contribution to the filing, and the scope of the attorney's limited representation. Failure to identify any such attorney will amount to a representation by the pro se litigant that the submission is the pro se litigant's submission for which no substantive assistance from an attorney was received.

CIVIL CASES
Pretrial Procedure

1. Pretrial Conferences. Judge Pratter regularly schedules an in-person initial pretrial conference (IPTC) pursuant to Rule 16 soon after the answer or other material response to the complaint is filed or soon after the case is transferred to her. Generally, a preliminary motion (such as a Rule 12(b)(6) motion to dismiss) will not prompt the scheduling of an IPTC. Prior to the IPTC, counsel may be required to submit to chambers an initial pretrial conference information or other status report. Generally, the conference will be held in chambers. In very rare cases the conference (or the participation of one or more counsel) may be by telephone. A written notice concerning the IPTC will be sent to counsel. Counsel should *not* wait to start discovery until after an IPTC has been held; the court expects that discovery will be underway in advance of the IPTC.

At the IPTC, counsel should be prepared to discuss those topics listed in Local Rule of Civil Procedure 16.1(a) and Fed.R.Civ.P. 16(b) and (c). Counsel should also be prepared to discuss the progress (and, preferably, the completion) of initial disclosures pursuant to Fed.R.Civ.P. 26(a)(1). In special management track cases, the parties should provide the court with a proposed case management plan pursuant to section 3:01 of the Civil Justice Expense and Delay Reduction Plan three days prior to the IPTC. Counsel taking part in the IPTC should be prepared to speak knowledgeably and with client authority on these subjects.

A scheduling order will be issued following the IPTC setting forth deadlines for the completion of discovery, the filing of dispositive motions, the filing of pretrial submissions, and a date when the case will be placed in the trial pool or specially listed for trial. Where appropriate, a date for another interim status conference or conferences may be set. In certain cases, particularly in special management track cases, the scheduling order may provide a date by which the parties will be required to prepare and submit to the court for approval a final pretrial order pursuant to Local Civil Rule 16.1(d)(2).

Typically, Judge Pratter will hold a final pretrial conference (FPTC) prior to the date the case will be placed in the trial pool or is scheduled for trial. At the FPTC, outstanding topics that were the subject of the IPTC and issues concerning the trial are typically discussed, as well as the subject of settlement possibilities. A final pretrial order or a final scheduling order in a complex case, as the case may be, will be issued at the conclusion of the FPTC.

Prior to attending any pretrial conference, counsel should confer with each other about the topics expected to be discussed at the conference, including a substantive discussion of potential settlement. Counsel are also expected to have discussed with their respective clients prior to the conference the issues to be addressed at any conference with the court and to come to the conference with all necessary authority.

Continuances and Extensions

1. General Policy. Counsel should expect the court to maintain the dates contained in the scheduling order, unless there is good cause to justify a change.

2. Requests for Extensions and Continuances. Generally, Judge Pratter will grant a short (i.e., two weeks or less) continuance or extension that will not affect the discovery cutoff or trial date (i.e., the date that a brief is due, the date of an evidentiary hearing, or the date of an oral argument on a nondispositive motion), if requested with the agreement of all parties. Any other request for a continuance or extension should set forth in detail the basis for the request and whether it is agreed to or opposed by the opposing party or parties. A request for an extension or continuance of longer than two weeks or of the trial date, discovery cutoff date, or the deadline for filing dispositive motions must be made sufficiently prior to the due date to allow time for the court to consider it and should set forth compelling reasons for the relief sought. An unopposed request may be made by letter to the court and should include the reasons for the request.

General Motion Practice

Except as set forth here, motion practice will be conducted in accordance with Local Rule 7.1. The originals of all motions and briefs should be filed with the Clerk's Office.

Every factual assertion considered by the submitting party to be important to that party's position in a motion, opposing papers, or brief must be supported by citation or other specific reference to the record where that fact may be found. Legal and record citations must be "pinpoint cites."

1. Oral Argument on Motions. If the court determines that oral argument will be helpful in deciding a matter, the judge will schedule it, particularly when it involves a dispositive motion. A party desiring oral argument should request it by letter or in the body of the motion or responsive pleading. The court is likely to hear oral argument on dispositive motions.

2. Reply and Surreply Briefs. Reply and surreply briefs are discouraged unless it is apparent on the face of the submission that it was necessary to rebut an issue or point of law not discussed in the initial briefs. Reply and surreply briefs may be filed and served within seven days of service of the brief to which the reply or surreply responds unless the court sets a different schedule. Reply and surreply submissions should not contain a repeat recitation of the facts of the case and, without leave of court for good cause shown, must not exceed 15 pages in toto. The court will *not* necessarily delay its decision while awaiting a reply or surreply brief.

No other briefs may be filed without leave of court for good cause shown.

3. Chambers Copies of Motions. Notwithstanding compliance with the court's procedure regarding use of ECF, counsel should send to chambers two courtesy copies of any motions (and related briefs) filed with the clerk of court.

4. Time to Respond to Rule 12(b) and Rule 56 Motions. For cases pending before Judge Pratter, parties have 21 days after service of a motion to dismiss under Fed.R.Civ.P. 12(b) or a motion for summary judgment under Fed.R.Civ.P. 56 to file their response.

Discovery Matters

1. Length of Discovery Period and Extensions. The length of time permitted for discovery depends upon the nature of the case. Generally, discovery will be permitted for up to six months from the date the complaint is responded to by answer or motion. In all employment cases alleging adverse action, parties must comply with the rules set forth in and use the Pilot Project Regarding Initial Discovery Protocols for Employment Cases Alleging Adverse Action.[*] Parties should *not* assume that the filing of a motion to dismiss will be sufficient reason to extend this six-month period, although the court will entertain a reasonable specific request by any party for an order staying discovery during the pendency of a motion to dismiss the complaint, provided that the request is made no later than *promptly* after the response to the motion is filed. In special management cases, Judge Pratter will permit additional time for discovery depending upon the need to do so identified by the parties at the IPTC, and any subsequent status conferences. A case will ordinarily be scheduled to be listed for trial or included in the trial pool approximately 60 days after the scheduled completion of all discovery without regard to the filing or nonfiling of a summary judgment motion.

2. Discovery Conferences and Dispute Resolution. When a discovery dispute occurs, Judge Pratter will consider a motion to compel under Local Civil Rule 26.1(g). Prior to submission of any discovery dispute to the court for resolution, counsel must consult Local Civil Rule 26.1(f), which requires counsel to make reasonable efforts to resolve the discovery dispute before submitting it to the court for resolution. The rule requires that the counsel who is submitting the dispute to the court include a certification that a good-faith resolution effort has been made by the counsel involved in the dispute. Judge Pratter expects that such certification will be substantive, specific, and meaningful. For example, it is not sufficient for the certification to simply recite that "reasonable efforts have been made but were unsuccessful," that "counsel have conferred in good faith," that "counsel repeatedly conferred with opposing counsel," or similar generalities. See, for example, *Naviant Mktg. Solutions, Inc. v. Larry Tucker, Inc.*, 339 F.3d 180, 186 (3d Cir. 2003); *Evans v. American Honda Motors Co.*, Civil Action No. 00-CV-2061 (E.D. Pa. November 26, 2003).

Accordingly, when counsel elect to submit a discovery dispute to Judge Pratter, the submission must include a Rule 26.1(f) certification that delineates with specificity the actual efforts made to resolve the discovery dispute amicably. Failure to include such a certification will subject the submission to summary denial without substantive consideration.

Once a motion to compel is filed, the court likely will schedule a telephone or in-person conference to resolve the dispute, to be held within 14 days or less of the court's receipt of the motion, with or without a formal written response from the non-moving

---

[*] See http://www.paed.uscourts.gov/documents/procedures/prapol3.pdf.

party. If the non-moving party wishes the court to consider the response in advance of ruling and/or a conference, such party should arrange to have the response delivered to chambers promptly or request a delay in the conference to permit the filing of a written response if the court has not requested one. If the court has not scheduled a conference to address a motion to compel, the non-moving party should submit a written response to the motion within seven days of service of the motion. If the parties work out the dispute amicably, they should notify the court and the scheduled conference, if any, will be canceled.

The motion and the response must each be accompanied by a form of order and a *brief not to exceed five pages* describing the disputed issue(s). Discovery motions and responses and the accompanying briefs should *not* recount the allegations of the complaint, the factual underpinnings of the defense, or the history of the case *except as absolutely necessary* for an understanding and resolution of the specific discovery dispute at issue. In many instances, the court expects to rule promptly on discovery motions and often decides such motions during the telephone conference if one is held. The court may act on discovery motions prior to receipt of responsive briefs by initiating a telephone conference for that purpose. A reminder: *All motions must contain the certification required under Local Civil Rule 26.1(f).*

Judge Pratter permits telephone conferences to resolve discovery disputes during depositions in cases where the deposition would otherwise have to be adjourned. However, counsel should resort to such efforts only sparingly and certainly only after making all appropriate efforts to resolve the impasse amicably, professionally, and realistically. Of course, counsel should not assume that last-minute efforts to reach the court for such disputes will be successful.

3. **Confidentiality Agreements.** Judge Pratter will consider entry of stipulated, narrowly fashioned confidentiality, protective, or seal orders if the proposed order includes a detailed statement demonstrating that good cause exists for the order. See *Pansy v. Borough of Stroudsburg,* 23 F.3d 772, 786 (3d Cir. 1994). All such orders must contain the following language (or language substantially similar): "The Court retains the right to allow, sua sponte or upon motion, disclosure of any subject covered by this [stipulation/order] or to modify this [stipulation/order] at any time in the interest of justice."

4. **Expert Witnesses.** The time for disclosure of the identity of experts, submission of curricula vitae, and for discovery pursuant to Fed.R.Civ.P. 26(a)(2)(B) will be set forth in the scheduling order issued at the conclusion of the IPTC. Requests after the conclusion of discovery for scheduling orders relating to expert witnesses will be entertained only upon a showing of good cause and an explanation as to why the need for experts was not anticipated earlier.

Settlement

Settlement will be discussed at the IPTC, at subsequent status conferences, and at the FPTC. However, settlement of a case is primarily the responsibility of the parties and, unless requested by all parties, Judge Pratter generally will not set required or mandatory settlement conferences. Judge Pratter will only very rarely participate in settlement negotiations in nonjury cases or cases where dispositive motions are pending. By agreement of the parties, a case in which settlement prospects are promising may be referred to a magistrate judge or to a senior district court judge for a settlement conference. Judge Pratter welcomes all reasonable suggestions by counsel with respect to options for the pursuit of potential settlement at any time during the pendency of the case.

Arbitration

Upon demand for trial de novo from an arbitration award, Judge Pratter will issue an order setting the date for trial at the earliest date available to the court. Ordinarily, neither discovery nor dispositive motions will be allowed after the arbitration hearing is held except that the parties are free to mutually agree to additional discovery, provided that there is no impact upon the court's scheduling of the case for trial.

Summary Judgment Motions

All summary judgment motions and oppositions to such motions *must* contain a numbered paragraph-by-paragraph recitation of facts with specific citations to the record for the support of all those facts. The court will not consider any assertion of a fact that is not supported by a citation to the record. A party opposing summary judgment must state in similar paragraph form whether that party agrees or disagrees that the fact(s) as stated by the moving party are undisputed. If a party contends that a fact is in dispute, citation must be made to the record evidence that supports the party's view of that particular fact. Failure to address the moving party's factual contentions in this manner will lead to the court's consideration of the moving party's factual assertion(s) as undisputed.

The filing of a motion for summary judgment will *not* operate to postpone or delay an arbitration in the absence of a specific order from the court.

Proposed Final Pretrial Memoranda

Unless otherwise ordered, each party must prepare its own pretrial memoranda and should include the topics addressed in Local Rule of Civil Procedure 16.1(c), and should also include the following items:
a. all stipulations of counsel;
b. any objection to: (1) the admissibility of any exhibit based on authenticity, (2) the admissibility for any reason (except relevancy) of any evidence expected to be offered, (3) the adequacy of the qualifications of an expert witness expected to testify, and (4) the admissibility of any opinion testimony from lay witnesses pursuant to Federal Rule of Evidence 701. Such objection must describe with particularity the ground(s) and the authority for the objection;
c. deposition testimony (including videotaped depositions) to be offered during a party's case-in-chief (with citations to the page and line number), including the opposing party's counter-designations.

The scheduling order, or any other orders that may be entered, will set forth the due date for the final pretrial memoranda.

Injunctions

Judge Pratter will list promptly any request for a temporary restraining order (TRO) or a preliminary injunction assigned to her. She will hold a prehearing conference to discuss discovery to narrow the issues in contention and to allocate time for the hearing. Expedited discovery will be discussed and, when appropriate, ordered at the conclusion of the prehearing conference.

Submission of proposed findings of fact and conclusions of law for TRO and injunction hearings will be required. The time for submission of these items will be set at the prehearing conference.

Trial Procedure

Counsel must read and review with clients and courtroom colleagues the court's "Guidelines for Trial and Other Proceedings in the Courtroom." Those guidelines will be applied by the court, and counsel is expected to be familiar with the guidelines.

1. **Scheduling.** Judge Pratter's practice is to assign either a date for placing the case in the trial pool or a specific trial date at the time of the IPTC. Once a case is placed in the trial pool, counsel, parties, and witnesses should be ready to start trial upon 48 hours telephone notice, although all reasonable efforts will be made to provide at least 72 hours notice. In general, an even longer lead time will be provided. The trial day typically will be from 9:30 a.m. until 4:30 p.m. so that the early morning and late afternoon periods can be used for addressing matters outside the presence of the jury. Questions relating to scheduling matters should be directed to Judge Pratter's deputy clerks (civil or criminal) as appropriate.

2. **Cases Involving Out-of-Town Parties or Witnesses.** Other than in rare and exceptional circumstances, Judge Pratter schedules the trial of cases involving out-of-town counsel, parties, or witnesses the same as all other cases, leaving the scheduling of witnesses to counsel.

3. **Conflicts of Counsel.** Counsel should notify the court and opposing counsel immediately upon hearing of any unavoidable and compelling professional or personal conflicts affecting the trial schedule. Once the trial date has been set the court expects that obligation to take precedence over other matters (except serious, unanticipated personal or professional emergencies).

4. **Note-taking by Jurors.** Judge Pratter decides whether to permit jurors to take notes on an ad hoc basis. Generally, it is permitted. Jurors are not permitted to pose questions to be asked of witnesses.

5. **Voir Dire.** Ordinarily, Judge Pratter will conduct voir dire. The parties are afforded an opportunity to submit proposed voir dire questions. After the court has concluded voir dire, in most cases, counsel may suggest or pose directly follow-up questions. If allowed, counsel should typically use generic questions of the entire panel unless, at the court's invitation, limited follow-up questions of specific jurors is permitted.

6. **Trial Briefs.** Judge Pratter requires the submission of trial briefs no later than seven days before the trial pool date or the specified trial date.

7. **In Limine Motions.** Except as may otherwise be ordered, Judge Pratter requires motions in limine to be submitted in writing no later than 14 days before the trial pool date or specified trial date.

8. **Examination of Witnesses Out of Sequence.** Generally, counsel will be permitted to examine his/her own witnesses out of turn for the convenience of a witness unless it is objected to by the opposing party and prejudice would result.

9. **Opening Statements and Summations.** Judge Pratter normally attempts to obtain the agreement of counsel regarding time limits on opening statements and closing arguments. However, in most cases 20 to 30 minutes should be adequate for an opening statement and 30 to 45 minutes should be adequate for summation.

10. **Examination of Witnesses or Argument by More Than One Attorney.** Judge Pratter will permit more than one attorney for a party to examine different witnesses or to argue different points of law before the court, but only one attorney may examine the same witness, and only one attorney per party may address the jury during the opening statement or summation.

Practice and Procedures of Judges and Judges' Forms and Orders

11. *Examination of Witnesses Beyond Redirect and Recross.* Redirect and recross will be strictly limited to matters not previously covered by direct or cross examinations or special circumstances. Where appropriate, a proffer may be requested before it is permitted.

12. *Videotaped Testimony.* Videotaped testimony should begin with the witness being sworn. Objections should be brought to the court's attention at the time of the FPTC. After the court rules on any objections (ordinarily at the FPTC), counsel must edit the tapes before offering the videotaped testimony at trial. All material objections should be resolved before offering the videotape as evidence.

13. *Reading Material Into the Record.* Judge Pratter has no special practice or policy regarding reading into the record stipulations, pleadings, or discovery material.

14. *Preparation of Exhibits.* Exhibits should be pre-marked and pre-exchanged in accordance with the final pretrial order. On the day trial is scheduled to commence, two binders containing a copy of each exhibit and a copy of a schedule of exhibits should be provided to the court by each party. Equipment and the smooth presentation of exhibits in video or other electronic form is the responsibility of counsel and should be attended to with care. Backup plans in the event of equipment failure should be available.

15. *Offering Exhibits Into Evidence.* Generally, unless the parties have an agreement as to the admissibility of a proposed exhibit, a witness may not testify as to its content until it has been admitted into evidence.

16. *Directed Verdict Motions.* Motions for judgment as a matter of law in jury trials and motions for an involuntary dismissal in nonjury trials should be in writing if at all possible. Oral argument on such motions is ordinarily permitted.

17. *Proposed Jury Instructions and Verdict Forms.* Proposed jury instructions on substantive issues and proposed verdict forms or special interrogatories to the jury should be submitted no later than seven days before the trial pool date. A courtesy copy of the proposed jury instructions (or findings of fact and conclusions of law) should be submitted to chambers by electronic filing in a format discussed ahead of time with the court's chambers staff. Jury instructions need only be submitted with respect to substantive issues in the case. Proposed instructions on procedural matters such as the burden of proof, unanimity, and credibility are not necessary.

Each proposed instruction should be on a separate sheet of paper, double-spaced, and *include citation to specific authority*. Proposed instructions without citation to specific legal authority will not be considered. Cases and model jury instructions that are cited should be accurately quoted and a pinpoint page reference should be provided.

If a model jury instruction is submitted, for instance, from Devitt & Blackmar, *Federal Jury Practice and Instructions,* or Sand, *Modern Federal Jury Instructions,* the submitting party should state whether the proposed jury instruction is unchanged or modified. If a party modifies a model jury instruction, additions should be underlined and deletions should be placed in brackets.

Counsel will have the opportunity to file supplemental points or proposed findings of fact and conclusions of law near the close of testimony, and prior to summations, Judge Pratter conducts a charging conference in all cases.

18. *Proposed Findings of Fact and Conclusions of Law.* Proposed findings of fact and conclusions of law in nonjury cases must be submitted at least seven days before the trial pool date. The parties may submit revised findings of fact and conclusions of law with specific reference to testimonial or documentary evidence that has been admitted at the close of testimony, unless otherwise provided for in the final pretrial order.

19. Offers of Proof. If any party desires an "offer of proof" as to any witness or exhibit expected to be offered, that party must inquire of opposing counsel prior to the start of trial for such information. If the inquiring party is dissatisfied with any offer provided, he or she must file a motion seeking relief prior to trial.

20. Unavailability of Witness. Because a witness may be unavailable at the time of trial, as defined in Fed.R.Civ.P. 32(a)(3), the court expects oral or videotaped depositions to be used at trial for *any witness* whose testimony the party believes essential to the presentation of that party's case, whether the witness is a party, a non-party, or an expert. The unavailability of such witness *will not be a ground to delay* the commencement or progress of trial.

21. Lay Witness Opinion. Any party expecting to offer opinion testimony from lay witnesses pursuant to Federal Rule of Evidence 701 with respect to issues of liability or damages must, at the time required for submission of expert reports, serve the opposing counsel with the same information and/or documents required with respect to such expert witnesses.

Jury Deliberations

1. Written Jury Instructions. In some cases, Judge Pratter may provide the jury with a copy of the instructions.

2. Exhibits in the Jury Room. Unless cause is shown, Judge Pratter will permit all exhibits containing substantive or real evidence to go out with the jury. Demonstrative exhibits ordinarily will not be permitted in the jury room. Counsel should confer with each other as to which exhibits should go into the jury room.

3. Handling Jury Requests to Read Back Testimony or Replay Tapes. At the jury's request, if the transcript is available, Judge Pratter may consider allowing the reading of the appropriate portions back to the jury and the replaying of audio and video tapes.

4. Availability of Counsel During Jury Deliberation. Unless excused by the court, counsel should remain in the courthouse during jury deliberations, and, in any event, be no more than 15 minutes away from the courthouse.

5. Taking the Verdict and Special Verdicts. Ordinarily, Judge Pratter will submit written interrogatories to the jury. The verdict form will be reviewed with counsel before it is provided to the jury.

6. Polling the Jury. Judge Pratter will poll the jury upon request.

7. Interviewing the Jury. Ordinarily, Judge Pratter will allow counsel to interview jurors following conclusion of the trial but will set certain conditions for the interviews. At a minimum, jurors will be told that they are under no obligation to talk with counsel.

CRIMINAL CASES

In general, policies and procedures for criminal cases are those set forth above for civil cases.

1. Oral Argument and Motions. If requested, Judge Pratter generally will permit oral argument on a substantive motion in a criminal case. Evidentiary hearings typically will be set to take place very promptly following the due date of papers opposing the motion.

2. Pretrial Conferences. Judge Pratter will hold a scheduling conference with counsel in criminal cases on an as-needed basis or if requested by counsel. At the conclusion of the conference, if trial seems likely, Judge Pratter will issue a scheduling order governing speedy trial issues, discovery, time for filing motions, and the trial date.

Practice and Procedures of Judges and Judges' Forms and Orders

3. Voir Dire. In criminal cases, the voir dire is conducted by Judge Pratter, based, in part, on questions submitted by counsel. After the voir dire is concluded, the judge will permit counsel to suggest follow-up questions. Counsel should plan for submission of proposed voir dire questions in writing seven days before the trial date.

4. Indictments and Informations. Generally, Judge Pratter does not permit the jury to have a copy of the indictment or information during deliberations.

5. Sentencing Memoranda. Judge Pratter requires the submission of objections to the presentence-investigation report and the submission of sentencing memoranda in accordance with the notice of sentencing issued shortly in conjunction with the entry of a guilty plea or judgment. The judge expects substantive memoranda from both counsel for the government and defense counsel.

6. Continuances. Defense counsel will be expected to consult with counsel's client and set forth in papers submitted to the court the client's position with respect to any request for a continuance. The defendant's written agreement with the request must be submitted to the court at the time of the defense motion.

OTHER GENERAL MATTERS

1. Briefs of Cases on Appeal. Judge Pratter welcomes copies of appellate briefs concerning decisions rendered by her.

2. Consultation with Opposing Counsel. In general, Judge Pratter expects counsel to bring matters to her attention only after they have been discussed with opposing counsel. When communicating with the court, counsel should be prepared to state the position of opposing counsel, e.g., opposing counsel does not oppose the continuance, opposing counsel opposes the request to show photographs to the jury during opening statements, etc.

3. Professionalism in the Courtroom. To repeat comments set forth above, Judge Pratter expects punctuality and courtesy from counsel to the court and to each other, both in the presence of the court and otherwise. The examination of witnesses during hearings or trials should be conducted from the lectern or from counsel's table. Counsel always should rise to address the court unless specifically instructed otherwise. In addition, counsel will direct all comments to the court or to the witness under examination and not to other counsel or to the jury. To the extent possible, the court should be alerted to issues that will need to be ruled upon during the day at the start of the day's proceedings, or during recess out of the jury's presence.

4. Miscellaneous Courtroom Conduct Issues
   a. Counsel must turn off and not operate (surreptitiously or otherwise) cell phones, electronic messaging devices ("Blackberries"), PDAs, pagers, and the like. All such equipment must remain off and unused for the duration of the proceeding. Counsel has the responsibility to advise their client(s), witnesses, and colleagues of the court's requirement in this regard.
   b. If counsel wishes to approach the witness, counsel should ask for permission to do so. If counsel needs to approach one witness many times, a single request for permission will suffice. When counsel approaches the witness, he or she should accomplish the reason for approaching and then return to the place from which he or she is questioning.
   c. If counsel wishes to make an objection, he or she should stand and state the objection along with the technical basis for the objection in a word or phrase, like "hearsay," without making a speech. If counsel wishes to have a sidebar

conference, the court usually will grant the request if counsel does not abuse this option. Counsel is encouraged to bring any evidentiary questions to the attention of the court outside the presence of the jury.

d. Counsel has the responsibility to advise witnesses that no witness may talk to the jury at any time during the pendency of the case. For example, if the witness has stepped down from the witness stand to testify from an exhibit, the witness should not have any private conversation whatsoever with any juror. The witness may, of course, direct his or her answers in the jury's direction, as long as the witness is still answering the lawyer's questions.

e. In opening statements or closing arguments, no lawyer may call a witness or opposing counsel a "liar" or say that the witness "lied." Such conclusions are for the jury to make. Using such language, including use of the phrases, "I believe," or "I think," is not appropriate during openings or closings.

f. There often will be a clerk in the courtroom during a jury trial who can give the jurors any exhibits or other items that counsel requests be given to them. Counsel should not walk up to the jury and start handing the jurors things unless specifically permitted by the court to do so. Likewise, counsel should not ask the jurors if they can see or hear something. If counsel is concerned, he or she should say something like: "Your Honor, would the court ask if the jury can see or hear."

g. A jury trial is a formal affair and all counsel are to act accordingly. Coats, coffee cups, crumpled papers, empty transit boxes, water bottles, candy wrappers, and the like should not be left within sight of the jury.

h. Opposing counsel should not have extended conversations with each other in front of the jury without the court's permission. The court will allow counsel to have a private conversation if requested and if it will move things along. Lawyers should not argue with either opposing counsel or the court.

i. It is counsel's obligation to make all necessary arrangements for securing a transcript of the proceedings.

5.   Additional Questions. If counsel has a specific question on a matter not addressed above, counsel is encouraged to contact the court's chambers staff.

Practice and Procedures of Judges and Judges' Forms and Orders

**UNITED STATES DISTRICT COURT
FOR THE EASTERN DISTRICT OF PENNSYLVANIA**

UNITED STATES OF AMERICA   Criminal No.

    vs.

    I, _____ (Defendant), have consulted with my counsel concerning my right under the Speedy Trial Act and my right to a speedy trial under the Sixth Amendment to the U.S. Constitution. I do not oppose a continuance of my trial, now scheduled for (**date**), and agree that the ends of justice served by a continuance outweigh the best interest of the public and myself in a speedy trial. I understand that the time between the filing of a Motion to Continue and the new trial date to be set by the Court will be excluded for purposes of computing the time within which my trial must commence under the Speedy Trial Act, and I also agree that this delay will not deprive me of my speedy trial rights under the Sixth Amendment. I understand that if I do not wish to sign this document, the Court will hold a hearing at which I will be present.

_____   _____
Witness signature   Defendant

                                                                       _____
                                                                       Date

Judge Gene E.K. Pratter

This Order will be modified as needed in cases involving Pro Se Defendants.

IN THE UNITED STATES DISTRICT COURT
FOR THE EASTERN DISTRICT OF PENNSYLVANIA

XXXXX	:	CIVIL ACTION
Plaintiff	:	
v.	:	
	:	
XXXXXXXXXX	:	
Defendant.	:	No. XX–XXXX

ORDER

AND NOW, on this ____ day of _____, 20__, upon consideration of Plaintiff's Complaint and *pro se* status, it is hereby **ORDERED** that:

1. Plaintiff is reminded that [his/her] status as a self-represented litigant does not insulate [him/her] from the obligations to follow the applicable rules, deadlines, requirements, and procedures relating to this case.

2. All original pleadings and other papers submitted for consideration to the Court in this case are to be filed with the Clerk of Court. Copies of papers filed in this Court are to be served upon counsel for all other parties (or directly on any party acting *pro se*). Service may be by first class, postage pre-paid mail, except as to the original Complaint, which must be served in compliance with Rule 4 of the Federal Rules of Civil Procedure. Proof that service has been made is provided by a certificate of service. This certificate should be filed in the case along with the original papers and should show the date and manner of service. If any pleading or other paper submitted for filing does not include a certificate of service upon the opposing party or counsel for opposing party, it may be disregarded by the Court.

3. Any request for court action shall be set forth in a motion, properly filed and served. The parties shall file all motions, including proof of service upon opposing parties, with the Clerk of Court. The Federal Rules of Civil Procedure, Local Rules, and this Court's General Policies and Procedures[*] are to be followed. Plaintiff is specifically directed to comply with Local Civil Rule 7.1 and this Court's Policies and Procedures and serve and file a proper response to all motions within the time specified therein. Failure to do so may result in dismissal of this action or other sanction.

4. If Plaintiff has received substantive assistance (i.e., help with the development of strategy or tactics, drafting pleadings or motions or briefs, etc.) from an attorney for any material filed with the Court, [he/she] shall, at the time the material is filed, identify the attorney, the attorney's contribution to the filing, and the scope of the attorney's limited representation.

5. Plaintiff is specifically directed to comply with Local Rule 26.1(f) which provides that "[n]o motion or other application pursuant to the Federal Rules of Civil Procedure governing discovery or pursuant to this rule shall be made unless it contains a certification of counsel that the parties, after reasonable effort,

---

[*] All counsel and unrepresented parties are expected to review the Court's General Policies and Procedures available on the Court's website at www.paed.uscourts.gov concerning the conduct of the litigation. Any counsel or unrepresented party desiring a hard copy of the Court's Policies and Procedures may call the Court's Civil Deputy, Ms. Rose A. Barber, at 267-299-7350, to request a copy.

are unable to resolve the dispute." Plaintiff shall attempt to resolve any discovery disputes by contacting defendant's counsel directly by telephone or through correspondence.

6. No direct communication is to take place with the District Judge or United States Magistrate Judge with regard to this case, unless explicitly instructed otherwise. All relevant information and papers are to be directed to the Clerk of Court.

7. Plaintiff is directed to provide to the Clerk of Court all addresses, fax numbers, email addresses or other contact points by which [he/she] can be contacted regarding this case. *See also* Local Rule of Civil Procedure 5.1. All parties have the obligation to provide current, accurate contact information to the Court and opposing counsel. Failure to do so could result in court orders or other information not being timely delivered, which could affect the parties' legal rights.

BY THE COURT:

_____
GENE E.K. PRATTER
UNITED STATES DISTRICT JUDGE

Judge Gene E.K. Pratter

GUIDELINES FOR TRIAL AND OTHER PROCEEDINGS IN THE COURTROOM
JUDGE GENE E.K. PRATTER

COUNSEL IS ALSO ADVISED TO READ JUDGE PRATTER'S GENERAL PRETRIAL AND TRIAL PROCEDURES

TRIAL COUNSEL: PLEASE READ CAREFULLY. SHARE THESE GUIDELINES WITH YOUR CLIENTS AND COLLEAGUES WHO WILL BE PARTICIPATING IN TRIAL.

Preface

Compliance with these Guidelines is expected. These Guidelines are not intended to be exhaustive; they may be curtailed or modified in some cases. Deviations, or requests for deviations, will be discussed at the pretrial conference(s).

Civility is the key to behavior in the court—that includes everyone: the Judge, staff, lawyers, parties, witnesses and observers. If there are complaints about anyone's civility, please bring the matter to the immediate attention of the Court by asking for a conference in Chambers.

Promptness

1. The Judge makes every effort to commence proceedings at the time set. Promptness is expected from counsel and witnesses. Known scheduling issues, or requests for scheduling changes should be raised with the Court at the earliest possible time. Schedule changes will be announced as soon as they are known.

2. During jury deliberations, counsel must be present or available in the Courtroom on 15 minutes' notice to counsel's office. Otherwise, the right to be present may be waived, and counsel's absence may be taken as counsel's consent for proceedings to take place in the courtroom during counsel's absence.

Courtroom Decorum

1. Keep the proceedings low-key and reasonably formal. It is not a circus, an audition or a stage for demonstrating dramatic ability; nor is it an oratorical contest. It should be a dignified proceeding at all times.

2. Rise when the jury or the Judge enter or leave the courtroom.

3. Address all remarks to the Judge, not to opposing counsel. Colloquy or argument between or among attorneys is prohibited.

4. Rise when addressing the Judge and when making objections. (This calls the Judge's attention to objecting counsel and makes it much easier for the court reporter to correctly note the speaker.)

5. When offering a stipulation in a jury case, first confer with opposing counsel so that there are no misunderstandings.

6. Do not exhibit excessive familiarity with witnesses, jurors, or opposing counsel. For example, do not use first names for witnesses, parties or opposing counsel. During jury argument, do not address any jury individually or by name.

7. Do not bring food or beverages into the courtroom without the Court's express advance permission. (During lengthy proceedings the Court will allow counsel to keep unobtrusive mints and the like at counsel table.) Do not allow witnesses, co-counsel, legal assistants or visitors to chew gum, bring in packaged snacks, bottled water, "designer" coffees, etc. Water will be available on the witness stand and on counsel tables.

8. When court is in session, do not address the reporter, ESR operator or Courtroom Deputy. All requests made of court personnel should be addressed to the Court.

9. Stand a respectful distance from the jury at all times.

10. Address the Court as "Your Honor," not "Ma'am".

11. TURN OFF all cell phones, Blackberries, pagers, PDA's or similar devices. These devices must remain off and unused in the courtroom unless the Court gives express permission to the contrary. Do not operate Blackberries, text messaging devices or similar equipment to transmit at any time during any proceeding in the courtroom. Both the Court and the jury can see when counsel or litigants are doing so,

and it is generally interpreted as being rude. It also causes counsel to miss important things happening in court.

Statement of the Case

Each party must submit a "statement of the case" for use by the Court at the beginning of voir dire to advise the jurors of the nature of the case and the issues to be decided by the jury. The statement should be brief (normally two or three paragraphs in length) and neutral in tone and content.

Opening Statements

Confine opening statements to what counsel expects the evidence to show. It is not proper to use the opening statement to argue the case, instruct as to the law, or explain the purpose of an opening statement. Presumably the Court has already done so. Unless the case is unusually complex, the average time for an opening statement should be less than 30 minutes.

Voir Dire

The Court will conduct voir dire of the jury. Counsel may be permitted to ask brief follow-up questions of the jurors. Counsel may suggest questions for the Court to pose to the whole panel. Do not attempt to question each juror or condition jurors unless the Court specifically authorizes such a procedure. Typically, individual follow-up voir dire at side bar with counsel and the specific juror will follow the general voir dire of the panel as a whole.

Witnesses

1. It is unnecessary to greet or introduce oneself to adverse witnesses. Commence cross-examination without preliminaries. The right to cross-examine is neither a right to examine crossly nor to ask the witness to pass on the credibility of another witness.

2. Examine witnesses while seated at counsel table, standing behind counsel table, or at the lectern, as directed by the Court. Generally, the Court expects counsel to use the lectern.

3. Do not approach a witness or the bench without leave of Court.

4. Do not hover over a witness, even when permission has been granted to approach the witness. Maintain a respectable distance from the witness.

5. If there is need to point to an exhibit or to use the easel when asking a question, return to counsel table or the lectern as soon as possible. Do not linger in the well of the court.

6. A whiteboard, white paper, chalk, pens, pointer, screen, TV and VCR are available. However, if counsel wants an x-ray viewing box, tape recorder, computer, power point or similar equipment, counsel must furnish it or make arrangements with the Courtroom Deputy in advance, preferably no later than the final pretrial conference.

7. Treat witnesses with fairness and consideration. Do not shout at, ridicule or otherwise abuse witnesses. Do not engage in argumentative "talking over" a witness who attempts to explain an answer. If appropriate, counsel should ask the Court to curtail the witness who is unresponsive.

8. Do not ever, by facial expression or other conduct, exhibit any opinion concerning any witness' testimony. Counsel are to admonish their clients and witnesses about this common occurrence.

9. Do not ask the stenography/ESR operator to mark testimony. Address all requests for re-reading of questions and answers to the Judge.

10. If a witness is on the stand at a recess or adjournment, have the witness back on the stand ready to proceed when the proceedings resume.

11. Do not delay proceedings by writing out witnesses' answers during questioning. Charts and diagrams, where possible, should be prepared in advance, but counsel may use the writing board for opening statements and closing arguments.

12. Where a party has more than one lawyer, only one lawyer may conduct the direct or cross-examination of a given witness.

Objections

1. When objecting, stand and state only that there is an objection and briefly specify the technical nature of the ground(s). Do not use objections to make a speech, recapitulate testimony, or to guide the witness.

2. Do not argue an objection until the Judge grants permission or requests argument.

3. Give the Judge advance notice if there is reason to anticipate that any question of law or evidence is difficult, unusual, obscure or will provoke an argument.

4. Sidebar or Chambers conferences during trial are not to be utilized for discussion of evidentiary issues that could be addressed during recesses. If the issue is important enough to justify interruption of the trial, the jury will be excused and the matter heard in open court.

Exhibits

1. Normally, all exhibits should be marked in advance.

2. If counsel desires to display exhibits to the jury, sufficient additional copies must be available to provide each juror with a copy. Alternatively, use enlarged photographic, projected copies or juror notebooks. When copies have been provided (as is expected), the law clerk or Courtroom Deputy will hand out copies to the jurors unless the Court expressly permits counsel to do so.

3. Each counsel is responsible for any exhibits secured from the Deputy. At each noon-time or end-of-the-day adjournment, return all admitted exhibits to the Deputy. It is strongly recommended that counsel work together to make sure at least one extra set of clean exhibits is available in the courtroom.

4. If at all possible, let the Deputy or the Court know in advance the exhibits your next witness will be using.

5. Do not approach the witness with an exhibit without permission from the Judge.

6. Show documents and other exhibits, where practical, to opposing counsel *before* their use in court.

7. In a rare case, when it is necessary to mark an exhibit in open court, ask that the reporter or Deputy mark it and briefly describe the nature of the exhibit.

8. Exhibits should be offered in evidence when they become admissible rather than as a group at the end of counsel's case.

9. When referring to an exhibit, mention the exhibit number so that the record will be clear.

10. Counsel must review and certify on the record that what goes to the jury is correct before closing arguments.

11. Ordinarily, exhibits will be returned to counsel at the end of trial.

Depositions

1. All depositions used at the trial must be in accordance with the Local Rules.

2. Portions of depositions used for impeachment may be read to the jury during cross-examination, with pages and lines indicated for the record before reading. The witness should be asked whether he or she was asked the question(s) and gave the answer(s) on the date of the deposition(s).

Closing Arguments

Counsel should never assert personal opinion of: 1) the credibility of a witness, 2) the culpability of a civil litigant, or 3) the guilt or innocence of an accused. Never assert personal knowledge of a fact in issue or a fact not in evidence; do not argue the "Golden Rule."

Jury Instructions

All requested instructions must be filed and served no later than the final pretrial conference or as otherwise ordered by the Court. Supplemental instructions must be filed and served as soon as the need for them becomes apparent. Attempt to agree on neutral instructions. Remember: less is better than more, and "advocacy" instructions will be rejected. Joint submissions of instructions may be required.

Professionalism

Remember—professionalism is paramount and helps everyone achieve a fair, expeditious and economical trial.

PILOT PROJECT REGARDING
INITIAL DISCOVERY PROTOCOLS
FOR EMPLOYMENT CASES ALLEGING ADVERSE ACTION

November 2011

The Federal Judicial Center is making this document available at the request of the Advisory Committee on Civil Rules, in furtherance of the Center's statutory mission to conduct and stimulate research and development for the improvement of judicial administration. While the Center regards the contents as responsible and valuable, it does not reflect policy or recommendations of the Board of the Federal Judicial Center.

TABLE OF CONTENTS

	Page
Introduction	218
Employment Protocols Committee Roster	220
Initial Discovery Protocols for Employment Cases Alleging Adverse Action	220
Standing Order for Certain Employment Cases	224
Model Protective Order	225

INTRODUCTION

The Initial Discovery Protocols for Employment Cases Alleging Adverse Action provide a new pretrial procedure for certain types of federal employment cases. As described in the Protocols, their intent is to "encourage parties and their counsel to exchange the most relevant information and documents early in the case, to assist in framing the issues to be resolved and to plan for more efficient and targeted discovery." Individual judges throughout the United States District Courts will pilot test the Protocols and the Federal Judicial Center will evaluate their effects.

This project grew out of the 2010 Conference on Civil Litigation at Duke University, sponsored by the Judicial Conference Advisory Committee on Civil Rules for the purpose of re-examining civil procedures and collecting recommendations for their improvement. During the conference, a wide range of attendees expressed support for the idea of case-type-specific "pattern discovery" as a possible solution to the problems of unnecessary cost and delay in the litigation process. They also arrived at a consensus that employment cases, "regularly litigated and [presenting] recurring issues,"* would be a good area for experimentation with the concept.

Following the conference, Judge Lee Rosenthal convened a nationwide committee of attorneys, highly experienced in employment matters, to develop a pilot project in this area. Judge John Koeltl volunteered to lead this committee. By design, the committee had a balance of plaintiff and defense attorneys.

---

* Civil Rules Advisory Committee, *Report to the Standing Committee*, 10 (May 17, 2010).

Joseph Garrison[*] (New Haven, Connecticut) chaired a plaintiff subcommittee, and Chris Kitchel[†] (Portland, Oregon) chaired a defense subcommittee. The committee invited the Institute for the Advancement of the American Legal System at the University of Denver (IAALS) to facilitate the process.

The group worked diligently over the course of one year. Committee members met at IAALS for valuable in-person discussions in March and July of 2011. Judge Koeltl was in attendance as well, to oversee the process and assist in achieving workable consensus. In addition, committee members exchanged hundreds of emails, held frequent telephone conferences, and prepared numerous drafts. The committee's final product is the result of rigorous debate and compromise on both sides, undertaken in the spirit of making constructive and even-handed improvements to the pretrial process.

The Protocols create a new category of information exchange, replacing initial disclosures with initial discovery specific to employment cases alleging adverse action. This discovery is provided automatically by both sides within 30 days of the defendant's responsive pleading or motion. While the parties' subsequent right to discovery under the F.R.C.P. is not affected, the amount and type of information initially exchanged ought to focus the disputed issues, streamline the discovery process, and minimize opportunities for gamesmanship. The Protocols are accompanied by a standing order for their implementation by individual judges in the pilot project, as well as a model protective order that the attorneys and the judge can use a basis for discussion.

The Federal Judicial Center will establish a framework for effectively measuring the results of this pilot project.[‡] If the new process ultimately benefits litigants, it is a model that can be used to develop protocols for other types of cases. **Please note**: Judges adopting the protocols for use in cases before them should inform FJC senior researcher Emery Lee, elee@fjc.gov, so that their cases may be included in the evaluation.

---

[*] Mr. Garrison was a panelist at the Duke Conference. He also wrote and submitted a conference paper, entitled *A Proposal to Implement a Cost-Effective and Efficient Procedural Tool Into Federal Litigation Practice*, which advocated for the adoption of model or pattern discovery tools for "categories of cases which routinely appear in the federal courts" and suggested the appointment of a task force to bring the idea to fruition.

[†] Ms. Kitchel serves on the American College of Trial Lawyers Task Force on Discovery and Civil Justice, which produced the *Final Report on the Joint Project of the American College of Trial Lawyers Task Force on Discovery and the Institute for the Advancement of the American Legal System*, 268 F.R.D. 407 (2009). As a result of her role on the ACTL Task Force, Ms. Kitchel had already begun discussing possibilities for improving employment litigation with Judge Rosenthal when she attended the Duke Conference.

[‡] Civil Rules Advisory Committee, *Draft Minutes of April 2011 Meeting*, 43 (June 8, 2011).

EMPLOYMENT PROTOCOLS COMMITTEE ROSTER

Fred Alvarez
Wilson Sonsini Goodrich & Rosati
Palo Alto, CA

Kathryn Burkett Dickson
Dickson Levy Vinick Burrell Hyams LLP
Oakland, CA

Herbert Eisenberg
Eisenberg & Schnell LLP
New York, NY

Joseph Garrison
Garrison, Levin-Epstein, Chimes,
Richardson & Fitzgerald, PC
New Haven, CT

Margaret Harris
Butler & Harris
Houston, TX

John Jansonius
Akin Gump Strauss Hauer & Feld LLP
Dallas, TX

Chris Kitchel
Stoel Rives LLP
Portland, OR

Jonathan Margolis
Rodgers, Powers & Schwartz, LLP
Boston, MA

Ellen Messing
Messing, Rudavsky & Weliky, PC
Boston, MA

Bettina (Betsy) Plevan
Proskauer Rose LLP
New York, NY

Felix Springer
Day Pitney LLP
Hartford, CT

INITIAL DISCOVERY PROTOCOLS
FOR EMPLOYMENT CASES ALLEGING ADVERSE ACTION

PART 1: INTRODUCTION AND DEFINITIONS.

(1) Statement of purpose.

    a. The Initial Discovery Protocols for Employment Cases Alleging Adverse Action is a proposal designed to be implemented as a pilot project by individual judges throughout the United States District Courts. The project and the product are endorsed by the Civil Rules Advisory Committee.

    b. In participating courts, the Initial Discovery Protocols will be implemented by standing order and will apply to all employment cases that challenge one or more actions alleged to be adverse, except:

        i. Class actions;

        ii. Cases in which the allegations involve <u>only</u> the following:

            1. Discrimination in hiring;

            2. Harassment/hostile work environment;

            3. Violations of wage and hour laws under the Fair Labor Standards Act (FLSA);

            4. Failure to provide reasonable accommodations under the Americans with Disabilities Act (ADA);

            5. Violations of the Family Medical Leave Act (FMLA);

            6. Violations of the Employee Retirement Income Security Act (ERISA).

    If any party believes that there is good cause why a particular case should be exempted, in whole or in part, from this pilot program, that party may raise such reason with the Court.

c. The Initial Discovery Protocols are not intended to preclude or to modify the rights of any party for discovery as provided by the Federal Rules of Civil Procedure (F.R.C.P.) and other applicable local rules, but they are intended to supersede the parties' obligations to make initial disclosures pursuant to F.R.C.P. 26(a)(1). The purpose of the pilot project is to encourage parties and their counsel to exchange the most relevant information and documents early in the case, to assist in framing the issues to be resolved and to plan for more efficient and targeted discovery.

d. The Initial Discovery Protocols were prepared by a group of highly experienced attorneys from across the country who regularly represent plaintiffs and/or defendants in employment matters. The information and documents identified are those most likely to be requested automatically by experienced counsel in any similar case. They are unlike initial disclosures pursuant to F.R.C.P. 26(a)(1) because they focus on the type of information most likely to be useful in narrowing the issues for employment discrimination cases.

(2) Definitions. The following definitions apply to cases proceeding under the Initial Discovery Protocols.

a. ***Concerning.*** The term "concerning" means referring to, describing, evidencing, or constituting.

b. ***Document.*** The terms "document" and "documents" are defined to be synonymous in meaning and equal in scope to the terms "documents" and "electronically stored information" as used in F.R.C.P. 34(a).

c. ***Identify (Documents).*** When referring to documents, to "identify" means to give, to the extent known: (i) the type of document; (ii) the general subject matter of the document; (iii) the date of the document; (iv) the author(s), according to the document; and (v) the person(s) to whom, according to the document, the document (or a copy) was to have been sent; or, alternatively, to produce the document.

d. ***Identify (Persons).*** When referring to natural persons, to "identify" means to give the person's: (i) full name; (ii) present or last known address and telephone number; (iii) present or last known place of employment; (iv) present or last known job title; and (v) relationship, if any, to the plaintiff or defendant. Once a person has been identified in accordance with this subparagraph, only the name of that person need be listed in response to subsequent discovery requesting the identification of that person.

(3) Instructions.

a. For this Initial Discovery, the relevant time period begins three years before the date of the adverse action, unless otherwise specified.

b. This Initial Discovery is not subject to objections except upon the grounds set forth in F.R.C.P. 26(b)(2)(B).

c. If a partial or incomplete answer or production is provided, the responding party shall state the reason that the answer or production is partial or incomplete.

d. This Initial Discovery is subject to F.R.C.P. 26(e) regarding supplementation and F.R.C.P. 26(g) regarding certification of responses.

e. This Initial Discovery is subject to F.R.C.P. 34(B)(2)(E) regarding form of production.

PART 2: PRODUCTION BY PLAINTIFF.

(1) Timing.

a. The plaintiff's Initial Discovery shall be provided within 30 days after the defendant has submitted a responsive pleading or motion, unless the court rules otherwise.

(2) Documents that Plaintiff must produce to Defendant.

a. All communications concerning the factual allegations or claims at issue in this lawsuit between the plaintiff and the defendant.

Practice and Procedures of Judges and Judges' Forms and Orders

    b.   Claims, lawsuits, administrative charges, and complaints by the plaintiff that rely upon any of the same factual allegations or claims as those at issue in this lawsuit.

    c.   Documents concerning the formation and termination, if any, of the employment relationship at issue in this lawsuit, irrespective of the relevant time period.

    d.   Documents concerning the terms and conditions of the employment relationship at issue in this lawsuit.

    e.   Diary, journal, and calendar entries maintained by the plaintiff concerning the factual allegations or claims at issue in this lawsuit.

    f.   The plaintiff's current resume(s).

    g.   Documents in the possession of the plaintiff concerning claims for unemployment benefits, unless production is prohibited by applicable law.

    h.   Documents concerning: (i) communications with potential employers; (ii) job search efforts; and (iii) offer(s) of employment, job description(s), and income and benefits of subsequent employment. The defendant shall not contact or subpoena a prospective or current employer to discover information about the plaintiff's claims without first providing the plaintiff 30 days notice and an opportunity to file a motion for a protective order or a motion to quash such subpoena. If such a motion is filed, contact will not be initiated or the subpoena will not be served until the motion is ruled upon.

    i.   Documents concerning the termination of any subsequent employment.

    j.   Any other document(s) upon which the plaintiff relies to support the plaintiff's claims.

(3) Information that Plaintiff must produce to Defendant.

    a.   Identify persons the plaintiff believes to have knowledge of the facts concerning the claims or defenses at issue in this lawsuit, and a brief description of that knowledge.

    b.   Describe the categories of damages the plaintiff claims.

    c.   State whether the plaintiff has applied for disability benefits and/or social security disability benefits after the adverse action, whether any application has been granted, and the nature of the award, if any. Identify any document concerning any such application.

PART 3: PRODUCTION BY DEFENDANT.

(1) Timing.

    a.   The defendant's Initial Discovery shall be provided within 30 days after the defendant has submitted a responsive pleading or motion, unless the court rules otherwise.

(2) Documents that Defendant must produce to Plaintiff.

    a.   All communications concerning the factual allegations or claims at issue in this lawsuit among or between:

        i.   The plaintiff and the defendant;

        ii.   The plaintiff's manager(s), and/or supervisor(s), and/or the defendant's human resources representative(s).

    b.   Responses to claims, lawsuits, administrative charges, and complaints by the plaintiff that rely upon any of the same factual allegations or claims as those at issue in this lawsuit.

    c.   Documents concerning the formation and termination, if any, of the employment relationship at issue in this lawsuit, irrespective of the relevant time period.

d. The plaintiff's personnel file, in any form, maintained by the defendant, including files concerning the plaintiff maintained by the plaintiff's supervisor(s), manager(s), or the defendant's human resources representative(s), irrespective of the relevant time period.

e. The plaintiff's performance evaluations and formal discipline.

f. Documents relied upon to make the employment decision(s) at issue in this lawsuit.

g. Workplace policies or guidelines relevant to the adverse action in effect at the time of the adverse action. Depending upon the case, those may include policies or guidelines that address:

   i. Discipline;

   ii. Termination of employment;

   iii. Promotion;

   iv. Discrimination;

   v. Performance reviews or evaluations;

   vi. Misconduct;

   vii. Retaliation; and

   viii. Nature of the employment relationship.

h. The table of contents and index of any employee handbook, code of conduct, or policies and procedures manual in effect at the time of the adverse action.

i. Job description(s) for the position(s) that the plaintiff held.

j. Documents showing the plaintiff's compensation and benefits. Those normally include retirement plan benefits, fringe benefits, employee benefit summary plan descriptions, and summaries of compensation.

k. Agreements between the plaintiff and the defendant to waive jury trial rights or to arbitrate disputes.

l. Documents concerning investigation(s) of any complaint(s) about the plaintiff or made by the plaintiff, if relevant to the plaintiff's factual allegations or claims at issue in this lawsuit and not otherwise privileged.

m. Documents in the possession of the defendant and/or the defendant's agent(s) concerning claims for unemployment benefits unless production is prohibited by applicable law.

n. Any other document(s) upon which the defendant relies to support the defenses, affirmative defenses, and counterclaims, including any other document(s) describing the reasons for the adverse action.

(3) Information that Defendant must produce to Plaintiff.

a. Identify the plaintiff's supervisor(s) and/or manager(s).

b. Identify person(s) presently known to the defendant who were involved in making the decision to take the adverse action.

c. Identify persons the defendant believes to have knowledge of the facts concerning the claims or defenses at issue in this lawsuit, and a brief description of that knowledge.

d. State whether the plaintiff has applied for disability benefits and/or social security disability benefits after the adverse action. State whether the defendant has provided information to any third party concerning the application(s). Identify any documents concerning any such application or any such information provided to a third party.

Practice and Procedures of Judges and Judges' Forms and Orders

UNITED STATES DISTRICT COURT
FOR THE _____ DISTRICT OF _____
_____ DIVISION

_____,)		
Plaintiff,)		
)		
vs.)	Case No. _____	
)		
_____,)	Judge _____	
)		
Defendant.)		

STANDING ORDER FOR CERTAIN EMPLOYMENT CASES

    This Court is participating in a Pilot Program for **INITIAL DISCOVERY PROTOCOLS FOR EMPLOYMENT CASES ALLEGING ADVERSE ACTION,** initiated by the Advisory Committee on Federal Rules of Civil Procedure (see "Discovery protocol for employment cases," under "Educational programs and materials," at www.fjc.gov).

    The Initial Discovery Protocols will apply to all employment cases pending in this court that challenge one or more actions alleged to be adverse, except:

      i. Class actions;
     ii. Cases in which the allegations involve <u>only</u> the following:

          1. Discrimination in hiring;
          2. Harassment/hostile work environment;
          3. Violations of wage and hour laws under the Fair Labor Standards Act (FLSA);
          4. Failure to provide reasonable accommodations under the Americans with Disabilities Act (ADA);
          5. Violations of the Family Medical Leave Act (FMLA);
          6. Violations of the Employee Retirement Income Security Act (ERISA).

    Parties and counsel in the Pilot Program shall comply with the Initial Discovery Protocols, attached to this Order. If any party believes that there is good cause why a particular case should be exempted from the Initial Discovery Protocols, in whole or in part, that party may raise the issue with the Court.

    Within 30 days following the defendant's submission of a responsive pleading or motion, the parties shall provide to one another the documents and information described in the Initial Discovery Protocols for the relevant time period. This obligation supersedes the parties' obligations to provide initial disclosures pursuant to F.R.C.P. 26(a)(1). The parties shall use the documents and information exchanged in accordance with the Initial Discovery Protocols to prepare the F.R.C.P. 26(f) discovery plan.

    The parties' responses to the Initial Discovery Protocols shall comply with the F.R.C.P. obligations to certify and supplement discovery responses, as well as the form of production standards for documents and electronically stored information. As set forth in the Protocols, this Initial Discovery is not subject to objections, except upon the grounds set forth in F.R.C.P. 26(b)(2)(B).

ENTER:

Dated: _____   _____
                                                                 [Name]
                                                                 United States [District/Magistrate] Judge

Judge Gene E.K. Pratter

The Initial Discovery Protocols for Employment Cases Alleging Adverse Action are designed to achieve the goal of more efficient and targeted discovery. If a protective order will be entered in a case to which the Initial Discovery Protocols applies, immediate entry of the order will allow the parties to commence discovery without delay. In furtherance of that goal, the Employment Protocols Committee offers the following Model Protective Order. Recognizing that the decision to enter a protective order, as well as the parameters of any such order, rests within the Court's sound discretion and is subject to local practice, the following provisions are options from which the Court might select.

MODEL PROTECTIVE ORDER

It is hereby ordered by the Court that the following restrictions and procedures shall apply to certain information, documents and excerpts from documents supplied by the parties to each other in response to discovery requests:

1. Counsel for any party may designate any document, information contained in a document, information revealed in an interrogatory response or information revealed during a deposition as confidential if counsel determines, in good faith, that such designation is necessary to protect the interests of the client. Information and documents designated by a party as confidential will be stamped "CONFIDENTIAL." "Confidential" information or documents may be referred to collectively as "confidential information."

2. Unless ordered by the Court, or otherwise provided for herein, the Confidential Information disclosed will be held and used by the person receiving such information solely for use in connection with the above-captioned action.

3. In the event a party challenges another party's confidential designation, counsel shall make a good faith effort to resolve the dispute, and in the absence of a resolution, the challenging party may thereafter seek resolution by the Court. Nothing in this Protective Order constitutes an admission by any party that Confidential Information disclosed in this case is relevant or admissible. Each party specifically reserves the right to object to the use or admissibility of all Confidential Information disclosed, in accordance with applicable law and Court rules.

4. Information or documents designated as "confidential" shall not be disclosed to any person, except:

    a. The requesting party and counsel, including in-house counsel;

    b. Employees of such counsel assigned to and necessary to assist in the litigation;

    c. Consultants or experts assisting in the prosecution or defense of the matter, to the extent deemed necessary by counsel;

    d. Any person from whom testimony is taken or is to be taken in these actions, except that such a person may only be shown that Confidential Information during and in preparation for his/her testimony and may not retain the Confidential Information; and

    e. The Court (including any clerk, stenographer, or other person having access to any Confidential Information by virtue of his or her position with the Court) or the jury at trial or as exhibits to motions.

5. Prior to disclosing or displaying the Confidential Information to any person, counsel shall:

    a. inform the person of the confidential nature of the information or documents; and

    b. inform the person that this Court has enjoined the use of the information or documents by him/her for any purpose other than this litigation and has enjoined the disclosure of that information or documents to any other person.

6. The Confidential Information may be displayed to and discussed with the persons identified in Paragraphs 4(c) and (d) only on the condition that prior to any such display or discussion, each such person shall be asked to sign an agreement to be bound by this Order in the form attached

hereto as Exhibit A. In the event such person refuses to sign an agreement in the form attached as Exhibit A, the party desiring to disclose the Confidential Information may seek appropriate relief from the Court.

7. The disclosure of a document or information without designating it as "confidential" shall not constitute a waiver of the right to designate such document or information as Confidential Information provided that the material is designated pursuant to the procedures set forth herein no later than that latter of fourteen (14) days after the close of discovery or fourteen (14) days after the document or information's production. If so designated, the document or information shall thenceforth be treated as Confidential Information subject to all the terms of this Stipulation and Order.

8. All information subject to confidential treatment in accordance with the terms of this Stipulation and Order that is filed with the Court, and any pleadings, motions or other papers filed with the Court disclosing any Confidential Information, shall be filed under seal to the extent permitted by law (including without limitation any applicable rules of court) and kept under seal until further order of the Court. To the extent the Court requires any further act by the parties as a precondition to the filing of documents under seal (beyond the submission of this Stipulation and Order Regarding Confidential Information), it shall be the obligation of the producing party of the documents to be filed with the Court to satisfy any such precondition. Where possible, only confidential portions of filings with the Court shall be filed under seal.

9. At the conclusion of litigation, the Confidential Information and any copies thereof shall be promptly (and in no event later than thirty (30) days after entry of final judgment no longer subject to further appeal) returned to the producing party or certified as destroyed, except that the parties' counsel shall be permitted to retain their working files on the condition that those files will remain confidential.

The foregoing is entirely without prejudice to the right of any party to apply to the Court for any further Protective Order relating to confidential information; or to object to the production of documents or information; or to apply to the Court for an order compelling production of documents or information; or for modification of this Order. This Order may be enforced by either party and any violation may result in the imposition of sanctions by the Court.

EXHIBIT A

 I have been informed by counsel that certain documents or information to be disclosed to me in connection with the matter entitled _____ have been designated as confidential. I have been informed that any such documents or information labeled "CONFIDENTIAL—PRODUCED PURSUANT TO PROTECTIVE ORDER" are confidential by Order of the Court.

 I hereby agree that I will not disclose any information contained in such documents to any other person. I further agree not to use any such information for any purpose other than this litigation.

_____ DATED:

Signed in the presence of:

_____

(Attorney)

Judge Nitza I. Quiñones Alejandro

Judge Quiñones Alejandro was born in 1951 in Puerto Rico, where she grew up in a military family. She received her B.B.A. in 1972 from the School of Business at the University of Puerto Rico and her J.D. in 1975 from the University of Puerto Rico School of Law. After graduating from law school, she moved to Philadelphia and began her career as a Staff Attorney for Community Legal Services, Inc., where she worked from 1975 to 1977. From 1977 to 1979, Judge Quiñones Alejandro worked as an attorney advisor for the Office of Hearings and Appeals of the Social Security Administration in the Department of Health and Human Services. From 1979 to 1991, she served as a staff attorney for the Office of District Counsel of the Department of Veterans Affairs. On November 5, 1991, she was elected as the first hispanic female judge to serve on the Philadelphia County Court of Common Pleas. Presiding over both criminal and civil cases, Judge Quiñones Alejandro served on the Court of Common Pleas until 2013. She became a judge of the United States District Court for the Eastern District of Pennsylvania on June 19, 2013.

At this time, Judge Quiñones Alejandro has no set judicial practices or procedures. Counsel and pro se litigants are advised to follow the Federal Rules of Civil Procedure and the Local Civil Rules. Consistent with this directive, letter motion practice is discouraged unless the matter has been discussed with all parties and there is no opposition to the request.

Judge Quiñones Alejandro's practices and procedures will appear on the website of the district court as soon as they are available. The website can be found at http://www.paed.uscourts.gov/us08001.asp.

Judge L. Felipe Restrepo

Judge Restrepo was born in Medellin, Colombia, raised in Northern Virginia, and sworn in as a United States citizen on September 7, 1993. He received his B.A. from the University of Pennsylvania in 1981 and his J.D. from Tulane Law School in 1986.

From 1993 to 2006, Judge Restrepo was in private practice with the firm of Krasner & Restrepo, concentrating in criminal defense and civil rights litigation. Prior to the formation of Krasner & Restrepo, he was an assistant federal defender for the Eastern District of Pennsylvania, and prior to that he was an assistant defender with the Defender Association of Philadelphia. Judge Restrepo is currently an adjunct professor at the University of Pennsylvania and Temple University law schools.

Judge Restrepo served as a magistrate judge of the United States District Court for the Eastern District of Pennsylvania from June 2006 until June 2013. By appointment of President Obama, he began service as a United States district court judge for the Eastern District of Pennsylvania on June 19, 2013.

PRELIMINARY GENERAL MATTERS

1. Correspondence with the Court. Counsel or pro se parties may correspond with the court concerning scheduling, routine matters, or to advise the court that a case has been settled or dismissed. Any written communication requesting action by the court should include a description of the situation requiring the court's attention, the position of the opposing party, and the specific relief sought. Otherwise, all communications with the court should be made by the filing of a pleading, motion, application, brief, or legal memorandum. Counsel should make themselves familiar with the electronic case filing (ECF) system available in the Office of the Clerk of Court. Pursuant to Local Rule 5.1.2, all filings must be made on ECF, unless excepted under that rule. Counsel should not send the judge copies of letters sent to each other unless specifically invited to do so.

2. Communications with Law Clerks and Deputy Clerks. Law clerks may not render advice to counsel and have no authority to grant continuances or to give advice on substantive or procedural matters. Therefore, unless directly contacted by a law clerk, or instructed by the court to do so, counsel should not communicate with the law clerks.

Counsel may contact chambers by telephone when a written communication is insufficient to timely address an issue. The court also permits counsel to telephone chambers to schedule conferences or proceedings, including pretrial or discovery-related conferences, or to make arrangements for the attendance of witnesses, exhibit handling, or video replay.

Telephone inquiries should be directed as appropriate to one of the following:

Civil Deputy Clerk: Maryellen Fox—267-299-7741
Contact for matters relating to civil scheduling, case management, and general procedures.

Criminal Deputy Clerk: Juanita Davis—267-299-7691
Contact regarding all criminal matters, general procedures, courtroom procedures, trial setup, and transcripts.

Counsel should submit current telephone numbers, fax numbers, e-mail addresses and any changes to the Clerk's Office, the courtroom deputy, and the judicial secretary/deputy clerk.

3. **Telephone Conferences.** Judge Restrepo may hold telephone conferences to resolve scheduling matters or discovery disputes. The court will notify counsel of the date and time for the telephone conference. In a civil case, counsel for the moving party will be responsible for initiating the telephone conference and contacting Judge Restrepo through his secretary/deputy clerk after all parties are present on the call. In a criminal case, the United States Attorney's Office will be responsible for initiating the call.

4. **Oral Arguments and Evidentiary Hearings.** Judge Restrepo does not set aside certain days or times for oral argument, motions, or evidentiary hearings. Hearings and argument are scheduled when warranted.

5. **Pro Hac Vice Admissions.** To be admitted pro hac vice, associate counsel of record should submit a written motion for admission. The admission of out-of-the-jurisdiction counsel pro hac vice does not relieve associate counsel of responsibility for the matter before the court.

6. **Faxed and Electronic Mail.** Unless specifically requested or explicitly permitted by the court, parties should not transmit pleadings, motions, or other filings by fax or e-mail to chambers.

7. **Courtesy Copies.** Counsel should send one courtesy copy of a motion, brief, or memorandum to chambers at the time of filing.

CIVIL CASES
Pretrial Procedure

1. **Rule 16 Conference.** The court will schedule a preliminary pretrial conference as described in Federal Rule of Civil Procedure 16(b) and (c) shortly after a defendant has filed an appearance or pleading. At least three business days prior to the pretrial conference, *counsel must submit to chambers the report of the Rule 26(f) meeting with a proposed discovery plan.*

The court relies on counsels' good-faith compliance with Rule 26(f) *in all respects.* The Rule 26(f) meeting should take place as early in the case as possible. Outstanding motions will not excuse the requirements of holding the meeting and submitting the plan. The meeting should be a meaningful and substantive discussion to formulate the proposed discovery plan required by the rule. *Parties who do not comply will have no voice at the scheduling conference and may be subject to additional sanctions.*

At the initial pretrial conference, the parties should be prepared to address all topics listed in Local Rule of Civil Procedure 16.1(b) and Federal Rule of Civil Procedure 16(b) and (c), the progress of self-executing disclosure under Federal Rule of Civil Procedure 26(a), and any settlement or mediation proposals. The court will issue a Rule 16 scheduling order following the conference.

Lead trial counsel must attend the Rule 16 conference. Counsel taking part in any pretrial conference must be prepared to speak on every subject, including settlement, and have authority from their clients to do so. Counsel should be prepared to discuss all claims and defenses in detail, and must have a thorough understanding of the facts.

2. **Final Pretrial Conference.** There will be a final pretrial conference within 10 days of the trial date. Counsel must comply with Local Rule 16.1 regarding the submission of a pretrial memorandum. These memoranda should be filed, with a courtesy copy to chambers, no later than 7 days prior to the pretrial conference.

During this conference, the court will address factual and legal issues, the admissibility of exhibits, scheduling issues, and settlement. At the conclusion of the conference, the court will issue a final pretrial order or a final scheduling order in a complex case.

Continuances and Extensions

Unless there is good cause to justify a change, the parties are expected to adhere to the dates contained in the scheduling order. The court will grant a continuance or extension based on a stipulation of all parties if the continuance or extension does not affect the date dispositive motions are due. If a continuance or extension will affect the dispositive motion's date or trial date, counsel should make a written request that sets forth the basis for the continuance or extension and indicates whether the other party or parties agree to or oppose the request. A request for an extension or continuance of the trial date or the deadline for filing dispositive motions must be made sufficiently prior to the due date to allow time for the court to consider it. These requests should be made by motion, although an unopposed request may be made by letter to the court.

General Motion Practice

1. **Oral Argument on Motions.** If the judge believes oral argument will be helpful in deciding a matter, he will schedule it, particularly when it involves a dispositive motion. A party desiring oral argument should request it by letter or in the body of the motion or responsive pleading.

2. **Reply and Surreply Briefs.** Reply and surreply briefs are *not permitted* unless leave to file them is granted upon motion of a party.

3. **Length and Content of Briefs or Legal Memoranda.** All grounds for relief should be set forth in a single, comprehensive motion. A motion to dismiss, for example, should not be divided into separate motions for each count, but rather should include all bases for relief. *Any brief or memorandum filed in support of the motion should be limited to 20 double-spaced pages with text in 12-point type.* This includes the table of contents and any attachments or addenda. If a party requires more than 20 pages to explain its position to the court, a motion to exceed the page limit should be filed, setting forth good cause for granting an exception to this rule. Any reply brief should be limited to 10 pages.

4. **Rule 56 Motions.** All parties *must* comply with the following protocol as to summary judgment pleadings:

1. The movant must file, in support of the motion for summary judgment, a statement of undisputed facts that sets forth, in numbered paragraphs, all material facts that the movant contends are undisputed;

2. The respondent must file, in opposition to the motion for summary judgment, a separate statement of disputed facts, responding to the numbered paragraphs set forth in the movant's statement of undisputed facts, that the respondent contends present a genuine issue to be tried. The respondent must also set forth, in separate numbered paragraphs, any additional facts that the respondent contends preclude summary judgment.

3. All material facts set forth in the statement of undisputed facts required to be served by the movant will be admitted unless controverted by the opposing party.

4. Statements of material facts in support of or in opposition to a motion for summary judgment should include specific and not general references to the parts of the record that support each of the statements. Each stated fact and each statement that a material fact is disputed must cite the source relied upon, including the title, page, and line of the document supporting the statement.

5. For purposes of summary judgment, counsel should submit a joint appendix, including any and all exhibits that may be referenced in their respective motions, no later than the date the initial motion for summary judgment is docketed. All pages/exhibits of the appendix must be "Bates-stamped" and referenced in the motions consistent with the Bates number assigned each page. Judge Restrepo will not consider any document/exhibit not included in the appendix.

Failure of the movant to follow this procedure in all respects will result in the denial of the motion. Respondent's failure to comply will result in the court's considering the motion as uncontested.

Discovery Matters

1. Length of Discovery Period and Extensions. In standard track cases, the court usually allows up to 90 days from the date of the Rule 16 conference to complete discovery. In special management cases, the court will permit additional time to conduct discovery if the parties identify a need to do so at the Rule 16 conference, or any subsequent status conferences. A case will ordinarily be listed for trial 60 to 90 days after the completion of discovery.

2. Discovery Conferences and Dispute Resolution. When a discovery default occurs, the court will consider a motion to compel under Local Civil Rule 26.1(g). If the parties are unable to resolve the matter by themselves, after the reasonable efforts required by Local Civil Rule 26.1(f), the party seeking relief may file a motion to compel. *The motion should not exceed five double-spaced pages of text in 12-point type, and should not contain exhibits or include a brief or memorandum of law.*

Once a motion to compel is filed, the court will schedule a telephone or in-person conference to resolve the dispute as soon as possible. The responding party may file a response within five days. This response should also be limited to five double-spaced pages of text in 12-point type and should not include exhibits or a brief or memorandum of law. If the parties resolve the dispute, the conference will be canceled. If the court's intervention is required, the court may impose sanctions in favor of the prevailing party. Judge Restrepo permits telephone conferences to resolve disputes during depositions in cases where the deposition would otherwise have to be adjourned.

3. Confidentiality Agreements. The court will only approve confidentiality or sealing orders for good cause shown. See *Pansy v. Borough of Stroudsburg*, 23 F.3d 772 (3d Cir. 1994).

Settlement

Settlement will be discussed at the initial Rule 16 status conference and at any subsequent conference. The court will not participate in settlement negotiations in nonjury cases. A case may be referred to a magistrate judge for a settlement conference.

Arbitration

1. General Approach to Arbitration. Judge Restrepo will not hold a Rule 16 conference or issue a scheduling order in arbitration track cases unless there is a de novo appeal from an arbitration award. The parties are expected to complete all discovery prior to the date of the arbitration hearing.

2. **Scheduling of Trial De Novo from Arbitration.** Upon demand for trial de novo from an arbitration award, the court will issue a scheduling order setting the date for trial at the earliest date available to the court. Ordinarily, neither discovery nor dispositive motions will be allowed after the arbitration hearing is held.

Final Pretrial Memoranda

Unless otherwise ordered by the court, the pretrial memoranda should be prepared in accordance with the provisions of Local Rule of Civil Procedure 16.1(c), and should also include the following items:

   a. All stipulations of counsel.

   b. A statement of objection to: (1) the admissibility of any exhibit based on authenticity, (2) the admissibility of any evidence expected to be offered for any reason (except relevancy), (3) the adequacy of the qualifications of an expert witness expected to testify, and (4) the admissibility of any opinion testimony from lay witnesses pursuant to Federal Rule of Evidence 701. Such objection should describe with particularity the ground and the authority for the objection.

   c. Deposition testimony (including videotaped deposition testimony) that the party intends to offer during its case-in-chief. The statement should include citations to the page and line number and the opposing party's counter-designations.

Injunctions

1. **Scheduling and Expedited Discovery.** Judge Restrepo will promptly list any request for a temporary restraining order (TRO) or a preliminary injunction assigned to him.

2. **Pre-hearing Conference.** Judge Restrepo will hold a pre-hearing conference to discuss discovery issues, narrow the issues of contention, and allocate time for the hearing. Expedited discovery will be discussed and, when appropriate, ordered at the conclusion of the pre-hearing conference.

3. **Proposed Findings of Fact and Conclusions of Law.** Judge Restrepo requires submission of proposed findings of fact and conclusions of law for TRO and injunction hearings. The court will set the time for submission of these items at the pre-hearing conference.

Trial Procedure

1. **Scheduling Cases.** A date for trial will be determined at the initial Rule 16 conference. Once a case is listed for trial, counsel, parties, and witnesses should be ready to start trial on the date noted. Questions relating to scheduling matters should be directed to Judge Restrepo's deputy clerk.

2. **Cases Involving Out-of-Town Parties or Witnesses.** Judge Restrepo schedules the trial of cases involving out-of-town counsel, parties, or witnesses in the same manner as all other cases. Counsel are responsible for the scheduling of witnesses.

3. **Conflicts of Counsel.** Counsel should notify the court immediately upon hearing of any unavoidable and compelling professional or personal conflicts affecting the trial schedule.

4. **Jury Selection in Civil Cases.** After a brief introduction to the case and the importance of jury duty, Judge Restrepo will entertain cause and hardship strikes. The attorneys will then be permitted to conduct voir dire. The plaintiff will begin and be given no more than 35 minutes to voir dire the panel. The defense will follow and will be given no more than 35 minutes to voir dire the panel.

Peremptory challenges will be exercised by alternate strikes, plaintiff first, until each side has stricken three potential jurors or opts not to use any or all of their strikes. Judge Restrepo will typically seat eight jurors in a civil case.

5.   Note-taking by Jurors.   Judge Restrepo permits jurors to take notes.

6.   Trial Briefs.   Parties should submit a trial brief only if a new or unique point of law is involved.

7.   In Limine Motions.   The time for filing motions in limine will be determined at the Rule 16 conference and will be confirmed in the scheduling order.

8.   Examination of Witnesses Out of Sequence.   The court will permit counsel to examine his or her own witnesses out of turn for the convenience of a witness.

9.   Opening Statements and Summations.   Judge Restrepo does not put time limits on opening statements or closing arguments. Judge Restrepo will charge the jury prior to counsels' closing arguments.

10.   Examination of Witnesses or Argument by More Than One Attorney.   More than one attorney for a party may examine different witnesses or argue different points of law before the court. Only one attorney for each side may examine the same witness or address the jury during the opening statement or summation.

11.   Examination of Witnesses on Redirect and Recross.   The court will permit limited recross-examination on matters not previously covered by cross-examination or in special circumstances.

12.   Videotaped Testimony.   Videotaped testimony should begin with the witness being sworn. Counsel should bring objections to the court's attention at the time of the final pretrial conference. After the court rules on any objections, counsel should edit the tapes before offering the videotaped testimony at trial.

13.   Reading of Material into the Record.   Judge Restrepo has no special practice or policy regarding reading stipulations, pleadings, or discovery material into the record at trial.

14.   Preparation of Exhibits.   Exhibits should be pre-marked and exchanged in accordance with the final pretrial order. In civil cases, the parties will prepare one exhibit book with all exhibits that counsel may use at trial. Counsel should provide two copies of the joint exhibit book to the court.

15.   Offering Exhibits into Evidence.   Unless the parties have an agreement as to the admissibility of a proposed exhibit, a witness may not testify as to its content until it has been admitted into evidence.

16.   Directed Verdict Motions.   Motions for judgment as a matter of law in jury trials and motions for an involuntary dismissal in nonjury trials must be in writing. Oral argument on the motions is ordinarily permitted.

17.   Proposed Jury Instructions and Verdict Forms.   Judge Restrepo's scheduling order will note the date on which the parties must file with the clerk of court *joint* proposed jury instructions on substantive issues and proposed verdict forms or special interrogatories to the jury. Each party must also file proposed jury instructions, verdict forms, or special interrogatories on those issues not agreed upon by the parties in their joint submission. In submitting proposed points for charge, the parties are directed to the Model Civil Jury Instructions, which are available online at http://www.ca3.uscourts.gov/model-jury-instructions. Where applicable, the Court will use the Model Civil Jury Instructions to instruct the jury.

In submitting points for charge based on the Model Civil Jury Instructions, the parties need only refer to the model instruction by number and do not need to submit the text of the instruction.

Jury instructions should be submitted on a separate sheet of paper, double spaced, with accurate quotes from and citations to cases and pattern jury instructions where appropriate. The parties should also provide chambers with proposed jury instructions on a computer disk in Microsoft Word format.

18. *Proposed Findings of Fact and Conclusions of Law.* Proposed findings of fact and conclusions of law in nonjury cases should be submitted at least seven days before the trial or trial pool date. The parties should also provide them on a computer disk in Microsoft Word format. The parties may submit revised or supplemental findings of fact and conclusions of law with specific reference to trial evidence at the conclusion of the case. A schedule for the submission of revised findings and conclusions will be discussed at the conclusion of trial.

19. *Unavailability of Witness.* If a witness is unavailable at the time of trial, as defined in Federal Rule of Civil Procedure 32(a)(3), the court expects an oral or videotaped deposition to be used at trial for that witness, whether the witness is a party, a nonparty, or an expert. The unavailability of such witness will not be a ground to delay the commencement or progress of trial.

20. *Objections.* Judge Restrepo does not permit speaking objections. Objections should be made by reciting the appropriate rule number or a one-word basis.

21. *Lay Witness Opinion.* Any party expecting to offer lay opinion testimony pursuant to Federal Rule of Evidence 701 regarding issues of liability or damages must provide the opposing parties with information or documents supporting the testimony at the time required for submission of expert reports.

Jury Deliberations

1. *Written Jury Instructions.* The court will give the jury a copy of the written jury instructions.

2. *Exhibits in the Jury Room.* After the jury has been instructed and taken to the jury room to begin deliberations, the court and counsel will discuss which exhibits should go out with the jury for their consideration during deliberations.

3. *Handling of Jury Requests to Read Back Testimony or Replay Tapes.* At the jury's request, the court may permit the deputy clerk to read portions of testimony back to the jury or to replay the audiotaped or videotaped testimony.

4. *Availability of Counsel During Jury Deliberation.* Unless excused by the court, counsel must remain in the courthouse during jury deliberations.

5. *Taking the Verdict and Special Verdicts.* Ordinarily, the court will submit interrogatories to the jury. The courtroom deputy will take the verdict in the presence of the court, counsel, and the parties.

6. *Polling the Jury.* If requested by counsel, the court will poll the jury.

7. *Interviewing the Jury.* Judge Restrepo will allow counsel to interview jurors but will instruct the jury that they are not required to talk to the attorneys.

CRIMINAL CASES
Oral Argument and Motions

The court will generally permit oral argument on a substantive motion in a criminal case upon request.

Pretrial Conferences

Judge Restrepo will generally hold a telephone scheduling conference with counsel in criminal cases shortly after arraignment. At the conclusion of the conference, the court will issue a scheduling order governing speedy trial issues, discovery, time for filing motions, and the trial date.

Voir Dire

In criminal cases, Judge Restrepo will conduct voir dire, based, in part, on questions submitted by counsel. After the voir dire is concluded, the court will permit counsel to suggest follow-up questions. Counsel should submit proposed voir dire questions in writing seven days before the trial date.

Sentencing Memoranda

Judge Restrepo requires the parties to submit objections to the presentence-investigation report and sentencing memoranda in accordance with the notice of sentencing, which will be issued shortly after the entry of a guilty plea or conviction.

OTHER MATTERS
Briefs of Cases on Appeal

Judge Restrepo welcomes copies of appellate briefs when a decision he has made is appealed.

Consultation with Opposing Counsel

In general, Judge Restrepo expects counsel to bring matters to his attention only after they have been discussed with opposing counsel. When communicating with the court, counsel should be prepared to state the position of opposing counsel.

Professionalism

Judge Restrepo will insist on punctuality and courtesy from counsel to the court and to each other, both in the presence of the court and otherwise. The examination of witnesses should be conducted from the lectern or from counsel table. Counsel need not ask the court for permission before approaching witnesses. In addition, counsel will direct all comments to the court or to the witness under examination and not to other counsel or to the jury. To the extent possible, the parties should notify the court of any issues that will need to be ruled upon at the start of the day's proceedings, or during a recess out of the jury's presence. Sidebar conferences are discouraged but permitted when necessary.

Judge L. Felipe Restrepo

IN THE UNITED STATES DISTRICT COURT
FOR THE EASTERN DISTRICT OF PENNSYLVANIA

PLAINTIFF	:	CIVIL ACTION
v.	:	NO. xx--xxxx
DEFENDANT	:	

ORDER GOVERNING ELECTRONIC DISCOVERY

AND NOW, this _____ day of _____, 20__, in anticipation of the Rule 16 conference, it is **ORDERED** as follows:

1. **Introduction**. In the event the parties cannot reach an agreement on how to conduct electronic discovery ("e-discovery") before the Rule 16 scheduling conference, the following default standards shall apply until such time, if ever, the parties conduct e-discovery on a consensual basis.

2. **Exchange of e-discovery materials**. Prior to the Rule 26(f) conference, the parties shall exchange the following information:

    a. a list of the most likely custodians of relevant electronic materials, including a brief description of each person's title and responsibilities;

    b. a list of each relevant electronic system that has been in place at all relevant times and a general description of each system, including the nature, scope, character, organization, and formats employed in each system;

    c. the parties should also include other pertinent information about their electronic documents and whether those electronic documents are of limited accessibility, that is, those created or used by electronic media no longer in use, maintained in redundant electronic storage media, or for which retrieval involves substantial cost;

    d. the name of the individual responsible for the party's electronic document retention policies ("the retention coordinator");

    e. a general description of the party's electronic document retention policies;

    f. the name of the individual who shall serve as the party's "e-discovery liaison;"

    g. a description of any problems reasonably anticipated to arise in connection with e-discovery.

   To the extent that the state of the pleadings does not permit a meaningful discussion of the above issues by the time of the Rule 26(f) conference, the parties shall either agree on a date by which this information will be mutually exchanged or submit the issue for resolution by the court at the Rule 16 scheduling conference.

3. **E-discovery conference**. The parties shall discuss the parameters of their anticipated e-discovery at the Rule 26(f) conference and shall be prepared to address e-discovery at the Rule 16 scheduling conference with the court.

4. **E-discovery liaison**. To promote communication and cooperation between the parties, each party shall designate a single individual through whom all e-discovery requests and responses are made ("the e-discovery liaison"). Regardless of whether the e-discovery liaison is an attorney (in-house or outside counsel), a third party consultant, or an employee of the party, he or she must be:

    a. familiar with the party's electronic systems and capabilities in order to explain these systems and answer relevant questions;

b. knowledgeable about the technical aspects of e-discovery, including electronic document storage, organization, and format issues;

c. prepared to participate in e-discovery dispute resolutions; and,

d. responsible for organizing the party's e-discovery efforts to insure consistency and thoroughness and, generally, to facilitate the e-discovery process.

5. **Search methodology**. If the parties intend to employ an electronic search to locate relevant electronic documents, the parties shall disclose any restrictions as to scope and method which might affect their ability to conduct a complete electronic search of the electronic documents. The parties shall reach agreement as to the method of searching, and the words, terms, and phrases to be searched with the assistance of the respective e-discovery liaisons, who are charged with familiarity with the parties' respective systems. The parties also shall reach agreement as to the timing and conditions of any additional searches which may become necessary in the normal course of discovery. To minimize the expense, the parties may consider limiting the scope of the electronic search (e.g., time frames, fields, document types).

6. **Timing of e-discovery**. Discovery of electronic documents shall proceed in the following sequenced fashion:

a. after receiving requests for document production, the parties shall search their documents, other than those identified as limited accessibility electronic documents, and produce responsive electronic documents in accordance with FED. R. CIV. P. 26(b)(2);

b. electronic searches of documents identified as of limited accessibility shall not be conducted until the initial electronic document search has been completed;

c. requests for information expected to be found in limited accessibility documents must be narrowly focused with a factual basis supporting the request; and,

d. on-site inspections of electronic media under FED. R. CIV. P. 34(b) shall not be permitted, absent exceptional circumstances where good cause and specific need have been demonstrated.

7. **Format**. If, during the course of the Rule 26(f) conference, the parties cannot agree to the format for document production, electronic documents shall be produced to the requesting party as image files (e.g., PDF or TIFF). When the image file is produced, the producing party must preserve the integrity of the electronic document's contents, i.e., the original formatting of the document, its metadata and, where applicable, its revision history. After initial production in image file format is complete, a party must demonstrate particularized need for production of electronic documents in their native format.

8. **Retention**. Within the first thirty (30) days of discovery, the parties shall negotiate an agreement that outlines the steps each party shall take to segregate and preserve the integrity of all relevant electronic documents. In order to avoid later accusations of spoliation, a FED. R. CIV. P. 30(b)(6) deposition of each party's retention coordinator may be appropriate.

The retention coordinators shall:

a. take steps to ensure that e-mail of identified custodians shall not be permanently deleted in the ordinary course of business and that electronic documents maintained by the individual custodians shall not be altered;

b. provide notice as to the criteria used for spam and/or virus filtering of e-mails and attachments; Documents filtered out by such systems shall be deemed non-responsive so long as the criteria underlying the filtering are reasonable.

Within seven (7) days of identifying the relevant document custodians, the retention coordinators shall implement the above procedures and each party's counsel shall file a statement of compliance.

9. **Privilege**. Electronic documents that contain privileged information or attorney work product shall be immediately returned if the documents appear on their face to have been inadvertently produced

or if there is notice of the inadvertent production. All copies shall be returned or destroyed by the receiving party.

10. **Costs**. Generally, the costs of discovery shall be borne by each party. However, the court will apportion the costs of electronic discovery upon a showing of good cause.

_____
L. Felipe Restrepo
United States District Court

Judge Eduardo C. Robreno

Judge Robreno was born on July 28, 1945, in Havana, Cuba. He is a graduate of Massachusetts State College at Westfield (B.A. History, 1967), University of Massachusetts (M.S. Labor Relations, 1969), and Rutgers Law School (J.D., 1978). From 1978 to 1981, Judge Robreno served as a trial attorney in the Antitrust Division of the United States Department of Justice and as a special assistant United States attorney. From 1981 to 1992, he was in private practice in Philadelphia, Pennsylvania. Judge Robreno was appointed to the United States District Court for the Eastern District of Pennsylvania on June 30, 1992.

PRELIMINARY GENERAL MATTERS

1. *Correspondence with the Court.* Judge Robreno permits correspondence with the court concerning scheduling, other routine matters, and to advise the court that a case has been settled or dismissed. Any written communication requesting action by the court should include, at a minimum, a description of the situation requiring the court's attention, the position of the opposing party (i.e., consent or opposition), and the specific relief sought. Otherwise, all communications with the court should be made by the filing of pleadings, motions, applications, briefs, or legal memoranda. Counsel should not send Judge Robreno copies of letters sent to each other unless specifically invited to do so.

2. *Communications with Law Clerks.* Judge Robreno discourages communications with his law clerks. Counsel should not call upon law clerks for advice on substantive or procedural matters. Communications with the court about scheduling matters should be directed to Judge Robreno's courtroom deputy.

3. *Electronic Case Filing (ECF).* Judge Robreno requires that all documents are filed electronically by the attorney using the Electronic Case Filing (ECF) system. ECF provides greater efficiency and timeliness in the filing of pleadings, automatic e-mail notice of case activity, and electronic storage of documents for remote access by the court, the bar, and the litigants. Attorneys appearing before Judge Robreno are required to register as Electronic Case Filing (ECF) filing users at the Office of the Clerk of Court or at the court's website at http://www.paed.uscourts.gov. *Please be advised that Judge Robreno does not accept courtesy copies.*

4. *Telephone Conferences.* Judge Robreno may hold telephone conferences to resolve scheduling matters or discovery disputes. Counsel will be notified of the date and time for the telephone conference. It will be the responsibility of counsel for the moving party to initiate the telephone conference and to contact Judge Robreno through his secretary after all parties are present on the call.

5. *Oral Arguments and Evidentiary Hearings.* Judge Robreno does not set aside certain days or times for oral argument, motions, or evidentiary hearings. Hearings and argument are scheduled when warranted.

6. *Pro Hac Vice Admissions.* Judge Robreno prefers that a written motion for admission be made by associate counsel of record. The admission of out-of-the-jurisdiction counsel pro hac vice does not relieve associate counsel of responsibility for the matter before the court.

CIVIL CASES
Pretrial Procedure

1.   Pretrial Conferences. Judge Robreno regularly schedules an in-person initial pretrial conference (IPTC) soon after the answer is filed or the case is transferred to him. Prior to the IPTC, the parties should confer and prepare a joint report pursuant to Fed.R.Civ.P. 26(f). The joint report should be filed 72 hours prior to the IPTC.

At the IPTC, counsel should be prepared to discuss those topics listed in Local Rule of Civil Procedure 16.1(b), and Fed.R.Civ.P. 16(b) and (c). Counsel should also be prepared to discuss the progress of self-executing disclosure pursuant to section 4:01 of the Civil Justice Expense and Delay Reduction Plan. In special management track cases, the parties should provide the court with a proposed case management plan pursuant to section 3:01 of the expense and delay reduction plan three days prior to the IPTC. As provided in section 8:01 and chapter IX of the plan, Judge Robreno requires that counsel taking part in the IPTC be prepared to speak knowledgeably on these subjects.

A scheduling order will be issued at the conclusion of the IPTC, which will set forth deadlines for the completion of discovery, the filing of dispositive motions, the filing of pretrial submissions, and a date certain when the case will be placed in the trial pool. Where appropriate, a date for an interim status conference may be provided. In certain cases, particularly in special management track cases, Judge Robreno may provide a date by which the parties will be required to prepare and submit to the court for approval a final pretrial order pursuant to Local Civil Rule 16.1(d).

Judge Robreno typically holds a final pretrial conference (FPTC) within 10 days of the date the case will be placed in the trial pool. A final pretrial order or a final scheduling order in a complex case, as the case may be, will be issued at the conclusion of the FPTC. At that time, outstanding topics that were the subject of the IPTC, and issues concerning the trial are typically discussed, as well as possible settlement.

Continuances and Extensions

1.   General Policy. Judge Robreno has a general policy of adhering to the dates contained in the scheduling order, unless good cause is shown that justifies a change.

2.   Continuances and Extensions. Judge Robreno will grant a continuance or extension that will not affect the discovery cutoff or trial date (i.e., the date that a brief is due, the date of an evidentiary hearing, or the date of an oral argument on a nondispositive motion), if based on a stipulation agreed upon by all parties. Any other request for a continuance or extension should set forth in detail the basis for the request and whether it is agreed to or opposed by the opposing party. A request for an extension or continuance of the trial date, discovery cutoff date, or the deadline for filing dispositive motions must be made sufficiently prior to the due date to allow time for the court to consider it. An unopposed request may be made by letter to the court.

General Motion Practice

1.   Oral Argument on Motions. If Judge Robreno determines that oral argument will be helpful in deciding a matter, he will schedule it, particularly when it involves a dispositive motion. A party desiring oral argument should request it by letter or in the body of the motion or responsive pleading.

2. Reply and Surreply Briefs. Reply and surreply briefs are discouraged unless necessary to rebut an issue or point of law not discussed in the initial briefs. They should not be filed for motions of any nature without prior leave of the court. Any motion for leave should be filed of record with a copy of the proposed brief attached as an exhibit to the motion.

Discovery Matters

1. Length of Discovery Period and Extensions. In standard track cases, Judge Robreno usually allows up to 90 days from the date of the IPTC to complete discovery. In special management cases, Judge Robreno will permit additional time depending upon the need to do so identified by the parties at the IPTC, and any subsequent status conferences. A case will ordinarily be listed for trial 30 to 60 days after the completion of discovery.

2. Discovery Conferences and Dispute Resolution. When a discovery default occurs, Judge Robreno will consider a motion to compel under Local Civil Rule 26.1. When a discovery dispute occurs and the parties are unable to resolve the matter by themselves, after undertaking the reasonable efforts required by Local Civil Rule 26.1(f), the party seeking relief must file a motion to compel.

Once a motion to compel is filed, Judge Robreno will schedule a telephone or in-person conference to resolve the dispute within 10 days. The non-moving party will be allowed 9 days to file a response. If the parties work out the dispute, the conference will be canceled. If the court's intervention is required, the court customarily imposes sanctions upon the non-prevailing party unless the position of the non-prevailing party is found to have been substantially justified. Judge Robreno permits telephone conferences to resolve discovery disputes during depositions in cases where the deposition would otherwise have to be adjourned.

3. Confidentiality Agreements. Judge Robreno will not approve confidentiality or sealing orders unless good cause is shown.

4. Expert Witnesses. The time for disclosure of the identity of experts, submission of curricula vitae, and for discovery pursuant to Fed.R.Civ.P. 26(a)(2)(B), will be set forth in the scheduling order issued at the conclusion of the IPTC.

Settlement

1. General Approach to Settlement and Nonjury Cases. Settlement will be discussed at the IPTC, at subsequent status conferences, and at the FPTC. However, it is Judge Robreno's view that settlement of a case is the responsibility of the parties and, unless requested by all parties, he will not schedule settlement conferences. Judge Robreno will not participate in settlement negotiations in nonjury cases. By agreement of all parties, a case in which settlement prospects are promising may be referred to a magistrate judge or to another district court judge for a settlement conference.

Arbitration

1. General Approach to Arbitration Cases. Judge Robreno neither holds an IPTC nor issues a scheduling order in arbitration track cases, unless there is a de novo appeal from an arbitration award. The parties are expected to complete all discovery prior to the date of the arbitration hearing.

2. **Scheduling of Trial De Novo from Arbitration.** Upon demand for trial de novo from an arbitration award, Judge Robreno will issue a scheduling order setting the date for trial at the earliest date available to the court. Ordinarily, neither discovery nor dispositive motions will be allowed after the arbitration hearing is held.

Proposed Final Pretrial Memoranda

1. **Required Form of Pretrial Memoranda.** Unless otherwise ordered by Judge Robreno, the pretrial memorandum should be prepared in accordance with the provisions of Local Rule of Civil Procedure 16.1(c), and should also include the following items:
    a. All stipulations of counsel;
    b. Any objection to: (1) the admissibility of any exhibit based on authenticity, (2) the admissibility for any reason (except relevancy) of any evidence expected to be offered; (3) the adequacy of the qualifications of an expert witness expected to testify, and (4) the admissibility of any opinion testimony from lay witnesses pursuant to Federal Rule of Evidence 701. Such objection must describe with particularity the ground and the authority for the objection;
    c. Deposition testimony (including videotaped depositions) to be offered during a party's case-in-chief (with citations to the page and line number), including the opposing party's counter-designations.

Injunctions

1. **Scheduling and Expedited Discovery.** Judge Robreno will promptly list any request for a temporary restraining order (TRO) or a preliminary injunction assigned to him.

2. **Conference Held Prior to Hearing.** Judge Robreno will hold a prehearing conference to discuss discovery issues, narrow the issues of contention, and to allocate time for the hearing. Expedited discovery will be discussed and, when appropriate, ordered at the conclusion of the prehearing conference.

3. **Proposed Findings of Fact and Conclusions of Law.** Judge Robreno requires submission of proposed findings of fact and conclusions of law for TRO and injunction hearings. The time for submission of these items will be set at the prehearing conference.

Trial Procedure

1. **Scheduling Cases.** Judge Robreno's practice is to assign a date for placing the case in the trial pool at the time of the IPTC. Once a case is placed in the trial pool, counsel, parties, and witnesses should be ready to start trial upon 24 hours telephone notice. Ordinarily, a case will begin on or shortly after its trial pool date. Questions relating to scheduling matters should be directed to Judge Robreno's courtroom deputy.

2. **Conflicts of Counsel.** Judge Robreno requires that counsel notify the court immediately upon hearing of any unavoidable and compelling professional or personal conflicts affecting the trial schedule.

3. **Cases Involving Out-of-Town Parties or Witnesses.** Judge Robreno schedules the trial of cases involving out-of-town counsel, parties, or witnesses the same as all other cases. He leaves the scheduling of witnesses to counsel.

4. **Note-taking by Jurors.** Judge Robreno generally permits jurors to take notes.

5. **Trial Briefs.** Judge Robreno requires the submission of a trial brief no later than 10 days before the trial pool date.

6. Voir Dire. Ordinarily, Judge Robreno conducts voir dire in all cases. The parties are afforded an opportunity to submit proposed voir dire questions. After the court has concluded voir dire, counsel is afforded the opportunity to suggest follow-up questions.

7. In Limine Motions. Judge Robreno requires motions in limine to be submitted no later than 10 days before the trial pool date. The specific dates are set forth in the scheduling order.

8. Examination of Witnesses Out of Sequence. Judge Robreno generally will permit counsel to examine its own witnesses out of turn for the convenience of a witness unless it is objected to by the opposing party and prejudice would result.

9. Opening Statements and Summations. Judge Robreno normally attempts to obtain the agreement of counsel regarding time limits on opening statements and summations. However, he believes that in most cases 20 to 30 minutes is adequate for an opening statement and 30 to 45 minutes is adequate for summation.

10. Examination of Witnesses or Argument by More Than One Attorney. Judge Robreno will permit more than one attorney for a party to examine different witnesses or to argue different points of law before the court. He will not permit more than one attorney to examine the same witness, or to address the jury during the opening statement, or summation.

11. Examination of Witnesses Beyond Redirect and Recross. Judge Robreno disfavors redirect and recross unless it involves matters not previously covered by direct or cross examinations or special circumstances. Where appropriate, a proffer may be requested before it is permitted.

12. Videotaped Testimony. Videotaped testimony should begin with the witness being sworn. Objections should be brought to the court's attention at the time of the FPTC. After the court rules on any objections (ordinarily at the FPTC), counsel should edit the tapes before offering the videotaped testimony at trial.

13. Reading of Material Into the Record. Judge Robreno has no special practice or policy regarding reading into the record stipulations, pleadings, or discovery material.

14. Preparation of Exhibits. Judge Robreno requires that exhibits be pre-marked and pre-exchanged in accordance with the final pretrial order. On the day trial is scheduled to commence, one copy of each exhibit and a copy of a schedule of exhibits should be provided to the court.

15. Offering Exhibits Into Evidence. Generally, unless the parties have an agreement as to the admissibility of a proposed exhibit, a witness may not testify as to its content until it has been admitted into evidence.

16. Directed Verdict Motions. Judge Robreno prefers that motions for judgment as a matter of law in jury trials and motions for an involuntary dismissal in nonjury trials be in writing. Oral argument on the motions is ordinarily permitted.

17. Proposed Jury Instructions and Verdict Forms. In his scheduling order, Judge Robreno provides that proposed jury instructions on substantive issues and proposed verdict forms or special interrogatories to the jury be submitted no later than 10 days before the trial pool date. Jury instructions need only be submitted with respect to substantive issues in the case. Proposed instructions on procedural matters such as the burden of proof, unanimity, and credibility are not necessary.

Each proposed instruction should be on a separate sheet of paper, double-spaced, and *include citation to specific authority*. Proposed instructions without citation to specific legal authority will not be considered. Cases and model jury instructions that are cited should be accurately quoted and a pinpoint page reference should be provided.

Counsel will have the opportunity to file supplemental points, or proposed findings of fact and conclusions of law, near the close of testimony.

If a model jury instruction is submitted, for instance, from Devitt & Blackmar, *Federal Jury Practice and Instructions,* or Sand, *Modern Federal Jury Instructions,* the submitting party must state whether the proposed jury instruction is unchanged or modified. If a party modifies a model jury instruction, the modification should be set forth in the following manner: additions should be underlined and deletions should be placed in brackets.

18. Proposed Findings of Fact and Conclusions of Law. In his scheduling order, Judge Robreno provides that proposed findings of fact and conclusions of law in nonjury cases be submitted at least 10 days before the trial pool date. The parties may submit revised findings of fact and conclusions of law with specific reference to testimonial or documentary evidence that has been admitted at the close of testimony, unless otherwise provided for in the final pretrial order.

19. Offers of Proof. If any party desires an "offer of proof" as to any witness or exhibit expected to be offered, that party must inquire of counsel prior to the start of trial for such information. If the inquiring party is dissatisfied with any offer provided, he or she must file a motion seeking relief from the court prior to trial.

20. Unavailability of Witness. Because a witness may be unavailable at the time of trial, as defined in Fed.R.Civ.P. 32(a)(3), the court expects oral or videotaped depositions to be used at trial for *any witness* whose testimony the party believes essential to the presentation of that party's case, whether the witness is a party, a non-party, or an expert. The unavailability of such witness *will not be a ground to delay* the commencement or progress of trial.

21. Lay Witness Opinion. Any party expecting to offer opinion testimony from lay witnesses pursuant to Federal Rule of Evidence 701 with respect to issues of liability or damages should, at the time required for submission of expert reports, serve the opposing parties with the same information and/or documents required with respect to such expert witnesses.

Jury Deliberations

1. Written Jury Instructions. Judge Robreno generally provides the jury with a copy of the jury instructions.

2. Exhibits in the Jury Room. Unless cause is shown, Judge Robreno will permit all exhibits containing substantive or real evidence to go out with the jury. Demonstrative exhibits ordinarily will not be permitted in the jury room.

3. Handling of Jury Requests to Read Back Testimony or Replay Tapes. At the jury's request, if the transcript is available, Judge Robreno will consider allowing the reading of the appropriate portions back to the jury and the replaying of audiotapes and videotapes.

4. Availability of Counsel During Jury Deliberation. Unless excused by Judge Robreno, counsel must remain in the courthouse during jury deliberations.

5. Taking the Verdict and Special Interrogatories. Ordinarily, Judge Robreno will submit interrogatories to the jury.

6. Polling the Jury. Ordinarily, Judge Robreno will poll the jury.

7. Interviewing the Jury. Ordinarily, Judge Robreno will allow counsel to interview jurors but will set certain conditions for the interviews.

CRIMINAL CASES

1. **Approach to Oral Argument and Motions.** If requested, Judge Robreno will generally permit oral argument on a substantive motion in a criminal case.

2. **Pretrial Conferences.** Judge Robreno generally will hold a telephone scheduling conference with counsel in criminal cases shortly after arraignment. At the conclusion of the conference, Judge Robreno will issue a scheduling order governing speedy trial issues, discovery, time for filing motions, and the trial date.

3. **Voir Dire.** In criminal cases, the voir dire is conducted by Judge Robreno, based, in part, on questions submitted by counsel. After the voir dire is concluded, the judge will permit counsel to suggest follow-up questions. In his scheduling order, Judge Robreno provides for the submission of proposed voir dire questions by counsel in writing 10 days before the trial date.

4. **Sentencing Memoranda.** Judge Robreno requires the submission of objections to the presentence investigation report and the submission of sentencing memoranda in accordance with the notice of sentencing issued shortly after the entry of a guilty plea or judgment (in the case of a conviction).

OTHER GENERAL MATTERS

1. **Briefs of Cases on Appeal.** Judge Robreno welcomes copies of appellate briefs when a decision rendered by him is appealed.

2. **Consultation with Opposing Counsel.** In general, Judge Robreno expects counsel to bring matters to his attention only after they have been discussed with opposing counsel. When communicating with the court, counsel must be prepared to state the position of opposing counsel, for example, opposing counsel does not oppose the continuance, opposing counsel opposes my request to show photographs to the jury during opening statements, etc.

3. **Professionalism.** Judge Robreno will insist on punctuality and courtesy from counsel to the court and to each other, both in the presence of the court and otherwise. The examination of witnesses should be conducted from the lectern or from counsel's table. Counsel should rise to address the court and must seek permission of the court before approaching witnesses or the bench. In addition, counsel will direct all comments to the court or to the witness under examination and not to other counsel or to the jury. To the extent possible, the court should be alerted to issues that will need to be ruled upon during the day at the start of the day's proceedings, or during recess out of the jury's presence. Sidebar conferences are permitted when appropriate but are generally discouraged.

Judge Eduardo C. Robreno

JOINT STATUS REPORT PURSUANT TO RULE 26(f)

Caption: _____ Civil Action No:_____

Basis of Jurisdiction: _____

Jury Trial: _____ Non-Jury Trial: _____ Arbitration: _____

Plaintiff's counsel participating in the Rule 16 Conference: _____
Defendant's counsel participating in the Rule 16 Conference: _____
Do counsel have full authority to settle at a Rule 16 Conference?: _____

When did the parties hold the Rule 26 Conference? _____
When did the parties comply with Rule 26(a)'s duty of self-executing disclosure? _____

Does either side expect to file a case-dispositive motion? _____ (yes/no)
    If yes, under what Rule _____
    If yes, specify the issue _____
    Proposed deadline for filing dispositive motions: _____

Does either side anticipate the use of experts? _____
    If yes, what is the proposed deadline for expert discovery? _____

Approximate date case should be trial-ready: _____
    Time for Plaintiff's case: _____   Time for Defendant's case: _____

Is a settlement conference likely to be helpful? _____   If so, when:
    Early _____ (yes/no)   After Discovery _____ (yes/no)

What is the outcome of your discussions with your clients about proceeding before a Magistrate Judge for final disposition? _____

Plan for Discovery:

1. The parties anticipate that discovery should be completed within _____ days.
2. What is the minimum amount of time necessary to complete discovery prior to an ADR session, should one be ordered or agreed to? _____
3. Have the parties discussed issues relating to claims of privilege or of protection as trial-preparation material, as required by Rule 26(f)(3)(D)? _____
4. Identify any other discovery issues which should be addressed at the Rule 16 Conference, including limitations on discovery, protective Orders needed, or other elements which should be included in a particularized discovery plan. _____
5. If you contend the discovery period should exceed 90 days, please state reason: _____

Judge Cynthia M. Rufe

Judge Rufe was born in 1948 in Philadelphia, Pennsylvania. She received a B.A. from Adelphi University in 1970, and a J.D. from the Law School of the State University of New York in 1977. Judge Rufe served as deputy in the Bucks County Public Defender's Office and also served as coordinator in the Juvenile Division from 1977 to 1982. From 1982 to 1993, Judge Rufe was in private practice, during which time she served as a solicitor for the Bucks County Children and Youth Services Agency from 1984 to 1988. Judge Rufe served as a judge on the Bucks County Court of Common Pleas from 1994 to 2002. She was appointed to the United States District Court for the Eastern District of Pennsylvania on May 3, 2002.

PRELIMINARY GENERAL MATTERS

1. *Communications with Chambers.* Judge Rufe permits communications with chambers via telephone, regular mail, or facsimile (10-page limit) regarding scheduling and other non-substantive matters. All other issues must be addressed by an appropriate motion or other filing. Transmittal of pleadings, motions, or other filings by facsimile to chambers is not permitted.

Under no circumstances may any party or counsel communicate ex parte with any chambers personnel concerning substantive matters. Law clerks may not render advice to counsel and have no authority to grant continuances or any other relief. Telephone inquiries should be directed as appropriate to either of the following:

Judicial Secretary/Civil Courtroom Deputy: Velma T. White
Telephone: 267-299-7490
Facsimile: 267-299-5077
Contact for matters related to civil scheduling and case management, requesting telephone conferences, and general procedures.

ESR/Criminal Courtroom Deputy: Erica Pratt
Telephone: 267-299-7499
Facsimile: 267-299-7498
Contact for matters related to criminal scheduling and case management, and obtaining transcripts of civil and criminal proceedings.

2. *Telephone Conferences.* Counsel may arrange a telephone conference with Judge Rufe to resolve straightforward discovery disputes, but complicated matters should be resolved via formal motion and briefing. Counsel must exhaustively address all discovery disputes with opposing counsel before requesting Judge Rufe's assistance. Counsel for one of the parties must initiate all conference calls.

3. *Stipulations and Consent Decrees.* Any stipulations, consent decrees, or other documents requiring court approval or the judge's signature must be submitted using Electronic Case Filing (see item 4 below) in a form containing original signatures. Judge Rufe will not sign any document containing a duplicated signature of any counsel, party, or representative.

4. *Electronic Case Filing.* Judge Rufe requires the use of Electronic Case Filing (ECF). ECF provides greater efficiency and timeliness in the filing of pleadings, automatic e-mail notice of case activity, and electronic storage of documents for remote access by the court, the bar, and the litigants. Attorneys are urged to register as ECF users in accordance with

Rule 5.1.2 of the Local Rules of Civil Procedure, referencing the procedural order on electronic case filing. Stipulations and proposed orders must be filed on ECF; proposed orders should be attached to corresponding motions or memoranda of law.

5. **Standing Orders.** Judge Rufe has no standing orders.

CIVIL CASES
Pretrial Procedure

1. **Rule 26 Conferences.** Judge Rufe relies on counsels' good-faith compliance in all respects with Fed.R.Civ.P. 26(f). The Rule 26(f) meeting should take place as soon as possible and, in any event, at least 14 days before the Rule 16 scheduling conference. Outstanding motions will not excuse counsel from timely holding the meeting and submitting a Rule 26 plan. Compliance is mandatory. The meeting should not be viewed as perfunctory, but rather as a meaningful and substantive discussion among professionals to formulate the discovery plan required by the rule. Parties who do not comply will have no voice at the scheduling conference and may be subject to additional sanctions.

2. **Rule 16 Scheduling Conferences.** Judge Rufe will issue an order for a Rule 16 scheduling conference to be held in chambers. Counsel should read carefully all instructions contained therein. Attached to the order will be a scheduling information report, which must be completed and returned to chambers at least three business days before the conference. For the convenience of out-of-state counsel, in some very limited circumstances Judge Rufe may conduct Rule 16 conferences via telephone.

Lead trial counsel must attend the Rule 16 conference and must enter an appearance prior to the conference unless Judge Rufe approves a substitution. If lead trial counsel is appearing pro hac vice, local counsel must also attend the conference. All applications to appear pro hac vice must be approved prior to the conference.

Any attorney appearing at the conference should have evaluated the case for settlement purposes and have settlement authority from the client. Motions to dismiss, transfer, add parties, and other threshold motions should be filed before the conference. Counsel must be prepared to present argument at the conference on any pending motions.

After the conference, Judge Rufe will issue a scheduling order to govern further proceedings in the case. The scheduling order will usually include the requirements and deadlines set forth in the sample scheduling order shown on page 253 of this book.

Continuances and Extensions

1. **Requests for Extensions of Time.** Where compelling circumstances so require, counsel may request an extension of a filing or other deadline only if such request has no effect on other existing deadlines. Judge Rufe will extend the deadline for filing dispositive motions or a trial pool date only in very limited circumstances and where genuinely necessary. If a request for an extension is unopposed, counsel must so state and may submit the request via letter or joint stipulation. Opposed requests must so state and be filed as a motion.

General Motion Practice

1. **Oral Argument on Motions.** Unless oral argument is requested and may be useful, Judge Rufe regularly decides motions on the papers.

2. **Motions Practice.** In most cases, summary judgment motions filed pursuant to Federal Rule of Civil Procedure 56(b) will use the form and schedule outlined in attachment 1 to the sample scheduling order (see page 255 of this book), which is known as the "alternative method." In rare cases, however, Judge Rufe will permit the parties to file their Rule 56(b)

motions under the standard approach. Judge Rufe will notify the parties in the scheduling order governing their matter whether they must file their Rule 56(b) motions pursuant to the alternative method outlined in attachment 1 to the sample scheduling order.

Under the alternative method, motions for summary judgment under Rule 56(b) must not exceed five double-spaced pages. For the purposes of such a motion only, Local Rule of Civil Procedure 7.1(c) does not apply to require the submission of a memorandum of law in support of the initial motion. Rather, the motion should be in outline form, identifying the issues that form the basis of the party's request for relief. The plaintiff's response memoranda must not exceed 25 double-spaced pages. Likewise, the defendant's reply memoranda must not exceed 25 double-spaced pages. Any surreply memoranda must not exceed 10 double-spaced pages. For the purposes of a motion under the alternative method, the parties need not seek leave of the court to file their reply and surreply memoranda.

Under the traditional method, a defendant's motion for summary judgment should not exceed 25 double-spaced pages. The plaintiff's response must not exceed 25 double-spaced pages. Any reply and surreply must not exceed 10 pages and may be filed only after obtaining leave of the court.

For all other motions, Judge Rufe follows the requirements of Local Rule of Civil Procedure 7.1. Such motions and responses must not exceed 15 double-spaced pages. Reply and surreply memoranda may only be filed with leave of court and must not exceed 10 double-spaced pages. To file reply and/or surreply memoranda, counsel should file a motion requesting leave to file an additional memorandum and attach the proposed memorandum as an exhibit. The motion and attached reply or surreply should be filed within 10 days of the memorandum to which the reply or surreply responds.

3. **Chambers Copies of Motion Papers.** Judge Rufe appreciates courtesy copies of significant motions, memoranda of law, and other pleadings, but requests that counsel send to chambers only *one* courtesy copy. In the case of significant motions with voluminous attachments or exhibits, counsel should supply chambers with a courtesy copy of all relevant materials, arranged in an orderly fashion, upon filing. Transmittal of courtesy copies by facsimile is not permitted.

Settlement

1. **Settlement Conferences.** Judge Rufe addresses the possibility of settlement at all stages in the proceedings. In addition, consistent with Local Rule 53.3, Judge Rufe directs all parties to consider the use of an alternative-dispute-resolution process at an appropriate stage in the litigation. United States Magistrate Judge Carol Sandra Moore Wells is available to conduct settlement conferences in civil matters, and Judge Rufe strongly encourages litigants to avail themselves of Judge Wells's skillful assistance.

If for any reason counsel desires a continuance of a settlement conference listed before Judge Wells, counsel must contact Judge Wells's chambers directly. If, however, the requested continuance exceeds 14 days, counsel must receive Judge Rufe's approval before contacting Judge Wells's chambers.

2. **Pretrial Settlement.** Upon reaching a settlement, counsel must notify Judge Rufe's chambers immediately and request dismissal of the action pursuant to Local Rule of Civil Procedure 41.1 or some other procedure that will effectively terminate the litigation.

Pretrial Conferences and Proposed Pretrial Memoranda

1. **Pretrial Conferences.** Judge Rufe regularly lists a pretrial conference date in the scheduling order. Pretrial conferences are typically scheduled for the weeks preceding the trial pool to which a case is assigned. Counsel should read carefully all instructions contained in the scheduling order. Judge Rufe uses the pretrial conference to resolve any motions in limine and other pretrial matters, and to discuss voir dire and other trial procedures.

Trial Procedure

1. **Scheduling of Cases.** Judge Rufe's scheduling order will usually assign a case to a two-week trial pool. The list of matters to be tried is published in *The Legal Intelligencer*; however, that list is subject to modification. All parties, witnesses, and counsel can expect their case to be tried during the trial pool period and should arrange their schedules accordingly. Judge Rufe will make every effort to notify counsel at least three business days in advance of the day trial is to commence. At the request of counsel, Judge Rufe may list nonjury trials or complex matters for a special listing or date certain. Judge Rufe will use the pretrial conference to discuss specific trial procedures. Counsel should contact chambers three to four days in advance of trial for courtroom assignment.

CRIMINAL CASES

1. **Motions Practice.** All pretrial motions must be filed no later than 30 days in advance of the scheduled trial date, and except in rare circumstances will be heard on a date prior to the scheduled trial date. In multi-defendant proceedings, all motions will be heard jointly. Defendants may not join in co-defendants' pretrial motions without leave of the court. Counsel are advised to provide Judge Rufe with supporting memoranda no later than the date of the hearing. The supporting memoranda must not exceed 25 double-spaced pages.

All post-trial motions must be filed in accordance with the Federal and Local Rules of Criminal Procedure. Supporting memoranda for such motions and response memoranda should not exceed 25 double-spaced pages. Reply and surreply memoranda may only be filed with leave of court and should not exceed 10 double-spaced pages.

2. **Continuances of Trial.** Any request for a continuance must be filed no later than 14 days in advance of the scheduled trial date. Requests for a continuance must be filed as a motion stating the reasons for the request. Any such motion must be accompanied by a proposed form of order that, if approved by the court, would grant the relief sought by the motion. The proposed form of order *must* be consistent with the requirements of the Speedy Trial Act, 18 U.S.C. § 3161(h)(8) and include a proposed finding that explains in reasonable detail why the ends of justice served by granting the requested continuance outweigh the best interest of the public and the defendant in a speedy trial. Requests by letter are not permitted.

3. **Pretrial Conferences.** Judge Rufe will schedule a pretrial conference with counsel at least three days prior to the scheduled trial date and may be conducted by telephone in limited circumstances. Any issues related to voir dire, motions in limine, jury instructions, and jury verdict forms will be addressed at that time.

4. **Voir Dire.** Judge Rufe conducts extensive voir dire in criminal jury matters. Counsel are permitted to address the venire with follow-up questions.

5. **Sentencing.** Judge Rufe will schedule a speedy sentencing for a date selected at the time the court accepts a guilty plea or there is a conviction at trial. Judge Rufe discourages continuance of sentencing, and sentencing will be continued for good cause only. Judge Rufe will not consider any request for a continuance exceeding 90 days.

In the rare event of a 90-day continuance, if counsel for both the government and the defendant(s) believe that good cause exists for an additional continuance beyond the 90-day period, counsel may jointly request in writing an additional continuance. Any such request must state why good cause exists for an additional continuance. If Judge Rufe grants such a request, counsel are required to submit in writing a joint status update every 30 days until judgment of sentence is entered.

Sentencing motions and supporting memoranda must be filed at least 14 days prior to the scheduled sentencing date, and any response thereto must be filed at least seven days prior to the scheduled sentencing date.

Sentencing memoranda (exclusive of motions) must be filed no later than seven days prior to the scheduled sentencing date, and any response thereto must be filed at least three days prior to the scheduled sentencing date.

OTHER GENERAL MATTERS

For any civil litigation issues not addressed above, please consult the Local Rules of Civil Procedure for the Eastern District of Pennsylvania, available at http://www.paed.uscourts.gov/documents/locrules/civil/cvrules.pdf.

Judge Cynthia M. Rufe

Appendix A—Sample Scheduling Order

IN THE UNITED STATES DISTRICT COURT
FOR THE EASTERN DISTRICT OF PENNSYLVANIA

[JOHN DOE], Plaintiff	: : :	
v.	: :	CIVIL ACTION NO. 07-[_____]
[JANE ROE], Defendant	: : :	

SCHEDULING ORDER

AND NOW, this [___] day of [_____], 20___, after a Rule 16 conference with counsel, the Court hereby enters the following Scheduling Order to govern further proceedings in this case:

1. The parties are hereby granted leave to file any amended pleadings, including those adding or deleting parties, within [_____] ([___]) days of the date of this Scheduling Order;

2. Fact discovery shall be completed by [_____];

3. Plaintiff shall produce its expert report(s) by **[close of fact discovery]**; Defendant shall produce its expert report(s) by **[30 days after Plaintiff's service deadline]**; all expert discovery, including depositions, shall be completed by **[30 days after Defendant's service deadline]**;

4. All motions for summary judgment and partial summary judgment shall be filed on or before **[30 days after close of all discovery]**. The parties shall conform their motions and any responses, replies, or surreplies to the form and schedule outlined in Attachment 1;

5. The case shall be referred to Magistrate Judge Carol Sandra Moore Wells for a settlement conference. Counsel for the parties are directed to report to Judge Wells's Chambers (Suite 3016) on [_____]. The parties and/or persons with full authority to settle **must** accompany counsel unless excused in advance by Judge Wells.

6. The parties, through counsel, shall jointly report to the Court in writing on or before [_____] with respect to whether the case is settled. In the event the case is not settled on or before [_____], counsel shall include in their joint report a statement as to whether they believe a settlement conference before a magistrate judge, mediation under Local Civil Rule 53.3 (a copy of which is attached hereto as Attachment 2) and the Mediation Protocol Under Local Civil Rule 53.3, or some other form of alternative dispute resolution might be of assistance in resolving the case and, if so, on what form of alternative dispute resolution they agree and by what date they will be prepared to commence such proceedings;

7. A final pretrial conference will be held on [_____]. At least one of the attorneys for each party shall have the authority to enter into stipulations and to make admissions regarding all matters.

Final pretrial memoranda shall be filed pursuant to Local Rule of Civil Procedure 16.1(c) and shall contain all items listed in that rule, including the following: a jurisdictional statement; statement (or, in Defendant's memorandum, counterstatement) of the facts of the case; damages computation, or description of other relief sought; list of intended witnesses, designated separately for liability and damages; schedule of exhibits to be offered at trial; estimate of required trial time; and special comments regarding legal issues, stipulations, amendments of pleadings, or other appropriate matters. Plaintiff shall file its pretrial memorandum **[approximately two weeks prior to the final pretrial conference]**. Defendant shall file its pretrial memorandum by **[approximately seven days after Plaintiff files its pretrial memorandum]**.

In addition to the above, if applicable, each party is required to submit the following in conjunction with the pretrial memoranda: proposed *voir dire* questions, proposed jury instructions (one point per page), proposed jury interrogatories, a trial memorandum on the legal issues involved in the case, and any motions *in limine*. The failure to submit proposed jury instructions may result in the forfeiture of your right to object to omissions in jury charge. If possible, counsel should provide the Court with copies of the proposed jury instructions and jury interrogatories on 3.5" IBM compatible computer diskettes, in a format readable by WordPerfect 12. If this is a non-jury trial, each party is required to submit proposed findings of fact and conclusions of law on the date on which its pretrial memorandum is due.

In preparation for the final pretrial conference, counsel are expected to communicate with each other on the following matters in an effort to reach agreement or, if agreement is not possible, to submit, the precise points in dispute, in writing, in a joint statement on the following: (a) agreed upon and disputed facts; (b) objections to any proposed witnesses; (c) objections to any proposed exhibits (including objections to genuineness and authenticity); (d) objections to any depositions to be read at trial; (e) disputed legal issues; (f) amendments to pleadings; (g) stipulated to and disputed points for charge; (h) verdict sheet and special interrogatories; and (i) number of days required for trial.

8. Trial is scheduled for the [_____] trial pool.

It is so **ORDERED**.

BY THE COURT:

CYNTHIA M. RUFE, J.

Scheduling Order Attachment 1

Judge Rufe's Required Procedure on Summary Judgment for Those Moving under Rule 56(b)

1. **Initial Filing of Moving Party**: A party referred to in Rule 56(b) and moving under Rule 56(b) may move without reference to supporting affidavits or other evidence and, in doing so, the party making the motion shall:

    (1) identify in outline form the issue(s) and/or sub-issue(s) as to which the Motion is directed;

    (2) provide a separate, short and concise <u>Statement of Stipulated Material Facts</u>, as described below;

    (3) affirm, on the basis prescribed in Rule 11, that there is no legally sufficient evidentiary basis to support the issues so identified; and

    (4) request judgment as provided in Rule 56(c).

    The initial filing by the moving party should not exceed <u>five (5) double-spaced, type-written pages</u>, excluding the Statement of Stipulated Material Facts.

    No later than fourteen (14) days prior to the case dispositive motion deadline outlined in the Court's scheduling order, the parties shall meet and confer as to the facts material to the case. The initial filing of the moving party must include a short and concise Statement of Stipulated Material Facts, which sets forth, in numbered paragraphs, the material facts that the parties agree are not in dispute. Only the facts that bear on material issues shall be included.

2. **Response of Non-Moving Party**: The non-moving party may file a Response within twenty-one (21) days after the Motion for Summary Judgment is served. The Response, subject to the provisions of Rule 56(e) and (f), shall be supported with affidavits, depositions, documents or other evidence permitted by those provisions. Where applicable, references to such evidence must include specific citations to exhibit, page, and line number. The Response may not exceed <u>twenty-five (25) pages</u>.

3. **Reply of Moving Party**: The movant shall file a Reply as permitted by Rule 56(c). Such a Reply must be filed not later than fourteen (14) days after receipt of the Response from the non-moving party. The Reply must specify the relevant exhibit, page, and line numbers when referring to the record. The Reply may not exceed <u>twenty-five (25) pages</u>.

4. **Sur-Reply of Non-Moving Party (Optional)**: The non-moving party may, within seven (7) days after the Reply is received, file a Sur-reply to the Reply described in paragraph 3 above. The Sur-reply must specify the relevant exhibit, page, and line numbers when referring to the record. The Sur-reply may not exceed <u>ten (10) pages</u>.

The purpose of this procedure is to encourage the parties in their dispositive motion to track the natural order of trial where the plaintiff sets forth its cause and the defendant then responds.

Scheduling Order Attachment 2

LOCAL RULE OF CIVIL PROCEDURE 53.3: ALTERNATIVE DISPUTE RESOLUTION

I. Litigants in all civil actions, exempting only social security appeals, pro se prisoner civil rights actions, and petitions for habeas corpus, shall be required to consider the use of an alternative dispute resolution process (the "ADR process") at an appropriate stage in the litigation.

II. ADR processes may include mediation and settlement conferences and such other ADR processes as the judge to whom the case is assigned (the "assigned judge") may designate.

III. All ADR processes subject to this Rule shall be confidential, and disclosure by any person of confidential dispute resolution communications is prohibited unless confidentiality has been waived by all participants in the ADR process, or disclosure is ordered by the assigned judge for good cause shown.

IV. Nothing in the Rule shall be construed to limit the assigned judge from (a) conducting settlement conferences or referring a matter to a magistrate judge for a settlement conference, or (b) ordering the litigants to participate in an ADR process, or (c) approving or disapproving of an ADR process selected by the litigants.

V. The Alternative Dispute Resolution ("ADR") Committee of the court shall administer, oversee, and evaluate the court's ADR program in accordance with the Alternative Dispute Resolution Act of 1998. The Clerk of Court, or such other person as may be designated from time to time by the Chief Judge, shall serve as the ADR coordinator. Under the direction of the ADR committee, the coordinator shall administer a program for recruitment, screening and training of attorneys to serve as neutrals.

VI. The Rule is intended to be flexible so as to permit the court to adopt, from time to time, guidelines and policies for the administration of the ADR program. The procedures promulgated by the court for the implementation of the ADR program shall be maintained on file in the office of the Clerk.

VII. Nothing in the Rule shall be construed to amend or modify the provisions of Local Civil Rule 53.2 (compulsory and voluntary arbitration with right of trial *de novo*). Local Civil Rule 53.2.1 (compulsory mediation) is repealed by separate order.

<u>Explanatory Note</u>

The Rule is intended to implement the provisions of the Alternative Dispute Resolution Act of 1998 and to demonstrate the long-standing commitment of the court and its bar to non-binding alternative dispute resolution, without, however, limiting the authority and discretion of the assigned judge. Certain civil actions are exempted from the Rule as cases not appropriate for ADR process pursuant to the Alternative Dispute Resolution Act of 1998.

Effective July 1, 2003

Judge Juan R. Sánchez

Judge Sánchez was born in Vega Baja, Puerto Rico, and graduated from DeWitt Clinton High School in the Bronx, New York City. Judge Sánchez received his Bachelor of Arts degree, cum laude, from City College of the City University of New York, and his Juris Doctor from the University of Pennsylvania Law School, where he received the Benjamin R. Jones Award for commitment to humanity and the law. After a career with Chester County Legal Aid and the Public Defender's Office of Chester County, Judge Sánchez was elected to the Chester County Court of Common Pleas in 1997, where he served until President George W. Bush nominated him to a seat on the District Court for the Eastern District of Pennsylvania. Judge Sánchez was inducted on July 9, 2004.

PRELIMINARY GENERAL MATTERS

1. Communications with Chambers. Judge Sánchez permits communications with chambers by telephone, letter, or facsimile regarding scheduling and other non-substantive matters. All other issues, except discovery disputes, must be addressed by motion or other filing. Under no circumstances may any party or counsel communicate ex parte with any chambers personnel concerning substantive matters.

Telephone inquiries should be directed to Judge Sánchez's civil or criminal deputy, as appropriate, at the telephone numbers listed below. If the appropriate deputy is unavailable, attorneys may speak to Judge Sánchez's law clerks regarding scheduling matters; however, law clerks may not render advice to counsel.

Civil Deputy: Nancy DeLisle
Telephone: 267-299-7780
Facsimile: 267-299-5067
Contact for matters related to civil scheduling and case management, requesting telephone conferences, and general court procedures.

ESR/Criminal Courtroom Deputy: Adrienne Mann
Telephone: 267-299-7789
Facsimile: 267-299-7788
Contact for matters related to criminal scheduling and case management.

2. Stipulations and Consent Decrees. Any stipulations, consent decrees, or other documents requiring court approval or signature must be submitted in a form containing original signatures. Judge Sánchez will not sign any document containing a duplicated signature of any counsel, party, or representative.

3. Electronic Filing. Judge Sánchez expects attorneys practicing before him to use electronic case filing and to comply with the court's Electronic Case Filing (ECF) procedures pursuant to Local Civil Rule 5.1.2, unless excused from ECF registration. Pro se litigants are not required to file electronically. Courtesy copies are not required unless (1) the filing includes exhibits totaling more than 20 pages, or (2) the filing includes materials submitted under seal. In either of these instances, counsel should mail or hand-deliver to chambers a courtesy copy of the filing or, in the case of a filing containing sealed material, the portion or portions of the filing submitted under seal.

CIVIL CASES
Pretrial Procedure

1. Requests for Extensions of Time. Where compelling circumstances so require, counsel may request an extension of a filing or other deadline only if such request has no effect on other existing deadlines, particularly the trial date. Judge Sánchez will extend the deadline for filing dispositive motions or a trial pool date only in very limited circumstances and where genuinely necessary. If a request for an extension is unopposed, counsel must so state and may submit the request via letter or joint stipulation. Opposed requests must so state and be filed as a motion.

2. Rule 16 Scheduling Conferences. Judge Sánchez will schedule a Rule 16 conference once an answer is filed or, in some instances, while a motion to dismiss is pending. Unless Judge Sánchez approves a substitution in advance, lead trial counsel must attend the Rule 16 conference and must enter his or her appearance prior to the conference. If lead trial counsel is appearing pro hac vice, local counsel must also attend the Rule 16 conference. All applications to appear pro hac vice must be in writing and must be approved prior to the conference.

Judge Sánchez views the Rule 16 conference as an important step in the management of a case. He discourages requests to continue Rule 16 conferences or to conduct such conferences telephonically, and warns counsel a continuance may affect the time allowed for discovery before dispositive motions and trial.

Judge Sánchez relies on counsel's good-faith compliance in all respects with Rule 26(f). The Rule 26(f) meeting will take place as soon as possible, and should be viewed not as perfunctory but rather as a meaningful and substantive discussion among professionals to formulate the discovery plan required by the Rule. Outstanding motions will not excuse counsel from timely holding the meeting. Parties who do not comply will have no voice at the scheduling conference and may be subject to additional sanctions.

Before the Rule 16 conference, counsel will have discussed the nature and basis of the parties' claims and defenses, the possibility of a prompt settlement, and a discovery plan pursuant to Rule 26(f). The parties must also complete the joint Rule 16 conference information report included in Judge Sánchez's policies and procedures and must fax the completed report to chambers no later than one day before the Rule 16 conference. Counsel should expect a final pretrial conference to be scheduled approximately a month after the submission of any dispositive motion and a trial pool date approximately a week after the final pretrial conference.

Motions to dismiss, transfer, add parties, and other threshold motions should be filed before the Rule 16 conference. *Counsel must be prepared to present argument at the conference on any pending motions.*

At the conference, counsel should be prepared to discuss the strengths and weaknesses of the case and should therefore be conversant in the essential facts and issues involved. Counsel must have full authority to negotiate a settlement of the case or be accompanied by a client or client representative who has such authority. If necessary, Judge Sánchez will issue a scheduling order to govern further proceedings in the case after the conference.

3. Continuances. Judge Sánchez strongly disfavors requests for continuances. In civil cases, counsel must have good cause (for example, death or serious bodily injury) for the request. If good cause exists, a continuance must be sought as soon as possible. Requests for continuances must be in writing and should be faxed to chambers with a copy to opposing counsel. A formal motion is not required.

The party requesting a continuance must present the position of opposing counsel. If opposing counsel opposes the request, the requesting party must set up a conference call with Judge Sánchez to resolve the matter.

General Motion Practice

1. **Oral Argument.** Unless oral argument is requested and may be useful, Judge Sánchez regularly decides motions on the papers. If oral argument is scheduled, counsel should be prompt, professionally attired, and well prepared. During oral argument, counsel should refrain from simply repeating what the briefs assert. Judge Sánchez encourages counsel to bring their clients to oral argument on dispositive motions.

2. **General Policies.** Judge Sánchez advises counsel to carefully consider Rule 11 and notifies counsel that he will impose sanctions when a filing has no factual basis.

    Before any motion based on a curable defect under Rule 12 is filed, counsel must certify that opposing counsel has been given an opportunity to cure the defect.

    Any motion and its supporting memorandum of law *must not total more than 15 pages*. In those rare instances in which counsel believes additional pages are necessary, counsel should seek leave to exceed the page limit by motion.

3. **Motions for Injunctive Relief.** When a temporary restraining order is requested, Judge Sánchez will immediately schedule a conference to hear the motion. Unless the urgency of the circumstances preclude notice to opposing counsel, Judge Sánchez requires that all counsel be present.

    Judge Sánchez will schedule preliminary and permanent injunction hearings as soon as possible and will generally permit expedited discovery for injunctive matters.

4. **Dispositive Motions.** Counsel are advised to file any dispositive motions and oppositions to them in accordance with the deadlines established in the scheduling order entered in the case.

5. **Motions for Summary Judgment.** Any motion for summary judgment pursuant to Federal Rule of Civil Procedure 56 should be accompanied by a separate, short, and concise statement, in numbered paragraphs, of the material facts as to which the moving party contends there is no genuine issue to be tried. Only those facts that are material to the issues in dispute should be included in the enumerated statement of facts. Each factual assertion must be accompanied by a citation to the specific portion or portions of the record that support the assertion, including the exhibit, page, and line number. The court will not consider factual assertions not supported by a citation to the record.

    A party opposing a motion for summary judgment should file a separate, short, and concise statement responding to the numbered paragraphs set forth in the moving party's statement of undisputed facts and either conceding the facts as undisputed or stating a genuine dispute exists. If the opposing party asserts a genuine dispute exists as to any fact, the party must cite to the specific portion or portions of the record that create the dispute, including the exhibit, page, and line number. The opposing party should also set forth in enumerated paragraphs any additional facts that the party contends preclude summary judgment. All facts set forth in the moving party's statement of undisputed facts will be deemed admitted unless controverted by the opposing party.

6. **Reply Briefs.** Reply briefs may be submitted without leave of court in support of a motion for summary judgment or other dispositive motion, and with the court's permission in support of non-dispositive motions. Replies may not exceed 10 pages and should address *only* issues raised in the opposition to the motion, without repeating arguments

made in the initial brief. Replies must be submitted no later than 7 days after the opposition is filed. When referring to the record, the reply must *specify* the relevant exhibit, page, and line numbers.

A surreply may only be filed with permission of the court upon good cause shown and may not exceed five pages.

7.   Policies Regarding All Other Motions.   For all other motions, Judge Sánchez follows the requirements of Local Civil Rule 7.1.

Discovery Matters

1.   Discovery Conference and Dispute Resolution.   Parties are expected to manage discovery pursuant to Fed.R.Civ.P. 26 without involving Judge Sánchez, except in the rarest of cases.

2.   Discovery Disputes.   Counsel must exhaustively address all discovery disputes among themselves before requesting Judge Sánchez's assistance. In the event the parties are unable to resolve a discovery dispute on their own, counsel should request a teleconference with Judge Sánchez by faxing a letter to chambers briefly outlining the nature of the dispute. The letter must certify that counsel have made a good-faith effort to resolve the issue themselves. *Motions to compel or other discovery motions should not be filed until a teleconference has been held.* If a teleconference is scheduled, the requesting party or, in the event of a joint request, plaintiff's counsel should initiate the call.

3.   Expert Witnesses.   Judge Sánchez directs the exchange of expert reports and supporting documentation/information in advance of trial pursuant to Rule 26(a)(2)(B). A violation of the disclosure requirements of the rule may result in the barring of expert testimony at trial. Any deposition of an expert under Rule 26(b)(4)(A) must be conducted before the deadline for submission of dispositive motions.

Settlement

1.   Settlement Conferences.   Judge Sánchez addresses the possibility of settlement at all stages in the proceedings. In addition, consistent with Local Civil Rule 53.3, Judge Sánchez directs all parties to consider the use of an alternative dispute resolution process at an appropriate stage in the litigation. Judge Sánchez also encourages early referral to a magistrate judge for settlement discussions.

Upon reaching a settlement, counsel must notify Judge Sánchez's chambers immediately and request dismissal of the action pursuant to Local Civil Rule 41.1.

Trial Procedure

1.   General Procedures.   Civility is the foundation of Judge Sánchez's courtroom procedures. Rise when the judge and the jury enter and leave the courtroom.

Court normally begins at 9:00 a.m. The court will make every effort to commence proceedings on time. Counsel, parties, and witnesses must be on time.

Witnesses and parties should be instructed to wear proper attire to court. Shorts, tank tops, etc. are not permitted attire. Witnesses or parties not properly attired may be excluded from the courtroom.

Cell phones and other electronic devices must be turned off (not on silent or vibrate mode) before entering the courtroom. Recording or taking photographs in the courtroom is strictly prohibited. A violation of these rules may result in confiscation of the cell phone or device and prosecution. Attorneys are responsible for their own electronic devices and those of their witnesses and clients.

Food, drink, and chewing gum are prohibited in the courtroom and witnesses should be so instructed.

Requests concerning courtroom technology, including requests for an electronic courtroom, should be directed to Michael Hearn at 267-299-7039 or Ed Morrissy at 267-299-7044. Requests for an electronic courtroom should be submitted as far in advance of trial as possible.

2.   Decorum of Counsel.   Counsel should dress in an appropriate professional manner. The trial will at all times be conducted in a dignified and formal manner. Counsel should not raise their voices any louder than is necessary to be clearly heard by the court, witnesses, and the jury. All remarks should be addressed to the court. Counsel should never act or speak disrespectfully to the court or opposing counsel in any manner.

Counsel's demeanor should be one of courtesy and professionalism. Counsel should not exhibit familiarity with the parties, jurors, or opposing counsel, and should avoid using first names. During opening statements or closing arguments, no juror should be addressed individually or by name. Neither counsel nor the parties, by their body language or facial expression, should convey their reaction to the testimony of a witness.

Counsel must rise to address the court. Address the court as "Your Honor."

3.   Court Seating.   Under local practice, the plaintiff's table is closest to the jury box. Any requests concerning seating (such as requests for more than one counsel table for all plaintiffs or all defendants or special requests for seating, visual aids, etc.) should be submitted to Judge Sánchez's civil courtroom deputy, Nancy DeLisle, at least *one week* before trial.

Only counsel and parties, if desired, should sit at counsel table. Witnesses must sit in the spectator section only, unless otherwise authorized by the court. If any party desires sequestration, an appropriate motion should be made at the outset of the trial. If sequestration is ordered, all witnesses for all parties will be sequestered. Counsel will be responsible for informing their non-party witnesses that they should remain outside the courtroom until called, and that they should not discuss their testimony with other witnesses until the trial is concluded.

4.   Final Pretrial Conferences.   Judge Sánchez will use the pretrial conference to discuss specific trial procedures. Judge Sánchez regularly lists a pretrial conference date in the scheduling order. Generally, the final pretrial conference will be held not less than 30 days after the close of discovery. Pretrial conferences are typically scheduled for the week preceding the trial date or trial pool to which a case is assigned. Judge Sánchez uses the pretrial conference to resolve any outstanding motions and to discuss voir dire and other trial procedures.

5.   Scheduling of Cases.   Judge Sánchez's scheduling order will usually assign a case to a two-week trial pool. All parties, witnesses, and counsel can expect their cases to be tried during the trial pool period and should arrange their schedules accordingly. Judge Sánchez will make every effort to give counsel reasonable notice of a trial date within the trial pool period and will attempt to notify counsel at least 72 hours—and in no event less than 24 hours—before the day trial is to commence. Counsel may telephone chambers during the week before the trial pool for guidance. At the request of counsel, Judge Sánchez may list nonjury trials or complex matters for a special listing/date-certain. In appropriate cases, Judge Sánchez may impose time limits on the parties' trial presentations. See *Duquesne Light Co. v. Westinghouse Elec. Corp.* 66 F.3d 604, 609–10 (3d Cir. 1995).

6. **Designations of Depositions.** Judge Sánchez expects to decide disputes regarding deposition designations and preserved objections within depositions at the final pretrial conference. To facilitate the timely resolution of such disputes, the parties must exchange deposition designations at least one week prior to the pretrial conference and counter-designations must be exchanged at least three days prior to the pretrial conference. The parties must submit any objections to designations and counter-designations to the court in writing no later than one day before the pretrial conference. Objections should be raised by letter; a formal motion is not required.

7. **Requested Voir Dire, Points for Charge, and Verdict Slip.** Prior to the final pretrial conference, the parties must submit a *joint*, neutral statement of the facts for voir dire and *joint* questions for voir dire, highlighting only the disputed questions. Voir dire questions should not number more than 15.

    The parties must also submit *joint* requested points for charge and a *joint* verdict slip with only the disputed points highlighted. Judge Sánchez prefers the Third Circuit Model Jury Instructions but will hear argument on reasons for deviations. The joint requested points for charge and joint verdict slip should be filed on the docket, *one point to a page in sequence*, and should be sent by e-mail to sanchezdocs@paed.uscourts.gov in WordPerfect format. Unless requested by chambers, no other document should be e-mailed to Judge Sánchez. An e-mail to chambers does not constitute filing.

    Judge Sánchez will hear argument on disputed points for charge and the verdict slip at the final pretrial conference and, if necessary, for a total of 15 minutes at the close of testimony and before closing arguments.

    Counsel will have an automatic exception for any point not given as submitted. All other exceptions must be made known to the Court before the jury is dismissed for deliberations.

    Judge Sánchez typically conducts voir dire in civil cases. Counsel must submit joint proposed voir dire questions prior to the pretrial conference. No more than 15 questions will be asked.

8. **Sidebar Conferences.** Judge Sánchez discourages sidebar conferences; issues should be resolved at the final pretrial conference.

    Any matter arising during trial must be brought to the judge's attention between 8 a.m. and 9 a.m., during breaks, at lunchtime, or after the jury is dismissed for the day.

9. **In Limine Motions.** Motions in limine with respect to legal matters that the parties reasonably expect to arise during trial must be presented in accordance with the deadline established in the scheduling order. Motions in limine filed after the deadline will be considered only upon a showing of good cause.

10. **Opening Statements.** The purpose of the opening statement is to state briefly what counsel expects the evidence to show. Brief reference to the law will be permitted, to the extent such references will aid the jury in understanding what counsel expects to prove. It is not proper to use the opening statement to argue the case. Upon violation of any of these rules, the court may, sua sponte, interrupt the opening statement and admonish counsel. The court may also impose time limits on opening and closing statements. Counsel must seek the permission of the court to present an opening or closing statement in excess of 30 minutes.

11. **Exhibits.** So as to avoid duplication of exhibits and confusion regarding exhibit numbers, Judge Sánchez requires the parties to work together to prepare a single set of sequentially numbered trial exhibits, without regard for who will propound the exhibit at

trial. The parties need not agree on the admissibility of any exhibit in preparing the exhibit binders. The court will rule on the admissibility of individual exhibits in the course of trial. Exhibits may be moved for admission at any time during counsel's case.

Counsel should assemble all exhibits to be offered at trial and number those exhibits from 1 to 79 (or 790, as the case demands). The plaintiff's first exhibit should be numbered "1," and the defendant's first exhibit should have the number immediately following the number of the plaintiff's last exhibit, so that if the plaintiff has 29 exhibits, the defendant's first exhibit would be numbered "30." Only one copy of a document should be included in the exhibits. If a document the defendant intends to introduce is included among the plaintiff's exhibits, the defendant should not include a second copy of the document in its exhibits. All proposed exhibits should be placed in binders, accompanied by a table of contents. The table of contents should include the exhibit number, a brief description of the exhibit, and two columns with the headings "Admitted" and "Not Admitted" for the court's use during trial. In cases involving multiple exhibit binders, counsel should prepare a master table of contents that also specifies the volume in which each exhibit appears. One copy of the exhibit binders must be available for the court's use, and another copy must be available for use by witnesses. As exhibits are offered at trial, counsel should refer to the exhibit by the same number (and volume number, in cases involving multiple exhibit binders), as follows:

Direct: "Please look at the contract, exhibit 32, and tell the jury ...";

Cross: "Turning now to exhibit 32, the contract, isn't it true that ..."

At the close of evidence, the parties should edit the binders so that only those exhibits admitted into evidence are returned to the Court. (A binder of admitted exhibits hypothetically could be numbered 1–10, 14, 27, 33–39, and 45.) The Court will hear argument on whether particular exhibits go out with the jury at the close of the charge to the jury.

12. **Witnesses.** The rule of civility is absolute in addressing witnesses, whether on direct or cross-examination. Witnesses should be treated with fairness and consideration; they should not be shouted at, ridiculed, or abused in any manner. Counsel should not approach a witness without leave of court, and should not by facial expression or other conduct, exhibit an opinion concerning any witness.

Counsel on direct must ensure that a witness is speaking into the microphone for ease of recording and hearing.

If a witness was on the stand at a recess or adjournment, the witness should be on the stand ready to proceed when court is resumed. Counsel are reminded that they may not discuss a witness's testimony with him or her once that witness has begun testifying until the witness is excused.

Judge Sánchez expects trial to proceed smoothly without delay and counsel are advised to avoid running out of witnesses during a trial day. If there will be a problem with the scheduling of any witness, counsel should inform the court at the preliminary conference and at the beginning of that day's proceedings.

Counsel must provide opposing counsel and the court with a list of witnesses for the next day.

13. **Videotaped Testimony.** If a witness is testifying by way of videotape, counsel must resolve all issues of objections and redaction prior to or during the final pretrial conference. In no case will trial be delayed to argue about or edit a videotape. See also section 17 below, regarding other courtroom tools.

Any objection to any part of videotaped or written deposition testimony must be reviewed with the judge during the pretrial conference and presented with a transcript and with reference to page numbers and grounds for objection. Trial counsel should be sure any videotape is rewound. See also section 14 below, regarding objections.

14. Objections. When objecting, counsel should only state "objection" and cite to the evidentiary rule upon which the objection is based in a word or two. Counsel should not offer argument or explanation unless requested to do so by the court. Counsel will not be permitted to state additional reasons for an objection after the court has ruled. Additionally, counsel should not use objections for the purpose of making a speech, recapitulating testimony, or attempting to guide the witness.

For purposes of protecting the record, counsel may, outside of the hearing of the jury, request a more complete argument on an objection. Argument will be heard during a scheduled break or before or after trial for the day.

In a case involving multiple parties, an objection by one will be considered an objection by all *unless* a party specifically opts out of the objection.

Any objection to any part of videotaped or written deposition testimony must be reviewed with the judge during the pretrial conference and presented with a transcript and with reference to page numbers and grounds for objection.

15. Examination of Witnesses. Counsel should conduct examination of witnesses from the lectern unless counsel has obtained the court's permission to conduct witness examinations from another appropriate location in the courtroom.

When using an exhibit during the examination of a witness, counsel should be prepared through tabbing or other means to display only the relevant document to the witness.

Counsel should ask witnesses to state and spell their names for the benefit of the ESR operator.

If a witness is to be examined on the basis of prior written statements made by the witness, and these statements have not yet been received into evidence, the witness must first be shown the statement and asked whether he or she acknowledges having made it.

Counsel should avoid the use of argumentative questions when questioning an opposing party. Instead, questions should be kept clear and to the point.

16. Cross-examination. If counsel wishes to cross-examine a witness on the basis of a deposition, counsel must give a copy of the deposition to the witness, who will be permitted to read the deposition and to adopt or deny the testimony before counsel may proceed with cross-examination.

Judge Sánchez permits direct, cross, and redirect examination of a witness. Judge Sánchez generally permits recross-examination only "[w]here new evidence is opened up on redirect examination." *United States v. Riggi,* 951 F.2d 1368, 1375 (3d Cir. 1991) (explaining "the privilege of recross-examination as to matters not covered on redirect examination lies within the trial court's discretion" (citation omitted)).

17. Other Courtroom Tools. Admissions, pleadings, requests for admissions, admissions of parties contained in depositions, and interrogatories are not part of the evidence at trial unless counsel moves for their admission and they are admitted.

18. Summation and Jury Charge. Judge Sánchez allows only 30 minutes for closing argument, including rebuttal, unless leave is granted for additional time. Plaintiff's counsel should be sure to reserve time from his or her closing to use for rebuttal. Failure to do so will constitute a waiver of rebuttal.

Any objection to any point for charge will be resolved or noted before closing arguments begin. No further changes will be made to the points for charge after closing arguments begin.

During closing, counsel must refrain from expressing any opinion about the credibility of any witness, the culpability of the plaintiff or the defendant, personal knowledge of a fact in issue, or any fact not in evidence.

Judge Sánchez will not permit any personal attack or any closing argument that invokes gender, sexual orientation, ethnicity, race, religion, or politics.

Any objection during closing should be carefully considered, brief, and based on a rule in a word or two only.

19. **Proposed Findings of Fact and Conclusions of Law.** For all nonjury trials, the court requires the parties to submit proposed findings of fact and conclusions of law. Proposed findings and conclusions must be submitted within 21 days of receipt of the trial transcript, which will be ordered promptly.

20. **Miscellaneous.** For any civil litigation issues not addressed above, please consult the Local Rules of Civil Procedure for the Eastern District of Pennsylvania, available at http://www.paed.uscourts.gov.

Jury Deliberations

1. **Contact with the Jury.** From the time the jury is selected until it is discharged, counsel, the parties, and their witnesses must avoid all forms of contact with individual jurors. If the jury or any individual juror is entering an elevator, counsel and his or her clients are advised to take another elevator.

2. **Availability of Counsel During Jury Deliberations.** During jury deliberations, counsel and their clients should be available to return to the courtroom on 10 minutes' notice.

CRIMINAL MATTERS

Judge Sánchez's requirements for courtroom decorum and civility apply particularly in criminal matters. Counsel are advised to treat the jurors' time and every witness with respect.

At no time during trial will Judge Sánchez permit counsel to comment adversely on the silence of a defendant, make statements of personal belief, attack counsel, appeal to the self-interest or passions of the jury, or make comments based on gender, sexual orientation, race, ethnicity, religion, or politics. A violation of any of these rules will result in severe sanctions.

1. **Motions Practice.** All pretrial motions—including motions in limine and any motions challenging the indictment, seeking suppression of evidence, or raising any dispositive matters—must be filed in accordance with the deadlines set forth in the scheduling order entered in the case. Upon the filing of any motion, the parties must advise the court whether they intend to present testimony in support of or in opposition to the motion and the expected duration of any such testimony, so that the court can schedule a motion hearing, if necessary.

2. **Continuances of Trial.** Any request for a continuance must be filed no later than 14 days in advance of the scheduled trial date. Requests for a continuance must be filed as a motion stating the reasons for the request. Any such motion must be accompanied by a proposed form of order that, if approved by the court, would grant the relief sought by the motion. The proposed form of order *must* be consistent with the requirements of the Speedy Trial Act, 18 U.S.C. § 3161(h)(8), and must include a proposed finding that explains in reasonable detail why the ends of justice served by granting the requested continuance outweigh the best interest of the public and the defendant in a speedy trial.

Judge Sánchez requires a telephone conference before granting the first continuance of a trial. Any subsequent continuance is strongly discouraged, and, if further continuance is sought, counsel must appear in person to argue the matter.

3. **Pretrial Conferences.** Judge Sánchez may schedule a pretrial conference in appropriate cases. Any issues related to voir dire, motions in limine, jury instructions, and jury verdict forms must be submitted prior to the pretrial conference.

4. **Voir Dire.** Judge Sánchez conducts extensive voir dire in criminal jury matters. Counsel may submit follow-up questions for Judge Sánchez to ask.

5. **Testimonial Issues.** Judge Sánchez strongly encourages the disclosure of Jencks Act and Rule 26.2 statements prior to trial so that any dispute may be resolved at the pretrial conference without delaying the trial. If disclosure is withheld until after direct examination, the statements will be presumed to be relevant and the opposing party will be afforded a recess to prepare for cross-examination.

If the government expects to introduce Rule 404(b) evidence relating to other crimes, wrongs, or acts, it must file a notice of its intention to do so prior to the pretrial conference. The notice must include a brief summary of the proposed evidence, identifying the purpose for which the evidence will be offered, and a proposed jury instruction to precede the introduction of such evidence.

If tapes are used in a case, counsel will jointly resolve any dispute regarding the accuracy of transcripts prior to the pretrial conference. Any unresolved dispute must be raised at the pretrial conference.

6. **Guilty Pleas.** Before a defendant offers a guilty plea, the guilty plea memorandum, guilty plea agreement, and acknowledgment of rights must be completed and reviewed with the defendant, and must be provided to the court.

The guilty plea agreement must state whether the plea is a general plea of guilty, a conditional plea, or a plea of nolo contendere. The guilty plea agreement must also disclose to the defendant and the court whether the plea is entered pursuant to Fed.R.Crim.P. 11(c)(1)(A), (B), or (C), relating to the obligation of the government regarding other charges under subsection (A), a non-binding sentencing recommendation under subsection (B), or a binding sentencing recommendation under subsection (C). In addition, the plea agreement *must* inform the defendant and remind the court, pursuant to Rule 11(c)(3)(B), that the defendant has no right to withdraw the plea if the court does not follow the recommendation or request if the plea is entered under 11(c)(1)(B).

Form AO245B (Criminal Justice Work Sheet) must be completed for each defendant.

7. **Sentencing.** Judge Sánchez will schedule a sentencing on the day the court accepts a defendant's guilty plea or after a defendant is convicted at trial. Judge Sánchez discourages continuances of sentencing, and sentencing will be continued for good cause only. Judge Sánchez will not consider any request for a continuance exceeding 90 days.

If, after receiving a first continuance, both counsel for the government and defense counsel believe that good cause exists for an additional continuance beyond the 90-day period, counsel may jointly submit a written request for an additional continuance, explaining why good cause exists.

To avoid delay in sentencing, all objections to the presentence-investigation report (PSR) must be sent to the probation officer in advance of sentencing. In no event will counsel raise objections for the first time in a sentencing memorandum.

Sentencing motions and supporting memoranda must be filed at least 14 days prior to the scheduled sentencing date, and any response thereto must be filed at least 7 days prior to the scheduled sentencing date.

Sentencing memoranda (exclusive of motions) by both the government and the defense must be filed *no later than one week* before the scheduled sentencing date, and any response thereto must be filed at least three days prior to the scheduled sentencing date.

8. Miscellaneous. For any criminal litigation issues not addressed above, please consult the Local Rules of Criminal Procedure for the Eastern District of Pennsylvania, available at http://www.paed.uscourts.gov.

JOINT RULE 16 CONFERENCE INFORMATION REPORT

Caption: _____ Civil Action No: _____
Basis of Jurisdiction: _____ Jury Trial or Non-Jury Trial: _____

Plaintiff's lead trial counsel:_____
Defendant's lead trial counsel: _____
Do counsel have full authority to settle at Rule 16 conference?_____
    If not, client with such authority who will attend:_____

When did the parties exchange Rule 26(a) initial disclosures?_____

How much time do the parties need for fact discovery? _____
Identify any other discovery issues which should be addressed at the Rule 16 conference, including any need for sequencing of discovery, limitations on discovery, protective orders, or other elements which should be included in a particularized discovery plan:_____
_____
_____
_____

Does either side expect to file a case-dispositive motion? _____
    If yes, under what Rule? _____
    If yes, specify the issue(s):_____
    Proposed deadline for filing dispositive motions: _____

Does either side anticipate the use of experts? _____
    If yes, what is the proposed deadline for expert discovery?_____

Approximate date case should be trial-ready:_____
    Estimated trial time for Plaintiff's case:_____
    Estimated trial time for Defendant's case: _____

Has settlement been discussed? _____
    If not, why not?_____

Is a settlement conference likely to be helpful? _____
    If so, when? Early? After discovery? _____

Have you discussed consenting to proceed before a United States Magistrate Judge? _____

**This form should be faxed to Chambers at 267-299-5067
no later than one day before the Rule 16 conference.**

Judge Timothy J. Savage

Judge Savage received his A.B. from Assumption College in 1968, and his J.D. from Temple Law School in 1971. He was an associate with McCoy, Evans, and Lewis from 1971 until 1974, when he went into private practice, concentrating on criminal and civil litigation in the federal and state courts until his appointment to the federal bench. He also served as a hearing examiner for the Pennsylvania Liquor Control Board from 1977 until 2002. Judge Savage was appointed to the United States District Court for the Eastern District of Pennsylvania on August 2, 2002.

PRELIMINARY GENERAL MATTERS

1. Correspondence with the Court. Written communications concerning any case must be by the filing of a pleading, motion, application, or other similar filing provided for in the Federal Rules of Civil Procedure or Local Rules of Civil Procedure.

Correspondence is permitted only in the following instances:
   a. When counsel are specifically requested by the court to communicate information by letter;
   b. When there is an uncontested request for an extension of the Rule 16 scheduling order deadlines not affecting the dates for filing summary judgment motions; and
   c. When there is an unanticipated personal matter concerning counsel, a party, a witness, or counsel's immediate family, such as medical problems, vacation plans, or other personal problems; or
   d. To advise that a case has been settled.

Counsel should not send copies of correspondence among and between counsel to the court.

2. Communications with Law Clerks. Law clerks have no authority to grant continuances or to give advice on substantive or procedural matters. Therefore, unless contacted by a law clerk, counsel should not communicate with the law clerks.

3. Telephone Conferences. When a written communication concerning a case cannot timely address a problem, counsel may initiate necessary telephone communications with chambers. Issues appropriately addressed by telephone contact include scheduling of conferences or proceedings, including pretrial and trial conferences, attendance of witnesses, exhibit handling or arrangements for video replay, and arrangements for telephone conferences regarding discovery disputes.

Telephone inquiries should be directed as appropriate to either one of the following:

Judicial Assistant: Roseann Giangiordano—267-299-7480
   Contact for matters relating to civil scheduling, case management, and general procedures.

Courtroom Deputy: Harry E. Grace, Jr.—267-299-7599
   Contact for matters regarding all criminal cases, courtroom procedures, trial setup, and transcripts.

Counsel are advised to submit current telephone and fax numbers to the Clerk's Office, the courtroom deputy, and the judicial secretary.

4. Facsimiles. Facsimile transmittal of pleadings, motions, other filings, or correspondence to chambers is not permitted, unless requested.

5. ***Electronic Case Filing and Courtesy Copies.*** Counsel must file all pleadings electronically through ECF. Courtesy copies should not be provided to chambers unless the exhibits are voluminous or chambers requests them.

6. ***Pro Hac Vice Motions.*** Counsel moving for the pro hac vice admission of an attorney must file a motion setting forth the attorney's admissions, the reason why the party desires the attorney to participate, and why the attorney is especially qualified to do so. The form application provided by the clerk is inadequate. If the motion does not comply with this requirement, it will be denied.

CIVIL CASES
Pretrial Procedure

1. ***Pretrial Conferences.*** A preliminary pretrial conference as described in Fed.R.Civ.P. 16(b) and (c) will be scheduled shortly after a defendant has filed an appearance or pleading. At least *three business days* prior to the pretrial conference, counsel must file a comprehensive joint report of the Rule 26(f) meeting in the form of the sample shown on page 276 of this book.

The court relies on counsel's good-faith compliance in all respects with Rule 26(f). The Rule 26(f) meeting should take place as soon as possible. The meeting should not be viewed as perfunctory but rather as a meaningful and substantive discussion among professionals to formulate the proposed discovery plan required by the rule and to discuss the parties' factual and legal positions.

Outstanding motions will *not* excuse the requirements of holding the meeting and submitting the plan. Compliance is mandatory. *Parties who do not comply will have no voice at the scheduling conference and may be subject to additional sanctions.*

Topics addressed at the initial pretrial conference are those listed in Local Rule of Civil Procedure 16.1(b), Fed.R.Civ.P. 16(b) and (c), the progress of self-executing disclosure under Federal Rule of Civil Procedure 26(a), discovery, the preservation and production of electronically stored information, settlement, mediation proposals, and the facts regarding liability, damages, and relief sought. A Rule 16 scheduling order is issued at the conclusion of the conference.

Lead trial counsel, not an associate, must attend the Rule 16 conference. Counsel should have a thorough comprehension of the facts and must be prepared to discuss all claims and defenses in detail, including settlement, and have authority from their clients to do so.

2. ***Threshold Motions.*** Motions to dismiss, transfer, add parties, and other threshold motions should be filed before the Rule 16 conference. Counsel must be prepared to discuss the merits of any outstanding motions at the conference.

General Motion Practice

1. ***Oral Argument on Motions.*** Oral argument is not routinely scheduled. A party desiring oral argument should request it by letter or in the body of the motion or responsive pleading.

2. ***Reply Briefs.*** Reply briefs, addressing only issues raised in the brief in opposition and not repeating arguments in the brief, may be filed within seven days of service of the opponent's brief in opposition and should be limited to 10 pages. No further briefs may be filed.

3. Motions for Summary Judgment. Any motion for summary judgment filed pursuant to Fed.R.Civ.P. 56 must include a separate statement of undisputed facts that sets forth, in numbered paragraphs, the material facts that the moving party contends are undisputed and entitle the movant to judgment as a matter of law. Only those facts that bear on dispositive material issues should be included in the statement of undisputed facts.

The papers opposing a motion for summary judgment must include a separate statement of material facts, responding to the numbered paragraphs set forth in the statement of undisputed facts, which the respondent contends present genuine issues to be tried. The responding party also must set forth, in separate numbered paragraphs, any additional facts that the respondent contends preclude summary judgment. All material facts set forth in the statement required to be served by the moving party will be admitted unless controverted by the opposing party.

Statements of material facts in support of or in opposition to a motion for summary judgment should include specific and not general references to the parts of the record that support each of the statements. Each stated fact must cite the source relied upon, including the page and line of any document or deposition to which reference is made.

Discovery Matters

1. Discovery Period. The Federal Rules of Civil Procedure call for voluntary, cooperative discovery in a *timely* manner. The information required to be disclosed pursuant to Fed.R.Civ.P. 26(a) is required to be exchanged no later than 14 days after the date of the order scheduling the Rule 16 conference. Compliance with the rules is *mandatory*. Counsel are expected to act in accordance with both the *letter* and the *spirit* of the rules.

The parties are required to commence discovery *immediately* upon receipt of notice of the Rule 16 conference. Pending motions will not excuse counsel from proceeding with discovery. Counsel will be required to report on the progress of discovery at the Rule 16 conference.

2. Discovery Conferences and Dispute Resolution. When timely discovery is not forthcoming after a reasonable attempt has been made to obtain it, the immediate assistance of the court should be sought after compliance with Local Rule 26.1(f). The certification must state *in detail* what efforts were made to resolve the dispute.

The court encourages the submission of discovery disputes by telephone conference. If a discovery motion is filed, it may be acted upon before a response is filed either with or without a telephone conference.

3. Electronic Discovery. It is expected that the parties will reach an agreement on how to conduct electronic discovery. In the event the parties cannot reach such an agreement before the Rule 16 scheduling conference, the court will enter an order incorporating default standards. The default order can be viewed at www.paed.uscourts.gov.

The parties should discuss the parameters of their anticipated e-discovery at the Rule 26(f) conference and should be prepared to address e-discovery at the Rule 16 scheduling conference with the court.

Settlement and Mediation

1. Settlement Conferences. Counsel are required to schedule a settlement conference with Magistrate Judge M. Faith Angell as set forth in the scheduling order. Counsel must adhere to Magistrate Judge Angell's requirements regarding the conduct of the conference.

2. Mediation. In addressing settlement or early disposition of the case, counsel are reminded that participation in an early alternative dispute resolution effort is strongly encouraged. Counsel should be familiar with the court's mediation program and Local Rule 53.2. Counsel are required to explore the feasibility of ADR, including court-annexed mediation, not only between themselves, but with their clients as well. The specific reason for any decision not to participate in a form of early ADR should be delineated in the Rule 26(f) report.

Final Pretrial Conference

In the pretrial memoranda, counsel must detail the substance of the testimony of each witness. Identifying a witness as giving testimony on liability and/or damages is insufficient.

The parties must provide the court with one copy of each exhibit and two copies of a schedule of exhibits that briefly describes each exhibit. At trial, the parties must provide the court with an additional copy of each exhibit. Exhibits are to be arranged and tabbed in a three-ring binder.

Sidebar conferences and objections to evidence that should have been anticipated are discouraged and are to be avoided at trial. Consequently, one of the goals of the final pretrial conference, which counsel can expect to last two to four hours, is to resolve all evidentiary issues to avoid delay at trial and to provide counsel with advance notice of evidentiary requirements. Therefore, rulings on all outstanding motions and objections to witnesses and exhibits will be made at the final pretrial conference.

Counsel should be prepared to state their objections to witnesses and exhibits, and to respond to opposing counsel's objections. It is expected that counsel have discussed and have attempted to resolve all objections to exhibits and testimony prior to the final pretrial conference, leaving for the court only those objections the parties could not resolve.

Any party intending to use depositions, written or video, at trial must notify all other parties in the pretrial memorandum. Objections to deposition testimony must be made prior to the pretrial conference in writing, setting forth the page and line numbers of the challenged testimony and a clear statement for the basis of the objection. The objecting party must provide the court with a copy of the deposition transcript with the challenged testimony highlighted.

Trial Procedure

1. Scheduling of Cases. The scheduling order will set a date certain for trial or the date when the case will be placed in the trial pool. For cases in the trial pool, counsel must be prepared to commence trial upon 48 hours notice.

2. Voir Dire. Counsel must discuss voir dire questions and resolve any differences the day before jury selection. If they cannot agree, counsel must advise the deputy clerk that the judge must rule upon the disputed issues.

3. Trial Objections and Sidebars. Sidebar conferences are discouraged and are rarely permitted. Only unanticipated issues will necessitate a sidebar conference.

Speaking objections are not permitted. Objections should be made by reciting the appropriate rule number or a one-word basis.

4. Motions in Limine. Motions in limine must be filed by the deadline set in the scheduling order. Rulings upon such motions are usually made before or at the final pretrial conference.

5. Opening Statements and Summations. Time limits on opening statements and summations are generally not fixed. However, depending upon the issues in the case and the length of the trial, time limits may be imposed.

Rebuttal must not be a rehashing of closing argument.

6. Examination of Witnesses by More Than One Attorney. Only one attorney for a party may examine the same witness or argue the same legal point. More than one attorney for a party may examine different witnesses or argue different legal points.

7. Offers of Proof. Counsel must confer privately to resolve any unanticipated evidentiary issues that may arise during trial. Only if they are unable to reach agreement should counsel bring the matter to the deputy clerk's attention at the beginning of the day or during an appropriate break when the jury is not present.

8. Videotaped Testimony. Counsel must discuss in advance of the trial all objections to the presentation of videotaped testimony to resolve all conflicts. If counsel cannot resolve their disagreements, they should present any outstanding disagreements at least 10 days prior to the final pretrial conference by providing a transcript of the testimony with the challenged question and answer highlighted, and a list setting forth each objection by page and line numbers and the basis for the objection.

The videotape must be edited prior to trial to eliminate pauses and speed-ups so there are no interruptions. Counsel must arrange with the deputy clerk a date and time before the trial date to test and learn to operate the courtroom equipment.

9. Reading of Material Into the Record. There is no special practice or policy for reading stipulations, pleadings, or discovery material into the record. Reading of material into the record may be done in a manner agreed upon by Judge Savage and counsel.

10. Preparation of Exhibits. At the final pretrial conference, the parties must provide the court with one copy of each exhibit and two copies of a schedule of exhibits that briefly describes each exhibit. At the trial, the parties must provide the court with an additional copy of each exhibit. Exhibits should be arranged jointly and tabbed in a single three-ring binder containing all exhibits numbered consecutively.

11. Offering Exhibits Into Evidence. Exhibits are admitted into evidence at the close of each party's case-in-chief and not during testimony or after the exhibit is identified. Counsel should review the exhibits in advance so that agreed-upon exhibits can be admitted quickly and disputed exhibits ruled upon at the conclusion of the party's case.

Exhibits may be published to the jury at the end of the party's examination of the witness or prior to a break. If the exhibit is necessary to explain the testimony, Judge Savage may permit it to be published during the testimony. Permission must be sought prior to the witness taking the stand.

12. Proposed Jury Instructions and Verdict Forms. Counsel must meet and discuss proposed jury instructions for the purpose of submitting agreed-upon jury instructions and verdict forms. Proposed instructions should cover only the substantive issues regarding the elements of each cause of action and each defense. Basic instructions, such as the burden of proof, credibility, and procedure, should not be submitted. Counsel are expected to cooperate in the preparation of the joint proposed instructions. Failure to cooperate in the process will result in the imposition of sanctions.

Submitting a proposed point does *not* constitute a waiver of objection. Counsel are instructed to work on proposed instructions regardless of counsel's position with respect to a point's applicability. If the court sustains an objection to a particular joint instruction, it will not be submitted to the jury. Objections to jointly submitted points will be discussed and ruled upon at the charging conference.

If counsel cannot agree, proposed alternative instructions must be submitted with authority for each instruction. If a model jury instruction is used, the party submitting it must state whether the proposed instruction is unchanged or modified. If a party modifies a model instruction, additions should be underlined and deletions should be placed in brackets.

13. Proposed Findings of Fact and Conclusions of Law. In a nonjury trial, the parties must file a stipulation of uncontested facts. Each party must submit proposed findings of fact and conclusions of law.

Jury Deliberations

1. Exhibits in the Jury Room. After the jury has retired to deliberate, counsel must review the exhibits to determine which exhibits will go out with the jury. If counsel cannot agree, they should request a ruling immediately after the jury retires to the deliberations room.

2. Availability of Counsel During Jury Deliberations. Counsel must be available upon 15 minutes' notice during jury deliberations. As a practical matter, this means that counsel must stay in or near the courthouse.

3. Interviewing the Jury. After a verdict has been recorded and the jury has been discharged, counsel may request to interview jurors. The jurors are told that they are permitted to talk to counsel, if they desire, but they need not do so. Counsel must respect the jurors' desire not to speak to them.

CRIMINAL CASES

1. Oral Argument and Motions. Judge Savage will grant oral argument on motions if he believes it will assist him in deciding the motions. He usually considers and decides motions in limine prior to trial.

2. Pretrial Conferences. Pretrial conferences in criminal cases are held only in complex cases or those involving several attorneys.

3. Pretrial Hearings. Suppression, *Starks,* and *Daubert* hearings are typically held at least two weeks prior to trial. The government is required to file proposed findings of fact and conclusions of law prior to the commencement of the hearing. The parties may request leave to supplement proposed findings of fact after the hearing.

4. Voir Dire. Judge Savage conducts voir dire in criminal cases. Counsel may submit proposed voir dire questions.

5. Proposed Jury Instructions and Verdict Forms. Each party must submit to the court, and serve on opposing counsel, proposed points for charge and any proposed jury interrogatories no later than seven days prior to the trial date. Each point for charge and proposed jury interrogatory should be numbered and on a separate sheet of paper identifying the name of the requesting party. Each proposed instruction must be submitted with authority. If a model jury instruction is used, the party submitting it must state whether the proposed instruction is unchanged or modified. If a party modifies a model instruction, additions should be underlined and deletions should be placed in brackets.

6. Trial Memorandum. At least one week prior to the trial date, the government must file a trial memorandum setting forth the essential elements of the offenses, the facts that it intends to present, the identity of each witness it intends to call, a statement of the substance of each witness's testimony, and any legal issues. The defendant is not required to file a trial memorandum, but may do so.

7. **Guilty Plea Memorandum.** The government must submit a guilty plea memorandum at least two days prior to the change of plea hearing. The memorandum must include the elements of each offense to which the defendant is pleading guilty and legal citations for the elements, the maximum statutory penalties for each offense, the terms of any plea agreement, and the factual basis for the plea.

8. **Motions for Downward Departure.** A motion for downward departure, except a motion filed under section 5K1.1 of the United States Sentencing Guidelines, must be filed two weeks prior to the sentencing date. The motion should include legal and factual support for the proposed departure. A government motion pursuant to section 5K1.1 must be filed at least one week before sentencing.

9. **Sentencing Memoranda.** Judge Savage requires the submission of sentencing memoranda by both the government and the defendant no later than one week before sentencing. The memorandum must set forth any legal authority relied upon by the party. One copy of each sentencing memorandum, motion, and response must be served on the opposing party, the court (Chambers, Room 9614), and the United States Probation Office when the original is filed.

If a defendant is responsible for restitution, the government must submit sufficient information in its sentencing memorandum to enable the court to determine entitlement, the name and the address of each victim, the amount of loss for each victim, and documentary support for each amount. If liability for restitution is joint and several, the government must itemize the restitution amount for which each defendant is responsible.

IN THE UNITED STATES DISTRICT COURT
FOR THE EASTERN DISTRICT OF PENNSYLVANIA

PLAINTIFF	:	CIVIL ACTION
v.	:	NO.
DEFENDANT	:	

REPORT OF RULE 26(f) MEETING

In accordance with Federal Rule of Civil Procedure 26(f), counsel for the parties conferred on (date) and submit the following report of their meeting for the court's consideration:

1. **Discussion of Claims, Defenses and Relevant Issues**

   You should assume that the court has read the complaint and is familiar with the claims. However, the facts supporting those claims and defenses are unknown. Therefore, counsel shall set forth concisely the factual background that the parties contend support their claims and defenses.

   Summarize your discussion of primary issues, threshold issues and those issues on which the parties will need to conduct discovery. Identify what information each party needs in discovery as well as when and why. Also indicate likely motions and their timing.

2. **Informal Disclosures**

   State the parties' agreement on timing, form and scope of informal disclosures. Specifically identify not only the information listed in Rule 26(a)(1), but any additional information the parties agree to disclose informally.

   Keep in mind that self-executing discovery must not be delayed until the pretrial conference. If the parties have not made the Rule 26(a) initial disclosures within the time required by the Court's Order scheduling the pretrial conference, they should explain why not.

3. **Formal Discovery**

   Indicate nature, sequence and timing of formal discovery, as well as any need to conduct discovery in phases to prepare for the filing of motions or for settlement discussions. Specifically delineate what discovery will be conducted formally.

   The discovery deadline should normally be no more than 120–150 days from the date of the Rule 16 pretrial conference. If the parties believe there are compelling reasons for a longer period of discovery, state them.

   The parties are required to address procedures to preserve electronically stored information, to avoid inadvertent privilege waivers, and to determine the form in which electronic information will be produced. The cost of producing the information must be discussed.

4. **Electronic Discovery**

   It is expected that the parties will reach an agreement on how to conduct electronic discovery. In the event the parties cannot reach such an agreement before the Rule 16 scheduling conference, the court will enter an order incorporating default standards. The default order can be viewed at www.paed.uscourts.gov.

   The parties shall discuss the parameters of their anticipated e-discovery at the Rule 26(f) conference and shall be prepared to address e-discovery at the Rule 16 scheduling conference with the court.

Judge Timothy J. Savage

5. **Expert Witness Disclosures**

   Indicate agreement on timing and sequence of disclosure of the identity and anticipated testimony of expert witnesses, including whether depositions of experts will be needed.

   The parties should expect that the court requires expert reports to be exchanged simultaneously. If there are compelling reasons to stagger the production of expert reports, state them.

6. **Early Settlement or Resolution**

   The parties must familiarize themselves with Local Rule 53.3 before responding. Recite the parties' discussion about early resolution through ADR, motion or otherwise explain what steps were taken by counsel to advise the client of alternative dispute resolution options. Explain any decision not to seek early resolution and what mediation options the parties may consider and when mediation would be appropriate.

7. **Trial date**

   If a date certain is requested, state the reasons. Generally, if requested, a firm trial date will be scheduled.

8. **Other Matters**

   Indicate discussion and any agreement on matters not addressed above.

_____   _____
(Attorney Signature)   (Attorney Signature)

REV. 120711

IN THE UNITED STATES DISTRICT COURT
FOR THE EASTERN DISTRICT OF PENNSYLVANIA

PLAINTIFF	:	CIVIL ACTION
	:	
	:	
v.	:	NO.
	:	
DEFENDANT	:	

ORDER GOVERNING ELECTRONIC DISCOVERY

AND NOW, this _____ day of _____, 20____, in anticipation of the Rule 16 conference, it is **ORDERED** as follows:

1. Introduction. In the event the parties cannot reach an agreement on how to conduct electronic discovery ("e-discovery") before the Rule 16 scheduling conference, the following default standards shall apply until such time, if ever, the parties conduct e-discovery on a consensual basis.

2. Exchange of e-discovery materials. Prior to the Rule 26(f) conference, the parties shall exchange the following information:

   a. a list of the most likely custodians of relevant electronic materials, including a brief description of each person's title and responsibilities;

   b. a list of each relevant electronic system that has been in place at all relevant times and a general description of each system, including the nature, scope, character, organization, and formats employed in each system.

   c. the parties should also include other pertinent information about their electronic documents and whether those electronic documents are of limited accessibility, that is, those created or used by electronic media no longer in use, maintained in redundant electronic storage media, or for which retrieval involves substantial cost;

   d. the name of the individual responsible for the party's electronic document retention policies ("the retention coordinator");

   e. a general description of the party's electronic document retention policies.

   f. the name of the individual who shall serve as the party's "e-discovery liaison;"

   g. A description of any problems reasonably anticipated to arise in connection with e-discovery.

   To the extent that the state of the pleadings does not permit a meaningful discussion of the above issues by the time of the Rule 26(f) conference, the parties shall either agree on a date by which this information will be mutually exchanged or submit the issue for resolution by the court at the Rule 16 scheduling conference.

3. E-discovery conference. The parties shall discuss the parameters of their anticipated e-discovery at the Rule 26(f) conference and shall be prepared to address e-discovery at the Rule 16 scheduling conference with the court.

4. E-discovery liaison. To promote communication and cooperation between the parties, each party shall designate a single individual through whom all e-discovery requests and responses are made ("the e-discovery liaison"). Regardless of whether the e-discovery liaison is an attorney (in-house or outside counsel), a third party consultant, or an employee of the party, he or she must be:

   a. familiar with the party's electronic systems and capabilities in order to explain these systems and answer relevant questions;

   b. knowledgeable about the technical aspects of e-discovery, including electronic document storage, organization, and format issues;

   c. prepared to participate in e-discovery dispute resolutions; and,

   d. responsible for organizing the party's e-discovery efforts to insure consistency and thoroughness and, generally, to facilitate the e-discovery process.

5. Search methodology. If the parties intend to employ an electronic search to locate relevant electronic documents, the parties shall disclose any restrictions as to scope and method which might affect their ability to conduct a complete electronic search of the electronic documents. The parties shall reach agreement as to the method of searching, and the words, terms, and phrases to be searched with the

assistance of the respective e-discovery liaisons, who are charged with familiarity with the parties' respective systems. The parties also shall reach agreement as to the timing and conditions of any additional searches which may become necessary in the normal course of discovery. To minimize the expense, the parties may consider limiting the scope of the electronic search (e.g., time frames, fields, document types).

6. Timing of e-discovery. Discovery of electronic documents shall proceed in the following sequenced fashion:

    a.   after receiving requests for document production, the parties shall search their documents, other than those identified as limited accessibility electronic documents, and produce responsive electronic documents in accordance with Fed.R.Civ.P. 26(b)(2);

    b.   electronic searches of documents identified as of limited accessibility shall not be conducted until the initial electronic document search has been completed;

    c.   requests for information expected to be found in limited accessibility documents must be narrowly focused with a factual basis supporting the request; and,

    d.   on-site inspections of electronic media under Fed.R.Civ.P.34(b) shall not be permitted, absent exceptional circumstances where good cause and specific need have been demonstrated.

7. Format. If, during the course of the Rule 26(f) conference, the parties cannot agree to the format for document production, electronic documents shall be produced to the requesting party as image files (e.g., PDF or TIFF). When the image file is produced, the producing party must preserve the integrity of the electronic document's contents, i.e., the original formatting of the document, its metadata and, where applicable, its revision history. After initial production in image file format is complete, a party must demonstrate particularized need for production of electronic documents in their native format.

8. Retention. Within the first thirty (30) days of discovery, the parties shall negotiate an agreement that outlines the steps each party shall take to segregate and preserve the integrity of all relevant electronic documents. In order to avoid later accusations of spoliation, a Fed. R. Civ. P. 30(b)(6) deposition of each party's retention coordinator may be appropriate.

The retention coordinators shall:

    a.   take steps to ensure that e-mail of identified custodians shall not be permanently deleted in the ordinary course of business and that electronic documents maintained by the individual custodians shall not be altered;

    b.   provide notice as to the criteria used for spam and/or virus filtering of e-mails and attachments; documents filtered out by such systems shall be deemed nonresponsive so long as the criteria underlying the filtering are reasonable.

Within seven (7) days of identifying the relevant document custodians, the retention coordinators shall implement the above procedures and each party's counsel shall file a statement of compliance.

9. Privilege. Electronic documents that contain privileged information or attorney work product shall be immediately returned if the documents appear on their face to have been inadvertently produced or if there is notice of the inadvertent production. All copies shall be returned or destroyed by the receiving party.

10. Costs. Generally, the costs of discovery shall be borne by each party. However, the court will apportion the costs of electronic discovery upon a showing of good cause.

TIMOTHY J. SAVAGE, J.

Rev. 120711

Judge Berle M. Schiller

Judge Schiller was born in 1944 in Brooklyn, New York. He received a B.A. from Bowdoin College in 1965, and a J.D. from New York University School of Law in 1968. Judge Schiller was in private practice from 1968 to 1993. He served as chief counsel for the Federal Transit Administration from 1994 to 1996. He also served as an appellate judge for the Superior Court of Pennsylvania from 1996 to 2000. Judge Schiller was appointed to the United States District Court for the Eastern District of Pennsylvania on June 2, 2000. He assumed senior status on June 18, 2012.

PRELIMINARY GENERAL MATTERS

1.   Correspondence with the Court. Judge Schiller advises against correspondence with the court on scheduling matters. *Absent permission from the court, any faxes to chambers should not exceed 10 pages.* Additionally, communication with opposing counsel should be by the same means of communication with chambers. For example, if counsel faxes a letter to chambers, counsel must fax a copy of that letter to opposing counsel.

2.   Communications with Civil Deputy. Judge Schiller does permit counsel to communicate with his deputies on any matters that relate to their responsibilities. For matters regarding scheduling, case management, and general procedures in *civil* cases, counsel should contact Jean Pennie, Judge Schiller's civil deputy, at 267-299-7621.

3.   Magistrate Judge Assignment. Magistrate Judge Jacob P. Hart is assigned to Judge Schiller.

4.   Electronic Case Filing (ECF) Policy. Judge Schiller requires that all documents be filed electronically by the attorney through the Electronic Case Filing (ECF) system. ECF provides greater efficiency and timeliness in the filing of pleadings, automatic e-mail notice of case activity, and electronic storage of documents for remote access by the court, the bar, and the litigants. Attorneys appearing before Judge Schiller are *required* to register as Electronic Case Filing users at the Office of the Clerk of Court or at the court's website at www.paed.uscourts.gov.

5.   Potential Conflicts of Interest. Counsel is expected to inform the court of any change of ownership so that potential conflicts of interest can be avoided.

CIVIL CASES
Pretrial Procedure

1.   Pretrial Conferences. Judge Schiller orders Rule 16 scheduling conferences as soon as practicable after the defendant responds to the complaint. Counsel is expected to commence discovery immediately upon the joining of the case in order to have a substantial amount of discovery completed by the time they appear for the Rule 16 conference. Settlement invariably appears on the agenda of the Rule 16 conference. Counsel is directed to promptly *enter an appearance on the docket.* Unless counsel has entered his or her appearance on the docket, the court will not allow counsel to participate on behalf of any party or individual in any court proceeding or request. In addition, no later than five days prior to the conference, the parties are to submit to chambers their proposed discovery plan as required by Fed.R.Civ.P. 26(f).*

---

*   Judge Schiller requires counsel to submit proposed discovery plans pursuant to Fed.R.Civ.P. 26(f) in addition to the Rule 16 conference information report, a sample of which is shown on page 287 of this book.

Upon receiving a notice for Rule 16 conference, any counsel with prior commitment must notify the court within *three* days of such conflict. If such notice is not given to the court within three days, the conference will not be rescheduled and counsel will be expected to attend.

Absent compelling circumstances, counsel should file motions to dismiss, transfer, add parties, or seek other threshold action before the conference. Counsel should note the prospect of Rule 56 motions at the conference.

The conference usually takes 30 minutes. Absent extraordinary circumstances, the conference will not be held by telephone. Unless approval has been granted prior to the conference, trial counsel must attend.

2. *Discovery of Documents, Photographs, and Videographs in Digital Format.* The parties will meet and confer before the initial pretrial conference to be fully prepared to advise the court of the following matters:

    a. Whether, during discovery, the parties will exchange documents in digital format; whether there are any issues as to the format to be used; and whether there are any issues as to the alteration of documents that may routinely occur when paper documents are converted to digital format.

    b. Whether the parties contemplate the use of any photographs in digital format, and whether there are any issues as to how and when digital alteration of photos is to be disclosed.

    c. Whether the parties plan to create and exchange video in digital format; arrangements for the synchronization of audio and video for any videotaped depositions in digital format that may be shown at trial.

    d. Whether there are any issues as to the discovery of digital materials other than those identified in paragraphs (a) through (c) above (such as databases), and whether the parties have agreed on ground rules for the routine business practices that affect the retention of these digital materials.

Continuances and Extensions

Counsel should make requests for continuance by motion, with a concise explanatory memorandum appended. Judge Schiller will grant a continuance only for the most compelling reasons; in any event, Judge Schiller considers motions for continuances on their merits, whether opposed or unopposed. *If counsel for both parties consent to a continuance, they must submit a one-page stipulation signed by both parties with a signature line for the judge to sign and date, should Judge Schiller grant the continuance.*

General Motion Practice

1. *Chambers Copies of Motion Papers.* The parties must submit courtesy copies of any pleadings and/or motions listed in Fed.R.Civ.P. 7 unless the pleading or motion has been filed electronically. In the case of long documents or voluminous attachments filed electronically, a courtesy copy is appreciated. Legal memoranda should not exceed 25 pages unless specific permission has been granted by the court. Praecipe/motion to the court for permission is required before a party files a reply to a response to any motion.

Discovery Matters

1. *Length of Discovery Period and Extensions.* In an uncomplicated case, discovery should be completed within 90 to 120 days, with a trial listing shortly thereafter. In complex cases, longer periods of discovery may be permitted. The discovery deadline is in no sense a hypothetical date. Judge Schiller typically does not hold a further conference unless counsel requests one to discuss settlement or a special trial issue. It will only be changed for weighty cause shown.

Foreseeable discovery problems, including noncompliance or tardiness, will not constitute an acceptable ground for continuance of the trial. Counsel should act promptly to enforce the discovery schedule.

2.   Discovery Conferences and Dispute Resolution.   Judge Schiller *strongly disfavors* discovery motions. Counsel must make every effort to resolve discovery disputes on their own. If court intervention is required, prior to filing any motions, the parties should first contact Judge Schiller's civil deputy at 267-299-7621 to set up a telephone conference.

3.   Unexcused Violations of Scheduling Orders.   Unexcused violations of scheduling orders are subject to sanctions under Fed.R.Civ.P. 16(f), upon motion or the court's initiative. The court will normally sanction counsel's failure to appear at a Rule 16 pretrial conference by awarding costs to counsel who do appear.

Settlement

1.   General Approach to Settlement.   Judge Schiller always seeks to help the parties achieve the settlement of their disputes.

Proposed Final Pretrial Memoranda

A joint pretrial disclosure memorandum is required, signed by all counsel.[*] Although counsel should consult Local Rule 16.1(c) for guidance, they should tailor the memorandum to be commensurate with the needs of the case. The foregoing sentence is intended to encourage brevity and simplicity. The memorandum should be submitted at least 14 days before the trial date or as specified in the scheduling order. Absent cooperation, counsel may file a separate memorandum with the permission of the court. If the joint pretrial disclosure memorandum is not submitted on time or in proper form, the court may consider the imposition of sanctions in appropriate cases.

Trial Procedure

1.   Scheduling of Cases.   The trial listing will be for a *specific date* or as a *backup* to another trial as specified in the scheduling order. Trials typically begin on a Monday. These trial listings do not constitute a "pool." The case will be called for trial on the date assigned unless Speedy Trial Act constraints in a criminal case are preemptive. However, if a case is scheduled as a "backup," counsel should be prepared for trial in the event the specified case settles or is continued.

Counsel should direct all communications regarding the trial calendar to Judge Schiller's civil deputy clerk at 267-299-7621.

2.   Trial Depositions.   Trial depositions must be scheduled so as not to delay trial or disrupt trial preparation. They may not be taken later than 14 days before the trial date unless the parties agree or the court approves. Continuance applications because of refusal of an expert witness to appear for trial or to be available for trial deposition will not be granted if notice of the trial date was given to the witness at least 60 days in advance or at the earliest reasonable opportunity.

---

[*]   A joint pretrial disclosure memorandum is not required in arbitrations, but is required in arbitration appeals.

3. **Post-trial Motions.** Post-trial motions are to be governed by the Federal Rules of Civil Procedure generally and specifically by Judge Schiller's Guide for Post-trial Motions, which is available to counsel upon request by calling Judge Schiller's civil deputy clerk at 267-299-7621.

CRIMINAL CASES

1. **Communications with Criminal Deputy.** Judge Schiller does permit counsel to communicate with his deputies on any matters that relate to their responsibilities. For matters regarding scheduling, case management, and general procedures in criminal cases, counsel should contact Christopher Campoli at 267-299-7629.

2. **Motions to suppress.** Within 14 days prior to the commencement of trial, counsel should file any motions to suppress.

3. **Probation Report.** Judge Schiller does not permit the defendant or counsel to review the Probation Department's written recommendations as to sentence.

4. **Sentencing.** Within 48 hours prior to sentencing, counsel must file sentencing memoranda.

5. **Jury Instructions.** At least 14 days prior to the commencement of trial, counsel must file proposed jury instructions and proposed verdict sheets, with courtesy copies submitted to chambers in hard-copy form and on disk (in WordPerfect 10 format, if possible).

IN THE UNITED STATES DISTRICT COURT
FOR THE EASTERN DISTRICT OF PENNSYLVANIA

PARTY1,	:	CIVIL ACTION
Plaintiff,	:	
	:	
v.	:	
	:	
PARTY2,	:	No. [DOCKET NO.]
Defendant.	:	

SCHEDULING ORDER

AND NOW, this ____ day of MONTH, YEAR, following a Rule 16 conference on DATE with counsel for the parties, and pursuant to Federal Rule of Civil Procedure 16 and Local Rule of Civil Procedure 16.1(b), it is hereby ORDERED that:

1. Counsel for all parties are strongly encouraged to resolve discovery disputes by themselves. In the event a discovery dispute requires court intervention, the parties shall first seek a telephone conference with the Court before filing any motion.

2. Any motions for leave to amend the pleadings and any motions for leave to join other parties shall be filed by DATE.*

3. All fact discovery shall be completed by DATE.

4. Pursuant to Federal Rule of Civil Procedure 26(a)(2), plaintiff's experts' identities and their reports (including any curricula vitae) shall be disclosed by DATE; defendant's experts' identities and their reports (including any curricula vitae) shall be disclosed by DATE. In the event that a *Daubert* hearing results in the exclusion of an expert, an additional expert may not be substituted for the excluded expert unless good cause is shown.

5. Any motions for summary judgment shall be filed by DATE.† Responses to any motions for summary judgment shall be filed within the time permitted under Local Rule of Civil Procedure 7(c). Counsel are expected to communicate with each other and, if possible, to produce a joint appendix for submission to the court.

6. A Final Pretrial Conference will be held on DATE at TIME. Forty-eight hours prior to a pretrial conference, the parties may submit to chambers a list of issues, no longer than two pages, which they wish to discuss at the conference.

---

*   All requests for action by the Court shall be by motion, *see* Fed.R.Civ.P. 7(b), except for routine requests, which may be by letter to the Court with copies to all parties, indicating in such a letter whether the other parties consent to the request. The parties must submit courtesy copies of pleadings and/or motions. Responses to all motions are due no later than fourteen days from the date of filing, weekends included, court holidays excluded. Court permission, by motion, is required before a party files a reply to a response to any motion. Any reply brief is limited to the issues raised in the response, and may not raise theories or issues not discussed in the original motion.

†   Motions for summary judgment must provide specific citations to those portions of the record which show an absence of any genuine issue of material fact. Similarly, the papers opposing a motion for summary judgment should provide specific citations to those portions of the record which demonstrate the existence of a genuine issue of material fact. For claims arising under state law, counsel must brief the basis for choosing the applicable law, or submit a stipulation signed by all parties that the law of a particular state applies.

7. The parties will file a pretrial stipulation at least fourteen (14) days before the final pretrial conference that will advise the court fully with respect to the following:
   a. The equipment to be used by each party during trial, if any, including equipment already installed in the courtroom and equipment to be brought to the courtroom, and any arrangements for shared use of equipment.
   b. The presentation software to be used by each party during trial, if any, and whether each party is able to receive and use digital files of presentation materials prepared by the other.
   c. Any expected use of videoconferencing.
   d. The testing, inspection, compatibility, reliability, positioning, and backup for any equipment to be brought to the courtroom for trial. Each party will have adequate opportunity to inspect any equipment, except a computer containing privileged and work product materials, brought into the courtroom by the other party for use in making presentations during trial. Counsel will be expected to represent to the Court at the outset of trial that these matters have been dealt with satisfactorily. The Court expects no delays resulting from equipment failures that could have been anticipated.
8. In lieu of a Final Pretrial Order under Local Rules 16.1(d)(1) and (2), counsel shall submit a Joint Pretrial Disclosure Memorandum by the date of the final pretrial conference, containing:
   a. Agreed facts. Counsel should make a conscientious effort to narrow the areas of dispute;
   b. Each party's disputed facts;
   c. A list of each party's witnesses and exhibits, the subject matter of each witness's testimony, other disclosures required by Rule 26(a)(3), and a realistic, good faith estimate of the total time for trial. The parties should have pre-marked and exchanged all exhibits for trial. Any objections to the authenticity of evidence should be noted or will be considered waived. Objections pursuant to Rule 26(a)(3) are due seven days thereafter.
   d. Proposed voir dire questions (for jury trials only);
   e. A summary of the applicable law, including, in diversity cases, the basis for choosing the applicable law;
   f. An alert to the court of unusual legal issues which would serve as the basis for a motion for a judgment as a matter of law (Fed.R.Civ.Pro. 50) or other dispositive motion. The parties should state their contentions and the authority for those contentions;
   g. The signed approval of trial counsel for each party.
9. By DATE [generally, one week to two weeks before trial], counsel shall file the following, with courtesy copies submitted to chambers in hard copy form and on disk (in Word Perfect 8 format, if possible):
   a. For jury trials, proposed points for charge and verdict sheets OR, for nonjury trials, proposed findings of fact and conclusions of law. For all disputed legal issues, include citations to relevant authority or challenges on that point will be deemed waived;
   b. Proposed jury verdict sheets (for jury trials only).
10. Final pretrial motions are due DATE [generally, one week to two weeks before trial].*

---

* Such motions are not to exceed ten pages. Parties are encouraged to submit pretrial motions earlier, if possible.

11. [For trials with a date certain:] A [bench/jury] trial in the above captioned case is set for DATE in Courtroom 5C.

    [For backup trials:] A [bench/jury] trial in the above captioned case is set for DATE at TIME in Courtroom 5C to commence upon completion or other disposition of CASE NAME, E.D. Pa. docket no. ## ####.

12. At the outset of the first day of trial, all counsel must submit two sets of pre-marked and tabbed three ring binders containing all exhibits in the case. For physical ("real") evidence, simply insert a tabbed page listing an exhibit number and enclose a short description of the exhibit. If the documentation in the trial is so voluminous that the use of binders is impracticable, counsel should notify the court to make alternate arrangements. If any trial exhibits will be delivered to the courthouse by way of the courthouse loading dock, counsel shall provide Chambers with detailed information regarding the delivery, including the name of the trucking company delivering the exhibits, a description of the items to be delivered, the date the delivery will be made, and contact information for counsel responsible for the delivery. Such information must be provided to Chambers at least three business days prior to the commencement of the trial.

13. If agreeable to both parties, counsel for plaintiff shall telephone Chambers to schedule a settlement conference with a Magistrate Judge. Plaintiff's counsel shall promptly advise the court of settlement of the case.

Judge Berle M. Schiller

[*Counsel:* Please bring completed form to the conference. Do not mail.]

RULE 16 CONFERENCE INFORMATION REPORT

Caption: _____

Civil Action No._____ Jury trial _____ Bench trial _____ Arbitration_____

    Trial counsel _____

    Representing _____

    Law Firm _____

    Address _____

    Telephone _____ Fax _____

    Email _____

Are there threshold motions?_____
                                      (identify motion(s))

When will discovery be completed?_____
                                      (date)

Will motion for summary judgment be filed? _____
                                      (yes or no)

Ready for trial by? _____
                                      (date)

Has settlement been discussed?_____ If not, why not? _____
                              (yes or no)

Future settlement conference requested? _____
                                      (yes or no)

Novel issues or special problems? _____ Describe overleaf.
                              (yes or no)

Trial time estimates

    Time to present your case _____

    Time for entire trial _____

Date: _____

                                                      _____
                                                      Signature of counsel

                                                      _____
                                                      Typed or printed name

Judge Jeffrey L. Schmehl

Judge Schmehl was born in November 1955 in Reading, Pennsylvania. He received his B.A. from Dickinson College in 1977 and his J.D. from the University of Toledo College of Law in 1980. He served as an assistant public defender in Berks County, Pennsylvania, from 1980 to 1981. From 1981 to 1986, he served as an assistant district attorney in Berks County and also worked as a sole practitioner in Reading. Judge Schmehl joined the law firm of Rhoda, Stoudt & Bradley in 1986, becoming a partner in 1988 and serving with the firm until 1997. During much of that time, he also served as Berks County solicitor. He became a judge of the Berks County Court of Common Pleas in 1998 and served on the court until 2013. He served as president judge of the court from 2008 to 2013. Judge Schmehl became a judge of the United States District Court for the Eastern District of Pennsylvania on June 27, 2013.

PRELIMINARY GENERAL MATTERS

1. *Correspondence with the Court.* Law clerks have no authority to grant continuances or to give advice on substantive or procedural matters. Therefore, unless contacted by a law clerk, counsel should not communicate with the law clerk. Telephone inquiries regarding civil cases should be directed to Barbara A. Crossley, Judge Schmehl's civil deputy clerk, at 610-320-5099. Telephone inquiries regarding criminal cases should be directed to Teri Lefkowith, Judge Schmehl's criminal deputy clerk, at 610-320-5030.

2. *Telephone Conferences.* Judge Schmehl will hold telephone conferences to resolve scheduling matters, discovery disputes, and substantive motions. The court will also hold telephone conferences at any time to explore the possibility of settlements. The court will notify counsel of the date and time for the telephone conference. In a civil case, counsel for the moving party will be responsible for initiating the telephone conference and contacting Judge Schmehl through his secretary or civil deputy clerk after all parties are present on the call. In a criminal case, the United States Attorney's Office will be responsible for initiating the call and contacting Judge Schmehl through his criminal deputy clerk after all parties are present on the call.

3. *Oral Arguments and Evidentiary Hearings.* Judge Schmehl does not set aside certain days or times for oral argument, motions, or evidentiary hearings. Hearings and arguments are scheduled when warranted.

4. *Pro Hac Vice Admissions.* Counsel moving for the pro hac vice admission of an attorney must file a motion setting forth the attorney's admission, the reason why the party desires the attorney to participate, and why the attorney is especially qualified to do so. The form application provided by the clerk is inadequate. Moving counsel must also indicate that the filing fee has been paid.

5. *Faxes.* Unless specifically requested or explicitly permitted by the court, parties should not transmit pleadings, motions, or other filings by fax to chambers.

6. *Courtesy Copies.* Courtesy copies should not be provided to chambers unless the exhibits are voluminous or chambers requires them.

CIVIL CASES
Pretrial Procedure

1. *Rule 16 Conference.* The court will schedule a preliminary pretrial conference as described in Federal Rule of Civil Procedure 16(b) and (c) shortly after a defendant has filed an appearance or pleading. Counsel are expected to commence discovery immediately upon the joining of the case in order to have a substantive amount of discovery completed by the time they appear for the Rule 16 conference. At least three business days prior to the pretrial conference, *counsel must complete and submit to Judge Schmehl's Reading chambers by e-mail, fax, or hard copy the joint status report of the Rule 26(f) meeting.* A blank form for this report will be included with the Rule 16 conference notice. It will also be available on the court's website with Judge Schmehl's policies and procedures and is shown on page 295 of this book.

The court relies on counsel's good-faith compliance with Rule 26(f) *in all respects*. The Rule 26(f) meeting should take place as early in the case as possible, but no later than 21 days before the scheduled Rule 16 conference. Outstanding motions will *not* excuse the requirements of holding the meeting and submitting the plan. The meeting should be a meaningful and substantive discussion to formulate the proposed discovery plan required by the Rule. *Parties who do not comply will have no voice at the scheduling conference and may be subject to additional sanctions.* Initial disclosures pursuant to Rule 26(a) must be completed no later than seven days before the Rule 16 conference.

It is also expected that the parties will reach an agreement on how to conduct electronic discovery. The parties should discuss the parameters of their anticipated e-discovery at the Rule 26(f) conference and should be prepared to address e-discovery at the Rule 16 conference with the court. In the event the parties cannot reach such an agreement before the Rule 16 conference, the court will enter an order incorporating default standards.

At the initial pretrial conference, the parties should be prepared to address all topics listed in Local Rule of Civil Procedure 16.1(b) and Federal Rule of Civil Procedure 16(b) and (c), the progress of self-executing disclosure under Federal Rule of Civil Procedure 26(a), and any settlement or mediation proposals. The court will issue a Rule 16 scheduling order at the conclusion of the conference.

Lead trial counsel must attend the Rule 16 conference. Counsel taking part in any pretrial conference must be prepared to speak on every subject, including settlement, and have authority from their client to do so. Counsel must be prepared to discuss all claims and defenses in detail and should have a thorough comprehension of the facts.

2. **Final Pretrial Conference.** There will be a final pretrial conference within ten days of the trial date. Counsel must comply with Local Rule 16.1 regarding the submission of a pretrial memorandum. These memoranda must be filed no later than seven days prior to the pretrial conference.

During this conference, the court will address factual and legal issues, the admissibility of exhibits, scheduling issues, and settlement.

Continuances and Extensions

Unless there is good cause to justify a change, the parties are expected to adhere to the dates contained in the scheduling order. The court will grant a continuance or extension based on a stipulation of all parties if the continuance or extension does not affect the discovery cutoff or trial date. If a continuance or extension will affect the discovery cutoff or trial date, counsel should make a written request setting forth the basis for the continuance or extension and indicating whether the other party or parties agree to or oppose the request. A request for an extension or continuance of the trial date, discovery deadline, or the deadline for filing dispositive motions must be made sufficiently prior to the due date to allow time for the court to consider it. These requests should be made by motion, although an unopposed request may be made by letter to the court.

General Motion Practice

1.   Oral Argument on Motions.   If the judge believes oral argument will be helpful in deciding a matter, he will schedule it, particularly when it involves a dispositive motion. A party desiring oral argument should request it by letter or in the body of the motion or responsive pleading.

2.   Reply and Surreply Briefs.   Reply briefs, addressing only issues raised in the brief in opposition and not repeating arguments in the brief, may be filed within seven days of service of the opponent's brief in opposition and should be limited to 10 pages. No further briefs may be filed.

3.   Length and Content of Briefs or Legal Memoranda.   All grounds for relief should be set forth in a single, comprehensive motion. A motion to dismiss, for example, should not be divided into separate motions for each count, but rather should include all bases for relief. *Any brief or memorandum filed in support of the motion should be limited to 25 pages.* If a party requires more than 25 pages to explain its position to the court, a motion to exceed the page limit should be filed, setting forth good cause for granting an exception to this rule.

4.   Rule 56 Motions.   In most cases, Judge Schmehl will only entertain a motion for summary judgment pursuant to Rule 56 of the Federal Rules of Civil Procedure if the parties file a stipulation as to all the material facts that govern the resolution of the motion.

Discovery Matters

1.   Length of Discovery Period and Extensions.   In standard track cases, the court usually allows up to 90 days from the date of the Rule 16 conference to complete discovery. In special management cases, the court will permit additional time to conduct discovery if the parties identify a need to do so at the Rule 16 conference or any subsequent status conferences. A case will ordinarily be listed for trial 30 to 60 days after the completion of discovery.

2.   Discovery Conferences and Dispute Resolution.   Counsel for all parties are strongly encouraged to resolve discovery disputes by themselves. In the event that a discovery dispute requires court intervention, the party contemplating a motion should seek a telephone conference with the court before filing any motion. If the telephone conference fails to resolve the discovery dispute, the party seeking relief will be permitted to file an appropriate discovery motion. *The motion should not exceed five pages, should not contain exhibits, and should not include a brief or memorandum of law.*

The responding party may file a response within five days. This response should also be limited to five pages and should not include exhibits or a brief or memorandum of law. Judge Schmehl permits telephone conferences to resolve disputes during depositions in cases where the deposition would otherwise have to be adjourned.

3.   Confidentiality Agreements.   The court will only approve confidentiality or sealing orders for good cause shown.

Settlement

1.   General Approach to Settlement and Nonjury Cases.   Settlement will be discussed at the initial Rule 16 status conference and at any subsequent conference. The court will not participate in settlement negotiations in nonjury cases. A case may be referred to a magistrate judge for a settlement conference.

Arbitration

1. General Approach to Arbitration. Judge Schmehl will not hold a Rule 16 conference or issue a scheduling order in arbitration track cases unless there is a de novo appeal from an arbitration award. The parties are expected to complete all discovery prior to the date of the arbitration hearing.

2. Scheduling of Trial De Novo from Arbitration. Upon demand for trial de novo from an arbitration award, the court will issue a scheduling order setting the date for trial at the earliest date available to the court. Ordinarily, neither discovery nor dispositive motions will be allowed after the arbitration hearing is held.

Final Pretrial Memoranda

1. Required Form of Pretrial Memoranda. Unless otherwise ordered by the court, the pretrial memorandum should be prepared in accordance with the provisions of Local Rule of Civil Procedure 16.1(c), and should also include the following items:
   a. All stipulations of counsel.
   b. A statement of objection to (1) the admissibility of any exhibit based on authenticity, (2) the admissibility of any evidence expected to be offered for any reason (except relevancy), (3) the adequacy of the qualifications of an expert witness expected to testify, and (4) the admissibility of any opinion testimony from lay witnesses pursuant to Federal Rule of Evidence 701. Such objection should describe with particularity the ground and the authority for the objection.
   c. Deposition testimony (including videotaped deposition testimony) that the party intends to offer during its case-in-chief. The statement should include citations to the page and line number and the opposing party's counter-designations.

Injunctions

1. Scheduling and Expedited Discovery. Judge Schmehl will promptly list any request for a temporary restraining order (TRO) or a preliminary injunction assigned to him.

2. Pre-hearing Conference. Judge Schmehl will hold a pre-hearing telephone conference call to discuss discovery issues and possible resolution of the request for a TRO. Expedited discovery will be discussed and, when appropriate, ordered at the conclusion of the pre-hearing conference.

3. Proposed Findings of Fact and Conclusions of Law. Judge Schmehl requires submission of proposed findings of fact and conclusions of law for TRO and injunction hearings. The court will set the time for submission of these items at the pre-hearing conference.

Trial Procedure

1. Scheduling Cases. A date for trial will be determined at the initial Rule 16 conference. The trial listing will be for a date certain as specified in the scheduling order and not as part of a pool. Questions relating to scheduling matters should be directed to Judge Schmehl's civil deputy clerk.

2. Cases Involving Out-of-Town Parties or Witnesses. Judge Schmehl schedules the trial of cases involving out-of-town counsel, parties, or witnesses in the same manner as all other cases. Counsel are responsible for the scheduling of witnesses.

3. Conflicts of Counsel. Counsel should notify the court immediately upon hearing of any unavoidable and compelling professional or personal conflicts affecting the trial schedule.

4. **Note-taking by Jurors.** Note-taking by jurors may be permitted at the court's discretion.

5. **Voir Dire.** Judge Schmehl permits counsel to conduct all voir dire in civil cases. There is generally a limit of 30 minutes for each side for voir dire.

6. **Trial Briefs.** Parties should submit a trial brief only if a new or unique point of law is involved.

7. **Motions in Limine.** The time for filing motions in limine will be determined at the Rule 16 conference and will be confirmed in the scheduling order.

8. **Examination of Witnesses Out of Sequence.** The court will permit counsel to examine his or her own witnesses out of turn for the convenience of a witness.

9. **Opening Statements and Summations.** In most cases, the court permits up to 30 minutes for an opening statement and up to 45 minutes for a summation or closing argument.

10. **Examination of Witnesses or Argument by More Than One Attorney.** More than one attorney for a party may examine different witnesses or argue different points of law before the court. Only one attorney for each side may examine the same witness or address the jury during the opening statement or summation.

11. **Redirect and Recross-examination of Witnesses.** The court will permit limited redirect and recross-examination on matters not previously covered by cross-examination or in special circumstances.

12. **Videotaped Testimony.** Videotaped testimony should begin with the witness being sworn. Counsel should bring objections to the court's attention at the time of the final pretrial conference. After the court rules on any objections, counsel should edit the tapes before offering the videotaped testimony at trial.

13. **Reading of Material into the Record.** Judge Schmehl has no special practice or policy regarding reading stipulations, pleadings, or discovery material into the record at trial.

14. **Preparation of Exhibits.** Exhibits should be pre-marked and exchanged in accordance with the final pretrial order. On the day trial is scheduled to commence, counsel should provide one copy of each exhibit and a copy of a schedule of exhibits to the court.

15. **Offering Exhibits into Evidence.** Unless the parties have an agreement as to the admissibility of a proposed exhibit, a witness may not testify as to its content until it has been admitted into evidence.

16. **Directed Verdict Motions.** Motions for judgment as a matter of law in jury trials and motions for an involuntary dismissal in nonjury trials must be in writing. Oral argument on the motions is ordinarily permitted.

17. **Proposed Jury Instructions and Verdict Forms.** In his scheduling order, Judge Schmehl typically requires that the parties submit proposed jury instructions on substantive issues and proposed verdict forms or special interrogatories for the jury no later than 10 days before the trial. Counsel should submit a copy of the proposed jury instructions to chambers via electronic mail at Chambers_of_Judge_Jeffrey_L_Schmehl@paed.uscourts.gov. Jury instructions need only be submitted with respect to substantive issues in the case. Proposed instructions on procedural matters such as the burden of proof, unanimity, and credibility are not necessary.

Each proposed instruction should be on a separate sheet of paper, double-spaced, and should *include citation to specific authority*. The court will not consider proposed instructions without citation to specific legal authority. Cases and model jury instructions that are cited should be accurately quoted and a page reference should be provided.

Counsel will have the opportunity to file supplemental points or proposed findings of fact and conclusions of law during trial as necessary. If a model jury instruction is submitted, for instance, from Devitt and Blackmar's *Federal Jury Practice and Instructions*, the submitting party must state whether the proposed jury instruction is unchanged or modified. If a party modifies a model jury instruction, the additions should be underlined and deletions should be placed in brackets.

18. Proposed Findings of Fact and Conclusions of Law. Proposed findings of fact and conclusions of law in nonjury cases should be submitted at least seven days *before* the trial date. They should be submitted to chambers in hard copy and via electronic mail at Chambers_of_Judge_Jeffrey_L_Schmehl@paed.uscourts.gov. The parties may submit revised or supplemental findings of fact and conclusions of law with specific reference to trial evidence at the conclusion of the case. A schedule for the submission of revised findings and conclusions will be discussed at the conclusion of trial.

19. Unavailability of Witnesses. If a witness is unavailable at the time of trial, as defined in Federal Rule of Civil Procedure 32(a)(4), the court expects an oral or videotaped deposition to be used at trial for that witness, whether the witness is a party, a non-party, or an expert. The unavailability of a witness *will not be a ground to delay* the commencement or progress of trial.

20. Lay Witness Opinion. Any party expecting to offer lay opinion testimony pursuant to Federal Rule of Evidence 701 regarding issues of liability or damages must provide the opposing parties with information or documents supporting the testimony at the time required for submission of expert reports.

21. Bifurcation. In cases where the number of witnesses for damages greatly exceeds the number of witnesses for liability, Judge Schmehl may bifurcate the trial of the case.

22. Stipulations. Judge Schmehl strongly encourages counsel to stipulate to as many matters as possible before trial, including undisputed facts, exhibits, jury instructions, and special interrogatories.

Jury Deliberations

1. Exhibits in the Jury Room. After the jury has been instructed and taken to the jury room to begin deliberations, the court and counsel will discuss which exhibits should go out with the jury for their consideration during deliberations.

2. Handling of Jury Requests to Read Back Testimony or Replay Tapes. At the jury's request, the court may permit the deputy clerk to read portions of testimony back to the jury or to replay the audiotaped or videotaped testimony.

3. Availability of Counsel During Jury Deliberations. During jury deliberations, counsel may leave the courthouse, but they must leave cell phone numbers with the civil or criminal deputy clerk and be able to return to the courthouse within 10 to 15 minutes.

4. Taking the Verdict and Special Verdicts. Ordinarily, the court will submit interrogatories to the jury. The courtroom deputy will take the verdict in the presence of the court, counsel, and the parties.

5. Polling the Jury. If requested by counsel, the court will poll the jury.

6. Interviewing the Jury. Judge Schmehl will allow counsel to interview the jurors but will instruct the jury that they are not required to talk to the attorneys.

CRIMINAL CASES

1. Approach to Oral Argument and Motions. The court will generally permit oral argument on a substantive motion in a criminal case upon request.

2. Pretrial Conferences. Judge Schmehl does not generally hold a telephone scheduling conference with counsel in criminal cases unless counsel specifically request one. All scheduling of criminal matters is handled by the judge's criminal deputy clerk.

3. Voir Dire. In criminal cases, Judge Schmehl will conduct the initial voir dire regarding hardships, the general suitability of the jurors, etc. Counsel may then ask additional, preapproved questions. Counsel should submit proposed voir dire questions in writing seven days before the trial date.

4. Sentencing Memoranda. Judge Schmehl requires the parties to submit objections to the presentence-investigation report and sentencing memoranda in accordance with the notice of sentencing, which will be issued shortly after the entry of a guilty plea or conviction.

Other Matters

1. Briefs of Cases on Appeal. Judge Schmehl welcomes copies of appellate briefs when a decision he has made is appealed.

2. Consultation with Opposing Counsel. In general, Judge Schmehl expects counsel to bring matters to his attention only after they have been discussed with opposing counsel.

3. Professionalism. Judge Schmehl will insist on punctuality and courtesy from counsel to the court and to each other, both in the presence of the court and otherwise. The examination of witnesses should be conducted from the lectern or from counsel table. Counsel should rise to address the court and should seek permission of the court before approaching witnesses or the bench. In addition, counsel will direct all comments to the court or to the witness under examination and not to other counsel or to the jury. To the extent possible, the parties should notify the court of any issues that will need to be ruled upon at the start of the day's proceedings, or during a recess out of the jury's presence. Sidebar conferences are permitted when necessary.

Judge Jeffrey L. Schmehl

Joint Status Report Pursuant to Rule 26(f)

Caption: _____   Civil Action No: _____

Basis of Jurisdiction: _____

Jury Trial: _____   Non-Jury Trial: _____   Arbitration: _____

Plaintiff's counsel participating in the Rule 16 Conference: _____
Defendant's counsel participating in the Rule 16 Conference: _____
Do counsel have full authority to settle at Rule 16 Conference? _____
    If not, client with such authority who will attend conference: _____

When did the parties hold the Rule 26 Conference? _____
When did the parties comply with Rule 26(a)'s duty of self-executing disclosure? _____

Does either side expect to file a case-dispositive motion? _____ (yes/no)
    If yes, under what Rule? _____
    If yes, specify the issue: _____
    Proposed deadline for filing dispositive motions: _____

Does either side anticipate the use of experts? _____
    If yes, what is the proposed deadline for expert discovery? _____

Approximate date case should be trial-ready: _____
    Time for Plaintiff's case: _____   Time for Defendant's case: _____

Is a settlement conference likely to be helpful? _____   If so, when:
    Early _____ (yes/no)   After Discovery _____ (yes/no)

What is the outcome of your discussions with your clients about proceeding before a Magistrate Judge for final disposition? _____

Plan for Discovery:

1. The parties anticipate that discovery should be completed within _____ days.
2. What is the minimum amount of time necessary to complete discovery prior to an ADR session, should one be ordered or agreed to? _____
3. Have the parties discussed issues relating to claims of privilege or of protection as trial-preparation material, as required by Rule 26(f)(3)(D)? _____
4. Identify any other discovery issues which should be addressed at the Rule 16 Conference, including limitations on discovery, protective Orders needed, or other elements which should be included in a particularized discovery plan: _____
5. If you contend the discovery period should exceed 90 days, please state reason: _____

This form should be submitted to Chambers by email, fax, or hard copy.
Chambers_of_Judge_Jeffrey_L_Schmehl@paed.uscourts.gov
Fax: 610-320-5002
The Madison Building, Room 401, 400 Washington St., Reading, PA 19601

Judge Norma L. Shapiro

Judge Shapiro was born on July 27, 1928, in Philadelphia, Pennsylvania. She received a B.A. from the University of Michigan in 1948, and a J.D. from the University of Pennsylvania in 1951. Prior to her appointment to the bench, Judge Shapiro was in private practice in Philadelphia. Judge Shapiro was appointed to the United States District Court for the Eastern District of Pennsylvania in 1978. She assumed senior status on February 1, 2011.

PRELIMINARY GENERAL MATTERS

1. *Electronic Filing.* Judge Shapiro fully supports and encourages the use of the Electronic Case Filing (ECF) system for the submission of civil documents. The ECF system provides greater efficiency and timeliness in the filing of pleadings, and electronic storage of documents for remote access by the court, the bar, and the litigants. Applications are available from the Office of the Clerk of Court, 601 Market Street, Room 2609, Philadelphia, Pennsylvania 19106-1797 or 215-597-7704.

Counsel are advised that current telephone and fax number(s) and any changes thereto are to be submitted in writing to the clerk of court with a copy to the courtroom deputy clerk.

2. *Correspondence with the Court.* Counsel may write to Judge Shapiro (with copies to all other counsel) to request an extension of time or for other matters pertaining to scheduling; counsel should state whether the request is opposed. Counsel opposing such request should notify the court promptly in writing. Judge Shapiro does not permit correspondence in lieu of formal discovery, contested motions, or substantive matters that should be made of record; as to such matters, opposing counsel will be expected to respond within the time required by the Federal Rules of Civil Procedure unless otherwise notified by the court for compelling reasons.

3. *Communication with Law Clerks.* Contact with the deputy clerk is generally preferable, particularly to obtain copies of orders or discuss scheduling conflicts. However, Judge Shapiro permits communication with her law clerks regarding *administrative* matters such as scheduling, extensions of time, notice of settlement, etc., *if the deputy clerk is unavailable.* Joint calls by counsel for all parties are preferred. If counsel for all parties are not present on the phone call, the caller must state whether opposing counsel has been contacted regarding the subject of the call.

4. *Telephone Conferences.* Telephone conferences for preliminary pretrial conferences, scheduling changes, extensions of time, and similar matters are acceptable to Judge Shapiro by arrangement with the deputy clerk. *Telephone availability for final pretrial conferences is not acceptable unless leave of court has been granted. Leave is granted **only** when attendance would be unduly expensive or burdensome. Parties must remain on telephone availability until released by the court.* If more than five parties are involved in a telephone conference call, counsel or a conference call operator must place the call.

5. *Oral Arguments and Evidentiary Hearings.* Judge Shapiro generally sets aside *10:00 a.m.* as a preferred time for holding preliminary Rule 16 scheduling conferences, oral arguments on dispositive motions other than summary judgment, and sentencing hearings, and *4:00 p.m.* for arguments on motions for summary judgment and final pretrial or settlement conferences. Judge Shapiro is willing to vary such scheduling at the request of counsel, especially if persons from out of town must participate.

Judge Norma L. Shapiro

6. Civility Among Attorneys. Judge Shapiro expects counsel to abide by the Code of Civility adopted by the Pennsylvania Supreme Court on December 6, 2000, and the Working Rules of Professionalism adopted by the Philadelphia Bar Association on June 28, 1990, copies of which are shown starting at page 317 of this book.

Pretrial Procedure

1. Pretrial Conferences. Fed.R.Civ.P. 16 conferences will be scheduled within 60 days after a responsive pleading has been filed. Counsel will be expected to have complied with the requirements of Fed.R.Civ.P. 26 and Form 35, as amended December 1, 2006, as applicable, prior to this conference.

Judge Shapiro conducts status conferences on order or request, settlement conferences (except in nonjury cases), and pretrial conferences. A final pretrial conference normally will be held as close to the time of trial as reasonable in the circumstances, and, unless specially listed, the case will be deemed ready for trial at any time thereafter. *Trial counsel are required to be present at the final pretrial conference.* Copies of the pretrial conference order and order pursuant to Fed.R.Civ.P. 16 normally issued by Judge Shapiro in connection with the Rule 16 pretrial conferences, are shown on pages 303 and 307 of this book.* As explained in the pretrial conference order, counsel are required to complete and return a pretrial scheduling/status conference report to Judge Shapiro one week prior to a Rule 16 conference. The agenda normally used at Rule 16 conferences, as well as requirements pertaining to final pretrial conferences and information regarding possible sanctions for failure to comply with scheduling or pretrial orders, are set forth in the order pursuant to Fed.R.Civ.P. 16 and Local Rules 16.1 and 16.2, shown on page 307. Also shown are Judge Shapiro's standing pretrial order number 1 in special track cases (see page 312) and a case statement required if a claim is asserted under RICO (see page 315).

Continuances and Extensions

1. General Policy. Judge Shapiro will normally consult counsel concerning a briefing schedule, oral argument, evidentiary hearing, discovery deadline, final pretrial conference, or trial date and then grant one *reasonable* continuance only for good cause; minor changes to accommodate counsel will be granted when possible. However, continuances in arbitration cases are granted only in accord with Local Rule of Civil Procedure 53.2.

2. Requests for Extensions and Continuances. Requests for extensions or continuances should be submitted *before* the time previously ordered or imposed by rule has expired and well before, when possible. Judge Shapiro prefers that continuances or extensions be requested by submitting a stipulation or motion with a proposed order.

General Motion Practice

1. Oral Argument on Motions. Oral argument on motions to dismiss will be heard at the Fed.R.Civ.P. 16 conference; oral argument on motions for summary judgment will be heard at the final pretrial conference. Oral argument otherwise will not be held routinely but will be considered on request; oral argument will more likely be granted on dispositive motions.

2. Reply and Surreply Briefs. Reply and surreply briefs are not encouraged; where necessary, they may be allowed by the court's scheduling order or by leave of court on request, particularly on dispositive motions. If oral argument is granted, leave to reply will usually be denied.

---

* All forms referred to herein are available from the court's website: www.paed.uscourts.gov.

3.   Chambers Copies of Motion Papers. Judge Shapiro appreciates receiving a courtesy copy of all motion papers.

Discovery Matters

1.   Length of Discovery Period and Extensions. Judge Shapiro normally permits from 60 to 90 days for the completion of discovery; more time is allowed in complex cases or on a specific showing of need at the Rule 16 conference. Extensions of time are granted for a time certain on a specific showing of a need for that time for a specific purpose.

2.   Discovery Conferences and Dispute Resolution. After the Rule 16 conference, Judge Shapiro holds discovery conferences only if requested by counsel or required by the conduct of counsel. Judge Shapiro does not encourage telephone conferences to resolve discovery disputes arising during depositions, but permits them when necessary.

3.   Confidentiality Agreements. If it is necessary and appropriate that a confidentiality agreement be filed with the court, Judge Shapiro prefers that it be submitted for consideration by stipulation; if agreement cannot be reached, a party seeking such an order may move for a proposed form of order prior to the preliminary pretrial conference. Judge Shapiro will sign a confidentiality order, even if agreed to by the parties, only if it is not impermissibly restrictive or difficult to enforce and there is an adequate showing of good cause. Furthermore, no confidentiality agreement will be approved unless it is limited to pretrial discovery between and among counsel, does not restrict the dissemination of information obtained legally from sources other than the opposing party, does not contemplate return or destruction of documents filed with the court, and is subject to modification or dissolution by the court upon notice to all counsel.

4.   Witnesses. Counsel are expected to comply with Fed.R.Civ.P. 26(a)(2), as amended December 1, 2006. Counsel are also expected to offer only expert testimony complying with Federal Rule of Evidence 702, as amended December 1, 2000. Treating physicians offering opinions are considered expert witnesses.

Settlement

1.   General Approach to Settlement and Nonjury Cases. Judge Shapiro encourages settlement discussions and inquiries as to the status of such settlement discussions at each pretrial conference. Judge Shapiro becomes involved in the discussions only with the consent of all parties. She will refer settlement negotiations to a magistrate judge if the parties express such a preference or it is in the interest of the administration of justice. As a general rule, she does not participate in settlement discussions in nonjury cases, but she may suggest that the parties explore settlement possibilities. She may refer a case to a magistrate judge, propose a mediator, or suggest some form of alternative dispute resolution such as arbitration or a summary jury trial.

2.   Referral of Settlement Negotiations to Another District Court Judge. Judge Shapiro sometimes refers a matter for settlement to another district court judge if requested by the parties or if Judge Shapiro believes there is a potential that it may be productive, but only if, for some special reason, such a referral is preferable to referral to a magistrate judge.

Arbitration

1.   General Approach to Arbitration Cases. Judge Shapiro has no special practice or procedure for arbitration cases, except that pretrial memoranda are not required nor are pretrial conferences routinely held. Motions filed less than 30 days prior to the scheduled arbitration date will not be considered. Continuance of an arbitration date beyond the 30 days permitted by Local Rule 53.2(5)(A) is rarely granted; there must be a motion and showing of good cause other than a need for extended discovery.

2. **Scheduling of Trial De Novo from Arbitration.** Judge Shapiro schedules a final pretrial conference promptly after a demand for a trial de novo, and places the case in the trial pool as soon as possible.

Proposed Final Pretrial Memoranda

1. **Required Form of Final Pretrial Memoranda.** The order following the preliminary pretrial conference will specify whether the form provided in Local Rule 16.1(c) or 16.1(d) should be followed. In addition, Judge Shapiro requires counsel to have provided to opposing counsel all exhibits listed in proposed final pretrial memoranda, if not received from opposing counsel in discovery. Exhibits should be numbered for use at trial. It is helpful to list any stipulated facts to avoid the necessity of proof at trial. Admissibility of exhibits will be considered at the final pretrial conference. Therefore, strict compliance with Fed.R.Civ.P. 26, as amended December 1, 2006, is required.

Counsel are required to identify witnesses and documents, as required by Fed.R.Civ.P. 26(a)(2) and (3) in their final pretrial memoranda to aid in the conduct of the final pretrial conference. Testimony and exhibits will be limited at trial to the information timely disclosed in accordance with Fed.R.Civ.P. 26(a)(2) and (3).

2. **Common Deficiencies in Pretrial Memoranda.** Counsel frequently do not comply with Fed.R.Civ.P. 26 and the pretrial orders of the court. A party may not reserve the general right to offer witnesses or exhibits listed by its opponent, but must list the witnesses and exhibits it may present at trial in its case-in-chief; witnesses on rebuttal or exhibits to be used solely for impeachment purposes need not be listed. The lists of witnesses, documents, and exhibits in the final pretrial memorandum may be supplemented only for good cause as determined by Judge Shapiro. A lengthy statement of contested facts in the final pretrial memorandum is not necessary.

Injunctions

1. **Scheduling and Expedited Discovery.** Applications for temporary restraining orders will be heard ex parte only when required by the nature of the action. Preliminary injunction hearings are promptly scheduled upon request; permanent injunction hearings, as other final dispositive proceedings, are held when scheduled by the court after consultation with counsel.

2. **Proposed Findings of Fact and Conclusions of Law.** Judge Shapiro does not ordinarily require proposed findings of fact and conclusions of law for preliminary injunction hearings; if submitted, they should be submitted as promptly as possible.

Trial Procedure

1. **Scheduling of Cases.** In scheduling cases for trial, Judge Shapiro assigns a date certain to the extent possible, but she also places cases in the trial pool. In an unusual situation, there will be a special listing after consultation with counsel; a special listing is a firm date for trial.

2. **Conflicts of Counsel.** Judge Shapiro prefers that counsel notify her of professional or personal conflicts affecting her trial schedule by letter to her deputy clerk.

3. Cases Involving Out-of-Town Parties or Witnesses. Judge Shapiro makes an effort to assign a date certain for trial of cases involving numerous parties, out-of-town parties, or witnesses; otherwise, there will ordinarily be at least one week's notice of the trial date.

4. Note-taking by Jurors. Judge Shapiro permits note-taking by jurors.

5. Trial Briefs. Judge Shapiro encourages submission of trial briefs when necessary or likely to be helpful to the court, but she does not expect them to be filed in all cases.

6. Voir Dire. It is Judge Shapiro's usual practice to conduct the general voir dire herself. She permits counsel to submit proposed voir dire questions for the entire panel and to conduct supplemental individual voir dire following her questions of the panel as a group. Where a special voir dire panel is used, a written questionnaire may be used in consultation with counsel.

7. Sidebar Conferences. Judge Shapiro holds sidebar conferences when necessary to prevent improper argument before the jury; sidebar conferences are on the record.

8. In Limine Motions. Except in complex cases, few motions in limine are appropriate. Judge Shapiro will hear such motions at the final pretrial conference or immediately prior to trial unless an earlier ruling will assist settlement discussions.

9. Examination of Witnesses Out of Sequence. Judge Shapiro is willing to take witnesses out of turn for their convenience, particularly where there is no objection by opposing counsel.

10. Opening Statements and Summations. Judge Shapiro prefers that opening statements be limited to 30 minutes, but she will allow more time if really necessary. She strongly discourages the use of opening statements to provide an advance summary of all the evidence to be presented or to make closing argument from anticipated evidence. No exhibits or demonstrative evidence may be used in opening unless there has been an approved stipulation of admissibility on the record.

Judge Shapiro does not have an established time limit for summations, but expects counsel to respect the natural limits of jurors' ability to give undivided attention to argument. Only one attorney for each party may open, and only one attorney for each party may close.

11. Examination of Witnesses or Argument by More Than One Attorney. Judge Shapiro will permit more than one attorney for a party to examine different witnesses or to argue different points, but two attorneys may not examine the same witness. See Local Rule of Civil Procedure 43.1.

12. Examination of Witnesses Beyond Redirect and Recross. Judge Shapiro does not have a policy regarding examination of witnesses after redirect and recross have been completed; a policy is unnecessary because a request for such further examination is so rare.

13. Videotaped Testimony. Judge Shapiro requires that objections to videotaped testimony be ruled on in advance of trial.

14. Reading Material Into the Record. When reading stipulations, pleadings, or discovery materials into the record, counsel must follow the Federal Rules of Civil Procedure. If depositions are read into the record at trial, Judge Shapiro requires that the pertinent deposition testimony be offered as an exhibit to avoid transcription in the trial record.

15. Preparation of Exhibits. Exhibits must be pre-marked and pre-exchanged; counsel should provide Judge Shapiro with a copy of trial exhibits.

16. Offering Exhibits Into Evidence. Judge Shapiro has no preference regarding whether exhibits are offered into evidence when identified, at the close of testimony by the witness identifying the exhibit, at the close of the day, or at the close of each party's case-in-chief. She will not admit exhibits used in cross-examination if offered by the cross-examiner during an opponent's case.

17. Directed Verdict Motions. Judge Shapiro has no preference as to whether motions for judgment as a matter of law (or motions for judgment on partial findings in nonjury trials) are submitted in writing or orally. She does not regularly hear argument on such motions; she may occasionally hear argument on such motions in nonjury trials.

18. Proposed Jury Instructions and Interrogatories to the Jury. Judge Shapiro requires proposed jury instructions to be submitted in all cases prior to the start of trial. She holds a charging conference to discuss proposed jury instructions. She permits submission of supplemental proposed jury instructions prior to the charging conference.

If the case is to be submitted on special interrogatories, a proposed verdict form may be submitted. The final verdict form will be provided to counsel prior to closing argument. See number 5 under Jury Deliberations, below.

19. Proposed Findings of Fact and Conclusions of Law. Judge Shapiro requires submission of proposed findings of fact and conclusions of law in nonjury cases prior to the start of trial.

Jury Deliberations

1. Written Jury Instructions. Judge Shapiro will consider submitting written instructions to the jury.

2. Exhibits in the Jury Room. Judge Shapiro does not generally permit all trial exhibits to go to the jury room, but determines which exhibits go to the jury room after consultation with counsel for all parties.

3. Handling of Jury Requests to Read Back Testimony or Replay Tapes. Judge Shapiro will consult with counsel before allowing portions of testimony to be reheard by the jury.

4. Availability of Counsel During Jury Deliberations. Judge Shapiro does not require counsel to remain in the courthouse during deliberations; they must keep the deputy clerk advised of their whereabouts and remain reasonably available on telephone notice.

5. Taking the Verdict and Special Interrogatories. In a civil case, Judge Shapiro usually submits special interrogatories to the jury. Counsel may submit proposed special interrogatories in their final pretrial memoranda. Proposed special interrogatories are always submitted to counsel prior to closing arguments. See number 18 under Trial Procedure, above.

6. Polling the Jury. Judge Shapiro's general practice is to poll the jury, without request from counsel.

7. Interviewing the Jury. Judge Shapiro does not ordinarily permit counsel to initiate juror interviews after the verdict has been recorded and the jury has been discharged, except upon motion and good cause shown. See Local Rule of Criminal Procedure 24.1(c).

CRIMINAL CASES

1. Approach to Oral Argument and Motions. Judge Shapiro has no general preference regarding oral arguments on motions in criminal cases.

2. Pretrial Conferences. Judge Shapiro does not usually hold pretrial conferences except in multi-defendant criminal cases, or cases with potential speedy trial issues, but she will consider a request by counsel to do so.

3. Voir Dire. Judge Shapiro conducts the entire general voir dire in criminal cases, but she permits submission of proposed voir dire questions. Judge Shapiro generally questions the panel as a whole and then permits individual questioning by the attorneys; procedures may differ in a high-profile case. Juror questionnaires are favorably considered in complex criminal cases.

4. Sentencing Memoranda. Judge Shapiro permits submission of sentencing memoranda by both the government and defendants.

OTHER GENERAL MATTERS

Judge Shapiro appreciates receiving copies of appellate briefs if a decision she renders is appealed.

Judge Shapiro expects that all papers will be filed prior to the day they are to be considered by the court.

Judge Norma L. Shapiro

IN THE UNITED STATES DISTRICT COURT
FOR THE EASTERN DISTRICT OF PENNSYLVANIA

	:	CIVIL ACTION
	:	
v.	:	
	:	
	:	

PRETRIAL CONFERENCE ORDER

BEFORE THE HONORABLE NORMA L. SHAPIRO

    AND NOW, this _____ day of _____, 20___, it is **ORDERED** that a Fed.R.Civ.P. 16 pretrial conference in the above case will be held on _____, **20___**, at **9:30 A.M.,** in Chambers, Room 10614, United States Courthouse, 601 Market Street, Philadelphia, PA. **This conference may be held by telephone upon request of the parties to Madeline F. Ward, Deputy Clerk (267-299-7549).** If the conference is held by phone, the Court will initiate the call and <u>**counsel shall remain available for said telephone conference unless and until excused by the court**</u>.

    The attached form is to be completed and returned to Chambers **one week** prior to the conference; counsel for all parties are expected to discuss together the matters covered by this report form and be prepared to participate in accordance with the court's Order under Fed.R.Civ.P. 16, Local Rules 16.1 and 16.2. **Counsel are expected to comply with Fed.R.Civ.P. 16 and 26, the Code of Civility adopted by the Pennsylvania Supreme Court, as amended on April 21, 2005, and the Working Rules of Professionalism, adopted by the Philadelphia Bar Association on June 28, 1990.**

                                                                   _____
                                                                   Madeline F. Ward, Deputy Clerk to
                                                                   The Honorable Norma L. Shapiro

PRETRIAL SCHEDULING/STATUS CONFERENCE REPORT

DATE:_____

CIVIL ACTION NO.:_____ JURY TRIAL:_____ NON-JURY TRIAL:_____

Title of Case:_____

Name of **Trial** Counsel:_____

Representing:_____

Law Firm:_____

Address:_____

Phone Number (including area code):_____

Jurisdiction:_____

Proof of Service Filed as to Defendants*:   Yes_____   No_____

1a.   Fed.R.Civ.P. 16 conference date:_____

1b.   Fed.R.Civ.P. 26(f) discovery/settlement conference date (at least 21 days prior to above)*:_____

2.   Proposed Discovery Schedule:

   Plaintiff:_____

   Defendant:_____

   Third-Party Defendant:_____

If discovery of electronically stored information is proposed, information required by Form 35, as amended December 1, 2006 (adaptation attached), must be provided or the right to such discovery will be waived.

3.   Mandatory Disclosure under Fed.R.Civ.P. 26(a)(1) (due 14 days after Fed.R.Civ.P. 26(f) conference):_____

   _____

4.   What, if any, matters will require action by the court before trial?_____

   _____

5.   Case will be ready for trial on or about:_____

6.   Trial time: a) Estimate of total time to present your case:_____

            b) Estimate of total time for the entire trial:_____

7.   Prospect of Settlement: Likely _____   Possible _____   Unlikely_____

   Settlement conference desired?   Now_____   Later_____

   (State at what stage appropriate)_____

8.   Special comments:_____

   _____

                                                            _____
                                                            Counsel for

*   **Fed.R.Civ.P. 4(m):** If service of summons and complaint is not made upon a defendant within 120 days, the action shall be dismissed without prejudice as to that defendant.

Judge Norma L. Shapiro

Adaptation of Form 35. Report of Parties' Planning Meeting

Please insert caption of the case, listing all parties involved:

                            :   CIVIL ACTION
                            :
v.   :
                            :
                            :   NO.

1. Pursuant to Fed.R.Civ.P. 26(f), a meeting was held on _____ at _____ and was attended by the following attorneys (provide names only):

For plaintiff(s): _____

For defendant(s): _____

For third-parties: _____

2. **Pre-discovery disclosures:** the parties have exchanged [___] will exchange [___] by _____, _____, the information required by Fed.R.Civ.P. 26(a)(1).

3. **Discovery plan:** The parties jointly propose to the court the following discovery plan (use separate paragraphs or subparagraphs as necessary, if the parties disagree):

Discovery will be needed on the following subjects: _____
_____
_____.

All discovery will be commenced in time to be completed by _____.

Discovery on (name issue(s) for early discovery) _____
_____
to be completed by _____.

Maximum of ____ interrogatories by each party to any other party; responses due ___ days after service.

Maximum of ____ requests for admission by each party to any other party; responses due ____ days after service.

Maximum of ____ depositions by plaintiff(s) and ____ by defendant(s). Each deposition (other than of _____) limited to maximum of ___ hours unless extended by agreement of the parties.

Reports from retained experts under Rule 26(a)(2) due:
    from plaintiff(s) by _____;
    from defendant(s) by _____; and
    from third parties by _____.

Supplementations under Rule 26(e) due _____ (times or intervals).

4. **Other items:** Please use separate paragraphs or subparagraphs as necessary if the parties disagree.

Plaintiff(s) should be allowed ninety (90) days after service of the complaint to join additional parties and/or amend the pleadings. *See* Local Rule of Civil Procedure 14.1.

Defendant(s) should be allowed ninety (90) days after service of the answer to join additional parties or to amend the pleadings. *See* Local Rule of Civil Procedure 14.1.

All potentially dispositive motions shall be filed with the final pretrial memorandum.

Settlement is likely [____]; unlikely [____]; cannot be evaluated prior to the Fed.R.Civ.P. 16 conference [____]; or may be enhanced by use of the following alternative dispute resolution procedure: _____

_____ .

Final lists of witnesses and exhibits under Rule 26(a)(3) shall be due with each party's final pretrial memorandum.

Objections to the final lists of witnesses and exhibits under Fed.R.Civ.P. 26(a)(3) shall be made at the final pretrial conference.

The case will be ready for trial two (2) days after the final pretrial conference. Trial of this case is expected to take ____ days.

Other matters: _____
_____
_____
_____
_____ .

Date: _____   By: _____
                                                         Please print/type name of attorney submitting report

Judge Norma L. Shapiro

IN THE UNITED STATES DISTRICT COURT
FOR THE EASTERN DISTRICT OF PENNSYLVANIA

STANDARD MANAGEMENT TRACK

ORDER PURSUANT TO FEDERAL RULES OF CIVIL PROCEDURE 16 and 26
LOCAL CIVIL RULES 16.1 AND 16.2
and THE CIVIL JUSTICE EXPENSE AND DELAY REDUCTION PLAN
(effective December 31, 1991, as Amended January 12, 2001)

Rule 16(b) of the Federal Rules of Civil Procedure requires the court, except in categories of actions exempted by district court rule, to consult with all attorneys and any unrepresented parties, by a scheduling conference, telephone, mail or other suitable means, and within 90 days after the appearance of a defendant and within 120 days after the complaint has been served on a defendant, to take appropriate action with respect to:

   a. joining other parties and amending the pleadings (see Local Rule 14.1);

   b. filing and hearing motions;

   c. completing discovery;

   d. modifying the time for disclosure under Rules 26(a) and 26(e)(1) and the extent of discovery to be permitted;

   e. providing for disclosure or discovery of electronically stored information;

   f. including any agreements the parties reach for asserting claims of privilege or of protection as trial-preparation material after production;

   g. setting the date or dates for conferences before trial, a final pretrial conference and trial; and

   h. any other matters appropriate in the circumstances of the case.

The purpose of this Order is to implement these mandatory procedures by establishing a method for consulting with all attorneys and any unrepresented parties prior to issuing the scheduling order required by the Rule.

Counsel will be expected to have complied with Fed.R.Civ.P. 26. There will be a Fed.R.Civ.P. 16 conference scheduled within **60** days after a responsive pleading has been filed. This conference will be in Chambers or by telephone upon request of the parties to the Deputy Clerk (267-299-7549). The purpose of the conference will be to:

   i. expedite the disposition of the action;

   ii. establish early and continuing control so that the case will not be protracted because of lack of management;

   iii. discourage wasteful pretrial activities;

   iv. improve the quality of the trial through more thorough preparation; and

   v. facilitate settlement of the case. (Rule 16(c) permits the court to require a party or its representative to be present or reasonably available by telephone to consider possible settlement.)

The participants at any pretrial conference are on notice that the court may take action with respect to the:

   1. formulation and simplification of the issues, including the elimination of frivolous claims or defenses;

   2. necessity or desirability of amendments to the pleadings;

3. limitation of time to amend the pleadings or join other parties;
4. completion of discovery, particularly with regard to scheduling, including orders affecting disclosures under Fed.R.Civ.P. 26, and Fed.R.Civ.P. 29 through and including 37;
5. possibility of obtaining admissions of fact and of documents to avoid unnecessary proof and cumulative evidence, stipulations regarding the authenticity of documents, and advance rulings from the court on the admissibility of evidence;
6. identification of witnesses and documents;
7. need and schedule for filing and exchanging pretrial memoranda, and the date or dates for further conferences;
8. appropriateness and timing of summary adjudication under Fed.R.Civ.P. 56;
9. advisability of referring matters to a magistrate judge or master;
10. possibility of settlement or the use of extrajudicial procedures to resolve the dispute;
11. form and substance of the pretrial order;
12. disposition of pending motions;
13. need for adopting special procedures for managing potentially difficult or protracted actions that may involve complex issues, multiple parties, difficult legal questions, or unusual proof problems; and
14. any other matters that may aid in the disposition of the action.

At least one of the attorneys for each party participating in any conference before trial shall have authority to bind that party regarding all matters identified above and all reasonably related matters.

The Order following the preliminary pretrial conference will specify whether the pretrial memorandum form provided in Local Rule 16.1(c) or 16.1(d) should be followed. In addition, all exhibits listed in proposed final pretrial memoranda are to have been provided to opposing counsel if not received from opposing counsel in discovery. Exhibits should be numbered for use at trial. It is helpful to list any stipulated facts to avoid the necessity of proof at trial.

Counsel are required to identify witnesses in their final pretrial memoranda and as to each witness listed therein make the disclosure required by Fed.R.Civ.P. 26(a)(2). Testimony will be limited at trial to the information disclosed.

A final pretrial conference will be held as close to the time of trial as possible, and unless specially listed, the case will be deemed ready for trial at any time thereafter. Parties to the conference will formulate a plan for trial, including a program for facilitating the admission of evidence, for approval by the judge. The final pretrial conference shall be attended by trial counsel and by any unrepresented parties. Upon notice of the court in the final pretrial conference order, representatives of the parties with authority to bind them in settlement discussions shall be present or, with prior permission of the court, be available by telephone during the settlement conference. To accommodate this requirement, conference dates will be rescheduled once by the Deputy Clerk on request for good cause shown.

An Order will be entered reciting the action taken at a pretrial conference. This Order will control the subsequent course of the action unless modified by a subsequent Order. The Order following a final pretrial conference will be modified only to prevent manifest injustice.

If a party or party's attorney fails to obey a scheduling pretrial Order, or if no appearance is made on behalf of a party at a scheduling or pretrial conference, or if a party or party's attorney is substantially unprepared to participate in the conference, or if a party or party's attorney fails to participate in good faith, the judge, upon motion or her own initiative, may impose sanctions as provided by 28 U.S.C. § 1927, the Federal Rules of Civil Procedure and the Local Rules of this court. The judge may require the party or the attorney representing the party or both to pay the reasonable expenses, including attorneys' fees, incurred by opposing counsel because of any noncompliance with the rules, unless the judge finds that noncompliance was substantially justified or that other circumstances make an award of expenses unjust.

The schedule will not be modified except upon a showing of good cause, by leave of the judge, or the magistrate judge to whom a request may be referred.

IT IS SO ORDERED, this _____ day of _____, 20___.

_____
Norma L. Shapiro, S.J.

UNITED STATES DISTRICT COURT
FOR THE EASTERN DISTRICT OF PENNSYLVANIA

                                    :   CIVIL ACTION
                                    :
v.   :
                                    :
                                    :   NO.

SPECIAL MANAGEMENT TRACK CASE

CASE MANAGEMENT POLICY

    1. This case will be managed pursuant to the Manual on Complex Litigation, Fourth (the "Manual"). This case is exempt from mandatory disclosure; discovery will be managed by a separate order of this court consistent with the Federal Rules of Civil Procedure 16 and 26. (*See* Paragraph 6 below for anticipated interim procedure.)

    2. The **initial pretrial conference** will be held when defense counsel has entered an appearance or within thirty (30) days after the filing of the response to the complaint. In anticipation of receipt of the order scheduling the initial pretrial conference, all parties in this case and cases likely to be the subject of pretrial consolidation, shall familiarize themselves with the Manual, the provisions of which generally will guide the management of this case. In particular, it is expected that counsel shall anticipate the agenda items for the initial pretrial conference set forth in Part IV, § 40.1; and Form 41.2 of the Manual, in order to facilitate preparation for the conference.

    3. **Time and expense records**. All counsel who expect to make a claim for fees and costs are expected to make and maintain daily entries of time and expenses incurred in connection with this litigation. Subject to discussion at the initial pretrial conference, it is expected that the court will enter an order requiring that these records be made and maintained and filed with the court periodically during the litigation. These records shall be filed **under seal**. *See* Form 41.32 of the Manual.

    4. **Admission of counsel pro hac vice** by motion and order, and retention of local counsel pursuant to Local Rule of Civil Procedure 83.5, as amended October 1, 2002 (unless expressly waived by the court), will be required before an attorney who is not a member of the bar of this court takes any action in the case, including attending any conference with the court.

    5. **Pleadings**. The court expects to approve stipulations granting defendant(s) a reasonable extension to a date certain within which to answer or otherwise move or to file counterclaims, if the time to do so will expire before the date expected or set for the initial pretrial conference. It is anticipated that at the initial pretrial conference a time will be set for the filing of all subsequent pleadings and any necessary joinder of third parties.

    6. **Discovery**. Mandatory discovery may proceed, but it is expected that the court will stay all formal discovery in its order scheduling the initial pretrial conference, with formal discovery to be scheduled in the First Case Management Order following the initial conference.

    7. **Communications with the court** and its staff will be done in accordance with the Notice to Counsel which accompanies this policy statement. In addition, counsel will be expected to confer among themselves with respect to any and all disputes and attempt to resolve them before approaching the judge for resolution.

    8. **Duties of counsel**. Prior to the initial conference, it is expected that counsel will see that all appearances are on the docket and that the necessary consultation among the parties has taken place on all matters expected to be on the agenda for the initial pretrial conference, including the organization of counsel in multi-party or class actions. It is expected that a joint proposal for a case management order be prepared and presented at the initial pretrial conference, and that counsel of record attend the initial conference with the authority to agree and resolve all issues planned for the agenda of that conference.

9. To the extent that any provision of this policy statement conflicts with a specific case management or other order entered in this litigation, the case-specific order shall control.

10. Unexcused violations of scheduling or case management orders are subject to sanctions under Fed.R.Civ.P. 16(f), upon motion or the initiative of the court.

_____
Norma L. Shapiro, S.J.

Date: _____, 20___

IN THE UNITED STATES DISTRICT COURT
FOR THE EASTERN DISTRICT OF PENNSYLVANIA

	:	CIVIL ACTION
	:	
v.	:	
	:	
	:	NO.
	:	**SPECIAL MANAGEMENT TRACK**

PRETRIAL ORDER NO. 1

AND NOW, this _____ day of _____, 20___, it is **ORDERED** that:

1. This case is governed by the Special Management Track Case Management Policy of Judge Shapiro, a copy of which is attached hereto.

2. All parties shall appear for an **initial pretrial conference** with Judge Norma L. Shapiro on _____, **20**___, at **10:00 a.m.** in Courtroom 10-A, United States Courthouse, 601 Market Street, Philadelphia, Pennsylvania.

   a. **Attendance**. Each party represented by counsel shall appear through its attorney who will have primary responsibility for its interests in this litigation.

   b. **Service List**. Copies of this Order are being mailed or faxed to all attorneys whose names appear on the docket. Counsel are requested to advise the Deputy Clerk of any additions or corrections and to forward a copy of this Order to any other attorneys or parties who should be notified, including those in any additional related cases that may be filed in, removed to, or transferred to this court before the conference.

   c. **Other Participants**. Persons who are not named as parties in this litigation but may later be joined as parties or are parties in related litigation pending in other federal or state courts are invited to attend in person or by counsel.

3. **Purposes and Agenda**. The conference will be held for the purposes specified in Fed.R.Civ.P. 16(a), 16(b), 16(c), and 16(f) and subject to sanctions prescribed in Rule 16(f). Counsel are required to submit **in writing** to the court, in Chambers, no later than ten (10) working days prior to the scheduled conference, a list of any items that should be on the agenda.

4. **Preparations for the Conference.**

   a. **Procedures for Complex Litigation**. Counsel shall familiarize themselves with the *Manual for Complex Litigation, Fourth*, and be prepared at the conference to suggest procedures that will facilitate the expeditious, economical, and just resolution of this litigation.

   b. **Initial Duties of Counsel**. Before the conference, counsel shall confer and seek consensus with respect to the items on the agenda, including a proposed discovery plan under Rule 26(f) and a suggested schedule under Rule 16(b) for joinder of parties, amendment of pleadings, consideration of any class action allegations, and trial.

   c. **Preliminary Reports**. Counsel shall submit to the court, in Chambers, by _____, 20___, a brief written statement indicating their client's respective (or joint) preliminary understanding of the facts involved in the litigation and what they expect to be the critical factual and legal issues. These statements will not be binding, will not waive claims or defenses, and may not be offered in evidence against a party in later proceedings.

   d. **List of Affiliated Companies and Counsel**. To assist the court in identifying any problems of recusal or disqualification, each party shall submit to the court **in writing** by _____, **20**___, a list of all companies affiliated with the parties and all counsel associated in the litigation.

5. **Interim Measures**. Until otherwise ordered by the court:

   a. **Discovery**. Pending the conference, all outstanding discovery proceedings are **STAYED** and no further discovery shall be initiated. This directive does not preclude mandatory discovery regarding the identification and location of relevant documents and witnesses under Fed.R.Civ.P. 26(a). Relief from this stay may be granted for good cause shown, such as, *inter alia*, the ill health of a proposed deponent.

   b. If any party presently expects to seek a protective order regarding discovery for reasons of confidentiality or otherwise and counsel have not reached consensus when they confer before the conference, *see* ¶ 4b *infra,* the party who will seek such an order shall submit and serve a proposed order with the preliminary report, *see* ¶ 4c *infra.*

   c. **Preservation of records**. Each party shall preserve all documents and other records containing information potentially relevant to the subject matter of this litigation. Subject to further order of the court, parties may continue routine erasures of computerized data pursuant to existing programs, but they shall (1) immediately notify opposing counsel about such programs; and (2) preserve any printouts of such data. Requests for relief from this Order will receive prompt attention from the court.

                                                  _____
                                                  Norma L. Shapiro, S.J.

Attachment

IN THE UNITED STATES DISTRICT COURT
FOR THE EASTERN DISTRICT OF PENNSYLVANIA

	:	CIVIL ACTION
	:	
v.	:	
	:	
	:	NO.
	:	**SPECIAL MANAGEMENT TRACK**

SERVICE LIST

For Plaintiffs:

For Defendants:

Judge Norma L. Shapiro

IN THE UNITED STATES DISTRICT COURT
FOR THE EASTERN DISTRICT OF PENNSYLVANIA

v.	: CIVIL ACTION : : : : NO.

RICO CASE STANDING ORDER
18 U.S.C. §§ 1961–1968

The above-captioned case contains a civil RICO claim, which has been filed in this court pursuant to 18 U.S.C. §§ 1961-1968. This Standing Order has been designed to establish a uniform and efficient procedure for processing this case.

Plaintiff shall file, on or before _____, a RICO case statement; a copy shall be delivered to Chambers. This statement shall include the facts plaintiffs are relying upon to prove this RICO claim. In particular, this statement shall be in a form that uses the numbers and letters as set forth below, and shall provide the following information:

1. State whether the alleged unlawful conduct is in violation of 18 U.S.C. §§ 1962(a), (b), (c), and/or (d).
2. List each defendant and state the alleged misconduct and basis of liability of each defendant.
3. List the alleged victims and state how each victim was allegedly injured.
4. Describe in detail the pattern of racketeering activity or collection of unlawful debts alleged for each RICO claim. A description of the pattern of racketeering shall include the following information:
   a. List the alleged predicate acts and the specific statutes that were allegedly violated;
   b. If the RICO claim is based on the predicate offenses of wire fraud, mail fraud, or fraud in the sale of securities, the "circumstances of fraud or mistake shall be stated in particularity";
   c. Describe how the predicate acts form a "pattern of racketeering activity"; and
   d. State whether the alleged predicate acts relate to each other as part of a common plan. If so, describe.
5. Describe in detail the alleged enterprise for each RICO claim. A description of the enterprise shall include the following information:
   a. State the names of the individuals, partnerships, corporations, associations, or other legal entities that allegedly constitute the enterprise;
   b. Describe the structure, purpose, function and course of conduct of the enterprise;
   c. State whether any defendants are employees, officers or directors of the alleged enterprise;
   d. State whether any defendants are associated with the alleged enterprise; and
   e. State whether you are alleging that the defendants are individuals or entities separate from the alleged enterprise, or that the defendants are the enterprise itself; or members of the enterprise.
6. Describe the alleged relationship between the activities of the enterprise and the pattern of racketeering activity. Discuss how the racketeering activity differs from the usual and daily activities of the enterprise, if at all.
7. Describe the effect of the activities of the enterprise on interstate or foreign commerce.

8. If the complaint alleges a violation of 18 U.S.C. § 1962(a), provide the following information:
   a. State who received the income derived from the pattern of racketeering activity or through the collection of an unlawful debt; and
   b. Describe the use or investment of such income.
9. If the complaint alleges a violation of 18 U.S.C. § 1962(b), describe the acquisition or maintenance of any interest in or control of the alleged enterprise.
10. If the complaint alleges a violation of 18 U.S.C. § 1962(c), provide the following information:
    a. State who is employed by or associated with the enterprise; and
    b. State whether the same entity is both the liable "person" and the "enterprise" under § 1962(c).
11. If the complaint alleges a violation of 18 U.S.C. § 1962(d), describe the alleged conspiracy.
12. Describe the alleged injury to business or property.
13. Describe the direct causal relationship between the alleged injury and the violation of the RICO statute.
14. Provide any additional information that you feel would be helpful to the court in trying the RICO claim.

IT IS SO ORDERED.

_____
Norma L. Shapiro, S.J.

Date: _____

Judge Norma L. Shapiro

CODE OF CIVILITY

Preamble.

The hallmark of an enlightened and effective system of justice is the adherence to standards of professional responsibility and civility. Judges and lawyers must always be mindful of the appearance of justice as well as its dispensation. The following principles are designed to assist judges and lawyers in how to conduct themselves in a manner that preserves the dignity and honor of the judiciary and the legal profession. These principles are intended to encourage lawyers, judges and court personnel to practice civility and decorum and to confirm the legal profession's status as an honorable and respected profession where courtesy and civility are observed as a matter of course.

The conduct of lawyers and judges should be characterized at all times by professional integrity and personal courtesy in the fullest sense of those terms. Integrity and courtesy are indispensable to the practice of law and the orderly administration of justice by our courts. Uncivil or obstructive conduct impedes the fundamental goal of resolving disputes in a rational, peaceful and efficient manner.

The following principles are designed to encourage judges and lawyers to meet their obligations toward each other and the judicial system in general. It is expected that judges and lawyers will make a voluntary and mutual commitment to adhere to these principles. These principles are not intended to supersede or alter existing disciplinary codes or standards of conduct, nor shall they be used as a basis for litigation, lawyer discipline or sanctions.

A Judge's Duties to Lawyers and Other Judges.

1. A judge must maintain control of the proceedings and has an obligation to ensure that proceedings are conducted in a civil manner.

2. A judge should show respect, courtesy and patience to the lawyers, parties and all participants in the legal process by treating all with civility.

3. A judge should ensure that court-supervised personnel dress and conduct themselves appropriately and act civilly toward lawyers, parties and witnesses.

4. A judge should refrain from acting upon or manifesting racial, gender or other bias or prejudice toward any participant in the legal process.

5. A judge should always refer to counsel by surname preceded by the preferred title (Mr., Mrs., Ms. or Miss) or by the professional title of attorney or counselor while in the courtroom.

6. A judge should not employ hostile or demeaning words in opinions or in written or oral communications with lawyers, parties or witnesses.

7. A judge should be punctual in convening trials, hearings, meetings and conferences.

8. A judge should be considerate of the time constraints upon lawyers, parties and witnesses and the expenses attendant to litigation when scheduling trials, hearings, meetings and conferences to the extent such scheduling is consistent with the efficient conduct of litigation.

9. A judge should ensure that disputes are resolved in a prompt and efficient manner and give all issues in controversy deliberate, informed and impartial analysis and explain, when appropriate, the reasons for the decision of the court.

10. A judge should allow the lawyers to present proper arguments and to make a complete and accurate record.

11. A judge should not impugn the integrity or professionalism of any lawyer on the basis of the clients whom or the causes which he or she represents.

12. A judge should recognize that the conciliation process is an integral part of litigation and thus should protect all confidences and remain unbiased with respect to conciliation communications.

13. A judge should work in cooperation with all other judges and other jurisdictions with respect to availability of lawyers, witnesses, parties and court resources.

14. A judge should conscientiously assist and cooperate with other jurists to assure the efficient and expeditious processing of cases.

15. Judges should treat each other with courtesy and respect.

The Lawyer's Duties to the Court and to Other Lawyers.

1. A lawyer should act in a manner consistent with the fair, efficient and humane system of justice and treat all participants in the legal process in a civil, professional and courteous manner at all times. These principles apply to the lawyer's conduct in the courtroom, in office practice and in the course of litigation.

2. A lawyer should speak and write in a civil and respectful manner in all communications with the court, court personnel, and other lawyers.

3. A lawyer should not engage in any conduct that diminishes the dignity or decorum of the courtroom.

4. A lawyer should advise clients and witnesses of the proper dress and conduct expected of them when appearing in court and should, to the best of his or her ability, prevent clients and witnesses from creating disorder and disruption in the courtroom.

5. A lawyer should abstain from making disparaging personal remarks or engaging in acrimonious speech or conduct toward opposing counsel or any participants in the legal process and shall treat everyone involved with fair consideration.

6. A lawyer should not bring the profession into disrepute by making unfounded accusations of impropriety or personal attacks upon counsel and, absent good cause, should not attribute improper motive or conduct to other counsel.

7. A lawyer should refrain from acting upon or manifesting racial, gender or other bias or prejudice toward any participant in the legal process.

8. A lawyer should not misrepresent, mischaracterize, misquote or miscite facts or authorities in any oral or written communication to the court.

9. A lawyer should be punctual and prepared for all court appearances.

10. A lawyer should avoid ex parte communications with the court, including the judge's staff, on pending matters in person, by telephone or in letters and other forms of written communication unless authorized. Communication with the judge on any matter pending before the judge, without notice to opposing counsel, is strictly prohibited.

11. A lawyer should be considerate of the time constraints and pressures on the court in the court's effort to administer justice and make every effort to comply with schedules set by the court.

12. A lawyer, when in the courtroom, should make all remarks only to the judge and never to opposing counsel. When in the courtroom a lawyer should refer to opposing counsel by surname preceded by the preferred title (Mr., Mrs., Ms. or Miss) or the professional title of attorney or counselor.

13. A lawyer should show respect for the court by proper demeanor and decorum. In the courtroom a lawyer should address the judge as "Your Honor" or "the Court" or by other formal designation. A lawyer should begin an argument by saying "May it please the court" and identify himself/herself, the firm and the client.

14. A lawyer should deliver to all counsel involved in a proceeding any written communication that a lawyer sends to the court. Said copies should be delivered at substantially the same time and by the same means as the written communication to the court.

15. A lawyer should attempt to verify the availability of necessary participants and witnesses before hearing and trial dates are set or, if that is not feasible, immediately after such dates have been set and promptly notify the court of any anticipated problems.

16. A lawyer should understand that court personnel are an integral part of the justice system and should treat them with courtesy and respect at all times.

17. A lawyer should demonstrate respect for other lawyers, which requires that counsel be punctual in meeting appointments with other lawyers and considerate of the schedules of other participants in the legal process; adhere to commitments, whether made orally or in writing; and respond promptly to communications from other lawyers.

18. A lawyer should strive to protect the dignity and independence of the judiciary, particularly from unjust criticism and attack.

19. A lawyer should be cognizant of the standing of the legal profession and should bring these principles to the attention of other lawyers when appropriate.

Working Rules of Professionalism
Adopted by the Philadelphia Bar Association

1 Treat with civility opposing counsel, lawyers, and their staffs, witnesses, and the courts and court officers. Professional courtesy is a virtue, not a shortcoming. It is entirely compatible with vigorous advocacy and zealous representation.

2 Keep the lines of communication open. Telephone calls and correspondence should be answered promptly even if the answer is a simple acknowledgment with a promise to respond substantively later.

3 Be mindful of the schedules of others as you are of your own. Seek agreement in advance for the scheduling of meetings, depositions, hearings, and trials. Do not purposely wait until Friday afternoon to make hand deliveries and send telefaxes. Absent exigent circumstances, a reasonable request for a scheduling accommodation should be granted.

4 Be punctual in honoring scheduled appearances. Lateness is demeaning to others and to our profession.

5 If your adversary is entitled to something, provide it without unnecessary formalities. Discovery disputes and motion practice cost time and money. They should be a last resort.

6 Grant reasonable extensions of time when they will not adversely affect your client's interests. Explain to your client that the consequences of refusing a reasonable extension may be the filing of dilatory objections or motions and the creation of a hostile atmosphere in which your reasonable request will also be refused. Ultimately the hostility will escalate and so will the cost of legal services.

7 Attempt to reconcile differences through negotiation, expeditiously and without needless expense. Taking the initiative to settle a case or resolve a dispute is not a sign of weakness and should not be viewed as such.

Adopted June 28, 1990. All Philadelphia lawyers are encouraged to abide by these guidelines.

The quality of the profession will be as worthy as the character of the people who practice it. Self-esteem and shared respect for each other will ultimately be reflected in responsible professional conduct. The lawyers and law firms of our city are urged to subscribe to and actively promote these values so that the high standards of professionalism that have so long enhanced our professional lives will be preserved and passed on to future generations of Philadelphia lawyers.

Judge Joel H. Slomsky

Judge Slomsky received his B.A. from Brooklyn College of the City University of New York in 1967. He received his J.D. in 1970 from the New York Law School. Upon graduation from law school, Mr. Slomsky was selected through the Honors Program to be a Special Attorney with the U.S. Department of Justice, Criminal Division, Organized Crime and Racketeering Section, and was later assigned to the Philadelphia Strike Force. In 1973, Mr. Slomsky joined Lipschitz & Danella as an associate. In 1974, Mr. Slomsky started practicing as a sole practitioner and worked as a sole practitioner from 1974 to 1982 and again from 1990 to the present. He was a partner in a small firm from 1982 to 1990. His practice is mainly federal and includes racketeering cases, tax cases, securities fraud, health care and government contracting fraud, ERISA, antitrust matters, and tax matters.

PRELIMINARY GENERAL MATTERS

1. Written Communications with Chambers. Written communications with the court concerning any case assigned to Judge Slomsky's calendar should be by the filing of a pleading, motion, application, or other similar filing provided for in the Federal Rules of Civil Procedure or Local Rules of Civil Procedure.

Correspondence regarding the following is permitted, provided the letter states that counsel agrees or disagrees with the request:

(1) When counsel are specifically requested by the court to communicate some information to the court by letter;

(2) When there is an uncontested request for a continuance of the Rule 16 scheduling order deadlines not affecting the dates for filing a summary judgment motion and trial;

(3) When the participation of counsel in the case is expected to be affected by an unanticipated personal matter concerning counsel, a party, a witness, or counsel's immediate family, such as medical problems, vacation plans, or other personal problems; or

(4) To confirm or advise the court that a case has been settled, dismissed, or otherwise finally disposed.

Counsel should not send copies of correspondence among and between counsel to the court.

2. Telephone Calls. Law clerks may not render advice to counsel and have no authority to grant continuances or to give advice on substantive or procedural matters. Therefore, unless counsel is contacted by a law clerk, counsel should not communicate with the law clerks.

When a written communication concerning a case cannot timely address a problem, counsel may initiate necessary telephone communications with chambers. Issues appropriately addressed by telephone contact include scheduling of conferences or proceedings, including pretrial and trial conferences; attendance of witnesses; exhibit handling or arrangements for video replay; and arrangements for telephone conferences regarding discovery disputes.

Telephone inquiries should be directed as appropriate to either one of the following:

Judicial Secretary: Chris Murphy Casper—267-299-7341
Contact for matters relating to civil scheduling, case management, and general procedures.

Courtroom Deputy: Margaret Gallagher—267-299-7349
Contact for matters regarding all criminal matters, courtroom procedures, trial setup, and transcripts.

Counsel are advised to submit current telephone and fax numbers to the Clerk's Office, the courtroom deputy, and the judicial secretary.

4. **Faxes.** Facsimile transmittal of pleadings, motions, other filings, or correspondence to chambers is not permitted.

5. **Electronic Case Filing (ECF) and Courtesy Copies.** Counsel should file all pleadings electronically through ECF. Notwithstanding compliance with this procedure regarding use of ECF, counsel should send to chambers two courtesy copies of any motions (and related briefs) filed with the clerk of the court. In the unusual case where counsel does not file using ECF or counsel is requested to do so, two courtesy copies of all pleadings and motion papers should be delivered to Chambers, Room 5614, United States Courthouse, 601 Market Street, Philadelphia, PA 19106.

CIVIL CASES
Pretrial Procedure

1. **Rule 16 Conference and Rule 26(f) Meeting.** A preliminary pretrial conference as described in Fed.R.Civ.P. 16(b) and (c) will be scheduled shortly after a defendant has filed an appearance or pleading. At least *three business days* prior to the pretrial conference, counsel must file with the clerk a joint report of the Rule 26(f) meeting with a provisional discovery plan adopted at the conference in the form shown in the sample on page 330 of this book.

The court relies on counsel's good-faith compliance in all respects with Rule 26(f). The Rule 26(f) meeting should take place as soon as possible and, in any event, no later than 14 days after the date of the order scheduling the Rule 16 conference. The meeting should not be viewed as perfunctory but rather as a meaningful and substantive discussion among professionals to formulate the proposed discovery plan required by the rule.

Outstanding motions will *not* excuse the requirements of holding the meeting and submitting the plan. Compliance is mandatory. *Parties who do not comply will have no voice at the scheduling conference and may be subject to additional sanctions.*

Topics addressed at the initial pretrial conference are those listed in Local Rule of Civil Procedure 16.1(b), Federal Rule of Civil Procedure 16(b) and (c), the progress of self-executing disclosure under Federal Rule of Civil Procedure 26(a), discovery, the preservation and production of electronically stored information, settlement, and mediation proposals. A Rule 16 scheduling order is issued at the conclusion of the conference.

Lead trial counsel, not an associate, must attend the Rule 16 conference. Counsel should have a thorough comprehension of the facts and should be prepared to discuss all claims and defenses in detail, including settlement, and have authority from their clients to do so.

2. **Threshold Motions.** Motions to dismiss, amend, transfer, add parties, and other threshold motions should be filed before the Rule 16 conference. Counsel should be prepared to discuss the merits of any outstanding motions at the conference.

3. Settlement Conferences. Counsel are required to attend a settlement conference with Magistrate Judge Carol Sandra Moore Wells as set forth in the scheduling order. Counsel must adhere to Magistrate Judge Wells's requirements regarding the conduct of the conference. The parties and/or persons with full authority to settle must accompany counsel to the mediation before Judge Wells unless excused in advance by Judge Wells.

4. Mediation. In addressing settlement or early disposition of the case, counsel are reminded that participation in an early alternative dispute resolution effort is strongly encouraged. Counsel should be familiar with the court's mediation program and Local Rule 53.2. Counsel are required to explore the feasibility of ADR, including court-annexed mediation, not only between themselves but with their clients as well. The specific reason for any decision not to participate in a form of early ADR should be delineated in the Rule 26(f) report.

5. Pro Hac Vice Admissions. Counsel moving for the pro hac vice admission of an attorney must file a motion setting forth in detail the attorney's admissions, the reason why the party desires the attorney to participate, and why the attorney is especially qualified to do so. The form application provided by the clerk is inadequate.

6. Confidentiality Agreements. Judge Slomsky will consider entry of stipulated confidentiality or sealing orders if the proposed order includes a detailed statement demonstrating that good cause exists for the order. See *Pansy v. Borough of Stroudsburg*, 23 F.3d 772, 786 (3d Cir. 1994). All such orders must contain the following language (or language substantially similar):

> "The Court retains the right to allow disclosure of any subject covered by this stipulation or to modify this stipulation at any time in the interest of justice."

Discovery Matters

1. Length of Discovery Period and Extensions. The Federal Rules of Civil Procedure call for voluntary, cooperative discovery in a *timely* manner. The information required to be disclosed pursuant to Fed.R.Civ.P. 26(a) is required to be exchanged no later than 14 days after the date of the order scheduling the Rule 16 conference. Compliance with the rules is *mandatory*. Counsel are expected to act in accordance with both the *letter* and the *spirit* of the rules.

The parties are required to commence discovery *immediately* upon receipt of notice of the Rule 16 conference. Pending motions do not excuse counsel from proceeding with discovery. Counsel will be required to report on the progress of discovery at the Rule 16 conference.

When timely discovery is not forthcoming after a reasonable attempt has been made to obtain it, the immediate assistance of the court should be sought after compliance with Local Rule 26.1(f). The certification must state *in detail* what efforts were made to resolve the dispute.

The court encourages the submission of discovery disputes by telephone conference. If a discovery motion is filed, it may be acted upon before a response is filed either with or without a telephone conference.

2. Electronic Discovery. It is expected that the parties will reach an agreement on how to conduct electronic discovery. In the event the parties cannot reach such an agreement before the Rule 16 scheduling conference, the court will enter an order incorporating default standards. The default order can be viewed at www.paed.uscourts.gov.

The parties should discuss the parameters of their anticipated e-discovery at the Rule 26(f) conference and should be prepared to address e-discovery at the Rule 16 scheduling conference with the court.

Motions Practice

1.   Oral Arguments and Evidentiary Hearings. Oral argument is not routinely scheduled. A party desiring oral argument should request it by letter or in the body of the motion or responsive pleading.

2.   Reply Briefs. Reply briefs, addressing only issues raised in the brief in opposition and not repeating arguments in the initial brief, may be filed within seven days of service of the opponent's brief in opposition and should be limited to 10 pages. No further briefs may be filed.

Rule 56 Motions

Any motion for summary judgment filed pursuant to Fed.R.Civ.P. 56 should include a separate statement of undisputed facts that sets forth, in numbered paragraphs, the material facts that the moving party contends are undisputed and entitle the movant to judgment as a matter of law. Only those facts that bear on dispositive material issues should be included in the statement of undisputed facts.

The papers opposing a motion for summary judgment should include a separate statement of material facts, responding to the numbered paragraphs set forth in the statement of undisputed facts, which the respondent contends present genuine issues to be tried. The responding party also should set forth, in separate numbered paragraphs, any additional facts that the respondent contends preclude summary judgment. All material facts set forth in the statement required to be served by the moving party should be admitted unless controverted by the opposing party.

Statements of material facts in support of or in opposition to a motion for summary judgment should include specific and not general references to the parts of the record that support each of the statements. Each stated fact should cite the source relied upon, including the page and line of any document or deposition to which reference is made.

Final Pretrial Conference

The filing of a pretrial memorandum as described in Local Rule 16.1(c) will be required. In the pretrial memoranda, counsel must detail the substance of the testimony of each witness. Identifying a witness as giving testimony on liability and/or damages is insufficient.

The parties should provide the court with one copy of each exhibit and three copies of a schedule of exhibits that briefly describe each exhibit. At the trial, the parties should provide the court with two copies of each exhibit. Exhibits should be arranged and tabbed in a single three-ring binder containing all exhibits numbered consecutively.

Sidebar conferences and objections to evidence that should have been anticipated are discouraged and are to be avoided at trial. Consequently, one of the goals of the final pretrial conference, which counsel can expect to last two to four hours, is to resolve all evidentiary issues to avoid delay at trial and to provide counsel with advance notice of evidentiary requirements. Therefore, rulings on all outstanding motions and objections to witnesses and exhibits will be made at the final pretrial conference.

Counsel should be prepared to state their objections to witnesses and exhibits, and to respond to opposing counsel's objections. It is expected that counsel have discussed and have attempted to resolve all objections to exhibits and testimony prior to the final pretrial conference, leaving for the court only those objections the parties could not resolve.

Any party intending to use depositions, written or video, at trial must notify all other parties in the pretrial memorandum. Objections to deposition testimony should be made prior to the pretrial conference in writing, setting forth the page and line numbers of the challenged testimony and a clear statement for the basis of the objection. The objecting party must provide the court with a copy of the deposition transcript with the challenged testimony highlighted.

Courtroom and Trial Procedure

1. **Scheduling of Cases.** The scheduling order will set a date certain for trial or the date when the case will be placed in the trial pool. For cases in the trial pool, counsel should be prepared to commence trial upon 48 hours notice.

2. **Voir Dire.** Counsel must discuss voir dire questions and resolve any differences before the panel is brought to the courtroom. If they cannot agree, counsel must advise the deputy clerk that the judge must rule upon the disputed issues. Judge Slomsky permits counsel to conduct voir dire in civil cases. There is generally a time limit of 30 minutes for each side for voir dire. Judge Slomsky conducts voir dire in criminal cases.

3. **Trial Objections and Sidebars.** Sidebar conferences are discouraged and are rarely permitted. Only unanticipated issues will necessitate a sidebar conference.

    Judge Slomsky does not permit speaking objections. Objections should be made by reciting the appropriate rule number or a one-word basis.

4. **Motions in Limine.** Motions in limine must be filed by the deadline set in the scheduling order. Judge Slomsky will usually rule upon such motions before or at the final pretrial conference.

5. **Examination of Witnesses Out of Sequence.** The court will permit counsel to examine his/her own witnesses out of turn for the convenience of a witness.

6. **Opening Statements and Summations.** Judge Slomsky usually does not place a time limit on opening statements and summations. However, depending upon the issues in the case and the length of the trial, he may suggest time limits. He will discuss the time needed with counsel.

    Rebuttal should not take more than five minutes and must not be a rehashing of counsel's closing argument.

7. **Examination of Witnesses by More Than One Attorney.** Only one attorney for a party may examine the same witness or argue the same legal point. More than one attorney for a party may examine different witnesses or argue different legal points.

8. **Examination of Witnesses Beyond Redirect and Recross.** The court will permit limited recross-examination on matters not previously covered by cross-examination or in special circumstances.

9. **Offers of Proof.** Counsel should discuss privately any evidentiary issue that may have been unanticipated. Only after they have been unable to reach agreement, should counsel bring the matter to the deputy clerk's attention at the beginning of the day or during an appropriate break when the jury is not present.

10. **Videotaped Testimony.** Counsel must discuss in advance of trial all objections to the presentation of videotaped testimony to resolve all conflicts. If counsel cannot resolve their disagreements, they should present any outstanding disagreements at least 10 days prior to the final pretrial conference by providing a transcript of the testimony with the challenged question and answer highlighted, and a list setting forth each objection by page and line numbers and the basis for the objection.

The videotape must be edited prior to trial to eliminate pauses and speed-ups so there are no interruptions. Counsel should check with the deputy clerk to determine whether the courtroom is equipped for playback or whether counsel must provide playback equipment.

11. Reading of Material into the Record. Judge Slomsky has no special practice or policy for reading stipulations, pleadings, or discovery material into the record. Reading of material into the record may be done in a manner agreed upon by Judge Slomsky and counsel.

12. Preparation of Exhibits. At the final pretrial conference, the parties should provide the court with one copy of each exhibit and three copies of a schedule of exhibits that briefly describe each exhibit. At the trial, the parties should provide the court with two copies of each exhibit. Exhibits should be arranged and tabbed in a single three-ring binder containing all exhibits numbered consecutively.

13. Lay Witness Opinion. Any party expecting to offer lay opinion testimony pursuant to Federal Rule of Evidence 701 regarding issues of liability or damages should provide the opposing parties with information or documents supporting the testimony at the time required for submission of expert reports.

14. Offering Exhibits into Evidence. Exhibits are to be placed in evidence during testimony, at a convenient time during a party's case-in-chief, or at the close of each party's case-in-chief. If the latter, counsel should review the exhibits in advance so that agreed-upon exhibits can be admitted quickly and disputed exhibits ruled upon at a time that will not impose on the jury.

Exhibits may be published to the jury at the end of the party's examination of the witness or prior to a break. If the exhibit is necessary to explain the testimony, Judge Slomsky may permit it to be published during the testimony. Ordinarily, permission must be sought prior to the witness taking the stand.

15. Motions for Judgment as a Matter of Law. Motions for judgment as a matter of law and motions for judgment on partial findings may be oral or written. Oral argument will be permitted if counsel request it.

16. Proposed Jury Instructions and Verdict Forms. Counsel must meet and discuss proposed jury instructions and verdict forms for the purpose of submitting agreed-upon jury instructions and verdict forms. The proposed instructions should cover only the substantive issues regarding the elements of each cause of action and each defense. Basic instructions, such as the burden of proof, credibility, and procedure, should not be submitted.

Counsel are expected to cooperate in the preparation of the joint proposed instructions. Failure to cooperate in the process will result in the imposition of sanctions.

Submitting a proposed point does not constitute a waiver of objection. Counsel are instructed to work on proposed instructions regardless of counsel's position with respect to a point's applicability. If the court sustains an objection to a particular instruction, it will not be submitted to the jury. Objections to jointly submitted points will be discussed and ruled upon at the charging conference.

If counsel cannot agree, proposed alternative instructions must be submitted with authority for each instruction. If a model jury instruction is used, the party submitting it shall state whether the proposed instruction is unchanged or modified. If a party modifies a model instruction, additions should be underlined and deletions should be placed in brackets. Counsel should also submit proposed jury instructions and verdict forms on a disk in WordPerfect format.

17. **Proposed Findings of Fact and Conclusions of Law.** In a nonjury trial, counsel should submit findings of fact and conclusions of law upon which they agree. In addition, each party should submit any additional proposed findings of fact and conclusions of law for the consideration of the court.

Proposed findings of fact and conclusions of law in a nonjury trial should be submitted at least seven days *before* the trial or trial pool date. They should be on hard copy and on a disk in WordPerfect format. The parties may submit revised or supplemental findings of fact and conclusions of law with specific reference to trial evidence at the conclusion of the case. A schedule for the submission of revised findings/conclusions will be discussed at the conclusion of trial.

18. **Juror Note-taking.** As a general rule, Judge Slomsky does not allow the jury to take notes. In an appropriate case, he may permit note-taking.

19. **Written Jury Instructions.** Judge Slomsky does not give the jury a copy of the written jury instructions. However, he may do so in an appropriate case.

20. **Exhibits in the Jury Room.** After the jury has retired to deliberate, counsel should review the exhibits to determine which exhibits will go out with the jury. If counsel cannot agree, they should request a ruling immediately after the jury retires to the deliberations room.

21. **Handling of Jury Request to Read Back Testimony.** Judge Slomsky will advise the jury that testimony is usually not in transcript form to give them. However, if a transcript is available, he will consider having appropriate portions read if requested by the jury. He may allow tapes and videotapes to be replayed to the extent necessary.

22. **Availability of Counsel During Jury Deliberations.** Counsel must be available upon 15 minutes notice during jury deliberations. As a practical matter, this means that counsel must stay in or near the courthouse. Counsel must leave their office and cell phone numbers with the deputy clerk.

23. **Taking the Verdict and Special Interrogatories.** Judge Slomsky has no general practice for taking a special or general verdict. He usually submits interrogatories to the jury in civil cases. The courtroom deputy will take the verdict in the presence of the court, counsel, and the parties.

24. **Polling the Jury.** Judge Slomsky has no standard practice for polling the jury. He generally allows it if requested.

25. **Interviewing the Jury.** After a verdict has been recorded and the jury has been discharged, counsel may interview jurors. The jurors are told that they are permitted to talk to counsel and others, if they desire, but they need not do so. Counsel should respect the jurors' desire not to speak to them. Counsel is not permitted to disclose facts to the jury that were previously excluded by evidentiary rulings or would undermine the jury's confidence in its verdict.

26. **Courtroom Decorum and Professionalism.** Judge Slomsky will insist on punctuality and courtesy from counsel to the court and to each other, both in the presence of the court and otherwise. The examination of witnesses should be conducted from the lectern or from counsel table. Counsel should rise to address the court and should seek permission of the court before approaching witnesses or the bench. In addition, counsel will direct all comments to the court or to the witness under examination and not to other counsel or to the jury. Counsel are reminded that their own opinions regarding facts or issues in a case are irrelevant and should not be communicated to the jury (e.g., "I think ...., we believe ..."). To the extent possible, the parties should notify the court of any issues that will need to be

ruled upon at the start of the day's proceedings, or during a recess out of the jury's presence. Unless leave is otherwise given, counsel should make opening statements and closing arguments from the lectern and should speak into the microphone.

PROCEDURES IN CRIMINAL CASES

1.   Oral Argument and Motions.   Judge Slomsky will grant oral argument on motions if he believes it will assist him in deciding the motions. He usually considers and decides motions in limine prior to trial.

2.   Pretrial Conferences.   Pretrial conferences in criminal cases are held only in complex cases or those involving several attorneys.

3.   Pretrial Hearings.   Suppression, *Starks,* and *Daubert* hearings are typically held at least two weeks prior to trial. The government is required to file proposed findings of fact and conclusions of law prior to the commencement of the hearing. The parties may request leave to supplement proposed findings of fact after the hearing.

4.   Continuances.   In all criminal cases, before a continuance will be granted, defense counsel must obtain the defendant's written consent to a continuance. Such consent should be given using the court's Speedy Trial Act acknowledgment of rights form. This form must be signed by the defendant and docketed before any continuance is issued.

5.   Voir Dire.   Judge Slomsky conducts voir dire in criminal cases. Counsel may submit proposed voir dire questions.

6.   Proposed Jury Instructions and Verdict Forms.   Each party must submit to the court and serve on opposing counsel proposed points for charge and any proposed jury interrogatories no later than seven days prior to the trial date. Each point for charge and proposed jury interrogatory should be numbered and on a separate sheet of paper identifying the name of the requesting party. Each proposed instruction must be submitted with authority. If a model jury instruction is used, the party submitting it should state whether the proposed instruction is unchanged or modified. If a party modifies a model instruction, additions should be underlined and deletions should be placed in brackets.

7.   Trial Memorandum.   At least one week prior to the trial date, the government must file a trial memorandum setting forth the essential elements of the offenses, the facts that it intends to present, the identity of each witness it intends to call, a statement of the substance of each witness's testimony, and any legal issues. The defendant is not required to file a trial memorandum but may do so.

8.   Guilty Plea Memorandum.   The government must submit a guilty plea memorandum at least two days prior to the change of plea hearing. The memorandum should include the elements of each offense to which the defendant is pleading guilty and legal citations for the elements, the maximum statutory penalties for each offense, the terms of any plea agreement, and the factual basis for the plea.

9.   Motions for Downward Departure.   A motion for downward departure, except a motion filed under § 5K1.1 of the United States Sentencing Guidelines, must be filed two weeks prior to the sentencing date. The motion should include legal and factual support for the proposed departure. A government motion pursuant to § 5K1.1 must be filed at least one week before sentencing.

10.   Sentencing Memoranda.   Judge Slomsky requires the submission of sentencing memoranda by both the government and the defendant no later than one week before sentencing. The memorandum must set forth any legal authority relied upon by the party.

One copy of each sentencing memorandum, motion, and response should be served on the opposing party, the court (chambers, room 4000), and the United States Probation Office when the original is filed.

If a defendant is responsible for restitution, the government must submit sufficient information in its sentencing memorandum to enable the court to determine entitlement, the name and the address of each victim, the amount of loss for each victim, and documentary support for each amount. If liability for restitution is joint and several, the government should itemize the restitution amount for which each defendant is responsible.

IN THE UNITED STATES DISTRICT COURT
FOR THE EASTERN DISTRICT OF PENNSYLVANIA

	:	CIVIL ACTION
v.	:	NO.

REPORT OF RULE 26(f) MEETING

In accordance with Federal Rule of Civil Procedure 26(f), counsel for the parties conferred on (date) and submit the following report of their meeting for the court's consideration:

1. Discussion of Claims, Defenses and Relevant Issues

    You should assume that the court has read the complaint and is familiar with the claims. However, the facts supporting those claims and defenses are unknown. Therefore, **counsel shall set forth concisely the factual background that the parties contend support their claims and defenses.**

    Summarize your discussion of primary issues, threshold issues and those issues on which the parties will need to conduct discovery. Identify what information each party needs in discovery as well as when and why. Also indicate likely motions and their timing.

2. Informal Disclosures

    State the parties' agreement on timing, form and scope of informal disclosures. Specifically identify not only the information listed in Rule 26(a)(1), but any additional information the parties agree to disclose informally.

    Keep in mind that self-executing discovery must not be delayed until the pretrial conference. If the parties have not made the Rule 26(a) initial disclosures within the time required by the Court's Order scheduling the pretrial conference, they should explain why not.

3. Formal Discovery

    Indicate nature, sequence and timing of formal discovery, as well as any need to conduct discovery in phases to prepare for the filing of motions or for settlement discussions. Specifically delineate what discovery will be conducted formally.

    The discovery deadline should normally be no more than 120–150 days from the date of the Rule 16 pretrial conference. If the parties believe there are compelling reasons for a longer period of discovery, state them.

    The parties are required to address procedures to preserve electronically stored information, to avoid inadvertent privilege waivers, and to determine the form in which electronic information will be produced. The cost of producing the information must be discussed.

4. Electronic Discovery

    It is expected that the parties will reach an agreement on how to conduct electronic discovery. In the event the parties cannot reach such an agreement before the Rule 16 scheduling conference, the court will enter an order incorporating default standards. The default order can be viewed at www.paed.uscourts.gov.

    The parties shall discuss the parameters of their anticipated e-discovery at the Rule 26(f) conference and shall be prepared to address e-discovery at the Rule 16 scheduling conference with the court.

Judge Joel H. Slomsky

5. Expert Witness Disclosures

    Indicate agreement on timing and sequence of disclosure of the identity and anticipated testimony of expert witnesses, including whether depositions of experts will be needed.

    The parties should expect that the court requires expert reports to be exchanged simultaneously. If there are compelling reasons to stagger the production of expert reports, state them.

6. Early Settlement or Resolution

    The parties must familiarize themselves with Local Rule 53.3 before responding. Recite the parties' discussion about early resolution through ADR, motion or otherwise explain what steps were taken by counsel to advise the client of alternative dispute resolution options.

    Explain any decision not to seek early resolution and what mediation options the parties may consider and when mediation would be appropriate.

7. Trial

    If a date certain is requested, state the reasons. Generally, if requested, a firm trial date will be scheduled. Please provide the estimated length of trial.

    Please provide a statement whether all parties agree to a referral of this case to U.S. Magistrate Judge Carol Sandra Moore Wells for trial.[*]

8. Other Matters

    Indicate discussion and any agreement on matters not addressed above.

_____
(Attorney Signature)

_____
(Attorney Signature)

Rev 082106

---

[*] Magistrate judges are authorized, with agreement of the parties, to try any civil case, jury or non-jury, with appeals going directly to the Third Circuit. All cases assigned to Judge Wells are given a firm trial date.

IN THE UNITED STATES DISTRICT COURT
FOR THE EASTERN DISTRICT OF PENNSYLVANIA

	:	CIVIL ACTION
	:	
v.	:	NO. xx--xxxx
	:	
	:	

ORDER GOVERNING ELECTRONIC DISCOVERY

AND NOW, this _____ day of _____, 20___, in anticipation of the Rule 16 conference, it is **ORDERED** as follows:

1. **Introduction**. In the event the parties cannot reach an agreement on how to conduct electronic discovery ("e-discovery") before the Rule 16 scheduling conference, the following default standards shall apply until such time, if ever, the parties conduct e-discovery on a consensual basis.

2. **Exchange of e-discovery materials**. Prior to the Rule 26(f) conference, the parties shall exchange the following information:

   a. a list of the most likely custodians of relevant electronic materials, including a brief description of each person's title and responsibilities;

   b. a list of each relevant electronic system that has been in place at all relevant times and a general description of each system, including the nature, scope, character, organization, and formats employed in each system.

   c. the parties should also include other pertinent information about their electronic documents and whether those electronic documents are of limited accessibility, that is, those created or used by electronic media no longer in use, maintained in redundant electronic storage media, or for which retrieval involves substantial cost;

   d. the name of the individual responsible for the party's electronic document retention policies ("the retention coordinator");

   e. a general description of the party's electronic document retention policies.

   f. the name of the individual who shall serve as the party's "e-discovery liaison;"

   g. a description of any problems reasonably anticipated to arise in connection with e-discovery.

   To the extent that the state of the pleadings does not permit a meaningful discussion of the above issues by the time of the Rule 26(f) conference, the parties shall either agree on a date by which this information will be mutually exchanged or submit the issue for resolution by the court at the Rule 16 scheduling conference.

3. **E-discovery conference**. The parties shall discuss the parameters of their anticipated e-discovery at the Rule 26(f) conference and shall be prepared to address e-discovery at the Rule 16 scheduling conference with the court.

4. **E-discovery liaison**. To promote communication and cooperation between the parties, each party shall designate a single individual through whom all e-discovery requests and responses are made ("the e-discovery liaison"). Regardless of whether the e-discovery liaison is an attorney (in-house or outside counsel), a third party consultant, or an employee of the party, he or she must be:

   a. familiar with the party's electronic systems and capabilities in order to explain these systems and answer relevant questions;

   b. knowledgeable about the technical aspects of e-discovery, including electronic document storage, organization, and format issues;

c. prepared to participate in e-discovery dispute resolutions; and,

  d. responsible for organizing the party's e-discovery efforts to insure consistency and thoroughness and, generally, to facilitate the e-discovery process.

  5. **Search methodology.** If the parties intend to employ an electronic search to locate relevant electronic documents, the parties shall disclose any restrictions as to scope and method which might affect their ability to conduct a complete electronic search of the electronic documents. The parties shall reach agreement as to the method of searching, and the words, terms, and phrases to be searched with the assistance of the respective e-discovery liaisons, who are charged with familiarity with the parties' respective systems. The parties also shall reach agreement as to the timing and conditions of any additional searches which may become necessary in the normal course of discovery. To minimize the expense, the parties may consider limiting the scope of the electronic search (e.g., time frames, fields, document types).

  6. **Timing of e-discovery.** Discovery of electronic documents shall proceed in the following sequenced fashion:

  a. after receiving requests for document production, the parties shall search their documents, other than those identified as limited accessibility electronic documents, and produce responsive electronic documents, all in accordance with FED. R. CIV. P. 26(b)(2);

  b. electronic searches of documents identified as of limited accessibility shall not be conducted until the initial electronic document search has been completed;

  c. requests for information expected to be found in limited accessibility documents must be narrowly focused with a factual basis supporting the request; and,

  d. on-site inspections of electronic media under FED. R. CIV. P.34(b) shall not be permitted, absent exceptional circumstances where good cause and specific need have been demonstrated.

  7. **Format.** If, during the course of the Rule 26(f) conference, the parties cannot agree to the format for document production, electronic documents shall be produced to the requesting party as image files (e.g., PDF or TIFF). When the image file is produced, the producing party must preserve the integrity of the electronic document's contents, i.e., the original formatting of the document, its metadata and, where applicable, its revision history. After initial production in image file format is complete, a party must demonstrate particularized need for production of electronic documents in their native format.

  8. **Retention.** Within the first thirty (30) days of discovery, the parties shall negotiate an agreement that outlines the steps each party shall take to segregate and preserve the integrity of all relevant electronic documents. In order to avoid later accusations of spoliation, a FED. R. CIV. P. 30(b)(6) deposition of each party's retention coordinator may be appropriate.

  The retention coordinators shall:

  a. take steps to ensure that e-mail of identified custodians shall not be permanently deleted in the ordinary course of business and that electronic documents maintained by the individual custodians shall not be altered;

  b. provide notice as to the criteria used for spam and/or virus filtering of e-mails and attachments; Documents filtered out by such systems shall be deemed non-responsive so long as the criteria underlying the filtering are reasonable.

   Within seven (7) days of identifying the relevant document custodians, the retention coordinators shall implement the above procedures and each party's counsel shall file a statement of compliance.

  9. **Privilege.** Electronic documents that contain privileged information or attorney work product shall be immediately returned if the documents appear on their face to have been inadvertently produced or if there is notice of the inadvertent production. All copies shall be returned or destroyed by the receiving party.

10. **Costs**. Generally, the costs of discovery shall be borne by each party. However, the court will apportion the costs of electronic discovery upon a showing of good cause.

JOEL H. SLOMSKY, J.

Judge Joel H. Slomsky

FORM

**UNITED STATES DISTRICT COURT
FOR THE EASTERN DISTRICT OF PENNSYLVANIA**

UNITED STATES OF AMERICACriminal No._____

vs.

_____

I, _____ (Defendant), have consulted with my counsel concerning my right under the Speedy Trial Act and my right to a speedy trial under the Sixth Amendment to the U.S. Constitution. I do not oppose a continuance of my trial, now scheduled for _____, **20__ and the Hearing on Motions Scheduled for** _____, **20__**, and agree that the ends of justice served by a continuance outweigh the best interest of the public and myself in a speedy trial. I understand that the time between the filing of a Motion to continue and the new trial date to be set by the Court will be excluded for purposes of computing the time within which my trial must commence under the Speedy Trial Act, and I also agree that this delay will not deprive me of my speedy trial rights under the Sixth Amendment. I understand that if I do not wish to sign this document, the Court will hold a hearing at which I will be present.

_____
Witness SignatureDefendant Signature

_____
Date

Judge Lawrence F. Stengel

Judge Stengel was born in Lancaster, Pennsylvania, in 1952. He is a graduate of St. Joseph's University and the University of Pittsburgh School of Law. From 1980 to 1990, Judge Stengel was in private practice. In 1990, he was appointed by Governor Robert Casey to the Lancaster County Court of Common Pleas and was elected to that court in 1991. Judge Stengel was appointed to the United States District Court for the Eastern District of Pennsylvania on June 21, 2004.

PRELIMINARY GENERAL MATTERS

1. *Correspondence with the Court.* Judge Stengel requests counsel to please not write letters directly to the court, or send or designate copies of correspondence among and between counsel to the court, except:

(1) when letters of transmittal accompany documents required to be sent to, or filed with, the court or in another official office in the courthouse;

(2) when counsel are specifically requested by the court to communicate some information to the court by letter;

(3) when there is an uncontested request for a continuance of the Rule 16 scheduling order deadlines not affecting the trial date or pool placement;

(4) when the participation of counsel in the case is expected to be affected by a personal matter concerning counsel, a party, a witness, or counsel's immediate family, such as medical problems, vacation plans, or other similarly personal problems or questions; or

(5) to confirm or advise the court that a case has been settled, dismissed, or otherwise finally disposed.

All other written communications with the court concerning any case assigned to Judge Stengel's calendar should be by the filing of a pleading, motion, application, brief, legal memorandum, busy slip, or other similar filing provided for in the Federal Rules of Civil or Criminal Procedure or the Local Rules of Civil or Criminal Procedure. *Do not write letters to the court that are properly the subject of these filings.*

When a written communication concerning a case cannot timely address a problem, counsel may initiate necessary telephone communications with Judge Stengel's chambers. Issues appropriately addressed by telephone contact include:

(1) scheduling of conferences or proceedings, including pretrial and trial conferences and the attendance of witnesses;

(2) exhibit handling or arrangements for video replay;

(3) arrangements for telephone conferences regarding discovery disputes; and

(4) requests for absolutely necessary extensions of time to file any response, reply, brief, memorandum of law, or the like.

All such inquiries should be directed to the appropriate deputy clerk. Counsel should submit current telephone numbers, fax numbers, and any changes to the Clerk's Office, and to the appropriate deputy clerk.

2. *Communication with Law Clerks and Deputy Clerks.* Judge Stengel strongly discourages communication with law clerks. Telephone inquiries regarding civil cases should be directed to Patricia A. Cardella, Judge Stengel's civil deputy clerk, at 267-299-7760. Telephone inquiries regarding criminal cases should be directed to Laura L. Buenzle, Judge Stengel's criminal deputy clerk, at 267-299-7769.

3. **Telephone Conferences.** Judge Stengel will hold telephone conferences to resolve scheduling matters or discovery disputes. The court will notify counsel of the date and time for the telephone conference. In a civil case, counsel for the moving party will be responsible for initiating the telephone conference and contacting Judge Stengel through his secretary/deputy clerk after all parties are present on the call. In a criminal case, the United States Attorney's Office will be responsible for initiating the call and contacting Judge Stengel through his criminal deputy clerk after all parties are present on the call.

4. **Oral Arguments and Evidentiary Hearings.** Judge Stengel does not set aside certain days or times for oral argument, motions, or evidentiary hearings. Hearings and argument are scheduled when warranted.

5. **Pro Hac Vice Admissions.** To be admitted pro hac vice, associate counsel of record should submit a written motion for admission. The admission of out-of-the-jurisdiction counsel pro hac vice does not relieve associate counsel of responsibility for the matter before the court.

6. **Faxes.** Unless specifically requested or explicitly permitted by the court, parties should not transmit pleadings, motions, or other filings by fax to chambers.

7. **Courtesy Copies.** Counsel should send one courtesy copy of a motion, brief, or memorandum to chambers at the time of filing. If the motion, brief, or memorandum was electronically filed, you do not need to provide chambers with a courtesy copy.

CIVIL CASES
Pretrial Procedure

1. **Rule 16 Conference.** The court will schedule a preliminary pretrial conference as described in Fed.R.Civ.P. 16(b) and (c) shortly after a defendant has filed an appearance or pleading. At least three business days prior to the pretrial conference, *counsel must complete and submit to Judge Stengel's Philadelphia chambers the joint status report of the Rule 26(f) meeting.* A blank form for this report will be included with the Rule 16 conference notice. It will also be available on the website with Judge Stengel's policies and procedures.

The court relies on counsels' good-faith compliance with Rule 26(f) *in all respects.* The Rule 26(f) meeting should take place as early in the case as possible, but no later than 21 days before the scheduled Rule 16 conference. Outstanding motions will *not* excuse the requirements of holding the meeting and submitting the plan. The meeting should be a meaningful and substantive discussion to formulate the proposed discovery plan required by the rule. *Parties who do not comply will have no voice at the scheduling conference and may be subject to additional sanctions.* Initial disclosures pursuant to Rule 26(a) should be completed no later than seven days before the Rule 16 conference.

It is also expected that the parties will reach an agreement on how to conduct electronic discovery. The parties should discuss the parameters of their anticipated e-discovery at the Rule 26(f) conference and should be prepared to address e-discovery at the Rule 16 conference with the court. In the event the parties cannot reach such an agreement before the Rule 16 conference, the court will enter an order incorporating default standards, a sample of which is found on the website below Judge Stengel's policies and procedures.

At the initial pretrial conference, the parties should be prepared to address all topics listed in Local Rule of Civil Procedure 16.1(b) and Fed.R.Civ.P. 16(b) and (c), the progress of self-executing disclosure under Fed.R.Civ.P. 26(a), and any settlement or mediation proposals. The court will issue a Rule 16 scheduling order at the conclusion of the conference.

Lead trial counsel must attend the Rule 16 conference. Counsel taking part in any pretrial conference must be prepared to speak on every subject, including settlement, and have authority from their clients to do so. Counsel must be prepared to discuss all claims and defenses in detail, and should have a thorough comprehension of the facts.

2.   Final Pretrial Conference.   There will be a final pretrial conference within 10 days of the trial date or the date the case will be placed in the trial pool. Counsel must comply with Local Rule 16.1 regarding the submission of pretrial memoranda. These memoranda must be filed with a courtesy copy to chambers, no later than seven days prior to the pretrial conference.

During this conference, the court will address factual and legal issues, the admissibility of exhibits, scheduling issues, and settlement. At the conclusion of the conference, the court will then issue a final pretrial order or a final scheduling order in a complex case.

Continuances and Extensions

Unless there is good cause to justify a change, the parties are expected to adhere to the dates contained in the scheduling order. The court will grant a continuance or extension based on a stipulation of all parties if the continuance or extension does not affect the discovery cutoff or trial date. If a continuance or extension will affect the discovery cutoff or trial date, counsel should make a written request that sets forth the basis for the continuance or extension and indicates whether the other party or parties agree to or oppose the request. A request for an extension or continuance of the trial date, discovery deadline, or the deadline for filing dispositive motions must be made sufficiently prior to the due date to allow time for the court to consider it. These requests should be made by motion, although an unopposed request may be made by letter to the court.

General Motion Practice

1.   Oral Argument on Motions.   If the judge believes oral argument will be helpful in deciding a matter, he will schedule it, particularly when it involves a dispositive motion. A party desiring oral argument should request it by letter or in the body of the motion or responsive pleading.

2.   Reply and Surreply Briefs.   Reply and surreply briefs are *not permitted* unless leave to file them is granted upon motion of a party.

3.   Length and Content of Briefs or Legal Memoranda.   All grounds for relief should be set forth in a single, comprehensive motion. A motion to dismiss, for example, should not be divided into separate motions for each count, but rather should include all bases for relief. *Any brief or memorandum filed in support of the motion should be limited to 25 pages.* This includes the table of contents and any attachments or addenda. If a party requires more than 25 pages to explain its position to the court, a motion to exceed the page limit should be filed, setting forth good cause for granting an exception to this rule.

4.   Rule 56 Motions.   With any motion for summary judgment pursuant to Rule 56 of the Federal Rules of Civil Procedure, there should be filed a separate, short, and concise statement of the material facts, in numbered paragraphs, as to which the moving party contends there is no genuine issue to be tried.

The papers opposing a motion for summary judgment must include a separate, short, and concise statement of the material facts, responding to the numbered paragraphs set forth in the statement required in the previous paragraph, as to which it is contended there exists a genuine issue to be tried.

Statements of material facts in support of or in opposition to a motion must include references to the parts of the record that support the statements. All material facts set forth in the statement required to be served by the moving party may be taken by the court as admitted unless controverted by the opposing party.

Discovery Matters

1. Length of Discovery Period and Extensions. In standard track cases, the court usually allows up to 90 days from the date of the Rule 16 conference to complete discovery. In special management cases, the court will permit additional time to conduct discovery if the parties identify a need to do so at the Rule 16 conference, or any subsequent status conferences. A case will ordinarily be listed for trial 30 to 60 days after the completion of discovery.

2. Discovery Conferences and Dispute Resolution. When a discovery default occurs, the court will consider a motion to compel under Local Civil Rule 26.1(g). If the parties are unable to resolve the matter by themselves, after the reasonable efforts required by Local Civil Rule 26.1(f), the party seeking relief may file a motion to compel. *The motion must not exceed five pages, must not contain exhibits, and must not include a brief or memorandum of law.*

Once a motion to compel is filed, the court will schedule a telephone or in-person conference to resolve the dispute as soon as possible. The responding party may file a response within five days. This response should also be limited to five pages and should not include exhibits or a brief or memorandum of law. If the parties resolve the dispute, the conference will be canceled. If the court's intervention is required, the court may impose sanctions in favor of the prevailing party. Judge Stengel permits telephone conferences to resolve disputes during depositions in cases where the deposition would otherwise have to be adjourned.

3. Confidentiality Agreements. The court will only approve confidentiality or sealing orders for good cause shown.

Settlement

1. General Approach to Settlement and Nonjury Cases. Settlement will be discussed at the initial Rule 16 status conference and at any subsequent conference. The court will not participate in settlement negotiations in nonjury cases. A case may be referred to a magistrate judge for a settlement conference.

Arbitration

1. General Approach to Arbitration. Judge Stengel will not hold a Rule 16 conference or issue a scheduling order in arbitration track cases, unless there is a de novo appeal from an arbitration award. The parties are expected to complete all discovery prior to the date of the arbitration hearing.

2. Scheduling of Trial De Novo from Arbitration. Upon demand for trial de novo from an arbitration award, the court will issue a scheduling order setting the date for trial at the earliest date available to the court. Ordinarily, neither discovery nor dispositive motions will be allowed after the arbitration hearing is held.

Final Pretrial Memoranda

1. **Required Form of Pretrial Memoranda.** Unless otherwise ordered by the court, the pretrial memorandum should be prepared in accordance with the provisions of Local Rule of Civil Procedure 16.1(c), and should also include the following items:
   a. All stipulations of counsel.
   b. A statement of objection to (1) the admissibility of any exhibit based on authenticity, (2) the admissibility of any evidence expected to be offered for any reason (except relevancy), (3) the adequacy of the qualifications of an expert witness expected to testify, and (4) the admissibility of any opinion testimony from lay witnesses pursuant to Federal Rule of Evidence 701. Such objection must describe with particularity the ground and the authority for the objection.
   c. Deposition testimony (including videotaped deposition testimony) that the party intends to offer during its case-in-chief. The statement should include citations to the page and line number and the opposing party's counter-designations.

Injunctions

1. **Scheduling and Expedited Discovery.** Judge Stengel will promptly list any request for a temporary restraining order (TRO) or a preliminary injunction assigned to him.

2. **Prehearing Conference.** Judge Stengel will hold a prehearing conference to discuss discovery issues, narrow the issues of contention, and allocate time for the hearing. Expedited discovery will be discussed and, when appropriate, ordered at the conclusion of the prehearing conference.

3. **Proposed Findings of Fact and Conclusions of Law.** Judge Stengel requires submission of proposed findings of fact and conclusions of law for TRO and injunction hearings. The court will set the time for submission of these items at the prehearing conference.

Trial Procedure

1. **Scheduling Cases.** A date for trial or for placing the case in the trial pool will be determined at the initial Rule 16 conference. Once a case is placed in the trial pool, counsel, parties, and witnesses should be ready to start trial upon 48 hours telephone notice. Ordinarily, a case will begin on or shortly after its trial pool date. Questions relating to scheduling matters should be directed to Judge Stengel's civil deputy clerk.

2. **Cases Involving Out-of-Town Parties or Witnesses.** Judge Stengel schedules the trial of cases involving out-of-town counsel, parties, or witnesses in the same manner as all other cases. Counsel are responsible for the scheduling of witnesses.

3. **Conflicts of Counsel.** Counsel should notify the court immediately upon hearing of any unavoidable and compelling professional or personal conflicts affecting the trial schedule.

4. **Note-taking by Jurors.** Judge Stengel permits jurors to take notes.

5. **Voir Dire.** Judge Stengel permits counsel to conduct all voir dire in civil cases. There is generally a time limit of 30 minutes for each side for voir dire.

6. **Trial Briefs.** Parties should submit a trial brief only if a new or unique point of law is involved.

7. **Motions in Limine.** The time for filing motions in limine will be determined at the Rule 16 conference and will be confirmed in the scheduling order.

8. **Examination of Witnesses Out of Sequence.** The court will permit counsel to examine his or her own witnesses out of turn for the convenience of a witness.

9. **Opening Statements and Summations.** In most cases, the court permits 20 to 30 minutes for an opening statement and 30 to 45 minutes for a summation or closing argument.

10. **Examination of Witnesses or Argument by More Than One Attorney.** More than one attorney for a party may examine different witnesses or argue different points of law before the court. Only one attorney for each side may examine the same witness or address the jury during the opening statement or summation.

11. **Examination of Witnesses Beyond Redirect and Recross.** The court will permit limited redirect and recross-examination on matters not previously covered by cross-examination or in special circumstances.

12. **Videotaped Testimony.** Videotaped testimony should begin with the witness being sworn. Counsel should bring objections to the court's attention at the time of the final pretrial conference. After the court rules on any objections, counsel should edit the tapes before offering the videotaped testimony at trial.

13. **Reading of Material Into the Record.** Judge Stengel has no special practice or policy regarding reading stipulations, pleadings, or discovery material into the record at trial.

14. **Preparation of Exhibits.** Exhibits should be pre-marked and exchanged in accordance with the final pretrial order. On the day trial is scheduled to commence, counsel should provide one copy of each exhibit and a copy of a schedule of exhibits to the court.

15. **Offering Exhibits Into Evidence.** Unless the parties have an agreement as to the admissibility of a proposed exhibit, a witness may not testify as to its content until it has been admitted into evidence.

16. **Directed Verdict Motions.** Motions for judgment as a matter of law in jury trials and motions for an involuntary dismissal in nonjury trials must be in writing. Oral argument on the motions is ordinarily permitted.

17. **Proposed Jury Instructions and Verdict Forms.** In his scheduling order, Judge Stengel typically requires that the parties submit proposed jury instructions on substantive issues and proposed verdict forms or special interrogatories for the jury no later than 10 days before the trial or trial pool date. Counsel should submit a copy of the proposed jury instructions to chambers via electronic mail at Chambers_of_Judge_Lawrence_F_Stengel@paed.uscourts.gov. Jury instructions need only be submitted with respect to substantive issues in the case. Proposed instructions on procedural matters such as the burden of proof, unanimity, and credibility are not necessary.

Each proposed instruction should be on a separate sheet of paper, double-spaced, and should *include citation to specific authority*. The court will not consider proposed instructions without citation to specific legal authority. Cases and model jury instructions that are cited should be accurately quoted and a page reference should be provided.

Counsel will have the opportunity to file supplemental points or proposed findings of fact and conclusions of law during trial as necessary.

If a model jury instruction is submitted, for instance, from Devitt & Blackmar, *Federal Jury Practice and Instructions,* the submitting party must state whether the proposed jury instruction is unchanged or modified. If a party modifies a model jury instruction, the additions should be underlined and deletions should be placed in brackets.

18. **Proposed Findings of Fact and Conclusions of Law.** Proposed findings of fact and conclusions of law in nonjury cases should be submitted at least seven days *before* the trial or trial pool date. They should be submitted to chambers on hard copy and via electronic

mail at Chambers_of_Judge_Lawrence_F_Stengel@paed.uscourts.gov. The parties may submit revised or supplemental findings of fact and conclusions of law with specific reference to trial evidence at the conclusion of the case. A schedule for the submission of revised findings/conclusions will be discussed at the conclusion of trial.

19. **Unavailability of Witness.** If a witness is unavailable at the time of trial, as defined in Fed.R.Civ.P. 32(a)(3), the court expects an oral or videotaped deposition to be used at trial for that witness, whether the witness is a party, a non-party, or an expert. The unavailability of such witness *will not be a ground to delay* the commencement or progress of trial.

20. **Lay Witness Opinion.** Any party expecting to offer lay opinion testimony pursuant to Federal Rule of Evidence 701 regarding issues of liability or damages must provide the opposing parties with information or documents supporting the testimony at the time required for submission of expert reports.

Jury Deliberations

1. **Written Jury Instructions.** In the appropriate case, the court will give the jury a copy of the written jury instructions.

2. **Exhibits in the Jury Room.** After the jury has been instructed and taken to the jury room to begin deliberations, the court and counsel will discuss which exhibits should go out with the jury for their consideration during deliberations.

3. **Handling of Jury Requests to Read Back Testimony or Replay Tapes.** At the jury's request, the court may permit the deputy clerk to read portions of testimony back to the jury or to replay the audiotaped or videotaped testimony.

4. **Availability of Counsel During Jury Deliberation.** Unless excused by the court, counsel must remain in the courthouse during jury deliberations.

5. **Taking the Verdict and Special Verdicts.** Ordinarily, the court will submit interrogatories to the jury. The courtroom deputy will take the verdict in the presence of the court, counsel, and the parties.

6. **Polling the Jury.** If requested by counsel, the court will poll the jury.

7. **Interviewing the Jury.** Judge Stengel will allow counsel to interview jurors but will instruct the jury that they are not required to talk to the attorneys.

CRIMINAL CASES

1. **Approach to Oral Argument and Motions.** The court will generally permit oral argument on a substantive motion in a criminal case upon request.

2. **Pretrial Conferences.** Judge Stengel does not generally hold a telephone scheduling conference with counsel in criminal cases, unless counsel specifically request one. All scheduling of criminal matters is handled by the judge's criminal deputy clerk.

3. **Voir Dire.** In criminal cases, Judge Stengel will conduct voir dire, based, in part, on questions submitted by counsel. After the voir dire is concluded, the court will permit counsel to suggest follow-up questions. Counsel should submit proposed voir dire questions in writing seven days before the trial date.

4. **Sentencing Memoranda.** Judge Stengel requires the parties to submit objections to the presentence-investigation report and sentencing memoranda in accordance with the notice of sentencing, which will be issued shortly after the entry of a guilty plea or conviction.

OTHER MATTERS

1.   Briefs of Cases on Appeal.   Judge Stengel welcomes copies of appellate briefs when a decision he has made is appealed.

2.   Consultation with Opposing Counsel.   In general, Judge Stengel expects counsel to bring matters to his attention only after they have been discussed with opposing counsel. When communicating with the court, counsel should be prepared to state the position of opposing counsel.

3.   Professionalism.   Judge Stengel will insist on punctuality and courtesy from counsel to the court and to each other, both in the presence of the court and otherwise. The examination of witnesses should be conducted from the lectern or from counsel table. Counsel should rise to address the court and should seek permission of the court before approaching witnesses or the bench. In addition, counsel will direct all comments to the court or to the witness under examination and not to other counsel or to the jury. To the extent possible, the parties should notify the court of any issues that will need to be ruled upon at the start of the day's proceedings, or during a recess out of the jury's presence. Sidebar conferences are permitted when necessary.

Joint Status Report Pursuant to Rule 26(f)

Caption: _____   Civil Action No: _____

Basis of Jurisdiction: _____

Jury Trial: _____   Non-Jury Trial: _____   Arbitration: _____

Plaintiff's counsel participating in the Rule 16 Conference: _____
Defendant's counsel participating in the Rule 16 Conference: _____
Do counsel have full authority to settle at a Rule 16 Conference?: _____
    If not, client with such authority who will attend conference: _____

When did the parties hold the Rule 26 Conference? _____
When did the parties comply with Rule 26(a)'s duty of self-executing disclosure? _____

Does either side expect to file a case-dispositive motion? _____ (yes/no)
    If yes, under what Rule _____
    If yes, specify the issue _____
    Proposed deadline for filing dispositive motions: _____

Does either side anticipate the use of experts? _____
    If yes, what is the proposed deadline for expert discovery? _____

Approximate date case should be trial-ready: _____
    Time for Plaintiff's case: _____   Time for Defendant's case: _____

Is a settlement conference likely to be helpful? _____   If so, when:
    Early _____ (yes/no)   After Discovery _____ (yes/no)

What is the outcome of your discussions with your clients about proceeding before a Magistrate Judge for final disposition? _____

Plan for Discovery:

1. The parties anticipate that discovery should be completed within _____ days.
2. What is the minimum amount of time necessary to complete discovery prior to an ADR session, should one be ordered or agreed to? _____
3. Have the parties discussed issues relating to claims of privilege or of protection as trial-preparation material, as required by Rule 26(f)(3)(D)? _____
4. Identify any other discovery issues which should be addressed at the Rule 16 Conference, including limitations on discovery, protective Orders needed, or other elements which should be included in a particularized discovery plan. _____
5. If you contend the discovery period should exceed 90 days, please state reason: _____

This form should be faxed to Chambers at 267-299-5068,
mailed to Chambers, or hand-delivered to Chambers at
3809 U.S. Courthouse, 601 Market Street, Philadelphia, PA 19106

Judge Lawrence F. Stengel

IN THE UNITED STATES DISTRICT COURT
FOR THE EASTERN DISTRICT OF PENNSYLVANIA

Plaintiff	:	CIVIL ACTION
	:	
v.	:	NO.
	:	
Defendant	:	

ORDER GOVERNING ELECTRONIC DISCOVERY

AND NOW, this _____ day of _____, 20__, following a pretrial conference, it is hereby **ORDERED** that the following default standards shall apply until such time, if ever, the parties conduct e-discovery on a consensual basis:

1. **Exchange of e-discovery materials:** Prior to _____, the parties shall exchange the following information:

    a. A list of the most likely custodians of relevant electronic materials, including a brief description of each person's title and responsibilities;

    b. A list of each relevant electronic system that has been in place at all relevant times and a general description of each system, including the nature, scope, character, organization, and formats employed in each system;

    c. The parties should also include other pertinent information about their electronic documents and whether those electronic documents are of limited accessibility, that is, those created or used by electronic media no longer in use, maintained in redundant electronic storage media, or for which retrieval involves substantial cost;

    d. The name of the individual responsible for the party's electronic document retention policies ("the retention coordinator");

    e. A general description of the party's electronic document retention policies;

    f. The name of the individual who shall serve as the party's "e-discovery liaison;"

    g. A description of any problems reasonably anticipated to arise in connection with e-discovery.

2. **E-discovery liaison:** No later than _____, to promote communication and cooperation between the parties, each party shall designate a single individual through whom all e-discovery requests and responses are made ("the e-discovery liaison"). Regardless of whether the e-discovery liaison is an attorney (in-house or outside counsel), a third party consultant, or an employee of the party, he or she must be:

    a. Familiar with the party's electronic systems and capabilities in order to explain these systems and answer relevant questions;

    b. Knowledgeable about the technical aspects of e-discovery, including electronic document storage, organization, and format issues;

    c. Prepared to participate in e-discovery dispute resolutions; and,

    d. Responsible for organizing the party's e-discovery efforts to insure consistency and thoroughness and, generally, to facilitate the e-discovery process.

3. **Search methodology:** If the parties intend to employ an electronic search to locate relevant electronic documents, the parties shall disclose, within thirty days, any restrictions as to the scope and the method which might affect their ability to conduct a complete electronic search of the electronic

documents. The parties shall reach agreement as to the method of searching, and the words, terms, and phrases to be searched with the assistance of the respective e-discovery liaisons, who are charged with familiarity with the parties' respective systems. The parties also shall reach agreement as to the timing and conditions of any additional searches which may become necessary in the normal course of discovery. To minimize the expense, the parties may consider limiting the scope of the electronic search (e.g., time frames, fields, document types).

    4. **Timing of e-discovery:** Discovery of electronic documents shall proceed in the following sequenced fashion:

        a. After receiving requests for document production, the parties shall search their documents, other than those identified as limited accessibility electronic documents, and produce responsive electronic documents in accordance with Rule 26(b)(2) of the Federal Rules of Civil Procedure;

        b. Electronic searches of documents identified as of limited accessibility shall not be conducted until the initial electronic document search has been completed;

        c. Requests for information expected to be found in limited accessibility documents must be narrowly focused with a factual basis supporting the request; and,

        d. On-site inspections of electronic media under Rule 34(b) shall not be permitted, absent exceptional circumstances where good cause and specific need have been demonstrated.

    5. **Format:** If the parties cannot agree to the format for document production, electronic documents shall be produced to the requesting party as image files (e.g., PDF or TIFF). When the image file is produced, the producing party must preserve the integrity of the electronic document's contents, i.e., the original formatting of the document, its metadata and, where applicable, its revision history. After initial production in image file format is complete, a party must demonstrate particularized need for production of electronic documents in their native format.

    6. **Retention:** The parties shall negotiate an agreement that outlines the steps each party shall take to segregate and preserve the integrity of all relevant electronic documents. In order to avoid later accusations of spoliation, a Rule 30(b)(6) deposition of each party's retention coordinator may be appropriate. The retention coordinators shall:

        a. Take steps to ensure that e-mail of identified custodians shall not be permanently deleted in the ordinary course of business and that electronic documents maintained by the individual custodians shall not be altered;

        b. Provide notice as to the criteria used for spam and/or virus filtering of e-mails and attachments; documents filtered out by such systems shall be deemed non-responsive so long as the criteria underlying the filtering are reasonable.

Within seven days of identifying the relevant document custodians, the retention coordinators shall implement the above procedures and each party's counsel shall file a statement of compliance.

    7. **Privilege:** Electronic documents that contain privileged information or attorney work product shall be immediately returned if the documents appear on their face to have been inadvertently produced or if there is notice of the inadvertent production. All copies shall be returned or destroyed by the receiving party.

    8. **Costs:** Generally, the costs of discovery shall be borne by each party. However, the court will apportion the costs of electronic discovery upon a showing of good cause.

BY THE COURT:

LAWRENCE F. STENGEL, J.

Judge R. Barclay Surrick

Judge Surrick was born in Media, Pennsylvania, in 1937. He received a B.A. from Dickinson College in 1960, a J.D. from Dickinson College in 1965, and an LL.M. from the University of Virginia School of Law in 1982. Judge Surrick was in private practice from 1965 to 1977, where he also served as chief of the Appellate Division, Office of the Public Defender of Delaware County, Pennsylvania, from 1965 to 1974. From 1978 to 2000, he served as a judge on the Court of Common Pleas of Delaware County, Pennsylvania. Judge Surrick was appointed to the United States District Court for the Eastern District of Pennsylvania on June 5, 2000. He assumed senior status on February 1, 2011.

PRELIMINARY GENERAL MATTERS

1.   *Correspondence with the Court.* Judge Surrick permits correspondence with the court as long as the initiating attorney has discussed his or her request with other counsel.

2.   *Communication with Law Clerks.* Judge Surrick permits communication with law clerks concerning administrative aspects of the case. Counsel may not communicate with the law clerks on the merits of any case, and law clerks are not permitted to render advice to counsel and have no authority to grant continuances or to speak on behalf of the court.

3.   *Telephone Conferences.* Judge Surrick will handle disputes concerning discovery, scheduling, and requests for extensions of time by telephone conference. Prior to requesting a telephone conference, counsel should discuss the dispute with other counsel and send Judge Surrick a letter setting forth his or her position and the position of opposing counsel.

4.   *Oral Arguments and Evidentiary Hearings.* Judge Surrick will determine whether to schedule oral argument or an evidentiary hearing on a case-by-case basis. If counsel prefer either oral argument or an evidentiary hearing, they should request it by letter. Judge Surrick does not set aside any certain days or times for oral arguments or evidentiary hearings.

5.   *Pro Hac Vice Admissions.* Judge Surrick does not have a preference as to how counsel should submit a pro hac vice motion to the court. He will usually grant the motion if it is unopposed.

CIVIL CASES
Pretrial Procedure

1.   *Pretrial Conferences.* Judge Surrick regularly conducts pretrial conferences. Judge Surrick's civil deputy will initiate the scheduling of an initial pretrial conference. All pretrial conferences are held in chambers. Judge Surrick uses a standard pretrial order to notify counsel of the conference. The regular agenda topics at an initial pretrial conference include pleadings, service, joinder, settlement, jurisdictional defects, and the setting of discovery deadlines and a trial date. Judge Surrick uses a standard scheduling order pursuant to Rule 16, which is issued after the initial pretrial conference.

Judge Surrick will conduct settlement conferences if requested by all parties. Magistrate Judge Lynne A. Sitarski is Judge Surrick's assigned magistrate, and she will also conduct settlement conferences upon request of all parties.

Continuances and Extensions

1. **General Policy.** Judge Surrick has a general policy of adhering to originally scheduled dates unless a compelling reason is presented that justifies a change. This policy applies to briefing schedules, oral arguments, evidentiary hearings, pretrial conferences, discovery deadlines, and trial dates.

2. **Requests for Extensions and Continuances.** Counsel should advise Judge Surrick immediately, and before the date has run, of any compelling reason that justifies an extension or continuance of any originally scheduled date. Requests for continuances are preferably made by letter, setting forth the reasons and noting the agreement or disagreement of all other counsel. Original stipulations are to be submitted to chambers. Upon approval, the stipulation will be electronically filed. Requests may also be communicated by telephone conference with all counsel participating.

General Motion Practice

1. **Oral Argument on Motions.** Judge Surrick may schedule oral argument on motions when it is requested by counsel. Oral argument will be scheduled when Judge Surrick believes oral argument will be helpful in the decision-making process.

2. **Reply and Surreply Briefs.** Reply and surreply briefs should be filed only when absolutely necessary and only in circumstances where the parties wish to draw Judge Surrick's attention to controlling authority not previously cited by the parties.

3. **Chambers Copies of Motion Papers.** Judge Surrick requests that copies of motion papers be sent to chambers when the original is not wholly filed (with exhibits) on the ECF system and when the motion paper exceeds 50 pages.

Discovery Matters

1. **Length of Discovery Period.** In non-complex litigation, Judge Surrick regularly allows 120 days to complete discovery, which is measured from the entry of appearances by defense counsel. If counsel have been diligent and genuinely require additional time for discovery, Judge Surrick will usually grant additional time. In arbitration cases, discovery must be completed prior to the arbitration date.

2. **Discovery Conferences and Dispute Resolution.** The parties should make every effort to resolve discovery disputes without Judge Surrick's assistance. In the event that Judge Surrick decides a conference is necessary, the conference will be held by telephone or in chambers. In the event that the discovery dispute is complex, a motion should be filed.

3. **Confidentiality Agreements.** In the event that a confidentiality agreement is necessary, Judge Surrick prefers that counsel submit a stipulated order for consideration along with a memorandum setting forth proposed findings to meet the requirements of *Pansy v. Borough of Stroudsburg*, 23 F.3d 772 (3d Cir. 1994).

4. **Expert Witnesses.** Expert witness discovery is covered at the pretrial conference and is the subject of part of the scheduling order. In most cases, the plaintiff must serve expert reports and/or responses before the defendant. Generally, all expert witness discovery must be completed by the time all other discovery is completed.

Settlement

1. General Approach to Settlement and Nonjury Cases. Judge Surrick believes that the court's involvement in settlement conferences is generally helpful. At the request of all counsel in a jury case, a settlement conference will be scheduled before Judge Surrick or a magistrate judge. Settlement conferences in nonjury cases are referred to a magistrate judge.

2. Referral of Settlement Negotiations to Another District Court Judge. Judge Surrick will not refer settlement negotiations to another district court judge unless the parties present a compelling reason to do so and the judge to whom negotiations are to be referred consents.

Arbitration

1. General Approach to Arbitration Cases. Judge Surrick normally does not hold pretrial conferences nor does he issue scheduling orders in arbitration cases.

2. Scheduling of Trial De Novo from Arbitration. Upon demand for trial de novo after an arbitration award, the case will be scheduled for trial immediately. Judge Surrick's civil deputy will clear trial dates with counsel, and Judge Surrick will then issue a scheduling order setting deadlines for the parties' pretrial memoranda.

Injunctions

1. Scheduling and Expedited Discovery. Judge Surrick will promptly list any injunction matters assigned to him for a hearing. In appropriate cases, Judge Surrick will require expedited discovery.

When the plaintiff requests a temporary restraining order, plaintiff's counsel should contact Judge Surrick's civil deputy for a conference date and serve the motion, complaint, and notice of the conference date upon the opposing party and counsel prior to that date unless, for good cause shown, this is impossible.

2. Proposed Findings of Fact and Conclusions of Law. Judge Surrick requires submission of proposed findings of fact and conclusions of law in injunction cases as early as possible.

Trial Procedure

1. Scheduling of Cases. Judge Surrick schedules cases for a date certain. Complex, multi-party cases are specially listed.

2. Conflicts of Counsel. Counsel should notify Judge Surrick of any professional or personal conflicts affecting the trial schedule by telephone or in writing. Opposing counsel must also be notified promptly.

3. Cases Involving Out-of-Town Parties or Witnesses. Trial scheduling by Judge Surrick is not generally affected by the presence of out-of-town parties or witnesses. Judge Surrick leaves the scheduling of witnesses to counsel.

4. Note-taking by Jurors. Judge Surrick permits note-taking by jurors in complicated cases and in other cases in which it is deemed appropriate.

5. Trial Briefs. Judge Surrick encourages the submission of trial briefs in all cases.

6. Voir Dire. Judge Surrick sets a date for the submission of voir dire questions by scheduling order. In civil cases, Judge Surrick may conduct the voir dire or the attorneys may conduct voir dire out of the presence of Judge Surrick. This will be discussed at the final pretrial conference.

7. **Sidebars.** Judge Surrick permits sidebar conferences, but limits them if they become a distraction or interrupt the flow of the trial.

8. **In Limine Motions.** In limine motions should be presented in sufficient time so that they can be considered in advance of trial. Routine in limine motions will ordinarily be disposed of on the first day of trial or during the course of the trial.

9. **Examination of Witnesses Out of Sequence.** Judge Surrick will generally grant a request by counsel to take the testimony of a witness out of turn for the convenience of the witness subject to objection by opposing counsel.

10. **Opening Statements and Summations.** No time limits are placed on opening statements or summations by counsel. However, Judge Surrick believes that 30 to 45 minutes is usually adequate for an opening and 30 to 45 minutes is usually adequate for a summation in routine cases.

11. **Offers of Proof.** Judge Surrick requires that parties inquire of each other privately as to offers of proof regarding any witness or exhibit expected to be offered. If counsel cannot resolve such matters, Judge Surrick will rule on them upon application before a witness testifies or an exhibit is offered into evidence.

12. **Examination of Witnesses or Argument by More Than One Attorney.** More than one attorney for a party may examine different witnesses or argue different legal points before Judge Surrick. Ordinarily, more than one attorney for a party may not examine a single witness or argue the same legal point.

13. **Examination of Witnesses Beyond Redirect or Recross.** Judge Surrick has no general policy regarding further examination of a witness after redirect or recross has been completed. Where appropriate, he will allow it.

14. **Videotaped Testimony.** Judge Surrick requires that a list of all objections to videotaped trial testimony and a copy of the transcript be submitted to the court well in advance of the offering of such evidence. The videotape should then be edited to eliminate pauses and speed-ups to the maximum extent such final editing is possible. Videotape playback equipment should be brought into the courtroom at the beginning of the morning or afternoon session at which the videotape will be played. It should not block the view of counsel or the jury when not in use.

15. **Reading of Material Into the Record.** Judge Surrick does not have a special practice or policy regarding the reading of stipulations, pleadings, or discovery material into the record. He permits it when appropriate.

16. **Preparation of Exhibits.** Judge Surrick requires that exhibits be pre-marked and pre-exchanged. A bench copy of trial exhibits should be provided to the court on the first day of trial. The trial exhibits should be accompanied by an exhibit list that describes each exhibit.

17. **Offering of Exhibits Into Evidence.** Judge Surrick permits counsel to choose the timing of their offer of exhibits into evidence as long as each exhibit is offered and admitted into evidence before it is shown to the jury. At the conclusion of a party's case-in-chief, counsel should make sure that all exhibits intended to be offered into evidence either have been or are offered into evidence.

18. **Motions for Judgment as a Matter of Law and Motions for Judgment on Partial Findings.** Motions for judgment as a matter of law and motions for judgment on partial findings may be either oral or written. Oral argument will be permitted if counsel request it.

19. Proposed Jury Instructions and Verdict Forms. Judge Surrick requires proposed jury instructions and verdict forms to be filed with the clerk and a courtesy copy to be sent to chambers. He sets the deadline for submissions by scheduling order. Judge Surrick will permit submission of supplemental jury instructions up to the time he charges the jury.

20. Proposed Findings of Fact and Conclusions of Law. Judge Surrick requires that proposed findings of fact and conclusions of law be filed with the clerk and a courtesy copy be sent to chambers. He sets the deadline for submissions by scheduling order.

Jury Deliberations

1. Written Jury Instructions. Judge Surrick does not give the jury a copy of the written jury instructions, but may do so in an appropriate case.

2. Exhibits in the Jury Room. After the close of the charge, counsel will review the exhibits and to the extent possible reach agreement on which exhibits will go out to the jury. Any disputes will be resolved by Judge Surrick.

3. Handling of Jury Requests to Read Back Testimony or Replay Tapes. If the jury requests that testimony be read back or that tapes be replayed, Judge Surrick will confer with counsel with regard to the jury's request. Such requests are not granted as a matter of course.

4. Availability of Counsel During Jury Deliberations. Judge Surrick requires that counsel be available on 10 minutes' notice during the jury deliberations.

5. Taking the Verdict and Special Interrogatories. The courtroom deputy will take the verdict. Special interrogatories are submitted to the jury in most civil cases.

6. Polling the Jury. Judge Surrick will permit polling the jury when requested. Polling of the jury is allowed in all criminal cases.

7. Interviewing the Jury. After a verdict has been recorded and a jury has been discharged, counsel may interview jurors. The jurors are told that they are permitted to talk to counsel and others, if they desire, but they do not need to do so.

CRIMINAL CASES

1. Oral Argument on Motions. Judge Surrick will allow oral argument on motions in a criminal case upon the request of counsel.

2. Pretrial Conferences. Judge Surrick will hold pretrial conferences only in complex criminal cases.

3. Voir Dire. Judge Surrick conducts voir dire in criminal cases.

Judge William H. Yohn, Jr.

The Honorable William H. Yohn, Jr. received an A.B. from Princeton University in 1957, and a J.D. from Yale Law School in 1960. He was an assistant district attorney for Montgomery County from 1962 to 1965. Judge Yohn was a member of the Pennsylvania House of Representatives from 1968 to 1980, and a judge in the Montgomery County Court of Common Pleas from 1981 to 1991. He was engaged in private practice from 1961 to 1981. Judge Yohn was appointed United States district judge on September 16, 1991, and entered into duty on September 23, 1991. He assumed senior status on November 20, 2003.

PRELIMINARY GENERAL MATTERS

1. **Correspondence with the Court.** Correspondence with the court is permitted as long as the initiating attorney has discussed his or her request with other counsel and the letter notes their agreement or disagreement with the writer's request. See also the standard notice to counsel (shown on page 364 of this book) that is routinely sent to counsel promptly after assignment of a case to the judge.

2. **Communications with Law Clerks.** Communications are permitted with the law clerks concerning administrative aspects of cases, but they are discouraged. Counsel may not communicate with the law clerks on the merits of any case, and law clerks are not permitted to render advice to counsel and have no authority to grant continuances or to speak on behalf of the court.

3. **Telephone Conferences.** Telephone conferences with counsel are a preferred method of handling disputes concerning discovery, scheduling, and requests for extensions of time. However, prior to the telephone conference, initiating counsel should discuss the dispute with other counsel and send the court a letter setting forth his or her position and the position of opposing counsel.

4. **Oral Arguments and Evidentiary Hearings.** The judge determines in any given case whether to schedule oral argument or an evidentiary hearing. If counsel prefer oral argument or an evidentiary hearing, they should request it. The scheduling of all such matters is handled by the judge. The judge does not set aside any certain days for oral arguments or evidentiary hearings.

5. **Pro Hac Vice Admissions.** The judge does not have a preference as to how counsel should submit a pro hac vice motion to the court. He will usually grant the motion upon its presentation, subject to the right of other counsel to object at a later date.

CIVIL CASES
Pretrial Procedure

1. **Pretrial Conferences.** The judge regularly conducts a preliminary pretrial conference, and, if requested by all parties, he will conduct settlement conferences. Preliminary pretrial conferences are usually held early in a case. Among the regular agenda items at a preliminary pretrial conference are pleadings, service, joinder, settlement, jurisdictional defects, and the setting of discovery deadlines and a trial date. The judge uses a standard pretrial order to notify counsel of a conference. He also uses a standard scheduling order pursuant to Rule 16, which is issued at the conclusion of a preliminary pretrial conference. Sample copies of these orders are shown starting at page 358 of this book.

Continuances and Extensions

1. **General Policy.** The judge has a general policy of adhering to originally scheduled dates unless a compelling reason is presented that justifies a change and opposing counsel consents. This policy applies to briefing schedules, oral argument, evidentiary hearings, and discovery deadlines. Trial dates will be changed for a compelling reason, if the request is submitted in a timely manner.

2. **Requests for Extensions and Continuances.** Requests for extension of discovery deadlines or trial dates can be made by letter, stating the reasons and noting the agreement or disagreement of all other counsel and the period of delay requested, or by telephone conference with all counsel participating.

General Motion Practice

1. **Oral Argument on Motions.** Normally, oral argument on motions will be scheduled only when it is requested by counsel and the court believes it would be helpful in its decision-making process. Occasionally, the court will schedule oral argument without counsel's request.

2. **Reply and Surreply Briefs.** Reply and surreply briefs are discouraged and should be filed only on those rare occasions where the parties wish to draw the court's attention to controlling authority not previously cited by the parties.

3. **Chambers Copies of Motion Papers.** Although not required, the judge encourages counsel to send a courtesy copy of motion papers to chambers if the document has not been filed electronically.

Discovery Matters

1. **Length of Discovery Period of Extensions.** In non-complex litigation, the judge usually allows 120 days to complete discovery, measured from the entry of appearance by defense counsel. If counsel have been diligent and genuinely need more time for discovery, he will usually grant additional time as long as it does not interfere with the trial date. In arbitration cases, discovery must be completed prior to the arbitration date.

2. **Discovery Conferences and Dispute Resolution.** The parties should make every effort to resolve discovery disputes without the court's assistance. The judge will convene a discovery conference, usually by telephone, to assist if the parties are unable to resolve disputes without the court's assistance. Where the discovery dispute is complex, a motion should be filed.

3. **Confidentiality Agreements.** The judge does not favor confidentiality agreements, and begins consideration of any confidentiality agreement with a presumption that all litigation materials are open to the public. In the event that a confidentiality agreement becomes necessary, the judge prefers that counsel submit a stipulated order for consideration along with a memorandum setting forth proposed findings to meet the requirements of *Pansy v. Stroudsburg*.

4. **Expert Witnesses.** Expert witness discovery is covered at the pretrial conference and is the subject of a scheduling order. In most cases, the plaintiff must serve expert reports and/or responses to expert witness discovery before the defendant is required to do so. Generally, all expert witness discovery must be completed by the time all other discovery is concluded.

Settlement

1. General Approach to Settlement and Nonjury Cases. The judge believes that the court's involvement in settlement conferences is generally helpful and will become involved in jury cases at the request of counsel. In nonjury cases, he will refer settlement negotiations to Magistrate Judge Elizabeth Hey.

2. Referral of Settlement Negotiations to Another District Court Judge. The judge will not refer settlement negotiations to another district court judge unless the parties present a compelling reason to do so and the judge to whom the negotiations are to be referred consents.

Arbitration

1. General Approach to Arbitration Cases. Preliminary pretrial conferences normally are not held in cases eligible for arbitration, and, except in unusual cases, scheduling orders are not issued. An order will be issued, however, prohibiting discovery after the arbitration hearing except upon order of the court upon good cause shown as to why the discovery requested could not have been reasonably anticipated and completed prior to the arbitration.

2. Scheduling of Trial De Novo from Arbitration. Upon demand for trial de novo after an arbitration award, the case will be scheduled for trial immediately. Plaintiff's pretrial memorandum will be filed within 7 days of the filing of the demand for trial de novo, and defendant's pretrial memorandum is to be filed within 14 days of the demand.

Proposed Final Pretrial Memoranda

1. Required Form of Pretrial Memoranda. All pretrial memoranda must be in accordance with Local Rule of Civil Procedure 16.1(c) unless the scheduling order provides otherwise in a particular case.

Injunctions

1. Scheduling and Expedited Discovery. Any injunction matters assigned to the judge will be promptly listed for a hearing; however, the amount of time available for the hearing may be limited. The scheduling of the injunction hearing will be fixed at an initial conference attended by all counsel. In appropriate cases, expedited discovery will be required.

When plaintiff requests a temporary restraining order, plaintiff's counsel should contact the judge's secretary for a conference date and serve the motion, complaint, and notice of the conference date upon the opposing party and counsel prior to that date unless, for good cause shown, this is impossible.

2. Proposed Findings of Fact and Conclusions of Law. Proposed findings of fact and conclusions of law must be submitted at the start of an injunction hearing.

Trial Procedure

1. Scheduling of Cases. Cases are scheduled for a date certain. Generally cases will be set to commence on a Monday. Complex, multi-party cases are specially listed. The judge will review the cases listed for each week during the latter part of the prior week and determine which will proceed to trial first depending upon the needs of all parties, witnesses, and counsel.

2. Conflicts of Counsel. Counsel should notify the judge of any professional or personal conflicts affecting the trial schedule by telephoning or writing to his courtroom deputy. Opposing counsel must also be notified promptly.

3. **Cases Involving Out-of-Town Parties or Witnesses.** Trial scheduling does not generally change by the presence of out-of-town parties or witnesses, although counsel should notify the court of any particular problem. The scheduling of witnesses is normally left to counsel.

4. **Note-taking by Jurors.** Jurors are permitted to take notes.

5. **Trial Briefs.** The submission of trial briefs is encouraged, particularly in unusual or complex cases and in cases where unusual evidentiary problems are anticipated.

6. **Voir Dire.** The judge conducts voir dire in civil cases. He permits counsel to submit special questions to him before voir dire begins. At the conclusion of his questions, he usually will allow counsel themselves to direct additional questions to the panel or to any individual member of the panel.

7. **Sidebars.** The judge permits sidebar conferences, but tries to limit them because they distract the jury and interrupt the flow of the trial.

8. **In Limine Motions.** In limine motions involving complex legal issues should be presented in sufficient time so that they can be considered in advance of trial. Routine in limine motions will ordinarily be disposed of on the first day of trial or during the course of the trial.

9. **Examination of Witnesses Out of Sequence.** The judge will generally grant a request by counsel to take the testimony of a witness out of turn for the convenience of the witness subject to objection by opposing counsel.

10. **Opening Statements and Summations.** No time limits are placed on opening statements or summations by counsel. However, 15 minutes is usually adequate for an opening statement and 30 to 45 minutes is usually adequate for a summation. Opening statements are not for argument, but are for presentation of an outline of what the parties intend to prove.

11. **Examination of Witnesses or Argument by More Than One Attorney.** More than one attorney for a party may examine different witnesses or argue different legal points. Ordinarily, not more than one attorney for a party may examine a single witness or argue the same legal point.

12. **Offers of Proof.** The attorneys should inquire of each other privately as to anticipated offers of proof regarding any witness or exhibit. If counsel cannot resolve such matters, the court will rule on them before a witness testifies or an exhibit is offered into evidence and at a time when the jury will not be inconvenienced.

13. **Examination of Witnesses Beyond Redirect or Recross.** Examination of witnesses beyond redirect and recross will ordinarily not be allowed.

14. **Videotaped Testimony.** Counsel are required to discuss in advance of trial all objections to the presentation of videotaped testimony and to attempt to resolve all conflicts. If they cannot resolve their disagreements, counsel should present any outstanding disagreements to the court for decision, well in advance of the offering of such evidence. The videotape should then be edited to eliminate pauses and speed-ups to the maximum extent such final editing is possible. Videotape playback equipment should be brought into the courtroom at the beginning of the morning or afternoon session at which the videotape will be played. It must never block the view of counsel or the jury when not in use.

15. **Reading of Material Into the Record.** There is no special practice or policy for reading stipulations, pleadings, or discovery material into the record.

16. Preparation of Exhibits. Exhibits must be pre-marked and pre-exchanged. A bench copy of trial exhibits should be provided to the court on the first day of trial. The trial exhibits should be accompanied by an exhibit list that describes each exhibit.

17. Offering Exhibits Into Evidence. As long as each exhibit is offered and admitted into evidence before it is shown to the jury, the judge has no particular preference as to when counsel should offer exhibits into evidence. At the conclusion of a party's case-in-chief, counsel should make sure that all exhibits intended to be offered into evidence either have been or are offered into evidence. Counsel who wait until the end of their case-in-chief to offer all of their exhibits into evidence should review them with opposing counsel in advance so that the agreed-upon exhibits can be admitted into evidence quickly and the disputed exhibits can be presented to the court at a time that will not impose on the jury.

18. Motions for Judgment as a Matter of Law and Motions for Judgment on Partial Findings. Motions for judgment as a matter of law and motions for judgment on partial findings may be either oral or written. Oral argument will be permitted if counsel requests it.

19. Proposed Jury Instructions and Verdict Forms. Counsel will meet and discuss proposed jury instructions and verdict forms and submit to the court at least 10 business days before the trial date a complete set of agreed-upon jury instructions and verdict forms.

If counsel cannot agree, proposed alternatives must be submitted to the court at least five business days before the trial date.

20. Proposed Findings of Fact and Conclusions of Law. Counsel will meet and discuss proposed findings of fact and conclusions of law and submit to the court at least 10 business days before the trial date a complete set of agreed-upon proposed findings of fact and conclusions of law. If counsel cannot agree, proposed alternatives are to be submitted to the court at least five business days before the trial date.

Jury Deliberations

1. Written Jury Instructions. The judge does not give the jury a copy of the written jury instructions, but may do so in an appropriate case.

2. Exhibits in the Jury Room. After the close of the charge, counsel will review the exhibits to determine which exhibits will go out with the jury. Any disputes will be resolved by the court.

3. Handling of Jury Requests to Read Back Testimony or Replay Tapes. If the jury requests that testimony be read back or that tapes be replayed, the judge will confer with counsel, consider the extent of the jury's request, and, if it is reasonable, comply with it.

4. Availability of Counsel During Jury Deliberations. Counsel should be available on 15 minutes notice during jury deliberations. As a practical matter, this means that counsel must stay in or very near the courthouse or have an associate present.

5. Taking the Verdict and Special Interrogatories. The courtroom deputy will take the verdict. Special interrogatories are submitted to the jury in most civil cases.

6. Polling the Jury. Polling of the jury is normally unnecessary in a civil case, but will be permitted if requested. Polling of the jury is always allowed in criminal cases.

7. Interviewing the Jury. After a verdict has been recorded and a jury has been discharged, counsel may interview jurors. The jurors are told that they are permitted to talk to counsel and others, if they desire, but they need not do so.

CRIMINAL CASES

1.   Oral Argument on Motions. Oral argument on motions in a criminal case is permitted upon request of counsel.

2.   Pretrial Conferences. Pretrial conferences will be held only in complex criminal cases.

3.   Voir Dire. The judge conducts voir dire in criminal cases. Counsel may suggest questions to him in advance of voir dire. At the conclusion of his questions, he usually will allow counsel to direct additional questions to the panel or any individual member of the panel.

4.   Sentencing Memoranda. The judge permits and encourages the submission of sentencing memoranda by both the government and the defense. Letters from others on behalf of the defendant should not be sent to chambers. Rather, such letters should be accumulated by defendant's counsel, shown to the government's attorney, and offered into evidence at the sentencing hearing.

OTHER GENERAL MATTERS

At the close of counsel's business with the court, it is not necessary that counsel request permission to be excused.

Copies of appellate briefs should not be sent to the judge in the event of an appeal.

The judge expects punctuality and courtesy from counsel regarding each other, both in the presence of the court and otherwise. He is of the view that vigorous, robust advocacy need not be rude.

IN THE UNITED STATES DISTRICT COURT
FOR THE EASTERN DISTRICT OF PENNSYLVANIA

:   CIVIL ACTION

v.   :   NO.

                               :

SCHEDULING ORDER

AND NOW, this _____ day of _____, 20___, **IT IS ORDERED** as follows:

1. Counsel are encouraged to request a voluntary settlement conference as early in the discovery process as they feel it will be productive. A settlement conference will be scheduled upon agreement of all counsel. Unless the court authorizes an exception, such agreement constitutes counsel's certification that there is a reasonable possibility of settlement and that the party represented by counsel will engage in good faith negotiations to resolve the litigation. All settlement conferences in non-jury cases will be conducted by Magistrate Judge Elizabeth T. Hey.

If a settlement conference has not been previously requested, plaintiff's counsel is directed to contact Magistrate Judge Elizabeth T. Hey in the week prior to the close of discovery to schedule a mandatory settlement conference which will be held within the two (2) weeks after the close of discovery. All settlement conferences in prisoner pro se cases will be conducted by telephone.

At any settlement conference, counsel shall have his/her client or a person authorized by his/her client with unlimited authority to settle at the conference or available by telephone during the entire conference.

Discovery

2. All discovery shall proceed forthwith and continue in such manner as will assure that all requests for, and responses to, discovery will be noticed, served and completed by _____. Discovery may take place thereafter by agreement of the parties without court approval, so long as the trial will not be delayed and trial preparation will not unreasonably be disrupted. No discovery may take place during the trial unless directed by the court.

In all pro se cases, the defendant shall, within thirty (30) days from the date of this order, take the oral deposition of the pro se plaintiff, unless the court excuses such discovery upon motion made and good cause shown by any defendant governed by this requirement. The taking of this preliminary deposition of a pro se plaintiff shall not preclude a defendant from taking a later deposition if it is otherwise permissible under the Federal Rules of Civil Procedure.

3. Plaintiff shall comply with the requirements of Fed.R.Civ.Proc. 26(a)(2) for disclosure of expert testimony forty (40) days prior to the close of the discovery period.

4. Defendant shall comply with the requirements of Fed. R. Civ. Proc. 26(a)(2) for disclosure of expert testimony twenty (20) days prior to the close of the discovery period.

5. All parties shall file with the Clerk of Court and opposing counsel the pretrial disclosure required by Fed. R. Civ. Proc. 26(a)(3)(A)(i) and (C)(iii) by the close of the discovery period. No witness, expert or fact, not listed may be called to testify during the party's case in chief.

Motions

6. All motions to amend the complaint, join or add additional defendants or name John Doe defendants shall be filed within 60 days of the date of this order. All motions for summary judgment or partial summary judgment shall be filed and served on or before _____. All motions in limine shall be filed and served at least five (5) business days before the trial date. All other motions shall be filed and served prior to the close of the discovery period. Any motions filed in violation of this order shall be deemed waived unless good cause is shown.

Judge William H. Yohn, Jr.

No brief filed in support of or in opposition to <u>any</u> motion shall exceed twenty-five (25) pages in length without prior leave of court. The moving party may file a reply brief, limited to a maximum of seven (7) pages, within five (5) business days of the filing of the opposing party's response.

7. In addition to a brief, any party filing a motion for summary judgment or partial summary judgment shall file a separate, short and concise statement, in numbered paragraphs, of the material facts as to which the party contends there is no genuine issue to be tried. The party must support each of the material facts with specific citations to the underlying record, and attach a copy of the relevant portions of that record, if practicable and not already of record. Failure to submit such a statement of material facts with citations may constitute ground for denial of the motion.

The opposing party shall file a separate, short and concise statement, responding to the numbered paragraphs in the moving party's statement, of the material facts as to which the opposing party contends there is a genuine issue to be tried and shall conform to the record citation requirements listed above. All factual assertions set forth in the statement required to be served by the moving party shall be deemed admitted unless controverted by the statement required to be served by the opposing party.

Trial

8. All parties shall prepare and file with the Clerk of Court and opposing counsel their pretrial memoranda, in accordance with Local Rule 16.1(c)(1)(2)(3)(6) and (7) as follows:

    A. Plaintiff—at least twenty (20) days prior to the trial date.

    B. Defendant—at least ten (10) days prior to the trial date.

9. Any party having an objection to the admissibility of any exhibit based on authenticity or the adequacy of the qualifications of an expert witness expected to testify, shall set forth separately each such objection in their pretrial memorandum. Such objection shall describe with particularity the ground and the authority for the objection.

10. The case is scheduled for trial on _____, <u>at 10:00 a.m</u>. This scheduling order will be the <u>only</u> written notice counsel will receive of the date this case will be tried. Counsel and all parties shall be prepared to commence trial on this date and the court will make every effort to commence trial on this date consistent with its other obligations. The order in which cases are listed in the *Legal Intelligencer* for that date has no relevancy to the order in which they will be called for trial.

Ordinarily cases will begin trial on the date scheduled. In the event the court is unable to begin the trial within two (2) weeks of that date, counsel will be given the option of remaining on the standby list until the case can proceed to trial or continuing the case to a new fixed date in the future. A copy of the court's trial guidelines is available from the courtroom deputy upon request.

11. Because a witness may be unavailable at the time of trial as defined in Federal Rule of Civil Procedure 32(a)(4), the court expects use of oral or videotape depositions at trial of any witness whose testimony a party believes is essential to the presentation of that party's case, whether that witness is a party, a non-party or an expert. The unavailability of any such witness <u>will not be a ground to delay</u> the commencement or progress of the trial. Any oral or videotape deposition for use at trial shall be held at least five (5) business days before the trial date.

12. Any party who contends or will contend that the proposed testimony of any expert witness requires a *Daubert* hearing shall notify the court by letter at least thirty (30) days prior to the trial date so that the hearing can be held prior to trial and without impinging upon the jury's time.

In the event a deposition is to be offered at trial, the offering party shall file with the court, prior to the commencement of the trial, a copy of the deposition transcript, but only after all efforts have been made to resolve objections with other counsel. Portions of the deposition offered by the plaintiff shall be marked in blue; portions offered by the defendant, in red. Where a court ruling is necessary, the basis for unresolved objections shall be stated in five (5) words or less in the margin of the deposition page(s) and a covering list of such objections supplied therewith.

Practice and Procedures of Judges and Judges' Forms and Orders

13. **(JURY CASES ONLY)** All proposed jury instructions shall be numbered and shall have citations of authority for each point (one point per page). If a model jury instruction is submitted, for instance, from the *Third Circuit Model Jury Instructions* or O'Malley, *Federal Jury Practice and Instructions* (6th Edition) or *Pennsylvania Suggested Standard Civil Jury Instructions,* counsel shall state whether the proposed jury instruction is modified or unchanged. If counsel modifies a model jury instruction, additions shall be underlined and deletions shall be placed in brackets. If a model jury instruction is unchanged, it may be submitted by title and paragraph reference only.

At least fifteen (15) business days before the trial date, counsel shall exchange proposed jury instructions and proposed jury interrogatories. Counsel for the plaintiff is directed to initiate the scheduling of a meeting of all counsel to be held at least ten (10) business days before the trial date, at which counsel shall meet, discuss and submit to the court one complete set of agreed upon jury instructions and jury interrogatories. The original shall be filed with the Clerk of Court. If a good faith effort is not made to comply with this directive, the trial may be continued or sanctions imposed on individual counsel.

If the parties are unable to agree upon certain jury instructions or jury interrogatories, at least five (5) business days before the trial date, the party proposing the instruction or interrogatory shall submit to the court one (1) copy of the proposed instruction or interrogatory and its citation of authority and the party opposing the instruction or interrogatory shall submit to the court one (1) copy of its specific objection, citation of authority and proposed alternative. The originals shall be filed with the Clerk of Court.

At least five (5) business days before the trial date, each party shall file a trial memorandum on the legal issues involved in the case and that party's proposed voir dire questions. The originals shall be filed with the Clerk of Court.

At least five (5) business days before the trial date, each party shall submit to the court a *one page or less* summary in non-legalese language of its contentions with reference to the facts, theories of liability and damages. Prior to the beginning of voir dire, the other party may file objections or alternatives to this summary. The summary will be used by the court in its preliminary and final instructions to the jury to familiarize the jurors with the general framework of the factual issues in the case.

14. **(NON-JURY CASES ONLY)** At least fifteen (15) business days before the trial date, counsel shall exchange proposed findings of fact and conclusions of law.

Counsel for the plaintiff is directed to initiate the scheduling of a meeting of all counsel to be held at least ten (10) business days before the trial date at which counsel shall meet, discuss and submit to the court one (1) complete set of agreed upon findings of fact and conclusions of law. The original shall be filed with the Clerk of Court. If a good faith effort is not made to comply with this directive, the trial may be continued or sanctions imposed on individual counsel.

With reference to those findings of fact and conclusions of law upon which the parties are not able to agree, at least five (5) business days before the trial date each party shall submit to the court two (2) copies of that party's proposed disputed findings of fact and conclusions of law, and a trial memorandum on the legal issues involved in the case. The original shall be filed with the Clerk of Court.

15. All trial exhibits, except for impeaching documents, shall be premarked and exchanged by counsel prior to the commencement of trial. Defense counsel shall not mark or use any exhibit which is an additional copy of an exhibit which has been listed by plaintiff's counsel. Defense counsel shall use plaintiff's exhibit throughout the trial. At the commencement of trial, counsel shall supply the court with a bench copy of each exhibit, the duplication of which is practicable (two (2) copies in non-jury trials), and two (2) copies of a schedule of all exhibits which shall briefly describe each exhibit. Counsel shall also prepare a binder of their exhibits to be placed on the witness stand and used by all witnesses.

At the time of its use, counsel shall supply the court and opposing counsel with a copy of each impeaching document, the duplication of which is practicable.

William H. Yohn, Jr., Judge

Judge William H. Yohn, Jr.

TRIAL GUIDELINES

1. Daily Schedule

Unless notified to the contrary, the jury portion of the trial will be conducted each trial day from 9:30 a.m. (10:00 a.m. on Mondays) to 12:15 p.m. and from 1:30 p.m. to 4:15 p.m. Trials will convene promptly at the designated time on each trial day.

Matters to be discussed outside the presence of the jury will not ordinarily be considered during the hours designated for a jury trial, and side-bar discussions are discouraged. Any matters to be considered outside the presence of the jury should be scheduled for 9:00 a.m. with notice given on the preceding trial day to the court and all counsel.

2. Motions

Undisposed of motions and other pretrial issues will be resolved at or prior to the beginning of the trial. However, it is the responsibility of counsel to bring them to the attention of the court.

3. Voir Dire

The judge conducts voir dire in civil and criminal cases. He permits counsel to submit special questions to him before voir dire begins. At the conclusion of his questions, he usually will allow counsel to ask additional questions directly to the panel or to any individual member of the panel.

4. Openings and Closings

No time limits are placed on opening statements or summations by counsel. However, fifteen (15) minutes is usually adequate for an opening statement and thirty (30) to forty-five (45) minutes is usually adequate for a summation. Opening statements are not for argument, but are for presentation of an outline of what the parties intend to prove.

5. Witnesses

The court intends to start on time and expects counsel, witnesses and parties to be available when needed. Do not run out of witnesses. Failure to have witnesses available during trial may result in the preclusion of their testimony.

The judge will generally grant a request by counsel to take the testimony of a witness out of turn for the convenience of the witness subject to objection by opposing counsel. A doctor's testimony will be taken, whenever possible, at a time convenient to the doctor, even if it means interrupting the testimony of another witness.

More than one attorney for a party may examine different witnesses or argue different legal points. Ordinarily, not more than one attorney for a party may examine a single witness or argue the same legal point.

Examination of witnesses beyond redirect and recross will be allowed only rarely.

6. Objections and Side-bars

Objections should be stated in just a few words or by rule number. Extensive argument on objections in the presence of the jury is forbidden. If counsel feels that extensive argument will be needed, he or she should advise the court in advance so that it can be scheduled for argument outside the presence of the jury at 9:00 a.m. on one of the trial days.

The judge permits, but tries to limit, side-bar conferences because they distract the jury and interrupt the flow of the trial.

7. Offers of Proof

The attorneys should inquire of each other privately as to offers of proof regarding any witness or exhibit expected to be offered. If counsel cannot resolve such matters, the court will rule on them before a witness testifies or an exhibit is offered into evidence and at a time when the jury will not be inconvenienced.

8. Stipulations

Offers to stipulate shall not be made in the presence of the jury, unless they have previously been agreed to informally between the attorneys in the absence of the jury. Stipulations may be oral, but preferably they should be in writing and received as an exhibit.

9. Videotaped Testimony

Counsel are required to discuss in advance of trial all objections to the presentation of videotaped testimony and attempt to resolve all conflicts. If they cannot resolve their differences, counsel should present any outstanding disagreements to the court in accordance with the procedure established in the scheduling order. The videotape should then be edited to eliminate pauses and speed-ups to the maximum extent such final editing is possible. Videotape playback equipment should be brought into the courtroom at the beginning of the morning or afternoon session at which the videotape will be played. It must never block the view of counsel or the jury when not in use.

10. Reading to the Jury

There is no special practice or policy for reading stipulations, pleadings, or discovery material into the record.

11. Exhibits

Exhibits must be pre-marked and pre-exchanged. A bench copy of trial exhibits should be provided to the court on the first day of trial. The trial exhibits should be accompanied by an exhibit list which describes each exhibit.

As long as each exhibit is offered and admitted into evidence before it is shown to the jury, the judge has no particular preference as to when counsel should offer exhibits into evidence. At the conclusion of a party's case-in-chief, counsel should make sure that all exhibits intended to be offered into evidence either have been or are offered into evidence.

Once an exhibit has been admitted into evidence, it must remain on the evidence table accessible to all counsel and witnesses. To the extent practicable, the court also prefers that all exhibits which have been identified by a witness also remain on the exhibit table.

Once an exhibit has been admitted into evidence, all parts of the exhibit may be referred to throughout the trial and during summations. However, the court will consider separately whether or not the exhibit will be sent out with the jury during deliberations.

Unless there is objection from opposing counsel placed on the record, exhibits are released at the close of trial to the custody of the party who offered them and must be picked up within 48 hours or they will be destroyed.

12. Comments to the Jury

Except during opening statements, closing statements and, where warranted, voir dire, counsel may not speak directly to the jury without the permission of the judge.

13. Courtroom Movement

Counsel may move about the courtroom freely without asking permission. It is specifically not necessary to ask permission to approach a witness or to move the lectern, easel or a blackboard. If counsel is standing near a witness for the purpose of pointing something out on an exhibit, opposing counsel may also be present to observe firsthand what is being pointed out. However, neither counsel should stand between the witness and the jury.

14. Exhibits to the Jury

After the close of the charge, counsel will review the exhibits among themselves to determine which exhibits will go out with the jury. Any disputes will be resolved by the court.

15. Jury Requests

If the jury requests that testimony be read back or that tapes be replayed, the judge will confer with counsel, consider the extent of the jury's request, and, if it is reasonable, comply with it.

16. Deliberations

Counsel should be available on fifteen (15) minutes' notice during jury deliberations. As a practical matter, this means that counsel must stay in or very near the courthouse or have an associate present.

17. Verdict

The courtroom deputy will take the verdict. Special interrogatories are submitted to the jury in most civil cases.

18. Polling the Jury

Polling of the jury is normally unnecessary in a civil case, but will be permitted if requested. Polling of the jury is always allowed in criminal cases.

19. Interviewing the Jury

After a verdict has been recorded and a jury has been discharged, counsel may interview jurors. The jurors are told that they are permitted to talk to counsel and others, if they desire, but they need not do so.

THE JUDGE EXPECTS PUNCTUALITY FROM COUNSEL AND COURTESY REGARDING EACH OTHER, BOTH IN THE PRESENCE OF THE COURT AND OTHERWISE. HE IS OF THE VIEW THAT VIGOROUS, ROBUST ADVOCACY NEED NOT BE RUDE.

JUDGE WILLIAM H. YOHN, JR.
(COURTROOM 14-B)
ROOM 14613
U.S. COURTHOUSE
601 MARKET ST.
PHILA., PA 19106

October, 2011

NOTICE TO COUNSEL REGARDING THE COURT'S SCHEDULING AND DISCOVERY POLICY

1. Pursuant to Fed.R.Civ.P. 16(b) and (c), the court will schedule a preliminary pretrial conference shortly after a defendant has filed an appearance or pleading, or shortly after a case has been reassigned to its calendar.

2. Threshold motions such as to amend, to transfer, to remand, or to add parties should be filed, whenever possible, before the pretrial conference.

3. The conference will usually be held in chambers and last 15–30 minutes. The court may decide to conduct the conference by telephone or via mail. In complex cases, the court requires trial counsel to be present or, in extraordinary situations and where counsel are located significantly outside the greater metropolitan Philadelphia area, to be available by telephone.

4. At the conference, the following matters, among others, will be considered and acted upon:

    A. Jurisdictional defects;

    B. Time limits for the joinder of parties and/or the amendment of pleadings;

    C. Prospects of an amicable settlement;

    D. Establishment of a schedule for remaining pretrial proceedings such as discovery, additional motions, pretrial filings, the exchange of exhibits, and the exchange of expert reports; and

    E. Setting a date for trial.

5. A mandatory settlement conference will be held at the close of discovery. No other conferences will be held unless requested by counsel for the exploration of settlement, for trial management, or for preparation purposes. Conferences are encouraged provided counsel believe they will be useful.

6. In most cases, discovery should be completed within 120 days after service of the complaint. Counsels' joint proposed discovery plan under Fed.R.Civ.P. 26(f)(3) should set forth the dates, time intervals, and subject of discovery to be completed by the discovery deadline.

7. All reasonably foreseeable discovery must be noticed, served, and completed by the discovery deadline. Discovery may take place thereafter by agreement of the parties without court approval so long as the trial is not delayed and trial preparation is not unreasonably disrupted. The court will not entertain motions to compel discovery after the date of the discovery deadline except upon the showing of good cause for the failure to timely file or serve such motions.

8. When timely discovery is not forthcoming after a reasonable attempt has been made to obtain it, parties should first seek to resolve disputes under Local Rule 26.1(f), then seek the assistance of the court. The court encourages the submission of discovery disputes by telephone conference. If a discovery motion is filed, it may be acted upon before a response is filed with or without a telephone conference.

9. Requests for extension of discovery deadlines or trial dates may be made by letter or telephone conference. A letter must state the reasons an extension is required, note the agreement or disagreement of all other counsel, and specify the period of delay requested. A telephone conference requires the participation of all counsel. Requests not in compliance with these requirements will be denied. Requests will not ordinarily be granted unless made within 30 days of the date of the scheduling order.

10. The filing of a Pretrial Memorandum as described in Local Rule 16.1(c) is required. Local Rule 16.1(d)(2) will only be utilized when specially ordered by the court.

11. After arbitration, requests for trial *de novo* will result in a prompt date for trial. No discovery or motions, except motions *in limine*, will be allowed after arbitration except as ordered by the court upon the showing of good cause as to why the discovery or motion requested could not have been reasonably anticipated and completed before arbitration.

12. Unexcused violations of scheduling orders are subject to sanctions under Fed.R.Civ.P. 16(f), upon either the motion of a party or the initiative of the court.

13. Letters or other written communication shall be directed to the court and not to law clerks. Telephone calls to law clerks are strongly discouraged. Law clerks are not permitted to render advice to counsel and have no authority to grant continuances or to speak on behalf of the court.

14. This court urges the use of Electronic Case Filing ("ECF"). ECF provides greater efficiency and timeliness in the filing of pleadings, automatic e-mail notice of case activity, as well as electronic storage of documents for remote access by the Court, the bar and the litigants. Attorneys are urged to register for Electronic Case Filing ("ECF") Filing Users in accordance with Rule 5.1.2 of the Local Rules of Civil Procedure, referencing the Procedural Order on Electronic Case Filing.

Counsel are advised that changes to their telephone and FAX number(s) are to be submitted both to the Clerk's Office and to Thomas J. McCann, Deputy Clerk to the Honorable William H. Yohn, Jr., Room 14613 U.S. Courthouse, 601 Market Street, Philadelphia, PA 19106.

15. All inquiries concerning the status of cases as trial dates approach should be directed to Rita L. Polkowski, Secretary to the Honorable William H. Yohn, Jr., at (215) 597-4361.

William H. Yohn, Jr., Judge

Bankruptcy Judges

Chief Bankruptcy Judge Eric L. Frank

Judge Frank received his J.D. in 1976 from the University of Pennsylvania Law School and his B.A. in 1973 from the State University of New York at Binghamton. Judge Frank assumed office on February 14, 2006. He became Chief Bankruptcy Judge on March 1, 2013.

PRELIMINARY GENERAL MATTERS

1.   Correspondence with the Court.   Judge Frank discourages unsolicited correspondence from counsel. He will, however, occasionally invite and/or direct counsel to report on the status of matters via letter. Otherwise, Judge Frank will not consider matters raised via correspondence that should be raised properly by motion practice. All correspondence that relates to Judge Frank's calendar must be directed to the courtroom deputy, Pamela Blalock, by telephone at 215-408-2801, or e-mail at pamela_blalock@paeb.uscourts.gov.

2.   Communications with Law Clerk.   Judge Frank permits counsel to speak directly with his law clerk, subject to the limitations that law clerks are not permitted to give legal advice or discuss the merits of pending matters. Scheduling matters should be first taken up with the judge's courtroom deputy, or, in the alternative, with his judicial assistant.

3.   Telephone Conferences and Use of Facsimile Machines.   Judge Frank welcomes the use of telephone conferences, provided that all pertinent parties are available to participate. The judge's courtroom deputy generally handles the scheduling of telephone conferences. *Parties participating in telephone conferences must use a land line telephone; use of cell phones is not permitted.*

Judge Frank does not accept facsimile correspondence or pleadings from counsel unless it is requested and approved in advance.

4.   Pro Hac Vice Admissions.   Judge Frank prefers written requests for admission pro hac vice, but will allow such requests to be made orally or in writing at the time of hearing, when in keeping with local rule.

5.   Chambers Copies of Filed Papers.   Except when requested, Judge Frank discourages counsel from submitting chambers copies of pleadings. However, counsel may submit courtesy copies of memoranda of law to chambers.

LITIGATION GENERALLY
Continuances and Extensions

1.   General Policy.   Judge Frank is generally liberal with requests for continuances, provided that all parties consent. Such requests should be made to the courtroom deputy by letter if time permits, or by telephone, if necessary. Counsel are advised that Judge Frank's courtroom deputy is not in the office on Fridays and counsel with hearings scheduled for a Monday should plan accordingly. In emergencies, on Fridays, such requests should be directed to Judge Frank's ESR operator (who serves as his backup courtroom deputy), judicial assistant, or law clerk.

2.   Need for Filing Formal Stipulation or Motion.   If all parties consent, requests for continuances will be granted ordinarily as of course without the need for filing a formal stipulation or motion (except in adversary or other matters subject to a scheduling or pretrial order). If a request for a continuance is opposed, the judge favors resolution of the dispute by conference call arranged by the parties. Depending upon the nature of the case and its posture, the judge may require that a written motion be filed in lieu of a conference. The parties should contact the judge's courtroom deputy to ascertain the judge's preference in a particular case.

3. *Need for Court Appearance.* If Judge Frank determines that a written motion is required, he may dispose of a contested continuance request on the papers alone without awaiting a response. He may require a response. Counsel will be advised in advance if a court appearance will be necessary.

Proposed Findings of Fact and Conclusions of Law

Judge Frank requires proposed findings of fact and conclusions of law in contested matters or adversary proceedings, unless otherwise indicated at the conclusion of the proceedings in court. Memoranda of law from the parties are welcome and the judge may, depending upon the circumstances, refrain from deciding matters from the bench if parties wish an opportunity to brief certain issues.

Reading of Material Into the Record

Judge Frank will usually not permit the reading of substantial material into the record.

Settlements

1. *General Approach and Philosophy.* Judge Frank actively encourages settlement discussions and will participate in telephone conferences or chambers settlement conferences if all parties in interest agree. Judge Frank will participate in such conferences only to the extent that his role as fact finder will not be jeopardized if such discussions are unsuccessful. Requests for settlement conferences, whether by telephone or in chambers, should be directed to the judge's courtroom deputy. *Parties participating in telephone conferences must use a land line telephone; use of cell phones is not permitted.*

2. *Referral of Settlement Negotiations to Another Bankruptcy Judge.* When all parties in interest are in agreement and mediation is either inappropriate or has been unsuccessful, a request for a settlement conference with another bankruptcy judge will be entertained.

3. *Need for Court Appearance.* Settlements should be reported to Judge Frank's courtroom deputy and the necessary motions for court approval filed in accordance with Fed.R.Bankr.P. 9019 and local rule, as applicable. An objection to a proposed settlement will require a court appearance. Otherwise, a court appearance is not required unless counsel are advised to the contrary.

UNCONTESTED MATTERS

When a motion or application is uncontested because no responsive pleading was filed by the deadline set forth in the notice of motion, counsel for the moving party should file a certificate of no response and notify Judge Frank's courtroom deputy by telephone that the matter is uncontested. If, however, a moving party is aware that the respondent intends to appear and contest the request for relief, notwithstanding the failure to file a timely response, the moving party is expected to appear at the scheduled hearing.

APPEARANCE IN COURT

The following are matters in which appearance by counsel is *always* required, even in the absence of objection or response:

1. Motions to withdraw as debtor's counsel;
2. Motions requesting that a dismissal order or order granting relief from the automatic stay include provisions that restrict the filing of new bankruptcy cases or that provide in rem relief;
3. Motions to reconsider or to vacate orders dismissing or closing a case;
4. Motions to impose a stay under 11 U.S.C. § 105 (but not under § 362(c)(4));
5. Motions for sale of property pursuant to 11 U.S.C. § 363; and
6. Motions for default judgments in adversary proceedings.

Counsel may request permission to appear by telephone on such uncontested matters, particularly if counsel is located away from the general vicinity of the courthouse. Such requests should be directed to Judge Frank's courtroom deputy well in advance of the scheduled hearing date, and will be considered on a case-by-case basis. *Parties participating by telephone must use a land line telephone; use of cell phones is not permitted.*

APPEARANCE BY TELEPHONE OR VIDEO CONFERENCE

Counsel are generally expected to appear in person at scheduled trials, hearings, and conferences. However, there are sometimes circumstances under which counsel may be permitted to appear via telephone or video conference, such as at pretrial conferences when one or both counsel are not located in the general vicinity of the courthouse, or on a matter that the court itself has scheduled for hearing because of questions Judge Frank may wish to direct to counsel, see L.B.R. 9076-1. Requests for appearance by telephone should be directed to the courtroom deputy, Pamela Blalock, by telephone at 215-408-2801, or by e-mail at pamela_blalock@paeb.uscourts.gov.

CONTESTED MATTER PRACTICE AND PROCEDURE
Filing Memoranda of Law/Briefs

1. Before Hearing. Judge Frank ordinarily does not require that memoranda of law be filed prior to a hearing. If a party chooses to file a prehearing memorandum of law, a copy should be served on other interested parties. If the memorandum is filed less than three business days before the hearing, a courtesy copy should be delivered to chambers prior to the hearing, if possible. Service on other parties should be effected in a manner that is at least as fast as service of the courtesy copy to chambers.

2. After Hearing. Memoranda are required only if so indicated at the conclusion of proceedings in court. Parties desiring to submit post-hearing memoranda will be permitted generally to do so.

3. Reply and Surreply Memoranda/Briefs. Reply and surreply memoranda/briefs generally will be permitted if requested and will be included in any briefing order entered by the court. If a briefing schedule has been established and does not include reply or surreply memoranda, requests to file such memoranda should be directed initially to Judge Frank's courtroom deputy and will be considered on a case-by-case basis.

Scheduling of Expedited Hearings

Local Bankruptcy Rule 9014-2 governs requests for expedited hearings. Upon the filing of a motion for expedited hearing with the Clerk's Office, Judge Frank's courtroom deputy will consult with the judge to determine the appropriate course of action, and counsel will be so advised. *In matters in which relief is requested that directly affects one or more specific respondents, consistent with the Local Rule, Judge Frank ordinarily will not grant or schedule an expedited hearing unless the movant's counsel confers with the respondents' counsel regarding their consent to an expedited hearing and their availability for the requested expedited hearing.*

When submitting a proposed order for the scheduling of an expedited hearing, counsel are encouraged to use the form of order posted on the court website at http://www.paeb.uscourts.gov/content/chief-judge-eric-l-frank.

Rule 52(c) Motions

Such motions are permitted under Fed.R.Bankr.P. 7052 and 9014, and may be made orally or in writing.

Examination of Witnesses or Argument by More Than One Counsel

Judge Frank will permit more than one attorney for a party to examine different witnesses or argue different points of law if permission is asked in advance of any such examination and the circumstances warrant.

Examination of Witnesses Beyond Redirect and Recross

If Judge Frank chooses to direct questions to a witness, he will usually do so after direct and cross-examination has been completed and before counsel is offered the opportunity for redirect and recross-examination. Judge Frank does not favor examination of a witness after redirect and recross.

Presentation of Evidence

1. *Use of Rule 43(c) Affidavits.* Judge Frank permits the use of Rule 43(c) affidavits in lieu of testimony if the parties consent to their use. With the consent of all parties, Judge Frank also will (1) accept an offer of proof in lieu of actual testimony and (2) permit an expert appraiser's written report to be substituted for direct examination of the appraiser if the report has been served upon opposing parties prior to the hearing and if the appraiser is available for cross-examination and redirect examination.

2. *Marking of Exhibits and Number of Copies.* Exhibits should be pre-marked and exchanged with opposing counsel *prior* to the hearing. The original exhibit should be given to the witness during his or her testimony, and counsel should have sufficient copies of each exhibit for all parties as it is being used. Judge Frank does not require, but does encourage, counsel to provide a courtesy copy of an exhibit for his review on the bench during the testimony. However, if any party objects to the court viewing exhibits or a particular exhibit during the trial, Judge Frank will refrain from doing so until it is admitted into evidence or until an objection over its admission must be resolved, except to the extent necessary to make evidentiary rulings or to rule on the admissibility of the document.

When the exhibits are particularly numerous, Judge Frank encourages the use of a binder and index so as to facilitate the trial.

3. *Offering Exhibits Into Evidence.* Exhibits should ordinarily be offered into evidence at the conclusion of the party's case, rather than during the midst of the presentation of the case, unless otherwise justified by the circumstances.

4. **Need for Presentation of Evidence if Uncontested.** If the moving party must demonstrate "cause" for relief, or if the moving party requests that findings be made, evidence may be required even if the motion is uncontested, if the court is unable to make such findings on the basis of the pleadings alone. In appropriate circumstances, Judge Frank will accept a proffer or affidavit.

5. **Need for Joint Pretrial Statement.** Counsel are expected to advise the court well in advance of the scheduled hearing date if any contested matter (including objections to a claim) will likely involve multiple witnesses, extensive use of documentary evidence, or complex legal issues. Upon receipt of such advice from counsel, Judge Frank may engage in more active prehearing management of the matter, which may include requiring the submission of a joint pretrial statement in the form prescribed by his pretrial order (shown on page 376 of this book).

ADVERSARY PROCEEDINGS
Discovery Matters

1. **Length of Discovery Period and Extensions.** After the answer to the complaint is filed, a pretrial order will be entered establishing discovery deadlines, setting a date for submission of a joint pretrial statement, and scheduling a pretrial/settlement conference date. A copy of Judge Frank's standard pretrial order is shown on page 376 of this book. Extensions of deadlines that do not affect a scheduled trial date, and to which the parties agree, may be made by stipulation, which must be submitted to the court for approval. Otherwise, a motion will be required. The court may decide the motion on the papers, schedule a conference call, or set the matter for hearing.

2. **Discovery Conferences and Dispute Resolution.** Judge Frank will entertain conference calls for the purpose of resolving discovery disputes. Requests for sanctions may be made only by written motion.

3. **Confidentiality Agreements.** Judge Frank will consider approval of confidentiality agreements within the bounds of section 107 of the Bankruptcy Code and federal common law.

4. **Expert Witnesses.** Judge Frank requires the advance identification of expert witnesses in the joint pretrial statement as provided in the pretrial order.

Pretrial Conferences

Typically a final pretrial/settlement conference will be scheduled in the pretrial order. However, if circumstances warrant, Judge Frank may schedule an initial pretrial conference or status hearing early in the proceeding. Judge Frank will entertain requests for other pretrial conferences by telephone directed to the courtroom deputy or judicial assistant. Usually, such telephone requests will be granted only if all parties agree. Otherwise, a written request should be filed.

Filing of Memoranda and Briefs

1. **Pretrial.** Each party may file a trial memorandum with the clerk of court, provided it is served on opposing counsel and a copy delivered to chambers five days prior to the trial date.

2. **Post-trial.** Post-trial memoranda are necessary only when specifically requested by the court. However, Judge Frank will normally approve requests from the parties to submit them.

3. Reply and Surreply Memoranda and Briefs. The complete briefing schedule will ordinarily be established at the conclusion of the trial. If a briefing schedule has been established and does not include reply and surreply memoranda, requests to file such memoranda should be directed initially to Judge Frank's courtroom deputy and will be considered on a case-by-case basis.

Mediation

The pretrial order will ask counsel to consider participation in the mediation program. If all parties agree, a mediator will be assigned. If parties do not identify a proposed mediator in their communication to the court indicating their willingness to mediate, the court will appoint a mediator from among the approved list of mediators. *Mediation will not suspend any of the deadlines established in the pretrial order.*

ARBITRATION

1. General Approach to Arbitration Cases. Adversary proceedings will be assigned to compulsory arbitration in accordance with Local Bankruptcy Rule 9019-2.

2. Scheduling of Trial De Novo from Arbitration. Once a trial de novo is demanded, Judge Frank will generally issue a pretrial order directing the filing of a joint pretrial statement and setting a date for trial.

TRIAL PROCEDURE

1. Scheduling of Cases. Proceedings will be scheduled for trial at a pretrial conference.

2. Matters Involving Out-of-Town Parties or Witnesses. Judge Frank will try to accommodate out-of-town parties or witnesses when scheduling trials. Counsel should make the court aware of such circumstances at the pretrial/settlement conference.

3. Sidebars. Sidebar conferences will be entertained when necessary.

4. In Limine Motions. Judge Frank's pretrial order contains a deadline for the filing of in limine motions.

5. Opening Statements and Summations. Opening statements and summations should be brief and concise and limited to discussion of facts in evidence and applicable law.

6. Examinations of Witnesses Out of Sequence. Judge Frank will permit counsel to examine witnesses out of turn if all parties consent or for the legitimate convenience of the witnesses.

7. Videotaped Testimony. Judge Frank will permit the use of videotaped testimony to the extent agreed to by all parties or as allowed by the Federal Rules of Bankruptcy Procedure. Arrangement to have equipment set up in the courtroom and/or cleared through security should be done in advance by contacting his courtroom deputy.

INJUNCTIONS

1. Scheduling and Expedited Discovery. Hearings on motions for temporary restraining orders or preliminary injunctions are scheduled in the same manner as requests for expedited hearings in contested matters.

Requests for expedited discovery should be filed and served upon opposing parties. Courtesy copies of all documents seeking expedited relief should be sent to chambers. The requests will be determined summarily after opposing parties have had a reasonable opportunity to respond.

2.   *Proposed Findings of Fact and Conclusions of Law.*   Judge Frank usually requires the submission of proposed findings of fact and conclusions of law.

COURTROOM DECORUM AND CONDUCT OF COUNSEL IN MATTERS PENDING BEFORE JUDGE FRANK

Judge Frank believes that the resolution of disputes, whether by agreement or by the court after a matter is ripe for decision, and the progress of a case under title 11 U.S.C., can be either greatly aided or impeded by the attitudes and behavior of counsel and the parties involved in the proceeding. Judge Frank, therefore, subscribes to the Code of Civility, adopted by the Supreme Court of Pennsylvania by order dated December 6, 2000. In August 1998, the American Bar Association House of Delegates adopted "Guidelines for Litigation Conduct." The names of the websites where these are reproduced in full follow. Counsel are encouraged to read each of these and become familiar with them.

- Pennsylvania Supreme Court Code of Civility
  http://www.pacode.com/secure/data/204/chapter99/subchapDtoc.html

- American Bar Association Guidelines for Litigation Conduct
  http://www.abanet.org/litigation/conductguidelines/

UNITED STATES BANKRUPTCY COURT
FOR THE EASTERN DISTRICT OF PENNSYLVANIA

In re : Chapter

Debtor(s) : Bky. No.

Plaintiff(s) :

v. :

Defendant(s) : Adv. No.

PRETRIAL ORDER #1

AND NOW, it is hereby **ORDERED** that:

1. If not already filed, any party that is subject to Fed. R. Bankr. P. 7007.1 shall file the required disclosure on or before **(7 days)**.

2. On or before **(21 days)**, the parties shall file a joint statement whether they consent to participate in the court-annexed mediation program and transmit a copy of the joint statement to chambers. The joint statement may include up to three suggested mediators from the list of certified mediators, which list may be obtained from the Clerk. If the joint statement requests mediation but contains no suggested mediator(s), then the Court will choose one.

3. On or before **(21 days)**, counsel shall have held and concluded the mandatory discovery conference pursuant to Fed. R. Civ. P. 26(f), incorporated into these proceedings by Fed. R. Bankr. P. 7026. During said conference, the parties shall discuss how to proceed with general discovery and electronic discovery and shall consider whether the discovery and pretrial schedule detailed below in this order is appropriate in this proceeding.

4. On or before **(35 days)**, after the conclusion of the parties' discovery conference, should the parties propose a discovery or pretrial schedule that differs from the one below, they shall file with the bankruptcy court a report on discovery, as mandated by Fed. R. Civ. P. 26(f). The parties shall detail those differences in their Rule 26(f) Report, along with the reasons therefor. The court may, when appropriate, order a hearing based on the information found in the Rule 26(f) Report. If the parties are in agreement with the discovery schedule outlined herein, no report need be filed unless there are objections to the initial discovery disclosures.

5. On or before **(35 days)**, after the conclusion of the Rule 26(f) conference, the parties shall provide the initial disclosures detailed in Fed. R. Civ. P. 26(a)(1). Any objections to the propriety of requiring the initial discovery disclosures required by Fed. R. Civ. P. 26(a)(1), see Fed. R. Civ. P. 26(a)(1) (subparagraph following subparagraph (E)) shall be set forth in the parties' Rule 26(f) Report.

6. The following discovery and trial schedule shall be considered by the parties in their deliberations at their discovery conference:

    a. All expert witnesses shall be identified and a copy of each expert's report shall be provided to every other party, in accordance with Fed. R. Civ. P. 26(a)(2) **on or before (70 days)**.

Chief Bankruptcy Judge Eric L. Frank

b. All discovery shall be completed **on or before (91 days)**.

c. All motions to amend the pleadings, or for summary judgment, shall be filed on or before **(118 days)**. If such a motion or motions is/are filed, the parties are **not relieved** of their obligation to comply with the terms of the balance of this Pretrial Order.

d. All discovery disclosures pursuant to Fed. R. Civ. P. 26(a)(3) shall be served on opposing parties and filed with the bankruptcy court **on or before (132 days)**.

e. Any objections to Rule 26(a)(3) disclosures shall be served on opposing counsel and filed with the bankruptcy court **on or before (139 days)**.

f. **On or before (153 days)**, the parties shall file a joint pretrial statement. The joint pretrial statement shall be signed by all counsel. *It is the obligation of the Plaintiff's counsel to initiate the procedures for its preparation and to assemble and submit the proposed pretrial statement to the court.* Plaintiff's counsel shall submit a proposed joint pretrial statement to Defendant's counsel not less than 7 days prior to the deadline for its submission. Counsel are expected to make a diligent effort to prepare a proposed pretrial statement in which will be noted all of the issues on which the parties are in agreement and all of those issues on which they disagree. The proposed pretrial statement shall govern the conduct of the trial and shall supersede all prior pleadings in the case. Amendments will be allowed only in exceptional circumstances and to prevent manifest injustice.

7. The joint pretrial statement shall be in the following form:

    A. Basis of jurisdiction (including a statement whether this matter is core or noncore). If the matter is noncore, the parties shall state whether they consent to the court's entry of a final order pursuant to 28 U.S.C. § 157(c)(2). If the parties disagree, they shall each cite to relevant authority to support their positions.

    B. Statement of uncontested facts.

    C. Statement of facts which are in dispute. [No facts should be disputed unless opposing counsel expects to present contrary evidence on the point at trial, or genuinely challenges the fact on credibility grounds.]

    D. Damages or other relief. A statement of damages claimed or relief sought. A party seeking damages shall list each item claimed under a separate descriptive heading, shall provide a detailed description of each item and state the amount of damages claimed. A party seeking relief other than damages shall list the exact form of relief sought with precise designations of persons, parties, places and things expected to be included in any order providing relief.

    E. Legal issues presented and the constitutional, statutory, regulatory and decisional authorities relied upon. (Counsel should include a brief statement regarding which party has the burden of proof on each legal issue.)

    F. Witnesses listed along with a brief statement of the evidence the witness will give. Witnesses shall be classified between those who any party expects to present and those whom any party may call if the need arises. If not already provided to all parties, the address and telephone number of each witness shall be disclosed.

    G. A list of all exhibits to be offered into evidence which shall be serially numbered and physically marked before trial in accordance with the schedule. Documents which a party may offer if the need arises shall be separately identified.

    H. Motion(s) *In Limine*: The parties shall identify any Motions *In Limine* that they believe need to be resolved prior to trial. The nature of the issue shall be described in sufficient detail to facilitate a discussion of the issue(s) at the final pretrial/settlement conference and to permit the court to issue an appropriate scheduling order, if necessary, for the filing and resolution of such Motion(s).

      I. <u>A list of each discovery item</u> and trial deposition to be offered into evidence. (Counsel shall designate by page portion of deposition testimony and by number the interrogatories which shall be offered in evidence at trial.)

      J. <u>Estimated trial time</u>.

      K. <u>A certification</u> that the parties have attempted good faith settlement discussions without success.

8. A mandatory final pretrial/settlement conference shall be held on **(Date) at (time) in Bankruptcy Courtroom No. 1, Robert N.C. Nix Federal Building & Courthouse, 900 Market Street, Second Floor, Philadelphia, Pennsylvania.**

9. If the adversary proceeding is not resolved prior to the conclusion of the final pretrial/settlement conference, the adversary proceeding shall be scheduled for trial at the Court's first available date.

10. Each party may file, no later than five (5) days prior to the date of trial, a trial memorandum with service on the opposing part(y)(ies) and a courtesy copy delivered to Chambers.

11. All trial exhibits shall be pre-marked and exchanged by counsel at least three (3) business days prior to the date of trial.

12. **The trial may be continued only in exceptional circumstances on Motion and leave of Court.**

Date: _____   _____
                                                                        ERIC L. FRANK
                                                                        U.S. BANKRUPTCY JUDGE

Chief Bankruptcy Judge Eric L. Frank

**UNITED STATES BANKRUPTCY COURT
EASTERN DISTRICT OF PENNSYLVANIA**

IN RE: : **Chapter**
:
Debtor(s) : **Bky. No.**

ORDER

AND NOW, upon consideration of the _____ ("the Motion"), and the request for an expedited hearing thereon, and sufficient cause being shown, it is hereby **ORDERED** that:

1. The request for an expedited hearing is **GRANTED**.

2. A hearing to consider the Motion shall be and hereby is scheduled on _____, 20__, at _____, **in the United States Bankruptcy Court, 900 Market Street, 2nd Floor, Courtroom No. 1, Philadelphia, Pennsylvania, 19107.**

3. Written objections or other responsive pleadings to the Motion (while not required) may be filed up to the time of the hearing and all will be considered at the hearing.

4. The Movant shall serve the Motion and this Order on the U.S. Trustee, the case Trustee (if any), the individual Respondent(s) (if any), counsel to the Official Committee of Unsecured Creditors (if any), all secured creditors and all priority creditors by overnight mail, facsimile transmission or e-mail transmission **no later than 5:00 p.m. on** _____. Service under this Paragraph is effective if made to each party identified above through the court's CM/ECF system.

5. The Movant shall serve this Order and a Notice of the Motion in conformity with Local Bankruptcy Form 9014-3 on all other parties in interest, including creditors, by regular mail no later than 5:00 p.m. on _____.

6. Prior to the hearing, the Movant shall file a Certification setting forth compliance with the service requirements of Paragraphs 5 and 6 above as applicable.

Date: _____

_____
**ERIC L. FRANK
U.S. BANKRUPTCY JUDGE**

UNITED STATES BANKRUPTCY COURT
EASTERN DISTRICT OF PENNSYLVANIA

IN RE: : Chapter
 :
Debtor(s) : Bky. No.

ORDER

AND NOW, upon consideration of the Debtor(s)' Motion to Extend the Automatic Stay under 11 U.S.C. § 362(c)(3)(B) ("the Motion"), and after notice and hearing, and there being no opposition to the Motion,

It is hereby **ORDERED** that:

1. The Motion is **GRANTED**.

2. The automatic stay is extended with respect to all creditors who were served with the Motion or Notice of the Motion and shall remain in effect unless modified by the court in accordance with 11 U.S.C. § 362(d) and Fed. R. Bankr. P. 4001(a).

Date: _____

_____
ERIC L. FRANK
U.S. BANKRUPTCY JUDGE

Chief Bankruptcy Judge Eric L. Frank

UNITED STATES BANKRUPTCY COURT
EASTERN DISTRICT OF PENNSYLVANIA

IN RE:	:	Chapter 13
	:	
	:	
Debtor(s)	:	Bky. No.

ORDER

AND NOW, upon consideration of the Application for Compensation ("the Application") filed by the Debtor(s)' counsel ("the Applicant") and upon the Applicant's certification that proper service has been made on all interested parties and upon the Applicant's certification of no response,

It is hereby **ORDERED** that:

1. The Application is **GRANTED**.

2. Compensation is **ALLOWED** in favor of the Applicant in the amount of $_____.

3. The Chapter 13 Trustee chapter 13 is authorized to distribute to the Applicant as an administrative expense pursuant to 11 U.S.C. § 1326(b), 11 U.S.C. § 507, 11 U.S.C. § 503(b) and 11 U.S.C. § 330(a)(4)(B), the allowed compensation set forth in ¶ 2 less $_____ which was paid by the Debtor(s) prepetition, to the extent such distribution is authorized under the terms of the confirmed chapter 13 plan.

Date: _____

_____
ERIC L. FRANK
U.S. BANKRUPTCY JUDGE

UNITED STATES BANKRUPTCY COURT
EASTERN DISTRICT OF PENNSYLVANIA

IN RE: : Chapter
:
Debtor(s) : Bky. No.

ORDER

AND NOW, upon consideration of the Motion of **[name #1]** for Leave to Conduct Rule 2004 Examination of **[name #2]** ("the Motion"), and there being no response thereto, and after notice and hearing,

It is hereby **ORDERED** that:

1. The Motion is **GRANTED**.
2. **[name #1]** may conduct a Rule 2004 Examination of **[name #2]**.
3. The scope of the examination shall be that set forth in the Motion and Fed. R. Bankr. P. 2004(b).
4. Attendance at the Rule 2004 Examination shall be governed by Fed. R. Bankr. P. 2004(c) and 9016.

Date: _____
_____
ERIC L. FRANK
U.S. BANKRUPTCY JUDGE

Chief Bankruptcy Judge Eric L. Frank

UNITED STATES BANKRUPTCY COURT
EASTERN DISTRICT OF PENNSYLVANIA

IN RE: : **Chapter 7**
:
:
Debtor(s) : Bky. No.   ELF

ORDER CONVERTING CASE UNDER CHAPTER 7 TO CASE UNDER CHAPTER 13

WHEREAS, the Debtor(s) has/have filed a Motion to Convert Case from Chapter 7 to Chapter 13, see 11 U.S.C. § 706(a), and there being no objection thereto, and the court having considered the record and finding that the case has not been converted previously under 11 U.S.C. § 1112, § 1208, or § 1307,

It is hereby **ORDERED** that:

1. This chapter 7 case is converted to a case under chapter 13.

2. Within twenty-eight (28) days of the entry of this order, the chapter 7 Trustee shall file:

    a. An account of all receipts and disbursements made in the chapter 7 case, and
    b. A report on the administration of the case pursuant to 11 U.S.C. § 704(9).

3. The trustee forthwith shall turn over to the Debtor(s) all records and property of the estate remaining in the trustee's custody and control.

4. The trustee or any other party entitled to compensation may within twenty-eight (28) days of the date of this order file an application for compensation and reimbursement of expenses.

5. On or before fourteen (14) days from the entry of this order, the Debtor(s) shall file the statements and schedules required by Bankruptcy Rule 1007(b), if such have not already been filed.

6. On or before fourteen (14) days from the entry of this order, the Debtor(s) shall file a chapter 13 plan.

Date: _____   _____
                                                    ERIC L. FRANK
                                                    U.S. BANKRUPTCY JUDGE

UNITED STATES BANKRUPTCY COURT
EASTERN DISTRICT OF PENNSYLVANIA

IN RE: :   Chapter 13
                                      :
        Debtor(s)   :   Bky. No. ELF

ORDER

AND NOW, upon consideration of the Debtor(s)' Motion to Modify Confirmed Plan **(Doc. #)**, and after a hearing, and with the consent of the Chapter 13 Trustee, and for the reasons stated in court,

It is hereby **ORDERED** that:

1. The Motion is **GRANTED**.
2. The Debtor(s)' Amended Chapter 13 Plan **(Doc. #)** is **APPROVED**.

Date: _____

                                                                 ERIC L. FRANK
                                                                 U.S. BANKRUPTCY JUDGE

Chief Bankruptcy Judge Eric L. Frank

UNITED STATES BANKRUPTCY COURT
EASTERN DISTRICT OF PENNSYLVANIA

IN RE:	:	Chapter
	:	
Debtor(s)	:	Bky. No. ELF

ORDER

AND NOW, upon Motion of the Debtor(s) to avoid a judicial lien held by _____ ("the Respondent") in personal property and/or real property of the Debtor(s) located at **[address]**,

And, the Debtor(s) having asserted that the alleged lien arising from the judgment entered at **[court and docket #]** is subject to avoidance pursuant to 11 U.S.C. § 522(f),

And, the Debtor(s) having certified that adequate notice of the Motion was sent to the Respondent and that no answer or other response to the Motion has been filed,

It is hereby **ORDERED** that the Motion is **GRANTED** by default and the judicial lien held by the Respondent, if any, in:

    (a) the real property of the Debtor(s) and/or

    (b) the personal property of the Debtor(s)

listed and claimed as exempt in Schedule C of the Debtor(s)' bankruptcy schedules is **AVOIDED**.

Date: _____

                                          ERIC L. FRANK
                                          U.S. BANKRUPTCY JUDGE

Bankruptcy Judge Magdeline D. Coleman

Judge Coleman received her J.D. in 1981 from the University of Pennsylvania Law School and her B.A. in 1978 from Chestnut Hill College. Judge Coleman was appointed to the United States Bankruptcy Court for the Eastern District of Pennsylvania on April 12, 2010.

PRELIMINARY GENERAL MATTERS

1. *Correspondence with the Court.* Judge Coleman generally discourages unsolicited correspondence from counsel and will not consider correspondence that should be the subject of motion practice. Judge Coleman will, however, occasionally invite and/or direct counsel to report on the status of matters via letters. Otherwise, all correspondence that relates to Judge Coleman's calendar must be directed to the courtroom deputy.

2. *Communications with Law Clerk.* Judge Coleman does not permit her law clerk to give legal advice or discuss the merits of pending cases. The scheduling of trials, hearings, and most conferences is the responsibility of Judge Coleman's courtroom deputy or, in the alternative, her judicial assistant.

3. *Telephone Conferences and Use of Facsimile Machines.* Judge Coleman welcomes telephone conferences. A request for a telephone conference generally will not be granted in the absence of a filed pleading, motion, or other communication from all of the parties. Unless a request for a telephone conference is being made in lieu of an appearance at a scheduled hearing (in which event Judge Coleman's courtroom deputy should be consulted), the judge's judicial assistant handles the scheduling of all telephone conferences. All requests for telephonic conferences and/or appearances must be made at least 24 hours in advance.

Judge Coleman does not accept facsimile transmissions unless they are requested and approved in advance.

4. *Pro Hac Vice Admissions.* Judge Coleman prefers that written requests for admission pro hac vice be submitted in accordance with Local Bankruptcy Rule 2090-1(c). Oral motion may be made in open court at the time of the hearing or trial. The fee required under Local Bankr. R. 2090-1(c) must be paid whether the request for admission pro hac vice is made by written application and motion or by oral motion in open court.

5. *Chambers Copies of Filed Papers.* In adversary proceedings and chapter 11 cases, Judge Coleman would appreciate receiving chambers copies of documents filed when the exhibits are voluminous. In all other situations, Judge Coleman will accept courtesy or chambers copies of filed papers, but stresses to the bar that this is in no way required without specific request on her part.

LITIGATION GENERALLY
Continuances and Extensions

1. *General Policy.* Judge Coleman generally is liberal with requests for continuances where all parties are in agreement. The request must be made through the judge's courtroom deputy by letter, if time permits, or by telephone (except for a request for an extension of the dates in a pretrial order which should be made by stipulation with the consent of all parties or upon motion of the court). The request must be made no later than 5:00 p.m. the day prior to the event being continued, otherwise counsel must appear at the scheduled hearing.

2. Where the Request for a Continuance is Opposed. If a request for a continuance is opposed or the matter has been specially listed, Judge Coleman expects counsel to raise the issue via a telephone conference call. Otherwise, the request for a continuance should be presented by written motion sufficiently in advance of the hearing to allow the motion to be disposed of prior to the originally scheduled date. If necessary, a request for expedited consideration should be made.

3. Need for Court Appearance. If written motions were required, Judge Coleman may dispose of a contested continuance request on the papers alone and counsel will be advised in advance if a court appearance will be necessary. Otherwise, a court appearance will be required when a postponement cannot be obtained through communication with her courtroom deputy.

Proposed Findings of Fact and Conclusions of Law

Judge Coleman does not require proposed findings of fact and conclusions of law unless she specifically indicates so at the conclusion of the matter or proceeding in court. Judge Coleman will generally permit filing them, upon request. Similarly, the judge welcomes memoranda of law from the parties, and will generally refrain from deciding matters from the bench if the parties desire an opportunity to brief certain issues.

Reading of Material Into the Record

Judge Coleman usually will not permit the reading of substantial material into the record.

Settlements

1. Settlement Conferences. Judge Coleman encourages settlement discussions and will entertain chambers settlement conferences if all parties in interest agree. However, Judge Coleman will participate in such conferences only to the extent it will not jeopardize her role as a fact finder should a settlement not be reached successfully.

2. Referral of Settlement Negotiations to Another Bankruptcy Judge. When all parties in interest are in agreement and mediation is either inappropriate or has been unsuccessful, a request for a settlement conference with another bankruptcy judge will be entertained.

3. Need for Court Appearances. Settlements should be reported promptly to Judge Coleman's courtroom deputy and, if the matter is under advisement, also to her law clerk. The necessary motions to seek court approval must be filed pursuant to Federal Bankruptcy Rule 9019 and local rule, as applicable. An objection to a proposed settlement will require a court appearance. Otherwise, a court appearance is not required unless counsel are advised to the contrary.

UNCONTESTED MATTERS

Judge Coleman will enter orders in response to a timely filed certificate of no objection. To avoid appearance at the scheduled hearing, counsel should contact the courtroom deputy at least 24 hours prior to the hearing.

APPEARANCE IN COURT

Certain matters require an appearance notwithstanding the absence of a filed answer or other response. They include:

1. Motions to withdraw as debtor's counsel;
2. Motions to reconsider or vacate orders;

3. Motions to extend or impose the automatic stay pursuant to § 362(c)(3) or (c)(4). The debtor seeking such relief must also appear in connection with such motion;
4. Objections to proofs of claim. Depending on the nature of the objection, the applicable burden of proof may require a record to be made notwithstanding the absence of a response by the claimant;
5. Motions to sell property pursuant to § 363;
6. Motions under Fed.R.Bankr.P. 9019 to approve a settlement or compromise;
7. Motions requesting that a dismissal order include provisions that restrict the filing of a new bankruptcy case or that provide in rem relief;
8. Motions for default judgments in adversary proceedings.

Counsel may request permission to appear by phone on such uncontested matters, particularly if counsel is located away from the vicinity of the courthouse. Such requests should be directed to the judge's courtroom deputy well in advance of the scheduled hearing date, and will be considered on a case-by-case basis.

CONTESTED MATTER PRACTICE AND PROCEDURE
Filing Memoranda of Law/Briefs

1. **Before Hearing.** Judge Coleman will consider prehearing briefs but they are not required. If prepared, all parties in interest must be provided with copies of prehearing briefs.

2. **After Hearing.** Memoranda are required only if a briefing schedule has been established at the conclusion of the proceedings in court. Parties desiring to submit posthearing memoranda ordinarily will be permitted to do so.

3. **Reply and Surreply Memoranda/Briefs.** Reply and surreply memoranda/briefs will be permitted if approved in advance, generally at the time a briefing schedule is established. Judge Coleman will not consider any unsolicited reply memoranda filed without prior permission of the court.

Scheduling of Expedited Hearings

Local Bankruptcy Rule 5070-1 governs motions for expedited hearings. Counsel are strongly encouraged to notify Judge Coleman's courtroom deputy by telephone that a motion for expedited consideration will be filed. If the request is approved, the courtroom deputy will notify the movant's counsel of the hearing date and time.

Rule 52(c) Motions

Such motions are permitted under Fed.R.Bankr.P. 7052 and 9014, and may be made orally or in writing.

Examination of Witnesses or Argument by More Than One Counsel

Judge Coleman will permit more than one attorney for a party to examine a witness or argue different points of law if permission is asked in advance and under appropriate circumstances.

Examination of Witnesses Beyond Redirect and Recross

Judge Coleman does not favor further examination of a witness after redirect and recross have been completed.

Presentation of Evidence

1.   Use of Rule 43(c) Affidavits. When an expert witness will be providing an appraisal, Judge Coleman permits counsel to submit the expert's written report in lieu of direct examination where (1) the party offering it served a copy upon opposing counsel prior to the hearing, and (2) the expert is available at the hearing for cross-examination and redirect examination. See *In re Adair*, 965 F.2d 777 (9th Cir.1992).

For other witnesses, Judge Coleman will generally permit the use of Rule 43(c) affidavits in lieu of testimony when (1) all parties in interest consent, (2) out-of-town witnesses are involved, and (3) cross-examination can be held via telephone or video conference call.

2.   Marking of Exhibits and Number of Copies. When any party intends to offer more than five exhibits, Judge Coleman requires counsel to pre-mark and exchange exhibits prior to the start of the hearing. Otherwise, Judge Coleman appreciates counsel pre-marking exhibits and exchanging copies in advance.

Counsel needs the original for the witness and should have a copy of the exhibit for every other party present. When the exhibits are particularly numerous, a binder and index may facilitate the trial.

If any party objects to the court viewing an exhibit during the trial, the court will refrain from doing so until the objection is resolved or the exhibit's admission is resolved.

3.   Offering Exhibits Into Evidence. Exhibits should be offered at the conclusion of the party's case-in-chief, unless justified by the circumstances.

4.   Need for Presentation of Evidence if Uncontested. If a moving party must demonstrate "cause" for relief, or if the moving party requests that findings be made, evidence may be required even though the motion is uncontested if the court is unable to make such findings on the basis of the pleadings alone. In appropriate circumstances, the judge will accept a proffer or affidavit.

ADVERSARY PROCEEDINGS
Discovery Matters

1.   Length of Discovery Period and Extensions. A pretrial order will be entered in all adversary proceedings and certain contested matters establishing a discovery deadline. A copy of Judge Coleman's standard pretrial order is shown on page 392 of this book. Extensions of the deadlines generally will be given upon submission of a stipulation by consent of all parties or cause shown. Otherwise, a motion will be required. The court may decide the motion on the papers, schedule a conference call, or set the matter for hearing.

2.   Discovery Conferences and Dispute Resolution. Judge Coleman will entertain conference calls for the purpose of resolving discovery disputes. Requests for sanctions may be made only by written motion.

3.   Confidentiality Agreements. Judge Coleman will approve confidentiality agreements or orders subject to the limitations of statutory and common law.

4.   Expert Witnesses. Judge Coleman requires the advance identification of expert witnesses in the joint pretrial statement to be prepared in conformity with her standard pretrial order, shown on page 392 of this book.

5.   e-Discovery. The pretrial order entered by Judge Coleman requires that all electronic discovery issues be addressed by the parties as part of the Rule 26 discovery conferences.

Pretrial Conferences

Final pretrial/settlement conferences will typically be scheduled in the pretrial order. However, Judge Coleman may enter a form of pretrial order that schedules an initial pretrial conference or status hearing. The judge will entertain requests for other pretrial conferences by phone or otherwise as the circumstances warrant.

Filing of Memoranda and Briefs

1. *Pretrial.* Each party may file a pretrial memorandum with the clerk of court, provided it is served on opposing counsel and a courtesy copy is delivered to chambers five business days prior to the trial date.

2. *Post-trial.* Post-trial memoranda are necessary only when specifically requested by the court; however, Judge Coleman will liberally approve requests from the parties to submit them. The schedule for briefing will generally be established at the conclusion of the trial. In cases in which a transcript is being ordered by a party or parties, Judge Coleman will generally permit the briefing schedule to commence after receipt of the transcript in the regular course of business.

3. *Reply and Surreply Memoranda and Briefs.* The complete briefing schedule will ordinarily be established at the conclusion of trial proceedings. Briefs not otherwise identified at that time should not be submitted.

Mediation

The pretrial order will ask counsel to consider participation in the mediation program. If all parties agree, a mediator will be assigned. If parties do not identify a proposed mediator in their communication to the court indicating their willingness to mediate, the court will appoint a mediator from the approved list of mediators. Judge Coleman will not insist that the parties attempt mediation against their will, nor does she require parties to explain a decision not to participate in mediation. Mediation will not suspend any of the deadlines established in the pretrial order.

ARBITRATION

1. *General Approach to Arbitration.* Adversary proceedings will be assigned to compulsory arbitration in accordance with Local Bankruptcy Rule 9019-2.

2. *Scheduling of Trial De Novo from Arbitration.* Once a trial de novo is demanded, Judge Coleman will generally issue a pretrial order directing the filing of a joint pretrial statement and setting a date for trial.

TRIAL PROCEDURE

1. *Scheduling of Cases.* Motions are assigned a hearing date in accordance with Local Bankruptcy Rule 5070-1. Adversary proceedings are assigned a trial date after the pretrial/settlement conference in accordance with the pretrial order.

2. *Matters Involving Out-of-Town Parties or Witnesses.* Judge Coleman endeavors to be as flexible as possible in matters involving out-of-town parties or witnesses when scheduling trials. Counsel should make the court aware of such circumstances in the joint pretrial statement as required by the pretrial order.

3. *Sidebars.* Sidebar conferences are discouraged but will be entertained when necessary.

4. **_In Limine Motions._** Judge Coleman's pretrial order contains a deadline for the filing of in limine motions.

5. **_Opening Statements and Summations._** Judge Coleman will permit opening and closing statements, but will sometimes suggest that they be waived where pretrial memoranda have been submitted and/or post-trial memoranda are contemplated.

6. **_Examinations of Witnesses Out of Sequence._** Judge Coleman will permit counsel to examine witnesses out of turn if all parties consent or for the legitimate convenience of the witness.

7. **_Videotaped Testimony._** Judge Coleman will permit the use of videotaped testimony to the extent agreed to by all parties or as allowed by the Federal Rules of Bankruptcy Procedure. Arrangements to have equipment set up in the courtroom and/or cleared through security should be done in advance by contacting the courtroom deputy.

INJUNCTIONS

1. **_Hearings on Motions for Temporary Restraining Orders or Preliminary Injunctions._** Hearings on motions for temporary restraining orders or preliminary injunctions are viewed and scheduled in the same manner as requests for expedited consideration in contested matters. Requests for expedited discovery are treated in the same fashion. Requests for expedited discovery should be filed and served upon opposing parties.

Courtesy copies of all filed documents seeking expedited relief should be sent to chambers. The requests will be determined summarily after opposing parties have had a reasonable opportunity to respond.

2. **_Proposed Findings of Fact and Conclusions of Law._** Judge Coleman usually requires the submission of proposed facts and conclusions of law unless the parties are informed otherwise.

COURTROOM DECORUM AND CONDUCT OF COUNSEL IN MATTERS PENDING BEFORE JUDGE COLEMAN

Judge Coleman believes that the resolution of disputes, whether by agreement or by the court after a matter is ripe for decision, and the progress of a case under title 11 U.S.C., can be either greatly aided or impeded by the attitudes and behavior of counsel and the parties involved in the proceeding. Judge Coleman, therefore, subscribes to the Code of Civility, adopted by the Supreme Court of Pennsylvania by order dated December 6, 2000. In August 1998, the American Bar Association House of Delegates adopted "Guidelines for Litigation Conduct." The names of the websites where these are reproduced in full follow. Counsel are encouraged to read each of these and become familiar with them.

- Pennsylvania Supreme Court Code of Civility
  http://www.pacode.com/secure/data/204/chapter99/subchapDtoc.html
- American Bar Association Guidelines for Litigation Conduct
  http://www.abanet.org/litigation/conductguidelines/

IN THE UNITED STATES BANKRUPTCY COURT
FOR THE EASTERN DISTRICT OF PENNSYLVANIA

In re	:	**Chapter**
,	:	
Debtor.	:	**Bankruptcy No. -mdc**
	:	
,	:	
Plaintiff,	:	
v.	:	
	:	
,	:	
Defendant.	:	**Adversary No. -mdc**

PRETRIAL SCHEDULING ORDER

AND NOW, this _____ day of _____, 20__, the plaintiff(s) having filed an adversary proceeding and the defendant(s) having filed a responsive pleading, it is hereby **ORDERED** that:

1. On or before **[21 days from the entry of the Order]**, the parties shall comply with Fed. R. Bankr. P. 7007.1, if the rule is applicable thereto, and the required disclosure statement has not yet been filed.

2. On or before **[21 days from the entry of the Order]**, the parties shall submit to chambers a joint statement indicating whether they consent to participate in the court-annexed mediation program. The joint statement may include up to three suggested mediators from the list of certified mediators, which list may be obtained from the Clerk. If the joint statement contains no suggested mediator(s), then the Court will choose one.

3. On or before **[21 days from the entry of this Order]**, counsel shall have held and concluded the mandatory discovery conference pursuant to Fed. R. Civ. P. 26(f), incorporated into these proceedings by Fed. R. Bankr. P. 7026. During said conference, the parties shall consider, as part of their deliberations on how to proceed with discovery (including electronic discovery), the discovery and pretrial schedule detailed in paragraph 6 below in this Order.

4. **Within fourteen days of the conclusion of the parties' discovery conference,** should the parties propose a discovery or pretrial schedule that _differs from the one below_, they shall file with the Bankruptcy Court a report on discovery as mandated by Fed. R. Civ. P. 26(f). The parties shall detail those differences in their Rule 26(f) report, along with the reasons therefore. The Court may, when appropriate, order a hearing based upon the information found in the Rule 26(f) report. If the parties are in agreement with the discovery schedule as outlined herein, no report need be filed unless there are objections to the initial discovery disclosures.

5. **Within fourteen days after the conclusion of the Rule 26(f) conference,** the parties shall provide the initial disclosures detailed in Fed. R. Civ. P. 26(a)(1). Any objections to the initial discovery disclosures required by Fed. R. Civ. P. 26(a)(1) shall be clearly raised in the Rule 26(f) report.

6. The following discovery and pretrial schedule shall be considered by the parties in their deliberations at their discovery conference:

    A. All discovery shall be completed on or before **[90 days from the date of this Order]**.

B. All expert witnesses shall be identified and a copy of each expert's report shall be provided to every other party, in accordance with Fed. R. Civ. P. 26(a)(2) on or before **[60 days from the date of this Order]**.

C. All motions to amend the pleadings or for summary judgment shall be filed on or before **120 days from this Order]**.

D. All discovery disclosures pursuant to Fed. R. Civ. P. 26(a)(3) shall be served on opposing parties and filed with the bankruptcy court on or before **[2 weeks after C above]**.

E. Any objections to the Rule 26(a)(3) disclosures shall be served on opposing parties and filed with the bankruptcy court on or before **[2 weeks after D above]**.

F. On or before **[30 days after E above]**, the parties shall file a joint pretrial statement consistent with the form set forth in paragraph 7 below and file a copy with chambers. The joint pretrial statement shall be signed by all counsel. It is the obligation of the plaintiff's counsel to initiate, assemble and submit the proposed pretrial statement. Plaintiff's counsel shall submit a proposed joint pretrial statement to defendant's counsel not less than 7 days prior to the deadline for its submission.

Counsel are expected to make a diligent effort to prepare a proposed pretrial statement in which will be noted all of the issues on which the parties are in agreement and all of those issues on which they disagree. The proposed pretrial statement shall supersede all pleadings in the case. Amendments will be allowed only in exceptional circumstances and to prevent manifest injustice.

G. All motions *in limine* shall be filed on or before **[30 days after E above]**.

7. The joint pretrial statement shall be in the following form:

    A. <u>Basis of jurisdiction</u>. A statement setting forth the basis of jurisdiction and whether the matter is core or noncore. If the matter is noncore, the parties shall state whether they consent to the Court's entry of a final order pursuant to 28 U.S.C. § 157(c)(2). If the parties disagree, they shall each cite to relevant authority to support their positions.

    B. <u>Statement of uncontested facts</u>. A statement of the uncontested facts.

    C. <u>Statement of facts which are in dispute</u>. A statement of the facts in dispute. No facts should be disputed unless opposing counsel expects to present contrary evidence on the point at trial, or genuinely challenges the fact on credibility grounds.

    D. <u>Damages or other relief</u>. A statement of damages claimed or relief sought. A party seeking damages shall provide, for each cause of action being pursued: (a) a detailed description of each item of damages claimed; (b) the legal authority for such damages and (c) the specific amount of damages claimed. A party seeking relief other than damages shall, for each cause of action being pursued, list the exact form of relief sought with precise designation of persons, parties, places and things expected to be included in any order for relief and the legal authority for such relief.

    E. <u>Legal issues</u>. For the causes of action being pursued, identify the following: (i) the constitutional, statutory, regulatory and decisional authorities being relied upon for each cause of action; (ii) the elements which must be satisfied to prevail on each cause of action; and (iii) which party bears the burden of proof on each element. Also list any additional legal issues (*e.g.*, affirmative defenses) that will be relevant to the court's disposition of the matter, the authority pertinent to each legal issue, and the party which bears the burden on the issue.

    F. <u>Witnesses</u>. A list of witnesses in the order in which they will be called, along with a brief statement of the evidence the witness will give. Witnesses shall be classified between those whom any party expected to present and those whom any party may call if the need arises. If not already provided to all parties, the address and telephone number of each witness shall be disclosed.

G. <u>A list of all exhibits</u>. A list of all exhibits to be offered into evidence which shall be serially numbered and physically marked before trial in accordance with the schedule. Documents which a party may offer if the need arises shall be separately identified.

H. <u>A list of each discovery item and trial deposition</u>. A list of each discovery item and trial deposition to be offered into evidence. Counsel shall designate by page portion of deposition testimony and by number the interrogatories/request for admissions which shall be offered into evidence.

I. <u>Estimated trial time and scheduling issues</u>. A statement of: (1) the estimated time which the trial will require; and (2) any issues that should be considered in setting a trial date (<u>e.g.</u>, witnesses traveling from out-of-state who will need notice of the trial date to make their travel plans).

J. <u>Certification</u>. A certification that the parties have attempted good faith settlement discussions without success.

8. A mandatory pretrial/settlement conference shall be held on _____ ____, 20__, at 1:00 p.m. **[change time if necessary]** in Bankruptcy Courtroom No. 5, Robert N.C. Nix Federal Building & Courthouse, 900 Market Street, 2nd Floor, Philadelphia, Pennsylvania.

9. IF the adversary proceeding is not resolved prior to the conclusion of the final pretrial/settlement conferences, the adversary proceeding shall be set down for trial at the Court's first available trial date. The trial may be continued only in exceptional circumstances on motion to and leave of Court.

10. Seven (7) or more days prior to the date of the trial, each party is required to provide: (i) a copy of exhibits to the opposing parties; and (ii) two copies of exhibits to chambers.

11. The court may require each party to file (and, if not directed by the Court, each party may choose to file), five (5) days prior to the date of the trial, a pretrial memorandum with service on the opposing party and a courtesy copy delivered to chambers.

_____
MAGDELINE D. COLEMAN
UNITED STATES BANKRUPTCY JUDGE

Copies to:

Plaintiff's Counsel

Defendant's Counsel

Courtroom Deputy
Ms. Eileen Godfrey

Bankruptcy Judge Richard E. Fehling

Judge Fehling was born in Reading, Pennsylvania, in 1952. He received a B.A. from Yale University in 1974 and a J.D. from Dickinson School of Law in 1979. Judge Fehling was appointed to the United States Bankruptcy Court for the Eastern District of Pennsylvania on February 14, 2006. Since his appointment, Judge Fehling has presided in the Reading Division of the court.

PRELIMINARY GENERAL MATTERS

1. Correspondence with the Court. Judge Fehling discourages communications, including correspondence, from counsel to the court and will not consider communications that address any issue that should properly be raised in a pleading. Judge Fehling's courtroom deputy is responsible for scheduling all hearings and trials. Consequently, all communications that relate to Judge Fehling's calendar must be directed to his courtroom deputy.

2. Communications with Law Clerks. Judge Fehling permits counsel to speak directly with his law clerk, subject to the obvious limitations that law clerks are not permitted to give legal advice or discuss legal issues. Any questions concerning the status of a matter under advisement should be directed to the Clerk's Office or should be put in writing to the judge, with a copy of the correspondence sent to all opposing parties. Any questions concerning the general status of a case or the status of an uncontested matter should be directed to the Clerk's Office.

3. Telephone Conferences and Use of Facsimile Machines. Judge Fehling welcomes the use of telephone conferences, particularly when they relate to pretrial matters. The judge's judicial assistant handles the scheduling of all telephone conferences and, therefore, all inquiries regarding the scheduling of telephone conferences should be directed to Judge Fehling's judicial assistant.

4. Pro Hac Vice Admissions. Judge Fehling prefers that written requests for admission pro hac vice be submitted in accordance with Local Bankr. R. 2090-1(c). As a matter of professional courtesy and in keeping with a "national practice," however, Judge Fehling liberally grants oral motions made in open court at the time of the hearing or trial. The fee required under Local Bankr. R. 2090-1(c) must be paid whether the request for admission pro hac vice is made by written application and motion or by oral motion in open court.

5. Chambers Copies of Filed Papers. Parties should not submit to the chambers so-called "courtesy" copies of pleadings, memoranda of law, or any other filed documents.

6. Proposed Orders. In the certain specific types of motions listed below, counsel should provide a proposed order substantially in the form set forth on pages 405–406.

    a. Expedited consideration (page 405).
    b. Avoidance of a lien pursuant to 11 U.S.C. § 522(f) (page 406).

LITIGATION GENERALLY

The following practices and procedures pertain to litigation generally, whether contested matters in motion practice or trials in adversary proceedings or any other matter that results in a court appearance.

Continuances and Extensions

1. General Policy. Counsel must first contact opposing counsel to seek consent to the requested continuance. Requests with consent for a continuance should be made by letter, telephone, or e-mail to the courtroom deputy. As a matter of professionalism and civility, counsel should liberally consent to a reasonable request for a continuance, unless such a request materially prejudices their client. If all parties consent, a request for a continuance will usually be granted.

2. Need for Filing Formal Stipulation or Motion. All contested requests for a continuance must be made by written motion to the courtroom deputy. After receiving a motion for a continuance, the courtroom deputy will forward the motion to chambers. Ordinarily, Judge Fehling will then have his judicial assistant schedule a telephone conference. Judge Fehling will decide on a case-by-case basis whether cause exists to grant a motion for a continuance. Counsel are urged to file their motions for the continuance as soon as they become aware of the need for a continuance and well in advance of a specially listed hearing or trial so that the court may schedule another matter in the reserved time.

3. Need for Court Appearance. A party's appearance (both counsel and party) in court is required when a continuance cannot be arranged.

Settlements

1. Philosophy. Judge Fehling actively encourages settlement discussions and will participate in telephone settlement conferences if the parties so request. Occasionally, when the nature of the case requires, Judge Fehling will conduct settlement conferences in his chambers. Requests for a settlement conference, whether by telephone or in chambers, should be directed to Judge Fehling's judicial assistant by letter or telephone.

2. Referral of Settlement Negotiations to a Mediator or to Another Bankruptcy Judge. If a settlement conference is held in a case assigned to Judge Fehling, he is ordinarily the judge who will preside over the conference. If the nature of the case so requires, however, Judge Fehling will entertain a party's (or the parties') request to substitute a mediator or another judge in the district to preside over the settlement conference.

3. Need for Court Appearance for a Settlement. To the extent court approval of any settlement is sought, the provisions of Fed.R.Bankr.P. 9019 must be followed if applicable. If an objection is filed to a settlement motion, a court appearance will be necessary.

Opening Statements and Summations

Judge Fehling prefers that opening statements and summations, if necessary, be brief and concise.

Filing Memoranda and Proposed Findings of Fact and Conclusions of Law

1. Before Hearing or Trial. Unless specifically ordered to the contrary, memoranda of law need not be filed prior to a hearing or trial. If a party chooses to file a prehearing or pretrial memorandum, the party may do so.

2. After Hearing or Trial. Counsel may be directed by bench order following a hearing or trial to file memoranda of law.

3. Reply and Surreply Memoranda/Briefs. Judge Fehling discourages the parties from filing reply and surreply memoranda of law. If a party desires to file a reply memorandum, he or she must first submit a written request to Judge Fehling. Judge Fehling will not consider any unsolicited reply memorandum without prior permission of the court. If Judge Fehling permits a party to file a reply memorandum, however, he will permit the opposing party to file a surreply memorandum.

4. Proposed Findings of Fact and Conclusions of Law. Judge Fehling will sometimes request that the parties file proposed findings of fact and conclusions of law with a memorandum of law following the conclusion of a hearing or trial. If Judge Fehling does not order the parties to file these submissions, however, the parties are not obligated to file them.

5. Maximum Page Length for Memoranda of Law. No memorandum of law may exceed 25 pages without express permission of Judge Fehling.

Rule 52(c) Motions

Rule 52(c) motions are permitted under Fed.R.Bankr.P. 7052 and 9014.

Witnesses

1. Examination of Witnesses or Argument by More Than One Attorney. Judge Fehling will only occasionally approve the examination of a witness by more than one attorney representing a party; he will consider requests to do so in appropriate circumstances.

2. Examination of Witnesses Beyond Redirect and Recross. Judge Fehling discourages the examination of witnesses beyond redirect and recross.

3. Examination of Witnesses Out of Sequence. Judge Fehling will permit counsel to examine witnesses out of turn if all parties consent or if required for the legitimate convenience of the witnesses or otherwise.

4. Testimony by Telephone. Refer to the section below titled "Testimony of a Party or Other Person as a Witness in Court by Telephone or Video Conferencing," on page 398.

Presentation of Evidence

1. Use of Rule 43(e) Affidavits. Judge Fehling permits the use of Rule 43(e) affidavits in lieu of testimony if the parties consent to their use. In addition, Judge Fehling will permit an expert appraiser's written report to be substituted for direct examination of the appraiser if the report has been served upon opposing parties prior to the hearing or trial and if the appraiser is available for cross-examination.

2. Marking of Exhibits and Number of Copies. Exhibits must be pre-marked and exchanged with opposing counsel prior to the hearing. The original exhibit should be given to the witness during his or her testimony, and counsel should come to court with sufficient copies of each exhibit to provide Judge Fehling, his law clerk, and all parties with a copy of each exhibit as it is being used. NOTE: Failure to follow this rule may result in the exclusion of nonconforming exhibits from the court's consideration. If the exhibits are particularly numerous, a binder and index of tabbed exhibits will facilitate the hearing or trial.

3. Offering Exhibits in Evidence. Exhibits should ordinarily be offered in evidence at the conclusion of the party's case-in-chief, unless otherwise justified by the circumstances of the case.

4. Need for Presentation of Evidence if Uncontested. The moving party always bears the risk of carrying their burden, even in uncontested matters. Judge Fehling does not presume to advise counsel regarding presentation of their case.

5.   Reading of Material Into the Record. Judge Fehling generally will not permit the parties to read lengthy material into the record. Instead, Judge Fehling will direct counsel to stipulate to the documentary submission.

6.   Audiovisual Evidence, Including Videotaped Testimony. Judge Fehling will permit the use of audiovisual evidence, including videotaped testimony, to the extent agreed upon by all parties or as allowed by the Federal Rules of Bankruptcy Procedure and the Federal Rules of Evidence. Arrangements to have appropriate equipment cleared through security and set up in the courtroom must be made in advance by contacting Judge Fehling's courtroom deputy.

7.   Confidentiality Stipulations and Documents Under Seal. Judge Fehling will consider requests by a party or a stipulation of all parties to establish a procedure for asserting claims of privilege or protection as trial preparation material after production of discovery. Any requests for documents to be sealed must accord with Local Bankr. R. 5003-1.

Matters Involving Out-of-Town Parties or Witnesses

1.   Generally. Judge Fehling will attempt to accommodate out-of-town counsel, parties, and witnesses when scheduling and conducting hearings and trials. Counsel are requested to make the court aware of such circumstances as early in the proceeding as possible.

2.   Participation in Court of Counsel or Parties by Telephone or Video Conferencing. Judge Fehling will allow counsel and parties to participate in preliminary matters, hearings on contested matters, and in trials in adversary proceedings in certain circumstances in accordance with Local Bankr. R. 9076-1. Any requests by counsel or a party to participate in court by telephone or video conference should be brought to the attention of Judge Fehling's courtroom deputy and counsel for all opposing parties at the earliest possible opportunity. The nature and extent of such participation may vary from case to case, and special procedures for each case may be set forth in a pretrial procedural order, if necessary. If any party intends to testify remotely in any such hearing or trial, the party must comply with the requirements set forth below.

3.   Testimony of a Party or Other Person as a Witness in Court by Telephone or Video Conferencing. Judge Fehling will allow a witness, including a party, to testify in preliminary matters, hearings on contested matters, and trials in adversary proceedings under the following conditions:

1. Appropriate (in the sole discretion of court personnel) technical arrangements for remote testimony should be made in advance of the hearing or trial;

2. Appropriate (in the sole discretion of court personnel) arrangements should be made to verify the identity of a remote witness, to assure that no person is coaching or otherwise assisting the remote witness, and to administer the oath to the remote witness;

3. If the connection to the remote witness fails or if the remote witness's testimony becomes unintelligible (in the sole discretion of court personnel), the hearing or trial will proceed without the remote witness's testimony, which may not be rescheduled to another day or time (unless the difficulty is caused by a malfunction of court equipment); and

4. All exhibits to which the remote witness will refer in his or her testimony should be pre-marked with copies provided (whether as hard copies or in a suitable electronic format) to opposing counsel at least two days in advance of the hearing or trial.

Sidebars

Requests for sidebar conferences will be granted when necessary.

In Limine Motions

The pretrial order entered by Judge Fehling in every adversary proceeding contains a deadline for the filing of in limine motions. (A copy of Judge Fehling's form pretrial order is shown on page 402 of this book.)

UNCONTESTED MATTERS

When a motion or application is uncontested because no responsive pleading was filed by the deadline set forth in the notice of motion, counsel for the moving party should file a certificate of no response, notify Judge Fehling's courtroom deputy by telephone that the matter is uncontested, and request that she remove it from the hearing list. Even in uncontested matters, the moving party continues to bear the risk of satisfying its burden, whether through the unopposed averments in the pleadings or through testimony and exhibits if necessary.

ADVERSARY PROCEEDINGS
Discovery Matters

1. **Length of Discovery Period and Extensions.** After a responsive pleading to the complaint is filed, a pretrial order will be entered establishing a discovery schedule. (A copy of Judge Fehling's form pretrial order is shown on page 402 of this book.) If all parties consent to an extension, a stipulation extending discovery may be filed, accompanied by a proposed order approving the stipulation. In these situations, the discovery schedule will usually be extended pursuant to the consented request. If a party requests an extension to which objection is raised, a motion to extend the discovery deadline must be filed. Judge Fehling will usually decide such a matter without the parties' court appearance, although he may schedule a telephone conference about it. The parties should be aware and take into account that changing the discovery schedule could and often will affect all subsequent scheduled dates in the pretrial order.

2. **Discovery Conferences and Dispute Resolution.** If any discovery dispute arises, the parties should immediately call Judge Fehling's chambers requesting the scheduling of a telephone conference with Judge Fehling. If the dispute is not resolved in the telephone conference, the dispute must be resolved by motion practice. If neither party desires to present evidence relating to a discovery dispute, the parties may contact Judge Fehling's courtroom deputy and arrange to file a scheduling order to submit the matter on stipulated facts and memoranda of law (if necessary).

3. **Confidentiality Agreements.** Confidentiality agreements will be considered by Judge Fehling pursuant to 11 U.S.C. § 107 and federal common law. For documents filed under seal, refer to Local Bankr. R. 5003-1.

4. **Expert Witnesses.** The pretrial order entered by Judge Fehling requires that expert witnesses be identified in the pretrial statement. The pretrial statement must also include a brief summary of the testimony the expert is expected to present at trial. (A copy of Judge Fehling's form pretrial order is shown on page 402.)

5. **e-Discovery.** The pretrial order entered by Judge Fehling requires that all electronic discovery issues be addressed by the parties as part of the Rule 26 discovery conferences. (A copy of Judge Fehling's form pretrial order is shown on page 402.)

Pretrial Conferences

1. Scheduling Telephone Conference. Upon the closing of the pleadings in an adversary proceeding, Judge Fehling's office will contact counsel about participating in a scheduling telephone conference. In such a conference, the parties will discuss which pretrial activities (mediation, discovery, exchange of experts, dispositive motions, etc.) will be necessary and which will not be necessary.

2. Pretrial Conference. Based upon the scheduling telephone conference, Judge Fehling will prepare and enter a pretrial order that will set the dates by which all pretrial activities must be completed. The pretrial order will also set the date and time of the pretrial conference, which will ordinarily be held in open court, without a compelling request to the contrary. (A copy of Judge Fehling's form pretrial order is shown on page 402.) Counsel may request to appear by telephone at a pretrial conference by contacting Judge Fehling's courtroom deputy in advance of the conference, but personal appearance is greatly preferred.

Scheduling of Cases

Proceedings will be scheduled for trial during the pretrial conference.

Briefing Schedules for Motions

Motions in an adversary proceeding (dismissal, summary judgment, etc.) other than motions for expedited consideration, which are discussed below, will not be scheduled in accordance with the system for self-scheduling motions in contested matters. Counsel for the moving party, immediately upon the filing of the motion, must contact Judge Fehling's courtroom deputy, to notify her about the filing of the motion. Judge Fehling will then enter a scheduling order setting the dates by which supporting and opposing briefs must be filed and, if warranted, setting the date and time for oral argument.

Mediation and Arbitration

1. Pretrial Orders. Judge Fehling will enter a pretrial order in all adversary cases except those assigned to compulsory arbitration. (A copy of Judge Fehling's form pretrial order is shown on page 402.) The pretrial order requests that the parties inform Judge Fehling in writing whether they consent to participate in mediation, which participation Judge Fehling encourages. If all parties consent, a mediator will be appointed promptly.

2. General Approach to Arbitration Cases. Adversary proceedings will be assigned to compulsory arbitration in accordance with Local Bankr. R. 9019-2.

3. Scheduling of Trial De Novo from Arbitration. If a trial de novo is demanded following arbitration, Judge Fehling will issue a pretrial order that contains a discovery schedule, a date for the filing of a joint pretrial statement, and the date and time of the pretrial conference. (A copy of Judge Fehling's form pretrial order is shown on page 402.) Judge Fehling will schedule the trial during the pretrial conference.

Expedited Contested Matters

1. Expedited Consideration Generally. Local Bankr. Rules 5070-1(f) and 9014-2 govern requests for expedited hearings. Upon the filing of a motion for expedited hearing with the Clerk's Office, and service of such a motion on other parties in interest, Judge Fehling's courtroom deputy will consult with the judge to determine the appropriate course of action, including the scheduling of a hearing or telephone conference. (The proposed order granting expedited consideration should be in substantial compliance with the form of order shown on page 405.)

2. **Certificate of Consultation and Service.** All motions for expedited consideration must include a statement of counsel that certifies that counsel has consulted, or has attempted to consult, with all interested parties and the results of such consultation, as required by Local Bankr. Rule 5070-1(f)(1), and that certifies a list of all parties who have been served with the motion for expedited consideration.

INJUNCTIONS
Scheduling and Expedited Discovery

1. **Preliminary Injunctions.** Motions for temporary restraining orders or for preliminary injunctions must be filed with the Clerk's Office with notice given to opposing parties in compliance with Fed.R.Bankr.P. 7065. Upon filing of the motion, Judge Fehling's courtroom deputy will consult with the judge to determine the appropriate course of action, including the scheduling of a hearing or telephone conference.

2. **Expedited Discovery.** Motions for expedited discovery must be filed with the Clerk's Office and served upon opposing parties. Such a motion will be determined summarily after opposing parties have had an opportunity to respond.

Proposed Findings of Fact and Conclusions of Law

Judge Fehling does not require the filing of proposed findings of fact and conclusions of law when a temporary restraining order or preliminary injunction is sought unless the parties are advised otherwise.

APPENDIX "A"

UNITED STATES BANKRUPTCY COURT
FOR THE EASTERN DISTRICT OF PENNSYLVANIA

In re: :
                                      : Bankruptcy No. ____-_____
    Debtor(s)   : Chapter _____

    Plaintiff(s)   :
    v.   :
    Defendant(s)   : Adversary No. ____-_____

PRE-TRIAL ORDER #1
(See Paragraph H. for date of Mandatory Courtroom Conference)

AND NOW, this _____ day of _____, 20___, the Plaintiff(s) having filed an adversary proceeding and the Defendant(s) having filed a responsive pleading thereto, it is hereby ORDERED that:

1. On or before _____, the parties shall file a Joint Jurisdictional Statement in which they state whether this matter is core or non-core. If the matter is non-core, the parties shall also state whether they consent to this Court's entry of a final order under 28 U.S.C. § 157(c)(2) or otherwise.

2. On or before _____, the parties shall submit to the clerk a Joint Statement indicating whether they consent to participate in the court-annexed mediation program. If a party declines to so participate, said party shall state the reason(s) for such declination in the Joint Statement.

3. On or before _____, counsel shall have held and concluded the mandatory discovery conference pursuant to Fed. R. Civ. P. 26(f), which is incorporated into these proceedings by Fed. R. Bankr. P. 7026.

    A. Prior to the Rule 26(f) conference, counsel shall review the client's information management systems including computer-based and other digital systems, to understand how information is stored and how it can be retrieved, including currently maintained computer files as well as historical archival backup and legacy computer files. Counsel shall also determine the person or persons with knowledge about the client's information management systems, including computer-based and other digital systems, with the ability to facilitate, through counsel, reasonably anticipated discovery.

    B. During the Rule 26(f) conference, the parties shall review, as part of their deliberations, how to proceed with general discovery, electronic discovery, and the pre-trial schedule detailed below in paragraph 5 of this Order.

4. Within fourteen (14) days after the conclusion of the Rule 26(f) discovery conference, the parties shall file a discovery plan as mandated by Fed. R. Civ. P. 26(f) only in the event that:

Bankruptcy Judge Richard E. Fehling

    A.   any party proposes a discovery or pre-trial schedule that differs from the one outlined in paragraph 5 below,

    B.   any party objects that Rule 26(a)(1) initial disclosures are not appropriate in the circumstances of the action, or

    C.   disputes arise about electronic discovery.

In the event of (A), (B), or (C) above, a formal pleading shall be filed pursuant to motion practice under L.B.R. 9014-3.

5.   Within fourteen (14) days after the conclusion of the Rule 26(f) discovery conference, the parties shall provide each other with the initial disclosures detailed in Fed. R. Civ. P. 26(a)(1).

6.   The following discovery and trial schedule shall be reviewed by the parties in their deliberations at their Rule 26(f) discovery conference:

    A.   All expert witnesses shall be identified and a copy of each expert's report shall be provided to every other party, in accordance with Fed. R. Civ. P. 26(a)(2), on or before _____.

    B.   Any electronic discovery issues or proposed stipulations and orders relating to claims of privilege and attorney work product arising after production of electronic discovery pursuant to Rule 26(f)(4) shall be filed on or before _____, using Official Form 35.

    C.   All discovery shall be completed on or before _____.

    D.   All motions to amend the pleadings, or for summary judgment, shall be filed on or before _____.

    E.   All motions *in limine* (other than motions objecting to initial disclosures) shall be filed on or before _____.

    F.   All discovery disclosures pursuant to Fed. R. Civ. P. 26(a)(3) shall be served on opposing parties and filed with the bankruptcy court on or before _____.

    G.   Any objections to the Rule 26(a)(3) disclosures shall be served on opposing counsel and filed with the bankruptcy court pursuant to motion practice under L.B.R. 9014-3 on or before _____.

    H.   On or before _____, the parties shall file a Joint Pre-trial Statement. The Joint Pre-trial Statement shall be signed by all counsel. It is the obligation of the Plaintiff's counsel to initiate the preparation of the Joint Pre-trial Statement and to assemble and file the Joint Pre-trial Statement. Plaintiff's counsel shall submit a proposed Joint Pre-trial Statement to Defendant's counsel not less than 7 days prior to the deadline for its submission.

The Joint Pre-trial Statement shall set forth all of the issues on which the parties agree and disagree and shall contain the following:

    I.   <u>Basis of jurisdiction</u>. (including a statement whether this matter is core or non-core). If the matter is non-core, the parties shall state whether they consent to the court's entry of a final order pursuant to 28 U.S.C. § 157(c)(2). If the parties disagree, they shall each cite relevant authority to support their positions.

    II.   <u>Statement of uncontested facts</u>.

    III.   <u>Statement of facts that are in dispute</u>. No facts should be disputed unless opposing counsel expects to present contrary evidence on the point at trial, or genuinely challenges the fact on credibility grounds.

    IV.   <u>Damages or other relief</u>. A statement of damages claimed or relief sought. A party seeking damages shall list each item claimed under a separate descriptive heading, shall provide a detailed description of each item and shall state the amount of damages claimed. A party seeking relief other than damages shall list the exact form of relief sought with precise designations of persons, parties, places and things expected to be included in any order providing relief.

V. Legal issues presented and the constitutional, statutory, regulatory, and decisional authorities relied upon. Counsel shall include a brief statement regarding which party has the burden of proof on each legal issue.

VI. Witnesses, listed in the order they will be called, with a brief statement of the evidence the witness will give. Witnesses shall be classified to include those whom any party expects to present and those whom any party may call if the need arises. If not already provided to all parties, the address and telephone number of each witness shall be disclosed.

VII. Exhibits listed in the order they will be offered into evidence. Exhibits shall be serially numbered and physically marked before trial in the order of their intended presentation. Documents that a party may offer if the need arises shall be separately identified.

VIII. A list of each discovery item and trial deposition to be offered into evidence. Counsel shall designate by page and line the portion of deposition testimony and by number the interrogatories that shall be offered in evidence at trial.

IX. Estimated trial time.

X. A certification that the parties have attempted good faith settlement discussions without success.

I. A mandatory final pre-trial/settlement conference shall be held on **Wednesday, _____, 20__, at ___ A.M., in Bankruptcy Courtroom #1, Third Floor, The Madison, 400 Washington Street, Reading, PA.**

> **If the parties desire to continue the pre-trial/settlement conference, they shall provide the court with written notice of the request for a continuance at least three (3) business days prior to the date set for the pre-trial/settlement conference. No party shall be excused from attendance at the pre-trial/settlement conference unless the court approves the written request for a continuance.**
>
> **(a). Failure of counsel for Plaintiff to attend the pre-trial/settlement conference without obtaining court approval for a continuance by providing the court with three (3) business days written notice of a request for a continuance may result in dismissal of the complaint without prejudice.**
>
> **(b). Failure of counsel for Defendant to attend the pre-trial/settlement conference without obtaining court approval for a continuance by providing the court with three (3) business days written notice of a request for a continuance may result in entry of judgment against Defendant on the complaint.**

J. If the adversary proceeding is not resolved prior to the conclusion of the conference, the court shall enter an Order Setting Adversary Trial Date and serve a copy of same on each party at said conference.

K. If any party violates any of these provisions, the court shall consider imposition of sanctions on the offending party and their counsel.

BY THE COURT

_____
RICHARD E. FEHLING
United States Bankruptcy Judge

Bankruptcy Judge Richard E. Fehling

APPENDIX "B-1"

UNITED STATES BANKRUPTCY COURT
FOR THE EASTERN DISTRICT OF PENNSYLVANIA

In re: :
                          :   Case No. _____ – _____ REF
         Debtor(s)   :   Chapter _____

ORDER SETTING EXPEDITED HEARING TO CONSIDER MOTION

AND NOW, this _____ day of _____, 20__, the Movants having requested expedited consideration of their Motion _____ [describe Motion] _____ _____ (the "Motion"), IT IS HEREBY ORDERED that an expedited hearing for my consideration of the Movants' Motion shall be held at:

**United States Bankruptcy Court—E.D. Pa.
Courtroom Number 1
Third Floor, The Madison
400 Washington Street**
Reading, Pennsylvania on _____ ___, 20___, at __:__ _.m. prevailing time.

IT IS HEREBY FURTHER ORDERED that any party opposing the Motion shall file an answer or response at or before the time and date of the hearing set above and that any party opposing the Motion shall appear at the hearing on the Motion or it may be granted without further notice.

IT IS HEREBY FURTHER ORDERED that Movants' counsel shall immediately both (1.) notify by telephone and (2.) serve copies of this signed Order and the Motion on the following parties by e-mail or facsimile: Counsel for the United States Trustee and either the Chapter 7 or the Chapter 13 Trustee, counsel for the Debtors [if the motion is not filed by the Debtors], all secured creditors with liens on Movants' property (by serving their counsel if known), all other parties affected by the Motion (by serving their counsel if known), and all other interested parties.

                                        BY THE COURT

                                        _____
                                        RICHARD E. FEHLING
                                        United States Bankruptcy Judge

APPENDIX "B-2"

UNITED STATES BANKRUPTCY COURT
FOR THE EASTERN DISTRICT OF PENNSYLVANIA

In re: _____ :
　　　　_____, : Chapter __
Debtors　　　　　　　　　　　 : Bankruptcy No. __-2____REF

ORDER

　　　AND NOW, this __ day of _____, 20__, upon the motion of Debtor[s] to avoid an alleged judicial lien (DOCKET NUMBER and COURT) or nonpossessory, nonpurchase money security interest of _____ NAME OF CREDITOR _____ in Debtor[s's] exempt real or personal property located at _____ LOCATION OF PROPERTY SUBJECT TO THE LIEN _____, and upon Debtor[s] having asserted that the alleged lien is subject to avoidance pursuant to Section 522(f)(1), 11 U.S.C. § 522(f)(1), and upon Debtor[s] having certified that adequate notice of the motion was sent to the lienholder and that no answer or other response to the motion has been filed,

　　　IT IS HEREBY ORDERED that the motion is granted by default and the above judicial lien and/or a nonpossessory, nonpurchase money security interest of _____ NAME OF CREDITOR _____, if any, in Debtor[s's] real or personal property located in _____ LOCATION _____ is avoided to the extent it impairs Debtor[s's] exemption.

　　　IT IS FURTHER ORDERED, pursuant to Section 349(b)(1)(B), 11 U.S.C. §349(b)(1)(B), that dismissal of this case reinstates and lien voided under Section 522.

　　　　　　　　　　　　　　　　　　　　　　　BY THE COURT

　　　　　　　　　　　　　　　　　　　　　　　_____
　　　　　　　　　　　　　　　　　　　　　　　RICHARD E. FEHLING
　　　　　　　　　　　　　　　　　　　　　　　United States Bankruptcy Judge

Bankruptcy Judge Jean K. FitzSimon

Judge FitzSimon was appointed to the United States Bankruptcy Court for the Eastern District of Pennsylvania on June 28, 2006. She received her B.A. from St. John's College and J.D. from Notre Dame Law School.

PRELIMINARY GENERAL MATTERS

1. Correspondence with the Court. Judge FitzSimon generally discourages unsolicited correspondence from counsel and will not consider correspondence that addresses any issue that should properly be raised by motion practice. Judge FitzSimon will, however, occasionally invite and/or direct counsel to report on the status of matters via letters. Counsel may not, by letter, raise or answer substantive issues or seek advice from the court. Judge FitzSimon's courtroom deputy is responsible for scheduling all hearings and trials. Consequently, all correspondence that relates to Judge FitzSimon's calendar must be directed to her deputy.

2. Communications with Law Clerks. Judge FitzSimon permits counsel to speak directly with her law clerk, subject to the limitation that law clerks are not permitted to give legal advice or discuss the merits of pending cases. The scheduling of trials, hearings, and most conferences is the responsibility of Judge FitzSimon's courtroom deputy or, in the alternative, her judicial assistant.

3. Telephone Conferences and Use of Facsimile Machines. Judge FitzSimon welcomes telephone conferences. A request for a telephone conference generally will not be granted in the absence of a filed pleading, motion, or other communication from all of the parties. Unless a request for a telephone conference is being made in lieu of an appearance at a scheduled hearing (in which event Judge FitzSimon's courtroom deputy should be consulted), the judge's judicial assistant handles the scheduling of all telephone conferences. All requests for telephonic conferences and/or appearances must be made at least 24 hours in advance. Parties participating in telephone conferences must use a land line telephone; use of cell phones is not permitted.

Judge FitzSimon does not accept facsimile transmissions unless they are requested and approved in advance.

4. Pro Hac Vice Admissions. Judge FitzSimon prefers that written requests for admission pro hac vice be submitted in accordance with Local Bankruptcy Rule 2090-1(c). Oral motion may be made in open court at the time of the hearing or trial. The fee required under Local Bankr. R. 2090-1(c) must be paid whether the request for admission pro hac vice is made by written application and motion or by oral motion in open court.

5. Chambers Copies of Filed Papers. In adversary proceedings and chapter 11 cases, Judge FitzSimon would appreciate receiving chambers copies of documents filed when the exhibits are voluminous. In all other situations, Judge FitzSimon will accept courtesy or chambers copies of filed papers, but stresses to the bar that this is in no way required without specific request on her part.

LITIGATION GENERALLY
Continuances and Extensions

1. General Policy Where Parties Are In Agreement. Judge FitzSimon generally is liberal with requests for continuances where all parties are in agreement. The request should be made through the judge's courtroom deputy by letter, if time permits, or by telephone (except for a request for an extension of the dates in a pretrial order, which must be made by stipulation with the consent of all parties or upon motion to the court).

2. Where the Request for a Continuance Is Opposed. If a request for a continuance is opposed or the matter has been specially listed, Judge FitzSimon expects counsel to raise the issue via a telephone conference call. Otherwise, the request for a continuance should be presented by written motion sufficiently in advance of the hearing to allow the matter to be disposed of prior to the originally scheduled date. If necessary, a request for expedited consideration should be made.

3. Need for Court Appearance. Judge FitzSimon may sometimes dispose of a contested continuance request on the papers alone. Counsel will be advised in advance if a court appearance will be necessary.

Proposed Findings of Fact and Conclusions of Law

Judge FitzSimon does not require proposed findings of fact and conclusions of law unless she specifically indicates so at the conclusion of the matter or proceeding in court. Judge FitzSimon will generally permit such filings, upon request. Similarly, the judge welcomes memoranda of law from the parties, and will generally refrain from deciding matters from the bench if the parties desire an opportunity to brief certain issues.

Reading of Material Into the Record

Judge FitzSimon usually will not permit the reading of substantial material into the record.

Settlements

1. Settlement Conferences. Judge FitzSimon encourages settlement discussions and will entertain chambers settlement conferences if all parties in interest agree. However, Judge FitzSimon will participate in such conferences only to the extent it will not jeopardize her role as a fact finder should a settlement not successfully be reached.

2. Referral of Settlement Negotiations to Another Bankruptcy Judge. When all parties in interest are in agreement and mediation is either inappropriate or has been unsuccessful, a request for a settlement conference with another bankruptcy judge will be entertained.

3. Need for Court Appearances. Settlements should be reported promptly to Judge FitzSimon's courtroom deputy and, if the matter is under advisement, also to her law clerk. The necessary motions to seek court approval must be filed pursuant to Federal Bankruptcy Rule 9019 and local rule, as applicable. An objection to a proposed settlement will require a court appearance.

Form Orders

When a debtor files a motion either for expedited consideration of a matter or to avoid a lien pursuant to 11 U.S.C. § 522(f)(1)(A) or (B), the proposed order granting the relief should be in the form as set forth on page 417.

UNCONTESTED MATTERS

Judge FitzSimon will enter orders in response to a timely filed certificate of no objection. To avoid appearance at the scheduled hearing, counsel should contact the courtroom deputy at least 24 hours prior to the hearing.

Certain matters require an appearance, notwithstanding the absence of a filed answer or other response. They include:

1. Motions to withdraw as debtor's counsel;

2. Motions to reconsider or vacate orders;

3. Motions to extend or impose the automatic stay pursuant to § 362(c)(3) or (c)(4). The debtor seeking such relief must also appear in connection with such motion;

4. Objections to proofs of claim. Depending on the nature of the objection, the applicable burden of proof may require a record to be made notwithstanding the absence of a response by the claimant;

5. Motions to sell property pursuant to § 363;

6. Motions under Fed.R.Bankr.P. 9019 to approve a settlement or compromise;

7. Motions requesting that a dismissal order include provisions that restrict the filing of a new bankruptcy case or that provide in rem relief;

8. Motions for default judgments in adversary proceedings.

Counsel may request permission to appear by phone on such uncontested matters, particularly if counsel is located away from the vicinity of the courthouse. Such requests should be directed to the judge's courtroom deputy well in advance of the scheduled hearing date, and will be considered on a case-by-case basis. Parties participating telephonically must use a land line telephone; use of cell phones is not permitted.

CONTESTED MATTER PRACTICE AND PROCEDURE
Filing Memoranda of Law/Briefs

1. **Before Hearing.** Judge FitzSimon will consider prehearing briefs, but they are not required.

2. **After Hearing.** Memoranda are required only if a briefing schedule has been established at the conclusion of the proceedings in court. Parties desiring to submit post-hearing memoranda ordinarily will be permitted to do so.

3. **Reply and Surreply Memoranda/Briefs.** Reply and surreply memoranda or briefs will be permitted if approved in advance, generally at the time a briefing schedule is established. Judge FitzSimon will not consider any unsolicited reply memoranda filed without prior permission of the court.

4. **Length of Memoranda/Briefs.** Unless otherwise permitted by the court prior to filing, memoranda and briefs must be no more than 25 pages long.

Scheduling of Contested Matters

Upon the filing of a motion and answer or response to the motion in a contested matter, if presenting evidence or argument is anticipated to take 30 minutes or longer, the parties are required to notify Judge FitzSimon's courtroom deputy of the need to schedule a specially listed hearing. The matter will then be taken off the regular docket and be specially listed by the judge's courtroom deputy or by court order.

Scheduling of Expedited Hearings

Local Bankruptcy Rule 5070-1 governs motions for expedited hearings. In matters in which relief is requested that directly affects one or more specific respondents, consistent with the local rule, Judge FitzSimon ordinarily will not grant or schedule an expedited hearing unless the movant's counsel confers with the respondents' counsel regarding their consent to an expedited hearing and their availability for the requested expedited hearing. Counsel should submit an order in the form set forth in the sample expedited form order on page 418. Counsel are strongly encouraged to notify the courtroom deputy by telephone that a motion for expedited consideration will be filed. If the request is approved, the courtroom deputy will notify movant's counsel of the hearing date.

Rule 52(c) Motions

Rule 52(c) motions are permitted under Fed.R.Bankr.P. 7052 and 9014.

Examination of Witnesses or Argument by More Than One Counsel

Judge FitzSimon will permit more than one attorney for a party to examine a witness or argue different points of law if permission is asked in advance and under appropriate circumstances.

Examination of Witnesses Beyond Redirect and Recross

Judge FitzSimon rarely will permit further examination of a witness after direct and recross have been completed.

Presentation of Evidence

1.   Use of Rule 43(e) Affidavits. When an expert witness will be providing an appraisal, Judge FitzSimon generally requires counsel to submit the expert's written report in lieu of direct examination. See *In re Adair,* 965 F.2d 777 (9th Cir. 1992). The expert report must be served upon opposing counsel prior to the hearing or proceeding and the expert must be available at the hearing or proceeding for cross-examination and redirect examination.

For other witnesses, Judge FitzSimon will generally permit the use of Rule 43(e) affidavits in lieu of testimony (1) upon agreement of counsel or (2) where out-of-town witnesses are involved and cross-examination can be held via telephone conference call.

2.   Marking of Exhibits and Number of Copies. Exhibits must be pre-marked and exchanged with opposing counsel *prior* to the hearing. Counsel needs the original for the witness and should have a copy of the exhibit for every other party present. When the exhibits are particularly numerous, a binder and index may facilitate the trial. A bench copy of exhibits is appreciated, but is not required without advance notice. If any party objects to the court viewing an exhibit during the trial, the court will refrain from doing so until the objection is resolved or the exhibit's admission is resolved.

3.   Offering Exhibits in Evidence. Exhibits should be offered at the conclusion of the party's case-in-chief.

4.   Need for Presentation of Evidence if Uncontested. If the moving party must demonstrate cause for relief, or if the moving party requests that findings be made, evidence may be required even though the motion is uncontested if the court is unable to make such findings on the basis of the pleadings alone. In appropriate circumstances, the judge will accept a proffer or affidavit.

ADVERSARY PROCEEDINGS
Discovery Matters

1.   Length of Discovery Period and Extensions. A pretrial order will be entered in all adversary proceedings and certain contested matters establishing a discovery deadline. A copy of Judge FitzSimon's standard pretrial order is shown on page 414. Extensions of the deadlines generally will be given upon submission of a stipulation by consent of all parties or cause shown.

2. Discovery Conferences and Dispute Resolution. Judge FitzSimon will entertain conference calls for the purpose of resolving discovery disputes. Requests for sanctions may be made only by written motion.

3. Confidentiality Agreements. Judge FitzSimon will approve confidentiality agreements or orders subject to the limitations of statutory and common law.

4. Expert Witnesses. Judge FitzSimon requires the advance identification of expert witnesses in the joint pretrial statement to be prepared in conformity with her standard pretrial order (a copy is shown on page 414 of this book). When an expert witness will be providing an appraisal, Judge FitzSimon requires counsel to submit the expert's written report in lieu of direct examination. See *In re Adair,* 965 F.2d 777 (9th Cir. 1992). The expert must be available at the hearing or proceeding for cross-examination and redirect examination.

5. e-Discovery. The pretrial order entered by Judge FitzSimon requires that all electronic discovery issues be addressed by the parties as part of the Rule 26 discovery conferences.

Pretrial Conferences

Final pretrial/settlement conferences will typically be scheduled in the pretrial order. However, Judge FitzSimon may enter a form of pretrial order that schedules an initial pretrial conference or status hearing. The judge will entertain requests for other pretrial conferences by phone or otherwise as the circumstances warrant.

Joint Pretrial Statement

Prior to the final pretrial/settlement conference, and by a date specified in the pretrial order, the parties are directed to submit a joint pretrial statement. Judge FitzSimon's pretrial order sets forth detailed and specific instructions for completing the joint pretrial statement, which should be completed cooperatively and timely. Failure to submit a timely or adequate joint pretrial statement may result in delay in the adversary proceeding's trial calendar and/or in the court ordering the parties to revise the joint pretrial statement.

Filing of Trial Memoranda and Briefs

1. Pretrial. Each party may file a pretrial memorandum with the clerk of court, provided it is served on opposing counsel and a courtesy copy is delivered to chambers five business days prior to the trial date.

2. Post-trial. Post-trial memoranda are necessary only when specifically requested by the court; however, Judge FitzSimon liberally will approve requests from the parties to submit them. The schedule for briefing will generally be established at the conclusion of the trial. In cases in which a transcript is being ordered by a party or parties, Judge FitzSimon will generally permit the briefing schedule to commence after receipt of the transcript in the regular course of business.

3. Reply and Surreply Memoranda and Briefs. The complete briefing schedule ordinarily will be established at the conclusion of trial proceedings. Briefs not otherwise identified at that time should not be submitted.

Mediation

The pretrial order will ask counsel to consider participation in the mediation program. If all parties agree, a mediator will be assigned. If the parties do not identify a proposed mediator in their communication to the court indicating their willingness to mediate, the court will appoint a mediator from the approved list of mediators. Judge FitzSimon will not insist that the parties attempt mediation against their will, nor does she require parties to explain a decision not to participate in mediation. Mediation will not suspend any of the deadlines established in the pretrial order.

Briefing Schedule for Motions

Dispositive motions in an adversary proceeding (dismissal, summary judgment, etc.), other than motions for expedited consideration, which are discussed above, will not be scheduled in accordance with the system for self-scheduling motions in contested matters. When filing a dispositive motion in an adversary proceeding, counsel should not assign a hearing date to the motion. After a response to the motion is filed, a hearing date will be assigned by the judge and counsel will be notified.

ARBITRATION

1. General Approach to Arbitration. Proceedings will be assigned to compulsory arbitration in accordance with Local Bankruptcy Rule 9019-2.

2. Scheduling of Trial De Novo from Arbitration. Once a trial de novo is demanded, Judge FitzSimon generally will issue a pretrial order directing the filing of a joint pretrial statement and setting a date for trial.

TRIAL PROCEDURE

1. Scheduling of Cases. Motions are assigned a hearing date in accordance with Local Bankruptcy Rule 5070-1. Adversary proceedings are assigned a trial date after the pretrial/settlement conference in accordance with the pretrial order.

2. Matters Involving Out-of-Town Parties or Witnesses. Judge FitzSimon endeavors to be as flexible as possible in matters involving out-of-town parties or witnesses when scheduling trials. Counsel should make the court aware of such circumstances in the joint pretrial statement as required by the pretrial order.

3. Sidebars. Sidebar conferences are discouraged, but will be entertained when necessary.

4. In Limine Motions. Judge FitzSimon's pretrial order contains a deadline for filing in limine motions.

5. Opening Statements and Summations. Judge FitzSimon will permit opening and closing statements, but will sometimes suggest that they be waived where pretrial memoranda have been submitted and/or post-trial memoranda are contemplated.

6. Examination of Witnesses Out of Sequence. Judge FitzSimon will permit counsel to examine witnesses out of turn if all parties consent or for the legitimate convenience of the witness.

7. Videotaped Testimony. Judge FitzSimon will permit the use of videotaped testimony to the extent agreed to by all parties or as allowed by the Federal Rules of Bankruptcy Procedure. Arrangements to have equipment set up in the courtroom and/or cleared through security should be done in advance by contacting the courtroom deputy.

INJUNCTIONS

1. Hearings on Motions for Temporary Restraining Orders or Preliminary Injunctions. Hearings on motions for temporary restraining orders or preliminary injunctions are viewed and scheduled in the same manner as requests for expedited consideration in contested matters. Requests for expedited discovery are treated in the same fashion.

Requests for expedited discovery should be filed and served upon opposing parties. Courtesy copies of all filed documents seeking expedited relief should be sent to chambers. The requests will be determined summarily after opposing parties have had a reasonable opportunity to respond.

2.   Proposed Facts and Conclusions of Law. Judge FitzSimon generally requires the submission of proposed facts and conclusions of law unless the parties are informed otherwise.

IN THE UNITED STATES BANKRUPTCY COURT
FOR THE EASTERN DISTRICT OF PENNSYLVANIA

In re	:	**Chapter**
,	:	
Debtor.	:	**Case No. (JKF)**
,	:	
Plaintiff,	:	
v.	:	
,	:	
Defendant.	:	**Adversary No.**

PRETRIAL SCHEDULING ORDER

AND NOW, this _____ day of _____, 20___, the plaintiff(s) having filed an adversary proceeding and the defendant(s) having filed a responsive pleading, it is hereby **ORDERED** that:

1. On or before **[21 days from the entry of the Order]**, the parties shall submit to chambers a joint statement indicating whether they consent to participate in the court-annexed mediation program. The joint statement may include up to three suggested mediators from the list of certified mediators, which list may be obtained from the Clerk. If the joint statement contains no suggested mediator(s), then the Court will choose one.

2. On or before **[21 days from the entry of this Order]**, counsel shall have held and concluded the mandatory discovery conference pursuant to Fed.R.Civ.P. 26(f), incorporated into these proceedings by Fed.R.Bankr.P. 7026. During said conference, the parties shall consider, as part of their deliberations on how to proceed with discovery (including electronic discovery), the discovery and pretrial schedule detailed in paragraph 5 below in this Order.

3. **Within fourteen days of the conclusion of the parties' discovery conference,** should the parties propose a discovery or pretrial schedule that *differs from the one below*, they shall file with the Bankruptcy Court a report on discovery as mandated by Fed.R.Civ.P. 26(f). The parties shall detail those differences in their Rule 26(f) report, along with the reasons therefor. The Court may, when appropriate, order a hearing based upon the information found in the Rule 26(f) report. If the parties are in agreement with the discovery schedule as outlined herein, no report need be filed unless there are objections to the initial discovery disclosures.

4. **Within fourteen days after the conclusion of the Rule 26(f) conference,** the parties shall provide the initial disclosures detailed in Fed.R.Civ.P. 26(a)(1). Any objections to the initial discovery disclosures required by Fed.R.Civ.P. 26(a)(1) shall be clearly raised in a Rule 26(f) report.

5. The following discovery and pretrial schedule shall be considered by the parties in their deliberations at their discovery conference:

    A. All discovery shall be completed on or before **[90 days from the date of this Order]**.

    B. All expert witnesses shall be identified and a copy of each expert's report shall be provided to every other party, in accordance with Fed.R.Civ.P. 26(a)(2) on or before **[60 days from the date of this Order]**.

    C. All motions to amend the pleadings or for summary judgment shall be filed on or before **[120 days from this Order]**.

D. All discovery disclosures pursuant to Fed.R.Civ.P. 26(a)(3) shall be served on opposing parties and filed with the bankruptcy court on or before **[2 weeks after C above]**.

E. Any objections to the Rule 26(a)(3) disclosures shall be served on opposing parties and filed with the bankruptcy court on or before **[2 weeks after D above]**.

F. On or before **[30 days after E above]**, the parties shall file a joint pretrial statement consistent with the form set forth in paragraph 7 below and file a copy with chambers. The joint pretrial statement shall be signed by all counsel. It is the obligation of the plaintiff's counsel to initiate, assemble and submit the proposed pretrial statement. Plaintiff's counsel shall submit a proposed joint pretrial statement to defendant's counsel not less than 7 days prior to the deadline for its submission.

Counsel are expected to make a diligent effort to prepare a proposed pretrial statement in which will be noted all of the issues on which the parties are in agreement and all of those issues on which they disagree. The proposed pretrial statement shall supersede all pleadings in the case. Amendments will be allowed only in exceptional circumstances and to prevent manifest injustice.

G. All motions *in limine* shall be filed on or before **[30 days after E above]**.

6. The joint pretrial statement shall be in the following form:

    A. <u>Basis of jurisdiction</u>. A statement setting forth the basis of jurisdiction and whether the matter is core or noncore. If the matter is noncore, the parties shall state whether they consent to the Court's entry of a final order pursuant to 28 U.S.C. § 157(c)(2). If the parties disagree, they shall each cite to relevant authority to support their positions.

    B. <u>Statement of uncontested facts</u>. A statement of the uncontested facts.

    C. <u>Statement of facts which are in dispute</u>. A statement of the facts in dispute. No facts should be disputed unless opposing counsel expects to present contrary evidence on the point at trial, or genuinely challenges the fact on credibility grounds.

    D. <u>Damages or other relief</u>. A statement of damages claimed or relief sought. A party seeking damages shall provide, for each cause of action being pursued: (a) a detailed description of each item of damages claimed; (b) the legal authority for such damages and (c) the specific amount of damages claimed. A party seeking relief other than damages shall, for each cause of action being pursued, list the exact form of relief sought with precise designation of persons, parties, places and things expected to be included in any order for relief and the legal authority for such relief.

    E. <u>Legal issues</u>. For the causes of action being pursued, identify the following: (i) the constitutional, statutory, regulatory and decisional authorities being relied upon for each cause of action; (ii) the elements which must be satisfied to prevail on each cause of action; and (iii) which party bears the burden of proof on each element. Also list any additional legal issues (*e.g.*, affirmative defenses) that will be relevant to the court's disposition of the matter, the authority pertinent to each legal issue, and the party which bears the burden on the issue.

    F. <u>Witnesses</u>. A list of witnesses in the order in which they will be called, along with a brief statement of the evidence the witness will give. Witnesses shall be classified between those whom any party expected to present and those whom any party may call if the need arises. If not already provided to all parties, the address and telephone number of each witness shall be disclosed.

    G. <u>A list of all exhibits</u>. A list of all exhibits to be offered into evidence which shall be serially numbered and physically marked before trial in accordance with the schedule. Documents which a party may offer if the need arises shall be separately identified.

H. <u>A list of each discovery item and trial deposition</u>. A list of each discovery item and trial deposition to be offered into evidence. Counsel shall designate by page portion of deposition testimony and by number the interrogatories/request for admissions which shall be offered into evidence.

I. <u>Estimated trial time and scheduling issues</u>. A statement of: (i) the estimated time which the trial will require; and (2) any issues that should be considered in setting a trial date (<u>e.g.</u> witnesses traveling from out-of-state who will need notice of the trial date to make their travel plans).

J. <u>Certification</u>. A certification that the parties have attempted good faith settlement discussions without success.

7. A mandatory pretrial/settlement conference shall be held on _____, 20__, at 2:00 p.m. **[change time if necessary]** in Bankruptcy Courtroom No. 3, Robert N.C. Nix Federal Building & Courthouse, 900 Market Street, 2nd Floor, Philadelphia, Pennsylvania.

8. If the adversary proceeding is not resolved prior to the conclusion of the final pretrial/settlement conferences, the adversary proceeding shall be set down for trial at the Court's first available trial date. The trial may be continued only in exceptional circumstances on motion to and leave of Court.

9. Seven (7) or more days prior to the date of the trial, each party is required to provide: (i) a copy of exhibits to the opposing parties; and (ii) two copies of exhibits to chambers.

10. The Court may require each party to file (and, if not directed by the Court, each party may choose to file), five (5) days prior to the date of the trial, a pretrial memorandum with service on the opposing party and a courtesy copy delivered to chambers.

                                              HONORABLE JEAN K. FITZSIMON
                                              United States Bankruptcy Judge

Copies to:

Plaintiff's Counsel

Defendant's Counsel

Courtroom Deputy
Ms. Joan Ranieri

Bankruptcy Judge Jean K. FitzSimon

**IN THE UNITED STATES BANKRUPTCY COURT
FOR THE EASTERN DISTRICT OF PENNSYLVANIA**

In re   :   **Chapter**

,   :

            Debtor. :   **Case No.   (JKF)**

_ _ _ _ _ _ _ _ _ _ _ _ _ _ _ _ _ _ _ _

ORDER

This _____ day of _____, 20__, upon motion of the debtor to avoid an alleged judicial lien and/or nonpossessory, nonpurchase money security interest in exempt real or personal property held by [lienholder] and identified as located at [court & lien no.]. The real property is known as [address].

And the debtor having asserted that the alleged lien is subject to avoidance pursuant to 11 U.S.C. § 522(f)(1)(A) or (B),

And the debtor having certified that adequate notice of the motion was sent to the lienholder and that no answer or other response to the motion has been filed,

Accordingly, it is hereby ordered that the motion is granted by default and the judicial lien and/or a nonpossessory, nonpurchase money security interest in real or personal property held by [lienholder], if any, on aforementioned property is avoided.

_____
JEAN K. FITZSIMON
United States Bankruptcy Judge

Copies to:

debtor

debtor's counsel

creditor

IN THE UNITED STATES BANKRUPTCY COURT
FOR THE EASTERN DISTRICT OF PENNSYLVANIA

In re   :   Chapter

                                       :

         Debtor   :   Case No.   (JKF)

ORDER

AND NOW, upon consideration of the ***[NAME OF MOTION]*** ("the Motion"), and the request for an expedited hearing thereon, and sufficient cause being shown, it is hereby **ORDERED** that:

1. The request for an expedited hearing is **Granted**.
2. A hearing to consider the Motion shall be held on _____, 20___, at _____, in Bankruptcy Courtroom #5, Robert N.C. Nix, Sr., Federal Building & Post Office, 900 Market Street, 2nd Floor, Philadelphia, Pennsylvania.
3. Written objections or other responsive pleadings to the Motion (while not required) may be filed up to the time of the hearing and all will be considered at the hearing.
4. The Movant shall serve the Motion and this Order on the U.S. Trustee, the case Trustee (if any), the individual Respondent(s) (if any), counsel to the Official Committee of Unsecured Creditors (if any), all secured creditors and all priority creditors by overnight mail, facsimile transmission or e-mail transmission no later than 5:00 p.m. on _____. If the hearing is scheduled less than 48 hours after the Movant receives this Order, Movant shall give immediate telephonic notice of the hearing to the above as well.
5. The Movant shall serve this Order and the Notice of the Motion in conformity with Local Bankruptcy Form 9014-3 on all other parties in interest, including all creditors, by regular mail no later than 5:00 p.m. on _____.
6. Prior to the hearing, the Movant shall file a Certification setting forth compliance with the service requirements of Paragraphs 4 and 5 above as applicable.

Dated: _____

                                                            _____
                                                            HONORABLE JEAN K. FITZSIMON
                                                            United States Bankruptcy Judge

Bankruptcy Judge Bruce Fox

Judge Fox was born on October 22, 1949. He received a B.S. from the State University of New York at Stony Brook in 1971 and a J.D. from Harvard University Law School in 1975. He was appointed United States Bankruptcy Judge for the Eastern District of Pennsylvania on October 1, 1986.

PRELIMINARY GENERAL MATTERS

1. Correspondence with the Court. Judge Fox discourages correspondence from counsel to the court, and generally will not consider correspondence that should properly be the subject of motion practice. Counsel should not, by letter, raise or answer substantive issues or seek advice from the court.

2. Communications with Law Clerk. Judge Fox does not permit his law clerk to provide legal advice, to discuss legal issues, or to schedule matters. The scheduling of trials, hearings, and most conferences is the responsibility of Judge Fox's courtroom deputy.

3. Telephone Conferences and Use of Facsimile Machines. Judge Fox does not accept facsimile transmissions. He will on occasion hold telephone conferences when the issues warrant.

4. Pro Hac Vice Admissions. Judge Fox prefers that written requests for admission pro hac vice be submitted in accordance with Local Bankruptcy Rule 2090-1(c). Oral motions may be made in open court at the time of the hearing or trial.

5. Chambers Copies of Filed Papers. Judge Fox prefers that no chambers copies of pleadings or memoranda be submitted unless he specifically requests copies.

GENERAL LITIGATION
Continuances and Extensions

1. General Policy. If *all* parties in interest agree, requests for a continuance will be granted and can be arranged by telephone through the courtroom deputy, unless the trial or hearing has been specially listed by the court, or unless multiple continuances have already been granted.

2. Need for Filing Formal Stipulation or Motion. If all parties in interest will not agree to a postponement, or if the matter has been specially listed or postponed more than twice, a written request, or an oral request at the hearing, will be required. A postponement will only be granted if statutorily permissible, if it is genuinely necessary, and if the delay is unlikely to cause prejudice.

3. Need for Court Appearance. A court appearance will be required when a postponement cannot be obtained through communication with the courtroom deputy.

Proposed Findings of Fact and Conclusions of Law

1. Contested Matters. Judge Fox does not require proposed findings and conclusions unless he so requests at the conclusion of the hearing, or unless the parties so request at that time.

2. Adversary Proceedings. Judge Fox does not require proposed findings and conclusions unless he so requests at the conclusion of the trial or unless the parties so request at that time.

Reading of Material Into the Record

Judge Fox will usually not permit the reading of substantial material into the record.

Settlements

1. General Approach. Judge Fox will generally not become involved in settlement discussions, except where all parties in interest so request at a pretrial conference or during a hearing.

2. Referral of Settlement Negotiations to Another Bankruptcy Judge. When all parties in interest so request, and mediation is either inappropriate or has been unsuccessful, settlement conferences can be arranged with another bankruptcy judge.

3. Need for Court Appearance. To the extent court approval of any settlement is sought, the provisions of Fed.R.Bankr.P. 9019 must be followed, if applicable. An objection to a settlement motion will require a court appearance.

CONTESTED MATTER PRACTICE AND PROCEDURE
General

Hearing dates for contested matters are obtained by using the procedure found in Local Bankruptcy Rule 5070-1(a). In many, but not all, instances, the courtroom deputy will have recorded a message informing counsel of available hearing dates.

Filing Memoranda of Law/Briefs

1. Before Hearing. Memoranda are necessary only if Judge Fox has requested. Otherwise, the parties may file memoranda if they so choose.

2. After Hearing. Memoranda are necessary only if a briefing schedule has been established at the conclusion of the hearing. If a party desires to submit a post-hearing memorandum, that request will normally be approved.

3. Reply and Surreply Memoranda/Briefs. The intent of a party to file a reply memorandum will usually be determined at the conclusion of the hearing. Surreply memoranda will rarely be included in a post-hearing briefing schedule.

Scheduling of Expedited Hearings

A request for an expedited hearing should conform with Local Bankruptcy Rule 5070-1(f). If granted, the courtroom deputy will inform movant's counsel of the hearing date, the parties upon whom movant's counsel should provide notice, and the deadline for providing service to other parties in interest. Generally, the content of the notice will not be addressed in advance, as it is anticipated that the moving party will provide adequate notice.

Rule 52(c) Motions

Such motions are permitted under Fed.R.Bankr.P. 7052 and 9014.

Examination of Witnesses or Argument by More Than One Attorney

Judge Fox will permit more than one attorney for a party to examine different witnesses or argue different points of law in complex matters.

Examination of Witnesses Beyond Redirect and Recross

Judge Fox will rarely permit the examination of a witness after redirect and recross.

Presentation of Evidence

1. **Use of Rule 43(e) Affidavits.** Judge Fox does not use affidavits in lieu of testimony in contested matters unless the parties so agree. However, he may suggest in certain instances that an expert appraiser's written report serve in lieu of direct examination, where the report has been served upon opposing parties prior to the hearing and where the expert appraiser is available for cross-examination and redirect examination. See *In re Adair,* 965 F.2d 777 (9th Cir. 1992).

2. **Marking of Exhibits and Number of Copies.** Exhibits may, but need not, be pre-marked. Counsel need the original exhibit for the witness and should have a copy of the exhibit for every other party present. Unless requested, no copy for the court is necessary.

3. **Offering Exhibits in Evidence.** Exhibits should be offered in evidence just prior to the conclusion of the party's case-in-chief.

4. **Need for Presentation of Evidence if Uncontested.** If the moving party must demonstrate cause for relief, or if the moving party requests that findings be made (as in section 363 motions), evidence may be required even if the motion is uncontested.

ADVERSARY PROCEEDINGS
Discovery Matters

1. **Length of Discovery Period and Extensions.** A pretrial order will be entered establishing a discovery deadline. That deadline will usually be extended when all parties believe an extension is warranted.

2. **Discovery Conferences and Dispute Resolution.** In limited circumstances, discovery disputes may be resolved by telephone conference. In most instances, they will be resolved upon written motion after a hearing. See Local Bankruptcy Rule 7026-1(c).

3. **Confidentiality Agreements.** Judge Fox will only approve confidentiality agreements in those extremely narrow circumstances permitted by section 107 of the Bankruptcy Code and by federal common law. See, for example, *Pansy v. Borough of Stroudsburg,* 23 F.3d 772 (3d Cir. 1994).

4. **Expert Witnesses.** Judge Fox will require that expert witnesses be identified in a joint pretrial statement along with a brief summary of the testimony the expert is likely to present at trial. In addition, Fed.R.Bankr.P. 7026 incorporates Fed.R.Civ.P. 26(a)(2) and (b)(4).

Pretrial Conferences

Judge Fox will schedule a pretrial conference in adversary proceedings. The date and time of the conference will be fixed by a pretrial order entered shortly after defendant's answer is filed. The parties will usually be directed to file a joint pretrial statement (in the form established by Local Bankruptcy Rule 7016-1, one week prior to the conference).

Filing of Memoranda and Briefs

1. **Pretrial.** Memoranda are necessary only if Judge Fox has requested them. Otherwise, the parties may file memoranda if they so choose.

2. Post-trial. Memoranda are necessary only if a briefing schedule has been established at the conclusion of the trial. If a party desires to submit a post-trial memorandum, that request will generally be approved.

3. Reply and Surreply Memoranda and Briefs. The intent of a party to file a reply memorandum will usually be determined at the conclusion of the trial. Surreply memoranda will rarely be included in a post-trial briefing schedule.

Mediation

Judge Fox will request, as part of a pretrial order entered in almost all adversary proceedings, that the parties inform him in writing whether they will agree to participate in mediation. If all parties agree, a mediator will be assigned. Mediation will then proceed in accordance with Local Bankruptcy Rule 9019-3.

ARBITRATION

1. General Approach to Arbitration Cases. Proceedings will be assigned to compulsory arbitration in accordance with Local Bankruptcy Rule 9019-2.

2. Scheduling of Trial De Novo from Arbitration. Once a trial de novo is demanded, Judge Fox will usually issue an order directing the parties to file a joint pretrial statement within 14 days. Thereafter, the proceeding will be considered ready for trial.

TRIAL PROCEDURE

1. Scheduling of Cases. Proceedings will either be scheduled for trial at a pretrial conference or upon notice shortly after the conclusion of the conference.

2. Matters Involving Out-of-Town Parties or Witnesses. Judge Fox will attempt to accommodate out-of-town parties, counsel, and witnesses when scheduling trials. Video conferencing equipment is available for such situations.

3. Sidebars. Sidebar conferences may be sought when necessary.

4. In Limine Motions. A deadline for in limine motions will be established by pretrial order so as not to delay trial.

5. Opening Statements and Summations. Generally, no time limits are placed on opening statements or summations by counsel.

6. Examination of Witnesses Out of Sequence. Judge Fox will permit counsel to examine witnesses out of turn at the request of all parties or for the legitimate convenience of the witnesses.

7. Videotaped Testimony. Judge Fox will permit the use of videotaped testimony to the extent agreed to by all parties or as allowed by the Federal Rules of Bankruptcy Procedure.

INJUNCTIONS

1. Scheduling and Expedited Discovery. Hearings on motions for temporary restraining orders or preliminary injunctions are scheduled in the same manner as requests for expedited hearings in contested matters. Requests for expedited discovery should be filed and served upon opposing parties. They will be determined summarily after opposing parties have had reasonable opportunity to respond.

2. Proposed Findings of Fact and Conclusions of Law. Judge Fox does not require such submissions unless the parties are informed otherwise.

Bankruptcy Judge Stephen Raslavich

Judge Raslavich assumed his position as a bankruptcy judge for the Eastern District of Pennsylvania on October 29, 1993. Judge Raslavich is a former certified public accountant and practicing attorney. Prior to his appointment, he served for many years on the private panel of Chapter 7 Bankruptcy Trustees for the Bankruptcy Court of the Eastern District of Pennsylvania. Judge Raslavich is a graduate of the Villanova University School of Law (1980) and he received his undergraduate degree from the Wharton School of the University of Pennsylvania (1975).

PRELIMINARY GENERAL MATTERS

1. Correspondence with the Court. Judge Raslavich generally discourages unsolicited correspondence from counsel. Judge Raslavich will, however, occasionally invite and/or direct counsel to report on the status of matters via letter. Judge Raslavich discourages correspondence from counsel beyond this and in particular prefers counsel not to raise, via correspondence, matters that should otherwise be the subject of motion practice.

2. Communications with Law Clerks. Judge Raslavich permits counsel to speak directly with his law clerk subject to the limitations that law clerks are not permitted to give legal advice or discuss the merits of pending cases. Scheduling matters should ordinarily be taken up in the first instance with the judge's courtroom deputy, or in the alternative, with his judicial assistant.

3. Telephone Conferences and Use of Facsimile Machines. Judge Raslavich will liberally entertain requests for telephone conference calls, provided all pertinent parties are available to participate. Judge Raslavich insists that counsel not correspond with him via facsimile unless requested and approved in advance.

4. Pro Hac Vice Admissions. Judge Raslavich is very liberal with pro hac vice admissions, and will allow such request to be made orally or in writing.

5. Chambers Copies of Filed Papers. Judge Raslavich will accept courtesy or chambers copies of filed papers, but stresses to the bar that copies are in no way required unless specifically requested on his part.

GENERAL LITIGATION
Continuances and Extensions

1. General Policy. Judge Raslavich is generally liberal with requests for continuances where all parties are in agreement. Such requests should be made in the first instance via letter (if time permits) or telephone through the judge's courtroom deputy, and in the alternative to the judge's judicial assistant.

2. Need for Filing of Formal Stipulation or Motion. If all parties are in agreement, requests for continuances will ordinarily be granted as of course without the need for the filing of a formal stipulation or motion. If a request for a continuance is opposed, the judge expects counsel to raise the issue via conference call. Barring that, a written motion should be presented sufficiently in advance of the hearing to allow it to be disposed of prior to the originally scheduled date. If necessary, a request for expedited consideration should be made.

3. Need for Court Appearance. Judge Raslavich may sometimes dispose of a contested continuance request on the papers alone. Counsel will be advised in advance if a court appearance will be necessary.

Proposed Findings of Fact and Conclusions of Law

1.   Contested Matters/Adversary Proceedings. Judge Raslavich does not require proposed findings of fact and conclusions of law unless specifically so indicated at the conclusion of proceedings in court. Judge Raslavich will generally permit the filing of them, upon request. Similarly, the judge welcomes memoranda of law from the parties, and will generally refrain from deciding matters from the bench, if the parties desire an opportunity to brief certain issues.

Reading of Material Into the Record

Judge Raslavich will usually not permit the reading of substantial material into the record.

Settlements

1.   General Approach. Judge Raslavich will only become involved in settlement discussions at the request of all parties in interest. Upon such request, he will do so, but only to the limited extent that it will not jeopardize his role as fact finder if settlement discussions are unsuccessful.

2.   Referral of Settlement Negotiations to Another Bankruptcy Judge. When all parties in interest are in agreement and mediation is either inappropriate or has been unsuccessful, settlement conferences can usually be arranged with another bankruptcy judge.

3.   Need for Court Appearances. Settlements can usually be reported to Judge Raslavich's courtroom deputy, or in the alternative, to his judicial assistant, and the necessary motions to seek court approval, pursuant to Federal Bankruptcy Rule 9019, can be filed without a court appearance. Counsel will be advised of any exceptions.

CONTESTED MATTER PRACTICE AND PROCEDURE
Filing Memoranda of Law/Briefs

1.   Before Hearing. Judge Raslavich will consider prehearing briefs; however, counsel are again advised that they are not required.

2.   After Hearing. Memoranda are required only if so indicated at the conclusion of proceedings in court. Parties desiring to submit post-hearing memoranda will ordinarily be permitted to do so.

3.   Reply and Surreply Memoranda/Briefs. Reply and surreply memoranda or briefs will be permitted if approved in advance at the time a briefing schedule is established. Unsolicited extra briefs are viewed as improper.

Scheduling of Expedited Hearings

Judge Raslavich requires conformity with Local Bankruptcy Rule 5070-1(f) in connection with the presentation of requests for expedited consideration. If approved, counsel will generally be advised of the expedited hearing date via telephone conference from the courtroom deputy or the judge's judicial assistant in order to permit counsel to promptly make service on opposing parties.

Rule 52(c) Motions

Rule 52(c) motions may be made orally or in writing.

Examination of Witnesses or Argument by More Than One Counsel

Judge Raslavich will ordinarily permit more than one attorney for a party to examine different witnesses or argue different points of law if there is a valid reason for this approach.

Examination of Witnesses Beyond Redirect and Recross

Judge Raslavich generally permits further examination of witnesses after redirect and recross have been completed, but will curtail examinations that become repetitive or that are simply cumulative.

Presentation of Evidence

1.   Use of Rule 43(e) Affidavits. Judge Raslavich does not generally favor use of affidavits in lieu of testimony, but he may consider them upon agreement of counsel or where out-of-town witnesses are concerned, and cross-examination can be held via telephone conference call.

2.   Marking of Exhibits and Number of Copies. Judge Raslavich appreciates counsel pre-marking exhibits and exchanging copies in advance. A bench copy of exhibits is appreciated, but is not required absent advance notice.

3.   Offering Exhibits in Evidence. Judge Raslavich prefers that all of a party's exhibits be offered at the conclusion of that party's case, but is flexible on this point.

4.   Need for Presentation of Evidence if Uncontested. Judge Raslavich will rarely require presentation of evidence in support of uncontested matters. There are certain exceptions, however, such as when the moving party must affirmatively demonstrate "cause for relief" or when the moving party requests that certain findings be included in a proposed form of order, when the court is unable to make those findings on the basis of the pleadings alone. In these instances the judge will normally accept a proffer or affidavit.

ADVERSARY PROCEEDINGS
Discovery Matters

1.   Length of Discovery Period and Extensions. It is Judge Raslavich's practice to establish a discovery schedule via a pretrial order. The deadlines set forth in such order are meant to apply, but extensions will normally be granted given consent and cause shown.

2.   Discovery Conferences and Dispute Resolution. Judge Raslavich will entertain conference calls for the purpose of resolving discovery disputes. Monetary sanctions, however, will always require the presentation of a formal motion.

3.   Confidentiality Agreements. Judge Raslavich will approve confidentiality agreements or orders subject to the limitations of statutory and common law.

4.   Expert Witnesses. Judge Raslavich requires the advance identification of expert witnesses in the joint pretrial statement to be prepared in conformity with his standard pretrial order (see page 428 of this book).

Pretrial Conferences

Judge Raslavich infrequently schedules pretrial conferences at his own initiative, but will entertain requests for them for cause shown.

Filing of Memoranda and Briefs

1. Pretrial. Pretrial memoranda are appreciated; however, counsel are advised that they are unnecessary unless specifically requested.

2. Post-trial. Post-trial memoranda are necessary only where specifically requested by the court; however, Judge Raslavich will liberally approve requests from the parties to submit them. Judge Raslavich will generally permit the briefing schedule to commence after receipt of the transcript in the regular course of business.

3. Reply and Surreply Memoranda and Briefs. The complete briefing schedule will ordinarily be established at the conclusion of trial proceedings. Briefs not otherwise identified at that time should not be submitted.

Mediation

Judge Raslavich will liberally assign disputes to mediation at the request of the parties. Barring that, he reviews matters before him for possible referral to mediation on a case-by-case basis. Judge Raslavich will not insist that parties attempt mediation against their will, nor does he require parties to explain a decision not to participate in mediation.

Settlement of Adversary Proceedings

When a matter has been reported as settled, a written stipulation memorializing it will ordinarily be required to be filed within 30 days. Absent such filing or the request for an extension of time, the litigation will ordinarily be dismissed for failure to prosecute pursuant to L.B.R. 7041.

ARBITRATION

1. General Approach to Arbitration. Proceedings will be assigned to compulsory arbitration in accordance with Local Bankruptcy Rule 9019.2.

2. Scheduling of Trial De Novo. Once a trial de novo is demanded, Judge Raslavich will generally issue a pretrial order directing the filing of a joint pretrial statement and setting a date for trial.

TRIAL PROCEDURE

1. Scheduling of Cases. Motions are assigned a hearing date in accordance with Local Bankruptcy Rule 5070-1. Adversary proceedings are assigned a trial date via a pretrial scheduling order after the pleadings are closed. The lead time for trial fluctuates depending upon the size of the judge's calendar; however, every attempt is made to provide counsel with a prompt hearing date.

2. Matters Involving Out-of-Town Parties or Witnesses. Judge Raslavich endeavors to be as flexible as possible in matters involving out-of-town parties or witnesses.

3. Sidebars. Sidebar conferences are discouraged but will be entertained when necessary.

4. In Limine Motions. Judge Raslavich has no fixed practice regarding in limine motions and handles them instead on a case-by-case basis.

5. Opening Statements and Summations. Judge Raslavich will permit opening and closing statements, but will sometimes suggest that they be waived where pretrial memoranda have been submitted and/or post-trial memoranda are contemplated.

6. Examination of Witnesses Out of Sequence. Judge Raslavich is very flexible in allowing witnesses to be called out of turn for convenience.

7.   *Videotaped Testimony.* Judge Raslavich will permit the use of videotaped testimony to the extent agreed to by all parties or as allowed by the Federal Rules of Bankruptcy Procedure.

INJUNCTIONS

1.   *Hearings on Motions for Temporary Restraining Orders or Preliminary Injunctions.* Hearings on motions for temporary restraining orders or preliminary injunctions are viewed and scheduled in the same manner as requests for expedited consideration in contested matters. Requests for expedited discovery are treated in the same fashion.

2.   *Proposed Facts and Conclusions of Law.* As in contested matters, the judge does not generally require such submissions absent specific advice to the parties at the conclusion of trial proceedings.

IN THE UNITED STATES BANKRUPTCY COURT
FOR THE EASTERN DISTRICT OF PENNSYLVANIA

IN RE   : CHAPTER
                                           :
                                           :
                    DEBTOR   : BANKRUPTCY NO. SR
_____
:
:   PLAINTIFF   :
:   v.   :
:
:   DEFENDANT   : ADVS.
_____

PRETRIAL ORDER

AND NOW, this _____ day of _____ 20__, the Plaintiff(s) having filed an adversary proceeding and the Defendant(s) having filed a responsive pleading which warrants the entry of a pretrial scheduling order, it is hereby:

ORDERED, that:

1. On or before <u>a date 21 days after entry of this order</u>, counsel shall have held and concluded the mandatory discovery conference pursuant to Fed.R.Civ.P. 26(f), incorporated into these proceedings by Fed.R.Bankr.Pro. 7026. The parties shall consider, as part of their deliberations on how to proceed with discovery, the discovery and pretrial schedule detailed below in this order.

2. Within 14 days after the conclusion of the parties' discovery conference, should the parties propose a discovery or pretrial schedule that differs from the one below, they shall file with the Bankruptcy Court a report on discovery, as mandated by Fed.R.Civ.P. 26(f). The parties shall detail those differences in their Rule 26(f) report, along with the reasons therefor. The Court may, when appropriate, order a hearing based upon the information found in the Rule 26(f) report. If the parties are in agreement with the discovery schedule outlined herein, no report need be filed unless there are objections to the initial discovery disclosures.

3. Within 14 days after the conclusion of their Rule 26(f) conference, the parties shall provide the initial disclosures detailed in Fed.R.Civ.P. 26(a)(1). Any objections to the initial discovery disclosures required by Fed.R.Civ.P. 26(a)(1) shall be clearly raised in a Rule 26(f) report.

4. The following discovery and trial schedule shall be considered by the parties in their deliberations at their discovery conference:

    A. All discovery shall be completed on or before <u>65 days after Order</u>;

    B. All motions for summary judgment, shall be filed on or before <u>2 weeks after A above</u>;

    C. All motions *in limine* (other than motions objecting to initial disclosures) shall be filed on or before <u>2 weeks after A above</u>;

    D. All expert witnesses shall be identified and a copy of each expert's report shall be provided to every other party, in accordance with Fed.R.Civ.P. 26(a)(2) on or before <u>1 week after B & C</u>;

    E. All discovery disclosures pursuant to Fed.R.Civ.P. 26(a)(3) shall be served on opposing parties and filed with the bankruptcy court on or before <u>1 week after B & C</u>;

    F. Any objections to the Rule 26(a)(3) disclosures shall be served on opposing counsel and filed with the Bankruptcy Court on or before <u>2 weeks after E</u>;

G. On or before <u>30 days after F above</u>, the parties shall file a joint pretrial statement and file a copy with chambers. The joint pretrial statement shall be signed by all counsel. It is the obligation of the plaintiff's counsel to initiate the procedures for its preparation and to assemble and submit the proposed pretrial statement to the court. Plaintiff's counsel shall submit a proposed joint pretrial statement to defendant's counsel not less than 7 days prior to the deadline for its submission.

Counsel are expected to make a diligent effort to prepare a proposed pretrial statement in which will be noted all of the issues on which the parties are in agreement and all of those issues on which they disagree. The proposed pretrial order shall govern the conduct of the trial and shall supersede all prior pleadings in the case. Amendments will be allowed only in exceptional circumstances and to prevent manifest injustice.

The joint pretrial statement shall be in the following form:

I. <u>Basis of jurisdiction</u>. (including a statement whether this matter is core or non-core). If the matter is non-core, the parties shall state whether they consent to the court's entry of a final order pursuant to 28 U.S.C. § 157(c)(2). If the parties disagree, they shall each cite to relevant authority to support their positions.

II. <u>Statement of uncontested facts</u>.

III. <u>Statements of facts which are in dispute</u>. [No facts should be disputed unless opposing counsel expects to present contrary evidence on the point at trial, or genuinely challenges the fact on credibility grounds.]

IV. <u>Damages or other relief</u>. A statement of damages claimed or relief sought. A party seeking damages shall list each item claimed under a separate descriptive heading, shall provide a detailed description of each item and state the amount of damages claimed. A party seeking relief other than damages shall list the exact form of relief sought with precise designations of persons, parties, places and things expected to be included in any order providing relief.

V. <u>Legal issues presented</u> and the constitutional, statutory, regulatory and decisional authorities relied upon. (Counsel should include a brief statement regarding which party has the burden of proof on each legal issue.)

VI. <u>Witnesses</u> listed in the order they will be called along with a brief statement of the evidence the witness will give. Witnesses shall be classified between those who any party expects to present and those whom any party may call if the need arises. If not already provided to all parties, the address and telephone number of each witness shall be disclosed.

VII. <u>A list of all exhibits</u> to be offered into evidence which shall be serially numbered and physically marked before trial in accordance with the schedule. Documents which a party may offer if the need arises shall be separately identified.

VIII. <u>A list of each discovery item</u> and trial deposition to be offered into evidence. (Counsel shall designate by page portion of deposition testimony and by number the interrogatories which shall be offered in evidence at trial.)

IX. <u>Estimated trial time</u>.

X. <u>A certification</u> that the parties have attempted good faith settlement discussions without success.

5. No pretrial conferences with the Court will be scheduled unless one is requested by counsel or the Court deems it necessary.

6. Trial will be held on _____20____, 1:30 P.M. in Bankruptcy Courtroom No. 4, Second Floor, Robert C. Nix Courthouse, 900 Market Street, Philadelphia, Pennsylvania 19107. The trial may be continued only in exceptional circumstances with the permission of the Court.

By the Court:

_____
STEPHEN RASLAVICH
United States Bankruptcy Judge

Counsel for Plaintiff:

Counsel for Defendant:

Joseph J. McMahon, Esquire
Office Of The U.S. Trustee
950 W Curtis Center
7th & Sansom Streets
Philadelphia PA 19106

Nancy Mulvehill, Courtroom Deputy to Judge Raslavich

Magistrate Judges

Chief Magistrate Judge Carol Sandra Moore Wells

Judge Wells was born in 1949, and is a graduate of the University of Pennsylvania School of Law (J.D. 1985). From 1978 to 1984, she served the dual role of founder and teacher at Lotus Academy. During that time, Judge Wells also served as a law clerk/office manager with Nichols, Nichols, Clark & New Kirk. From 1985 to 1987, she was in private practice as an associate attorney with Pincus, Verlin, Hahn & Reich, P.C. From 1987 until 1996, Judge Wells worked for the City of Philadelphia as an assistant city solicitor, deputy city solicitor, and senior attorney. She was appointed as a magistrate judge of the United States District Court for the Eastern District of Pennsylvania on June 3, 1996, and was reappointed in 2004. She became Chief Magistrate Judge on October 1, 2011.

PRELIMINARY GENERAL MATTERS

1. **Correspondence with the Court.** Judge Wells permits correspondence from counsel on all matters, but prefers to resolve disputes via joint telephone conference.

2. **Communication with Law Clerks.** Judge Wells permits counsel to speak directly with her law clerks on procedural matters. However, her law clerks should never be contacted regarding substantive matters, including the merits of pending matters.

3. **Telephone Conferences.** Judge Wells prefers to hold conferences in chambers. However, when counsel cannot be present, or when time is of the essence, she encourages joint telephonic conferences. It is the responsibility of counsel to arrange mutually agreeable times for such conferences and to call chambers once counsel for all parties are on the line.

4. **Oral Arguments and Evidentiary Hearings.** Judge Wells does not set aside any special days or times for oral arguments or evidentiary hearings. These matters are scheduled by her deputy clerk, who will attempt to accommodate counsel's schedules.

CIVIL CASES

1. **Pretrial Conferences.** Judge Wells regularly conducts pretrial/status and settlement conferences in cases pending before her. Pretrial/status conferences, where appropriate, are scheduled promptly upon referral of the case to Judge Wells. The standard agenda for such conferences tracks federal rules.

Additionally, at pretrial conferences, attorneys from both sides should be prepared to discuss settlement possibilities.

Judge Wells expects opposing counsel to attempt to resolve disputes prior to bringing them to her attention, pursuant to Local Rule 26.1(f).

Continuances and Extensions

1. **General Policy.** Judge Wells's general policy on continuances for briefing schedules, oral arguments, evidentiary hearings, and discovery deadlines is to be flexible during the initial stages of litigation, but strict as the trial date approaches.

2. **Requests for Extensions and Continuances.** Judge Wells does not impose any specific requirement as to how far in advance of a scheduled event counsel must request a continuance or extension. However, she expects such a request to be made as soon as the need becomes apparent and sufficiently in advance for the court to schedule a matter.

A joint continuance or extension request of the parties may be made by letter or conference call. A contested request for a continuance or extension of a court-ordered deadline should be in a letter (faxed to chambers) or requested via formal motion.

General Motion Practice

1.   Oral Argument of Motions. Judge Wells will schedule oral arguments on a motion if it appears likely to be helpful to the court. One or all counsel should request oral argument if they consider it vital to a fair disposition of the issues before the court.

2.   Reply and Supplemental Briefs. If a telephone conference does not resolve an issue, Judge Wells may instruct the parties to file briefs. The parties must seek permission to file supplemental briefs.

3.   Chambers Copies of Motion Papers. The delivery of courtesy copies of all motion papers to Judge Wells's chambers, especially via electronic means, is encouraged.

Discovery Matters

1.   Length of Discovery Period and Extensions. Judge Wells has no general policy regarding the length of time allowed for discovery. The length of the discovery period is dictated by the complexity of the case and is determined at the Rule 26 discovery conference. At such a conference, both parties should provide input as realistic time limits.

2.   Discovery Conferences and Dispute Resolution. Judge Wells expects the parties to resolve most discovery disputes without court intervention, per Local Rule 26.1(f). If this is not possible, counsel should request a telephone conference by letter or initiate a *joint* telephone conference call. It should be noted that a telephone conference is not encouraged if pro se litigants are involved. In appropriate cases, Judge Wells will convene discovery conferences in chambers.

Judge Wells may initiate a discovery conference sua sponte. Furthermore, she broaches settlement negotiations at any stage of litigation.

3.   Confidentiality Agreements. Judge Wells encourages counsel to develop confidentiality agreements, when appropriate. However, she rarely will entertain stipulated confidentiality orders submitted for court approval.

4.   Expert Witnesses. Disclosure of the identity of experts who are to testify at trial is required as soon as they are known to the respective parties and no later than the end of the discovery period. In complex cases, Judge Wells may lengthen the time permitted for expert discovery.

Expert reports should be exchanged on or before the dates set by the scheduling order.

Judge Wells permits depositions of expert witnesses in accordance with the Federal Rules of Civil Procedure.

Settlement

1.   General Approach to Settlement and Nonjury Cases. Judge Wells conducts settlement conferences upon request of all parties, upon referral from a district court judge, or sua sponte. She actively encourages settlement and makes herself available for in-depth settlement discussions in referred cases.

Each attorney appearing for a party at a settlement conference *must* have full authority to negotiate and settle the case on behalf of his or her client. Judge Wells expects the parties to be present or available by telephone, unless expressly excused by her prior to the conference.

2.   Referral of Settlement Negotiations to Another Judge. In nonjury cases where the parties have consented to trial before Judge Wells, she will refer in-depth settlement negotiations to another magistrate judge.

Arbitration

1. **General Approach to Arbitration Cases.** Judge Wells has no special practices or procedures for arbitration cases, except for an accelerated discovery process.

2. **Scheduling of Trial De Novo from Arbitration.** When a demand for trial de novo is filed after arbitration, Judge Wells promptly schedules a status conference to explore the possibility of settlement and/or schedule a prompt, but mutually convenient trial date.

Proposed Final Pretrial Memoranda

1. **Required Form of Pretrial Memoranda.** Unless specifically provided for by a separate order, Judge Wells requires counsel to use the short-form pretrial memorandum described in Local Rule of Civil Procedure 16.1(c). A stipulation of uncontested facts, as set forth in Local Rule 16.1(d)(2)(b)(2)(A)–(E) should accompany this memorandum.

The judge also requires counsel to comply with the rules set forth in her scheduling order, which at a minimum, requires counsel, on a specific date, to file with the clerk and serve on opposing counsel (1) a list of all exhibits to be used at trial, (2) a list of all witnesses to be called at trial, as well as a brief summary of each witness's testimony, (3) memoranda of law on all legal and evidentiary issues expected to arise at trial, and (4) requests for instructions to the jury.

Trial Procedure

1. **Scheduling of Cases.** Judge Wells assigns a date certain for trial, after consulting with counsel. Counsel should be prepared during any pretrial conference and/or settlement conference to advise the judge as to when discovery and expert reports are expected to be complete.

2. **Conflicts of Counsel.** If a conflict of counsel will affect the trial schedule, Judge Wells requires that counsel file a written request for a joint telephone conference in order to resolve the issue. If pro se litigants are involved, Judge Wells may hold a conference on the record.

3. **Cases Involving Out-of-Town Parties or Witnesses.** When possible, Judge Wells will adjust the trial schedule to give consideration to out-of-town attorneys, parties, or witnesses.

4. **Note-taking by Jurors.** Judge Wells will allow jurors, in complex or otherwise appropriate cases, to take notes for personal use only.

5. **Trial Briefs.** Counsel should not submit trial briefs unless requested to do so by the court.

6. **Voir Dire.** Judge Wells requires counsel to submit proposed voir dire questions at the final pretrial conference. She permits counsel to conduct voir dire in civil cases, but personally presides over all such proceedings. Judge Wells conducts in-depth voir dire, at sidebar, in appropriate cases. There is no predetermined time limit for voir dire.

7. **Sidebars.** Judge Wells strongly discourages sidebars and encourages counsel to raise foreseeable issues before trial commences, during recesses, or after adjournments.

8. **Motions in Limine.** Motions in limine should be filed with a party's final pretrial memorandum and will usually be ruled upon at the final pretrial conference, unless it is appropriate to defer a ruling until some time during the trial.

9. **Examination of Witnesses Out of Sequence.** Subject to objections by opposing counsel, Judge Wells generally will allow witnesses to be examined out of sequence for the convenience of the witnesses and counsel.

10. Opening Statements and Summations. Judge Wells generally does not impose any predetermined time constraints in opening statements and summations.

11. Examination of Witnesses or Argument by More Than One Attorney. Judge Wells will permit only one attorney to examine a witness, but will allow more than one attorney to argue motions before the court.

12. Examination of Witnesses Beyond Redirect and Recross. Judge Wells has no fixed policy regarding the examination of a witness beyond redirect and recross. She will permit reasonable examination of a witness in areas that are not repetitive or beyond the scope of previous questioning by opposing counsel.

13. Videotaped Testimony. Judge Wells requires counsel to jointly view all videotaped depositions before the final pretrial conference in order to raise and resolve all material objections prior to the commencement of trial. The attorney sponsoring the videotape witness bears the responsibility for timely setting up playback equipment in the courtroom.

14. Reading Material Into the Record. Judge Wells encourages counsel to submit a stipulation of all undisputed facts and, whenever possible, to verify the authenticity of documents in order to expedite the trial process.

15. Preparation of Exhibits. All exhibits must be pre-marked and pre-exchanged prior to trial. Counsel must present to the court, in a looseleaf binder, a list and copy of all exhibits before trial.

16. Offering Exhibits Into Evidence. Judge Wells has no preference as to when exhibits should be offered into evidence.

17. Motions for Judgment as a Matter of Law and Motion for Judgment on Partial Findings. Motions for judgment as a matter of law or for judgment on partial findings may be submitted either orally or in writing. The court or any party may request oral argument.

18. Proposed Jury Instructions and Verdict Forms. As set forth in her standard scheduling order, Judge Wells requires counsel to submit joint proposed jury instructions, noting areas of agreement as well as objections. Counsel must also jointly submit a proposed verdict form or proposed special interrogatories to be submitted to the jury. At the final pretrial conference, Judge Wells will rule on any evidentiary objections. Prior to giving the jury charge, a copy of final jury instructions and verdict sheet (or special interrogatories) will be provided to counsel, who will be given an opportunity to take exception, make corrections, or suggest additions. Supplemental or amended jury instructions may be offered.

All jury verdicts must be unanimous, unless otherwise stipulated by the court and counsel prior to or during trial.

19. Proposed Findings of Fact and Conclusions of Law. Judge Wells requires counsel to submit proposed findings of fact and conclusions of law in nonjury cases at the final pretrial conference. She will permit supplementation of that submission (at the close of the trial or, in a complex matter, after trial) as necessary.

Jury Deliberations

1. Written Jury Instructions. Judge Wells will submit a copy of instructions to the jury in particularly complex cases or upon request of all counsel.

2. Exhibits in Jury Room. Judge Wells will ask counsel to stipulate what evidence will go out to the jury. Should counsel be unable to reach a consensus, Judge Wells will determine the issue.

3. Handling of Jury Requests to Read Back Testimony or Replay Tapes. Judge Wells will permit portions of the record to be reviewed by the jury; however, in the interest of fairness, she will consult counsel in attempting to provide a balanced, contextual review of the record.

4. Availability of Counsel During Jury Deliberations. Judge Wells requires counsel to spend the first hour of jury deliberations in or near the courthouse. Thereafter, counsel will be permitted to leave, provided they are available by phone or remain in close proximity to the courthouse. Cell phone numbers should be provided to her deputy clerk.

5. Taking the Verdict and Special Interrogatories. Judge Wells has no policy for special or general verdicts and she will, if appropriate, submit special interrogatories to the jury.

6. Polling the Jury. Judge Wells will, upon request of counsel, direct her deputy clerk to poll the jury.

7. Interviewing the Jury. After a civil verdict is taken, Judge Wells will permit jurors to be interviewed should they elect to participate, and with the admonition that counsel not inquire about specific votes.

CRIMINAL CASES

1. Approach to Oral Arguments and Motions. Judge Wells encourages oral argument or motions in criminal cases.

2. Pretrial Conferences and Motions. Judge Wells does not generally conduct pretrial conferences in criminal cases, but will do so, upon request of counsel.

3. Voir Dire. Judge Wells conducts all voir dire in criminal cases; counsel should submit proposed voir dire questions to the court in advance of trial.

4. Sentencing Memoranda. Judge Wells permits submission of sentencing memoranda.

OTHER GENERAL MATTERS

Counsel must be present at all duty week proceedings.

No party or their counsel may review pretrial service's recommendations regarding detention or release.

Judge Wells looks upon a single attorney representing multiple defendants in one case with disfavor, with the possible exception of the initial appearance. She prefers that counsel avoid all potential conflicts of interest by representing one defendant only in related criminal proceedings.

The court prefers having the opportunity to review all proposed orders prior to any hearing.

Judge Wells, while lacking the power to define the precise location and circumstances of detention, within her authority will be flexible in developing an appropriate detention or release package for defendants, particularly in regard to minors and those in need of psychological or medical assessment or treatment.

Judge Wells expects counsel to comply with Local Rules of Civil Procedure and to attempt to resolve any and all conflicts among themselves before bringing a matter before the court.

Judge Wells wishes to receive a courtesy copy of any briefs filed in appeal of her decisions. Further questions as to Judge Wells's policies should be directed to her deputy clerk.

Magistrate Judge M. Faith Angell

Magistrate Judge Angell is a graduate of Mount Holyoke College (A.B. 1959), Bryn Mawr College (M.S.S. 1965), and Temple University School of Law (J.D. 1971). She began her professional career as a social worker in child welfare, primarily in medical and community organization settings. While attending evening law school, she worked as the director of the Social Service Department at Wills Eye Hospital and later as chief social worker for the newly created Family Court Division of the Defender Association of Philadelphia.

In 1971, Judge Angell was appointed as an assistant district attorney for the City of Philadelphia. In 1972, she was appointed as an assistant attorney general and, in 1974, as a deputy attorney general and chief of the Division of Civil Litigation for the Eastern Regional Office of the Pennsylvania Department of Justice. In 1978, Judge Angell joined the Interstate Commerce Commission as regional counsel. In 1980, she became regional director and a member of the United States Senior Executive Service. In 1988, Judge Angell was appointed as an administrative law judge in the Office of Hearings and Appeals of the Social Security Administration. From 1973 to 1994, she taught in the clinical program at Temple University School of Law as an adjunct professor.

On May 14, 1990, Judge Angell was appointed as a United States magistrate judge of the United States District Court for the Eastern District of Pennsylvania, and she was reappointed in May 1998. From 2004 to 2006, Judge Angell was designated as Chief Magistrate Judge. She is currently on recall status.

Judge Angell is a member of the Academy of Certified Social Workers, the Philadelphia Bar Association, the Federal Magistrate Judges Association, and the National Association of Women Judges. Judge Angell is a former president of the Philadelphia Chapter of the Federal Bar Association and master in the Temple American Inn of Court. She is the chair of the Awards Committee. She served as co-chair of the Commission on Gender of the Third Circuit Task Force on Equal Treatment in the Courts. Judge Angell was a member of the Temple Law Alumni Executive Board from 1994 to 1999, and was the 1996 Women's Law Caucus Honoree. She served on the Supreme Court of Pennsylvania Committee on Racial and Gender Bias in the Justice System from 2000 to 2002. Judge Angell is a member of the board of advisors of the Bryn Mawr School of Social Work and Social Research and the executive board of the Temple Law Alumni Association.

PRELIMINARY GENERAL MATTERS

1. Correspondence with the Court. Judge Angell permits correspondence from counsel on all matters. If the occasion demands, counsel will be instructed to file a formal motion in lieu of prior correspondence.

2. Communication with Law Clerks. Judge Angell permits counsel to speak directly with her law clerks with the understanding that counsel must carefully observe ethical considerations and avoid discussion of the merits of a pending case. Attorneys should not attempt ex parte communication on matters of substance. Joint calls by counsel for all parties are preferred.

3. Telephone Conferences. Judge Angell encourages the use of telephone conferences for handling matters such as discovery disputes, scheduling changes, and extensions of time. It is counsel's responsibility to arrange such conference calls and to contact Judge Angell when all counsel are on the line. However, Judge Angell conducts in-chambers conferences for settlement discussions and complex issues.

4. *Oral Arguments and Evidentiary Hearings.* Judge Angell permits oral arguments and nonjury evidentiary hearings to be scheduled by her law clerks, who will attempt to accommodate the schedules of counsel.

5. *Pro Hac Vice Admissions.* Judge Angell prefers that an application for pro hac vice admission be made by formal motion filed prior to the day the attorney to be admitted first appears in court. She will permit an oral motion to be made at the time of the attorney's first appearance, but counsel will be directed to prepare an appropriate order to memorialize the pro hac vice admission.

CIVIL CASES
Pretrial Procedure

1. *Pretrial/Status Conferences.* Judge Angell regularly conducts pretrial/status and settlement conferences in cases pending before her.

Pretrial/status conferences, where appropriate, are scheduled promptly upon referral of the case to Judge Angell. One day every month is reserved for initial pretrial conferences in civil cases. The agenda for an initial pretrial/status conference usually includes (1) establishing dates for the completion of discovery, the filing of dispositive motions, the final pretrial conference, and trial; (2) discussion of outstanding motions and problems and encouragement of practical solutions to any disputes; and (3) exploration of settlement possibilities. A sample of the form of a scheduling order often used by Judge Angell is shown on page 444 of this book; however, Judge Angell will sometimes use the pretrial orders of the various district court judges to whom the case is assigned.

Settlement conferences are encouraged and will be scheduled at the request of the parties.

Continuances and Extensions

1. *General Policy.* Judge Angell will normally consult counsel before establishing a briefing schedule, oral argument, evidentiary hearing, discovery deadline, or trial date. When possible, Judge Angell tries to accommodate counsel with regard to requests for reasonable changes.

2. *Requests for Extensions and Continuances.* Judge Angell does not impose any specific requirement as to how far in advance of a scheduled event counsel must request a continuance or extension. However, she expects such a request to be made as soon as the need becomes apparent.

If counsel have agreed on a continuance or an extension, ordinarily a letter to Judge Angell will suffice. The letter should state that all parties agree to the extension, the reasons for the request, and the reasonable amount of additional time that counsel believe is necessary.

When a request for a continuance or extension is contested, the letter must state this fact.

General Motion Practice

1. *Oral Argument on Motions.* Judge Angell will schedule oral argument on a motion if it appears likely to be helpful to the court. Counsel should request oral argument if they consider it necessary.

2. *Reply and Surreply Briefs.* Judge Angell does not permit the filing of reply and surreply briefs, unless leave of court is granted. Before requesting permission to file a reply or surreply brief, counsel should evaluate carefully whether such a brief is necessary.

3. **Chamber Copies of Motion Papers.** Judge Angell expects a courtesy copy of all motion papers to be sent directly to her chambers.

Discovery Matters

1. **Length of Discovery Period and Extensions.** Judge Angell normally permits from 90 to 120 days for the completion of discovery; however, she will consider the informed view of counsel as to the time that will be required for discovery in a particular case. More time is allowed in complex cases or on a specific showing of need at the initial pretrial/status conference.

2. **Discovery Conferences and Dispute Resolution.** Judge Angell expects the parties to resolve most discovery disputes without court intervention. If, however, counsel are unable, in good faith, to resolve their dispute, Judge Angell encourages the use of telephone conferences or a letter to chambers to identify discovery disputes.

The use of motion practice in discovery is strongly discouraged. When a discovery dispute is identified, Judge Angell will promptly schedule a telephone conference, in-person conference, or hearing, as appropriate.

3. **Confidentiality Agreements.** Judge Angell encourages counsel to develop confidentiality agreements, when appropriate. As a general rule, she will not entertain stipulated confidentiality orders submitted for court approval.

4. **Expert Witnesses.** The disclosure of the identity of experts who are to testify at trial is required as soon as they are known to the respective parties, and no later than the end of the discovery period. If necessary, Judge Angell will allow additional time for expert discovery for good cause.

Expert reports are to be exchanged on or before the dates set by the scheduling order.

Beyond the requirements of the Federal Rules of Civil Procedure, Judge Angell does not have a special policy as to when the depositions of expert witnesses will be permitted.

Settlement

1. **General Approach to Settlement and Nonjury Cases.** Judge Angell actively encourages settlement discussions and makes herself available to discuss settlement if all parties wish her to be involved.

Each attorney appearing for a party at a settlement conference must have authority to settle on behalf of his/her client. The parties are expected to be present or available by telephone.

2. **Referral of Settlement Negotiations to Another Judge.** In nonjury cases where the parties have consented to trial before Judge Angell, she will refer settlement negotiations to another magistrate judge.

Arbitration

1. **General Approach to Arbitration Cases.** Judge Angell has no special practices or procedures for arbitration cases that differ from those set forth in Local Rule 53.2(3).

2. **Scheduling of Trial De Novo from Arbitration.** When a demand for trial de novo is filed after arbitration, Judge Angell promptly schedules a status conference to explore the possibility of settlement and, if necessary, to schedule a trial date.

Proposed Final Pretrial Memoranda

1. *Required Form of Pretrial Memoranda.* Unless specifically provided for by separate order in a particular case, Judge Angell requires the use of the short-form pretrial memorandum described in Rule 16.1 of the Local Rules of Civil Procedure. In addition, she requires a stipulation of uncontested facts as described in Local Rule 16.1(d)(2)(b)(2)(A) through (E).

Injunctions

Judge Angell will promptly list any injunction matters assigned to her. The scheduling of injunction matters will depend upon the circumstances of the case and will be determined at an initial conference to be attended by all counsel.

Trial Procedure

1. *Scheduling of Cases.* Judge Angell's normal practice is to assign a date certain for trial.

2. *Conflicts of Counsel.* Counsel should notify Judge Angell, and opposing counsel, promptly of any professional or personal conflicts that may affect the trial schedule. Such notice may be given by telephone.

3. *Parties or Witnesses.* When possible, Judge Angell attempts to adjust the trial schedule as necessary to give consideration to out-of-town attorneys, parties, and witnesses.

4. *Note-taking by Jurors.* Judge Angell generally discourages note-taking by jurors, but will consider permitting it in an appropriate case.

5. *Trial Briefs.* Judge Angell generally discourages the submission of trial briefs, except in unusual or complex cases and in cases where novel evidentiary problems are anticipated.

6. *Voir Dire.* Judge Angell conducts voir dire in civil cases. Counsel may submit proposed voir dire questions at the final pretrial conference and may, when appropriate, conduct supplemental voir dire following Judge Angell's questions.

7. *Sidebars.* Judge Angell prefers to avoid sidebar conferences and encourages counsel to raise issues before trial begins or during recesses or adjournments. However, she will hold sidebar conferences as the need arises.

8. *In Limine Motions.* Motions in limine should be submitted at the final pretrial conference.

9. *Examination of Witnesses Out of Sequence.* Judge Angell will generally grant a request by counsel to take the testimony of a witness out of turn for the convenience of the witness, subject to objection by opposing counsel.

10. *Opening Statements and Summations.* Judge Angell encourages brevity in opening statements and summations. She will usually discuss with counsel the time needed and secure from all counsel an understanding as to an appropriate length of time.

11. *Examination of Witnesses or Argument by More Than One Attorney.* Judge Angell will permit more than one attorney to examine different witnesses; however, only one attorney for a party may examine a particular witness. More than one attorney for a party may argue different points in a motion before Judge Angell.

12. *Examination of Witnesses Beyond Redirect and Recross.* Permission to examine witnesses beyond redirect and recross depends on the particular facts and circumstances of the case. Judge Angell will sustain an appropriate objection to such further examination if it goes beyond the scope of the previous examination of opposing counsel.

13. Videotaped Testimony. Before the final pretrial conference, Judge Angell requires counsel to view all videotaped depositions that will be offered at trial for the purposes of editing the videotape and resolving material objections. All objections to videotaped testimony that cannot be resolved between counsel must be raised at the final pretrial conference and will be ruled upon by Judge Angell at that time.

14. Reading of Material Into the Record. Judge Angell has no special practice or policy for reading pleadings or discovery material into the record. She will permit it when necessary; however, she encourages counsel to minimize the necessity for this by stipulating to as many facts as possible.

15. Preparation of Exhibits. Judge Angell requires all exhibits to be pre-marked and pre-exchanged. Counsel should provide the court with one copy of each trial exhibit as well as an exhibit list.

16. Offering Exhibits Into Evidence. Judge Angell prefers to have all exhibits offered into evidence at the close of the party's case-in-chief.

17. Motions for Judgment as a Matter of Law and Motions for Judgment on Partial Findings. Judge Angell has no particular preference as to whether motions for judgment as matter of law (or motions for judgment on partial findings in nonjury trials) are submitted in writing or orally. Oral argument, if necessary, will be requested by the court.

18. Proposed Jury Instructions and Verdict Forms. As set forth in her standard scheduling order, Judge Angell requires counsel to submit *joint* proposed jury instructions, noting areas of agreement as well as any objections. Counsel are also required to *jointly* submit a proposed verdict form or proposed special interrogatories to be submitted to the jury. At the final pretrial conference, Judge Angell will rule on any objections.

Prior to giving the jury charge, counsel will be provided with a copy of the final jury instructions and verdict sheet (or special interrogatories) and will be given an opportunity to take exception, make corrections, or suggest additions.

19. Proposed Findings of Fact and Conclusions of Law. Judge Angell requires counsel to submit proposed findings of fact and conclusions of law in nonjury cases at the final pretrial conference. She will permit supplementation later (at the close of trial or, in a complex matter, after trial) as necessary.

Jury Deliberations

1. Written Jury Instructions. Judge Angell has never given the jury a copy of the jury instructions.

2. Exhibits in the Jury Room. Unless the parties request otherwise, Judge Angell generally permits all of the trial exhibits that have been admitted into evidence to go out with the jury.

3. Handling of Jury Requests to Read Back Testimony or Replay Tapes. Judge Angell permits testimony to be read back where the jurors identify the requested testimony with reasonable precision. Judge Angell recalls no instance where a jury has asked to have a videotape or audiotape replayed; however, she would probably permit replaying if such a request was made.

4. Availability of Counsel During Jury Deliberations. Judge Angell does not require counsel to remain in the courthouse during deliberations, but she does require that they be available on telephone notice.

5. Taking the Verdict and Special Interrogatories. Judge Angell has no usual practice regarding special or general verdicts. Judge Angell frequently submits interrogatories to the jury.

6. Polling the Jury. Upon request, Judge Angell will permit the jury to be polled.

7. Interviewing the Jury. Judge Angell does not usually permit counsel to interview jurors after the verdict is recorded and the jury has been discharged.

CRIMINAL CASES

1. Sentencing Memoranda. When a pretrial sentencing report is used, Judge Angell permits the submission of sentencing memoranda by both counsel.

2. Additional Matters. At all "criminal duty week" proceedings, counsel, once appointed or retained, must be present to permit the proceeding to go forward.

Once the court has ordered that a defendant be detained or has set conditions of release, any proposed changes thereto must be submitted to the court by written motion.

While Judge Angell has no power to designate the pretrial detention facility, she does encourage counsel to alert her to any special needs, especially a defendant's medical needs, which may be addressed by order.

Judge Angell does not favor the dual representation of defendants by a single attorney at any criminal proceeding, apart, perhaps, from the initial appearance.

Judge Angell requires that all relevant documents be delivered to chambers in advance of court. Counsel may contact her clerk if there are questions regarding the matters before the court.

OTHER GENERAL MATTERS

Unless requested, Judge Angell prefers not to receive copies of appellate briefs when a decision rendered by her is appealed.

Judge Angell expects counsel to be on time when appearing before her and to be courteous with each other, both in the presence of the court and otherwise.

In general, Judge Angell expects counsel to discuss matters with opposing counsel before bringing them to her attention.

Counsel should not hesitate to contact Judge Angell's law clerks if they have a question about her courtroom practices or procedures.

IN THE UNITED STATES DISTRICT COURT
FOR THE EASTERN DISTRICT OF PENNSYLVANIA

	)	CIVIL ACTION
	)	
vs.	)	
	)	
	)	NO.

SCHEDULING ORDER

AND NOW, this _____ day of _____, 20___, it is ORDERED:

1. Pretrial procedure will follow the Federal Rule of Civil Procedure 16 and the Local Rule of Civil Procedure (LRCP) 16.1.

2. Discovery, consistent with LRCP 26.1, is to be completed by _____. (30, 60 or 90 days from date of Order).

3. Expert interrogatories and depositions are to be completed by _____. (30 days from the close of discovery).

4. All dispositive motions are to be filed by _____. (30 days from the close of expert discovery). All responses to dispositive motions are to be filed by _____. (30 days from the filing of dispositive motions).

5. Pretrial Memoranda, prepared consistent with LRCP 16.1(c), are to be filed with the Court by _____. (2 weeks before trial date). The listing of witnesses will be subject to LRCP 16.1(d)1(b).

6. Trial exhibits are to be pre-marked and exchanged by _____ (at least 5 days prior to trial) with the authenticity subject to LRCP 16.1(d)1(a).

7. A final pre-trial Order, if required, will be prepared consistent with LRCP 16.1(d)2 and submitted by counsel for plaintiff to Chambers at least three (3) days prior to the scheduled final pretrial conference.

8. The final pretrial conference will be held on _____ (2–4 days before trial) and conducted consistent with LRCP 16.1(d)3.

9. The trial will be held on _____, in Courtroom _____.

10. In a jury trial, the parties shall submit proposed voir dire questions, _joint_ proposed jury instructions and _joint_ proposed verdict forms on or before _____, (at least 5 days prior to trial) consistent with LRCP 16.1(d)4.

11. In a non-jury trial the proposed findings of fact and conclusions of law are to be submitted by all parties at the final pre-trial conference.

12. A joint stipulation of uncontested facts consistent with LRCP 16.1(d)2(b)(2) is to be submitted at the final pre-trial conference, unless a final pre-trial Order which includes the stipulation has been required for submission prior to the conference.

13. All requests by counsel are to be in writing, filed with the Clerk of Court and in Motion form, consistent with LRCP 7.1, unless directed otherwise by the Court.

BY THE COURT:

_____
M. FAITH ANGELL
UNITED STATES MAGISTRATE JUDGE

Magistrate Judge Linda K. Caracappa

Judge Caracappa was born on June 20, 1950, in Norristown, Pennsylvania. She received a B.A. from The Pennsylvania State University in 1971 and a J.D. from Villanova Law School in 1974. From 1975 until 1981, Judge Caracappa served in the Bucks County District Attorney's Office. From 1981 to 2000, Judge Caracappa was in private practice in Warrington, Bucks County, with the law firm Harris & Harris. From 1995 to 2000, Judge Caracappa served in the Bucks County Solicitor's Office. Judge Caracappa was appointed as a United States magistrate judge on November 17, 2000.

PRELIMINARY GENERAL MATTERS

1. Correspondence with the Court. Judge Caracappa permits correspondence from counsel on all matters.

2. Communications with Law Clerks. Judge Caracappa permits counsel to communicate with her deputy and law clerks on scheduling and administrative matters.

3. Telephone Conferences. Judge Caracappa prefers and encourages counsel to come to her chambers for conferences. When counsel cannot be present, she encourages the use of telephone conferences.

4. Oral Arguments and Evidentiary Hearings. Judge Caracappa does not set aside any special days or times for oral arguments or evidentiary hearings.

5. Pro Hac Vice Admissions. Judge Caracappa permits oral motions for pro hac vice admissions on the day that the attorney to be admitted first appears. A written motion before that time is not necessary. However, counsel should prepare an appropriate order to memorialize the pro hac vice admission. Evidence of payment of the pro hac vice fee must accompany the motion for admission. See Local Rule of Civil Procedure 83.5.2.

CIVIL CASES
Pretrial Procedure

1. Pretrial Conferences. Judge Caracappa will schedule status conferences, settlement conferences, and final pretrial conferences as required by the circumstance of each particular case. Judge Caracappa will work with counsel in the scheduling of either telephone conferences or conferences in chambers to resolve any issues that may arise during the progress of the case. Judge Caracappa does expect, however, that counsel will make all good-faith efforts to resolve any disputed matter between themselves before seeking involvement of the court.

Continuances and Extensions

1. General Policy. Judge Caracappa will normally consult counsel before establishing a briefing schedule, oral argument, evidentiary hearing, discovery deadline, or trial date. When possible, Judge Caracappa tries to accommodate counsel with regard to requests for reasonable changes.

2. Requests for Extensions and Continuances. For extensions and continuances, Judge Caracappa prefers a stipulation when possible. Judge Caracappa does not require a formal motion, and she will accept a letter for such requests. Judge Caracappa suggests that proposed orders of this type be submitted, and she prefers a joint request if possible. Judge Caracappa will often use telephone conferences to resolve such requests.

General Motion Practice

1. Oral Argument on Motions. Judge Caracappa will schedule oral argument on motions if it appears likely to be helpful to the court's resolution of the matter. Counsel may request oral argument if considered appropriate.

2. Reply and Surreply Briefs. Judge Caracappa permits reply briefs and surreply briefs, but she requests that counsel notify the court of the party's intention to file such a brief.

3. Chambers Copies of Motion Papers. Judge Caracappa prefers that a courtesy copy of all motion papers to be sent directly to her chambers.

Discovery Matters

1. Length of Discovery Period and Extensions. Judge Caracappa has no general policy on the amount of time allowed for discovery. The length of the discovery period is dictated by the complexity of the case and by the informed view of counsel.

2. Discovery Conferences and Dispute Resolution. Judge Caracappa encourages the parties to resolve discovery disputes without court intervention. Should counsel be unable, in good faith, to resolve their dispute, Judge Caracappa also encourages contact with the court so that telephone or chambers conferences may be set up to resolve outstanding issues.

3. Confidentiality Agreements. Judge Caracappa will permit confidentiality agreements subject to the requirements of *Pansy v. Borough of Stroudsburg,* 23 F.3d 772, 786 (3d Cir. 1994).

4. Expert Witnesses. The parties will identify expert witnesses and provide expert reports pursuant to Rule 26 and the Rule 16 scheduling order entered in each case.

Settlement

1. General Approach to Settlement. At the time a matter is referred for trial or settlement, and where practicable after consultation with counsel in advance of scheduling, an order will be sent to counsel scheduling a settlement conference and calling for the submission of a settlement conference summary by counsel (see the sample order for a settlement conference and settlement conference summary on pages 450 to 451 of this book). Judge Caracappa will require that a principal with settlement authority attend the conference in person. In exceptional circumstances, Judge Caracappa will permit that principal to participate in the conference by telephone. Depending on the circumstances, Judge Caracappa may schedule additional settlement conferences. Counsel and their clients should be prepared to devote a full day for any scheduled conference.

Arbitration

1. General Approach to Arbitration Cases. Judge Caracappa has no special practices or procedures for arbitration cases.

2. Scheduling of Trial De Novo from Arbitration. When a demand for trial de novo is filed after arbitration, Judge Caracappa promptly schedules a status conference to explore the possibility of settlement and, if necessary, to schedule a trial date.

Proposed Final Pretrial Memoranda

1.   ***Required Form of Pretrial Memoranda.***   Unless specifically provided for by separate order, Judge Caracappa will require the use of the short-form pretrial memorandum described in Local Civil Rule 16.1(c). Judge Caracappa encourages counsel to stipulate to uncontested facts as generally set out in Local Civil Rule 16.1.

2.   ***Common Deficiencies in Pretrial Memoranda.***   Judge Caracappa does not observe any significant deficiencies in the pretrial memoranda submitted to her.

Injunctions

1.   ***Scheduling and Expedited Discovery.***   Judge Caracappa will promptly list for a conference any injunction matters assigned to her. The scheduling of injunction matters will depend upon the circumstances of the case and will be determined at an initial conference to be attended by all counsel.

2.   ***Proposed Findings of Fact and Conclusions of Law.***   Judge Caracappa requires the submission of proposed findings of fact and conclusions of law in advance of the hearing in all injunction cases.

Trial Procedure

1.   ***Scheduling of Cases.***   Judge Caracappa's cases will be specially listed for trial based upon the availability of counsel and critical witnesses.

2.   ***Conflicts of Counsel.***   Counsel should notify Judge Caracappa, and opposing counsel, promptly of any professional or personal conflicts that may affect the trial schedule. Such notice may be given by telephone.

3.   ***Cases Involving Out-of-Town Parties or Witnesses.***   Judge Caracappa will make all reasonable attempts to accommodate the schedules and availability of all parties and witnesses.

4.   ***Note-taking by Jurors.***   Judge Caracappa permits the taking of notes by jurors.

5.   ***Trial Briefs.***   Judge Caracappa encourages the submission of trial briefs when they are necessary or likely to be helpful to the court.

6.   ***Voir Dire.***   It is Judge Caracappa's practice to preside over voir dire and jury selection. Judge Caracappa permits counsel to conduct voir dire in all civil cases. Counsel should exchange proposed voir dire questions at the final pretrial conference. Judge Caracappa may conduct supplemental voir dire when appropriate.

7.   ***Sidebars.***   Judge Caracappa discourages the use of sidebar conferences. Counsel are encouraged to raise evidentiary issues before trial or during recesses or adjournments.

8.   ***In Limine Motions.***   Judge Caracappa prefers to receive in limine motions at least one week before trial, but she will accept them up to the time of trial.

9.   ***Examination of Witnesses Out of Sequence.***   Judge Caracappa will permit counsel to take witnesses out of turn for the convenience of the witnesses, if no prejudice is caused to the opposing side.

10.   ***Opening Statements and Summations.***   Judge Caracappa has no fixed rule on the time limits for opening statements or summations. Judge Caracappa will grant a reasonable amount of time for counsel as dictated by the nature of the case.

11. Examination of Witnesses or Argument by More Than One Attorney. Judge Caracappa will not normally permit more than one attorney for the party to examine the same witness. However, more than one attorney for a party may argue different points in a motion before Judge Caracappa.

12. Examination of Witness Beyond Redirect and Recross. Judge Caracappa will generally restrict counsel from examining witnesses beyond redirect and recross.

13. Videotaped Testimony. Judge Caracappa requires counsel to review all videotaped depositions and to have them edited so as to fairly present only the essential evidence of the witness involved. With the assistance of the court, counsel are expected to resolve all matters pertaining to objections before offering the videotape into evidence.

14. Reading of Material Into the Record. Judge Caracappa has no special practice with regard to reading stipulations, pleadings, or discovery materials into the record.

15. Preparation of Exhibits. Judge Caracappa requires all exhibits to be pre-marked and pre-exchanged. Counsel should provide the court with two copies of each trial exhibit, as well as an exhibit list.

16. Offering Exhibits Into Evidence. Judge Caracappa expects counsel to reach agreement in advance as to the admission of exhibits. Judge Caracappa has no particular procedure as to when an exhibit may be formally offered into evidence.

17. Motions for Judgment as a Matter of Law and Motions for Judgment on Partial Findings. Judge Caracappa has no special policy or preference concerning whether motions for judgment as a matter of law (or motions for judgment on partial findings in nonjury trials) be written or oral. Judge Caracappa usually conducts oral arguments on these motions.

18. Proposed Jury Instructions and Verdict Forms. Judge Caracappa prefers to receive proposed jury instructions only for difficult or novel areas of law. She will accept supplemental points prior to the delivery of the charge. Judge Caracappa usually conducts a conference on proposed jury instructions.

19. Proposed Findings of Fact and Conclusions of Law. Judge Caracappa requires counsel to submit proposed findings of fact and conclusions of law in nonjury cases at the final pretrial conference. She will permit supplementation later (at the close of trial or, in a complex matter, after trial) as necessary.

Jury Deliberations

1. Written Jury Instructions. In most cases, Judge Caracappa gives a copy of her instructions to the jury.

2. Exhibits in the Jury Room. Judge Caracappa will consider what exhibits should be sent out to the jury during their deliberations on a case-by-case basis, but generally prefers all exhibits be given to the jury at the start of deliberations.

3. Handling of Jury Requests to Read Back Testimony or Replay Tapes. Judge Caracappa will seek the input of counsel and will then make a determination on a case-by-case basis when requests are made to read back testimony or replay tapes.

4. Availability of Counsel During Jury Deliberations. Judge Caracappa usually requires counsel to remain in the courthouse during jury deliberations.

5. Taking the Verdict and Special Interrogatories. Judge Caracappa normally submits special interrogatories to the jury. Judge Caracappa expects counsel to submit proposed special interrogatories to the jury, preferably in a joint submission.

6. Polling the Jury. Judge Caracappa will grant a request to poll the jury.

7. Interviewing the Jury. Judge Caracappa will permit counsel to interview jurors, but only after the verdict has been recorded and the jury has been discharged and told in clear terms that they have no obligation to speak with counsel.

CRIMINAL CASES

1. Approach to Oral Argument and Motions. Judge Caracappa permits oral argument when counsel request it and when it is necessary for an informed disposition of the motion.

2. Pretrial Conferences. Judge Caracappa does not routinely hold pretrial conferences in criminal cases.

3. Voir Dire. Judge Caracappa permits counsel to conduct the voir dire in criminal cases.

4. Sentencing Memoranda. Judge Caracappa permits, but does not require, submission of sentencing memoranda by both sides.

OTHER GENERAL MATTERS

When a decision rendered by Judge Caracappa is appealed, she prefers to receive copies of appellate briefs. Judge Caracappa expects counsel to be prompt in all appearances, to be professional and courteous to each other, both in the presence of the court and otherwise, and to have discussions with each other about any matter in dispute before it is brought to the attention of the court. Counsel should feel free to contact Judge Caracappa's deputy clerk or law clerks if they have any questions about her courtroom practices or procedures.

**IN THE UNITED STATES DISTRICT COURT
FOR THE EASTERN DISTRICT OF PENNSYLVANIA**

	:	CIVIL ACTION
	:	
	:	
v.	:	
	:	
	:	NO.
	:	

ORDER

A Settlement Conference in the above-captioned case will be held on _____, at _____, before the Honorable Linda K. Caracappa, United States Magistrate Judge, in Room 3042, U.S. Courthouse, 601 Market Street, Philadelphia, PA 19106.

The Court assumes that settlement of this case is a real possibility, and the Court has set aside the entire day for this conference. Parties are to remain present until expressly released by the Court.

Counsel are directed to have clients with ultimate authority to settle physically <u>PRESENT</u> in the courtroom for the duration of this conference.[*]

Counsel are further directed to complete the enclosed Settlement Conference Summary to be faxed or mailed to Chambers on or before _____.

BY THE COURT:

_____
Honorable Linda K. Caracappa
267-299-7640/267-299-5075 Fax

Date: _____

cc: _____

---

[*] Parties include all persons, corporations or other business entities, and insurance companies with an interest in the case, and each entity with an interest in the case *must* attend the conference. In the case of corporate or other business entities, the corporate official with ultimate settlement authority is required to attend. Where an insurance company is involved, a representative with ultimate settlement authority is also required to attend.

Magistrate Judge Linda K. Caracappa

IN THE UNITED STATES DISTRICT COURT
FOR THE EASTERN DISTRICT OF PENNSYLVANIA

v.

CIVIL ACTION

NO.

SETTLEMENT CONFERENCE SUMMARY

COUNSEL ATTENDING SETTLEMENT CONFERENCE:
    Name: _____
    Address: _____
    Phone: _____
    Client: _____

CLIENT ATTENDING SETTLEMENT CONFERENCE:
    Name of Individual with Ultimate Settlement Authority
    who will be present at the settlement conference: _____

MOTIONS PENDING:
_____
_____
_____

STATUS OF DISCOVERY:
_____
_____
_____

OTHER RELEVANT MATTERS:
_____
_____
_____

PRIOR OFFERS/DEMAND:
_____
_____
_____

ATTACH SYNOPSIS OF CASE

IDENTIFY: 1) CAUSES OF ACTION, 2) PROOFS OF SAME, AND 3) ITEMIZATION AND PROOF OF DAMAGES CLAIMED. COUNSEL SHOULD ALSO INCLUDE ANY OTHER INFORMATION THAT WOULD BE HELPFUL TO THE COURT IN EVALUATING THIS MATTER.

Magistrate Judge Jacob P. Hart

Judge Hart received a B.A. from the University of Pennsylvania in 1963 and an LL.B. from the University of Pennsylvania Law School in 1967. From 1967 to 1968, Judge Hart served as a law clerk to the Honorable Samuel J. Roberts of the Pennsylvania Supreme Court. Judge Hart was in private practice in Philadelphia from 1968 to 1971 and again from 1973 to 1995. He served as the director for the Enforcement Division of the Middle Atlantic Region of the United States Environmental Protection Agency in 1972. Judge Hart served as the director of the Appellate Mediation Program of the United States Court of Appeals for the Third Circuit from 1995 to 1997. He was appointed as a United States Magistrate Judge on November 17, 1997.

PRELIMINARY GENERAL MATTERS

1. **Correspondence with the Court.** Judge Hart permits correspondence with the court on scheduling and administrative matters.

2. **Communications with Law Clerks.** Judge Hart permits correspondence with his law clerks on procedural matters only.

CIVIL CASES
Pretrial Procedure

1. **Pretrial Conferences.** Upon the consent of the parties to trial before a magistrate judge and referral by the district court judge, Judge Hart holds a scheduling conference, usually by telephone. At that time, all deadlines are set and the case is listed for trial (see his scheduling order shown on page 458 of this book).

Settlement

1. **General Approach to Settlement and Nonjury Cases.** At the time a case is referred for settlement, an order will be sent to counsel, scheduling the conference (see the settlement schedule shown on page 461 of this book). Judge Hart requires that a principal with settlement authority attend the conference and requires counsel for all parties to submit *confidential* position papers. In *exceptional* circumstances, Judge Hart will permit the principal with settlement authority to participate by telephone.

Proposed Final Pretrial Memoranda

1. **Required Form of Pretrial Memoranda in Jury Cases.** In lieu of pretrial memoranda or a final pretrial order, under Local Rule 16.1(d)(1) and (2), a pretrial stipulation must be submitted containing the following:

(a) Agreed facts. A conscientious effort should be made to narrow the areas of dispute.

(b) Each party's disputed facts.

(c) Each party's exhibits, as marked for trial. (Any objections to authenticity should be noted or will be considered waived. Exhibits are to be provided to the court in the form of two jointly prepared, looseleaf exhibit books, each separately numbering Joint Exhibits, Plaintiff's Exhibits, and Defendant's Exhibits.)

(d) Each party's witnesses and the subject matter of the witness's testimony. *(Judge Hart requires parties who intend on using video equipment to present the testimony of a witness, to either supply that equipment or request, at least two weeks before trial, that the court reserve equipment for them.)*

(e) Unusual issues—contentions and authority.

(f) Proposed voir dire questions, request for jury instructions, and a proposed jury verdict form. Counsel must make a good-faith effort to agree upon as many of these items as possible. *(Judge Hart requires that these items be submitted on disk, in WordPerfect format, if possible, as well as on hard copy.)*

(g) The signed approval of trial counsel for each party.

It will be the responsibility of plaintiff's counsel to circulate a draft of this pretrial stipulation at least one week before it is due.

2. **Required Form of Pretrial Memoranda in Nonjury Cases.** In lieu of pretrial memoranda or a final pretrial order, under Local Rule 16.1(d)(1) and (2), a pretrial stipulation must be submitted containing the following:

(a) Agreed facts. A conscientious effort should be made to narrow the areas of dispute.

(b) Each party's disputed facts.

(c) Each party's exhibits, as marked for trial. (Any objections to authenticity should be noted or will be considered waived. Exhibits are to be provided to the court in the form of two jointly prepared, looseleaf exhibit books, each separately numbering Joint Exhibits, Plaintiff's Exhibits, and Defendant's Exhibits.)

(d) Each party's witnesses and the subject matter of the witness's testimony. *(Judge Hart requires parties who intend on using video equipment to present the testimony of a witness, to either supply that equipment or request, at least two weeks before trial, that the court reserve equipment for them.)*

(e) Unusual issues—contentions and authority.

(f) Proposed findings of fact and conclusions of law. *(Judge Hart requires that these items be submitted on disk, in WordPerfect format, if possible, as well as hard copy.)*

(g) The signed approval of trial counsel for each party.

It will be the responsibility of plaintiff's counsel to circulate a draft of this pretrial stipulation at least one week before it is due.

Trial Procedure

1. **Scheduling of Cases.** In most cases, Judge Hart will set a date certain for trial. However, due to Judge Hart's calendar, in some instances, a case is listed as a backup to another, but also given a "drop dead date" (see the backup scheduling order on page 459 of this book). If the first case is disposed of prior to two weeks before the trial date, the backup case will be tried at that time. If not, the case will be tried on the "drop dead date" previously set.

Practice and Procedures of Judges and Judges' Forms and Orders

2. Courtroom Procedures and Location. Judge Hart does not have an assigned courtroom for civil matters. As soon as the court is aware of the courtroom assignment, counsel will be notified. Subpoenas can direct witnesses to report to chambers, room 3041 U.S. Courthouse. Judge Hart's staff will then direct witnesses to the appropriate courtroom.

Jury selection ordinarily takes place at 2:00 p.m. Monday afternoon. Judge Hart will give his opening instructions to the jury the following morning. The judge sits from 9:30 a.m. until 4:30 p.m., with an hour break for lunch and a brief recess in the morning and in the afternoon.

3. Jury Selection. Once questioning has been completed, and challenges for cause ruled upon, the court will excuse all but the first 16 prospective jurors. Peremptory challenges will then be exercised by alternate strikes, plaintiff first, until each side has stricken three names. (The additional two jurors kept in the room during this phase are simply a precaution lest someone suddenly comes up with a reason why they must be excused.)

4. Approaching Witnesses. Unless it is necessary to show a document to a witness, counsel should question either from counsel table or from the lectern. A small courtroom is usually assigned, and movement around the floor during questioning can be distracting. Counsel need not ask permission to approach a witness each time they do so. Once per trial is enough.

5. Note-taking by Jurors. The jury may take notes.

6. Voir Dire. The court conducts voir dire. Counsel may ask additional questions, upon request, after the court has questioned the panel, and may ask follow-up questions to individual jurors who are called to the witness stand to answer private questions.

7. Sidebars. Sidebars are to be kept to an absolute minimum. During a trial, Judge Hart is always available, in chambers, both before and after court sessions, and during the lunch break.

8. Examination of Witnesses or Argument by More Than One Attorney. If more than one lawyer is representing a party, they must decide who will examine each witness. Only one lawyer may speak per witness. (Of course, the lawyers may choose which witnesses to examine and the lawyers may take turns.)

9. Examination of Witnesses Beyond Redirect and Recross. The court permits one redirect examination and one recross-examination. There is no such thing as re-redirect or re-recross.

10. Objections. If counsel wishes to object to a question, a simple "objection" is all that is necessary. No speeches, please. If the court needs more information in order to rule, it will ask.

11. Offering Exhibits Into Evidence. Counsel may move exhibits into evidence as they are identified, or at the close of a witness's testimony. Lawyers should not, however, wait until the end of their case and then move everything.

Jury Deliberations

1. Exhibits in the Jury Room. All exhibits that have been admitted into evidence are sent into the jury room during deliberations, together with a copy of the court's jury instructions.

2. Interviewing the Jury. After the jury has been discharged, the court permits jurors who wish to do so to speak with counsel.

CRIMINAL CASES

1. Practices and Procedures. When Judge Hart is assigned to criminal duty matters, he holds the hearings in Courtroom 5A at 1:30 p.m. Arraignments assigned by the district court are held on Thursday mornings at 10:30 a.m., in Courtroom 5A.

2. Probation Report. Where there is no waiver of the presentence report, Judge Hart permits the defendant or defense counsel to review the Probation Department's written recommendation as to sentence.

JUDGE HART'S STANDING ORDER RE PRETRIAL STIPULATION
(JURY TRIAL)

In lieu of pretrial memoranda or a Final Pretrial Order, under Local Rules 16.1(d)(1) and (2), a Pretrial Stipulation shall be submitted, containing the following:

1. Agreed facts. A conscientious effort should be made to narrow the areas of dispute.

2. Each party's disputed facts.

3. Each party's exhibits, as marked for trial. (Any objections to authenticity should be noted or will be considered waived. Exhibits shall be provided to the Court in the form of two, jointly prepared, loose leaf Exhibit Books, each separately numbering Joint Exhibits, Plaintiff's Exhibits, and Defendant's Exhibits.)

4. Each party's witnesses and the subject matter of the witness's testimony. (PLEASE NOTE: IF YOU WILL BE USING VIDEO EQUIPMENT TO PRESENT THE TESTIMONY OF A WITNESS, YOU MUST EITHER SUPPLY THAT EQUIPMENT OR REQUEST AT LEAST TWO WEEKS BEFORE TRIAL THAT THE COURT RESERVE EQUIPMENT FOR YOU)

5. Unusual issues—contentions and authority.

6. Proposed voir dire questions, requests for jury instructions, and a proposed jury verdict form. Counsel shall make a good faith effort to agree upon as many of these items as possible. (THESE ITEMS ARE TO BE SUBMITTED ON DISK—WORDPERFECT IF POSSIBLE—AS WELL AS IN HARD COPY.)

7. The signed approval of trial counsel for each party.

IT SHALL BE THE RESPONSIBILITY OF PLAINTIFF'S COUNSEL TO CIRCULATE A DRAFT OF THIS PRETRIAL STIPULATION AT LEAST ONE WEEK BEFORE IT IS DUE.

JUDGE HART'S STANDING ORDER RE PRETRIAL STIPULATION
(BENCH TRIAL)

In lieu of pretrial memoranda or a Final Pretrial Order, under Local Rules 16.1(d)(1) and (2), a Pretrial Stipulation shall be submitted, containing the following:

1. Agreed facts. A conscientious effort should be made to narrow the areas of dispute.

2. Each party's disputed facts.

3. Each party's exhibits, as marked for trial. (Any objections to authenticity should be noted or will be considered waived. Exhibits shall be provided to the Court in the form of two jointly prepared, loose leaf Exhibit Books, separately numbering Joint Exhibits, Plaintiff's Exhibits, and Defendant's Exhibits.)

4. Each party's witnesses and the subject matter of the witness's testimony. (PLEASE NOTE: IF YOU WILL BE USING VIDEO EQUIPMENT TO PRESENT THE TESTIMONY OF A WITNESS, YOU MUST EITHER SUPPLY THAT EQUIPMENT OR REQUEST AT LEAST TWO WEEKS BEFORE TRIAL THAT THE COURT RESERVE EQUIPMENT FOR YOU.)

5. Unusual issues—contentions and authority.

6. Proposed findings of fact and conclusions of law. (THESE ITEMS ARE TO BE SUBMITTED ON DISK—WORDPERFECT IF POSSIBLE—AS WELL AS IN HARD COPY.)

7. The signed approval of trial counsel for each party.

IT SHALL BE THE RESPONSIBILITY OF PLAINTIFF'S COUNSEL TO CIRCULATE A DRAFT OF THIS PRETRIAL STIPULATION AT LEAST ONE WEEK BEFORE IT IS DUE.

Practice and Procedures of Judges and Judges' Forms and Orders

**IN THE UNITED STATES DISTRICT COURT
FOR THE EASTERN DISTRICT OF PENNSYLVANIA**

Plaintiff   :   CIVIL ACTION

      v.   :

Defendant   :   NO.

O R D E R

AND NOW, this ____ day of _____, 20___, the following schedule is HEREBY ORDERED in the above captioned matter.

1. All discovery (including responses) is to be completed by _____.

2. All dispositive motions shall be filed on or before _____, with **courtesy copies hand delivered to chambers** on the day of filing.

3. All Motions in Limine shall be filed by _____, with **courtesy copies hand delivered to chambers** on the day of filing. Responses to Motions in Limine shall be filed by _____.

4. A Pretrial Stipulation, signed by all counsel, shall be filed by (*two weeks prior to trial*). (See Standing Order Re Pretrial Stipulation, attached hereto).

5. JURY SELECTION will take place at **2:00 p.m.** on **Monday,** _____.

6. TRIAL DATE: **Tuesday,** _____.

By (*two weeks prior to trial*), plaintiff will report in writing on counsels' serious settlement efforts. Any party may request a conference. A final conference in the above case will be held in chambers, Room 3041, U.S. Courthouse, 1:30 p.m., on the day of jury selection.

BY THE COURT:

_____
Jacob P. Hart
UNITED STATES MAGISTRATE JUDGE

cc: Faxed to:

Magistrate Judge Jacob P. Hart

IN THE UNITED STATES DISTRICT COURT
FOR THE EASTERN DISTRICT OF PENNSYLVANIA

Plaintiff	:	CIVIL ACTION
v.	:	
Defendant	:	NO.

ORDER

AND NOW, this ____ day of _____, 20___, the following schedule is HEREBY ORDERED in the above captioned matter.

1. All discovery (including responses) is to be completed by _____.

2. All dispositive motions shall be filed on or before _____, with **courtesy copies hand delivered to chambers** on the day of filing.

3. All Motions in Limine shall be filed by _____, with **courtesy copies hand delivered to chambers** on the day of filing. Responses to Motions in Limine shall be filed by _____.

4. A Pretrial Stipulation, signed by all counsel, shall be filed by (*two weeks prior to trial*). (See Standing Order Re Pretrial Stipulation, attached hereto).

5. JURY SELECTION will take place at **2:00 p.m.** on **Monday,** _____.

6. TRIAL DATE: **Tuesday,** _____. **Note: This case will be a back-up to a previously scheduled trial on this date.** If the Court has not disposed of the previously scheduled case on or before *two weeks prior to trial date*, counsel will be notified of that fact, and this case will then be tried on *drop dead date*.

By (*two weeks prior to trial*), plaintiff will report in writing on counsels' serious settlement efforts. Any party may request a conference. A final conference in the above case will be held in chambers, Room 3041, U.S. Courthouse, 1:30 p.m., on the day of jury selection.

BY THE COURT:

_____
Jacob P. Hart
UNITED STATES MAGISTRATE JUDGE

A DOZEN WAYS TO BE COMFORTABLE IN JUDGE HART'S COURTROOM

1. The Court conducts *voir dire*. Counsel may ask additional questions, upon request, after the Court has questioned the panel, and may ask follow up questions to individual jurors who are called to the witness stand to answer private questions.

2. Once questioning has been completed, and challenges for cause ruled upon, the Court will excuse all but the first 16 prospective jurors. Peremptory challenges will then be exercised by alternate strikes, plaintiff first, until each side has stricken three names. (The additional 2 jurors kept in the room during this phase is simply a precaution lest someone suddenly come up with a reason why they must be excused)

3. During trial, the Court sits from 9:30 a.m. to 4:30 p.m., with one hour for lunch, and at least two breaks.

4. Side bars are to be kept to an absolute minimum. During a trial Judge Hart is always available, in chambers, both before and after Court sessions, and during the lunch break.

5. Unless it is necessary to show a document to a witness, counsel should question either from counsel table or from the lectern. We are usually assigned to a small courtroom, and movement around the floor during questioning can be distracting. Counsel need not ask permission to approach a witness each time they do so. Once per trial is enough.

6. If counsel wishes to object to a question, a simple "objection." is all that is necessary. No speeches, please. If the Court needs more information in order to rule, it will ask.

7. The Court permits one redirect examination and one re-cross examination. There is no such thing as re-re direct or re-re cross.

8. If more than one lawyer is representing a party, please decide who will examine each witness. Only one lawyer may speak per witness. (Of course, it's your choice and feel free to take turns).

9. The jury may take notes.

10. Counsel may move exhibits into evidence as they are identified, or at the close of a witness's testimony. Do not, however, wait until the end of your case and then move everything.

11. All exhibits that have been admitted into evidence are sent into the jury room during deliberations, together with a copy of the Court's jury instructions.

12. After the jury has been discharged, the Court permits jurors who wish to do so to speak with counsel.

Magistrate Judge Jacob P. Hart

IN THE UNITED STATES DISTRICT COURT
FOR THE EASTERN DISTRICT OF PENNSYLVANIA

Plaintiff   :   CIVIL ACTION

v.

Defendant   :   NO.

ORDER

AND NOW, this _____ day of _____, 20___, pursuant to the Order of Judge (_____) in the above captioned matter, a settlement conference has been scheduled before the undersigned on *(day)* at *(time)*, in Room 3041, United States Courthouse, 601 Market St., Philadelphia, PA 19106.

The senior attorney in charge of the matter for each of the parties, **AND THE PARTIES THEMSELVES,** or if a corporation, an official of the corporation with settlement authority are required to attend the conference in person. If a party is more than one hundred miles from Philadelphia and prior permission is given by the court, the party may participate by telephone. The parties and counsel must be prepared to discuss settlement or other disposition of the matter.

Counsel are directed to fax confidential position papers not longer than 2 pages directly to Chambers (fax. no. 215-580-2163) not later than 2 business days prior to the date of the conference. The position paper should address the party's settlement position, as well as any other issue that counsel believes will be of assistance to the Court in helping the parties resolve this matter. **THIS DOCUMENT IS NOT TO BE SHARED WITH OPPOSING COUNSEL NOR FILED OF RECORD. THIS IS FOR JUDGE HART'S EYES ONLY.**

BY THE COURT:

_____
JACOB P. HART
UNITED STATES MAGISTRATE JUDGE

Copies faxed to: Copies mailed to:

Magistrate Judge Elizabeth T. Hey

Judge Hey received a B.A. from Vassar College in 1983. She graduated from the joint Law and Psychology Program at Hahnemann and Villanova, receiving a J.D. in 1989 from Villanova University School of Law and a Ph.D. from Hahnemann University Graduate School in 1991. She then clerked for Colins J. Seitz of the United States Court of Appeals for the Third Circuit, following which she spent four years as a litigation associate with Dechert Price and Rhoads. From 1995 to 2007 she was an assistant federal defender in the Federal Division of the Defender Association of Philadelphia. In April 2007, she was sworn in as a United States magistrate judge for the Eastern District of Pennsylvania.

PRELIMINARY GENERAL MATTERS

1. *Correspondence with the Court.* Judge Hey permits correspondence with the court on scheduling and administrative matters.

2. *Communications with Law Clerks.* Judge Hey permits communications, both written and oral, with her law clerks on procedural matters only.

CIVIL CASES
Consent Trials

1. *Scheduling of Cases.* Upon the consent of the parties to trial before a magistrate judge and referral by the district court judge, Judge Hey holds a scheduling conference, usually by telephone. At that time, all deadlines are set and the case is listed for trial (see Scheduling Order—Jury on page 465, and Scheduling Order—Bench on page 466). Rather than using a trial pool, Judge Hey sets a date certain for trial at the time of the scheduling conference. The deadlines that are set in the original scheduling order are subject to revision only by the court and only for good cause. A stipulation among counsel will not alter the court's calendar.

2. *Standing Orders.* Judge Hey has standing orders regarding the preparation of civil cases referred for jury and non-jury trials (see Standing Order—Jury on page 467, and Standing Order—Bench on page 468).

Courtroom Procedures

1. *Courtroom Assignments.* Judge Hey is assigned to Courtroom 6 of the Robert N.C. Nix Building at 9th and Market Streets.

2. *Final Pretrial Conference.* Judge Hey conducts a final pretrial conference approximately two weeks prior to trial.

3. *Jury Selection.* Judge Hey endeavors to hold jury selection as early as possible on the date the case is listed for trial. However, jury panels in the building are assigned on a seniority basis. Therefore, there are times when jury selection is not completed until the afternoon of the date the case is listed for trial.

4. *Voir Dire.* The judge conducts voir dire. Counsel may ask additional questions or follow-up questions once the court has concluded asking questions. Because some questions may involve private matters, the court welcomes the prospective jurors to answer such questions at sidebar.

Once questioning has been completed, and challenges for cause ruled upon, the court will excuse all but the first 16 prospective jurors. Peremptory challenges will then be exercised by alternate strikes, plaintiff first, until each side has stricken 3 names. (The additional 2 jurors kept in the room during this phase is simply a precaution in case someone suddenly comes up with a reason why he/she must be excused.) In the event of multiple plaintiffs or defendants, the judge ordinarily does not permit additional peremptory challenges.

5. **Sidebars.** Sidebars are to be kept to an absolute minimum.

6. **Instructions to the Jury and Opening Statements.** If time permits, Judge Hey will give her opening instructions to the jury immediately following jury selection and the case will proceed. Counsel should be prepared to present their opening statements on the day of jury selection.

7. **Note-taking by Jurors.** The jury is permitted to take notes once the opening statements are completed.

8. **General Policy on the Examination of Witnesses.** Unless it is necessary to show a document to a witness, counsel should question either from counsel table or from the lectern. Counsel need not ask permission to approach a witness each time they do so. Once per trial is sufficient.

9. **Objections.** If counsel wishes to object to a question, a simple "objection" with grounds in three words or less is all that is necessary. If the court needs more information in order to rule, it will ask.

The court permits one redirect and one recross-examination.

10. **Examination of Witnesses by More Than One Attorney.** If more than one lawyer is representing a party, please decide who will examine each witness. Only one lawyer may speak per witness. (Of course, it is your choice and feel free to take turns.)

11. **Examination of a Witness Beyond Redirect or Recross.** The court permits one redirect and one recross-examination.

12. **Offering Exhibits into Evidence.** Counsel may move exhibits into evidence as they are identified, or at the close of a witness's testimony. Do not, however, wait until the end of your case and then move everything.

13. **Exhibits in the Jury Room.** Judge Hey's general rule is that all exhibits that have been admitted into evidence are sent into the jury room during deliberations, together with a copy of the court's instructions.

14. **Interviewing the Jury.** After the jury has been discharged, the court permits jurors who wish to do so to speak with counsel.

Settlement Conferences

At the time a case is referred for settlement, an order will be sent to counsel, scheduling the conference (see settlement schedule on page 469). Judge Hey requires that a principal with settlement authority attend the conference and requires counsel for all parties to submit **confidential** position papers. In exceptional circumstances, Judge Hey will permit the principal with settlement authority to participate by telephone. However, such request should be made of the court prior to the conference, with a copy of the request sent to opposing counsel, and will not be considered until counsel has submitted the party's conference memorandum.

CRIMINAL/MISDEMEANOR CASES

1. **Criminal Duty Matters.** When Judge Hey is assigned to criminal duty matters, she holds the hearings in Courtroom 5A in the United States Courthouse at 6th and Market Streets, at 1:30 p.m.

2. **Pretrial Services Report.** Judge Hey permits counsel for the government and defense counsel to review the pretrial services report.

3. **Probation Report.** Where there is no waiver of the presentence report, Judge Hey permits the defendant or defense counsel to review the Probation Department's written recommendation as to sentence.

OTHER GENERAL MATTERS

The judge sits from 9:30 a.m. until 4:30 p.m., with an hour break for lunch and a brief recess in the morning and in the afternoon. During trial, Judge Hey is available, in chambers, both before and after court, and during the lunch break.

Magistrate Judge Elizabeth T. Hey

**IN THE UNITED STATES DISTRICT COURT
FOR THE EASTERN DISTRICT OF PENNSYLVANIA**

PLAINTIFF	:	CIVIL ACTION
v.	:	
DEFENDANT	:	NO.

ORDER

AND NOW, this _____ day of _____, 20___, the following schedule is HEREBY ORDERED in the above captioned matter.

1. All discovery (including responses) is to be completed by **DATE.**

2. All motions regarding expert witnesses shall be filed by **DATE.**
   Responses to such motions shall be filed by **DATE.**

3. All dispositive motions shall be filed on or before **DATE.**
   Responses to such motions shall be filed by **DATE.**

4. All Motions in Limine shall be filed by **DATE.**
   Responses to such motions shall be filed by **DATE.**

5. A Pretrial Stipulation, signed by all counsel, shall be filed by **DATE.**
   (See Standing Order Re Pretrial Stipulation, attached hereto).

6. A Final Pretrial Conference will be held in Courtroom 6 of the Robert N.C. Nix Building, 900 Market Street at **TIME**, on **DATE.**

7. JURY SELECTION will take place at **TIME** on **DATE,** with trial commencing immediately following jury selection.

By **DATE,** plaintiff will report in writing on counsels' serious settlement efforts. Any party may request a settlement conference.

If any of the documents required by this Order are not electronically filed, counsel shall have a copy hand-delivered to Chambers on the day of filing. The deadlines listed above are subject to revision only by the Court and only for good cause. A stipulation among counsel will not alter the Court's calendar.

BY THE COURT:

_____
Elizabeth T. Hey
UNITED STATES MAGISTRATE JUDGE

Practice and Procedures of Judges and Judges' Forms and Orders

IN THE UNITED STATES DISTRICT COURT
FOR THE EASTERN DISTRICT OF PENNSYLVANIA

PLAINTIFF	:	CIVIL ACTION
v.	:	
DEFENDANT	:	NO.

O R D E R

AND NOW, this _____ day of _____, 20___, the following schedule is HEREBY ORDERED in the above captioned matter.

1. All discovery (including responses) is to be completed by **DATE**.

2. All motions regarding expert witnesses shall be filed by **DATE**.
   Responses to such motions shall be filed by **DATE**.

3. All dispositive motions shall be filed on or before **DATE**.
   Responses to such motions shall be filed by **DATE**.

4. All Motions in Limine shall be filed by **DATE**.
   Responses to such motions shall be filed by **DATE**.

5. A Pretrial Stipulation, signed by all counsel, shall be filed by **DATE**.
   (See Standing Order Re Pretrial Stipulation, attached hereto).

6. A Final Pretrial Conference will be held in Courtroom 6 of the Robert N.C. Nix Building at 900 Market Street at **TIME**, on **DATE**.

7. Trial will commence on **TIME, at DATE.**

By **DATE,** plaintiff will report in writing on counsels' serious settlement efforts. Any party may request a settlement conference, and the court will arrange for such a conference with another Magistrate Judge.

If any of the documents required by this Order are not electronically filed, counsel shall have a copy hand-delivered to Chambers on the day of filing. The deadlines listed above are subject to revision only by the Court and only for good cause. A stipulation among counsel will not alter the Court's calendar.

BY THE COURT:

_____
Elizabeth T. Hey
UNITED STATES MAGISTRATE JUDGE

Magistrate Judge Elizabeth T. Hey

JUDGE HEY'S STANDING ORDER RE PRETRIAL STIPULATION
(JURY TRIAL)

In lieu of pretrial memoranda or a Final Pretrial Order, under Local Rules 16.1(d)(1) and (2), a Pretrial Stipulation shall be submitted, containing the following:

1. Agreed facts. A conscientious effort should be made to narrow the areas of dispute.

2. Each party's disputed facts.

3. Two copies of each party's exhibits, as marked for trial. (Any objections to authenticity should be noted or will be considered waived. Exhibits shall be provided to the Court in the form of two, jointly prepared, loose leaf Exhibit Books, each separately numbering Joint Exhibits, Plaintiff's Exhibits, and Defendant's Exhibits.) If counsel expect to utilize oversized exhibits, please make the court aware so that we may make arrangements with Court Security Officers.

4. Each party's witnesses and the subject matter of the witness's testimony.

5. Unusual issues—contentions and authority.

6. Proposed voir dire questions, requests for jury instructions, and a proposed jury verdict form. Counsel shall make a good faith effort to agree upon as many of these items as possible. (THESE ITEMS ARE TO BE SUBMITTED IN HARD COPY AND ON DISK OR EMAILED TO THE LAW CLERK ASSIGNED TO THE CASE.)

7. A statement of the electronic equipment that each side will be bringing for the presentation of its case and any request for additional electronic equipment that counsel will request the court to provide.

8. The signed approval of trial counsel for each party.

IT SHALL BE THE RESPONSIBILITY OF PLAINTIFF'S COUNSEL TO CIRCULATE A DRAFT OF THIS PRETRIAL STIPULATION AT LEAST ONE WEEK BEFORE IT IS DUE.

JUDGE HEY'S STANDING ORDER RE PRETRIAL STIPULATION
(BENCH TRIAL)

In lieu of pretrial memoranda or a Final Pretrial Order, under Local Rules 16.1(d)(1) and (2), a Pretrial Stipulation shall be submitted, containing the following:

1. Agreed facts. A conscientious effort should be made to narrow the areas of dispute.
2. Each party's disputed facts.
3. Each party's exhibits, as marked for trial. (Any objections to authenticity should be noted or will be considered waived. Exhibits shall be provided to the Court in the form of a jointly prepared, loose leaf Exhibit Book separately numbering Joint Exhibits, Plaintiff's Exhibits, and Defendant's Exhibits.) If counsel expect to utilize oversized exhibits, please make the court aware so that we may make arrangements with Court Security Officers.
4. Each party's witnesses and the subject matter of the witness's testimony.
5. Unusual issues—contentions and authority.
6. Proposed findings of fact and conclusions of law (THESE ITEMS ARE TO BE SUBMITTED IN HARD COPY AND ON DISK OR EMAILED TO THE LAW CLERK ASSIGNED TO THE CASE).
7. A statement of electronic equipment that each side will be bringing for the presentation of its case and any request for additional electronic equipment that counsel will request the court to provide.
8. The signed approval of trial counsel for each party.

IT SHALL BE THE RESPONSIBILITY OF PLAINTIFF'S COUNSEL TO CIRCULATE A DRAFT OF THIS PRETRIAL STIPULATION AT LEAST ONE WEEK BEFORE IT IS DUE

Magistrate Judge Elizabeth T. Hey

IN THE UNITED STATES DISTRICT COURT
FOR THE EASTERN DISTRICT OF PENNSYLVANIA

PLAINTIFF	:	CIVIL ACTION
	:	
v.	:	
	:	
DEFENDANT	:	NO.

ORDER

AND NOW, this _____ day of _____, 20___, this matter having been referred by the Honorable _____ for a settlement conference, IT IS HEREBY ORDERED that a settlement conference will be held on **date at time**, before the undersigned in Courtroom 6, 2nd floor, United States Courthouse, Robert N.C. Nix Building, 900 Market Street, Philadelphia, Pennsylvania.

The following are required to attend the conference in person: (1) the senior attorney in charge of the matter for each of the parties, (2) **the parties themselves,** or if a corporation, an official of the corporation with full settlement authority, (3) representatives with full settlement authority of all insurance carriers or other entities responsible for paying any portion of a settlement. The Court will grant an exception to this requirement **only** upon written request a week prior to the conference (with a copy to all counsel) showing good cause and exceptional circumstances.

Each party is directed to submit to Chambers (via facsimile at 267-299-5061) a **confidential** settlement memorandum of no more than four typed double-spaced pages, setting out the following in order:

1. The names, telephone numbers, facsimile numbers and e-mail addresses of counsel to appear at the conference on behalf of the party;

2. The name of the party or the party's representative, including insurer if applicable (with title or position) to appear at the conference;

3. The status of any pending motions;

4. The status of discovery;

5. A brief statement of the elements and manner of proof of the party's claims and/or defenses;

6. A brief statement of the party's damages and manner of proof of their damages or, as appropriate, its position on damages claimed by any opposing party;

7. The last demand and/or offer; and

8. Any other matters that counsel believe may be relevant to settlement discussions.

Counsel are directed to fax the position paper to Chambers not later than **four** business days prior to the date of the conference. The document is **not** to be shared with opposing counsel nor filed of record. This is for Judge Hey's eyes only. Counsel are encouraged to attach particularly relevant trial exhibits to their submissions. If such exhibits are lengthy, the relevant portions should be delineated. Counsel are also directed to exchange settlement offer and demand prior to the conference.

BY THE COURT:

_____
ELIZABETH T. HEY
UNITED STATES MAGISTRATE JUDGE

Magistrate Judge Henry S. Perkin

Magistrate Judge Perkin was born on December 27, 1947, in Trenton, New Jersey, and has lived in Allentown, Pennsylvania, for most of his life. He is a graduate of Duquesne University (1969) and the Duquesne University School of Law (1972), where he served as the comment editor of the *Duquesne Law Review*. Upon graduation from law school, he served a clerkship with the Honorable Alfred T. Williams, Jr., president judge of the Court of Common Pleas of Northampton County. He worked as an assistant public defender (1975–1977) and assistant district attorney (1977–1987) in Lehigh County. He served as the Lehigh County solicitor from 1995 through 2006. From 2006 to March 1, 2007, he served as the solicitor for the city of Allentown. During his years as an attorney, Judge Perkin maintained a private practice in which he handled a variety of commercial litigation. He was sworn in as a United States magistrate judge on March 2, 2007.

PRELIMINARY GENERAL MATTERS

1.   Correspondence with the Court. Judge Perkin permits correspondence from counsel on any matters as long as all other counsel in the matter are sent copies of such correspondence. Judge Perkin sometimes permits letter motions in lieu of formal motions.

2.   Communication with Law Clerks. Judge Perkin permits counsel to communicate with his law clerks on scheduling and administrative matters, but never on the merits of a case.

3.   Telephone Conferences. Judge Perkin prefers that counsel come to chambers for all conferences. Telephone conferences may be used, however, for dealing with matters such as scheduling changes and routine discovery disputes. It will be the responsibility of counsel requesting a conference to contact the judge's deputy clerk, Helen A. Nicholas.

4.   Oral Arguments and Evidentiary Hearings. To the extent deemed necessary by Judge Perkin, oral arguments and evidentiary hearings will be scheduled through his deputy clerk. All reasonable efforts will be made to accommodate the schedules of counsel.

5.   Pro Hac Vice Admissions. Judge Perkin will permit oral motions for pro hac vice admissions on the day that the attorney to be admitted first appears. On or before the date of the non-admitted attorney's first appearance, counsel must prepare an appropriate order to memorialize the pro hac vice admission.

CIVIL CASES—IN GENERAL
Pretrial Procedure

Judge Perkin regularly conducts pretrial/status and settlement conferences in cases pending before him. Pretrial/status conferences, where appropriate, are scheduled promptly upon referral of the case to Judge Perkin. *At pretrial conferences, attorneys from both sides should be prepared to discuss settlement possibilities.*

General Motions Practice

1.   Oral Argument on Motions. Judge Perkin will schedule oral argument on motions only if it appears likely to be helpful to the court's resolution of the matter.

2.   Reply and Supplemental Briefs. Judge Perkin will not normally permit reply or supplemental briefs except as may be permitted pursuant to Local R.Civ.P. 7.1(c). Counsel desiring to file a reply or supplemental brief must first seek permission of the court before such a brief will be accepted, and attach the proposed reply or supplemental brief as an exhibit.

3. **Chambers Copy of Motions Papers.** Judge Perkin encourages a courtesy copy of all motion papers to be sent directly to chambers.

Discovery Matters

1. **Discovery Disputes.** Judge Perkin expects counsel to attempt to resolve disputes prior to bringing them to his attention, pursuant to Rule 26.1(f) of the Local Rules of Civil Procedure for the Eastern District of Pennsylvania. Should counsel be unable, in good faith, to resolve their dispute, Judge Perkin permits contact with the court through his deputy clerk to set up telephone or chambers conferences to resolve outstanding issues. Generally, Judge Perkin prefers letter memoranda outlining the discovery dispute. Such memoranda should include the steps taken to resolve the dispute as well as the relief requested. The letter memoranda and the responses should be in Microsoft Word or WordPerfect format and sent to Judge Perkin's chambers by e-mail at Chambers_of_Judge_Henry_S_Perkin@paed.uscourts.gov.

Except for subpoenas issued to non-parties, the use of motion practice in discovery matters is discouraged. Matters involving the enforcement of subpoenas issued to non-parties should be handled through motion practice.

2. **Confidentiality Agreements.** Judge Perkin will permit confidentiality agreements subject to the requirements of *Pansy v. Borough of Stroudsburg,* 23 F.3d 772, 786 (3d Cir. 1994).

Settlement When Jurisdiction Remains with the District Court

1. **Preliminary Telephone Conference.** When a matter is referred to Judge Perkin for purposes of settlement, he will generally hold a chambers conference with the parties. In certain cases, he may choose to hold a preliminary telephone conference with counsel. At the time of the telephone conference, counsel will be expected to discuss: the status of settlement discussions (if any) and timing of the actual chambers conference. It is Judge Perkin's practice to hold settlement conferences as early as practicable and to stage discovery in order to facilitate settlement and control costs without contradiction to the referring judge's Rule 16 scheduling order. Counsel should read and be familiar with Judge Perkin's *Settlement Procedures* posted on the court's website at http://www.paed.uscourts.gov.

2. **Settlement Conference Memoranda.** Judge Perkin will normally require counsel to submit a brief written conference summary one week before the scheduled conference, including an offer/demand settlement proposal. This summary should not exceed two pages. Judge Perkin requires that counsel exchange their summaries, but counsel is not required to communicate their settlement proposals in the exchanged summaries. This information may be provided by a separate document to the court. The summaries are not to be filed with the Clerk's Office.

3. **Parties' Attendance and Participation.** Judge Perkin will require that a party or party's representative with knowledge of the case and *full and binding* settlement authority attend the chambers conference *in person*. **At the settlement conference, trial counsel must appear and bring with them all persons whose consent may be necessary to settle the case. "All persons" means: insurance adjustors with full and unlimited authority to settle the case, as well as clients. Persons present must have full and unlimited settlement authority and may not confer by telephone with anyone to seek additional authority. The defendant's settlement authority must be consistent with and not less than the plaintiff's last demand.** *Only* in exceptional circumstances, Judge Perkin will permit that person to participate in the conference by telephone. This will be the exception rather than the rule. Counsel seeking this relief must

contact chambers as soon as they are aware of a problem with attendance. A copy of Judge Perkin's settlement conference scheduling order is shown on page 476. Counsel and the parties must strictly adhere to this procedure.

At the conference, the judge will expect counsel to:

- Be prepared to discuss the weaknesses as well as the strengths of their case.
- Prepare their client. Judge Perkin will speak to them directly.
- Be patient. Settlement is a process. It takes time.
- Be flexible. Avoid bottom lines or top numbers.
- Realistically evaluate the case.
- Manage your client's expectations.
- Manage your own expectations.

4. Follow-up Contact. Judge Perkin will, if appropriate, continue to work with counsel after the settlement conference if the matter is not resolved at the conference.

5. Continuances. Settlement conferences are scheduled by order of the court and are not discretionary. Counsel and participants should use all efforts to be available for this conference. Due to the large number of cases scheduled for settlement conferences, any need to reschedule the conference could cause a delay of that conference for several weeks. For this reason, any continuance requests should be made within 14 days of receipt of the notice scheduling the conference. Continuance requests will only be granted for the most compelling reasons.

Settlement When Jurisdiction for All Purposes Has Been Referred to Judge Perkin

1. Jury Matters. Judge Perkin may, after discussion with counsel, conduct his own settlement conferences using the above-outlined procedures. If not appropriate, but a conference is deemed worthwhile, Judge Perkin may obtain the assistance of another magistrate judge to preside over settlement discussions.

2. Nonjury Matters. Judge Perkin will not take part in settlement discussions in a nonjury matter. A settlement conference may, however, be arranged with another magistrate judge.

CIVIL CASES—REFERRED TO JUDGE PERKIN FOR ALL PURPOSES
Arbitration

1. General Approach to Arbitration Cases. Judge Perkin has no special practices or procedures for arbitration cases.

2. Scheduling Trial De Novo from Arbitration. Judge Perkin will schedule trial promptly when a demand for trial de novo is filed following arbitration.

Pretrial Procedure

1. Length of Discovery Period. Judge Perkin normally permits 90 to 120 days for the completion of discovery. Additional time will be allowed in complex cases or upon a specific showing of need. *Judge Perkin will encourage that the most essential discovery be undertaken early in the case so as to foster early settlement and minimize the costs of litigation.*

2. Continuances and Extensions. In that counsel will have substantial input in the setting of dates in the Rule 16 order, Judge Perkin expects counsel to comply with the dates set out in that order. Extensions will be entertained upon a showing that circumstances beyond the reasonable expectation of counsel have hampered the progress of the case.

Judge Perkin will not require a formal motion seeking an extension and will consider requests for extensions brought to the attention of his deputy clerk, who will set up either a telephone or chambers conference. In most cases, extensions will only be considered after a conference with the judge.

3. **Expert Witnesses.** The parties will identify expert witnesses and provide expert reports pursuant to the Rule 16 scheduling order entered in the particular case. A failure to do so will normally bar the use of the expert's testimony at trial.

Pretrial Memoranda

Unless specifically provided for by separate order, Judge Perkin will require the use of the short-form pretrial memorandum described in Rule 16.1(c) of the Local Rules of Civil Procedure for the Eastern District of Pennsylvania. In certain cases, Judge Perkin may require counsel to stipulate to uncontested facts as generally set out in Local Rule 16.1(d)(2)(b)(2)(A–E).

Trial Procedure

1. **Scheduling of Cases.** Judge Perkin's cases will be specially listed for trial based upon the court's calendar and the availability of counsel, the parties, experts, and critical witnesses.

2. **Conflicts of Counsel.** Given the manner of scheduling, conflicts will normally not occur. Should counsel, however, have a professional or personal conflict that may affect the trial schedule, notice should be provided immediately to opposing counsel and the court.

3. **Parties or Witnesses.** Judge Perkin will make all reasonable attempts to accommodate the schedules and availability of parties, experts, and critical witnesses.

4. **Note-taking by Jurors.** Judge Perkin will consider note-taking by jurors on a case-by-case basis.

5. **Trial Briefs.** Judge Perkin encourages the submission of trial briefs when they are necessary or likely to be helpful to the court.

6. **Voir Dire.** Judge Perkin usually permits counsel to conduct all voir dire.

7. **Sidebar.** Judge Perkin discourages the use of sidebar conferences. Counsel are encouraged to raise particular evidentiary issues before trial or during recesses or adjournments.

8. **In Limine Motions.** Judge Perkin will accept in limine motions in advance of the final pretrial conference and in accordance with the scheduling order so as to give him an adequate opportunity to consider the merits of each motion.

9. **Examination of Witnesses Out of Sequence.** Judge Perkin will permit witnesses to be taken out of turn in appropriate circumstances.

10. **Opening Statements and Submission.** Judge Perkin will discuss with counsel the length of time necessary and appropriate for opening and closing statements, but will give counsel reasonable latitude.

11. **Examination of Witnesses or Argument by More than One Attorney.** Judge Perkin will not normally permit more than one attorney for the party to examine the same witness or more than one attorney to present argument on behalf of the party on the same issue.

12. **Examination of Witnesses Beyond Redirect or Recross.** Judge Perkin will generally restrict counsel from examining witnesses beyond redirect and recross.

13. Videotaped Testimony. Judge Perkin requires counsel to review all videotaped depositions and have them edited, after consultation with each other, so as to fairly present only the essential evidence of the witness involved. Counsel are expected to resolve all matters pertaining to objections before offering the videotape into evidence.

14. Reading of Material into the Record. Judge Perkin has no special practice with regard to reading stipulations, pleadings, or discovery materials into the record.

15. Preparation of Exhibits. Prior to commencement of trial, exhibits are to be premarked and exchanged by counsel. Counsel should provide Judge Perkin with two copies of each exhibit, together with a schedule of exhibits that briefly describes each exhibit. Counsel are encouraged, however, to provide the court with only the essential and relevant portions of bulky exhibits, together with sufficient material to provide context for the relevant portion of the exhibits.

16. Offering Exhibits into Evidence. Judge Perkin expects counsel to reach agreement in advance as to the admission of exhibits. Judge Perkin has no particular procedure as to when an exhibit may be formally offered into evidence.

17. Motions for Judgment as a Matter of Law and Motions for Judgment on Partial Findings. Motions for judgment as a matter of law or motions for judgment on partial findings in nonjury trials may be submitted in writing or orally. Judge Perkin will ordinarily request oral argument on these motions.

18. Proposed Jury Instructions and Verdict Forms. Judge Perkin requires counsel to submit joint proposed jury instructions, noting areas of agreement as well as objections. The points for charge should be submitted with appropriate citations of legal authority and must be provided to the court in accordance with the deadline set forth in the scheduling order. Counsel will submit a jointly prepared verdict form or proposed special interrogatories in accordance with the deadline set forth in the scheduling order. If counsel are unable to agree, they may submit separate proposed forms of interrogatories. Judge Perkin will encourage counsel to agree upon a less than unanimous verdict.

19. Proposed Findings of Fact and Conclusions of Law. Judge Perkin requires counsel to submit proposed findings of fact and conclusions of law in nonjury cases at the final pretrial conference or at a date set forth in the scheduling order. A supplementation will be permitted at the close of trial or, in an appropriate case, after trial.

Jury Deliberations

1. Written Jury Instructions. Judge Perkin has no particular practice or policy on submitting a copy of instructions to the jury.

2. Exhibits in the Jury Room. Judge Perkin will consider what exhibits should be sent out to the jury during their deliberations on a case-by-case basis.

3. Handling of Jury Requests to Read Back Testimony or Replay Tapes. Judge Perkin will seek the input of counsel and will then make a determination on a case-by-case basis when requests are made to read back testimony or replay tapes.

4. Availability of Counsel During Jury Deliberations. Judge Perkin will not require counsel to remain in the courthouse during deliberations but will require counsel to be available on short telephone notice. Counsel must provide the deputy clerk with their phone number.

5.   Taking the Verdict and Special Interrogatories. Judge Perkin has no usual practice with respect to taking a verdict. Judge Perkin will submit written interrogatories to the jury in the appropriate case. A copy of the interrogatories will be given to the jury during their deliberations.

6.   Polling the Jury. Judge Perkin will, if requested, permit the jury to be polled.

7.   Interviewing the Jury. Judge Perkin will permit counsel to interview jurors, but only after the verdict has been recorded, the jury has been discharged, *and* they have been told in clear terms that they have no obligation to speak with counsel.

CRIMINAL CASES

1.   Sentencing Memoranda. When a pretrial sentencing report is used, Judge Perkin permits the submission of sentencing memoranda by both counsel.

2.   Additional Matters. At all "criminal duty week" proceedings, counsel, once appointed or retained, must be present to permit the proceeding to go forward. Once the court has ordered that a defendant be detained or has set conditions of release, any proposed changes thereto must be submitted to the court by written motion. Judge Perkin does not favor the dual representation of defendants by a single attorney at any criminal proceeding, apart, perhaps, from the initial appearance. Judge Perkin requires that all relevant documents be delivered to chambers in advance of court. Counsel may contact the court's deputy clerk, Helen A. Nicholas, if there are questions regarding the matters before the court.

GENERAL MATTERS

When a decision rendered by the court is appealed, Judge Perkin prefers to receive copies of appellate briefs. Judge Perkin expects counsel to be prompt in all appearances, to be professional and courteous to each other, both in the presence of the court and otherwise, and to have discussions with each other about any matter in dispute before it is brought to the attention of the court. Counsel should feel free to contact Judge Perkin's deputy clerk or law clerks if they have any questions about his courtroom practices or procedures.

Practice and Procedures of Judges and Judges' Forms and Orders

IN THE UNITED STATES DISTRICT COURT
FOR THE EASTERN DISTRICT OF PENNSYLVANIA

Plaintiff   Civil Action No.

v.

Defendant

SETTLEMENT CONFERENCE SCHEDULING ORDER

Please be advised that an in person settlement conference in the above-captioned case will be held on _____ at _____ before the Honorable Henry S. Perkin, United States Magistrate Judge, in Suite 4401, United States Courthouse and Federal Building, 504 West Hamilton Street, Allentown, PA.

COUNSEL ARE DIRECTED TO REPORT TO CHAMBERS ON THE DATE AND TIME STATED ABOVE. PURSUANT TO LOCAL RULE 16.1 (d) 3, **TRIAL COUNSEL** SHALL APPEAR AND BRING WITH THEM ALL PERSONS WHOSE CONSENT MAY BE NECESSARY TO SETTLE THIS CASE. **ALL PERSONS SHALL MEAN INSURANCE ADJUSTORS WITH FULL AND UNLIMITED AUTHORITY TO SETTLE THE CASE, AS WELL AS CLIENTS. PERSONS PRESENT MUST HAVE FULL AND UNLIMITED SETTLEMENT AUTHORITY AND MAY NOT CONFER BY TELEPHONE WITH ANYONE TO SEEK ADDITIONAL AUTHORITY. DEFENDANT'S SETTLEMENT AUTHORITY MUST BE CONSISTENT WITH AND NOT LESS THAN THE PLAINTIFF'S LAST DEMAND.**

FAILURE TO COMPLY WITH THIS ORDER MAY RESULT IN THE IMPOSITION OF SANCTIONS.

PLEASE SEE JUDGE PERKIN'S SETTLEMENT PROCEDURES AT www.paed.uscourts.gov.

Counsel are further directed to provide a Conference Summary and Case Synopsis to Chambers, by Email on or before _____. The Email address is Chambers_of_Henry_S_Perkin@paed.uscourts.gov. The Conference Summary and Case Synopsis shall include:

1. The caption of the case
2. Whether case is a jury or nonjury trial
3. The trial counsel's name, address, phone number, fax number and client name
4. Identify any pending motions
5. Any other relevant matters
6. All prior demands and offers.
7. A case synopsis, **limited to two pages**, which shall be in **Microsoft Word** or **Wordperfect** Format
8. Should all parties so agree, they may consent to permit the court to have ex parte communication with counsel by sending the attached form to chambers by fax.

This Email address shall be used for no other purposes unless prior permission is granted.

BY THE COURT

/ss/ Henry S. Perkin
HENRY S. PERKIN

FOR INFORMATION CONTACT CHAMBERS
Phone: 610-434-3823
FAX: 610-434-5152

Date:

cc.

Magistrate Judge Henry S. Perkin

**IN THE UNITED STATES DISTRICT COURT
FOR THE EASTERN DISTRICT OF PENNSYLVANIA**

        Plaintiff   Civil Action No.

v.

        Defendant

**CONSENT TO HAVE EX PARTE COMMUNICATION
WITH UNITED STATES MAGISTRATE JUDGE**

Counsel for the parties to the above-captioned civil proceeding hereby consent to ex parte communication with the United States Magistrate Judge Henry S. Perkin for the purpose of assisting with settlement/discovery matters in the above-captioned case.

The undersigned represent all counsel in the above-captioned civil proceeding.

DATED:

_____   _____
_____   _____
_____   _____
_____   _____
        (Attorneys)   (Representing)

Magistrate Judge Arnold C. Rapoport

Judge Rapoport was born on April 4, 1931, in Allentown, Pennsylvania. He received a B.A. from Muhlenberg College in 1954 and a J.D. from Temple University School of Law in 1960. From 1962 to 1992, Judge Rapoport was in private practice in Allentown, Pennsylvania. Judge Rapoport was appointed a part-time United States magistrate judge for the Eastern District of Pennsylvania on May 22, 1975; he was appointed a full-time magistrate judge on May 4, 1992.

PRELIMINARY GENERAL MATTERS

1.   Correspondence with the Court.   Judge Rapoport permits correspondence from counsel on all matters. On occasion, correspondence will be treated as a motion. If the occasion demands, counsel will be instructed to file a formal motion in lieu of prior correspondence.

2.   Communications with Law Clerk.   Judge Rapoport permits counsel to speak directly with his law clerk with the understanding that counsel must carefully observe ethical considerations and avoid discussion of the merits of a pending case.

3.   Telephone Conferences.   Judge Rapoport encourages the use of telephone conferences.

4.   Oral Arguments and Evidentiary Hearings.   Judge Rapoport does not set aside specific days or times for oral arguments or evidentiary hearings.

CIVIL CASES
Pretrial Procedure

1.   Pretrial Conferences.   Judge Rapoport regularly conducts status conferences. Prior to the first status conference, Judge Rapoport sometimes issues a preliminary order establishing tentative dates for the completion of discovery, the final pretrial conference, and trial. The preliminary order also advises counsel of certain guidelines that probably will be followed by the court throughout the case. Settlement is also discussed and is done as soon as possible after the filing of the complaint and answer.

Judge Rapoport generally will schedule a pretrial conference and settlement conference at the request of counsel for a party. In complex cases, counsel are usually asked to prepare an agenda for pretrial and settlement conferences.

Continuances and Extensions

1.   General Policy.   Counsel will be given an opportunity to approve the dates for such matters as briefing schedules, oral arguments, evidentiary hearings, discovery deadlines, and trial dates. Once those dates are fixed by the court, counsel are expected to arrange their private and professional schedules to conform to those dates.

2.   Requests for Extensions and Continuances.   Judge Rapoport does not impose any specific requirement as to how far in advance of a scheduled event counsel must request a continuance or an extension. If the situation warrants granting such a request, the request will be granted. Judge Rapoport has no preference as to the method by which counsel may seek a continuance or an extension, and he will accept such requests by motion, letter, stipulation, or conference call.

General Motion Practice

1.   Oral Argument on Motions.   Judge Rapoport generally will grant oral argument on motions if it is requested by counsel.

2. **Reply and Surreply Briefs.** If requested by counsel, reply briefs and supplementary briefs will generally be allowed by Judge Rapoport. Emphasis is on *brief* briefs.

3. **Chambers Copies of Motion Papers.** Judge Rapoport encourages counsel to send courtesy copies of motion papers to his chambers.

Discovery Matters

1. **Discovery Conferences and Dispute Resolution.** If problems surface in discovery, Judge Rapoport will hold a discovery conference at the request of an attorney or, if the situation warrants, sua sponte. Judge Rapoport permits telephone conferences to resolve discovery disputes that arise during depositions, only after the parties have taken ego clashes out of the dispute, except when he is on the bench.

2. **Confidentiality Agreements.** Judge Rapoport has no specific policy concerning uncontested confidentiality orders. He usually does not require a conference for consideration of a stipulated confidentiality order.

3. **Expert Witnesses.** In cases involving expert witnesses, Judge Rapoport prefers that each expert prepare a written report and that the depositions of expert witnesses be taken by counsel. Judge Rapoport has no specific policy concerning the point in a case at which the parties should identify expert witnesses.

Settlement

1. **General Approach to Settlement and Nonjury Cases.** Judge Rapoport's general approach to settlement negotiations is to discuss settlement as soon as possible and throughout the pendency of a case. Mature, earnest professionals should understand and explain to their clients that the sequence of events is a settlement conference and, if that fails, then a trial. Actually, it is the settlement conference at which the parties will have their only chance to control the outcome of the case. The next settlement conference (often identified as a trial) wherein the outcome is decided by a jury, puts the outcome into the hands of strangers, thereby losing any ability to control the outcome.

In nonjury cases, Judge Rapoport will participate in settlement negotiations very rarely and only with the concurrence of all parties and counsel.

Proposed Final Pretrial Memoranda

1. **Required Form of Pretrial Memoranda.** In addition to the requirement of Local Civil Rule 16.1(c), Judge Rapoport normally requires counsel to comply with the requirements set forth in the scheduling order, which requires counsel, on a specific date, to file with the clerk and serve on opposing counsel: (a) a list of all exhibits to be used at trial, (b) a list showing each witness to be called at trial and setting forth the point or points to be established by the testimony of each witness, (c) memoranda of law on all legal and evidentiary issues expected to arise at trial, and (d) requests for instructions to the jury.

2. **Common Deficiencies in Pretrial Memoranda.** Judge Rapoport notes that late filing by counsel of proposed final pretrial memoranda is a deficiency that he commonly observes.

Trial Procedure

1. **Scheduling of Cases.** Each case on Judge Rapoport's calendar is assigned a date certain for trial with the understanding that more than one case may be scheduled on a particular date.

2. **Conflicts of Counsel.** When counsel become aware of professional or personal conflicts that may affect the trial schedule, they should notify Judge Rapoport and opposing counsel immediately. Such notice may be given to Judge Rapoport's deputy clerk by telephone, but it should be confirmed in writing.

3. **Cases Involving Out-of-Town Parties or Witnesses.** Although Judge Rapoport has no special policy for these matters, some consideration will be given to out-of-town attorneys, parties, and witnesses.

4. **Note-taking by Jurors.** Judge Rapoport generally allows note-taking by jurors, subject to limiting instructions as to the use for their personal recollection and not to be shown to or used by other jurors.

5. **Trial Briefs.** Judge Rapoport generally requires the submission of trial briefs.

6. **Voir Dire.** Judge Rapoport usually permits counsel to conduct all voir dire. Judge Rapoport's deputy clerk normally is present during voir dire, and she is familiar with legal matters involved in jury selection. If problems arise and the deputy clerk cannot achieve agreement among counsel, she will notify Judge Rapoport and Judge Rapoport or another available judge will come to the bench to resolve the dispute. Judge Rapoport does not place any time limits on voir dire as long as counsel do not abuse the privilege.

7. **Sidebars.** Judge Rapoport discourages sidebar conferences.

8. **In Limine Motions.** Counsel may submit motions in limine at any time, provided that the court has an adequate factual basis in the record and is not asked to rule in a vacuum or render an advisory opinion.

9. **Examination of Witnesses Out of Sequence.** Judge Rapoport permits counsel to call witnesses out of turn for the convenience of the witnesses.

10. **Opening Statements and Summations.** Judge Rapoport generally does not impose a time limit on opening statements. With regard to summations, time limits generally are not imposed, but Judge Rapoport discusses time limits for summations with counsel at the charging conference on jury instructions. As to opening statements and summations, brevity is a virtue.

11. **Examination of Witnesses or Argument by More Than One Attorney.** Judge Rapoport generally does not permit more than one attorney for a party to examine different witnesses or to argue different points before the court.

12. **Examination of Witnesses Beyond Redirect and Recross.** Judge Rapoport generally does not permit further examination of witnesses after redirect and recross have been completed.

13. **Videotaped Testimony.** With respect to the use of videotaped testimony, Judge Rapoport has no special procedures. He prefers that the equipment be set up in advance to avoid wasting time in the courtroom. It is the obligation of the attorneys to see that the equipment they need is in the courtroom.

14. **Reading of Material Into the Record.** Judge Rapoport has no special practice or policy about reading stipulations, pleadings, or discovery materials into the record.

15. **Preparation of Exhibits.** Judge Rapoport requires that all documentary and photographic exhibits be pre-marked and that counsel exchange copies of all such exhibits with each other and provide an opportunity for opposing counsel to view any models or videotapes. Counsel should provide one copy of all trial exhibits to Judge Rapoport.

16. **Offering Exhibits Into Evidence.** Judge Rapoport has no preference as to when counsel should offer exhibits into evidence.

17. Motions for Judgment as a Matter of Law and Motions for Judgment on Partial Findings. Motions for judgment as a matter of law (or motions for judgment on partial findings in nonjury trials) may be oral or written. Judge Rapoport rarely allows oral argument on such motions.

18. Proposed Jury Instructions and Verdict Forms. Judge Rapoport requires that counsel submit proposed jury instructions. Judge Rapoport permits submission of supplemental proposed jury instructions prior to the delivery of the charge. Judge Rapoport usually conducts a charging conference on proposed jury instructions.

19. Proposed Findings of Fact and Conclusions of Law. Judge Rapoport requires submission by counsel of proposed findings of fact and conclusions of law.

Jury Deliberations

1. Written Jury Instructions. Judge Rapoport gives the jury a copy of the instructions only when requested to do so.

2. Exhibits in the Jury Room. Judge Rapoport's general rule is that if an exhibit is admitted into evidence, it goes to the jury room.

3. Handling of Jury Requests to Read Back Testimony or Replay Tapes. If the jury requests to have portions of testimony read back, the testimony is played back on the court's electronic court reporting equipment. When audiotape or videotape recordings have been admitted into evidence, and the jury requests that they be replayed, Judge Rapoport permits this, and it is done in the courtroom.

4. Availability of Counsel During Jury Deliberations. Judge Rapoport permits counsel to return to their offices and be available on telephone notice during jury deliberations.

5. Taking the Verdict and Special Interrogatories. In most civil cases, Judge Rapoport submits written interrogatories to the jury.

6. Polling the Jury. If there is a request to poll the jury, the jury is polled by the courtroom deputy.

7. Interviewing the Jury. Judge Rapoport permits counsel to interview jurors after the verdict has been recorded and the jury has been discharged. Counsel are directed not to be abusive of jurors in such interviews. The jury is generally told that they may, but are not required to, speak with counsel.

Magistrate Judge Timothy R. Rice

United States Magistrate Judge Timothy R. Rice was appointed in March 2005. Chief Justice John Roberts appointed him in 2009 to the Criminal Rules Committee of the U.S. Judicial Conference. In 2010, he received the Philadelphia Bar Association's Justice William J. Brennan, Jr. Distinguished Jurist Award for his work on a reentry program to assist ex-offenders. In 2011, he received the Gideon Award from Temple University School of Law for his "dedication to the cause of justice for the indigent."

From 1988 to 2005, Judge Rice served as an assistant U.S. attorney for the Eastern District of Pennsylvania. He served as chief of the Criminal Division from 2002 to 2005, and previously supervised the Financial Institution Fraud Section and the Public Corruption Section at the U.S. Attorney's Office.

He has been an adjunct faculty member at Temple University School of Law since 1990, teaching courses in advanced criminal trial advocacy and evidence.

He graduated magna cum laude in 1986 from the Temple University School of Law, where he served as editor-in-chief of the *Temple Law Review*. He served as law clerk to the Honorable Anthony J. Scirica on the U.S. District Court for the Eastern District of Pennsylvania from 1986 to 1987, and on the U.S. Court of Appeals for the Third Circuit from 1987 to 1988. He is a member of the American Law Institute.

PRELIMINARY GENERAL MATTERS

1.   *Professionalism.* All counsel and parties are expected to conduct themselves in a civil, polite, and professional manner at all times. All proceedings will begin at the scheduled time, and punctuality is expected.

2.   *Courtroom Conduct.* All lawyers and parties are expected to stand when addressing the court, the jury, or any witness. Use of computer technology to display evidence and exhibits is strongly encouraged.

3.   *Electronic Case Filing and Courtesy Copies.* All pleadings should be filed electronically with the clerk of court. Courtesy copies are optional.

4.   *Correspondence with the Court.* Judge Rice permits correspondence from counsel on all matters.

5.   *Communications with Law Clerks.* Judge Rice permits counsel to speak directly with his law clerks with the understanding that counsel must carefully observe ethical considerations and avoid discussion of the merits of a pending case. Attorneys should not attempt ex parte communication on matters of substance. Joint calls by counsel for all parties are preferred.

6.   *Telephone Conferences.* Judge Rice encourages the use of telephone conferences for handling matters such as discovery disputes, scheduling changes, and extensions of time.

7.   *Oral Arguments and Evidentiary Hearings.* Oral arguments and evidentiary hearings may be scheduled through Judge Rice's deputy clerk. All reasonable efforts will be made to accommodate the schedules of counsel.

CIVIL CASES
Civil Consent Trials

1.   *Pretrial and Trial Procedure.* Upon referral of a civil consent trial, a pretrial conference will be conducted and an order entered advising counsel of the court's expectations with regard to any outstanding discovery, evidentiary, or scheduling issues. Trial memoranda highlighting anticipated factual, legal, or evidentiary issues are helpful. The parties must submit joint proposed voir dire questions, jury instructions, and either verdict slips or special interrogatories to the jury. Disputed points should be highlighted for resolution by the court. Judge Rice will conduct the voir dire. Computer imaging technology should be used whenever possible. The jury will be provided with a written copy of the jury charge, and the jury will be charged before the closing arguments of counsel. (See the sample Fed.R.Civ.P. 16 pretrial scheduling order for standard track cases on page 485 of this book.)

Pretrial Procedure

1. Pretrial Conferences. Judge Rice will schedule status conferences, settlement conferences, and final pretrial conferences as required by the circumstance of each case. Every effort will be made to accommodate the schedules of counsel.

Continuances and Extensions

1. General Policy. Judge Rice will normally consult with counsel before establishing a briefing schedule, oral argument, evidentiary hearing, discovery deadline, or trial date. When possible, Judge Rice tries to accommodate counsel with regard to requests for reasonable changes.

General Motion Practice

1. Chambers Copies of Motion Papers. If pleadings are electronically filed, counsel should not incur the additional expense of preparing and delivering courtesy copies.

Discovery Matters

1. Discovery Disputes. Discovery should be conducted in a voluntary, candid, cooperative, and timely manner. Written motions normally are not required. Discovery disputes will be resolved during pretrial conferences or, if necessary, on telephone conferences. Formal discovery motions should be filed only after court orders or directives are violated.

2. Confidentiality Agreements. Judge Rice will permit confidentiality agreements only if they comply with *Pansy v. Borough of Stroudsburg,* 23 F.3d 772, 786 (3d Cir. 1994).

Settlement

1. Settlement Conferences. Lead counsel must attend the settlement conference with the parties and with the person or persons having full authority to negotiate and settle the case in light of the recent demand, unless prior permission to participate via telephone has been granted. Prior to the conference, counsel should submit a conference summary on the forms provided with the order scheduling the settlement conference. A settlement conference should be held only if there is a realistic possibility of settlement. (See the sample conference order and settlement conference summary on pages 488 and 489 of this book.)

Trial Procedure

1. Scheduling of Cases. All of Judge Rice's cases are specially listed for trial.

2. Conflicts of Counsel. Professional and personal conflicts of counsel are normally not a problem, since all trials are specially listed by Judge Rice after consultation with counsel. Requests involving personal or family emergencies will be granted.

3. **Note-taking by Jurors.** Judge Rice allows note-taking by jurors. Judge Rice permits jurors to submit written questions for witnesses. See *Juries & Jury Trials,* American Bar Association, 2005.

4. **Trial Briefs.** Judge Rice requires the submission of trial briefs.

5. **Voir Dire.** Judge Rice conducts voir dire in civil cases. Counsel may submit joint proposed voir dire questions and request supplemental voir dire following Judge Rice's questions.

6. **Sidebars.** Judge Rice permits sidebars.

7. **Jury Questions.** Consistent with ABA procedures and the practice in the Third Circuit, jurors may submit written questions to a witness to clarify testimony. A copy of the protocol will be provided to all counsel.

8. **In Limine Motions.** Judge Rice encourages in limine motions.

9. **Examination of Witnesses Out of Sequence.** Judge Rice will permit counsel to take witnesses out of turn for the convenience of the witnesses.

10. **Opening Statements and Summations.** Judge Rice has no fixed rule on the time limits for opening statements or summations. Judge Rice will grant a reasonable amount of time for counsel as dictated by the nature of the case.

11. **Reading of Material Into the Record.** Judge Rice will request that counsel read stipulations and pleadings into the record. For depositions, he prefers that a witness respond to the questions of counsel in open court.

12. **Preparation of Exhibits.** Judge Rice requires that exhibits be pre-marked and pre-exchanged. At the commencement of trial, counsel must provide Judge Rice with two copies of all trial exhibits, along with two copies of a schedule of exhibits that briefly describes each exhibit.

13. **Proposed Jury Instructions and Verdict Forms.** Judge Rice requires counsel to submit joint proposed jury instructions, noting areas of agreement as well as objections. The points for charge should be submitted with appropriate citations of legal authority and are to be provided to the court as required by the pretrial scheduling order. Counsel will also submit a jointly prepared verdict form or proposed special interrogatories to the jury.

14. **Proposed Findings of Fact and Conclusions of Law.** In nonjury cases, Judge Rice prefers submission of proposed findings of fact and conclusions of law shortly after the trial, citing the trial transcript if it is available.

Jury Deliberations

1. **Written Jury Instructions.** Judge Rice will give the jury a written copy of his instructions. Judge Rice will normally charge the jury before closing arguments.

2. **Exhibits in the Jury Room.** Judge Rice permits all of the trial exhibits that have been admitted into evidence to go out with the jury.

3. **Availability of Counsel During Jury Deliberations.** Judge Rice will not require counsel to remain in the courthouse during deliberations but will require counsel to be available on short telephone notice.

4. **Polling the Jury.** Judge Rice will grant a request to poll the jury.

Magistrate Judge Timothy R. Rice

IN THE UNITED STATES DISTRICT COURT
FOR THE EASTERN DISTRICT OF PENNSYLVANIA

Plaintiff	:	CIVIL ACTION
	:	
v.	:	
	:	NO.
Defendant	:	

FEDERAL RULE OF CIVIL PROCEDURE 16 PRETRIAL SCHEDULING ORDER
STANDARD TRACK CASES

AND NOW, this _____ day of _____, following a telephone conference with all counsel, IT IS ORDERED as follows:

1. All discovery shall proceed forthwith and continue in such manner as will assure that all requests for and responses to discovery will be served, noticed, and completed by _____.

2. A settlement conference is scheduled to be held on _____, before the Honorable Timothy R. Rice, Magistrate Judge.

3. On or before _____, counsel for each party shall serve upon counsel for every other party the information referred to in Federal Rule of Civil Procedure 26(a)(2)(B) by expert report, deposition, or answer to expert interrogatory.

4. Dispositive motions shall be filed no later than _____. Any motion for summary judgment pursuant to Fed.R.Civ.P. 56, shall include a separate, short and concise statement of the material facts, in numbered paragraphs, as to which the moving party contends there is no genuine issue to be tried.

The papers opposing a motion for summary judgment shall include separate, short and concise statement of the material facts, responding to the numbered paragraphs set forth in the statement required in the foregoing paragraph, as to which it is contended that there exists a genuine issue to be tried.

Statements of material facts in support of or in opposition to a motion shall include references to the parts of the record that support the statements.

All material facts set forth in the statement required to be served by the moving party may be taken by the Court as admitted unless controverted by the opposing party.

5. On or before _____, counsel for each party shall serve upon counsel for every other party:

   (a) the original or a copy of each exhibit they expect to offer at trial in furtherance of their respective contentions. Each party shall mark its trial exhibits in advance of trial with consecutive numbers appropriate prefixed with an identifying letter of counsel's choice (*i.e.,* P-1, P-2, D-1, D-2);

   (b) curriculum vitae for each expert witness expected to testify; and

   (c) a specific identification of each discovery item expected to be offered into evidence.

6. All parties shall prepare and file with the Clerk of Court their pretrial memoranda in accordance with this Order and Local Rule of Civil Procedure 16.1(c), as follows:

Plaintiff—on or before _____.
Defendants—on or before _____.
All motions in limited shall be filed on or before _____.
Responses thereto are due on or before _____.

In addition to compliance with Local Rule of Civil Procedure 16.1(c), the parties shall include the following in, or attached to, their pretrial memoranda:

    a.   a listing of the identity of each expert witness to be called at trial by the party;

    b.   a curriculum vitae for each expert witness listed;

    c.   a listing of each fact witness to be called at trial with a brief statement of the nature of their expected testimony (witnesses not listed may not be called by that party in its case-in-chief);

    d.   an itemized statement of claimant's damages or other relief sought;

    e.   A statement of any anticipated important legal issues on which the Court will be required to rule, together with counsel's single best authority on each such issue.

One (1) copy of the pretrial memoranda shall be filed with the Clerk of Court and two (2) copies shall be sent to the Court (Chambers).

7. A final pretrial conference for this matter will be held on _____, at **9:30 a.m.** in Courtroom _____.

    (a) If a nonjury trial is scheduled, the parties shall file one (1) copy of proposed findings of fact and conclusions of law with the Clerk of Court on or before _____. One (1) copy of the proposed findings of fact and conclusions of law shall be sent to the Court (Chambers).

8. **No later than three (3) days** before the date trial is scheduled to commence if a date certain, or three (3) days before case appears in the trial pool, the parties shall file a complete and comprehensive stipulation of uncontested facts pursuant to paragraph (d)(2)(b)(2) of Local Rule of Civil Procedure 16.1; the original shall be filed with the Clerk of Court, and two (2) copies shall be submitted to the Court (Chambers).

9. At the commencement of trial, the parties shall provide the Court with three (3) copies of a schedule of exhibits which shall briefly describe each exhibit. At the trial, the parties shall provide the Court with two (2) copies of each exhibit at the time of its first use at trial.

10. This case will be listed for trial as follows:

Date Certain: _____, in Courtroom _____.

Counsel should consider themselves attached as of this date.

<u>COUNSEL PLEASE NOTE:</u> This Scheduling Order will be the only written notice counsel receive of the date this case will be tried. Counsel and all parties shall be prepared to commence trial on _____.

11. Any party having an objection to: (a) the admissibility of any exhibit based on authenticity; (b) the adequacy of the qualifications of an expert witness expected to testify; (c) the admissibility for any reason (except relevancy) of any item of evidence expected to be offered; or (d) the admissibility of any opinion testimony from law witnesses pursuant to Federal Rule of Evidence 701 shall set forth separately each such objection, clearly and concisely, in their pretrial memorandum. Such objection shall describe with particularity the ground and the authority for the objection. Unless the Court concludes at trial that manifest injustice will result, the Court can be expected to overrule any objection offered at trial in respect to any matter covered by (a), (b), (c) and/or (d) above, if the Court concludes that the objection should have been made as required by this Order.

12. Only those exhibits, discovery items, and expert witnesses identified in the manner set forth in this Order shall be considered by the Court for admission into evidence at trial, unless stipulated to by all affected parties and approved by the Court, <u>or</u> by Order of Court so as to avoid manifest injustice.

13. Because a witness may be unavailable at the time of trial in the manner defined in Federal Rule of Civil Procedure 32(a)(3), the Court expects use of oral or videotape depositions at trial of any witness whose testimony a party believes essential to the presentation of that party's case, whether that witness is a party, a non-party, or an expert. The unavailability of any such witness will not be a ground to delay

the commencement or progress of an ongoing trial. In the event a deposition is to be offered, the offering party shall file with the Court, prior to the commencement of the trial, a copy of the deposition, but only after all efforts have been made to resolve objections with other counsel. Unresolved objections shall be noted in the margin of the deposition page(s) where a Court ruling is necessary.

14. The parties will submit a joint neutral statement of the facts for *voir dire*. Prior to the final pretrial conference, no later than _____, the parties will submit joint questions for *voir dire,* highlighting only the disputed questions. *Voir dire* questions should not number more than fifteen (15).

15. The parties will also submit joint requested points for charge and a joint verdict slip with only the disputed points highlighted by _____. Requested points for charge and verdict slip shall be filed with the Clerk's Office, one point to a page in sequence, and by e-mail (Chambers_of_Magistrate_Judge_Timothy_Rice_@paed.uscourts.gov) or diskette. Please provide Judge Rice's Chambers with a hard copy as well as a diskette in Word Perfect format. No other document should be e-mailed to Judge Rice, and an e-mail to Chambers does not constitute filing.

HONORABLE TIMOTHY R. RICE
United States Magistrate Judge

Practice and Procedures of Judges and Judges' Forms and Orders

IN THE UNITED STATES DISTRICT COURT
FOR THE EASTERN DISTRICT OF PENNSYLVANIA

Plaintiff,	:	CIVIL ACTION
	:	
v.	:	
	:	
	:	NO.
Defendant,	:	

CONFERENCE NOTICE

A Settlement Conference in the above-captioned case will be held on _____, at _____, before the Honorable Timothy R. Rice, United States Magistrate Judge, in Room 3029, U.S. Courthouse, 601 Market Street, Philadelphia, PA 19106.

- Please notify the court if settlement is not a real possibility.

- **The conference will not be held unless counsel has clients with <u>full and complete</u> settlement authority physically present for the duration of the conference. Full and complete authority means the party's representative must possess authority consistent with the most recent demand.**[*]

Please complete the attached summary and fax it to Chambers (267) 299-5064 on or before _____.

Chavela M. Settles
Deputy Clerk to
Magistrate Judge Timothy R. Rice
(267) 299-7660

---

[*] Parties include all persons, corporations or other business entities, and insurance companies with an interest in the case, and each entity with an interest in the case <u>must</u> attend the conference. In the case of corporate or other business entities, the corporate official with ultimate settlement authority is required to attend. Where an insurance company is involved, a representative with full and complete settlement authority is also required to attend.

Magistrate Judge Timothy R. Rice

SETTLEMENT CONFERENCE SUMMARY

CAPTION: _____

DISTRICT COURT JUDGE: _____ **JURY / NONJURY**
                                                   (Circle One)

    TRIAL/POOL DATE: _____

COUNSEL ATTENDING SETTLEMENT CONFERENCE:

    Name: _____
    Address: _____
    Phone: _____
    Client: _____

CLIENT ATTENDING SETTLEMENT CONFERENCE:

Name of Individual with Ultimate Settlement Authority who will be present at the settlement conference (include company and position where applicable):

_____

MOTIONS PENDING:

_____
_____
_____

OTHER RELEVANT MATTERS:

_____
_____
_____

PRIOR OFFERS/DEMANDS:

_____
_____

ATTACH SYNOPSIS OF CASE (LIMITED TO ONE PAGE)

Magistrate Judge Thomas J. Rueter

Judge Rueter was born on July 12, 1955, in Philadelphia, Pennsylvania. He graduated summa cum laude from the University of Scranton in 1977, and in 1980 received a J.D. from Dickinson School of Law of the Pennsylvania State University, where he was Notes editor of the *Law Review*. From 1980 to 1982, he was a law clerk for the Honorable Joseph L. McGlynn, Jr., United States District Court for the Eastern District of Pennsylvania.

Judge Rueter was an associate of the Philadelphia law firm of White and Williams from 1982 to 1985. From 1985 to 1994, Judge Rueter was an assistant United States attorney in Philadelphia, and from 1990 to 1994, he served as chief of the Narcotics Section. Judge Rueter was appointed as a United States magistrate judge on February 22, 1994.

PRELIMINARY GENERAL MATTERS

1. Correspondence with the Court. Judge Rueter permits correspondence from counsel on all matters. Judge Rueter sometimes permits letter motions in lieu of formal motions.

2. Communications with Law Clerks. Judge Rueter permits counsel to talk with his law clerks regarding procedural matters, but never on the merits of the case. He encourages his law clerks to call counsel, for example, to determine whether a response will be filed to a motion.

3. Telephone Conferences. Judge Rueter prefers that counsel come to his chambers for conferences. When counsel cannot be present, he encourages the use of telephone conferences.

4. Oral Arguments and Evidentiary Hearings. Judge Rueter does not set aside any special days or times for oral arguments or evidentiary hearings.

5. Pro Hac Vice Admissions. Judge Rueter permits oral motions for pro hac vice admissions on the day that the attorney to be admitted first appears. A written motion before that time is not necessary. However, counsel should prepare an appropriate order to memorialize the pro hac vice admission.

CIVIL CASES
Pretrial Procedure

1. Pretrial Conferences. Judge Rueter conducts status conferences, settlement conferences, and final pretrial conferences, but not on any fixed schedule. He will normally schedule a pretrial conference at the request of counsel. The agenda for these conferences varies greatly and, therefore, Judge Rueter does not issue a standard agenda for them.

Judge Rueter uses a standard form of pretrial order that varies depending on the issues of each case.

Continuances and Extensions

1. General Policy. Judge Rueter's general policy on continuances for briefing schedules, oral arguments, evidentiary hearings, and discovery deadlines is to be accommodating at the initial stage of the case and to become less obliging as trial approaches. For trial dates, Judge Rueter is guided almost entirely by the district court judge to whom the case is assigned. He does not have any fixed requirements on how far in advance of a due date counsel should submit a request for an extension of time or a continuance.

2. Requests for Extensions and Continuances. For extensions and continuances, Judge Rueter prefers a stipulation when possible. Judge Rueter does not require a formal motion, and he will accept a letter for such requests. Judge Rueter suggests that letters of this type be submitted after an agreement is reached among counsel.

General Motion Practice

1.   Oral Argument on Motions. Judge Rueter generally will grant oral argument on motions if it is requested by counsel.

2.   Reply and Surreply Briefs. Judge Rueter permits reply briefs and surreply briefs, but requests counsel to notify the court of the party's intention to file such a brief.

3.   Chambers Copy of Motion Papers. Judge Rueter prefers to receive a courtesy copy of all motion papers.

Discovery Matters

1.   Length of Discovery Period and Extensions. Judge Rueter has no general policy on the amount of time allowed for discovery. The length of the discovery period is dictated by the complexity of the case.

2.   Discovery Conferences and Dispute Resolution. Judge Rueter will hold a discovery conference at the request of an attorney or the district court judge and initiates follow-up conferences when he believes they will be helpful. Judge Rueter will permit telephone conferences to resolve discovery disputes that arise during depositions.

3.   Confidentiality Agreements. Judge Rueter permits stipulated confidentiality agreements to be submitted for his approval when the reasons for these proposed agreements are clearly articulated.

4.   Expert Witnesses. Judge Rueter prefers written expert reports and expert depositions, but he neither requires nor prohibits either. He prefers that the parties identify experts as early as possible and, in any event, no later than the date of the final pretrial conference.

Settlement—Consent Cases

1.   General Approach to Settlement and Nonjury Cases. Judge Rueter will not take part in settlement discussions when there will be a nonjury trial. When the trial will be by jury, Judge Rueter will participate, but will not place undue pressure on counsel to settle.

2.   Settlement—Jurisdiction Remains with the District Court. When a case is referred to Judge Rueter for settlement only, he will conduct a settlement conference whether the trial is jury or nonjury. Judge Rueter does not require a pretrial memorandum or any written synopsis of the case by counsel for the conference, although he welcomes any submission by counsel. The clients need not be present. However, counsel is expected to attend the conference with settlement authority and have the client available by telephone.

3.   Referral of Settlement Negotiations to Another Magistrate Judge. Judge Rueter occasionally refers settlement negotiations to another magistrate judge, if it is a nonjury case in which he is the trial judge.

Arbitration

1.   General Approach to Arbitration Cases. Judge Rueter does not use any special practices or procedures for arbitration cases.

2.   Scheduling of Trial De Novo from Arbitration. Judge Rueter schedules a trial promptly when a demand for a trial de novo is filed after arbitration.

Proposed Final Pretrial Memoranda

1. Required Form of Pretrial Memoranda. Judge Rueter has no requirements for pretrial memoranda other than those set forth in Local Rule 16.1(c).

2. Common Deficiencies in Pretrial Memoranda. Judge Rueter does not observe any significant deficiencies in the pretrial memoranda submitted to him.

Trial Procedure

1. Scheduling of Cases. All of Judge Rueter's cases are specially listed for trial.

2. Conflicts of Counsel. Professional and personal conflicts of counsel are normally not a problem, since all trials are specially listed by Judge Rueter after consultation with counsel.

3. Cases Involving Out-of-Town Parties or Witnesses. Judge Rueter has no special policies for cases involving out-of-town parties or witnesses.

4. Note-taking of Jurors. Judge Rueter permits the taking of notes by jurors.

5. Trial Briefs. Judge Rueter encourages submission of trial briefs.

6. Voir Dire. Generally, Judge Rueter conducts voir dire himself after receiving proposed questions from counsel. After he has conducted voir dire, he affords counsel the opportunity to suggest questions he has not posed to the jury pool.

7. Sidebars. Judge Rueter permits sidebars, but on a complex motion or objection, he prefers to hold argument out of the hearing of the jury.

8. In Limine Motions. Judge Rueter prefers to receive in limine motions at least one week before trial, but he will accept them up to the time of trial.

9. Examination of Witnesses Out of Sequence. Judge Rueter will permit counsel to take witnesses out of turn for the convenience of the witnesses.

10. Opening Statements and Summations. Judge Rueter has no fixed rule on the time limits for opening statements or summations. Judge Rueter will grant a reasonable amount of time for counsel as dictated by the nature of the case.

11. Examination of Witnesses or Argument by More Than One Attorney. More than one attorney for a party may examine different witnesses or argue different points before Judge Rueter.

12. Examination of Witnesses Beyond Redirect and Recross. Judge Rueter generally does not permit further examination of witnesses after redirect and recross have been completed.

13. Videotaped Testimony. Judge Rueter has no special policy on the use of videotaped testimony.

14. Reading of Material Into the Record. Judge Rueter permits counsel to read stipulations and pleadings into the record. For depositions, he prefers that a witness respond to the questions of counsel in open court.

15. Preparation of Exhibits. Judge Rueter prefers that exhibits be pre-marked and he requires that they be pre-exchanged. Counsel should provide one copy of the exhibits to Judge Rueter.

16. Offering Exhibits Into Evidence. Judge Rueter has no preference as to when counsel should offer exhibits into evidence.

17. Motions for Judgment as a Matter of Law and Motions for Judgment on Partial Findings. A written motion for judgment as a matter of law or motion for judgment on partial findings is not required, and Judge Rueter permits oral argument on these motions if requested by either party.

18. Proposed Jury Instructions and Verdict Forms. Judge Rueter prefers to receive proposed jury instructions only for difficult or novel areas of law. He will accept supplemental points prior to the delivery of the charge. Judge Rueter usually conducts a conference on proposed jury instructions.

19. Proposed Findings of Fact and Conclusions of Law. In nonjury cases, Judge Rueter prefers submission of proposed findings of fact and conclusions of law shortly after the trial, citing the trial transcript if it is available.

Jury Deliberations

1. Written Jury Instructions. In most cases, Judge Rueter gives a copy of his instructions to the jury.

2. Exhibits in the Jury Room. Exhibits are not automatically sent out to the jury. Judge Rueter seeks agreement from counsel on what to send out to the jury. When there is no agreement, he rules on the requests.

3. Handling of Jury Requests to Read Back Testimony or Replay Tapes. If the jury requests to have portions of testimony read back, the testimony is played back on the court's electronic court-reporting equipment. When audiotape or videotape recordings have been admitted into evidence, and the jury requests that they be replayed, Judge Rueter permits this, and it is done in the courtroom.

4. Availability of Counsel During Jury Deliberations. Counsel may return to their offices during jury deliberations, but they must be available on telephone notice.

5. Taking the Verdict and Special Interrogatories. Whether Judge Rueter takes a general or special verdict depends on the nature and facts of the case.

6. Polling the Jury. Judge Rueter will grant a request to poll the jury.

7. Interviewing the Jury. In civil cases, jurors may be interviewed by counsel, but only after the verdict has been recorded and the jury has been discharged.

CRIMINAL CASES

1. Approach to Oral Argument and Motions. Oral argument in criminal cases is the rule rather than the exception for Judge Rueter.

2. Pretrial Conferences. Judge Rueter does not conduct pretrial conferences in criminal cases.

3. Voir Dire. Judge Rueter conducts all the voir dire in criminal cases.

4. Sentencing Memoranda. Judge Rueter permits, but does not require, submission of sentencing memoranda by both sides.

OTHER GENERAL MATTERS

Judge Rueter prefers to receive copies of the appellate briefs when a decision rendered by him is appealed.

Magistrate Judge Lynne A. Sitarski

Judge Lynne A. Sitarski was born in Philadelphia, Pennsylvania, in 1964. She graduated from St. Hubert's Catholic High School for Girls in 1982. Judge Sitarski attended the University of Scranton, graduating with honors in May 1986, earning a Bachelor of Science degree in economics/finance. Immediately after college, Judge Sitarski enrolled at the Temple University School of Law, where she became a member of the *Temple Law Review,* and served as note/comment editor on the *Law Review's* editorial board during her third year. Also during her third year of law school, Ms. Sitarski participated in Temple's Honors Clinical Program, serving as a legal intern to Judge Dolores K. Sloviter of the United States Court of Appeals for the Third Circuit. Judge Sitarski received her Juris Doctor, cum laude, in 1989. She was admitted to practice before both the Supreme Court of Pennsylvania and the Supreme Court of New Jersey in December 1989.

Beginning in the fall of 1989, Judge Sitarski worked at major law firms in Philadelphia as a litigation attorney. In October 2000, Judge Sitarski left private practice to join the public sector, accepting the position of deputy city solicitor in the City of Philadelphia Law Department's Civil Rights Unit. As a deputy city solicitor, Judge Sitarski represented the city of Philadelphia and its employees as defendants in civil rights actions arising out of the alleged violation of constitutionally protected rights. Judge Sitarski served as lead counsel in many jury trials in the United States District Court for the Eastern District of Pennsylvania. In January 2006, Judge Sitarski was appointed chief deputy city solicitor of the Civil Rights Unit. On October 29, 2007, Judge Sitarski was sworn in as a United States magistrate judge.

PRELIMINARY GENERAL MATTERS

1. ***Professionalism.*** Judge Sitarski expects counsel and parties to conduct themselves in a civil, polite, and professional manner at all times. All proceedings will begin at the scheduled time, and punctuality is expected.

2. ***Correspondence with the Court.*** Judge Sitarski permits correspondence from counsel on all matters. She sometimes permits letter motions in lieu of formal motions.

3. ***Communications with Law Clerks.*** Judge Sitarski permits counsel to talk with her law clerks regarding procedural matters, but never on the merits of the case. She encourages her law clerks to call counsel, for example, to determine whether a response will be filed to a motion.

4. ***Telephone Conferences.*** Judge Sitarski prefers that counsel come to chambers for all conferences. Telephone conferences may be used, however, for dealing with matters such as scheduling changes, extensions of time, and routine discovery disputes. Counsel seeking any such relief are responsible for initiating the conference by contacting Judge Sitarski's deputy clerk.

5. ***Oral Arguments and Evidentiary Hearings.*** Oral arguments and evidentiary hearings may be scheduled through Judge Sitarski's deputy clerk. All reasonable efforts will be made to accommodate the schedules of counsel.

6. ***Pro Hac Vice Admissions.*** Judge Sitarski will permit oral motions for pro hac vice admissions on the day that the attorney to be admitted first appears. On or before the date of the non-admitted attorney's first appearance, counsel must prepare an appropriate order to memorialize the pro hac vice admission.

CIVIL CASES
Pretrial Procedure

1. *Pretrial Status Conference.* Judge Sitarski will schedule status conferences, settlement conferences, and final pretrial conferences as required by the circumstance of each particular case. Judge Sitarski will schedule either telephone conferences or conferences in chambers to resolve any issues that may arise as the case progresses. Judge Sitarski does expect, however, that counsel will make all good-faith efforts to resolve any disputed matter between themselves before seeking involvement of the court. Counsel are expected to be mindful of the mandate of Fed.R.Civ.P. 1 that the procedural rules "should be construed and administered to secure the just, speedy, and inexpensive determination of every action and proceeding."

Continuances and Extensions

1. *General Policy.* Generally, Judge Sitarski will expect counsel to comply with the requirements set out in the court's initial Rule 16 order. A scheduling order will be issued after a conference with the parties. The court expects that counsel will provide all information necessary to set realistic and firm deadlines. Counsel will be encouraged to consider settlement at the earliest possible stage and, alternatively, to consider discovery staging agreements that permit productive settlement discussions before the parties are required to bear the extensive costs of protracted discovery. Extensions will be entertained upon a showing that circumstances beyond the reasonable expectation of counsel have hampered the progress of the case. Judge Sitarski will not require a formal motion seeking an extension and will consider requests for extensions brought to the attention of her deputy clerk, who will set up either a telephone or chambers conference.

General Motions Practice

1. *Oral Argument on Motions.* Judge Sitarski will schedule oral argument on motions if it appears likely to be helpful to the court's resolution of the matter. Counsel may request oral argument if considered appropriate.

2. *Reply and Surreply Briefs.* Judge Sitarski will permit reply briefs. Judge Sitarski will not normally permit surreply briefs, and counsel who wish to file a surreply must first seek permission of the court before such a brief will be accepted.

3. *Chambers Copy of Motions Papers.* Judge Sitarski expects a courtesy copy of all motion papers to be sent directly to chambers. Judge Sitarski expects that these papers will be submitted by hand delivery, overnight courier, or fax.

Discovery Matters

1. *Length of Discovery Period and Extensions.* Judge Sitarski normally permits from 90 to 120 days for the completion of discovery; however, she will consider the informed view of counsel as to the time that will be required for discovery in a particular case. Additional time will be allowed in complex cases or upon a specific showing of need. Judge Sitarski will also consider staged discovery. She will encourage that the most essential discovery be undertaken early in the case so that it will foster early settlement opportunities and minimize the costs of litigation.

2. *Discovery Conferences and Dispute Resolution.* Discovery should be conducted in a voluntary, candid, cooperative, and timely manner. Judge Sitarski expects the parties to resolve discovery disputes without court intervention. Should counsel be unable, in good faith, to resolve their dispute, Judge Sitarski permits contact with the court so that telephone or chambers conferences may be set up to resolve outstanding issues. Judge Sitarski prefers to resolve discovery disputes by the use of written motions.

3. Confidentiality Agreements. Judge Sitarski will permit confidentiality agreements subject to the requirements of *Pansy v. Borough of Stroudsburg,* 23 F.3d 772, 786 (3d Cir. 1994).

4. Expert Witnesses. The parties will identify expert witnesses and provide expert reports pursuant to the Rule 16 scheduling order entered in the particular case. A failure to do so may bar the use of the expert's testimony at trial.

Settlement When Jurisdiction Remains with the District Court

1. Settlement Conference Memoranda. Judge Sitarski will normally require counsel to submit a confidential settlement conference memorandum one week before the actual conference. Judge Sitarski permits each attorney to submit copies of up to five documents that he/she considers critical to resolution of the case. An order outlining the matters to be covered in the memorandum will be filed shortly after the conference is scheduled. These summaries should be submitted to the court only, and should *not* be filed with the Clerk's Office. Judge Sitarski expects that these submissions will include a candid discussion of the submitting party's strengths and weaknesses in the case.

2. Parties' Attendance and Participation. Judge Sitarski will require that each party or a representative of each party with knowledge of the case and settlement authority attend the conference in person. In very exceptional circumstances, with advance approval, Judge Sitarski will permit that person to participate in the conference by telephone.

3. Follow-up Contact. Judge Sitarski will, if appropriate, continue to work with counsel after the settlement conference if the matter is not resolved at the conference.

Settlement When Jurisdiction for All Purposes Has Been Referred to Judge Sitarski

1. Jury Matters. Judge Sitarski may, after discussion with counsel, conduct her own settlement conferences using the procedures referred to above. If that is not appropriate, and if a conference is deemed worthwhile, Judge Sitarski will seek the assistance of another magistrate judge to assist with settlement discussions.

2. Nonjury Matters. Judge Sitarski will not take part in settlement discussions in a nonjury matter. A settlement conference may, however, be arranged with another magistrate judge.

Arbitration

1. General Approach to Arbitration Cases. Judge Sitarski has no special practices or procedures for arbitration cases.

2. Scheduling Trial De Novo from Arbitration. Judge Sitarski will schedule trial promptly when a demand for trial de novo is filed following arbitration.

Proposed Pretrial Memoranda

1. *Required Form of Pretrial Memoranda.* Unless specifically provided for by separate order, Judge Sitarski will require the use of the short-form pretrial memorandum described in Rule 16.1(c) of the Local Rules of Civil Procedure for the Eastern District of Pennsylvania. In certain cases, Judge Sitarski may require counsel to stipulate to uncontested facts as generally set out in Local Rule 16.1(d)(2)(b)(2)(A–E).

Injunctions

1. *Scheduling and Expedited Discovery.* Judge Sitarski will promptly list for a conference any injunction matters assigned to her. The scheduling of injunction matters will depend upon the circumstances of the case and will be determined at an initial conference to be attended by all counsel.

2. *Proposed Findings of Fact and Conclusions of Law.* Judge Sitarski requires the submission of proposed findings of fact and conclusions of law in advance of the hearing in all injunction cases.

Trial Procedure

1. *Scheduling of Cases.* Judge Sitarski's cases will be specially listed for trial based upon the court's calendar and the availability of counsel, the parties, experts, and critical witnesses.

2. *Conflicts of Counsel.* Given the manner of scheduling, conflicts will normally not occur. Should a professional or personal conflict arise that may affect the trial schedule, counsel must immediately notify opposing counsel and the court. The court will hold a conference to address the conflict.

3. *Parties or Witnesses.* Judge Sitarski will make all reasonable attempts to accommodate the schedules and availability of parties and witnesses.

4. *Note-taking by Jurors.* Judge Sitarski will consider note-taking by jurors on a case-by-case basis.

5. *Trial Briefs.* Judge Sitarski encourages the submission of trial briefs when they are necessary or likely to be helpful to the court.

6. *Voir Dire.* It is Judge Sitarski's general practice to preside over voir dire and jury selection. Judge Sitarski permits counsel to conduct voir dire in all civil cases. Counsel should exchange proposed voir dire questions prior to the final pretrial conference. Judge Sitarski may conduct supplemental voir dire when appropriate.

7. *Sidebar.* Judge Sitarski strongly discourages the use of sidebar conferences. Counsel are encouraged to raise particular evidentiary issues before trial or during recesses or adjournments.

8. *In Limine Motions.* Judge Sitarski requires that in limine motions be filed and served in advance of the final pretrial conference so as to give her an opportunity to consider the merits of each motion.

9. *Examination of Witnesses Out of Sequence.* Judge Sitarski will permit witnesses to be taken out of turn in appropriate circumstances.

10. *Opening Statements and Submission.* Judge Sitarski will discuss with counsel the length of time necessary and appropriate for opening and closing statements, but will give counsel reasonable latitude.

11. Examination of Witnesses or Argument by More Than One Attorney. Judge Sitarski will normally not permit more than one attorney for the party to examine the same witness and will normally not permit more than one attorney to present argument on behalf of the party on the same point.

12. Examination of Witnesses Beyond Redirect or Recross. Judge Sitarski will generally restrict counsel from examining witnesses beyond redirect and recross.

13. Videotaped Testimony. Judge Sitarski requires counsel to review all videotaped depositions and to have them edited so as to fairly present only the essential evidence of the witness involved. Counsel are expected to resolve all matters pertaining to objections before offering the videotape into evidence.

14. Reading of Material Into the Record. Judge Sitarski will request that counsel read stipulations and pleadings into the record. Judge Sitarski discourages reading depositions into the record; she prefers that a witness respond to the questions of counsel in open court.

15. Preparation of Exhibits. Prior to commencement of trial, counsel should pre-mark and exchange exhibits. Counsel should provide Judge Sitarski with two sets of exhibits in a tabbed, three-ring binder, together with a schedule of exhibits that briefly describes each exhibit. Counsel are encouraged, however, to provide the court with only the essential and relevant portions of lengthy exhibits, together with sufficient material to provide context for the relevant portion of the exhibits.

16. Offering Exhibits Into Evidence. Judge Sitarski expects counsel to attempt in good faith to reach agreement in advance as to the admission of exhibits. Judge Sitarski has no particular procedure as to when an exhibit may be formally offered into evidence.

17. Motions for Judgment as a Matter of Law and Motions for Judgment on Partial Findings. Motions for judgment as a matter of law or motions for judgment on partial findings in nonjury trials may be submitted in writing or orally. Judge Sitarski will ordinarily request oral argument on these motions.

18. Proposed Jury Instructions and Verdict Forms. Judge Sitarski strongly encourages counsel to use the Third Circuit's Model Jury Instructions whenever possible. Judge Sitarski requires counsel to submit joint proposed jury instructions noting areas of agreement as well as objections. The points for charge should be submitted with appropriate citations of legal authority and must be provided to the court at least two business days prior to the commencement of trial.

Counsel will submit a jointly prepared verdict form or proposed special interrogatories at least two business days prior to the start of trial. If counsel are unable to agree, they may submit separate proposed forms of interrogatories. She will accept supplemental points prior to the delivery of the charge. Judge Sitarski usually conducts a conference on proposed jury instructions. The proposed jury instructions and verdict forms should be submitted on paper *and* electronically, either on a disk delivered to chambers, or via e-mail to chambers, in WordPerfect format.

19. Proposed Findings of Fact and Conclusions of Law. Judge Sitarski requires counsel to submit proposed findings of fact and conclusions of law in nonjury cases at the final pretrial conference. They should be submitted on paper *and* electronically, either on a disk delivered to chambers, or via e-mail to chambers, in WordPerfect format. Supplementation will be permitted at the close of trial or in an appropriate case after trial.

Jury Deliberations

1. Written Jury Instructions. Judge Sitarski has no particular practice or policy on submitting a copy of instructions to the jury.

2. Exhibits in the Jury Room. Judge Sitarski will consider what exhibits should be sent out to the jury during their deliberations on a case-by-case basis.

3. Handling of Jury Requests to Read Back Testimony or Replay Tapes. Judge Sitarski will seek the input of counsel and will then make a determination on a case-by-case basis when requests are made to read back testimony or replay tapes.

4. Availability of Counsel During Jury Deliberations. Judge Sitarski will not require counsel to remain in the courthouse during deliberations, but will require counsel to be available on short telephone notice and be able to be in the courtroom within 15 minutes.

5. Taking the Verdict and Special Interrogatories. Judge Sitarski has no usual practice with respect to taking a verdict. Judge Sitarski will submit written interrogatories to the jury. A copy of the interrogatories will be given to each juror.

6. Polling the Jury. Judge Sitarski will, if requested, permit the jury to be polled.

7. Interviewing the Jury. Judge Sitarski will permit counsel to interview jurors, but only after the verdict has been recorded, and the jury has been discharged and told in clear terms that they have no obligation to speak with counsel.

CRIMINAL DUTY WEEK
Practices and Procedures

When Judge Sitarski is assigned to criminal duty matters, she holds the hearings in Courtroom 5A at 1:30 p.m. Arraignments assigned by the district court are held on Thursday mornings at 10:30 a.m., in Courtroom 5A.

At all criminal duty week proceedings, counsel, once appointed or retained, must be present for all proceedings. Once the court has ordered that a defendant be detained or has set conditions of release, any proposed changes thereto must be submitted to the court by written motion.

Judge Sitarski requires that all relevant documents be delivered to chambers in advance of all hearings and other proceedings. Counsel may contact Judge Sitarski's deputy clerk if there are questions regarding the matters before the court.

OTHER GENERAL MATTERS

When a decision rendered by the court is appealed, Judge Sitarski prefers to receive copies of appellate briefs.

Judge Sitarski expects counsel to be prompt in all appearances, to be professional and courteous to each other, both in the presence of the court and otherwise, and to have discussions with each other about any matter in dispute before it is brought to the attention of the court.

Counsel should feel free to contact Judge Sitarski's deputy clerk or law clerks if they have any questions about her courtroom practices or procedures.

Practice and Procedures of Judges and Judges' Forms and Orders

IN THE UNITED STATES DISTRICT COURT
FOR THE EASTERN DISTRICT OF PENNSYLVANIA

XXXXXXXXXXXX	:	CIVIL ACTION
	:	
v.	:	
	:	
	:	
	:	NO: 00-cv-0000
XXXXXXXXXXXXXX	:	

ORDER

AND NOW, this _____ day of _____, 20___, IT IS HEREBY ORDERED that a **SETTLEMENT CONFERENCE** in the above-captioned case will be held on _____, 20___, **at 9:30 A.M.,** before the Honorable Lynne A. Sitarski, United States Magistrate Judge, in Courtroom 3E, U.S. Courthouse, 601 Market Street, Philadelphia, PA 19106.

- Please notify the court if settlement is not a real possibility.

- The conference will not be held unless counsel has clients with <u>full and complete</u> settlement authority physically present for the duration of the conference.[*] **Full and complete authority means the party's representative must possess authority consistent with the most recent demand.**

- Lead Trial Counsel for each party shall be physically present at the Settlement Conference. Counsel are expected to be fully familiar with the facts of the case, the legal theories supporting their client's claims or defenses, and the procedural posture of the case. **Failure to comply with this Order may result in the imposition of sanctions.**

Please complete the attached confidential summary and fax it to Chambers (267) 299-5060 on or before _____, 20___. These submissions shall be submitted to the Court only, and should include a candid discussion of the submitting party's strengths and weaknesses in the case.

BY THE COURT:

_____
LYNNE A. SITARSKI
UNITED STATES MAGISTRATE JUDGE

Date:

cc: XXXXXXXXX, Esquire (via facsimile)
XXXXXXXXX, Esquire (via facsimile)

---

[*] Parties include all persons, corporations or other business entities, and insurance companies with an interest in the case, and each entity with an interest in the case <u>must</u> attend the conference. In the case of corporate or other business entities, the corporate official with ultimate settlement authority is required to attend. Where an insurance company is involved, a representative with full and complete settlement authority is also required to attend.

Magistrate Judge Lynne A. Sitarski

CONFIDENTIAL SETTLEMENT CONFERENCE SUMMARY

Caption: _____

DISTRICT COURT JUDGE: _____   JURY/NONJURY
                                                                                                            (Circle One)

TRIAL POOL DATE: _____

COUNSEL ATTENDING SETTLEMENT CONFERENCE:

Name: _____

Address: _____

Phone: _____

Client: _____

CLIENT ATTENDING SETTLEMENT CONFERENCE:

    <u>Name of Individual with Full and Complete Settlement Authority who will be present at the settlement conference (include company and position where applicable):</u>

_____

MOTIONS PENDING:

_____
_____
_____

OTHER RELEVANT MATTERS:

_____
_____
_____

PRIOR OFFERS/DEMANDS:

_____
_____
_____

ATTACH SYNOPSIS OF CASE (<u>LIMITED TO ONE PAGE</u>)

Magistrate Judge David R. Strawbridge

Judge Strawbridge was born on August 19, 1945, in Abington, Pennsylvania. He is a graduate of Brown University (1967) and Villanova University School of Law (1971). He worked as an assistant district attorney in Philadelphia from 1971 through 1976 and as an assistant United States attorney for the Eastern District of Pennsylvania from 1976 through 1978. In 1978, he joined Cozen O'Connor, where he worked as a trial lawyer for nearly 27 years. At Cozen O'Connor, he handled a variety of insurance coverage, insurance defense, subrogation, and commercial cases. In 1998, he opened Cozen O'Connor's first international office in London. He returned to Cozen O'Connor's Philadelphia office in 2002. He was sworn in as a United States magistrate judge on April 26, 2005.

PRELIMINARY GENERAL MATTERS

1. Correspondence with the Court. Judge Strawbridge permits correspondence from counsel on all matters.

2. Communications with Law Clerks. Judge Strawbridge permits counsel to communicate with his law clerks on scheduling and administrative matters, but never on the merits of a case.

3. Telephone Conferences. Judge Strawbridge prefers that counsel come to chambers for all conferences. Telephone conferences may be used, however, for dealing with matters such as scheduling changes, extensions of time, and routine discovery disputes. It will be the responsibility of counsel seeking relief to initiate any such conference by contacting the judge's deputy clerk, Lori DiSanti.

4. Oral Arguments and Evidentiary Hearings. Oral arguments and evidentiary hearings may be scheduled through Judge Strawbridge's deputy clerk. All reasonable efforts will be made to accommodate the schedules of counsel.

5. Pro Hac Vice Admissions. Judge Strawbridge will permit oral motions for pro hac vice admissions on the day that the attorney to be admitted first appears. On or before the date of the non-admitted attorney's first appearance, counsel must prepare an appropriate order to memorialize the pro hac vice admission.

CIVIL CASES
Pretrial Procedure

1. Pretrial Status Conference. Judge Strawbridge will schedule status conferences, settlement conferences, and final pretrial conferences as required by the circumstance of each particular case. Judge Strawbridge will work with counsel in the scheduling of either telephone conferences or conferences in chambers to resolve any issues that may arise during the progress of the case. Judge Strawbridge does expect, however, that counsel will make all good-faith efforts to resolve any disputed matter between themselves before seeking involvement of the court. Counsel are expected to be mindful of the mandate of Fed.R.Civ.P. 1 that the procedural rules "should be construed and administered to secure the just, speedy, and inexpensive determination of every action and proceeding."

Continuances and Extensions

In that counsel will have substantial input in the setting of dates in the Rule 16 order, Judge Strawbridge expects counsel to comply with the dates set out in that order. Extensions will be entertained upon a showing that circumstances beyond the reasonable expectation of counsel have hampered the progress of the case. Judge Strawbridge will not require a formal motion seeking an extension and will consider requests for extensions to be brought to the attention of his deputy clerk, who will set up either a telephone or chambers conference.

General Motions Practice

1.   Oral Argument on Motions.   Judge Strawbridge will schedule oral argument on motions if it appears likely to be helpful to the court's resolution of the matter. Counsel may request oral argument if considered appropriate.

2.   Reply and Surreply Briefs.   Judge Strawbridge will permit reply briefs. Judge Strawbridge will not normally permit surreply briefs, and counsel desiring to file a surreply must first seek permission of the court before such a brief will be accepted.

3.   Chambers Copy of Motions Papers.   Judge Strawbridge requires a courtesy copy of all motion papers to be sent directly to chambers.

Discovery Matters

1.   Length of Discovery Period and Extensions.   Judge Strawbridge normally permits from 90 to 120 days for the completion of discovery; however, he will consider the informed view of counsel as to the time that will be required for discovery in a particular case. Additional time will be allowed in complex cases or upon a specific showing of need. Judge Strawbridge will also consider staged discovery. He will encourage that the most essential discovery be undertaken early in the case so that it will foster early settlement opportunities and minimize the costs of litigation.

2.   Discovery Disputes.   Judge Strawbridge expects the parties to resolve discovery disputes without court intervention. Should counsel be unable, in good faith, to resolve their dispute, Judge Strawbridge permits contact with the court through his deputy clerk to set up telephone or chambers conferences to resolve outstanding issues. The use of motion practice in discovery matters is discouraged.

3.   Confidentiality Agreements.   Judge Strawbridge will permit confidentiality agreements subject to the requirements of *Pansy v. Borough of Stroudsburg*, 23 F.3d 772, 786 (3d Cir. 1994).

4.   Expert Witnesses.   The parties will identify expert witnesses and provide expert reports pursuant to the Rule 16 scheduling order entered in the particular case. A failure to do so may bar the use of the expert's testimony at trial.

Settlement

1.   When Jurisdiction Remains with the District Court

    a.   Preliminary Telephone Conference.   When a matter is referred to Judge Strawbridge for purposes of settlement, he will normally hold a preliminary telephone conference with counsel. At the time of the telephone conference, counsel will be expected to discuss the status of settlement discussions (if any) and the timing of the actual face-to-face conference. In the interest of streamlining the litigation, Judge Strawbridge will encourage counsel to participate in settlement discussions as early as practicable and to stage discovery so as to facilitate settlement and control costs without doing violence to the referring judge's Rule 16 requirements.

    b.   Settlement Conference Memoranda.   Judge Strawbridge will normally require counsel to submit a brief conference memorandum one week before the actual conference. Judge Strawbridge will enter an order following the preliminary telephone conference that outlines the matters to be covered in the conference memorandum. Judge Strawbridge will encourage counsel to agree to exchange their memoranda. The memoranda are not to be filed with the Clerk's Office.

    c.   **Demands and Offers.** Judge Strawbridge requires the plaintiff (and the defendant to any affirmative claim) to set out a written good-faith demand prior to the conference. The defendant (or the other responding party) is required to respond to that demand in writing. The dates of the demands and offers will be set out in Judge Strawbridge's settlement conference order in each case.

    d.   **Parties' Attendance and Participation.** Judge Strawbridge will require that each party or party's representative with knowledge of the case and settlement authority attend the conference in person. In exceptional circumstances, Judge Strawbridge will permit that person to participate in the conference by telephone. Counsel seeking this relief must contact chambers as soon as they are aware of a problem with attendance.

    At the conference, the judge will expect counsel to:

- Be prepared to discuss the weaknesses as well as the strengths of their case.
- Prepare their client. Judge Strawbridge will speak to them directly.
- Organize and bring the critical documents. The judge will want to see them.
- Attach relevant summary expert reports to the conference memos. The judge will review them.
- Bring any photographs, sketches, diagrams, and charts. The judge will review them.
- Be patient. Settlement is a process. It takes time.
- Be flexible. Avoid bottom lines or top numbers.
- Be creative.
- Manage your client's expectations.
- Manage your own expectations.

    e.   **Follow-up Contact.** Judge Strawbridge will, if appropriate, continue to work with counsel after the settlement conference if the matter is not resolved at the conference.

2.   **When Jurisdiction for All Purposes Has Been Referred to Judge Strawbridge**

    a.   **Jury Matters.** Judge Strawbridge may, after discussion with counsel, conduct his own settlement conferences using the procedures referred to above. If that is not appropriate, and if a conference is deemed worthwhile, Judge Strawbridge will obtain the assistance of another magistrate judge to assist with settlement discussions.

    b.   **Nonjury Matters.** Judge Strawbridge will not take part in settlement discussions in a nonjury matter. A settlement conference may, however, be arranged with another magistrate judge.

Arbitration

1.   **General Approach to Arbitration Cases.** Judge Strawbridge has no special practices or procedures for arbitration cases.

2.   **Scheduling Trial De Novo from Arbitration.** Judge Strawbridge will schedule trial promptly when a demand for trial de novo is filed following arbitration.

Proposed Pretrial Memoranda

Unless specifically provided for by separate order, Judge Strawbridge will require the use of the short-form pretrial memorandum described in Rule 16.1(c) of the Local Rules of

Civil Procedure for the Eastern District of Pennsylvania. In certain cases, Judge Strawbridge may require counsel to stipulate to uncontested facts as generally set out in Local Rule 16.1(d)(2)(b)(2)(A–E).

Trial Procedure

1. **Scheduling of Cases.** Judge Strawbridge's cases will be specially listed for trial based upon the court's calendar and the availability of counsel, the parties, experts, and critical witnesses.

2. **Conflicts of Counsel.** Given the manner of scheduling, conflicts will normally not occur. Should counsel, however, have a professional or personal conflict that may affect the trial schedule, notice should be provided immediately to opposing counsel and the court.

3. **Parties or Witnesses.** Judge Strawbridge will make all reasonable attempts to accommodate the schedules and availability of parties, experts, and critical witnesses.

4. **Note-taking by Jurors.** Judge Strawbridge will consider note-taking by jurors on a case-by-case basis.

5. **Trial Briefs.** Judge Strawbridge encourages the submission of trial briefs when they are necessary or likely to be helpful to the court.

6. **Voir Dire.** Judge Strawbridge will normally conduct voir dire in civil cases. Counsel may submit proposed voir dire questions at the final pretrial conference and may, when appropriate, conduct supplemental voir dire.

7. **Sidebar.** Judge Strawbridge discourages the use of sidebar conferences. Counsel are encouraged to raise particular evidentiary issues before trial or during recesses or adjournments.

8. **In Limine Motions.** Judge Strawbridge will accept in limine motions in advance of the final pretrial conference and in accordance with his scheduling order so as to give him an opportunity to consider the merits of the motion.

9. **Examination of Witnesses Out of Sequence.** Judge Strawbridge will permit witnesses to be taken out of turn in appropriate circumstances.

10. **Opening Statements and Submission.** Judge Strawbridge will discuss with counsel the length of time necessary and appropriate for opening and closing statements, but will give counsel reasonable latitude.

11. **Examination of Witnesses or Argument by More Than One Attorney.** Judge Strawbridge will not normally permit more than one attorney for the party to examine the same witness or more than one attorney to present argument on behalf of the party on the same point.

12. **Examination of Witnesses Beyond Redirect or Recross.** Judge Strawbridge will generally restrict counsel from examining witnesses beyond redirect and recross.

13. **Videotaped Testimony.** Judge Strawbridge requires counsel to review all videotaped depositions and to have them edited so as to fairly present only the essential evidence of the witness involved. Counsel are expected to resolve all matters pertaining to objections before offering the videotape into evidence.

14. **Reading of Material Into the Record.** Judge Strawbridge has no special practice with regard to reading stipulations, pleadings, or discovery materials into the record.

15. Preparation of Exhibits. Prior to commencement of trial, exhibits are to be premarked and exchanged by counsel. Counsel should provide Judge Strawbridge with two copies of each exhibit, together with a schedule of exhibits that briefly describes each exhibit. Counsel are encouraged, however, to provide the court with only the essential and relevant portions of bulky exhibits, together with sufficient material to provide context for the relevant portion of the exhibits.

16. Offering Exhibits Into Evidence. Judge Strawbridge expects counsel to reach agreement in advance as to the admission of exhibits. Judge Strawbridge has no particular procedure as to when an exhibit may be formally offered into evidence.

17. Motions for Judgment as a Matter of Law and Motions for Judgment on Partial Findings. Motions for judgment as a matter of law or motions for judgment on partial findings in nonjury trials may be submitted in writing or orally. Judge Strawbridge will ordinarily request oral argument on these motions.

18. Proposed Jury Instructions and Verdict Forms. Judge Strawbridge requires counsel to submit joint proposed jury instructions noting areas of agreement as well as objections. The points for charge should be submitted with appropriate citations of legal authority and must be provided to the court in accordance with the deadline set forth in his scheduling order.

Counsel will submit a jointly prepared verdict form or proposed special interrogatories in accordance with the deadline set forth in his scheduling order. If counsel are unable to agree, they may submit separate proposed forms of interrogatories. Judge Strawbridge will encourage counsel to agree upon a less than unanimous verdict.

19. Proposed Findings of Fact and Conclusions of Law. Judge Strawbridge requires counsel to submit proposed findings of fact and conclusions of law in nonjury cases at the final pretrial conference or at another date set forth in a scheduling order. A supplementation will be permitted at the close of trial or, in an appropriate case, after trial.

Jury Deliberations

1. Written Jury Instructions. Judge Strawbridge has no particular practice or policy on submitting a copy of instructions to the jury.

2. Exhibits in the Jury Room. Judge Strawbridge will consider what exhibits should be sent out to the jury during their deliberations on a case-by-case basis.

3. Handling of Jury Requests to Read Back Testimony or Replay Tapes. Judge Strawbridge will seek the input of counsel and will then make a determination on a case-by-case basis when requests are made to read back testimony or replay tapes.

4. Availability of Counsel During Jury Deliberations. Judge Strawbridge will not require counsel to remain in the courthouse during deliberations, but will require counsel to be available on short telephone notice.

5. Taking the Verdict and Special Interrogatories. Judge Strawbridge has no usual practice with respect to taking a verdict. Judge Strawbridge will submit written interrogatories to the jury in the appropriate case. A copy of the interrogatories will be given to the jurors during their deliberation.

6. Polling the Jury. Judge Strawbridge will, if requested, permit the jury to be polled.

7. Interviewing the Jury. Judge Strawbridge will permit counsel to interview jurors, but only after the verdict has been recorded, the jury has been discharged, *and* they have been told in clear terms that they have no obligation to speak with counsel.

CRIMINAL CASES

1. **Sentencing Memoranda.** When a pretrial sentencing report is used, Judge Strawbridge permits the submission of sentencing memoranda by both counsel.

2. **Additional Matters.** At all "criminal duty week" proceedings, counsel, once appointed or retained, must be present to permit the proceeding to go forward.

Once the court has ordered that a defendant be detained or has set conditions of release, any proposed changes thereto must be submitted to the court by written motion.

Judge Strawbridge does not favor the dual representation of defendants by a single attorney at any criminal proceeding, apart, perhaps, from the initial appearance.

Judge Strawbridge requires that all relevant documents be delivered to chambers in advance of court. Counsel may contact the court's deputy clerk, Lori DiSanti (267-299-7790), if there are questions regarding the matters before the court.

OTHER GENERAL MATTERS

When a decision rendered by the court is appealed, Judge Strawbridge prefers to receive copies of appellate briefs.

Judge Strawbridge expects counsel to be prompt in all appearances, to be professional and courteous to each other, both in the presence of the court and otherwise, and to have discussions with each other about any matter in dispute before it is brought to the attention of the court.

Counsel should feel free to contact Judge Strawbridge's deputy clerk or law clerks if they have any questions about his courtroom practices or procedures.

Part II

Standing Orders

Court Approval of Reporters Required for Taking of Depositions   *511*

Calendar Control   *511*

Civil Suspense Docket   *512*

Bankruptcy Administration Orders   *512*

Assignment Procedure for Habeas Corpus and Social Security Cases for United States Magistrates   *513*

Order Adopting Civil Justice Expense and Delay Reduction Plan   *514*

Order Extending Civil Justice Expense and Delay Reduction Plan   *514*

Approval of Pre-Judgment Notice of 28 U.S.C. § 3101(d)   *515*

Standing Orders Re: 1993 Amendments to Federal Rules of Civil Procedure   *516*

Presentence Investigations and Time Limits   *517*

Standing Order Re: Sentencing Reform Act of 1984   *518*

COURT APPROVAL OF REPORTERS REQUIRED FOR TAKING OF DEPOSITIONS

Adopted June 30, 1959

Depositions taken within the jurisdiction of this Court, upon oral examination, will not be considered by the Court for any purpose unless the testimony taken therein has been stenographically reported by a qualified reporter whom the Court has first approved. Reporters so approved are authorized to administer oaths to the persons brought before them as witnesses.

The Clerk of this Court shall keep a list of approved reporters, which list shall include the official court reporters. Copies of the list shall be available to litigants and their counsel.

The rule adopted June 9, 1955 (effective August 1, 1955) is hereby revoked.

CALENDAR CONTROL

The following order, relating to calendar control, was adopted on January 1, 1970, and is effective as of January 1, 1970.

1. Each judge will maintain a list of cases that are genuinely ready for trial, and genuinely likely to be tried.

   a. While there is no limit on the number of cases which may be listed, it should seldom be necessary to have more than 15 cases on any such list at any given time.

   b. No one lawyer may be included more than once in the first five cases on any such list.

   c. Each such list should include both jury and non-jury cases. For purposes of compiling these lists, realistic estimates of the probably duration of trial will be found very helpful.

2. At least one week before the scheduled start of a series of trials, each judge's list shall be published in the Legal Intelligencer.

   a. Publication of such list should continue during that session of trials, adding cases as appropriate, and deleting cases disposed of.

3. As among judges scheduled for trials, whenever there is conflict among the engagements of counsel, the oldest case will normally have priority (unless other arrangements are worked out in advance by the judges involved). The age of a case is to be determined by reference to the date of filing (i.e., the lowest number).

4. Once a trial has started, none of the lawyers involved may commence another trial before the same judge if the lawyer involved has another case listed among the first five cases on the list of any other judge then conducting trials or scheduled to begin or resume trials within seven (7) days thereafter.

   (Exception: A lawyer may start another trial before the same judge with the consent of all the other judges on whose lists he has other cases in the first five; such consent shall be freely given whenever it appears likely that such other judge will be unable to commence trial of such other case within the next seven (7) days).

5. Busy slips shall be recognized during all periods in which counsel is attached for trial.

   a. Counsel shall be deemed "attached" until the expiration of one business day after the conclusion of the trial. A trial shall be deemed concluded when the verdict is rendered or when finally terminated otherwise than by verdict.

   b. In his discretion, a judge may "attach" one case in addition to the case on trial, provided the trial of such "back-up" case actually commences promptly at the conclusion of the trial in progress.

      (1) Ordinarily, no such "back-up" attachment should commence more than seven (7) days before the anticipated conclusion of the trial in progress.

   c. Counsel may not remain "attached" for more than one business day for purposes of settlement negotiations or for purposes of awaiting confirmation of settlement, or related purposes.

Standing Orders

    6.   Advance special listings. In cases involving several busy lawyers, key witnesses from distant points, especially important issues, or other special circumstances, a judge may grant a special listing in advance. Such advance special listing shall take priority over all other trial engagements thereafter scheduled, but only if the following requirements are met:

        a.   Such listing shall be established at least thirty (30) days in advance, by notice to all counsel involved, and by notice to all active judges.

        b.   All judges shall be notified as early as practicable, and not later than thirty (30) days in advance, of the names of all counsel involved and the probable duration of the scheduled trial.

        c.   Not more than one such special listing shall be granted by the same judge to any one lawyer in any period of six (6) months, except for good cause shown.

CIVIL SUSPENSE DOCKET

Adopted June 24, 1975

    1.   There shall be established a special docket entitled "Civil Suspense Docket" in which shall be listed all civil actions which for reasons beyond the Court's control are unable to proceed to trial without delay. The "Civil Suspense Docket" shall be administered as follows:

        a.   The judge to whom the case is assigned shall enter an order transferring the case from his current case list to the Civil Suspense Docket. In the Order of Transfer the judge shall set forth the reason for the transfer. (Suggested form of order attached).

        b.   The Judge shall review the status of the civil action from time to time and transfer the case to his regular trial list as soon as the condition which required transfer to the Civil Suspense Docket has been removed.

        c.   A civil action shall not remain in the Civil Suspense Docket for more than six months from date of order, unless continued in suspense status by further order of the court.

        d.   On receipt of an order transferring an action to the Civil Suspense Docket, the Clerk of Court shall take appropriate action to remove the case as an open one for statistical purposes.

        e.   The transfer to the Civil Suspense Docket and the removal of the action as an open case for statistical purposes shall not constitute or be considered a dismissal or disposition of the matter; jurisdiction is retained and should further proceedings in the action become necessary or desirable, any party may initiate it in the same manner as if the Order of Transfer had not been entered.

        f.   Copies of all orders transferring cases between the suspense and active dockets or continuing cases in the suspense docket shall be delivered to the Calendar Committee which shall have supervisory authority over the Civil Suspense Docket.

        g.   On the first day of January and July of each year, each judge shall submit to the Calendar Committee a report, in such form as the Committee may determine, of all the cases in his Civil Suspense Docket.

BANKRUPTCY ADMINISTRATION ORDERS

ORDER

    This 25th day of July, 1984, pursuant to authorization provided in 28 U.S.C. § 157, as amended, and pursuant to Resolution approved by the judges of this court, it is

    ORDERED that any and all cases under Title 11 and any and all proceedings arising under Title 11 or arising in or related to a case under Title 11 are and shall be referred to the Bankruptcy Judges for the district, and it is

    FURTHER ORDERED that the Bankruptcy judges of the district are authorized to perform the duties to the full extent set forth in 28 U.S.C. § 157, as amended, and subject to the review procedures set forth in 28 U.S.C. §§ 157(c)(1) and 158. It is

FURTHER ORDERED that personal injury tort and wrongful death claims in bankruptcy cases pending in this district shall be tried in this district court or in the district court in the district in which the claims arose, as determined by a judge of this district.

This Order shall not be deemed to affect the status of any case, matter or proceeding presently pending before a district judge.

ORDER OF REFERENCE

And now this 8th day of November, 1990, pursuant to a Resolution approved by the judges of this Court, it is hereby Ordered that:

    1. The order dated July 25, 1984, referring cases under the Bankruptcy Code to the Bankruptcy Judges for this district is amended by deleting the following paragraph of that order:

ORDERED that any and all cases under Title 11 and any and all proceedings arising under Title 11 or arising in or related to a case under Title 11 are and shall be referred to the Bankruptcy Judges for the district.

And substituting for that paragraph the following:

ORDERED that any and all cases under chapter 7, 11, 12, and 13 of Title 11 and any and all proceedings arising under Title 11 or arising in or related to a chapter 7, 11, 12, or 13 case under Title 11 are and shall be referred to the Bankruptcy Judges for the district.

    2. This order shall not be deemed to affect the status of any case, proceeding or matter previously referred to the Bankruptcy Judges for the district.

ORDER OF REFERENCE

AND NOW, this 29th day of June, 1992, upon Resolution adopted at a duly noticed meeting of the Board of Judges, it is

ORDERED that the Local Bankruptcy Rules (attached hereto as "Exhibit A") are adopted effective July 31, 1992, and shall supersede any prior Local Bankruptcy Rules.

ASSIGNMENT PROCEDURE FOR HABEAS CORPUS AND SOCIAL SECURITY CASES FOR UNITED STATES MAGISTRATES

    A. All Habeas Corpus and Social Security cases upon filing shall be assigned by the Clerk of Court pursuant to Local Civil Rule 3 to the calendar of a judge of this court.

    B. Upon the entry of an Order of Referral of a Habeas Corpus or a Social Security case to a magistrate of this court, the following assignment procedures shall apply:

    1. *Assignment of Habeas Corpus and Social Security Cases.* There shall be a separate block of assignment cards for Habeas Corpus and Social Security cases. In each block of assignment cards for each category, the names of each magistrate shall appear an equal number of times in a non-sequential manner. The sequence of magistrates' names within each block shall be kept secret and no person shall directly or indirectly ascertain or divulge or attempt to ascertain or divulge the name of the magistrate to whom any case may be assigned before the assignment, and all assignment cards shall be preserved.

    2. *Assignment of Related Cases.* If the fact of relationship is indicated on the appropriate form at the time of filing, the assignment clerk shall assign the case to the same magistrate to whom the earlier numbered related case is assigned, and shall note such assignment by means of a separate block of cards on which he shall place the case number and the category and the name of the magistrate.

    a. All Habeas Corpus petitions filed by the same individual shall be deemed related.

    b. All Social Security petitions filed by the same individual shall be deemed related.

C. This procedure shall apply to all cases filed on or after June 1, 1990, except for related cases.

Approved by the Judges of this Court, May 29, 1990.

ORDER ADOPTING CIVIL JUSTICE EXPENSE
AND DELAY REDUCTION PLAN

AND NOW, this 25th day of October, 1991, pursuant to the Resolution approved by the judges of this court on October 7, 1991, it is hereby

ORDERED that the attached Civil Justice Expense and Delay Reduction Plan is hereby adopted, effective December 31, 1991, and shall apply to all civil action cases filed on or after that day and may, in the discretion of the court, apply to civil action cases pending on that date; it is further

ORDERED, that the Civil Justice Expense and Delay Reduction Plan is promulgated by this court pursuant to Title 28, United States Code Sections 471 and 472, and this Plan, as it may be amended from time to time, shall be maintained on file in the office of the Clerk of Court for public inspection; it is further

ORDERED that the Civil Justice Expense and Delay Reduction Plan shall be published by the Clerk of Court to inform members of the bar and public of its adoption and to afford opportunity for public notice and comment.

ORDER EXTENDING CIVIL JUSTICE EXPENSE
AND DELAY REDUCTION PLAN

AND NOW, to wit, this 11th day of December, 1995, it appearing that on October 25, 1991, this Court entered an Order adopting the attached Civil Justice Expense and Delay Reduction Plan, effective December 31, 1991, and,

it further appearing that the said Plan was adopted by this Court as a pilot program and is currently scheduled to lapse on December 31, 1995, and,

it further appearing that authorization for this pilot program has been extended by 28 U.S.C. § 471, as amended, and that the Congress has authorized promulgation and extension of the Civil Justice Expense and Delay Reduction Plans and,

it further appearing to the Court that when the Plan was adopted, the duty of self-executing disclosure was only made applicable to cases on the Standard Management Track, it is hereby

ORDERED that the court hereby clarifies that the duties of self executing disclosure prescribed by this Plan at the time of its adoption do not apply to cases on the Special Management Track, and it is further

ORDERED that the attached Civil Justice Expense and Delay Reduction Plan shall remain in effect until December 31, 1997, and it is further

ORDERED that the Civil Justice Expense and Delay Reduction Plan is promulgated by this Court pursuant to 28 U.S.C. §§ 471, 472 and that this Plan, as it may be amended from time to time, shall be maintained in the Office of the Clerk of Court for public inspection, and, it is further

ORDERED that the fact of the Civil Justice Expense and Delay Reduction Plan's extension shall be published by the Clerk of Court to inform members of the bar and public of its adoption and extension and to afford opportunity for public notice and comment.

Approval of Pre-Judgment Notice of 28 U.S.C. § 3101(d)

APPROVAL OF PRE-JUDGMENT NOTICE OF 28 U.S.C. § 3101(d)

PROCEDURAL ORDER

In accordance with Section 3101(d) of the Federal Debt Collections Procedures Act of 1990, 28 U.S.C. § 3101(d), the form and content of the pre-judgment notice to be provided to the debtors when the government seeks a pre-judgment remedy under Section 3101, et seq. as set forth below, is hereby APPROVED:

IN THE UNITED STATES DISTRICT COURT
FOR THE EASTERN DISTRICT OF PENNSYLVANIA

United States of America,)
   Plaintiff,)
)
  v.) Case No. :_____
)
)
Defendant(s))

CLERK'S NOTICE OF PREJUDGMENT (_____)
[Attachment, Garnishment, Receivership, Sequestration]

You are hereby notified that this [property] is being taken by the United States Government ("the Government"), which believes that [name of debtor] owes it a debt of $ [amount] for [reason for debt]. The Government has filed a lawsuit to collect this debt. The Government has determined that it must take possession of this property at this time because [recite the pertinent ground or grounds from section 3101(b)]. The Government wants to be sure [name of debtor] will satisfy any indebtedness the court determines is due.

You are hereby notified that there are exemptions under the law which may protect some of the property from being taken by the Government if [name of debtor] can show that the exemptions apply. Attached is a summary of the major exemptions which apply in most situations in the State of [State where property is located]:

 [A statement summarizing in plain and understandable English the election available with respect to such State under Section 3014 and the types of property that may be exempted under each of the alternatives specified in paragraphs (1) and (2) of Section 3014(a), and a statement that different property may be so exempted with respect to the State in which the debtor resides.]

If you are [name of debtor] and you disagree with the reason the Government has given for taking your property at this time, or if you think you do not owe the money to the Government that it says you do, or if you think the property the Government is taking qualifies under one of the above exemptions, you have a right to ask the court to convene a hearing so it can consider your views, including returning your property to you.

If you want a hearing, you must promptly notify the court. You must make your request in writing, and either mail it or deliver it in person to the Clerk of the Court at [address]. If you wish, you may use this notice to request the hearing by checking the box below and mailing or delivering this notice to the court clerk. You must also send a copy of your request to the Government at [address], so the Government will know that you want a hearing and can be present at the hearing. The hearing will take place seven (7) days after the clerk receives your request, if you ask for it to take place that quickly and if the court can hear you that soon. Under all circumstances the hearing will take place as soon as possible.

At the hearing you may explain to the judge why you think you do not owe the money to the Government, why you disagree with the reason given by the Government for having to take your property, or why you believe the property the Government has taken is exempt or is owned by someone else. You may present any or all of these claims at the hearing.

If you think you live outside the Federal judicial district in which the court is located, you may request, within twenty-one (21) days after you receive this notice, that this proceeding to take your property be transferred by the court to another court located in the Federal judicial district in which you reside.

Standing Orders

You must make this request in writing, and either mail it or deliver it in person to the Clerk of the Court at [address]. You must also send a copy of your request to the Government at [address], so the Government will know you want the proceeding to be transferred to another court location.

Be sure to keep a copy of this notice for your own records. If you have any questions about your rights or about this procedure, you should contact a lawyer, an office of public legal assistance, or the Clerk of the Court. The Clerk is not permitted to give legal advice, but can refer you to other sources of information.

                                      CLERK
                                      UNITED STATES DISTRICT COURT

It is further Ordered that a copy of the Pre-Judgment Notice shall accompany all Pre-Judgment Writs issues by the Court.

Dated: May 7, 1992

STANDING ORDERS RE: 1993 AMENDMENTS TO FEDERAL RULES OF CIVIL PROCEDURE

STANDING ORDER

AND NOW, this 1st day of December, 1993, the Judges of this Court having determined that:

Some of the new provisions in the Federal Rules of Civil Procedure included in the amendments that became effective on December 1, 1993, authorize each United States district court, by order, to direct that the provisions shall not be followed in the district;

Some of the new provisions are inconsistent with this Court's Civil Justice Expense and Delay Reduction Plan (referred to in this Standing Order as "the Plan"), adopted in accordance with the Civil Justice Reform Act of 1990, 28 U.S.C. §§ 471–482.

Efficient judicial administration to secure the just, speedy, and inexpensive determination of civil litigation mandated by Rule 1 of the Federal Rules of Civil Procedure requires the Court to allow adequate time for its Judges, its Civil Justice Reform Act Advisory Group, the Federal Courts Committee of the Philadelphia Bar Association, the Local Civil Rules Advisory Committee, other interested groups and members of its bar in general to evaluate the new provisions in light of the Plan and other aspects of established practice in the Court; and

After its evaluation, the Court will decide which of the optional provisions, if any, will be followed in this district and what changes, if any, will be made in the Local Rules of Civil Procedure.

NOW, THEREFORE, in accordance with the resolution approved by the Judges of this Court on November 8, 1993, it is

ORDERED as follows:

    1. Until further action by this Court, the following provisions in the Federal Rules of Civil Procedure will not be in effect in this district:

        a. The requirement in Rule 26(a)(1) for Initial Disclosures. The provisions for Self-Executing Disclosure in section 4:01 of the Plan will continue to be in effect.

        b. The requirement in Rule 26(a)(4) that disclosures be filed. Demands for disclosure under the Plan, disclosures under Rules 26(a)(2) and (3) of the Federal Rules of Civil Procedure and stipulations under Rule 29 of those rules that do not require court approval will be subject to all of the provisions in paragraphs (a) through (e) in Local Rule of Civil Procedure 26.1.

c. The requirements in Rule 26(f) for a meeting of the parties, the development of a proposed discovery plan and a written report to the court and the prohibition in the first sentence of Rule 26(d) against seeking discovery before the occurrence of a 26(f) meeting.

The provisions in Sections 3:01 and 7:01 of the Plan, requiring the parties to confer, and the provision in Section 4:01(b) on timing and Sequence of Discovery will continue to be in effect except that, notwithstanding the provision in Section 4:01(b), a party may take a deposition before the time specified in that section if the notice contains a certification in accordance with Rule 30(a)(2)(c) of the Federal Rules of Civil Procedure.

2. Nothing in this Standing Order shall be construed to limit the discretion of any judicial officer to take whatever steps he or she decides are appropriate in the interest of just and speedy disposition of a case assigned to him or her, including steps identical with or similar to provisions in rules that this Standing Order provides are not in effect in this district.

3. References in this Standing Order to specific provisions of the Plan as continuing to be in effect are solely for clarification. The Plan in its entirety, except as expressly stated in paragraph 1(c) of this Standing Order, continues to be in effect.

4. The requirements and limitations in the Federal Rules of Civil Procedure identified in paragraphs 1(a), (b), and (c) of this Standing Order as not being in effect in this district shall not be in effect in the United States Bankruptcy Court for the Eastern District of Pennsylvania.

5. Suggestions for consideration by the court in its evaluation of the new provisions in the Federal Rules of Civil Procedure should be submitted in writing to the Clerk of Court, 2609 United States Courthouse, Philadelphia, Pennsylvania 19106-1797, on or before January 31, 1994.

AS AMENDED OCTOBER 1, 1997

NOTICE

On September 22, 1997, the Court amended its Standing Order of December 1, 1993, so as to rescind Section 1(c), by which the Court opted out of the limitations of Federal Rules of Civil Procedure 30(a)(2), 31(a)(2), concerning depositions, and 33(a) concerning interrogatories. The Court also retitled Section 1(d) as Section 1(c). These amendments will apply to all cases filed on or after October 1, 1997. All members of our bar should familiarize themselves with this revised Standing Order.

A copy of the revised Standing Order is reproduced below. Additional copies of the revised Standing Order may be obtained from the office of the Clerk of Court by submitting a written or faxed request. The fax numbers are as follows: 215-597-6390 or 215-580-2167. The proposed amendment can also be downloaded from an Electronic Bulletin Board which may be reached at 215-597-0646 or 215-597-5384 and is available on the Internet at http://www.paed.uscourts.gov.

STANDING ORDER

AND NOW, this 22nd day of September, 1997, pursuant to the Resolution of the Judges of this Court on this date, it is hereby Ordered that effective October 1, 1997, the Court's Standing Order of December 1, 1993 dealing with the 1993 Amendments to the Federal Rules of Civil Procedure is amended to rescind Section 1(c) and to renumber Section 1(d) as Section 1(c).

PRESENTENCE INVESTIGATIONS AND TIME LIMITS

AND NOW, this 13th day of JUNE, 1994, in accordance with the resolution approved by the Judges of this court this same day, it is hereby

ORDERED that the following standing order is adopted for use in criminal cases in which sentences are imposed under the Sentencing Reform Act of 1984:

1. Sentencing will occur without unnecessary delay and not less than eighty (80) days following the date on which a defendant pleads guilty, nolo contendere, or is found guilty, unless an individual judge directs that the sentence be imposed on an earlier or later date.

2. At the time the presentence investigation and report are ordered, a sentencing hearing date will be fixed by the sentencing judge; and, the attorney for the Government will make available to the probation officer all investigative and file material relevant to the case. The sentencing hearing date may be continued if necessary.

3. Not less than thirty-five (35) days before the sentencing hearing, the probation officer must furnish the presentence report to the defendant, the defendant's counsel, and the attorney for the Government. The probation officer's recommendation for sentence will not be disclosed unless directed by an individual judge.

4. Within fourteen (14) days after receiving the presentence report, the parties shall deliver in writing to the probation officer, and to each other, any objections to any material information, sentencing classifications, sentencing guideline ranges, and policy statements contained in or omitted from the presentence report. If no objections will be filed, the probation officer shall be so notified in writing within the aforesaid time limits. Any objection not filed will be deemed waived unless the Court finds good cause for allowing it to be raised.

5. Should the attorney for the Government intend to file a motion for a downward departure under United States Sentencing Guideline Section 5K1.1, or from a statutory mandatory minimum, the probation officer will be notified in writing on or before the submission date set for the filing of objections, and be provided with whatever information supports the motion.

6. Not later than seven (7) days before the sentencing hearing, the probation officer must submit the presentence report to the Court, together with an addendum setting forth any unresolved objections, the grounds for those objections, and the probation officer's comments on the objections. At the same time, the probation officer must furnish the revisions of the presentence report and the addendum to the defendant, the defendant's counsel, and the attorney for the Government.

(This standing order takes into account the amendments to Rule 32 of the Federal Rules of Criminal Procedures which have an effective date of December 1, 1994).

STANDING ORDER
RE: SENTENCING REFORM ACT OF 1984

STAGE 1. Unless otherwise ordered by an individual judge, sentencing will occur without unnecessary delay not less than eighty (80) days after a defendant pleads guilty, nolo contendere, or is found guilty.

STAGE 2. Not less than thirty-five (35) days before the sentencing hearing, the probation officer must furnish the presentence report to the defendant, the defendant's counsel, and the attorney for the Government. The probation officer's recommendation for sentence will not be disclosed unless directed by an individual judge.

STAGE 3. Within fourteen (14) days after receiving the presentence report, the parties shall deliver in writing to the probation officer, and to each other, any objections to any material information, sentencing classifications, sentencing guideline ranges, and policy statements contained in or omitted from the presentence report. If no objections will be filed, the probation officer shall be so notified in writing within the aforesaid time limits. Any objection not filed will be deemed waived unless the Court finds good cause for allowing it to be raised.

STAGE 4. Should the attorney for the Government intend to file a motion for a downward departure under United States Sentencing Guideline Section 5K1.1, or from a statutory mandatory minimum, the probation officer will be notified in writing on or before the submission date set for the filing of objections, and be provided with whatever information supports the motion.

STAGE 5. Not later than seven (7) days before the sentencing hearing, the probation officer must submit the presentence report to the Court, together with an addendum setting forth any unresolved objections, the grounds for those objections, and the probation officer's comments on the objections. At the same time, the probation officer must furnish the revisions of the presentence report and the addendum to the defendant, the defendant's counsel, and the attorney for the Government.

STAGE 6. The presentence report is a confidential document. Rule 32(b)(3)(A) provides that copies of the presentence report are provided to prosecution and the defense attorneys for the purpose of the sentencing hearing. The attorneys may retain these copies. The attorney for the Government may also retain the presentence report for use in collecting financial penalties. 18 U.S.C. § 3552(d).

Defendant: _____   Criminal No. _____

Date of Plea: _____

Date of Sentencing: _____

Time of Sentencing: _____ o'clock ____ m.

(To be distributed to each defendant and each counsel at time presentence report is ordered)

cc: Pretrial Services (via FAX)

Cr. 37 (2/96)

Part III

Clerk's Office Procedural Handbook

UNITED STATES DISTRICT COURT
FOR THE
EASTERN DISTRICT OF PENNSYLVANIA

CLERK'S OFFICE PROCEDURAL HANDBOOK

June 2013

Clerk's Office Procedural Handbook

This handbook has been prepared as a supplement to the Local Rules of the United States District Court for the Eastern District of Pennsylvania. It is intended to provide administrative information and act as a guide for specific procedural areas. However, if there is a conflict between this supplemental guide and the Local or Federal Rules of Procedure, the Rules govern.

I greatly acknowledge Marlene McHugh Anderson, Thomas Clewley, Kevin Dunleavy and Lucy Chin of my staff for their efforts in the production of this handbook.

We welcome any comments or suggestions for improving this handbook. Please forward your comments to: The Office of the Clerk of Court, United States District Court, Eastern District of Pennsylvania, 2609 United States Courthouse, Philadelphia, Pennsylvania 19106-1797 or FAX them to: (215) 597-6390.

Michael E. Kunz
Clerk of Court

http://www.paed.uscourts.gov

TABLE OF CONTENTS

ELECTRONIC CASE FILING SYSTEM 529
- A. Rule 5.1.2 Electronic Case Filing Procedures..........................529
- B. Eligibility, Registration and Password.......................................531
- C. Signature..531
- D. Excluded Cases and Documents 532
- E. Training Seminars..532

FILING A CIVIL ACTION 532
- A. Civil Justice Delay and Expense Reduction Plan 533
- B. Designation Form 533
  - Instructions for Completing the Designation Form 533
- C. Civil Cover Sheet (Form JS 44) 534
  - Instructions for Completing Civil Cover Sheet.........................534
- D. Case Management Track Designation Form 536
- E. Verifications..536
- F. Filing an Amended Complaint..536
- G. Class Action Complaints—Local Rule 23.1.............................536
- H. Copies of Complaints 536
- I. Service of Process 537
- J. Waiver of Service of Summons..537

DOCUMENTS 537
- A. Copies of Paper Documents..538
- B. Certificate of Service..538
- C. Third-Party Complaint..539
- D. Excluded Personal Identifiers—Local Rule of Civil Procedure 5.1.3..............539
- E. Electronic Case File Privacy—Local Rule of Criminal Procedure 53.2..........539
- F. Sealed Pleadings 539
- G. False Claims Act Cases 540
- H. Pleadings that are NOT Filed 540
- I. Facsimile Transmission of Notice of Orders in Civil and Criminal Cases 540
- J. Mail 541

MOTIONS 542

SUMMONS 542

JURISDICTION 542

SUBPOENAS 543
- A. Civil 543
- B. Criminal 544

FOREIGN SUBPOENAS...544
- A. Filing Procedure in Out-Of-State Court...................................544
- B. Service 544
- C. To Contest..544
- D. Attendance 544

525

Clerk's Office Procedural Handbook

DISCOVERY 544

TEMPORARY RESTRAINING ORDER (T.R.O.) 545

WRIT OF GARNISHMENT, ATTACHMENT AND EXECUTION 545

FILING OF JUDGMENT BY DEFAULT 545
    A.   Rule 55(a), Federal Rules of Civil Procedure 545
    B.   Rule 55(b), Federal Rules of Civil Procedure 545

MULTIDISTRICT LITIGATION 545

ARBITRATION 546
    A.   Procedure For Cases Eligible For Arbitration 546
    B.   Trial Procedure 546
    C.   Arbitrators 546
    D.   Arbitrators' Award 547
    E.   Demand for Trial De Novo 547

APPEALS 547
    A.   Civil 547
    B.   Criminal 547
    C.   Report and Recommendation of U.S. Magistrate Judge 547
    D.   Bankruptcy 547
    E.   Patent—"Little Tucker Act" Cases and Claims Court Transfer Cases 547
    F.   Service 548
    G.   Filing Fee 548
    H.   Preparation of the Record on Appeal 548

CERTIFICATION OF JUDGMENT (AO 451) 548

REFERRAL TO UNITED STATES MAGISTRATE JUDGE 548

POST JUDGMENT INTEREST RATE 549

TAXATION OF COSTS 549
    A.   Normally Allowable District Court Costs (sought pursuant to
          28 U.S.C. § 1920) in General 549
    B.   Normally Unallowable District Court Costs in General 551
    C.   Burden of Proof Regarding Normally Allowable District Court Costs
          (sought pursuant to 28 U.S.C. § 1920) 552
    D.   General Objections to Normally Allowable District Court Costs
          (sought pursuant to 28 U.S.C. § 1920) in their Entirety 553
    E.   Specific Objections to Normally Allowable District Court Costs
          (sought pursuant to 28 U.S.C. § 1920) 557
    F.   Special Procedures for Allowance of District Court Costs in Situations
          Involving Federal Rule of Civil Procedure 68 (and not involving
          28 U.S.C. § 1920) 563
    G.   Taxation of Appellate Court Costs by the Clerk of the District Court 563

COURTROOM DEPUTY CLERKS 589
    A.   New Case Procedures 589

Table of Contents

B.	Pretrial Practices	589
C.	Scheduling Cases	589
D.	Trial List	590
E.	Judicial Schedule of Trials—Automated System Inquiry (JUST-ASK)	590
F.	Lobby Kiosk Information System	591
G.	Busy Slips	591
H.	Attachments for Trial	591
I.	Continuances—Criminal Cases	591
J.	Motions	591
K.	Exhibits	591
L.	Other Duties	592

Listing of Courtroom Deputy Clerks. 592

STANDING ORDER RE: SENTENCING REFORM ACT OF 1984 594

AFTER-HOURS CONTACT FOR EMERGENCY MATTERS 594

AFTER-HOURS FILING DEPOSITORY 594

OPINIONS/CORRESPONDENCE CLERK 594

HOW TO FIND A CASE NUMBER 594

CLERK'S INDEX FILE BY NATURE OF SUIT. 595

COPYWORK 595

RECORDS ROOM. 595

CREDIT CARD COLLECTION NETWORK. 595

REQUIRED CHECK CONVERSION DISCLOSURE. 596

DEPOSITING/WITHDRAWING MONIES 596

A.	Deposits	596
B.	Registry Fund, Deposit Fund, Interest-Bearing Accounts	596

FINES 597

CENTRAL VIOLATIONS BUREAU (CVB). 597

BAIL BONDS 597

ATTORNEY ADMISSIONS 598

COURT REPORTING/RECORDING SERVICES 598

ELECTRONIC TRANSCRIPTS OF COURT PROCEEDINGS 598

DIGITAL AUDIO FILE ELECTRONIC ACCESS PROGRAM 599

VIDEOTAPE SERVICES 599

Clerk's Office Procedural Handbook

VIDEO TELECONFERENCING 599

COURTROOM TECHNOLOGY 599

INTERPRETERS' SERVICES 599

JURY SELECTION 600
    A.   Term of Jury Service 600
    B.   Excuse from Jury Service on Request 600
    C.   Payment 600

INCLEMENT WEATHER 600

PACER—PUBLIC ACCESS TO COURT ELECTRONIC RECORDS 600

INTERNET WEBSITE 601

LOCAL RULES 602

PORTABLE ELECTRONIC DEVICES AND PUBLIC TELEPHONE LOCATIONS 602

DIRECTORY OF PUBLIC TELEPHONE LOCATIONS 602

PERSONNEL DIRECTORY 604

LIST OF APPENDICES 613

INDEX 615

ELECTRONIC CASE FILING SYSTEM

The United States District Court for the Eastern District of Pennsylvania utilizes an automated civil docketing system, Case Management/Electronic Case Filing ("CM/ECF").

Effective May 27, 2003, dockets for all civil cases filed since July 1, 1990 and dockets for all criminal cases filed since July 1, 1992 will be available for viewing and printing from the CM/ECF system.

All new civil cases filed in this court are entered into this court's Electronic Case Filing ("ECF") system in accordance with provisions of the Electronic Case Filing Procedures **(Appendix A)**. CM/ECF provides a new, easy-to-use electronic case filing feature that will allow users to file and view court documents over the Internet. Documents are automatically docketed as part of the filing process and are immediately available electronically. CM/ECF also offers the following benefits:

- 24-hour access to filed documents over the Internet;
- automatic e-mail notice of case activity to attorneys of record and judges;
- ability to download and print documents directly from the court system;
- concurrent access to case files by multiple parties;
- secure storage of documents.

A. **Rule 5.1.2 Electronic Case Filing Procedures.** All cases and documents filed in this court are required to be filed on the ECF system in accordance with provisions of the ECF Procedures, as set forth below unless excepted under these procedures.

   1. **Definitions**

      (a) *"ECF Filing User"* means those who have Court-issued log-ins and passwords to file documents electronically.

      (b) *"Notice of Electronic Case Filing"* means the notice generated by the ECF system when a document has been filed electronically, stating that the document has been filed.

      (c) *"Judge"* means the District Judge assigned to the case, or the Magistrate Judge to whom all or any part of a case has been referred pursuant to 28 U.S.C. § 636.

      (d) *"Court"* shall mean the United States District Court for the Eastern District of Pennsylvania.

   2. **Scope of Electronic Case Filing**

      (a) All civil and criminal cases filed in this court are required to be entered into the court's ECF system in accordance with these ECF Procedures. **Unless an attorney is excused from ECF registration under Section 3 of these ECF Procedures or except** as expressly provided in **Section 16 and other sections** of these ECF Procedures, or as ordered by the judge, all pleadings, documents, motions, memoranda of law, petitions, certificates of service and other documents required to be filed with the clerk of court in connection with a case must be electronically filed.

      (b) The filing of all initial papers in civil cases, such as the complaint and the issuance and service of the summons, and, in criminal cases, the indictment or information, warrant for arrest or summons, will be accomplished by paper copy filed in the traditional manner rather than electronically. Parties must concurrently provide the clerk of court with a computer disk, in PDF format **(Appendix B)** containing a copy of all documents provided in paper form at the time of filing. All subsequent documents and pleadings must be filed electronically, except as provided in these ECF Procedures or as ordered by the judge. Under this paragraph, all attorneys are required to complete the ECF Validation of Signature form **(Appendix C)**, as described in Section 3**(c)** below.

Parties are invited to participate in a pilot program to file complaints electronically on the CM/ECF system. If you are interested in this program, please complete an information form (Appendix EE) and you will be contacted by the Clerk's Office for training.

(c) Once registered, an ECF Filing User may request to withdraw from participation in the ECF System by providing the clerk of court with written notice of the request which shall be forwarded to the Chief Judge for approval.

(d) Nothing in these ECF Procedures shall be construed to nullify or contradict the provisions set forth in Rule 26.1 of the Local Rules of Civil Procedure, *Discovery,* directing that interrogatories, requests for production and inspection and requests for admission under Fed. R.Civ.P. 33, 34 and 36 that answers, responses and objections to interrogatories and to Rules 34 and 36, and that requests, notices of depositions and depositions under Fed.R.Civ.P. 30 and 31, shall not be filed with the court.

(e) Nothing in these ECF Procedures shall be construed to nullify or contradict the provisions set forth in Rule 39.3 of the Local Rules of Civil Procedure, *Records, Files and Exhibits,* directing that the clerk of court maintain custody of all records, files and exhibits in all cases filed in this court until such time as the case is finally resolved, dismissed or abandoned, as set forth in paragraph (e) of Rule 39.3.

(f) All cases filed in the ECF System in which a notice of appeal is filed shall be governed by Rule 10 of the Federal Rules of Appellate Procedure and relevant Local Rules and internal operating procedures of the United States Court of Appeals for the Third Circuit, with any differences about whether the record truly discloses what occurred in the district court to be submitted to and settled by the judge. Cases in which there is a right of direct appeal to the United States Supreme Court shall be governed by the rules of the United States Supreme Court.

3. **Excuse From Registration; Format of Documents in Electronic Form**

An attorney who believes he or she should be excused from registering as an ECF Filing User may apply for an exception to this rule by detailed letter to the clerk of court, who shall forward the letter to the chief judge for decision. Thereafter, attorneys and others who are excused from registering as ECF Filing Users in accordance with this section are required to comply with the procedures set forth below.

(a) All complaints must be submitted on disk in portable document format (PDF) at the time of filing, so that the complaint may be entered into the District Court's ECF system, and must be accompanied by a courtesy copy of the complaint in paper format for use by the court; under this paragraph, all attorneys are required to complete the ECF Validation of Signature form **(Appendix C)**, as described in Paragraph (c) below.

(b) All documents filed by an attorney who has been excused from registering as an ECF Filing User, as defined under this rule, must be submitted on disk in PDF, so that the filings may be entered into the District Court's ECF system, and must be accompanied by a courtesy copy of the document in paper format for use by the court; under this paragraph, all attorneys are required to complete the ECF Validation of Signature form, as described in Paragraph (c) below.

(c) Attorneys who complete the ECF Validation of Signature form will receive a signature code which must be used by the attorney on the signature line of all courtesy copies submitted with a disk for purposes of signature validation pursuant to Rule 11 of the Federal Rules of Civil Procedure; the document as submitted under Section 3 of this rule will constitute the original document, except for those documents which are excluded from the provisions of rule as set forth in Section 16 of the rule; attorneys are required to have submitted a completed ECF Validation of Signature form just once in order to file all complaints and documents in all subsequent cases in this court.

Electronic Case Filing System

(d) Service of process will continue to be made in accordance with those provisions set forth in Rule 5 of the Federal Rules of Civil Procedure.

(e) For convenience of attorneys who do not have access to compatible hardware or software, a computer with PDF conversion capability is available in the Clerk's Offices at Philadelphia and Allentown, with assistance for PDF conversion provided by Clerk's Office staff as needed; attorneys who have reason for not providing this material on disk are required to notice the Clerk's Office in writing attached to the document, explaining the reason for not providing this material on disk.

(f) Attorneys who have been excused under this section from registering as ECF Filing Users are requested to register and participate in the court's Program for Facsimile Service of Notice to Counsel or Litigants in Civil and Criminal Cases.

(g) Those documents and categories of cases which are now excluded from the provisions of this section consistent with the policy of the Judicial Conference of the United States, as may be amended from time to time, are set forth in this rule **(Appendix A, Section 16)**.

B. **Eligibility, Registration and Password.**

(a) Unless otherwise excused, attorneys admitted to the bar of this court, including those admitted pro hac vice, are required to register as ECF Filing Users of the court's ECF system. Registration is in a form prescribed by the clerk of court **(Appendix D)** and requires the Filing User's name, address, telephone number, Internet e-mail address and a declaration that the attorney is admitted to the bar of this court and is a member in good standing.

(b) Upon the approval of the judge, a party to a case who is not represented by an attorney may register as an ECF Filing User in the ECF System solely for purposes of the action. Registration is in a form prescribed by the clerk of court and requires identification of the case as well as the name, address, telephone number and Internet e-mail address of the party. If, during the course of the case, the party retains an attorney who appears on the party's behalf, the attorney must advise the clerk of court to terminate the party's registration as a Filing User upon the attorney's appearance.

(c) Registration as an ECF Filing User constitutes agreement to receive and consent to make electronic service of all documents as provided in these ECF Procedures in accordance with Rule 5(b)(2)(D) of the Federal Rules of Civil Procedure and the Federal Rules of Criminal Procedure, as referenced in Rule 49(b) of the Federal Rules of Criminal Procedure. This agreement and consent is applicable to all future cases until revoked by the ECF Filing User.

(d) Once registration is completed, the ECF Filing User will receive notification of the user log-in and password. ECF Filing Users agree to protect the security of their passwords and immediately notify the clerk of court by telephone, with said notification confirmed immediately thereafter in writing delivered by e-mail, facsimile or hand-delivery to the attention of the clerk of court, if they learn that their password has been compromised. Users may be subject to sanctions by the judge for failure to comply with this provision. For security reasons, the court recommends that ECF Filing Users periodically change their passwords, which shall be done by notifying the clerk of the court who shall implement the change.

C. **Signature.**

(a) The user log-in and password required to submit documents to the ECF System serve as the ECF Filing User's signature on all electronic documents filed with the court. They also serve as a signature for purposes of Rule 11(a) of the Federal Rules of Civil Procedure, the Local Rules of this court, and any other purpose for which a signature is required in connection with proceedings before the court. Each document filed electronically must, if possible, indicate that it has been electronically filed. Electronically filed documents must include a signature block and must set forth the name, address, telephone number and the attorney's state bar

Clerk's Office Procedural Handbook

identification number, if applicable. In addition, the name of the ECF Filing User under whose log-in and password the document is submitted must be preceded by an "s/" and typed in the space where the signature would otherwise appear.

(b) No ECF Filing User or other person may knowingly permit or cause to permit a Filing User's password to be used by anyone other than an authorized agent of the Filing User.

(c) Documents requiring signatures of more than one party must be electronically filed either by: (1) submitting a scanned document containing all necessary signatures; (2) representing the consent of the other parties on the document; (3) identifying on the document the parties whose signatures are required and by the submission of a notice of endorsement by the other parties no later than three business days after filing; or (4) any other manner approved by the court.

D. **Excluded Cases and Documents.** A list of types of documents and categories of cases, which are presently excluded from the provisions of ECF Procedures, as may be amended from time to time, is attached hereto and made a part of ECF Procedures **(Appendix A, Section 16)**.

E. **Training Seminars.** ECF training is available to members of the bar, paralegals, secretaries and automation support staff. For information regarding participation in the court's CM/ECF system, see **Appendix E**.

FILING A CIVIL ACTION

The filing of **all** initial papers in civil cases, such as the complaint and the issuance and service of the summons, and, in criminal cases, the indictment or information, warrant for arrest or summons, will be accomplished by paper copy filed in the traditional manner rather than electronically. Parties must concurrently provide the clerk of court with a computer disk, PDF format containing a copy of all documents provided in paper form at the time of filing. All subsequent documents and pleadings must be filed electronically, except as provided in ECF Procedures or as ordered by the judge. Under this paragraph, all attorneys are required to complete the ECF Validation of Signature form, as described in Section 3(c) of the ECF Procedures.

All new civil actions are to be filed on 8½" x 11" paper in the Clerk's Office, Room 2609, second floor of the Federal Courthouse, or in the divisional office in Allentown, Pennsylvania between the hours of 8:30 a.m. and 5:00 p.m. Filings are accepted by mail, as well as in person. The addresses are:

United States District Court
Eastern District of Pennsylvania
U.S. Courthouse
601 Market Street, Room 2609
Philadelphia, PA 19106-1797
(215) 597-7704

United States District Court
U.S. Courthouse and Federal Building
504 West Hamilton Street, Suite 1601
Allentown, PA 18101-1500
(610) 434-3896

Parties are invited to participate in a pilot program to file complaints electronically on the CM/ECF system. If you are interested in this program, please complete an information form (Appendix EE) and you will be contacted by the Clerk's Office for training.

The cost for filing a civil action is $400.00 (A $350.00 filing fee established by 28 U.S.C. § 1914(A), plus a $50.00 administrative fee established by the Judicial Conference. The $50.00 administrative fee shall not be charged to petitioners in civil actions seeking Habeas Corpus relief pursuant to 28 U.S.C.

§§ 2241-2266). Payment may be made in three forms: cash, credit card, or checks made payable to **"Clerk, U.S. District Court"**.

All subsequent filings, motions, pleadings and other papers are to be filed electronically by the ECF system or on disk in PDF format accompanied by a courtesy copy, by mail or in person in Room 2609 at the courthouse in Philadelphia or Suite 1601 at the divisional office in Allentown.

Counsel should include the following in the drafting of the complaint or petition: (a) name of court; (b) name and address of both parties, in caption form; (c) title of action; (d) a short and plain statement of the grounds upon which the court's jurisdiction depends; (e) a short and plain statement of the claim showing that the pleader is entitled to relief; (f) a demand for judgment for the relief to which the plaintiff deems himself entitled; (g) jury demand; and (h) name, address, Pennsylvania attorney identification number and signature of plaintiff's attorney.

A. Civil Justice Expense and Delay Reduction Plan

In response to a mandate by the Civil Justice Reform Act of 1990 and in an effort to reduce the cost and delay of civil litigation in the federal courts, this district adopted The Civil Justice Expense and Delay Reduction Plan with an effective date of December 31, 1991. A copy of the plan can be obtained by contacting Aida Ayala at 267-299-7099. This district was selected as a pilot district and was required to implement a plan by December 31, 1991. An Advisory Group was appointed in April 1991 to prepare a report and recommendation on the status of the Eastern District of Pennsylvania. Based on this report, the judges adopted the expense and delay reduction plan.

B. Designation Form

The designation form **(Appendix F)** is to be used by counsel to designate the category of the cause of action for the purpose of assignment to the appropriate calendar. It is to be completed by plaintiff's counsel and submitted at the time of filing.

The court requires two (2) copies of the designation form. Additional forms are not required for additional defendants, nor are additional forms required when the United States Government or an officer or agency thereof is involved.

Instructions for Completing the Designation Form

1. **Address of Plaintiff and Defendant.** House or apartment address, street, city, county and zip code are required in this section.

2. **Place of Accident.** The place of the accident, incident, or transaction; house or apartment address, street, city, county and zip code are required in this section. Note: Counsel should continue on reverse side if additional space is needed to fully explain this matter.

3. **Disclosure Statement.** In accordance with Federal Rule of Civil Procedure 7.1(a), *Disclosure Statement,* a nongovernmental corporate party to an action or proceeding in a district court must file copies of a statement that identifies any parent corporation and any publicly held corporation that owns 10% or more of its stock or state that there is no such corporation **(Appendix G)**.

    A party must file the Rule 7.1(a) statement with its first appearance, pleading, petition, motion, response, or other request addressed to the court, and promptly file a supplemental statement upon any change in the information that the statement requires.

4. **Related Cases.** This refers to pending cases or cases disposed of in the United States District Court for the Eastern District of Pennsylvania within *a one-year period.*

    If the case is related, counsel must indicate the case number, the presiding judge, and the date terminated.

5. **Civil Category Checklist.** Counsel are required to determine whether the action arises under: (a) federal question, Title 28 U.S.C. § 1331; or (b) diversity, Title 28 U.S.C. § 1332. Counsel must check off the one specific category within the appropriate classification to which that case pertains. This is for the purpose of proper case assignment by classification.

6. **Arbitration Certification.** The arbitration certification is used to determine whether or not the case exceeds the damages threshold of $150,000, which is the maximum amount for any arbitration proceeding. Counsel are advised to refer to Local Civil Rule 53.2, Section 3, Paragraph C, which states that damages will be presumed to be less than $150,000 and thus eligible for arbitration unless counsel, at the time of filing, states that the damages exceed that amount. The effect of this certification is to remove the case from eligibility for arbitration. Date and signature must be included in this section.

7. **Date and Signature.** The date of filing and signature of counsel is required in this section.

C. Civil Cover Sheet (Form JS 44)

The Civil Cover Sheet **(Appendix H)** is required by the Clerk of Court for the purpose of initiating the civil docket sheet. It is completed by plaintiff's counsel and submitted at the time of filing. Only one civil cover sheet is required by the court to accompany the complaint, regardless of whether or not the United States of America, or an officer of an agency thereof, is a party.

Instructions for Completing a Civil Cover Sheet

1. **Parties.** The complete name(s) and address(es) of plaintiff(s) and defendant(s) are required in this section.

2. **Attorneys.**

    Plaintiff's Attorney: Firm name, address, Pennsylvania bar identification number and telephone number is required.

    Defendant's Attorney: Firm name, address, Pennsylvania bar identification number and telephone number, if known.

3. **Jurisdiction.** Counsel should place an "X" in the appropriate box corresponding to the jurisdictional basis of the action.

    The following order of priority should be utilized in cases where more than one basis of jurisdiction is set out in the complaint.

    (a) United States Plaintiff. Jurisdiction is based on 28 U.S.C. §§ 1345 and 1348. Suits by agencies and officers of the United States are in this category.

    (b) United States Defendant. Jurisdiction is based on 28 U.S.C. § 1346 and includes suits against agencies and officers of the United States.

    (c) Federal Question. Various statutes give the district court jurisdiction to hear and determine controversies where federal rights between parties are covered by statute or Constitution.

    (d) Diversity of Citizenship. This refers to suits under 28 U.S.C. § 1332. In this situation, parties are residents of different states.

    Note: If diversity is checked, it must be further categorized in the box to the right.

4. **Nature of Suit.** Counsel must indicate the general description of the suit by placing an "X" in the appropriate box. If more than one possible category applies, select the most explicit and specific classification.

    Note: Only one check mark is to be made in this area.

Filing a Civil Action

Explanatory information for social security. In the section for Social Security, six possible types of claims or actions are listed.

Suit Code Number	Abbreviation for Cause of Action	Substantive Statement Explaining Type
861	HIA	All claims for health insurance benefits (Medicare) under Title XVIII, Part A, of the Social Security Act, as amended. Also includes claims by hospitals, skilled nursing facilities, etc. for certification as providers of services under the program. (42 U.S.C. § 395f(b)).
862	BL	All claims for "black lung" benefits under Title IV, Part B, of the Federal Coal Mine Health and Safety Act of 1969 (30 U.S.C. § 923).
863	DIWC	All claims filed by insured workers for disability insurance benefits under Title II of the Social Security Act, as amended; plus all claims filed for child's insurance benefits based on disability (42 U.S.C. § 405(g)).
863	DIWW	All claims filed for widows' or widowers' insurance benefits based on disability under Title XVI of the Social Security Act, as amended (42 U.S.C. § 405(g)).
864	SSID	All claims for supplemental security income payments based upon disability filed under Title XVI of the Social Security Act, as amended.
865	RSI	All claims for retirement (old age) and survivors' benefits under Title II of the Social Security Act, as amended. (42 U.S.C. § 405(g)).

5. **Origin.** Counsel are required to indicate which one of the seven possible categories is applicable to the case being filed. The following explanatory guidelines should be consulted in this matter.

    (a) Original Proceeding—This category will be the appropriate one for most cases.

    (b) Removed from State Court—Proceedings initiated in the State Courts may be removed to the District Court under Title 28 U.S.C. § 1441.

    (c) Remanded from Appellate Court—Use the date of remand as the filing date.

    (d) Reinstated or Reopened—Use the reopening date as the filing date.

    (e) Transferred from Another District—Self-explanatory.

    (f) Multidistrict Litigation—Use when a multidistrict case is transferred into this district (Title 28 U.S.C. § 1407).

    (g) Appeal to District Judge from Magistrate Judgment—Self-explanatory.

6. **Cause of Action.** In this section, a citation must be used for the U.S. civil statute under which the filing is made. In addition, a brief statement of the cause of action must also be included by counsel.

7. **Class Action.** This item should be checked if the case is alleged to be a class action under Fed. R. Civ. P. 23.

    Demand: The dollar amount which is sought in the case should be inserted in this space.

Clerk's Office Procedural Handbook

Jury Demand: Counsel should check "yes" in this section only if a jury trial is demanded in the complaint.

8. **Related Case(s), if any.** This section is used to reference related pending cases, if any. If there are related pending cases or cases disposed of within a one-year period, insert the docket numbers and the corresponding judges' names for such cases.

9. **Date and Signature.** The date of filing and the signature should be the final insertion on the civil cover sheet.

D. Case Management Track Designation Form

Each civil case will be assigned to one of the following tracks **(Appendix I):**

1. **Habeas Corpus**—Cases brought under 28 U.S.C. § 2241 through § 2255.
2. **Social Security**—Cases requesting review of a decision of the Secretary of Health and Human Services denying the plaintiff Social Security benefits.
3. **Arbitration**—Cases designated for arbitration under Local Civil Rule 53.2.
4. **Asbestos**—Cases involving claims for personal injury or property damage from exposure to asbestos.
5. **Special Management**—Cases that do not fall into tracks 1 through 4 or that need special or intense management by the court due to one or more of the following factors:
    (a) large number of parties;
    (b) large number of claims;
    (c) complex factual issues;
    (d) large volume of evidence;
    (e) problems locating or preserving evidence;
    (f) extensive discovery;
    (g) exceptionally long time needed to prepare for disposition;
    (h) decision needed within an exceptionally short time;
    (i) need to decide preliminary issues before final disposition.
6. **Standard Management**—Cases that do not fall into any of the other tracks.

E. Verifications

Verifications or affidavits are not required to be filed with a complaint, except: (a) where the complaint seeks entry of a temporary restraining order [Federal Rule of Civil Procedure 65(b)]; and (b) in shareholder derivative actions (Federal Rule of Civil Procedure 23.1). In lieu of a verification or an affidavit, it is appropriate to submit an unsworn declaration in the form set forth in 28 U.S.C. § 1746.

F. Filing an Amended Complaint

A party may amend its pleading once as a matter of course within: (A) 21 days after serving it, or (B) if the pleading is one to which a responsive pleading is required, 21 days after service of a responsive pleading or 21 days after service of a motion under Rule 12(b), (e) or (f), whichever is earlier.

G. Class Action Complaints—Local Rule 23.1

Class action complaints must bear next to their caption the legend, "Complaint—Class Action". In addition, they must set forth certain "Class Action Allegations" which are described in Local Civil Rule 23.1.

H. Copies of Complaints

It is not necessary to deliver multiple copies of the complaint and amended complaint to the Clerk's Office to be served on the defendants. It is only necessary to deliver an original complaint or an original amended complaint for filing. The Clerk's Office will process all completed summonses and return them to counsel for service on the opposing party.

I. Service of Process

Defendants have 21 days after the service of the summons and complaint to file an answer to the complaint unless otherwise ordered by the court.

The U.S. Attorney has 60 days after service to file an answer to the complaint in actions against the United States of America, an officer or agency thereof.

J. Waiver of Service of Summons

Rule 4 of the Federal Rules of Civil Procedure requires certain parties to cooperate in saving cost of the service of the summons and complaint. A defendant who, after being notified of an action and asked to waive service of summons, fails to do so will be required to bear the cost of such service unless good cause is shown for its failure to sign and return the waiver.

It is not good cause for a failure to waive service that a party believes that the complaint is unfounded, or that the action has been brought in an improper place or in a court that lacks jurisdiction over the subject matter of the action or over its person or property. A party who waives service of the summons retains all defenses and objections (except relating to the summons or to the service of the summons), and may later object to the jurisdiction of the court or to the place where the action has been brought.

A defendant who waives service must, within the time specified on the waiver form, serve on the plaintiff's attorney (or unrepresented party) a response to the complaint and must also file a signed copy of the response with the court. If the answer or motion is not served within this time, a default judgment may be taken against the defendant. By waiving service, a defendant is allowed more time to answer than if the summons had been actually served when the request for waiver of service was received.

If you need additional information on filing complaints contact Rick Sabol, Operations Manager, at 267-299-7011.

DOCUMENTS

The original docket sheets, record files, and indices to all cases are available for inspection in the Clerk's Office, Room 2609, in Philadelphia or in Suite 1601 of the divisional office in Allentown. The civil dockets are divided among ten clerks and the last digit of each case number determines the docket clerk to whom the case is assigned for processing.

The following personnel perform case processing duties in the civil section in the Philadelphia Clerk's Office:

(#1)	Rob Fehrle	267-299-7001
(#2)	Kirk Kopacz	267-299-7002
(#3)	Tom Giambrone	267-299-7003
(#4)	Tashia Irving	267-299-7004
(#5)	Kimberly Williams	267-299-7005
(#6)	Michele Helmer	267-299-7006
(#7)	Joseph Lavin	267-299-7007
(#8)	Ashley Mastrangelo	267-299-7008
(#9)	Steve Gill	267-299-7009
(#10)	Frank DelCampo	267-299-7010

At the divisional office in Allentown, Pennsylvania, contact Evelyn Renner at 610-434-3896, Matthew A. Sheetz at 610-776-6116, Kris Yerry at 610-776-6115 or Lauren Sampson at 610-776-6121.

Criminal case processing is divided among clerks—Angelo Peso, 267-299-7160, James Hamilton, 267-299-7024, Kevin Eibel, 267-299-7035 and Mark Ciamaichelo, 267-299-7145. Carlos Cardona, 267-299-7023, reviews overall compliance with the Speedy Trial Act. The Magistrate Judges' Docket Clerk is Mark Ciamaichelo, 267-299-7145.

Rule 11 of the Federal Rules of Civil Procedure requires that every pleading, motion and other paper of a party represented by an attorney be signed by the attorney. Please be sure to date the pleadings, attach a certificate of service, and include the address and phone number of counsel. It is not necessary to send a cover letter when filing routine pleadings. However, if you are filing a pleading which requires special attention please include a cover letter.

The user log-in and password required to submit documents to the ECF system serve as the ECF Filing User's signature on all electronic documents filed with the court. They also serve as a signature for purposes of Rule 11(a) of the Federal Rules of Civil Procedure, the Local Rules of this court, and any other purpose for which a signature is required in connection with proceedings before the court. Each document filed electronically must, if possible, indicate that it has been electronically filed.

Electronically filed documents must include a signature block and must set forth the name, address, telephone number and the attorney's state bar identification number, if applicable. In addition, the name of the ECF Filing User under whose log-in and password the document is submitted must be preceded by an "**s/**" and typed in the space where the signature would otherwise appear. Documents requiring signatures of more than one party must be electronically filed either by: (1) submitting a scanned document containing all necessary signatures; (2) representing the consent of the other parties on the document; (3) identifying on the document the parties whose signatures are required and by the submission of a notice of endorsement by the other parties no later than three business days after filing; or (4) any other manner approved by the court.

A.   Copies of Paper Documents

For filing paper documents, a disk in PDF format of all motions, memoranda and briefs is needed, accompanied by a courtesy copy. We suggest you do not combine pleadings but file a separate pleading for each action in which a resolution is sought. When filing individual pleadings, it is easier and more efficient for the judge to have the option to sign an order ruling on the individual pleading rather than have to prepare an order.

It is important that pleadings be assembled with all documents in support thereof attached in sets. This ensures proper filing and also enables the judge to have complete sets. Note: The Clerk's Office does not date-stamp copies of pleadings unless accompanied by self-addressed, stamped envelopes.

B.   Certificate of Service

When filing pleadings, it is necessary to attach a certificate of service indicating the names of all counsel and/or parties you have served.

When an ECF Filing User electronically files a pleading or other document using the ECF system, a Notice of Electronic Case Filing shall automatically be generated by the system, and shall be sent automatically to all parties entitled to service under the Federal Rules of Civil Procedure, the Federal Rules of Criminal Procedure and the Local Rules of the Eastern District of Pennsylvania who have consented to electronic service. Electronic service of the Notice of Electronic Case Filing constitutes service of the filed document to all such parties and shall be deemed to satisfy the requirements of Rule 5(b)(2)(D) of the Federal Rules of Civil Procedure and Rule 49 of the Federal Rules of Criminal Procedure.

All documents filed using the ECF system shall contain a Certificate of Service stating that the document has been filed electronically and is available for viewing and downloading from the ECF system. The Certificate of Service must identify the manner in which service on each party was accomplished, including any party who has not consented to electronic service.

C. Third-Party Complaint

Leave of court is not necessary to file a third-party complaint if it is filed by the defendant within 14 days after service of the original answer to the complaint. However, leave of court is necessary if the defendant files the third-party complaint after the expiration of 14 days of the service of the answer. Counsel must file a <u>Motion for Leave to File a Third-Party Complaint</u>, together with a memorandum, proposed order and the proposed third-party complaint. When the judge signs the order, the clerk will process the complaint. (See Rule 14, Federal Rules of Civil Procedure.)

D. Excluded Personal Identifiers—Local Rule of Civil Procedure 5.1.3

As documents in civil cases may be available for personal inspection in the office of the clerk at the United States Courthouse, or, if filed electronically, may be made available on the court's Electronic Case Filing system, such personal identifiers as Social Security numbers, dates of birth, financial account numbers and names of minor children should be modified or partially redacted in all documents filed either in traditional paper form or electronically **(Appendix J)**.

E. Electronic Case File Privacy—Local Rule of Criminal Procedure 53.2

In compliance with the policy of the Judicial Conference of the United States and the E-Government Act of 2002, and in order to promote electronic access to documents in the criminal case files while also protecting personal privacy and other legitimate interests, parties shall refrain from including, or shall partially redact where inclusion is necessary, the following personal data identifiers from all documents filed with the court, including exhibits thereto, whether filed electronically or in paper, unless otherwise ordered by the court:

(1) **Social Security numbers.** If an individual's Social Security number must be included, only the last four digits of that number should be used.

(2) **Names of minor children.** If the involvement of a minor child must be mentioned, only the initials of the child should be used.

(3) **Dates of birth.** In an individual's date of birth must be included, only the year should be used.

(4) **Financial account numbers.** If financial account numbers are relevant, only the last four digits of the number should be used.

(5) **Home addresses.** If a home address must be included, only the city and state should be listed.

In compliance with the E-Government Act of 2002, a party wishing to file a document containing the personal data identifiers listed above may file an unredacted document under seal. This document shall be retained by the court as part of the record. The court may, however, still require the party to file a redacted copy for the public file. Trial exhibits may be safeguarded by means other than redaction, and the court may modify this rule to fit the requirements of particular cases.

The responsibility for redacting these personal identifiers rests solely with counsel and the parties. The Clerk need not review filings for compliance with this rule.

F. Sealed Pleadings

Sealed cases and documents ordered to be placed under seal are excluded from the provisions of the ECF Procedures **(Appendix A)** and must be filed in paper format filed in the traditional manner and not electronically. A motion to file documents under seal may be filed electronically unless prohibited by law. The order of the court authorizing the filing of documents under seal may be filed electronically unless prohibited by law. A paper copy of the order must be attached to the documents under seal and be delivered to the clerk of court. Include a cover letter identifying the contents of the envelope and information pertaining to the sealing of the document and/or case. The envelope containing the sealed pleading should reflect the caption and case number and should also identify the type of pleading contained in the envelope. If a document is being filed and sealed pursuant to a protective order or other order, refer to the sealed document in your cover letter. Please include the word "SEALED" near the top margin of the letter to alert the person opening the mail to exercise caution in processing the envelope.

Local Rule of Civil Procedure 5.1.5 provides that a document in a civil action may be filed under seal only if:

(1)   the civil action is brought pursuant to a federal statute that prescribes the sealing of the record or of certain specific documents; or

(2)   the Court orders the document sealed.

Where a document is sealed pursuant to § 5.1.5(a)(1), the continued status of the document under seal shall be governed by the relevant federal statute. If no federal statute governs, §§ 5.1.5(b)(2) and (c) shall apply.

When a document is sealed pursuant to § 5.1.5(a)(2), the document, if it remains in the custody of the Court, shall not be unsealed for two years after the conclusion of the civil action including all appeals, unless the Court orders otherwise.

If a document is still sealed at the conclusion of the two-year period and the Court has not entered an order continuing its sealed status beyond that time, the Clerk of Court shall notify the attorney for the party having submitted the sealed document at the attorney's address on the docket that the document will be unsealed unless the attorney or the submitting party advises the Clerk within sixty (60) days that said attorney or submitting party objects. If the attorney or submitting party objects to the unsealing of the document or if the Clerk's notification is returned unclaimed, the Court will make a determination, on a case-by-case basis, whether to maintain the document under seal, to unseal it, or to require further notification.

G.   False Claims Act Cases

All False Claims Act cases are opened by the docket clerk and filed **under seal**. The Complaint is docketed and no summons is issued. The Complaint is impounded and sent to the assigned Judge.

The Government may file a number of motions for an extension of the seal on the False Claims Act cases. If the Government files a Notice of Election to Decline Intervention or Election to Intervene, it is docketed and forwarded to the Court. If there is a complaint or an amended complaint attached to the notice, it is also docketed and forwarded to the Court. A summons is never issued unless directed by the court.

Only upon Court order is the complaint unsealed. At this point, the court will issue an order directing the Clerk's Office and the U.S. Attorney's Office how to proceed.

H.   Pleadings that are NOT Filed

The following pleadings are not filed pursuant to Local Civil Rule 26.1—Discovery:

- Requests for Production of Documents;
- Requests for Admissions;
- Interrogatories;
- Answers to Interrogatories;
- Notices of Deposition;
- Depositions.

I.   Facsimile Transmission of Notice of Orders in Civil and Criminal Cases

Attorneys who do not register to participate in the ECF program are requested to register and participate in the court's Program for Facsimile Service of Notice to Counsel or Litigants in Civil and Criminal Cases (the "Fax Noticing Program"). This program allows attorneys and pro se litigants to waive the provisions of Federal Rule of Civil Procedure 77(d) or Federal Rule of Criminal Procedure 49(c), which requires service of Notice of Orders and Judgments by means of mail, and instead consent to receive Notice of Orders and Judgments by means of facsimile transmission.

Forms of Consent to Receive Notice of Orders and Judgments by means of Facsimile Transmission and Waiver of the Provisions of Fed.R.Civ.P. 77(d) or Fed.R.Crim.P. 49(c) Providing for said Notice by means of Mail are available through the Clerk's Office **(Appendix K)**. Execution of the Facsimile Transmission Authorization form authorizes the Clerk of Court to serve notice of the entry of Orders or Judgments pursuant to Fed.R.Civ.P. 77(d) or Fed.R.Crim.P. 49(c) by facsimile in lieu of notice by means of mail. The Facsimile Transmission Authorization form also serves as Notice to and Authorization for the Clerk of Court to keep your name and the relevant information on file so that the Facsimile Transmission Authorization form will apply to all pending and future civil and criminal cases in which the attorney or pro se litigant is, or will be, either counsel or a party to litigation.

The waiver of the provisions providing for notice of the entry of Orders or Judgments by mail will include all pending civil and criminal cases in the Eastern District of Pennsylvania for the pro se litigant and all pending civil and criminal cases in the Eastern District of Pennsylvania in which the attorney either represents a party or is a party to the litigation, except for grand jury proceedings and impounded cases.

The Clerk of Court will make three attempts to transmit the Notice of Entry of Orders and Judgments by means of Facsimile. If after three attempts facsimile transmission is unsuccessful, Notice shall be made by means of mail pursuant to Fed.R.Civ.P. 77(d) or Fed.R.Crim.P. 49(c).

J.   Mail

The court in its ongoing commitment to provide more timely notice and enhance the level of service to members of the bar, litigants and the public, has joined efforts with the U.S. Postal Service to implement procedures to streamline and facilitate the delivery and processing of mail directed to and from the U.S. Courthouse.

Mail Sent to Counsel

In order to expedite delivery of notices from judicial officers and the clerk of court, members of the bar are requested to furnish the following information by completing an Information Form **(Appendix L)**: Name; Bar I.D. number; Firm, Address; City; State; **Zip Code and 4-digit extension number** and Facsimile number. Please return the completed form to the clerk of court at:

> Michael E. Kunz, Clerk of Court
> United States District Court
>   for the Eastern District of Pennsylvania
> U.S. Courthouse
> 601 Market Street, Room 2609
> Philadelphia, PA 19106-1797

or, by facsimile to: (215) 597-6390, (267) 299-7135 or (610) 434-6174.

Mail Sent to the Court

In order to take full advantage of these procedures, all mail sent to the United States District Court for the Eastern District of Pennsylvania at 601 Market Street, Philadelphia, PA and divisional office locations should include both the **zip code and 4-digit extension number.** Accordingly, all mail submitted to a judicial officer should be addressed as follows:

Name of Judicial Officer
United States District Court
   for the Eastern District of Pennsylvania
U.S. Courthouse
601 Market Street, Room #____
Philadelphia, PA 19106-1797

Michael E. Kunz, Clerk of Court
United States District Court
   for the Eastern District of Pennsylvania
U.S. Courthouse
601 Market Street, Room 2609
Philadelphia, PA 19106-1797

The use of bar coding technology currently available in word processing software packages in addressing envelopes is encouraged. A listing of the room numbers and Zip Code and 4-digit extension numbers of the judicial officers is available in the Clerk's Office **(Appendix M).**

MOTIONS

An application to the court for an order (unless made during a hearing or trial) shall be made in writing stating with particularity the grounds therefor, and shall set forth the relief sought. [See Federal Rule of Civil Procedure 7(b)(1) and Local Civil Rule 7.1(a).]

All motions shall contain a caption setting forth the name of the court, the title of the action, the file number, and a designation. [See Federal Rule of Civil Procedure 10(a).]

Every motion not certified as uncontested must be accompanied by a brief containing a concise statement of the legal contentions and authorities relied upon in support of the motion. Every motion shall be accompanied by a form of order which, if approved by the court, would grant the relief sought by the motion. Uncontested motions must be accompanied by a written statement as to the date and manner of service of the motion and supporting brief.

Every motion of a party represented by an attorney shall be signed by at least one attorney of record in the attorney's individual name, whose address shall be stated. A party who is not represented by an attorney shall sign each motion and state their correct address as indicated. [See Federal Rule of Civil Procedure 7(b)(3).]

A brief in opposition to the motion, together with such answer or other response as may be appropriate, is required if the served party opposes the motion.

The response to the motion must be made within 14 days after service of the motion and supporting brief, except that in the case of a motion under Fed. R. Civ. P. 12(b) or 56, the opposing party shall respond within twenty-one (21) days. [See Local Civil Rule 7.1(c).]

SUMMONS

Summonses shall be prepared by counsel **(Appendix N).** At the time of the filing of a complaint, all summonses shall be submitted to the Clerk of Court's office for signature and seal. Each defendant's name as it appears on the complaint (without its addresses) is to be typed on a summons and submitted to the deputy clerk. The original and sufficient copies for each defendant will be returned to counsel. To issue a second summons, file a Praecipe to Issue Alias Summons, naming the defendants.

JURISDICTION

The Eastern District of Pennsylvania includes the counties of Berks, Bucks, Chester, Delaware, Lancaster, Lehigh, Montgomery, Northampton, and Philadelphia. Please take note that effective April 19, 1999, jurisdiction of the county of Schuylkill was transferred to the U.S.D.C. Middle District of Pennsylvania.

Court for the Eastern District is held at Philadelphia, Reading, Allentown and Easton. When it appears from the designation form filed by counsel, or from the complaint, petition, motion, answer, response, indictment, information or other pleading in a civil or criminal case, that a plaintiff or defendant resides in or that the accident, incident, or transaction occurred in the counties of Berks, Lancaster, Lehigh, or Northampton, said case shall be assigned or reassigned for trial and pretrial procedures to a judge assigned to hear cases from Reading, Allentown or Easton.

All other cases, unless otherwise directed by the court, shall be tried in Philadelphia, and as each case is filed, assigned to a judge, who shall thereafter have charge of the case for all purposes. (See Local Civil Rule 40.1)

The Office of the Clerk of Court maintains two Clerk's Offices and accepts all filings in Philadelphia and Allentown, Pennsylvania at the following addresses:

United States District Court
Eastern District of Pennsylvania
United States Courthouse
601 Market Street, Room 2609
Philadelphia, PA 19106-1797
(215) 597-7704

United States District Court
Edward N. Cahn United States
Courthouse & Federal Building
504 West Hamilton Street, Suite 1601
Allentown, PA 18101-1500
(601) 434-3896

SUBPOENAS

(Rule 45, Federal Rules of Civil Procedure as amended December, 1991 and Rule 17, Federal Rules of Criminal Procedure)

A. Civil

Under Rule 45 of the Federal Rules of Civil Procedure, attorneys are authorized to issue subpoenas in the name of any court in which they are authorized to practice, and in the case of a deposition or a production of documents taking place in another district, in the name of the court where the deposition or the production is to take place. Attorneys issuing subpoenas must comply with the appropriate Federal Rules and with Local Rules.

Although it is no longer necessary that subpoenas be issued by the Clerk, the Clerk still has the authority to do so. In those instances in which counsel elects to have the Clerk of Court issue the subpoena, an original and one copy is needed for each witness to be served. The requirement that a subpoena be issued under seal has been abolished.

For a foreign deposition (deposition being taken in a state other than Pennsylvania), subpoenas are issued in blank by the Clerk's office, completed and served by counsel. They are not signed by the court where the original notice to take the deposition is filed.

All subpoenas may be served by a person who is not a party and is not less than 18 years of age. There is no provision in the rules for subpoenas to be served by mail.

Pursuant to F.R.C.P. 45 (b) (2), a subpoena may be served anywhere within the district. However, subpoenas may only be served outside the district if they are within 100 miles of the place designated in the subpoena for the deposition, trial, production of documents, hearing, or inspection. The federal rules also permit the service of a subpoena that is outside of the district but within the state if certain conditions are met. See, F.R.C.P. 45(b)(2). All subpoenas must be accompanied by a check made payable to the witness for the witness fee ($40 per day) and mileage (.555 cents per mile, round trip).

A copy of the subpoena is left with the witness and the original subpoena is returned to counsel.

B. Criminal

Under Rule 17 of the Federal Rules of Criminal Procedure, the Clerk of Court or the Magistrate Judge hearing the matter shall issue subpoenas. An original and one copy is needed for each witness to be served. All subpoenas issued by the Clerk are: 1) completed by counsel; 2) signed by the Clerk of Court; and 3) have the seal of the court over the name of the Clerk of Court before being served on the witness.

All subpoenas may be served by a person who is not a party and is not less than 18 years of age. There is no provision in the rules for subpoenas to be served by mail.

All subpoenas must be accompanied by a check made payable to the witness for the witness fee ($40.00 per day) and mileage (.555 cents per mile, round trip) unless the subpoena was issued on behalf of the United States or the court has determined upon an *ex parte* motion that the defendant is financially unable to pay.

A criminal subpoena requiring the attendance of a witness at a hearing or trial may be served at any place within the United States. Subpoenas which are directed at witnesses in a foreign country shall be issued in accordance with 28 U.S.C. § 1783.

For more detailed information on criminal subpoenas, refer to Federal Rule of Criminal Procedure 17.

FOREIGN SUBPOENAS
(Rule 45, Federal Rules of Civil Procedure)

A foreign subpoena is one issued out of a court other than where the original case is pending. For example, a case is pending in California but counsel would like to take the deposition of someone in the Eastern District of Pennsylvania.

A. Filing Procedure in Out-Of-State Court

Counsel should complete the subpoena forms, attach a check for the witness fee and mileage in the sum of $40.00 per day, plus .555 cents per mile, round trip, and send them, together with the stamped copy of the notice to take the deposition, to the United States District Court nearest where the deponent resides. The referred court where the deposition shall issue will stamp the name of the clerk, have the form signed by a deputy and affix the seal of its court over the signature.

B. Service

Service of the deposition subpoena must be by process server. There is no provision for service by mail. The subpoena is left with the witness, together with the witness fee. Counsel should make arrangements with a special process server for serving the subpoena.

C. To Contest

To contest a foreign (deposition) subpoena, file a motion to quash the deposition subpoena in the district where the subpoena was issued. File an original motion with the court. The case is filed as a miscellaneous case, with an associated filing fee of $46.00.

D. Attendance

A person to whom a civil subpoena for the taking of a deposition is directed may be required to attend at any place within 100 miles from the place where the person resides, is employed or transacts business in person, is served, or at such other convenient place as is fixed by an order of court.

DISCOVERY

In accordance with Local Civil Rule 26.1, discovery material is not filed with the court. The party serving the discovery material or taking the deposition shall retain the original and be the custodian of it. Every motion governing discovery shall identify and set forth, verbatim, the relevant parts of the interrogatory, request, answer, response, objection, notice, subpoena or deposition. Any party responding to the motion shall set forth, verbatim, in that party's memorandum any other part that the party believes necessary to the court's consideration of the motion.

TEMPORARY RESTRAINING ORDER (T.R.O.)

The assigned judge will set a time (usually the same day you file the T.R.O.) to meet with you and opposing counsel, if any. File the case in the Clerk's Office and give the clerk sufficient time to assemble the case for the judge and prepare the docket. If the judge grants the temporary restraining order, it is the responsibility of counsel for plaintiff to make service of the T.R.O. on the defendants.

We suggest you call Rick Sabol, the Operations Manager, at 267-299-7011 with any questions.

WRITS OF GARNISHMENT, ATTACHMENT AND EXECUTION

Writs of Garnishment and Attachment are prepared by counsel, filed with the Clerk's Office for processing and served by the U.S. Marshal. Counsel is responsible for Notice to opposing counsel. Notice must be given to all Owners of the Property **(Appendix O).**

You must wait 14 days before you can execute on a judgment, unless a Motion to Vacate, Motion to Stay, Motion for Reconsideration, or Motion for a New Trial is pending. If counsel requests, we will process the Praecipe for a Writ of Garnishment or Execution immediately, referring the matter to the assigned judge, if available, or to the judge's chambers for guidance (See, Rule 62, Federal Rules of Civil Procedure).

FILING OF JUDGMENT BY DEFAULT

A.   Rule 55(a), Federal Rules of Civil Procedure

You must file a request with the Clerk for the entry of a default for want of answer or other defense. Set forth the following information: (1) defendant was properly served on a particular date; (2) the time for defendant to file an answer to the complaint has expired; (3) that as of the date of the filing of the request for entry of the default, no answer (or motion to dismiss or motion for summary judgment) has been filed; (4) instruct the Clerk to enter a default against the defendant (name the defendant if more than one in a case) for want of answer or other defense.

If the defendant is an individual, be sure that the defendant was served a copy of the complaint by either special process server, or waiver of service provisions of the Federal Rules of Civil Procedure Rule 4(d) or otherwise in accordance with Federal Rules of Civil Procedure Rule 4.

B.   Rule 55(b), Federal Rules of Civil Procedure

To file a request for judgment by default for an individual, file an affidavit indicating the individual is (1) not an infant; (2) not incompetent; (3) not in the military; (4) amount due and owing; and (5) form of judgment.

To file a request for judgment by default for a corporation, file only an affidavit of amount due. If the amount asked for in the complaint differs from that asked for in the proposed judgment, the affidavit of amount due should explain the discrepancy.

MULTIDISTRICT LITIGATION

Due to the volume of litigation and the complexity of procedural requirements, those cases that are classified as being multidistrict litigation are governed by a separate and unique set of procedural rules. These rules are contained in the Procedural Manual for Multidistrict Litigation. Counsel may review this manual in the Clerk's Office, Room 2609, or may purchase copies from the Multidistrict Litigation Panel in Washington, D.C. Specific requests for information and related inquiries should be directed to Jeffrey N. Luthi, Clerk of the Panel, Multidistrict Litigation Panel, One Columbus Circle, N.E., Suite G-255, North Lobby, Washington, D.C. 20002-8004 or at (202) 502-2800.

The deputy clerk with general responsibility for local involvement in multidistrict litigation matters is Tom Dempsey, at (267-299-7018).

On July 29, 1991, the Judicial Panel on Multidistrict Litigation entered an opinion and order transferring all asbestos cases that were not on trial and were pending outside the Eastern District of Pennsylvania to this Court and assigning them to the late Honorable Charles R. Weiner for coordinated or consolidated pretrial proceedings pursuant to 28 U.S.C. § 1407, MDL 875, In Re: Asbestos Product Liability Litigation. MDL 875 has been reassigned to the Honorable Eduardo C. Robreno. The deputy clerk with general responsibility is Tom Dempsey (267-299-7018).

ARBITRATION

Our arbitration program provides litigants with a more prompt and less expensive alternative to the traditional courtroom trial. It has been in operation since 1978 and includes all civil cases (except social security cases, cases in which a prisoner is a party, cases alleging a violation of a constitutional right and cases where jurisdiction is based on 28 U.S.C. § 1343) where money damages only are sought in an amount not exceeding $150,000. Counsel are advised to refer to Local Civil Rule 53.2 for the specific types and categories of cases that are considered to be eligible for arbitration.

A. Procedure for Cases Eligible for Arbitration

When a complaint is filed, our local civil rule provides that damages are presumed to be not in excess of $150,000 unless counsel certifies that the damages exceed that amount. Immediately after the answer is filed, the attorneys receive a letter from the Clerk's Office advising them of the date for the arbitration hearing and also notifying them that discovery must be completed within 90 days. The clerk schedules the arbitration hearing for a specific day, usually a date about four months after an answer has been filed. In the event a party files a motion for judgment on the pleadings, summary judgment, or similar relief, our local rule provides that the case may not be heard until the court has ruled on the motion. However, the filing of a motion after the judge designates the arbitrators who will hear the case (usually about 30 days prior to the arbitration hearing) shall not stay the arbitration unless the judge so orders.

B. Trial Procedure

Although the Federal Rules of Evidence are designated as guides for the admissibility of evidence at the arbitration hearing, copies or photographs of exhibits must be marked for identification and delivered to the adverse party at least ten days prior to arbitration. The arbitrators shall receive such exhibits in evidence without formal proof, unless counsel has been notified at least five days prior to the hearing that their opponent intends to raise an issue concerning the authenticity of the exhibit. The arbitration hearing is not recorded unless a party at their own expense arranges for a recording. The arbitrators are authorized to change the date of the arbitration hearing, provided it takes place within 30 days of the date originally scheduled.

C. Arbitrators

We currently have over 1500 lawyers certified as arbitrators. In order to qualify for certification, the lawyer must be admitted to practice before our court, be a member of the bar for at least five years, and be determined by our Chief Judge to be competent to perform the duties of an arbitrator. An arbitrator receives $150 for each case arbitrated. Three arbitrators are appointed for each case. They are randomly selected by the Clerk and each panel of three arbitrators is composed of one whose practice is primarily representing plaintiffs, one whose practice is primarily representing defendants, and one whose practice does not fit either category. The arbitrators are scheduled for hearing dates several months in advance. However, it is not until the judge signs the order designating the arbitrators who will hear the case (approximately 30 days prior to the arbitration hearing) that counsel learn the identity of the arbitrators and the arbitrators become aware of the case assigned to them.

D. Arbitrators' Award

Immediately after the hearing, the arbitrators make a simple award, e.g., "Award in favor of defendant" or "Award in favor of plaintiff in the amount of $X against (naming one or more defendants)." The arbitrators are instructed that they should not file findings of fact, conclusions of law nor opinions of any kind. The arbitrators' award shall be entered as the final judgment of the Court, unless within 30 days of the filing of the award a party demands a trial de novo.

E. Demand for Trial De Novo

Upon the filing of a demand for trial de novo, the case proceeds as if it had never been heard by the arbitrators.

APPEALS

A. Civil

In civil cases, you have 30 days to file an appeal, unless the government is a party, in which case you have 60 days. The time commences from the date the order or judgment is entered on the docket (calendar days, not working days). A cross appeal should be filed 14 days from the filing of the first appeal.

All cases filed in the ECF System in which a notice of appeal is filed shall be governed by Rule 10 of the Federal Rules of Appellate Procedure and relevant Local Rules and internal operating procedures of the United States Court of Appeals for the Third Circuit, with any differences about whether the record truly discloses what occurred in the district court to be submitted to and settled by the judge. Cases in which there is a right of direct appeal to the United States Supreme Court shall be governed by the rules of the United States Supreme Court.

For cases filed in paper format, an original notice of appeal, a copy for each counsel of record, a copy for the Third Circuit Court of Appeals and a copy for the District Court Judge are needed.

B. Criminal

In criminal cases you have 14 days to file an appeal. Cross appeals should also be filed within 14 days.

For cases filed in paper format, an original notice of appeal, a copy for all counsel of record, a copy for the Third Circuit Court of Appeals and a copy for the District Court Judge are needed. Also needed is the Clerk's Information Sheet concerning criminal cases in which a notice of appeal is filed.

If the attorney is court-appointed, pursuant to the provisions of the Criminal Justice Act, a filing fee is not required.

C. Report and Recommendation of U.S. Magistrate Judge

A party has 14 days to file objections. An original and one copy is required.

D. Bankruptcy

A party has 14 days to file a bankruptcy appeal to the District Court. This appeal is filed in the Bankruptcy Court. An original and copies for all counsel of record are required. Counsel must file designation of record on appeal (Bankruptcy Rule 8006).

E. Patent, "Little Tucker Act" and Claims Court Transfer Cases

Appeals in patent and "Little Tucker Act" cases [28 U. S. C. §§ 1295 (a) (1)–(2)] from certain interlocutory orders in these cases [28 U.S.C. § 1295(c)], and from orders transferring or refusing to transfer cases to the United States Claims Court [28 U.S.C. § 1292 (d)(4)(B)], go to the United States Court of Appeals for the Federal Circuit. Federal Circuit Rules, practice notes, and appendix of forms are found in the *Rules of*

Practice Before the United States Court of Appeals for the Federal Circuit, available from the Clerk of that Court upon request. Call (202) 633-6550 or write to 717 Madison Place, N.W., Washington, DC 20439.

F. Service

Appellate Rule 25(c) outlines the procedures for service of the notice of appeal.

The Clerk of Court is responsible for serving a copy of the notice of appeal by mail/e-mail to counsel of record other than the appellant. The date the notice of appeal was filed is noted on each copy served. A notation is made on the docket by the clerk of the names of the parties to whom copies are mailed and the date of mailing.

G. Filing Fee

The $5 filing fee for the notice of appeal and the $450 docket fee for the Court of Appeals are tendered to the Clerk of Court at the time of filing the notice of appeal. If the fee is not paid within 14 days after docketing, the clerk is authorized to dismiss the appeal.

H. Preparation of the Record on Appeal

Rule 11 of the Federal Rules of Appellate Procedure provide for certification and transmittal of the original district court records file and exhibits to the Court of Appeals. However, the United States Court of Appeals for the Third Circuit has initiated an experimental program for retention of records in the district courts. In order to monitor record and case management, the district courts have been directed to retain the court records and to transmit to the Court of Appeals a certified copy of the docket entries in lieu of the entire record.

However, Rule 11 of the Third Circuit Rules provides that all reinstated parts of the record are to be transmitted if any party or the court requests such at any time during the pendency of the proceeding.

Rule 11 requires the appellant within 14 days after filing of the notice of appeal, to order from the court reporter, a transcript of the proceedings not already on file that the appellant deems necessary for inclusion in the record **(Appendix P)**. Rule 11 of the Third Circuit Rules also requires that a deposit be made with the court reporter of the estimated cost of transcript.

Any questions you may have concerning appeals should be directed to Orlando Medina, Jr., 267-299-7015.

CERTIFICATION OF JUDGMENT (AO 451)

Check Appellate Rule 4(a)(4) before issuing an AO 451. Also check the docket sheet for any post-judgment motions which may have the effect of "staying" the execution on the judgment.

The clerk does not have the authority to issue an AO 451 if a Motion to Vacate the Judgment, Motion for Reconsideration, or Motion to Stay is pending or unless the "appeal time" has expired except when ordered by the court that entered the judgment for good cause shown. (28 U.S.C. § 1963, as amended.) The appeal time commences to run from the date the judgment is entered on the docket, unless otherwise ordered by the Court. The clerk is not authorized to issue an AO 451 before the expiration of the appeal time because the case may be "reversed" on appeal and result in substantial loss to plaintiff because of the executions on the property of the defendant.

Normally, all civil cases may be appealed within 30 days from the date of entry of the final judgment on the docket. The United States always has 60 days within which to file an appeal. Be sure to attach a certified copy of the judgment to the AO 451 form.

REFERRAL TO UNITED STATES MAGISTRATE JUDGE

In accordance with the provisions of 28 U.S.C. § 636(c) and Local Civil Rule 72.1, U.S. Magistrate Judges may conduct, upon consent of all the parties in a civil case, any or all proceedings, including a jury or non-jury trial, and order the entry of a final judgment.

Taxation of Costs

Your decision to consent, or not to consent, to the referral of your case to a U.S. Magistrate Judge for disposition is entirely voluntary and should be communicated solely to the Clerk of Court. Appropriate consent forms for this purpose are available from the Clerk's Office **(Appendix Q)**.

Only if all the parties in the case consent to the referral to a magistrate judge will either the district court judge or the magistrate judge be informed of your decision. The judge will then decide whether or not to refer the case to a magistrate judge for disposition, but no action eligible for arbitration will be referred by consent of the parties until the arbitration has been concluded and trial de novo demanded pursuant to Local Civil Rule 53.2. The court may, for good cause shown on its motion, or under extraordinary circumstances shown by any party, vacate a referral of a civil matter to a magistrate judge.

When a case is referred to a magistrate judge for all further proceedings, including the entry of final judgment, the final judgment may be appealed directly to the Court of Appeals for the Third Circuit, unless the parties elect to have the case reviewed by the appropriate district judge (in which event any further appeal to the Court of Appeals would only be by petition for leave to appeal). (See Local Civil Rule 72.1).

POST JUDGMENT INTEREST RATE

In accordance with 28 U.S.C. § 1961 and 40 U.S.C. § 258, interest shall be allowed on any money judgment in a civil case recovered in a district court. Execution therefor may be levied by the marshal, in any case where, by the law of the State in which such court is held, execution may be levied for interest on judgments recovered in the courts of the State. Such interest shall be calculated from the date of the entry of the judgment, at a rate equal to the weekly average 1-year constant maturity Treasury yield, as published by the Board of Governors of the Federal Reserve System, for the calendar week preceding the date of the judgment. Requests for the current rate and any questions should be directed to Richard Sabol, Operations Manager, at (267-299-7011) or Terry Milano, Assistant Operations Manager, at (267-299-7013). Current rates are available through a link to the Federal Reserve from our website, http://www.paed.uscourts.gov.

TAXATION OF COSTS BY THE CLERK OF THE UNITED STATES DISTRICT COURT FOR THE EASTERN DISTRICT OF PENNSYLVANIA (AUGUST 7, 2012)

TABLE OF CONTENTS:

- A. Normally Allowable District Court Costs in General
- B. Normally Unallowable District Court Costs in General
- C. Burden of Proof Regarding Normally Allowable District Court Costs
- D. General Objections to Normally Allowable District Court Costs in their Entirety
- E. Specific Objections to Normally Allowable District Court Costs
- F. Special Procedures for Allowance of District Court Costs in Situations Involving Federal Rule of Civil Procedure 68
- G. Taxation of Appellate Court Costs and Supreme Court Costs by the Clerk of the District Court

A.   Normally Allowable District Court Costs in General.

It is well-established that district court costs may not be imposed in federal district courts except where they are authorized by either a statute or a rule of court.[1] Excluding from the discussion those district court costs taxable pursuant to Federal Rule of Civil Procedure 68 (which will be discussed in Section F of this manual), and certain narrowly-defined appellate court costs which are taxable by the district court (which will be discussed in Section G of this manual), federal district court costs are governed by Federal

Rule of Civil Procedure 54(d).[2] The text of Federal Rule of Civil Procedure 54(d) is divided into two sections:

- Federal Rule of Civil Procedure 54(d)(2), which by its own terms governs **"_Attorney's Fees_"**; and

- Federal Rule of Civil Procedure 54(d)(1), which by its own terms governs **"_(District Court) Costs Other Than Attorney's Fees_."**

All of those "(District Court) Costs Other Than Attorney's Fees" made taxable by Federal Rule of Civil Procedure 54(d)(1) are listed in 28 U.S.C. § 1920,[3] and the Clerk[4] has authority to tax those types of district court costs which are listed in 28 U.S.C. § 1920 in favor of the prevailing party or parties, and against the non-prevailing party or parties.[5] (Federal Rule of Civil Procedure 54(d)(1) costs may be assessed by the Clerk even when attorney fees pursuant to Federal Rule of Civil Procedure 54(d)(2) are disallowed by the presiding judge[6]).

Those items of district court costs taxable in the first instance by the Clerk, as listed in 28 U.S.C. § 1920, are:

"(1)   Fees of the clerk or marshal;

"(2)   Fees for printed or electronically recorded transcripts necessarily obtained for use in the case;

"(3)   Fees and disbursements for printing and witnesses;

"(4)   Fees for exemplification and the cost of making copies of any materials where the copies are necessarily obtained for use in the case;

"(5)   Docket fees under (28 U.S.C. § 1923); (and)

"(6)   Compensation of court appointed experts, compensation of interpreters, and salaries, fees, expenses, and costs of special interpretation services under (28 U.S.C. § 1828)."

The prevailing party, having had judgment entered in its favor, may file a bill of costs seeking any of the items authorized by 28 U.S.C. § 1920.

A bill of costs must be supported by an affidavit pursuant to 28 U.S.C. § 1924, stating that the costs sought were both actually incurred and necessarily incurred.[7]

It is generally advisable for the prevailing party to not file a bill of costs until after any appeals are decided, or until after any period for filing appeals, or for filing post trial motions, expires, so that if any additional costs are incurred, the bill of costs will not have to be amended.[8]

The bill of costs will then be forwarded to the deputy clerk responsible for taxation of costs.

The section of Federal Rule of Civil Procedure 54(d)(1) requiring fourteen days' notice simply means that <u>at least fourteen days</u> must elapse between the filing of the bill of costs and the taxing of costs; as a practical matter, it is usually necessary in the Eastern District of Pennsylvania for much more than fourteen days to process a taxation of costs request pursuant to § 1920 and these procedures. Costs will not be taxed until the underlying litigation is completed, and until after any period in which an appeal may be raised has lapsed; this is based on the simple principle that until the underlying litigation is over, the issue of who is the ultimately "prevailing party" has not yet been determined.[9] Once the issue of who is the ultimately prevailing party has been finally determined, the clerk shall send letters to both parties (or their counsel) asking for objections in writing from the non-prevailing party within fourteen (14) days, with the prevailing party then having fourteen (14) days to respond in writing. Local Rule of Civil Procedure 5.1(b) requires all counsel and any pro se litigants to provide the Clerk with an address for purposes of notices and service; the aforesaid letter will therefore be mailed to counsel (or to a pro se litigant) at their last known addresses, which constitutes proper and valid service upon them (pursuant to Federal Rule of Civil Procedure 5(b)(2)(C)) (it is for this reason that in the event that any of these letters are returned to the Clerk by the Postal Service as undeliverable, that the Clerk will not conduct any further investigation to find a current address for any of these persons).

All of the aforesaid objections and all of the aforesaid responses to the objections must be made by means of a court filing (letters shall not suffice).

In order to avoid the possibility of this Clerk entering a taxation opinion which may possibly have to be vacated at a later point in time, the Clerk will delay the taxing of costs until after all appeals have been exhausted[10] (or, until after the time period for filing an appeal has lapsed).[11]

The clerk will make a determination based on the bill of costs itself, and the arguments made in writing (if any); in addition, any relevant statutes, rules of court, and/or caselaw may play a role in the Clerk's determination of whether district court costs should be taxed and, if warranted, in what amount.

After making his determination, the clerk will thereafter enter a written taxation of costs opinion, accompanied, if warranted, by a judgment. A true and correct copy of the taxation opinion and any attached judgment shall be forwarded to all parties of record, or their counsel. Costs are effective as of the date the Clerk's judgment is entered on the docket. Either party can appeal the Clerk's taxation opinion and/or judgment to the presiding Article III judicial officer within seven days, pursuant to F.R.C.P. 54(d)(1) (this seven day period is not jurisdictional, and the court has discretion to consider an untimely appeal of a Clerk's taxation opinion and/or judgment in the event of "excusable neglect" on the part of the appealing party).[12]

B. Normally Unallowable District Court Costs in General.

Normally, the Clerk will tailor his taxation of costs opinion around the items requested and the actual objections raised by the losing party or parties, and will not raise issues *sua sponte*; however, as stated previously, since the Clerk's power is strictly limited by 28 U.S.C. § 1920, a necessary corollary is that if a requested item is never authorized by 28 U.S.C. § 1920 under any circumstances, the Clerk may not tax that item as a 28 U.S.C. § 1920 cost, even where the losing party or parties have not raised any objections to the item or items in question.[13]

Congress has provided for the assessment of attorney fees by means of Federal Rule of Civil Procedure 54(d)(2); as they are not specifically listed in 28 U.S.C. § 1920, attorney fees are clearly not taxable pursuant to Federal Rule of Civil Procedure 54(d)(1).[14] Pursuant to the language of Federal Rule of Civil Procedure 54(d) itself, attorney fees are only recoverable from the presiding judge pursuant to Federal Rule of Civil Procedure 54(d)(2), and not from the Clerk pursuant to Federal Rule of Civil Procedure 54(d)(1). An award or disallowance of attorney fees pursuant to Federal Rule of Civil Procedure 54(d)(2) is totally separate and distinct from an award of statutory costs pursuant to Federal Rule of Civil Procedure 54(d)(1).[15] The rationale supporting this standard is that unlike attorney fees, an assessment of 28 U.S.C. § 1920 costs is considered to be purely ministerial, and is not considered to be punitive toward the non-prevailing party, but merely as reimbursement to the prevailing party for their costs in bringing a successful civil action[16] (whereas an assessment of attorney fees *is* considered to be punitive[17]).

In addition, those litigation costs which are more closely associated with the routine overhead of practicing law than with the types of district court costs listed in 28 U.S.C. § 1920 are not taxable by pursuant to Federal Rule of Civil Procedure 54(d)(1), as they are seen as analogous to attorney fees.[18] (The fact that counsel did not perform the actual work leading to an unallowable item of cost, but was charged with it by an "evidence" provider as a condition of obtaining evidence, or by a stenographer, as a condition of obtaining a transcript, does not change the fact that the item is not listed in 28 U.S.C. § 1920 and is therefore unallowable).[19]

By this standard, costs which are not, even arguably, among those types of district court costs listed in 28 U.S.C. § 1920, include:

(1) the costs of attorney work product, such as pleadings, motions, memoranda and briefs, as well as case-related correspondence.[20] (Although costs related to the production of exact copies[21] of original documentary evidence[22] such as records[23] as taxable under 28 U.S.C. § 1920, we repeat once again that costs of attorney work product are not taxable under that statute; therefore, the prevailing party must be able to explain what types of documents were copied when requesting the taxing of these types of costs).[24]

(2) the costs of attorney court-admission fees (including court fees for admission "pro hac vice").[25] "Mediation fees" are also not taxable pursuant to 28 U.S.C. § 1920.[26]

(3) the costs of law firm rent, the costs of law firm utilities and costs for any and all non-attorney law firm staffing,[27] such as the costs of paralegals[28] and the costs of secretarial services[29] (including the costs of typing[30] and the costs of word processing[31]).

(4) attorney travel expenses[32] (including attorney airfare,[33] attorney meals,[34] attorney lodging,[35] attorney parking[36] and attorney car rentals[37]). Accordingly, these costs are prohibited in a Clerk's Taxation of Costs. *(Travel expenses for a witness, unlike travel expenses for an attorney, are, at least arguably, taxable by the Clerk pursuant to 28 U.S.C. § 1920(3)).*[38]

(5) costs related to legal research.[39]

(6) telephone expenses[40] (including both long distance and local telephone calls).[41]

(7) costs related to the use of facsimile machines.[42]

(8) costs of courier, local delivery and/or messenger services.[43] (We hasten to point out that this standard does not apply to costs for governmental service of process or private service of process, which may be taxed pursuant to 28 U.S.C. § 1920(1)).[44]

(9) postage costs.[45]

(10) costs of shipping and handling (including shipping and handling by means of the "United Parcel Service" or by means of "Federal Express").[46]

(11) fees paid to a special master.[47]

(12) the costs of investigative services.[48]

(13) costs related to the preparation of an expert's testimony or report,[49] including costs related to an Independent Medical Examination.[50] (although expert witness fees may be allowable in some situations pursuant to 28 U.S.C. § 1920(3) and/or 28 U.S.C. § 1920(6)).

(14) case-related work performed by accounting professionals.[51]

(15) the cost of telegrams.[52]

(16) unexplained requests for "miscellaneous" costs.[53]

C. Burden of Proof Regarding Normally Allowable District Court Costs.

Federal Rule of Civil Procedure 54 (d)(1) directs that "(district court) costs—other than attorney fees" (i.e. those costs authorized by 28 U.S.C. § 1920[54]) "*should* be allowed to the prevailing party (emphasis added)." This language is evidence of "specific intent"[55] on the part of Congress that there should be a heavy presumption[56] that "the 'prevailing party' *automatically* is entitled to costs"[57] as a matter of course, once it has been shown that the costs sought are, at least arguably, of those types of costs listed in 28 U.S.C. § 1920,[58] provided that those costs were both *actually incurred* (as evidenced by a sworn affidavit)[59] and *necessarily incurred* ("necessarily" meaning that the costs were reasonably incurred for the prevailing party's effective preparation, judged in light of the situation existing when the costs in question were actually incurred, without regard to whether the costs relate to items which were actually used).[60]

The rationale supporting this heavy presumption is that unlike attorney fees, an assessment of 28 U.S.C. § 1920 costs is considered to be purely ministerial, and is not considered to be punitive toward the non-prevailing party or parties, but merely as reimbursement to the prevailing party or parties for their costs in bringing or pursuing a successful civil action[61] (whereas an assessment of attorney fees *is* considered to be punitive[62]). A consequence of this heavy presumption is that the non-prevailing party or parties bear the burden of proof, and must overcome the aforesaid heavy presumption in favor of the taxing of district court costs against that non-prevailing party or parties.[63] Because of this heavy presumption, it is considered punitive towards the prevailing party or parties to deny to that prevailing party or parties district court costs which are ordinarily automatically taxed under 28 U.S.C. § 1920,[64] and it is not necessary for the prevailing party or parties to argue that the non-prevailing party or parties did something that was wrong or inappropriate.[65]

As a further result of the aforesaid heavy presumption, in the event taxable district court costs are denied to the prevailing party or parties, the Clerk must specifically state what defect, bad act or impropriety on the part of that prevailing party or parties leads the Clerk to deny to that prevailing party or parties otherwise allowable costs.[66]

As the United States Court of Appeals for the Third Circuit appropriately noted in 2010, it is for precisely these reasons that counsel should always advise each client, before commencing the litigation process, that in the event that their litigation is unsuccessful, that there is a risk of taxation of district court costs against that client pursuant to 28 U.S.C. § 1920.[67]

D.   General Objections to Normally Allowable District Court Costs in their Entirety.

(1)   **Alleged pretrial stipulation.** It is well-settled law that if the parties to a civil action have stipulated prior to the final judgment in the underlying lawsuit as to how district court costs will be apportioned or taxed, that stipulation is controlling, if a bill of costs is ultimately filed.[68] In situations where the parties disagree on this issue, it is important to recall that the Clerk has no fact-finding mechanism; accordingly, the Clerk must not address this general objection, and will proceed to tax costs as if there was no pre-judgment stipulation between the parties as to how these costs would be apportioned; if any party is not satisfied with this result, they can appeal the Taxation Opinion and the accompanying Judgment to the trial judge.[69] (A Clerk's Taxation of Costs proceeding is not a forum for re-examining the underlying facts of the lawsuit or for re-litigating the underlying lawsuit).[70]

(2)   **Alleged Economic Disparity between the parties.** According to a 2010 decision of the United States Court of Appeals for the Third Circuit, economic disparity between the parties is an objection that this clerk and/or this court "***may not consider.***"[71]

To go into further detail, we note that Federal Rule of Civil Procedure 54(d)(1) directs that "costs—other than attorney fees" (i.e. those costs authorized by 28 U.S.C. § 1920) "***should*** be allowed to the prevailing party (emphasis added)." This language is evidence of "specific intent"[72] on the part of Congress that there should be a heavy presumption[73] that "the 'prevailing party' automatically is entitled to costs[74] as a matter of course, once it has been shown that the costs sought are, at least arguably, of those types of costs listed in 28 U.S.C. § 1920.[75] We are therefore of the view that the Clerk has no discretion to disallow otherwise allowable costs based on an argument rooted in economics; economic disparity between the parties is not a basis for disallowing costs, and a very strong presumption exists that consideration of the equities does not favor a disallowance of costs by the court.[76] The Clerk may tax costs not only where the losing party is less affluent than the prevailing party, but also where the losing party is actually indigent.[77] Even complete and utter inability to pay is not grounds for a disallowance of costs.[78] Likewise, even the granting of in forma pauperis status to the losing party does not rebut this heavy presumption.[79]

(3)   **Bankruptcy.**

   i.   ***Bills of costs filed against a debtor in bankruptcy.***
        Judicial proceedings relating to a claim against a debtor who has filed for bankruptcy are void *ab initio* absent relief from the automatic stay.[80] As a result of the automatic stay, all formal and informal actions taken against a debtor in bankruptcy are stayed.[81] Accordingly, costs may not be taxed against a debtor in bankruptcy because of the automatic stay provision of the Bankruptcy Code.[82]

   ii. ***Bills of costs filed by, or on behalf of, a debtor in bankruptcy.***
        "Within one action, claims ***against a debtor*** will be suspended by the automatic stay, even though closely related claims asserted ***by the debtor*** may continue."[83] Accordingly, a debtor in bankruptcy, or the debtor's estate in bankruptcy, may have 28 U.S.C. § 1920 costs taxed in his, or hers or its favor.

(4)   **Alleged Chilling Effect.** According to a 2010 decision of the United States Court of Appeals for the Third Circuit, the objection that awarding costs would have a "chilling effect" on litigation which is

allegedly socially important is always "***unpersuasive***,"[84] since "(t)he fact that a prevailing party prosecutes its rights under the Federal Rules of Civil Procedure to an award of costs ***cannot*** be seen as chilling the flow of litigation."[85]

To go into further detail, a Clerk's Taxation of Costs proceeding is not a forum for re-examining the facts of the underlying lawsuit;[86] therefore, as stated previously, there is a ***heavy presumption***[87] in favor of "***automatically***"[88] taxing those types of costs which are listed in 28 U.S.C. § 1920[89] which the prevailing party both ***actually incurred*** (as evidenced by a sworn affidavit)[90] and ***necessarily incurred*** ("necessarily" meaning that the costs were reasonably incurred for the prevailing party's effective preparation, judged in light of the situation existing when the costs in question were actually incurred, without regard to whether the costs relate to items which were actually used).[91]

(5)   **Alleged Good Faith by Non-prevailing party.** According to a 2010 decision of the United States Court of Appeals for the Third Circuit, the alleged good faith of the non-prevailing party is an objection that the clerk and/or the court "***may not consider***."[92]

To go into further detail, the bare allegation that an action was brought in good faith and was neither frivolous, unreasonable nor without foundation is not sufficient to overcome the presumption inherent in Fed. P. Civ. P. 54(d) that "costs ... ***should*** be allowed to the prevailing party (emphasis added)."[93] As the court explained in Popeil Brothers v. Schick Electric, 516 F.2d 772 (7th Cir. 1975), "(i)f the awarding of costs could be thwarted every time the unsuccessful party is a normal, average party and not a knave, Rule 54(d) would have little substance remaining." 516 F.2d at 776. Hence, "good faith litigation does not absolve a party from imposition of costs."[94] If costs were only taxable in those situations where the losing party acted in bad faith, 28 U.S.C. § 1920 would have very little meaning.[95] A Clerk's Taxation of Costs proceeding is simply not a forum for re-examining, or for re-litigating, the underlying facts of the lawsuit.[96] Therefore, it is not a valid objection that the issues in the underlying case were closely contested and that the final judgment allegedly could have, or allegedly should have, gone in the other direction; the alleged complexity or closeness of the issues litigated is not relevant to the taxing of costs by the Court or Clerk.[97]

There is a ***heavy presumption***[98] in favor of "***automatically***"[99] taxing those types of costs listed in 28 U.S.C. § 1920[100] which the prevailing party both ***actually incurred*** (as evidenced by a sworn affidavit)[101] and ***necessarily incurred*** ("necessarily" meaning that the costs were reasonably incurred for the prevailing party's effective preparation, judged in light of the situation existing when the costs in question were actually incurred, without regard to whether the costs relate to items which were actually used).[102]

(6)   **The issues in the underlying case were allegedly close.** The general objection that the facts and/or issues in this case were closely contested and allegedly could have, or should have, gone in the other direction and resulted in a victory for the non-prevailing party is an objection that this clerk and/or this court "***may not consider***."[103]

A Clerk's Taxation of Costs proceeding is simply not a forum for re-examining, or for re-litigating, the underlying facts of the lawsuit.[104] Therefore, it is not a valid objection that the issues in the underlying case were closely contested and that the final judgment allegedly could have, or allegedly should have, gone in the other direction; the complexity or closeness of the issues litigated is not relevant to the taxing of costs by the Court or Clerk.[105]

There is a ***heavy presumption***[106] in favor of "***automatically***"[107] taxing those types of costs which are listed in 28 U.S.C. § 1920[108] which the prevailing party both ***actually incurred*** (as evidenced by a sworn affidavit)[109] and ***necessarily incurred*** ("necessarily" meaning that the costs were reasonably incurred for the prevailing party's effective preparation, judged in light of the situation existing when the costs in question were actually incurred, without regard to whether the costs relate to items which were actually used).[110]

(7)   **Allegedly Untimely Filing of the Bill of Costs.** The Eastern District of Pennsylvania is one of very few districts in the federal system that has no local rule governing the time for filing a bill of costs. In the absence of any local rule, courts have held that bills of cost must be filed within a "reasonable" time after the conclusion of the litigation.[111] It is generally advisable for the prevailing party to not file a bill of

costs until after any appeals are decided, or until after any period for filing appeals expires, so that if any additional costs are incurred, that bill of costs will not have to be amended.[112]

To avoid the possibility of the Clerk entering a taxation opinion which may possibly have to be vacated at a later point in time, the Clerk will delay the taxing of costs until after all appeals have been exhausted[113] (or, until after the time period for filing an appeal has lapsed).[114]

(8) **Alleged Misconduct.**

   A. *Alleged Misconduct by the Prevailing Party.*
   Often a general objection to the bill of costs in its entirety is made which alleges that costs were allegedly incurred as a result of bad faith on the part of the prevailing party and/or their counsel during the underlying litigation.

   A request for taxation of 28 U.S.C. § 1920 costs may be disallowed where there has been misconduct by the prevailing party during the litigation process which led to excessive costs; however, there is a strong presumption in taxation situations that the prevailing party *did not* act in bad faith,[115] and the heavy burden of proving such bad faith rests with the non-prevailing party.[116]

   For purposes of taxation of district court costs, allegedly bad conduct must be analyzed in the light of the situation as it appeared to exist at the time the said allegedly bad act was undertaken (and not in the light of the situation as it appears with the benefit of hindsight).[117] The Third Circuit has stated that a lawyer's act of making an argument which could be construed as "well-intentioned zeal" on their client's behalf cannot be construed as evidence of such bad faith,[118] even where the prevailing party did not win regarding every argument made in the underlying litigation.[119] The fact that the prevailing party may have incurred some costs relating to a line of argument in the underlying litigation that was ultimately unsuccessful is irrelevant in a taxation matter,[120] as is the relative degree of complexity of the various issues in the underlying litigation.[121]

   The determination of whether such misconduct has occurred must be made by the presiding judicial officer, as the Clerk has no fact-finding procedure, and as a Clerk's Taxation of Costs proceeding is not a forum for re-examining the underlying facts of the lawsuit or for re-litigating the underlying lawsuit.[122] Therefore, the Clerk may not consider this general objection; if there is an appeal of the taxation opinion by any party, the court may consider this argument pursuant to Federal Rule of Civil Procedure 54(d)(1).

   B. *Alleged Misconduct by the Non-prevailing party.*
   The prevailing party may allege that the non-prevailing parties acted in bad faith during the litigation process. We note that it is considered punitive towards a prevailing party to deny to that prevailing party district court costs which are ordinarily automatically[123] taxed under 28 U.S.C. § 1920,[124] and it is not necessary for the prevailing party to argue that the non-prevailing party did something that was wrong or inappropriate;[125] however, although not necessary, a finding of bad faith on the part of the non-prevailing would be grounds for **not** reducing costs and/or grounds for **not** disallowing costs.[126] This determination must be made by the presiding judicial officer, as the Clerk has no fact-finding procedure, and a Clerk's Taxation of Costs proceeding is not a forum for re-examining the underlying facts of the lawsuit or for re-litigating the underlying lawsuit.[127] If there is an appeal of the taxation opinion by any party, the court may consider this argument pursuant to Federal Rule of Civil Procedure 54(d)(1).

   C. *Alleged Malice on the part of the Prevailing Party.*
   Often a non-prevailing party will argue that filing of the bill of costs against it was allegedly motivated by malice on the part of the prevailing party. We note that the prevailing party's state of mind is irrelevant to the taxing of costs.

(9) **Prevailing Party in the Underlying Lawsuit.** A general objection to the bill of costs is often made stating that the prevailing party allegedly prevailed on some issues at the trial, even though judgment was entered in favor of his opponent. The relevant rule of court, Federal Rule of Civil Procedure 54(d)(1),

directs the taxing of costs in favor of "the prevailing party." In order to determine the issue of which party, or parties, prevailed, "the court must (first) identify the relief plaintiff sought,"[128] then, after that, the court must read the text of the final entry of judgment in the underlying lawsuit,[129] and then, after that, the court must ask itself "whether the plaintiff achieved 'some of the benefit sought' by the party bringing the suit."[130] Applying this standard, it is clear that although it is not necessary for a plaintiff to receive **all** of the relief sought, the plaintiff must still receive at least **some** of the relief sought in order to be considered a prevailing party.[131] The plaintiff is considered the prevailing party and the defendants are considered the non-prevailing parties in those situations where a favorable judgment is entered for plaintiff on any of the claims plaintiff asserted, even if plaintiff is only successful on a fraction of the claims asserted and even if plaintiff obtains only a fraction of the relief sought.[132]

Likewise, the law is clear that where a reading of the text of the judgment indicates that plaintiff has not prevailed on any of its claims or obtained any relief, defendant is considered to be the prevailing party.[133] This rule applies and a defendant is considered to be the prevailing party, even where the defendant does not prevail on its counterclaims.[134] The law is also clear that costs incurred by a defendant may be taxed against a plaintiff who ultimately withdraws an action, even where the withdrawal was voluntary.[135]

If a situation is presented to the Clerk in which plaintiff is either wholly or partially successful on its claims, and defendant is are also either wholly or partially successful on a its counterclaims, the issue of who is the prevailing party must be decided by the court on a case-by-case basis, and not by the Clerk of Court,[136] since it requires consideration of the unique facts of the underlying lawsuit and since the Clerk of Court has no fact-finding mechanism for re-examining the underlying facts of the lawsuit or for re-litigating the underlying lawsuit.[137]

It is irrelevant to the taxing of costs that the matter was disposed of by means of summary judgment and no trial took place.[138] It is irrelevant to the taxing of costs that this matter was disposed of by means of a directed verdict.[139] It is also irrelevant to the taxing of costs that this matter was disposed of by means of a judgment NOV.[140]

It is also merits comment that the party who has prevailed at the final stage a lawsuit reaches is considered the prevailing party for the entire lawsuit and may recover costs related to all stages of the lawsuit; this includes earlier stages at which the ultimately prevailing party did not prevail.[141]

(10)   **Itemization.** A general objection to the bill of costs in its entirety is often raised which claims that the costs sought are allegedly not sufficiently explained. Provided that the bill of costs is neat and legible, there is no need for counsel to use the court's official bill of costs form;[142] there is likewise no requirement for the prevailing party to supply receipts[143] (even in a situation where receipts or a more detailed itemization would be useful to the court and/or opposing counsel),[144] rather, caselaw holds that the standard is that costs must be sufficiently explained to the extent that opposing counsel can make informed objections and the Clerk or Court can make an informed determination of whether requested costs are allowable.[145]

The bill of costs must be accompanied by an affidavit from prevailing party or its counsel stating, under penalty of perjury, that the costs are correct and were actually and necessarily incurred; the existence of such an affidavit in a Clerk's Taxation of Costs proceeding is given very great weight with respect to the aforesaid burden of proof in favor of the taxation of those types of costs listed in the taxation statute.[146]

(11)   **Alleged failure of the prevailing party to actually pay requested costs.** The objection is sometimes raised of whether costs can be taxed for items which the prevailing party has not paid, which the prevailing party admits are overdue but nevertheless claims are taxable. Research by this Clerk has uncovered no precedential caselaw on this issue, either in this court or in any federal district or circuit court.

28 U.S.C. § 1924 establishes the standard that an amount sought in a bill of costs must be "correct" and must have been "necessarily incurred." This manual has already addressed the subject of "correctness." Concerning the subject of whether these costs have been "necessarily incurred," and with no caselaw on this issue, the Clerk of the Eastern District of Pennsylvania sought a solution to this issue in the *Webster's II New Riverside University Dictionary* (1984). This dictionary defines the word "incur" as "to become liable or subject to, especially because of one's own actions." The standard for taxing costs,

therefore, is not whether costs have already been paid by the prevailing party; rather, the standard is whether the prevailing party is liable for these costs. The word "incurred" is not synonymous with the words "already paid."

(12) **Alleged Actions of the trial court and alleged interaction with attorney fees.** Where the court has expressly allowed or disallowed district court costs ***pursuant to 28 U.S.C. § 1920*** (that is, district court costs other than attorney fees and attorney costs) in the final order or judgement, the Clerk is bound to comply with that Order;[147] however, an award or disallowance of attorney fees and attorney costs pursuant to Federal Rule of Civil Procedure 54(d)(2) is totally separate and distinct from an award of statutory costs pursuant to Federal Rule of Civil Procedure 54(d)(1);[148] accordingly, if there is a court Order in the underlying case denying "attorney fees and costs," it does not preclude the taxing of § 1920 costs,[149] and Federal Civil Rule 54(d)(1) costs may be assessed even when attorney fees are disallowed.[150] (Parenthetically, statutes mentioning "attorney fees and costs" mean "attorney fees and attorney costs," and do not relate to § 1920 costs).[151]

(13) **Alleged Failure to Make Use of the Official Bill of Costs form.** Although there is a standard form provided by the Administrative Office of the United States Courts, use of this form is optional; where the official form is not used, district court costs may yet be taxed where the request for costs is neat, legible and understandable.[152]

(14) **Allegedly Joint and Several Liability.** In a case where multiple parties on one side of the bar do not prevail, costs against those multiple losing parties are presumptively joint and several, and any losing party or parties who want costs to be taxed against them in any way other than jointly and severally bears the burden of proving that these costs should be so taxed.[153]

(15) **Cases brought in federal court pursuant to 28 U.S.C. § 1332 (commonly known as "diversity jurisdiction").** Where an action is brought in federal court pursuant to 28 U.S.C. § 1332 and there are both state and federal cost-shifting statutes or rules of court that may possibly apply, the federal statute or rule trumps the state statute or rule, so that the state procedures may be disregarded, and district court costs may be taxed in diversity jurisdiction cases pursuant to 28 U.S.C. § 1920 and Federal Rule of Civil Procedure 54(d)(1).[154]

(16) **United States as a party.** Title 28 U.S.C. § 2412 permits taxation against the United States or any agency or official thereof. The Federal Courts Administration Act of 1992[155] provides that the United States may recover filing fees when it prevails in a civil action.

(17) **State governments as party.** The Eleventh Amendment to the Constitution does not bar taxation of district court costs against a state government, its agencies or officials.[156]

(18) **Costs in Admiralty Cases.** District court clerks may tax 28 U.S.C. 1920 costs in admiralty cases.[157]

(19) **Interveners.** The prevailing practice is that interveners in agency actions are treated like any other prevailing or losing party.[158]

(20) **Language on costs in Jurisdictional Statute.** In any case brought under a specific statute, the clerk's office must check to see if that statute has provisions concerning costs; if there is a statutotry provision concerning costs, that statutory rule, and not 28 U.S.C. § 1920, applies.[159] Statutes mentioning "attorney fees and costs" mean "attorney fees and attorney costs," and do not relate to § 1920 costs.[160]

E. **Specific Objections to Normally Allowable District Court Costs.**

The following is a discussion of the manner in which the Clerk of the United States District Court for the Eastern District of Pennsylvania addresses issues regarding specific items of district court costs which are listed in 28 U.S.C. § 1920.

(1) ***28 U.S.C. § 1920(1)***
  i. **Fees of the Clerk.** The relevant statute, 18 U.S.C. § 1920(1) directs the taxing of fees of the Clerk.[161] Costs related to both fees of a state clerk and costs for removal to federal court are recoverable in federal court pursuant to 28 U.S.C. § 1920(1).[162] (The Federal Courts Admin-

istration Act of 1992 provides that when the United States is a plaintiff that prevails in a civil action, it may recover fees of the Clerk).[163]

There is a heavy presumption[164] in favor of "***automatically***"[165] taxing those types of costs listed in 28 U.S.C. § 1920[166] which the prevailing party both ***actually incurred*** (as evidenced by a sworn affidavit)[167] and ***necessarily incurred*** ("necessarily" meaning that the costs were reasonably incurred for the prevailing party's effective preparation, judged in light of the situation existing when the costs in question were actually incurred, without regard to whether the costs relate to items which were actually used).[168]

ii. **Fees of the Marshal.** The relevant statute, 28 U.S.C. § 1920(1), directs the taxing of fees of the Marshal, which includes the costs of service of process, including subpoena service.[169] Federal courts interpret this provision of 28 U.S.C. § 1920(1) as permitting the taxing of costs for both governmental process servers and private process servers.[170] Federal courts also interpret this provision of 28 U.S.C. § 1920(1) as permitting the taxing of costs for a process server's mileage in connection with that service.[171] It is irrelevant to the taxing of costs whether the non-prevailing party offered to waive service, or whether the prevailing party did or did not request a waiver of service pursuant to Federal Rule of Civil Procedure 4.[172] Costs related to the production of exact copies of an original copy of documentary evidence, including the costs of a subpoena duces tecum (also known as a records subpoena or a records deposition)[173] are seen as taxable costs pursuant to 28 U.S.C. § 1920(4), and will be discussed later in this taxation opinion.

There is a heavy presumption[174] in favor of "***automatically***"[175] taxing those types of costs listed in 28 U.S.C. § 1920[176] which the prevailing party both ***actually incurred*** (as evidenced by a sworn affidavit)[177] and ***necessarily incurred*** ("necessarily" meaning that the costs were reasonably incurred for the prevailing party's effective preparation, judged in light of the situation existing when the costs in question were actually incurred, without regard to whether the costs relate to items which were actually used).[178]

(2) ***28 U.S.C. § 1920(2)***

i. **Deposition Costs.** The relevant statute, 28 U.S.C. § 1920(2), directs the taxing of costs for "transcripts necessarily obtained for use in the case." This provision governing "transcripts" applies to deposition transcripts;[179] and modern caselaw states that both stenographic depositions and videotaped depositions are considered "transcripts" for the purposes of 28 U.S.C. § 1920(2);[180] by this standard, a prevailing party may also recover costs associated with the playback of videotaped depositions.[181]

The Clerk also notes that deposition costs are taxable for the depositions of both fact witnesses and expert witnesses.[182]

There is a heavy presumption[183] in favor of "***automatically***"[184] taxing those types of costs listed in 28 U.S.C. § 1920[185] which the prevailing party both ***actually incurred*** (as evidenced by a sworn affidavit)[186] and ***necessarily incurred*** ("necessarily" meaning that the costs were reasonably incurred for the prevailing party's effective preparation, judged in light of the situation existing when the costs in question were actually incurred, without regard to whether the costs relate to items which were actually used).[187] Examples of situations where deposition transcripts are seen as necessary for a party's effective preparation, even where they were not used, ***include, but are not limited to***, situations involving deponents who ultimately do not testify at a trial;[188] situations involving deponents who ultimately are not permitted by the court to testify at a trial;[189] and situations where deposition transcripts were necessary to support, or to oppose, pre-trial motions[190] and/or post-trial motions[191] (including motions seeking the entry of summary judgment,[192] and/or motions seeking the entry of a default judgment[193] and/or motions seeking the entry of a judgment NOV[194]). ***Both*** stenographic copies of deposition transcript ***and*** videotaped copies of transcripts of the exact same testimony are taxable[195] where both copies were necessary to counsel's effective preparation (judged in light of the situation existing when the costs in question were actually incurred, without regard to whether the costs relate to items which were actually used).[196]

However, even if a deposition transcript is "necessarily obtained," counsel may not always recover costs incurred in having it prepared on an expedited basis. Expedited rates for deposition transcripts have been allowed where circumstances justify such a schedule, judged in light of the situation existing at the time of the taking of the testimony in question.[197]

ii. **Costs of Other Types of Transcripts.** The relevant statute, 28 U.S.C. § 1920(2), directs the taxing of costs for "transcripts necessarily obtained for use in the case." This provision governing "transcripts" applies to trial transcripts and allows for their taxation.[198] This provision governing "transcripts" also applies to transcripts of hearings and other pre-trial proceedings, and allows for their taxation.[199] This provision governing "transcripts" also applies to transcripts of extra-judicial, non-judicial, or other out-of-court proceedings or conferences, and allows for their taxation.[200]

There is a heavy presumption[201] in favor of "***automatically***"[202] taxing those types of costs listed in 28 U.S.C. § 1920[203] which the prevailing party both ***actually incurred*** (as evidenced by a sworn affidavit)[204] and ***necessarily incurred*** ("necessarily" meaning that the costs were reasonably incurred for the prevailing party's effective preparation, judged in light of the situation existing when the costs in question were actually incurred, without regard to whether the costs relate to items which were actually used).[205] Examples of situations where transcripts are seen as necessarily obtained, even where they were not used, ***include, but are not limited to***, situations where the transcripts were needed to support, or to oppose, pre-trial motions[206] and/or post-trial motions.[207]

However, even if such a transcript is "necessarily obtained," counsel may not always recover costs incurred in having it prepared on an expedited basis. Expedited rates have been allowed where circumstances justify such a schedule, judged in light of the situation existing at the time of the taking of the testimony in question.[208]

(3) ***28 U.S.C. § 1920(3)***

i. **Printing costs.** The relevant statute, 28 U.S.C. § 1920(3), directs the taxing of "printing" costs[209] (although typing costs are not taxable under this statute[210]).

There is a heavy presumption[211] in favor of "***automatically***"[212] taxing those types of costs listed in 28 U.S.C. § 1920[213] which the prevailing party both ***actually incurred*** (as evidenced by a sworn affidavit)[214] and ***necessarily incurred*** ("necessarily" meaning that the costs were reasonably incurred for the prevailing party's effective preparation, judged in light of the situation existing when the costs in question were actually incurred, without regard to whether the costs relate to items which were actually used.[215]

ii. **Witness Attendance Fees.** The relevant statute, 28 U.S.C. § 1920(3), directs the taxing of witness fees. Witness fees are capped by the witness fee statute, 28 U.S.C. § 1821.[216] The United States Supreme Court has held that the witness fee statute (28 U.S.C. § 1821 or its direct predecessor statute) is incorporated by reference into 28 U.S.C. § 1920(3) (or its direct predecessor statute).[217]

28 U.S.C. § 1821(b) limits witness attendance fees to $40.00 per witness per day. Witness attendance fees actually incurred by the prevailing party or parties are taxable for every day a witness is either present in court, or present at a deposition hearing,[218] with a reasonable "good faith" expectation on the part of the prevailing party's counsel that the witness may have to testify, even where the witness does not actually testify.[219] (Authority also permits the taxing of attendance costs pursuant to 28 U.S.C. § 1821(b) for "travel days," where reasonable[220]).

This limit of $40.00 per witness per day of attendance applies to both fact and expert witnesses,[221] except where the expert witness in question was court-appointed pursuant to 28 U.S.C. § 1920(6).[222] Costs related to an expert's preparation, or to the creation of an expert report, are not set forth in 28 U.S.C. § 1920, and are therefore not taxable.[223]

In addition, although no witness fees are taxable for witnesses who are parties to the litigation,[224] witness fees are taxable for employees of a corporate party as long as they are not real parties in interest to the litigation.[225]

There is a heavy presumption[226] in favor of "***automatically***"[227] taxing those types of costs listed in 28 U.S.C. § 1920[228] which the prevailing party both ***actually incurred*** (as evidenced by a sworn affidavit)[229] and ***necessarily incurred*** ("necessarily" meaning that the costs were reasonably incurred for the prevailing party's effective preparation, judged in light of the situation existing when the costs in question were actually incurred, without regard to whether the costs relate to items which were actually used).[230]

iii. **Witness Travel Costs Fees.** The relevant statute, 28 U.S.C. § 1920(3) directs the taxing of witness fees. Witness fees are capped by the witness fee statute, 28 U.S.C. § 1821.[231] The United States Supreme Court has held that the witness fee statute (28 U.S.C. § 1821 or its direct predecessor statute) is incorporated by reference into 28 U.S.C. § 1920(3) (or its direct predecessor statute).[232]

28 U.S.C. § 1821(c) sets limits, based on reasonableness, on witness travel and mileage costs.

Travel costs are taxable pursuant to 28 U.S.C. § 1920(3) where the need to travel was reasonable, judged in light of the situation existing at the time the travel costs were incurred.[233] (Although travel costs for a witness are, at least arguably, taxable pursuant to 28 U.S.C. § 1920, we hasten to point out that travel costs for an attorney are not taxable pursuant to 28 U.S.C. § 1920[234]).

There is a heavy presumption[235] in favor of "***automatically***"[236] taxing those types of costs listed in 28 U.S.C. § 1920[237] which the prevailing party both ***actually incurred*** (as evidenced by a sworn affidavit)[238] and ***necessarily incurred*** ("necessarily" meaning that the costs were reasonably incurred for the prevailing party's effective preparation, judged in light of the situation existing when the costs in question were actually incurred, without regard to whether the costs relate to items which were actually used).[239]

iv. **Witness Subsistence Fees.** The relevant statute, 28 U.S.C. § 1920(3) directs the taxing of witness fees. Witness fees are capped by the witness fee statute, 28 U.S.C. § 1821.[240] The United States Supreme Court has held that the witness fee statute (28 U.S.C. § 1821 or its direct predecessor statute) is incorporated by reference into 28 U.S.C. § 1920(3) (or its direct predecessor statute).[241]

28 U.S.C. § 1821(d) limits witness subsistence (meals and lodging) allowances in "high cost" areas such as the Eastern District of Pennsylvania to $328.50 per day when the traveling witness can supply ***all*** of his or her receipts for their requested subsistence allowance (and $219.00 per day when that witness cannot supply ***all*** of his or her receipts for their requested subsistence allowance); the witness can also recover a flat rate of $49.50 in subsistence for the last day of their trip.

Witness subsistence fees are taxable pursuant to 28 U.S.C. § 1920(3) where the need to travel was reasonable, judged in light of the situation existing at the time the costs were incurred.[242] (Although subsistence fees for a witness are, at least arguably, taxable pursuant to 28 U.S.C. § 1920, we hasten to point out that subsistence fees for an attorney are not taxable pursuant to 28 U.S.C. § 1920[243]).

There is a heavy presumption[244] in favor of "***automatically***"[245] taxing those types of costs listed in 28 U.S.C. § 1920[246] which the prevailing party both ***actually incurred*** (as evidenced by a sworn affidavit)[247] and ***necessarily incurred*** ("necessarily" meaning that the costs were reasonably incurred for the prevailing party's effective preparation, judged in light of the situation existing when the costs in question were actually incurred, without regard to whether the costs relate to items which were actually used).[248]

(4) **_28 U.S.C. § 1920(4)_**

    i. **Documentary Evidence.** The relevant statute, 28 U.S.C. § 1920(4) directs the taxing of "fees for exemplification and the cost of making copies of any materials where the copies are necessarily obtained for use in the case(.)" The United States Court of Appeals for the Third Circuit spoke on 28 U.S.C. § 1920(4) in Race Tires America, Inc. v. Hoosier Racing Tire Corp., 674 F.3d 158 (3d Cir. 2012).

    Citing *Webster's Third International Dictionary 504* (3d edition 1993) as authority, the Race Tires America court noted that the word "copy" means "***an imitation, transcript or reproduction of an original work.***"

    The Race Tires America court applied this dictionary definition to conclude that for purposes of 28 U.S.C. § 1920(4), ***the word "copying" means the "scanning," "conversion" or "reproduction" of an "original" item of "evidence" so as to create a "duplicate" copy of that "evidence.***" The Race Tires America court also applied this dictionary definition to conclude that ***the word "copying" also means the "scanning," "conversion" or "reproduction" of an "original" "transcript," so as to create a "duplicate" copy of that "transcript.***"

    Accordingly, a duplicate copy of original records,[249] or a duplicate copy of other original documents produced in discovery,[250] as well as the costs of a subpoena duces tecum (also known as a records subpoena or a records deposition)[251] are taxable costs pursuant to 28 U.S.C. § 1920(4).

    The Race Tires America court also found that the creation of "digital duplicates" of original evidence are also, at least arguably, taxable pursuant to 28 U.S.C. § 1920(4).[252]

    There is a heavy presumption[253] in favor of "***automatically***"[254] taxing those types of costs listed in 28 U.S.C. § 1920[255] which the prevailing party both ***actually incurred*** (as evidenced by a sworn affidavit)[256] and ***necessarily incurred*** ("necessarily" meaning that the costs were reasonably incurred for the prevailing party's effective preparation, judged in light of the situation existing when the costs in question were actually incurred, without regard to whether the costs relate to items which were actually used).[257]

    Situations where costs of exact duplicate copies of original evidence are seen as "necessary" pursuant to 28 U.S.C. § 1920(4) (even where the duplicate copies in question were not used) ***include, but are not limited to***, situations where such exact duplicate copies of original evidence are attached to any deposition transcript,[258] and/or situations where such exact duplicate copies of original evidence are attached to any pleading[259] and/or situations where such exact duplicate copies of original evidence are attached to any motion[260] (including a motion for summary judgment).[261]

    ii. **Demonstrative Evidence.** The relevant statute, 28 U.S.C. § 1920(4), directs the taxing of "fees for exemplification and the cost of making copies of any materials where the copies are necessarily obtained for use in the case(.)" The United States Court of Appeals for the Third Circuit spoke on 28 U.S.C. § 1920(4) in Race Tires America, Inc. v. Hoosier Racing Tire Corp., 674 F.3d 158 (3d Cir. 2012). The Race Tires America court held that the word "copies" means an exact copy, or an exact duplicate, of an original piece of evidence. The Race Tires America court also found that because, in drafting 28 U.S.C. § 1920(4), Congress had specifically used two different words in the same statute ("copies" and "exemplification"), that the word "copies" and the word "exemplification" presumptively do not have the same meaning (although the Race Tires America court pointedly declined to offer a definition of the word "exemplification").

    With no guidance from the Third Circuit in Race Tires America, the only ***controlling*** guidance in ***this*** jurisdiction regarding a definition of the word "exemplification" for purposes of 28 U.S.C. § 1920(4) is found in In re: Kulicke and Soffa Industries Securities Litigation, 747 F.Supp. 1136 (E.D. Pa. 1990); aff'd without comment, 944 F.2d 897 (3rd Cir. 1991), which held that the concept of "exemplification" incorporates the concept "demonstrative evidence."

Federal courts in other jurisdictions have reached the same conclusion.[262] Examples of such taxable costs relating to demonstrative evidence include the costs of photos,[263] models,[264] maps,[265] blow-ups,[266] charts,[267] diagrams,[268] computer graphics,[269] and the like; however, costs related to an expert's preparation or to the creation of an expert report are a prohibited item which cannot be allowed as exemplification).[270]

There is a heavy presumption[271] in favor of "**_automatically_**"[272] taxing those types of costs listed in 28 U.S.C. § 1920[273] which the prevailing party both **_actually incurred_** (as evidenced by a sworn affidavit)[274] and **_necessarily incurred_** ("necessarily" meaning that the costs were reasonably incurred for the prevailing party's effective preparation, judged in light of the situation existing when the costs in question were actually incurred, without regard to whether the costs relate to items which were actually used).[275] Examples of situations where such costs are seen as necessary pursuant to 28 U.S.C. § 1920(4), even where the demonstrative evidence in question was not used, **_include, but are not limited to_**, situations where such demonstrative evidence is attached to any deposition transcript,[276] and/or situations where such demonstrative evidence is attached to any pleading[277] and/or situations where such demonstrative evidence is attached to any motion[278] (including a motion for summary judgment).[279]

(5) **_28 U.S.C. § 1920(5)_**

    i. **Docket fees.** The relevant statute, 28 U.S.C. § 1920(5) directs the taxing of those types of docket fees authorized by under 28 U.S.C. § 1923.[280]

    There is a heavy presumption[281] in favor of "**_automatically_**"[282] taxing those types of costs listed in 28 U.S.C. § 1920[283] which the prevailing party both **_actually incurred_** (as evidenced by a sworn affidavit)[284] and **_necessarily incurred_** ("necessarily" meaning that the costs were reasonably incurred for the prevailing party's effective preparation, judged in light of the situation existing when the costs in question were actually incurred, without regard to whether the costs relate to items which were actually used).[285]

(6) **_28 U.S.C. § 1920(6)_**

    i. **Court Appointed Experts.** The relevant statute, 28 U.S.C. § 1920(6), authorizes the taxing of costs of "court appointed experts." Costs related to the preparation of an expert's testimony or report are not mentioned in 28 U.S.C. § 1920 and are therefore not taxable[286] (although we note that costs incurred for an expert's preparation of an exhibit may be taxable in a situation where the prevailing party can demonstrate that these costs are strictly limited to exhibit preparation and do not involve preparation of testimony or a report[287]). Such unallowable costs also include costs related to an Independent Medical Examination.[288]

    There is a heavy presumption[289] in favor of "**_automatically_**"[290] taxing those types of costs listed in 28 U.S.C. § 1920[291] which the prevailing party both **_actually incurred_** (as evidenced by a sworn affidavit)[292] and **_necessarily incurred_** ("necessarily" meaning that the costs were reasonably incurred for the prevailing party's effective preparation, judged in light of the situation existing when the costs in question were actually incurred, without regard to whether the costs relate to items which were actually used).[293]

    ii. **Interpreters.** The relevant statute, 28 U.S.C. § 1920(6), authorizes "(the) compensation of interpreters." These costs are limited to the cost of oral translation, and do not include the cost of document translation (based on ordinary definition of the word "interpreters").[294]

    In addition, the fees and the salaries, expenses, and costs of special interpretation services under 28 U.S.C. § 1818 are recoverable pursuant to 28 U.S.C. § 1920(6).

    There is a heavy presumption[295] in favor of "**_automatically_**"[296] taxing those types of costs listed in 28 U.S.C. § 1920[297] which the prevailing party both **_actually incurred_** (as evidenced by a sworn affidavit)[298] and **_necessarily incurred_** ("necessarily" meaning that the costs were reasonably incurred for the prevailing party's effective preparation, judged in light of the situation existing when the costs in question were actually incurred, without regard to whether the costs relate to items which were actually used).[299]

F. Special Procedures for Allowance of District Court Costs in Situations Involving Federal Rule of Civil Procedure 68.

As previously stated, it is well-established that costs may not be imposed in federal district courts except where they are authorized by either a statute or a rule of court.[300]

Federal Rule of Civil Procedure 68 provides that:

> "(A) party defending against a claim may serve on an opposing party an offer to allow judgment on specified terms, with the costs then accrued . . . (if this offer is not accepted, and the subsequent) judgment that the offeree finally obtains is not more favorable than the unaccepted offer, the offeree must pay the costs incurred after the offer was made."

The policy supporting Rule 68 is the societal interest in encouraging settlement of cases, thereby saving the litigants and the court from unnecessary costs and effort.[301]

Rule 68 costs are taxable only by a district court judge, not the Clerk of the District Court.

Rule 68 costs may include attorney fees where the substantive statute at the heart of the case defines "costs" as including attorney fees; however, where the substantive statute at the heart of the case does not define "costs" as including attorney fees, then attorney fees are customarily not taxable pursuant to Rule 68.[302] According to this rule, where the offer does not specifically mention attorney fees as part of costs, such an offer does not necessarily exclude an allowance of attorney fees: the key factor is the language of the substantive statute at the heart of the case.[303]

Rule 68 does not apply in situations where a defendant serves upon the adverse party an offer to allow judgment to be taken against the defendant, and the final judgment is entered **in favor of the defendant, not the plaintiff.**[304]

G. Taxation of Appellate Court Costs and Supreme Court Costs by the Clerk of the District Court.

It is well-established that costs may not be imposed by the clerk of the district court except where they are authorized by either a statute or a rule of court.[305] As previously stated, Federal Rule of Civil Procedure 54(d)(1) expressly makes those items of district court costs which are listed in 28 U.S.C. § 1920[306] taxable by the clerk of the district court.[307] In addition, Federal Rule of Appellate Procedure 39(e) "expressly"[308] makes certain items of appellate court costs which are listed in that rule taxable by the clerk of the district court.[309] Those items of appellate court costs made taxable by the district court clerk by Federal Rule of Appellate Procedure 39(e) are:

(1) the preparation and transmission of the record;

(2) the reporter's transcript, if needed to determine the appeal;

(3) premiums paid for a supersedeas bond, or other bond to preserve rights pending appeal; and

(4) the fee for filing the notice of appeal.

We note that those types of costs listed in F.R.A.P. 39(e) are plainly not the same types of costs listed in the taxation statute, 28 U.S.C. § 1920;[310] however, we also note that F.R.A.P. 39(e) "_expressly_"[311] states that the types of costs listed in that appellate rule of court are taxable by the clerk of the district court.[312] In resolving this apparent conflict, it must be noted that since the adoption of the procedures created by F.R.A.P. 39(e) postdates the adoption of the procedures created by 28 U.S.C. § 1920, that to the extent that there is any apparent conflict, the district court clerk must give F.R.A.P. 39(e) more weight than 28 U.S.C. § 1920 when taxing appellate court costs.[313] **Accordingly, appellate court costs which are listed in F.R.A.P. 39(e) are taxable by the clerk of the district court, "regardless of whether § 1920 authorizes an award of those (appellate court) costs**."[314] The rationale behind this procedure directing the district court clerk, rather than the appellate court clerk, to tax appellate court costs pursuant to F.R.A.P. 39(e) is "general convenience."[315]

Once the appellate court has entered a final judgment in the underlying litigation, the clerk of the district court may tax these F.R.A.P. 39(e) costs without the need to wait for an instruction from the appellate court or from the appellate clerk directing the district clerk to tax them[316] (except where there is dispute between the parties pursuant to Federal Rule of Appellate Procedure 39(a)(4) as to who exactly is the prevailing party in the appellate court).[317] In addition, the district clerk has the discretion to tax costs even where the appellate court orders that both sides shall bear their own costs.[318]

In addition to these procedures, it bears noting that one of the most firmly established constitutional principles is the mandate principle, which hold that when a higher court issues a mandate, lower courts must obey it with regard to all issues which that higher court addressed.[319] In addition, mandate costs imposed by an appellate court leave no discretion in the hands of the district court or its Clerk; the Clerk of the district court **must** tax costs as shown on mandate of a United States Court of Appeals[320] (the rationale behind this procedure is that a federal district court is the only federal court with the authority to actually execute on a judgment[321]).

This document will now address the request for costs incurred before the United States Supreme Court.

It is well-established that costs may not be imposed in federal district courts except where they are authorized by either a statute or a rule of court.[322] Costs taxable by the United States Supreme Court are limited pursuant to Supreme Court Rule 43.3 to fees of the Clerk of the United States Supreme Court and costs of printing the joint appendix; the Clerk of the United States Supreme Court shall include these costs in the mandate; when a higher court issues a mandate, lower courts must obey it with regard to all issues which that higher court addressed.[323] Accordingly, the Clerk of the district court **must** tax costs as shown on mandate of the United States Supreme Court[324] (the rationale behind this procedure is that a federal district court is the only federal court with the authority to actually execute on a judgment[325]).

Endnotes:

1   Taniguchi v. Kan Pacific Saipan, Ltd., 132 S.Ct. 1997 (2012); Alyeska Pipeline Service Co. v. Wilderness Society, 421 U.S. 240 (1975); Fleischmann Distilling Co. v. Maier Brewing Co., 386 U.S. 714 (1967); Reger v. The Nemours Foundation, 599 F.3d 285 (3d Cir. 2010); Abrams v. Lightolier, Inc., 50 F.3d 1204 (3d Cir. 1995).

2   Reger v. The Nemours Foundation, 599 F.3d 285 (3d Cir. 2010); Abrams v. Lightolier, Inc., 50 F.3d 1204 (3d Cir. 1995).

3   Taniguchi v. Kan Pacific Saipan, Ltd., 132 S.Ct. 1997 (2012); Buchanan v. Stanships, Inc., 485 U.S. 265 (1988); Alyeska Pipeline Service Co. v. Wilderness Society, 421 U.S. 240 (1975); Fleischmann Distilling Co. v. Maier Brewing Co., 386 U.S. 714 (1967); Reger v. The Nemours Foundation, 599 F.3d 285 (3d Cir. 2010); In re: Paoli Railroad Yard PCB Litigation, 221 F.3d 449 (3d Cir. 2000); Adams v. Teamsters Local 115, 678 F.Supp.2d 314 (E.D. Pa. 2007).

4   Taniguchi v. Kan Pacific Saipan, Ltd., 132 S.Ct. 1997 (2012); Buchanan v. Stanships, Inc., 485 U.S. 265 (1988); Reger v. The Nemours Foundation, 599 F.3d 285 (3d Cir. 2010); McKenna v. City of Philadelphia, 582 F.3d 447 (3d Cir. 2009).

5   Greene v. Fraternal Order of Police, 183 F.R.D. 445 (E.D. Pa. 1998); Lacovara v. Merrill Lynch, Pierce, Fenner & Smith, 102 F.R.D. 959 (E.D. Pa. 1984).

6   Buchanan v. Stanships, Inc., 485 U.S. 265 (1988); Friedman v. Ganassi, 853 F.2d 207 (3d Cir. 1988); Adams v. Teamsters Local 115, 678 F.Supp.2d 314 (E.D. Pa. 2007); Greene v. Fraternal Order of Police, 183 F.R.D. 445 (E.D. Pa. 1998).

7   Brazos Valley Coalition for Life, Inc. v. City of Bryan, Texas, 421 F.3d 314 (5th Cir. 2005); Trepel v. Roadway Express, Inc., 266 F.3d 418 (6th Cir. 2001); Holmes v. Cessna Aircraft Co., 11 F.3d 63 (5th Cir. 1994); Dovenmuehle v. Gilldorn Mortgage Midwest Corp., 871 F.2d 697 (7th Cir. 1989); Mason v. Belieu, 543 F.2d 215 (D.C. Cir. 1976); Wahl v. Carrier Manufacturing Co., 511 F.2d 209 (7th Cir. 1975); McInnis v. Town of Weston, 458 F.Supp.2d 7 (D. Conn. 2006); Sullivan v. Cheshier, 991 F.Supp. 999 (N.D. Ill. 1998); Hollenbeck v. Falstaff Brewing Corp., 605 F.Supp. 421 (E.D. Mo. 1984); Morrissey v. County Tower Corp., 568 F.Supp. 980 (E.D. Mo. 1983).

8   Crawford Fitting Company v. J. T. Gibbons, Inc., 482 U.S. 437 (1987); Reger v. The Nemours Foundation,599 F.3d 285 (3d Cir. 2010); In re: Paoli Railroad Yard PCB Litigation, 221 F.3d 449 (3d Cir. 2000); Abrams v. Lightolier, Inc., 50 F.3d 1204 (3d Cir. 1995); Institutionalized Juveniles v. Secretary of Public Welfare, 758 F.2d 897 (3d Cir. 1985); Nugget Distributors Cooperative of America v. Mr. Nugget, Inc.,

Endnotes

145 F.R.D. 54 (E.D.Pa. 1992). Accord, Perry v. Metro Suburban Bus Authority; 236 FRD 110 (EDNY 2006); Schmitz-Werke GMBH v. Rockland Industries, 271 F.Supp. 2d 734 (D. Maryland 2003); Roberts v. Interstate Distrib. Co., 242 F.Supp. 2d 850 (D. Oregon 2002); In Re: Glacier Bay, 746 F.Supp. 1379 (D. Alaska 1990).

9   Brazos Valley Coalition for Life, Inc. v. City of Bryan, Texas, 421 F.3d 314 (5th Cir. 2005); Trepel v. Roadway Express, Inc., 266 F.3d 418 (6th Cir. 2001); Holmes v. Cessna Aircraft Co., 11 F.3d 63 (5th Cir. 1994); Dovenmuehle v. Gilldorn Mortgage Midwest Corp., 871 F.2d 697 (7th Cir. 1989); Mason v. Belieu, 543 F.2d 215 (D.C. Cir. 1976); Wahl v. Carrier Manufacturing Co., 511 F.2d 209 (7th Cir. 1975); McInnis v. Town of Weston, 458 F.Supp.2d 7 (D. Conn. 2006); Sullivan v. Cheshire, 991 F.Supp. 999 (N.D. Ill. 1998); Hollenbeck v. Falstaff Brewing Corp., 605 F.Supp. 421 (E.D. Mo. 1984); Morrissey v. County Tower Corp., 568 F.Supp. 980 (E.D. Mo. 1983).

10   Brown v. American Enka Corp., 452 F.Supp. 154 (ED Tenn. 1976).

11   Brown v. American Enka Corp., 452 F.Supp. 154 (ED Tenn. 1976).

12   In re: Paoli Railroad Yard PCB Litigation, 221 F.3d 449 (3rd Cir. 2000). Accord, Soberay Mach. & Equip. Co. v. MRF Ltd., 181 F.3d 759 (6th Cir. 1999); Lorenz v. Valley Forge Insurance Co., 23 F.3d 1259 (7th Cir. 1994); McGuigan v. Cae Link Corp., 155 FRD 31 (NDNY 1994); American Key Corp. v. Cumberland Associates, 102 FRD 496 (NDGa 1984); and Dorothy K. Winston & Co. v. Town Heights Dev., Inc., 68 FRD 431 (DDC 1975).

13   Northbrook Excess and Surplus Insurance Co. v. Procter & Gamble Co., 924 F.2d 633 (7th Cir. 1991).

14   Alyeska Pipeline Service Co. v. Wilderness Society, 421 U.S. 240 (1975); Adams v. Teamsters Local 115, 678 F.Supp.2d 314 (E.D. Pa. 2007); Nugget Distributors Cooperative of America v. Mr. Nugget, Inc., 145 F.R.D. 54 (E.D.Pa. 1992). Accord, Cook Children's Medical Center v. New England PPO Plan of Gen. Consol. Management, 491 F.3d 266 (5th Cir. 2007); Perry v. Metro Suburban Bus Authority; 236 F.R.D. 110 (EDNY 2006); Schmitz-Werke GMBH v. Rockland Industries, 271 F.Supp. 2d 734 (D. Maryland 2003); Roberts v. Interstate Distrib. Co., 242 F.Supp. 2d 850 (D. Oregon 2002); US v. Bedford Associates, 548 F.Supp. 748 (SDNY 1982).

15   Buchanan v. Stanships, Inc., 485 U.S. 265 (1988); Friedman v. Ganassi, 853 F.2d 207 (3d Cir. 1988); Adams v. Teamsters Local 115, 678 F.Supp.2d 314 (E.D. Pa. 2007).

16   Abrams v. Lightolier, Inc., 50 F.3d 1204 (3d Cir. 1995); Smith v. SEPTA, 47 F.3d 97 (3d Cir. 1995); Friedman v. Ganassi, 853 F.2d 207 (3d Cir. 1988); Institutionalized Juveniles v. Secretary of Public Welfare, 758 F.2d 897 (3rd Cir. 1985); Pearlstine v. United States, 649 F.2d 194 (3rd Cir. 1981); Delaney v. Capone, 642 F.2d 57 (3d Cir. 1981); Samuel v. University of Pittsburgh, 538 F.2d 991 (3d Cir. 1976); ADM Corp. v. Speedmaster Packing Corp., 525 F.2d 662 (3d Cir. 1975); Greene v. Fraternal Order of Police, 183 F.R.D. 445 (E.D.Pa. 1998). Accord, In Re: Air Crash Disaster at John F. Kennedy International Airport on June 24, 1975, 687 F.2d 626 (2nd Cir. 1982); In Re: Glacier Bay, 746 F.Supp. 1379 (D. Alaska 1990).

17   Chambers v. NASCO, Inc., 501 U.S. 32 (1991); Alyeska Pipeline Service Co. v. Wilderness Society, 421 U.S. 240 (1975); Fleischmann Distilling Co. v. Maier Brewing Co., 386 U.S. 714 (1967).

18   Nugget Distributors Cooperative of America v. Mr. Nugget, Inc., 145 F.R.D. 54 (E.D.Pa. 1992). Accord, Alyeska Pipeline Service Co. v. Wilderness Society, 421 U.S. 240 (1975); In re: Paoli Railroad Yard PCB Litigation, 221 F.3d 449 (3d Cir. 2000); Abrams v. Lightolier, Inc., 50 F.3d 1204 (3d Cir. 1995). See, also, Harkins v. Riverboat Services, 286 F. Supp. 2d 976 (ND Ill. 2003), aff'd, 385 F.3d 1099 (7th Cir. 2004); and In Re: Glacier Bay, 746 F.Supp. 1379 (D. Alaska 1990).

19   Race Tires America, Inc. v. Hoosier Racing Tire Corp., 2012 WL 887593 (3d Cir. March 16, 2012).

20   In re: Paoli Railroad Yard PCB Litigation, 221 F.3d 449 (3d Cir. 2000); Levin v. Parkhouse, 484 F.Supp. 1091 (E.D. Pa. 1980). Accord, In Re: San Juan Dupont Plaza Hotel Fire Litigation, 994 F.2d 956 (1st Cir. 1993); Krouse v. American Sterilizer Co., 928 F.Supp. 543 (W.D. Pa. 1996); In Re: Glacier Bay, 746 F.Supp. 1379 (D. Alaska 1990); Stacy v. Williams, 50 F.R.D. 52 (N.D. Miss. 1970); Bourazak v. North River Insurance Co., 280 F.Supp. 89 (S.D. Ill. 1968).

21   Race Tires America, Inc. v. Hoosier Racing Tire Corp., 2012 WL 887593 (3d Cir. March 16, 2012).

22   Smith v. Tenet Healthsystems SL, Inc., 436 F.3d 879 (8th Cir. 2006); Helms v. WalMart Stores, Inc., 808 F.Supp. 1568 (ND Ga. 1992), aff'd 998 F.2d 1023 (11th Cir. 1993); Soler v. McHenry, 771 F.Supp. 252 (ND Ill. 1991), aff'd, 989 F.2d 251 (7th Cir. 1993); Haagen-Dazs Co. v. Rainbow Gourmet Ice Creams, Inc., 920 F.2d 587 (9th Cir. 1990); Rodriguez-Garcia v. Davila, 904 F.2d 90 (1st Cir. 1990); Allen v. United States Steel Corp., 665 F.2d 689 (5th Cir. 1982); McGuigan v. CAE Link Corp., 155 FRD 31 (NDNY 1994); Nelson v. Darragh Co., 120 FRD 517 (WD Ark. 1988); Radol v. Thomas, 113 FRD 172 (SD Ohio 1986); Roche

	v. Normandy, 566 F.Supp. 37 (ED Mo. 1983); Meadows v. Ford Motor Co., 62 FRD 98 (WD Ky. 1973); Gillam v. A. Shyman, Inc., 31 FRD 271 (D. Alaska 1962).
23	Smith v. Tenet Healthsystems SL, Inc., 436 F.3d 879 (8th Cir. 2006).
24	Yasui v. Maui Electric Co., 78 F.Supp. 2d 1124 (D. Hawaii 1999); Garonzik v. Whitman Diner, 910 F.Supp 167 (D.N.J. 1995); Corsair Asset Management, Inc. v. Moskovitz, 142 FRD 347 (N.D. Ga. 1992).
25	Montgomery County v. Microvote Corp., 2004 WL 1087196 (EDPA 2004); Sun Media Systems, Inc. v. KDSM, LLC, 587 F.Supp. 2d 1059 (S.D. Iowa 2008).
26	Gary Brown and Associates v. Ashdon, Inc., 268 Fed.Appx. 837 (11th Cir. 2008); Jensen v. Lawler, 338 F.Supp. 2d 739 (SD Texas 2004).
27	Nugget Distributors Cooperative of America v. Mr. Nugget, Inc., 145 F.R.D. 54 (E.D.Pa. 1992). Accord, In Re: San Juan Dupont Plaza Hotel Fire Litigation, 994 F.2d 956 (1st Cir. 1993); United States Football League v. National Football League, 887 F.2d 408 (2nd Cir. 1989); Wahl v. Carrier Manufacturing Co., 511 F.2d 209 (7th Cir. 1975); In Re: Glacier Bay, 746 F.Supp. 1379 (D. Alaska 1990); Hollenbeck v. Falstaff Brewing Corp., 605 F.Supp. 421 (ED Mo. 1984).
28	United States Football League v. National Football League, 887 F.2d 408 (2nd Cir. 1989); Allen v. United States Steel Corp., 665 F.2d 689 (5th Cir. 1982).
29	Nugget Distributors Cooperative of America v. Mr. Nugget, Inc., 145 F.R.D. 54 (E.D.Pa. 1992). Accord, Avirgan v. Hull, 705 F.Supp. 1544 (SD Fla 1989), aff'd, 932 F.2d 1572 (11th Cir. 1991); Wahl v. Carrier Manufacturing Co., 511 F.2d 209 (7th Cir. 1975); Corsair Asset Management, Inc. v. Moskovitz, 142 F.R.D. 347 (ND Ga 1992); In Re: Glacier Bay, 746 F.Supp. 1379 (D. Alaska 1990).
30	Wahl v. Carrier Manufacturing Co., 511 F.2d 209 (7th Cir. 1975); In Re: Glacier Bay, 746 F.Supp. 1379 (D. Alaska 1990).
31	Corsair Asset Management, Inc. v. Moskovitz, 142 F.R.D. 347 (ND Ga 1992); Litton Systems, Inc. V. American Telephone & Telegraph Co., 613 F.Supp. 824 (SDNY 1985).
32	Nugget Distributors Cooperative of America v. Mr. Nugget, Inc., 145 F.R.D. 54 (E.D.Pa. 1992). Accord, Gary Brown and Associates v. Ashdon, Inc., 268 Fed.Appx. 837 (11th Cir. 2008); Avirgan v. Hull, 705 F.Supp. 1544 (SD Fla 1989), aff'd, 932 F.2d 1572 (11th Cir. 1991); Wahl v. Carrier Manufacturing Co., 511 F.2d 209 (7th Cir. 1975); Sun Media Systems, Inc. v. KDSM, LLC, 587 F.Supp. 2d 1059 (S.D. Iowa 2008); Yasui v. Maui Electric Co., 78 F.Supp.2d 1124 (D. Hawaii 1999); Royal Palace Hotel Associates v. International Resort Classics, 178 FRD 595 (MD Fl. 1998); Corsair Asset Management, Inc. v. Moskovitz, 142 FRD 347 (ND Ga 1992); In Re: Glacier Bay, 746 F.Supp. 1379 (D. Alaska 1990); Central Delaware Branch of the NAACP v. City of Dover, Delaware, 123 FRD 85 (D. Delaware 1988); Hollenbeck v. Falstaff Brewing Corp., 605 F.Supp. 421 (ED Mo. 1984); Evans v. Fuller, 94 F.R.D. 311, 314 (W.D. Ark. 1982); Neely v. General Electric Co., 90 F.R.D. 627, 630 (N.D. Ga. 1981); United States v. Bexar County, 89 F.R.D. 391, 394 (W.D. Tex. 1981).
33	Sun Media Systems, Inc. v. KDSM, LLC, 587 F.Supp. 2d 1059 (S.D. Iowa 2008).
34	Gary Brown and Associates v. Ashdon, Inc., 268 Fed.Appx. 837 (11th Cir. 2008); Sun Media Systems, Inc. v. KDSM, LLC, 587 F.Supp. 2d 1059 (S.D. Iowa 2008); Central Delaware Branch of the NAACP v. City of Dover, Delaware, 123 F.R.D. 85 (D. Delaware 1988).
35	Sun Media Systems, Inc. v. KDSM, LLC, 587 F.Supp. 2d 1059 (S.D. Iowa 2008); Central Delaware Branch of the NAACP v. City of Dover, Delaware, 123 F.R.D. 85 (D. Delaware 1988).
36	Sun Media Systems, Inc. v. KDSM, LLC, 587 F.Supp. 2d 1059 (S.D. Iowa 2008); Yasui v. Maui Electric Co., 78 F.Supp.2d 1124 (D. Hawaii 1999); Cody v. Private Agencies Collaborating Together, Inc., 911 F.Supp. 1 (D.D.C. 1995).
37	Sun Media Systems, Inc. v. KDSM, LLC, 587 F.Supp. 2d 1059 (S.D. Iowa 2008).
38	Central Delaware Branch of the NAACP v. City of Dover, Delaware, 123 F.R.D. 85 (D. Delaware 1988).
39	Nugget Distributors Cooperative of America v. Mr. Nugget, Inc., 145 F.R.D. 54 (E.D.Pa. 1992); See, also, Gary Brown and Associates v. Ashdon, Inc., 268 Fed.Appx. 837 (11th Cir. 2008); Duckworth v. Whisenant, 97 F.3d 1393 (11th Cir. 1993); Avirgan v. Hull, 705 F.Supp. 1544 (SD Fla 1989), aff'd, 932 F.2d 1572 (11th Cir. 1991); Sun Media Systems, Inc. v. KDSM, LLC, 587 F.Supp. 2d 1059 (S.D. Iowa 2008); DiBella v. Hopkins, 407 F.Supp.2d 537 (SDNY 2005); Yasui v. Maui Electric Co., 78 F.Supp.2d 1124 (D. Hawaii 1999); Royal Palace Hotel Associates v. International Resort Classics, 178 FRD 595 (MD Fl. 1998); Corsair Asset Management, Inc. v. Moskovitz, 142 FRD 347 (ND Ga 1992); Aloha Towers Associates v. Millenium Aloha, Inc., 938 F. Supp. 646 (D. Hawaii 1996); U.S. v. Bedford Associates, 548 F.Supp. 748, 753 (S.D.N.Y. 1982).

Endnotes

40 Nugget Distributors Cooperative of America v. Mr. Nugget, Inc., 145 F.R.D. 54 (E.D.Pa. 1992). Accord, In Re: San Juan Dupont Plaza Hotel Fire Litigation, 994 F.2d 956 (1st Cir. 1993); Wahl v. Carrier Manufacturing Co., 511 F.2d 209 (7th Cir. 1975); Avirgan v. Hull, 705 F.Supp. 1544 (SD Fla 1989), aff'd, 932 F.2d 1572 (11th Cir. 1991); Massachusetts Fair Share v. Law Enforcement Assistance Association, 776 F.2d 1066, 1070 (D.C. Cir. 1985); Sun Media Systems, Inc. v. KDSM, LLC, 587 F.Supp. 2d 1059 (S.D. Iowa 2008); Yasui v. Maui Electric Co., 78 F.Supp.2d 1124 (D. Hawaii 1999); Royal Palace Hotel Associates v. International Resort Classics, 178 FRD 595 (MD Fl. 1998); Cody v. Private Agencies Collaborating Together, Inc., 911 F.Supp. 1 (D.D.C. 1995); Corsair Asset Management, Inc. v. Moskovitz, 142 FRD 347 (ND Ga 1992); In Re: Glacier Bay, 746 F.Supp. 1379 (D. Alaska 1990); General Drivers and Dairy Employees, Local 563 v. Bake Rite Baking Co., 580 F.Supp. 426, 440 (E.D. Wisc. 1984); Hollenbeck v. Falstaff Brewing Corp., 605 F.Supp. 421 (ED Mo. 1984).

41 In Re: Glacier Bay, 746 F.Supp. 1379 (D. Alaska 1990); Hollenbeck v. Falstaff Brewing Corp., 605 F.Supp. 421 (ED Mo. 1984).

42 Nugget Distributors Cooperative of America v. Mr. Nugget, Inc., 145 F.R.D. 54 (E.D.Pa. 1992). Accord, Avirgan v. Hull, 705 F.Supp. 1544 (SD Fla 1989), aff'd, 932 F.2d 1572 (11th Cir. 1991); Sun Media Systems, Inc. v. KDSM, LLC, 587 F.Supp. 2d 1059 (S.D. Iowa 2008); Cody v. Private Agencies Collaborating Together, Inc., 911 F.Supp. 1 (D.D.C. 1995); Corsair Asset Management, Inc. v. Moskovitz, 142 F.R.D. 347 (ND Ga 1992); In re: San Juan DuPont Plaza Hotel Fire Litigation, 142 F.R.D. 41 (D.P.R. 1992); Hollenbeck v. Falstaff Brewing Corp., 605 F.Supp. 421 (ED Mo. 1984).

43 Nugget Distributors Cooperative of America v. Mr. Nugget, Inc., 145 F.R.D. 54 (E.D.Pa. 1992). Accord, Gary Brown and Associates v. Ashdon, Inc., 268 Fed.Appx. 837 (11th Cir. 2008); Avirgan v. Hull, 705 F.Supp. 1544 (SD Fla 1989), aff'd, 932 F.2d 1572 (11th Cir. 1991); Yasui v. Maui Electric Co., 78 F.Supp.2d 1124 (D. Hawaii 1999); Corsair Asset Management, Inc. v. Moskovitz, 142 FRD 347 (ND Ga 1992); In Re: Glacier Bay, 746 F.Supp. 1379 (D. Alaska 1990); Hollenbeck v. Falstaff Brewing Corp., 605 F.Supp. 421 (ED Mo. 1984).

44 McGuigan v. CAE Link Corp., 155 FRD 31 (NDNY 1994).

45 In the Matter of Penn Central Transportation Co., 630 F.2d 183 (3d Cir. 1980); Nugget Distributors Cooperative of America v. Mr. Nugget, Inc., 145 F.R.D. 54 (E.D.Pa. 1992). Accord, Gary Brown and Associates v. Ashdon, Inc., 268 Fed.Appx. 837 (11th Cir. 2008); Duckworth v. Whisenant, 97 F.3d 1393 (11th Cir. 1993); Avirgan v. Hull, 705 F.Supp. 1544 (SD Fla 1989), aff'd, 932 F.2d 1572 (11th Cir. 1991); Wahl v. Carrier Manufacturing Co., 511 F.2d 209 (7th Cir. 1975); Zeuner v. Rare Hospitality Int'l, 386 F.Supp. 2d 635 (MDNC 2005); Yasui v. Maui Electric Co., 78 F.Supp.2d 1124 (D. Hawaii 1999); Royal Palace Hotel Associates v. International Resort Classics, 178 FRD 595 (MD Fl. 1998); Cody v. Private Agencies Collaborating Together, Inc., 911 F.Supp. 1 (D.D.C. 1995); Corsair Asset Management, Inc. v. Moskovitz, 142 FRD 347 (ND Ga 1992); In Re: Glacier Bay, 746 F.Supp. 1379 (D. Alaska 1990); Hollenbeck v. Falstaff Brewing Corp., 605 F.Supp. 421 (ED Mo. 1984).

46 Wahl v. Carrier Manufacturing Co., 511 F.2d 209 (7th Cir. 1975); Sun Media Systems, Inc. v. KDSM, LLC, 587 F.Supp. 2d 1059 (S.D. Iowa 2008); In Re: Glacier Bay, 746 F.Supp. 1379 (D. Alaska 1990); Hollenbeck v. Falstaff Brewing Corp., 605 F.Supp. 421 (ED Mo. 1984).

47 Nelson v. Darragh Co., 120 F.R.D. 517 (W.D. Ark. 1988); Mallonee v. Fahey, 117 F.Supp. 259 (S.D. Cal. 1953).

48 Marquez v. American Export Lines, 41 FRD 386 (SDNY 1967).

49 Sierra Club v. EPA, 769 F.2d 796 (DC Cir. 1985); In Re: Air Crash Disaster at John F. Kennedy International Airport on June 24, 1975, 687 F.2d 626 (2nd Cir. 1982); Griffith v. Mt. Carmel Medical Center, 157 F.R.D. 499 (D. Kansas 1994); Radol v. Thomas, 113 FRD 172 (SD Ohio 1986); Marquez v. American Export Lines, 41 FRD 386 (SDNY 1967).

50 Jensen v. Lawler, 338 F.Supp. 2d 739 (SD Texas 2004).

51 In re: San Juan DuPont Plaza Hotel Fire Litigation, 142 F.R.D. 41 (D.P.R. 1992); Parts & Electric Motors, Inc. v. Sterling Electric, 123 FRD 584 (ND Ill. 1988).

52 Corsair Asset Management, Inc. v. Moskovitz, 142 FRD 347 (ND Ga 1992)

53 Wahl v. Carrier Manufacturing Co., 511 F.2d 209 (7th Cir. 1975); Hollenbeck v. Falstaff Brewing Corp., 605 F.Supp. 421 (ED Mo. 1984).

54 Buchanan v. Stanships, Inc., 485 U.S. 265 (1988); Reger v. The Nemours Foundation, 599 F.3d 285 (3d Cir. 2010); In re: Paoli Railroad Yard PCB Litigation, 221 F.3d 449 (3d Cir. 2000).

55 Delta Air Lines, Inc. v. August, 450 U.S. 346, 353 (1981).

56 Reger v. The Nemours Foundation, 599 F.3d 285 (3d Cir. 2010); In re: Paoli Railroad Yard PCB Litigation, 221 F.3d 449 (3d Cir. 2000); Abrams v. Lightolier, Inc., 50 F.3d 1204 (3d Cir. 1995); Smith v. SEPTA, 47 F.3d 97 (3d Cir. 1995); Friedman v. Ganassi, 853 F.2d 207 (3d Cir. 1988); Institutionalized Juveniles v. Secretary of Public Welfare, 758 F.2d 897 (3d Cir. 1985); Pearlstine v. United States, 649 F.2d 194 (3rd Cir. 1981); Delaney v. Capone, 642 F.2d 57 (3d Cir. 1981); Samuel v. University of Pittsburgh, 538 F.2d 991 (3d Cir. 1976); ADM Corp. v. Speedmaster Packing Corp., 525 F.2d 662 (3d Cir. 1975); City of Rome, Italy v. Glanton, 184 F.R.D. 547 (E.D. Pa. 1999); Greene v. Fraternal Order of Police, 183 F.R.D. 445 (E.D. Pa. 1998); Action Alliance for Senior Citizens of Greater Philadelphia v. Shapp, 74 F.R.D. 617 (E.D. Pa. 1977).

57 Buchanan v. Stanships, Inc., 485 U.S. 265, 268 (1988)(emphasis added). Accord, Delta Air Lines, Inc. v. August, 450 U.S. 346 (1981). See, also, Reger v. The Nemours Foundation, 599 F.3d 285 (3d Cir. 2010); In re: Paoli Railroad Yard PCB Litigation, 221 F.3d 449 (3d Cir. 2000); Abrams v. Lightolier, Inc., 50 F.3d 1204 (3d Cir. 1995); Smith v. SEPTA, 47 F.3d 97 (3d Cir. 1995); Friedman v. Ganassi, 853 F.2d 207 (3d Cir. 1988); Institutionalized Juveniles v. Secretary of Public Welfare, 758 F.2d 897 (3d Cir. 1985); Pearlstine v. United States, 649 F.2d 194 (3rd Cir. 1981); Delaney v. Capone, 642 F.2d 57 (3d Cir. 1981); Samuel v. University of Pittsburgh, 538 F.2d 991 (3d Cir. 1976); ADM Corp. v. Speedmaster Packing Corp., 525 F.2d 662 (3d Cir. 1975); City of Rome, Italy v. Glanton, 184 F.R.D. 547 (E.D. Pa. 1999); Greene v. Fraternal Order of Police, 183 F.R.D. 445 (E.D. Pa. 1998); Action Alliance for Senior Citizens of Greater Philadelphia v. Shapp, 74 F.R.D. 617 (E.D. Pa. 1977).

58 Buchanan v. Stanships, Inc., 485 U.S. 265 (1988); Delta Air Lines, Inc. v. August, 450 U.S. 346 (1981). Accord, Reger v. The Nemours Foundation, 599 F.3d 285 (3d Cir. 2010); In re: Paoli Railroad Yard PCB Litigation, 221 F.3d 449 (3d Cir. 2000); Abrams v. Lightolier, Inc., 50 F.3d 1204 (3d Cir. 1995); Smith v. SEPTA, 47 F.3d 97 (3d Cir. 1995); Friedman v. Ganassi, 853 F.2d 207 (3d Cir. 1988); Institutionalized Juveniles v. Secretary of Public Welfare, 758 F.2d 897 (3d Cir. 1985); Pearlstine v. United States, 649 F.2d 194 (3rd Cir. 1981); Delaney v. Capone, 642 F.2d 57 (3d Cir. 1981); Samuel v. University of Pittsburgh, 538 F.2d 991 (3d Cir. 1976); ADM Corp. v. Speedmaster Packing Corp., 525 F.2d 662 (3d Cir. 1975); City of Rome, Italy v. Glanton, 184 F.R.D. 547 (E.D. Pa. 1999); Greene v. Fraternal Order of Police, 183 F.R.D. 445 (E.D. Pa. 1998); Action Alliance for Senior Citizens of Greater Philadelphia v. Shapp, 74 F.R.D. 617 (E.D. Pa. 1977).

59 Brazos Valley Coalition for Life, Inc. v. City of Bryan, Texas, 421 F.3d 314 (5th Cir. 2005); Trepel v. Roadway Express, Inc., 266 F.3d 418 (6th Cir. 2001); Holmes v. Cessna Aircraft Co., 11 F.3d 63 (5th Cir. 1994); Dovenmuehle v. Gilldorn Mortgage Midwest Corp., 871 F.2d 697 (7th Cir. 1989); Mason v. Belieu, 543 F.2d 215 (D.C. Cir. 1976); Wahl v. Carrier Manufacturing Co., 511 F.2d 209 (7th Cir. 1975); McInnis v. Town of Weston, 458 F.Supp.2d 7 (D. Conn. 2006); Sullivan v. Cheshier, 991 F.Supp. 999 (N.D. Ill. 1998); Hollenbeck v. Falstaff Brewing Corp., 605 F.Supp. 421 (E.D. Mo. 1984); Morrissey v. County Tower Corp., 568 F.Supp. 980 (E.D. Mo. 1983).

60 In Re: Kulicke & Soffa Industries Inc. Securities Litigation, 747 F.Supp. 1136 (E.D.Pa. 1990), aff'd, 944 F.2d 897 (3rd Cir. 1991); ADM Corp. v. Speedmaster Packing Corp., 525 F.2d 662 (3d Cir. 1975); Nugget Distributors Cooperative of America v. Mr. Nugget, Inc., 145 F.R.D. 54 (E.D.Pa. 1992). Accord, Charter Medical Corp v. Cardin, 127 F.R.D. 111 (D. Maryland 1989); Women's Federal Savings and Loan Association of Cleveland v. Nevada National Bank, 108 F.R.D. 396 (D. Nevada 1985); International Wood Processors v. Power Dry, Inc., 598 F. Supp. 299 (D.S.C. 1984); Morrissey v. County Tower Corp., 568 F.Supp. 178 (ED Mo. 1983).

61 Delta Air Lines, Inc. v. August, 450 U.S. 346 (1981); Reger v. The Nemours Foundation, 599 F.3d 285 (3d Cir. 2010); Abrams v. Lightolier, Inc., 50 F.3d 1204 (3d Cir. 1995); Smith v. SEPTA, 47 F.3d 97 (3d Cir. 1995); Friedman v. Ganassi, 853 F.2d 207 (3d Cir. 1988); Institutionalized Juveniles v. Secretary of Public Welfare, 758 F.2d 897 (3rd Cir. 1985); Pearlstine v. United States, 649 F.2d 194 (3rd Cir. 1981); Delaney v. Capone, 642 F.2d 57 (3d Cir. 1981); Samuel v. University of Pittsburgh, 538 F.2d 991 (3d Cir. 1976); ADM Corp. v. Speedmaster Packing Corp., 525 F.2d 662 (3d Cir. 1975); Greene v. Fraternal Order of Police, 183 F.R.D. 445 (E.D.Pa. 1998). Accord, In Re: Air Crash Disaster at John F. Kennedy International Airport on June 24, 1975, 687 F.2d 626 (2nd Cir. 1982); In Re: Glacier Bay, 746 F.Supp. 1379 (D. Alaska 1990).

62 Chambers v. NASCO, Inc., 501 U.S. 32 (1991); Alyeska Pipeline Service Co. v. Wilderness Society, 421 U.S. 240 (1975).

63 Reger v. The Nemours Foundation, 599 F.3d 285 (3d Cir. 2010); In re: Paoli Railroad Yard PCB Litigation, 221 F.3d 449 (3d Cir. 2000); Friedman v. Ganassi, 853 F.2d 207 (3d Cir. 1988); Adams v. Teamsters Local 115, 678 F.Supp.2d 314 (E.D. Pa. 2007); Montgomery County v. Microvote Corp., 2004 WL 1087196 (EDPA 2004); Greene v. Fraternal Order of Police, 183 F.R.D. 445 (E.D.Pa. 1998). Accord, McGuigan v. CAE Link Corp., 155 F.R.D. 31 (NDNY 1994).

Endnotes

64 Reger v. The Nemours Foundation, 599 F.3d 285 (3d Cir. 2010); Smith v. SEPTA, 47 F.3d 97 (3d Cir. 1995); Friedman v. Ganassi, 853 F.2d 207 (3d Cir. 1988); Institutionalized Juveniles v. Secretary of Public Welfare, 758 F.2d 897, 926 (3rd Cir. 1985); Pearlstine v. United States, 649 F.2d 194 (3rd Cir. 1981); Delaney v. Capone, 642 F.2d 57 (3d Cir. 1981); Samuel v. University of Pittsburgh, 538 F.2d 991 (3d Cir. 1976); ADM Corp. v. Speedmaster Packing Corp., 525 F.2d 662 (3d Cir. 1975); Adams v. Teamsters Local 115, 678 F.Supp.2d 314 (E.D. Pa. 2007).

65 Reger v. The Nemours Foundation, 599 F.3d 285 (3d Cir. 2010).

66 Reger v. The Nemours Foundation, 599 F.3d 285 (3d Cir. 2010); Friedman v. Ganassi, 853 F.2d 207 (3d Cir. 1988); Pearlstine v. United States, 649 F.2d 194 (3rd Cir. 1981); ADM Corp. v. Speedmaster Packaging Corp., 525 F.2d 662, (3rd Cir. 1975); Adams v. Teamsters Local 115, 678 F.Supp.2d 314 (E.D. Pa. 2007). Accord, In Re Olympia Brewing Co. Securities Litigation, 613 F.Supp. 1286, 1302 (N.D.Ill. 1985).

67 Reger v. The Nemours Foundation, 599 F.3d 285 (3d Cir. 2010).

68 Thomas v. Duralite Co., Inc., 524 F.2d 577 (3rd Cir. 1975). Accord, Dail v. George A. Arab, Inc., 391 F.Supp. 2d 1142 (M.D. Fla 2005); DiCecco v. The Dillard House, Inc., 149 F.R.D. 239 (N.D.Ga. 1993); Frigiquip Corp. v. Parker-Hannifin Corp., 75 F.R.D. 605 (W.D. Okla. 1977).

69 See, Federal Rule of Civil Procedure 54(d)(1).

70 Buchanan v. Stanships, Inc., 485 U.S. 265 (1988); Samaad v. City of Dallas, 922 F.2d 216 (5th Cir. 1991).

71 Reger v. The Nemours Foundation, 599 F.3d 285, 289 Footnote 3 (3d Cir. 2010) (emphasis added).

72 Delta Air Lines, Inc. v. August, 450 U.S. 346, 353 (1981).

73 Reger v. The Nemours Foundation, 599 F.3d 285 (3d Cir. 2010); In re: Paoli Railroad Yard PCB Litigation, 221 F.3d 449 (3d Cir. 2000); Abrams v. Lightolier, Inc., 50 F.3d 1204 (3d Cir. 1995); Smith v. SEPTA, 47 F.3d 97 (3d Cir. 1995); Friedman v. Ganassi, 853 F.2d 207 (3d Cir. 1988); Institutionalized Juveniles v. Secretary of Public Welfare, 758 F.2d 897 (3d Cir. 1985); Pearlstine v. United States, 649 F.2d 194 (3rd Cir. 1981); Delaney v. Capone, 642 F.2d 57 (3d Cir. 1981); Samuel v. University of Pittsburgh, 538 F.2d 991 (3d Cir. 1976); ADM Corp. v. Speedmaster Packing Corp., 525 F.2d 662 (3d Cir. 1975); City of Rome, Italy v. Glanton, 184 F.R.D. 547 (E.D. Pa. 1999); Greene v. Fraternal Order of Police, 183 F.R.D. 445 (E.D. Pa. 1998); Action Alliance for Senior Citizens of Greater Philadelphia v. Shapp, 74 F.R.D. 617 (E.D. Pa. 1977).

74 Buchanan v. Stanships, Inc., 485 U.S. 265, 268 (1988)(emphasis added). Accord, Delta Air Lines, Inc. v. August, 450 U.S. 346 (1981).

75 Buchanan v. Stanships, Inc., 485 U.S. 265 (1988); Delta Air Lines, Inc. v. August, 450 U.S. 346 (1981); Reger v. The Nemours Foundation, 599 F.3d 285 (3d Cir. 2010); In re: Paoli Railroad Yard PCB Litigation, 221 F.3d 449 (3d Cir. 2000); Abrams v. Lightolier, Inc., 50 F.3d 1204 (3d Cir. 1995); Smith v. SEPTA, 47 F.3d 97 (3d Cir. 1995); Friedman v. Ganassi, 853 F.2d 207 (3d Cir. 1988); Institutionalized Juveniles v. Secretary of Public Welfare, 758 F.2d 897 (3d Cir. 1985); Pearlstine v. United States, 649 F.2d 194 (3rd Cir. 1981); Delaney v. Capone, 642 F.2d 57 (3d Cir. 1981); Samuel v. University of Pittsburgh, 538 F.2d 991 (3d Cir. 1976); ADM Corp. v. Speedmaster Packing Corp., 525 F.2d 662 (3d Cir. 1975); City of Rome, Italy v. Glanton, 184 F.R.D. 547 (E.D. Pa. 1999); Greene v. Fraternal Order of Police, 183 F.R.D. 445 (E.D. Pa. 1998); Action Alliance for Senior Citizens of Greater Philadelphia v. Shapp, 74 F.R.D. 617 (E.D. Pa. 1977).

76 Reger v. The Nemours Foundation, 599 F.3d 285 (3d Cir. 2010); In re: Paoli Railroad Yard PCB Litigation, 221 F.3d 449 (3d Cir. 2000); Smith v. SEPTA, 47 F.3d 97 (3d Cir. 1995); Friedman v. Ganassi, 853 F.2d 207 (3d Cir. 1988); Adams v. Teamsters Local 115, 678 F.Supp.2d 314 (E.D. Pa. 2007); Action Alliance for Senior Citizens of Greater Philadelphia v. Shapp, 74 F.R.D. 617 (ED Pa. 1977). Accord, Matthew v. Crosby, 480 F.3d 1265 (11th Cir. 2007); Weaver v. Toombs, 948 F.2d 1004 (6th Cir. 1991); Perry v. Metro Suburban Bus Authority, 236 FRD 110 (EDNY 2006).

77 Reger v. The Nemours Foundation, 599 F.3d 285 (3d Cir. 2010); Adams v. Teamsters Local 115, 678 F.Supp.2d 314 (E.D. Pa. 2007); Action Alliance for Senior Citizens of Greater Philadelphia v. Shapp, 74 F.R.D. 617 (ED Pa. 1977).

78 Reger v. The Nemours Foundation, 599 F.3d 285 (3d Cir. 2010); In re: Paoli Railroad Yard PCB Litigation, 221 F.3d 449 (3d Cir. 2000); Adams v. Teamsters Local 115, 678 F.Supp.2d 314 (E.D. Pa. 2007); Greene v. Fraternal Order of Police, 183 F.R.D. 445 (ED Pa. 1998).

79 Adams v. Teamsters Local 115, 678 F.Supp.2d 314 (E.D. Pa. 2007). Accord, Washington v. Patlis, 916 F.2d 1036 (5th Cir. 1990); Chevrette v. Marks, 558 F.Supp. 1133 (M.D. Pa. 1983).

80 Constitution Bank v. Tubbs, 68 F.3d 685 (3rd Cir. 1995).

81 Association of St. Croix Condominium Owners v. St. Croix Hotel Corp., 682 F.2d 446 (3rd Cir 1982).

82   Franklin Savings Association v. Office of Thrift Supervision, 31 F.3d 1020 (10th Cir. 1994); Aerotech Resources Inc. v. Dodson Aviation, Inc., 237 F.R.D. 659 (D. Kansas 2005).

83   Maritime Electric Co. v. United Jersey Bank, 959 F.2d 1194, 1205 (3rd Cir. 1991) (emphasis added). See, also, Jefferson Ward Stores, Inc. v. Doody Co., 48 BR 276 (ED Pa 1985). Accord, Farley v. Henson, 2 F.3d 273 (8th Cir. 1993); Martin-Trigona v. Champion Federal Savings and Loan Association, 892 F.2d 575 (7th Cir. 1989); Carley Capital Group v. Fireman's Fund Insurance Co., 889 F.2d 1126 (DC Cir 1989).

84   Reger v. The Nemours Foundation, 599 F.3d 285, 289 (3d Cir. 2010)(emphasis added).

85   Reger v. The Nemours Foundation, 599 F.3d 285 (3d Cir. 2010)(emphasis added).

86   Buchanan v. Stanships, Inc., 485 U.S. 265 (1988). Accord, Samaad v. City of Dallas, 922 F.2d 216 (5th Cir. 1991).

87   Reger v. The Nemours Foundation, 599 F.3d 285 (3d Cir. 2010); In re: Paoli Railroad Yard PCB Litigation, 221 F.3d 449 (3d Cir. 2000); Abrams v. Lightolier, Inc., 50 F.3d 1204 (3d Cir. 1995); Smith v. SEPTA, 47 F.3d 97 (3d Cir. 1995); Friedman v. Ganassi, 853 F.2d 207 (3d Cir. 1988); Institutionalized Juveniles v. Secretary of Public Welfare, 758 F.2d 897 (3d Cir. 1985); Pearlstine v. United States, 649 F.2d 194 (3rd Cir. 1981); Delaney v. Capone, 642 F.2d 57 (3d Cir. 1981); Samuel v. University of Pittsburgh, 538 F.2d 991 (3d Cir. 1976); ADM Corp. v. Speedmaster Packing Corp., 525 F.2d 662 (3d Cir. 1975); Adams v. Teamsters Local 115, 678 F.Supp.2d 314 (E.D. Pa. 2007); City of Rome, Italy v. Glanton, 184 F.R.D. 547 (E.D. Pa. 1999); Greene v. Fraternal Order of Police, 183 F.R.D. 445 (E.D. Pa. 1998); Action Alliance for Senior Citizens of Greater Philadelphia v. Shapp, 74 F.R.D. 617 (E.D. Pa. 1977).

88   Buchanan v. Stanships, Inc., 485 U.S. 265, 268 (1988)(emphasis added). Accord, Delta Air Lines, Inc. v. August, 450 U.S. 346 (1981). See, also, Reger v. The Nemours Foundation, 599 F.3d 285 (3d Cir. 2010); In re: Paoli Railroad Yard PCB Litigation, 221 F.3d 449 (3d Cir. 2000); Abrams v. Lightolier, Inc., 50 F.3d 1204 (3d Cir. 1995); Smith v. SEPTA, 47 F.3d 97 (3d Cir. 1995); Friedman v. Ganassi, 853 F.2d 207 (3d Cir. 1988); Institutionalized Juveniles v. Secretary of Public Welfare, 758 F.2d 897 (3d Cir. 1985); Pearlstine v. United States, 649 F.2d 194 (3rd Cir. 1981); Delaney v. Capone, 642 F.2d 57 (3d Cir. 1981); Samuel v. University of Pittsburgh, 538 F.2d 991 (3d Cir. 1976); ADM Corp. v. Speedmaster Packing Corp., 525 F.2d 662 (3d Cir. 1975); City of Rome, Italy v. Glanton, 184 F.R.D. 547 (E.D. Pa. 1999); Greene v. Fraternal Order of Police, 183 F.R.D. 445 (E.D. Pa. 1998); Action Alliance for Senior Citizens of Greater Philadelphia v. Shapp, 74 F.R.D. 617 (E.D. Pa. 1977).

89   Buchanan v. Stanships, Inc., 485 U.S. 265 (1988); Delta Air Lines, Inc. v. August, 450 U.S. 346 (1981). Accord, Reger v. The Nemours Foundation, 599 F.3d 285 (3d Cir. 2010); In re: Paoli Railroad Yard PCB Litigation, 221 F.3d 449 (3d Cir. 2000); Abrams v. Lightolier, Inc., 50 F.3d 1204 (3d Cir. 1995); Smith v. SEPTA, 47 F.3d 97 (3d Cir. 1995); Friedman v. Ganassi, 853 F.2d 207 (3d Cir. 1988); Institutionalized Juveniles v. Secretary of Public Welfare, 758 F.2d 897 (3d Cir. 1985); Pearlstine v. United States, 649 F.2d 194 (3rd Cir. 1981); Delaney v. Capone, 642 F.2d 57 (3d Cir. 1981); Samuel v. University of Pittsburgh, 538 F.2d 991 (3d Cir. 1976); ADM Corp. v. Speedmaster Packing Corp., 525 F.2d 662 (3d Cir. 1975); City of Rome, Italy v. Glanton, 184 F.R.D. 547 (E.D. Pa. 1999); Greene v. Fraternal Order of Police, 183 F.R.D. 445 (E.D. Pa. 1998); Action Alliance for Senior Citizens of Greater Philadelphia v. Shapp, 74 F.R.D. 617 (E.D. Pa. 1977).

90   Brazos Valley Coalition for Life, Inc. v. City of Bryan, Texas, 421 F.3d 314 (5th Cir. 2005); Trepel v. Roadway Express, Inc., 266 F.3d 418 (6th Cir. 2001); Holmes v. Cessna Aircraft Co., 11 F.3d 63 (5th Cir. 1994); Dovenmuehle v. Gilldorn Mortgage Midwest Corp., 871 F.2d 697 (7th Cir. 1989); Mason v. Belieu, 543 F.2d 215 (D.C. Cir. 1976); Wahl v. Carrier Manufacturing Co., 511 F.2d 209 (7th Cir. 1975); McInnis v. Town of Weston, 458 F.Supp.2d 7 (D. Conn. 2006); Sullivan v. Cheshier, 991 F.Supp. 999 (N.D. Ill. 1998); Hollenbeck v. Falstaff Brewing Corp., 605 F.Supp. 421 (E.D. Mo. 1984); Morrissey v. County Tower Corp., 568 F.Supp. 980 (E.D. Mo. 1983).

91   In Re: Kulicke & Soffa Industries Inc. Securities Litigation, 747 F.Supp. 1136 (E.D.Pa. 1990), aff'd, 944 F.2d 897 (3rd Cir. 1991); ADM Corp. v. Speedmaster Packing Corp., 525 F.2d 662 (3d Cir. 1975); Nugget Distributors Cooperative of America v. Mr. Nugget, Inc., 145 F.R.D. 54 (E.D.Pa. 1992). Accord, Charter Medical Corp v. Cardin, 127 F.R.D. 111 (D. Maryland 1989); Women's Federal Savings and Loan Association of Cleveland v. Nevada National Bank, 108 F.R.D. 396 (D. Nevada 1985); International Wood Processors v. Power Dry, Inc., 598 F. Supp. 299 (D.S.C. 1984); Morrissey v. County Tower Corp., 568 F.Supp. 178 (ED Mo. 1983).

92   Reger v. The Nemours Foundation, 599 F.3d 285, 289 Footnote 3 (3d Cir. 2010) (emphasis added).

93   Reger v. The Nemours Foundation, 599 F.3d 285 (3d Cir. 2010); Friedman v. Ganassi, 853 F.2d 207 (3d Cir.1988). Accord, McGuigan v. CAE Link Corp., 155 F.R.D. 31 (NDNY 1994).

Endnotes

94 Maldonado v. Parasole, 66 F.R.D. 388,390 (EDNY 1975). Accord, Buchanan v. Stanships, Inc., 485 U.S. 265 (1988); Reger v. The Nemours Foundation, 599 F.3d 285 (3d Cir. 2010); In re: Paoli Railroad Yard PCB Litigation, 221 F.3d 449 (3d Cir. 2000); Smith v. SEPTA, 47 F.3d 97 (3d Cir. 1995); Friedman v. Ganassi, 853 F.2d 207 (3d Cir. 1988); Greene v. Fraternal Order of Police, 183 F.R.D. 445 (ED Pa. 1998). See, also, McGuigan v. Cae Lank Corp., 155 F.R.D. 31 (NDNY 1994); Phillips v. Cameron Tool Corp., 131 F.R.D. 151 (SD Ind. 1990).

95 Friedman v. Ganassi, 853 F.2d 207 (3d Cir. 1988). See, also, Popeil Brothers v. Schick Electric, 516 F.2d 772 (7th Cir. 1975); McGuigan v. Cae Lank Corp., 155 F.R.D. 31 (NDNY 1994); Phillips v. Cameron Tool Corp., 131 F.R.D. 151 (S D. Ind. 1990); Maldonado v. Parasole, 66 F.R.D. 388,390 (EDNY 1975).

96 Buchanan v. Stanships, Inc., 485 U.S. 265 (1988); Reger v. The Nemours Foundation, 599 F.3d 285 (3d Cir. 2010). Accord, Samaad v. City of Dallas, 922 F.2d 216 (5th Cir. 1991).

97 Buchanan v. Stanships, Inc., 485 U.S. 265 (1988); Reger v. The Nemours Foundation, 599 F.3d 285 (3d Cir. 2010); In re: Paoli Railroad Yard PCB Litigation, 221 F.3d 449 (3d Cir. 2000); Smith v. SEPTA, 47 F.3d 97 (3d Cir. 1995); Friedman v. Ganassi, 853 F.2d 207 (3d Cir. 1988); Greene v. Fraternal Order of Police, 183 F.R.D. 445 (ED Pa. 1998). Accord, McGuigan v. Cae Lank Corp., 155 F.R.D. 31 (NDNY 1994); Phillips v. Cameron Tool Corp., 131 F.R.D. 151 (S D. Ind. 1990); Maldonado v. Parasole, 66 F.R.D. 388,390 (EDNY 1975).

98 Reger v. The Nemours Foundation, 599 F.3d 285 (3d Cir. 2010); In re: Paoli Railroad Yard PCB Litigation, 221 F.3d 449 (3d Cir. 2000); Abrams v. Lightolier, Inc., 50 F.3d 1204 (3d Cir. 1995); Smith v. SEPTA, 47 F.3d 97 (3d Cir. 1995); Friedman v. Ganassi, 853 F.2d 207 (3d Cir. 1988); Institutionalized Juveniles v. Secretary of Public Welfare, 758 F.2d 897 (3d Cir. 1985); Pearlstine v. United States, 649 F.2d 194 (3rd Cir. 1981); Delaney v. Capone, 642 F.2d 57 (3d Cir. 1981); Samuel v. University of Pittsburgh, 538 F.2d 991 (3d Cir. 1976); ADM Corp. v. Speedmaster Packing Corp., 525 F.2d 662 (3d Cir. 1975); Adams v. Teamsters Local 115, 678 F.Supp.2d 314 (E.D. Pa. 2007); City of Rome, Italy v. Glanton, 184 F.R.D. 547 (E.D. Pa. 1999); Greene v. Fraternal Order of Police, 183 F.R.D. 445 (E.D. Pa. 1998); Action Alliance for Senior Citizens of Greater Philadelphia v. Shapp, 74 F.R.D. 617 (E.D. Pa. 1977).

99 Buchanan v. Stanships, Inc., 485 U.S. 265, 268 (1988)(emphasis added). Accord, Delta Air Lines, Inc. v. August, 450 U.S. 346 (1981). See, also, Reger v. The Nemours Foundation, 599 F.3d 285 (3d Cir. 2010); In re: Paoli Railroad Yard PCB Litigation, 221 F.3d 449 (3d Cir. 2000); Abrams v. Lightolier, Inc., 50 F.3d 1204 (3d Cir. 1995); Smith v. SEPTA, 47 F.3d 97 (3d Cir. 1995); Friedman v. Ganassi, 853 F.2d 207 (3d Cir. 1988); Institutionalized Juveniles v. Secretary of Public Welfare, 758 F.2d 897 (3d Cir. 1985); Pearlstine v. United States, 649 F.2d 194 (3rd Cir. 1981); Delaney v. Capone, 642 F.2d 57 (3d Cir. 1981); Samuel v. University of Pittsburgh, 538 F.2d 991 (3d Cir. 1976); ADM Corp. v. Speedmaster Packing Corp., 525 F.2d 662 (3d Cir. 1975); City of Rome, Italy v. Glanton, 184 F.R.D. 547 (E.D. Pa. 1999); Greene v. Fraternal Order of Police, 183 F.R.D. 445 (E.D. Pa. 1998); Action Alliance for Senior Citizens of Greater Philadelphia v. Shapp, 74 F.R.D. 617 (E.D. Pa. 1977).

100 Buchanan v. Stanships, Inc., 485 U.S. 265 (1988); Delta Air Lines, Inc. v. August, 450 U.S. 346 (1981). Accord, Reger v. The Nemours Foundation, 599 F.3d 285 (3d Cir. 2010); In re: Paoli Railroad Yard PCB Litigation, 221 F.3d 449 (3d Cir. 2000); Abrams v. Lightolier, Inc., 50 F.3d 1204 (3d Cir. 1995); Smith v. SEPTA, 47 F.3d 97 (3d Cir. 1995); Friedman v. Ganassi, 853 F.2d 207 (3d Cir. 1988); Institutionalized Juveniles v. Secretary of Public Welfare, 758 F.2d 897 (3d Cir. 1985); Pearlstine v. United States, 649 F.2d 194 (3rd Cir. 1981); Delaney v. Capone, 642 F.2d 57 (3d Cir. 1981); Samuel v. University of Pittsburgh, 538 F.2d 991 (3d Cir. 1976); ADM Corp. v. Speedmaster Packing Corp., 525 F.2d 662 (3d Cir. 1975); City of Rome, Italy v. Glanton, 184 F.R.D. 547 (E.D. Pa. 1999); Greene v. Fraternal Order of Police, 183 F.R.D. 445 (E.D. Pa. 1998); Action Alliance for Senior Citizens of Greater Philadelphia v. Shapp, 74 F.R.D. 617 (E.D. Pa. 1977).

101 Brazos Valley Coalition for Life, Inc. v. City of Bryan, Texas, 421 F.3d 314 (5th Cir. 2005); Trepel v. Roadway Express, Inc., 266 F.3d 418 (6th Cir. 2001); Holmes v. Cessna Aircraft Co., 11 F.3d 63 (5th Cir. 1994); Dovenmuehle v. Gilldorn Mortgage Midwest Corp., 871 F.2d 697 (7th Cir. 1989); Mason v. Belieu, 543 F.2d 215 (D.C. Cir. 1976); Wahl v. Carrier Manufacturing Co., 511 F.2d 209 (7th Cir. 1975); McInnis v. Town of Weston, 458 F.Supp.2d 7 (D. Conn. 2006); Sullivan v. Cheshier, 991 F.Supp. 999 (N.D. Ill. 1998); Hollenbeck v. Falstaff Brewing Corp., 605 F.Supp. 421 (E.D. Mo. 1984); Morrissey v. County Tower Corp., 568 F.Supp. 980 (E.D. Mo. 1983).

102 In Re: Kulicke & Soffa Industries Inc. Securities Litigation, 747 F.Supp. 1136 (E.D.Pa. 1990), aff'd, 944 F.2d 897 (3rd Cir. 1991); ADM Corp. v. Speedmaster Packing Corp., 525 F.2d 662 (3d Cir. 1975); Nugget Distributors Cooperative of America v. Mr. Nugget, Inc., 145 F.R.D. 54 (E.D.Pa. 1992). Accord, Charter Medical Corp v. Cardin, 127 F.R.D. 111 (D. Maryland 1989); Women's Federal Savings and Loan Association of Cleveland v. Nevada National Bank, 108 F.R.D. 396 (D. Nevada 1985); International Wood Pro-

cessors v. Power Dry, Inc., 598 F. Supp. 299 (D.S.C. 1984); Morrissey v. County Tower Corp., 568 F.Supp. 178 (ED Mo. 1983).

103 Reger v. The Nemours Foundation, 599 F.3d 285, 289 Footnote 3 (3d Cir. 2010) (emphasis added).

104 Buchanan v. Stanships, Inc., 485 U.S. 265 (1988); Reger v. The Nemours Foundation, 599 F.3d 285 (3d Cir. 2010). Accord, Samaad v. City of Dallas, 922 F.2d 216 (5th Cir. 1991).

105 Buchanan v. Stanships, Inc., 485 U.S. 265 (1988); Reger v. The Nemours Foundation, 599 F.3d 285 (3d Cir. 2010); In re: Paoli Railroad Yard PCB Litigation, 221 F.3d 449 (3d Cir. 2000); Smith v. SEPTA, 47 F.3d 97 (3d Cir. 1995); Friedman v. Ganassi, 853 F.2d 207 (3d Cir. 1988); Greene v. Fraternal Order of Police, 183 F.R.D. 445 (ED Pa. 1998). Accord, McGuigan v. Cae Lank Corp., 155 F.R.D. 31 (NDNY 1994); Phillips v. Cameron Tool Corp., 131 F.R.D. 151 (S D. Ind. 1990); Maldonado v. Parasole, 66 F.R.D. 388,390 (EDNY 1975).

106 Reger v. The Nemours Foundation, 599 F.3d 285 (3d Cir. 2010); In re: Paoli Railroad Yard PCB Litigation, 221 F.3d 449 (3d Cir. 2000); Abrams v. Lightolier, Inc., 50 F.3d 1204 (3d Cir. 1995); Smith v. SEPTA, 47 F.3d 97 (3d Cir. 1995); Friedman v. Ganassi, 853 F.2d 207 (3d Cir. 1988); Institutionalized Juveniles v. Secretary of Public Welfare, 758 F.2d 897 (3d Cir. 1985); Pearlstine v. United States, 649 F.2d 194 (3rd Cir. 1981); Delaney v. Capone, 642 F.2d 57 (3d Cir. 1981); Samuel v. University of Pittsburgh, 538 F.2d 991 (3d Cir. 1976); ADM Corp. v. Speedmaster Packing Corp., 525 F.2d 662 (3d Cir. 1975); Adams v. Teamsters Local 115, 678 F.Supp.2d 314 (E.D. Pa. 2007); City of Rome, Italy v. Glanton, 184 F.R.D. 547 (E.D. Pa. 1999); Greene v. Fraternal Order of Police, 183 F.R.D. 445 (E.D. Pa. 1998); Action Alliance for Senior Citizens of Greater Philadelphia v. Shapp, 74 F.R.D. 617 (E.D. Pa. 1977).

107 Buchanan v. Stanships, Inc., 485 U.S. 265, 268 (1988)(emphasis added). Accord, Delta Air Lines, Inc. v. August, 450 U.S. 346 (1981). See, also, Reger v. The Nemours Foundation, 599 F.3d 285 (3d Cir. 2010); In re: Paoli Railroad Yard PCB Litigation, 221 F.3d 449 (3d Cir. 2000); Abrams v. Lightolier, Inc., 50 F.3d 1204 (3d Cir. 1995); Smith v. SEPTA, 47 F.3d 97 (3d Cir. 1995); Friedman v. Ganassi, 853 F.2d 207 (3d Cir. 1988); Institutionalized Juveniles v. Secretary of Public Welfare, 758 F.2d 897 (3d Cir. 1985); Pearlstine v. United States, 649 F.2d 194 (3rd Cir. 1981); Delaney v. Capone, 642 F.2d 57 (3d Cir. 1981); Samuel v. University of Pittsburgh, 538 F.2d 991 (3d Cir. 1976); ADM Corp. v. Speedmaster Packing Corp., 525 F.2d 662 (3d Cir. 1975); City of Rome, Italy v. Glanton, 184 F.R.D. 547 (E.D. Pa. 1999); Greene v. Fraternal Order of Police, 183 F.R.D. 445 (E.D. Pa. 1998); Action Alliance for Senior Citizens of Greater Philadelphia v. Shapp, 74 F.R.D. 617 (E.D. Pa. 1977).

108 Buchanan v. Stanships, Inc., 485 U.S. 265 (1988); Delta Air Lines, Inc. v. August, 450 U.S. 346 (1981). Accord, Reger v. The Nemours Foundation, 599 F.3d 285 (3d Cir. 2010); In re: Paoli Railroad Yard PCB Litigation, 221 F.3d 449 (3d Cir. 2000); Abrams v. Lightolier, Inc., 50 F.3d 1204 (3d Cir. 1995); Smith v. SEPTA, 47 F.3d 97 (3d Cir. 1995); Friedman v. Ganassi, 853 F.2d 207 (3d Cir. 1988); Institutionalized Juveniles v. Secretary of Public Welfare, 758 F.2d 897 (3d Cir. 1985); Pearlstine v. United States, 649 F.2d 194 (3rd Cir. 1981); Delaney v. Capone, 642 F.2d 57 (3d Cir. 1981); Samuel v. University of Pittsburgh, 538 F.2d 991 (3d Cir. 1976); ADM Corp. v. Speedmaster Packing Corp., 525 F.2d 662 (3d Cir. 1975); City of Rome, Italy v. Glanton, 184 F.R.D. 547 (E.D. Pa. 1999); Greene v. Fraternal Order of Police, 183 F.R.D. 445 (E.D. Pa. 1998); Action Alliance for Senior Citizens of Greater Philadelphia v. Shapp, 74 F.R.D. 617 (E.D. Pa. 1977).

109 Brazos Valley Coalition for Life, Inc. v. City of Bryan, Texas, 421 F.3d 314 (5th Cir. 2005); Trepel v. Roadway Express, Inc., 266 F.3d 418 (6th Cir. 2001); Holmes v. Cessna Aircraft Co., 11 F.3d 63 (5th Cir. 1994); Dovenmuehle v. Gilldorn Mortgage Midwest Corp., 871 F.2d 697 (7th Cir. 1989); Mason v. Belieu, 543 F.2d 215 (D.C. Cir. 1976); Wahl v. Carrier Manufacturing Co., 511 F.2d 209 (7th Cir. 1975); McInnis v. Town of Weston, 458 F.Supp.2d 7 (D. Conn. 2006); Sullivan v. Cheshier, 991 F.Supp. 999 (N.D. Ill. 1998); Hollenbeck v. Falstaff Brewing Corp., 605 F.Supp. 421 (E.D. Mo. 1984); Morrissey v. County Tower Corp., 568 F.Supp. 980 (E.D. Mo. 1983).

110 In Re: Kulicke & Soffa Industries Inc. Securities Litigation, 747 F.Supp. 1136 (E.D.Pa. 1990), aff'd, 944 F.2d 897 (3rd Cir. 1991); ADM Corp. v. Speedmaster Packing Corp., 525 F.2d 662 (3d Cir. 1975); Nugget Distributors Cooperative of America v. Mr. Nugget, Inc., 145 F.R.D. 54 (E.D.Pa. 1992). Accord, Charter Medical Corp v. Cardin, 127 F.R.D. 111 (D. Maryland 1989); Women's Federal Savings and Loan Association of Cleveland v. Nevada National Bank, 108 F.R.D. 396 (D. Nevada 1985); International Wood Processors v. Power Dry, Inc., 598 F. Supp. 299 (D.S.C. 1984); Morrissey v. County Tower Corp., 568 F.Supp. 178 (ED Mo. 1983).

111 United States v. Hoffa, 497 F.2d 294 (7th Cir. 1974); Radol v. Thomas, 113 F.R.D. 172 (SD Ohio 1986).

112 Radol v. Thomas, 113 F.R.D. 172 (SD Ohio 1986).

113 Brown v. American Enka Corp., 452 F.Supp. 154 (ED Tenn. 1976).

Endnotes

114 Brown v. American Enka Corp., 452 F.Supp. 154 (ED Tenn. 1976).

115 In re: Paoli Railroad Yard PCB Litigation, 221 F.3d 449 (3d Cir. 2000); Institutionalized Juveniles v. Secretary of Public Welfare, 758 F.2d 897, 926 (3rd Cir. 1985).

116 In re: Paoli Railroad Yard PCB Litigation, 221 F.3d 449 (3d Cir. 2000); Institutionalized Juveniles v. Secretary of Public Welfare, 758 F.2d 897, 926 (3rd Cir. 1985).

117 ADM. Corp. v. Speedmaster Packaging Corp., 525 F.2d 662, 664 (3rd Cir. 1975).

118 Race Tires America, Inc. v. Hoosier Racing Tire Corp., 2012 WL 887593 (3d Cir. March 16, 2012).

119 Institutionalized Juveniles v. Secretary of Public Welfare, 758 F.2d 897, 926 (3rd Cir. 1985).

120 In re: Paoli Railroad Yard PCB Litigation, 221 F.3d 449 (3d Cir. 2000); Institutionalized Juveniles v. Secretary of Public Welfare, 758 F.2d 897, 926 (3rd Cir. 1985); Montgomery County v. Microvote Corp., 2004 WL 1087196 (EDPA 2004); Lacovara v. Merrill Lynch, 102 F.R.D. 959 (ED Pa. 1984). Accord, Zackaroff v. Koch Transfer Co., 862 F.2d 1263 (6th Cir. 1988); First Community Traders, Inc. v. Heinold Commodities, Inc., 766 F.2d 1007 (7th Cir. 1985); Friends for All Children v. Lockheed Aircraft Corp., 725 F.2d 1392 (DC Cir. 1984); Superturf, Inc. v. Monsanto Co., 660 F.2d 1275 (8th Cir. 1981); Jones v. Diamond, 594 F.2d 997 (4th Cir. 1979); U.S. v. Mitchell, 580 F.2d 789 (5th Cir. 1978); K-2 Ski Co. v. Head Ski Co., 506 F.2d 47 (9th Cir. 1974); Garonzik v. Whitman Diner, 910 F.Supp. 167 (D.N.J. 1995); Weseloh-Hurtig v. Hepker, 152 F.R.D. 198 (D. Kansas 1993); Bruno v. Western Electric Co., 618 F.Supp. 398 (D. Colorado 1985); Seber v. Daniels Transfer Co., 618 F.Supp. 1311 (W.D. Pa. 1985); Wade v. Mississippi Cooperative Extension Service, 64 F.R.D. 102 (N.D.Miss. 1974); Sperry Rand Corp. v. A-T-O, Inc., 58 F.R.D. 132 (E.D.Va. 1973).

121 In re: Paoli Railroad Yard PCB Litigation, 221 F.3d 449 (3d Cir. 2000); Institutionalized Juveniles v. Secretary of Public Welfare, 758 F.2d 897, 926 (3rd Cir. 1985).

122 Buchanan v. Stanships, Inc., 485 U.S. 265 (1988); Samaad v. City of Dallas, 922 F.2d 216 (5th Cir. 1991).

123 Buchanan v. Stanships, Inc., 485 U.S. 265, 268 (1988)(emphasis added). Accord, Delta Air Lines, Inc. v. August, 450 U.S. 346 (1981). See, also, Reger v. The Nemours Foundation, 599 F.3d 285 (3d Cir. 2010); In re: Paoli Railroad Yard PCB Litigation, 221 F.3d 449 (3d Cir. 2000); Abrams v. Lightolier, Inc., 50 F.3d 1204 (3d Cir. 1995); Smith v. SEPTA, 47 F.3d 97 (3d Cir. 1995); Friedman v. Ganassi, 853 F.2d 207 (3d Cir. 1988); Institutionalized Juveniles v. Secretary of Public Welfare, 758 F.2d 897 (3d Cir. 1985); Pearlstine v. United States, 649 F.2d 194 (3rd Cir. 1981); Delaney v. Capone, 642 F.2d 57 (3d Cir. 1981); Samuel v. University of Pittsburgh, 538 F.2d 991 (3d Cir. 1976); ADM Corp. v. Speedmaster Packing Corp., 525 F.2d 662 (3d Cir. 1975); City of Rome, Italy v. Glanton, 184 F.R.D. 547 (E.D. Pa. 1999); Greene v. Fraternal Order of Police, 183 F.R.D. 445 (E.D. Pa. 1998); Action Alliance for Senior Citizens of Greater Philadelphia v. Shapp, 74 F.R.D. 617 (E.D. Pa. 1977).

124 Reger v. The Nemours Foundation, 599 F.3d 285 (3d Cir. 2010); Smith v. SEPTA, 47 F.3d 97 (3d Cir. 1995); Friedman v. Ganassi, 853 F.2d 207 (3d Cir. 1988); Institutionalized Juveniles v. Secretary of Public Welfare, 758 F.2d 897, 926 (3rd Cir. 1985); Pearlstine v. United States, 649 F.2d 194 (3rd Cir. 1981); Delaney v. Capone, 642 F.2d 57 (3d Cir. 1981); Samuel v. University of Pittsburgh, 538 F.2d 991 (3d Cir. 1976); ADM Corp. v. Speedmaster Packing Corp., 525 F.2d 662 (3d Cir. 1975).

125 Reger v. The Nemours Foundation, 599 F.3d 285 (3d Cir. 2010).

126 Reger v. The Nemours Foundation, 599 F.3d 285 (3d Cir. 2010).

127 Buchanan v. Stanships, Inc., 485 U.S. 265 (1988); Samaad v. City of Dallas, 922 F.2d 216 (5th Cir. 1991).

128 Institutionalized Juveniles v. Secretary of Public Welfare, 758 F.2d 897, 911 (3rd Cir. 1985). The Third Circuit in Institutionalized Juveniles first applied this standard to attorney fees, and then held that it also applies to 28 U.S.C. § 1920 costs. Accord, Montgomery County v. Microvote Corp., 2004 WL 1087196 (E.D.Pa. 2004).

129 Montgomery County v. Microvote Corp., 2004 WL 1087196 (E.D.Pa. 2004); Greene v. Fraternal Order of Police, 183 F.R.D. 445 (E.D. Pa. 1998); Lacovara v. Merrill Lynch, Pierce, Fenner & Smith, 102 F.R.D. 959 (E.D. Pa. 1984). See, also, Hines v. Perez, 242 F.2d 459 (9th Cir. 1957); Garonzik v. Whitman Diner, 910 F.Supp. 167 (D.N.J. 1995); Sperry Rand Corp. v. A-T-O, Inc., 58 F.R.D. 132 (E.D.Va. 1973).

130 Institutionalized Juveniles v. Secretary of Public Welfare, 758 F.2d 897, 910 (3rd Cir. 1985). The Third Circuit in Institutionalized Juveniles first applied this standard to attorney fees, and then held that it also applies to 28 U.S.C. § 1920 costs. Accord, Montgomery County v. Microvote Corp., 2004 WL 1087196 (E.D.Pa. 2004).

131 Institutionalized Juveniles v. Secretary of Public Welfare, 758 F.2d 897 (3rd Cir. 1985); Montgomery County v. Microvote Corp., 2004 WL 1087196 (EDPA 2004); Greene v. Fraternal Order of Police, 183 F.R.D. 445 (ED Pa. 1998). Accord, Roberts v. Interstate Distrib. Co., 242 F.Supp. 2d 850 (D. Oregon

2002); Garonzik v. Whitman Diner, 910 F.Supp. 167 (D.N.J. 1995); Green Construction Co. v. Kansas Power and Light Co., 153 F.R.D. 670 (D. Kansas 1994); Weseloh-Hurtig v. Hepker, 152 F.R.D. 198 (D. Kansas 1993).

132   Institutionalized Juveniles v. Secretary of Public Welfare, 758 F.2d 897 (3d Cir. 1985); Montgomery County v. Microvote Corp., 2004 WL 1087196 (EDPA 2004). Accord, Zackaroff v. Koch Transfer Co., 862 F.2d 1263 (6th Cir. 1988); First Community Traders, Inc. v. Heinold Commodities, Inc., 766 F.2d 1007 (7th Cir. 1985); Friends for All Children v. Lockheed Aircraft Corp., 725 F.2d 1392 (DC Cir. 1984); Superturf, Inc. v. Monsanto Co., 660 F.2d 1275 (8th Cir. 1981); Jones v. Diamond, 594 F.2d 997 (4th Cir. 1979); U.S. v. Mitchell, 580 F.2d 789 (5th Cir. 1978); K-2 Ski Co. v. Head Ski Co., 506 F.2d 47 (9th Cir. 1974); Garonzik v. Whitman Diner, 910 F.Supp. 167 (D.N.J. 1995); Weseloh-Hurtig v. Hepker, 152 F.R.D. 198 (D. Kansas 1993); Bruno v. Western Electric Co., 618 F.Supp. 398 (D. Colorado 1985); Seber v. Daniels Transfer Co., 618 F.Supp. 1311 (W.D. Pa. 1985); Wade v. Mississippi Cooperative Extension Service, 64 F.R.D. 102 (N.D.Miss. 1974); Sperry Rand Corp. v. A-T-O, Inc., 58 F.R.D. 132 (E.D.Va. 1973).

133   Greene v. Fraternal Order of Police, 183 F.R.D. 445 (ED Pa. 1998); Lacovara v. Merrill Lynch, 102 F.R.D. 959 (ED Pa. 1984). Accord, Scientific Holding Co. v. Plessey, 510 F.2d 15 (2nd Cir. 1974).

134   Lacovara v. Merrill Lynch, 102 F.R.D. 959 (ED Pa. 1984). Accord, Scientific Holding Co. v. Plessey, 510 F.2d 15 (2nd Cir. 1974).

135   Brandt v. Schal Associates, 854 F.2d 948 (7th Cir. 1988); Bishop v. West American Insurance Co., 95 F.R.D. 494 (N.D.Ga. 1982).

136   City of Rome, Italy v. Glanton, 184 F.R.D. 547 (ED Pa. 1999); Lacovara v. Merrill Lynch, 102 F.R.D. 959 (ED Pa. 1984).

137   Buchanan v. Stanships, Inc., 485 U.S. 265 (1988); Samaad v. City of Dallas, 922 F.2d 216 (5th Cir. 1991).

138   Mitchell v. City of Moore, Oklahoma, 218 F.3d 1190 (10th Cir. 2000); Stearns Airport Equipment Co., Inc. v. FMC Corporation, 170 F.3d 518 (5th Cir. 1999); Cengr v. Fusibond Piping Systems, Inc., 135 F.3d 445 (7th Cir. 1998); Johnson v. Henderson, 67 F.3d 299 (6th Cir. 1995); Sevenson Environmental Services, Inc. v. Shaw Environmental, Inc., 246 F.R.D. 154 (WDNY 2007); Yasui v. Maui Electric Company, 78 F.Supp.2d 1124 (D. Hawaii 1999); Woolfson v. Doyle, 180 F.Supp. 86 (SDNY 1960).

139   LaVay Corporation v. Dominion Federal Savings and Loan, 830 F.2d 522 (4th Cir. 1987).

140   Neumann v. Reinforced Earth Company, 109 FRD 698 (DDC 1986).

141   Furman v. Cirrito, 782 F.2d 353 (2d Cir. 1986); Knox v. Schweiker, 567 F.Supp. 959 (D.Del. 1983).

142   Women's Federal Savings and Loan Association of Cleveland v. Nevada National Bank, 108 F.R.D. 396 (D. Nevada 1985).

143   McInnis v. Town of Weston, 458 F.Supp.2d 7 (D. Conn 2006); Sullivan v. Cheshire, 991 F.Supp. (ND Ill. 1998); McGuigan v. CAE Link Corp., 155 F.R.D. 31 (NDNY 1994).

144   McInnis v. Town of Weston, 458 F.Supp.2d 7 (D. Conn 2006).

145   Harkins v. Riverboat Services, 286 F.Supp. 2d 976 (ND Ill. 2003), aff'd, 385 F.3d 1099 (7th Cir. 2004); McGuigan v. CAE Link Corp., 155 F.R.D. 31 (N.D.N.Y. 1994); Morrissey v. County Tower Corp., 568 F. Supp. 980 (E.D. Mo. 1983); Harceg v. Brown, 536 F.Supp. 125 (N.D. Ill. 1982). Accord, Seidman v. American Mobile Systems, 965 F.Supp. 612 (E.D. Pa. 1997).

146   Brazos Valley Coalition for Life, Inc. v. City of Bryan, Texas, 421 F.3d 314 (5th Cir. 2005); Trepel v. Roadway Express, Inc., 266 F.3d 418 (6th Cir. 2001); Holmes v. Cessna Aircraft Co., 11 F.3d 63 (5th Cir. 1994); Dovenmuehle v. Gilldorn Mortgage Midwest Corp., 871 F.2d 697 (7th Cir. 1989); Mason v. Belieu, 543 F.2d 215 (D.C. Cir. 1976); Wahl v. Carrier Manufacturing Co., 511 F.2d 209 (7th Cir. 1975); McInnis v. Town of Weston, 458 F.Supp.2d 7 (D. Conn. 2006); Sullivan v. Cheshire, 991 F.Supp. 999 (N.D. Ill. 1998); Hollenbeck v. Falstaff Brewing Corp., 605 F.Supp. 421 (E.D. Mo. 1984); Morrissey v. County Tower Corp., 568 F.Supp. 980 (E.D. Mo. 1983).

147   Friedman v. Ganassi, 853 F.2d 207 (3d Cir. 1988).

148   Buchanan v. Stanships, Inc., 485 U.S. 265 (1988); Friedman v. Ganassi, 853 F.2d 207 (3d Cir. 1988); Adams v. Teamsters Local 115, 678 F.Supp.2d 314 (E.D.Pa, 2007).

149   Friedman v. Ganassi, 853 F.2d 207 (3d Cir. 1988); Dr. Bernard Heller Foundation v. Lee, 847 F.2d 83 (3rd Cir. 1988); Dominic v. Hess Oil V.I. Corp., 841 F.2d 513 (3rd Cir. 1988).

150   Buchanan v. Stanships, Inc., 485 U.S. 265 (1988); Abrams v. Lightolier, Inc., 50 F.3d 1204 (3d Cir. 1995); Friedman v. Ganassi, 853 F.2d 207 (3d Cir. 1988); Adams v. Teamsters Local 115, 678 F.Supp.2d 314 (E.D.Pa, 2007); Greene v. Fraternal Order of Police, 183 F.R.D. 445 (E.D. Pa. 1998).

Endnotes

151 Friedman v. Ganassi, 853 F.2d 207 (3d Cir. 1988); Dr. Bernard Heller Foundation v. Lee, 847 F.2d 83 (3rd Cir. 1988); Dominic v. Hess Oil V.I. Corp., 841 F.2d 513 (3rd Cir. 1988).

152 Women's Federal Savings and Loan Association of Cleveland v. Nevada National Bank, 108 F.R.D. 396 (D. Nevada 1985).

153 In re: Paoli Railroad Yard PCB Litigation, 221 F.3d 449 (3d Cir. 2000). Accord, Tubbs v. Sacramento County Jail, 258 F.R.D. 657 (E.D. Cal. 2009); Electronic Specialty Co. v. International Controls Corp., 47 F.R.D. 158 (SDNY 1969).

154 Abrams v. Lightolier, Inc., 50 F.3d 1204 (3d Cir. 1995).

155 P.L. 102-572.

156 Samuel v. University of Pittsburgh, 538 F.2d 991 (3rd Cir. 1976); Halderman v. Pennhurst State School and Hospital, 533 F.Supp. 631, 639 (E.D. Pa. 1981). See, also, Gay Students Services v. Texas A&M University, 612 F.2d 160, 165 (5th Cir. 1980); Gary W. v. Louisiana, 601 F.2d 240 (5th Cir. 1979); Kovats v. Rutgers, 633 F.Supp. 1469, 1475 (D.N.J. 1986).

157 Copperweld Steel Co. v. DeMag-Mannesmann-Bohler, 624 F.2d 7 (3rd Cir. 1980).

158 American Truck Assoc., Inc. v. I.C.C., 666 F.2d 167, 169 (5th Cir. 1982); American Railway Supervisors Association v. United States, 582 F.2d 1066, 1067 (7th Cir. 1978); Delta Airlines, Inc. v. Civil Aeronautics Board, 505 F.2d 386 (D.C. Cir.1974); Smith v. Board of School Commissioners of Mobile County, 119 F.R.D. 440, 443 (S.D. Ala. 1988); Monroe v. United Air Lines, Inc., 565 F.Supp. 274 (N.D.Ill 1983).

159 Buchanan v. Stanships, Inc., 485 U.S. 265 (1988); Friedman v. Ganassi, 853 F.2d 207 (3d Cir. 1988).

160 Friedman v. Ganassi, 853 F.2d 207 (3d Cir. 1988); Dr. Bernard Heller Foundation v. Lee, 847 F.2d 83 (3rd Cir. 1988); Dominic v. Hess Oil V.I. Corp., 841 F.2d 513 (3rd Cir. 1988).

161 Proffitt v. Municipal Authority of Borough of Morrisville, 716 F.Supp. 845 (E.D. Pa. 1989), aff'd, 897 F.2d 523 (3d Cir. 1990); Nugget Distributors Cooperative of America v. Mr. Nugget, Inc., 145 F.R.D. 54 (E.D.Pa. 1992). Accord, East v. Barnhart, 377 F.Supp. 2d 1170 (MD Alabama 2003); United States v. Orenic, 110 F.R.D. 584 (W.D. Va. 1986); Bishop v. West American Insurance Co., 95 F.R.D. 494 (N.D.Ga. 1982).

162 McGuigan v. CAE Link Corp., 155 F.R.D. 31 (N.D.N.Y. 1994); Bishop v. West American Insurance Co., 95 F.R.D. 494 (N.D.Ga. 1982).

163 United States Public Law 102-572.

164 Reger v. The Nemours Foundation, 599 F.3d 285 (3d Cir. 2010); In re: Paoli Railroad Yard PCB Litigation, 221 F.3d 449 (3d Cir. 2000); Abrams v. Lightolier, Inc., 50 F.3d 1204 (3d Cir. 1995); Smith v. SEPTA, 47 F.3d 97 (3d Cir. 1995); Friedman v. Ganassi, 853 F.2d 207 (3d Cir. 1988); Institutionalized Juveniles v. Secretary of Public Welfare, 758 F.2d 897 (3d Cir. 1985); Pearlstine v. United States, 649 F.2d 194 (3rd Cir. 1981); Delaney v. Capone, 642 F.2d 57 (3d Cir. 1981); Samuel v. University of Pittsburgh, 538 F.2d 991 (3d Cir. 1976); ADM Corp. v. Speedmaster Packing Corp., 525 F.2d 662 (3d Cir. 1975); City of Rome, Italy v. Glanton, 184 F.R.D. 547 (E.D. Pa. 1999); Greene v. Fraternal Order of Police, 183 F.R.D. 445 (E.D. Pa. 1998); Action Alliance for Senior Citizens of Greater Philadelphia v. Shapp, 74 F.R.D. 617 (E.D. Pa. 1977).

165 Buchanan v. Stanships, Inc., 485 U.S. 265, 268 (1988)(emphasis added). Accord, Delta Air Lines, Inc. v. August, 450 U.S. 346 (1981). See, also, Reger v. The Nemours Foundation, 599 F.3d 285 (3d Cir. 2010); In re: Paoli Railroad Yard PCB Litigation, 221 F.3d 449 (3d Cir. 2000); Abrams v. Lightolier, Inc., 50 F.3d 1204 (3d Cir. 1995); Smith v. SEPTA, 47 F.3d 97 (3d Cir. 1995); Friedman v. Ganassi, 853 F.2d 207 (3d Cir. 1988); Institutionalized Juveniles v. Secretary of Public Welfare, 758 F.2d 897 (3d Cir. 1985); Pearlstine v. United States, 649 F.2d 194 (3rd Cir. 1981); Delaney v. Capone, 642 F.2d 57 (3d Cir. 1981); Samuel v. University of Pittsburgh, 538 F.2d 991 (3d Cir. 1976); ADM Corp. v. Speedmaster Packing Corp., 525 F.2d 662 (3d Cir. 1975); City of Rome, Italy v. Glanton, 184 F.R.D. 547 (E.D. Pa. 1999); Greene v. Fraternal Order of Police, 183 F.R.D. 445 (E.D. Pa. 1998); Action Alliance for Senior Citizens of Greater Philadelphia v. Shapp, 74 F.R.D. 617 (E.D. Pa. 1977).

166 Buchanan v. Stanships, Inc., 485 U.S. 265 (1988); Delta Air Lines, Inc. v. August, 450 U.S. 346 (1981). Accord, Reger v. The Nemours Foundation, 599 F.3d 285 (3d Cir. 2010); In re: Paoli Railroad Yard PCB Litigation, 221 F.3d 449 (3d Cir. 2000); Abrams v. Lightolier, Inc., 50 F.3d 1204 (3d Cir. 1995); Smith v. SEPTA, 47 F.3d 97 (3d Cir. 1995); Friedman v. Ganassi, 853 F.2d 207 (3d Cir. 1988); Institutionalized Juveniles v. Secretary of Public Welfare, 758 F.2d 897 (3d Cir. 1985); Pearlstine v. United States, 649 F.2d 194 (3rd Cir. 1981); Delaney v. Capone, 642 F.2d 57 (3d Cir. 1981); Samuel v. University of Pittsburgh, 538 F.2d 991 (3d Cir. 1976); ADM Corp. v. Speedmaster Packing Corp., 525 F.2d 662 (3d Cir. 1975); City of Rome, Italy v. Glanton, 184 F.R.D. 547 (E.D. Pa. 1999); Greene v. Fraternal Order of Police, 183 F.R.D.

445 (E.D. Pa. 1998); Action Alliance for Senior Citizens of Greater Philadelphia v. Shapp, 74 F.R.D. 617 (E.D. Pa. 1977).

167 Brazos Valley Coalition for Life, Inc. v. City of Bryan, Texas, 421 F.3d 314 (5th Cir. 2005); Trepel v. Roadway Express, Inc., 266 F.3d 418 (6th Cir. 2001); Holmes v. Cessna Aircraft Co., 11 F.3d 63 (5th Cir. 1994); Dovenmuehle v. Gilldorn Mortgage Midwest Corp., 871 F.2d 697 (7th Cir. 1989); Mason v. Belieu, 543 F.2d 215 (D.C. Cir. 1976); Wahl v. Carrier Manufacturing Co., 511 F.2d 209 (7th Cir. 1975); McInnis v. Town of Weston, 458 F.Supp.2d 7 (D. Conn. 2006); Sullivan v. Cheshier, 991 F.Supp. 999 (N.D. Ill. 1998); Hollenbeck v. Falstaff Brewing Corp., 605 F.Supp. 421 (E.D. Mo. 1984); Morrissey v. County Tower Corp., 568 F.Supp. 980 (E.D. Mo. 1983).

168 In Re: Kulicke & Soffa Industries Inc. Securities Litigation, 747 F.Supp. 1136 (E.D.Pa. 1990), aff'd, 944 F.2d 897 (3rd Cir. 1991); ADM Corp. v. Speedmaster Packing Corp., 525 F.2d 662 (3d Cir. 1975); Nugget Distributors Cooperative of America v. Mr. Nugget, Inc., 145 F.R.D. 54 (E.D.Pa. 1992). Accord, Charter Medical Corp v. Cardin, 127 F.R.D. 111 (D. Maryland 1989); Women's Federal Savings and Loan Association of Cleveland v. Nevada National Bank, 108 F.R.D. 396 (D. Nevada 1985); International Wood Processors v. Power Dry, Inc., 598 F. Supp. 299 (D.S.C. 1984); Morrissey v. County Tower Corp., 568 F.Supp. 178 (ED Mo. 1983).

169 Proffitt v. Municipal Authority of Borough of Morrisville, 716 F.Supp. 845 (ED Pa. 1989), aff'd, 897 F.2d 523 (3d Cir. 1990); Montgomery County v. Microvote Corp., 2004 WL 1087196 (EDPA 2004). Accord, Long v. Howard University, 561 F.Supp.2d 85 (D.D.C. 2008); Shared Medical System v. Ashford Presbyterian Community Hospital, 212 F.R.D. 50 (D.P.R. 2002); McGuigan v. CAE Link Corp., 155 F.R.D. 31 (NDNY 1994).

170 Montgomery County v. Microvote Corp., 2004 WL 1087196 (EDPA 2004). Accord, Shared Medical System v. Ashford Presbyterian Community Hospital, 212 F.R.D. 50 (D.P.R. 2002); Griffith v. Mt. Carmel Medical Center, 157 F.R.D. 499 (D. Kansas 1994); McGuigan v. CAE Link Corp., 155 F.R.D. 31 (NDNY 1994).

171 Movitz v. First National Bank of Chicago, 982 F.Supp. 571 (ND Ill 1997).

172 Montgomery County v. Microvote Corp., 2004 WL 1087196 (EDPA 2004).

173 Montgomery County v. Microvote Corp., 2004 WL 1087196 (EDPA 2004); McGuigan v. CAE Link Corp., 155 FRD 31 (NDNY 1994).

174 Reger v. The Nemours Foundation, 599 F.3d 285 (3d Cir. 2010); In re: Paoli Railroad Yard PCB Litigation, 221 F.3d 449 (3d Cir. 2000); Abrams v. Lightolier, Inc., 50 F.3d 1204 (3d Cir. 1995); Smith v. SEPTA, 47 F.3d 97 (3d Cir. 1995); Friedman v. Ganassi, 853 F.2d 207 (3d Cir. 1988); Institutionalized Juveniles v. Secretary of Public Welfare, 758 F.2d 897 (3d Cir. 1985); Pearlstine v. United States, 649 F.2d 194 (3rd Cir. 1981); Delaney v. Capone, 642 F.2d 57 (3d Cir. 1981); Samuel v. University of Pittsburgh, 538 F.2d 991 (3d Cir. 1976); ADM Corp. v. Speedmaster Packing Corp., 525 F.2d 662 (3d Cir. 1975); City of Rome, Italy v. Glanton, 184 F.R.D. 547 (E.D. Pa. 1999); Greene v. Fraternal Order of Police, 183 F.R.D. 445 (E.D. Pa. 1998); Action Alliance for Senior Citizens of Greater Philadelphia v. Shapp, 74 F.R.D. 617 (E.D. Pa. 1977).

175 Buchanan v. Stanships, Inc., 485 U.S. 265, 268 (1988)(emphasis added). Accord, Delta Air Lines, Inc. v. August, 450 U.S. 346 (1981). See, also, Reger v. The Nemours Foundation, 599 F.3d 285 (3d Cir. 2010); In re: Paoli Railroad Yard PCB Litigation, 221 F.3d 449 (3d Cir. 2000); Abrams v. Lightolier, Inc., 50 F.3d 1204 (3d Cir. 1995); Smith v. SEPTA, 47 F.3d 97 (3d Cir. 1995); Friedman v. Ganassi, 853 F.2d 207 (3d Cir. 1988); Institutionalized Juveniles v. Secretary of Public Welfare, 758 F.2d 897 (3d Cir. 1985); Pearlstine v. United States, 649 F.2d 194 (3rd Cir. 1981); Delaney v. Capone, 642 F.2d 57 (3d Cir. 1981); Samuel v. University of Pittsburgh, 538 F.2d 991 (3d Cir. 1976); ADM Corp. v. Speedmaster Packing Corp., 525 F.2d 662 (3d Cir. 1975); City of Rome, Italy v. Glanton, 184 F.R.D. 547 (E.D. Pa. 1999); Greene v. Fraternal Order of Police, 183 F.R.D. 445 (E.D. Pa. 1998); Action Alliance for Senior Citizens of Greater Philadelphia v. Shapp, 74 F.R.D. 617 (E.D. Pa. 1977).

176 Buchanan v. Stanships, Inc., 485 U.S. 265 (1988); Delta Air Lines, Inc. v. August, 450 U.S. 346 (1981). Accord, Reger v. The Nemours Foundation, 599 F.3d 285 (3d Cir. 2010); In re: Paoli Railroad Yard PCB Litigation, 221 F.3d 449 (3d Cir. 2000); Abrams v. Lightolier, Inc., 50 F.3d 1204 (3d Cir. 1995); Smith v. SEPTA, 47 F.3d 97 (3d Cir. 1995); Friedman v. Ganassi, 853 F.2d 207 (3d Cir. 1988); Institutionalized Juveniles v. Secretary of Public Welfare, 758 F.2d 897 (3d Cir. 1985); Pearlstine v. United States, 649 F.2d 194 (3rd Cir. 1981); Delaney v. Capone, 642 F.2d 57 (3d Cir. 1981); Samuel v. University of Pittsburgh, 538 F.2d 991 (3d Cir. 1976); ADM Corp. v. Speedmaster Packing Corp., 525 F.2d 662 (3d Cir. 1975); City of Rome, Italy v. Glanton, 184 F.R.D. 547 (E.D. Pa. 1999); Greene v. Fraternal Order of Police, 183 F.R.D. 445 (E.D. Pa. 1998); Action Alliance for Senior Citizens of Greater Philadelphia v. Shapp, 74 F.R.D. 617 (E.D. Pa. 1977).

Endnotes

177 Brazos Valley Coalition for Life, Inc. v. City of Bryan, Texas, 421 F.3d 314 (5th Cir. 2005); Trepel v. Roadway Express, Inc., 266 F.3d 418 (6th Cir. 2001); Holmes v. Cessna Aircraft Co., 11 F.3d 63 (5th Cir. 1994); Dovenmuehle v. Gilldorn Mortgage Midwest Corp., 871 F.2d 697 (7th Cir. 1989); Mason v. Belieu, 543 F.2d 215 (D.C. Cir. 1976); Wahl v. Carrier Manufacturing Co., 511 F.2d 209 (7th Cir. 1975); McInnis v. Town of Weston, 458 F.Supp.2d 7 (D. Conn. 2006); Sullivan v. Cheshire, 991 F.Supp. 999 (N.D. Ill. 1998); Hollenbeck v. Falstaff Brewing Corp., 605 F.Supp. 421 (E.D. Mo. 1984); Morrissey v. County Tower Corp., 568 F.Supp. 980 (E.D. Mo. 1983).

178 In Re: Kulicke & Soffa Industries Inc. Securities Litigation, 747 F.Supp. 1136 (E.D.Pa. 1990), aff'd, 944 F.2d 897 (3rd Cir. 1991); ADM Corp. v. Speedmaster Packing Corp., 525 F.2d 662 (3d Cir. 1975); Nugget Distributors Cooperative of America v. Mr. Nugget, Inc., 145 F.R.D. 54 (E.D.Pa. 1992). Accord, Charter Medical Corp v. Cardin, 127 F.R.D. 111 (D. Maryland 1989); Women's Federal Savings and Loan Association of Cleveland v. Nevada National Bank, 108 F.R.D. 396 (D. Nevada 1985); International Wood Processors v. Power Dry, Inc., 598 F. Supp. 299 (D.S.C. 1984); Morrissey v. County Tower Corp., 568 F.Supp. 178 (ED Mo. 1983).

179 In Re: Kulicke & Soffa Industries, Inc. Securities Litigation, 747 F.Supp. 1136 (ED Pa. 1990) aff'd 944 F.2d 897 (3rd Cir. 1991); Montgomery County v. Microvote Corp., 2004 WL 1087196 (EDPA 2004); Nugget Distributors Cooperative v. Mr. Nugget, Inc., 145 F.R.D. 54 (ED Pa. 1992). Accord, McGuigan v. CAE Link Corp., 155 F.R.D. 31 (NDNY 1994).

180 BDT Products, Inc. v. Lexmark International, Inc., 405 F.3d 415 (6th Cir. 2005); Tilton v. Capital Cities/ABC Inc., 115 F.3d 1471 (10th Cir. 1997); Morrison v. Reichhold Chems., 97 F.3d 460 (11th Cir. 1996); Commercial Credit Equipment Corp. v. Stamps, 920 F.2d 1361 (7th Cir. 1990); Rio Props v. Stewart Annoyances, Ltd., 420 F.Supp. 2d 1127 (D. Nevada 2006); United International Holdings v. Wharf, Ltd., 174 F.R.D. 479 (D. Colo. 1997); Garonzik v. Whitman Diner, 910 F.Supp 167 (D.N.J. 1995); McGuigan v. CAE Link Corp., 155 F.R.D. 31 (NDNY 1994); Weseloh-Hurtig v. Hepker, 152 F.R.D. 198 (D. Kansas 1993); Deaton v. Dreis & Krump Mfg. Co. (ND Ohio 1991).

181 Garonzik v. Whitman Diner, 910 F.Supp. 167 (D.N.J. 1995).

182 Although 28 U.S.C. § 1920 does limit the payment of fees to an expert witness, 28 U.S.C. § 1920 does not contain a limit on the payment of fees to a court reporter in connection to the testimony of an expert witness.

183 Reger v. The Nemours Foundation, 599 F.3d 285 (3d Cir. 2010); In re: Paoli Railroad Yard PCB Litigation, 221 F.3d 449 (3d Cir. 2000); Abrams v. Lightolier, Inc., 50 F.3d 1204 (3d Cir. 1995); Smith v. SEPTA, 47 F.3d 97 (3d Cir. 1995); Friedman v. Ganassi, 853 F.2d 207 (3d Cir. 1988); Institutionalized Juveniles v. Secretary of Public Welfare, 758 F.2d 897 (3d Cir. 1985); Pearlstine v. United States, 649 F.2d 194 (3rd Cir. 1981); Delaney v. Capone, 642 F.2d 57 (3d Cir. 1981); Samuel v. University of Pittsburgh, 538 F.2d 991 (3d Cir. 1976); ADM Corp. v. Speedmaster Packing Corp., 525 F.2d 662 (3d Cir. 1975); City of Rome, Italy v. Glanton, 184 F.R.D. 547 (E.D. Pa. 1999); Greene v. Fraternal Order of Police, 183 F.R.D. 445 (E.D. Pa. 1998); Action Alliance for Senior Citizens of Greater Philadelphia v. Shapp, 74 F.R.D. 617 (E.D. Pa. 1977).

184 Buchanan v. Stanships, Inc., 485 U.S. 265, 268 (1988)(emphasis added). Accord, Delta Air Lines, Inc. v. August, 450 U.S. 346 (1981). See, also, Reger v. The Nemours Foundation, 599 F.3d 285 (3d Cir. 2010); In re: Paoli Railroad Yard PCB Litigation, 221 F.3d 449 (3d Cir. 2000); Abrams v. Lightolier, Inc., 50 F.3d 1204 (3d Cir. 1995); Smith v. SEPTA, 47 F.3d 97 (3d Cir. 1995); Friedman v. Ganassi, 853 F.2d 207 (3d Cir. 1988); Institutionalized Juveniles v. Secretary of Public Welfare, 758 F.2d 897 (3d Cir. 1985); Pearlstine v. United States, 649 F.2d 194 (3rd Cir. 1981); Delaney v. Capone, 642 F.2d 57 (3d Cir. 1981); Samuel v. University of Pittsburgh, 538 F.2d 991 (3d Cir. 1976); ADM Corp. v. Speedmaster Packing Corp., 525 F.2d 662 (3d Cir. 1975); City of Rome, Italy v. Glanton, 184 F.R.D. 547 (E.D. Pa. 1999); Greene v. Fraternal Order of Police, 183 F.R.D. 445 (E.D. Pa. 1998); Action Alliance for Senior Citizens of Greater Philadelphia v. Shapp, 74 F.R.D. 617 (E.D. Pa. 1977).

185 Buchanan v. Stanships, Inc., 485 U.S. 265 (1988); Delta Air Lines, Inc. v. August, 450 U.S. 346 (1981). Accord, Reger v. The Nemours Foundation, 599 F.3d 285 (3d Cir. 2010); In re: Paoli Railroad Yard PCB Litigation, 221 F.3d 449 (3d Cir. 2000); Abrams v. Lightolier, Inc., 50 F.3d 1204 (3d Cir. 1995); Smith v. SEPTA, 47 F.3d 97 (3d Cir. 1995); Friedman v. Ganassi, 853 F.2d 207 (3d Cir. 1988); Institutionalized Juveniles v. Secretary of Public Welfare, 758 F.2d 897 (3d Cir. 1985); Pearlstine v. United States, 649 F.2d 194 (3rd Cir. 1981); Delaney v. Capone, 642 F.2d 57 (3d Cir. 1981); Samuel v. University of Pittsburgh, 538 F.2d 991 (3d Cir. 1976); ADM Corp. v. Speedmaster Packing Corp., 525 F.2d 662 (3d Cir. 1975); City of Rome, Italy v. Glanton, 184 F.R.D. 547 (E.D. Pa. 1999); Greene v. Fraternal Order of Police, 183 F.R.D. 445 (E.D. Pa. 1998); Action Alliance for Senior Citizens of Greater Philadelphia v. Shapp, 74 F.R.D. 617 (E.D. Pa. 1977).

186 Brazos Valley Coalition for Life, Inc. v. City of Bryan, Texas, 421 F.3d 314 (5th Cir. 2005); Trepel v. Roadway Express, Inc., 266 F.3d 418 (6th Cir. 2001); Holmes v. Cessna Aircraft Co., 11 F.3d 63 (5th Cir. 1994); Dovenmuehle v. Gilldorn Mortgage Midwest Corp., 871 F.2d 697 (7th Cir. 1989); Mason v. Belieu, 543 F.2d 215 (D.C. Cir. 1976); Wahl v. Carrier Manufacturing Co., 511 F.2d 209 (7th Cir. 1975); McInnis v. Town of Weston, 458 F.Supp.2d 7 (D. Conn. 2006); Sullivan v. Cheshire, 991 F.Supp. 999 (N.D. Ill. 1998); Hollenbeck v. Falstaff Brewing Corp., 605 F.Supp. 421 (E.D. Mo. 1984); Morrissey v. County Tower Corp., 568 F.Supp. 980 (E.D. Mo. 1983).

187 In Re: Kulicke & Soffa Industries Inc. Securities Litigation, 747 F.Supp. 1136 (E.D.Pa. 1990), aff'd, 944 F.2d 897 (3rd Cir. 1991); ADM Corp. v. Speedmaster Packing Corp., 525 F.2d 662 (3d Cir. 1975); Nugget Distributors Cooperative of America v. Mr. Nugget, Inc., 145 F.R.D. 54 (E.D.Pa. 1992). Accord, Charter Medical Corp v. Cardin, 127 F.R.D. 111 (D. Maryland 1989); Women's Federal Savings and Loan Association of Cleveland v. Nevada National Bank, 108 F.R.D. 396 (D. Nevada 1985); International Wood Processors v. Power Dry, Inc., 598 F. Supp. 299 (D.S.C. 1984); Morrissey v. County Tower Corp., 568 F.Supp. 178 (ED Mo. 1983).

188 In Re: Kulicke & Soffa Industries, Inc. Securities Litigation, 747 F.Supp. 1136 (ED Pa. 1990) aff'd 944 F.2d 897 (3rd. Cir. 1991).

189 Sullivan v. Cheshire, 991 F.Supp. 999 (ND Ill. 1998).

190 In Re: Kulicke & Soffa Industries Inc. Securities Litigation, 747 F.Supp. 1136 (E.D.Pa. 1990), aff'd, 944 F.2d 897 (3rd Cir. 1991).

191 In Re: Kulicke & Soffa Industries Inc. Securities Litigation, 747 F.Supp. 1136 (E.D.Pa. 1990), aff'd, 944 F.2d 897 (3rd. Cir. 1991).

192 Mitchell v. City of Moore, Oklahoma, 218 F.3d 1190 (10th Cir. 2000); Stearns Airport Equipment Co., Inc. v. FMC Corporation, 170 F.3d 518 (5th Cir. 1999); Cengr v. Fusibond Piping Systems, Inc., 135 F.3d 445 (7th Cir. 1998); Sevenson Environmental Services, Inc. v. Shaw Environmental, Inc., 246 F.R.D. 154 (WDNY 2007); Yasui v. Maui Electric Company, 78 F.Supp.2d 1124 (D. Hawaii 1999).

193 LaVay Corporation v. Dominion Federal Savings and Loan, 830 F.2d 522 (4th Cir. 1987).

194 Neumann v. Reinforced Earth Company, 109 FRD 698 (DDC 1986).

195 BDT Products, Inc. v. Lexmark International, Inc., 405 F.3d 415 (6th Cir. 2005); Tilton v. Capital Cities/ABC, Inc., 115 F.3d 1471 (10th Cir. 1997); Garonzik v. Whitman Diner, 910 F.Supp. 167 (D.N.J. 1995).

196 In re: Paoli Railroad Yard PCB Litigation, 221 F.3d 449 (3rd Cir. 2000); In Re: Kulicke & Soffa Industries Inc. Securities Litigation, 747 F.Supp. 1136 (E.D.Pa. 1990), aff'd, 944 F.2d 897 (3rd Cir. 1991); ADM Corp. v. Speedmaster Packing Corp., 525 F.2d 662 (3d Cir. 1975); Nugget Distributors Cooperative of America v. Mr. Nugget, Inc., 145 F.R.D. 54 (E.D.Pa. 1992). Accord, Charter Medical Corp v. Cardin, 127 F.R.D. 111 (D. Maryland 1989); Women's Federal Savings and Loan Association of Cleveland v. Nevada National Bank, 108 FRD 396 (D. Nevada 1985); International Wood Processors v. Power Dry, Inc., 598 F. Supp. 299 (D.S.C. 1984); Morrissey v. County Tower Corp., 568 F.Supp. 178 (ED Mo. 1983).

197 McGuigan v. CAE Link Corp., 155 F.R.D. 31 (NDNY 1994).

198 In Re: Kulicke & Soffa Industries Inc. Securities Litigation, 747 F.Supp. 1136 (E.D.Pa. 1990), aff'd, 944 F.2d 897 (3rd. Cir. 1991); Montgomery County v. Microvote Corp., 2004 WL 1087196 (E.D.Pa 2004). Accord, Holmes v. Cessna Aircraft Co., 11 F.3d 63 (5th Cir. 1994).

199 Montgomery County v. Microvote Corp., 2004 WL 1087196 (E.D.Pa. 2004). Accord, Weeks v. Samsung Heavy Industries, 126 F.3d1997); Karsian v. Inter Regional Financial Group, Inc., 13 F.Supp.2d 1085 (D. Colorado 1998); Movitz v. First National Bank of Chicago, 982 F.Supp. 571 (ND Ill. 1997); Marcoin, Inc. v. Edwin K. Williams & Co., Inc., 88 FRD 588 (E.D.Va. 1980); Electronic Specialty Co. v. International Controls Corp., 47 FRD 158 (SDNY 1969).

200 Morrissey v. County Tower Corp., 568 F.Supp. 980 (ED Mo. 1983).

201 Reger v. The Nemours Foundation, 599 F.3d 285 (3d Cir. 2010); In re: Paoli Railroad Yard PCB Litigation, 221 F.3d 449 (3d Cir. 2000); Abrams v. Lightolier, Inc., 50 F.3d 1204 (3d Cir. 1995); Smith v. SEPTA, 47 F.3d 97 (3d Cir. 1995); Friedman v. Ganassi, 853 F.2d 207 (3d Cir. 1988); Institutionalized Juveniles v. Secretary of Public Welfare, 758 F.2d 897 (3d Cir. 1985); Pearlstine v. United States, 649 F.2d 194 (3rd Cir. 1981); Delaney v. Capone, 642 F.2d 57 (3d Cir. 1981); Samuel v. University of Pittsburgh, 538 F.2d 991 (3d Cir. 1976); ADM Corp. v. Speedmaster Packing Corp., 525 F.2d 662 (3d Cir. 1975); City of Rome, Italy v. Glanton, 184 F.R.D. 547 (E.D. Pa. 1999); Greene v. Fraternal Order of Police, 183 F.R.D. 445 (E.D. Pa. 1998); Action Alliance for Senior Citizens of Greater Philadelphia v. Shapp, 74 F.R.D. 617 (E.D. Pa. 1977).

Endnotes

202 Buchanan v. Stanships, Inc., 485 U.S. 265, 268 (1988)(emphasis added). Accord, Delta Air Lines, Inc. v. August, 450 U.S. 346 (1981). See, also, Reger v. The Nemours Foundation, 599 F.3d 285 (3d Cir. 2010); In re: Paoli Railroad Yard PCB Litigation, 221 F.3d 449 (3d Cir. 2000); Abrams v. Lightolier, Inc., 50 F.3d 1204 (3d Cir. 1995); Smith v. SEPTA, 47 F.3d 97 (3d Cir. 1995); Friedman v. Ganassi, 853 F.2d 207 (3d Cir. 1988); Institutionalized Juveniles v. Secretary of Public Welfare, 758 F.2d 897 (3d Cir. 1985); Pearlstine v. United States, 649 F.2d 194 (3rd Cir. 1981); Delaney v. Capone, 642 F.2d 57 (3d Cir. 1981); Samuel v. University of Pittsburgh, 538 F.2d 991 (3d Cir. 1976); ADM Corp. v. Speedmaster Packing Corp., 525 F.2d 662 (3d Cir. 1975); City of Rome, Italy v. Glanton, 184 F.R.D. 547 (E.D. Pa. 1999); Greene v. Fraternal Order of Police, 183 F.R.D. 445 (E.D. Pa. 1998); Action Alliance for Senior Citizens of Greater Philadelphia v. Shapp, 74 F.R.D. 617 (E.D. Pa. 1977).

203 Buchanan v. Stanships, Inc., 485 U.S. 265 (1988); Delta Air Lines, Inc. v. August, 450 U.S. 346 (1981). Accord, Reger v. The Nemours Foundation, 599 F.3d 285 (3d Cir. 2010); In re: Paoli Railroad Yard PCB Litigation, 221 F.3d 449 (3d Cir. 2000); Abrams v. Lightolier, Inc., 50 F.3d 1204 (3d Cir. 1995); Smith v. SEPTA, 47 F.3d 97 (3d Cir. 1995); Friedman v. Ganassi, 853 F.2d 207 (3d Cir. 1988); Institutionalized Juveniles v. Secretary of Public Welfare, 758 F.2d 897 (3d Cir. 1985); Pearlstine v. United States, 649 F.2d 194 (3rd Cir. 1981); Delaney v. Capone, 642 F.2d 57 (3d Cir. 1981); Samuel v. University of Pittsburgh, 538 F.2d 991 (3d Cir. 1976); ADM Corp. v. Speedmaster Packing Corp., 525 F.2d 662 (3d Cir. 1975); City of Rome, Italy v. Glanton, 184 F.R.D. 547 (E.D. Pa. 1999); Greene v. Fraternal Order of Police, 183 F.R.D. 445 (E.D. Pa. 1998); Action Alliance for Senior Citizens of Greater Philadelphia v. Shapp, 74 F.R.D. 617 (E.D. Pa. 1977).

204 Brazos Valley Coalition for Life, Inc. v. City of Bryan, Texas, 421 F.3d 314 (5th Cir. 2005); Trepel v. Roadway Express, Inc., 266 F.3d 418 (6th Cir. 2001); Holmes v. Cessna Aircraft Co., 11 F.3d 63 (5th Cir. 1994); Dovenmuehle v. Gilldorn Mortgage Midwest Corp., 871 F.2d 697 (7th Cir. 1989); Mason v. Belieu, 543 F.2d 215 (D.C. Cir. 1976); Wahl v. Carrier Manufacturing Co., 511 F.2d 209 (7th Cir. 1975); McInnis v. Town of Weston, 458 F.Supp.2d 7 (D. Conn. 2006); Sullivan v. Cheshier, 991 F.Supp. 999 (N.D. Ill. 1998); Hollenbeck v. Falstaff Brewing Corp., 605 F.Supp. 421 (E.D. Mo. 1984); Morrissey v. County Tower Corp., 568 F.Supp. 980 (E.D. Mo. 1983).

205 In Re: Kulicke & Soffa Industries Inc. Securities Litigation, 747 F.Supp. 1136 (E.D.Pa. 1990), aff'd, 944 F.2d 897 (3rd Cir. 1991); ADM Corp. v. Speedmaster Packing Corp., 525 F.2d 662 (3d Cir. 1975); Nugget Distributors Cooperative of America v. Mr. Nugget, Inc., 145 F.R.D. 54 (E.D.Pa. 1992). Accord, Charter Medical Corp v. Cardin, 127 F.R.D. 111 (D. Maryland 1989); Women's Federal Savings and Loan Association of Cleveland v. Nevada National Bank, 108 F.R.D. 396 (D. Nevada 1985); International Wood Processors v. Power Dry, Inc., 598 F. Supp. 299 (D.S.C. 1984); Morrissey v. County Tower Corp., 568 F.Supp. 178 (ED Mo. 1983).

206 In Re: Kulicke & Soffa Industries Inc. Securities Litigation, 747 F.Supp. 1136 (E.D.Pa. 1990), aff'd, 944 F.2d 897 (3rd Cir. 1991).

207 In Re: Kulicke & Soffa Industries Inc. Securities Litigation, 747 F.Supp. 1136 (E.D.Pa. 1990), aff'd, 944 F.2d 897 (3rd Cir. 1991).

208 In re: Paoli Railroad Yard PCB Litigation, 221 F.3d 449 (3d Cir. 2000); Montgomery County v. Microvote Corp., 2004 WL 1087196 (EDPA 2004); Tracy v. Goldberg, 203 F.Supp. 188 (E.D. Pa. 1962). See, also, Charter Medical Corp. v. Cardin, 127 F.R.D. 111 (D. Maryland 1989); Harrisburg Coalition Against Ruining the Environment v. Volpe, 65 F.R.D. 608 (M.D. Pa. 1974).

209 Proffitt v. Municipal Authority of Borough of Morrisville, 716 F.Supp. 845 (E.D. Pa. 1989), aff'd, 897 F.2d 523 (3d Cir. 1990); Shannon v. United States Department of Housing and Urban Development, 433 F.Supp. 249 (E.D. Pa. 1977).

210 In Re: Glacier Bay, 746 F.Supp. 1379 (D. Alaska 1990).

211 Reger v. The Nemours Foundation, 599 F.3d 285 (3d Cir. 2010); In re: Paoli Railroad Yard PCB Litigation, 221 F.3d 449 (3d Cir. 2000); Abrams v. Lightolier, Inc., 50 F.3d 1204 (3d Cir. 1995); Smith v. SEPTA, 47 F.3d 97 (3d Cir. 1995); Friedman v. Ganassi, 853 F.2d 207 (3d Cir. 1988); Institutionalized Juveniles v. Secretary of Public Welfare, 758 F.2d 897 (3d Cir. 1985); Pearlstine v. United States, 649 F.2d 194 (3rd Cir. 1981); Delaney v. Capone, 642 F.2d 57 (3d Cir. 1981); Samuel v. University of Pittsburgh, 538 F.2d 991 (3d Cir. 1976); ADM Corp. v. Speedmaster Packing Corp., 525 F.2d 662 (3d Cir. 1975); City of Rome, Italy v. Glanton, 184 F.R.D. 547 (E.D. Pa. 1999); Greene v. Fraternal Order of Police, 183 F.R.D. 445 (E.D. Pa. 1998); Action Alliance for Senior Citizens of Greater Philadelphia v. Shapp, 74 F.R.D. 617 (E.D. Pa. 1977).

212 Buchanan v. Stanships, Inc., 485 U.S. 265, 268 (1988)(emphasis added). Accord, Delta Air Lines, Inc. v. August, 450 U.S. 346 (1981). See, also, Reger v. The Nemours Foundation, 599 F.3d 285 (3d Cir. 2010); In re: Paoli Railroad Yard PCB Litigation, 221 F.3d 449 (3d Cir. 2000); Abrams v. Lightolier, Inc., 50 F.3d

1204 (3d Cir. 1995); Smith v. SEPTA, 47 F.3d 97 (3d Cir. 1995); Friedman v. Ganassi, 853 F.2d 207 (3d Cir. 1988); Institutionalized Juveniles v. Secretary of Public Welfare, 758 F.2d 897 (3d Cir. 1985); Pearlstine v. United States, 649 F.2d 194 (3rd Cir. 1981); Delaney v. Capone, 642 F.2d 57 (3d Cir. 1981); Samuel v. University of Pittsburgh, 538 F.2d 991 (3d Cir. 1976); ADM Corp. v. Speedmaster Packing Corp., 525 F.2d 662 (3d Cir. 1975); City of Rome, Italy v. Glanton, 184 F.R.D. 547 (E.D. Pa. 1999); Greene v. Fraternal Order of Police, 183 F.R.D. 445 (E.D. Pa. 1998); Action Alliance for Senior Citizens of Greater Philadelphia v. Shapp, 74 F.R.D. 617 (E.D. Pa. 1977).

213 Buchanan v. Stanships, Inc., 485 U.S. 265 (1988); Delta Air Lines, Inc. v. August, 450 U.S. 346 (1981). Accord, Reger v. The Nemours Foundation, 599 F.3d 285 (3d Cir. 2010); In re: Paoli Railroad Yard PCB Litigation, 221 F.3d 449 (3d Cir. 2000); Abrams v. Lightolier, Inc., 50 F.3d 1204 (3d Cir. 1995); Smith v. SEPTA, 47 F.3d 97 (3d Cir. 1995); Friedman v. Ganassi, 853 F.2d 207 (3d Cir. 1988); Institutionalized Juveniles v. Secretary of Public Welfare, 758 F.2d 897 (3d Cir. 1985); Pearlstine v. United States, 649 F.2d 194 (3rd Cir. 1981); Delaney v. Capone, 642 F.2d 57 (3d Cir. 1981); Samuel v. University of Pittsburgh, 538 F.2d 991 (3d Cir. 1976); ADM Corp. v. Speedmaster Packing Corp., 525 F.2d 662 (3d Cir. 1975); City of Rome, Italy v. Glanton, 184 F.R.D. 547 (E.D. Pa. 1999); Greene v. Fraternal Order of Police, 183 F.R.D. 445 (E.D. Pa. 1998); Action Alliance for Senior Citizens of Greater Philadelphia v. Shapp, 74 F.R.D. 617 (E.D. Pa. 1977).

214 Brazos Valley Coalition for Life, Inc. v. City of Bryan, Texas, 421 F.3d 314 (5th Cir. 2005); Trepel v. Roadway Express, Inc., 266 F.3d 418 (6th Cir. 2001); Holmes v. Cessna Aircraft Co., 11 F.3d 63 (5th Cir. 1994); Dovenmuehle v. Gilldorn Mortgage Midwest Corp., 871 F.2d 697 (7th Cir. 1989); Mason v. Belieu, 543 F.2d 215 (D.C. Cir. 1976); Wahl v. Carrier Manufacturing Co., 511 F.2d 209 (7th Cir. 1975); McInnis v. Town of Weston, 458 F.Supp.2d 7 (D. Conn. 2006); Sullivan v. Cheshier, 991 F.Supp. 999 (N.D. Ill. 1998); Hollenbeck v. Falstaff Brewing Corp., 605 F.Supp. 421 (E.D. Mo. 1984); Morrissey v. County Tower Corp., 568 F.Supp. 980 (E.D. Mo. 1983).

215 In Re: Kulicke & Soffa Industries Inc. Securities Litigation, 747 F.Supp. 1136 (E.D.Pa. 1990), aff'd, 944 F.2d 897 (3rd Cir. 1991); ADM Corp. v. Speedmaster Packing Corp., 525 F.2d 662 (3d Cir. 1975); Nugget Distributors Cooperative of America v. Mr. Nugget, Inc., 145 F.R.D. 54 (E.D.Pa. 1992). Accord, Charter Medical Corp v. Cardin, 127 FRD 111 (D. Maryland 1989); Women's Federal Savings and Loan Association of Cleveland v. Nevada National Bank, 108 FRD 396 (D. Nevada 1985); International Wood Processors v. Power Dry, Inc., 598 F. Supp. 299 (D.S.C. 1984); Morrissey v. County Tower Corp., 568 F.Supp. 178 (ED Mo. 1983).

216 Kansas v. Colorado, 129 S.Ct. 1294 (2009).

217 Crawford Fitting Company v. J. T. Gibbons, Inc., 482 U.S. 437 (1987); Henkel v. Chicago, St. Paul, Minneapolis and Omaha Railroad Company, 284 U.S. 444 (1932).

218 Griffith v. Mt. Carmel Medical Center, 157 F.R.D. 499 (D. Kansas 1994).

219 Brazos Valley Coalition for Life, Inc. v. City of Bryan, Texas, 421 F.3d 314 (5th Cir. 2005); Trepel v. Montgomery County v. Microvote Corp., 2004 WL 1087196 (EDPA 2004); Greene v. Fraternal Order of Police, 183 F.R.D. 445 (E.D. Pa. 1998). Accord, Nissho-Iwai Co. v. Occidental Crude Sales, 729 F.2d 1530 (5th Cir. 1984); Quy v. Air America, Inc., 667 F.2d 1059 (D.C. Cir. 1981); Karsian v. Inter Regional Financial Group, Inc., 13 F.Supp.2d 1085 (D. Colorado 1998); Marino v. Town of Kirkland, 146 F.R.D. 49 (N.D.N.Y. 1993); Morrissey v. County Tower Corp., 568 F. Supp. 980 (E.D. Mo. 1983); Independence Tube Corp. v. Copperweld Corp., 543 F.Supp. 706 (N.D.Ill. 1982); Christian v. Tackett, 86 F.R.D. 220 (N.D. Miss. 1979); Gillam v. A. Shyman, Inc., 31 F.R.D. 271 (D. Alaska 1962).

220 Dr. Bernard Heller Foundation v. Lee, 847 F.2d 83 (3rd Cir. 1988); Greene v. Fraternal Order of Police, 183 F.R.D. 445 (E.D. Pa. 1998). See, also, Louisiana Power and Light Co. v. Kellstrom, 50 F.3d 319 (5th Cir. 1995); McGuigan v. CAE Link Corp., 155 F.R.D. 31 (NDNY 1994).

221 Kansas v. Colorado, 129 S.Ct. 1294 (2009); Crawford Fitting Company v. J. T. Gibbons, Inc., 482 U.S. 437 (1987); In re Philadelphia Mortgage Trust, 930 F.2d 306 (3rd Cir. 1990); Friedman v. Ganassi, 853 F.2d 207 (3rd Cir. 1988); Dr. Bernard Heller Foundation v. Lee, 847 F.2d 83 (3rd Cir. 1988); Dominic v. Hess Oil V.I. Corp., 841 F.2d 513 (3rd Cir. 1988).

222 Crawford Fitting Company v. J. T. Gibbons, Inc., 482 U.S. 437 (1987); In re Philadelphia Mortgage Trust, 930 F.2d 306 (3rd Cir. 1990); Friedman v. Ganassi, 853 F.2d 207 (3rd Cir. 1988); Dr. Bernard Heller Foundation v. Lee, 847 F.2d 83 (3rd Cir. 1988); Dominic v. Hess Oil V.I. Corp., 841 F.2d 513 (3rd Cir. 1988).

223 Sierra Club v. EPA, 769 F.2d 796 (DC Cir. 1985); In Re: Air Crash Disaster at John F. Kennedy International Airport on June 24, 1975, 687 F.2d 626 (2nd Cir. 1982); Griffith v. Mt. Carmel Medical Center, 157 F.R.D. 499 (D. Kansas 1994); Radol v. Thomas, 113 F.R.D. 172 (SD Ohio 1986); Marquez v. American Export Lines, 41 F.R.D. 386 (SDNY 1967).

Endnotes

224 Greene v. Fraternal Order of Police, 183 F.R.D. 445 (E.D. Pa. 1998). See, also, Bee v. Greaves, 910 F.2d 686 (10th Cir. 1990); Jensen v. Lawler, 338 F.Supp. 2d 739 (SD Texas 2004); Heverly v. Lewis, 99 F.R.D. 135, 136 (D.Nev. 1983); Gillam v. Shyman, Inc., 31 F.R.D. 271 (D. Alaska 1962).

225 Greene v. Fraternal Order of Police, 183 F.R.D. 445 (E.D. Pa. 1998). See, also, Griffith v. Mt. Carmel Medical Center, 157 F.R.D. 499 (D. Kansas 1994); Todd Shipyards Corp. v. Turbine Services, Inc., 592 F.Supp. 380 (E.D. La. 1984); Morrison v. Alleluia Cushion Co., 73 F.R.D. 70, 71 (N.D. Miss. 1976); Sperry Rand Corp. v. A-T-O Co., 58 F.R.D. 132 (E.D. Va. 1973).

226 Reger v. The Nemours Foundation, 599 F.3d 285 (3d Cir. 2010); In re: Paoli Railroad Yard PCB Litigation, 221 F.3d 449 (3d Cir. 2000); Abrams v. Lightolier, Inc., 50 F.3d 1204 (3d Cir. 1995); Smith v. SEPTA, 47 F.3d 97 (3d Cir. 1995); Friedman v. Ganassi, 853 F.2d 207 (3d Cir. 1988); Institutionalized Juveniles v. Secretary of Public Welfare, 758 F.2d 897 (3d Cir. 1985); Pearlstine v. United States, 649 F.2d 194 (3rd Cir. 1981); Delaney v. Capone, 642 F.2d 57 (3d Cir. 1981); Samuel v. University of Pittsburgh, 538 F.2d 991 (3d Cir. 1976); ADM Corp. v. Speedmaster Packing Corp., 525 F.2d 662 (3d Cir. 1975); City of Rome, Italy v. Glanton, 184 F.R.D. 547 (E.D. Pa. 1999); Greene v. Fraternal Order of Police, 183 F.R.D. 445 (E.D. Pa. 1998); Action Alliance for Senior Citizens of Greater Philadelphia v. Shapp, 74 F.R.D. 617 (E.D. Pa. 1977).

227 Buchanan v. Stanships, Inc., 485 U.S. 265, 268 (1988)(emphasis added). Accord, Delta Air Lines, Inc. v. August, 450 U.S. 346 (1981). See, also, Reger v. The Nemours Foundation, 599 F.3d 285 (3d Cir. 2010); In re: Paoli Railroad Yard PCB Litigation, 221 F.3d 449 (3d Cir. 2000); Abrams v. Lightolier, Inc., 50 F.3d 1204 (3d Cir. 1995); Smith v. SEPTA, 47 F.3d 97 (3d Cir. 1995); Friedman v. Ganassi, 853 F.2d 207 (3d Cir. 1988); Institutionalized Juveniles v. Secretary of Public Welfare, 758 F.2d 897 (3d Cir. 1985); Pearlstine v. United States, 649 F.2d 194 (3rd Cir. 1981); Delaney v. Capone, 642 F.2d 57 (3d Cir. 1981); Samuel v. University of Pittsburgh, 538 F.2d 991 (3d Cir. 1976); ADM Corp. v. Speedmaster Packing Corp., 525 F.2d 662 (3d Cir. 1975); City of Rome, Italy v. Glanton, 184 F.R.D. 547 (E.D. Pa. 1999); Greene v. Fraternal Order of Police, 183 F.R.D. 445 (E.D. Pa. 1998); Action Alliance for Senior Citizens of Greater Philadelphia v. Shapp, 74 F.R.D. 617 (E.D. Pa. 1977).

228 Buchanan v. Stanships, Inc., 485 U.S. 265 (1988); Delta Air Lines, Inc. v. August, 450 U.S. 346 (1981). Accord, Reger v. The Nemours Foundation, 599 F.3d 285 (3d Cir. 2010); In re: Paoli Railroad Yard PCB Litigation, 221 F.3d 449 (3d Cir. 2000); Abrams v. Lightolier, Inc., 50 F.3d 1204 (3d Cir. 1995); Smith v. SEPTA, 47 F.3d 97 (3d Cir. 1995); Friedman v. Ganassi, 853 F.2d 207 (3d Cir. 1988); Institutionalized Juveniles v. Secretary of Public Welfare, 758 F.2d 897 (3d Cir. 1985); Pearlstine v. United States, 649 F.2d 194 (3rd Cir. 1981); Delaney v. Capone, 642 F.2d 57 (3d Cir. 1981); Samuel v. University of Pittsburgh, 538 F.2d 991 (3d Cir. 1976); ADM Corp. v. Speedmaster Packing Corp., 525 F.2d 662 (3d Cir. 1975); City of Rome, Italy v. Glanton, 184 F.R.D. 547 (E.D. Pa. 1999); Greene v. Fraternal Order of Police, 183 F.R.D. 445 (E.D. Pa. 1998); Action Alliance for Senior Citizens of Greater Philadelphia v. Shapp, 74 F.R.D. 617 (E.D. Pa. 1977).

229 Brazos Valley Coalition for Life, Inc. v. City of Bryan, Texas, 421 F.3d 314 (5th Cir. 2005); Trepel v. Roadway Express, Inc., 266 F.3d 418 (6th Cir. 2001); Holmes v. Cessna Aircraft Co., 11 F.3d 63 (5th Cir. 1994); Dovenmuehle v. Gilldorn Mortgage Midwest Corp., 871 F.2d 697 (7th Cir. 1989); Mason v. Belieu, 543 F.2d 215 (D.C. Cir. 1976); Wahl v. Carrier Manufacturing Co., 511 F.2d 209 (7th Cir. 1975); McInnis v. Town of Weston, 458 F.Supp.2d 7 (D. Conn. 2006); Sullivan v. Cheshier, 991 F.Supp. 999 (N.D. Ill. 1998); Hollenbeck v. Falstaff Brewing Corp., 605 F.Supp. 421 (E.D. Mo. 1984); Morrissey v. County Tower Corp., 568 F.Supp. 980 (E.D. Mo. 1983).

230 In Re: Kulicke & Soffa Industries Inc. Securities Litigation, 747 F.Supp. 1136 (E.D.Pa. 1990), aff'd, 944 F.2d 897 (3rd Cir. 1991); ADM Corp. v. Speedmaster Packing Corp., 525 F.2d 662 (3d Cir. 1975); Nugget Distributors Cooperative of America v. Mr. Nugget, Inc., 145 F.R.D. 54 (E.D.Pa. 1992). Accord, Charter Medical Corp v. Cardin, 127 FRD 111 (D. Maryland 1989); Women's Federal Savings and Loan Association of Cleveland v. Nevada National Bank, 108 FRD 396 (D. Nevada 1985); International Wood Processors v. Power Dry, Inc., 598 F. Supp. 299 (D.S.C. 1984); Morrissey v. County Tower Corp., 568 F.Supp. 178 (ED Mo. 1983).

231 Kansas v. Colorado, 129 S.Ct. 1294 (2009).

232 Crawford Fitting Company v. J. T. Gibbons, Inc., 482 U.S. 437 (1987); Henkel v. Chicago, St. Paul, Minneapolis and Omaha Railroad Company, 284 U.S. 444 (1932).

233 Greene v. Fraternal Order of Police, 183 F.R.D. 445 (E.D. Pa. 1998); Raio v. American Airlines, 102 F.R.D. 608 (E.D. Pa. 1984). See, also, Women's Federal Savings and Loan Association of Cleveland v. Nevada National Bank, 108 F.R.D. 396 (D. Nevada 1985).

234 Central Delaware Branch of the NAACP v. City of Dover, Delaware, 123 FRD 85 (D. Delaware 1988).

235 Reger v. The Nemours Foundation, 599 F.3d 285 (3d Cir. 2010); In re: Paoli Railroad Yard PCB Litigation, 221 F.3d 449 (3d Cir. 2000); Abrams v. Lightolier, Inc., 50 F.3d 1204 (3d Cir. 1995); Smith v. SEPTA, 47 F.3d 97 (3d Cir. 1995); Friedman v. Ganassi, 853 F.2d 207 (3d Cir. 1988); Institutionalized Juveniles v. Secretary of Public Welfare, 758 F.2d 897 (3d Cir. 1985); Pearlstine v. United States, 649 F.2d 194 (3rd Cir. 1981); Delaney v. Capone, 642 F.2d 57 (3d Cir. 1981); Samuel v. University of Pittsburgh, 538 F.2d 991 (3d Cir. 1976); ADM Corp. v. Speedmaster Packing Corp., 525 F.2d 662 (3d Cir. 1975); City of Rome, Italy v. Glanton, 184 F.R.D. 547 (E.D. Pa. 1999); Greene v. Fraternal Order of Police, 183 F.R.D. 445 (E.D. Pa. 1998); Action Alliance for Senior Citizens of Greater Philadelphia v. Shapp, 74 F.R.D. 617 (E.D. Pa. 1977).

236 Buchanan v. Stanships, Inc., 485 U.S. 265, 268 (1988)(emphasis added). Accord, Delta Air Lines, Inc. v. August, 450 U.S. 346 (1981). See, also, Reger v. The Nemours Foundation, 599 F.3d 285 (3d Cir. 2010); In re: Paoli Railroad Yard PCB Litigation, 221 F.3d 449 (3d Cir. 2000); Abrams v. Lightolier, Inc., 50 F.3d 1204 (3d Cir. 1995); Smith v. SEPTA, 47 F.3d 97 (3d Cir. 1995); Friedman v. Ganassi, 853 F.2d 207 (3d Cir. 1988); Institutionalized Juveniles v. Secretary of Public Welfare, 758 F.2d 897 (3d Cir. 1985); Pearlstine v. United States, 649 F.2d 194 (3rd Cir. 1981); Delaney v. Capone, 642 F.2d 57 (3d Cir. 1981); Samuel v. University of Pittsburgh, 538 F.2d 991 (3d Cir. 1976); ADM Corp. v. Speedmaster Packing Corp., 525 F.2d 662 (3d Cir. 1975); City of Rome, Italy v. Glanton, 184 F.R.D. 547 (E.D. Pa. 1999); Greene v. Fraternal Order of Police, 183 F.R.D. 445 (E.D. Pa. 1998); Action Alliance for Senior Citizens of Greater Philadelphia v. Shapp, 74 F.R.D. 617 (E.D. Pa. 1977).

237 Buchanan v. Stanships, Inc., 485 U.S. 265 (1988); Delta Air Lines, Inc. v. August, 450 U.S. 346 (1981). Accord, Reger v. The Nemours Foundation, 599 F.3d 285 (3d Cir. 2010); In re: Paoli Railroad Yard PCB Litigation, 221 F.3d 449 (3d Cir. 2000); Abrams v. Lightolier, Inc., 50 F.3d 1204 (3d Cir. 1995); Smith v. SEPTA, 47 F.3d 97 (3d Cir. 1995); Friedman v. Ganassi, 853 F.2d 207 (3d Cir. 1988); Institutionalized Juveniles v. Secretary of Public Welfare, 758 F.2d 897 (3d Cir. 1985); Pearlstine v. United States, 649 F.2d 194 (3rd Cir. 1981); Delaney v. Capone, 642 F.2d 57 (3d Cir. 1981); Samuel v. University of Pittsburgh, 538 F.2d 991 (3d Cir. 1976); ADM Corp. v. Speedmaster Packing Corp., 525 F.2d 662 (3d Cir. 1975); City of Rome, Italy v. Glanton, 184 F.R.D. 547 (E.D. Pa. 1999); Greene v. Fraternal Order of Police, 183 F.R.D. 445 (E.D. Pa. 1998); Action Alliance for Senior Citizens of Greater Philadelphia v. Shapp, 74 F.R.D. 617 (E.D. Pa. 1977).

238 Brazos Valley Coalition for Life, Inc. v. City of Bryan, Texas, 421 F.3d 314 (5th Cir. 2005); Trepel v. Roadway Express, Inc., 266 F.3d 418 (6th Cir. 2001); Holmes v. Cessna Aircraft Co., 11 F.3d 63 (5th Cir. 1994); Dovenmuehle v. Gilldorn Mortgage Midwest Corp., 871 F.2d 697 (7th Cir. 1989); Mason v. Belieu, 543 F.2d 215 (D.C. Cir. 1976); Wahl v. Carrier Manufacturing Co., 511 F.2d 209 (7th Cir. 1975); McInnis v. Town of Weston, 458 F.Supp.2d 7 (D. Conn. 2006); Sullivan v. Cheshire, 991 F.Supp. 999 (N.D. Ill. 1998); Hollenbeck v. Falstaff Brewing Corp., 605 F.Supp. 421 (E.D. Mo. 1984); Morrissey v. County Tower Corp., 568 F.Supp. 980 (E.D. Mo. 1983).

239 In Re: Kulicke & Soffa Industries Inc. Securities Litigation, 747 F.Supp. 1136 (E.D.Pa. 1990), aff'd, 944 F.2d 897 (3rd Cir. 1991); ADM Corp. v. Speedmaster Packing Corp., 525 F.2d 662 (3d Cir. 1975); Nugget Distributors Cooperative of America v. Mr. Nugget, Inc., 145 F.R.D. 54 (E.D.Pa. 1992). Accord, Charter Medical Corp v. Cardin, 127 F.R.D. 111 (D. Maryland 1989); Women's Federal Savings and Loan Association of Cleveland v. Nevada National Bank, 108 F.R.D. 396 (D. Nevada 1985); International Wood Processors v. Power Dry, Inc., 598 F. Supp. 299 (D.S.C. 1984); Morrissey v. County Tower Corp., 568 F.Supp. 178 (ED Mo. 1983).

240 Kansas v. Colorado, 129 S.Ct. 1294 (2009).

241 Crawford Fitting Company v. J. T. Gibbons, Inc., 482 U.S. 437 (1987); Henkel v. Chicago, St. Paul, Minneapolis and Omaha Railroad Company, 284 U.S. 444 (1932).

242 Greene v. Fraternal Order of Police, 183 F.R.D. 445 (E.D. Pa. 1998); Raio v. American Airlines, 102 F.R.D. 608 (E.D. Pa. 1984). See, also, Women's Federal Savings and Loan Association of Cleveland v. Nevada National Bank, 108 F.R.D. 396 (D. Nevada 1985).

243 Central Delaware Branch of the NAACP v. City of Dover, Delaware, 123 FRD 85 (D. Delaware 1988).

244 Reger v. The Nemours Foundation, 599 F.3d 285 (3d Cir. 2010); In re: Paoli Railroad Yard PCB Litigation, 221 F.3d 449 (3d Cir. 2000); Abrams v. Lightolier, Inc., 50 F.3d 1204 (3d Cir. 1995); Smith v. SEPTA, 47 F.3d 97 (3d Cir. 1995); Friedman v. Ganassi, 853 F.2d 207 (3d Cir. 1988); Institutionalized Juveniles v. Secretary of Public Welfare, 758 F.2d 897 (3d Cir. 1985); Pearlstine v. United States, 649 F.2d 194 (3rd Cir. 1981); Delaney v. Capone, 642 F.2d 57 (3d Cir. 1981); Samuel v. University of Pittsburgh, 538 F.2d 991 (3d Cir. 1976); ADM Corp. v. Speedmaster Packing Corp., 525 F.2d 662 (3d Cir. 1975); City of Rome, Italy v. Glanton, 184 F.R.D. 547 (E.D. Pa. 1999); Greene v. Fraternal Order of Police, 183 F.R.D.

Endnotes

445 (E.D. Pa. 1998); Action Alliance for Senior Citizens of Greater Philadelphia v. Shapp, 74 F.R.D. 617 (E.D. Pa. 1977).

245   Buchanan v. Stanships, Inc., 485 U.S. 265, 268 (1988)(emphasis added). Accord, Delta Air Lines, Inc. v. August, 450 U.S. 346 (1981). See, also, Reger v. The Nemours Foundation, 599 F.3d 285 (3d Cir. 2010); In re: Paoli Railroad Yard PCB Litigation, 221 F.3d 449 (3d Cir. 2000); Abrams v. Lightolier, Inc., 50 F.3d 1204 (3d Cir. 1995); Smith v. SEPTA, 47 F.3d 97 (3d Cir. 1995); Friedman v. Ganassi, 853 F.2d 207 (3d Cir. 1988); Institutionalized Juveniles v. Secretary of Public Welfare, 758 F.2d 897 (3d Cir. 1985); Pearlstine v. United States, 649 F.2d 194 (3rd Cir. 1981); Delaney v. Capone, 642 F.2d 57 (3d Cir. 1981); Samuel v. University of Pittsburgh, 538 F.2d 991 (3d Cir. 1976); ADM Corp. v. Speedmaster Packing Corp., 525 F.2d 662 (3d Cir. 1975); City of Rome, Italy v. Glanton, 184 F.R.D. 547 (E.D. Pa. 1999); Greene v. Fraternal Order of Police, 183 F.R.D. 445 (E.D. Pa. 1998); Action Alliance for Senior Citizens of Greater Philadelphia v. Shapp, 74 F.R.D. 617 (E.D. Pa. 1977).

246   Buchanan v. Stanships, Inc., 485 U.S. 265 (1988); Delta Air Lines, Inc. v. August, 450 U.S. 346 (1981). Accord, Reger v. The Nemours Foundation, 599 F.3d 285 (3d Cir. 2010); In re: Paoli Railroad Yard PCB Litigation, 221 F.3d 449 (3d Cir. 2000); Abrams v. Lightolier, Inc., 50 F.3d 1204 (3d Cir. 1995); Smith v. SEPTA, 47 F.3d 97 (3d Cir. 1995); Friedman v. Ganassi, 853 F.2d 207 (3d Cir. 1988); Institutionalized Juveniles v. Secretary of Public Welfare, 758 F.2d 897 (3d Cir. 1985); Pearlstine v. United States, 649 F.2d 194 (3rd Cir. 1981); Delaney v. Capone, 642 F.2d 57 (3d Cir. 1981); Samuel v. University of Pittsburgh, 538 F.2d 991 (3d Cir. 1976); ADM Corp. v. Speedmaster Packing Corp., 525 F.2d 662 (3d Cir. 1975); City of Rome, Italy v. Glanton, 184 F.R.D. 547 (E.D. Pa. 1999); Greene v. Fraternal Order of Police, 183 F.R.D. 445 (E.D. Pa. 1998); Action Alliance for Senior Citizens of Greater Philadelphia v. Shapp, 74 F.R.D. 617 (E.D. Pa. 1977).

247   Brazos Valley Coalition for Life, Inc. v. City of Bryan, Texas, 421 F.3d 314 (5th Cir. 2005); Trepel v. Roadway Express, Inc., 266 F.3d 418 (6th Cir. 2001); Holmes v. Cessna Aircraft Co., 11 F.3d 63 (5th Cir. 1994); Dovenmuehle v. Gilldorn Mortgage Midwest Corp., 871 F.2d 697 (7th Cir. 1989); Mason v. Belieu, 543 F.2d 215 (D.C. Cir. 1976); Wahl v. Carrier Manufacturing Co., 511 F.2d 209 (7th Cir. 1975); McInnis v. Town of Weston, 458 F.Supp.2d 7 (D. Conn. 2006); Sullivan v. Cheshier, 991 F.Supp. 999 (N.D. Ill. 1998); Hollenbeck v. Falstaff Brewing Corp., 605 F.Supp. 421 (E.D. Mo. 1984); Morrissey v. County Tower Corp., 568 F.Supp. 980 (E.D. Mo. 1983).

248   In Re: Kulicke & Soffa Industries Inc. Securities Litigation, 747 F.Supp. 1136 (E.D.Pa. 1990), aff'd, 944 F.2d 897 (3rd Cir. 1991); ADM Corp. v. Speedmaster Packing Corp., 525 F.2d 662 (3d Cir. 1975); Nugget Distributors Cooperative of America v. Mr. Nugget, Inc., 145 F.R.D. 54 (E.D.Pa. 1992). Accord, Charter Medical Corp v. Cardin, 127 FRD 111 (D. Maryland 1989); Women's Federal Savings and Loan Association of Cleveland v. Nevada National Bank, 108 FRD 396 (D. Nevada 1985); International Wood Processors v. Power Dry, Inc., 598 F. Supp. 299 (D.S.C. 1984); Morrissey v. County Tower Corp., 568 F.Supp. 178 (ED Mo. 1983).

249   Smith v. Tenet Healthsystems SL, Inc., 436 F.3d 879 (8th Cir. 2006).

250   Helms v. WalMart Stores, Inc., 808 F.Supp. 1568 (ND Ga. 1992), aff'd 998 F.2d 1023 (11th Cir. 1993); Haagen-Dazs Co. v. Rainbow Gourmet Ice Creams, Inc., 920 F.2d 587 (9th Cir. 1990); Rodriguez-Garcia v. Davila, 904 F.2d 90 (1st Cir. 1990); Allen v. United States Steel Corp., 665 F.2d 689 (5th Cir. 1982); McGuigan v. CAE Link Corp., 155 FRD 31 (NDNY 1994); Nelson v. Darragh Co., 120 FRD 517 (WD Ark. 1988); Meadows v. Ford Motor Co., 62 FRD 98 (WD Ky. 1973); Gillam v. A. Shyman, Inc., 31 FRD 271 (D. Alaska 1962).

251   Montgomery County v. Microvote Corp., 2004 WL 1087196 (EDPA 2004); McGuigan v. CAE Link Corp., 155 FRD 31 (NDNY 1994).

252   Race Tires America, Inc. v. Hoosier Racing Tire Corp., 674 F.3d 158 (3d Cir. 2012).

253   Reger v. The Nemours Foundation, 599 F.3d 285 (3d Cir. 2010); In re: Paoli Railroad Yard PCB Litigation, 221 F.3d 449 (3d Cir. 2000); Abrams v. Lightolier, Inc., 50 F.3d 1204 (3d Cir. 1995); Smith v. SEPTA, 47 F.3d 97 (3d Cir. 1995); Friedman v. Ganassi, 853 F.2d 207 (3d Cir. 1988); Institutionalized Juveniles v. Secretary of Public Welfare, 758 F.2d 897 (3d Cir. 1985); Pearlstine v. United States, 649 F.2d 194 (3rd Cir. 1981); Delaney v. Capone, 642 F.2d 57 (3d Cir. 1981); Samuel v. University of Pittsburgh, 538 F.2d 991 (3d Cir. 1976); ADM Corp. v. Speedmaster Packing Corp., 525 F.2d 662 (3d Cir. 1975); City of Rome, Italy v. Glanton, 184 F.R.D. 547 (E.D. Pa. 1999); Greene v. Fraternal Order of Police, 183 F.R.D. 445 (E.D. Pa. 1998); Action Alliance for Senior Citizens of Greater Philadelphia v. Shapp, 74 F.R.D. 617 (E.D. Pa. 1977).

254   Buchanan v. Stanships, Inc., 485 U.S. 265, 268 (1988)(emphasis added). Accord, Delta Air Lines, Inc. v. August, 450 U.S. 346 (1981). See, also, Reger v. The Nemours Foundation, 599 F.3d 285 (3d Cir. 2010); In re: Paoli Railroad Yard PCB Litigation, 221 F.3d 449 (3d Cir. 2000); Abrams v. Lightolier, Inc., 50 F.3d

1204 (3d Cir. 1995); Smith v. SEPTA, 47 F.3d 97 (3d Cir. 1995); Friedman v. Ganassi, 853 F.2d 207 (3d Cir. 1988); Institutionalized Juveniles v. Secretary of Public Welfare, 758 F.2d 897 (3d Cir. 1985); Pearlstine v. United States, 649 F.2d 194 (3rd Cir. 1981); Delaney v. Capone, 642 F.2d 57 (3d Cir. 1981); Samuel v. University of Pittsburgh, 538 F.2d 991 (3d Cir. 1976); ADM Corp. v. Speedmaster Packing Corp., 525 F.2d 662 (3d Cir. 1975); City of Rome, Italy v. Glanton, 184 F.R.D. 547 (E.D. Pa. 1999); Greene v. Fraternal Order of Police, 183 F.R.D. 445 (E.D. Pa. 1998); Action Alliance for Senior Citizens of Greater Philadelphia v. Shapp, 74 F.R.D. 617 (E.D. Pa. 1977).

255 Buchanan v. Stanships, Inc., 485 U.S. 265 (1988); Delta Air Lines, Inc. v. August, 450 U.S. 346 (1981). Accord, Reger v. The Nemours Foundation, 599 F.3d 285 (3d Cir. 2010); In re: Paoli Railroad Yard PCB Litigation, 221 F.3d 449 (3d Cir. 2000); Abrams v. Lightolier, Inc., 50 F.3d 1204 (3d Cir. 1995); Smith v. SEPTA, 47 F.3d 97 (3d Cir. 1995); Friedman v. Ganassi, 853 F.2d 207 (3d Cir. 1988); Institutionalized Juveniles v. Secretary of Public Welfare, 758 F.2d 897 (3d Cir. 1985); Pearlstine v. United States, 649 F.2d 194 (3rd Cir. 1981); Delaney v. Capone, 642 F.2d 57 (3d Cir. 1981); Samuel v. University of Pittsburgh, 538 F.2d 991 (3d Cir. 1976); ADM Corp. v. Speedmaster Packing Corp., 525 F.2d 662 (3d Cir. 1975); City of Rome, Italy v. Glanton, 184 F.R.D. 547 (E.D. Pa. 1999); Greene v. Fraternal Order of Police, 183 F.R.D. 445 (E.D. Pa. 1998); Action Alliance for Senior Citizens of Greater Philadelphia v. Shapp, 74 F.R.D. 617 (E.D. Pa. 1977).

256 Brazos Valley Coalition for Life, Inc. v. City of Bryan, Texas, 421 F.3d 314 (5th Cir. 2005); Trepel v. Roadway Express, Inc., 266 F.3d 418 (6th Cir. 2001); Holmes v. Cessna Aircraft Co., 11 F.3d 63 (5th Cir. 1994); Dovenmuehle v. Gilldorn Mortgage Midwest Corp., 871 F.2d 697 (7th Cir. 1989); Mason v. Belieu, 543 F.2d 215 (D.C. Cir. 1976); Wahl v. Carrier Manufacturing Co., 511 F.2d 209 (7th Cir. 1975); McInnis v. Town of Weston, 458 F.Supp.2d 7 (D. Conn. 2006); Sullivan v. Cheshier, 991 F.Supp. 999 (N.D. Ill. 1998); Hollenbeck v. Falstaff Brewing Corp., 605 F.Supp. 421 (E.D. Mo. 1984); Morrissey v. County Tower Corp., 568 F.Supp. 980 (E.D. Mo. 1983).

257 In Re: Kulicke & Soffa Industries Inc. Securities Litigation, 747 F.Supp. 1136 (E.D.Pa. 1990), aff'd, 944 F.2d 897 (3rd Cir. 1991); ADM Corp. v. Speedmaster Packing Corp., 525 F.2d 662 (3d Cir. 1975); Nugget Distributors Cooperative of America v. Mr. Nugget, Inc., 145 F.R.D. 54 (E.D.Pa. 1992). Accord, Charter Medical Corp v. Cardin, 127 F.R.D. 111 (D. Maryland 1989); Women's Federal Savings and Loan Association of Cleveland v. Nevada National Bank, 108 F.R.D. 396 (D. Nevada 1985); International Wood Processors v. Power Dry, Inc., 598 F. Supp. 299 (D.S.C. 1984); Morrissey v. County Tower Corp., 568 F.Supp. 178 (ED Mo. 1983).

258 Johnson v. Holway, 522 F.Supp. 2d 12 (DDC 2007).

259 Johnson v. Holway, 522 F.Supp. 2d 12 (DDC 2007).

260 Johnson v. Holway, 522 F.Supp. 2d 12 (DDC 2007).

261 Haroco, Inc. v. American National Bank and Trust Company of Chicago, 38 F.3d 1429 (7th Cir. 1994); Johnson v. Holway, 522 F.Supp. 2d 12 (DDC 2007).

262 Accord, Soler v. McHenry, 771 F.Supp. 252 (ND Ill. 1991), aff'd, 989 F.2d 251 (7th Cir. 1993); Maxwell v. Hapag-Lloyd Aktiengesellschaft, 862 F.2d 767 (9th Cir. 1988); Nissho-Iwai Co. v. Occidental Crude Sales, Ltd., 729 F.2d 1530 (5th Cir. 1984); DiBella v. Hopkins, 407 F.Supp. 2d 537 (SDNY 2005); Jensen v. Lawler, 338 F.Supp. 2d 739 (SD Texas 2004); United Intern. Holdings, Inc. v. Wharf (Holdings) Ltd., 174 FRD 479 (D. Colo. 1997); Phillips v. Cameron Tool Corp., 131 F.R.D. 151 (SD Ind. 1990).

263 Soler v. McHenry, 771 F.Supp. 252 (ND Ill. 1991), aff'd, 989 F.2d 251 (7th Cir. 1993); Maxwell v. Hapag-Lloyd Aktiengesellschaft, 862 F.2d 767 (9th Cir. 1988); In Re: Air Crash Disaster at John F. Kennedy International Airport on June 24, 1975, 687 F.2d 626 (2nd Cir. 1982); Jensen v. Lawler, 338 F.Supp. 2d 739 (SD Texas 2004); United Intern. Holdings, Inc. v. Wharf (Holdings) Ltd., 174 FRD 479 (D. Colo. 1997).

264 Jensen v. Lawler, 338 F.Supp. 2d 739 (SD Texas 2004).

265 In Re: Air Crash Disaster at John F. Kennedy International Airport on June 24, 1975, 687 F.2d 626 (2nd Cir. 1982).

266 Soler v. McHenry, 771 F.Supp. 252 (ND Ill. 1991); aff'd, 989 F.2d 251 (7th Cir. 1993); Nissho-Iwai Co. v. Occidental Crude Sales, Ltd., 729 F.2d 1530 (5th Cir. 1984); DiBella v. Hopkins, 407 F.Supp. 2d 537 (SDNY 2005); Jensen v. Lawler, 338 F.Supp. 2d 739 (SD Texas 2004).

267 In Re: Air Crash Disaster at John F. Kennedy International Airport on June 24, 1975, 687 F.2d 626 (2nd Cir. 1982); DiBella v. Hopkins, 407 F.Supp.2d 537 (SDNY 2005); United Intern. Holdings, Inc. v. Wharf (Holdings) Ltd., 174 F.R.D. 479 (D. Colo. 1997).

268 Phillips v. Cameron Tool Corp., 131 F.R.D. 151 (SD Ind. 1990).

269 DiBella v. Hopkins, 407 F.Supp.2d 537 (SDNY 2005).

Endnotes

270   Sierra Club v. EPA, 769 F.2d 796 (DC Cir. 1985); In Re: Air Crash Disaster at John F. Kennedy International Airport on June 24, 1975, 687 F.2d 626 (2nd Cir. 1982); Griffith v. Mt. Carmel Medical Center, 157 F.R.D. 499 (D. Kansas 1994); Radol v. Thomas, 113 F.R.D. 172 (SD Ohio 1986); Marquez v. American Export Lines, 41 F.R.D. 386 (SDNY 1967).

271   Reger v. The Nemours Foundation, 599 F.3d 285 (3d Cir. 2010); In re: Paoli Railroad Yard PCB Litigation, 221 F.3d 449 (3d Cir. 2000); Abrams v. Lightolier, Inc., 50 F.3d 1204 (3d Cir. 1995); Smith v. SEPTA, 47 F.3d 97 (3d Cir. 1995); Friedman v. Ganassi, 853 F.2d 207 (3d Cir. 1988); Institutionalized Juveniles v. Secretary of Public Welfare, 758 F.2d 897 (3d Cir. 1985); Pearlstine v. United States, 649 F.2d 194 (3rd Cir. 1981); Delaney v. Capone, 642 F.2d 57 (3d Cir. 1981); Samuel v. University of Pittsburgh, 538 F.2d 991 (3d Cir. 1976); ADM Corp. v. Speedmaster Packing Corp., 525 F.2d 662 (3d Cir. 1975); City of Rome, Italy v. Glanton, 184 F.R.D. 547 (E.D. Pa. 1999); Greene v. Fraternal Order of Police, 183 F.R.D. 445 (E.D. Pa. 1998); Action Alliance for Senior Citizens of Greater Philadelphia v. Shapp, 74 F.R.D. 617 (E.D. Pa. 1977).

272   Buchanan v. Stanships, Inc., 485 U.S. 265, 268 (1988)(emphasis added). Accord, Delta Air Lines, Inc. v. August, 450 U.S. 346 (1981). See, also, Reger v. The Nemours Foundation, 599 F.3d 285 (3d Cir. 2010); In re: Paoli Railroad Yard PCB Litigation, 221 F.3d 449 (3d Cir. 2000); Abrams v. Lightolier, Inc., 50 F.3d 1204 (3d Cir. 1995); Smith v. SEPTA, 47 F.3d 97 (3d Cir. 1995); Friedman v. Ganassi, 853 F.2d 207 (3d Cir. 1988); Institutionalized Juveniles v. Secretary of Public Welfare, 758 F.2d 897 (3d Cir. 1985); Pearlstine v. United States, 649 F.2d 194 (3rd Cir. 1981); Delaney v. Capone, 642 F.2d 57 (3d Cir. 1981); Samuel v. University of Pittsburgh, 538 F.2d 991 (3d Cir. 1976); ADM Corp. v. Speedmaster Packing Corp., 525 F.2d 662 (3d Cir. 1975); City of Rome, Italy v. Glanton, 184 F.R.D. 547 (E.D. Pa. 1999); Greene v. Fraternal Order of Police, 183 F.R.D. 445 (E.D. Pa. 1998); Action Alliance for Senior Citizens of Greater Philadelphia v. Shapp, 74 F.R.D. 617 (E.D. Pa. 1977).

273   Buchanan v. Stanships, Inc., 485 U.S. 265 (1988); Delta Air Lines, Inc. v. August, 450 U.S. 346 (1981). Accord, Reger v. The Nemours Foundation, 599 F.3d 285 (3d Cir. 2010); In re: Paoli Railroad Yard PCB Litigation, 221 F.3d 449 (3d Cir. 2000); Abrams v. Lightolier, Inc., 50 F.3d 1204 (3d Cir. 1995); Smith v. SEPTA, 47 F.3d 97 (3d Cir. 1995); Friedman v. Ganassi, 853 F.2d 207 (3d Cir. 1988); Institutionalized Juveniles v. Secretary of Public Welfare, 758 F.2d 897 (3d Cir. 1985); Pearlstine v. United States, 649 F.2d 194 (3rd Cir. 1981); Delaney v. Capone, 642 F.2d 57 (3d Cir. 1981); Samuel v. University of Pittsburgh, 538 F.2d 991 (3d Cir. 1976); ADM Corp. v. Speedmaster Packing Corp., 525 F.2d 662 (3d Cir. 1975); City of Rome, Italy v. Glanton, 184 F.R.D. 547 (E.D. Pa. 1999); Greene v. Fraternal Order of Police, 183 F.R.D. 445 (E.D. Pa. 1998); Action Alliance for Senior Citizens of Greater Philadelphia v. Shapp, 74 F.R.D. 617 (E.D. Pa. 1977).

274   Brazos Valley Coalition for Life, Inc. v. City of Bryan, Texas, 421 F.3d 314 (5th Cir. 2005); Trepel v. Roadway Express, Inc., 266 F.3d 418 (6th Cir. 2001); Holmes v. Cessna Aircraft Co., 11 F.3d 63 (5th Cir. 1994); Dovenmuehle v. Gilldorn Mortgage Midwest Corp., 871 F.2d 697 (7th Cir. 1989); Mason v. Belieu, 543 F.2d 215 (D.C. Cir. 1976); Wahl v. Carrier Manufacturing Co., 511 F.2d 209 (7th Cir. 1975); McInnis v. Town of Weston, 458 F.Supp.2d 7 (D. Conn. 2006); Sullivan v. Cheshier, 991 F.Supp. 999 (N.D. Ill. 1998); Hollenbeck v. Falstaff Brewing Corp., 605 F.Supp. 421 (E.D. Mo. 1984); Morrissey v. County Tower Corp., 568 F.Supp. 980 (E.D. Mo. 1983).

275   In Re: Kulicke & Soffa Industries Inc. Securities Litigation, 747 F.Supp. 1136 (E.D.Pa. 1990), aff'd, 944 F.2d 897 (3rd Cir. 1991); ADM Corp. v. Speedmaster Packing Corp., 525 F.2d 662 (3d Cir. 1975); Nugget Distributors Cooperative of America v. Mr. Nugget, Inc., 145 F.R.D. 54 (E.D.Pa. 1992). Accord, Charter Medical Corp v. Cardin, 127 FRD 111 (D. Maryland 1989); Women's Federal Savings and Loan Association of Cleveland v. Nevada National Bank, 108 FRD 396 (D. Nevada 1985); International Wood Processors v. Power Dry, Inc., 598 F. Supp. 299 (D.S.C. 1984); Morrissey v. County Tower Corp., 568 F.Supp. 178 (ED Mo. 1983).

276   Johnson v. Holway, 522 F.Supp. 2d 12 (DDC 2007).

277   Johnson v. Holway, 522 F.Supp. 2d 12 (DDC 2007).

278   Johnson v. Holway, 522 F.Supp. 2d 12 (DDC 2007).

279   Haroco, Inc. v. American National Bank and Trust Company of Chicago, 38 F.3d 1429 (7th Cir. 1994); Johnson v. Holway, 522 F.Supp. 2d 12 (DDC 2007).

280   Winniczek v. Nagelberg, 400 F.3d 503 (7th Cir. 2005).

281   Reger v. The Nemours Foundation, 599 F.3d 285 (3d Cir. 2010); In re: Paoli Railroad Yard PCB Litigation, 221 F.3d 449 (3d Cir. 2000); Abrams v. Lightolier, Inc., 50 F.3d 1204 (3d Cir. 1995); Smith v. SEPTA, 47 F.3d 97 (3d Cir. 1995); Friedman v. Ganassi, 853 F.2d 207 (3d Cir. 1988); Institutionalized Juveniles v. Secretary of Public Welfare, 758 F.2d 897 (3d Cir. 1985); Pearlstine v. United States, 649 F.2d 194 (3rd Cir. 1981); Delaney v. Capone, 642 F.2d 57 (3d Cir. 1981); Samuel v. University of Pittsburgh,

538 F.2d 991 (3d Cir. 1976); ADM Corp. v. Speedmaster Packing Corp., 525 F.2d 662 (3d Cir. 1975); City of Rome, Italy v. Glanton, 184 F.R.D. 547 (E.D. Pa. 1999); Greene v. Fraternal Order of Police, 183 F.R.D. 445 (E.D. Pa. 1998); Action Alliance for Senior Citizens of Greater Philadelphia v. Shapp, 74 F.R.D. 617 (E.D. Pa. 1977).

282   Buchanan v. Stanships, Inc., 485 U.S. 265, 268 (1988)(emphasis added). Accord, Delta Air Lines, Inc. v. August, 450 U.S. 346 (1981). See, also, Reger v. The Nemours Foundation, 599 F.3d 285 (3d Cir. 2010); In re: Paoli Railroad Yard PCB Litigation, 221 F.3d 449 (3d Cir. 2000); Abrams v. Lightolier, Inc., 50 F.3d 1204 (3d Cir. 1995); Smith v. SEPTA, 47 F.3d 97 (3d Cir. 1995); Friedman v. Ganassi, 853 F.2d 207 (3d Cir. 1988); Institutionalized Juveniles v. Secretary of Public Welfare, 758 F.2d 897 (3d Cir. 1985); Pearlstine v. United States, 649 F.2d 194 (3rd Cir. 1981); Delaney v. Capone, 642 F.2d 57 (3d Cir. 1981); Samuel v. University of Pittsburgh, 538 F.2d 991 (3d Cir. 1976); ADM Corp. v. Speedmaster Packing Corp., 525 F.2d 662 (3d Cir. 1975); City of Rome, Italy v. Glanton, 184 F.R.D. 547 (E.D. Pa. 1999); Greene v. Fraternal Order of Police, 183 F.R.D. 445 (E.D. Pa. 1998); Action Alliance for Senior Citizens of Greater Philadelphia v. Shapp, 74 F.R.D. 617 (E.D. Pa. 1977).

283   Buchanan v. Stanships, Inc., 485 U.S. 265 (1988); Delta Air Lines, Inc. v. August, 450 U.S. 346 (1981). Accord, Reger v. The Nemours Foundation, 599 F.3d 285 (3d Cir. 2010); In re: Paoli Railroad Yard PCB Litigation, 221 F.3d 449 (3d Cir. 2000); Abrams v. Lightolier, Inc., 50 F.3d 1204 (3d Cir. 1995); Smith v. SEPTA, 47 F.3d 97 (3d Cir. 1995); Friedman v. Ganassi, 853 F.2d 207 (3d Cir. 1988); Institutionalized Juveniles v. Secretary of Public Welfare, 758 F.2d 897 (3d Cir. 1985); Pearlstine v. United States, 649 F.2d 194 (3rd Cir. 1981); Delaney v. Capone, 642 F.2d 57 (3d Cir. 1981); Samuel v. University of Pittsburgh, 538 F.2d 991 (3d Cir. 1976); ADM Corp. v. Speedmaster Packing Corp., 525 F.2d 662 (3d Cir. 1975); City of Rome, Italy v. Glanton, 184 F.R.D. 547 (E.D. Pa. 1999); Greene v. Fraternal Order of Police, 183 F.R.D. 445 (E.D. Pa. 1998); Action Alliance for Senior Citizens of Greater Philadelphia v. Shapp, 74 F.R.D. 617 (E.D. Pa. 1977).

284   Brazos Valley Coalition for Life, Inc. v. City of Bryan, Texas, 421 F.3d 314 (5th Cir. 2005); Trepel v. Roadway Express, Inc., 266 F.3d 418 (6th Cir. 2001); Holmes v. Cessna Aircraft Co., 11 F.3d 63 (5th Cir. 1994); Dovenmuehle v. Gilldorn Mortgage Midwest Corp., 871 F.2d 697 (7th Cir. 1989); Mason v. Belieu, 543 F.2d 215 (D.C. Cir. 1976); Wahl v. Carrier Manufacturing Co., 511 F.2d 209 (7th Cir. 1975); McInnis v. Town of Weston, 458 F.Supp.2d 7 (D. Conn. 2006); Sullivan v. Cheshier, 991 F.Supp. 999 (N.D. Ill. 1998); Hollenbeck v. Falstaff Brewing Corp., 605 F.Supp. 421 (E.D. Mo. 1984); Morrissey v. County Tower Corp., 568 F.Supp. 980 (E.D. Mo. 1983).

285   In Re: Kulicke & Soffa Industries Inc. Securities Litigation, 747 F.Supp. 1136 (E.D.Pa. 1990), aff'd, 944 F.2d 897 (3rd Cir. 1991); ADM Corp. v. Speedmaster Packing Corp., 525 F.2d 662 (3d Cir. 1975); Nugget Distributors Cooperative of America v. Mr. Nugget, Inc., 145 F.R.D. 54 (E.D.Pa. 1992). Accord, Charter Medical Corp v. Cardin, 127 FRD 111 (D. Maryland 1989); Women's Federal Savings and Loan Association of Cleveland v. Nevada National Bank, 108 F.R.D. 396 (D. Nevada 1985); International Wood Processors v. Power Dry, Inc., 598 F. Supp. 299 (D.S.C. 1984); Morrissey v. County Tower Corp., 568 F.Supp. 178 (ED Mo. 1983).

286   Sierra Club v. EPA, 769 F.2d 796 (DC Cir. 1985); In Re: Air Crash Disaster at John F. Kennedy International Airport on June 24, 1975, 687 F.2d 626 (2nd Cir. 1982); Griffith v. Mt. Carmel Medical Center, 157 F.R.D. 499 (D. Kansas 1994); Radol v. Thomas, 113 F.R.D. 172 (SD Ohio 1986); Marquez v. American Export Lines, 41 F.R.D. 386 (SDNY 1967).

287   In Re: Air Crash Disaster at John F. Kennedy International Airport on June 24, 1975, 687 F.2d 626 (2nd Cir. 1982).

288   Jensen v. Lawler, 338 F.Supp. 2d 739 (SD Texas 2004).

289   Reger v. The Nemours Foundation, 599 F.3d 285 (3d Cir. 2010); In re: Paoli Railroad Yard PCB Litigation, 221 F.3d 449 (3d Cir. 2000); Abrams v. Lightolier, Inc., 50 F.3d 1204 (3d Cir. 1995); Smith v. SEPTA, 47 F.3d 97 (3d Cir. 1995); Friedman v. Ganassi, 853 F.2d 207 (3d Cir. 1988); Institutionalized Juveniles v. Secretary of Public Welfare, 758 F.2d 897 (3d Cir. 1985); Pearlstine v. United States, 649 F.2d 194 (3rd Cir. 1981); Delaney v. Capone, 642 F.2d 57 (3d Cir. 1981); Samuel v. University of Pittsburgh, 538 F.2d 991 (3d Cir. 1976); ADM Corp. v. Speedmaster Packing Corp., 525 F.2d 662 (3d Cir. 1975); City of Rome, Italy v. Glanton, 184 F.R.D. 547 (E.D. Pa. 1999); Greene v. Fraternal Order of Police, 183 F.R.D. 445 (E.D. Pa. 1998); Action Alliance for Senior Citizens of Greater Philadelphia v. Shapp, 74 F.R.D. 617 (E.D. Pa. 1977).

290   Buchanan v. Stanships, Inc., 485 U.S. 265, 268 (1988)(emphasis added). Accord, Delta Air Lines, Inc. v. August, 450 U.S. 346 (1981). See, also, Reger v. The Nemours Foundation, 599 F.3d 285 (3d Cir. 2010); In re: Paoli Railroad Yard PCB Litigation, 221 F.3d 449 (3d Cir. 2000); Abrams v. Lightolier, Inc., 50 F.3d 1204 (3d Cir. 1995); Smith v. SEPTA, 47 F.3d 97 (3d Cir. 1995); Friedman v. Ganassi, 853 F.2d 207 (3d

Cir. 1988); Institutionalized Juveniles v. Secretary of Public Welfare, 758 F.2d 897 (3d Cir. 1985); Pearlstine v. United States, 649 F.2d 194 (3rd Cir. 1981); Delaney v. Capone, 642 F.2d 57 (3d Cir. 1981); Samuel v. University of Pittsburgh, 538 F.2d 991 (3d Cir. 1976); ADM Corp. v. Speedmaster Packing Corp., 525 F.2d 662 (3d Cir. 1975); City of Rome, Italy v. Glanton, 184 F.R.D. 547 (E.D. Pa. 1999); Greene v. Fraternal Order of Police, 183 F.R.D. 445 (E.D. Pa. 1998); Action Alliance for Senior Citizens of Greater Philadelphia v. Shapp, 74 F.R.D. 617 (E.D. Pa. 1977).

291   Buchanan v. Stanships, Inc., 485 U.S. 265 (1988); Delta Air Lines, Inc. v. August, 450 U.S. 346 (1981). Accord, Reger v. The Nemours Foundation, 599 F.3d 285 (3d Cir. 2010); In re: Paoli Railroad Yard PCB Litigation, 221 F.3d 449 (3d Cir. 2000); Abrams v. Lightolier, Inc., 50 F.3d 1204 (3d Cir. 1995); Smith v. SEPTA, 47 F.3d 97 (3d Cir. 1995); Friedman v. Ganassi, 853 F.2d 207 (3d Cir. 1988); Institutionalized Juveniles v. Secretary of Public Welfare, 758 F.2d 897 (3d Cir. 1985); Pearlstine v. United States, 649 F.2d 194 (3rd Cir. 1981); Delaney v. Capone, 642 F.2d 57 (3d Cir. 1981); Samuel v. University of Pittsburgh, 538 F.2d 991 (3d Cir. 1976); ADM Corp. v. Speedmaster Packing Corp., 525 F.2d 662 (3d Cir. 1975); City of Rome, Italy v. Glanton, 184 F.R.D. 547 (E.D. Pa. 1999); Greene v. Fraternal Order of Police, 183 F.R.D. 445 (E.D. Pa. 1998); Action Alliance for Senior Citizens of Greater Philadelphia v. Shapp, 74 F.R.D. 617 (E.D. Pa. 1977).

292   Brazos Valley Coalition for Life, Inc. v. City of Bryan, Texas, 421 F.3d 314 (5th Cir. 2005); Trepel v. Roadway Express, Inc., 266 F.3d 418 (6th Cir. 2001); Holmes v. Cessna Aircraft Co., 11 F.3d 63 (5th Cir. 1994); Dovenmuehle v. Gilldorn Mortgage Midwest Corp., 871 F.2d 697 (7th Cir. 1989); Mason v. Belieu, 543 F.2d 215 (D.C. Cir. 1976); Wahl v. Carrier Manufacturing Co., 511 F.2d 209 (7th Cir. 1975); McInnis v. Town of Weston, 458 F.Supp.2d 7 (D. Conn. 2006); Sullivan v. Cheshier, 991 F.Supp. 999 (N.D. Ill. 1998); Hollenbeck v. Falstaff Brewing Corp., 605 F.Supp. 421 (E.D. Mo. 1984); Morrissey v. County Tower Corp., 568 F.Supp. 980 (E.D. Mo. 1983).

293   In Re: Kulicke & Soffa Industries Inc. Securities Litigation, 747 F.Supp. 1136 (E.D.Pa. 1990), aff'd, 944 F.2d 897 (3rd Cir. 1991); ADM Corp. v. Speedmaster Packing Corp., 525 F.2d 662 (3d Cir. 1975); Nugget Distributors Cooperative of America v. Mr. Nugget, Inc., 145 F.R.D. 54 (E.D.Pa. 1992). Accord, Charter Medical Corp v. Cardin, 127 FRD 111 (D. Maryland 1989); Women's Federal Savings and Loan Association of Cleveland v. Nevada National Bank, 108 F.R.D. 396 (D. Nevada 1985); International Wood Processors v. Power Dry, Inc., 598 F. Supp. 299 (D.S.C. 1984); Morrissey v. County Tower Corp., 568 F.Supp. 178 (ED Mo. 1983).

294   Taniguchi v. Kan Pacific Saipan, Ltd., 132 S.Ct. 1997 (2012).

295   Reger v. The Nemours Foundation, 599 F.3d 285 (3d Cir. 2010); In re: Paoli Railroad Yard PCB Litigation, 221 F.3d 449 (3d Cir. 2000); Abrams v. Lightolier, Inc., 50 F.3d 1204 (3d Cir. 1995); Smith v. SEPTA, 47 F.3d 97 (3d Cir. 1995); Friedman v. Ganassi, 853 F.2d 207 (3d Cir. 1988); Institutionalized Juveniles v. Secretary of Public Welfare, 758 F.2d 897 (3d Cir. 1985); Pearlstine v. United States, 649 F.2d 194 (3rd Cir. 1981); Delaney v. Capone, 642 F.2d 57 (3d Cir. 1981); Samuel v. University of Pittsburgh, 538 F.2d 991 (3d Cir. 1976); ADM Corp. v. Speedmaster Packing Corp., 525 F.2d 662 (3d Cir. 1975); City of Rome, Italy v. Glanton, 184 F.R.D. 547 (E.D. Pa. 1999); Greene v. Fraternal Order of Police, 183 F.R.D. 445 (E.D. Pa. 1998); Action Alliance for Senior Citizens of Greater Philadelphia v. Shapp, 74 F.R.D. 617 (E.D. Pa. 1977).

296   Buchanan v. Stanships, Inc., 485 U.S. 265, 268 (1988)(emphasis added). Accord, Delta Air Lines, Inc. v. August, 450 U.S. 346 (1981). See, also, Reger v. The Nemours Foundation, 599 F.3d 285 (3d Cir. 2010); In re: Paoli Railroad Yard PCB Litigation, 221 F.3d 449 (3d Cir. 2000); Abrams v. Lightolier, Inc., 50 F.3d 1204 (3d Cir. 1995); Smith v. SEPTA, 47 F.3d 97 (3d Cir. 1995); Friedman v. Ganassi, 853 F.2d 207 (3d Cir. 1988); Institutionalized Juveniles v. Secretary of Public Welfare, 758 F.2d 897 (3d Cir. 1985); Pearlstine v. United States, 649 F.2d 194 (3rd Cir. 1981); Delaney v. Capone, 642 F.2d 57 (3d Cir. 1981); Samuel v. University of Pittsburgh, 538 F.2d 991 (3d Cir. 1976); ADM Corp. v. Speedmaster Packing Corp., 525 F.2d 662 (3d Cir. 1975); City of Rome, Italy v. Glanton, 184 F.R.D. 547 (E.D. Pa. 1999); Greene v. Fraternal Order of Police, 183 F.R.D. 445 (E.D. Pa. 1998); Action Alliance for Senior Citizens of Greater Philadelphia v. Shapp, 74 F.R.D. 617 (E.D. Pa. 1977).

297   Buchanan v. Stanships, Inc., 485 U.S. 265 (1988); Delta Air Lines, Inc. v. August, 450 U.S. 346 (1981). Accord, Reger v. The Nemours Foundation, 599 F.3d 285 (3d Cir. 2010); In re: Paoli Railroad Yard PCB Litigation, 221 F.3d 449 (3d Cir. 2000); Abrams v. Lightolier, Inc., 50 F.3d 1204 (3d Cir. 1995); Smith v. SEPTA, 47 F.3d 97 (3d Cir. 1995); Friedman v. Ganassi, 853 F.2d 207 (3d Cir. 1988); Institutionalized Juveniles v. Secretary of Public Welfare, 758 F.2d 897 (3d Cir. 1985); Pearlstine v. United States, 649 F.2d 194 (3rd Cir. 1981); Delaney v. Capone, 642 F.2d 57 (3d Cir. 1981); Samuel v. University of Pittsburgh, 538 F.2d 991 (3d Cir. 1976); ADM Corp. v. Speedmaster Packing Corp., 525 F.2d 662 (3d Cir. 1975); City of Rome, Italy v. Glanton, 184 F.R.D. 547 (E.D. Pa. 1999); Greene v. Fraternal Order of Police, 183 F.R.D.

445 (E.D. Pa. 1998); Action Alliance for Senior Citizens of Greater Philadelphia v. Shapp, 74 F.R.D. 617 (E.D. Pa. 1977).

298   Brazos Valley Coalition for Life, Inc. v. City of Bryan, Texas, 421 F.3d 314 (5th Cir. 2005); Trepel v. Roadway Express, Inc., 266 F.3d 418 (6th Cir. 2001); Holmes v. Cessna Aircraft Co., 11 F.3d 63 (5th Cir. 1994); Dovenmuehle v. Gilldorn Mortgage Midwest Corp., 871 F.2d 697 (7th Cir. 1989); Mason v. Belieu, 543 F.2d 215 (D.C. Cir. 1976); Wahl v. Carrier Manufacturing Co., 511 F.2d 209 (7th Cir. 1975); McInnis v. Town of Weston, 458 F.Supp.2d 7 (D. Conn. 2006); Sullivan v. Cheshire, 991 F.Supp. 999 (N.D. Ill. 1998); Hollenbeck v. Falstaff Brewing Corp., 605 F.Supp. 421 (E.D. Mo. 1984); Morrissey v. County Tower Corp., 568 F.Supp. 980 (E.D. Mo. 1983).

299   In Re: Kulicke & Soffa Industries Inc. Securities Litigation, 747 F.Supp. 1136 (E.D.Pa. 1990), aff'd, 944 F.2d 897 (3rd Cir. 1991); ADM Corp. v. Speedmaster Packing Corp., 525 F.2d 662 (3d Cir. 1975); Nugget Distributors Cooperative of America v. Mr. Nugget, Inc., 145 F.R.D. 54 (E.D.Pa. 1992). Accord, Charter Medical Corp v. Cardin, 127 FRD 111 (D. Maryland 1989); Women's Federal Savings and Loan Association of Cleveland v. Nevada National Bank, 108 FRD 396 (D. Nevada 1985); International Wood Processors v. Power Dry, Inc., 598 F. Supp. 299 (D.S.C. 1984); Morrissey v. County Tower Corp., 568 F.Supp. 178 (ED Mo. 1983).

300   Reger v. The Nemours Foundation, 599 F.3d 285 (3d Cir. 2010); Abrams v. Lightolier, Inc., 50 F.3d 1204 (3d Cir. 1995).

301   Delta Air Lines, Inc. v. August, 450 U.S. 346 (1981).

302   Sea Coast Foods, Inc. v. Lu-Mar Lobster & Shrimp, 260 F.3d 1054 (9th Cir. 2001).

303   Sea Coast Foods, Inc. v. Lu-Mar Lobster & Shrimp, 260 F.3d 1054 (9th Cir. 2001).

304   Delta Air Lines, Inc. v. August, 450 U.S. 346 (1981).

305   Abrams v. Lightolier, Inc., 50 F.3d 1204 (3d Cir. 1995).

306   Buchanan v. Stanships, Inc., 485 U.S. 265 (1988); Alyeska Pipeline Service Co. v. Wilderness Society, 421 U.S. 240 (1975); Fleischmann Distilling Co. v. Maier Brewing Co., 386 U.S. 714 (1967); Reger v. The Nemours Foundation, 599 F.3d 285 (3d Cir. 2010); In re: Paoli Railroad Yard PCB Litigation, 221 F.3d 449 (3d Cir. 2000); Adams v. Teamsters Local 115, 678 F.Supp.2d 314 (E.D. Pa. 2007).

307   Buchanan v. Stanships, Inc., 485 U.S. 265 (1988); Reger v. The Nemours Foundation, 599 F.3d 285 (3d Cir. 2010); McKenna v. City of Philadelphia, 582 F.3d 447 (3d Cir. 2009).

308   Buchanan v. Stanships, Inc., 485 U.S. 265 (1988); Reger v. The Nemours Foundation, 599 F.3d 285 (3d Cir. 2010); McKenna v. City of Philadelphia, 582 F.3d 447 (3d Cir. 2009).

309   SNA, Inc. v. Array, 173 F.Supp.2d 347 (E.D.Pa. 2001). Accord, L-3 Communications Corp. v. OSI Systems, Inc., 607 F.3d 24, 30 (2d Cir. 2010); Republic Tobacco Co. v. North Atlantic Trading Co., 481 F.3d 442 (7th Cir. 2007); Emmenegger v. Bull Moose Tube Co., 324 F.3d 616 (8th Cir. 2003); Berthelsen v. Kane, 907 F.2d 617 (6th Cir. 1990); Choice Hotels International, Inc. v. Kaushik, 203 F.Supp.2d 1281 (M.D. Ala. 2002).

310   Republic Tobacco Co. v. North Atlantic Trading Co., 481 F.3d 442 (7th Cir. 2007).

311   Republic Tobacco Co. v. North Atlantic Trading Co., 481 F.3d 442, 448 (7th Cir. 2007)(emphasis added).

312   Republic Tobacco Co. v. North Atlantic Trading Co., 481 F.3d 442 (7th Cir. 2007).

313   Republic Tobacco Co. v. North Atlantic Trading Co., 481 F.3d 442 (7th Cir. 2007).

314   Republic Tobacco Co. v. North Atlantic Trading Co., 481 F.3d 442, 448 (7th Cir. 2007)(emphasis added).

315   Advisory Committee Notes on the 1967 adoption of Federal Rule of Appellate Procedure 39(e).

316   L-3 Communications Corp. v. OSI Systems, Inc., 607 F.3d 24 (2d Cir. 2010).

317   L-3 Communications Corp. v. OSI Systems, Inc., 607 F.3d 24 (2d Cir. 2010).

318   Republic Tobacco Co. v. North Atlantic Trading Co., 481 F.3d 442 (7th Cir. 2007).

319   Casey v. Planned Parenthood of Southeastern Pennsylvania, 14 F.3d 848 (3rd Cir. 1994).

320   Briggs v. Pennsylvania Railroad Co., 334 U.S. 304 (1948). Although it is over sixty years old, the United States Supreme Court's decision in Briggs has never been reversed and remains vital law to this date. Accord, Casey v. Planned Parenthood of Southeastern Pennsylvania, 14 F.3d 848 (3rd Cir. 1994).

321   Pease v. Rathbun-Jones Engineering Co., 243 U.S. 273 (1917).

322   Abrams v. Lightolier, Inc., 50 F.3d 1204 (3d Cir. 1995).

323   Casey v. Planned Parenthood of Southeastern Pennsylvania, 14 F.3d 848 (3rd Cir. 1994).

324   Briggs v. Pennsylvania Railroad Co., 334 U.S. 304 (1948). Although it is over sixty years old, the United States Supreme Court's decision in Briggs has never been reversed and remains vital law to this date. Accord, Casey v. Planned Parenthood of Southeastern Pennsylvania, 14 F.3d 848 (3rd Cir. 1994).

325   Pease v. Rathbun-Jones Engineering Co., 243 U.S. 273 (1917).

COURTROOM DEPUTY CLERKS

Each judge is assigned a courtroom deputy clerk who is responsible for scheduling and monitoring cases on the judge's calendar. The courtroom deputy clerk acts as a liaison between the judge and counsel, scheduling dates and times for hearings on motions, pretrial hearings and trials, and conferring with attorneys on any special trial procedures.

A.   New Case Procedures

The Eastern District of Pennsylvania operates on an individual calendar system, as opposed to a master calendar system, which means that the assigned judge is responsible for all cases assigned, from filing to disposition.

After a case is filed, the courtroom deputy clerk checks the docket for timely service of process and the filing of an answer. If service has not been made within 90 days, a letter will be sent by the courtroom deputy clerk asking that service be made by the 120th day. If service has been made but the complaint has not been answered, again a letter will be sent by the courtroom deputy requesting counsel to motion for judgment by default. Please do not ignore these notices. If you do, it could result in dismissal of the case for lack of prosecution. [See Federal Rule of Civil Procedure 12(a)].

Counsel may receive a status request form by contacting the courtroom deputy to the judge to whom the case is assigned. This form contains questions relating to the scheduling of the case, such as, length of time needed for discovery and estimated length of time for trial.

B.   Pretrial Practices

After a complaint is filed, service has been made, and an answer is filed, an order is prepared which sets forth a discovery schedule. The order will specify a date by which all discovery must be completed and schedules a final pretrial conference, generally four to six weeks after the discovery deadline. Usually the case is put in the civil pool for trial in one month. However, not all judges follow the same pretrial practices. If you have any questions, call the courtroom deputy clerk of the judge to whom the case is assigned, or check the court's website at http://www.paed.uscourts.gov for judges' policies and procedures.

C.   Scheduling Cases

When discovery has been completed and pretrial conferences have been held, there are three ways in which a case can be scheduled for trial:

1. **Civil Trial Pool**—Most judges have the majority of cases in this pool.

2. **Date Certain**—This is a target date set weeks or months in advance and depends on the judge's calendar and availability of attorneys for the date to be met.

3. **Special Listing**—An agreement exists between the District Court judges and the State Court judges in the nine county area of Bucks, Chester, Delaware, Montgomery, Philadelphia, Berks, Lancaster, Lehigh and Northampton **(Appendix S)**.

    These special listings take precedence over all other trial engagements provided the following requirements are met:

    - the listing is established 30 days in advance by notice to counsel involved and all active judges;
    - all district court judges and the judges in the 9-county area are notified at least 30 days in advance of counsel involved and of probable duration of trial;

Clerk's Office Procedural Handbook

- that not more than one such special listing shall be granted by the same judge to one lawyer in a six-month period, except for good cause.

The notice which is sent to district court judges and to court administrators in other courts must contain the name of the case, the date the case is scheduled, name of counsel, and the approximate amount of time required for trial.

D. Trial List

Each judge maintains a trial list of cases generally ready for trial. The federal trial list is published in the *Legal Intelligencer* from Monday through Friday. Below is a sample listing:

J. Curtis Joyner, C.J.
Courtroom 17A
Deputy Clerk: Sharon Carter
Phone: 267-299-7419

MON., MARCH 5, 2007
On Trial
Civil Jury Trial
10:00 A.M.
2006-8995   J. Smith
Becker v. ABC Company
M. Doe; J.P. Stewart

Trial Pool
2005-7213   p.p.
Jones v. Friedman
D. Wood

The following notice is published each day in the *Legal Intelligencer* and explains the policy of the Judges of the United States District Court for listing cases in the Eastern District of Pennsylvania.

1. Counsel shall promptly notify the deputy clerk to each judge before whom he/she has a case listed upon becoming attached for trial in another court. To be accorded recognition, a busy slip, using the designated form, MUST be filed in Room 2609 before 1:00 p.m. on the day after counsel becomes attached.

2. Cases in the trial pools do not necessarily appear in the order in which they will be called. Counsel should therefore be ready to begin trial upon receiving telephone call notice, subject to the following:

    (a) Counsel whose cases are in the pools will be given 48 hours' notice, if feasible, but not less than 24 hours notice to be ready for trial with witnesses.

    (b) It is counsel's responsibility to check with each judge's deputy clerk on the status and movement of criminal and civil cases in that judge's pool.

    (c) Counsel will not be required to commence trial less than 24 hours after completing trial of another case.

E. Judicial Schedule of Trials—Automated System Inquiry (JUST-ASK)

The Judicial Schedule of Trials—Automated System Inquiry (JUST-ASK) system provides up-to-date information on the status of trials scheduled in the United States District Court seven days a week, twenty-four hours a day. JUST-ASK is offered free of charge and is accessible to any individual or office with a PC and internet access.

Events, such as verdicts, settlements, and continuances constantly change the status of cases on the Court's trial list. JUST-ASK immediately reflects the daily status of listings as the information becomes available to the Clerk of Court.

All cases scheduled for trial, presently on trial, in the trial pool and special notices from the Court are included on the system. JUST-ASK also provides the capability of viewing a report on the disposition of cases previously listed on the system. For user convenience, all information contained in this system is available by judge, date, case number, party name and/or attorney name. The user may choose the option which is most convenient to view listings. For example, JUST-ASK allows the user to retrieve a list of cases in which a specified attorney is involved, then the information can be printed at the user's computer. If you have any questions on scheduling, please contact the courtroom deputy.

The JUST-ASK system can be accessed through the District Court's website at http://www.paed.uscourts.gov.

F. Lobby Kiosk Information System

An automated informational kiosk system, located in the U.S. Courthouse lobby, includes current information on district court and court of appeals hearings, as well as a directory of judges and court clerks, location of other government agencies and general information. The kiosk provides touch screen technology, as well as mapping techniques to guide visitors to their destinations.

G. Busy Slips

It is important that busy slips **(Appendix T)** be filed promptly so that cases can be properly scheduled. Busy slips can be obtained at the front counter of the Clerk's Office, Room 2609, and should be filed in the Clerk's Office by 1:00 p.m. the day after counsel becomes attached. If a conflict arises before a particular judge, priority is given to the oldest case by date of filing. Please advise the courtroom deputy when the attorney is again available, or if the case was settled.

H. Attachments for Trial

Attorneys can only be attached three business days prior to a date of trial and can only be held for attachment for three business days.

I. Continuances—Criminal Cases

The Speedy Trial Act requires that defendants be brought to trial within a 70-day period after indictment or initial appearance before a judicial officer. This 70-day period can be extended only by a judge for specific reasons set forth in the Speedy Trial Act Plan which is on file and available for inspection in the Clerk's Office.

J. Motions

When filing a motion, please include a proposed order for the judge's signature. Since courtroom deputies are responsible for tracking motions, it is important that a certificate of service be attached to the motion so that they can calculate the date the response is due. If the parties have reached an agreement, notify us by stipulation. If a motion has been filed and the parties have settled their dispute, let the courtroom deputy know as soon as possible.

K. Exhibits

At the completion of trial, either the courtroom deputy clerk will keep exhibits or the Court will have counsel maintain custody until all appeals are exhausted or the appeal time has expired. If the courtroom deputy clerk has custody, the exhibits will be returned to counsel. If the exhibits are too large or too bulky to mail, the courtroom deputy will send a letter to the attorney requesting that the exhibits be picked up. If the exhibits are not picked up, they will be deemed abandoned and will then be destroyed (see Local Civil Rule 39).

L. Other Duties

Some additional duties performed by courtroom deputy clerks are:

- noting the appearance of counsel in matters before the court;
- impaneling the jury and administering oaths to jurors; providing liaison with the jury clerk as to ordering and canceling of juries; and keeping required records on other jury matters;
- administering oaths to witnesses, interpreters, attorneys on admission, and oaths of allegiance to applicants for citizenship;
- recording proceedings and rulings for minutes of the court; filing, marking, storing, and returning exhibits; and composing minute orders to carry out expressed intention of the judge;
- preparing verdict forms and judgments;
- advising the financial section of the Clerk's Office on matters affecting that section, particularly the imposition of fines and orders of restitution by the judge in criminal cases.

The following charts list the courtroom deputy clerks according to their assigned judge, along with their telephone numbers.

DISTRICT COURT JUDGE	COURTROOM DEPUTY	PHONE NUMBER
J. Curtis Joyner, Ch. J.	Sharon Carter	267-299-7419
Stewart Dalzell	Eileen Adler	267-299-7399
Eduardo C. Robreno	Ronald Vance	267-299-7429
Mary A. McLaughlin	Dennis Hartman	267-299-7609
Petrese B. Tucker	Michael Owens	267-299-7619
Legrome D. Davis	Donna Croce	267-299-7659
Cynthia M. Rufe	Velma White (Civil) Erica Pratt (Criminal)	267-299-7491 267-299-7499
Timothy J. Savage	Harry Grace	267-299-7489
James Knoll Gardner	Cheryl Sinclair (Civil) Jennifer Fitzko (Criminal)	610-434-3457 610-391-7019
Gene E. K. Pratter	Michael Coyle	267-299-7359
Lawrence F. Stengel	Patricia Cardella (Civil) Laura Buenzle (Criminal)	267-299-7761 267-299-7769
Paul S. Diamond	Marian Scarengelli	267-299-7739
Juan R. Sánchez	Nancy DeLisle (Civil) Adrienne Mann (Criminal)	267-299-7781 267-299-7789
Joel H. Slomsky	Margaret Gallagher	267-299-7349
C. Darnell Jones, II	A'iShah El-Shabazz	267-299-7759
Mitchell S. Goldberg	Steve Sonnie	267-299-7509

Courtroom Deputy Clerks

SENIOR JUDGE	COURTROOM DEPUTY	PHONE NUMBER
J. William Ditter, Jr.	Stephen Iannacone	267-299-7211
Norma L. Shapiro	Madeline Ward	267-299-7549
Thomas N. O'Neill, Jr.	Charles Ervin	267-299-7559
Edmund V. Ludwig	Kathryne Crispell	267-299-7589
Robert F. Kelly	Thomas Garrity	267-299-7319
Jan E. DuBois	Milahn Hull	267-299-7339
Ronald L. Buckwalter	Matthew Higgins	267-299-7369
William H. Yohn, Jr.	Thomas McCann	267-299-7379
Harvey Bartle III	Katherine Gallagher	267-299-7389
John R. Padova	Geraldine Keane (Civil) Michael Beck (Criminal)	215-597-1178 267-299-7409
Anita B. Brody	Marie O'Donnell (Civil) James Scheidt (Criminal)	267-299-7431 267-299-7439
Berle M. Schiller	Jean Pennie (Civil) Christopher Campoli (Criminal)	267-299-7621 267-299-7629
R. Barclay Surrick	Christina Franzese	267-299-7639
Michael M. Baylson	JoAnne Bryson (Civil) Janice Lutz (Criminal)	267-299-7571 267-299-7291

MAGISTRATE JUDGE	COURTROOM DEPUTY	PHONE NUMBER
Carol Sandra Moore Wells, Ch. J.	Edward Andrews	215-597-7833
Thomas J. Rueter	Lisa Tipping	215-597-0048
Linda K. Caracappa	Ian Broderick	267-299-7640
Timothy R. Rice	Chavela Settles	267-299-7660
David R. Strawbridge	Lorraine DiSanti	267-299-7790
L. Felipe Restrepo	Juanita Davis	267-299-7690
Henry S. Perkin	Helen Nicholas	610-434-3823
Elizabeth T. Hey	Lara Karlson	267-299-7670
Lynne A. Sitarski	Regina Zarnowski	267-299-7810
Arnold C. Rapoport	Carlene Jones	610-391-7032
M. Faith Angell	Shelli MacElderry	215-597-6079
Jacob P. Hart	Deborah Stevenson	215-597-2733

STANDING ORDER RE: SENTENCING REFORM ACT OF 1984

In accordance with the resolution approved by the Judges of this court on January 19, 1988, a standing order **(Appendix U)** was adopted for use in criminal cases in which sentences are imposed under the Sentencing Reform Act of 1984 (Chapter II of the Comprehensive Crime Control Act, Public Law No. 98473, 98 Stat. 1837, 1976 (enacted October 12, 1984).

AFTER-HOURS CONTACT FOR EMERGENCY MATTERS

A deputy clerk is on duty in the Clerk's Office each weekday from 8:00 a.m. to 5:30 p.m. Attorneys who wish to contact the United States District Court for the Eastern District of Pennsylvania during the evenings after 5:30 p.m. or on weekends may do so by calling (215) 597-0374 or toll-free at (800) 525-5726 or (877) 437-7411. These numbers connect with the Court Security Office and Federal Protective Service which is staffed 24 hours a day, 7 days a week. Attorneys who call these numbers will be referred to the clerk or a deputy clerk on duty. This service is available for attorneys who have to file an injunction, ship attachment, or other emergency business during non-business hours.

AFTER-HOURS FILING DEPOSITORY

An After-Hours Filing Depository is provided in the lobby of the courthouse past the metal detectors and is able to receive documents for filing after 5:00 p.m. A time recorder is affixed to the depository which enables the person submitting documents for filing to note the time and date the documents are placed in the depository. If the documents are submitted after the doors are locked, access to the building may be gained by activating the buzzer adjacent to the main entrance on Market Street.

OPINIONS/CORRESPONDENCE CLERK

Margaret Stipa and Matthew Cocci are responsible for answering general correspondence inquiries. Margaret can be reached at 267-299-7047; Matthew can be contacted at 267-299-7094.

We maintain civil case files for calendar years 2008 to the present year and criminal case files from 2007 to the present, in addition to all open cases, in the Clerk's Office. Files for previous years are stored at the Federal Records Center. Send a letter to the attention of the correspondence clerks specifying the case number of the file you need and the documents in which you are interested. They will obtain the file and send you a copy of the papers that you need at a cost of $.50 per page. There is an additional fee of $11 for a certified copy. The cost of retrieving a file from the Federal Records Center is $53.

Any inquiries to search the index for case numbers, judgment, decrees, etc., will be handled by the correspondence clerks. The fee is $30 per name searched.

Judicial opinions filed in the Eastern District since June 1, 1997, as well as opinions filed in Civil Action Number 96-963, A.C.L.U. et al. v. Janet Reno, Attorney General of the U.S., in Civil Action Number 96-1458, American Library et al. v. U.S. Department of Justice, in Civil Action Number 96-2486, Cyber Promotions, Inc. v. America Online, Inc., and in Civil Action Number 96-5213, America Online, Inc. v. Cyber Promotions, Inc., may be obtained through the opinion section on the Eastern District of Pennsylvania's Internet website at http://www.paed.uscourts.gov.

HOW TO FIND A CASE NUMBER

Cases are indexed using the microfiche system, public access computers and **PACER** (see section on **PACER**). At the computers located in the Clerk's Office, you will find printed explanations on the procedure to locate a case number in order to find the docket sheet for that case. Every microfiche index is labeled with the filing time frames for each category. Information on cases filed prior to the specified time frames may be obtained from the Records Room.

CLERK'S INDEX FILE BY NATURE OF SUIT

The Clerk's Office makes this service available at no cost. It is an Index to Civil Actions by Subject prior to March 21, 1994, and is arranged under these main topics: Persons, Property, Contract, Torts & Other Statutes. Subject headings are exactly the same as those specified on the Civil Cover Sheet.

Refer to the Table of Contents under the appropriate main heading and find the page number on which reference is made to civil actions on the desired subject. Copy down the case number(s) shown and draw the case file jackets or docket sheets to see if the cases listed are helpful.

COPYWORK

Adjacent to Room 2609 is the Reproduction Room. To have copies made, you must complete a request form and prepay the cost either in person or by mail.

It is possible to obtain copywork the same day. However, it depends on the quantity of work and the time constraints of the photocopy operator.

RECORDS ROOM

Adjacent to the Reproduction Room is the Records Room where all open case files for civil and criminal cases are maintained. In addition to all open case files, all civil files from 2008 to the present year, and all criminal cases from 2007 to the present year are located in the file room. Individual files and papers may be inspected in this area by the general public. Files are available from the Federal Records Center through our office. There is a $53 fee for this service. If you have questions, you may contact the records room at 267-299-7082.

CREDIT CARD COLLECTION NETWORK

In September of 1987, the Department of Treasury established a government credit card collection network to enable federal agencies to accept credit cards (Visa, MasterCard, American Express, Discover and Diners Club) for the collection of receipts due the government.

Credit cards are accepted as payment for the following transactions in the Clerk's Office:

- filing fees;
- copywork (docket sheets, opinions, etc.);
- copies of ESR-taped proceedings;
- attorney admission fees;
- searches and certifications;
- retrieval fees for case files maintained at the Federal Records Center.

1. **Counter Transactions.** Submit the charge card at the counter for recording, validating, and imprinting onto a bank charge slip. The amount of the charge, transaction code, date and time appear on the bank charge slip and cash register receipt. The original cash register receipt and bank charge slip are given to the customer, and the copies are kept on file in the Clerk's Office.

2. **Telephone Requests.** Give your name, credit card number and its expiration date to the Clerk's office receptionist. Your requested work will be returned to you with a cash register receipt and a bank charge slip, which will have the words "TELEPHONE REQUEST" inserted in the signature block.

3. **Mail Requests.** The following information must be provided in your request letter: credit card number, expiration date, and specified amount to be charged. The letter must be signed by the same person whose signature appears on the credit card. You will receive a cash register receipt and a bank charge slip, which will have the words "MAIL REQUEST" inserted in the signature block.

For those law firms which are concerned with the safekeeping of the actual credit card, the Clerk's Office will maintain the firm's credit card number, expiration date, and the signature of one of the firm's partners after completion of an authorization form **(Appendix V)**. The courier will reference the authorization form and the transaction will be processed. On the bank charge slip, "AUTHORIZATION ON FILE" would appear in the signature block.

REQUIRED CHECK CONVERSION DISCLOSURE

When you provide a check as payment, you authorize us either to use information from your check to make a one-time electronic fund transfer from your account or to process the payment as a check transaction. When we use information from your check to make an electronic fund transfer, funds may be withdrawn from your account as soon as the same day we receive your payment, and you will not receive your check back from your financial institution. For inquiries, please call 267-299-7107.

If the electronic fund transfer cannot be completed because there are insufficient funds in your account, we may impose a one-time fee of $53.00 against your account, which we will also collect by electronic fund transfer.

A Privacy Act Statement required by 5 U.S.C., Section 552a(e)(3) stating our authority for soliciting and collecting the information from your check, and explaining the purposes and routine uses which will be made of your check information, is available from our internet site at www.paed.uscourts.gov or call toll free at 866-945-7920 to obtain a copy by mail. Furnishing the check information is voluntary, but a decision not to do so may require you to make payment by some other method.

DEPOSITING/WITHDRAWING MONIES

The Fiscal Department is responsible for coordinating all financial transactions involving the district court. All court-related fees are paid and disbursements made through this department. In order to deposit or withdraw monies from the registry, you must submit a proposed order. Please call Lucy Chin, the Financial Manager, at 267-299-7112 with any questions on this procedure.

A. Deposits

All checks should be made payable to **"Clerk, U.S. District Court"**. This is the only form of check that will be accepted. It is recommended that all deposits made into the registry of the court for subsequent disbursement be accomplished by a treasurers' check or a certified check in order to allow for prompt disbursement.

B. Registry Fund, Deposit Fund, Interest-Bearing Accounts

Disbursements are made from the registry fund upon order of the court only. The case docket is reviewed to determine if disbursement is appropriate, then the financial ledger sheet is pulled from the registry binder and compared with the court order. A voucher is prepared by the financial deputy and a check is drawn and mailed to the payee.

As a result of a new appropriation authority approved by the Judicial Conference, a fee in the amount of 10% of the annual interest has been established to cover the costs to the Judiciary for handling registry funds placed in interest-bearing accounts. The fee shall apply to all money and property held in the Court's registry and invested in interest-bearing accounts, except unclaimed monies held in accounts for individuals or persons whose whereabouts are unknown. Assessment of this fee will commence on all case payments (withdrawals) from the registry of the Court made on or after December 1, 1988. However, fees will be assessed only for the holding of funds after September 30, 1988. As to previously existing accounts, September 30 will be considered the original date of deposit with respect to the starting case balance and the number of days held. The fee will be computed at the time of withdrawal from the date of receipt into the registry through the date of withdrawal based on the average daily balance in the account. Payment of the fee will be deducted from the balance on deposit at the time of distribution.

Disbursements from the deposit fund, i.e., court-appointed counsel fees, are accomplished by preparing a voucher and forwarding it to the certifying officer. When the certified voucher is returned, a check is drawn on the voucher and mailed to the payee.

Upon order of the court, an interest-bearing account is closed with the local bank and deposited into the registry fund as a bank transfer. A U.S. Treasury check is drawn and handled the same as a registry disbursement.

FINES

Fine payments received through the mail are checked for the case number. If the individual is on probation, the receipt for payment is processed and sent to the Probation Office to credit the proper account. If the individual is not on probation, the payment is checked against the Case Master File to assure the proper amount is received without any overpayment. Overpayment is discouraged and the Probation Office is made aware of overpayment and asked to have the correct amount resubmitted. When it is impossible to have the check reissued for the correct amount, the overpayment is deposited into the Deposit Fund and disbursed at a later time to the probationer.

After the payments are verified as correct, a receipt is issued. The money is deposited into the U.S. Treasury (General and Special Fund) and postal fines are deposited into the deposit fund and disbursed quarterly. The original receipts are forwarded to the Probation Office.

Fines to be paid in person are sent to the Fiscal Department, where the Fine Case Account is checked. The financial deputy fills out a form indicating the case caption and number, the account number (FUND), and the amount to be paid. The form is given to the individual, who is sent to the cashier for issuance of a receipt.

Fines received from the Probation Office are hand-delivered by probation personnel. If the fine is a first payment, a letter is attached stating the defendant's name, case number, and the amount to be paid. The criminal or magistrate docket is checked to obtain the total amount and a new account is set up on the automated financial system.

If there was a prior payment, the Probation Office attaches a card with the payment, indicating the case number.

CENTRAL VIOLATIONS BUREAU (CVB)

In the district courts, the CVB provides a case management system for petty offenses (and some misdemeanors) which originate with the filing of a violation notice sent by the issuing government agency directly to the CVB. If collateral is forfeited to the CVB within the specified time, the date and amount is entered and the case is closed. In cases which are not disposed of through forfeiture of collateral, the CVB schedules a hearing before a Magistrate Judge, notifies the defendant, and records the Magistrate Judge's disposition of the case.

BAIL BONDS

Bail is generally set by the court from one of the following categories:

1. **Own Recognizance**—In this instance, the defendant signs an Appearance Bond in the amount fixed by the court without posting any security.

2. **In An Amount Equal to 10% of Total Amount of Bond**—In this instance, the defendant or someone on their behalf deposits 10% of the amount of the bond. If it is the defendant's cash, only the defendant signs the appearance bond. If it is the surety's cash, then both must sign. Local Civil Rule 67.1(a) states that "no attorney, or officer of this court shall be acceptable as surety bail, or security of any kind in any proceeding in this court."

3. **In An Amount with Good Security**—In this instance, both the defendant and the surety must sign the appearance bond with acceptable security being posted. Security may be one of the following:

    - **cash**—only cash, certified or cashiers check, or money order are acceptable;
    - **corporate surety**—with power of attorney;

Clerk's Office Procedural Handbook

- **individual sureties—Real Estate**—explained on sample form "Bail Bond Secured by Property or Real Estate Bail" **(Appendix W)**;
- **securities**—only negotiable securities are acceptable.

ATTORNEY ADMISSIONS

Applications for admission to the bar of our court for those attorneys who are currently members in good standing of the bar of the Supreme Court of Pennsylvania pursuant to Local Rule of Civil Procedure 83.5(a) may be obtained at the front counter of the Clerk's Office. Admission ceremonies are held once a week. The fee for attorney admission is $201.00. There is an $18.00 fee for a duplicate certificate of admission or certificate of good standing. For further information on attorney admissions, call Aida Ayala, the attorney admissions clerk at 267-299-7099.

Pursuant to Local Rule of Civil Procedure 83.5.2(b), for attorneys who are not currently admitted to either the bar of this court or the bar of the Supreme Court of Pennsylvania shall not actively participate in the conduct of any trial or pre-trial or post-trial proceeding before this court unless, upon motion of a member of the bar of this court containing a verified application, leave to do so is granted **(Appendix X)**. A $40 fee is assessed for such admissions.

COURT REPORTING/RECORDING SERVICES

Orders for transcripts produced by court reporters can be accomplished through the Court Reporter Supervisor, Joan Carr (267-299-7104), by means of a Transcript Order Form **(Appendix Y)**.

Orders for transcripts produced by electronic sound recording can be accomplished through the Transcript Coordinator, David Hayes (267-299-7041) by means of a Transcript Order Form **(Appendix Y)**. Orders for tapes or CDs produced by ESR can be accomplished by means of the Tape Order Form **(Appendix Z)**.

ELECTRONIC TRANSCRIPTS OF COURT PROCEEDINGS

With the exception of sealed transcripts which are excluded from electronic filing, effective June 2, 2008 electronic transcripts of court proceedings in the United States District Court, Eastern District of Pennsylvania, will be made available to the public as follows:

- Transcripts of civil court proceedings will be placed on CM/ECF or **PACER** unless the presiding judge otherwise directs.
- Transcripts of criminal court proceedings will not be placed on CM/ECF or **PACER** unless the presiding judge otherwise directs after giving the prosecution and defense counsel an opportunity to be heard.

If electronic transcripts are to be made available to the public upon approval of the assigned judge:

- A transcript provided to the court by a court reporter or transcriber will be available at the office of the clerk for inspection for a period of 90 days after it is delivered to the clerk.
- During the 90-day period a copy of the transcript may also be obtained by purchase from the court reporter or transcriber through the office of the clerk. An attorney who obtains the transcript from the office of the clerk will be allowed remote electronic access to the transcript through the court's CM/ECF system.
- After the 90-day period has expired, the filed transcript will be available for inspection and copying in the clerk's office and for download from the court's CM/ECF system through the **PACER** system.

In addition, amendments to the Federal Civil and Criminal Rules of Procedure (Civil Rule 5.2 and Criminal Rule 49.1) require that personal identification information be redacted from documents filed with the court, including Social Security numbers, names of minor children, financial account numbers, dates of birth, and in criminal cases, home addresses.

Interpreters' Services

For more information on electronic transcripts, please contact Joan Carr, Supervisor of Court Reporters (267-299-7104) or Michael Hearn, Electronic Sound Recording Coordinator (267-299-7039). (See **Appendix AA**.)

DIGITAL AUDIO FILE ELECTRONIC ACCESS

Digital audio recordings of courtroom proceedings will be publicly available on **PACER** upon the approval of the presiding judge. The project enables **PACER** users to download, in MP3 format, court proceedings that have been recorded using electronic sound recording technology. (See **Appendix BB**.)

For more information contact Michael Hearn, Electronic Sound Recording Coordinator, at 267-299-7039.

VIDEOTAPE SERVICES

The Clerk's Office has videotape facilities for the taking of depositions of witnesses. These services are provided at the discretion of the assigned judge. To request videotaping of witnesses, contact Edward Morrissy at 267-299-7044. There is no charge for the use of the videotape service, but counsel is required to supply the necessary videotapes.

Counsel is required to give notice to the opposing party as to their intention to utilize the videotape procedure.

VIDEO TELECONFERENCING

On June 1, 1995 the Eastern District of Pennsylvania started a video teleconferencing pilot program sponsored by the United States Marshal Service and the Federal Bureau of Prisons. This program establishes a closed circuit television link between the United States District Court in Philadelphia and the Federal Correctional Institute at Fairton, New Jersey. In May 1998, this program was expanded to include links between the District Court and State Correctional Institutions, including Graterford, Greene and Camp Hill. The program allows criminal defendants incarcerated at these institutions to fully participate in court appearances, interviews and conferences. The equipment and facilities are also available to the Office of Pretrial Services, the United States Probation Office, the Federal Defender, the United States Attorney, and the defense bar when not in use by the Court. All requests to use the VTC equipment for conferences are to be submitted to the VTC Coordinator who may be reached at 267-299-7039.

The VTC program has not been limited to only cases in which defendants are incarcerated. For visiting judge cases in which judges of this court sit by designation in Middle or Western District Court cases, this program has been successfully utilized to conduct conferences between this court and counsel from outside districts which are similarly equipped with VTC equipment. For further information on this service, contact the VTC Coordinator.

COURTROOM TECHNOLOGY

Several courtrooms provide an array of technical components that support evidence presentation, remote site interactions, language interpreting and audio enhancement. The state-of-the-art technologies include assisted listening systems, integrated court interpreting systems, video teleconferencing systems, document/video presentation systems, evidence trolleys, annotation pads, document cameras, as well as connectivity at counsel tables for use with court- or attorney- provided PCs. The court welcomes the bar to make use of these technologies and training is available at the courthouse. For further information, contact Michael Hearn at 267-299-7039 or Edward Morrissy at 267-299-7044.

INTERPRETERS' SERVICES

Effective September 1, 1997, the Clerk's Office became responsible for scheduling interpreters for all criminal proceedings and for all civil cases initiated by the government. The interpreter coordinator, Larry Bowman (267-299-7029) will schedule all interpreters required for court appearances.

Once the need for an interpreter has been established, the courtroom deputy to the assigned judge will be responsible for notifying the interpreter coordinator of all court proceedings requiring the use of an interpreter.

JURY SELECTION

The jury section is responsible for selecting and maintaining a pool of citizens qualified to serve as grand and petit jurors in this district and summoning these individuals for jury service. Jurors are selected pursuant to the *Plan of the Random Selection of Grand and Petit Jurors of 1968 for the Eastern District of Pennsylvania*. A copy of this plan is available for inspection in the Office of the Clerk of Court. The jury section is also responsible for preparation of vouchers and documentation required to reimburse jurors for their service.

A. Term of Jury Service

In our district, jurors are called for either a two-day/one trial term of service each Monday or a three-day/one trial term of service on Wednesdays. If selected for a case where the trial extends beyond one week, jurors are required to serve until the completion of the trial.

B. Excuse from Jury Service on Request

In addition to members of groups and occupational classes subject to excuse from jury service pursuant to 28 U.S.C. §§ 1863(b)(5) and (7), any person summoned for jury service may, on request, be excused temporarily by a judge of this court. The person must show undue hardship or extreme inconvenience by reason of great distance, either in miles or travel time, from the place of holding court, grave illness in the family or any other emergency which outweighs in urgency the obligation to serve as a juror when summoned, or any other factor which the court determines to constitute an undue hardship or to create an extreme inconvenience to the juror. Additionally, in situations where it is anticipated that a trial or grand jury proceeding may require more than thirty days of service, the court may consider, as a further basis for temporary excuse, severe economic hardship to an employer which would result from the absence of a key employee during the period of such service.

The period for which such prospective jurors may be excused shall be the period of time which the judge deems necessary under the circumstances, which shall be fixed in the order granting the excuse. At the expiration of the period so fixed, such persons shall be summoned again for jury service within a reasonable time.

C. Payment

Jurors receive $40 for each day in attendance, plus .555 cents per mile (eff. 4/17/2012) as measured from their residence to the courthouse (round trip). The court calculates the computation of this fee. If a juror lives more than 50 miles from the courthouse and remains overnight, the juror will be reimbursed for room and living expenses. Subsistence allowance is $209 per night (from 9/1 through 11/30) and $203 per night (from 12/1 through 8/31) in Philadelphia, $142 per night in Reading, and $134 per night in Allentown or Easton. If you have any questions regarding jury matters, you may call 267-299-7299.

INCLEMENT WEATHER

In the event of inclement or otherwise extreme weather conditions, the public is urged to call the court's **Code-A-Phone** line for a special announcement on whether the courthouse will be closed or if trials have been canceled for that day. A recorded message on the toll-free number **1-800-829-0189** will be accessible from about 5:30 a.m. Attorneys and jurors are requested to call this number before leaving their office or residence to attend court. It is also suggested that the public tune into radio and television news stations, which will also broadcast announcements if jury trials have been adjourned or if the courthouse will be closed for that day. If no announcement is made by 6:00 a.m. and there is no special message on the recording, it should be assumed that court will be in session and jurors are to report for jury duty as scheduled.

PACER—PUBLIC ACCESS TO COURT ELECTRONIC RECORDS

The **PACER** system provides improved access to court records for attorneys and other members of the public. This electronic access system allows any member of the public to access information contained in the court's civil/criminal docket database via internet access. The user is able to access a search of information either through a case name or a case number and can request docket reports. The information is either saved on the user's PC or the report is printed during online access.

All civil cases filed since July 1, 1990 and all criminal cases filed since July, 1992 are contained on the **PACER** system. In addition, the **PACER** system will allow an end-user to check recent activity. If there has been no recent activity, the **PACER** system will confirm that fact in seconds.

The **PACER** system is available 24 hours a day, 7 days a week. Electronic case filings and updates to the docket are available for immediate view.

The Eastern District of Pennsylvania **PACER** system is administered by the **PACER** Service Center. The center provides all support services as well as billing services for **PACER** access.

Many Eastern District of Pennsylvania **PACER** users are already registered with the **PACER** Service Center for access to **PACER** systems throughout the federal court system. If you are currently registered with the **PACER** Service Center, please call the center at 1-800-676-6856 to add the Eastern District of Pennsylvania to your account.

If you are not registered with the center, complete a **PACER** Registration Form **(Appendix CC)** available on the court's website at http://www.paed.uscourts.gov and forward it to the **PACER** Service Center, P.O. Box 780549, San Antonio, TX 78278-0549, or fax it to (201) 301-6441, or a completed application may be submitted via e-mail. The address for **PACER** is http://www.pacer.gov. Users may access **PACER** by using their **PACER** login and password. The fee for accessing **PACER** is $.10 per page.

Should you have any questions concerning **PACER** service or registration, please contact the center at (800) 676-6856.

INTERNET WEBSITE

Information on multiple services and all judicial opinions filed since June 1, 1997 in the United States District Court for the Eastern District of Pennsylvania, as well as e-mail capabilities are available on the Internet at http://www.paed.uscourts.gov. The site contains the following:

- Judicial opinions filed since June 1, 1997, including a Recent Opinions section;
- E-mail capabilities with the Office of the Clerk of Court;
- Directory of automated services **(Appendix DD)**;
- Local civil, criminal and bankruptcy rules;
- Court notices;
- Electronic Case Filing;
- Forms;
- Report of cases specially listed for U.S. District Court and surrounding county courts;
- Multidistrict litigation information;
- Criminal documents;
- Frequently asked questions;
- Clerk's Office Procedural Handbook containing information on: filing civil actions/documents, general motion practice and pretrial procedures, fees, judicial chambers information (phone numbers, addresses, staff), forms (appendices), Clerk's Office directory, appeals, bill of costs and after hours filing;
- Telephone directory and address information;
- Judicial Schedule of Trials—Automated System Inquiry (JUST-ASK);

- Search capabilities;
- Link to **PACER**;
- Judicial policies and procedures;
- Juror information;
- Federal holidays;
- Arbitrator and mediator applications.

LOCAL RULES

The local rules of court—civil, criminal, admiralty, and bankruptcy—are available from the Clerk's Office, and also on the Internet at http://www.paed.uscourts.gov. Inquiries should be directed to Aida Ayala, 267-299-7099, Room 2625.

PORTABLE ELECTRONIC DEVICES AND PUBLIC TELEPHONE LOCATIONS

Visitors to the U.S. Courthouse are permitted to carry portable electronic devices, such as cell phones and laptops into the courthouse, but all equipment will be subject to x-ray and visual inspection by the Court Security Officers at the security screening station. All equipment must be turned off before entering courtrooms and chambers, unless otherwise authorized by the presiding judge. Failure to follow this restriction may result in sanctions by the judge.

While cell phones are permitted in the courthouse, there are also numerous pay telephones available for use by the public located on every floor of the building, except on the 21st and 22nd floors. A directory of public telephone locations and numbers follows.

DIRECTORY OF PUBLIC TELEPHONE LOCATIONS
U.S. Courthouse
Philadelphia, PA

FLOOR	TELEPHONE #	LOCATION OF PHONE
Lobby	215-922-8886	Hallway adjacent to public elevators
Lobby	215-922-8668	Hallway adjacent to public elevators
Lobby	215-922-8673	Hallway adjacent to public elevators
Lobby	215-922-8683	Hallway adjacent to public elevators
Lobby	215-922-8682	Hallway adjacent to public elevators
Lobby	215-922-8671	Hallway adjacent to public elevators
2nd Floor	215-922-8048	Adjacent to public elevators
3rd Floor	215-922-8690	Hallway adjacent to secured corridor
4th Floor	215-922-8797	Hallway adjacent to secured corridor
4th Floor	215-922-8796	Hallway adjacent to secured corridor
5th Floor	215-922-8798	Hallway adjacent to secured corridor
5th Floor	215-922-8855	Hallway adjacent to secured corridor

Directory of Public Telephone Locations

6th Floor	215-922-8863	Hallway adjacent to secured corridor
6th Floor	215-922-8860	Hallway adjacent to secured corridor
7th Floor	215-922-8870	Hallway adjacent to secured corridor
7th Floor	215-922-8864	Hallway adjacent to secured corridor
8th Floor	215-922-8874	Hallway adjacent to secured corridor
8th Floor	215-922-8873	Hallway adjacent to secured corridor
9th Floor	215-922-8728	Hallway adjacent to secured corridor
10th Floor	215-922-8987	Hallway adjacent to secured corridor
10th Floor	215-922-8882	Hallway adjacent to secured corridor
11th Floor	215-922-8883	Hallway adjacent to secured corridor
11th Floor	215-925-8884	Hallway adjacent to secured corridor
12th Floor	215-922-9199	Hallway adjacent to secured corridor
12th Floor	215-922-9193	Hallway adjacent to secured corridor
13th Floor	215-922-9222	Hallway adjacent to secured corridor
13th Floor	215-922-9203	Hallway adjacent to secured corridor
14th Floor	215-922-9315	Hallway adjacent to secured corridor
14th Floor	215-922-9335	Hallway adjacent to secured corridor
15th Floor	215-922-9431	Hallway adjacent to secured corridor
15th Floor	215-922-9437	Hallway adjacent to secured corridor
16th Floor	215-922-9459	Hallway adjacent to secured corridor
16th Floor	215-922-9480	Hallway adjacent to secured corridor
17th floor	215-922-9491	Hallway adjacent to secured corridor
17th Floor	215-922-9488	Hallway adjacent to secured corridor
18th Floor	215-922-9335	Hallway adjacent to secured corridor
19th Floor	215-922-9542	South end of hallway
20th Floor	215-922-9551	Hallway adjacent to secured corridor

Clerk's Office Procedural Handbook

April 22, 2013

UNITED STATES DISTRICT COURT
EASTERN DISTRICT OF PENNSYLVANIA
CLERK'S OFFICE EMPLOYEE LIST

INFORMATION DESK—Chris Kurek (215) 597-7704

CLERK OF COURT
Michael E. Kunz	215-597-9221
Miriam Coco, Secretary	267-299-7085
Lauren Boyer	267-299-7086

CASE REASSIGNMENTS/ TAXATION OF COSTS
Susan Renz	267-299-7218

STAFF ATTORNEY
Ken Wilson	267-299-7088
Kevin Dunleavy	267-299-7087

HUMAN RESOURCES
Human Resources Administrator
Donna L. Diaz	267-299-7089

Human Resources Coordinator
Deana Drobonick	267-299-7091

Personnel Specialists
Jamie L. Wilson	267-299-7092
Diane Michalik	267-299-7242

MDL 875 LAW CLERK
Michele Ventura	267-299-7422

CHIEF DEPUTY
Susan Matlack	267-299-7051

ADMINISTRATIVE SERVICES MANAGER
Thomas Clewley	267-299-7036

ASSISTANT ADMINISTRATIVE SERVICES MANAGER
Michael Sienkiewicz	267-299-7030

ELECTRONIC SOUND RECORDING COORDINATOR
Michael Hearn	267-299-7039

TRANSCRIPTION COORDINATOR
David Hayes	267-299-7041

ESR OPERATORS
James Beck	267-299-7196
Jimmy Cruz	267-299-7224
Michael DelRossi	267-299-7219
Inna Goldshteyn	267-299-7222
Patrick Kelly	267-299-7236
Jerry LaRosa	267-299-7129
Jeffrey Lucini	267-299-7214
Andrea Mack	267-299-7179
Nelson Malave	267-299-7213
Joseph Matkowski	267-299-7220
Mark Rafferty	267-299-7221
Dennis Taylor	267-299-7121
Crystal Wardlaw	267-299-7212
Jessica Whitfield	267-299-7161

COURTROOM TECHNOLOGY COORDINATOR
Michael Hearn	267-299-7039
Edward Morrissy	267-299-7044

COURTROOM DEPUTY SUPERVISORS
Donna Bozzelli	267-299-7539
Stephen Iannacone	267-299-7211

COURTROOM DEPUTY CLERKS
Eileen Adler - SD	267-299-7399
Rosalind Burton-Hoop	267-299-7459
Sharon Carter - JCJ	267-299-7419
Kathryne Crispell - EL	267-299-7589
Katherine Gallagher - HB	267-299-7389
Harry Grace - TJS	267-299-7489
Dennis Hartman - MAM	267-299-7609
Milahn V. Hull (JED)	267-299-7069
Michael Owens - PBT	267-299-7619
Elizabeth Purnell	267-299-7579
Ronald Vance - ER	267-299-7429
Madeline Ward - NS	267-299-7549

COURTROOM DEPUTY CLERKS/ESR OPERATORS
Michael Beck - JRP	267-299-7409
Laura Buenzle - LFS	267-299-7769
Christopher Campoli - BMS	267-299-7629
Michael Coyle - GEKP	267-299-7359
Donna Croce - LDD	267-299-7659
A'iShah El-Shabazz - DJ	267-299-7759
Charles Ervin - TON	267-299-7559
Jennifer Fitzko - JKG	610-391-7019
Connie Flores	267-299-7191
Christina Franzese - RBS	267-299-7639
Margaret Gallagher - JHS	267-299-7349

Personnel Directory

Thomas Garrity - RK	267-299-7319
Matthew Higgins -RB	267-299-7369
Teri Lefkowith	610-320-5030
Janice Lutz- MMB	267-299-7291
Kristin R. Makely	267-299-7330
Adrienne Mann - JRS	267-299-7789
Thomas McCann - WY	267-299-7379
Erica Pratt - CMR	267-299-7499
Marion Scarengelli - PD	267-299-7739
James Scheidt - AB	267-299-7439
Steve Sonnie - MG	267-299-7509
Anthony Tumminello	610-252-7548
Andrew Follmer	267-299-7226
Lenora Kashner Wittje	267-299-7529

SECRETARY/COURTROOM DEPUTY CLERKS

Lisa Brady	267-299-7158
Patricia Feldman	267-299-7441
Sharon Hall	267-299-7591
Sheila Jeffers	267-299-7169
Judy Mack	610-320-5006
Carol Sampson	267-299-7174
Marcie Silfies	610-320-9821

MAGISTRATE JUDGES DEPUTY CLERKS

Edward Andrews - CSMW	267-299-7771
Ian Broderick - LKC	267-299-7641
Juanita Davis - LFR	267-299-7690
Lorraine DiSanti - DRS	267-299-7790
Maryellen Fox	267-299-7741
Carlene Jones - ACR	610-391-7032
Lara Karlson - ETH	267-299-7670
Shelli MacElderry - MFA	215-597-6079
Helen Nicholas - HSP	610-391-7025
Chavela Settles - TRR	267-299-7660
Deborah Stevenson - JPH	267-299-7721
Lisa Tipping - TJR	267-299-7701
Regina M. Zarnowski - LAS	267-299-7810

OPINION/CORRESPONDENCE CLERKS

Matt Cocci	267-299-7094
Margaret Stipa	267-299-7047

JURY ADMINISTRATOR

Paul Lombardi	267-299-7078

JURY SELECTION

Main Number	267-299-7299

JURY SELECTION

Elizabeth Cleek	267-299-7049
Jean Conboy	267-299-7050
Carolanne Goss	267-299-7077
Jo-Anne Hohenstein	267-299-7076
Marilou Masters	267-299-7079
AnnaMarie Prudente	267-299-7081

Shelia Ward	267-299-7080

ARCHIVAL SPECIALIST

Frederick Druding, Jr.	267-299-7046

RECORDS ROOM SUPERVISOR

Michael Finney	267-299-7084

FILE/MAIL METERING CLERKS

Ken Campbell	267-299-7082/83
Steven Carey	267-299-7082/83
Carl J. Hauger	267-299-7082/83
Michael P. Sweeney	267-299-7082/83
Brian Weissman	267-299-7082/83

XEROX OPERATOR

Kenneth E. Duvak	267-299-7082/83

ADMINISTRATIVE SERVICES SUPERVISOR

Michael Hutelmyer	267-299-7095

ADMINISTRATIVE SERVICES CLERKS
Telecommunications Specialist

John Szymanski	267-299-7186
James Finegan	267-299-7097
Richard Struble	267-299-7100

Technical Support Specialist

Gregg Keller	267-299-7194

Property & Procurement Specialist

Trevor McDermott	267-299-7096

Property Officer

Charles Parkinson	267-299-7144

Procurement Specialists

Casey Fretz - Supplies	267-299-7142
Lori Stutz	267-299-7098
Raymond Wolf	267-299-7223

Procurement Assistants

Donna Bakker	267-299-7171
Jordan Todd	267-299-7170

NATURALIZATION / ATTORNEY ADMISSIONS

Aida Ayala	267-299-7099

INTERPRETER COORDINATOR

Larry Bowman	267-299-7029

AUTOMATION TRAINER

William Jones	267-299-7063

CASE OPENING/DOCUMENT SCANNING CLERKS

Christopher Ehly	267-299-7245
Brian Johnson	267-299-7277

Clerk's Office Procedural Handbook

Patrick McLaughlin	267-299-7215

FISCAL

Financial Manager
Lucy Chin	267-299-7112

Financial Officer
Joseph Hall	267-299-7107

Financial Supervisor
Maria Andrews	267-299-7108

Voucher/Disbursements
Terryl Richardson	267-299-7109

CJA Vouchers
Peter Mordeczko	267-299-7110

Financial Assistant
Zachary Robinson	267-299-7111

Receivable Checks
Michael O'Reilly	267-299-7131
Kelly Stratton	267-299-7113

BUDGET ANALYST
Joseph Hall	267-299-7107

DOCUMENT SCANNING CLERK
Liana Lui	267-299-7243
Greg Williams	267-299-7244

AUTOMATION SUPPORT 267-299-7240

SYSTEMS MANAGER
Mark Boraske	267-299-7052

ASSISTANT SYSTEMS MANAGER
Dan De Cerchio	267-299-7055

SYSTEMS ADMINISTRATORS
Raymond Gilchrist	267-299-7057
Sean O'Connor	267-299-7056

ANALYST
Mary Grace O'Connor	267-299-7066

SYSTEMS TECHNOLOGY ADMINISTRATORS
Daniel Baback	267-299-7153
Dan DeLuca	267-299-7054

AUTOMATION SUPPORT TECHNICIANS
Bryant Jones	267-299-7172
Omar Lee	267-299-7154
Dawn Molony	267-299-7247
Jon Montovani	267-299-7053

ALLENTOWN OFFICE AUTOMATION SUPPORT TECHNICIAN
Craig R. Kroznuski	610-776-6117

AUTOMATION SUPPORT SPECIALIST
James McGovern	267-299-7059

DATA QUALITY ANALYSTS
Gail Olson	267-299-7060
Karen Vample	267-299-7061

SYSTEMS ANALYST PROGRAMMER
Ronald Sochanski	267-299-7065

STATISTICAL ANALYST
Stanislaw Furtek	267-299-7058
May Kim	267-299-7143
Kyle John Noll	267-299-7064
Suzy Roman	267-299-7020

STATISTICAL CLERK
Britney Butler	267-299-7234

OPERATIONS MANAGER
Richard Sabol	267-299-7011

ASSISTANT OPERATIONS MANAGER
Theresa Milano	267-299-7013

CASE PROCESSING SUPERVISOR
Jane Firestone	267-299-7014

CASE PROCESSING QUALITY CONTROL CLERK
Michele DiNapoli	267-299-7147

PRISONER DOCKET CLERKS
# 1-3 Fernando Benitez	267-299-7025
# 4-6 Linda Jerry	267-299-7026
# 7-9 Jim Deitz	267-299-7022
# 1-0 Peggy Rosser	267-299-7062

MDL/CASE PROCESSING CLERK
Thomas Dempsey	267-299-7018

CASE PROCESSING/DOCUMENT SCANNING CLERKS
Vincent Alia	267-299-7238
Alex Eggert	267-299-7216
Jenna Frigo	267-299-7248
Ulie Hevener	267-299-7296
Kristen Pepin	267-299-7233
Nicole Phillippi	267-299-7288
Eric Sobieski	267-299-7241
Stacy Wertz	267-299-7289

MDL/CASE PROCESSING COORDINATOR
Linda Jerry	267-299-7026

ASSIGNMENT CLERK
Gregg Swierczynski	267-299-7230

CASE PROCESSING SUPERVISOR
Nicole D'Urso	267-299-7017

CASE PROCESSING CLERKS
#1 Robert D. Fehrle	267-299-7001
#2 Kirk Kopacz	267-299-7002
#3 Eric Sobieski	267-299-7003
#4 Tashia Irving	267-299-7004
#5 Kimberly Williams	267-299-7005
#6 Michele Helmer	267-299-7006
#7 Joseph Lavin	267-299-7007
#8 Ashley Mastrangelo	267-299-7008
#9 Steve Gill	267-299-7009
#10 Frank DelCampo	267-299-7010
#1-10 Jenniffer Cabrera	267-299-7227
#1-10 Lisa DeAngelo	267-299-7043
#1-10 Amanda Frazier	267-299-7177
#1-10 Ann Murphy	267-299-7068
#1-10 Danielle Puchon	267-299-7048

CASE OPENING/ARBITRATION and MEDIATION SUPERVISOR
Sherry Bowman	267-299-7067

CASE OPENING/ARBITRATION CLERKS
#1-2 Michael Mani	267-299-7071
#3-4 Patricia Jones	267-299-7072
#5-6 Joseph Walton	267-299-7073
#7-8 Janet M. Vecchione	267-299-7074
#9-0 Kimberly Scott-Hayden	267-299-7075
#0-9 Richard Thieme	267-299-7285

MEDIATION CLERK
Sherry Bowman	267-299-7067

CASE OPENING/DOCUMENT SCANNING CLERKS
Shawn A. Cammy	267-299-7282
Michael Cosgrove	267-299-7284
Katie Furphy	267-299-7286
Kelly Ann Haggerty	267-299-7283
Christian Henry	267-299-7193
Julie Leva	267-299-7193
Nelly Lu	267-299-7195
Peter O'Driscoll	267-299-7173
Heather Stolinski	267-299-7159
Justin Wood	267-299-7280

CASE PROCESSING SUPERVISOR
Kevin Eibel	267-299-7035

SPEEDY TRIAL COORDINATOR/ QUALITY CONTROL CLERK
Carlos Cardona	267-299-7023

CRIMINAL DOCKETING CLERKS
#1-3 Thomas Giambrone	267-299-7160
#4-6 James Hamilton	267-299-7024
#7-9 Kevin Eibel	267-299-7035
#0 Mark Ciamaichelo	267-299-7145

GRAND JURY CLERK
Eileen Bobb	267-299-7016

APPEALS CASE PROCESSING CLERK
Orlando Medina, Jr.	267-299-7015

ASSIGNMENT CLERK
Steve B. Tomas	267-299-7028

MAGISTRATE DOCKETING CLERK
Mark Ciamaichelo	267-299-7145

PRO SE WRIT CLERK
Daniel McCormack	267-299-7021

CASE PROCESSING/DOCUMENT SCANNING CLERK
John Arrow	267-299-7235

ALLENTOWN CASE PROCESSING CLERKS
Evelyn Renner	610-776-6114
Lauren B. Sampson	610-776-6121
Matthew A. Sheetz	610-776-6116
Kris Yerry	610-776-6115

SUPERVISOR OF COURT REPORTERS
Joan Carr	267-299-7104

OFFICIAL COURT REPORTERS
Kathleen Feldman	215-779-5578
Lynn McCloskey	856-649-4774
Suzanne White	215-627-1882
Gregg Wolfe	215-925-6409

COMPUTER ROOM
267-299-7070

ALLENTOWN OFFICE
Michael E. Kunz, Clerk of Court
U.S. District Court, ED of PA
504 W. Hamilton Street, Suite 1601
Allentown, PA 18101-1500

Craig R. Kroznuski	610-776-6117
Evelyn Renner	610-776-6114
Lauren B. Sampson	610-776-6121
Matthew A. Sheetz	610-776-6116
Kris Yerry	610-776-6115

PRO SE LAW
HABEAS CORPUS CLERK
Leslie Marant   267-299-7511

PRO SE LAW CLERKS
Elaine Battle   267-299-7034
Miriam Silberstein   267-299-7033

Adler, Eileen	267-299-7399
Alia, Vincent	267-299-7238
Andrews, Edward	267-299-7771
Andrews, Maria	267-299-7108
Arrow, John	267-299-7235
Ayala, Aida	267-299-7099
Baback, Daniel	267-299-7153
Bakker, Donna	267-299-7171
Battle, Elaine	267-299-7034
Beck, James	267-299-7196
Beck, Michael	267-299-7409
Benitez, Fernando	267-299-7025
Bobb, Eileen J.	267-299-7016
Boraske, Mark	267-299-7052
Bowman, Larry	267-299-7029
Bowman, Sherry	267-299-7067
Boyer, Lauren	267-299-7086
Bozzelli, Donna	267-299-7539
Brady, Lisa	267-299-7158
Broderick, Ian	267-299-7641
Buenzle, Laura	267-299-7769
Burton-Hoop, Rosalind	267-299-7459
Butler, Britney	267-299-7234
Cabrera, Jenniffer	267-299-7227
Campbell, Ken	267-299-7082/83
Campoli, Christopher	267-299-7629
Cammy, Shawn A.	267-299-7282
Carey, Steven	267-299-7082/83
Cardona, Carlos	267-299-7023
Carr, Joan	267-299-7104
Carter, Sharon	267-299-7419
Chin, Lucy	267-299-7112
Ciamaichelo, Mark	267-299-7145
Cleek, Elizabeth	267-299-7049
Clewley, Thomas	267-299-7036
Cocci, Matthew	267-299-7278
Coco, Miriam	267-299-7085
Conboy, Jean	267-299-7050
Cosgrove, Michael	267-299-7284
Coyle, Michael	267-299-7359
Crispell, Kathryne	267-299-7589
Croce, Donna	267-299-7659
Cruz, Jimmy	267-299-7224
D'Urso, Nicole	267-299-7017
Davis, Juanita	267-299-7690
De Angelo, Lisa	267-299-7043
De Cerchio, Dan	267-299-7055
Deitz, James	267-299-7022
DelCampo, Frank	267-299-7010
DelRossi, Michael	267-299-7219
DeLuca, Dan	267-299-7054
Dempsey, Thomas	267-299-7018
Diaz, Donna L.	267-299-7089
DiNapoli, Michele	267-299-7147
DiSanti, Lorraine	267-299-7790
Drobonick, Deana	267-299-7091
Druding, Jr., Frederick	267-299-7046
Dunleavy, Kevin	267-299-7087
Duvak, Kenneth E.	267-299-7082/83
Eggert, Alex	267-299-7216
Ehly, Christopher	267-299-7245
Eibel, Kevin	267-299-7035
El-Shabazz, A'iShah	267-299-7759
Ervin, Charles	267-299-7559
Fehrle, Robert D.	267-299-7001
Feldman, Kathleen	215-779-5578
Feldman, Patricia	267-299-7441
Finegan, James	267-299-7097
Finney, Michael	267-299-7084
Firestone, Jane	267-299-7014
Fitzko, Jennifer	610-391-7019
Flores, Constantine	267-299-7191
Follmer, Andrew	267-299-7226
Fox, Maryellen	267-299-7741
Franzese, Christina	267-299-7639
Frazier, Amanda	267-299-7177
Fretz, Casey	267-299-7142
Frigo, Jenna	267-299-7248
Furphy, Katie	267-299-7286
Furtek, Stanislaw	267-299-7058
Gallagher, Katherine	267-299-7389
Gallagher, Margaret	267-299-7349
Garrity, Thomas	267-299-7319
Giambrone, Thomas	267-299-7160
Gilchrist, Raymond	267-299-7057
Gill, Stephen	267-299-7009
Goldshteyn, Inna	267-299-7222
Goss, Carolanne	267-299-7077
Grace, Harry	267-299-7489
Haggerty, Kelly Ann	267-299-7283
Hall, Joseph	267-299-7107
Hall, Sharon	267-299-7591
Hamilton, James	267-299-7024
Hartman, Dennis	267-299-7609
Hauger, Carl J.	267-299-7082/83
Hayes, David	267-299-7041
Hearn, Michael	267-299-7039
Helmer, Michele	267-299-7006
Henry, Christian	267-299-7193
Hevener, Ulie	267-299-7296
Higgins, Matthew	267-299-7369
Hohenstein, Jo-Anne	267-299-7076
Hull, Milahn V.	267-299-7069
Hutelmyer, Michael	267-299-7095
Iannacone, Stephen	267-299-7211
Irving, Tashia	267-299-7004

Personnel Directory

Jeffers, Sheila	267-299-7169	O'Connor, Mary Grace	267-299-7066
Jerry, Linda	267-299-7026	O'Connor, Sean	267-299-7056
Johnson, Brian E.	267-299-7277	O'Driscoll, Peter	267-299-7173
Jones, Bryant	267-299-7172	O'Reilly, Michael J.	267-299-7131
Jones, Carlene	610-391-7032	Olson, Gail	267-299-7060
Jones, Patricia	267-299-7072	Owens, Michael	267-299-7619
Jones, William	267-299-7063		
		Parkinson, Charles	267-299-7144
Karlson, Lara L.	267-299-7670	Pepin, Kristen	267-299-7233
Keller, Gregg	267-299-7194	Phillippi, Nicole	267-299-7288
Kelly, Patrick	267-299-7236	Pratt, Erica	267-299-7499
Kim, May	267-299-7143	Prudente, AnnaMarie	267-299-7081
Kopacz, Kirk	267-299-7002	Puchon, Danielle	267-299-7048
Kroznuski, Craig R.	610-776-6117	Purnell, Elizabeth	267-299-7579
Kunz, Michael E.	215-597-9221		
Kurek, Chris	215-597-7704	Rafferty, Mark	267-299-7221
		Renner, Evelyn	610-776-6114
LaRosa, Jerry	267-299-7129	Renz, Susan L.	267-299-7218
Lavin, Joseph	267-299-7007	Richardson, Terryl	267-299-7109
Lee, Omar	267-299-7154	Robinson, Zachary	267-299-7111
Lefkowith, Teri	610-320-5030	Roman, Suzy	267-299-7020
Leva, Julie	267-299-7193	Rosser, Peggy	267-299-7062
Lombardi, Paul	267-299-7078		
Lu, Nelly	267-299-7195	Sabol, Richard	267-299-7011
Lucini, Jeffrey	267-299-7214	Sampson, Carol	267-299-7174
Lui, Liana	267-299-7243	Sampson, Lauren B.	610-776-6121
Lutz, Janice	267-299-7291	Scarengelli, Marion	267-299-7739
		Scheidt, James	267-299-7439
MacElderry, Shelli	215-597-6079	Scott-Hayden, Kimberly	267-299-7075
Mack, Andrea	267-299-7179	Settles, Chavela	267-299-7660
Mack, Judy	610-320-5006	Sheetz, Matthew A.	610-776-6116
Makely, Kristin R.	267-299-7330	Sienkiewicz, Michael	267-299-7030
Malave, Nelson	267-299-7213	Silberstein, Miriam	267-299-7033
Mani, Michael	267-299-7071	Silfies, Marcie	610-320-9821
Mann, Adrienne	267-299-7789	Sobieski, Eric	267-299-7241/267-299-7003
Marant, Leslie	267-299-7511	Sochanski, Ronald	267-299-7065
Masters, Marilou	267-299-7079	Sonnie, Stephen	267-299-7509
Mastrangelo, Ashley	267-299-7232	Stevenson, Deborah	267-299-7721
Matkowski, Joseph	267-299-7220	Stipa, Margaret	267-299-7047
Matlack, Susan	267-299-7051	Stolinski, Heather	267-299-7159
McCann, Thomas	267-299-7379	Stratton, Kelly	267-299-7113
McCloskey, Lynn	856-649-4774	Struble, Richard	267-299-7100
McCormack, Daniel	267-299-7021	Stutz, Lori	267-299-7098
McDermott, Trevor	267-299-7096	Sweeney, Michael P.	267-299-7082/83
McGovern, James	267-299-7059	Swierczynski, Gregg	267-299-7230
McLaughlin, Patrick	267-299-7215	Szymanski, John	267-299-7186
Medina, Jr., Orlando	267-299-7015		
Michalik, Diane	267-299-7242	Taylor, Dennis	267-299-7121
Milano, Theresa	267-299-7013	Thieme, Richard	267-299-7285
Molony, Dawn	267-299-7247	Tipping, Lisa	267-299-7701
Montovani, Jon	267-299-7053	Tomas, Steve	267-299-7028
Mordeczko, Peter	267-299-7110	Todd, Jordan	267-299-7170
Morrissy, Edward	267-299-7044	Tumminello, Anthony	610-252-7548
Murphy, Ann	267-299-7068		
		Vample, Karen	267-299-7061
Nicholas, Helen	610-391-7025	Vance, Ronald	267-299-7429
Noll, Kyle John	267-299-7064	Vecchione, Janet M.	267-299-7074
		Ventura, Michele	267-299-7422

Walton, Joseph	267-299-7073
Ward, Madeline	267-299-7549
Ward, Shelia	267-299-7080
Wardlaw, Crystal	267-299-7212
Weissman, Brian	267-299-7082/83
Wertz, Stacy	267-299-7289
White, Suzanne	215-627-1882
Whitfield, Jessica	267-299-7161
Williams, Greg	267-299-7244
Williams, Kimberly	267-299-7005
Wilson, Jamie L.	267-299-7092
Wilson, Ken	267-299-7088
Wittje, Lenora Kashner	267-299-7529
Wolf, Raymond	267-299-7223
Wolfe, Gregg	215-925-6409
Wood, Justin	267-299-7280
Yerry, Kris	610-776-6115
Zarnowski, Regina M.	267-299-7810

LIST OF APPENDICES[1]

APPENDIX A	ELECTRONIC CASE FILING PROCEDURES
APPENDIX B	**PDF** FILE INFORMATION
APPENDIX C	VALIDATION OF SIGNATURE FORM, LOCAL RULE 5.1.2
APPENDIX D	ELECTRONIC CASE FILING ACCOUNT REGISTRATION FORM
APPENDIX E	ELECTRONIC CASE FILING TRAINING REGISTRATION
APPENDIX F	DESIGNATION FORM
APPENDIX G	DISCLOSURE STATEMENT FORM
APPENDIX H	CIVIL COVER SHEET
APPENDIX I	CIVIL CASE MANAGEMENT TRACK DESIGNATION FORM
APPENDIX J	MODIFICATION OR REDACTION OF PERSONAL IDENTIFIERS, LOCAL RULE 5.1.3
APPENDIX K	CONSENT TO FACSIMILE TRANSMISSION OF NOTICES OF ORDERS
APPENDIX L	MAIL INFORMATION FORM
APPENDIX M	JUDGES' ROOM NUMBERS AND ZIP CODE + 4-DIGIT EXTENSION NUMBERS
APPENDIX N	SUMMONS IN A CIVIL ACTION
APPENDIX O	WRIT OF EXECUTION
APPENDIX P	APPELLATE TRANSCRIPT PURCHASE ORDER
APPENDIX Q	CONSENT TO PROCEED BEFORE A UNITED STATES MAGISTRATE JUDGE
APPENDIX R	BILL OF COSTS
APPENDIX S	SPECIAL LISTING AGREEMENT
APPENDIX T	BUSY SLIP
APPENDIX U	STANDING ORDER RE: SENTENCING REFORM ACT OF 1984
APPENDIX V	CREDIT CARD COLLECTION NETWORK AUTHORIZATION FORM
APPENDIX W	BAIL BOND SECURED BY PROPERTY OR REAL ESTATE BOND
APPENDIX X	ATTORNEY ADMISSIONS APPLICATION
APPENDIX Y	TRANSCRIPT ORDER FORM
APPENDIX Z	TAPE ORDER FORM
APPENDIX AA	AMENDMENT TO LOCAL RULE 5.1.2 AND NOTICE OF ELECTRONIC AVAILABILITY OF TRANSCRIPTS
APPENDIX BB	DIGITAL AUDIO FILE ELECTRONIC ACCESS PILOT PROGRAM

---

1. [Note: Appendices are reproduced at page 617 of this book and are available online at http://www.paed.uscourts.gov/us03005.asp.]

Clerk's Office Procedural Handbook

APPENDIX CC . . . . **PACER** - PUBLIC ACCESS TO COURT ELECTRONIC RECORDS REGISTRATION FORM
APPENDIX DD . . . . DIRECTORY OF COURT-AUTOMATED SERVICES
APPENDIX EE . . . . ELECTRONIC CASE FILING ELECTRONIC FILING OF COMPLAINTS INFORMATION FORM

INDEX

Admissions, SEE ATTORNEY ADMISSIONS
After-Hours Contact for Emergency Matters, 594
After-Hours Filing Depository, 594
Amended Complaint (Filing an), 536
Appeals, SEE NOTICE OF APPEAL
Appendices (List of), 613
Arbitration, 546
Attachments for Trial, 591
Attorney Admissions, 598

Bail Bonds, 597
Busy Slips, 591

Case Management Track Designation Form, 536
Case Number (How to Find a), 594
Cause of Action, 535, 535
Cell Phones, 602
Central Violations Bureau (CVB), 597
Certificate of Service, 538
Certification of Judgment (AO 451), 548
Civil Action (Procedure for Filing), 532
Civil Category, 534
Civil Cover Sheet, 534
Civil Justice Expense
    and Delay Reduction Plan, 533
Class Action Complaints, 536
Clerk's Index File by Nature of Suit, 595
Complaints,
    Amended, 536
    Class Action, 536
    Copies of, 536
    Filing, 532
    Third-Party, 539
Copies of Paper Documents (Number of), 538
Copywork, 595
Continuances, 591
Court Reporting/Recording Services, 598
Courtroom Deputy Clerks, 589, 592
Credit Card Collection Network, 595

Default Judgment, 545
Demand for Trial De Novo, 547
Depositing/Withdrawing Monies, 596
Designation Form, 533
Digital Audio File Electronic Access, 599
Directory,
    Personnel, Office of the Clerk of Court, 604
    Public Telephone Locations, 602
Disclosure Statement, 533
Discovery, 544
Documents, 537

ECF (Electronic Case Filing), 529
ECF Password, 531
ECF Registration, 531
ECF Training, 532
Electronic Case Filing (ECF), 529
Electronic Sound Recording, 599
Electronic Transcripts, 598
Emergency Matters, After-Hours Contact, 594
Excluded Cases and Documents, 540
Excluded Personal Identifiers, 539
Excuse from Jury Service on Request, 600
Exhibits, 591

Facsimile Transmission of Notices of Orders and
    Judgments, 540
False Claims Act Cases, 540
Fees,
    Attorney Admission, 598
    Certificate of Admission, Duplicate, 598
    Certificate of Good Standing, Duplicate, 598
    Civil Action, 532
    Federal Records Center, 594, 595
    Foreign Subpoenas, 544
    Name Search, 594
    Notice of Appeal, 548
    PACER access, 601
    Witness, 543, 544
File Room, SEE RECORDS ROOM
Filing,
    Amended Complaint, 536
    Civil Action, 532
    Default, 545
    Subpoenas, 543, 544
Fines, 597
Foreign Subpoenas, 544

Index to Civil Actions by Subject, 595
Internet Website, 601
Interpreters' Services, 599

Judgment by Default, 545
Judicial Opinions, 594, 601
Jurisdiction, 542
Jury Selection, 600
Jury Service (Term of), 600
JUST-ASK (Judicial Schedule of Trials -
    Automated System Inquiry), 590

Kiosk, 591

Lobby Kiosk Information System, 591
Local Rules, 602

615

Locate a Case Number, 594

Mail, 541
MDL (Multidistrict Litigation), 545
Motions, 542, 591
Multidistrict Litigation (MDL), 545

Nature of Suit, 534
Notice of Appeal, 547

Opinions/Correspondence, 594

PACER - Public Access to Court Electronic
  Records, 600
Patent,
  "Little Tucker Act" Cases, 547
PDF (Portable Document Format), 529
Personal Identifiers, Excluded, 539
Pleadings, 540
Portable Document Format (**PDF**), 529
Post Judgment Interest Rate, 549
Pretrial Practices, 589
Privacy, Electronic Case File, 539
Privacy Act, 596

Records Room, 595
Referral to U.S. Magistrate Judge, 548
Registration,
    ECF Filing User, 531
    Excuse From, 530
Registry Fund, Deposit Fund, Interest-Bearing
    Accounts, 596
Related Cases, 533

Scheduling Cases, 589
Sealed Pleadings, 539
Sentencing Reform Act of 1984, 594
Service of Process, 537
Signature (ECF), 531
Social Security (Explanatory Information), 535
Special Listing, 589
Special Management Case, 536
Subpoenas, 543, 544
    Foreign, 544
Summons, 542

Taxation of Costs, 549
    Allowable District Court Costs, 549
    Burden of Proof re: Normally Allowable
        Costs, 552
    General Objections, 553
    Normally Unallowable District Court
        Costs, 551
    Specific Objections, 557
    Special Procedures, 563
    Taxation of Appellate Court Costs, 563
Telephone (Public, Directory of Locations), 602

Temporary Restraining Order (T.R.O.), 545
Third-Party Complaint, 539
Transcripts Order, 598
Transcripts, Electronic, 598
Trial De Novo Demand, 547
Trial List (Publication of), 590
Trial Pool, 589
T.R.O. (Temporary Restraining Order), 545

Validation of Signature (ECF), 531
Verifications, 536
Video Teleconferencing, 599
Videotape Services, 599

Waiver of Service, 537
Weather (Inclement), 600
Website, 601
Writs of Garnishment, Attachment and
    Execution, 545

Rule 5.1.2 Electronic Case Filing - All cases and documents filed in this court are required to be filed on the Electronic Case Filing ("ECF") System in accordance with provisions of the *Electronic Case Filing ("ECF") Procedures,* as set forth below unless excepted under these procedures.

Rule 5.1.2 Electronic Case Filing ("ECF") Procedures

1. **Definitions**

    (a) "ECF Filing User" means those who have Court-issued log-ins and passwords to file documents electronically.

    (b) "Notice of Electronic Case Filing" means the notice generated by the ECF system when a document has been filed electronically, stating that the document has been filed.

    (c) "Judge" means the District Judge assigned to the case, or the Magistrate Judge to whom all or any part of a case has been referred pursuant to 28 U.S.C. § 636.

    (d) "Court" shall mean the United States District Court for the Eastern District of Pennsylvania.

2. **Scope of Electronic Case Filing**

    (a) All civil and criminal cases filed in this court are required to be entered into the court's Electronic Case Filing ("ECF") System in accordance with these Electronic Case Filing ("ECF") Procedures. Unless an attorney is excused from ECF registration under Section 3 of these ECF Procedures or except as expressly provided in Section 16 and other sections of these ECF Procedures, or as ordered by the judge, all pleadings, documents, motions, memoranda of law, petitions, certificates of service and other documents required to be filed with the clerk of court in connection with a case must be electronically filed.

    (b) The filing of all initial papers in civil cases, such as the complaint and the issuance and service of the summons, and, in criminal cases, the indictment or information, warrant for arrest or summons, will be accomplished by paper copy filed in the traditional manner rather than electronically. Parties must concurrently provide the clerk of court with a computer disk, in PDF format containing a copy of all documents provided in paper form at the time of filing. All subsequent documents and pleadings must be filed electronically, except as provided in these ECF Procedures or as ordered by the judge. Under this paragraph, all attorneys are required to complete the ECF Validation of Signature form, as described in Section 3(c) below.

    (c) Once registered, an ECF Filing User may request to withdraw from participation in the ECF System by providing the clerk of court with written notice of the request which shall be forwarded to the Chief Judge for approval.

    (d) Nothing in these ECF Procedures shall be construed to nullify or contradict the provisions set forth in Rule 26.1 of the Local Rules of Civil Procedure, *Discovery,* directing that interrogatories, requests for production and inspection and requests for admission under Fed. R.Civ.P. 33, 34 and 36 that answers, responses and objections to interrogatories and to Rules 34 and 36, and that requests, notices of depositions and depositions under Fed.R.Civ.P. 30 and 31, shall not be filed with the court.

    (e) Nothing in these ECF Procedures shall be construed to nullify or contradict the provisions set forth in Rule 39.3 of the Local Rules of Civil Procedure, *Records, Files and Exhibits,* directing that the clerk of court maintain custody of all records, files and exhibits in all cases filed in this court until such time as the case is finally resolved, dismissed or abandoned, as set forth in paragraph (e) of Rule 39.3.

    (f) All cases filed in the ECF System in which a notice of appeal is filed shall be governed by Rule 10 of the Federal Rules of Appellate Procedure and relevant Local Rules and internal operating pro-

Clerk's Office Procedural Handbook

cedures of the United States Court of Appeals for the Third Circuit, with any differences about whether the record truly discloses what occurred in the district court to be submitted to and settled by the judge. Cases in which there is a right of direct appeal to the United States Supreme Court shall be governed by the rules of the United States Supreme Court.

3. **Excuse From Registration; Format of Documents in Electronic Form**

   An attorney who believes he or she should be excused from registering as an ECF Filing User may apply for an exception to this rule by detailed letter to the clerk of court, who shall forward the letter to the chief judge for decision. Thereafter, attorneys and others who are excused from registering as ECF Filing Users in accordance with this section are required to comply with the procedures set forth below.

   (a) All complaints must be submitted on disk in portable document format (PDF) at the time of filing, so that the complaint may be entered into the District Court's ECF system, and must be accompanied by a courtesy copy of the complaint in paper format for use by the court; under this paragraph, all attorneys are required to complete the ECF Validation of Signature form, as described in Paragraph (c) below.

   (b) All documents filed by an attorney who has been excused from registering as an ECF Filing User, as defined under this rule, must be submitted on disk in PDF, so that the filings may be entered into the District Court's ECF system, and must be accompanied by a courtesy copy of the document in paper format for use by the court; under this paragraph, all attorneys are required to complete the ECF Validation of Signature form, as described in Paragraph (c) below.

   (c) Attorneys who complete the ECF Validation of Signature form will receive a signature code which must be used by the attorney on the signature line of all courtesy copies submitted with a disk for purposes of signature validation pursuant to Rule 11 of the Federal Rules of Civil Procedure; the document as submitted under Section 3 of this rule will constitute the original document, except for those documents which are excluded from the provisions of rule as set forth in Section 16 of the rule; attorneys are required to have submitted a completed ECF Validation of Signature form just once in order to file all complaints and documents in all subsequent cases in this court.

   (d) Service of process will continue to be made in accordance with those provisions set forth in Rule 5 of the Federal Rules of Civil Procedure.

   (e) For convenience of attorneys who do not have access to compatible hardware or software, a computer with PDF conversion capability is available in the Clerk's Offices at Philadelphia and Allentown, with assistance for PDF conversion provided by Clerk's Office staff as needed; attorneys who have reason for not providing this material on disk are required to notice the Clerk's Office in writing attached to the document, explaining the reason for not providing this material on disk.

   (f) Attorneys who have been excused under this section from registering as ECF Filing Users are requested to register and participate in the court's Program for Facsimile Service of Notice to Counsel or Litigants in Civil and Criminal Cases (the "Fax Noticing Program").

   (g) Those documents and categories of cases which are now excluded from the provisions of this section consistent with the policy of the Judicial Conference of the United States, as may be amended from time to time, are set forth in Section 16 of this rule.

4. **Eligibility, Registration and Password**

   (a) Unless otherwise excused, attorneys admitted to the bar of this court, including those admitted pro hac vice, are required to register as ECF Filing Users of the court's ECF system. Registration is in a form prescribed by the clerk of court and requires the Filing User's name, address, telephone number, Internet e-mail address and a declaration that the attorney is admitted to the bar of this court and is a member in good standing.

   (b) Upon the approval of the judge, a party to a case who is not represented by an attorney may register as an ECF Filing User in the ECF System solely for purposes of the action. Registration is in

Appendix A

a form prescribed by the clerk of court and requires identification of the case as well as the name, address, telephone number and Internet e-mail address of the party. If, during the course of the case, the party retains an attorney who appears on the party's behalf, the attorney must advise the clerk of court to terminate the party's registration as a Filing User upon the attorney's appearance.

(c) Registration as an ECF Filing User constitutes agreement to receive and consent to make electronic service of all documents as provided in these ECF Procedures in accordance with Rule 5(b)(2)(D) of the Federal Rules of Civil Procedure and the Federal Rules of Criminal Procedure, as referenced in Rule 49(b) of the Federal Rules of Criminal Procedure. This agreement and consent is applicable to all future cases until revoked by the ECF Filing User.

(d) Once registration is completed, the ECF Filing User will receive notification of the user log-in and password. ECF Filing Users agree to protect the security of their passwords and immediately notify the clerk of court by telephone, with said notification confirmed immediately thereafter in writing delivered by e-mail, facsimile or hand-delivery to the attention of the clerk of court, if they learn that their password has been compromised. Users may be subject to sanctions by the judge for failure to comply with this provision. For security reasons, the court recommends that ECF Filing Users periodically change their passwords, which shall be done by notifying the clerk of the court who shall implement the change.

5. **Consequences of Electronic Filing**

    (a) Electronic transmission of a document to the ECF System consistent with these ECF Procedures, together with the transmission of a notice of electronic case filing from the court, constitutes filing of the document for all purposes of the Federal Rules of Civil Procedure, the Federal Rules of Criminal Procedure and the Local Rules of this court, and constitutes entry of the document on the docket maintained by the clerk of court pursuant to Rules 58 and 79 of the Federal Rules of Civil Procedure and Rules 49 and 55 of the Federal Rules of Criminal Procedure.

    (b) A document that has been filed electronically is the official record of the document, and the filing party is bound by the document as filed. Except in the case of documents first filed in paper form and subsequently submitted electronically under Section 2 above, a document filed electronically is deemed filed at the time and date stated on the notice of electronic case filing from the court.

    (c) Filing a document electronically does not change any filing deadline set by the Federal Rules of Civil Procedure, the Federal Rules of Criminal Procedure, the Local Rules of the court, or an order of the judge.

    (d) All pleadings and documents filed electronically must be transmitted in the form prescribed by Rule 10(a) of the Federal Rules of Civil Procedure. All transmissions for electronic case filings of pleadings and documents to the ECF system shall be titled in accordance with the approved directory of civil and criminal events of the ECF system.

6. **Attachments and Exhibits**

    ECF Filing Users may submit all documents identified as exhibits or attachments in either paper copy filed in the traditional manner or electronic form. If using electronic form, an ECF Filing User must submit as exhibits or attachments only those excerpts of the identified documents that are relevant to the matter under consideration by the court. Excerpted material must be clearly and prominently identified as such. ECF Filing Users who file excerpts of documents as exhibits or attachments electronically pursuant to these ECF Procedures do so without prejudice to their right to file timely additional excerpts or the complete document, provided however, that the total number of pages of attachments and exhibits electronically filed shall not exceed 50 without prior approval of the judge. Pages of attachments and exhibits in excess of 50 may be filed in paper copy filed in the traditional manner. Responding parties who choose to file exhibits and attachments electronically may also timely file additional excerpts or the complete document, subject to the same page limitations as set forth above.

Clerk's Office Procedural Handbook

7. Sealed Documents

Documents ordered to be placed under seal must be filed in paper copy filed in the traditional manner and not electronically. A motion to file documents under seal may be filed electronically unless prohibited by law. The order of the court authorizing the filing of documents under seal may be filed electronically unless prohibited by law. A paper copy of the order must be attached to the documents under seal and be delivered to the clerk of court.

8. Service of Documents by Electronic Means

(a) When an ECF Filing User electronically files a pleading or other document using the ECF system, a Notice of Electronic Case Filing shall automatically be generated by the system, and shall be sent automatically to all parties entitled to service under the Federal Rules of Civil Procedure, the Federal Rules of Criminal Procedure and the Local Rules of the Eastern District of Pennsylvania who have consented to electronic service. Electronic service of the Notice of Electronic Case Filing constitutes service of the filed document to all such parties and shall be deemed to satisfy the requirements of Rule 5(b)(2)(D) of the Federal Rules of Civil Procedure and Rule 49 of the Federal Rules of Criminal Procedure.

(b) All documents filed using the ECF system shall contain a Certificate of Service stating that the document has been filed electronically and is available for viewing and downloading from the ECF system. The Certificate of Service must identify the manner in which service on each party was accomplished, including any party who has not consented to electronic service.

(c) Parties who have not consented to electronic service are entitled to receive a paper copy of any electronically filed pleading or other document. Service of such paper copy must be made according to the Federal Rules of Civil Procedure, the Federal Rules of Criminal Procedure and the Local Rules of the Eastern District of Pennsylvania.

(d) As set forth in Section 4 of these ECF Procedures, registration as an ECF Filing User constitutes agreement to receive and consent to make electronic service of all documents as provided in these ECF Procedures in accordance with Rule 5(b)(2)(D) of the Federal Rules of Civil Procedure and Rule 49 of the Federal Rules of Criminal Procedure. This agreement and consent is applicable to all pending and future actions assigned to the ECF System until revoked by the ECF Filing User.

(e) In accordance with Rule 6(d) of the Federal Rules of Civil Procedure, service by electronic means is treated the same as service by mail for the purpose of adding three (3) days to the prescribed period to respond.

(f) In accordance with Rule 77(d) of the Federal Rules of Civil Procedure, the court may serve notice of entry of orders or judgments by electronic means as provided in Rule 5(b) and Section 4 of this Procedural Order.

(g) In civil cases, the provisions of this Section 8 apply to service of documents covered by Rule 5(a) of the Federal Rules of Civil Procedure. Service of Original Process under Rule 4 of the Federal Rules of Civil Procedure is not authorized under these ECF Procedures to be accomplished electronically. This Section 8 does not apply to service of an arrest warrant, summons or subpoena in criminal cases.

9. Signature

(a) The user log-in and password required to submit documents to the ECF System serve as the ECF Filing User's signature on all electronic documents filed with the court. They also serve as a signature for purposes of Rule 11(a) of the Federal Rules of Civil Procedure, the Local Rules of this court, and any other purpose for which a signature is required in connection with proceedings before the court. Each document filed electronically must, if possible, indicate that it has been electronically filed. Electronically filed documents must include a signature block and must set forth the name, address, telephone number and the attorney's state bar identification number, if applicable. In addition,

Appendix A

the name of the ECF Filing User under whose log-in and password the document is submitted must be preceded by an "s/" and typed in the space where the signature would otherwise appear.

(b) No ECF Filing User or other person may knowingly permit or cause to permit a Filing User's password to be used by anyone other than an authorized agent of the Filing User.

(c) Documents requiring signatures of more than one party must be electronically filed either by: (1) submitting a scanned document containing all necessary signatures; (2) representing the consent of the other parties on the document; (3) identifying on the document the parties whose signatures are required and by the submission of a notice of endorsement by the other parties no later than seven (7) days after filing; or (4) any other manner approved by the court.

10. Submission of Stipulations and Proposed Orders

An ECF Filing User electronically submitting stipulations or proposed orders which may require a judge's signature must promptly deliver on computer disk or e-mail the stipulation or proposed order to the clerk of court for delivery to the judge unless the judge orders otherwise. An ECF Filing User who electronically submits a stipulation or proposed order is bound by all signature requirements set forth in Section 9 of these ECF Procedures and Rule 11(a) of the Federal Rules of Civil Procedure.

11. Retention Requirements

Documents that are electronically filed and require original signatures other than that of the Filing User must be maintained in paper form by the ECF Filing User until three (3) years after the time period for appeal expires. The ECF Filing User must provide original documents for review upon request of the judge.

12. Public Access

(a) Any person or organization, other than one registered as an ECF Filing User under Section 4 of these rules, may access the ECF Filing System at the court's Internet site, www.paed.uscourts.gov, by obtaining a PACER log-in and password. Those who have PACER access but who are not Filing Users may retrieve docket sheets and those documents which the court makes available on the Internet for the fee normally charged for this service as set by the fee schedule authorized by the Administrative Office of United States Courts, but they may not file documents.

(b) Documents should be made available electronically to the same extent that they are available for personal inspection in the office of the clerk of court at the U.S. Courthouse. Social Security numbers, dates of birth, financial account numbers and names of minor children should be modified or partially redacted in electronically filed documents.

(c) In connection with the electronic filing of any material, any person may apply by motion for an order limiting electronic access to, or prohibiting the electronic filing of, certain specifically identified materials on the grounds that such material is subject to privacy interests and that electronic access or electronic filing in the action is likely to prejudice those privacy interests. In further protection of privacy, reference is made to the provisions of Rule 5.1.3 of the Local Rules of Civil Procedure, *Excluded Personal Identifiers,* mandating the modification or redaction of such personal identifiers as Social Security numbers, dates of birth, financial account numbers and names of minor children in all documents filed either in traditional paper form or electronically.

13. Entry of Court Order

All orders, decrees, judgments and proceedings of the court will be filed in accordance with these rules which will constitute entry on the docket maintained by the clerk of court pursuant to Fed.R.Civ.P. 58 and 79, and Rules 49 and 55 of the Federal Rules of Criminal Procedure. All signed orders will be filed electronically by the clerk of court. Any order filed electronically without the original signature of a judge has the same force and effect as if the judge had affixed the judge's signature to a paper copy of the order and it had been entered on the docket in paper copy filed in the traditional manner.

14. Notice of Court Order and Judgment

Immediately upon the entry of an order or judgment, the clerk of court will transmit to ECF Filing Users in the case, in electronic form, a notice of electronic filing. Electronic transmission of the Notice of Electronic Case Filing constitutes the notice required by Rule 77(d) of the Federal Rules of Civil Procedure and Rule 49(c) of the Federal Rules of Criminal Procedure. In accordance with the Federal Rules of Civil Procedure, the clerk of court must give notice in paper form to a person who has been excused under Section 3 of Local Rule 5.1.2 from registering as ECF Filing User.

15. Technical Failure

An ECF Filing User whose filing is determined to be untimely as the result of a technical failure may seek appropriate relief from the judge, provided that the User immediately notifies the clerk of court of the technical failure by telephone, with said notification confirmed immediately thereafter in writing delivered by e-mail, facsimile or by hand to the attention of the clerk of court. The clerk of the court shall forthwith notify the chambers of the judge.

16. Categories of Cases and Types of Documents in Civil and Criminal Cases Excluded from Electronic Case Filing

As provided in Section 2(b) above, all initial papers in civil and criminal cases, including the complaint, amended complaint, third-party complaint, notice of removal, the issuance and service of the summons, and the indictment and information in criminal cases, cannot be electronically filed on the court's CM/ECF system, but must be filed on paper accompanied by a copy of the document on disk in PDF format. Additionally, the following types of documents and categories of cases, as may be amended from time to time, can neither be electronically filed on the court's CM/ECF system nor submitted on disk in PDF format by an attorney excused from participation from ECF pursuant to Section 3 of these procedures, but must be filed in paper copy filed in the traditional manner, consistent with the policy of the Judicial Conference of the United States:

A. EXCLUDED CASES

1. Grand jury matters
2. Qui tam cases
3. Sealed cases

B. EXCLUDED DOCUMENTS

CIVIL CASES

1. Administrative records.
2. All documents filed by prisoners and pro se litigants, including the initial complaint and initial habeas corpus petitions, and death penalty habeas corpus petitions.
3. Bankruptcy appeal records.
4. Sealed documents.
5. State court records.
6. Transcript of civil proceedings shall be placed on CM/ECF or PACER, unless the presiding judge otherwise directs.
7. Discovery material, as set forth in Rule 26.1 of the Local Rules of Civil Procedure, *Discovery*, including:

    a) interrogatories, requests for production and inspection and requests for admission under Rules 33, 34 and 36 of the Federal Rules of Civil Procedure;

    b) answers, responses and objections to interrogatories and to Rules 34 and 36 of the Federal Rules of Civil Procedure;

    c) requests, notices of depositions and depositions under Rules 30 and 31 of the Federal Rules of Civil Procedure.

Appendix A

8. Praecipe for Writ of Execution.
9. Applications for Writ of Continuing Garnishment.
10. Praecipe to Issue Writ of Revival.
11. Praecipe for Writ of Seizure.
12. Praecipe for Writ to Restore.
13. Civil Jury Verdict Sheets.
14. Civil Minute Sheets.
15. Ex Parte Motions.

CRIMINAL CASES

1. Sealed documents.
2. Transcript of criminal proceedings shall not be placed on CM/ECF or PACER, unless the presiding judge otherwise directs after giving the prosecution and defense counsel an opportunity to be heard.
3. All documents requiring the signature of a defendant in a criminal or magistrate proceeding, such as wavier of indictment, waiver of presentence report, waiver of a jury trial, plea agreement, appearance bond, affidavit, and financial affidavit.
4. Criminal Jury Verdict Sheets.
5. Presentence Reports and any objections or other documents filed related to the Presentence Reports.
6. Criminal Minute Sheets.
7. Judgment and Commitment Orders.
8. Ex parte Motions.

What is a PDF file?

Portable Document Format (PDF) is a universal file format that preserves all fonts, formats, graphics and other typesetting attributes of a source (original) document, regardless of what application was used to create the source document. PDF files are most easily viewed using *Adobe Acrobat Reader®*, which is a free download available from www.adobe.com.

Why Convert Word and WordPerfect Documents to a PDF File?

PDF files are compact and are easily and quickly transmitted via the Web or through electronic mail. Although PDF files can be shared, viewed, navigated and printed, PDF files cannot be edited or altered by the recipient, thus preserving the integrity of the source document.

You must convert all of your documents to PDF format before submitting the documents to the District Clerk's Office through the Electronic Case Filing (ECF) system.

How Do You Convert a Word Processing Document to a PDF File?

1. **WordPerfect 9 or later versions:**

    WordPerfect 9 and later versions have a built-in capability to convert any document to a PDF file:
    1. Open the source document in WordPerfect.
    2. While the source document is on the screen, choose **FILE** from the menu bar.
    3. From the drop-down **FILE** menu, select **PUBLISH TO PDF.**
    4. To save the source document as a PDF file, type the document name where prompted in the PDF window. To save the PDF file to a floppy disk, place floppy disk in appropriate hardware slot, and type **A:*[document name]* in the "Publish To PDF" pop-up window. Press **"OK".**

    The source document is now saved in PDF format either on the hard drive or on a floppy disk.

2. **All other WordPerfect versions, MS Word, or other Applications:**

    To convert a source document from an application other than WordPerfect 9, Adobe Acrobat 5.0® (which contains a "writer" function) must be installed on your computer. Adobe Acrobat 5.0® is available for purchase from www.adobe.com.
    1. Open the source document.
    2. From the menu bar, select **PRINT.**
    3. In the "Printer" window, select **CURRENT PRINTER.**
    4. At the drop-down menu in the **CURRENT PRINTER** window, select **ACROBAT DISTILLER.**
    5. Press "OK" to print the file to your hard drive or floppy disk, instead of to the printer.
    6. After you press "OK", verify that the *SAVED FILE TYPE* is **PDF,** and press the **SAVE** button.

Appendix B

UNITED STATES DISTRICT COURT
EASTERN DISTRICT OF PENNSYLVANIA

OFFICE OF THE CLERK OF COURT

Rule 5.1.2 of the Local Rules of Civil Procedure
Electronic Case Filing

Validation of Signature Form

Pursuant to Rule 5.1.2, Electronic Case Filing, all attorneys who have been excused from registering as an ECF Filing User, as defined in the ECF Procedures set forth in Rule 5.1.2, are required to complete this *Validation of Signature* form validating his or her signature for submission of filings on disk in portable document format (PDF), so that the filings may be entered into the District Court's ECF system. The document on disk must be accompanied by a courtesy copy of the document in paper format for use by the court. Attorneys who complete this form will receive a signature code which must be used by the attorney on the signature line of all courtesy copies submitted with a disk. The document as submitted on the disk will constitute the original document under Section 3 of Local Civil Rule 5.1.2.

(Please Print or Type)

First Name: _____ Middle Initial/Name: _____

Last Name: _____ Generation (i.e., Sr., Jr.) _____

Firm: _____ Bar Id No. and State: _____

Address: _____

Address: _____

City: _____ State: _____ Zip Code _____

Telephone No: (___) _____ FAX No: (___) _____

E-mail Address: _____

Are you admitted to practice in the Eastern District of Pennsylvania?
☐ Yes   ☐ No

If yes, are you a member in good standing?
☐ Yes   ☐ No

Are you admitted to practice pro hac vice in the Eastern District of Pennsylvania?
☐ Yes   ☐ No

Are you registered as an ECF Filing User in the Eastern District of Pennsylvania?
☐ Yes   ☐ No

If no, would you like to also register as an ECF Filing User in the Eastern District of Pennsylvania?
☐ Yes   ☐ No

By submitting this registration form, the undersigned agrees/consents to the following:

1. I have read and understood the provisions of Rule 5.1.2 of the Local Rules of Civil Procedure, *Electronic Case Filing,* and the court's *ECF Procedures* set forth in Rule 5.1.2, and I agree to abide by all provisions set forth therein.

2. I agree that this form constitutes my signature for filings which must be submitted on disk in portable document format (PDF), as required by Section 3 of Rule 5.1.2, *Electronic Case Filing.* I

Appendix C

understand that I will be provided with a signature code which I must use on the signature line of all courtesy copies submitted with a disk. I have read and understood the provisions of Rule 11 of the Federal Rules of Civil Procedure, and I agree that my signature code used on the signature line of all courtesy copies submitted with a disk will serve as my signature for purposes of Rule 11. I further understand that the document as submitted on the disk will constitute the original document under Section 3 of Local Civil Rule 5.1.2.

3. I understand and agree that service of process will be made in accordance with those provisions set forth in Rule 5 of the Federal Rules of Civil Procedure.

I hereby certify that the above information is true and correct and I am a member in good standing of the United States District Court for the Eastern District of Pennsylvania.

_____ _____
                Signature   Date

Please return completed form by U.S. Mail to: Michael E. Kunz
U.S. District Court
2609 U.S. Courthouse
601 Market Street
Philadelphia, PA 19106-1797

DOCUMENTS
Forms

Download

ECF Registration/Notification Forms

To complete and submit an Electronic Case Filing (ECF) Account Registration Form and Notification of Case Activity Request Form, perform the following four (4) steps.

Step #1: Download the forms using your browser. The Electronic Case Filing (ECF) Account Registration Form and Notification of Case Activity Request Form can be found here. The forms are interactive and allow most fields to be completed on-line.

Step #2: Depending upon your preference, either (a) complete the forms on-line and then print the forms, or (b) print the forms and then complete them manually (i.e., by typing or hand, in ink). Where applicable, please use print settings that allow the forms to be printed on three (3) pages with no loss of text due to font and/or margin settings.

Step #3: (Optional) To help expedite processing, the Electronic Case Filing (ECF) Account Registration Form and Notification of Case Activity Request Form can also be submitted on-line if desired. Click on the Submit Forms button, located at the bottom of the forms, to submit on-line. If you submit the forms in this fashion, you must then complete step 4 so that the court receives your signature.

Step #4: Sign the printed forms & mail them to:

Michael E. Kunz, Clerk of Court
United States District Court for the Eastern District of Pennsylvania
U.S. Courthouse
601 Market Street, Room 2609
Philadelphia, PA 19106-1797
ATTN: ECF

ECF Registration Form

ECF Notification Form

Appendix D

Clerk's Office Procedural Handbook

UNITED STATES DISTRICT COURT
EASTERN DISTRICT OF PENNSYLVANIA

Office of the Clerk of Court

Electronic Case Filing (ECF)
Account Registration Form

This Electronic Case Filing (ECF) Account Registration Form shall be used to register for an account with the U.S.D.C. for the Eastern District of Pennsylvania's Electronic Case Filing (ECF) system. ECF Registered attorneys will have privileges to electronically submit documents in accordance with Local Civil Rule 5.1.2 and Local Criminal Rule 1.2.

(Please Print or Type)

First Name: _____ Middle Initial/Name: _____

Last Name: _____ Generation (i.e., Sr., Jr.): _____

Firm: _____ Bar Id No. and State: _____

Address: _____

Address: _____

City: _____ State: _____ Zip Code: _____

Telephone No: _____ FAX No: _____

E-Mail Address: _____

Last 4 digits of your Social Security number (to be used for the log-in code): _____

Are you admitted to practice in the Eastern District of Pennsylvania?
☐ Yes   ☐ No

If yes, are you a member in good standing?
☐ Yes   ☐ No

Are you admitted to practice pro hac vice in the Eastern District of Pennsylvania?
☐ Yes   ☐ No

Are you a registered ECF Filer in another U.S. District or Bankruptcy Court?
☐ Yes   ☐ No

If yes, please provide the district in which you are a registered ECF User and the log-in and password if you would like to have the same log-in and password. (Passwords must be at least eight characters long, include both upper and lower case and at least one digit or special character.)

District: _____ Log-in: _____ Password: _____

3/2012

Appendix D

By submitting this account registration form, the undersigned agrees/consents to the following:

1. I have read and understood the provisions of Rule 5.1.2 of the Local Rules of Civil Procedure, "Electronic Case Filing," amended Rule 1.2 of the Local Rules of Criminal Procedure, "Applicability and Effect of Local Rules," and the court's ECF Procedures set forth in Rule 5.1.2, and I agree to abide by all provisions set forth therein.

2. I agree that the combination of the user log-in and password will serve as my signature for purposes of the Federal Rules of Civil and Criminal Procedure. I further agree to protect the security of my password and to immediately notify the clerk of court by telephone, with said notification confirmed immediately thereafter in writing delivered by e-mail, facsimile or hand-delivery to the attention of the clerk of court, as soon as I learn that my password may have been compromised.

3. In accordance with the provisions of Rule 5(b)(2)(D) of the Federal Rules of Civil Procedure and Section 8 of the ECF Procedures, I agree that service may be given to me by electronic transmission and I consent to make electronic service of all documents.

4. I have read and understood the provisions of Rule 11 of the Federal Rules of Civil Procedure, particularly as referenced in Sections 9 and 10 of the ECF Procedures, and I agree to abide by the provisions set forth therein.

5. I agree to waive the provisions of Rule 77(d) of the Federal Rules of Civil Procedure and Rule 49(c) of the Federal Rules of Criminal Procedure, providing for service of notice by mail, and I consent that such notice may be served by electronic transmission in accordance with Section 14 of the ECF Procedures.

6. All transmissions for electronic case filings of pleadings and documents to the ECF system shall be titled in accordance with the approved directory of civil and criminal events of the ECF system in a case in which an attorney is counsel of record or on any document which is construed as an entry of appearance in accordance with Local Civil Rule 5.1.

I hereby certify that the above information is true and correct and I am a member in good standing of the United States District Court for the Eastern District of Pennsylvania.

_____   _____
Signature   Date

Please return completed form by U.S. Mail to: Michael E. Kunz
U.S. District Court
2609 U.S. Courthouse
601 Market Street
Philadelphia, PA 19106-1797
Attn: ECF

You will be notified of your user log-in and password by electronic mail. If you have any questions on the ECF registration process or the use of the electronic filing system, you may contact the Electronic Filing Information Center toll-free at 1-866-ECF-4ECF.

**UNITED STATES DISTRICT COURT
EASTERN DISTRICT OF PENNSYLVANIA**

Electronic Case Filing (ECF)
Notification of Case Activity Request Form

As a registered Electronic Case Filing User, I am requesting that the following e-mail address(es) receive electronic notification of case activity on any case in which I have entered my appearance. I understand that the e-mail address(es) listed below will receive the electronic notification of case activity, in addition to the e-mail address that I listed on my ECF Registration Form.

(Please print or type the e-mail address(es))

E-Mail Address(es)
Maximum of 3

_____

_____

_____

_____   _____
Attorney Name (Printed)   Attorney Signature

_____   _____
Telephone No.   Date

If there are any future changes to the information listed above, an amended *Notification of Case Activity Request Form* must be submitted. If more than 3 e-mail addresses are required, please submit a request to the Clerk of Court.

Please return this completed form to: Michael E. Kunz, Clerk of Court, 601 Market Street, Room 2609, Philadelphia, PA 19106-1797, ATTN: ECF or FAX (215) 597-6390.

NOTICE

I am pleased to announce that the Clerk's Office for the United States District Court for the Eastern District of Pennsylvania will be conducting hands-on training sessions for Civil and Criminal on the Electronic Case Filing System (ECF). This training will be held at the United States Courthouse, 601 Market Street, Philadelphia, PA and is available to members of the bar, paralegals, secretaries and automation support staff.

CM/ECF will allow attorneys to file and view documents from their office, home or anywhere they have access to the Internet, 24 hours a day. Documents are automatically docketed as part of the filing process and are immediately available electronically. CM/ECF also provides the following benefits:

- 24-hour access to filed documents over the Internet
- Automatic email notice of case activity
- The ability to download and print documents directly from the court system
- Concurrent access to case files by multiple parties
- Secure storage of documents

If you are interested in attending a training session, please complete the attached registration form indicating three date preferences. The training sessions are held every Tuesday and Thursday at 10:30 am. The training sessions will last approximately two hours. You will be notified of the date you are scheduled for training.

Thank you for your interest in the ECF system and if you have any questions on the ECF system, please call the toll-free number 1-866-ECF-4ECF (1-866-323-4323).

Michael E. Kunz
Clerk of Court

Appendix E

**UNITED STATES DISTRICT COURT
EASTERN DISTRICT OF PENNSYLVANIA**

**Office of the Clerk of Court
ECF Training Registration**

Name: _____ Title: _____

Firm: _____

Address: _____

Address: _____

City: _____ State: _____ Zip Code: _____

Telephone: _____ Fax: _____

E-Mail Address: _____

1st Date Preference: _____ 10:30 am
2nd Date Preference: _____ 10:30 am
3rd Date Preference: _____ 10:30 am

Please FAX the completed form to (215) 597-6390

-or by e-mail to-

PAED_clerksoffice@paed.uscourts.gov

- or by mail to -

Office of the Clerk of Court
2609 United States Courthouse
601 Market Street
Philadelphia, PA 19106
Attn: ECF Training Registration Form

UNITED STATES DISTRICT COURT

FOR THE EASTERN DISTRICT OF PENNSYLVANIA — DESIGNATION FORM to be used by counsel to indicate the category of the case for the purpose of assignment to appropriate calendar.

Address of Plaintiff: _____

Address of Defendant: _____

Place of Accident, Incident or Transaction: _____
(Use Reverse Side For Additional Space)

Does this civil action involve a nongovernmental corporate party with any parent corporation and any publicly held corporation owning 10% or more of its stock?
(Attach two copies of the Disclosure Statement Form in accordance with Fed.R.Civ.P. 7.1(a)) Yes ☐ No ☐

Does this case involve multidistrict litigation possibilities? Yes ☐ No ☐

RELATED CASE, IF ANY:

Case Number: _____ Judge: _____ Date Terminated: _____

Civil cases are deemed related when yes is answered to any of the following questions:

1. Is this case related to property included in an earlier numbered suit pending or within one year previously terminated action in this court? Yes ☐ No ☐

2. Does this case involve the same issue of fact or grow out of the same transaction as a prior suit pending or within one year previously terminated action in this court? Yes ☐ No ☐

3. Does this case involve the validity or infringement of a patent already in suit or any earlier numbered case pending or within one year previously terminated action in this court? Yes ☐ No ☐

4. Is this case a second or successive habeas corpus, social security appeal, or pro se civil rights case filed by the same individual? Yes ☐ No ☐

CIVIL: (Place ✔ in ONE CATEGORY ONLY)

A. *Federal Question Cases:*

1. ☐ Indemnity Contract, Marine Contract, and All Other Contracts
2. ☐ FELA
3. ☐ Jones Act-Personal Injury
4. ☐ Antitrust
5. ☐ Patent
6. ☐ Labor-Management Relations
7. ☐ Civil Rights
8. ☐ Habeas Corpus
9. ☐ Securities Act(s) Cases
10. ☐ Social Security Review Cases
11. ☐ All other Federal Question Cases
    (Please specify) _____

B. *Diversity Jurisdiction Cases:*

1. ☐ Insurance Contract and Other Contracts
2. ☐ Airplane Personal Injury
3. ☐ Assault, Defamation
4. ☐ Marine Personal Injury
5. ☐ Motor Vehicle Personal Injury
6. ☐ Other Personal Injury (Please specify)
7. ☐ Products Liability
8. ☐ Products Liability — Asbestos
9. ☐ All other Diversity Cases
    (Please specify) _____

ARBITRATION CERTIFICATION
(Check Appropriate Category)

I, _____, counsel of record do hereby certify:

☐ Pursuant to Local Civil Rule 53.2, Section 3(c)(2), that to the best of my knowledge and belief, the damages recoverable in this civil action case exceed the sum of $150,000.00 exclusive of interest and costs;

☐ Relief other than monetary damages is sought.

DATE: _____ _____ _____
             Attorney-at-Law   Attorney I.D.#

NOTE: A trial de novo will be a trial by jury only if there has been compliance with F.R.C.P. 38.

I certify that, to my knowledge, the within case is not related to any case now pending or within one year previously terminated action in this court except as noted above.

DATE: _____ _____ _____
             Attorney-at-Law   Attorney I.D.#

CIV. 609 (5/2012)

Appendix F

UNITED STATES DISTRICT COURT
EASTERN DISTRICT OF PENNSYLVANIA

:
:
V.   :   Civil Action
                                :   No: _____
:

DISCLOSURE STATEMENT FORM

Please check one box:

☐ The nongovernmental corporate party, _____, in the above listed civil action does not have any parent corporation and publicly held corporation that owns 10% or more of its stock.

☐ The nongovernmental corporate party, _____, in the above listed civil action has the following parent corporation(s) and publicly held corporation(s) that owns 10% or more of its stock:

_____

_____

_____

_____

_____   _____
Date   Signature

                              Counsel for: _____

Federal Rule of Civil Procedure 7.1 Disclosure Statement

(a) WHO MUST FILE; CONTENTS. A nongovernmental corporate party must file two copies of a disclosure statement that:

 (1) identifies any parent corporation and any publicly held corporation owning 10% or more of its stock; or

 (2) states that there is no such corporation.

(b) TIME TO FILE; SUPPLEMENTAL FILING. A party must:

 (1) file the disclosure statement with its first appearance, pleading, petition, motion, response, or other request addressed to the court; and

 (2) promptly file a supplemental statement if any required information changes.

Appendix G

Appendix G

**UNITED STATES DISTRICT COURT
EASTERN DISTRICT OF PENNSYLVANIA**

USA : Criminal Action
:
v. :
:
: No.

DISCLOSURE STATEMENT FORM

Please check one box:

- ☐ The nongovernmental corporate party, _____, in the above listed criminal action does not have any parent corporation and publicly held corporation that owns 10% or more of its stock.

- ☐ The nongovernmental corporate party, _____, in the above listed criminal action has the following parent corporation(s) and publicly held corporation(s) that owns 10% or more of its stock:

_____

_____

_____

_____

_____   _____
Date   Signature

Counsel for: _____

Federal Rule of Criminal Procedure 12.4 Disclosure Statement

(a) WHO MUST FILE

    (1) NONGOVERNMENTAL CORPORATE PARTY. Any nongovernmental corporate party to a proceeding in a district court must file a statement that identifies any parent corporation and any publicly held corporation that owns 10% or more of its stock or states that there is no such corporation.

    (2) ORGANIZATIONAL VICTIM. If an organization is a victim of the alleged criminal activity, the government must file a statement identifying the victim. If the organizational victim is a corporation, the statement must also disclose the information required by Rule 12.4(a)(1) to the extent that it can be obtained through due diligence.

(b) TIME FOR FILING; SUPPLEMENTAL FILING. A party must:

    (1) file the Rule 12.4(a) statement upon the defendant's initial appearance; and

    (2) promptly file a supplemental statement upon any change in the information that the statement requires.

JS 44 (Rev. 12/12)

CIVIL COVER SHEET

The JS 44 civil cover sheet and the information contained herein neither replace nor supplement the filing and service of pleadings or other papers as required by law, except as provided by local rules of court. This form, approved by the Judicial Conference of the United States in September 1974, is required for the use of the Clerk of Court for the purpose of initiating the civil docket sheet. *(SEE INSTRUCTIONS ON NEXT PAGE OF THIS FORM.)*

I. (a) PLAINTIFFS

DEFENDANTS

(b) County of Residence of First Listed Plaintiff _____
(EXCEPT IN U.S. PLAINTIFF CASES)

County of Residence of First Listed Defendant _____
(IN U.S. PLAINTIFF CASES ONLY)
NOTE: IN LAND CONDEMNATION CASES, USE THE LOCATION OF THE TRACT OF LAND INVOLVED.

(c) Attorneys *(Firm Name, Address, and Telephone Number)*

Attorneys *(If Known)*

II. BASIS OF JURISDICTION *(Place an "X" in One Box Only)*

- ❏ 1 U.S. Government Plaintiff
- ❏ 2 U.S. Government Defendant
- ❏ 3 Federal Question *(U.S. Government Not a Party)*
- ❏ 4 Diversity *(Indicate Citizenship of Parties in Item III)*

III. CITIZENSHIP OF PRINCIPAL PARTIES *(Place an "X" in One Box for Plaintiff and One Box for Defendant)*
(For Diversity Cases Only)

	PTF	DEF		PTF	DEF
Citizen of This State	❏ 1	❏ 1	Incorporated *or* Principal Place of Business In This State	❏ 4	❏ 4
Citizen of Another State	❏ 2	❏ 2	Incorporated *and* Principal Place of Business In Another State	❏ 5	❏ 5
Citizen or Subject of a Foreign Country	❏ 3	❏ 3	Foreign Nation	❏ 6	❏ 6

IV. NATURE OF SUIT *(Place an "X" in One Box Only)*

CONTRACT	TORTS		FORFEITURE/PENALTY	BANKRUPTCY	OTHER STATUTES
❏ 110 Insurance	**PERSONAL INJURY**	**PERSONAL INJURY**	❏ 625 Drug Related Seizure of Property 21 USC 881	❏ 422 Appeal 28 USC 158	❏ 375 False Claims Act
❏ 120 Marine	❏ 310 Airplane	❏ 365 Personal Injury - Product Liability	❏ 690 Other	❏ 423 Withdrawal 28 USC 157	❏ 400 State Reapportionment
❏ 130 Miller Act	❏ 315 Airplane Product Liability	❏ 367 Health Care/ Pharmaceutical Personal Injury Product Liability			❏ 410 Antitrust
❏ 140 Negotiable Instrument				**PROPERTY RIGHTS**	❏ 430 Banks and Banking
❏ 150 Recovery of Overpayment & Enforcement of Judgment	❏ 320 Assault, Libel & Slander			❏ 820 Copyrights	❏ 450 Commerce
❏ 151 Medicare Act	❏ 330 Federal Employers' Liability	❏ 368 Asbestos Personal Injury Product Liability		❏ 830 Patent	❏ 460 Deportation
❏ 152 Recovery of Defaulted Student Loans (Excludes Veterans)	❏ 340 Marine			❏ 840 Trademark	❏ 470 Racketeer Influenced and Corrupt Organizations
❏ 153 Recovery of Overpayment of Veteran's Benefits	❏ 345 Marine Product Liability	**PERSONAL PROPERTY**	**LABOR**	**SOCIAL SECURITY**	❏ 480 Consumer Credit
❏ 160 Stockholders' Suits	❏ 350 Motor Vehicle	❏ 370 Other Fraud	❏ 710 Fair Labor Standards Act	❏ 861 HIA (1395ff)	❏ 490 Cable/Sat TV
❏ 190 Other Contract	❏ 355 Motor Vehicle Product Liability	❏ 371 Truth in Lending	❏ 720 Labor/Management Relations	❏ 862 Black Lung (923)	❏ 850 Securities/Commodities/ Exchange
❏ 195 Contract Product Liability	❏ 360 Other Personal Injury	❏ 380 Other Personal Property Damage	❏ 740 Railway Labor Act	❏ 863 DIWC/DIWW (405(g))	❏ 890 Other Statutory Actions
❏ 196 Franchise	❏ 362 Personal Injury - Medical Malpractice	❏ 385 Property Damage Product Liability	❏ 751 Family and Medical Leave Act	❏ 864 SSID Title XVI	❏ 891 Agricultural Acts
			❏ 790 Other Labor Litigation	❏ 865 RSI (405(g))	❏ 893 Environmental Matters
REAL PROPERTY	**CIVIL RIGHTS**	**PRISONER PETITIONS**	❏ 791 Employee Retirement Income Security Act	**FEDERAL TAX SUITS**	❏ 895 Freedom of Information Act
❏ 210 Land Condemnation	❏ 440 Other Civil Rights	**Habeas Corpus:**		❏ 870 Taxes (U.S. Plaintiff or Defendant)	❏ 896 Arbitration
❏ 220 Foreclosure	❏ 441 Voting	❏ 463 Alien Detainee		❏ 871 IRS—Third Party 26 USC 7609	❏ 899 Administrative Procedure Act/Review or Appeal of Agency Decision
❏ 230 Rent Lease & Ejectment	❏ 442 Employment	❏ 510 Motions to Vacate Sentence			❏ 950 Constitutionality of State Statutes
❏ 240 Torts to Land	❏ 443 Housing/ Accommodations	❏ 530 General			
❏ 245 Tort Product Liability	❏ 445 Amer. w/Disabilities - Employment	❏ 535 Death Penalty	**IMMIGRATION**		
❏ 290 All Other Real Property		**Other:**	❏ 462 Naturalization Application		
	❏ 446 Amer. w/Disabilities - Other	❏ 540 Mandamus & Other	❏ 465 Other Immigration Actions		
	❏ 448 Education	❏ 550 Civil Rights			
		❏ 555 Prison Condition			
		❏ 560 Civil Detainee - Conditions of Confinement			

V. ORIGIN *(Place an "X" in One Box Only)*

- ❏ 1 Original Proceeding
- ❏ 2 Removed from State Court
- ❏ 3 Remanded from Appellate Court
- ❏ 4 Reinstated or Reopened
- ❏ 5 Transferred from Another District *(specify)*
- ❏ 6 Multidistrict Litigation

VI. CAUSE OF ACTION

Cite the U.S. Civil Statute under which you are filing *(Do not cite jurisdictional statutes unless diversity)*:

Brief description of cause:

VII. REQUESTED IN COMPLAINT:

❏ CHECK IF THIS IS A **CLASS ACTION** UNDER RULE 23, F.R.Cv.P.

DEMAND $

CHECK YES only if demanded in complaint:
JURY DEMAND: ❏ Yes ❏ No

VIII. RELATED CASE(S) IF ANY

(See instructions):
JUDGE _____   DOCKET NUMBER _____

DATE _____   SIGNATURE OF ATTORNEY OF RECORD _____

FOR OFFICE USE ONLY

RECEIPT # _____   AMOUNT _____   APPLYING IFP _____   JUDGE _____   MAG. JUDGE _____

Appendix H

Appendix H

JS 44 Reverse (Rev. 12/12)

INSTRUCTIONS FOR ATTORNEYS COMPLETING CIVIL COVER SHEET FORM JS 44

Authority For Civil Cover Sheet

The JS 44 civil cover sheet and the information contained herein neither replaces nor supplements the filings and service of pleading or other papers as required by law, except as provided by local rules of court. This form, approved by the Judicial Conference of the United States in September 1974, is required for the use of the Clerk of Court for the purpose of initiating the civil docket sheet. Consequently, a civil cover sheet is submitted to the Clerk of Court for each civil complaint filed. The attorney filing a case should complete the form as follows:

I.(a) **Plaintiffs-Defendants.** Enter names (last, first, middle initial) of plaintiff and defendant. If the plaintiff or defendant is a government agency, use only the full name or standard abbreviations. If the plaintiff or defendant is an official within a government agency, identify first the agency and then the official, giving both name and title.

(b) **County of Residence.** For each civil case filed, except U.S. plaintiff cases, enter the name of the county where the first listed plaintiff resides at the time of filing. In U.S. plaintiff cases, enter the name of the county in which the first listed defendant resides at the time of filing. (NOTE: In land condemnation cases, the county of residence of the "defendant" is the location of the tract of land involved.)

(c) **Attorneys.** Enter the firm name, address, telephone number, and attorney of record. If there are several attorneys, list them on an attachment, noting in this section "(see attachment)".

II. **Jurisdiction.** The basis of jurisdiction is set forth under Rule 8(a), F.R.Cv.P., which requires that jurisdictions be shown in pleadings. Place an "X" in one of the boxes. If there is more than one basis of jurisdiction, precedence is given in the order shown below.
United States plaintiff. (1) Jurisdiction based on 28 U.S.C. 1345 and 1348. Suits by agencies and officers of the United States are included here.
United States defendant. (2) When the plaintiff is suing the United States, its officers or agencies, place an "X" in this box.
Federal question. (3) This refers to suits under 28 U.S.C. 1331, where jurisdiction arises under the Constitution of the United States, an amendment to the Constitution, an act of Congress or a treaty of the United States. In cases where the U.S. is a party, the U.S. plaintiff or defendant code takes precedence, and box 1 or 2 should be marked.
Diversity of citizenship. (4) This refers to suits under 28 U.S.C. 1332, where parties are citizens of different states. When Box 4 is checked, the citizenship of the different parties must be checked. (See Section III below; **NOTE: federal question actions take precedence over diversity cases.**)

III. **Residence (citizenship) of Principal Parties.** This section of the JS 44 is to be completed if diversity of citizenship was indicated above. Mark this section for each principal party.

IV. **Nature of Suit.** Place an "X" in the appropriate box. If the nature of suit cannot be determined, be sure the cause of action, in Section VI below, is sufficient to enable the deputy clerk or the statistical clerk(s) in the Administrative Office to determine the nature of suit. If the cause fits more than one nature of suit, select the most definitive.

V. **Origin.** Place an "X" in one of the six boxes.
Original Proceedings. (1) Cases which originate in the United States district courts.
Removed from State Court. (2) Proceedings initiated in state courts may be removed to the district courts under Title 28 U.S.C., Section 1441. When the petition for removal is granted, check this box.
Remanded from Appellate Court. (3) Check this box for cases remanded to the district court for further action. Use the date of remand as the filing date.
Reinstated or Reopened. (4) Check this box for cases reinstated or reopened in the district court. Use the reopening date as the filing date.
Transferred from Another District. (5) For cases transferred under Title 28 U.S.C. Section 1404(a). Do not use this for within district transfers or multidistrict litigation transfers.
Multidistrict Litigation. (6) Check this box when a multidistrict case is transferred into the district under authority of Title 28 U.S.C. Section 1407. When this box is checked, do not check (5) above.

VI. **Cause of Action.** Report the civil statute directly related to the cause of action and give a brief description of the cause. **Do not cite jurisdictional statutes unless diversity.** Example: U.S. Civil Statute: 47 USC 553 Brief Description: Unauthorized reception of cable service

VII. **Requested in Complaint.** Class Action. Place an "X" in this box if you are filing a class action under Rule 23, F.R.Cv.P.
Demand. In this space enter the actual dollar amount being demanded or indicate other demand, such as a preliminary injunction.
Jury Demand. Check the appropriate box to indicate whether or not a jury is being demanded.

VIII. **Related Cases.** This section of the JS 44 is used to reference related pending cases, if any. If there are related pending cases, insert the docket numbers and the corresponding judge names for such cases.

Date and Attorney Signature. Date and sign the civil cover sheet.

**IN THE UNITED STATES DISTRICT COURT
FOR THE EASTERN DISTRICT OF PENNSYLVANIA**

CASE MANAGEMENT TRACK DESIGNATION FORM

	:	CIVIL ACTION
v.	:	
	:	
	:	NO.

In accordance with the Civil Justice Expense and Delay Reduction Plan of this court, counsel for plaintiff shall complete a Case Management Track Designation Form in all civil cases at the time of filing the complaint and serve a copy on all defendants. (See § 1:03 of the plan set forth on the reverse side of this form.) In the event that a defendant does not agree with the plaintiff regarding said designation, that defendant shall, with its first appearance, submit to the clerk of court and serve on the plaintiff and all other parties, a Case Management Track Designation Form specifying the track to which that defendant believes the case should be assigned.

SELECT ONE OF THE FOLLOWING CASE MANAGEMENT TRACKS:

(a) Habeas Corpus – Cases brought under 28 U.S.C. § 2241 through § 2255. ( )

(b) Social Security – Cases requesting review of a decision of the Secretary of Health and Human Services denying plaintiff Social Security Benefits. ( )

(c) Arbitration – Cases required to be designated for arbitration under Local Civil Rule 53.2. ( )

(d) Asbestos – Cases involving claims for personal injury or property damage from exposure to asbestos. ( )

(e) Special Management – Cases that do not fall into tracks (a) through (d) that are commonly referred to as complex and that need special or intense management by the court. (See reverse side of this form for a detailed explanation of special management cases.) ( )

(f) Standard Management – Cases that do not fall into any one of the other tracks. ( )

_____   _____   _____
Date   **Attorney-at-law**   **Attorney for**

_____   _____   _____
Telephone   **FAX Number**   **E-Mail Address**

(Civ. 660) 10/02

Appendix I

Appendix I

Civil Justice Expense and Delay Reduction Plan
Section 1:03 - Assignment to a Management Track

(a) The clerk of court will assign cases to tracks (a) through (d) based on the initial pleading.

(b) In all cases not appropriate for assignment by the clerk of court to tracks (a) through (d), the plaintiff shall submit to the clerk of court and serve with the complaint on all defendants a case management track designation form specifying that the plaintiff believes the case requires Standard Management or Special Management. In the event that a defendant does not agree with the plaintiff regarding said designation, that defendant shall, with its first appearance, submit to the clerk of court and serve on the plaintiff and all other parties, a case management track designation form specifying the track to which that defendant believes the case should be assigned.

(c) The court may, on its own initiative or upon the request of any party, change the track assignment of any case at any time.

(d) Nothing in this Plan is intended to abrogate or limit a judicial officer's authority in any case pending before that judicial officer, to direct pretrial and trial proceedings that are more stringent than those of the Plan and that are designed to accomplish cost and delay reduction.

(e) Nothing in this Plan is intended to supersede Local Civil Rules 40.1 and 72.1, or the procedure for random assignment of Habeas Corpus and Social Security cases referred to magistrate judges of the court.

SPECIAL MANAGEMENT CASE ASSIGNMENTS
(See §1.02 (e) Management Track Definitions of the
Civil Justice Expense and Delay Reduction Plan)

Special Management cases will usually include that class of cases commonly referred to as "complex litigation" as that term has been used in the Manuals for Complex Litigation. The first manual was prepared in 1969 and the Manual for Complex Litigation Second, MCL 2d was prepared in 1985. This term is intended to include cases that present unusual problems and require extraordinary treatment. See §0.1 of the first manual. Cases may require special or intense management by the court due to one or more of the following factors: (1) large number of parties; (2) large number of claims or defenses; (3) complex factual issues; (4) large volume of evidence; (5) problems locating or preserving evidence; (6) extensive discovery; (7) exceptionally long time needed to prepare for disposition; (8) decision needed within an exceptionally short time; and (9) need to decide preliminary issues before final disposition. It may include two or more related cases. Complex litigation typically includes such cases as antitrust cases; cases involving a large number of parties or an unincorporated association of large membership; cases involving requests for injunctive relief affecting the operation of large business entities; patent cases; copyright and trademark cases; common disaster cases such as those arising from aircraft crashes or marine disasters; actions brought by individual stockholders; stockholder's derivative and stockholder's representative actions; class actions or potential class actions; and other civil (and criminal) cases involving unusual multiplicity or complexity of factual issues. See §0.22 of the first Manual for Complex Litigation and Manual for Complex Litigation Second, Chapter 33.

Rule 5.1.3 Modification or Redaction of Personal Identifiers

As documents in civil cases may be made available for personal inspection in the office of the clerk of court at the United States Courthouse, or, if filed electronically, may be made available on the court's Electronic Case Filing system, such personal identifiers as Social Security numbers, dates of birth, financial account numbers and names of minor children should be modified or partially redacted in all documents filed either in traditional paper form or electronically.

NOTICE

PROGRAM FOR FACSIMILE SERVICE OF NOTICE
TO COUNSEL OR LITIGANTS IN CIVIL AND CRIMINAL CASES

The Court has authorized the Clerk of Court to implement a pilot program in civil and criminal cases to allow attorneys and pro se litigants to waive the provisions of Federal Rule of Civil Procedure 77(d) or Federal Rule of Criminal Procedure 49(c), which requires service of Notice of Orders and Judgments by means of mail, and instead consent to receive Notice of Orders and Judgments by means of facsimile transmission.

This notice is being sent to you because you either represent a party or are a party to litigation currently pending in this district. Enclosed please find a form of Consent to Receive Notice of Orders and Judgments by means of Facsimile Transmission and Waiver of the Provisions of Fed.R.Civ.P. 77(d) or Fed.R.Crim.P. 49(c) Providing for said Notice by means of Mail. Execution of this enclosed Facsimile Transmission Authorization form authorizes the Clerk of Court to serve notice of the entry of Orders or Judgments pursuant to Fed.R.Civ.P. 77(d) or Fed.R.Crim.P. 49(c) by facsimile in lieu of notice by means of mail. Please be advised that this enclosed Facsimile Transmission Authorization form also serves as Notice to and Authorization for the Clerk of Court to keep your name and the relevant information on file so that the Facsimile Transmission Authorization form will apply to all pending and future civil and criminal cases in which you are, or will be, either counsel or a party to litigation.

You are requested to complete the enclosed Facsimile Transmission Authorization form and return it to this office. Please be advised that waiver of the provisions providing for notice of the entry of Orders or Judgments by mail will include all pending civil and criminal cases in the Eastern District of Pennsylvania in which you either represent a party or are a party to the litigation, except for grand jury proceedings and impounded cases.

Please also be advised that the Clerk of Court shall make no more than three attempts to transmit the Notice of Entry of Orders and Judgments by means of facsimile. If after three attempts facsimile transmission is unsuccessful, Notice shall be made by means of mail pursuant to Fed.R.Civ.P. 77(d) or Fed.R.Crim.P. 49(c).

Thank you for your willingness to consider participating in this program. Should you have any questions concerning this notice, please contact Susan Matlack at (267) 299-7051.

Michael E. Kunz
Clerk of Court

UNITED STATES DISTRICT COURT
EASTERN DISTRICT OF PENNSYLVANIA

CONSENT TO RECEIVE NOTICE OF ORDERS AND JUDGMENTS IN CIVIL AND CRIMINAL CASES BY MEANS OF FACSIMILE TRANSMISSION AND WAIVER OF PROVISIONS OF FED.R.CIV.P. 77(d) OR FED.R. CRIM.P. 49(c) PROVIDING FOR SAID NOTICE BY MEANS OF MAIL

TO THE CLERK OF COURT:

I hereby waive the provisions of Fed.R.Civ.P. 77(d) or Fed.R.Crim.P. 49(c) providing for notice of the entry of Orders or Judgments by mail in the manner provided by Fed.R.Civ.P. 5 or Fed.R.Crim.P. 49(c), and consent that notice may be given to me, in all pending and future civil or criminal cases in which I enter my appearance, by the Clerk of Court by facsimile in lieu of notice by means of mail. I understand that this form, when executed, will serve as Notice to and Authorization for the Clerk of Court to keep this information on file for all pending and future civil or criminal cases in which I enter my appearance.

I hereby confirm, by execution of this form, that I understand that it is my responsibility to notify the Clerk of Court, in writing, of my current address and facsimile number.

_____   _____
Name (Printed)   Bar Id Number

_____   _____
Address (Printed)   Telephone Number

_____   _____
Address (Printed)   FAX Number

_____   _____
Signature   Date

Appendix K

SERVICES

MORE SERVICES

Fax Service of Notice of Orders and Judgments

The Court has authorized the Clerk of Court to implement a pilot program in civil and criminal cases to allow attorneys and pro se litigants to waive the provisions of Federal Rule of Civil Procedure 77(d) or Federal Rule of Criminal Procedure 49(c), which requires service of Notice of Orders and Judgments by means of mail, and instead consent to receive Notice of Orders and Judgments by means of facsimile transmission.

This notice is being sent to you because you either represent a party or are a party to litigation currently pending in this district. Enclosed please find a form of Consent to Receive Notice of Orders and Judgments by means of Facsimile Transmission and Waiver of the Provisions of Fed.R.Civ.P. 77(d) or Fed.R.Crim.P. 49(c) Providing for said Notice by means of Mail. Execution of this enclosed Facsimile Transmission Authorization form authorizes the Clerk of Court to serve notice of the entry of Orders or Judgments pursuant to Fed.R.Civ.P. 77(d) or Fed.R.Crim.P. 49(c) by facsimile in lieu of notice by means of mail. Please be advised that this enclosed Facsimile Transmission Authorization form also serves as Notice to and Authorization for the Clerk of Court to keep your name and the relevant information on file so that the Facsimile Transmission Authorization form will apply to all pending and future civil and criminal cases in which you are, or will be, either counsel or a party to litigation.

Please be advised that waiver of the provisions providing for notice of the entry of Orders or Judgments by mail will include all pending civil and criminal cases in the Eastern District of Pennsylvania in which you either represent a party or are a party to the litigation, except for grand jury proceedings and impounded cases.

Please also be advised that the Clerk of Court shall make no more than three attempts to transmit the Notice of Entry of Orders and Judgments by means of facsimile. If after three attempts facsimile transmission is unsuccessful, Notice shall be made by means of mail pursuant to Federal Rule of Civil Procedure 77(d) or Federal Rule of Criminal Procedure 49(c).

You are requested to complete the enclosed Facsimile Transmission Authorization form and return it to this office. Thank you for your willingness to consider participating in this program. Should you have any questions concerning this notice, please contact Susan Matlack at (267) 299-7051.

The information provided through this site is not intended to be nor should it be considered legal advice.

UNITED STATES DISTRICT COURT
EASTERN DISTRICT OF PENNSYLVANIA

INFORMATION FORM

Name: _____ Bar Id No.: _____

Firm: _____

Address: _____

_____

City: _____ State: _____ **Zip Code*:** _____ - _____

Facsimile No: _____

Please return completed form to:

Michael E. Kunz
Clerk of Court
United States District Court
for the Eastern District of Pennsylvania
U.S. Courthouse
601 Market Street, Room 2609
Philadelphia, PA 19106-1797

- or -

FAX to:

(215) 597-6390
(267) 299-7135
(610) 434-6174

* Please include zip code and 4-digit extension number

☐ Indicate here if you would like to receive information on the Pilot Fax Notice Program

☐ Indicate here if you would like to receive a Directory of Automated Services

Appendix L

Appendix L

Mail Sent to Counsel

Please see the Mail Sent to Counsel form.

Philadelphia Location

District Court Judges	Room No.	Zip Code
J. Curtis Joyner, Chief Judge	17614	19106-1709
Stewart Dalzell	15613	19106-1710
Eduardo C. Robreno	15614	19106-1720
Mary A. McLaughlin	13614	19106-1723
Petrese B. Tucker	9613	19106-1717
Legrome D. Davis	6614	19106-1714
Cynthia M. Rufe	12614	19106-1721
Timothy J. Savage	9614	19106-1718
James Knoll Gardner *(see Allentown Divisional Office Location)*		
Gene E. K. Pratter	10613	19106-1718
Lawrence F. Stengel	3809	19106-1727
(for Reading - see Divisional Office Location)		
Paul S. Diamond	6613	19106-1714
Juan R. Sánchez	8613	19106-1716
(for Reading - see Divisional Office Location)		
Joel H. Slomsky	5614	19106-1726
C. Darnell Jones, II	5613	19106-1714
Mitchell S. Goldberg	7614	19106-1712

Senior Judges	Room No.	Zip Code
Donald W. VanArtsdalen	3040	19106-1725
J. William Ditter, Jr.	3040	19106-1725
Norma L. Shapiro	10614	19106-1719
Thomas N. O'Neill, Jr.	4007	19106-1714
Edmund V. Ludwig	5118	19106-1714
Robert F. Kelly	11613	19106-1720
Jan E. DuBois	12613	19106-1721
Ronald L. Buckwalter	14614	19106-1724
William H. Yohn, Jr.	14613	19106-1731
Harvey Bartle III	16614	19106-1710
John R. Padova	17613	19106-1708
Anita B. Brody	7613	19106-1712
Berle M. Schiller	13613	19106-1723
R. Barclay Surrick	8614	19106-1716
Michael M. Baylson	3810	19106-1727

U.S. Magistrate Judges	Room No.	Zip Code
Carol Sandra Moore Wells, Chief Magistrate Judge	3016	19106-1730
Thomas J. Rueter	3000	19106-1727
Linda K. Caracappa	3042	19106-1725
Timothy R. Rice	3029	19106-1725
David R. Strawbridge	3030	19106-1725
L. Felipe Restrepo	3038	19106-1725
Henry S. Perkin	*(see Allentown Divisional Office Location)*	
Elizabeth T. Hey	*(see Nix Building Divisional Office Location)*	
Lynne A. Sitarski	3015	19106-1730
Arnold C. Rapoport	*(see Allentown Divisional Office Location)*	
M. Faith Angell	*(see Nix Building Divisional Office Location)*	
Jacob P. Hart	3006	19106-1727

Divisional Office Locations

Nix Building

Honorable Elizabeth T. Hey
Magistrate Judge
Robert N. C. Nix Federal Building
900 Market Street
Suite 219
Philadelphia, PA 19107

Honorable M. Faith Angell
Magistrate Judge
Robert N. C. Nix Federal Building
900 Market Street
Suite 211
Philadelphia, PA 19107

Allentown

Honorable James Knoll Gardner
Edward N. Cahn Courthouse & Federal Building
504 W. Hamilton Street
Room 4701
Allentown, PA 18101-1514

Honorable Henry S. Perkin
Magistrate Judge
Edward N. Cahn Courthouse & Federal Building
504 W. Hamilton Street
Room 4401
Allentown, PA 18101-1533

Honorable Arnold C. Rapoport
Magistrate Judge
Edward N. Cahn Courthouse & Federal Building
504 W. Hamilton Street
Room 3401
Allentown, PA 18101-1514

Reading

Honorable Lawrence F. Stengel
The Madison Building
400 Washington Street
Suite 201
Reading, PA 19601-3933

Honorable Juan R. Sánchez
The Madison Building
400 Washington Street
Suite 201
Reading, PA 19601-3933

Appendix M

Appendix M

Mail Sent to the Court

All mail sent to the United States District Court for the Eastern District of Pennsylvania at 601 Market Street, Philadelphia, PA and divisional office locations should include both the zip code and 4-digit extension number. The use of bar coding technology currently available in word processing software packages in addressing envelopes is encouraged.

James A. Byrne U.S. Courthouse – Philadelphia, PA

All mail submitted to a judicial officer or the Clerk of Court at the James A. Byrne U.S. Courthouse in Philadelphia, PA should be addressed as follows:

Name of Judicial Officer
United States District Court, Eastern District of Pennsylvania
U.S. Courthouse
601 Market Street, Room _____ (Room No. from below)
Philadelphia, PA _____ (Zip Code+Extension No. from below)

Michael E. Kunz, Clerk of Court
United States District Court, Eastern District of Pennsylvania
U.S. Courthouse
601 Market Street, Room 2609
Philadelphia, PA 19106-1797

AO 440 (Rev. 06/12) Summons in a Civil Action

UNITED STATES DISTRICT COURT
for the

Eastern District of Pennsylvania

_____	)))))	
Plaintiff(s)	))	
v.	))	Civil Action No.
	))))	
_____	))	
Defendant(s)	)	

SUMMONS IN A CIVIL ACTION

To: *(Defendant's name and address)*

A lawsuit has been filed against you.

Within 21 days after service of this summons on you (not counting the day you received it) — or 60 days if you are the United States or a United States agency, or an officer or employee of the United States described in Fed. R. Civ. P. 12 (a)(2) or (3) — you must serve on the plaintiff an answer to the attached complaint or a motion under Rule 12 of the Federal Rules of Civil Procedure. The answer or motion must be served on the plaintiff or plaintiff's attorney, whose name and address are:

If you fail to respond, judgment by default will be entered against you for the relief demanded in the complaint. You also must file your answer or motion with the court.

CLERK OF COURT

Date: _____   _____
                                   Signature of Clerk or Deputy Clerk

Appendix N

Appendix N

AO 440 (Rev. 06/12) Summons in a Civil Action (Page 2)

Civil Action No.

PROOF OF SERVICE
(This section should not be filed with the court unless required by Fed. R. Civ. P. 4 (l))

This summons for *(name of individual and title, if any)* _____
was received by me on *(date)* _____ .

☐ I personally served the summons on the individual at *(place)* _____
_____ on *(date)* _____ ; or

☐ I left the summons at the individual's residence or usual place of abode with *(name)* _____
_____ , a person of suitable age and discretion who resides there,
on *(date)* _____ , and mailed a copy to the individual's last known address; or

☐ I served the summons on *(name of individual)* _____ , who is
designated by law to accept service of process on behalf of *(name of organization)* _____
_____ on *(date)* _____ ; or

☐ I returned the summons unexecuted because _____ ; or

☐ Other *(specify)*:

My fees are $ _____ for travel and $ _____ for services, for a total of $ _____ .

I declare under penalty of perjury that this information is true.

Date: _____   _____
                                            Server's signature

                            _____
                                            Printed name and title

                            _____
                                            Server's address

Additional information regarding attempted service, etc:

649

**IN THE UNITED STATES DISTRICT COURT
FOR THE EASTERN DISTRICT OF PENNSYLVANIA**

:   CIVIL ACTION
:
:
:
:   NO.

PRAECIPE FOR WRIT OF EXECUTION

TO THE CLERK:

ISSUE WRIT OF EXECUTION in the above matter, directed to the United States Marshal for the Eastern District of Pennsylvania, and against _____ and against

_____
(Name and Address of Garnishee)

garnishee, and index this writ against* _____

_____ and against _____

_____ as garnishee, as a lis pendens against real property of the judgment debtor in the name of the garnishee, as follows:

_____

_____

    Amount Due $ _____

    Interest From _____ $ _____

                                 _____
                                 Attorney for

Date:_____

*Applicable to real estate only (Rule 3104(c)Pa. R.C.P.).

Civ. 637 (3/82)

Appendix O

Appendix O

IN THE UNITED STATES DISTRICT COURT
FOR THE EASTERN DISTRICT OF PENNSYLVANIA

: CIVIL ACTION
:
: NO.

WRIT OF EXECUTION

TO THE UNITED STATES MARSHAL FOR THE EASTERN DISTRICT OF PENNSYLVANIA:

To satisfy judgment, interest, and costs against _____
_____, defendant
(Name of Defendant)

(1) You are directed to levy upon the property of the defendant and to sell his interest therein:

(2) You are also directed to attach the property of the defendant not levied upon in the possession of

_____
(Name of Garnishee)

as garnishee.

_____
(Specifically Describe Property)

and to notify the garnishee that

    (a) an attachment has been issued;
    (b) the garnishee is enjoined from paying any debt to or for the account of the defendant and from delivering any property of the defendant or otherwise disposing thereof;

(3) If property of the defendant not levied upon and subject to attachment is found in the possession of anyone other than a named garnishee, you are directed to notify him that he has been added as a garnishee and is enjoined as above stated.

    Amount Due $ _____
    Interest From _____ $ _____
    (Cost to be Added) $ _____

                            MICHAEL E. KUNZ
                            Clerk of Court

                            BY: _____
                                                  (Deputy Clerk)

Seal of the Court:

MAJOR EXEMPTIONS UNDER PENNSYLVANIA AND FEDERAL LAW

1. 5300 statutory exemption
2. Bibles, school books, sewing machines, uniforms and equipment
3. Most wages and unemployment compensation
4. Social security benefits
5. Certain retirement funds and accounts
6. Certain veteran and armed forces benefits
7. Certain insurance proceeds.
8. Such other exceptions as may be provided by law.

Civ. 638 (3/82)

IN THE UNITED STATES DISTRICT COURT
FOR THE EASTERN DISTRICT OF PENNSYLVANIA

: CIVIL ACTION
:
:
:
:
: NO.

WRIT OF EXECUTION

NOTICE

This paper is a Writ of Execution. It has been issued because there is a judgment against you. It may cause your property to be held or taken to pay the judgment. You may have legal rights to prevent your property from being taken. A lawyer can advise you more specifically of these rights. If you wish to exercise your rights, you must act promptly.

The law provides that certain property cannot be taken. Such property is said to be exempt. There is a debtor's exemption of $300. There are other exemptions which may be applicable to you. Attached is a summary of some of the major exemptions. You may have other exemptions or other rights.

If you have an exemption, you should do the following promptly: (1) Fill out the attached claim form and demand for a prompt hearing. (2) Deliver the form or mail it to the United States Marshal's office at the address noted.

You should come to court ready to explain your exemption. If you do not come to court and prove your exemption, you may lose some of your property.

YOU SHOULD TAKE THIS PAPER TO YOUR LAWYER AT ONCE. IF YOU DO NOT HAVE A LAWYER OR CANNOT AFFORD ONE, GO TO OR TELEPHONE THE OFFICE SET FORTH BELOW TO FIND OUT WHERE YOU CAN GET LEGAL HELP.

LAWYER REFERRAL AND INFORMATION SERVICE
1101 Market Street
11th Floor
Philadelphia, PA 19107-2911

(215) 238-6333

Civ. 639 (3/82)

Appendix O

**IN THE UNITED STATES DISTRICT COURT
FOR THE EASTERN DISTRICT OF PENNSYLVANIA**

:	CIVIL ACTION
:	
:	
:	
:	
:	
:	NO.

CLAIM FOR EXEMPTION

TO THE U.S. MARSHAL:

I, the above named defendant, claim exemption of property from levy or attachment:

(1) From my personal property in my possession which has been levied upon,

    (a) I desire that my $300 statutory exemption be

        (i) set aside in kind (specify property to be set aside in kind):

            _____;

        (ii) paid in cash following the sale of the property levied upon; or

    (b) I claim the following exemption (specify property and basis of exemption):

        _____

(2) From my property which is in the possession of a third party, I claim the following exemptions:

    (a) My $300 statutory exemption: in cash;   in kind

(specify property): _____

    (b) Social security benefits on deposit in the amount of $_____

    (c) Other (specify amount and basis of exemption: _____

_____

I request a prompt court hearing to determine the exemption. Notice of the hearing should be given to me at

_____, _____
           (Address)   (Telephone number)

I declare under penalty of perjury that the foregoing statements made in this claim for exemption are true and correct.

Date: _____   _____
                                                                         (Signature of Defendant)

THIS CLAIM TO BE FILED WITH THE OFFICE OF THE U.S. MARSHAL FOR THE EASTERN DISTRICT OF PENNSYLVANIA:

2110 United States Courthouse
601 Market Street
Philadelphia, Pennsylvania 19106
(215) 597-7272

NOTE: Under paragraphs (1) and (2) of the writ, a description of specific property to be levied upon or attached may be set forth in the writ or included in a separate direction to the United States Marshal.

Under Paragraph (2) of the writ, if the attachment of a named garnishee is desired, his name should be set forth in the space provided.

Under Paragraph (3) of the writ, the United States Marshal may, as under prior practice, add as a garnishee any person not named in this writ who may be found in possession of property of the defendant. See Rule 3111(a). For limitations on the power to attach tangible personal property, see Rule 3108(a).

(b) Each court shall by local rule designate the officer, organization or person to be named in the notice.

Civ. 640 (10/99)

Appendix O

UNITED STATES DISTRICT COURT
FOR THE EASTERN DISTRICT OF PENNSYLVANIA

UNITED STATES OF AMERICA :
        Plaintiff :
                              :
v.   : CIVIL ACTION NO. _____
_____ :
        Defendant :
                              :
_____ :
        Garnishee :

TO: _____

      _____

      _____

Date of Notice: _____

IMPORTANT NOTICE

You are in default because you failed to take action required of you in this case. Unless you act within ten days from the date of this notice, a judgment may be entered against you without a hearing and you may lose your property or other important rights. You should take this Notice to a lawyer at once. If you do not have a lawyer or cannot afford one, go to or telephone the following office to find out where you can get legal help.

Lawyer Referral and Information Service
1101 Market Street, 11th Floor
Philadelphia, PA 19107-2911
(215) 238-6333

                                                _____
                                                Attorney for

Civ. 641 (9/91)

TRANSCRIPT PURCHASE ORDER
for Third Circuit Court of Appeals

District Court _____ Court of Appeals Docket No. _____

District Court Docket No. _____

Short Case Title _____

Date Notice of Appeal Filed by Clerk of District Court _____

Part I.

A. (To be completed by party responsible for ordering transcript) NOTE: A SEPARATE FORM IS TO BE TYPED FOR EACH COURT REPORTER IN THIS CASE.
Check one of the following and serve ALL COPIES:

TRANSCRIPT:

_____ None _____ Unnecessary for appeal purposes.

_____ Already on file in the District Court Clerk's office.

_____ This is to order a transcript of the proceedings heard on the date listed below from _____ (Court Reporter)
(Specify on lines below exact date of proceedings to be transcribed). If requesting only partial transcript of the proceedings, specify exactly what portion or what witness testimony is desired.

_____

_____

If proceeding to be transcribed was a trial, also check any appropriate box below for special requests; otherwise, this material will NOT be included in the trial transcripts.

_____ Voir dire _____ Open Statement of Plaintiff _____ Opening Statement of Defendant

_____ Closing Argument of Plaintiff _____ Closing Argument of Defendant

_____ Jury Instructions _____ Sentencing Hearings

FAILURE TO SPECIFY IN ADEQUATE DETAIL THOSE PROCEEDINGS TO BE TRANSCRIBED OR FAILURE TO MAKE PROMPT SATISFACTORY FINANCIAL ARRANGEMENTS FOR TRANSCRIPT ARE GROUNDS FOR DISMISSAL OF THE APPEAL OR IMPOSITION OF SANCTIONS

B. This is to certify that satisfactory financial arrangements have been completed with the court reporter for payment of the cost of the transcript. The method of payment will be:

_____ CJA Form submitted to District Court Judge _____ Motion for Transcript has been submitted to District Court

_____ CJA Form submitted to Court of Appeals _____ Private Funds

Signature _____ Date _____

Print Name _____ Counsel for _____

Address _____ Telephone _____

Part II. COURT REPORTER ACKNOWLEDGEMENT (To be completed by the Court Reporter and forwarded to the Court of Appeals on the same day transcript order is received.)

Date transcript order received	Estimated completion date; if not within 30 days of date financial arrangements made, motion for extension to be made to Court of Appeals	Estimated number of pages

_____ Arrangements for payment were made on _____

_____ Arrangements for payment have not been made pursuant to FRAP 10(b)

_____ _____ _____
Date Name of Court Reporter Telephone

Part III. NOTIFICATION THAT TRANSCRIPT HAS BEEN FILED IN THE DISTRICT COURT (To be completed by court reporter on date of filing transcript in District Court. Notification must be forwarded to the Court of Appeals on the same date.)

Actual Number of Pages _____ Actual Number of Volumes _____

_____ _____
Date Signature of Court Reporter

Appendix P

UNITED STATES DISTRICT COURT
FOR THE EASTERN DISTRICT OF PENNSYLVANIA

_____)		
Plaintiff)		
)		
v.)	*Civil Action No.*	
_____)		
Defendant)		

NOTICE, CONSENT, AND REFERENCE OF A CIVIL ACTION TO A MAGISTRATE JUDGE

<u>Notice of a magistrate judge's availability.</u> A United States magistrate judge of this court is available to conduct all proceedings in this civil action (including a jury or nonjury trial) and to order the entry of a final judgment. The judgment may then be appealed directly to the United States court of appeals like any other judgment of this court. A magistrate judge may exercise this authority only if, firstly, all parties voluntarily consent, and then the assigned Article III judicial officer approves.

You may consent to have your case referred to a magistrate judge, or you may withhold your consent without adverse substantive consequences. The name of any party withholding consent will not be revealed to any judge who may otherwise be involved with your case.

<u>Consent to a magistrate judge's authority.</u> The following parties consent (subject to approval by the assigned Article III judicial officer) to have a United States magistrate judge conduct all proceedings in this case including trial, the entry of final judgment, and all post-trial proceedings.

Parties' Printed Names: Signatures of Parties or Attorneys: Dates:

_____   _____   _____
_____   _____   _____
_____   _____   _____
_____   _____   _____

Reference Order

IT IS ORDERED: This case is referred to a United States magistrate judge _____ to conduct all proceedings and order the entry of a final judgment in accordance with 28 U.S.C. § 636(c) and Fed. R. Civ. P. 73.

_____
District Judge's signature

Date: _____   _____
                              (Printed Name and Title)

Note: Return this form to the clerk of court only if you are consenting to the exercise of jurisdiction by a United States magistrate judge.
Do not return this form to a judge.

Appendix Q

Clerk's Office Procedural Handbook

**United States District Court
Eastern District of Pennsylvania
United States Courthouse
Independence Mall West
601 Market Street
Philadelphia, PA 19106-1797**

*Chambers of
J. Curtis Joyner
Chief Judge*

*Michael E. Kunz
Clerk of Court*

*Clerk's Office
Room 2609
Telephone
(215) 597-7704*

**NOTICE OF RIGHT TO CONSENT TO EXERCISE OF JURISDICTION
BY A UNITED STATES MAGISTRATE JUDGE**

The district judges of this Court have found that the United States magistrate judges are experienced judicial officers who have regularly handled the disposition of hundreds of civil cases through motions and trials and are fully qualified to try any civil cases arising before this Court.

In accordance with the provisions of 28 U.S.C. §636(c), you are hereby notified that pursuant to Local Rule 72.1(h), the United States magistrate judges of this district, in addition to their other duties, may, upon the consent of all the parties in a civil case, conduct any or all proceedings in a civil case, including a jury or non-jury trial, and order the entry of a final judgment. Appropriate consent forms for this purpose are available from the clerk of court.

Your decision to consent, or not to consent, to the referral of your case to a United States magistrate judge for disposition is entirely voluntary and should be communicated solely to the clerk of the district court. Only if all the parties in the case consent to the reference to a magistrate judge will either the judge or magistrate judge be informed of your decision. **If you decide to consent, your case will receive a date certain for trial**.

No action eligible for arbitration will be referred by consent of the parties until the arbitration has been concluded and trial *de novo* demanded pursuant to Local Rule 53.2, Paragraph 7. The Court may, for good cause shown, on its own motion, or under extraordinary circumstances shown by any party, vacate a reference of a civil matter to a magistrate judge.

When a case is referred to a magistrate judge for all further proceedings, including the entry of final judgment, the final judgment shall be appealed directly to the Court of Appeals for the Third Circuit in the same manner as an appeal from any other judgment of a district court.

Nothing herein shall be construed to be a limitation of any party's right to seek review by the Supreme Court of the United States.

J. CURTIS JOYNER
CHIEF JUDGE

MICHAEL E. KUNZ
CLERK OF COURT

Civ. 635 (6/2011)

AO 133 (Rev. 12/09) Bill of Costs

UNITED STATES DISTRICT COURT
for the
Eastern District of Pennsylvania

)
)
v.) Case No.:
)
)

BILL OF COSTS

Judgment having been entered in the above entitled action on _____ against _____ ,
the Clerk is requested to tax the following as costs: Date

Fees of the Clerk...	$ _____
Fees for service of summons and subpoena	_____
Fees for printed or electronically recorded transcripts necessarily obtained for use in the case	_____
Fees and disbursements for printing...	_____
Fees for witnesses *(itemize on page two)*..	_____
Fees for exemplification and the costs of making copies of any materials where the copies are necessarily obtained for use in the case..	_____
Docket fees under 28 U.S.C. 1923..	_____
Costs as shown on Mandate of Court of Appeals.......................................	_____
Compensation of court-appointed experts	_____
Compensation of interpreters and costs of special interpretation services under 28 U.S.C. 1828 ...	_____
Other costs *(please itemize)*	_____
TOTAL	$ _____

SPECIAL NOTE: Attach to your bill an itemization and documentation for requested costs in all categories.

Declaration

I declare under penalty of perjury that the foregoing costs are correct and were necessarily incurred in this action and that the services for which fees have been charged were actually and necessarily performed. A copy of this bill has been served on all parties in the following manner:

☐   Electronic service   ☐   First class mail, postage prepaid

☐   Other: _____

s/ Attorney: _____

Name of Attorney: _____

For: _____   Date: _____
     Name of Claiming Party

Taxation of Costs

Costs are taxed in the amount of _____ and included in the judgment.

_____   By: _____   _____
   Clerk of Court   Deputy Clerk   Date

Appendix R

UNITED STATES DISTRICT COURT

NAME, CITY AND STATE OF RESIDENCE	ATTENDANCE		SUBSISTENCE		MILEAGE		Total Cost Each Witness
	Days	Total Cost	Days	Total Cost	Miles	Total Cost	
				TOTAL			

Witness Fees (computation, cf. 28 U.S.C. 1821 for statutory fees)

NOTICE

Section 1924, Title 28, U.S. Code (effective September 1, 1948) provides:
"Sec. 1924. Verification of bill of costs."

"Before any bill of costs is taxed, the party claiming any item of cost or disbursement shall attach thereto an affidavit, made by himself or by his duly authorized attorney or agent having knowledge of the facts, that such item is correct and has been necessarily incurred in the case and that the services for which fees have been charged were actually and necessarily performed."

See also Section 1920 of Title 28, which reads in part as follows:
"A bill of costs shall be filed in the case and, upon allowance, included in the judgment or decree."

The Federal Rules of Civil Procedure contain the following provisions:
RULE 54(d)(1)

Costs Other than Attorneys' Fees

Unless a federal statute, these rules, or a court order provides otherwise, costs — other than attorney's fees — should be allowed to the prevailing party. But costs against the United States, its officers, and its agencies may be imposed only to the extent allowed by law. The clerk may tax costs on 14 days' notice. On motion served within the next 7 days, the court may review the clerk's action.

RULE 6

(d) Additional Time After Certain Kinds of Service.

When a party may or must act within a specified time after service and service is made under Rule 5(b)(2)(C), (D), (E), or (F), 3 days are added after the period would otherwise expire under Rule 6(a).

RULE 58(e)

Cost or Fee Awards:

Ordinarily, the entry of judgment may not be delayed, nor the time for appeal extended, in order to tax costs or award fees. But if a timely motion for attorney's fees is made under Rule 54(d)(2), the court may act before a notice of appeal has been filed and become effective to order that the motion have the same effect under Federal Rule of Appellate Procedure 4(a)(4) as a timely motion under Rule 59.

GENERAL COURT REGULATION NO. 73-2
COURT OF COMMON PLEAS

D. **Conflicts in the Engagement of Counsel**

(1) **Common Pleas Court**

Common Pleas Court will recognize as engaged all counsel appearing of record in any case actually on trial before a Judge in the United States District Court in Philadelphia and one back-up case as published in the Legal Intelligencer. The engagement in the case actually on trial shall be effective until the trial terminates by verdict or otherwise and in the back-up case for a period of three (3) days including the day said case is first published.

(2) **United States District Court in Philadelphia**

The District Court will recognize as engaged all counsel of record in any case actually on trial before a Common Pleas Court Judge and in cases appearing in the first 20 cases on the Major case List and in the first 15 cases published on the General Jury Trial List. The engagement in the case actually on trial shall be effective until the trial terminates by verdict or otherwise and the case appearing in the first 20 or 15 for a period of three (3) days after said case reaches that position on the respective list.

(3) Both the Common Pleas Court and the United States District Court will observe the procedure of alternating assignments, i.e. counsel assigned to trial in the Common Pleas Court must upon completion be available for assignment in the United States District Court before accepting another assignment in the Common Pleas Court and visa versa.

No Counsel shall try successive cases in either court except by agreement between the respective judges involved as set forth in Paragraph 3 of Section "D" (4) hereof.

(4) **General**

Counsel Must Report Case Terminations to Appropriate Clerks

Counsel must immediately report the termination of all trials (by verdict or settlement conference) to the appropriate Clerk of the United States District Court or the Common Pleas Court. Failure to do so will result in the imposition of appropriate sanctions.

Engagement of Counsel in Non-Jury and Arbitration Cases

The United States District Court will not recognize engagements of counsel on the Non-Jury list of the Common Pleas Court or in Arbitration Cases, and conflicts encountered by counsel in this type of case shall be handled on an ad hoc basis as heretofore.

Problems of a Particular Case to be Taken Up With Appropriate Judge

Problems not otherwise covered in this regulation regarding the listing or assignment of a case for trial shall be taken up in the United States District Court with the Judge on whose individual calendar the case appears and in the Common Pleas Court with the Calendar Judge.

Appendix S

**IN THE UNITED STATES DISTRICT COURT
FOR THE EASTERN DISTRICT OF PENNSYLVANIA**

BUSY SLIP

I, _____

of _____
(Address)

_____, do hereby certify that I am engaged in trial or appellate
(Telephone Number)

argument before _____, in
(Name of Judge or Judges)

_____. _____
(Title or Name of Court of Record)   (Room Number)

in the case of _____

vs. _____. _____
                                            (Court Term & No.)

The case is expected to take approximately _____ trial days.

My case is number _____ on Judge _____ list in the U.S. District Court. Caption and number is as follows:

_____

I will notify that Judge's respective court clerk immediately upon the conclusion of this engagement.

Busy slips must be filed in Room 2609 on the designated form no later than 1:00 p.m. on the day after the day counsel becomes attached. If counsel is listed in the Legal Intelligencer on any Judge's trial list, counsel shall call that Judge's respective court clerk promptly so the attachment may be noted before the filing of a busy slip. It will be the duty of counsel to notify the Judge's respective court clerk immediately upon the conclusion of his engagement.

Failure to comply, including failure to use the designated form, will result in non-recognition of counsel's engagement.

_____
Attorney for (name of party)

Date Filed:
Date Withdrawn:
cc: All Counsel
C.V. 17(8/80)

Appendix T

IN THE UNITED STATES DISTRICT COURT
FOR THE EASTERN DISTRICT OF PENNSYLVANIA

STANDING ORDER
RE: SENTENCING REFORM ACT OF 1984

STAGE 1. Unless otherwise ordered by an individual judge, sentencing will occur without unnecessary delay not less than eighty (80) days after a defendant pleads guilty, nolo contendere, or is found guilty.

STAGE 2. Not less than thirty-five (35) days before the sentencing hearing, the probation officer must furnish the presentence report to the defendant, the defendant's counsel, and the attorney for the Government. The probation officer's recommendation for sentence will not be disclosed unless directed by an individual judge.

STAGE 3. Within fourteen (14) days after receiving the presentence report, the parties shall deliver in writing to the probation officer, and to each other, any objections to any material information, sentencing classifications, sentencing guideline ranges, and policy statements contained in or omitted from the presentence report. If no objections will be filed, the probation officer shall be so notified in writing within the aforesaid time limits. Any objection not filed will be deemed waived unless the Court finds good cause for allowing it to be raised.

STAGE 4. Should the attorney for the Government intend to file a motion for a downward departure under United States Sentencing Guideline Section 5K1.1, or from a statutory mandatory minimum, the probation officer will be notified in writing on or before the submission date set for the filing of objections, and be provided with whatever information supports the motion.

STAGE 5. Not later than seven (7) days before the sentencing hearing, the probation officer must submit the presentence report to the Court, together with an addendum setting forth any unresolved objections, the grounds for those objections, and the probation officer's comments on the objections. At the same time, the probation officer must furnish the revisions of the presentence report and the addendum to the defendant, the defendant's counsel, and the attorney for the Government.

STAGE 6. The presentence report is a confidential document. Rule 32(b)(3)(A) provides that copies of the presentence report are provided to prosecution and the defense attorneys for the purpose of the sentencing hearing. The attorneys may retain these copies. The attorney for the Government may also retain the presentence report for use in collecting financial penalties. 18 U.S.C. § 3552(d).

Defendant: _____   Criminal No. _____

Date of Plea: _____

Date of Sentencing: _____

Time of Sentencing: _____ o'clock ____ m.

(To be distributed to each defendant and each counsel at time presentence report is ordered)

cc: Pretrial Services (via FAX)

Cr. 37 (2/96)

Appendix U

UNITED STATES DISTRICT COURT
EASTERN DISTRICT OF PENNSYLVANIA

CREDIT CARD COLLECTION NETWORK PROCEDURES

In September of 1987, the Department of Treasury through its Financial Management Service (FMS), established a government credit card collection network to enable federal agencies to accept credit cards (Visa and MasterCard) for the collection of receipts due the government. (Effective August 30, 1999, Discover and American Express in addition to Visa and MasterCard credit cards were accepted for financial transactions by the Office of the Clerk of Court. Now, most other major credit cards, including American Express, Discover and Diners Club are accepted for financial transactions by the Office of the Clerk of Court.)

As a follow-up to the request of the Clerk of Court for the Eastern District of Pennsylvania in August of 1986, the Administrative Office of the United States Courts approved it as the pilot district for implementation of the credit card network within the Judiciary. Subsequently, the Administrative Office on behalf of the United States Courts, entered into a contract with a bank which provides clerks' offices with processing services for Visa and MasterCard transactions.

To implement the program in the Clerk's Office, we first identified potential transactions which we felt were conducive to the use of credit cards, as follows:

- filing fees
- copywork (including docket sheets, documents, judicial opinions)
- copies of ESR-taped proceedings
- fines and restitution
- bail
- attorney admission fees
- searches and certifications
- retrieval fees for records maintained at FRC, and
- CVB payments

Next, we selected 25 law firms and 10 sole practitioners in the Philadelphia and surrounding areas to participate in a pilot program, prior to announcing this service to the general bar and public. We conducted a one-day seminar for members of those law firms and outlined the program to them with a series of presentations from members of the Clerk's Office staff and bank representatives.

We believe the use of credit cards by members of the bar and the public facilitates the processing of financial transactions at the district court. From the government's perspective, the use of credit cards provides next-day availability of funds, reduces the amount of cash handled each day by cashiers, thereby minimizing the possibility of error, and facilitates the bookkeeping process for both the Clerk's Office and participating customers. Conservative estimates place the volume of charges of government transactions at $3 to $10 billion annually. By providing next-day availability of funds to the government, savings of at least $2 million a year will be realized.

From the law firms' perspective, the benefits are even greater. Using a credit card for payment of transactions in the Clerk's Office means that legal couriers no longer are required to carry cash to pay filing or copy fees; blank checks are no longer drawn because amounts are unknown; and the billing procedures fit easily into any internal accounting method used.

For those law firms which are concerned with the safekeeping of the actual credit card, the Clerk's Office will maintain the firm's credit card number, expiration date, and the signature of one of the firm's partners after completion of an authorization form (Attachment 1). The courier will reference the authorization form and the transaction will be processed. On the bank charge slip, "AUTHORIZATION ON FILE" would appear in the signature block. Attachment 2 is a list of the law firms that originally participated in our program.

Credit card transactions are handled in the same manner as transactions paid for by check or cash.

Appendix V

Appendix V

For counter transactions, the charge card is obtained from the customer for recording, validating, and imprinting onto a bank charge slip. The customer's card is then "swiped" through the terminal and the amount of sale is entered on the keyboard. The bank is contacted electronically through the terminal and an authorization number is obtained.

Once authorization is received, the slip is given to the payor for signature. The amount of the charge is entered into the register and it records the sale and payment data on the receipt in the slip printer. The bank charge slip is then inserted into the register printer and this action records the transaction code, date, time, charge, and amount onto the bank charge slip and matches the data recorded on the cash register receipt.

The original cash register receipt and bank charge slip are given to the customer and the copies are kept on file in the Clerk's Office.

For those requests received via telephone, the customer simply gives the name, credit card number, and its expiration date to the deputy clerk. The requested work is returned to the customer with two receipts -- a cash register receipt and a bank charge slip, which has the words "TELEPHONE REQUEST" inserted in the signature block.

Clerk's Office Procedural Handbook

ATTACHMENT 1

UNITED STATES DISTRICT COURT
EASTERN DISTRICT OF PENNSYLVANIA

CREDIT CARD COLLECTION NETWORK
AUTHORIZATION FORM

_____
(Name of Company/Firm)

hereby authorizes the United States District Court for the Eastern District of Pennsylvania to charge the following bank credit card number for payment of filing fees and other court-related expenses.

PLEASE PRINT:

Visa No. _____ Exp. Date _____ Security Code _____

MasterCard No. _____ Exp. Date _____ Security Code _____

Discover _____ Exp. Date _____ Security Code _____

American Express _____ Exp. Date _____ Security Code _____

Name: _____

Address: _____

City: _____ State: _____ Zip Code _____

Phone No. _____ Fax No. _____

This form, which will be kept on file in the Clerk's Office, shall remain in effect until specifically revoked in writing. It is the responsibility of the firm/company named herein to notify the Clerk's Office of the new expiration date when a credit card has been renewed, or if a credit card has been canceled or revoked.

Signature: _____ Date: _____

Appendix V

ATTACHMENT 2

CREDIT CARD PROGRAM LAW FIRM ORIGINAL PARTICIPANTS

Blank, Rome, Comisky & McCauley

Drinker, Biddle & Reath

Duane, Morris & Heckscher

Freedman & Lorry, P.C.

Hoyle, Morris & Kerr

Kittredge, Kaufman & Donley

Kohn, Savett, Klein & Graf

Krusen, Evans & Byrne

Pepper, Hamilton & Scheetz

MacElree, Harvey, Gallagher, O'Donnell & Featherman

Mesirov, Gelman, Jaffee, Cramer & Jamieson

Rawle & Henderson

Schnader, Harrison, Segal & Lewis

Stradley, Ronon, Stevens & Young

White & Williams

Wolfe, Block, Schorr & Solis-Cohen

SERVICES
Credit Card Collection Network

MORE SERVICES

Any law firm, legal agency, or company can arrange to use a Visa, MasterCard, Discover, or American Express card when making payment to the United States District Court for the Eastern District of Pennsylvania, Office of the Clerk of Court, for filing fees and other district-court-related expenses. Credit card payment provides for an alternative to cash/checks that easily accommodates any internal accounting procedure. The network supports in-person, telephone and mail requests.

In September of 1987, the Department of Treasury through its Financial Management Service (FMS), established a government credit card collection network to enable federal agencies to accept credit cards (Visa and MasterCard) for the collection of receipts due the government. Effective August 30, 1999, Discover and American Express in addition to Visa and MasterCard credit cards are accepted for financial transactions by the Office of the Clerk of Court.

As a follow-up to the request of the Clerk of Court for the Eastern District of Pennsylvania in August of 1986, the Administrative Office of the United States Courts approved it as the pilot district for implementation of the credit card network within the Judiciary. Subsequently, the Administrative Office, on behalf of the United States Courts, entered into a contract with a bank which provides clerks' offices with processing services for Visa and MasterCard transactions.

To implement the program in the Clerk's Office, we identified potential transactions (see Notice below) which we felt were conducive to the use of credit cards. Next, we selected 25 law firms and 10 sole practitioners in the Philadelphia and surrounding areas to participate in the pilot program, prior to announcing the service to the bar and general public. We conducted a one-day seminar for members of those law firms and outlined the program to them with a series of presentations from members of the Clerk's Office staff and bank representatives.

We believe the use of credit cards by members of the bar and the public facilitates the processing of financial transactions at the district court. From the government's perspective, the use of credit cards provides next-day availability of funds, reduces the amount of cash handled each day by cashiers, thereby minimizing the possibility of error, and facilitates the bookkeeping process for both the Clerk's Office and participating customers. Conservative estimates place the volume of charges of government transactions at $3 to $10 billion annually. By providing next-day availability of funds to the government, savings of at least $2 million a year will be realized.

From the law firms' perspective, the benefits are even greater. Using a credit card for payment of transactions in the Clerk's Office means that legal couriers no longer are required to carry cash to pay filing or copy fees; blank checks are no longer drawn because amounts are unknown; and the billing procedures fit easily into any internal accounting method used.

For those firms which are concerned with the safekeeping of the actual credit card, the Clerk's Office will maintain the firm's credit card number, expiration date and the signature of one of the firm's partners, after completion of an Authorization Application which can also be found here.

Please view this Notice concerning the Credit Card Collection Network. For additional information, please contact Lucy Chin at (267) 299-7112 or Joseph Hall at (267) 299-7107.

**IN THE UNITED STATES DISTRICT COURT
FOR THE EASTERN DISTRICT OF PENNSYLVANIA**

BAIL BOND SECURED BY PROPERTY OR REAL ESTATE BAIL

1. The deed to the property must be presented and all titled owners must sign the bail bond and affidavit of surety.

2. Proof of equity is required and if the real estate or property is located in Philadelphia a bail certificate issued by the City Controller's Office must be presented. If real estate or property located outside the City of Philadelphia is posted as security the following are required unless otherwise ordered by the Court:

    (a) An appraisal by a qualified real estate appraiser located in the area.

    (b) A copy of the settlement sheet evidencing the assessed valuation of the premises, if the property has been purchased within three years.

    (c) A lien search statement by a title company.

    (d) The latest receipt for taxes paid.

3. The justification of surety affidavit attached to the bail bond must be completed.

4. The deed is returned to surety unless special circumstances require that it be held by the Clerk during the pendency of the case.

5. A bail bond secured by real estate or property is entered as an outstanding encumbrance against the real estate or property posted as security in the judgment index of the Clerk of the United States District Court for the Eastern District of Pennsylvania.

6. Counsel for defendant or surety is required to file a certified copy of the bail bond with the Recorder of Deeds and the Prothonotary of the Court of Common Pleas or Court of general jurisdiction of the county wherein the real estate or property which is posted as security is located. The filing of a certified copy of the bail bond with the Prothonotary enters judgment by confession and records the bail bond as an outstanding encumbrance against the real estate or property during the pendency of the case or until exoneration of surety by the United States District Court.

    Within ten (10) business days counsel for the defendant or surety is required to return to the Clerk's office time-stamped copies of the local filings together with a verification that this requirement has been satisfied. A copy of the verification is to be served upon the Assistant U.S. Attorney assigned to the case.

7. The certified copy of the bail bond filed with the Prothonotary must be accompanied by a form of notice to defendant of entry of judgment and properly stamped envelopes addressed to the defendant and Clerk of the United States District Court for the Eastern District of Pennsylvania.

8. Upon termination of proceedings or upon entry of an Order exonerating surety in the United States District Court counsel for defendant or surety is required to file a certified copy of the judgment of the United States District Court or a certified copy of an Order exonerating surety with the Recorder of Deeds and the Prothonotary of the Court of the county where the bail bond is recorded as an outstanding encumbrance against the property posted as security.

CIV. 611
10/00

Appendix W

JUSTIFICATION OF SURETY REAL ESTATE OR PROPERTY BAIL

AFFIDAVIT

The undersigned, about to become Surety in the case cited herein, being duly sworn (or affirmed) deposes and says:

1. (I/We) reside at _____ .

2. (I/We) have no undisposed of criminal cases against me (us) pending in any Court, except as follows: _____

   _____

   _____

3. (I am/ We are) free from any trust,

   _____ the sole owner(s) of   )

   _____ joint tenant(s) in   )

   _____ tenant(s) by the entirety in   ) _____ ,
   (address of property)

   real estate situated in the said County of _____ ,

   as follows, viz.: a parcel of ground in size _____

   _____ , situated at _____

   _____ , in the _____ Ward,

   in the _____ Boro, _____ Twp., _____ City of _____ ,

   which is improved with the following buildings: _____

   _____ .

   (all other joint tenants or tenants by the entirety must co-sign this bond and state their addresses on the last page of this form or on an attachment hereto.)

4. The said property was obtained by _____ Deed _____ Will.

5. The _____ Deed _____ Will is dated _____ , and is recorded in the office of the _____ Recorder of Deeds _____ Register of Wills, of _____ County, _____ , Deed _____ Will Book, Vol. _____ , Page _____ , and the title is in _____ my name _____ and my spouse's name.

   Also, a parcel of ground, in size _____ ,

   situated at _____ ,

   in the _____ Ward, in the _____ Boro, _____ Twp. _____ City of _____

   which is improved with the following buildings: _____

   _____

   _____ .

   The said property was obtained by me by _____ Deed _____ Will. The _____ Deed _____ Will is dated _____ and is recorded in

Appendix W

_____ Deed _____ Will book, Vol. _____, Page _____ of _____ County, and is in _____ my name _____ and my spouse's name.

6   I am not Surety on any kind except as follows:

Date	Amount	Defendant

7. (I am /We are) not surety, guarantor, nor indorser for anyone, except as follows: _____

8. There are no mortgages, or other liens or encumbrances of any kind or description, upon the said premises, and there are no judgments against me, except as follows: _____

Mortgages as set forth in the Recorder of Deeds on first property

Mortgages as set forth in the Recorder of Deeds on second property

Judgements and Liens _____

Real estate taxes have been paid except: _____

9. The assessed valuation of said premises is _____.
10. No judgment has been entered or action instituted against me upon a forfeited recognizance except: _____.
11. There are no negotiations pending for the sale of any part of the said real estate or property; that there are no foreclosure proceedings now pending against me or the real estate or property herein described; that I have not acquired, taken, or received, the title to the said real estate or property, or any part thereof, with any design or intention to make any false, fraudulent, or deceptive showing of my sufficiency as surety in this behalf or otherwise than in good faith, but with the intention of holding and using the said real estate and property as my own.
12. I (we) promise not to transfer or encumber said property until final disposition of this case and exoneration of the subject bond.
13. I (we) further state that I (we) have read the bond of the defendant named above to which this affidavit is attached and made a part of, and I (we) acknowledge that I (we) and my (our) personal representatives are bound, jointly and severally with the defendant and any other sureties, to pay to the United States of America the bond amount specified in the event the bond is forfeited.
14. And further in accordance with law, we do hereby empower any attorney of any court of record within the United States District Court for the Eastern District of Pennsylvania or elsewhere to appear for us at any time, and with or without declarations filed, and whether or not the said ob-

ligation be in default, to confess judgment against us, and in favor of the United States of America for use of the aforesaid government, for the above sum and costs, with release of all errors, without stay of execution, and inquisition on and extension upon any levy or real estate is hereby waived, and condemnation agreed to, and the exemption of personal property from levy and sale on any execution hereon is also hereby expressly waived, and no benefit of exemption is claimed under and by virtue of any exemption law now in force or which may be passed hereafter. And for so doing this shall be sufficient warrant. A copy of this bond and warrant being filed in said action, it shall not be necessary to file the original as a warrant of attorney, any law or rule of the Court to the contrary, notwithstanding.

15. I (we) agree to pay the fees and costs of the Prothonotary of the Common Pleas Court or the Court of general jurisdiction wherein the real estate or property posted as security is located for recording the lien, notifying the Clerk of the United States Court for the Eastern District of Pennsylvania of the entry of the lien, and for recording of the satisfaction after proceedings have been terminated or surety is otherwise exonerated by the United States District Court.

16. I (we) have read carefully the foregoing affidavit and know that it is true and correct.

_____ (Seal) _____
(Surety)   Address

_____ (Seal) _____
(Surety)   Address

_____ (Seal) _____
(Co-Surety*)   Address

Sworn (affirmed) and subscribed before me this

_____ day of , _____ , _____ .

_____

*Co-Surety, if any, co-joint tenant or co-tenant by the entirety

Appendix X — Attorney Admissions Application (Pro Hac Vice)

To complete and submit an Attorney Admissions Application (Pro Hac Vice), perform the following three (3) steps.

Step #1: Download the form using your browser. The Attorney Admissions Application (Pro Hac Vice) can be found here. The form is interactive and allows most fields to be completed on-line. Adobe Reader is required to access the form and can be obtained through Document Tips.

Step #2: Depending upon your preference, either (a) complete the form on-line and then print the form, or (b) print the form and then complete it manually (i.e., by typing or hand, in ink).

Step #3: Have the form signed and notarized as required & submit it with a disk in PDF format along with the admission fee to:

Michael E. Kunz, Clerk of Court
United States District Court for the Eastern District of Pennsylvania
U.S. Courthouse
601 Market Street, Room 2609
Philadelphia, PA 19106-1797
ATTN: Attorney Admissions Application

**IN THE UNITED STATES DISTRICT COURT
FOR THE EASTERN DISTRICT OF PENNSYLVANIA**

	:	CIVIL ACTION NO. _____
v.	:	
	:	NO.

ORDER

AND NOW, this _____ Day of _____ , 20__ , it is hereby

ORDERED that the application of _____ , Esquire, to practice in this court pursuant to Local Rule of Civil Procedure 83.5.2(b) is

☐ GRANTED.
☐ DENIED.

_____
J.

Appendix X

IN THE UNITED STATES DISTRICT COURT
FOR THE EASTERN DISTRICT OF PENNSYLVANIA

Civil Action No# _____

APPLICATION FORM FOR THOSE ATTORNEYS SEEKING TO PRACTICE IN THIS COURT PURSUANT TO LOCAL RULE OF CIVIL PROCEDURE 83.5.2(b)

I. APPLICANT'S STATEMENT

I, _____ the undersigned, am an attorney who is not currently admitted to either the bar of this court or the bar of the Supreme Court of Pennsylvania, and I hereby apply for admission to practice in this court pursuant to Local Rule of Civil Procedure 83.5.2(b), and am submitting a check, number _____, for the $40.00 admission fee.

A. I state that I am currently admitted to practice in the following state jurisdictions:

(State where admitted)	(Admission date)	(Attorney Identification Number)
(State where admitted)	(Admission date)	(Attorney Identification Number)
(State where admitted)	(Admission date)	(Attorney Identification Number)

B. I state that I am currently admitted to practice in the following federal jurisdictions:

(Court where admitted)	(Admission date)	(Attorney Identification Number)
(Court where admitted)	(Admission date)	(Attorney Identification Number)
(Court where admitted)	(Admission date)	(Attorney Identification Number)

C. I state that I am at present a member of the aforesaid bars in good standing, and that I will demean myself as an attorney of this court uprightly and according to law, and that I will support and defend the Constitution of the United States.

I am entering my appearance for _____

_____
(Applicant's Signature)

_____
(Date)

APPLICANT'S OFFICE ADDRESS AND TELEPHONE NUMBER:

_____
_____
_____

Sworn and subscribed before me this
___ Day of _____, 200___

_____
Notary Public

II. SPONSOR'S STATEMENT, MOTION AND CERTIFICATE OF SERVICE

The undersigned member of the bar of the United States District Court for the Eastern District of Pennsylvania hereby moves for the admission of _____ to practice in said court pursuant to Local Rule of Civil Procedure 83.5.2(b), and certify that I know (or after reasonable inquiry believe) that the applicant is a member in good standing of the above-referenced state and federal courts and that the applicant's private and personal character is good. I certify that this application form was on this date mailed, with postage prepaid, to all interested counsel.

_____   _____   _____   _____
Sponsor's Name   Sponsor's Signature   Admission date   Attorney
                                                                              Identification No.

SPONSOR'S OFFICE ADDRESS AND TELEPHONE NUMBER:

_____
_____
_____

Sworn and subscribed before me this

___ Day of _____ , 200___

_____
Notary Public

Appendix X

**IN THE UNITED STATES DISTRICT COURT
FOR THE EASTERN DISTRICT OF PENNSYLVANIA**

	:	CIVIL ACTION
v.	:	
	:	NO.

CERTIFICATE OF SERVICE

I declare under penalty of perjury that a copy of the application of _____ Esquire, to practice in this court pursuant to Local Rule of Civil Procedure 83.5.2(b) and the relevant proposed Order which, if granted, would permit such practice in this court was mailed today with postage prepaid to:

_____

_____

_____

_____
Signature of Attorney

_____
Name of Attorney

_____
Name of Moving Party

_____
Date

AO 435 (Rev. 03/08)	Administrative Office of the United States Courts		FOR COURT USE ONLY
Please Read Instructions:	**TRANSCRIPT ORDER**		**DUE DATE:**

1. NAME		2. PHONE NUMBER	3. DATE	
4. MAILING ADDRESS		5. CITY	6. STATE	7. ZIP CODE

8. CASE NUMBER	9. JUDGE	DATES OF PROCEEDINGS	
		10. FROM	11. TO
12. CASE NAME		LOCATION OF PROCEEDINGS	
		13. CITY	14. STATE

15. ORDER FOR
- ☐ APPEAL
- ☐ NON-APPEAL
- ☐ CRIMINAL
- ☐ CIVIL
- ☐ CRIMINAL JUSTICE ACT
- ☐ IN FORMA PAUPERIS
- ☐ BANKRUPTCY
- ☐ OTHER *(Specify)*

16. TRANSCRIPT REQUESTED (Specify portion(s) and date(s) of proceeding(s) for which transcript is requested)

PORTIONS	DATE(S)	PORTION(S)	DATE(S)
☐ VOIR DIRE		☐ TESTIMONY (Specify Witness)	
☐ OPENING STATEMENT (Plaintiff)			
☐ OPENING STATEMENT (Defendant)			
☐ CLOSING ARGUMENT (Plaintiff)		☐ PRE-TRIAL PROCEEDING (Spcy)	
☐ CLOSING ARGUMENT (Defendant)			
☐ OPINION OF COURT			
☐ JURY INSTRUCTIONS		☐ OTHER (Specify)	
☐ SENTENCING			
☐ BAIL HEARING			

17. ORDER

CATEGORY	ORIGINAL (Includes Certified Copy to Clerk for Records of the Court)	FIRST COPY	ADDITIONAL COPIES	NO. OF PAGES ESTIMATE	COSTS
ORDINARY	☐	☐	NO. OF COPIES		
EXPEDITED	☐	☐	NO. OF COPIES		
DAILY	☐	☐	NO. OF COPIES		
HOURLY	☐	☐	NO. OF COPIES		
REALTIME	☐	☐			

CERTIFICATION (18. & 19.) By signing below, I certify that I will pay all charges (deposit plus additional).	ESTIMATE TOTAL	$ 0.00
18. SIGNATURE	PROCESSED BY	
19. DATE	PHONE NUMBER	

TRANSCRIPT TO BE PREPARED BY			COURT ADDRESS
	DATE	BY	
ORDER RECEIVED			
DEPOSIT PAID			DEPOSIT PAID
TRANSCRIPT ORDERED			TOTAL CHARGES	$ 0.00
TRANSCRIPT RECEIVED			LESS DEPOSIT	$ 0.00
ORDERING PARTY NOTIFIED TO PICK UP TRANSCRIPT			TOTAL REFUNDED	
PARTY RECEIVED TRANSCRIPT			TOTAL DUE	$ 0.00

DISTRIBUTION: COURT COPY   TRANSCRIPTION COPY   ORDER RECEIPT   ORDER COPY

Appendix Y

Appendix Y

AO 435
(Rev. 03/08)

INSTRUCTIONS

GENERAL

Use. Use this form to order the transcription of proceedings. Complete a separate order form for each case number for which transcripts are ordered.

Completion. Complete Items 1-19. Do *not* complete shaded areas which are reserved for the court's use.

Order Copy. Keep a copy for your records.

Mailing or Delivering to the Court. Mail or deliver the original, and two copies of this form to the Clerk of Court.

Deposit Fee. The court will notify you of the amount of the required deposit fee which may be mailed or delivered to the court. Upon receipt of the deposit, the court will process the order.

Deliver Time. Delivery time is computed from the date of receipt of the deposit fee or for transcripts ordered by the federal government from the date of receipt of the signed order form.

Completion of Order. The court will notify you when the transcript is completed.

Balance Due. If the deposit fee was insufficient to cover all charges, the court will notify you of the balance due which must be paid prior to receiving the completed order.

SPECIFIC

Items 1-19.	These items should always be completed.
Item 8.	Only one case number may be listed per order.
Item 15.	Place an "X" in each box that applies.
Item 16.	Place an "X" in the box for each portion requested. List specific date(s) of the proceedings for which transcript is requested. Be sure that the description is clearly written to facilitate processing. Orders may be placed for as few pages of transcript as are needed.
Item. 17.	*Categories.* There are five (5) categories of transcripts which may be ordered. These are:

> *Ordinary.* A transcript to be delivered within thirty (30) calendar days after receipt of an order. (Order is considered received upon receipt of the deposit.)
>
> *Expedited.* A transcript to be delivered within seven (7) calendar days after receipt of an order.
>
> *Daily.* A transcript to be delivered following adjournment and prior to the normal opening hour of the court on the following morning whether or not it actually is a court day.
>
> *Hourly.* A transcript of proceedings ordered under unusual circumstances to be delivered within two (2) hours.
>
> *Realtime.* A draft unedited transcript produced by a certified realtime reporter as a byproduct of realtime to be delivered electronically during proceedings or immediately following adjournment.

NOTE: Full price may be charged only if the transcript is delivered within the required time frame. For example, if an order for expedited transcript is not completed and delivered within seven (7) calendar days, payment would be at the ordinary delivery rate.

> *Ordering.* Place an "X" in each box that applies. Indicate the number of additional copies ordered.
>> *Original.* Original typing of the transcript. An original must be ordered and prepared prior to the availability of copies. The original fee is charged only once. The fee for the original includes the copy for the records of the court.
>>
>> *First Copy.* First copy of the transcript after the original has been prepared. All parties ordering copies must pay this rate for the first copy ordered.
>>
>> *Additional Copies.* All other copies of the transcript ordered by the same party.

Item 18.	Sign in this space to certify that you will pay all charges. (This includes the deposit plus any additional charges.)
Item 19.	Enter the date of signing.

Shaded Area. Reserved for the court's use.

AO 436 (Rev. 12/04)

Administrative Office of the United States Courts

CD/TAPE ORDER

Read Instructions on Next Page.

1. NAME	2. PHONE NUMBER	3. DATE	
4. MAILING ADDRESS	5. CITY	6. STATE	7. ZIP CODE

8. CASE NUMBER	9. CASE NAME	DATES OF PROCEEDINGS	
		10. FROM	11. TO
12. PRESIDING JUDGE		LOCATION OF PROCEEDINGS	
		13. CITY	14. STATE

15. ORDER FOR
☐ APPEAL   ☐ CRIMINAL   ☐ CRIMINAL JUSTICE ACT   ☐ BANKRUPTCY
☐ NON-APPEAL ☐ CIVIL   ☐ IN FORMA PAUPERIS   ☐ OTHER (Specify)

16. TAPE REQUESTED (Specify portion(s) and date(s) of proceeding(s) for which duplicate cd/tape(s) are requested.)

PORTION(S)	DATE(S)	PORTION(S)	DATE(S)
☐ VOIR DIRE		☐ TESTIMONY (Specify Witness)	
☐ OPENING STATEMENT (Plaintiff)			
☐ OPENING STATEMENT (Defendant)			
☐ CLOSING ARGUMENT (Plaintiff)		☐ PRE-TRIAL PROCEEDING (Spcy)	
☐ CLOSING ARGUMENT (Defendant)			
☐ OPINION OF COURT			
☐ JURY INSTRUCTIONS		☐ OTHER (Specify)	
☐ SENTENCING			
☐ BAIL HEARING			

17. ORDER

	NO. OF COPIES REQUESTED	COSTS
☐ REFORMATTED DUPLICATE TAPE(S) FOR PLAYBACK ON A STANDARD CASSETTE RECORDER AT 1-7/8 INCHES PER SECOND		
☐ UNREFORMATTED DUPLICATE TAPE(S) FOR PLAYBACK ON A 4-TRACK CASSETTE RECORDER AT 1-7/8 INCHES PER SECOND		
☐ UNREFORMATTED DUPLICATE TAPE(S) FOR PLAYBACK ON A 4-TRACK CASSETTE RECORDER AT 15/16 INCHES PER SECOND		
☐ RECORDABLE COMPACT DISC - CD		

CERTIFICATION (18. & 19.) By signing below, I certify that I will pay all charges (deposit plus additional) upon completion of the order.	ESTIMATE TOTAL	
18. SIGNATURE	19. DATE	

PROCESSED BY			PHONE NUMBER	
	DATE	BY		
ORDER RECEIVED			DEPOSIT PAID	
DEPOSIT PAID			TOTAL CHARGES	
TAPE / CD DUPLICATED			LESS DEPOSIT	
ORDERING PARTY NOTIFIED TO PICK UP TAPE			TOTAL REFUNDED	
PARTY RECEIVED TAPE / CD			TOTAL DUE	

DISTRIBUTION: COURT COPY   ORDER RECEIPT   ORDER COPY

Appendix Z

**IN THE UNITED STATES DISTRICT COURT
FOR THE EASTERN DISTRICT OF PENNSYLVANIA**

**IN RE: AMENDMENT TO LOCAL CIVIL RULE 5.1.2,
Electronic Case Filing ("ECF") Procedures**

ORDER

AND NOW, this 5th day of June 2008, it appearing that this Court is vested with authority, pursuant to 28 U.S.C. §§ 2071(e), 2077 and Federal Rule of Civil Procedure 83, to promulgate Local Civil Rules not inconsistent with the Federal Rules of Civil Procedure and applicable statutes, and

HAVING been notified that the Judicial Conference of the United States at its September, 2007 session approved a new policy regarding the electronic availability of transcripts of court proceedings and has directed the Administrative Office of the United States Courts to issue guidance to the courts on the implementation of the new policy, and

HAVING been advised that the new Judicial Conference policy authorizes the courts to make transcripts of court proceedings available electronically through the Case Management/Electronic Case Files (CM/ECF) system, and

HAVING determined that there is an immediate need pursuant to 28 U.S.C. § 2071(e) to amend the *Electronic Case Filing ("ECF") Procedures,* as set forth in Rule 5.1.2 of the Local Rules of Civil Procedure, to comply with the directive of the new Judicial Conference policy, it is hereby

ORDERED that Section 16B of the ECF Procedures set forth in Rule 5.1.2, *Excluded Documents, Civil Cases,* Item 6, *"Transcript of any proceeding,"* is deleted in its entirety and that the following is inserted in lieu thereof: *"Transcript of civil proceedings shall be placed on CM/ECF or PACER, unless the presiding judge otherwise directs."* It is further

ORDERED that Section 16B of the ECF Procedures set forth in Rule 5.1.2, *Excluded Documents, Criminal Cases,* Item 2, *"Transcript of any proceeding,"* is deleted in its entirety and the following is inserted in lieu thereof: *"Transcript of criminal proceedings shall not be placed on CM/ECF or PACER, unless the presiding judge otherwise directs after giving the prosecution and defense counsel an opportunity to be heard."* It is further

ORDERED that the above-described amendments to Rule 5.1.2 of the Local Rules of Civil Procedure are approved and adopted, effective June 2, 2008, with public notice and an opportunity for comment on the amended rule afforded in accordance with 28 U.S.C. § 2071(e). It is further

ORDERED that the Clerk of Court transmit a copy of amended Local Civil Rule 5.1.2 to the Director of the Administrative Office of the United States Courts and the Judicial Council of the Third Circuit Court of Appeals and make said Rule available to the bar and public.

FOR THE COURT: /s _____
HARVEY BARTLE III
Chief Judge

UNITED STATES DISTRICT COURT
EASTERN DISTRICT OF PENNSYLVANIA
OFFICE OF THE CLERK OF COURT

Notice of Electronic Availability of Transcripts in Case Management/Electronic Case Files (CM/ECF) and Transcript Redaction

At its September 2007 session, the Judicial Conference of the United States approved a new policy to make electronic transcripts of court proceedings available to the public. **Effective immediately,** this new policy will be implemented in the Office of the Clerk, United States District Court, Eastern District of Pennsylvania, as follows:

- Transcripts of civil court proceedings will be placed on CM/ECF or **PACER** unless the presiding judge otherwise directs.

- Transcripts of criminal court proceedings will not be placed on CM/ECF or **PACER** unless the presiding judge otherwise directs after giving the prosecution and defense counsel an opportunity to be heard.

If electronic transcripts are to be made available to the public upon approval of the assigned judge:

- A transcript provided to the court by a court reporter or transcriber will be available at the office of the clerk for inspection for a period of 90 days after it is delivered to the clerk.

- During the 90-day period a copy of the transcript may also be obtained by purchase from the court reporter or transcriber through the office of the clerk. An attorney who obtains the transcript from the office of the clerk will be allowed remote electronic access to the transcript through the court's CM/ECF system.

- After the 90-day period has expired, the filed transcript will be available for inspection and copying in the clerk's office and for download from the court's CM/ECF system through the **PACER** system.

In addition, amendments to the Federal Civil and Criminal Rules of Procedure (Civil Rule 5.2 and Criminal Rule 49.1) require that personal identification information be redacted from documents filed with the court, including Social Security numbers, names of minor children, financial account numbers, dates of birth, and in criminal cases, home addresses. Under the new transcripts access policy, procedures for applying redaction requirements to transcripts of court proceedings are outlined in the attachment to this Notice. It is important to note that it is *not* the responsibility of the court reporter nor transcriber to identify material in the transcript that should be redacted. The Judicial Conference policy imposes that responsibility on counsel.

Should you require clarification or additional information on this new policy, please contact Joan Carr, Supervisor of Court Reporters (267-299-7104) or Michael Hearn, Electronic Sound Recording Coordinator (267-299-7039).

Attachment

Appendix AA

United States District Court for the Eastern District of Pennsylvania
Electronic Availability of Transcripts and Transcript Redaction Procedures

- The requirement of the court reporter and transcriber to provide a certified copy of a transcript to the clerk for the records of the court has not changed, i.e. when a transcript is originally produced, a certified copy must be promptly delivered to the clerk. The Guide to Judiciary Policies and Procedures states that the transcript copy should be delivered to the clerk concurrently with—but not later than three working days after—delivery to the requesting party. Sealed transcripts are excluded from electronic filing.

- Transcripts of civil court proceedings will be placed on CM/ECF or **PACER** unless the presiding judge otherwise directs.

- Transcripts of criminal court proceedings will not be placed on CM/ECF or **PACER** unless the presiding judge otherwise directs after giving the prosecution and defense counsel an opportunity to be heard.

- If electronic transcripts are to be made available, a certified transcript provided to the court by a court reporter or transcriber will be available for review and inspection at the court's public terminal in the office of the clerk for a period of 90 days after it is delivered to the clerk.

- If electronic transcripts are to be made available, during the 90-day period a copy of the transcript may also be obtained by purchase from the court reporter or transcriber through the office of the clerk. An attorney who obtains the transcript from the office of the clerk will be allowed remote electronic access to the transcript through the court's CM/ECF system. Counsel of record in a case who have not purchased a copy of the transcript will not have access to the transcript through CM/ECF until they purchase it from the court reporter or transcriber through the office of the clerk or until the 90-day period has expired.

- If electronic transcripts are to be made available, after the 90-day period has expired, the filed transcript will be available for inspection and copying in the clerk's office and for download from the court's CM/ECF system through the **PACER** system.

- If electronic transcripts are to be made available, members of the public, including the news media, who purchase a transcript from the court reporter or transcriber through the clerk's office within the 90-day period, will not be granted remote electronic access during the restriction period. At the end of the restriction period, the public will be provided remote electronic access through **PACER** to the transcript originally submitted, or, if redaction was made, to the redacted transcript, unless it is under seal.

- The redaction of transcripts will be requested by counsel to a case. Even if the court reporter or transcriber notices that redactions will be necessary as he/she is preparing a transcript, he/she does not have the responsibility to redact information unless there is a redaction request made by the parties to the case. Court reporters and transcribers also do not have a responsibility to notify the parties of material that should be redacted. The Judicial Conference policy imposes the responsibility on counsel to identify material in the transcript that should be redacted.

- **Personal identifiers that a party may request be redacted:** Social Security numbers (or taxpayer identification numbers) to the last four digits, financial account numbers to the last four digits, dates of birth, individuals known to be minor children to the initials, and in criminal cases, any home addresses stated in court to the city and state. Information other than these specified identifiers may be redacted only if the moving party receives a ruling of the court to do so.

- The portion of a transcript that includes the voir dire or other juror information will not be made available through electronic access.

- Unless otherwise ordered by the court, the attorney must review the following portions of the transcripts:

    (a) opening and closing statements made on the party's behalf;

- (b) statements of the party;
- (c) the testimony of any witness called by the party;
- (d) sentencing proceedings; and
- (e) any other portion of the transcript as ordered by the court.

- Counsel is to file a Notice of Intent to Request Redaction with the clerk within seven business days of the transcript being delivered to the clerk (or filing in CM/ECF). Counsel is then to follow up, within 21 calendar days of initial delivery of the transcript to the clerk, with a specific request for redaction noting the page numbers and line numbers where redaction is required.

- If an attorney files a Notice of Intent to Request Redaction or a motion for extension of time to file this notice, and then does not submit a Redaction Request, the court may take action, either to have the attorney withdraw the Notice of Intent to Request Redaction or to issue a show cause order as to why the attorney has not met the redaction requirements.

- Once a court reporter or transcriber receives the list of redactions (Redaction Requests) from the clerk's office, he/she has ten days after the deadline for receipt of the attorneys' redaction request to redact the transcript and file the redacted transcript with the clerk. The original unredacted electronic transcript will be retained by the clerk of court as a restricted document.

- The court reporter or transcriber does not have the obligation to notify the parties that the certified copy of the transcript has been filed, nor is the court reporter or transcriber required to send a copy of the redacted transcript to the parties who originally ordered the transcript. The Clerk of Court notifies the parties that the transcript has been filed so that the parties are aware that the 7-day period within which to request redaction has begun.

- Statements of redaction (Redaction Requests) are to be filed by attorneys with the clerk. The statement should be worded in such a way that the personal information at issue is not repeated (i.e. Redact the Social Security number on page 12, line 9 to read xxx-xx-6789.) since the document is publicly available. There is no requirement that the redaction statements should be served on opposing counsel or parties.

UNITED STATES DISTRICT COURT
Eastern District of Pennsylvania
U.S. Courthouse
Independence Mall West
601 Market Street
Philadelphia, PA 19106-1797

Michael E. Kunz
Clerk of Court

Clerk's Office - Room 2609
Telephone: (215) 597-7704

Audio File Electronic Access Program

NOTICE

The United States District Court for the Eastern District of Pennsylvania participated in a national Digital Audio File Electronic Access Pilot Program. The pilot program was authorized by the Judicial Conference of the United States and provided digital audio files of court proceedings through the Public Access to Court Electronic Records (PACER) system. The Judicial Conference of the United States Committee on Court Administration and Case Management selected five pilot courts. The Eastern District of Pennsylvania and the District of Nebraska were the district courts selected to participate in the project. The Eastern District of North Carolina, the Northern District of Alabama and the District of Maine are the bankruptcy courts that were selected to participate in this project.

During the pilot project digital audio recordings of courtroom proceedings were publicly available on PACER upon the approval of the presiding judge. The project enables PACER users to download, in MP3 format, court proceedings that have been recorded using electronic sound recording technology. During the pilot program, access to the digital audio files cost 16 cents; 8 cents for accessing the docket sheet and another 8 cents for selecting the audio file. More than 840,000 subscribers already use PACER to access docket and case information from federal appellate, district and bankruptcy courts.

Digital audio recording has been an authorized method of making an official record of court proceedings since 1999, when it was approved by the Judicial Conference of the United States. Digital audio recording is used in district and bankruptcy courts in the federal court system. A majority of Eastern District of Pennsylvania district court judges and all magistrate judges use digital audio recordings of court proceedings.

At its March 2010 meeting, the Judicial Conference of the United States voted to allow courts, at the discretion of the presiding judge, to make digital audio recordings of court hearings available online to the public through PACER, for $2.40 per audio file. Should you have any questions concerning the program, please contact Michael Hearn, Electronic Sound Recording Coordinator, at 267-299-7039.

MICHAEL E. KUNZ
Clerk of Court

Appendix BB

EXTERNAL LINKS

You are about to leave the Web site of the U.S. District Court for the Eastern District of Pennsylvania, Office of the Clerk of Court. The hypertext links below lead to other federal-court Web sites and contain information created and maintained by other organizations within the federal judiciary. These links are provided for the user's convenience.

The U.S. District Court for the Eastern District of Pennsylvania, Office of the Clerk of Court does not control or guarantee the accuracy, relevance, timeliness, or completeness of this information.

Please click here to go to the PACER Service Center.

The information provided through this site is not intended to be nor should it be considered legal advice.

UNITED STATES DISTRICT COURT
EASTERN DISTRICT OF PENNSYLVANIA

DIRECTORY OF COURT-AUTOMATED SERVICES

DISTRICT COURT
Internet Web Site - <http://www.paed.uscourts.gov>

✔ *Case Management/Electronic Case Filing (CM/ECF)*

The Eastern District of Pennsylvania has been selected by the Administrative Office of the United States Courts (AO) from among several court applicants to be an alpha court site for implementation in and testing in of the Case Management/Electronic Case Files (CM/ECF) initiative currently under development by the AO. The system was implemented for civil cases on May 1, 2002 and for criminal cases on May 27, 2003. Through Internet technology attorneys can file documents from their offices via a Web browser and have immediate access to other documents filed electronically. CM/ECF provides the capability to view filings after normal court business hours and file documents 24 hours a day. Information and training is available by calling toll-free 1-866-ECF-4ECF.

✔ *Courtroom Technology*

Several courtrooms provide a wide array of technical components that support evidence presentation, remote site interactions, language interpreting and audio enhancement. The state-of-the-art technologies include assisted listening systems, integrated court interpreting systems, video conferencing systems, document/video presentation systems, evidence trolleys, annotation pads, document cameras, as well as connectivity at counsel tables for use with court or attorney provided PCs. The court welcomes the bar to make use of these technologies and training is available at the courthouse. For further information, contact Michael Hearn or Ed Morrissy at (267) 299-7039.

Appendix DD

✓ *Public Access to Court Electronic Records (PACER)*

The PACER system allows any member of the bar or the public who has access to a computer to obtain civil and criminal docket records and documents. The user can obtain the complete electronic history of all civil cases filed since July 1, 1990, and all pending civil cases as of July 1, 1990, except asbestos and prisoner cases, filed prior to July 1, 1990, and all criminal cases filed since July 1, 1992. Also available on the PACER system are civil documents filed in electronic form since May 1, 2002 and criminal documents filed in electronic form since May 27, 2003. To register for the PACER system call (800) 676-6856 or the form may be completed on-line at <http://pacer.psc.uscourts.gov>. The PACER system is available through the Internet at <https://ecf.paed.uscourts.gov>. The fee for accessing PACER on the Internet is $.10 per page with the charge capped at the cost for 30 pages for accessing any single document. Internet PACER provides access to an unlimited number of users.

✓ *Lobby Kiosk Information System*

The redesign of the US. Courthouse lobby was completed in December 2001. The district and circuit courts included in the redesign the installation of an automated informational kiosk and the development of a liaison relationship with the new Constitution Center on Independence Mall. The kiosk system includes a daily information on district court and court of appeals hearings, as well as a directory of judges and court clerks, a directory of other government agencies, and general information. The kiosk includes touch screen technology, as well as mapping techniques to guide visitors to their destinations.

✓ *Internet - Web Site*

Information on available services and judicial opinions filed since June 1, 1997 in the United States District Court for the Eastern District of Pennsylvania, as well as court notices, local rules, multidistrict litigation information, Clerk's Office Procedure Handbook, Frequently Asked Questions, Judicial Procedures, e-mail capabilities and more are available on the Internet <http://www.paed.uscourts.gov>.

Appendix DD

✓ *Pilot Program for Facsimile Service of Notice of Orders and Judgments*

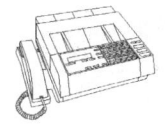

The court has authorized the Clerk of Court to implement a pilot program in civil and criminal cases to allow attorneys and pro se litigants to waive the provisions of Federal Rule of Civil Procedure 77(d) or Federal Rule of Criminal Procedure 49(c), which requires service of Notice of Orders and Judgments by means of mail, and instead consent to receive Notice of Orders and Judgments by means of facsimile transmission.

✓ *FAX Ordering of Docket/Document Copies and/or Searches*

Any member of a law firm, legal agency, or the public can FAX a request to obtain the following: (1) copies of dockets; (2) copies of documents; (3) name searches performed on records.

✓ *Judicial Schedule of Trials - Automated System Inquiry (JUST-ASK)*

JUST-ASK provides up-to-date information on the status of trials scheduled in the U.S. District Court seven days a week, twenty-four hours a day. All cases scheduled for trial, presently on trial, in the trial pool and special notices are included on the system. All information in JUST-ASK is available by judge, case number, party, attorney or entire listing. Events, such as verdicts, settlements, and continuances constantly change the status of cases on the court's trial list. JUST-ASK immediately reflects the daily status of listings as the information becomes available to the Clerk of Court.

✔ Credit Card Collection Network

Any law firm, legal agency, company or individual can arrange to use a Visa, MasterCard, Discover, American Express or Diners Club when making payment for filing fees and other district-court–related expenses.

Credit card payment provides for an alternative to cash/checks that easily accommodates any internal accounting procedure. The network supports in-person, telephone, and mail requests.

✔ Telephone Access for the Hearing and/or Speech Impaired

A hearing and/or speech impaired individual equipped with a Telecommunications Device for the Deaf (TDD) can contact the Office of the Clerk of Court by calling the General Service Administration's (GSA's) Federal Information Relay Service (FIRS) at (800) 877-8339.

✔ Mail Directed To and From the U.S. Courthouse

In order to expedite delivery of notices from judicial officers and the clerk of court, members of the bar are requested to furnish their zip code and 4-digit extension number. In order to take full advantage of these procedures, all mail sent to the courthouse should include the zip code and 4-digit extension number. Forms for supplying the full zip code and listings of the full zip codes for all judicial officers are available in the Office of the Clerk of Court or on the internet.

✔ *Video Teleconferencing Pilot Program (VTC)*

Video Teleconferencing is available between the U.S. District Court in Philadelphia and FCI Fairton, as well as several state correctional institutions. The program was initiated in 1995 with FCI Fairton for the video teleconferencing of criminal proceedings and expanded in 1998 to state correctional institutions primarily for use in prisoner civil rights pretrial proceedings. The system is available for court proceedings and for use by counsel when available. All requests to use the VTC system are to be directed to the VTC Coordinators at (267) 299-7039.

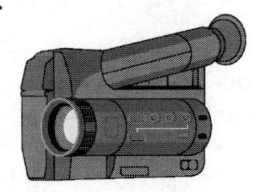

BANKRUPTCY COURT

✔ *Public Access to Court Electronic Records (PACER)*

The PACER system allows any member of the bar or the public who has access to a computer to obtain bankruptcy docket records. The fee for accessing PACER on the Internet is $.08 per page with the charge capped at the cost for 30 pages for accessing any single document. Internet PACER provides access to an unlimited number of users.

✔ *Voice Case Information System (VCIS)*

The VCIS system allows the general public to obtain voice BANCAP information from any standard touch-tone telephone.

Access VCIS by dialing (215) 597-2244.

Hello, and welcome to VCIS. What information would you like?

Appendix DD

FOR MORE INFORMATION...

Please check the appropriate service(s) listed below and provide the indicated address information:

District Court
- ☐ Case Management/Electronic Case Filing (CM/ECF)
- ☐ Courtroom Technology
- ☐ PACER (Civil/Criminal)
- ☐ Kiosk Information System
- ☐ Internet - Web Site
- ☐ Pilot FAX Program for Service of Orders and Judgments
- ☐ FAX Ordering
- ☐ JUST-ASK
- ☐ Credit Card Collection Network
- ☐ Telephone Access for Hearing/Speech-Impaired
- ☐ Mail Delivered to and From the Courthouse

Bankruptcy Court
- ☐ PACER (Bankruptcy)
- ☐ Voice Case Information System

☐ ALL OF THE ABOVE

ADDRESS INFORMATION

NAME _____

FIRM _____

ADDRESS _____

CITY _____ STATE _____ ZIP _____

PHONE ( ) _____ FAX ( ) _____

E-MAIL ADDRESS _____

Send this completed form to...

MICHAEL E. KUNZ, CLERK OF COURT
United States District Court
2609 U.S. Courthouse
601 Market Street
Philadelphia, PA 19106-1797

FAX: (215) 597-6390
or
<http://www.paed.uscourts.gov>

Clerk's Office Procedural Handbook

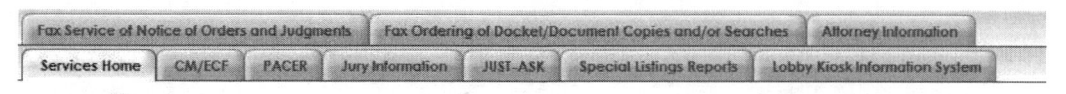

Fax Service of Notice of Orders and Judgments	Fax Ordering of Docket/Document Copies and/or Searches	Attorney Information

Services Home	CM/ECF	PACER	Jury Information	JUST-ASK	Special Listings Reports	Lobby Kiosk Information System

SERVICES

MORE SERVICES

The U.S. District Court for the Eastern District of Pennsylvania, Office of the Clerk of Court, currently offers these services to provide the bar, litigants and the general public with convenient and inexpensive access to court records.

**IN THE UNITED STATES DISTRICT COURT
FOR THE EASTERN DISTRICT OF PENNSYLVANIA**

NOTICE

**Electronic Case Filing (ECF)
Electronic Filing of Complaints**

The United States District Court for the Eastern District of Pennsylvania has authorized a pilot program to file complaints electronically on the CM/ECF system. If you are interested in filing complaints electronically, please complete the information below and you will be contacted to arrange a mutually convenient time for training.

If you have any questions on filing complaints electronically on the CM/ECF system, please do not hesitate to contact this office at 1-866-ECF-4ECF.

Michael E. Kunz
Clerk of Court

Name: _____ Phone: _____

Address: _____

Email: _____ FAX: _____

**Please return the completed form to the Clerk of Court by fax to
215-597-6390 or 267-299-7130.**

Appendix EE